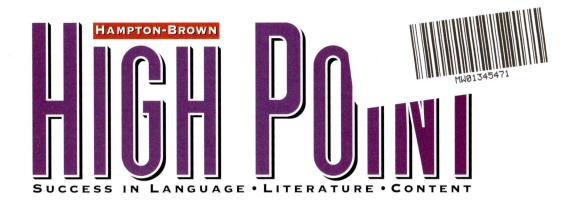

SUCCESS IN LANGUAGE • LITERATURE • CONTENT

Teacher's Edition

ALFREDO SCHIFINI
DEBORAH SHORT
JOSEFINA VILLAMIL TINAJERO

Copyright © Hampton-Brown
All rights reserved. No part of this book may be reproduced or transmitted in any form or by any means, electronic or mechanical, including photocopying, recording, or by an information storage and retrieval system without permission from the publisher.

Hampton-Brown
P.O. Box 223220
Carmel, California 93922
1-800-333-3510

Printed in the United States of America
0-7362-1224-8
03 04 05 06 07 08 09 10 10 9 8 7 6 5 4

Contents

Program Overview 4

Program Guide for Assessment and Instruction 15

Carlos Comes to Lakeside School T10a

UNIT 1   *Glad to Meet You!* T40h

UNIT 2   *Set the Table* T56a

UNIT 3   *On the Job* T70a

UNIT 4   *Numbers Count* T84a

UNIT 5   *City Sights* T98a

UNIT 6   *Welcome Home!* T114a

UNIT 7   *Pack Your Bags!* T128a

UNIT 8   *Friend to Friend* T142a

UNIT 9   *Let's Celebrate!* T156a

UNIT 10   *Here to Help* T170a

UNIT 11   *Make a Difference!* T184a

UNIT 12   *Our Living Planet* T198a

UNIT 13   *Past and Present* T212a

UNIT 14   *Tell Me More* T228a

UNIT 15   *Personal Best* T242a

UNIT 16   *This Land is Our Land* T256a

UNIT 17   *Harvest Time* T270a

UNIT 18   *Superstars* T284a

High Point Handbook T298

Bibliography of Related Literacy Research T305

Decoding Skills Sequence and High Frequency Words in The Basics T307

Partner Checklists T310

Partner Prompts T311

Audio Scripts T312

Scope and Sequence T330

Staff Development: Teaching English Learners T337

Phonics Transfer Chart and Articulation of Sounds in English T338

Language Structure Transfer Chart T346

Index T352

Program Authors

Outstanding authors, experts in second-language acquisition, literacy, and content, turn research into practice for your classroom!

Dr. Alfredo Schifini assists schools across the nation and internationally in developing comprehensive ESL programs. He has worked as a high school ESL teacher, elementary reading specialist, and school administrator. Dr. Schifini directs the Southern California Professional Development Institute for teachers of ELD. Through an arrangement with Cal Poly at Pomona, he also serves as program consultant to two large teacher-training efforts in the area of reading for struggling older students. His research interests include literacy development for older second-language learners and the integration of language and content-area instruction.

CURRICULUM REVIEWERS

Tedi Armet
Fort Bend Independent School District
Sugar Land, Texas

Suzanne Barton
International Newcomer Academy
Fort Worth Independent School District
Fort Worth, Texas

Maggie Brookshire
Emerald Middle School
Cajon Valley Unified School District
El Cajon, California

Raina Cannard
Elk Grove Unified School District
El Cajon, California

Lily Dam
Dallas Independent School District
Dallas, Texas

Judy Doss
Burbank High School
Burbank Unified School District
Burbank, California

Rossana Font-Carrasco
Paul W. Bell Middle School
Miami-Dade County School District 5
Miami, Florida

Jillian Friedman
Howard Middle School
Orange County Public Schools
Orlando, Florida

Vivian Kahn
Halsey Intermediate School 296
Community School District 32
New York, New York

Suzanne Lee
Josiah Quincy School
Boston, Massachusetts

Mary McBride
Monroe Middle School
Inglewood Unified School District
Los Angeles, California

Carolyn McGavock
Rafael Cordero Bilingual Academy, Junior High School 45
Community School District 4
New York, New York

Dr. Deborah Short is a division director at the Center for Applied Linguistics (CAL) in Washington, D.C. She has worked as a teacher, trainer, researcher, and curriculum/materials developer. Her work at CAL has concentrated on the integration of language learning with content-area instruction. Through several national projects, she has conducted research and has provided professional development and technical assistance to local and state education agencies across the United States. She currently directs the ESL Standards and Assessment Project for TESOL.

Dr. Josefina Villamil Tinajero specializes in staff development and school–university partnership programs, and consulted with school districts in the U.S. to design ESL, bilingual, literacy, and bi-literacy programs. She has served on state and national advisory committees for standards development, including English as a New Language Advisory Panel of the National Board of Professional Teaching Standards. She is currently Professor of Education and Associate Dean at the University of Texas at El Paso, and was President of the National Association for Bilingual Education, 1997–2000.

Juan Carlos Méndez
Community School District 9
Bronx, New York

Cynthia Nelson-Mosca
Cicero School District 99
Cicero, Illinois

Kim-Anh Nguyen
Franklin McKinley School District
San Jose, California

Ellie Paiewonsky
Technical Assistance Center of Nassau
Board of Cooperative Educational Services
Massapequa Park, New York

Jeanne Perrin
Boston Public Schools
Boston, Massachusetts

Becky Peurifoy
Rockwall Independent School District
Rockwall, Texas

Marjorie Rosenberg
Montgomery County Public Schools
Rockville, Maryland

Harriet Rudnit
Grades 6–8
Lincoln Hall Middle School
Lincolnwood, Illinois

Olga Ryzhikov
Forest Oak Middle School
Montgomery County, Maryland

Dr. Wageh Saad, Ed.D.
Dearborn Public Schools
Dearborn, Michigan

Gilbert Socas
West Miami Middle School
Miami-Dade County Public Schools
Miami, Florida

HIGH POINT

Standards-Based with Specialized Instructional Strategies

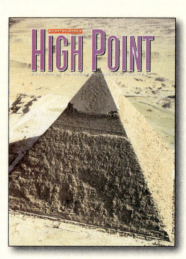

The Basics

Motivates
Struggling Readers and English Learners

➤ High interest, multicultural selections

➤ Significant themes

➤ Real-world appeal

➤ Engaging activities

PROGRAM OVERVIEW

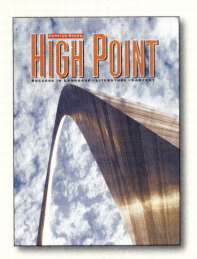
Level A

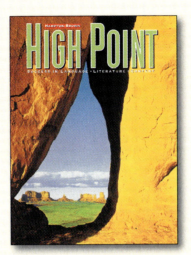
Level B

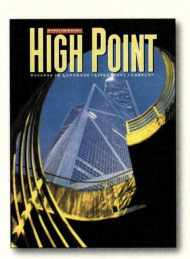
Level C

Closes Gaps
in Language and Literacy

➤ Extensive vocabulary development and skills practice

➤ Complete learning to read strand

➤ Direct instruction in reading strategies

➤ Abundant use of expository text

➤ Comprehensive grammar instruction

➤ Fully supported Writing Projects

Equips
Teachers for Effective Instruction

➤ Multi-level teaching strategies to address diverse needs

➤ Full array of assessment to diagnose, plan instruction, and measure progress

➤ Varied teaching tools—from transparencies to technology to tapes and theme books!

➤ Family newsletters in 7 languages to increase home involvement

Components

Integrated content across components creates a rich and contextualized learning environment. The variety of instructional tools keeps students engaged.

RESOURCES FOR STANDARDS-BASED INSTRUCTION	The Basics	LEVEL A	LEVEL B	LEVEL C
Student Books — Literature selected especially for struggling readers and English learners, instructional activities, and useful Handbooks all in one place (The Basics, Level A, Level B, Level C)	●	●	●	●
The Basics Bookshelf — 18 read-aloud Theme Books for building basic vocabulary and language patterns and for developing concepts of print, listening comprehension, and knowledge of text structures	●	●	●	●
Language Tapes/CDs — Recordings of songs, poems, stories, interviews, and speeches to develop vocabulary and language		●	●	●
Selection Tapes/CDs — Readings of the Student Book selections at Levels A–C and of the Theme Books in The Basics Bookshelf	●	●	●	●
Instructional Overheads — For group instruction in grammar skills, reading strategies, and the writing process	●	●	●	●
Reading Basics — Transparencies to teach phonics and word structure plus teacher scripts, letter tiles for word building, and word tiles for high frequency word instruction.	●			

8

PROGRAM OVERVIEW

RESOURCES FOR STANDARDS-BASED INSTRUCTION		The Basics	LEVEL A	LEVEL B	LEVEL C
Practice Books	Student workbooks for skills practice The Basics Level A Level B Level C	•	•	•	•
Teacher's Resource Books	Reproducible activity sheets that match the instructional overheads at Levels A–C and offer handwriting practice at The Basics, as well as family newsletters in seven languages	•	•	•	•
Diagnosis and Placement Inventory	Group-administered test for placing students into the appropriate *High Point* level based on reading and writing skills, along with a Teacher's Edition	•	•	•	•
Assessment Handbooks	A complete array of assessment tools including Language Acquisition Assessments, Selection Tests, Unit Tests, Writing Assessments, and Peer- and Self-Assessments The Basics Level A Level B Level C	•	•	•	•
CD-ROM Technology	*Inspiration* Visual Learning software for making graphic organizers and mind maps	•	•	•	•
Theme Libraries A–C (addition)	10 books per level coordinated with unit themes and targeted to beginning, intermediate, and advanced levels		•	•	•
Teacher's Edition	Your complete resource for planning and instruction The Basics Level A Level B Level C	•	•	•	•

Program Overview **9**

Motivational, Real-World Content

For The Basics, 18 themes with related read-aloud Theme Books motivate students as they build a foundation in vocabulary, English structures, and early literacy skills.

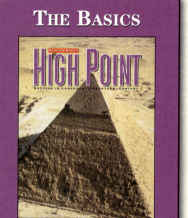

UNIT 1	Glad to Meet You!	UNIT 7	Pack Your Bags!	UNIT 13	Past and Present
UNIT 2	Set the Table	UNIT 8	Friend to Friend	UNIT 14	Tell Me More
UNIT 3	On the Job	UNIT 9	Let's Celebrate!	UNIT 15	Personal Best
UNIT 4	Numbers Count	UNIT 10	Here to Help	UNIT 16	This Land is Our Land
UNIT 5	City Sights	UNIT 11	Make a Difference!	UNIT 17	Harvest Time
UNIT 6	Welcome Home!	UNIT 12	Our Living Planet	UNIT 18	Superstars

PROGRAM OVERVIEW

Relevant, Curriculum-Connected Themes

At Levels A–C, significant themes speak to issues of interest for students, connect to middle school content, and offer instructional choices for teachers.

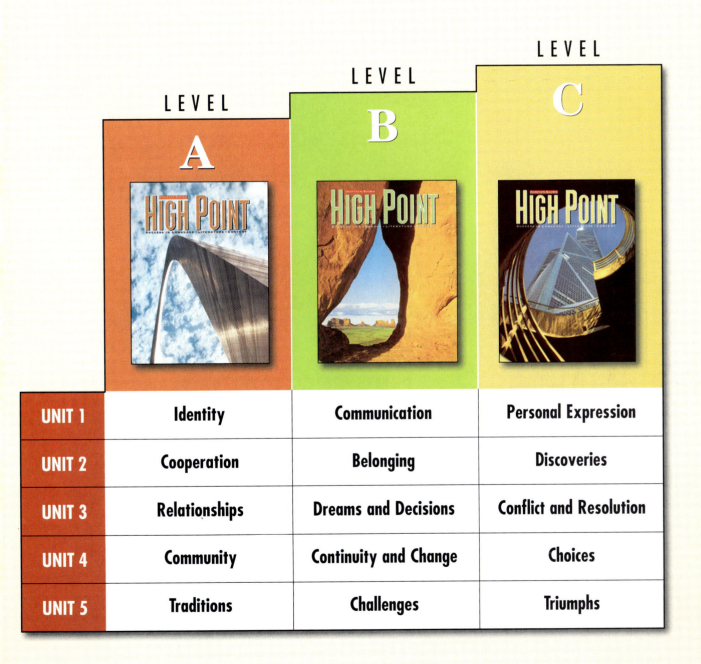

	LEVEL A	LEVEL B	LEVEL C
UNIT 1	Identity	Communication	Personal Expression
UNIT 2	Cooperation	Belonging	Discoveries
UNIT 3	Relationships	Dreams and Decisions	Conflict and Resolution
UNIT 4	Community	Continuity and Change	Choices
UNIT 5	Traditions	Challenges	Triumphs

Standards-Based Instruction for All Students

Curriculum Standards provide the foundation for **High Point**. Carefully selected readings and specially designed lessons with Multi-Level Strategies ensure standards-based instruction for struggling readers and English learners!

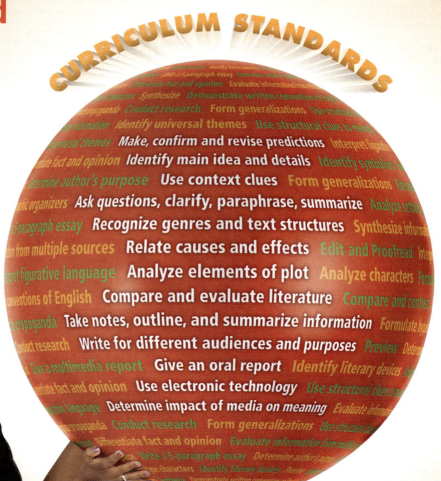

DIFFERENTIATED INSTRUCTION FOR EACH STANDARD

Multi-Level Strategies
ACTIVITY OPTIONS FOR ANALYZING ELEMENTS OF PLOT

BEGINNING Read the myth aloud, pausing after each event to clarify meaning. Have students sketch the event. Select and save one sketch per event. After reading, draw a rising-and-falling action map. Review the myth as you place the sketches on the map. Create a group sentence about each step in the plot: *A conflict happens when Hades steals Demeter's daughter.*

INTERMEDIATE Read the myth aloud or play its recording. Pause after key events to elicit steps in the plot: *What is the conflict about?* Work as a group to record events on the rising-and-falling action map on **Transparency 72**. After reading, partners retell the myth to each other.

ADVANCED As partners read the myth or listen to its recording, have them complete the plot diagram on **Master 72**. After reading, students retell the myth to each other. Then have students change an event and revise the plot diagram before telling the story again to see how events in the plot affect the final outcome.

PROGRAM OVERVIEW

Complete Skills Coverage

The **High Point** Scope and Sequence covers the full range of skills English learners need for academic success.

SCOPE AND SEQUENCE	The Basics	LEVEL A	LEVEL B	LEVEL C
Language Development and Communication	•	•	•	•
Language Functions	•	•	•	•
Language Patterns and Structures	•	•	•	•
Concepts and Vocabulary	•	•	•	•
Reading	•	•	•	•
Learning to Read: concepts of print, phonemic awareness, phonics, decoding, and word recognition	•			
Reading Strategies	•	•	•	•
Comprehension	•	•	•	•
Literary Analysis and Appreciation		•	•	•
Speaking, Listening, Viewing, Representing	•	•	•	•
Cognitive Academic Skills	•	•	•	•
Learning Strategies	•	•	•	•
Critical Thinking	•	•	•	•
Research Skills	•	•	•	•
Writing	•	•	•	•
Handwriting	•			
Writing Modes and Forms	•	•	•	•
Writing Process		•	•	•
Writer's Craft		•	•	•
Grammar, Usage, Mechanics, Spelling	•	•	•	•
Technology / Media		•	•	•
Cultural Perspectives	•	•	•	•

Program Overview **13**

Assessment To Inform Instruction

High Point includes a comprehensive array of assessment tools to place students at the appropriate level, to monitor students' progress, and to assess mastery of the Language Arts standards.

DIAGNOSIS AND PLACEMENT

Diagnosis and Placement Inventory
This group-administered test places students into the appropriate *High Point* level based on reading and writing skills. A Teacher's Edition contains additional diagnostic tools, including reading fluency assessments, and provides guidance on administering the test, scoring, and interpreting results.

PROGRESS MONITORING AND SUMMATIVE EVALUATION

These assessments appear in the Assessment Handbook for each level.

Language Acquisition Assessment
Identifies Performance Assessment opportunities in each unit and offers scoring rubrics to monitor the student's progress through the stages of language proficiency.

Selection Tests
At Levels A–C, multiple-choice items and short-answer questions measure mastery of the reading strategies and the vocabulary, comprehension, and language arts skills taught with each reading selection.

Unit Tests in Standardized Test Format
The multiple-choice sections of these tests for all levels measure students' cumulative understanding of skills and language. Writing Prompts for all levels measure progress in writing skills and fluency. At Levels A–C, the Read, Think, and Explain sections offer open-ended items to measure strategies and comprehension.

Writing Assessment
A Writing Progress Checklist is used to evaluate writing in The Basics. At Levels A–C, scoring rubrics offer guidance in evaluating students' work for the Writing Project in each unit. These rubrics assist teachers in assessing how students might score on a similar task if it were encountered on a standardized test by looking at content, form, and written conventions.

Self-Assessment and Peer-Assessment Forms
Students use these forms to evaluate their work and offer feedback to their classmates.

Portfolio Evaluation Form
Students and teachers use this form to evaluate progress shown by the work collected in the portfolio.

Diagnosis and Placement Inventory

Student Test

Teacher's Edition

Assessment Handbooks

The Basics

Level A

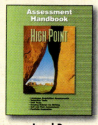
Level B

Level C

PROGRAM GUIDE FOR Assessment and Instruction

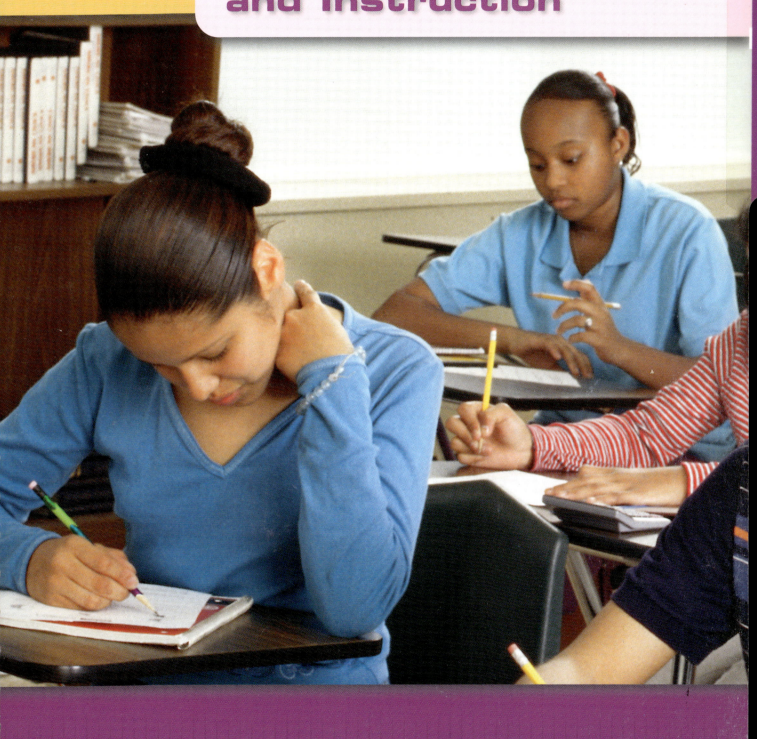

ASSESSMENT / INSTRUCTION

ASSESSMENT / INSTRUCTION

PROGRAM GUIDE FOR
Assessment and Instruction

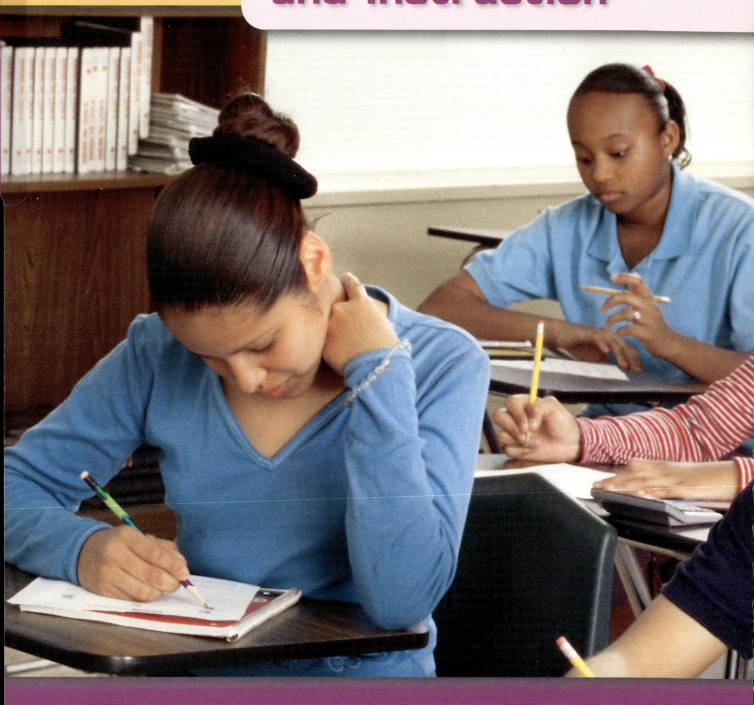

HIGH POINT

Program Guide for Assessment and Instruction

Program Goals and Organization

High Point offers standards-based instruction in reading and language arts. The program is carefully designed for English learners and struggling readers to accelerate their growth in language and literacy.

Four overlapping levels proceed on a continuum from The Basics, a beginning language and literacy level, to Level C, the most advanced level. From Level C, students move to study in mainstream materials.

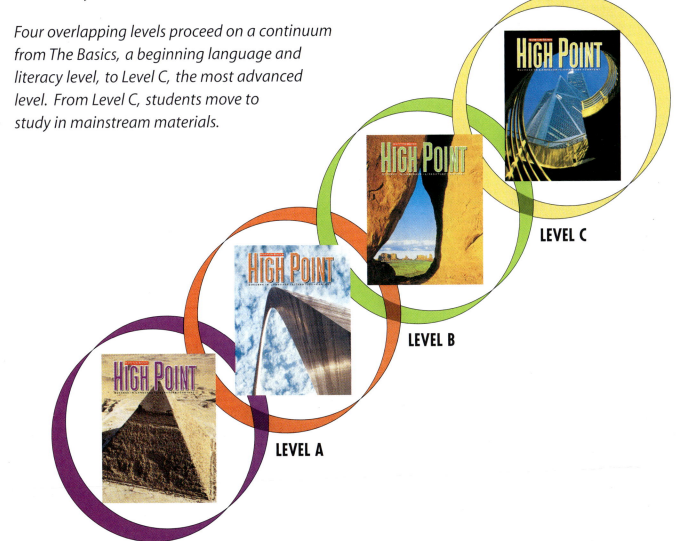

LEVEL C

LEVEL B

LEVEL A

THE BASICS

Program Guide

Identifying Students Who Need *High Point*

INITIAL IDENTIFICATION

High Point addresses the needs of struggling readers and English learners. To identify students who should study in *High Point*, consider information from assessments, such as the following:

- Standardized tests measure student performance in relation to a national norm. These tests report a student's percentile rank. Students scoring below the percentile rank set by your district, generally the 25th percentile, need the intervention program.

- Other tests report a student's reading level. Students whose reading level is two or more years below their grade level need the intervention program.

- A reading fluency measure, such as Edformation's *Standard Benchmark Reading Fluency Assessment Passages* available through Hampton-Brown, can also be used to determine reading level. Start by giving the student the fluency measure for the grade two years lower than the student's actual grade. If the number of words read correctly per minute by the student is lower than the mean for that grade level, the student should receive the intervention program.

- For English learners, districts are required to give a test that measures language proficiency level. Use the information from this test to identify students who need English language development.

The students identified for instruction in *High Point* come from a variety of backgrounds and educational experiences. Some have not yet learned to decode or have basic decoding skills but have not yet learned to apply them to multisyllabic words. Others possess decoding skills, but need to learn about text structures and the strategies of reading so that they can access grade-level materials and be successful in academic tasks.

Some English learners bring a solid educational foundation from their native country. In their home language they have developed academic skills that are on a par with their native English-speaking counterparts. Even if these students are literate in a language with a non-Roman alphabet and have the challenge of a new written code to crack, they already bring many of the skills and experiences they need to succeed in a structured academic setting.

Other English learners come from a patchwork of academic and life experiences. War, epidemics, natural disasters, or economic conditions may have caused students and their families to relocate within their home country or in other countries even before arriving in the U.S. School attendance may have been sporadic, with acquisition of skills and content more random than systematic. Limited academic experiences and the lack of formal literacy skills create special challenges for these students and their teachers.

High Point will help you meet these challenges. The Basics level teaches students how to decode and comprehend text up to a third-grade level. The direct, spiraling instruction in text structures, reading strategies, and comprehension skills in Levels A–C builds reading power, moving students to a sixth grade reading level. Coupled with the reading instruction is a complete language development strand to support English learners as well as struggling readers who may also need to broaden their vocabularies and to gain facility with the structures of English.

> **Correct placement is crucial to students' success in the program.**

DIAGNOSIS AND PLACEMENT

Correct placement is crucial to students' success in the program. The *Diagnosis and Placement Inventory* that accompanies *High Point* provides for six placement points into the materials. Students who need decoding skills will begin in The Basics level. See page 17 for the scope and sequence of decoding skills and the three placement points:

1. Non-readers and newly-arrived English learners will be placed at the beginning of the level.

2. Students with some literacy skills will be placed before the work on long vowels begins in Unit 5.

3. Students who can decode but still need to learn to apply their skills to multisyllabic words will be placed at Unit 14.

Students who have mastered decoding skills will be placed at the beginning of Level A, Level B, or Level C according to their reading level and the array of skills mastered on the *Diagnosis and Placement Inventory*.

16 Assessment

ASSESSMENT

Placement Points in *High Point*

The *Diagnosis and Placement Inventory* surveys students' reading and writing skills to present a student profile of strengths and weaknesses and place students into **High Point**. Students who are reading severely below grade level are likely to place in The Basics level because they need the phonics and decoding skills shown below. These are listed for the purpose of clarifying the placement points. The Basics level, like Levels A–C, contains a balance of skills in vocabulary development, reading comprehension, writing strategies and applications, and written and oral English conventions. The Student Profile that is generated from the administration of the *Diagnosis and Placement Inventory* presents a picture of where students stand in all these skills areas.

		THE BASICS Reading/Lexile Levels: Grades 1-3
Placement Point 1 →	LAKESIDE SCHOOL	Letters and Sounds
	UNIT 1	Short Vowels
	UNIT 2	Short Vowels and Digraphs
	UNIT 3	Short Vowels, Digraphs, and Double Consonants
	UNIT 4	Blends and Digraphs
Placement Point 2 →	UNIT 5	Long Vowels, Word Patterns, and Multisyllabic Words
	UNIT 6	Long Vowels and Word Patterns
	UNIT 7	Long Vowels and Word Patterns
	UNIT 8	Inflections
	UNIT 9	Inflections
	UNIT 10	Long Vowels
	UNIT 11	*R*-controlled Vowels
	UNIT 12	Multisyllabic Words
	UNIT 13	Words with *y*
Placement Point 3 →	UNIT 14	Diphthongs and Variant Vowels
	UNIT 15	Variant Vowels and Consonants
	UNIT 16	Multisyllabic Words
	UNIT 17	Multisyllabic Words (Suffixes and Prefixes)
	UNIT 18	Multisyllabic Words
Placement Point 4 →		**LEVEL A** Reading/Lexile Level: Grade 4
Placement Point 5 →		**LEVEL B** Reading/Lexile Level: Grade 5
Placement Point 6 →		**LEVEL C** Reading/Lexile Level: Grade 6

Program Guide **17**

Assessment to Inform Instruction

ASSESSMENT TOOLS

High Point offers a comprehensive array of assessment tools to inform instruction. These tools will help you place students into the program, monitor their progress, and evaluate their achievement both in language acquisition and in the language arts standards. These tools and the spiraling curriculum work together to ensure that students receive the instruction they need to accelerate their growth in language and literacy.

Assessment Tool	Description	Entry Level and Placement	Progress Monitoring	Summative Evaluation
Standard Benchmark Reading Fluency Assessment Passages	Three graded and equivalent passages are provided for each grade and are designed for administration at the beginning, middle, and end of the year. Administration of the passages identifies the student's fluency rate measured in words read correctly per minute (wcpm). This fluency rate can be compared to normative performance in order to identify students who need instruction in *High Point* or to assess their progress and achievement. Passages are available for license and downloading at www.edformation.com/hampton-brown .	✔	✔	✔
Diagnosis and Placement Inventory	This inventory surveys the skills taught in each level. It provides for six placement points into the program and gives a picture of the student's strengths and weaknesses in specific skills areas.	✔		
Language Acquisition Assessments	These assessments identify opportunities in each unit for performance assessments in which you can evaluate how well students demonstrate the language functions and structures targeted in the unit.		✔	
Decoding Progress Checks	At The Basics level, these word lists can be used on a weekly basis to monitor attainment of the targeted phonics skills.		✔	
Selection Tests	At Levels A–C, twenty tests, one per main selection, measure students' progress in reading strategies and vocabulary, comprehension, and language arts skills taught with the main selection.		✔	

ASSESSMENT

Assessment Tool	Description	Entry Level and Placement	Progress Monitoring	Summative Evaluation
Standard Progress Monitoring Reading Fluency Assessment Passages	Weekly graded and equivalent passages are provided for each grade. By measuring the number of words read correctly on the passages across several weeks, you can monitor a student's progress and plan effective instruction. Passages are available for license and downloading at www.edformation.com/hampton-brown .		✔	
Writing Assessments	At Levels A–C, these assessments, one per unit, provide rubrics and scoring guidelines for evaluating a student's writing in the mode and form targeted in each unit's writing project.		✔	
Writing Checklist / Writing Progress and Conference Form	These forms can be used to evaluate any writing done by the students and to hold writing conferences.		✔	
Self-Assessment Forms	These forms enable students to evaluate their own work.		✔	
Peer-Assessment Form	This form provides a vehicle for peer feedback on a variety of student work.		✔	
Portfolio Evaluation Form	This form serves as a record of both teacher- and student-selected samples in the portfolio and provides for summarizing performance.		✔	
Unit Tests	These tests, one for every three units at The Basics level and one for every unit at Levels A, B, or C, measure students' achievement.			✔
Student-Profile: Year-End	This form organizes information obtained from both formal and informal assessment and provides a permanent record of performance.			✔

Program Guide **19**

Reading Instruction in *High Point*

Learning to Read in The Basics

In each unit, students learn high frequency words, phonics skills, and decoding strategies, then apply them in decodable text.

❶ **The Basics** introduces 264 high frequency words. Students see them, hear them, say them, spell them, and use them in word work activities to help commit them to memory. They then read the words in context to develop automatic recognition.

High Frequency Word Instruction from Unit 11 of The Basics Student Book

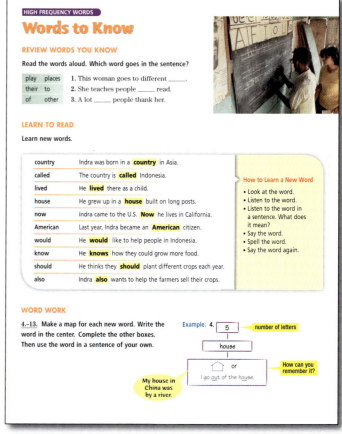

Practice

The **Reading Practice Book** and additional reinforcement activities in the Teacher's Edition provide sufficient repetitions to build skills mastery.

High Frequency Word Practice in the Reading Practice Book

20 Reading Instruction

❷ **Transparencies** help you build the meaning of words used in decoding activities, introduce phonics skills, model decoding strategies, and direct the guided practice. **Teacher Scripts** are in the Teacher's Edition and in a separate booklet to facilitate instruction at the overhead.

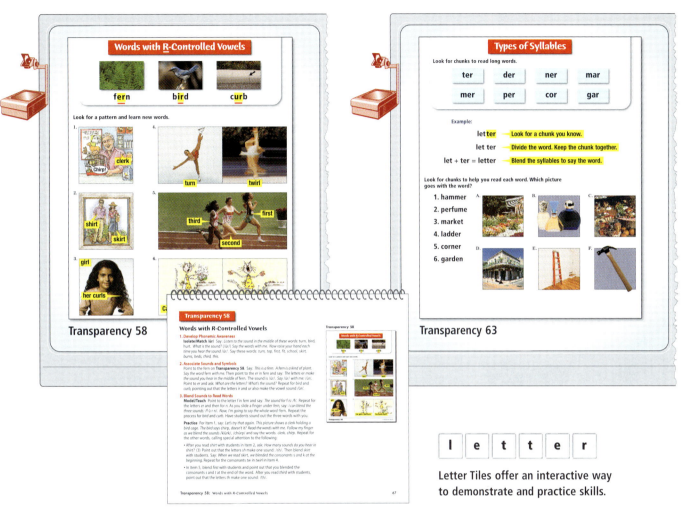

Transparency 58

Teacher Scripts

Transparency 63

Letter Tiles offer an interactive way to demonstrate and practice skills.

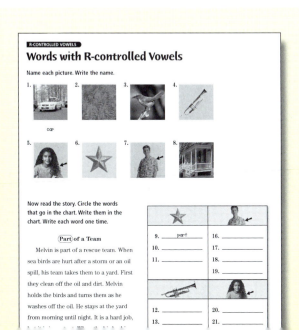

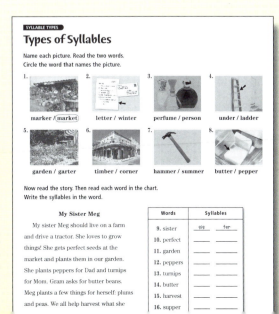

Phonics Practice and Decodable Text in the Reading Practice Book

Program Guide **21**

Learning to Read in The Basics, continued

❸ Next, in the Student Book, students review the skills, try the decoding strategy on their own, read decodable text, spell words with the new phonetic element, and participate in hands-on activities that anchor their understanding of the new skills.

Reading and Spelling Pages from Unit 11 of The Basics Student Book

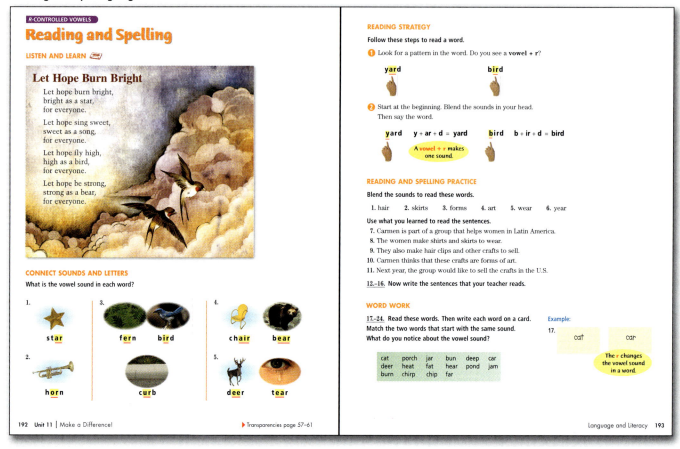

Practice

*The **Reading Practice Book** offers plenty of opportunities to read decodable text and build reading fluency.*

Unit 11 Decodable Book
(made from pages of the
Reading Practice Book)

22 Reading Instruction

READING INSTRUCTION

4 Students then apply phonics skills and read the pretaught high frequency words as they read and respond to a decodable selection.

Read on Your Own Pages from Unit 11 of The Basics Student Book

COMPREHENSION: CLASSIFY INFORMATION

Read on Your Own

Nadja Halilbegovich is from Bosnia.

Hafsat Abiola is from Nigeria.

Craig Kielburger is from Canada.

Kids Are Helping Kids

Kids can help other kids in important ways. Nadja, Hafsat, and Craig show us how.

Nadja helped kids in Bosnia. When Nadja was a girl, ethnic groups in Bosnia started a war. Kids lived in fear. A lot of them were hurt. Nadja started a radio show. She sang on the air to give children courage. She also published two books. They tell how hard it is to live through a war. She hopes her books will help end fighting in the world.

Hafsat helps kids in Nigeria. She formed a group called KIND. The group teaches children their rights. It shows kids how to be leaders. KIND also helps women and children get fair treatment.

Craig was 12 years old when he read that many kids were made to work in hard jobs for no pay. People treated them very badly. He had to help these kids. He formed a group called Free the Children. Now, his group speaks out for children's rights in 27 countries.

194 Unit 11 | Make a Difference!

CHECK YOUR UNDERSTANDING

1.–3. Copy the chart and then complete it.

Who Helped Others?	Where?	What Group of People Did He or She Help?	How?
1. Nadja Halilbegovich	Bosnia	children	She published two books. She started a radio show.

EXPAND YOUR VOCABULARY

4.–6. Tell a partner about each person on page 194. Use information from your chart and some of these words and phrases.

brings hope	fair treatment	hard jobs
sang on the air	rights	formed a group
war	published	Free the Children

Example: 4. Nadja published two books.
     The books tell about the war in Bosnia.

WRITE ABOUT PEOPLE

7. Choose one of the kids from page 194 or another person you know. Tell how the person makes a difference.

Example: 7. Craig helps kids who were made to work in hard jobs.
     He formed a group called Free the Children.

Language and Literacy 195

COMPREHENSION

Build Reading Fluency

Read the article. Stop when the timer goes off. Mark your score.
Then try it again two more times on different days.

Another Kid Helps Kids

Kimmie Weeks started making a difference when he was 10. The year was 1991. His country, Liberia, was at war. Many homes and schools were destroyed. Hundreds of children had no food. Many were sick. The fighting was so bad, children were trained to be soldiers. No one seemed to know what to do. Kimmie felt he had to help.

He and other kids started cleaning the streets. They picked up bricks, stones, and other trash left after the fighting. Then he started speaking on the radio. He said that children should not fight in war. His speeches helped. In 1996, Liberia stopped training children to fight.

Kimmie is now a young man. He is still helping the children of his country. He raises money to open more schools. Today, many children have better lives thanks to Kimmie Weeks.

Timed Passage for Reading Fluency from Unit 11 of the Reading Practice Book

Building Reading Power in Levels A–C

Once students have learned to decode in The Basics, they build reading power through the increasingly more difficult selections in Levels A–C.

Within and across levels:

- Reading level advances
- Length of selections increases
- Text density builds
- Picture/text correspondence decreases
- Vocabulary and concept loads progress
- Sentence structure and verb tenses increase in complexity

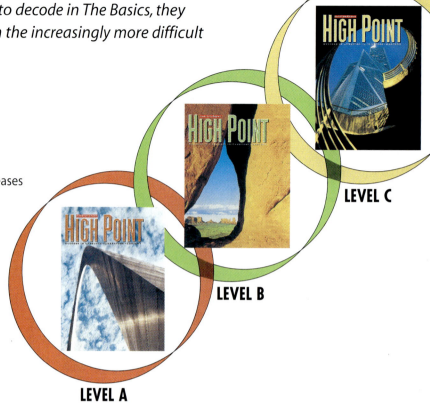

Level A

Level A Student Book

READING INSTRUCTION

Level B

1
THE SILENT YEARS

The twins' parents discover that Suzy and Neshy are deaf. They all learn sign language so everyone in the family can communicate with each other.

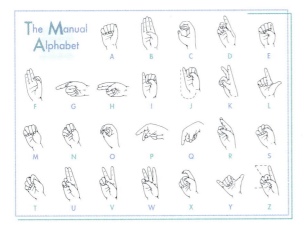

Early on they knew they were different from other children, because they were the only ones who shared a face. "They loved that about themselves," says Maria Aguayo, mother of Neshmayda and Suzette. "They had a way of communicating that no one else understood. One of them would point at something or make some noise and the other would go and get what she wanted." Two kids **cavorting through** a happy world of their own, experiencing life's surprises as one—in other words, twins.

But Suzy and Neshy were different for a much greater reason—they were born **deaf**.

"We did not know it for their first two-and-a-half years," says Maria, who **contracted** German measles during her first **trimester**. The technology in her native Puerto Rico was not as **advanced** as it is today, so her twins' deafness was not **diagnosed** until they were nearly three. "And when we first discovered they were deaf, I did not want to believe it. It was a mother's denial."

Maria soon accepted her daughters' **condition,** and as soon as she and her husband, Joaquin, heard about the Gallaudet school for the deaf in Washington, D.C., they moved their family and enrolled the twins, then five years old. "We all learned **sign language** so we could communicate with the girls," says Maria. "We started to talk about all the things that had happened to them in their first five years. I learned all these things that I had not known. For instance, Suzette had once been with her grandmother and **wound up** in the emergency room **getting stitches**. Her grandmother didn't know how she got hurt. Suzy later told me that she had fallen, that she was scared, that she wanted me there with her in the hospital **so badly**. When I discovered these things, I cried and cried."

Suzette (left) and Neshmayda (right) at age six. The twins are wearing hearing aids strapped to their chests as they enjoy a day at Baltimore's Inner Harbor.

BEFORE YOU MOVE ON...
1. **Inference** What do you think helped the twins form their own way of communicating?
2. **Cause and Effect** What caused the twins' deafness, and why did it take so long to diagnose?
3. **Prediction** Do you think the twins will remain close as they grow up? Why or why not?

cavorting through having fun in
deaf without the ability to hear

contracted got, caught
trimester three months of being pregnant
diagnosed discovered by doctors
sign language a way to communicate with our hands

wound up in the end was
getting stitches having her cut or wound closed by sewing
so badly so much

160 Unit 3 | Dreams and Decisions

Twins 161

Level B Student Book

Level C

3
CINQUÉ PLEADS FOR FREEDOM

Instead of Africa, the *Amistad* arrives in America. The Africans remain prisoners until Cinqué and his ally, John Adams, win their freedom in court.

But they had **claimed victory** too soon. Cinqué ordered the Spaniards to steer the ship toward the rising sun. They obeyed and sailed the ship east toward Africa during the day, but then at night turned the ship around and sailed northwest toward North America.

Then on August 27, 1839, the *Amistad* was **escorted** by an American ship into the harbor of New London, Connecticut. Weary, hungry, and hopelessly lost, Cinqué and the others were forced to come ashore.

An American naval lieutenant saw the possibility for quick **profits** in the Africans. But this was the North, and a group of whites and free blacks **campaigning against** the **institution of slavery** was gaining popularity. They called themselves **abolitionists**, and they took on Cinqué and the other Africans as their most important **case**.

The Africans were sent to prison in New Haven, Connecticut, until a decision could be made.

The abolitionists managed to find a translator, and Cinqué told his story in a U.S. court. He was only twenty-five years old, but his experience on the *Amistad* had given him the confidence of a much older man.

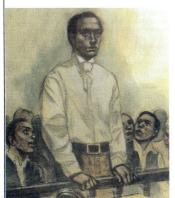

The courtroom was crowded, and many were moved by Cinqué's **impassioned words**.

"I am not here to argue the case against slavery," Cinqué said, "though I will say it is a sin against man and God. I am here to argue the facts. The **indisputable**, international law is that the stealing of slaves from Africa is now **illegal**."

"The men who kidnapped us, who beat and tortured us, were—and are—guilty of this crime," Cinqué continued.

"We are a peaceful people. We regret the loss of life caused by our **mutiny**. But we are not savages. We took over the ship to save our lives. We have done no wrong. Allow us to go home."

The weekend before the judge made his decision, Cinqué and his companions waited in the New Haven jail, their hearts filled with fear and hope. The judge held the power to make the Africans slaves or to set them free. On Monday morning, January 13, 1840, they worried no longer. He had decided they should be returned home.

They were free.

But as Cinqué was soon to learn, the passage to freedom was as winding as the *Amistad*'s journey across the sea. President Martin Van Buren, concerned that freeing the Mende would enrage southern slave holders, ordered the district attorney to **file an appeal** so the case would be heard in the U.S. Supreme Court. And because of this, Cinqué gained his greatest American **ally**: former president John Quincy Adams.

Having heard about the mutineers, Adams came out of **retirement** to argue Cinqué's case. He was seventy-two years old. It had been more than thirty years since he had argued a case in a courtroom, and the thought of bearing the responsibility for this one worried the elderly statesman deeply.

But inspired by Cinqué, whom many of the abolitionists had begun to refer to as the Black Prince, Adams tirelessly prepared his **defense**. In court he spoke on behalf of the Mende for eight and a half hours. Sweat poured from his brow, and his voice filled the packed courtroom as he presented his case.

claimed victory thought they won
pitched rocked
escorted guided, led, accompanied

profits earned money, income
campaigning against trying to convince others to stop
institution of slavery tradition of keeping slaves

impassioned words speech full of emotion
indisputable not-to-be-questioned
mutiny fight to take over the ship

file an appeal request a new trial
ally friend, supporter
retirement the private life he had since he quit working

170 Unit 3 | Conflict and Resolution

Amistad Rising 171

Level C Student Book

Program Guide 25

Explicit Skills Instruction

Instructional Overheads allow the teacher to present instruction explicitly.

TEXT FEATURES

This Overhead explains how to read for information. The Teacher's Edition tells the teacher how to model the skill and conduct guided practice. Students then apply the skill immediately as they read the article in the Student Book.

How to Read for Information

Directions: Use these strategies when you look at photos, maps, and diagrams.

Photos and Captions
1. Look at the photo. Ask yourself: What does it show?
2. Read the caption. Think about how it explains the photo.

Much of San Francisco was in ruins after the 1906 earthquake.

Maps
1. Use the compass rose to see which direction is north, south, east, and west on the map.
2. Use the legend to find out what symbols on the map mean.
3. Use the scale of miles to estimate distance.
4. Read titles or captions, to help you understand what the map shows.

California's San Andreas Fault

Diagrams
1. Look at the picture.
2. Read the labels, captions, and other text.
3. Describe what you see. Explain what the picture shows in your own words.

When plates move against each other, pressure is created.

Transparency 68   Level A, Unit 4 | Community   © Hampton-Brown

Level A Instructional Overhead

Level A Student Book

Hurricane in the Caribbean, 1998

Monday, September 21, 1998
Hurricane Georges Hits Puerto Rico

Hurricane Georges slammed into the island of Puerto Rico at around 6 p.m. today. Winds **reached** over 115 miles per hour. Airplanes flipped over like toys. Trees were **uprooted** and flew through the air like missiles. Over 80 percent of the island is without electricity. Seventy percent of all homes are without water.

Inside a Hurricane

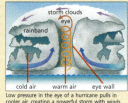

Low pressure in the eye of a hurricane pulls in cooler air, creating a powerful storm with winds over 74 miles per hour.

The path of Hurricane Georges

Tuesday, September 22, 1998
Georges Blasts Dominican Republic—Rescue Efforts Begin

Hurricane Georges spreads its destruction to the Dominican Republic. **Mudslides** and **flooding** kill over 200 people. More than 100,000 people are left **homeless**.

Meanwhile, rescue workers bring aid to Puerto Rico. More than 20,000 people **crowd into shelters** in San Juan and other cities.

Friday, September 25, 1998
Hurricane Relief Underway

Rescue workers in the Dominican Republic and Haiti **struggle** to bring food, water, and shelter to people. House after house **lies in ruins** or without a roof.

"There's no water. There's no power. There is nothing," says Domingo Osvaldo Fortuna as he fills a plastic jug with water from the garbage-filled Ozama River in Santo Domingo.

Aid from the United States begins to arrive. A French cargo plane brings **relief workers**, food, and medicine. Sixty-three firefighters from New York help to search for survivors.

Sunday, September 27, 1998
Hurricane Continues—Tons of Food On the Way

Tons of food and supplies begin to arrive in the Dominican Republic and Haiti. Volunteers fly in with tons of bottled water and enough **plastic sheeting** to repair 15,000 houses. Members of the U.S. military carry aid to towns **cut off by** flooding and mudslides.

Although it will take weeks or even years for the islands to **repair** the **damage**, **recovery** has slowly begun.

POINT-BY-POINT

HOW COMMUNITIES RESPOND TO DISASTERS

After a Hurricane:
- Emergency shelters are set up for people who are left homeless.
- Rescue workers bring food, water, and medicine to disaster victims.
- Rescue workers search for survivors.
- The international community sends aid to help victims recover and rebuild.

BEFORE YOU MOVE ON...

1. **Vocabulary** What words or phrases describe the strength of the hurricane?
2. **Cause and Effect** What problems did the hurricane cause?
3. **Details** How did other countries help the people on the islands?

---

reached got as fast as
uprooted pulled from the ground
Mudslides Rushing rivers of mud and rain
flooding water overflowing the banks of rivers
homeless without homes, with nowhere to live
crowd into are pushed together in
lies in ruins sits on the ground in pieces
Tons Several thousands of pounds
plastic sheeting waterproof covering
cut off by unable to have contact with the outside world because of
repair fix, correct

READING INSTRUCTION

TEXT STRUCTURES

This Overhead outlines the structures of different kinds of text and the corresponding reading strategies. The Teacher's Edition tells the teacher how to model the strategies and conduct guided practice. Students immediately apply the strategies to paired selections about ancient China, one fictional and one informational.

Level A Student Book: Fiction and Nonfiction

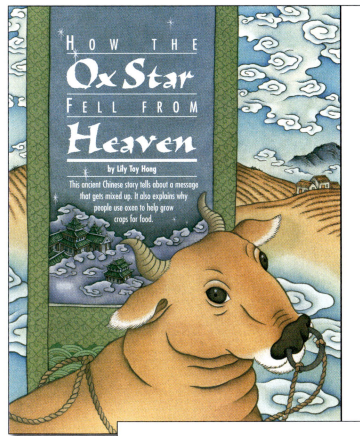

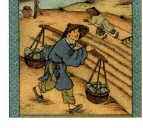

Level A Instructional Overhead

In the beginning, on Earth. They could o the heavens, among th with the Emperor of Al his Imperial Palace.

Clothed in robes of the finest **silk**, they **reclined** on **billowy** clouds. They never had to work, and their lives were easy.

Life on Earth was hard, especially hard since oxen did not live here. Farmers had no **beast of burden** to help with the planting of vegetables and rice in the spring, or with the gathering of **crops** at **harvest time**.

People were always tired and hungry. They **labored** from **sunup** to **sundown**, yet they could never finish all their work.

Because there was so little food, they sometimes went three, four, even five days without **one single meal**.

---

the heavens the sky
silk soft, shiny cloth
reclined leaned back, rested
billowy soft and fluffy
beast of burden animal used for heavy work
one single meal one meal to eat, anything to eat

BEFORE YOU MOVE ON...

1. **Details** What made life on Earth difficult for the farmers?
2. **Comparisons** How were the lives of the oxen and the humans different?
3. **Prediction** This story describes what life was like "in the beginning." How do you think the story may change by the end?

A Peasant's Life in
ANCIENT CHINA
an article by Shirleyann Costigan

Ancient China during the Zhou Dynasty, 1050 BCE–256 CE

Life was never easy for the peasant farmers of ancient China. They worked the earth, planted, and **harvested** the crops by hand. It was slow, **backbreaking** work. Around 700 BCE, many farmers began to use oxen or water buffalo to pull the plows and seed the fields. **Food production increased**. Everyone ate better. Life got a little easier, but not by much.

Most peasants lived in small villages near the **manor houses** of their **lords**. Their small huts were made of **packed earth** with dirt floors. Peasants rented the land they lived and worked on

In ancient China, the lords and scholars

Emperor
the Son of Heaven

Lords & Scholars
rulers of the land

Knights
protectors of the land

CLASSES OF SOCIETY IN ANCIENT CHINA, 700 BCE

There were three classes of people under the Emperor of ancient China. The people of each class had a place to fill in the Chinese order of life. The order rarely changed.

Peasant farmers worked from sunup to sundown all year long. They also had to work on roads and canals that ran through the countryside.

 Rice

Peasants grew their own food, as well as food for the ruling classes. Rice, soybeans, and millet were all common crops.

 Soybeans

 Millet

Spiraling Instruction

Instruction in **High Point** spirals across the levels and is tailored to students' increasing literacy and language skills.

Level A

This level introduces self-monitoring strategies. Teachers use the Instructional Overhead to model the strategy and conduct guided practice. Students then use a simple Note-Taking Chart to apply the strategy as they read.

Level A Instructional Overhead

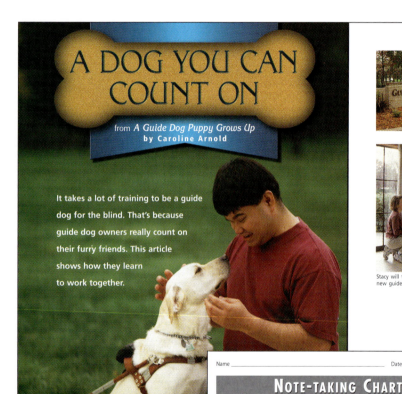

Level A Student Book

Level A Note-Taking Chart

Reading Instruction

READING INSTRUCTION

Levels B and C

These examples show the spiraling instruction. The Instructional Overhead introduces new aspects of the self-monitoring strategy—summarizing and predicting. Students use more advanced Note-Taking Charts as they read.

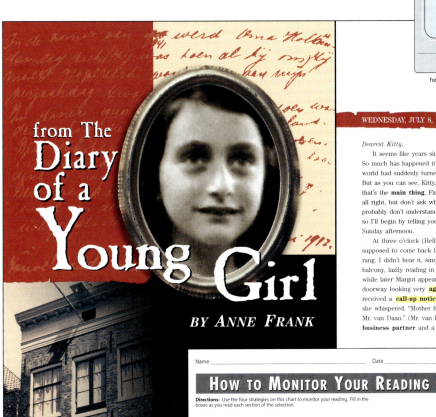

Level B Instructional Overhead

Level B Student Book

Level C Note-Taking Chart

Program Guide **29**

Extensive Practice

After reading, the Respond activities provide followup to the pretaught strategies and ensure ample skills practice.

Theme Book for Listening Comprehension and Main Idea Practice in The Basics

Reading Selection and Main Idea Practice in Level A

**MAIN IDEA AND DETAILS
The Basics**

**MAIN IDEA AND DETAILS
Level A**

Practice

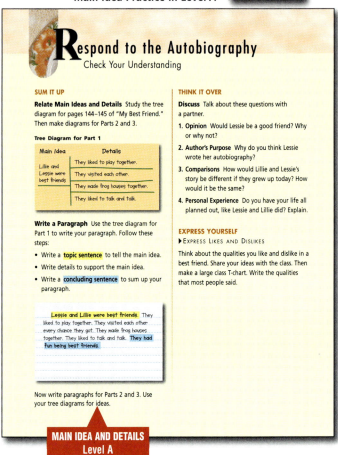

Main Idea Practice in the Reading Practice Book

30 Reading Instruction

READING INSTRUCTION

**Reading Selection and
Main Idea Practice in Level B**

**Reading Selection and
Main Idea Practice in Level C**

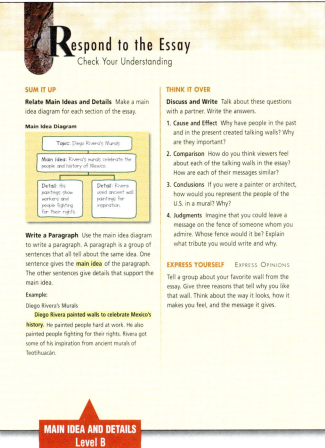

**MAIN IDEA AND DETAILS
Level B**

**MAIN IDEA AND DETAILS
Level C**

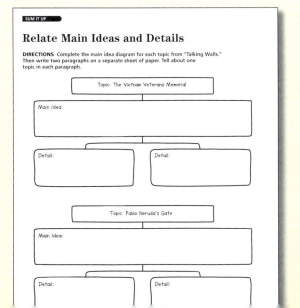

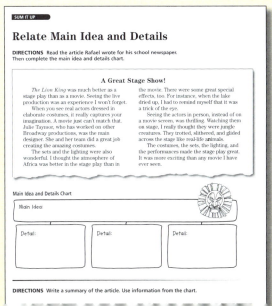

31

Language Development in *High Point*

Natural Language Models

Each theme begins with a song, poem, chant, story, or speech on tape. These interactive, motivational experiences spark language, model specific language functions or structures, and provide context for developing vocabulary and grammar skills.

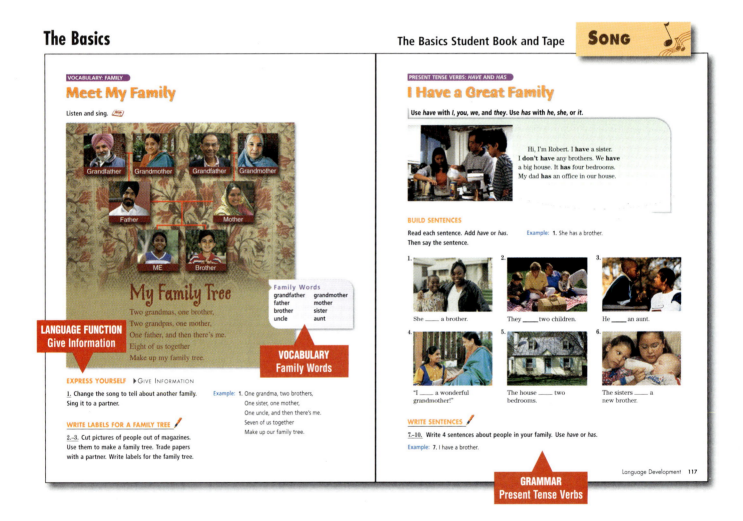

Level A

Level A Student Book and Tape **CHANT**

Build Language and Vocabulary
DESCRIBE

Listen to this rap about the gods and goddesses of ancient Greece.

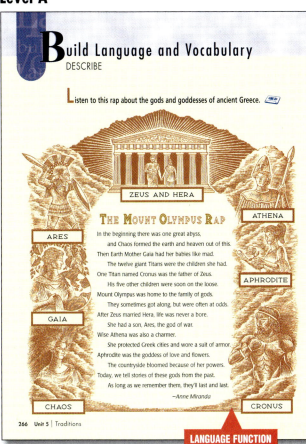

THE MOUNT OLYMPUS RAP

In the beginning there was one great abyss,
    and Chaos formed the earth and heaven out of this.
Then Earth Mother Gaia had her babies like mad.
    The twelve giant Titans were the children she had.
One Titan named Cronus was the father of Zeus.
    His five other children were soon on the loose.
Mount Olympus was home to the family of gods.
    They sometimes got along, but were often at odds.
After Zeus married Hera, life was never a bore.
    She had a son, Ares, the god of war.
Wise Athena was also a charmer.
    She protected Greek cities and wore a suit of armor.
Aphrodite was the goddess of love and flowers.
    The countryside bloomed because of her powers.
Today, we tell stories of these gods from the past.
    As long as we remember them, they'll last and last.

—Anne Miranda

266 Unit 5 | Traditions

LANGUAGE FUNCTION: Describe

MAKE A CHARACTER CHART
Work with the group to list all the characters in the poem on a chart. Also record what each character did. Follow this model:

Name	What Character Did
Chaos	formed earth and heaven
Gaia	had the 12 Titans

BUILD YOUR VOCABULARY
Describing Words Look at the pictures of the gods and goddesses on page 266. Think of a word to describe each one, or choose one from the **Word Bank**. Add a third column to your chart. In it, write a word to describe each character:

Name	What Character Did	What Character Was Like
Chaos	formed earth and heaven	powerful
Gaia	had the 12 Titans	strong

Word Bank
beautiful
big
dark
fierce
powerful
strong
tall
ugly

VOCABULARY: Describing Words

USE LANGUAGE STRUCTURES ▶ COMPLETE SENTENCES
Writing: Describe Greek Gods Choose a Greek god or goddess. Use the information from the character chart to write two complete sentences. Tell what the god or goddess did, and what he or she was like. Be sure each sentence includes a subject and a predicate.

Example:
Athena protected Greek cities. She was powerful.

GRAMMAR: Complete Sentences

Build Language and Vocabulary 267

Level B

Level B Student Book and Tape **STORY**

Build Language and Vocabulary
TELL A STORY

Listen to this tale from Vietnam about a rooster who learns what matters most to him.

The Rooster and the Jewel
A VIETNAMESE TALE

144 Unit 3 | Dreams and Decisions

LANGUAGE FUNCTION: Tell a Story

MAKE A STORY MAP
Work with a group to plan a story about something that matters most to you. Choose the object or event. Then fill out a story map to name the characters, tell the setting, and outline the events in the plot.

Characters — Setting
Beginning
Middle
Ending

BUILD YOUR VOCABULARY
Descriptive Words Think of words you will use to describe the story's characters and setting. Collect them in the charts.

Character	What is the character like?	What does the character do?	How, when, and where does the character do things?
Yolanda	young, smart	She skates. She seems to fly.	quickly, before dark, through the park

Setting	What can you see?	What can you hear?	What can you smell?	What can you taste?	What can you touch?
an afternoon in a park	trees, lake	birds, traffic	smoke, food cooking	hamburger	earth, grass

VOCABULARY: Describing Words, Story Elements

USE LANGUAGE STRUCTURES
▶ ADJECTIVES, ADVERBS, AND PREPOSITIONAL PHRASES

Speaking: Tell a Story Use your story map and the descriptive words in your charts to tell your story. Divide the story into parts so that each member of your group will have a part to tell.

Example:
Yolanda **quickly** gathered her skates and went **to the park**. She wanted to skate all **around the lake before dark**. She seemed to fly **through the park**, but then made a **sudden** stop. There **in the trees** she saw flames and smelled smoke. . . .

GRAMMAR: Adjectives, Adverbs, Prepositions

Build Language and Vocabulary 145

Program Guide 33

Systematic Grammar Instruction

The Instructional Overhead for Build Language and Vocabulary introduces the grammar skill. Followup lessons build skills in a logical sequence.

Instructional Overhead

ADD DETAILS TO SENTENCES

You can add adjectives, adverbs, or prepositional phrases to a sentence to make it more interesting.

A squirrel scrambles.

A <u>red</u> squirrel scrambles **quickly** across the garden.
  adjective   adverb   prepositional phrase

1. An **adjective** describes a noun or pronoun.
   The **huge** barn has a **blue** door. It is **full** of animals.

2. An **adverb** tells "how," "where," or "when." Adverbs usually tell more about a verb.
   We pet the bull **carefully**. The chickens live **outside**.

3. A prepositional phrase also tells "where" or "when." It starts with a **preposition** and ends with a noun or pronoun.
   The pigs live **across** the barnyard.
                         prepositional phrase

Try It!

Add details to these sentences. Use adjectives, adverbs, and prepositional phrases.

1. The rooster ran home.   3. The chicks found nothing to eat.
2. I lost the jewel.   4. I saw the animals.

GRAMMAR INTRODUCTION
Adjectives
Adverbs
Prepositions

Level B Student Book: Unit 3

Build Language and Vocabulary
TELL A STORY

Listen to this tale from Vietnam about a rooster who learns what matters most to him.

The Rooster and the Jewel
A VIETNAMESE TALE

MAKE A STORY

Work with a group... to you. Choose the... the characters, tel...

BUILD YOUR VO...

Descriptive Words Think of words you will use to describe the story's characters and setting. Collect them in the charts.

Character	What is the character like?	What does the character do?	How, when, and where does the character do things?
Yolanda	young, smart	She skates. She seems to fly.	quickly, before dark, through the park

Setting	What can you see?	What can you hear?	What can you smell?	What can you taste?	What can you touch?
an afternoon in a park	trees, lake	birds, traffic	smoke, food cooking	hamburger	earth, grass

USE LANGUAGE STRUCTURES
▶ ADJECTIVES, ADVERBS, AND PREPOSITIONAL PHRASES

Speaking: Tell a Story Use your story map and the descriptive words in your charts to tell your story. Divide the story into parts so that each member of your group will have a part to tell.

Example:
Yolanda **quickly** gathered her skates and went **to the park**. She wanted to skate all **around the lake before dark**. She seemed to fly **through the park**, but then made a **sudden** stop. There **in the trees** she saw flames and smelled smoke....

144   Unit 3 | Dreams and Decisions   Build Language and Vocabulary   145

Practice

*Abundant practice for each grammar skill in the **Language Practice Book** helps students master the complexities of English and transfer skills to writing.*

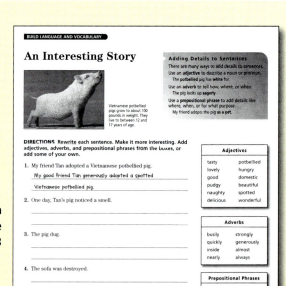

Grammar Practice in the Language Practice Book, Level B Unit 3

34   Language Development

LANGUAGE DEVELOPMENT

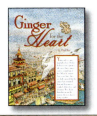

Level B Student Book: Unit 3

Level B Student Book: Unit 3

Respond to the Story, continued
Language Arts and Literature

GRAMMAR IN CONTEXT
USE ADJECTIVES

Learn About Adjectives An **adjective** is a word that describes, or tells about, a noun.

Adjectives can tell how many or how much.
  Yenna waited **four** years.
  Yenna had **little** interest in marrying.

Adjectives can tell which one.
  Yenna shook out the **first** shirt.

Adjectives can tell what something is like.
  The ginger was **fragrant** and **moist**.
  The **young** man asked Yenna to marry him.

Proper adjectives come from proper nouns. They begin with a capital letter.
  Chang was from China. He was **Chinese**.

Add Adjectives Expand these sentences with adjectives.
1. Yenna sewed with _____ needles and _____ thread.
2. The _____ man held the _____ ginger in his _____ hand.

Practice Write this paragraph. Add an adjective in each blank.

The _____ streets of Chinatown are interesting to see. There are _____ buildings. Some have _____ walls and _____ windows. One building has a _____ tower with _____ roof.

WRITING/SPEAKING
WRITE AN OUTCOME

Think of the new endings to the story you discussed with your group in the Sum It Up activity on page 155. How would the characters' actions change in order to cause a new outcome? Would their goals also change? Make a chart to organize your ideas. Then write the new outcome.

1. **Complete a Chart** Fill in a new Goal-and-Outcome Chart like the one you made on page 155.
2. **Write a Draft** Write the main events of the beginning, middle, and end of the new story. Include dialogue that shows what the characters' goals are.
3. **Edit Your Work** Add, change, or take out text to make your story more interesting. Do the characters have believable goals? What is the final outcome? Finally, check for correct spelling, punctuation, and grammar.
4. **Read and Discuss** Read your work in a group. Discuss the goals and actions that caused the new outcomes.

For more about the **writing process**, see Handbook pages 408–413.

GRAMMAR REVIEW
Adjectives

Respond to the Article, continued
Language Arts and Literature

GRAMMAR IN CONTEXT
USE ADJECTIVES THAT COMPARE

Learn About Comparative Adjectives A **comparative adjective** compares two things. To make the comparison, add **–er** to the adjective and use the word **than**.

  Neshy's hair is **longer than** Suzy's.

If the adjective is a long word, use **more** or **less**.
  Neshy is **more independent than** Suzy.

Learn About Superlative Adjectives A **superlative adjective** compares three or more things. Add **–est** to the adjective. Use **the** before the adjective.
  Suzy is **the fastest** runner in her class.

If the adjective is long, use **the most** or **the least**.
  The most important thing to the twins is staying in touch.

Practice Write these sentences. Use the correct form of the adjective in parentheses.
1. Some hearing-impaired people have a (great) hearing loss than others do.
2. Gallaudet is perhaps the (fine) school in the world for hearing-impaired students.
3. When they learned sign language, the twins were (confident) than before.
4. The (difficult) time of all came after the twins were separated.

TECHNOLOGY/MEDIA
WRITING
WRITE TO A TWIN

With a partner, take the roles of Suzy and Neshy. Pretend that you have been apart for one month. Write a series of letters or e-mails to each other.

1. **Choose a Topic** Here are some possible topics for your first letters:
   • future dreams or plans
   • life in your new city or home
   • an upcoming visit
   • family and friends
2. **Start the Series** One partner writes the first letter or e-mail. The other partner reads it and writes back. Write several more letters or e-mails back and forth.
3. **Check Your Work** Check your work before sending it to your "twin." Check for correct spelling and punctuation.

For more about **e-mail**, see Handbook page 382.

SEQUENTIAL GRAMMAR SKILL
Comparative Adjectives

GRAMMAR: ADJECTIVES

Historic Letters

Adjectives
An **adjective** describes a noun or pronoun. Adjectives can tell how many, how much, which one, or what something is like.
  The **second** letter describes the important rooms in the **grand** Empire Hotel.
A **proper adjective** comes from a proper noun.
  The letters bring **American** history to life.

DIRECTIONS Work with a small group. Read the article. Circle the adjectives. Write each adjective in the correct column of the chart.

In 1850, a boat sailed into the (crowded) harbor in San Francisco. On the boat were Louise Clappe, her husband, and her two sisters. They had come all the way from (central) Massachusetts. Leaving his wife in San Francisco, Dr. Fayette Clappe traveled to a rough camp in the Sierras to open a medical practice. Eventually, Louise joined him.

Over fifteen months, Louise wrote twenty-three letters from the camps. Her first letter describes her wild journey to the camp. The letters describe a distant time in American history. They tell about the French and Spanish miners and people from around the world. They describe the steep mountains, the brilliant river, and the crude buildings.

Louise wrote her last letter in November, 1852. After that, she returned to San Francisco and taught school for twenty-four years. She died in New Jersey in 1906.

How Many/ How Much	Which One	What Something Is Like	Proper Adjectives
1. ___	5. central	9. crowded	16. ___
2. ___	6. ___	10. ___	17. ___
3. ___	7. ___	11. ___	18. ___
4. ___	8. ___	12. ___	
		13. ___	
		14. ___	
		15. ___	

GRAMMAR: ADJECTIVES THAT COMPARE

Family Comparisons

Whitewater rafting is a thrilling adventure for many.

Adjectives That Compare
A **comparative adjective** compares two things.
  My sister is **quieter** than I am.
  She is **less sociable** than me, too.
A **superlative adjective** compares three or more things.
  I am the **friendliest** person in the family.
  I am the **most sociable** person in my home!
Use **–er** and **–est** for most two-syllable adjectives. Use **less** / **more** and **least** / **most** for words with three or more syllables.

DIRECTIONS Complete each sentence. Write the correct form of the adjective in parentheses.

1. Jayesh is ___more adventurous___ than his twin brother, Kuval. (**adventurous**)
2. He wants to raft down the _____ river in the West. (**wild**)
3. He wants to climb the _____ peak on the continent. (**high**)
4. Jayesh is _____ than Kuval. (**studious**)
5. Kuval is _____ than his brother. (**calm**)
6. To Kuval, drawing is the _____ thing in the world! (**exciting**)

DIRECTIONS Write sentences to compare people you know. Use the correct forms of the adjectives in the box or some of your own.

7. My sister is less confident than I am.
8. _____
9. _____
10. _____

creative
independent
tidy
nice
confident
funny
strong

More Practice on Adjectives in the Language Practice Book, Level B Unit 3

35

Writing Instruction in *High Point*

Fundamentals of Writing

The Basics level addresses the fundamentals of writing—from sentences to an expository paragraph.

The Basics Student Book

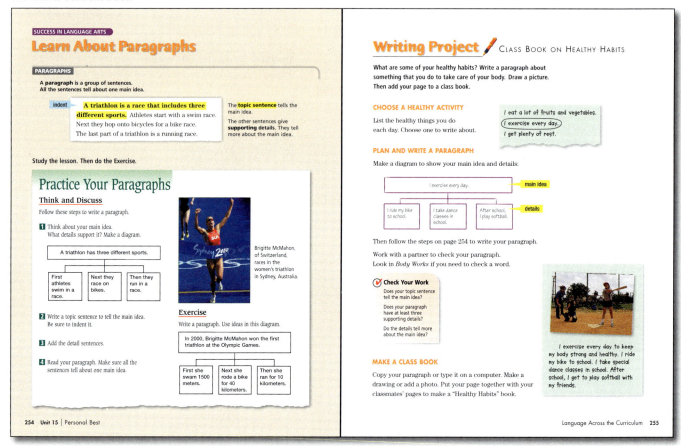

Writing Support

Writing instruction is scaffolded to ensure success.

Drafting Support

Writing Strategies and Applications

Writing Projects in each unit give experience with the modes and forms of writing represented in the standards and assessed on standardized tests.

THE WRITING PROCESS AT LEVELS A–C

- Students first study the writing mode through professional and student models and explore ways to organize their writing.

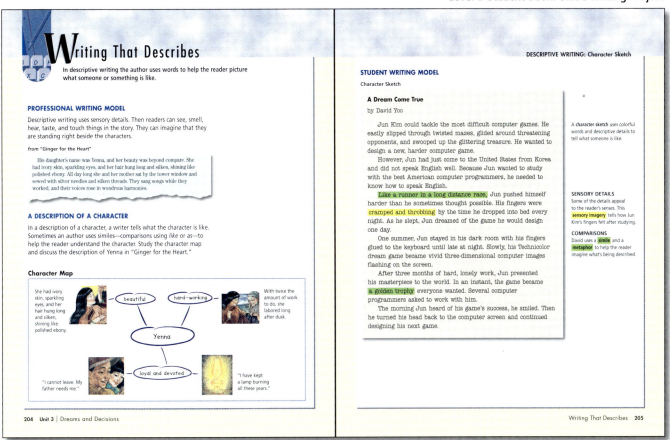

Level B Student Book: Unit 3 Writing Project

Support for Studying Writing Models

Writing Strategies and Applications, continued

THE WRITING PROCESS AT LEVELS A–C

- Next, students are guided step-by-step through the entire writing process with visual support.
- The Reflect and Evaluate features challenge students to self-assess so they can continually improve their writing.
- The Writer's Craft teaches such skills as word choice and elaboration to help students shape their writing. Language models illustrate quality differences.

Level B Student Book: Unit 3 Writing Project

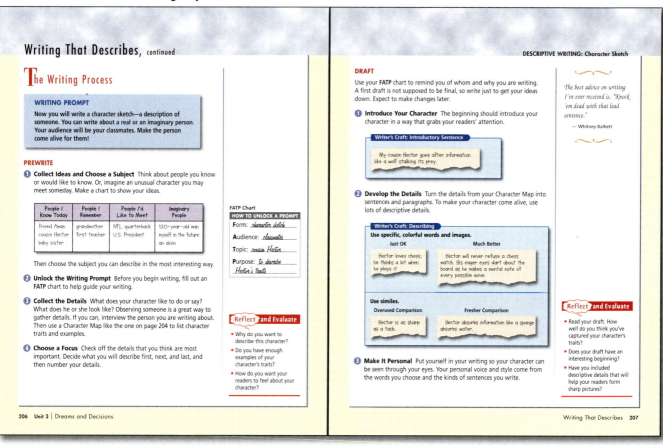

Prewriting Support

Level B

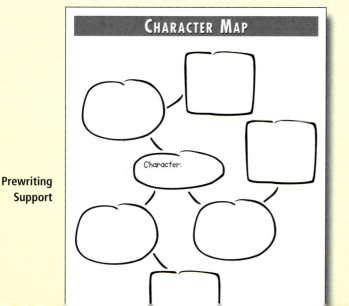

Writer's Craft Support

Level B

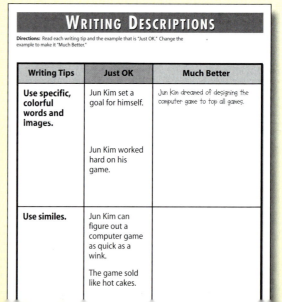

WRITING INSTRUCTION

THE WRITING PROCESS AT LEVELS A–C

- Revising strategies model language for effective participation in peer conferences.
- Technology features help students learn to write and revise their work on the computer.
- Grammar in context relates the unit's grammar focus to the writing.

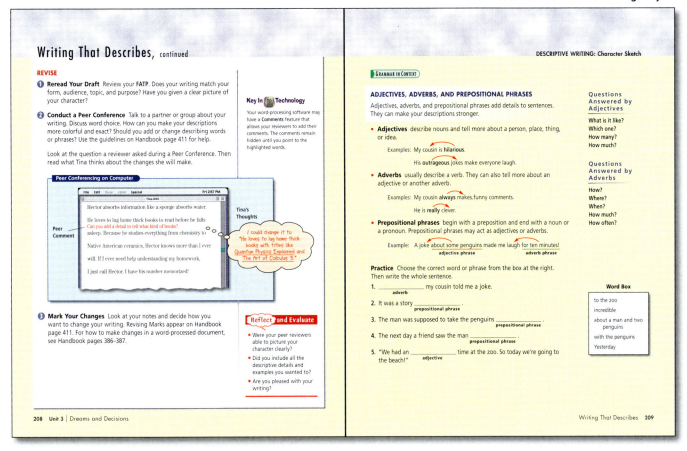

Level B Student Book: Unit 3 Writing Project

Level B

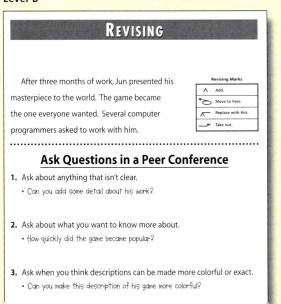

Revising Support

Writing Strategies and Applications, continued

THE WRITING PROCESS IN LEVELS A–C

- Editing and proofreading strategies help students achieve accuracy in written conventions.
- Technology features help students edit and publish work on the computer.

Level B Student Book: Unit 3 Writing Project

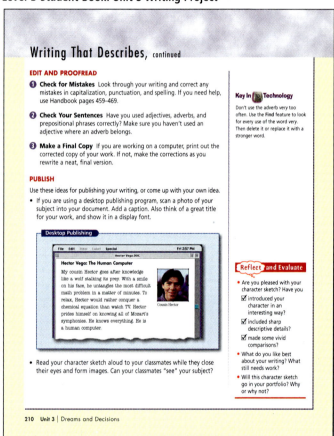

Practice in Written Conventions

Editing and Proofreading Support

WRITING INSTRUCTION

Written Conventions

Handbooks at each level support students in applying the written conventions of English.

Grammar Support in Handbook

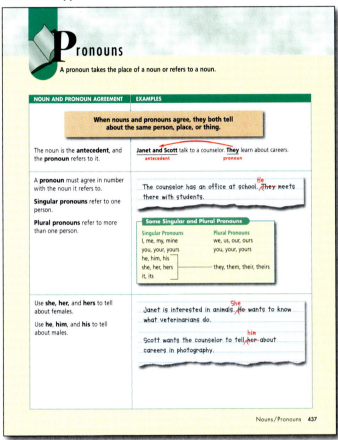

Punctuation Support in Handbook

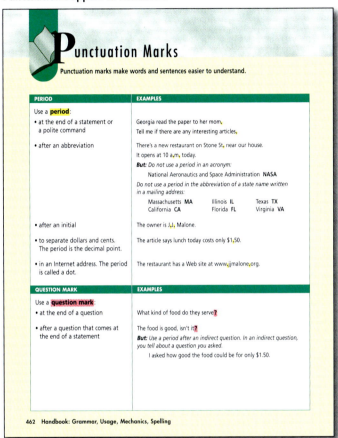

Level A

Level A

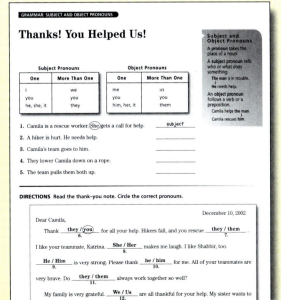

Extensive Pronoun Practice in the Practice Books

Program Guide **41**

Pacing Options

High Point is a flexible program whose pacing can be adjusted to one-hour, two-hour, or three-hour sessions.

The Basics

This level of *High Point* contains 18 units and an optional unit called Lakeside School. See page T10e of The Basics Teacher's Edition for the recommended pacing of Lakeside School.

3-HOUR INTERVENTION PACING
In this model, each unit takes one week. (Number of lessons in a unit varies from 13 to 16.)

UNIT 11	Day 1	Day 2	Day 3	Day 4	Day 5
Language Development (1 hour)	**Lesson 1** Introduce the Unit **Lesson 2** Vocabulary or Grammar Lesson	**Lessons 3–4** Vocabulary or Grammar Lessons	**Lesson 5** Vocabulary or Grammar Lesson **Lesson 12** Content Area Connection	**Lesson 13** Writing Project	**Lesson 13 (cont.)** Writing Project
Language and Literacy (2 hours)	**Lesson 6** The Basics Bookshelf: Theme Book Read-Alouds	**Lesson 8** High Frequency Words **Lesson 9 (Part 1)** Phonemic Awareness and Phonics	**Lesson 7** The Basics Bookshelf: Theme Book Comprehension and Retelling **Lesson 9 (Part 2)** Phonemic Awareness and Phonics	**Lesson 10** Reading and Spelling with Practice in Decodable Text	**Lesson 11** Independent Reading (decodable text), Comprehension, and Reading Fluency

DAILY PERIOD PACING
In this model, each unit takes about two weeks to complete.

UNIT 11 (Week 1)	Day 1	Day 2	Day 3	Day 4	Day 5
Language Development and Literacy (1 hour)	**Lesson 1** Introduce the Unit **Lesson 2** Vocabulary or Grammar Lesson	**Lessons 3–4** Vocabulary or Grammar Lessons	**Lesson 5** Vocabulary or Grammar Lesson **Lesson 6** The Basics Bookshelf: Theme Book Read-Alouds	**Lesson 7** The Basics Bookshelf: Theme Book Comprehension and Retelling	**Lesson 8** High Frequency Words **Lesson 9 (Part 1)** Phonemic Awareness and Phonics

UNIT 11 (Week 2)	Day 6	Day 7	Day 8	Day 9	Day 10
Language Development and Literacy (1 hour)	**Lesson 9 (Part 2)** Phonemic Awareness and Phonics	**Lesson 10** Reading and Spelling with Practice in Decodable Text	**Lesson 11** Independent Reading (decodable text), Comprehension, and Reading Fluency	**Lesson 12** Content Area Connection **Lesson 13** Writing Project	**Lesson 13 (cont.)** Writing Project

BLOCK SCHEDULE PACING
In this model, two or three sessions occur each week, so each unit takes about two weeks.

UNIT 11	Session 1	Session 2	Session 3	Session 4	Session 5	Session 6
Language Development (1 hour)	**Lesson 1** Introduce the Unit **Lesson 2** Vocabulary or Grammar Lesson	**Lessons 3–4** Vocabulary or Grammar Lessons	**Lesson 5** Vocabulary or Grammar Lesson	**Lesson 12** Language Across the Curriculum	**Lesson 13** Writing Project	**Lesson 13 (cont.)** Writing Project
Language and Literacy (1 to 1 ½ hours)	**Lesson 6** The Basics Bookshelf: Theme Book Read-Alouds	**Lesson 7** The Basics Bookshelf: Theme Book Comprehension and Retelling **Lesson 8** High Frequency Words	**Lesson 9 (Part 1)** Phonemic Awareness and Phonics	**Lesson 9 (Part 2)** Phonemic Awareness and Phonics	**Lesson 10** Reading and Spelling with Practice in Decodable Text	**Lesson 11** Independent Reading (decodable text), Comprehension, and Reading Fluency

PACING OPTIONS

Levels A–C

Levels A–C of *High Point* each contain 5 units. Each unit contains 2 themes.

3-HOUR INTERVENTION PACING

In this model, each unit takes approximately 3 weeks. (Number of lessons per theme varies.)

LEVEL A, UNIT 1	Day 1	Day 2	Day 3	Day 4	Day 5
THEME 1	**THEME 1** **Lesson 1** • Introduce the Theme **Lesson 2** • Build Language and Vocabulary	**Lesson 3** Prepare to Read • Vocabulary • Reading Strategy **Lessons 4–5** Read the Selection	**Lesson 6** Respond to the Selection • Check Your Understanding activities **Lesson 7** Respond to the Selection • Language Arts and Literature activities	**Lesson 8** Respond to the Selection • Content Area Connections **Conduct Grammar Minilesson**	**Lesson 9** Build Language and Vocabulary **Lesson 10** Prepare to Read • Vocabulary • Reading Strategy

LEVEL A, UNIT 1	Day 6	Day 7	Day 8	Day 9	Day 10
THEME 1 and THEME 2	**Lessons 11–12** Read the Selection **Lesson 13** Respond to the Selection • Check Your Understanding activities	**Lesson 14** Respond to the Selection • Language Arts and Literature activities **Conduct Grammar Minilesson**	**Lesson 15** Respond to the Selection • Content Area Connections **Conduct Research Skills Minilesson**	**THEME 2** **Lesson 1** • Introduce the Theme **Lesson 2** Build Language and Vocabulary **Lesson 3** Prepare to Read • Vocabulary • Reading Strategy	**Lessons 4–5** Read the Selection **Lesson 6** Respond to the Selection • Check Your Understanding activities **Conduct Grammar Minilesson**

LEVEL A, UNIT 1	Day 11	Day 12	Day 13	Day 14	Day 15
THEME 2	**Lesson 7** Respond to the Selection • Language Arts and Content Area Connections **Conduct Grammar Minilesson**	**Lesson 8** Build Language and Vocabulary **Lesson 9** Prepare to Read • Vocabulary • Reading Strategy **Lessons 10–11** Read the Selection	**Lesson 12** Respond to the Selection • Check Your Understanding activities **Lesson 13** Respond to the Selection • Language Arts and Literature	**Lesson 14** Respond to the Selection • Content Area Connections **Conduct Grammar Minilesson**	**Lesson 15** Prepare to Read • Vocabulary • Reading Strategy **Lesson 16** Read and Respond to the Poem **Unit Debrief and Assessment**
Writing Project		Study Writing Models Write Together	Prewrite Draft	Revise Grammar in Context	Edit and Proofread Publish

The intervention program will last two years for the student who places at the beginning of The Basics.

YEAR 1 33–36 weeks	**The Basics**	18-21 weeks
	Level A	15 weeks
YEAR 2 30 weeks	**Level B**	15 weeks
	Level C	15 weeks

DAILY PERIOD PACING

In this model, each unit takes 6-7 weeks to complete. The Activity Planners at the start of each unit in the Levels A–C Teacher's Editions show how to divide the units into daily periods. In general, each lesson takes about a day and the Writing Project is spread across the last week of each unit.

BLOCK SCHEDULE OR 2-HOUR SESSION PACING

In this model, two or three block schedule sessions occur each week such that each unit takes 6-7 weeks to complete. The Activity Planners at the start of each unit in the Levels A–C Teacher's Editions show how to divide the units into block schedule sessions. In general, two lessons can be completed per session and the Writing Project is spread across the last two weeks of the unit.

Program Guide **43**

Practice Book Contents and Homework Opportunities

Unit 1 Glad to Meet You!

RPB
- High Frequency Words **38**
- Short *a*, Short *o* **39, 40**
- Comprehension: Reading Fluency **41**

LPB
- Pronouns **40, 41**
- Present Tense Verbs: *am, is,* and *are* **42**
- Vocabulary: Communication **43**
- Statements and Exclamations **44**
- Writing Project: Postcard **45**

Unit 2 Set the Table

RPB
- High Frequency Words **42**
- Short *i*, Short *u* **43, 44**
- Comprehension: Reading Fluency **45**

LPB
- Vocabulary: Colors, Shapes, and Sizes **46**
- Vocabulary: Foods **47**
- Action Verbs **48**
- Negative Sentences **49**
- Writing Project: Exhibit Card **50**

Unit 3 On the Job

RPB
- High Frequency Words **46**
- Short *e* and *ck* **47**
- *ck* and Double Consonants **48**
- Comprehension: Reading Fluency **49**

LPB
- Vocabulary: Actions/Careers **51**
- Present Tense Verbs **52**
- Vocabulary: Tools and Careers **53**
- Questions **54**
- Writing Project: Job Handbook **55**

Unit 4 Numbers Count

RPB
- High Frequency Words **50**
- Blends **51**
- Digraphs **52**
- Comprehension: Reading Fluency **53**

LPB
- Questions with *Do* and *Does* **56**
- Vocabulary: Cardinal Numbers **57**
- Negative Sentences **58**
- Vocabulary: Ordinal Numbers **59**
- Contractions with *not* **60**
- Writing Project: Fact Sheet **61**

Unit 5 City Sights

RPB
- High Frequency Words **54**
- Word Patterns: CV, CVC, CVCC **55**
- Word Patterns and Multisyllabic Words **56**
- Comprehension: Reading Fluency **57**

LPB
- Vocabulary: Location Words **62**
- Vocabulary: Neighborhood **63**
- Regular Past Tense Verbs **64, 65**
- Statements with *There is* and *There are* **66**
- Pronoun-Verb Contractions **67**
- Writing Project: Journal Entry **68**

Unit 6 Welcome Home!

RPB
- High Frequency Words **58**
- Long Vowels: *a, i, o, u* **59**
- Long and Short Vowels: *a, i, o, u* **60**
- Comprehension: Reading Fluency **61**

LPB
- Vocabulary: Family **69**
- Present Tense Verbs: *has* and *have* **70**
- Vocabulary: Household Objects **71**
- Plural Nouns **72**
- Writing Project: Class Travel Book **73**

Unit 7 Pack Your Bags!

RPB
- High Frequency Words **62**
- Long Vowels: *ai, ay; ee, ea; oa, ow* **63**
- Word Patterns: CV, CVC, CVCC **64**
- Multisyllabic Words; Compound Words **65**
- Comprehension: Reading Fluency **66**

LPB
- Commands **74**
- Vocabulary: Landforms and Transportation **75**
- Vocabulary: Weather and Clothing **76**
- Verbs: *can* **77**
- Capitalization: Proper Nouns **78**
- Writing Project: Class Travel Book **79**

Unit 8 Friend to Friend

RPB
- High Frequency Words **67**
- Verb Ending: *-ed* **68, 69**
- Comprehension: Reading Fluency **70**

LPB
- Regular Past Tense Verbs **80**
- Vocabulary: Feelings **81**
- Irregular Past Tense Verbs: *was* and *were* **82**
- Negative Sentences and Contractions with *not* **83**
- Possessive Nouns **84**
- Writing Project: Friendship Book **85**

Unit 9 Let's Celebrate!

RPB
- High Frequency Words **71**
- Verb Ending: *-ing* **72**
- Comprehension: Reading Fluency **73**

LPB
- Adverbs **86**
- Present Progressive Verbs **87**
- Vocabulary: Country Words **88**
- Phrases with *like to* and *want to* **89**
- Writing Project: Celebration Poster **90**

Unit 10 Here to Help

RPB
- High Frequency Words **74**
- Long Vowels: *ie, igh, ui, ue* **75**
- Comprehension: Reading Fluency **76**

LPB
- Verbs: *may, might,* and *could* **91**
- Vocabulary: Time **92**
- Phrases with *have to* and *need to* **93**
- Possessive Pronouns **94**
- Writing Project: Job Advertisement **95**

Unit 11 Make a Difference!

RPB
- High Frequency Words **77**
- R-Controlled Vowels **78, 79**
- Comprehension: Reading Fluency **80**

LPB
- Irregular Past Tense Verbs **96**
- Vocabulary: Direction Words **97**
- Vocabulary: Civil Rights **98**
- Irregular Past Tense Verbs **99**
- Writing Project: Mandala **100**

Unit 12 Our Living Planet

RPB
- High Frequency Words **81**
- Syllable Types **82**
- Comprehension: Reading Fluency **83**

LPB
- Vocabulary: Opinion Words **101**
- Vocabulary: Animals and Habitats **102**
- Vocabulary: Plants and Habitats **103**
- Sensory Adjectives **104**
- Writing Project: Fact-and-Opinion Poster **105**

Unit 13 Past and Present

RPB
- High Frequency Words **84**
- Words with *y* **85, 86**
- Comprehension: Reading Fluency **87**

LPB
- Vocabulary: Historical Records **106**
- Nouns **107**
- Present and Past Tense Verbs **108**
- Object Pronouns **109**
- Writing Project: Comparison Poster **110**

Unit 14 Tell Me More

RPB
- High Frequency Words **88**
- Diphthongs **89**
- Variant Vowels **90**
- Comprehension: Reading Fluency **91**

LPB
- Vocabulary: Story Elements **111**
- Vocabulary: Opposites **112**
- Vocabulary: Phrases for Times and Places **113**
- Commands **114**
- Writing Project: New Story Ending **115**

Unit 15 Personal Best

RPB
- High Frequency Words **92**
- Variant Consonants **93**
- Variant Vowels and Silent Consonants **94**
- Comprehension: Reading Fluency **95**

LPB
- Vocabulary: The Body **116**
- Present Tense Verbs **117**
- Vocabulary: Sports **118**
- Pronouns **119**
- Writing Project: Class Book **120**

Unit 16 This Land Is Our Land

RPB
- High Frequency Words **96**
- Multisyllabic Words **97, 98**
- Comprehension: Reading Fluency **99**

LPB
- Vocabulary: American History **121**
- Questions with *How?* and *Why?* **122**
- Vocabulary: Landforms and Bodies of Water **123**
- Capitalization: Proper Nouns **124**
- Writing Project: Biographical Sketch **125**

Unit 17 Harvest Time

RPB
- High Frequency Words **100**
- Suffixes **101, 102**
- Prefixes **103**
- Comprehension: Reading Fluency **104**

LPB
- Questions: *How many? How much?* **126**
- Vocabulary: Farming **127**
- Vocabulary: At the Restaurant **128**
- Sensory Adjectives **129**
- Writing Project: Crop Report **130**

Unit 18 Superstars

RPB
- High Frequency Words **105**
- Multisyllabic Words **106, 107, 108**
- Comprehension: Reading Fluency **109**
- Timed Reading Chart **110**

LPB
- Vocabulary: Idioms **131**
- Future Tense Verbs and Contractions **132**
- Vocabulary: Space **133**
- Verb Tenses: Present, Past, and Future **134, 135**
- Writing Project: Diamante Poem **136**

RPB: Reading Practice Book
LPB: Language Practice Book

• **Homework Opportunity**

LESSON PLANS FOR Carlos Comes to Lakeside School

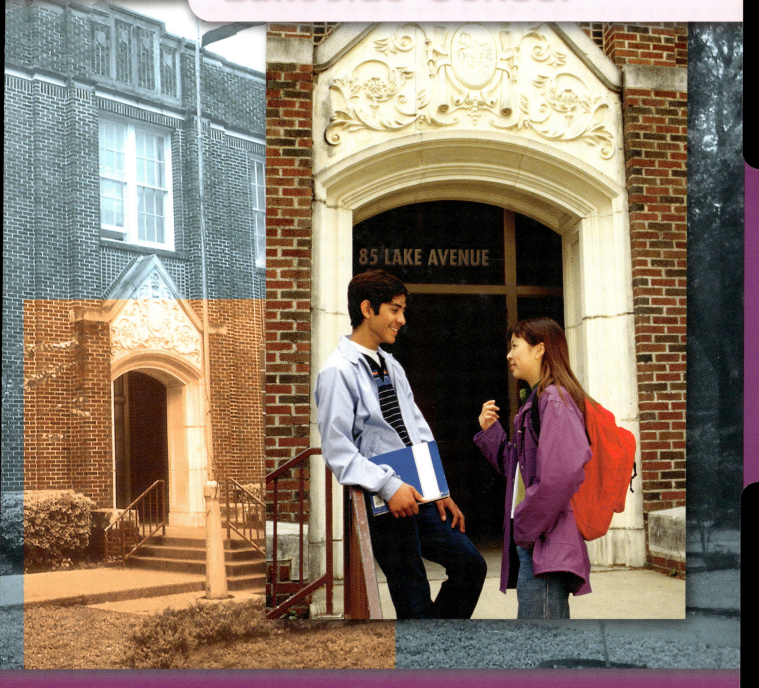

LAKESIDE SCHOOL

LESSON PLANS FOR
Carlos Comes to Lakeside School

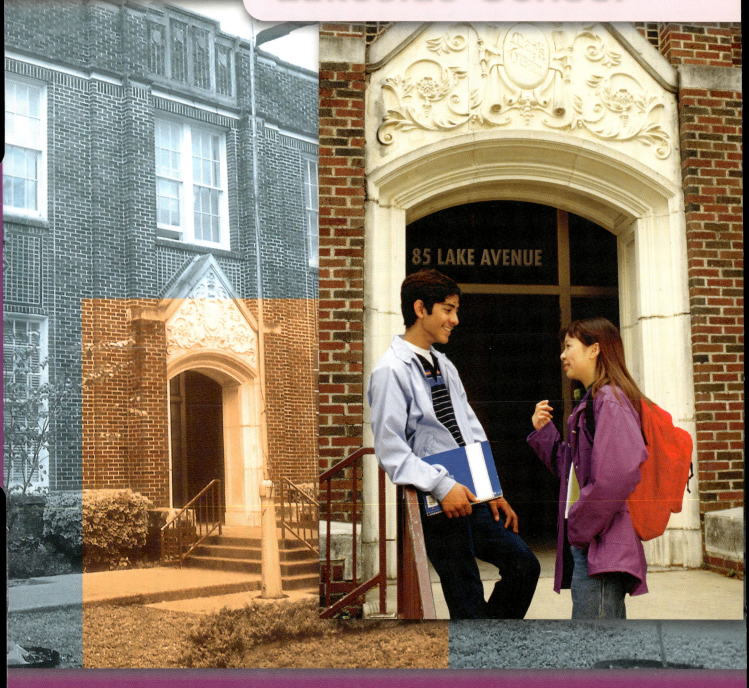

LAKESIDE SCHOOL

Resources

For Success in Language and Literacy

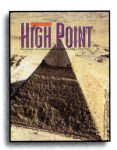

Student Book pages 10–39

For Language Skills Practice

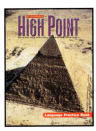

Language Practice Book pages 1–39

For Reading Skills Practice

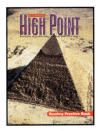

Reading Practice Book pages 1–37

For Vocabulary and Language Development

Posters (front)

Posters (back)

Listen and Learn Tape
Listen and Learn CD

For Phonics and High Frequency Word Instruction

Transparencies 1–10

Word Tiles
170 tiles with high frequency words and punctuation marks

Letter Tiles

For Comprehensive Assessment

Language Acquisition Assessment and Unit Test

For Planning and Instruction

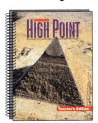

Teacher's Edition
pages T10a–T39z

Lakeside Planner **T10a**

LAKESIDE SCHOOL

Activity and Assessment Planner

LAKESIDE PAGES

Carlos Comes to Lakeside School

	BASIC VOCABULARY AND LANGUAGE DEVELOPMENT			LANGUAGE AND LITERACY	
11–13 **13a–13b**	**LESSON 1** Vocabulary Numbers **LESSON 2** Vocabulary T School Locations and Objects **LESSON 3** Vocabulary Greetings and Introductions	**LESSON 3** Functions Give Information Express Social Courtesies	**LESSON 3** Patterns and Structures T This is _____. T I am _____.	**LESSON 4** T High Frequency Words am I is school the this you	
14–15 **15a–15b**	**LESSON 5** Vocabulary T Classroom Objects and School Tools **LESSON 6** Vocabulary Greetings and Introductions	**LESSON 5** Function Ask and Answer Questions **LESSON 6** Function Express Social Courtesies	**LESSON 5** Patterns and Structures T Is this _____? T Here is _____. **LESSON 6** Patterns and Structures This is _____.	**LESSON 7** T High Frequency Words a an here my no yes	**LESSON 8** Phonics T Ss, Mm, Ff, Hh, Tt, Aa
16–17 **17a–17b**	**LESSON 9** Vocabulary T School Locations	**LESSON 10** Functions Express Social Courtesies Ask Questions	**LESSON 10** Patterns and Structures T Where is _____?	**LESSON 11** T High Frequency Words at it look of on see show where	**LESSON 12** Phonics T Blending short *a* words
18–19 **19a–19b**	**LESSON 13** Vocabulary T School Subjects T Telling Time	**LESSON 13** Function Give Information **LESSON 14** Functions Ask and Answer Questions Give Information	**LESSON 13** Patterns and Structures T What time is it? T It is _____. It is time for _____. **LESSON 14** Patterns and Structures T Where is _____? T Who is _____? T Here is _____. T Here are _____.	**LESSON 15** T High Frequency Words are good he she some time who your	**LESSON 16** Phonics T Nn, Ll, Pp, Gg, Ii

T10b Lakeside Planner

LAKESIDE PAGES	BASIC VOCABULARY AND LANGUAGE DEVELOPMENT			LANGUAGE AND LITERACY	
20–21 **21a–21b**	**LESSON 17** **Vocabulary** **T** Classroom Activities **LESSON 18** **Vocabulary** **T** Shapes **T** Commands	**LESSON 18** **Functions** Give and Carry Out Commands	**LESSON 18** **Patterns and Structures** *Show me _____.* *Point to _____.*	**LESSON 19** **T** **High Frequency Words** answer point read to with work write	**LESSON 20** **Phonics** Blending short *i* words
22–23 **23a–23b**	**LESSON 21** **Vocabulary** **T** School Objects and Personnel Personal Information	**LESSON 21** **Function** Give Personal Information **LESSON 22** **Functions** Ask for Information Express Needs	**LESSON 21** **Patterns and Structures** *My name is _____.* *My phone number is _____.* **LESSON 22** **Patterns and Structures** **T** *Where is _____?* **T** *What is _____?* **T** *I need to _____.*	**LESSON 23** **T** **High Frequency Words** call name need number to what	**LESSON 24** **Phonics** Rr, Dd, Cc, Vv, Oo
24–25 **25a–25b**	**LESSON 25** **Vocabulary** **T** Library Objects	**LESSON 25** **Function** Ask for and Give Information **LESSON 26** **Functions** Express Likes Ask and Answer Questions	**LESSON 25** **Patterns and Structures** *What is in the _____?* *A _____ is in the _____.* *Some _____ are in the _____.* **LESSON 26** **Patterns and Structures** *Do you like _____?* **T** *I like _____.* *Will you _____?* **T** *Does _____?*	**LESSON 27** **T** **High Frequency Words** do does for help in like me picture will	**LESSON 28** **Phonics** Blending short *o* words
26–27 **27a–27b**	**LESSON 29** **Vocabulary** **T** Sports	**LESSON 29** **Function** Express Likes **LESSON 30** **Function** Ask and Answer Questions	**LESSON 29** **Patterns and Structures** **T** *I like _____.* **LESSON 30** **Patterns and Structures** **T** *Can you _____?* **T** *I can _____.* **T** *You can _____.*	**LESSON 31** **T** **High Frequency Words** around can play too we	**LESSON 32** **Phonics** **T** Jj, Bb, Ww, Kk, Ee
28–29 **29a–29b**	**LESSON 33** **Vocabulary** **T** Body Parts	**LESSON 33** **Function** Give Information **LESSON 34** **Functions** Ask and Answer Questions Express Feelings	**LESSON 33** **Patterns and Structures** **T** *He/She has _____.* **T** *I/They have _____.* **LESSON 34** **Patterns and Structures** *How do you/they feel?* **T** *How does he/she feel?* *I/They feel _____.* **T** *He/She feels _____.* *My _____ hurts.*	**LESSON 35** **T** **High Frequency Words** feel has have how put they	**LESSON 36** **Phonics** Blending short *e* words

Lakeside Planner **T10c**

Activity and Assessment Planner, *Continued*

Carlos Comes to Lakeside School

LAKESIDE PAGES	BASIC VOCABULARY AND LANGUAGE DEVELOPMENT			LANGUAGE AND LITERACY	
30–31 31a–31b	**LESSON 37** Vocabulary T Food **LESSON 38** Vocabulary T Money	**LESSON 37** Function Express Likes and Dislikes **LESSON 38** Function Ask for and Give Information	**LESSON 37** Patterns and Structures I like _____. T I do not like _____. **LESSON 38** Patterns and Structures What is this/that? T This/That is _____.	**LESSON 39** T High Frequency Words and don't food not that	**LESSON 40** Writing T Write a Statement
32–33 33a–33b	**LESSON 41** Vocabulary Science Materials and Processes	**LESSON 42** Function Express Needs and Thoughts	**LESSON 42** Patterns and Structures T I need _____. I think _____.	**LESSON 43** T High Frequency Words give take think	**LESSON 44** Phonics T Zz, Yy, Uu, QU, qu, Xx
34–35 35a–35b	**LESSON 45** Vocabulary T Clothing T Colors	**LESSON 46** Function Ask and Answer Questions	**LESSON 46** Patterns and Structures Which _____ do you like? I like this/that _____. I like these/those _____.	**LESSON 47** T High Frequency Words both get little old them these things those very which	**LESSON 48** Phonics Blending short *u* words
36–37 37a–37b	**LESSON 49** Vocabulary Days of the Week Abbreviations for Days of the Week	**LESSON 50** Function Express Social Courtesies	**LESSON 50** Patterns and Structures See you _____.	**LESSON 51** T High Frequency Words great later soon tomorrow	**LESSON 52** Writing T Write a Question
38–39 39a–39b	**LESSON 53** Vocabulary Months of the Year **LESSON 54** Vocabulary T Action Verbs	**LESSON 54** Function Describe Actions	**LESSON 54** Patterns and Structures T Present Tense Verbs	**LESSON 55** T High Frequency Words book boy day girl group letters night year	**LESSON 56** Writing T Write an Exclamation

T10d Lakeside Planner

ASSESSMENT OPTIONS

The **Teacher's Edition** and the **Assessment Handbook** include these comprehensive assessment tools:

▶ **Ongoing, Informal Assessment**
Check for understanding and achieve closure for every lesson with the targeted questions and activities in the **Close and Assess** boxes in your Teacher's Edition.

▶ **Language Acquisition Assessment**
To verify students' ability to use the language functions and grammar structures taught in Lakeside, conduct this performance assessment.

▶ **Unit Test in Standardized Test Format**
This multiple-choice test measures students' cumulative understanding of the vocabulary, grammar structures, and phonics skills taught in Lakeside. It also evaluates students on writing a statement, question, and exclamation.

LAKESIDE ASSESSMENT OPPORTUNITIES	Assessment Handbook Pages
Language Acquisition Assessment	1c–1d
Lakeside Unit Test	1e

PACING OPTIONS

Lakeside School is designed for use with English learners and struggling readers. For those students who need language development as well as literacy, use Plan 1. For those who need only the literacy lessons, use Plan 2.

PACING OPTIONS: Plan 1

LESSONS	PERIODS	BLOCK SCHEDULE OR INTERVENTION SESSIONS
1–56	56 periods, 1 lesson per period	15 sessions, approximately 1 session for every 4 lessons

PACING OPTIONS: Plan 2

LESSONS	PERIODS	BLOCK SCHEDULE OR INTERVENTION SESSIONS
4, 7–8, 11–12, 15–16, 19–20, 23–24, 27–28, 31–32, 35–36, 39–40, 43–44, 47–48, 51–52, 55–56	27 periods, 1 lesson per period	13 sessions, approximately 1 session for every 2 lessons

LAKESIDE SCHOOL **OVERVIEW**

BASIC VOCABULARY AND LANGUAGE DEVELOPMENT

OBJECTIVES

Reading and Learning Strategies: Activate Prior Knowledge; Relate to Personal Experience; Build Background

Viewing: Interpret a Visual Image

LEARN ABOUT LAKESIDE SCHOOL

1. **Introduce Lakeside School** Read the title on page 11 and point to the picture of Carlos. Explain: *These pages tell about a boy named Carlos. He is new at Lakeside School.*

   Point out the sign on the building: *Lakeside School.* Tell students that the picture shows Carlos outside his new school. Explain that he is meeting a girl named Maylin, who will help him through his first day.

2. **Preview the Book** Point out the clock on page 12 and explain: *Carlos's story starts at the beginning of the school day. We will go with Carlos to his classes. We will see what he does during the day. These clocks tell us what time it is.* Have students page through the book to point out the clock on each left-hand page. Then read aloud the sentence that appears next to the clock and allow students time to look through the photographs.

REACHING ALL STUDENTS

HOME CONNECTION

At Home with Numbers To reinforce number concepts, encourage students to take home completed **Language Practice Book** pages 1 and 2. Students can read the number words aloud to family members. Then students and family members can list or draw home items containing numerals. Students can write the number words and bring their lists or drawings to school to share.

T10 Lakeside School

Carlos Comes to LAKESIDE SCHOOL

LAKESIDE SCHOOL LESSON 1

BASIC VOCABULARY AND LANGUAGE DEVELOPMENT

OBJECTIVES
Functions:
Listen Actively; Repeat Spoken Language
Concepts and Vocabulary: Numbers

USE NUMBERS

1 Introduce Numbers Point out the number 85 in the address for Lakeside School. Tell students that Carlos will see and use many numbers at school. Brainstorm places to find numbers: room numbers, schedules, clocks, buses, uniforms.

2 Identify Numbers Use **Language Practice Book** page 1 or make a chart to teach numbers and number words:

1 one		25	twenty-five
2 two		26	twenty-six
3 three		27	twenty-seven
4 four		28	twenty-eight
5 five		29	twenty-nine
6 six		30	thirty
7 seven		40	forty
8 eight		50	fifty
9 nine		60	sixty
10 ten		70	seventy
11 eleven		80	eighty
12 twelve		90	ninety
13 thirteen		100	one hundred
14 fourteen		101	one hundred one
15 fifteen		110	one hundred ten
16 sixteen		120	one hundred twenty
17 seventeen		130	one hundred thirty
18 eighteen		140	one hundred forty
19 nineteen		150	one hundred fifty
20 twenty		160	one hundred sixty
21 twenty-one		170	one hundred seventy
22 twenty-two		180	one hundred eighty
23 twenty-three		190	one hundred ninety
24 twenty-four		200	two hundred

Point to each number, say it, and have students echo-read. Next, call out numbers at random and have students point to them.

▶ **Language Practice Book** pages 1, 2

CLOSE AND ASSESS

Make two sets of cards, one with numerals and one with number words. Have students match the cards and say the numbers.

Language Development
NUMBERS

Play number bingo. Show students how to make a 5 x 5 grid and have them copy numbers from **Language Practice Book** page 1 onto their grids. Call out numbers and have students mark them off on their grids until someone fills a row, a column, or a diagonal. Invite the student who wins the first round to call the numbers for the second round. As a variation, use only numbers from 1–50 or 51–100.

Language Development **T11**

LAKESIDE SCHOOL **LESSON 2**

BASIC VOCABULARY AND LANGUAGE DEVELOPMENT

OBJECTIVES

Concepts and Vocabulary:
- School Locations and Objects

Viewing: Interpret a Visual Image
Representing: Drawing

USE NAMES OF SCHOOL LOCATIONS AND OBJECTS

1 Look at the Photographs Point out the clock and explain: *It's 8:20 a.m. Time for school! Carlos is just going in. These photos show what Lakeside School looks like.*

Have students look at the main building on page 12. Say: *This is the front of the school. It is the outside of the building.* Point to each labeled item as you read its name. As you discuss the second photo, explain: *The entrance hall is inside the school. This is what you see when you go in the front door.*

Repeat the procedure with the photos on page 13. Explain that both photos show areas outside.

2 Sketch a School Building If possible, lead the class outside to face the main building of your school. Have students sketch the exterior in the space provided on page 3 of the **Language Practice Book**. (If it is not possible to go outside, students can sketch from memory.) Encourage them to include details such as windows, doors, and steps.

3 Label the Sketches In class, have students use the photos on this page as a model for labeling their own sketches. Supply specific words for your school, as necessary.

▶ **Language Practice Book** page 3

CLOSE AND ASSESS

Call out school locations and objects for students to identify on their sketches.

T12 Lakeside School

Time: 8:20 a.m.

This is Lakeside School.

This is the main building.

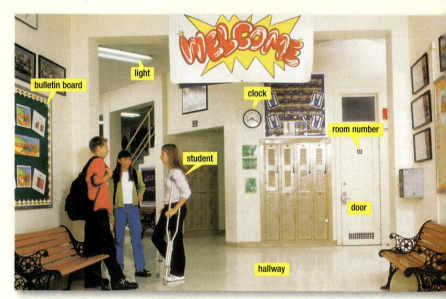

This is the entrance hall.

12

REACHING ALL STUDENTS

Vocabulary
SCHOOL LOCATIONS

Sort Photos Take snapshots of several locations and objects around your school. Invite volunteers to label the items they know. Then work together to arrange the photos into two categories: *Inside the School* and *Outside the School*.

Inside the School	Outside the School
light	street
clock	field

This is the parking lot.

This is the field.

Pronunciation of Names
Maylin mā **lin**
Carlos **car** lōs

Listen and Learn

Maylin: Hi, I'm Maylin.
Carlos: Hello. I am Carlos. Nice to meet you.

Language Development

GIVE INFORMATION

Divide the class into small groups and have the members share their sketches from **Language Practice Book** page 3. The group combines the information from each sketch to create a large, labeled drawing of the main school building. Provide the sentence frame: *This is the ____.* Then invite group members to act as tour guides to give information about the building: *This is the front door of our school.*

LAKESIDE SCHOOL **LESSON 3**

BASIC VOCABULARY AND LANGUAGE DEVELOPMENT

OBJECTIVES
Functions: Listen Actively; Repeat Spoken Language; Give Information; Express Social Courtesies
Concepts and Vocabulary: Greetings and Introductions
Patterns and Structures:
🅣 *I am ____.;* 🅣 *This is ____.*
Speaking: Introductions

GIVE INFORMATION

1 Introduce the Pattern: *This is ____.* Read aloud the captions. Then use the pattern to tell about objects on these pages: *This is the flag.* Have students describe the features in your classroom: *This is the door.*

2 Take a School Tour As you walk, pause for students to check off and label on **Language Practice Book** page 4 the objects they see. Provide vocabulary for additional items. Back in class, have volunteers tell about the items they found.

▶ **Language Practice Book** page 4

EXPRESS SOCIAL COURTESIES

3 Introduce the Pattern: *I am ____.* Play the "Listen and Learn" conversation on the **Lakeside Language Tape/CD.** Students will listen twice to the conversation, then echo the lines, and chime in on Carlos's part. Ask volunteers to role-play the conversation.

Side A
CD Track 1

4 Practice Introductions Organize students into an Inside-Outside Circle (see page T337d). Students in the inside circle say: *Hi, I'm ____.* Students in the outside circle say: *Hello. I am ____. Nice to meet you.* Rotate the circles for more practice.

CLOSE AND ASSESS

Have one partner point to an item on pages 12–13; the other describes it with this pattern: *This is ____.*

Language Development **T13**

LAKESIDE SCHOOL **LESSON 4**

LANGUAGE AND LITERACY: HIGH FREQUENCY WORDS

OBJECTIVES
Learning to Read:
- Recognize High Frequency Words

INTRODUCE

1 Learn New Words Place a word and its letter tiles on the screen as you work through the Strategy for Learning a New Word. For example, for *this,* say:

1. *First, look at the word.* (Display the word tile for *this.*)

2. *Now listen to the word:* this, this.

3. *Listen to the word in a sentence:* What school is this? This is Lakeside School. *What does the word* this *mean? It means "the one we are talking about."*

4. *Say the word after me:* this.

5. *Spell the word:* t-h-i-s. (As you say each letter, place the corresponding letter tile below the word tile. Have students spell the word again in unison as you point to each tile.)

6. *Say the word again:* this.

Repeat the process for each new word. Good sentences for the third step are:

- What **is** your name?
- Read **the** book.
- We go to **school**.
- **I** like our class.
- I **am** the teacher.
- **You** are students.

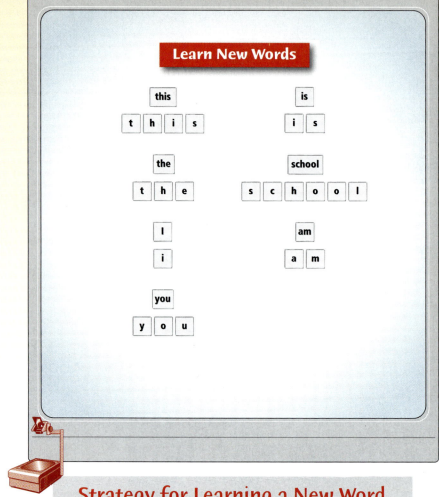

Strategy for Learning a New Word

1. Look at the word.
2. Listen to the word.
3. Listen to the word in a sentence.
4. Say the word.
5. Spell the word.
6. Say the word again.

REACHING ALL STUDENTS

Reading Fluency
RECOGNIZE HIGH FREQUENCY WORDS

To build automaticity with the new words, create a classroom word chart for display throughout the year. First, demonstrate printing each new word on a card. After the first word or two, print just the first letter and have students tell you the next. Model how to post a card on the chart by the first letter in the word. Have volunteers post the rest.

Students can use the classroom chart to practice together. For example:

- One student can say a word for another to find on the chart.
- Partners can match their word cards against the words on the chart.
- Small groups can challenge one another in hunts; for example, find three words with three letters each.

T13a Lakeside School

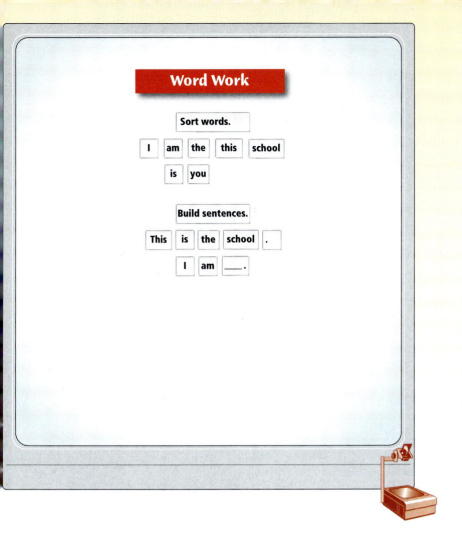

PRACTICE

2 Sort Words Place the direction tile on the screen and then place the word tiles in a random arrangement. Have students sort the words by the number of letters. Ask: *Which word has one letter?* (I) *Which words have two letters?* (am, is), etc. As students name the words, arrange them in groups. Finally, lead a choral reading of the words in each group.

3 Build Sentences Place the direction tile and then the word tiles on the screen to create the sentences shown. As you place each word, say it. Explain the placement of the periods: *This sentence tells something, so we use a period at the end.*

Model reading the text and filling in the blank: *This is the school. I am [your name].* Have partners read the sentences aloud, inserting their names.

APPLY

4 Read New Words Have students apply the skill by turning to pages 12–13 and finding each of the new words in the text.

▶ **Reading Practice Book** page 1

CLOSE AND ASSESS

Place the high frequency words one at a time on the screen. Call on volunteers to read them; have the group repeat them.

Multi-Level Strategies
LANGUAGE DEVELOPMENT

PRELITERATE The sentences you built in Step 3 can be used to check students' command of basic print concepts and classroom vocabulary (*word, letter, point,* etc.). Display the sentences on the overhead as shown. Then ask students to:

- count the number of words in each sentence.
- point to the first word in the sentence.
- point to the first letter in that word.
- show where to start reading again after the first sentence.

If students have difficulty with the tasks, use a classroom book with simple text to develop these concepts of print as well as the basic vocabulary students will need to participate in instruction.

Language and Literacy **T13b**

LAKESIDE SCHOOL **LESSON 5**

BASIC VOCABULARY AND LANGUAGE DEVELOPMENT

> **OBJECTIVES**
>
> **Functions:** Listen Actively; Repeat Spoken Language; Ask and Answer Questions
>
> **Concepts and Vocabulary:**
> 🅣 Classroom Objects; 🅣 School Tools
>
> **Patterns and Structures:**
> 🅣 *Here is* _____.; *Is this* _____?
>
> **Viewing:** Interpret a Visual Image

USE NAMES OF CLASSROOM OBJECTS AND SCHOOL TOOLS

1 Introduce the Pattern: *Here is* _____. Point to the clock and say: *Now it is 8:30. Carlos is in class. There are many things that he can use.* Use the pattern to introduce each classroom object: *Here is a pencil. I use a pencil to write.*

Turn to **Language Practice Book** page 5 and model how to complete the diminishing sentences in the first column. Have partners complete the remaining sentences.

▶ **Language Practice Book** page 5

ASK AND ANSWER QUESTIONS

2 Introduce the Patterns: *Is this* _____? and *This is* _____. Play the "Listen and Learn" conversation on the **Lakeside Language Tape/CD**. Students listen to the conversation as they follow along, and then echo it. On a last reading, they chime in with Carlos.

Then turn to **Language Practice Book** page 6 and help students prepare game spinners. Invite volunteers to model the game, then have small groups play together to practice the skill.

▶ **Language Practice Book** page 6

> **CLOSE AND ASSESS**
>
> Have one partner hold up a school tool and ask a question with the pattern *Is this* _____? The other partner answers with a statement: *This is* _____.

T14 Lakeside School

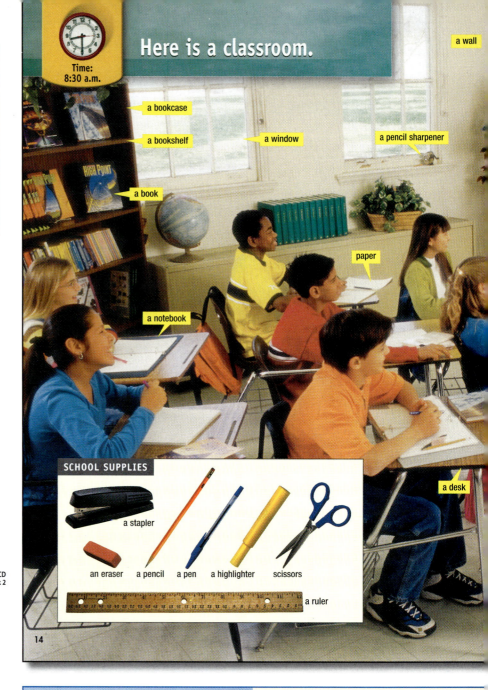

Here is a classroom.

Time: 8:30 a.m.

a wall • a bookcase • a bookshelf • a window • a pencil sharpener • a book • paper • a notebook • a desk

SCHOOL SUPPLIES
a stapler • an eraser • a pencil • a pen • a highlighter • scissors • a ruler

REACHING ALL STUDENTS

Vocabulary
CLASSROOM OBJECTS AND TOOLS

Labels, Labels Divide the classroom into several areas and assign a team to each area. Have each team identify the objects in their area and write the words on separate self-stick notes. The teams then trade their areas and notes and work together to affix the labels to the correct objects. Invite students to give information to the class: *This is a pencil sharpener.* Advanced students can tell more: *I use a pencil sharpener when my pencil is dull.*

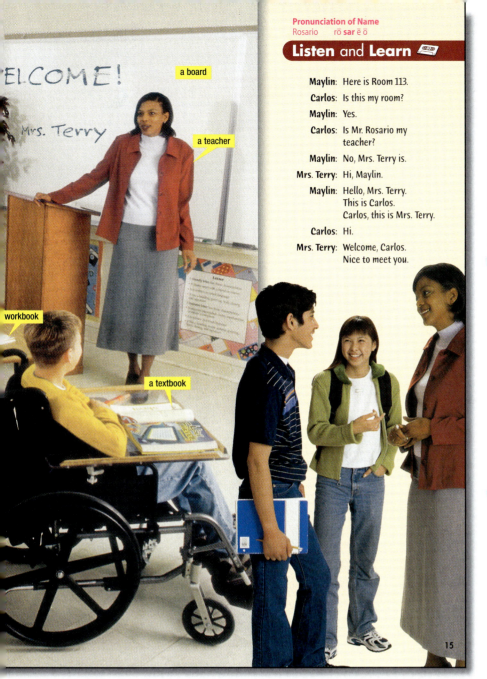

Pronunciation of Name
Rosario rō **sar** ē ō

Listen and Learn

Maylin:	Here is Room 113.
Carlos:	Is this my room?
Maylin:	Yes.
Carlos:	Is Mr. Rosario my teacher?
Maylin:	No, Mrs. Terry is.
Mrs. Terry:	Hi, Maylin.
Maylin:	Hello, Mrs. Terry. This is Carlos. Carlos, this is Mrs. Terry.
Carlos:	Hi.
Mrs. Terry:	Welcome, Carlos. Nice to meet you.

15

LAKESIDE SCHOOL LESSON 6

BASIC VOCABULARY AND LANGUAGE DEVELOPMENT

OBJECTIVES

Functions: Listen Actively; Repeat Spoken Language; Express Social Courtesies

Concepts and Vocabulary: Greetings and Introductions

Patterns and Structures: *This is _____.*

EXPRESS SOCIAL COURTESIES

1 Use Introductions Review the greetings from page 13: *hi, hello,* and *nice to meet you.* Then explain: *When you want two people to meet, you can gesture to one person and say: "This is ___."*

Replay the first reading of the conversation on the **Lakeside Language Tape/CD**. Have students listen for where Maylin introduces Carlos and Mrs. Terry. Invite them to repeat after you: *Carlos, this is Mrs. Terry.*

Side A
CD Track 2

2 Make Introductions Work together to match the speech balloons to the correct person on **Language Practice Book** page 7. Then make a chart to review words and phrases that are used in introductions. Have groups of three role-play one student introducing a new student to a teacher.

First Student:	Hi, _____. This is _____. _____, this is my friend _____.
New Student:	Hi, _____.
Teacher:	Welcome, _____. Nice to meet you.

▶ Language Practice Book page 7

CLOSE AND ASSESS

Have partners take turns introducing each other to you.

CULTURAL PERSPECTIVES

World Cultures: *Hello* in Many Languages Point out that every language has greetings. Invite students to teach the class how to say hello in languages they know. Then have the group make a poster with the title *"Hello" in Many Languages.* Invite students to add the names of their native languages and include the words and phrases they use to greet friends and family.

Language Development **T15**

LAKESIDE SCHOOL **LESSON 7**

LANGUAGE AND LITERACY: HIGH FREQUENCY WORDS

OBJECTIVES

Learning to Read:
❶ Recognize High Frequency Words

INTRODUCE

1 Learn New Words Place a word and its letter tiles on the screen as you work through the Strategy steps. For *yes,* say:

1. *First, look at the word.* (Display the word tile for *yes.*)

2. *Now listen to the word:* yes, yes.

3. *Listen to the word in a sentence:* Yes, this is an English class.

4. *Say the word after me:* yes.

5. *Spell the word:* y-e-s. (Say each letter as you place the tile. Point to each tile and have students spell the word.)

6. *Say the word again:* yes.

Repeat the process for the other words, using these context sentences:

• Is this **an** English class?
• **No**, this is homeroom.
• Is **my** teacher here?
• Yes. **Here** is the teacher.
• Here is **a** desk for you.

PRACTICE

2 Build Sentences Say each word as you place its tile on the screen: *Is this a _____? Is this an _____? Yes, this is _____ _____. No. This is _____ _____.* Model reading the text and filling in the blanks with classroom objects: *Is this a pen? No. This is an eraser.* Then have one partner ask the question; the other gives the answer.

APPLY

3 Read New Words Have students find the new words on pages 14–15.

▶ **Reading Practice Book** page 2

CLOSE AND ASSESS
Display the words for students to read.

T15a Lakeside School

Learn New Words

yes			an	
y	e	s	a	n

no			my	
n	o		m	y

here			a	
h	e	r	e	a
				a

Strategy for Learning a New Word

1. Look at the word.
2. Listen to the word.
3. Listen to the word in a sentence.

4. Say the word.
5. Spell the word.
6. Say the word again.

REACHING ALL STUDENTS

Reading Fluency
RECOGNIZE HIGH FREQUENCY WORDS

To build automaticity with the new high frequency words:

• Display the words. Have pairs make a word card set. Then have them sort the cards by number of letters in each word. Volunteers can tell how many words have one, two, three, or four letters, and say the word or words.

• Partners can use the word cards to practice together and test each other. One holds up a card and the other reads the word. Have them add the previous set of words (page 13a) to the card set for review.

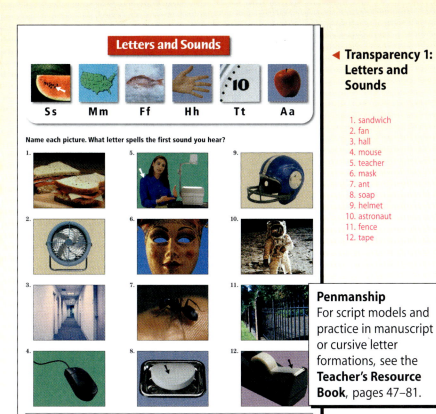

◀ Transparency 1: Letters and Sounds

1. sandwich
2. fan
3. hall
4. mouse
5. teacher
6. mask
7. ant
8. soap
9. helmet
10. astronaut
11. fence
12. tape

Penmanship For script models and practice in manuscript or cursive letter formations, see the **Teacher's Resource Book**, pages 47–81.

▼ Script for Transparency 1

Letters and Sounds

1. Develop Phonemic Awareness
Count Words in Sentences/Match Initial Sounds Say a sentence and have students count each word they hear: *Tom makes soup.* Then ask: *How many words are in this sentence?* (3) Repeat for: *Tom makes soup at home.* (5) Next, say: *Listen to these two words:* seed, soup. *Say the words with me:* seed, soup. *Do they begin with the same sound?* (yes) Repeat with these word pairs: *mud, hot; fast, fish; hit, home; ten, men; ask, apple; table, teacher.*

2. Associate Letters and Sounds
Learn Consonant Names, Sounds, and Formations Point to the seed on **Transparency 1**. Say: *This is a seed. Plants grow from seeds. Say* seed *with me:* seed. Then point to *Ss* and say: *This is capital* S, *and this is lowercase* s. *The letter* s *spells the first sound you hear in* seed. *The first sound is* /s/. *Say* /sss/ *with me:* /sss/. Point to the *s* and ask: *What is the letter? What is its sound?* Trace the *Ss* on the transparency as you explain how to form the letters and have students "write" the letters in the air. Repeat the process for *m, f, h,* and *t*. Then explain: *The letters* s, m, f, h, *and* t *are called* **consonants**—*they spell consonant sounds.*

Learn the Name, Sound, and Formation for the Vowel Aa Point to *Aa* and say: *This is the letter* a—*capital* A *and lowercase* a. *The letter* a *is a* **vowel**. Point to the apple and say: *Say* apple *with me:* apple. *Say its first sound:* /aaa/. *The sound* /aaa/ *is a vowel sound. When you say a vowel sound, you keep your mouth open and let the air flow out. Try it:* /aaa/. Then say: *The letter* a *spells the vowel sound* /a/ *you hear in* apple. Point to the *a* and ask: *What is the letter? What is its sound?* Then teach students how to form capital and lowercase *a*.

Practice Have students number a paper from 1–12. For Item 1, say: *What is in this picture? Let's say the word and then its first sound:* sandwich, /sss/. *What letter spells* /sss/ *as in* sandwich? *That's right,* s. Point to the *Ss* on the transparency. Have students write a capital and lowercase *s* by Item 1 on their papers. Repeat the process for Items 2–12.

LAKESIDE SCHOOL **LESSON 8**

LANGUAGE AND LITERACY: PHONICS

OBJECTIVES
Learning to Read: Build Oral Vocabulary; Develop Phonemic Awareness; ⊤ Associate Letters and Sounds

TEACH LETTERS AND SOUNDS

1 Build Oral Vocabulary Display Transparency 1. Play "I Spy." For example, for Item 10, say:

- *I spy an astronaut. An astronaut wears a special suit and travels in space. This astronaut is on the moon.*

When students find the astronaut, say: *Yes,* **this is an astronaut** (point). Repeat for the other words.

2 Develop Phonemic Awareness Remove the transparency and work through Step 1 of the script.

3 Associate Letters and Sounds Display Transparency 1 again. Work through Step 2 of the script.

▶ **Reading Practice Book** pages 3, 4

CLOSE AND ASSESS
Say the words *soap, hall, apple, mask, tape, fence* one at a time. Have the group write the letter that stands for the first sound in the word on a card and hold it up.

Review and Reteaching
PHONEMIC AWARENESS AND PHONICS

- **Match Initial Sounds** Say a sound and two words. Ask students to say which word begins with the sound you name. Some sounds and words to use are: /s/ *fan, soap;* /m/ *mask, hall;* /f/ *tape, fence;* /h/ *hand, mouse;* /t/ *tape, girl.*

- **Match Letters and Sounds** Give one letter card for *s, m, f, h, t,* or *a* (see pages 83–88 of the **Teacher's Resource Book**) to six students. Have the others each draw a picture from the transparency. Then students form groups to match the letters to the first sound in the picture names.

Language and Literacy **T15b**

LAKESIDE SCHOOL **LESSON 9**

BASIC VOCABULARY AND LANGUAGE DEVELOPMENT

> **OBJECTIVES**
> **Concepts and Vocabulary:**
> ⓣ School Locations
> **Viewing:** Interpret a Visual Image
> **Representing:** Map

USE NAMES OF SCHOOL LOCATIONS

1 View the Map Explain: *This is a map of Lakeside School. It shows the location of all the rooms in the building.*

Point out the room labeled "library" on the map. Then direct students' attention to the photo of the library on page 17. Ask: *What do you see in the library?* (books, students) *What do students do there?* (read, study, research) Continue to make connections between the map locations and the photos.

2 Start Maps of Your School Begin by drawing a large outline of your school floor plan on a chart, explaining: *We can draw a map of our school, too. Here is the main building.* Divide your outline into rooms. Then have students copy the map onto page 8 of the **Language Practice Book**.

3 Go on a Tour and Complete the School Maps Conduct a tour of the places in your school. Have students label the locations you visit on their maps, using the vocabulary in the box on the **Language Practice Book** page. Supply additional place names for your particular school, as necessary.

▶ **Language Practice Book** page 8

> **CLOSE AND ASSESS**
> Back in the classroom, have students tell you what words to write on the large floor plan to label the locations.

REACHING ALL STUDENTS

Vocabulary
SCHOOL LOCATIONS

Map Puzzles Have small groups choose a group member's map to turn into a puzzle. Make a copy of the map and cut it apart so that each room is one piece. Groups should mix up the pieces and then work to put them back together. Encourage students to name each room as they place it in the puzzle.

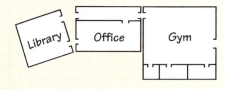

T16 Lakeside School

WHERE IS IT ON THE MAP?

THE MAIN OFFICE

THE COUNSELOR'S OFFICE

THE LIBRARY

THE GIRLS' BATHROOM

THE AUDITORIUM

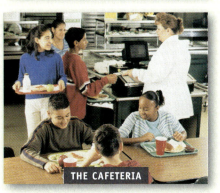
THE CAFETERIA

Language Development

ASK QUESTIONS

Have students use the map of their school that they made in Lesson 9. In an Inside-Outside Circle (see Cooperative Learning Structures, page T337d), students can ask each other questions about where places are on the map. Provide this question starter:

    Where is _____?

To answer, students point to the location on the map. Then the inside circle rotates and new partners repeat the process.

LAKESIDE SCHOOL **LESSON 10**

BASIC VOCABULARY AND LANGUAGE DEVELOPMENT

OBJECTIVES

Functions: Listen Actively; Repeat Spoken Language; Express Social Courtesies; Ask Questions

Patterns and Structures:
🅣 *Where is _____?*

EXPRESS SOCIAL COURTESIES

1 **Use *Please, Thank You,* and *You're Welcome*** Play the "Listen and Learn" conversation on the **Lakeside Language Tape/CD**. Students will listen twice to the conversation. On the second reading, have them raise their hands when they hear the words *please, thank you,* and *you're welcome*. As the tape continues, students will echo lines and then chime in on Carlos's part. Afterwards, use the terms in a simple role-play with a volunteer: *Please give me a pencil. Okay. Thank you. You're welcome.*

ASK QUESTIONS

2 **Introduce the Pattern: *Where is _____?*** Read what Carlos says first on page 16. Then say: *When you need to find out where something is, ask a question with* Where.

Model with the pictures on page 17: *Where is the main office?* Challenge the group to ask more questions about places and objects in your school. Collect the questions in a chart.

Where is _____?
Where is the gym?
Where is the nurse's office?

▶ **Language Practice Book** page 9

CLOSE AND ASSESS

Have partners work together to ask questions: one partner points to a location on page 17 and the other asks where it is.

Language Development **T17**

LAKESIDE SCHOOL **LESSON 11**

LANGUAGE AND LITERACY: HIGH FREQUENCY WORDS

OBJECTIVES
Learning to Read:
- Recognize High Frequency Words

INTRODUCE

1 Learn New Words Place a word and its letter tiles on the screen as you work through the Strategy steps. For example, for *of*, say:

1. *First, look at the word.* (Display the word tile for *of*.)

2. *Now listen to the word:* of, of.

3. *Listen to the word in a sentence:* This is a map of the school.

4. *Say the word after me:* of.

5. *Spell the word:* o-f. (Say each letter as you place the tile. Point to each tile and have students spell the word.)

6. *Say the word again:* of.

Repeat the process for the other words, using these context sentences:

- Please **show** me the map.
- **Where** is Room 124?
- Is Room 124 **on** the map?
- Yes, **look at** the map.
- Now I **see it** on the map.

PRACTICE

2 Build Sentences Say each word as you place its tile on the screen: *Where is the _____? I see it on the _____.* Model reading the text and filling in the blanks with classroom objects: *Where is the book? I see it on the table.* Then have one partner ask the question; the other gives the answer.

APPLY

3 Read New Words Have students find the new words on pages 16–17.

▶ Reading Practice Book page 5

CLOSE AND ASSESS
Display the words one at a time for students to read.

T17a Lakeside School

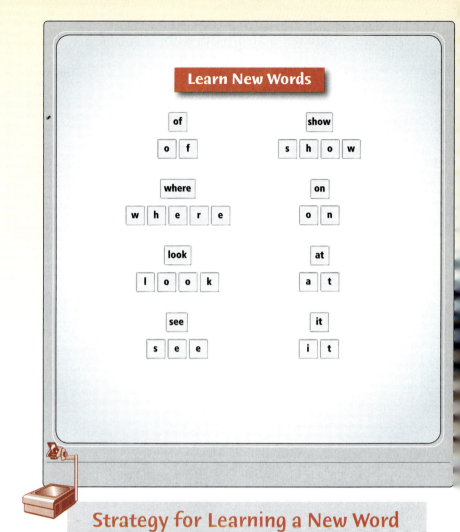

Strategy for Learning a New Word

1. Look at the word.
2. Listen to the word.
3. Listen to the word in a sentence.
4. Say the word.
5. Spell the word.
6. Say the word again.

REACHING ALL STUDENTS

Reading Fluency
RECOGNIZE HIGH FREQUENCY WORDS

To build automaticity with the new high frequency words:

- Have a volunteer look at the classroom chart of words, choose a word, and begin spelling it slowly. The rest of the group should try to guess the word in as few letters as possible.

- Have students list the new and review words by number of letters, on a chart like the one shown. Ask questions about the lists; for example: *Which list has the most words in it? How would you arrange each list in alphabetical order?*

1	2	3	4	5	6
I	is	the	this	where	school
a	am	you	here		
	an	yes	look		
	my	see	show		
	no				
	of				
	at				
	it				
	on				

Transparency 2: Blending

Blend Words with Short _a_

Blend the sounds to read each word.

am	at	at
Sam	hat	fat
ham	sat	mat

Read each word. Which picture goes with the word?

1. hat
2. ham
3. mat

A.   B.   C.

Transparency 2   © Hampton-Brown

Penmanship
For script models and practice in writing words in manuscript or cursive with correct letter spacing, see the **Teacher's Resource Book**, pages 47–81.

Materials
Letter tiles for:

a	f	h	m

s	S	t

▼ Script for Transparency 2

Blend Words with Short _a_

1. Develop Phonemic Awareness
Match Initial Sounds/Match Final Sounds Say: _Listen to these two words:_ at, am. _Say the words with me:_ at, am. _The first sound in these words is the same:_ /aaa/. _Now listen to these two words:_ an, it. _Say the words with me:_ an, it. _Is the first sound in each word the same?_ (no) Continue with word pairs _Sam, sat; ham, hat; fat, mat; at, hat._ Then say: _Now listen to these two words:_ hot, mat. _Say the words with me:_ hot, mat. _They end with the same sound:_ /t/. _Here are two more words:_ ham, hat. _Say the words with me:_ ham, hat. _Is the last sound in each word the same?_ (no) Continue with word pairs _hit, cat; pass, bus; ham, dot; if, in._

2. Blend Sounds to Read Words
Model Set letter tile _a_ at the left in the box on **Transparency 2** and letter tile _m_ at the right. Point to _a_ and say: _The sound for this letter is_ /aaa/. As you say the sound, slide _a_ next to _m_, and then put your finger under _m_. Say: _I can blend the sound_ /aaa/ _with the sound of the letter_ m: /aaammm/. _Now I am going to say the word fast:_ am. Summarize: _You can blend sounds like this to read a word. Just say the sound for the first letter, and blend it into the sound for the next letter._ Demonstrate again: Point to _a_ and say: _Say the sound for_ a _with me:_ /aaa/. Repeat for _m:_ /mmm/. Then slide a finger below the letters _am_ and say: _Help me blend the two sounds:_ /aaammm/. _Now let's say the word:_ am. Then leave _am_ at the right in the box, add letter tile _S_ at the left, and repeat the process to read _Sam._ Remove the _S,_ add _h,_ and repeat the process to read _ham._

Practice Have students read the words _am, Sam,_ and _ham_ below the box. Then repeat Model and Practice for the other two word sets.

3. Match Words and Pictures
Point to Item 1. Say: _Let's read this word._ Slide a finger slowly under the letters to lead students in sounding out the word: /haaat/, _hat._ Then say: _Which of these pictures—A, B, or C—shows a hat?_ (B) Repeat the process for Items 2 and 3.

LAKESIDE SCHOOL **LESSON 12**

LANGUAGE AND LITERACY: PHONICS

OBJECTIVES

Learning to Read: Build Oral Vocabulary; Develop Phonemic Awareness; Blend Sounds to Decode Words

TEACH BLENDING

1 **Build Oral Vocabulary** Display Transparency 2. Use _am, at, sat,_ and _fat_ in sentences to build meaning:

- _I **am** (your name). You are **at** your desks. You **sat** there yesterday. If you eat too much, you will get **fat**._

Use the pictures to develop the meaning of the words _ham, hat,_ and _mat._ For example:

- _This is a **mat**. A **mat** is soft. It is like a cushion. Gymnasts practice on a **mat**._

2 **Develop Phonemic Awareness** Remove the transparency and work through Step 1 of the script.

3 **Blend Sounds to Read Words** Display Transparency 2 again. Work through Steps 2 and 3 of the script.

▶ **Reading Practice Book** pages 6, 7

CLOSE AND ASSESS

Display _hat, sat, ham,_ and _fat._ Have students identify the sound of each letter and blend the sounds to read the word.

Review and Reteaching
PHONEMIC AWARENESS AND PHONICS

- **Listen for Initial and Final Sounds** Say a sound (e.g., /s/) and a word that begins or ends with the sound. Have students tell you whether they hear the sound at the beginning or at the end of the word. Some words to use are: _gas, map, ham, sit, net, ten._

- **Blend Sounds to Decode Words** Distribute letter cards for _a, h, s, f, m,_ and _t_ (see pages 83–88 in the **Teacher's Resource Book**). Have students spell and blend _at,_ then add a letter or change a letter to spell and blend _hat, sat, fat,_ and _mat._

Language and Literacy **T17b**

LAKESIDE SCHOOL LESSON 13

BASIC VOCABULARY AND LANGUAGE DEVELOPMENT

OBJECTIVES

Function: Give Information

Concepts and Vocabulary:
- School Subjects; - Telling Time

Patterns and Structures: - *What time is it?;* - *It is _____.; It is time for _____.*

Viewing: Interpret a Visual Image

TELL TIME

1 Introduce Clock Time Say: *It is now 8:45 a.m. and Carlos is getting ready to go to his classes. Soon we will meet some of his teachers, but first we'll practice telling time.* Turn to **Language Practice Book** page 10 and read the clocks. (Or just show various times on a clock and read them.) Explain that *a.m.* means "after midnight, but before 12 noon," and that *p.m.* means "after 12 noon, but before midnight." Ask volunteers to read different times you set on a clock.

2 Introduce the Patterns: *What time is it?* **and** *It is _____.* Model talking about time. Ask: *What time is it?* Point to a clock and use the pattern to answer: *It is 9:15 a.m.*

▶ **Language Practice Book** page 10

GIVE INFORMATION

3 Learn About Schedules Point to the Class Schedule and say: *The schedule shows Carlos when and where to go. It also tells the teacher for each class.* Read aloud the schedule and have students point to the matching photos.

4 Introduce the Pattern: *It is time for _____.* Relate the Class Schedule to the time. Point to the first line and say: *At 8:30 a.m., it is time for homeroom.* Have students give more information from the schedule.

CLOSE AND ASSESS

Call out a time: *It's 2:10 p.m.* and have the volunteers tell about their classes: *It's time for math.*

T18 Lakeside School

Time: 8:45 a.m.

Here are some teachers.

light switch — transparency — overhead projector — dictionary

MS. CHANDANI, ESL TEACHER

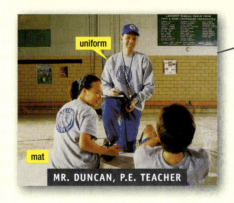

uniform — mat

MR. DUNCAN, P.E. TEACHER

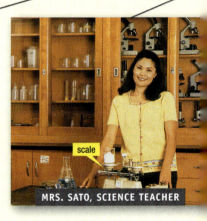

scale

MRS. SATO, SCIENCE TEACHER

18

REACHING ALL STUDENTS

Language Development
TELLING TIME

Play Clock Concentration Draw clock faces with different times on index cards. On separate cards write the corresponding times. Mix the cards and arrange them face down in several rows. Divide the class into two teams. Have a student from Team A turn over two cards. If the cards match, the player says the time and the team keeps the cards. Continue play until all cards have been matched. The team with the most matches wins.

MR. ROSARIO, MATH TEACHER

homework assignment

Class Schedule

Class	Time	Room	Teacher
Homeroom	8:30 a.m.	113	Mrs. Terry
Math	8:45 a.m.	124	Mr. Rosario
ESL, Lang. Arts	9:45 a.m.	118	Ms. Chandani
ESL, Reading	10:45 a.m.	121	Mr. Motts
P.E.	11:45 a.m.	Gym	Mr. Duncan
Lunch	12:40 p.m.		
Science	1:10 p.m.	116	Mrs. Sato
Social Studies	2:10 p.m.	233	Mrs. Varela
Band practice	3:10 p.m.	Auditorium	Mrs. Cally

map
globe

MRS. VARELA, SOCIAL STUDIES TEACHER

HOME CONNECTION

Class Schedule Have students take home a copy of their class schedules to show family members. Suggest that they draw a clock face to show the times of their classes. Provide frames for students to practice in school:

Math class is at 8:45 a.m.
It is in Room 124.
Mr. Rosario is my teacher.

Pronunciation of Names
Rosario   rō **sar** ē ō
Chandani chahn **dahn** ē
Sato   **sah** tō
Varela   var **el** ah

Listen and Learn

Maylin: It is time for math class. Who is your math teacher?
Carlos: Mr. Rosario.
Maylin: He is a good teacher.
Carlos: Where is your ESL class?
Maylin: It's in Room 118.
Carlos: Who is your teacher?
Maylin: Ms. Chandani. She is really nice!

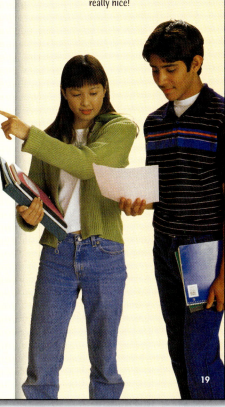

LAKESIDE SCHOOL **LESSON 14**

BASIC VOCABULARY AND LANGUAGE DEVELOPMENT

OBJECTIVES

Functions: Listen Actively; Repeat Spoken Language; Ask and Answer Questions; Give Information

Patterns and Structures:

🅣 *Where is* _____?; 🅣 *Who is* _____?;
🅣 *Here is* _____.; 🅣 *Here are* _____.

ASK AND ANSWER QUESTIONS

1 Introduce the Patterns: *Where/Who is* _____?
Play the "Listen and Learn" conversation on the **Lakeside Language Tape/CD**. Students follow along with the conversation, then listen to segments and echo lines. Finally, they chime in with Carlos.

2 Talk About Schedules Have students write their class schedules on **Language Practice Book** page 11. Explain how to ask and answer questions:

- Use *Where is* to ask about a place:
  Where is *P.E. class?*

- Answer with *It's:* **It's** *in the gym.*

- Use *Who is* to ask about a person:
  Who is *the math teacher?*

- Answer with the teacher's name:
  Mr. Rosario *is the math teacher.*

▶ **Language Practice Book** page 11

GIVE INFORMATION

3 Introduce the Patterns: *Here is/are* _____. Arrange combinations of objects around the room. Hold up a book and explain: Use *Here is* to tell about one thing: "Here is a book." Next hold up three pencils and explain: Use *Here are* to tell about more than one thing: "Here are three pencils."

▶ **Language Practice Book** page 12

CLOSE AND ASSESS

Have partners move around the room and say sentences about different objects: *Here is a map. Here are four pens.*

Language Development **T19**

LAKESIDE SCHOOL **LESSON 15**

LANGUAGE AND LITERACY: HIGH FREQUENCY WORDS

OBJECTIVES
Learning to Read:
- Recognize High Frequency Words

INTRODUCE

1 Learn New Words Place a word and its letter tiles on the screen as you work through the Strategy steps. For *your*, say:

1. *First, look at the word.* (Display the word tile for *your*.)
2. *Now listen to the word:* your, your.
3. *Listen to the word in a sentence:* Where is your science class?
4. *Say the word after me:* your.
5. *Spell the word:* y-o-u-r. (Say each letter as you place the tile. Point to each tile and have students spell the word.)
6. *Say the word again:* your.

Repeat the process for the other words, using these context sentences:

- **She** is in Room 121.
- **He** is Mr. Duncan.
- **Who are some good** teachers?
- Now it is **time** for class.

PRACTICE

2 Build Sentences Set out the word tiles at random and read aloud a sentence: *Who is she?* Place the tile for the first word to the left. Have students say which tiles to place next. Place the punctuation tile. Have students read the question. Continue with: *Who is he? Who are you? Where is your school?*

APPLY

3 Read New Words Have students find the new words on pages 18–19.

▶ Reading Practice Book page 8

CLOSE AND ASSESS
Display the words one at a time for students to read.

T19a Lakeside School

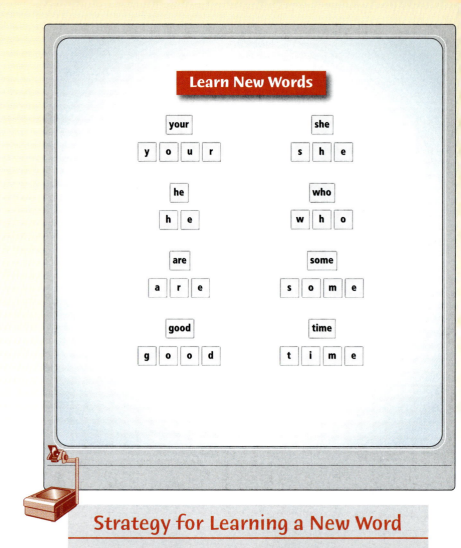

Learn New Words

your · she · he · who · are · some · good · time

Strategy for Learning a New Word

1. Look at the word.
2. Listen to the word.
3. Listen to the word in a sentence.
4. Say the word.
5. Spell the word.
6. Say the word again.

REACHING ALL STUDENTS

Multimodal Practice
RECOGNIZE HIGH FREQUENCY WORDS

Distribute sets of cards with the words printed lightly in pencil. Also display the words on a chart. Then provide coaching for each activity:

Kinesthetic One group of students carefully outlines the shapes of the words on the cards and then erases the letters.

Visual Other students match the outline shapes with the words on display.

Auditory Then one student can reprint the words inside the shapes, pronounce each word correctly, and have the group echo it.

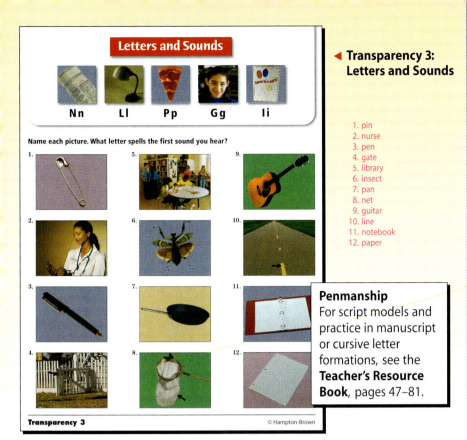

◀ Transparency 3: Letters and Sounds

1. pin
2. nurse
3. pen
4. gate
5. library
6. insect
7. pan
8. net
9. guitar
10. line
11. notebook
12. paper

Penmanship For script models and practice in manuscript or cursive letter formations, see the **Teacher's Resource Book**, pages 47–81.

▼ Script for Transparency 3

Letters and Sounds

1. Develop Phonemic Awareness

Count Words in Sentences/Match Initial Sounds Say a sentence and have students count each word they hear: *Nora likes pink gum.* Then ask: *How many words are in this sentence?* (4) Repeat for: *Len eats pizza for lunch.* (5) Next, say: *Listen to these two words:* nurse, net. *Say the words with me:* nurse, net. *Do they begin with the same sound?* (yes) Repeat with these word pairs: *note, lamp; pin, pencil; gate, insect; line, library; girl, guitar; in, on; line, net; pan, nurse.*

2. Associate Letters and Sounds

Learn Consonant Names, Sounds, and Formations Point to the newspaper on **Transparency 3**. Say: *This is a newspaper.* Say *newspaper* with me: *newspaper.* Then point to *Nn* and say: *This is capital* N, *and this is lowercase* n. *The letter* n *spells the first sound you hear in* newspaper. *The first sound is /n/.* Say /nnn/ *with me:* /nnn/. Point to the *n* and ask: *What is the letter? What is its sound?* Trace the *Nn* on the transparency as you explain how to form the letters and have students "write" the letters in the air. Repeat for *l, p,* and *g.* Then explain: *The letters* n, l, p, *and* g *are* **consonants**—*they spell consonant sounds.*

Learn the Name, Sound, and Formation for the Vowel *Ii* Point to *Ii* and say: *This is the letter* i—*capital* I *and lowercase* i. *The letter* i *is a* **vowel**. Point to the invitation and say: *Say* invitation *with me:* invitation. *Say its first sound:* /iii/. *The sound* /iii/ *is a vowel sound. When you say a vowel sound, you keep your mouth open and let the air flow out. Try it:* /iii/. Then say: *The letter* i *spells the vowel sound* /i/ *you hear in* invitation. Point to the *i* and ask: *What is the letter? What is its sound?* Then teach students how to form capital and lowercase *i.*

Practice Have students number a paper from 1–12. For Item 1, say: *What is in this picture? Let's say the word and then its first sound:* pin, /p/. *What letter spells* /p/ *as in* pin? *That's right,* p. Point to the *Pp* on the transparency. Have students write a capital and lowercase *p* by Item 1 on their papers. Repeat for Items 2–12.

LAKESIDE SCHOOL **LESSON 16**

LANGUAGE AND LITERACY: PHONICS

OBJECTIVES
Learning to Read: Build Oral Vocabulary; Develop Phonemic Awareness; 🅣 Associate Letters and Sounds

TEACH LETTERS AND SOUNDS

1 **Build Oral Vocabulary** Display Transparency 3. Play a game of "I Spy," giving clues until students find the picture. For example, for Item 9, say:

• *I spy a guitar. You play music with a guitar. It has strings and a long neck.*

When students find the guitar, say: *Yes,* **this is a guitar** (point). Repeat the game to build context for the other words.

2 **Develop Phonemic Awareness** Remove the transparency and work through Step 1 of the script.

3 **Associate Letters and Sounds** Display Transparency 3 again. Work through Step 2 of the script.

▶ **Reading Practice Book** pages 9, 10

CLOSE AND ASSESS
Say the words *net, pencil, gate, line,* and *insect* one at a time. Have students write the letter that stands for the first sound in the word on a card and hold it up.

Review and Reteaching
PHONEMIC AWARENESS AND PHONICS

• **Match Initial Sounds** Say a sound and two words. Ask students to tell you which word begins with the sound you name. Some sounds and words to use are: /n/ *girl, net;* /l/ *lamp, pen;* /p/ *nurse, pizza;* /g/ *gate, line;* /i/ *insect, apple.*

• **Match Letters and Sounds** Set out classroom objects or pictures whose names begin with the sounds taught to date. Distribute corresponding letter cards (see pages 83–88 in the **Teacher's Resource Book**). Have students name each object, say its first sound, and attach the appropriate letter card.

Language and Literacy **T19b**

LAKESIDE SCHOOL **LESSON 17**

BASIC VOCABULARY AND LANGUAGE DEVELOPMENT

OBJECTIVES
Concepts and Vocabulary:
- Classroom Activities
Viewing: Interpret a Visual Image

USE WORDS FOR CLASSROOM ACTIVITIES

1. **Identify Actions** Direct attention to pages 20–21. Explain: *Now it is 9:10 a.m. Carlos is in math class. Let's look at some of the things he does in math class.* Look at the photos and read aloud the captions.

2. **Present Words for Classroom Activities** Post a chart of common classroom actions:

Classroom Activities

answer	find	sit
ask	listen	stand
carry	look	talk
close	open	type
cut	point to	use
draw	read	work
erase	sharpen	write

As you read aloud the list, act out each action and have students copy you and say the word.

3. **Pantomime** Have volunteers pantomime a classroom activity from the chart for other students to guess.

▶ **Language Practice Book** page 13

CLOSE AND ASSESS
Call on students to show and tell about two actions they do at school.

Time: 9:10 a.m.

Here is a math class.

I work at my desk.

I raise my hand.

I write a problem on the board.

I write the answer to the problem. I show my work.

I work with a group.

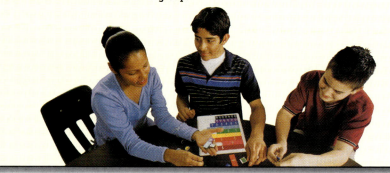

20

REACHING ALL STUDENTS

Vocabulary
CLASSROOM ACTIVITIES

Photo Captions Have small groups page through the text to find photographs of people doing classroom activities. Provide self-stick notes for students to create first-person captions for the individuals in the pictures. To model this activity, turn to pages 14–15 and write captions for the teacher: *I talk to the students. I stand in front of the board.* Affix the label near the teacher. Afterwards page through the book and ask the groups to share their captions.

T20 Lakeside School

I read my textbook.

I write my name on my worksheet.

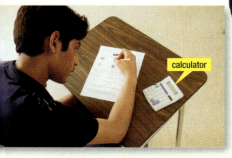
I read my worksheet. I write the answers.

Pronunciation of Name
Rosario   rō **sar** ē ō

Listen and Learn

Mr. Rosario:	Which circle shows 25% of 4? Show me.
Carlos:	Here is the circle. It is Circle C.
Mr. Rosario:	Good. Point to the circle that shows 50% of 4.
Carlos:	Here is the circle. It is Circle A.
Mr. Rosario:	Good. Now show me the circle that shows 75% of 4.
Carlos:	Here is the circle. It is Circle D.
Mr. Rosario:	Good job, Carlos!

Language Development

GIVE AND CARRY OUT COMMANDS

Divide the class into four teams and assign one shape—circle, triangle, rectangle, or square—to each team. Have each team locate all items in the classroom that have their assigned shape. Students from each group can give commands for a student in another group to follow: *Point to a circle. Show me a square.* Give each group the opportunity to give and carry out commands.

LAKESIDE SCHOOL   LESSON 18

BASIC VOCABULARY AND LANGUAGE DEVELOPMENT

OBJECTIVES

Functions: Listen Actively; Repeat Spoken Language; Give and Carry Out Commands
Concepts and Vocabulary:
🅣 Shapes; 🅣 Commands
Patterns and Structures:
Show me _____.; Point to _____.

USE NAMES OF SHAPES

1 Introduce Shapes Draw a circle, a square, a triangle, and a rectangle. Trace the outline as you name and describe each shape: *A triangle has three sides.*

2 Identify Shapes Use chart paper to draw a large pattern that includes combinations of the four shapes. Give instructions for volunteers to follow: *Color a square red. Count the circles.*

GIVE AND CARRY OUT COMMANDS

3 Introduce Commands Explain: *When you give a command, you tell someone what to do.* Then play the "Listen and Learn" conversation on the **Lakeside Language Tape/CD**. It contains good modeling of commands and responses to commands.

Side A   CD Track 5

4 Introduce the Patterns: *Point to _____.* and *Show me _____.* Post these sentence frames:

> Point to _____.
> Show me _____.

Use the patterns to give commands: *Point to Carlos's teacher. Show me a calculator.* Then have partners give and carry out commands.

▶ **Language Practice Book** pages 14, 15

CLOSE AND ASSESS

Write commands on several slips of paper; for example: *Point to Jan's desk. Show me a blue pen.* Volunteers can pick up a slip and carry out the command.

Language Development   **T21**

LAKESIDE SCHOOL **LESSON 19**

LANGUAGE AND LITERACY: HIGH FREQUENCY WORDS

OBJECTIVES
Learning to Read:
- Recognize High Frequency Words

INTRODUCE

1 Learn New Words Place a word and its letter tiles on the screen as you work through the Strategy steps. For example, for *work,* say:

1. *First, look at the word.* (Display the word tile for *work*.)
2. *Now listen to the word:* work, work.
3. *Listen to the word in a sentence:* I work at my desk.
4. *Say the word after me:* work.
5. *Spell the word:* w-o-r-k. (As you say each letter, place the corresponding letter tile. Point to each tile and have students spell the word.)
6. *Say the word again:* work.

Repeat the process for the other words, using these context sentences:

- I **read** a problem.
- I work **with** my teacher.
- I **write** an **answer**.
- I **point to** my worksheet.

PRACTICE

2 Build Sentences Say each word as you place its tile on the screen: *Point to the _____. Here is the _____. Here are the _____.* Model reading the text and filling in the blanks: *Point to the worksheet. Here is the worksheet. Here are the pencils.* Have one partner give the command and the other respond.

APPLY

3 Read New Words Have students find the new words on pages 20–21.

▶ **Reading Practice Book** page 11

CLOSE AND ASSESS
Display the words one at a time for students to read.

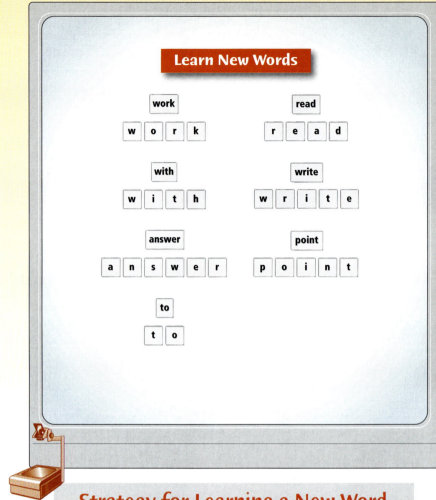

Strategy for Learning a New Word

1. Look at the word.
2. Listen to the word.
3. Listen to the word in a sentence.
4. Say the word.
5. Spell the word.
6. Say the word again.

REACHING ALL STUDENTS

Reading Fluency
RECOGNIZE HIGH FREQUENCY WORDS

To build automaticity with the new high frequency words:

- Display the word tiles on the overhead, one at a time. Scramble the letter tiles for the word below it. (Add distractor letters, for more of a challenge). Have volunteers rearrange the letter tiles and read the word.

- Use letter tiles on the overhead to spell out words from the list. Pause after each letter to see if students can identify the word you are spelling. After a word is identified, ask a volunteer to complete it.

T21a Lakeside School

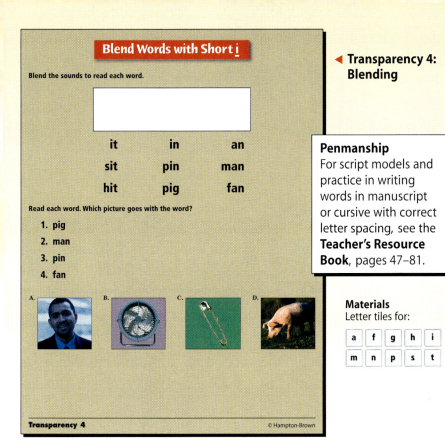

▼ Script for Transparency 4

Blend Words with Short *i*

1. Develop Phonemic Awareness
Match Initial Sounds/Match Final Sounds Say: *Listen to these two words:* it, in. *Say the words with me:* it, in. *The first sound in these words is the same:* /iii/. *Now listen to these two words:* it, at. *Say the words with me:* it, at. *Is the first sound in each word the same?* (no) Continue with word pairs *sit, lid; if, is; pig, hit; gift, girl.* Then say: *Now listen to these two words:* pin, man. *Say the words with me:* pin, man. *They end with the same sound:* /n/. *Here are two more words:* pig, in. *Say the words with me:* pig, in. *Is the last sound in each word the same?* (no) Continue with word pairs *lip, pit; sit, hat; pan, fin; big, fig; if, in.*

2. Blend Sounds to Read Words
Model Set letter tile *i* at the left in the box on **Transparency 4** and letter tile *t* at the right. Point to *i* and say: *The sound for this letter is* /iii/. As you say the sound, slide *i* next to *t*, and then put your finger under *t*. Say: *I can blend the sound* /iii/ *with the sound of the letter* t: /iiit/. *Now I'm going to say the word fast:* it. Summarize: *You can blend sounds like this to read a word. Just say the sound for the first letter, and blend it into the sound for the next letter.* Demonstrate again: Point to *i* and say: *Say the sound for* i *with me:* /iii/. Repeat for *t:* /t/. Then slide a finger below the letters *it* and say: *Help me blend the two sounds:* /iiit/. *Now let's say the word:* it. Then leave *it* at the right in the box, add letter tile *s* at the left, and repeat the process to read *sit*. Remove the *s*, add *h*, and repeat the process to read *hit*.

Practice Have students read the words *it, sit,* and *hit* below the box. Then repeat Model and Practice for the other two word sets.

3. Match Words and Pictures
Point to Item 1. Say: *Let's read this word.* Slide a finger slowly under the letters to lead students in sounding out the word: /piiig/, *pig.* Then say: *Now let's look at the pictures. Which of these pictures—A, B, C, or D—shows a pig?* (D) Repeat the process for Items 2, 3, and 4.

LAKESIDE SCHOOL **LESSON 20**

LANGUAGE AND LITERACY: PHONICS

OBJECTIVES
Learning to Read: Build Oral Vocabulary; Develop Phonemic Awareness; Blend Sounds to Decode Words

TEACH BLENDING

1 Build Oral Vocabulary Display Transparency 4. Use *it, sit,* and *hit* in sentences to build meaning.

- I **sit** in a chair (pantomime). **It** is big. Can you **hit** a ball? (pantomime)

Use the pictures to develop the meaning of the words *pin, fan, man,* and *pig*. For example:

- This is a **fan**. When a **fan** is on, it spins and blows air. It makes us feel cool.

2 Develop Phonemic Awareness Remove the transparency and work through Step 1 of the script.

3 Blend Sounds to Read Words Display Transparency 4 again. Work through Steps 2 and 3 of the script.

▶ **Reading Practice Book** pages 12, 13

CLOSE AND ASSESS
Display *hit, pin, sit, fan,* and *pig*. Have students identify the sounds in each word and blend them to read the word.

Review and Reteaching
PHONEMIC AWARENESS AND PHONICS

- **Listen for Initial and Final Sounds** Say a sound (e.g., /p/) and a word that begins or ends with the sound. Have students tell you whether they hear the sound at the beginning or at the end of the word. Some words to use are: p̲in, ma̲p, l̲amp, pil̲l, b̲ig, g̲et, pen̲, not̲e.

- **Blend Sounds to Decode Words** Distribute letter cards for *i, t, h, s, p, a,* and *f* (see pages 83–88 in the **Teacher's Resource Book**). Have students spell and blend *it*, then add a letter or change a letter to spell and blend *hit, sit, pit, fit, fat,* and *pat*.

Language and Literacy **T21b**

LAKESIDE SCHOOL **LESSON 21**

BASIC VOCABULARY AND LANGUAGE DEVELOPMENT

OBJECTIVES

Function: Give Personal Information
Concepts and Vocabulary:
🅣 School Objects; Personnel; Personal Information
Patterns and Structures: *My name is _____.; My phone number is _____.*
Viewing: Interpret a Visual Image

USE NAMES OF SCHOOL OBJECTS AND PERSONNEL

1 Introduce School Objects and Personnel Explain: *It's now 9:40 a.m. Carlos goes to the main office.* Point to the school workers and explain their jobs; for example: *The principal is in charge of the school.* Then point out the objects and explain how each object is used.

GIVE PERSONAL INFORMATION

2 Introduce the Pattern: *My name is _____.* Explain that students can introduce themselves by saying: *Hi. My name is _____.* Have partners practice introducing themselves.

3 Introduce the Pattern: *My phone number is _____.* Explain: *To call someone on the telephone, you need the phone number.* Write the school number and say: *At work, my phone number is 555-2467.* To tell someone your phone number, you can say: *"My phone number is _____."*

▶ **Language Practice Book** page 16

CLOSE AND ASSESS

Have students introduce themselves and give a fictitious phone number.

REACHING ALL STUDENTS

COMMUNITY CONNECTION

Community Service Numbers
Provide telephone books and brochures, or use local government Internet Web sites. Have groups find information for community services, such as the fire department, the police station, libraries, hospitals, and community centers. Groups can add the information to a class telephone directory. Make copies for students to use at home.

T22 Lakeside School

Pronunciation of Name
Cruz   krüz

Listen and Learn

Carlos:	Hi, Mrs. Cruz, my name is Carlos Parra. Where is the telephone? I need to call my mom.
Mrs. Cruz:	What is her phone number?
Carlos:	555-3298.
Mrs. Cruz:	Is this a work number?
Carlos:	Yes. My mom is at work. She is a secretary, like you.

Language Development

ASK FOR INFORMATION

Invite pairs of volunteers to role-play a talk show interview, with one student as the host and another as the guest. The class can represent the audience. The host asks questions with *what* and *where*: What is your name? Where is your home? The guest can answer with personal information, or take the role of a fictional character or famous person. Later, have the audience pose questions for the guest to answer.

LAKESIDE SCHOOL **LESSON 22**

BASIC VOCABULARY AND LANGUAGE DEVELOPMENT

OBJECTIVES

Functions: Listen Actively; Repeat Spoken Language; Ask for Information; Express Needs

Patterns and Structures:
❶ Where is _____ ?; ❶ What is _____ ?;
❶ I need to _____ .

ASK FOR INFORMATION

1 Introduce the Patterns: *Where/What is _____ ?* Side A / CD Track 6
Play the "Listen and Learn" conversation on the **Lakeside Language Tape/CD**. Students will listen twice to the conversation, then echo lines and chime in with Carlos.

2 Ask and Answer Questions Turn to **Language Practice Book** page 17 and explain: *When a question asks "What is," the answer tells about a thing. When the question asks "Where is," the answer tells about a place.*

▶ **Language Practice Book** page 17

EXPRESS NEEDS

3 Introduce the Pattern: *I need to _____ .* Post sentence pairs to model completing the pattern with a verb:

> My pencil is dull. I need to <u>sharpen</u> it.
> The class is starting. I need to <u>sit</u>.

Give scenarios and have students create sentences with the pattern.
- I am tired. (I need to rest.)
- I have a test. (I need to study.)

4 Use the Pattern: *I need to _____ .* Have partners find pictures of people in various settings. Help them add speech balloons that express each person's needs.

▶ **Language Practice Book** page 18

CLOSE AND ASSESS

Partners can role-play a school worker on pages 22–23. Have them ask a question or express a need.

LAKESIDE SCHOOL **LESSON 23**

LANGUAGE AND LITERACY: HIGH FREQUENCY WORDS

OBJECTIVES

Learning to Read:
- Recognize High Frequency Words

INTRODUCE

1 Learn New Words Place a word and its letter tiles on the screen as you work through the Strategy steps. For example, for *what,* say:

1. *First, look at the word.* (Display the word tile for *what.*)

2. *Now listen to the word:* what, what.

3. *Listen to the word in a sentence:* What is your name?

4. *Say the word after me:* what.

5. *Spell the word:* w-h-a-t. (As you say each letter, place the corresponding letter tile. Point to each tile and have students spell the word.)

6. *Say the word again:* what.

Repeat the process for the other words, using these context sentences. Point out the new meaning for the word *to:*

- My **name** is Maylin.
- I **need to** work with Carlos.
- I will **call** Carlos.
- The phone **number** is 555-9907.

PRACTICE

2 Sort Words Place the word tiles on the screen in a random arrangement. Have students sort the words to make this group: words that start with *n.*

APPLY

3 Read New Words Have students find the new words on pages 22–23.

▶ **Reading Practice Book** page 14

CLOSE AND ASSESS

Display the words one at a time for students to read.

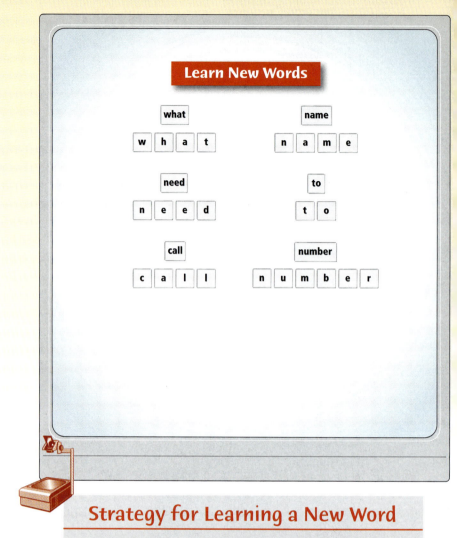

Strategy for Learning a New Word

1. Look at the word.
2. Listen to the word.
3. Listen to the word in a sentence.
4. Say the word.
5. Spell the word.
6. Say the word again.

REACHING ALL STUDENTS

Reading Fluency
RECOGNIZE HIGH FREQUENCY WORDS

To build automaticity with the new high frequency words:

- Provide copies of an emergency procedures page from a telephone directory or other source. Have small groups look for the new words on it, and highlight the ones they find.

- Go over the procedure for reporting an emergency. Write the steps. Write over the new high frequency words in another color. Read the sentences aloud and pause at each new word for students to supply it.

1. **Call** the emergency **number**: 911.
2. Tell the person your **name**.
3. Tell **what** is wrong.
4. Say the address. You **need to** give the town, too.
5. Give the phone **number**.

IMPORTANT: Verify that 911 is the emergency number for your area. This can vary.

T23a Lakeside School

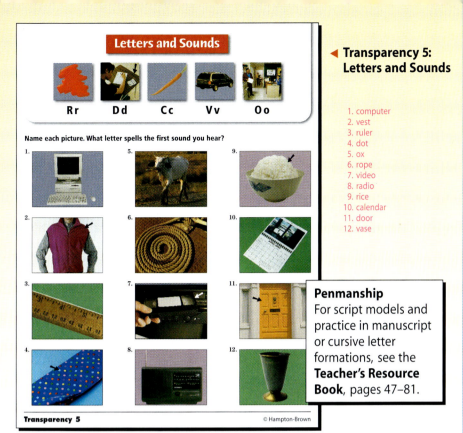

▼ Script for Transparency 5

Letters and Sounds

1. Develop Phonemic Awareness
Count Words in Sentences/Match Initial Sounds Say a sentence and have students count each word they hear: *Who drives the red van?* Then ask: *How many words are in the sentence?* (5) Repeat for: *Who drives the red van down the street?* (8) Next, say: *Listen to these two words:* red, run. *Say the words with me:* red, run. *Do they begin with the same sound?* (yes) Repeat with these word pairs: *dot, door; cup, vest; rope, ruler; ox, on; van, vine; computer, calendar.*

2. Associate Letters and Sounds
Learn Consonant Names, Sounds, and Formations Point to the swatch of red on **Transparency 5**. Say: *This is the color red. Say red with me:* red. Then point to *Rr* and say: *This is capital R, and this is lowercase r. The letter r spells the first sound you hear in* red. *The first sound is /r/. Say /rrr/ with me: /rrr/.* Point to the *r* and ask: *What is the letter? What is its sound?* Trace the *Rr* on the transparency as you explain how to form the letters and have students "write" the letters in the air. Repeat the process for *d, c,* and *v*. Then explain: *The letters r, d, c, and v are called* **consonants**—*they spell consonant sounds.*

Learn the Name, Sound, and Formation for the Vowel *Oo* Point to *Oo* and say: *This is the letter* o—*capital O and lowercase* o. *The letter* o *is a* **vowel**. Point to the office and say: *Say* office *with me:* office. *Say its first sound: /ooo/. The sound /ooo/ is a vowel sound. When you say a vowel sound, you keep your mouth open and let the air flow out. Try it: /ooo/.* Then say: *The letter* o *spells the vowel sound /o/ you hear in* office. Point to the *o* and ask: *What is the letter? What is its sound?* Then teach students how to form capital and lowercase *o*.

Practice Have students number a paper from 1–12. For Item 1, say: *What is in this picture? Let's say the word and then its first sound:* computer, /k/. *What letter spells /k/ as in* computer? *That's right,* c. Point to the *Cc* on the transparency. Have students write a capital and lowercase *c* by Item 1 on their papers. Repeat the process for Items 2–12.

LAKESIDE SCHOOL **LESSON 24**

LANGUAGE AND LITERACY: PHONICS

OBJECTIVES
Learning to Read: Build Oral Vocabulary; Develop Phonemic Awareness; 🅣 Associate Letters and Sounds

TEACH LETTERS AND SOUNDS

1 Build Oral Vocabulary Display Transparency 5. Play "I Spy," giving clues until students find the picture. For example, for Item 8, say:

• *I spy a radio. You can listen to music or the news on a radio. Some radios are small. You can carry them with you.*

When students find the radio, say: *Yes, this is a radio* (point). Repeat the game to build context for the other words.

2 Develop Phonemic Awareness Remove the transparency and work through Step 1 of the script.

3 Associate Letters and Sounds Display Transparency 5 again. Work through Step 2 of the script.

▶ **Reading Practice Book** pages 15, 16

CLOSE AND ASSESS
Say the words *carrot, ox, rope, desk,* and *video* one at a time. Have the group write the letter that stands for the first sound in the word on a card and hold it up.

Review and Reteaching
PHONEMIC AWARENESS AND PHONICS

- **Isolate Sounds** Say words that begin with the sounds taught to date and ask students to tell you the first sound they hear in the word.

- **Match Letters and Sounds** Display transparencies for the letters and sounds taught to date. Have students name each picture at the top, say the first sound, and tell the name of the letter. Then distribute letter cards (see pages 83–88 in the **Teacher's Resource Book**). Say words that begin with the sounds taught to date, and have students hold up the letter that spells the first sound in the word.

Language and Literacy **T23b**

LAKESIDE SCHOOL **LESSON 25**

BASIC VOCABULARY AND LANGUAGE DEVELOPMENT

> **OBJECTIVES**
>
> **Function:** Ask for and Give Information
> **Concepts and Vocabulary:**
> ⓣ Library Objects
> **Patterns and Structures:** *What is in the _____?; A _____ is in the _____.; Some _____ are in the _____.; Plurals with -s*
> **Viewing:** Interpret a Visual Image

USE NAMES OF LIBRARY OBJECTS

1 Introduce Library Objects Say: *At 11:00 a.m., Carlos goes to the school library. A library has books, magazines, and computers. A librarian helps you find books and materials.* Go over the labeled objects and show examples from your classroom.

ASK FOR AND GIVE INFORMATION

2 Introduce Plurals with -s Explain: *We add -s to show that there is more than one object.* Have students review the library scene and make a chart:

What is in the Library?

one	more than one
a globe	two chair**s**
a table	two door**s**

3 Introduce the Patterns: *What is in the _____?; A _____ is in the _____.; Some _____ are in the _____.*
Explain: *We use the question to ask what objects are in a place. We use the word* some *when we don't know how many objects there are or if the number is not important.*

4 Visit the School Library Ask the librarian to give a brief tour. Have students identify library objects.

▶ **Language Practice Book** page 19

> **CLOSE AND ASSESS**
>
> Assign groups different areas of the school. Have each group complete a chart headed "What is in the _____?" by listing items that are found in that place.

T24 Lakeside School

REACHING ALL STUDENTS

Vocabulary
LIBRARY OBJECTS

Library Tour Maps Have small groups make and label a drawing of the school library. Have groups compare drawings and make sure they have included all library objects. Then have group members take turns using the drawing to give a "tour" of the library. Encourage students to ask and answer questions about the library during the "tour."

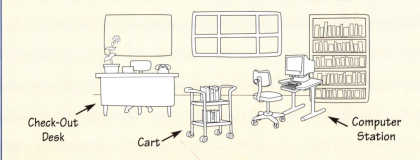

LAKESIDE SCHOOL **LESSON 26**

BASIC VOCABULARY AND LANGUAGE DEVELOPMENT

OBJECTIVES

Functions: Listen Actively; Repeat Spoken Language; Express Likes; Ask and Answer Questions

Patterns and Structures: *Will you _____?;* ❶ *Does _____?; Do you like _____?;* ❶ *I like _____.*

EXPRESS LIKES

1. **Introduce the Patterns:** *Do you like _____?* **and** *I like _____.* Play the "Listen and Learn" conversation on the **Lakeside Language Tape/CD**. Students will listen to the conversation, then echo one line at a time, and chime in on Carlos's part.

2. **People Hunt** Post sentence frames:

   > I like _____.
   > Do you like _____?

   Have students draw something they like, such as a sport, a food, or a hobby. Then have students mingle and ask other students if they like the same thing: *I like books. Do you like books?* Students who answer "yes" can sign the picture.

▶ **Language Practice Book** page 20

ASK AND ANSWER QUESTIONS

3. **Introduce the Patterns:** *Will you _____?* **and** *Does _____?* Review the conversation and explain: *You can start questions with* Will you *or* Does.

   Set out several books and pose questions: *Will you help me find a book about sports? Does it tell about baseball?* Students can answer, then ask new questions.

▶ **Language Practice Book** page 21

CLOSE AND ASSESS

Display the four language patterns presented and have partners role-play a conversation between a student and a librarian.

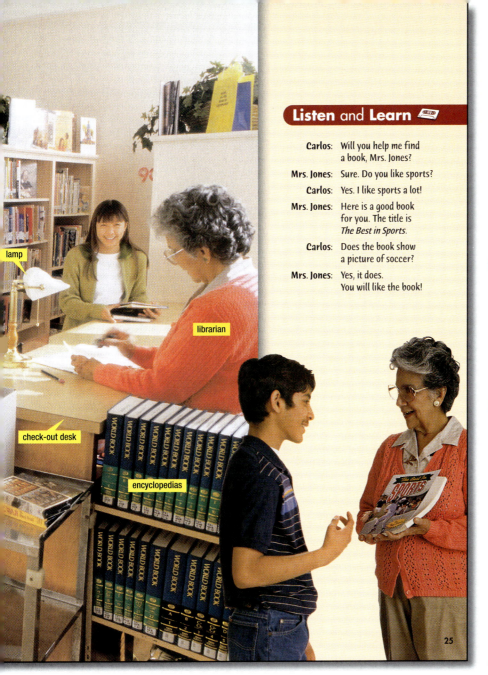

Listen and Learn

Carlos: Will you help me find a book, Mrs. Jones?
Mrs. Jones: Sure. Do you like sports?
Carlos: Yes. I like sports a lot!
Mrs. Jones: Here is a good book for you. The title is *The Best in Sports*.
Carlos: Does the book show a picture of soccer?
Mrs. Jones: Yes, it does. You will like the book!

Multimodal Practice

QUESTIONS AND ANSWERS

Visual Have students copy the first three lines of the conversation onto sentence strips, and then cut them apart to create word and end-mark cards.

Kinesthetic Students study the printed conversation and then use the cards to rebuild the lines.

Auditory Students can read the reconstructed conversation aloud for the group.

Language Development **T25**

LAKESIDE SCHOOL **LESSON 27**

LANGUAGE AND LITERACY: HIGH FREQUENCY WORDS

OBJECTIVES

Learning to Read:
- Recognize High Frequency Words

INTRODUCE

1 Learn New Words Place a word and its letter tiles on the screen as you work through the Strategy steps. For *for*, say:

1. *First, look at the word.* (Display the word tile for *for*.)
2. *Now listen to the word:* for, for.
3. *Listen to the word in a sentence:* I have a book for you.
4. *Say the word after me:* for.
5. *Spell the word:* f-o-r. (Say each letter as you place the tile. Point to each tile and have students spell the word.)
6. *Say the word again:* for.

Repeat the process for the other words, using these context sentences:

- Look **in** the library.
- **Does** it have a good book for **me**?
- I **will help** you.
- **Do** you **like** the **picture**?

PRACTICE

2 Build Sentences Set out the word tiles at random and read aloud a question: *Do you like this picture?* Place the tile for the first word to the left. Then have students tell you which tiles to place next. Place the punctuation tile. Have students read the question in unison. Continue with: *Does he help you? Does she see it?*

APPLY

3 Read New Words Have students find the new words on pages 24–25.

▶ **Reading Practice Book** page 17

CLOSE AND ASSESS

Display the words one at a time for students to read.

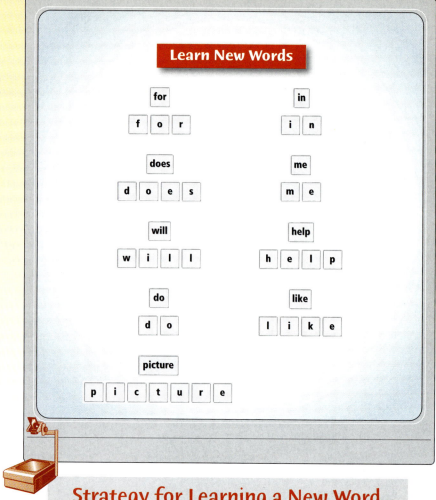

Strategy for Learning a New Word

1. Look at the word.
2. Listen to the word.
3. Listen to the word in a sentence.
4. Say the word.
5. Spell the word.
6. Say the word again.

REACHING ALL STUDENTS

Reading Fluency

RECOGNIZE HIGH FREQUENCY WORDS

To build automaticity with the new high frequency words:

- Display the word list. Give two clues for each word—the number of letters in it, and the letter it starts with—and have students guess it. Say: *Which word has two letters and starts with* d? (*do*) If students guess an incorrect word, go over why it doesn't work: *The word* does *starts with* d, *but it has more than two letters, doesn't it?*

- Give small groups the letter tiles for three of the words. Have them unscramble the letters to "find" their words. Groups can take turns leading the class in reading their words.

T25a Lakeside School

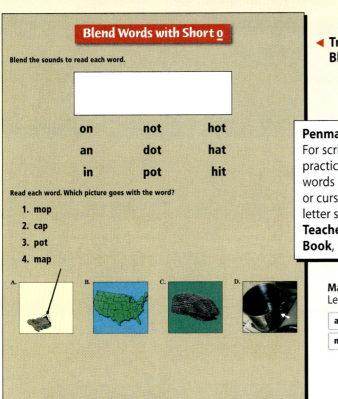

◀ Transparency 6: Blending

Penmanship
For script models and practice in writing words in manuscript or cursive with correct letter spacing, see the **Teacher's Resource Book**, pages 47–81.

Materials
Letter tiles for:
a d h i
n o p t

▼ Script for Transparency 6

Blend Words with Short o

1. Develop Phonemic Awareness
Match Initial Sounds/Match Final Sounds Say: *Listen to these two words: on, ox. Say the words with me: on, ox. The first sound in these words is the same: /ooo/. Now listen to these two words: on, it. Say the words with me: on, it. Is the first sound in each word the same?* (no) Continue with word pairs *ask, an; on, pot; top, not; hot, hit; in, if.* Then say: *Now listen to these two words: hop, map. Say the words with me: hop, map. They end with the same sound: /p/. Here are two more words: ham, hot. Say the words with me: ham, hot. Is the last sound in each word the same?* (no) Continue with word pairs *dot, run; rod, lid; van, on; mop, cap.*

2. Blend Sounds to Read Words
Model Set letter tile *o* at the left in the box on **Transparency 6** and letter tile *n* at the right. Point to *o* and say: *The sound for this letter is /ooo/.* As you say the sound, slide *o* next to *n*, and then put your finger under *n*. Say: *I can blend the sound /ooo/ with the sound of the letter n: /ooonnn/. Now I'm going to say the word fast: on.* Summarize: *You can blend sounds like this to read a word. Just say the sound for the first letter, and blend it into the sound for the next letter.* Demonstrate again: Point to *o* and say: *Say the sound for o with me: /ooo/.* Repeat for *n: /nnn/.* Then slide a finger below the letters *on* and say: *Help me blend the two sounds: /ooonnn/. Now let's say the word:* on. Then remove *o* and leave *n* at the right in the box. Add letter tile *a* at the left, and repeat the process to read *an*. Replace the *a* with *i* and repeat the process to read *in*.

Practice Have students read the words *on, an,* and *in* below the box. Then repeat Model and Practice for the other two word sets.

3. Match Words and Pictures
Point to Item 1. Say: *Let's read this word.* Slide a finger slowly under the letters to lead students in sounding out the word: */mmmooop/, mop.* Then say: *Now let's look at the pictures. Which of these pictures—A, B, C, or D—shows a mop?* (A) Repeat the process for Items 2, 3, and 4.

LAKESIDE SCHOOL **LESSON 28**

LANGUAGE AND LITERACY: PHONICS

OBJECTIVES
Learning to Read: Build Oral Vocabulary; Develop Phonemic Awareness; Blend Sounds to Decode Words

TEACH BLENDING

1 Build Oral Vocabulary Display Transparency 6. Use *on, dot,* and *hot* in sentences to build meaning:

• *I put my hand on the book* (pantomime). *A dot is a small circle with the color filled in* (demonstrate). *When it is hot, I like to swim.*

Use the pictures to develop the meaning of *mop, map, cap,* and *pot*:

• *This is a mop. You use a mop to clean a floor. You push the mop.*

2 Develop Phonemic Awareness
Remove the transparency and work through Step 1 of the script.

3 Blend Sounds to Read Words
Display Transparency 6 again. Work through Steps 2 and 3 of the script.

▶ Reading Practice Book pages 18, 19

CLOSE AND ASSESS
Display *pot, map, hot, mop,* and *hit*. Have students identify the sounds in each word and blend them to read the word.

Review and Reteaching
PHONEMIC AWARENESS AND PHONICS

• **Create Rhyming Words** Arrange students in a circle. Choose a word from Transparencies 1–6, for example: *vest*. The two students to your right must agree on a word that rhymes with yours. Go around the circle, encouraging partners to add more rhyming words.

• **Blend Sounds to Decode Words** Distribute letter cards for *h, o, t, g, n, d, p, i,* and *a* (see pages 83–88 in the **Teacher's Resource Book**). Have students spell and blend *hot*, then change a letter to spell and blend *got, not, dot, pot, pit,* and *pat*.

Language and Literacy **T25b**

LAKESIDE SCHOOL **LESSON 29**

BASIC VOCABULARY AND LANGUAGE DEVELOPMENT

OBJECTIVES

Functions: Listen Actively; Repeat Spoken Language; Express Likes
Concepts and Vocabulary: 🅣 Sports
Patterns and Structures: 🅣 *I like _____.*
Viewing: Interpret a Visual Image

USE SPORTS WORDS

1. **Introduce Sports Words** Explain: *It is now 12:00 p.m., or noon. Carlos is in P.E. class. "P.E." stands for physical education. Here, students play sports and exercise.* Use the photos to introduce sports words. Have students point to various objects as you say sentences: *Show me a softball glove.*

2. **Visit the School Gym** Ask a P.E. teacher to show sports equipment and demonstrate its use.

EXPRESS LIKES

3. **Review the Pattern:** *I like _____.* Play the "Listen and Learn" conversation on the **Lakeside Language Tape/CD**. Students will listen once to the conversation, and then listen again, clapping each time they hear the word *like* or *likes*. Then they'll echo the lines, and finally chime in on Carlos's part.

   Side B
   CD Track 8

▶ **Language Practice Book** page 22

CLOSE AND ASSESS

Have volunteers pantomime sports they like for the class to guess. The student doing the pantomime confirms correct guesses: *Yes, I like tennis.*

What do you do in P.E.?

You can play basketball.

You can play softball.

26

REACHING ALL STUDENTS

HOME CONNECTION

Sports Booklets Model how to create a booklet by folding two sheets of paper in half and stapling them together at the center. Have students add the title: *We Like Sports.* On each of the four inner pages, have students copy the sentence frame: *I like _____.* Students can complete the first page with a favorite sport: *I like judo.* Encourage them to draw or use pictures from magazines and newspapers, writing labels for the people and equipment.

Then have students interview three family members about their favorite sports. The family can work together to create a new page for each sport. Have the family members sign their names and complete the sentence with the name of the sport. In class, students can decorate the cover of their booklet to reflect the contents.

T26 Lakeside School

You can run around the track.

You can play volleyball.

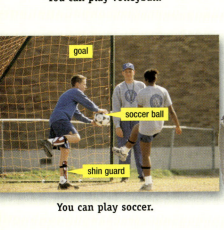

You can play soccer.

Listen and Learn

Dan: What sports do you like?
Carlos: I like soccer.
Dan: My friend Ron likes soccer, too. We also play basketball. Can you play basketball?
Carlos: Yes, I can play basketball. I like lots of sports.

Language Development

ASK AND ANSWER QUESTIONS

In small groups, have students show the drawings and sentences they made on **Language Practice Book** page 22. Encourage them to hold discussions. Provide frames:

> Do you like ____?
> I like ____.
> Can you ____?
> I can ____.

Students may record their discussions and play them for the class.

LAKESIDE SCHOOL **LESSON 30**

BASIC VOCABULARY AND LANGUAGE DEVELOPMENT

OBJECTIVES

Functions: Listen Actively; Ask and Answer Questions

Patterns and Structures:

🔊 Can you ____?;

🔊 I can ____.; 🔊 You can ____.

ASK AND ANSWER QUESTIONS

1. **Introduce the Pattern:** *You can ____.* Read the captions on pages 26–27 and have students follow along. Then have students use the pattern to tell about a sport at your school: *At Lakeside, you can play volleyball.*

2. **Introduce the Patterns:** *Can you ____?* and *I can ____.* Post sentence frames:

   > Can you ____?
   > I can ____.

   Then reread the caption for the bottom photo on page 26 and model adapting the text to form a new question and answer: *Can you play softball? I can play softball.* Use the scene for more ideas: *Can you hit the ball? Can you catch the ball?* Have partners work together to form more questions and answers.

3. **Talk About Sports** Turn to **Language Practice Book** page 23 and help students complete the sentences in Items 1–4 using the pattern *You can ____.* For the second activity, have partners complete questions with the pattern *Can you ____?*, then trade books to fill in the answers.

▶ **Language Practice Book** page 23

CLOSE AND ASSESS

Have partners use the patterns to ask and answer questions about sports or other activities.

LAKESIDE SCHOOL **LESSON 31**

LANGUAGE AND LITERACY: HIGH FREQUENCY WORDS

OBJECTIVES

Learning to Read:
- Recognize High Frequency Words

INTRODUCE

1 Learn New Words Place a word and its letter tiles on the screen as you work through the Strategy steps. For example, for *play*, say:

1. *First, look at the word.* (Display the word tile for *play*.)

2. *Now listen to the word:* play, play.

3. *Listen to the word in a sentence:* Do you play soccer?

4. *Say the word after me:* play.

5. *Spell the word:* p-l-a-y. (As you say each letter, place the corresponding letter tile. Point to each tile and have students spell the word.)

6. *Say the word again:* play.

Repeat the process for the other words, using these context sentences:

- Where **can we** run?
- We can run **around** the track.
- We can play soccer, **too**.

PRACTICE

2 Build Sentences Say each word as you place its tile on the screen: *Can you play _____? No. I play _____.*

Model reading the text and filling in the blanks with the names of sports: *Can you play basketball? No. I play soccer.* Then one partner asks the question; the other answers.

APPLY

3 Read New Words Have students find the new words on pages 26–27.

▶ **Reading Practice Book** page 20

CLOSE AND ASSESS

Display the words one at a time for students to read.

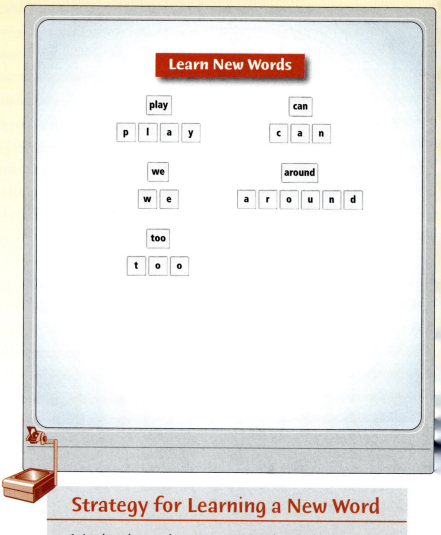

Strategy for Learning a New Word

1. Look at the word.
2. Listen to the word.
3. Listen to the word in a sentence.
4. Say the word.
5. Spell the word.
6. Say the word again.

REACHING ALL STUDENTS

Multimodal Practice

RECOGNIZE HIGH FREQUENCY WORDS

Display the sentences from Step 2. Then do the following activities.

Kinesthetic Students copy the sentences onto strips and cut them apart to make word and punctuation cards.

Visual Students reassemble the sentences to match those displayed.

Auditory Partners practice saying the sentences (filling in the blanks with sports), and then perform or tape their final reading.

T27a Lakeside School

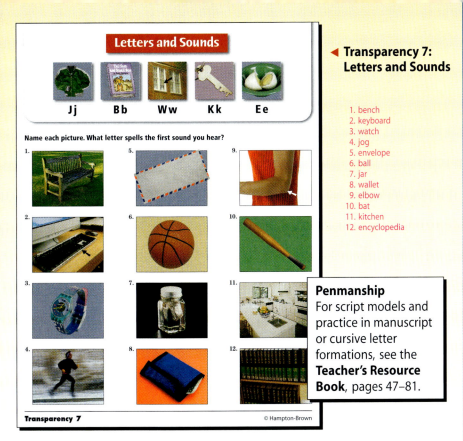

LAKESIDE SCHOOL **LESSON 32**

LANGUAGE AND LITERACY: PHONICS

OBJECTIVES

Learning to Read: Build Oral Vocabulary; Develop Phonemic Awareness; ⓣ Associate Letters and Sounds

TEACH LETTERS AND SOUNDS

1 **Build Oral Vocabulary** Display Transparency 7. Play "I Spy," giving clues until students find the picture. For example, for Item 3, say:

- *I spy a watch. You use a watch to see what time it is. You wear a watch on your wrist* (encircle your wrist).

When students find the watch, say: *Yes,* **this is a watch** (point). Repeat the game to build context for the other words.

2 **Develop Phonemic Awareness** Remove the transparency and work through Step 1 of the script.

3 **Associate Letters and Sounds** Display Transparency 7 again. Work through Step 2 of the script.

▶ **Reading Practice Book** pages 21, 22

CLOSE AND ASSESS

Say the words *jar, bench, window, key,* and *egg* one at a time. Have the group write the letter that stands for the first sound in the word on a card and hold it up.

Review and Reteaching
PHONEMIC AWARENESS AND PHONICS

- **Isolate Sounds** Say words that begin with the sounds taught to date and ask students to tell you the first sound they hear in the word. Choose picture names from Transparencies 1, 3, 5, and 7.

- **Match Letters and Sounds** Give one letter card for *j, b, w, k,* or *e* (see pages 83–88 of the **Teacher's Resource Book**) to five students. Have the other students each draw a picture from the transparency. Then students form groups to match the letters to the first sound in the picture names.

▶ Transparency 7: Letters and Sounds

1. bench
2. keyboard
3. watch
4. jog
5. envelope
6. ball
7. jar
8. wallet
9. elbow
10. bat
11. kitchen
12. encyclopedia

Penmanship
For script models and practice in manuscript or cursive letter formations, see the **Teacher's Resource Book**, pages 47–81.

▼ Script for Transparency 7

Letters and Sounds

1. Develop Phonemic Awareness
Match Initial Sounds Say: *Listen to these two words:* jog, jar. *Say the words with me:* jog, jar. *Do they begin with the same sound?* (yes) Repeat with these word pairs: *jacket, kitchen; book, bench; key, kitchen; egg, ant; watch, window; envelope, egg; ball, basket; book, jog.*

2. Associate Letters and Sounds
Learn Consonant Names, Sounds, and Formations Point to the jacket on **Transparency 7**. Say: *This is a jacket. You can wear a jacket to keep warm. Say* jacket *with me:* jacket. Then point to *Jj* and say: *This is capital* J, *and this is lowercase* j. *The letter* j *spells the first sound you hear in* jacket. *The first sound is* /j/. *Say* /j/ *with me:* /j/. Point to the *j* and ask: *What is the letter? What is its sound?* Trace the *Jj* on the transparency as you explain how to form the letters and have students "write" the letters in the air. Repeat the process for *b, w,* and *k*. Point out that the letter *k* makes the same sound as the letter *c*: /k/. Then explain: *The letters* j, b, w, *and* k *are called* **consonants**—*they spell consonant sounds.*

Learn the Name, Sound, and Formation for the Vowel *Ee* Point to *Ee* and say: *This is the letter* e—*capital* E *and lowercase* e. *The letter* e *is a* **vowel**. Point to the egg and say: *Say* egg *with me:* egg. *Say its first sound:* /eee/. *The sound* /e/ *is a vowel sound. When you say a vowel sound, you keep your mouth open and let the air flow out. Try it:* /eee/. Then say: *The letter* e *spells the vowel sound* /e/ *you hear in* egg. Point to the *e* and ask: *What is the letter? What is its sound?* Then teach students how to form capital and lowercase *e*.

Practice Have students number a paper from 1–12. For Item 1, say: *What is in this picture? Let's say the word and then its first sound:* bench, /b/. *What letter spells* /b/ *as in* bench? *That's right,* b. Point to the *Bb* on the transparency. Have students write a capital and lowercase *b* by Item 1 on their papers. Repeat the process for Items 2–12.

Language and Literacy **T27b**

LAKESIDE SCHOOL **LESSON 33**

BASIC VOCABULARY AND LANGUAGE DEVELOPMENT

> **OBJECTIVES**
>
> **Function:** Give Information
> **Concepts and Vocabulary:** 🅣 Body Parts
> **Patterns and Structures:**
> 🅣 *He/She has _____.;*
> 🅣 *I/They have _____.*
> **Viewing:** Interpret a Visual Image

USE NAMES FOR BODY PARTS

1 Look at the Photo Explain: *It's 12:35 p.m. Carlos is in the nurse's office because he hurt his foot. When you feel sick or get hurt, you can go see the nurse.* Describe the objects in the office: *A cold ice pack can make you feel better.*

2 Identify Body Parts Point to the *Parts of the Body* poster in the nurse's office. As you say each word, have students indicate the part on their own bodies.

▶ Language Practice Book page 24

GIVE INFORMATION

3 Introduce the Patterns: *He/She has _____.; I/They have _____.* Read aloud the photo captions. Then use a chart to explain the patterns:

Use	To Tell About
I have	yourself
He has	a boy or man
She has	a girl or woman
They have	more than one person

4 Role-Play Call on individuals or partners to pantomime the actions in the photos. Then have students use the patterns to describe the feelings: *She has a fever.*

▶ Language Practice Book page 25

> **CLOSE AND ASSESS**
>
> Have students use self-stick notes to write speech balloons for the students on page 29. Model how to convert the caption: *I have a toothache.*

T28 Lakeside School

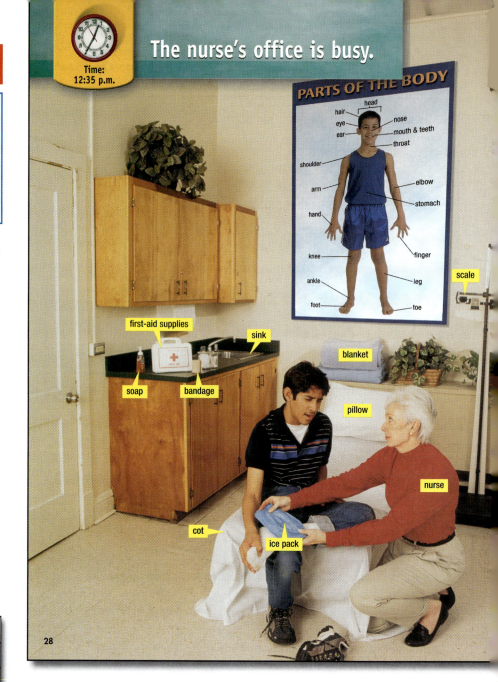

REACHING ALL STUDENTS

Vocabulary
BODY PARTS

Hokey Pokey Teach students the gestures to accompany the song "The Hokey Pokey" and sing it together a few times. Then invite students to imitate your actions as you give directions. Sing together a few times and then have student volunteers call out the names of the body parts as the class does the dance.

HOW DO THEY FEEL?

I feel sick.

He has a toothache.

She has a headache.

He has an earache.

She has a stomachache.

thermometer

They have colds. They have fevers, too.

Listen and Learn

Mrs. Kent:	How do you feel?
Carlos:	My foot hurts. I hurt it in P.E. class.
Mrs. Kent:	I'll put ice on it. You'll feel better tomorrow.
Carlos:	Thank you, Mrs. Kent.

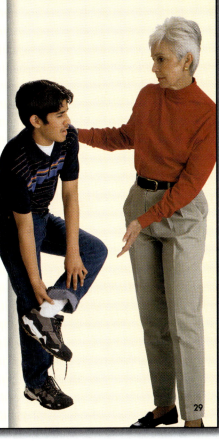

29

Language Development

EXPRESS FEELINGS (HEALTH)

Have small groups create skits about going to the school nurse's office. One student can be the nurse and ask: *How do you feel?* The others can use the health-related vocabulary and patterns to express their feelings.

Nurse: *How do you feel?*
Student: *I feel bad. I have a headache.*
Nurse: *Here is an ice pack.*
Student: *Thank you. I feel better.*

LAKESIDE SCHOOL **LESSON 34**

BASIC VOCABULARY AND LANGUAGE DEVELOPMENT

OBJECTIVES

Functions: Listen Actively; Repeat Spoken Language; Ask and Answer Questions; Express Feelings (health)

Patterns and Structures:
How do you/they feel?; ❶ *How does he/she feel? I/They feel _____.;* ❶ *He/She feels _____.; My _____ hurt(s).*

Speaking and Representing: Role-Play

ASK QUESTIONS AND EXPRESS FEELINGS (HEALTH)

Side B
CD Track 9

1 Introduce the Pattern: *How do you feel?* Play the "Listen and Learn" conversation on the **Lakeside Language Tape/CD**.

2 Introduce the Patterns: *I feel _____.* and *My _____ hurt(s).* Ask students: *How do you feel?* Then post a chart of possible responses:

How Do You Feel?

I feel _____.	My _____ hurt(s).
I feel fine.	My head hurts.
I feel sick.	My ears hurt.
I feel better.	My eyes hurt.

3 Introduce the Patterns: *How do(es) he/she/they feel?* and *He/She/They feel(s) _____.* Point to the pictures and model how to ask and answer questions: *How does the girl feel? She feels bad.* Point out that for one other person, you use *does*; for more than one, you use *do*.

4 Use the Patterns Have volunteers role-play feelings. Then have three students ask and answer questions:

Student 1: *How do you feel?*
Student 2: *My head hurts.*
Student 3: *She feels sick.*

▶ **Language Practice Book** pages 26, 27

CLOSE AND ASSESS

Call on a student: *Erika, how do you feel?* The student role-plays a feeling and explains: *I feel bad. I have a toothache.*

Language Development **T29**

LAKESIDE SCHOOL **LESSON 35**

LANGUAGE AND LITERACY: HIGH FREQUENCY WORDS

OBJECTIVES
Learning to Read:
❶ Recognize High Frequency Words

INTRODUCE

1 Learn New Words Place a word and its letter tiles on the screen as you work through the Strategy steps. For example, for *how,* say:

1. *First, look at the word.* (Display the word tile for *how.*)
2. *Now listen to the word:* how, how.
3. *Listen to the word in a sentence:* How do you feel?
4. *Say the word after me:* how.
5. *Spell the word:* h-o-w. (As you say each letter, place the corresponding letter tile. Point to each tile and have students spell the word.)
6. *Say the word again:* how.

Repeat the process for the other words, using these context sentences:

- I **have** a sore foot.
- The nurse **has** ice packs.
- **They** are good for my foot.
- I **put** an ice pack on my foot.
- I **feel** better.

PRACTICE

2 Sort Words Place the word tiles on the screen in a random arrangement. Have students first sort the words by number of letters, and then do a second sort of words that start with *h.*

APPLY

3 Read New Words Have students find the new words on pages 28–29.

▶ **Reading Practice Book** page 23

CLOSE AND ASSESS
Display the words one at a time for students to read.

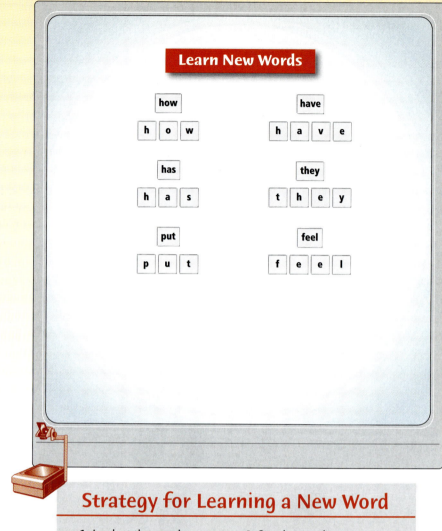

Strategy for Learning a New Word

1. Look at the word.
2. Listen to the word.
3. Listen to the word in a sentence.
4. Say the word.
5. Spell the word.
6. Say the word again.

REACHING ALL STUDENTS

Reading Fluency
RECOGNIZE HIGH FREQUENCY WORDS

To build automaticity with the new high frequency words:

- Use word tiles for new and review words to build sentences on the overhead; for example: *How do they feel? We have a good time. She has a picture of me.* Have students identify the new words and read the sentences.

- Give a volunteer letter tiles for one of the new words. Guide the student in placing one letter at a time to spell the word on the overhead. Others guess the word in as few letters as possible. Whoever guesses finishes the spelling.

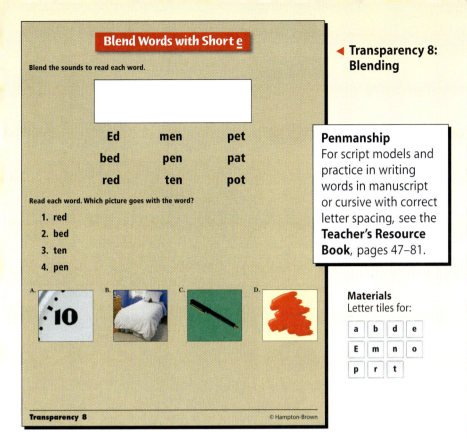

LAKESIDE SCHOOL **LESSON 36**

LANGUAGE AND LITERACY: PHONICS

OBJECTIVES

Learning to Read: Build Oral Vocabulary; Develop Phonemic Awareness; Blend Sounds to Decode Words

TEACH BLENDING

1 Build Oral Vocabulary Display Transparency 8. Use *men, pet,* and *pat* in sentences to build meaning:

- *One man can lift a chair. Two* **men** *can lift a table. Do you have a* **pet***? I have two* **pets***: a dog and a cat. The mother* **pats** *the baby's back* (pantomime).

Use the pictures to develop the meanings of *red, bed, ten,* and *pen:*

- *This is a* **pen***. A* **pen** *has ink. You write with a* **pen***.*

2 Develop Phonemic Awareness Remove the transparency and work through step 1 of the script.

3 Blend Sounds to Read Words Display Transparency 8 again. Work through Steps 2 and 3 of the script.

▶ **Reading Practice Book** pages 24, 25

CLOSE AND ASSESS

Display *pet, pen, pat, bed,* and *pot*. Call on students to identify the three sounds in each word and then blend the sounds to read the word.

Blend Words with Short *e*

1. Develop Phonemic Awareness
Create Rhyming Words Say: *Listen to these words:* pet, wet, net. *These words rhyme. They all have the same sounds at the end:* /et/. *Listen again:* pet, wet, net. *Now you say them. Here are three more words that rhyme:* pin, skin, spin. *Now you try. What are some words that rhyme with* nest? (rest, test, chest, best, vest, west) *What words rhyme with* bat? (hat, fat, rat, that, sat, mat, flat, pat)

2. Blend Sounds to Read Words
Model Set letter tile *E* at the left in the box on **Transparency 8** and letter tile *d* at the right. Point to *E* and say: *The sound for this letter is* /eee/. *As you say the sound, slide* E *next to* d, *and then put your finger under* d. *Say:* I can blend the sound /eee/ with the sound of the letter d: /eeed/. Now I'm going to say the word fast: Ed. Summarize: *You can blend sounds like this to read a word. Just say the sound for the first letter, and blend it into the sound for the next letter.* Demonstrate again: Point to *E* and say: *Say the sound for the letter* E *with me:* /eee/. Repeat for *d:* /d/. Then slide a finger below the letters *Ed* and say: *Help me blend the two sounds:* /eeed/. *Now let's say the word:* Ed. Then replace *E* with *e,* leave *d* at the right in the box, and add letter tile *b* at the left. Repeat the process to read *bed*. Remove the *b,* add *r,* and repeat the process to read *red*.

Practice Have students read the words *Ed, bed,* and *red* below the box. Then repeat Model and Practice for the other two word sets.

3. Match Words and Pictures
Point to Item 1. Say: *Let's read this word*. Slide a finger slowly under the letters to lead students in sounding out the word: /rrreeed/, red. Then say: *Now let's look at the pictures. Which of these pictures—A, B, C, or D—shows the color red?* (D) Repeat the process for Items 2, 3, and 4.

Review and Reteaching
PHONEMIC AWARENESS AND PHONICS

- **Create Rhyming Words** Arrange students in a circle. Choose a word from Transparencies 1–8, for example: *bed*. The two students to your right must agree on a word that rhymes with yours. Go around the circle, encouraging partners to add more rhyming words.

- **Blend Sounds to Decode Words** Distribute letter cards for *e, n, m, p, t, a, i,* and *o* (see pages 83–88 in the **Teacher's Resource Book**). Have students spell and blend *ten,* then change a letter to spell and blend *men, pen, pet, pat, pit,* and *pot*.

Language and Literacy **T29b**

LAKESIDE SCHOOL **LESSON 37**

BASIC VOCABULARY AND LANGUAGE DEVELOPMENT

OBJECTIVES

Functions: Listen Actively; Repeat Spoken Language; Express Likes and Dislikes
Concepts and Vocabulary: 🅣 Food
Patterns and Structures: *I like _____.;* 🅣 *I do not like _____.*
Viewing: Interpret a Visual Image

USE NAMES OF FOODS

1 Introduce Foods Explain: *At 12:45 p.m., Carlos buys lunch at the school cafeteria.* Briefly explain how a cafeteria works: *First, you choose your food. Then you pay the cashier. Then you take the tray to a table and you eat!* Read the food names and have students raise their hands to indicate foods they have tried.

2 Listen for Food Names Play the "Listen and Learn" conversation on the **Lakeside Language Tape/CD**. On the second reading, pause the tape and have students point to the foods as they are mentioned. Then have students echo the conversation and chime in on Carlos's part.

EXPRESS LIKES AND DISLIKES

3 Introduce the Patterns: *I like/do not like _____.* Point to a food on page 31 and model how to express likes and dislikes: *I like pizza. I do not like soup.* Then have volunteers express their preferences.

4 Think, Pair, Share Organize partners for Think, Pair, Share. (see page T337d) Students should first think about the foods on page 31, then pair to discuss their likes and dislikes, and share the information with the class.

▶ **Language Practice Book** page 28

CLOSE AND ASSESS

Name a food and call on students to tell whether or not they like that food.

T30 Lakeside School

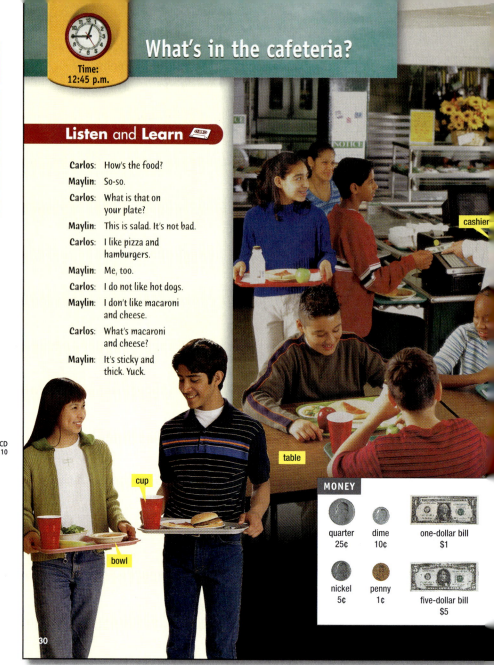

What's in the cafeteria?

Time: 12:45 p.m.

Listen and Learn

Carlos: How's the food?
Maylin: So-so.
Carlos: What is that on your plate?
Maylin: This is salad. It's not bad.
Carlos: I like pizza and hamburgers.
Maylin: Me, too.
Carlos: I do not like hot dogs.
Maylin: I don't like macaroni and cheese.
Carlos: What's macaroni and cheese?
Maylin: It's sticky and thick. Yuck.

MONEY

quarter 25¢
dime 10¢
one-dollar bill $1
nickel 5¢
penny 1¢
five-dollar bill $5

REACHING ALL STUDENTS

Vocabulary
FOOD

Food Posters Use the food categories on page 31 to label separate posters. (Hot Food, Salad, etc.) Then divide the class into groups and distribute one poster per group. Students will work together to draw or cut out pictures of foods which fall under their category. Then have group members show their poster and tell about the foods they found: *I like pasta. It is a hot food.*

A CAFETERIA TRAY

HOT FOOD

taco and beans   hot dog   soup   hamburger   macaroni and cheese   pizza

COLD FOOD

cake   apple sauce   bagel   egg   cottage cheese   ice cream

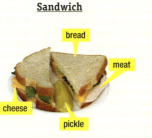

31

Language Development

EXPRESS LIKES AND DISLIKES

Use chart paper to set up a graph with the title "Foods We Like." Have each student choose a picture of a favorite food from **Language Practice Book** page 29. Sort the pictures and paste them in columns to form a bar graph. Repeat the procedure to create a bar graph for "Foods We Do Not Like." Help students interpret the graphs: *Many people like bagels. A lot of people do not like soup.*

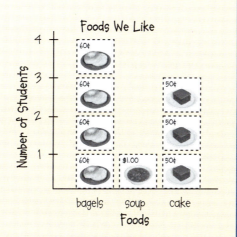

LAKESIDE SCHOOL **LESSON 38**

BASIC VOCABULARY AND LANGUAGE DEVELOPMENT

OBJECTIVES
Functions: Ask for and Give Information
Concepts and Vocabulary: ❶ Money
Patterns and Structures:
What is this/that?; ❶ *This/That is _____.*
Representing: Role-Play

IDENTIFY MONEY

1 Introduce Money Values Show actual coins and bills. Then explain the values:

Coin Name	Value	How Many Make $1.00?
penny	1¢	100

2 Build a Lunch Turn to **Language Practice Book** page 29 and help students use the pictures to create lunches costing under $2.00. Then ask volunteers to tell about their lunches: *My lunch costs $1.25. I can use a dollar and a quarter to pay.*

▶ **Language Practice Book** page 29

ASK FOR AND GIVE INFORMATION

3 Introduce the Patterns: *What is this/that?* and *This/That is _____.* Set food items around the room. Explain: *Use* this *to tell about something nearby. Use* that *to tell about something farther away.*

4 Role-Play Set up a cafeteria scene. Students can arrange food pictures from **Language Practice Book** page 29 to create a lunch on the tray of page 30. Students can ask questions about the food: *What is this food called? What is that?* Cafeteria workers can verify answers by turning over the pictures.

▶ **Language Practice Book** page 30

CLOSE AND ASSESS
Have partners ask questions such as *What is this food? How much does it cost?*

Language Development **T31**

LAKESIDE SCHOOL **LESSON 39**

LANGUAGE AND LITERACY: HIGH FREQUENCY WORDS

OBJECTIVES
Learning to Read:
- Recognize High Frequency Words

INTRODUCE

1 Learn New Words Place a word and its letter tiles on the screen for the Strategy steps. (See Teacher Note for *don't*.) For example, for *and*, say:

1. *First, look at the word.* (Display the word tile for *and*.)
2. *Now listen to the word:* and, and.
3. *Listen to the word in a sentence:* I like apples and bananas.
4. *Say the word after me:* and.
5. *Spell the word:* a-n-d. (Say each letter as you place the tile. Point to each tile and have students spell the word.)
6. *Say the word again:* and.

Repeat the process for the other words, using these context sentences:

- What **food** do you like to eat?
- **That** is yogurt.
- I do **not** like yogurt.
- I **don't** like beans.

PRACTICE

2 Build Sentences Set word tiles randomly and read aloud a sentence: *I like that food.* Place the tile for the first word to the left. Have students tell which tiles go next. Have students read the sentence. Continue with: *We don't like the food. That food is not good.*

APPLY

3 Read New Words Have students find the new words on pages 30–31.

▶ **Reading Practice Book** page 26

CLOSE AND ASSESS
Display the words one at a time for students to read.

T31a Lakeside School

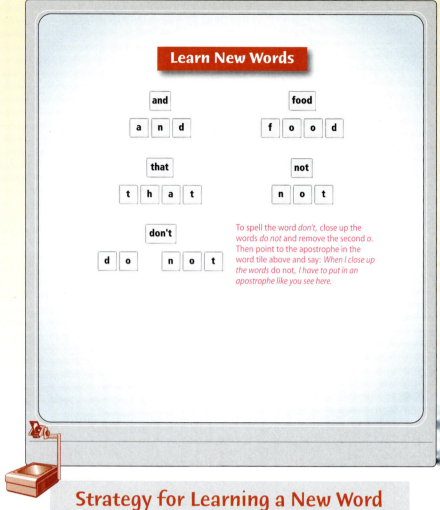

Strategy for Learning a New Word

1. Look at the word.
2. Listen to the word.
3. Listen to the word in a sentence.
4. Say the word.
5. Spell the word.
6. Say the word again.

REACHING ALL STUDENTS

Reading Fluency
RECOGNIZE HIGH FREQUENCY WORDS

To build automaticity with the new high frequency words:

- Display the new words. Have partners work together to find and write the three words with *o* or *oo*, the three words with *n*, the three words with *t* at the end, and the three words with *d*.
- Ask a volunteer to look at the classroom chart of new and review words, choose a word, and begin spelling it slowly. The rest of the group should try to guess the word in as few letters as possible.

How to Write a Statement

| The | school | is | good | . |

| Here | is | a | picture | . |

| That | is | the | answer | . |

| The | food | is | not | good | . |

Penmanship
For script models and practice in writing sentences in manuscript or cursive with correct word spacing, see the **Teacher's Resource Book**, pages 47–81.

Strategy for Statements

- A statement tells something.
- It starts with a capital letter.
- It ends with a period.

Multi-Level Strategies

CONCEPTS OF PRINT: CAPITAL LETTERS

NON-ROMAN ALPHABET

Students who speak Chinese or another language without capitalization may need practice to remember that a sentence starts with a capital letter. Point out the capital *T* at the beginning of *The school is good.* Display the letter tile for lowercase *t* to show the contrast. Then give partners lowercase letter tiles. Have them match the letters to capital letters at the beginning of sentences on a randomly selected page from pages 12–31.

LAKESIDE SCHOOL **LESSON 40**

LANGUAGE AND LITERACY: STATEMENTS

OBJECTIVES

Writing: ❶ Write a Statement

INTRODUCE

1 Learn About Statements Place the word tiles for the first sentence on the screen as you define a statement. Say:

1. *A statement is a sentence that tells something.* (Display *The school is good,* without the period.)

2. *Listen to the statement.* (As you read, point to each word.)

3. *What does it tell about?* (the school)

4. *The first word starts with a capital letter.* (Point to *T.*) *This is capital* T.

5. *A statement ends with a period.* (Place the period tile at the end.)

6. *Read the statement with me.*

Repeat for the other statements.

PRACTICE

2 Build Sentences Read a statement and place its word tiles randomly.

- They are here.
- We can play.
- It is time to call.
- This food is good.

Have students explain which tile to place first, how to order the rest of the words, and where to place the period. Have them read the statement in unison. Repeat for the other statements.

APPLY

3 Read Statements Have students find statements on pages 12–31.

▶ **Reading Practice Book** page 27

CLOSE AND ASSESS

Provide word tiles for the statements in Step 1. Read each statement and have a volunteer build it. Have other students tell what it is about, point to the capital letter, and point to the period.

Language and Literacy **T31b**

LAKESIDE SCHOOL **LESSON 41**

BASIC VOCABULARY AND LANGUAGE DEVELOPMENT

OBJECTIVES

Concepts and Vocabulary:
Science Materials and Processes
Viewing: Interpret a Visual Image

USE SCIENCE VOCABULARY

1. **Introduce Science Tools** View pages 32–33 and explain: *It's 1:15 p.m. Carlos is in science class. In the science lab, or laboratory, you can do experiments. They can show how plants grow and how things work.* Point to the objects and describe how they are used: *A model shows how something looks or works. This is a model of the sun and the planets.*

2. **Introduce Science Processes** Read the captions and explain or pantomime each action. Then call on volunteers to pantomime the actions for others to guess.

3. **Visit a School Science Lab** As you examine laboratory equipment, pause for students to check off and add items to the list of science materials at the top of **Language Practice Book** page 31. Then have them complete the rest of the page.

▶ **Language Practice Book** page 31

CLOSE AND ASSESS

Ask students questions about science tools and processes, for example:
- What tool do you use to observe something very small? (microscope)
- What do you do with a ruler? (measure)

Time: 1:15 p.m.

Science class is fun!

This is a science lab.

I listen to the teacher.   I do an experiment.

32

REACHING ALL STUDENTS

Vocabulary

SCIENCE TOOLS

Materials per group: one stalk of celery; one cup of water mixed with 2–3 drops of a dark food coloring; graph paper; ruler

Science Experiment Lead small groups in carrying out a simple experiment to show how plants absorb water. Post the following directions, pausing to reinforce the science terms, as needed:

1. **Measure** the level of the water.
2. Put the celery into the cup.
3. **Observe** the changes over time:
   - Measure the water in the cup.
   - Measure the color in the celery.
4. Take **notes**. Write the time, water level, and color level.
5. Show the changes in a line graph.
6. Write a **report**. Tell what you learned.

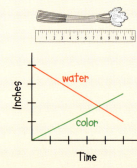

T32 Lakeside School

I measure.

microscope
I observe.

notes
I take notes.

Pronunciation of Name
Sato   sah tō

Listen and Learn

Carlos: Mrs. Sato, I need a tray for my plants. Can you give me one?
Mrs. Sato: I think you need more than one tray!
Carlos: Yes, I do.
Mrs. Sato: Then get two trays from the cabinet. Take them to the table.
Carlos: Thanks.

Language Development

EXPRESS NEEDS AND THOUGHTS

Have partners create dialog for one of the scenes on pages 20–33. Encourage them to use the new patterns and others they have learned:

   I think _____.

   I need _____.

   Do you like _____?

   I like _____.

   I do not like _____.

Encourage volunteers to role-play their dialogs for the group.

LAKESIDE SCHOOL **LESSON 42**

BASIC VOCABULARY AND LANGUAGE DEVELOPMENT

OBJECTIVES

Functions: Listen Actively; Repeat Spoken Language; Express Needs and Thoughts

Patterns and Structures:
I need _____.; I think _____.

EXPRESS NEEDS AND THOUGHTS

1 Introduce the Patterns: *I need _____.* and *I think _____.* Play the "Listen and Learn" conversation on the **Lakeside Language Tape/CD**. Students will listen to the conversation twice, then echo the conversation, and chime in on Carlos's part.

Side B
CD Track 11

2 Distinguish Between Needs and Thoughts Explain: *Use* I need *when you have to have something. Use* I think *when you want to share your ideas.* Pantomime measuring a plant, then model the patterns: *I think this plant is growing. Now I need a ruler to measure the plant.*

3 Think, Pair, Share Organize partners for Think, Pair, Share. (see page T337d) Have students tell about something they need and something they think. Pairs can use the patterns to create two sentences. Show examples in a chart.

I need _____.	I think _____.
some pens	you are smart
a book	science is fun

▶ Language Practice Book page 32

CLOSE AND ASSESS

Call on students to tell you something they need for school, and something they think about school.

LAKESIDE SCHOOL **LESSON 43**

LANGUAGE AND LITERACY: HIGH FREQUENCY WORDS

OBJECTIVES

Learning to Read:
- Recognize High Frequency Words

INTRODUCE

1 Learn New Words Place a word and its letter tiles on the screen as you work through the Strategy steps. For example, for *think*, say:

1. *First, look at the word.* (Display the word tile for *think*.)

2. *Now listen to the word:* think, think.

3. *Listen to the word in a sentence:* I think science is interesting.

4. *Say the word after me:* think.

5. *Spell the word:* t-h-i-n-k. (As you say each letter, place the corresponding letter tile. Point to each tile and have students spell the word.)

6. *Say the word again:* think.

Repeat the process for the other words, using these context sentences:

- Can you **give** me a tray?
- I **take** the tray to the table.

PRACTICE

2 Build Sentences Set out the word tiles at random and read aloud a sentence: *Take this to school.* Place the tile for the first word to the left. Then have students tell you which tile to place next to arrange the words in order. Have students read the sentence in unison. Continue with: *Can you give me some help? Yes. I think we can.*

APPLY

3 Read New Words Have students find the new words on pages 32–33.

▶ **Reading Practice Book** page 28

CLOSE AND ASSESS

Display the words one at a time for students to read.

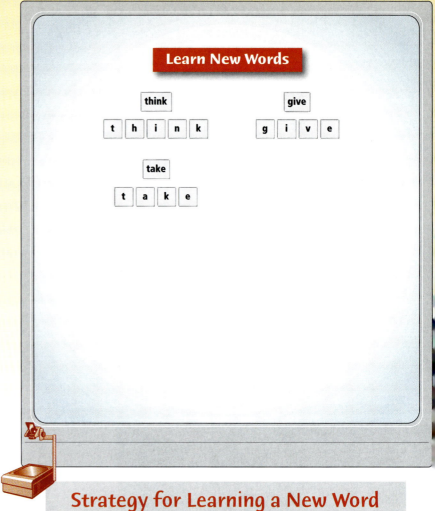

Strategy for Learning a New Word

1. Look at the word.
2. Listen to the word.
3. Listen to the word in a sentence.
4. Say the word.
5. Spell the word.
6. Say the word again.

REACHING ALL STUDENTS

Reading Fluency

RECOGNIZE HIGH FREQUENCY WORDS

To build automaticity with the new high frequency words:

- Use the letter tiles on the overhead to spell the new words, leaving a few letters missing from each one. Have volunteers complete the words and then call on a student to read each word. Repeat the activity, removing different letters from the words.

- Challenge students to create illustrations or pantomime to show the meaning of each new word. Ask them to present a drawing or a performance for the class to guess the word.

T33a Lakeside School

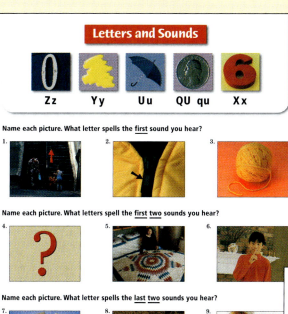

◀ Transparency 9: Letters and Sounds

1. upstairs
2. zipper
3. yarn
4. question (mark)
5. quilt
6. quiet
7. box
8. ox
9. ax

Penmanship
For script models and practice in manuscript or cursive letter formations, see the **Teacher's Resource Book**, pages 47–81.

▼ Script for Transparency 9

Letters and Sounds

1. Develop Phonemic Awareness
Match/Identify Sounds Say: *Listen to these two words:* zoo, zebra. *Do they begin with the same sound?* (yes) Repeat with: *yawn, yarn; zipper, zero; umbrella, envelope; up, yes.* Next, have students identify the first two sounds in *queen, quick, quilt.* (/kw/) Repeat for the last two sounds in *six, box, fix.* (/ks/)

2. Associate Letters and Sounds
Learn the Name, Sound, and Formation for the Vowel *Uu* Point to *Uu* on **Transparency 9** and say: *This is the letter* u—*capital* U *and lowercase* u. *The letter* u *is a vowel.* Point to the umbrella and say: *Say* umbrella *with me:* umbrella. *Say its first sound:* /uuu/. *The sound* /uuu/ *is a vowel sound.* Explain: *When you say a vowel sound, you keep your mouth open and let the air flow out. Try it:* /uuu/. *The letter* u *spells the vowel sound* /u/ *in* umbrella. Point to the *u* and ask: *What is the letter? What is its sound?* Then teach students how to form capital and lowercase *u*.

Learn Consonant Names, Sounds, and Formations Point to the zero. Say: *This is zero. Zero is a number that stands for none. Say* zero *with me:* zero. Then point to *Zz* and say: *This is capital* Z, *and this is lowercase* z. *The letter* z *spells the first sound you hear in* zero. *The first sound is* /z/. *Say* /zzz/ *with me:* /zzz/. Point to the *z* and ask: *What is the letter? What is its sound?* Trace the *Zz* as you explain how to form the letters. Students can "write" the letters in the air. Repeat for *y, qu,* and *x.* Explain: *The letters* z, y, q, *and* x *are called* **consonants**.

Practice Have students number a paper from 1–12. For Item 1, say: *Let's say this word and its first sound:* upstairs, /uuu/. *What letter spells* /uuu/ *as in* upstairs? (u) Point to the *Uu*. Have students write a capital and lowercase *u* by Item 1 on their papers. Repeat for Items 2–3. For Items 4–6, have students identify the first two sounds in each word (/kw/) and write the letters that stand for those sounds. Explain that *q* and *u* always come together. For Items 7–9, have students identify the last two sounds in each word (/ks/) and write the letter that stands for those sounds.

LAKESIDE SCHOOL **LESSON 44**

LANGUAGE AND LITERACY: PHONICS

OBJECTIVES
Learning to Read: Build Oral Vocabulary; Develop Phonemic Awareness;
🅣 Associate Letters and Sounds

TEACH LETTERS AND SOUNDS

1 Build Oral Vocabulary Display Transparency 9. Play "I Spy," giving clues until students find the picture. For example, for Item 2, say:

• *I spy a zipper. You move a zipper to open and close a jacket.*

Say: *Yes,* **this is the zipper** (point). Repeat the game for the other words.

2 Develop Phonemic Awareness Remove the transparency and work through Step 1 of the script.

3 Associate Letters and Sounds Display Transparency 9 again. Work through Step 2 of the script.

▶ **Reading Practice Book** pages 29, 30

CLOSE AND ASSESS

Say the words *zipper, umbrella* and *yarn* one at a time. Have the group write the letter that stands for the first sound in the word on a card and hold it up. Repeat for the letters that make the first two sounds in *quilt* (qu) and the letter that makes the last two sounds in *six.*

Review and Reteaching
PHONEMIC AWARENESS AND PHONICS

• **Isolate Sounds** Say words that begin with the sounds taught to date and ask students to tell you the first sound they hear in the word. Choose picture names from Transparencies 1, 3, 5, 7, and 9. For words with /kw/ *qu* or /ks/ *x,* ask students to tell you the first two or last two sounds they hear.

• **Match Letters and Sounds** Display Transparencies 1, 3, 5, 7, and 9 to reteach the letters and sounds. Help students create a word file where they collect words for each letter and sound.

Language and Literacy **T33b**

LAKESIDE SCHOOL **LESSON 45**

BASIC VOCABULARY AND LANGUAGE DEVELOPMENT

OBJECTIVES
Concepts and Vocabulary:
- Clothing; Colors

Viewing: Interpret a Visual Image

USE WORDS FOR COLORS AND CLOTHING

1. **Identify Colors** Explain: *It's 3:15 p.m., and Carlos is shopping in the school store. He can buy school supplies and clothes there.* Call attention to the color chart. Present the names of the colors, then have students name colors they see around the room.

2. **Identify Articles of Clothing** Say the name of each item of clothing on page 35. Have students give the name and color of items they can identify in the store display on page 34: *I see a tan sweatshirt.*

3. **Play "I Spy"** Give clues using words for colors and articles of clothing: *I spy blue socks.* All students wearing blue socks stand up. Ask a volunteer to give the next clue, and continue until all students have a chance to speak.

▶ **Language Practice Book** page 33

CLOSE AND ASSESS
Have students describe what their partner is wearing while the partner "models" or points to each item.

REACHING ALL STUDENTS

Vocabulary
COLORS AND CLOTHING

Fashion Show Have small groups organize fashion shows. Students can take turns modeling and describing the items of clothing: *This is a blue school sweatshirt. Here are some red pants.* Students may videotape the fashion shows and play them for families or other classes.

CULTURAL PERSPECTIVES

World Cultures: Traditional Costume Encourage students to describe traditional clothing from their home cultures. Students can bring in photos or articles of clothing to share with the class. Then invite family members to participate in a fashion show of regional, traditional, and ceremonial clothing. Encourage students to narrate as family members "model."

T34 Lakeside School

WHICH CLOTHES DO YOU LIKE?

gray sweatshirt

white cap

red jacket

tan T-shirt

blue shorts

green sweatpants

black sneakers

purple socks

Listen and Learn

Maylin: You can get good things at this store! Look at this little Lakeside lion.

Carlos: I like its T-shirt! I need a new T-shirt, too. Do you like this one?

Maylin: No, I don't like that color. I do like those blue shorts.

Carlos: I like them, too. My gym shorts are very old. I will get both the T-shirt and the shorts!

Maylin: I will just get my lion.

35

Language Development

ASK AND ANSWER QUESTIONS

Set up a simulation of a school store using personal and/or classroom objects. Students can take turns being the store clerk and customers. Provide sentence frames for students to ask and answer questions about sale items:

> Which _____ do you like?
> I like/do not like _____.
> I like this/that _____.
> I like these/those _____.
> I need/think _____.
> Here is/are _____.

LAKESIDE SCHOOL **LESSON 46**

BASIC VOCABULARY AND LANGUAGE DEVELOPMENT

OBJECTIVES

Functions: Listen Actively; Repeat Spoken Language; Ask and Answer Questions

Patterns and Structures: *Which _____ do you like?; I like this/that _____.; I like these/those _____.*

ASK AND ANSWER QUESTIONS

Materials: various articles of clothing in different colors

Side B
CD Track 12

1 Introduce the Patterns: *I like this/that ___.; I like these/those ___.* Play the "Listen and Learn" conversation on the **Lakeside Language Tape/CD**. Students will listen twice to the conversation, echo lines, and chime in with Carlos.

Use page 34 to explain how to choose the correct demonstrative adjective:

	one	more than one
near	**this** hat	**these** shoes
far	**that** shirt	**those** socks

Use the patterns to describe classroom objects: *I like that poster on the wall. I like these pens in my hand.*

2 Introduce the Pattern: *Which _____ do you like?* Explain that you use the pattern to get someone to choose from a group the things they like the most. Ask volunteers to choose clothes they like from page 35.

3 Use the Patterns to Ask and Answer Questions Set out several items of clothing. Have one partner ask questions: *Which cap do you like?* The other partner points and uses the patterns to answer: *I like this cap.*

▶ **Language Practice Book** page 34

CLOSE AND ASSESS

Divide students into groups of three. One student asks a question with *Which _____ do you like?* The others answer by naming objects that are near or farther away.

Language Development **T35**

LAKESIDE SCHOOL **LESSON 47**

LANGUAGE AND LITERACY: HIGH FREQUENCY WORDS

OBJECTIVES

Learning to Read:
- Recognize High Frequency Words

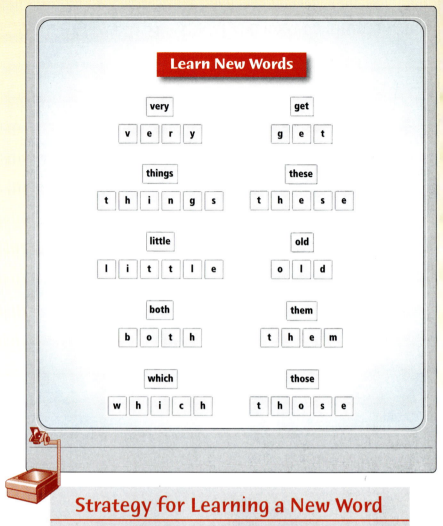

Strategy for Learning a New Word

1. Look at the word.
2. Listen to the word.
3. Listen to the word in a sentence.
4. Say the word.
5. Spell the word.
6. Say the word again.

INTRODUCE

1 Learn New Words Place a word and its letter tiles on the screen as you work through the Strategy steps. For example, for *very*, say:

1. *First, look at the word.* (Display the word tile for *very*.)
2. *Now listen to the word:* very, very.
3. *Listen to the word in a sentence:* This is a very good store.
4. *Say the word after me:* very.
5. *Spell the word:* v-e-r-y. (As you say each letter, place the corresponding letter tile. Point to each tile and have students spell the word.)
6. *Say the word again:* very.

Repeat the process for the other words, using these context sentences:

- I will **get** some **things** at the store.
- **These little** erasers are nicer than my **old** ones.
- I want **both** of **them**.
- **Which** bags do you like?
- I like **those** gray bags over there.

PRACTICE

2 Sort Words Place the word tiles on the screen in a random arrangement. Have students sort the words by the number of letters, and then do a second sort of words that start with the letters *th*.

APPLY

3 Read New Words Have students find the new words on pages 34–35.

▶ **Reading Practice Book** page 31

CLOSE AND ASSESS

Display the words one at a time for students to read.

REACHING ALL STUDENTS

Reading Fluency

RECOGNIZE HIGH FREQUENCY WORDS

To build automaticity with the new high frequency words:

- Have small groups secretly choose five words to make cards for, cut the letters apart, and scramble the letters for each word. Then groups trade sets of letters and compete to see which group can reassemble and read their words faster.

- Invite students to list the words in different ways; for example: alphabetical order or shortest to longest. Ask students to share their lists and have others guess the reason for the ordering.

T35a Lakeside School

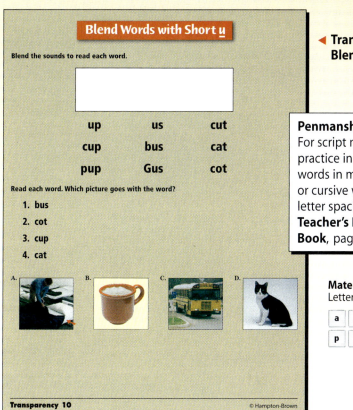

◀ **Transparency 10: Blending**

Penmanship
For script models and practice in writing words in manuscript or cursive with correct letter spacing, see the **Teacher's Resource Book**, pages 47–81.

Materials
Letter tiles for:

a	b	c	G	o
p	p	s	t	u

▼ Script for Transparency 10

Blend Words with Short u

1. Develop Phonemic Awareness
Match Initial Sounds/Match Final Sounds Say: *Listen to these two words:* up, us. *Say the words with me:* up, us. *The first sound in these words is the same:* /uuu/. *Now listen to these two words:* us, am. *Say the words with me:* us, am. *Is the first sound in each word the same?* (no) Continue with word pairs *us, is; yes, yell; cap, cut*. Then say: *Now listen to these two words:* cup, nap. *Say the words with me:* cup, nap. *They end with the same sound:* /p/. *Here are two more words:* bus, cut. *Say the words with me:* bus, cut. *Is the last sound in each word the same?* (no) Continue with word pairs *cup, cot; cut, cat; gas, bus; net, cab; bag, pig*.

2. Blend Sounds to Read Words
Model Set letter tile *u* at the left in the box on **Transparency 10** and letter tile *p* at the right. Point to *u* and say: *The sound for this letter is* /uuu/. As you say the sound, slide *u* next to *p*, and then put your finger under *p*. Say: *I can blend the sound* /uuu/ *with the sound of the letter* p: /uuup/. *Now I'm going to say the word fast:* up. Summarize: *You can blend sounds like this to read a word. Just say the sound for the first letter, and blend it into the sound for the next letter.* Demonstrate again: Point to *u* and say: *Say the sound for* u *with me:* /uuu/. Repeat for *p*: /p/. Then slide a finger below the letters *up* and say: *Help me blend the two sounds:* /uuup/. *Now let's say the word:* up. Then leave *up* at the right in the box and add letter tile *c* at the left. Repeat the process to read *cup*. Remove the *c*, add *p*, and repeat the process to read *pup*.

Practice Have students read the words *up, cup,* and *pup* below the box. Then repeat Model and Practice for the other two word sets.

3. Match Words and Pictures
Point to Item 1. Say: *Let's read this word*. Slide a finger slowly under the letters to lead students in sounding out the word: /buuusss/, *bus*. Then say: *Now let's look at the pictures. Which of these pictures—A, B, C, or D—shows a bus?* (C) Repeat the process for Items 2, 3, and 4.

LAKESIDE SCHOOL **LESSON 48**

LANGUAGE AND LITERACY: PHONICS

OBJECTIVES
Learning to Read: Build Oral Vocabulary; Develop Phonemic Awareness; Blend Sounds to Decode Words

TEACH BLENDING

1 **Build Oral Vocabulary** Display Transparency 10. Use *pup, us,* and *cut* in sentences to build meaning:

- *My friend's dog had puppies. She gave* **us**—*my sister and me*—*one* **pup**. *I use a knife to* **cut** *bread* (pantomime).

Use the pictures to develop the meaning of *cot, cup, bus,* and *cat*:

- *This is a* **cot**. *A* **cot** *is a small bed. When you are sick, you can lie down on a* **cot** *in the first aid room.*

2 **Develop Phonemic Awareness**
Remove the transparency and work through Step 1 of the script.

3 **Blend Sounds to Read Words**
Display Transparency 10 again. Work through Steps 2 and 3 of the script.

▶ **Reading Practice Book** pages 32, 33

CLOSE AND ASSESS
Display *bus, cup, cot, cut,* and *cap*. Have students identify the sound of each letter and blend the sounds to read the word.

Review and Reteaching
PHONEMIC AWARENESS AND PHONICS

- **Create Rhyming Words** Arrange students in a circle. Choose a word from Transparencies 1–10, for example: *cap, pet,* or *mop*. The two students to your right must agree on a word that rhymes with yours. Go around the circle, encouraging partners to add more rhyming words.

- **Blend Sounds to Decode Words** Distribute letter cards for *a, p, p, c, u, b, i,* and *t* (see pages 83–88 in the **Teacher's Resource Book**). Have students spell and blend *up*, then add a letter or change a letter to spell and blend *pup, cup, cut, but, bit,* and *bat*.

Language and Literacy **T35b**

LAKESIDE SCHOOL **LESSON 49**

BASIC VOCABULARY AND LANGUAGE DEVELOPMENT

OBJECTIVES

Concepts and Vocabulary: Days of the Week

Viewing: Interpret a Visual Image

USE NAMES FOR DAYS OF THE WEEK

1. **Introduce the Days of the Week** Use a calendar to explain: *There are seven days in one week. The weekdays are Monday through Friday. The weekend is Saturday and Sunday.* Write the days on separate index cards and invite volunteers to put them in order.

2. **Play a Game** Call out a day of the week: *Tuesday.* Then toss an object to a student, who names the day that follows: *Wednesday.* Play continues until the players review the days for one week.

3. **Discuss Daily Activities** Explain: *There are many things to do this week.* Point to the sign on page 36 and read the days and events. Ask: *When is the teacher meeting?* (Tuesday) *What will happen on Sunday?* (car wash)

4. **Introduce Abbreviations** Explain that, to save space in writing, people sometimes use a shorter form of a word, known as an **abbreviation**. Present the following abbreviations:

Sunday	Sun.	Thursday	Thurs.
Monday	Mon.	Friday	Fri.
Tuesday	Tue.	Saturday	Sat.
Wednesday	Wed.		

Point out that these abbreviations are formed from the first few letters of the word plus a period. To practice, write an abbreviation on the board and have a volunteer call out the day.

▶ Language Practice Book page 35

CLOSE AND ASSESS

Have students name a day of the week and tell something they do on that day: *I have piano lessons on Wednesday.*

T36 Lakeside School

REACHING ALL STUDENTS

Vocabulary
DAYS OF THE WEEK

School Signs Have small groups make school signs similar to the one on page 36. Suggest classroom or school-wide events they can include. Post the signs on a bulletin board and lead the class in reading each one aloud. At the end of each day, invite a student to tell about upcoming events: *On Wednesday, the science report is due. On Friday, we have a basketball game.*

Room 256
Mountain View School

This week in Room 256:
Monday: Report Cards
Tuesday: Soccer Game
Wednesday: Science Report due
Thursday: Library
Friday: Basketball Game
Saturday: School Dance
Sunday: Math Club Picnic

LAKESIDE SCHOOL **LESSON 50**

BASIC VOCABULARY AND LANGUAGE DEVELOPMENT

OBJECTIVES

Functions: Listen Actively; Repeat Spoken Language; Express Social Courtesies

Patterns and Structures: *See you _____.*

EXPRESS SOCIAL COURTESIES

1 Introduce Ways to Say Good-bye Point to the picture on pages 36–37 and explain: *The students are going home. They use different ways to say good-bye.* Read aloud the speech balloons. Then play the "Listen and Learn" conversation on the **Lakeside Language Tape/CD**. Students will listen to the conversation twice as they follow along. As the tape continues, students will echo the conversation and then chime in on Carlos's part.

Side B
CD Track 13

2 Use the Pattern: *See you _____.* Brainstorm ways to complete the pattern using time words or phrases:

> See you _____.
>
> See you soon.
> See you later.
> See you tomorrow.
> See you Monday.
> See you next week.

Use one of the phrases and call on students to answer by using another phrase that means good-bye.

▶ **Language Practice Book** page 36

CLOSE AND ASSESS

As students leave the room, have them say good-bye using the words, phrases, and patterns on the page.

Language Development **T37**

LAKESIDE SCHOOL LESSON 51

LANGUAGE AND LITERACY: HIGH FREQUENCY WORDS

OBJECTIVES
Learning to Read:
- Recognize High Frequency Words

INTRODUCE

1 **Learn New Words** Place a word and its letter tiles on the screen as you work through the Strategy steps. For example, for *soon*, say:

  1. *First, look at the word.* (Display the word tile for *soon*.)
  2. *Now listen to the word:* soon, soon.
  3. *Listen to the word in a sentence:* A basketball game will start soon.
  4. *Say the word after me:* soon.
  5. *Spell the word:* s-o-o-n. (As you say each letter, place the corresponding letter tile. Point to each tile and have students spell the word.)
  6. *Say the word again:* soon.

Repeat the process for the other words, using these context sentences:

- There is a soccer game **tomorrow**.
- I'll practice **later** this afternoon.
- Have a **great** game!

PRACTICE

2 **Build Sentences** Set out the word tiles at random and read aloud a sentence: *I can see you soon.* Place the tile for the first word to the left. Then have students tell you which tiles to place next. Have students read the sentence in unison. Continue with: *I can see you tomorrow. I can call you later. This school is great!*

APPLY

3 **Read New Words** Have students find the new words on pages 36–37.

▶ **Reading Practice Book** page 34

CLOSE AND ASSESS
Display the words one at a time for students to read.

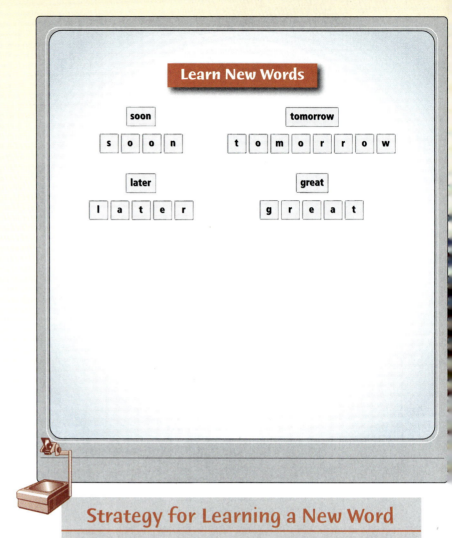

Strategy for Learning a New Word

1. Look at the word.
2. Listen to the word.
3. Listen to the word in a sentence.
4. Say the word.
5. Spell the word.
6. Say the word again.

REACHING ALL STUDENTS

Multimodal Practice

RECOGNIZE HIGH FREQUENCY WORDS

Display the sentences from Step 2. Then do the following activities.

Kinesthetic Students copy the sentences onto strips and cut them apart to make word and punctuation cards.

Visual Students reassemble the sentences to match those displayed.

Auditory Students work with partners to practice saying the sentences naturally, and then perform or tape a final reading for the class to hear.

How to Write a Question

| How | do | you | feel | ? |

| Where | is | the | picture | ? |

| What | time | is | it | ? |

| Can | you | play | tomorrow | ? |

Penmanship
For script models and practice in writing sentences in manuscript or cursive with correct word spacing, see the **Teacher's Resource Book**, pages 47–81.

Strategy for Questions

- A question asks something.
- It starts with a capital letter.
- It ends with a question mark.

- These words can start a question: *Are, Can, Do, Does, How, Is, What, Which, Where, Who, Will.*

Multi-Level Strategies
CONCEPTS OF PRINT: PUNCTUATION

LITERATE IN L1 Some languages follow different print conventions. For example: Spanish uses an inverted question mark before a question, as well as a question mark at the end. Arabic uses a question mark only at the beginning of a question. Have students work with a set of statements and questions copied out of Lakeside pages 12–37, without the end punctuation. Partners can add a period or a question mark to punctuate each sentence. Remind them that English uses a question mark only at the end of a question.

LAKESIDE SCHOOL **LESSON 52**

LANGUAGE AND LITERACY: QUESTIONS

OBJECTIVES

Writing: ❶ Write a Question

INTRODUCE

1 Learn About Questions Place the word tiles for the first sentence on the screen as you define a question. Say:

1. *A question is a sentence that asks something.* (Display *How do you feel,* without the question mark.)

2. *Listen to the question.* (Point to each word as you read *How do you feel?*)

3. *What does it ask about?* (feelings)

4. *The first word starts with a capital letter.* (Point to *H.*) *This is capital* H.

5. *A question ends with a question mark.* (Place the question mark.)

6. *Read the question with me.*

Repeat for the other questions.

PRACTICE

2 Build Questions Read a question and place its word tiles randomly: *What is your name? Who is she? Are they at school? Do you like the picture?*

Have students explain which word to place first, how to order the rest of the words, and where to place the question mark. Have them read the question in unison. Repeat for the other questions.

APPLY

3 Read Questions Have students find examples of questions on pages 14–37.

▶ **Reading Practice Book** page 35

CLOSE AND ASSESS

Provide word tiles for the questions in Step 1. Read each question and have a volunteer build it. Have other students tell what it asks about, point to the capital letter, and point to the question mark.

Language and Literacy **T37b**

LAKESIDE SCHOOL **LESSON 53**

BASIC VOCABULARY AND LANGUAGE DEVELOPMENT

OBJECTIVES

Concepts and Vocabulary:
Months of the Year

Critical Thinking:
Analyze Information; Generate Ideas

Representing: Graph; Calendar

USE NAMES FOR THE MONTHS OF THE YEAR

Materials: 12-month calendar

1. **Introduce the Months of the Year** Use a calendar to explain the months of the year: *There are twelve months in a year. January is the first month.* Say the names of the months in order as you page through the calendar.

2. **Conduct a Survey** Call out the names of the months in order and have students raise their hands to indicate the month of their birthdays. Have students help you tally the responses.

3. **Analyze Information** Display the results of the birthday survey in the form of a bar graph. Go over the data together; for example: *What month has the most/least birthdays? How many students were born in May?*

4. **Record Monthly Activities** Have students use **Language Practice Book** page 37 to make a personal calendar. Students should draw a picture and write a sentence describing something they do each month. Then they can share their work in small groups.

▶ **Language Practice Book** page 37

CLOSE AND ASSESS

Have partners alternate saying the names of the months in order.

Carlos has a great year!

September
Carlos meets lots of new friends.

October
Carlos sees a football game at night.

January
Carlos takes a picture of the snow.

February
Carlos gets a valentine from a girl in his class!

May
Carlos dances with a group at the school dance.

June
Carlos takes final exams.

38

REACHING ALL STUDENTS

HOME CONNECTION

Family Calendar Have students take home **Language Practice Book** page 37 and explain their drawings and sentences to family members. Then students can help create a family calendar containing important family dates and events. Students can report back to the class about how the family used the calendar, or bring the calendar in to share.

November
Carlos writes letters to his family.

December
Carlos sings songs from a book.

March
Carlos works in the school garden one day a week.

April
Carlos plays softball.

July
Carlos visits St. Louis.

August
Carlos swims at the city pool with a boy from his class.

39

Language Development

THIRD PERSON SINGULAR VERBS

Have small groups make up skits about what they do all year, using the months of the year and action verbs. One student narrates as the others act. Provide examples:

> In February, Miriam plays in the snow. Bao eats moon cakes.

You might also assign three months to each of four groups and put all the skits together to make one play.

LAKESIDE SCHOOL **LESSON 54**

BASIC VOCABULARY AND LANGUAGE DEVELOPMENT

OBJECTIVES

Functions: Listen Actively; Repeat Spoken Language; Describe Actions

Concepts and Vocabulary:
- Action Verbs

Patterns and Structures:
- Present Tense Verbs

USE THIRD PERSON SINGULAR VERBS

1 View the Photographs Explain: *These photos show what Carlos does each month of the year.* Call out the names of the months and read aloud the captions as students point to the correct picture.

2 Introduce Action Verbs Ask students to perform actions such as *run, walk, sit, stand, sing, read*. As students complete the actions, write sentences to describe them:

> Mai run<u>s</u>.
> Ali talk<u>s</u>.
> Javier sit<u>s</u>.
> Gina stand<u>s</u>.

Underline the *-s* at the end of each verb and explain: *When you describe one person's actions, use an -s at the end of the action word.* Read the sentences aloud and have students echo.

3 Use Action Verbs Have students take the role of Carlos and pantomime an action from one of the pages. Others should guess the action, to complete the sentence *Carlos _____*.

▶ **Language Practice Book** pages 38, 39

CLOSE AND ASSESS

Have volunteers show their drawings and read their sentences from the bottom of **Language Practice Book** page 39. Call on someone else to tell the action word in each sentence.

Language Development **T39**

LAKESIDE SCHOOL **LESSON 55**

LANGUAGE AND LITERACY: HIGH FREQUENCY WORDS

OBJECTIVES
Learning to Read:
- Recognize High Frequency Words

INTRODUCE

1 Learn New Words Place a word and its letter tiles on the screen as you work through the Strategy steps. For example, for *boy*, say:

1. *First, look at the word.* (Display the word tile for *boy*.)
2. *Now listen to the word:* boy, boy.
3. *Listen to the word in a sentence:* Carlos is a boy.
4. *Say the word after me:* boy.
5. *Spell the word:* b-o-y. (Say each letter as you place the tile. Point to each tile and have students spell the word.)
6. *Say the word again:* boy.

Repeat the process for the other words, using these context sentences:

- Every **day** Carlos reads a **book**.
- He does his homework at **night** with a **group** of friends.
- He writes **letters** to a **girl**.
- May is the best time of the **year**!

PRACTICE

2 Sort Words Place the word tiles randomly. Have students sort the words into words that name a person, words that name a time, and words that name one or more things. (person: *boy, girl*; time: *day, night, year*; thing or things: *book, letters, group*)

APPLY

3 Read New Words Have students find the new words on pages 38–39.

▶ Reading Practice Book page 36

CLOSE AND ASSESS
Display the words one at a time for students to read.

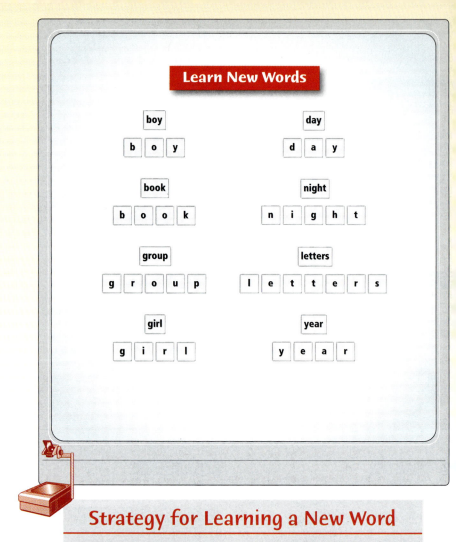

Strategy for Learning a New Word

1. Look at the word.
2. Listen to the word.
3. Listen to the word in a sentence.
4. Say the word.
5. Spell the word.
6. Say the word again.

REACHING ALL STUDENTS

Reading Fluency
RECOGNIZE HIGH FREQUENCY WORDS

To build automaticity with the new high frequency words:

- Have students create memory aids to cue meaning and/or pronunciation of the words. For example, for *day*, they might show the sun rising to cue meaning or write "d-A-y" to help with pronunciation.

- The words in this lesson often appear on charts, signs, lists, posters, and bulletin boards around school. Invite partners to go on a high frequency word hunt. Have them record the number of times and where they find each word. Later, sets of partners can compare their findings.

T39a Lakeside School

How to Write an Exclamation

| You | do | great | work | ! |

| I | like | this | book | ! |

| I | see | some | good | food | ! |

| They | play | day | and | night | ! |

Penmanship
For script models and practice in writing sentences in manuscript or cursive with correct word spacing, see the **Teacher's Resource Book**, pages 47–81.

Strategy for Exclamations

- An exclamation shows a strong feeling.
- It starts with a capital letter.
- It ends with an exclamation mark.

Multi-Level Strategies
CONCEPTS OF PRINT: PUNCTUATION

LITERATE IN L1 Some languages follow different print conventions. For example: Spanish uses an inverted exclamation mark before an exclamation, as well as an exclamation mark at the end. Have students work with a set of statements, questions, and exclamations copied out of Lakeside pages 12–39, without the end punctuation. Partners can add a period, a question mark, or an exclamation mark to punctuate each sentence. Remind them that English uses these marks only as end punctuation.

LAKESIDE SCHOOL **LESSON 56**

LANGUAGE AND LITERACY: EXCLAMATIONS

OBJECTIVES

Writing:
❶ Write an Exclamation

INTRODUCE

1 **Learn About Exclamations** Place the word tiles for the first sentence on the screen. Say:

1. *An exclamation is a sentence that shows a strong feeling.* (Display *You do great work,* without the exclamation mark.)

2. *Listen to the exclamation:* (Point to each word as you read: *You do great work!*)

3. *Does this sentence show a strong feeling?* (yes)

4. *The first word starts with a capital letter.* (Point to *Y.*) *This is capital Y.*

5. *An exclamation ends with an exclamation mark.* (Place the tile for the exclamation mark at the end.)

6. *Read the exclamation with me.*

Repeat for the other exclamations.

PRACTICE

2 **Build Sentences** Read a sentence and place its word tiles and exclamation mark randomly: *I think you are great! This book is very old! I need help! We can play here!* Have students tell you how to arrange the words and exclamation mark. Then have them read the exclamation in unison. Repeat for the other sentences.

APPLY

3 **Read Exclamations** Have students find exclamations on pages 18–39.

▶ **Reading Practice Book** page 37

CLOSE AND ASSESS

Provide word tiles for the exclamations in Step 1. Read each exclamation and have a volunteer build it. Have other students name the feeling and point to the capital letter and exclamation mark.

Language and Literacy **T39b**

Contents

▶ *Language Practice Book for* Lakeside School

Page	Concepts/Vocabulary	Language Functions	Patterns and Structures
1, 2	**Numbers and Number Words**		
3	**School Locations**	Give Information	
4	**School Locations**	Give Information	This is _____.
5	**Classroom Objects, School Tools**	Give Information	Here is a/an _____.
6	**Classroom Objects, School Tools**	Ask and Answer Questions	Is this _____? Yes/No. This is a/an _____.
7	**Greetings and Introductions**	Express Social Courtesies	This is _____. Nice to meet you.
8	**School Locations**	Give Information	
9	**School Locations**	Ask and Answer Questions	Where is _____?
10	**Telling Time**	Give Information	What time is it? It is _____.
11	**School Subjects; Schedules**	Ask and Answer Questions	Where is _____? Who is _____?
12	**Classroom Objects**	Give Information	Here is/are _____.
13	**Classroom Activities**	Give Information	
14	**Shapes**	Give and Carry Out Commands	
15	**Shapes; Letters; Classroom Objects**	Give and Carry Out Commands	Show me _____. Point to _____.
16	**Personal Information**	Give Information	My name is _____. My phone number is _____.
17	**Personal Information; School Schedules; School Locations**	Ask for Information	What is _____? Where is _____?
18	**Classroom Activities**	Express Needs	I need to _____.
19	**Library Objects**	Ask for and Give Information	A _____ is in the _____. Some _____ are in the _____.
20	**Basic/General**	Express Likes	Do you like _____? I like _____.
21	**School Vocabulary**	Ask for Information	Will you _____? Does _____?
22	**Sports**	Express Likes	I like _____.
23	**Sports**	Ask and Answer Questions	Can you _____? I/You can _____.
24	**Parts of the Body**	Give Information	
25	**Sickness and Injury**	Give Information	He/She has _____. They have _____.
26	**Parts of the Body; Sickness and Injury**	Express Feelings	How do you feel? My _____ hurt(s).
27	**Feeling Words (Health)**	Ask and Answer Questions	How does he/she feel? He/She feels _____. How do they feel? They feel _____.
28	**Food**	Express Likes and Dislikes	I like _____. I do not like _____.
29	**Money**	Ask for and Give Information	
30	**Food**	Ask for and Give Information	What is this/that? This/That is _____.
31	**Science Materials and Activities**	Give Information	
32	**School Activities**	Express Needs and Thoughts	I need _____. I think _____.
33	**Clothing/Colors**	Give Information	
34	**Clothing**	Ask and Answer Questions	Which _____ do you like? I like this/that/these/those _____.
35	**Days of the Week**	Give Information	On _____, I _____.
36	**Good-byes**	Express Social Courtesies	See you _____.
37	**Months of the Year**	Describe	
38, 39	**Actions**	Describe	Third-person singular action verbs (-s)

Language Practice Book: Lakeside School **T39d**

In the Language Practice Book

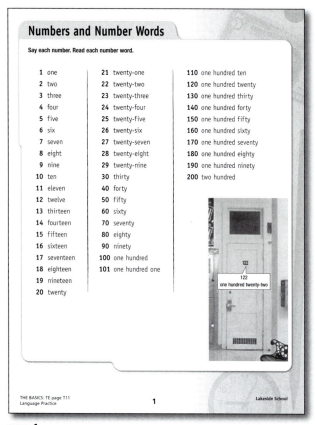
page 1

page 2

page 3

page 4

page 5

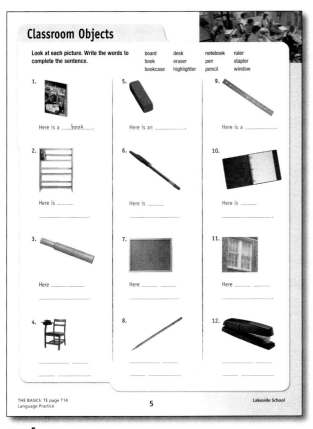

page 6

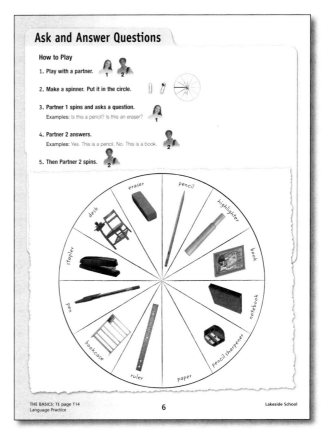

page 7

page 8

Language Practice Book: Lakeside School **T39f**

In the Language Practice Book, continued

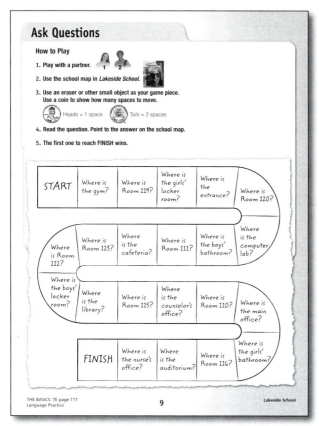

page 9

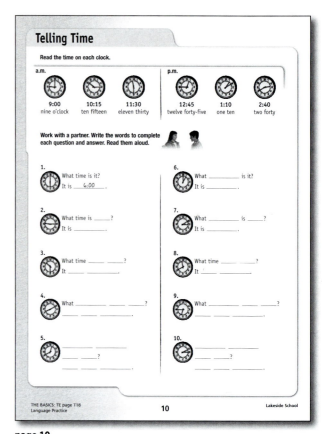

page 10

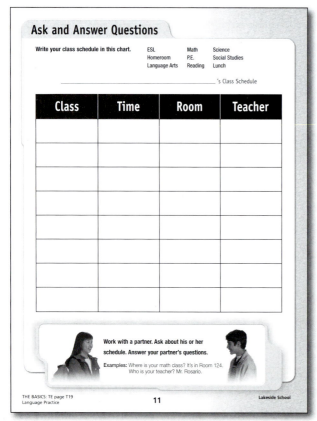

page 11

page 12

T39g Language Practice Book: Lakeside School

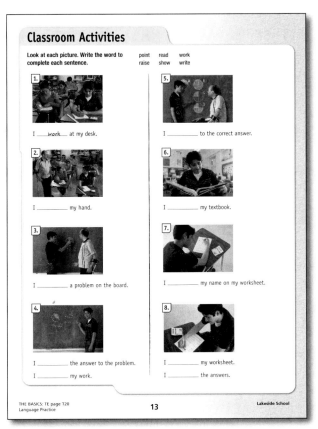

page 13

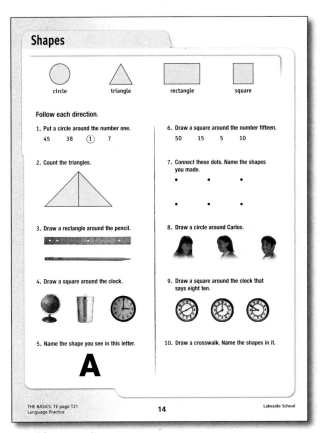

page 14

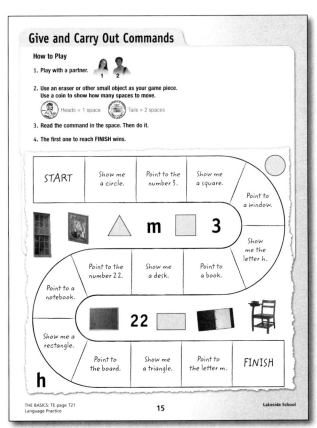

page 15

page 16

Language Practice Book: Lakeside School T39h

In the Language Practice Book, continued

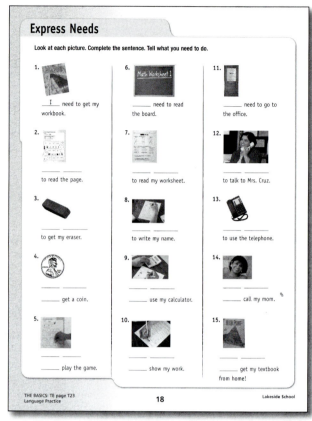

page 17

page 18

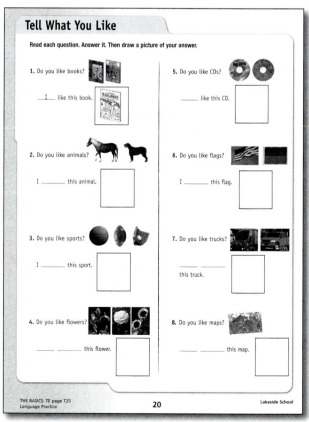

page 19

page 20

T39i Language Practice Book: Lakeside School

page 21

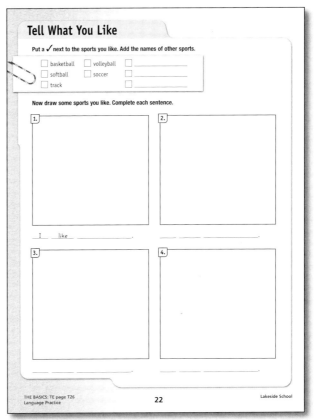
page 22

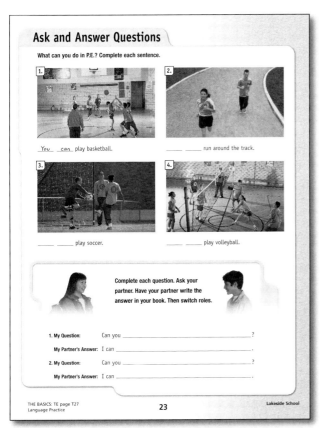
page 23

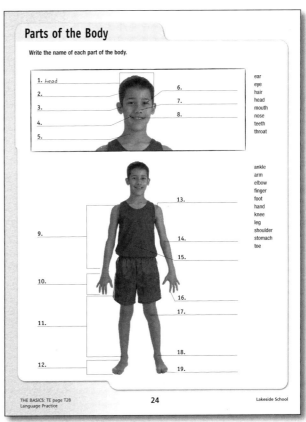
page 24

Language Practice Book: Lakeside School **T39j**

In the Language Practice Book, continued

page 25

page 26

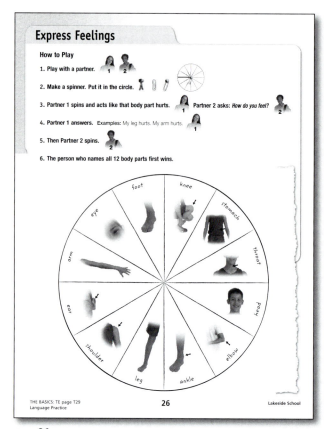

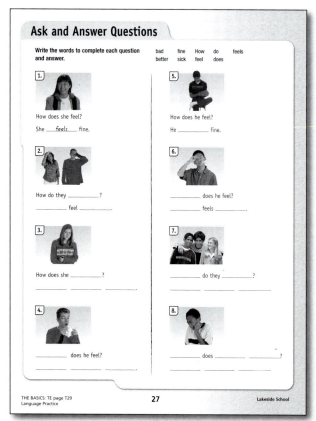

page 27

page 28

page 29

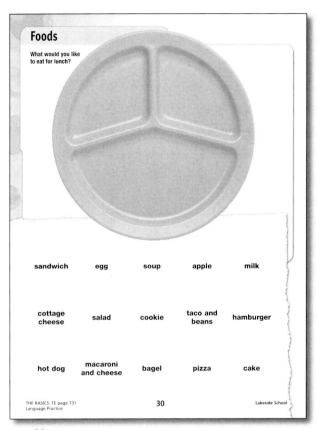

page 30

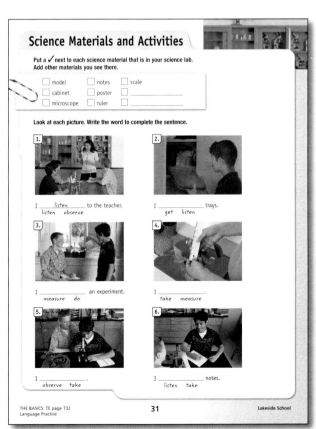

page 31

page 32

Language Practice Book: Lakeside School **T391**

In the Language Practice Book, continued

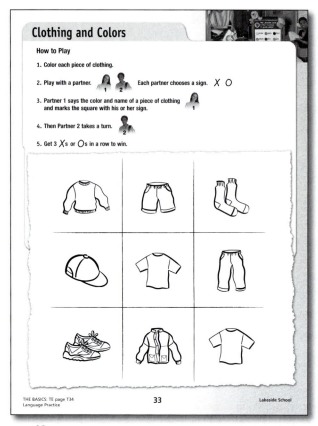

page 33

page 34

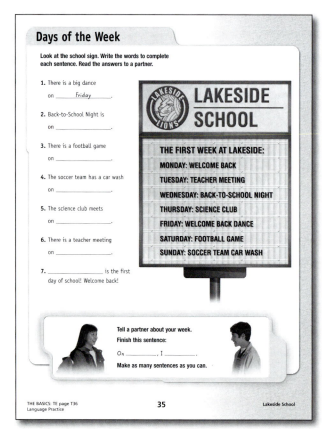

page 35

page 36

T39m Language Practice Book: Lakeside School

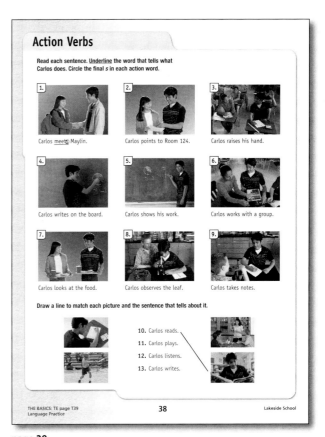
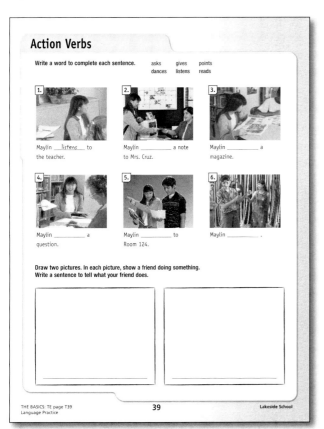

Contents

▶ *Reading Practice Book for* Lakeside School

High Frequency Words: *am, I, is, school, the, this, you* 1

High Frequency Words: *a, an, here, my, no, yes* 2

Letters and Sounds: *Ss, Mm, Ff, Hh, Tt, Aa* 3, 4

High Frequency Words: *at, it, look, of, on, see, show, where* 5

Blend Words with Short *a* 6, 7

High Frequency Words: *are, good, he, she, some, time, who, your* 8

Letters and Sounds: *Nn, Ll, Pp, Gg, Ii* 9, 10

High Frequency Words: *answer, point, read, to, with, work, write* 11

Blend Words with Short *a* and *i* 12, 13

High Frequency Words: *call, name, need, number, to, what* 14

Letters and Sounds: *Rr, Dd, Cc, Vv, Oo* 15, 16

High Frequency Words: *do, does, for, help, in, like, me, picture, will* 17

Blend Words with Short *a, i,* and *o* 18, 19

High Frequency Words: *around, can, play, too, we* 20

Letters and Sounds: *Jj, Bb, Ww, Kk, Ee* 21, 22

High Frequency Words: *feel, has, have, how, put, they* 23

Blend Words with Short *a, i, o,* and *e* 24, 25

High Frequency Words: *and, don't, food, not, that* 26

How to Write a Statement 27

High Frequency Words: *give, take, think* 28

Letters and Sounds: *Zz, Yy, Uu, Qu qu, Xx* 29, 30

High Frequency Words: *both, get, little, old, them, these, things, those, very, which* 31

Blend Words with Short *a, i, o, e,* and *u* 32, 33

High Frequency Words: *great, later, soon, tomorrow* 34

How to Write a Question 35

High Frequency Words: *book, boy, day, girl, group, letters, night, year* 36

How to Write an Exclamation 37

Reading Practice Book: Lakeside School **T39p**

In the Reading Practice Book

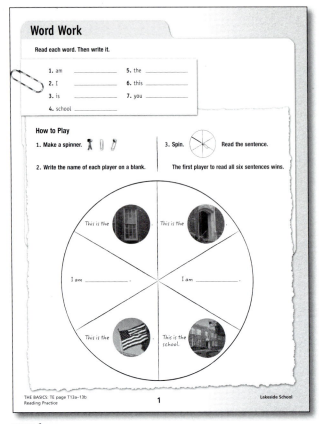

page 1

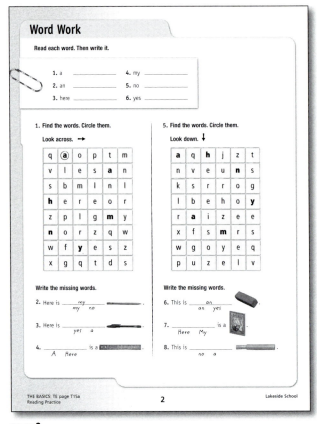

page 2

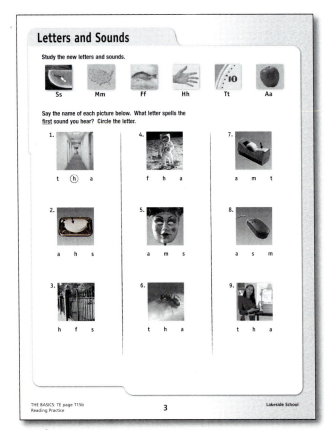

page 3

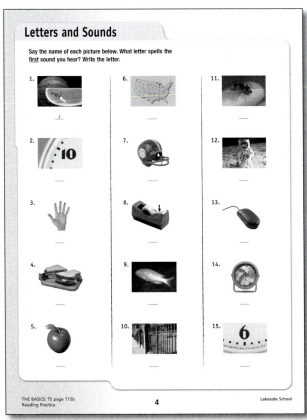

page 4

T39q Reading Practice Book: Lakeside School

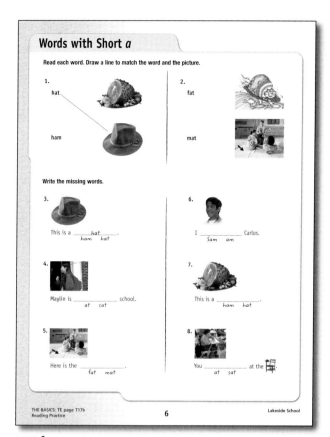

page 5

page 6

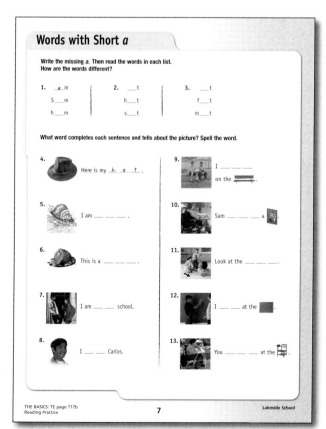

page 7

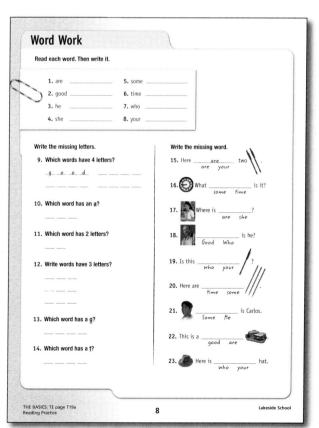

page 8

Reading Practice Book: Lakeside School **T39r**

In the Reading Practice Book, continued

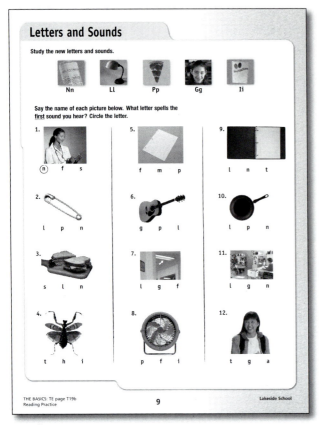

page 9

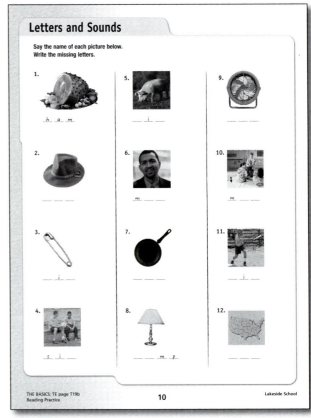

page 10

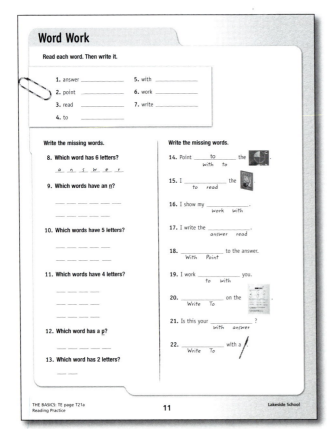

page 11

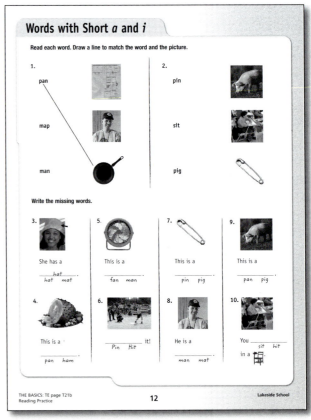

page 12

T39s Reading Practice Book: Lakeside School

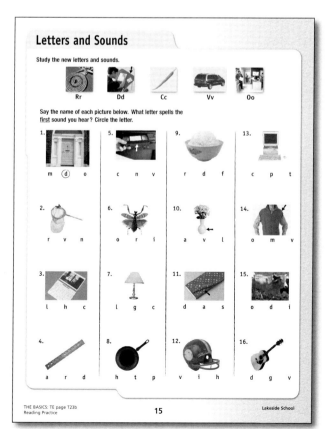

page 13

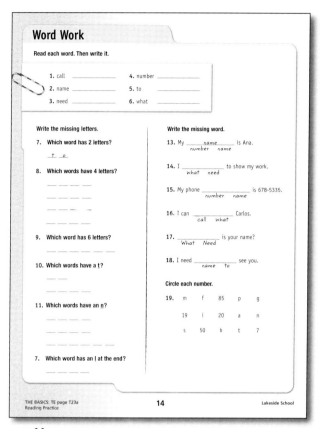

page 14

page 15

page 16

Reading Practice Book: Lakeside School **T39†**

In the Reading Practice Book, continued

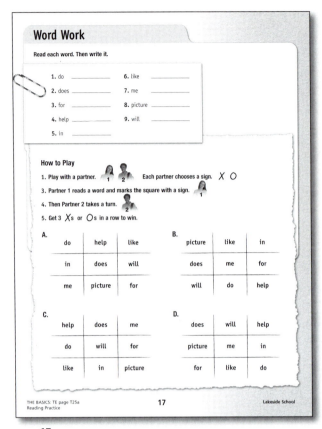

page 17

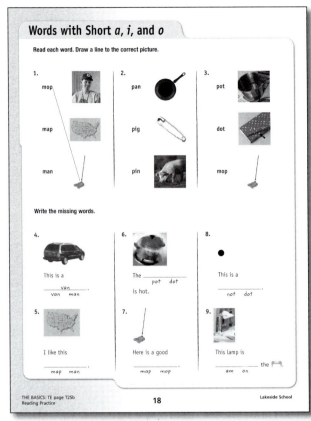

page 18

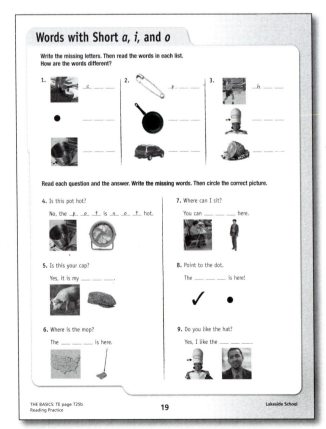

page 19

page 20

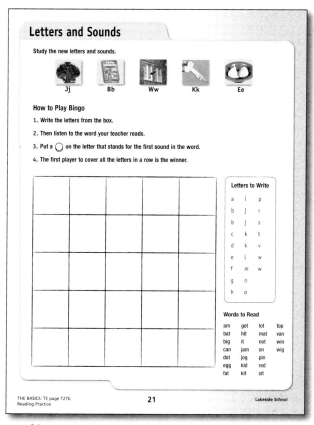
page 21

page 22

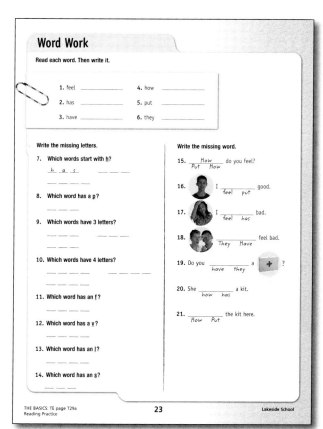
page 23

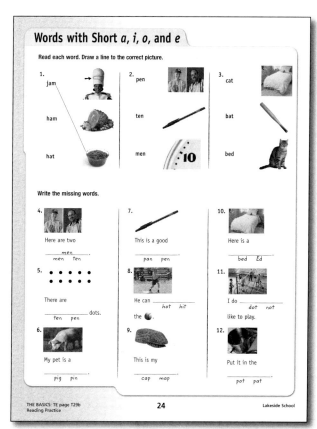
page 24

Reading Practice Book: Lakeside School T39v

In the Reading Practice Book, continued

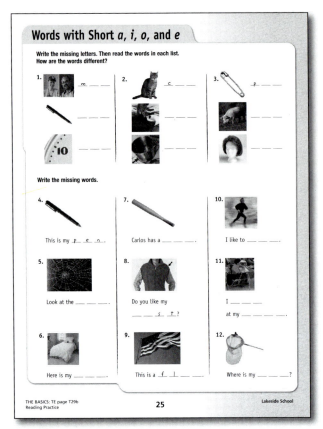

page 25

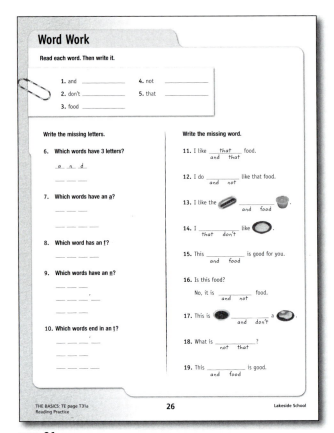

page 26

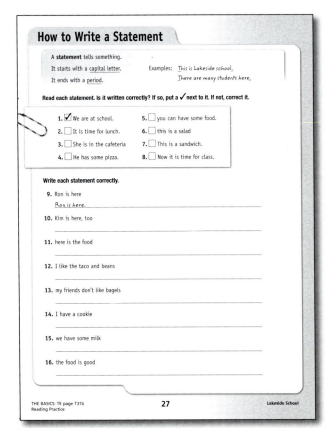

page 27

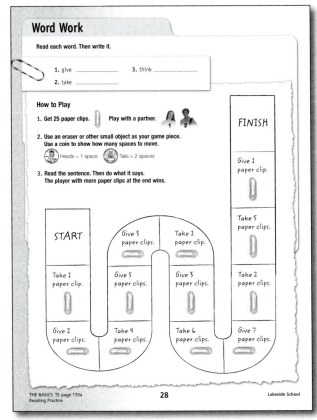

page 28

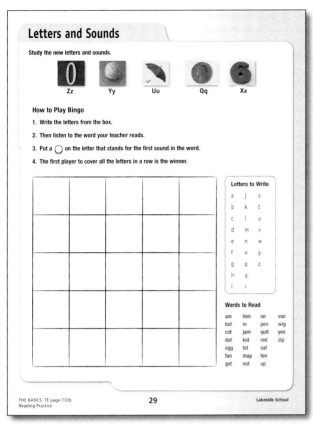

page 29

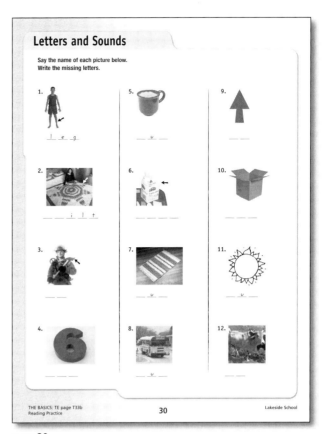

page 30

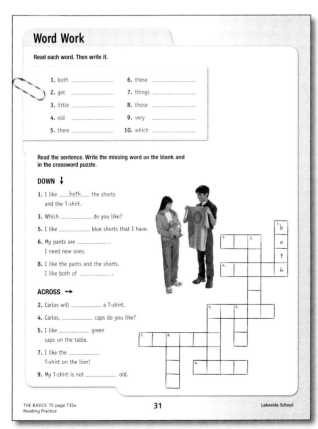

page 31

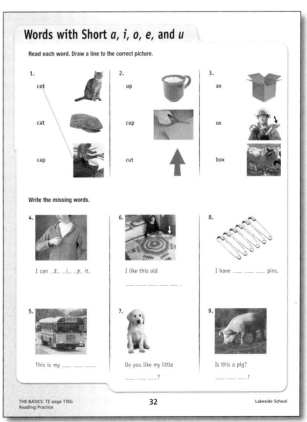

page 32

Reading Practice Book: Lakeside School **T39x**

In the Reading Practice Book, continued

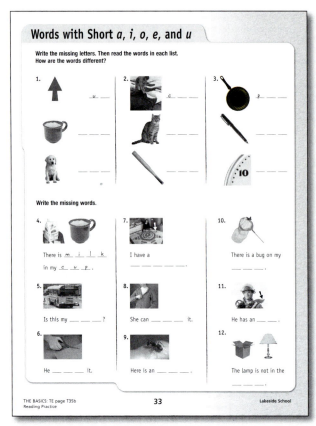

page 33

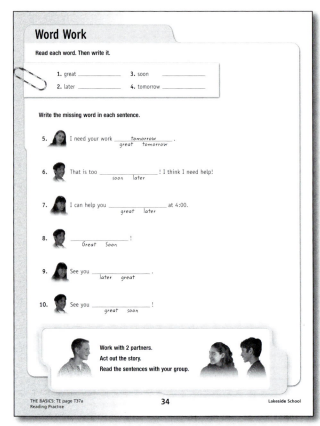

page 34

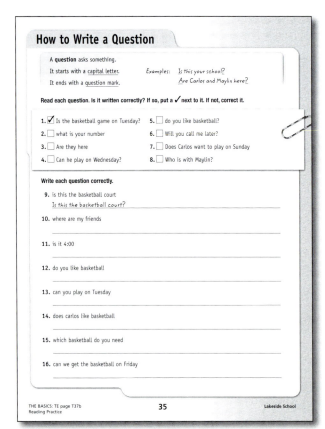

page 35

page 36

T39y Reading Practice Book: Lakeside School

How to Write an Exclamation

An **exclamation** shows a strong feeling.

It starts with a <u>capital letter</u>.

It ends with an <u>exclamation mark</u>.

Examples: <u>Help me</u>!

<u>Look at that</u>!

Read each exclamation. Is it written correctly? If so, put a ✓ next to it. If not, correct it.

1. ✓ See you soon!

2. ☐ listen

3. ☐ Here they are

4. ☐ This is good work!

5. ☐ I like that food

6. ☐ call me tomorrow

7. ☐ Carlos is here

8. ☐ great!

Write each exclamation correctly.

9. we can do that in October

<u>We can do that in October!</u>

10. this book is great

_____

11. see you later

_____

12. Carlos likes this one

_____

13. this is great work

_____

14. call me on Friday

_____

15. he looks great

_____

16. June will be fun

_____

THE BASICS: TE page T39b
Reading Practice

37

Lakeside School

page 37

Reading Practice Book: Lakeside School **T39z**

LESSON PLANS FOR Units 1-18

LESSON PLANS FOR Units 1-18

UNITS 1-18

Contents for Your Teacher's Edition

Unit Planner **T40h**

UNIT 1 Glad to Meet You! Unit Launch T40

Language Development

Pronouns **T42, T43**

Present Tense Verbs: *am* and *are* **T44**

Present Tense Verbs: *is* and *are* **T45**

Vocabulary: Personal Information **T46**

Vocabulary: Communication **T47**

Language and Literacy

Read and Think Together: Sequence
Good News .... REALISTIC FICTION **T48**

Words to Know **T49**

Reading and Spelling: short *a*, short *o* **T50**

Read on Your Own: Sequence
New at School .... REALISTIC FICTION **T52**

Statements and Exclamations **T53**

Language Across the Curriculum

Success in Mathematics: Basic Operations **T54**

Writing Project ✏ POSTCARD **T55**

THEME BOOK 📼

Unit Planner **T56a**

UNIT 2 Set the Table Unit Launch T56

Language Development

Adjectives **T58**

Vocabulary: Colors, Shapes, and Sizes **T59**

Vocabulary: Foods **T60**

Action Verbs **T61**

Language and Literacy

Read and Think Together: Steps in a Process
I Make Pictures Move! .... CAREER SKETCH **T62**

Words to Know **T63**

Reading and Spelling: short *i*, short *u*, *ch*, and *tch* **T64**

Read on Your Own: Steps in a Process
Something Good for Lunch .... REALISTIC FICTION.... **T66**

Negative Sentences................................ **T67**

Language Across the Curriculum

Success in Science: Food Pyramid **T68**

Writing Project ✏ EXHIBIT CARD **T69**

THEME BOOK 📼

T40a

Contents for Your Teacher's Edition, continued

UNIT 3 On the Job

Unit Planner T70a
Unit Launch T70

Language Development
Vocabulary: Actions/Careers T72
Present Tense Verbs............................. T73
Yes-or-No Questions T74
Vocabulary: Tools and Careers T75

Language and Literacy
Read and Think Together: Details
  What Is It? ....FANTASY T76
Words to Know T77
Reading and Spelling:
  short e, sh, ck, and double consonants........... T78
Read on Your Own: Details
  Let Ben Take It ....REALISTIC FICTION T80
Questions with *Who?*, *What?*, *Where?*, and *When?* T81

Language Across the Curriculum
Success in Science and Mathematics:
  Scientific Processes; Measurement T82
Writing Project / JOB HANDBOOK.................... T83

THEME BOOK

UNIT 4 Numbers Count

Unit Planner T84a
Unit Launch T84

Language Development
Questions with *Do* and *Does* T86
Vocabulary: Cardinal Numbers...................... T87
Negative Sentences............................... T88
Vocabulary: Ordinal Numbers...................... T89

Language and Literacy
Read and Think Together: Problems and Solutions
  A Year Without Rain ....HISTORICAL FICTION T90
Words to Know T91
Reading and Spelling: blends and digraphs T92
Read on Your Own: Details
  Rush! ....REALISTIC FICTION T94
Contractions with *not*............................ T95

Language Across the Curriculum
Success in Social Studies: Geography; Charts........ T96
Writing Project / FACT SHEET T97

THEME BOOK

UNIT 5 City Sights

Unit Planner T98a
Unit Launch T98

Language Development
Vocabulary: Location Words....................... T100
Vocabulary: Neighborhood T101, T102
Regular Past Tense Verbs.................. T103, T104
Statements with *There is* and *There are* T105

Language and Literacy
Read and Think Together: Details
  More Than a Meal ....REALISTIC FICTION.......... T106
Words to Know T107
Reading and Spelling:
  word patterns and multisyllabic words T108
Read on Your Own: Details
  Meet Jo ....NEWSPAPER ARTICLE.................. T110
Pronoun-Verb Contractions T111

Language Across the Curriculum
Success in Social Studies: Communities; Maps T112
Writing Project / JOURNAL ENTRY T113

THEME BOOK

T40b

Unit Planner T114a

UNIT 6 Welcome Home! Unit Launch T114

Language Development
Vocabulary: Family **T116**
Present Tense Verbs: *have* and *has* **T117**
Vocabulary: Rooms in a House **T118**
Vocabulary: Household Objects **T119**

Language and Literacy
Read and Think Together: Main Idea and Details
   Families .... PHOTO ESSAY **T120**
Words to Know **T121**
Reading and Spelling: long vowels (*a, i, o, u*) **T122**
Read on Your Own: Main Idea and Details
   When We Came To Wisconsin .. REALISTIC FICTION ... **T124**
Plural Nouns **T125**

Language Across the Curriculum
Success in Mathematics: Fractions, Decimals,
   and Percents **T126**
Writing Project / FAMILY ALBUM **T127**

THEME BOOK

Unit Planner T128a

UNIT 7 Pack Your Bags! Unit Launch T128

Language Development
Commands **T130**
Vocabulary: Landforms and Transportation **T131**
Vocabulary: Weather and Clothing **T132**
Verbs: *can* **T133**

Language and Literacy
Read and Think Together: Classify
   Explore! .... TRAVEL ESSAY **T134**
Words to Know **T135**
Reading and Spelling:
   long vowels (*ai, ay; ee, ea; oa, ow*) **T136**
Read on Your Own: Classify
   Explore a Wetland .... SCIENCE ARTICLE **T138**
Capitalization: Proper Nouns **T139**

Language Across the Curriculum
Success in Science: Cycles; Diagrams **T140**
Writing Project / CLASS TRAVEL BOOK **T141**

THEME BOOK

T40c

Contents for Your Teacher's Edition, continued

Unit Planner **T142a**

UNIT 8 Friend to Friend Unit Launch **T142**

Language Development

Regular Past Tense Verbs **T144**

Vocabulary: Feelings **T145**

Irregular Past Tense Verbs: *was* and *were* **T146**

Negative Sentences and Contractions with *not* **T147**

Language and Literacy

Read and Think Together: Cause and Effect
Friends Are Like That .... FICTIONAL JOURNAL **T148**

Words to Know **T149**

Reading and Spelling: verb ending (*-ed*) **T150**

Read on Your Own: Cause and Effect
Eva's Lesson .... REALISTIC FICTION **T152**

Possessive Nouns **T153**

Language Across the Curriculum

Success in Mathematics: Bar Graphs **T154**

Writing Project ✏ FRIENDSHIP BOOK **T155**

THEME BOOK 📼

Unit Planner **T156a**

UNIT 9 Let's Celebrate! Unit Launch **T156**

Language Development

Adverbs **T158**

Present Progressive Verbs **T159**

Vocabulary: Country Words **T160**

Phrases with *like to* and *want to* **T161**

Language and Literacy

Read and Think Together: Classify
Let's Dance! .... PHOTO ESSAY **T162**

Words to Know **T163**

Reading and Spelling: verb ending (*-ing*) **T164**

Read on Your Own: Details
Dance to Celebrate! .... SOCIAL STUDIES ARTICLE ... **T166**

Language Across the Curriculum

Success in Social Studies: World Cultures; Maps **T168**

Writing Project ✏ CELEBRATION POSTER **T169**

THEME BOOK 📼

Unit Planner **T170a**

UNIT 10 Here to Help Unit Launch **T170**

Language Development

Verbs: *may, might,* and *could* **T172**

Vocabulary: Time **T173**

Phrases with *have to* and *need to* **T174**

Possessive Pronouns **T175**

Language and Literacy

Read and Think Together: Cause and Effect
Power Out! .... REALISTIC FICTION **T176**

Words to Know **T177**

Reading and Spelling: long vowels (*ie, igh, ui, ue*) ... **T178**

Read on Your Own: Cause and Effect
Hot Crumbs Cause Fire .... NEWSPAPER ARTICLE ... **T180**

Language Across the Curriculum

Success in Social Studies: Local Government **T182**

Writing Project ✏ JOB ADVERTISEMENT **T183**

THEME BOOK 📼

T40d

Unit Planner T184a

UNIT 11 Make a Difference! Unit Launch T184

Language Development

Irregular Past Tense Verbs **T186**

Vocabulary: Direction Words **T187**

Vocabulary: Civil Rights **T188**

Irregular Past Tense Verbs **T189**

Language and Literacy

Read and Think Together: Sequence
Who Was Martin Luther King, Jr.?
BIOGRAPHY **T190**

Words to Know **T191**

Reading and Spelling: *r*-controlled vowels **T192**

Read on Your Own: Classify Information
Kids Are Helping Kids .... BIOGRAPHIES **T194**

Language Across the Curriculum

Success in Mathematics:
U. S. Elections; Tables and Circle Graphs **T196**

Writing Project ✏ PERSONAL NARRATIVE **T197**

THEME BOOK 📼

Unit Planner T198a

UNIT 12 Our Living Planet Unit Launch T198

Language Development

Vocabulary: Opinion Words **T200**

Vocabulary: Animals and Habitats **T201**

Vocabulary: Plants and Habitats **T202**

Sensory Adjectives **T203**

Language and Literacy

Read and Think Together: Sequence
Rachel Carson .... BIOGRAPHY **T204**

Words to Know **T205**

Reading and Spelling: *r*-controlled syllable types **T206**

Read on Your Own: Details, Cause and Effect
Animals in the Wild .... SCIENCE ARTICLE **T208**

Language Across the Curriculum

Success in Science and Mathematics:
Endangered Animals; Line Graphs **T210**

Writing Project ✏ FACT-AND-OPINION POSTER **T211**

THEME BOOK 📼

Unit Planner T212a

UNIT 13 Past and Present Unit Launch T212

Language Development

Vocabulary: History **T214**

Vocabulary: Historical Records **T215**

Nouns **T216**

Present and Past Tense Verbs **T217**

Object Pronouns **T218, T219**

Language and Literacy

Read and Think Together: Comparisons
The Children We Remember
HISTORICAL ACCOUNT **T220**

Words to Know **T221**

Reading and Spelling: words with *y* **T222**

Read on Your Own: Comparisons
Kidworks For Peace .... WEB PAGE: CHAT ROOM ... **T224**

Language Across the Curriculum

Success in Social Studies: U. S. Government **T226**

Writing Project ✏ COMPARISON POSTER **T227**

THEME BOOK 📼

T40e

Contents for Your Teacher's Edition, continued

Unit Planner T228a

UNIT 14 Tell Me More   Unit Launch T228

Language Development
Vocabulary: Story Elements T230
Vocabulary: Opposites T231
Vocabulary: Phrases for Times and Places T232
Commands T233

Language and Literacy
Read and Think Together: Characters
  The Eagle and the Moon Gold .... FABLE T234
Words to Know T235
Reading and Spelling:
  diphthongs and variant vowels T236
Read on Your Own: Story Elements
  A Chill in the Air .... REALISTIC FICTION T238

Language Across the Curriculum
Success in Language Arts: Myths; Characters,
  Setting, and Plot T240
Writing Project 🖋 NEW STORY ENDING T241

THEME BOOK

Unit Planner T242a

UNIT 15 Personal Best   Unit Launch T242

Language Development
Vocabulary: The Body T244
Present Tense Verbs T245
Vocabulary: Sports T246
Pronouns T247

Language and Literacy
Read and Think Together: Main Idea and Details
  Body Works .... SCIENCE ESSAY T248
Words to Know T249
Reading and Spelling:
  variant vowels and consonants T250
Read on Your Own: Main Idea and Details
  Summer Games Are a Big Hit
  NEWSPAPER ARTICLE T252

Language Across the Curriculum
Success in Language Arts:
  How to Build a Paragraph T254
Writing Project 🖋 CLASS BOOK ON HEALTHY HABITS T255

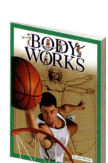

THEME BOOK

Unit Planner T256a

UNIT 16 This Land Is Our Land   Unit Launch T256

Language Development
Vocabulary: American History T258
Questions with *How?* and *Why?* T259
Vocabulary: Landforms and
  Bodies of Water T260
Capitalization: Proper Nouns T261

Language and Literacy
Read and Think Together: Classify
  All Across America .... SONG T262
Words to Know T263
Reading and Spelling: multisyllabic words T264
Read on Your Own: Classify
  Deep Canyon .... TRAVEL ARTICLE T266

Language Across the Curriculum
Success in Social Studies: Regions of the U.S.; Maps .. T268
Writing Project 🖋 BIOGRAPHICAL SKETCH T269

THEME BOOK

T40f

Unit Planner **T270a**

UNIT 17 Harvest Time   Unit Launch **T270**

Language Development
Questions: *How many?* and *How much?*. **T272**
Vocabulary: Farming. **T273**
Vocabulary: At the Restaurant. **T274**
Sensory Adjectives **T275**

Language and Literacy
Read and Think Together: Comparisons
Crops .... INFORMATIONAL TEXT **T276**
Words to Know **T277**
Reading and Spelling: prefixes and suffixes. **T278**
Read on Your Own: Comparisons
Many Places to Plant a Plant
INFORMATIONAL TEXT **T280**

Language Across the Curriculum
Success in Science: Plants **T282**
Writing Project ✏ CROP REPORT **T283**

THEME BOOK

Unit Planner **T284a**

UNIT 18 Superstars   Unit Launch **T284**

Language Development
Vocabulary: Idioms **T286**
Future Tense Verbs and Contractions **T287**
Vocabulary: Space. **T288**
Verb Tenses: Present, Past, Future. **T289**

Language and Literacy
Read and Think Together: Goal and Outcome
Sunny and Moonshine .... FANTASY. **T290**
Words to Know **T291**
Reading and Spelling: multisyllabic words. **T292**
Read on Your Own: Goal and Outcome
Fifth Moon's Story .... LEGEND **T294**

Language Across the Curriculum
Success in Science: Space **T296**
Writing Project ✏ DIAMANTE POEM **T297**

THEME BOOK

▸ *Handbook* **T298**

T40g

Resources

For Success in Language and Literacy

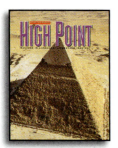

Student Book pages 40–55

For Language Skills Practice

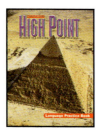

Language Practice Book pages 40–45

For Reading Skills Practice

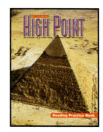

Reading Practice Book pages 38–41

For Vocabulary, Language Development, and Reading Fluency

Language Tape 1, Side A
Language CD 1, Tracks 1–5

For Reading Together

Theme Book *Good News* from The Basics Bookshelf

For Audio Walk-Throughs and Selection Readings

Selection Tape 1A
Selection CD 1, Tracks 1–2

For Phonics Instruction

Transparencies 11–15

Transparency Scripts 11–15

Letter Tiles

For Comprehensive Assessment

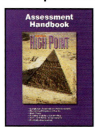

Language Acquisition Assessment, Units 1–3 Test, Writing Assessment, Self-Assessment

For Home-School Connections

High Point Newsletter 1 in seven languages

For Planning and Instruction

Teacher's Edition pages T40h–T55

T40h Unit Planner

UNIT 1

Glad to Meet You!

In This Unit

Vocabulary
- Personal Information
- Communication
- Numbers and Basic Operations

Language Functions
- Exchange Greetings and Good-byes
- Give Information
- Use the Telephone

Patterns and Structures
- Pronouns
- Present Tense Verbs
- Statements and Exclamations

Reading
- Phonics: Short a, Short o
- Comprehension: Identify Sequence (sequence chain)

Writing
- Sentences
- Postcard

Content Area Connection
- Mathematics (basic operations)

UNIT 1
Activity and Assessment Planner

UNIT 1: Glad to Meet You!

LESSONS

1

UNIT 1 LAUNCH
▶ *pages T40–T41*

LESSON 1: INTRODUCE UNIT 1 pages T40–T41

Vocabulary
T Personal Information

Viewing
Respond to
Self-Portraits

Learning Strategies
Preview

Build Background

Relate to Personal
Experience

Critical Thinking
Generate Ideas

2–7

LANGUAGE DEVELOPMENT
▶ *pages T42–T47*

**LESSON 2
PRONOUNS**
page T42

Function
Exchange Greetings
and Good-byes

**Patterns and
Structures**
T Pronouns

Writing
T Sentences

**LESSON 3
PRONOUNS**
page T43

Function
Give Information

**Patterns and
Structures**
T Pronouns

Writing
T Sentences

**LESSON 4
VERBS**
page T44

Function
Give Information

**Patterns and
Structures**
T Present Tense Verbs
(*am, are*)

Writing
Sentences

**LESSON 5
VERBS**
page T45

Function
Give Information

**Patterns and
Structures**
T Present Tense Verbs
(*is, are*)

Writing
T Sentences

**LESSON 6
PERSONAL
INFORMATION**
page T46

Function
Give Information

Vocabulary
T Personal information

Writing
Order Form

**LESSON 7
COMMUNICATION**
page T47

Functions
Use the Telephone

Express Social
Courtesies

Vocabulary
T Communication

Speaking
Role-Play

8–14

LANGUAGE AND LITERACY
▶ *pages T48a–T53*

**LESSON 8
BASICS BOOKSHELF**
pages T48a–T48d

Function
Listen to a Book

Vocabulary
T Communication Words

Reading Strategies
Activate Prior
Knowledge

Preview

Learning to Read
Hold a Book and Turn
Pages

Use Left-to-Right
Directionality

Track Print

Identify Words

**Critical Thinking and
Comprehension**
T Identify Sequence

**LESSON 9
BASICS BOOKSHELF:
COMPREHENSION**
page T48

Function
Retell a Story

Learning Strategy
Use Graphic Organizers
(sequence chain)

**Critical Thinking and
Comprehension**
T Identify Sequence

**LESSON 10
HIGH FREQUENCY
WORDS**
page T49

Learning to Read
T Recognize High
Frequency Words

**LESSON 11
PHONICS**
pages T50a–T50d

Learning to Read
Build Oral Vocabulary

Develop Phonemic
Awareness

T Associate Sounds and
Symbols: /a/ *a;* /o/ *o;*
phonograms *-an, -ag,
-at, -ap, -ad;
-ot, -op, -og*

Blend Sounds to
Decode Words

**LESSON 12
READING AND
SPELLING**
pages T50–T51

Learning to Read
Develop Phonemic
Awareness

T Associate Sounds and
Symbols: /a/ *a;* /o/ *o*

Blend Sounds to
Decode Words

Spelling
T Words with Short *a* and
Short *o*

**LESSON 13
INDEPENDENT
READING**
page T52

Function
Read a Selection

Learning to Read
T Recognize High
Frequency Words

T Decode Words
(short *a* and *o*)

Reading Strategies
Predict

Set a Purpose for
Reading

Retell

**Critical Thinking and
Comprehension**
T Identify Sequence

**LESSON 14
STATEMENTS AND
EXCLAMATIONS**
page T53

Function
Write

**Patterns and
Structures**
Statements and
Exclamations

Writing
Sentences with Correct
Capitalization and End
Marks

15–16

LANGUAGE ACROSS THE CURRICULUM
▶ *pages T54–T55*

**LESSON 15
MATHEMATICS: MATH PROBLEMS**
page T54

Function
Give Information

Vocabulary
Numbers and Basic
Operations

Critical Thinking
Solve Problems

**LESSON 16
WRITING PROJECT: POSTCARD**
page T55

Functions
Express Social
Courtesies

Give Information

Write

**Learning Strategies
and Critical Thinking**
Plan

Generate and Organize
Ideas

Self-Assess

Writing
Postcard

T40j Unit 1 | Glad to Meet You!

T = Objective Tested on Unit Test

ASSESSMENT OPTIONS

The **Teacher's Edition** and the **Assessment Handbook** include these comprehensive assessment tools:

▶ **Ongoing, Informal Assessment**
Check for understanding and achieve closure for every lesson with the targeted questions and activities in the **Close and Assess** boxes in your Teacher's Edition.

▶ **Decoding Progress Check**
These word lists for each unit provide a quick way to check on mastery of the phonics or word structure skills taught in the unit.

▶ **Language Acquisition Assessments**
To verify students' ability to use the language functions and grammar structures taught in Units 1–3, conduct these performance assessments.

▶ **Unit Test in Standardized Test Format**
This multiple-choice test measures students' cumulative understanding of the skills and language developed in Units 1–3.

▶ **Self- and Peer-Assessment**
Students use the Self-Assessment Form to evaluate their own work and develop learning strategies appropriate to their needs. Students offer feedback to their classmates with the Peer-Assessment Form.

▶ **Writing Assessment/Portfolio Opportunities**
You can evaluate students' writing in the Writing Projects using the Writing Progress Checklist. Then collaborate with students to choose work for their portfolios.

UNITS 1–3 ASSESSMENT OPPORTUNITIES	Assessment Handbook Pages
Decoding Progress Check	1a
Language Acquisition Assessments	2
Units 1–3 Test	3–8
Self-Assessment Form	9
Peer-Assessment Form	50
Writing Progress Checklist	51
Portfolio Evaluation Form	52

RELATED RESOURCES

Talking Walls
by Margy Burns Knight
Essays about walls that "talk" through words and pictures. Followed by the sequel *Talking Walls: The Stories Continue*. (Available from Hampton-Brown)
Theme Book: Read Aloud

Apples in a Box
by Juan Quintana
A farmer sells his produce at an open-air market. With photos. (Available from Hampton-Brown)
Phonics Reinforcement: Short o

Just Like Me
edited by Harriet Rohmer
Fourteen artists use words and pictures to tell about themselves, their work, and their lives. (Available from Hampton-Brown)
Easy Reading

At the Beach
by Huy Voun Lee
With his mother, Xiao Ming draws Chinese characters in the sand, many of which resemble the objects they stand for. (Available from Hampton-Brown)
Language Development: Present Tense Verbs

Puff . . . Flash . . . Bang!
by Gail Gibbons
A book about traffic lights, Morse code, hand gestures, and a host of other signals. (Available from Hampton-Brown)
Vocabulary: Communication Words

Unit Planner **T40k**

UNIT 1 **LESSON 1**

INTRODUCE UNIT 1: GLAD TO MEET YOU

OBJECTIVES

Concepts and Vocabulary:
🅣 Personal Information
Viewing: Respond to Self-Portraits
Learning Strategies:
Preview; Build Background; Relate to Personal Experience
Critical Thinking: Generate Ideas

START WITH A COMMON EXPERIENCE

1. **Introduce "Glad to Meet You!"** Read the unit title. Explain that people say this when they are introduced to somebody for the first time. It means "I am happy to know you now." Talk about how people can get to know each other when they meet. (give their names; tell about their schools, favorite music, hobbies, etc.)

2. **Meet Imran and Lupe** View the cards and self-portraits on page 40. Read the first sentence on each card and have students point to the picture it goes with. Read the rest of the information and talk about how it helps you get to know Imran and Lupe.

3. **Create Trading Cards** Read the activity directions on page 41. Model the steps by making your own card first. Then have students make their cards. Provide sentence frames:

```
I am _____.
        name
I am from _____.
              country
I am _____ years old.
        age
I go to _____.
           name of school
I like _____.
I also like _____.
```

REACHING ALL STUDENTS

HOME CONNECTION

Family Cards Send home a copy of *High Point Newsletter 1* in the **Teacher's Resource Book**. In the home activity, students create a card about a family member, drawing the person's picture on one side and writing the person's name and three sentences about him or her on the back. Students bring the cards to class to share.

Pronunciation of Names
Lupe — lü pe
Imran — im ran

Glad to Meet You!

Make a card about yourself.
Put your photo on one side.
Write about yourself on the other side.
Trade cards with a classmate.
Tell your class about the card.

In This Unit

Vocabulary
- Personal Information
- Communication
- Numbers and Basic Operations

Language Functions
- Exchange Greetings and Good-byes
- Give Information
- Use the Telephone

Patterns and Structures
- Pronouns
- Present Tense Verbs
- Statements and Exclamations

Reading
- Phonics: Short a, Short o
- Comprehension:
  Identify Sequence (sequence chain)

Writing
- Sentences
- Postcard

Content Area Connection
- Mathematics (basic operations)

41

PREVIEW THE UNIT

4 Look for Activities and Ways to Share Information Leaf through the unit, previewing activities students will do, for example:

page 42—learning a chant about saying hello and good-bye to a friend

page 46—filling in an order form

page 48—listening to the Bookshelf book (Display a copy of the book.)

page 52—reading about someone new at school who meets new friends

page 55—making a postcard to send to a friend or relative

Also ask students to look for kinds of personal information and ways to share it. Highlight the order form on page 46 and the ways to communicate on page 47, for example. Then sum up what the preview reveals: *People communicate in lots of ways to share personal information.*

5 Set Your Goals Start a class mind map on sharing information. Prompt students for pictures or words to add, and have them act out and describe other ideas for you to put into words. Talk together about what they want to learn about sharing information in this unit.

CLOSE AND ASSESS

Ask students to tell or show you something they are interested in learning in this unit.

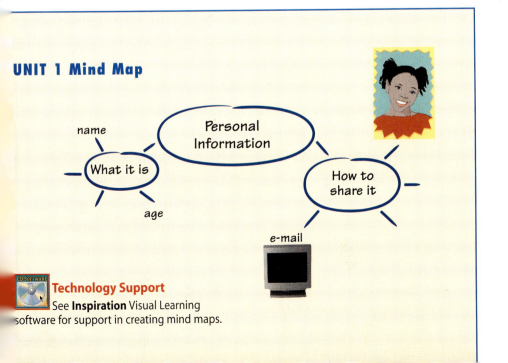

UNIT 1 Mind Map

Technology Support
See **Inspiration** Visual Learning software for support in creating mind maps.

Unit Launch **T41**

UNIT 1 LESSON 2
LANGUAGE DEVELOPMENT: PRONOUNS

OBJECTIVES

Functions: Listen Actively; Repeat Spoken Language; Recite; 🅣 Express Social Courtesies (greetings, good-byes)

Patterns and Structures: 🅣 Pronouns

Writing: 🅣 Sentences

INTRODUCE

1 Listen and Chant Play "Hello, Good-bye" on the **Language Tape/CD**. Students will listen and follow along with the words, echo the lines, and then chime in on the entire chant.

Tape 1A / CD 1 Track 1

2 Learn About Pronouns Read aloud the chart for pronouns and find examples in the chant. To ensure understanding, ask questions such as *How are you? How are you and [another student]?*

PRACTICE

3 Conduct "Express Yourself" Model the use of greetings and good-byes. Then have partners complete the activity.

How to Exchange Greetings and Good-byes

- If I see [student's name], I can say: *Hello, [name]* or *Hi, [name]*.
- Next, we ask about each other: *How are you?* Usually we answer: *I am fine.*
- When we leave, we say: *Good-bye, so long,* or *see you later.*

APPLY

4 Write Cards Encourage students to check their answers with a partner. Distribute Partner Checklist 1 on page T310.

▶ **Language Practice Book** page 40

CLOSE AND ASSESS

Greet a student by name and ask how he or she is. After the student replies, have him or her greet another student and ask how he or she is.

T42 Unit 1 | Glad to Meet You!

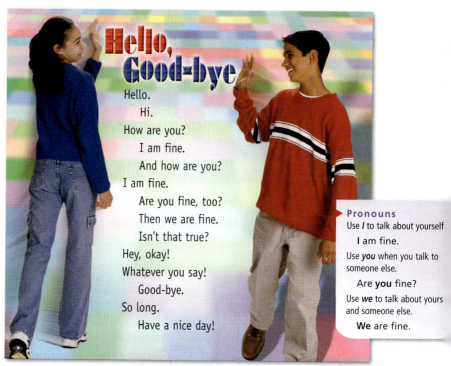

PRONOUNS
Nice to Meet You

Listen and chant.

Pronunciation of Names
Juan — wahn
Nikolai — nē kō li

Hello.
Hi.
How are you?
I am fine.
And how are you?
I am fine.
Are you fine, too?
Then we are fine.
Isn't that true?
Hey, okay!
Whatever you say!
Good-bye.
So long.
Have a nice day!

Pronouns
Use *I* to talk about yourself.
I am fine.
Use *you* when you talk to someone else.
Are **you** fine?
Use *we* to talk about yours and someone else.
We are fine.

EXPRESS YOURSELF ▶ EXCHANGE GREETINGS AND GOOD-BYES

1. Work with a partner. Say the chant and act it out. Add your names to the first 2 lines.

Example: 1. Hello, Juan.
Hi, Nikolai.

WRITE CARDS

2.–4. Work with a partner. Write each sentence below on a card. Mix your cards. Then choose a card. Finish the sentence.

| I am ___ . | You are ___ . | We are ___ . |

Example: 2. I am Nikolai.

Sample Responses
Students may complete sentences using their names or ages. They may tell how they feel (*I am fine.*) or where they are (*We are in English class.*). They might describe a person (*You are a girl.*).

42 Unit 1 | Glad to Meet You!

REACHING ALL STUDENTS

Language Development
PRONOUNS

Have students work in an Inside-Outside Circle (see Cooperative Learning Structures, page T337d) to practice sentences with *I* and *you*. Display these sentence starters:

I am _____ .
You are _____ .

To start, one student says: *I am <student's own name>. You are <partner's name>.* The partner repeats the sentences, substituting the correct names. Then the Inside Circle rotates and new partners repeat the process.

Language Practice Book page 40

PRONOUNS

They Are Friends

Pronunciation of Names
Lupe — lü pe
Imran — im ran

When you talk about other people or things, use the correct **pronoun**.

For a girl or a woman, use *she*. For a boy or man, use *he*.
   Today **she** is 14 years old.
   He is a great friend.
For a thing, use *it*.
   It is a birthday cake.
Use *they* to talk about more than one person or thing.
   They are ready to eat!

BUILD SENTENCES

Say each sentence. Add the correct pronoun.   Example: 1. He is 12 years old.

1.
   <u>He</u> is 12 years old.

2.
   <u>She</u> is from Nicaragua.

3.
   <u>They</u> are friends.

4.
   They eat soup.
   <u>It</u> is hot.

5.
   They share a sandwich.
   <u>It</u> is big.

6.
   Here are 2 bottles of milk.
   <u>They</u> are for the friends.

WRITE SENTENCES

7.–10. Write 4 sentences to tell about this picture.
Use *He is*, *She is*, *It is*, and *They are*.

Example: 7. He is Imran.
Sample Responses:
 7. He is Imran.
 8. She is Lupe.
 9. It is time for lunch.
10. They are in the cafeteria

In the Cafeteria — Lupe, tray, Imran

Language Development 43

UNIT 1 **LESSON 3**

LANGUAGE DEVELOPMENT: PRONOUNS

OBJECTIVES
Function: Give Information
Patterns and Structures: Pronouns
Writing: Sentences

INTRODUCE

1 Learn About Pronouns Read the page title and introduction. Next, direct students' attention to the photo and read the first rule and examples. As you read the sentences again, ask students to point to what the words *he* and *she* refer to in the photo.

Read the next rule and example. Have students point to what *It* refers to in the photo.

Finally, read the last rule and example. Have students point to the people that go with the word *they*. Offer additional examples: *He is tall. She is happy. It is going to taste great! They are friends.*

PRACTICE

2 Build Sentences Explain that Items 1–6 tell about two friends eating lunch. Work through the Example. Then assign the roles to two volunteers. Have them role-play the scene as the group works together to complete and say the sentences.

APPLY

3 Write Sentences In the Example, point out that you use *He* because you are talking about Imran, who is a boy. Have students work independently or with a partner to write their sentences.

▶ **Language Practice Book** page 41

CLOSE AND ASSESS

Have volunteers read aloud a sentence they wrote. Call on students to tell you who the pronoun refers to in the picture.

Language Development **T43**

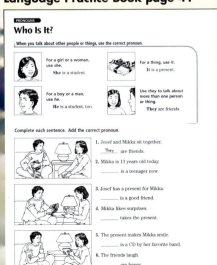
Language Practice Book page 41

Multi-Level Strategies

LANGUAGE DEVELOPMENT

LITERATE IN L1 Students who speak Spanish, Portuguese, or Thai, among other languages, may omit subject pronouns in English. Speakers of Farsi, Chinese, and other languages may make mistakes in gender for third-person pronouns.

To reinforce English pronoun usage, display sentences from page 43 on sentence strips, replacing the pronouns with nouns. Then distribute card sets with the pronouns. Ask students to take turns using their pronoun cards to replace the subjects.

UNIT 1 LESSON 4
LANGUAGE DEVELOPMENT: VERBS—AM AND ARE

OBJECTIVES
Function: Give Information
Patterns and Structures:
- Present Tense Verbs (am, are)

Writing: Sentences

INTRODUCE

1 Learn About Verbs Read the page title and introduction. Use the chart to establish that the verb *am* goes with *I* and that the verb *are* goes with *you* and *we*. Then give several examples. Point to yourself and say *I am a teacher.* Point to a student and say *You are a student.* Make a sweeping motion with your arms and say *We are in class.* Continue with more examples.

Then identify the boy on the left of the photo as Ron and the boy on the right as Juan. Read the examples in the book and have students point to the boy who is talking. Continue by substituting other examples, such as *I am Juan. You are Ron.*

PRACTICE

2 Build Sentences Read the directions and work through the Example. Explain that Items 1–3 show new students meeting. Assign the roles to volunteers and have them role-play the scene. Work together to complete each sentence, and then have the person playing the role repeat it.

APPLY

3 Write Sentences Read the directions and work through the Example. For students who need additional support in writing, guide them in modeling their sentences on the examples in this section or on the sentences with the photos above.

CLOSE AND ASSESS

Have volunteers read their sentences. The class should repeat each sentence, pointing to themselves as they say *I am*, to someone else as they say *you are*, and back and forth as they say *we are*.

T44 Unit 1 | Glad to Meet You!

PRESENT TENSE VERBS: AM AND ARE

We Are Friends

Pronunciation of Names
Juan   wahn

Use the **verbs** *am* and *are* correctly.

Pronoun	Verb	Example
I	am	I **am** Ron.
you	are	You **are** Juan.
we	are	We **are** friends.

BUILD SENTENCES

Look at each picture below. Add the correct verb. Say the new sentence.

Example: 1. You are Anna.

1. You __are__ Anna.
2. I __am__ glad to meet you.
3. We __are__ new to this school.

WRITE SENTENCES

4.–9. Work with a partner. Write 6 sentences. Tell about yourself, your partner, and both of you. Use *I am*, *You are*, and *We are*.

Example: 4. I am 13 years old.

Sample Responses
Students may complete sentences using their names or ages. They may tell how they feel (*I am sick.*) or where they are (*We are in P.E. class.*). They might describe a person (*You are a boy.*).

44 Unit 1 | Glad to Meet You!

REACHING ALL STUDENTS

CULTURAL PERSPECTIVES

U.S. Culture: Football/Soccer Point out that in the photo on page 44, the two boys have a soccer ball. Ask volunteers to describe or demonstrate differences between soccer and American-style football. Explain that soccer is popular in the U.S., too, but not as popular as football! Encourage interested students to gather facts about the two sports and to present the information to the class through art, drama, or another medium.

PRESENT TENSE VERBS: IS AND ARE

They Are Ready for Class

Pronunciation of Names
Lupe   lü pe
Juan   wahn
Huan   hü an

Use the **verbs** *is* and *are* correctly.

Pronoun	Verb	Example
he she it	is	He **is** on the steps. She **is** in front of the door. It **is** closed.
they	are	They **are** ready for class.

BUILD SENTENCES

Look at each sentence below. Add the correct verb. Say the new sentence.

Example: 1. Lupe is in P.E. class.

1. Lupe __is__ in P.E. class.
2. She wears sneakers. They __are__ white.
3. She wears a sweatshirt. It __is__ gray.
4. Now Lupe __is__ in the cafeteria.
5. Juan __is__ at the table.
6. They __are__ ready for lunch.

WRITE SENTENCES

7.–9. Where are your friends now? Write 3 sentences about them. Use *is* and *are*.

Example: 7. Huan is in the gym.
Sample Responses:
7. Huan is in the gym.
8. Marcos is 14 years old.
9. They are great friends.

Language Development **45**

Language Practice Book page 42

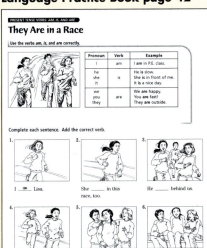

Multi-Level Strategies
LANGUAGE DEVELOPMENT

LITERATE IN L1 Students who speak Russian, Chinese, or Vietnamese, among other languages, may omit *am, is, are*. Hindi speakers may substitute *are* for *is* in some contexts.

For practice using forms of *be,* play an introduction game. Sit in a circle. Say to the person next to you: *I am (your name). You are (student's name). He/She is (next student's name).* The person next to you does the same, and so on around the circle. Add sentences with predicate adjectives: *They are happy.*

UNIT 1 **LESSON 5**

**LANGUAGE DEVELOPMENT:
VERBS—*IS* AND *ARE***

OBJECTIVES
Function: Give Information
Patterns and Structures:
● Present Tense Verbs (*is, are*)
Writing: ● Sentences

INTRODUCE

1 Learn About Verbs Read the page title and introduction, and then the entries across the chart. Direct students' attention to the photo as you say the example sentences again. Have students point to the people and things in the photo that the sentences tell about.

Offer additional examples, pointing to people and things as you describe them: *He is at school. She is at her desk. It is made of wood. They are in class.*

PRACTICE

2 Build Sentences Read the directions and work through the Example. Then discuss the photos before having students suggest a verb to complete each sentence. Decide on the correct verb together, read the completed sentence aloud yourself, and have the class repeat it.

APPLY

3 Write Sentences Read the directions and work through the Example. As students write their sentences, have them focus on choosing the correct verb, but help as necessary in naming and writing the locations they need.

▶ **Language Practice Book** page 42

CLOSE AND ASSESS

Ask volunteers to read aloud one of their sentences. Write the sentence out, and then erase the subject and verb. Call on students to come up and write a new subject and verb for the sentence.

Language Development **T45**

UNIT 1 LESSON 6
LANGUAGE DEVELOPMENT: PERSONAL INFORMATION

OBJECTIVES
Functions: Listen Actively; Give Information
Concepts and Vocabulary:
- Personal Information

Writing: Order Form

INTRODUCE

1 Learn Words for Personal Information Explain that people give personal information when they fill out an order form. Have students study the catalog and order forms to answer questions such as: *What names are on the forms? What is Lupe's address? What does Maylin want to buy?*

2 Make a Personal Information Chart Work with students to list and explain kinds of personal information. (For privacy, allow made-up addresses.)

> **Name:** your first and last name
> **Address:** the number and name of your street; also your apartment number

PRACTICE

3 Conduct "Who's Talking?" Play "Who's Talking?" on the **Language Tape/CD** to model how to give information. Have students listen to a speaker, then pause the tape and replay it, if necessary, before students point to the correct order form.

APPLY

4 Write Personal Information Have students copy and complete an order form, then describe the item to a partner, using information in the catalog (color, size, price).

CLOSE AND ASSESS
Ask questions about the orders, such as: *What did you write on the name line? What item do you want?*

T46 Unit 1 | Glad to Meet You!

VOCABULARY: PERSONAL INFORMATION

Fill In an Order Form

Pronunciation of Names
Maylin Yee — mā lin yē
Lupe Valle — lü pe vah ye

Two people want to buy some things. Read each order form.

WHO'S TALKING? ▶ GIVE INFORMATION

1.–2. Listen.
Point to the correct order form. Tell the name of the person.

Answers:
1. Lupe Valle
2. Maylin Yee

WRITE PERSONAL INFORMATION

3. Choose an item from the catalog. Copy an order form and complete it for yourself. Tell a partner about the item you want.

Sample Response
Students should include their names, an address and telephone number, the name, quantity, color, and price of the item, and size, if appropriate.

46 Unit 1 | Glad to Meet You!

REACHING ALL STUDENTS

Language Development
ABBREVIATIONS

Explain that an *abbreviation* is a shortened form of a word. Present the following abbreviations, along with a listing of the state postal abbreviations (Alaska = AK, etc.):

Street	St.	North	N.
Avenue	Ave.	South	S.
Road	Rd.	East	E.
Apartment	Apt.	West	W.

Write some abbreviated addresses on the board and have volunteers read them aloud. Then have students write their own address using the abbreviations they have just learned.

Vocabulary
PERSONAL INFORMATION

Word Sort Make a chart with these headings: *Name, Address, Item, Size, Color, Price.* Prepare index cards with information for each category. Hand out the cards to partners. One partner should read the card aloud, and the other should put it under the correct heading in the chart.

VOCABULARY: COMMUNICATION

How Can You Communicate?

Pronunciation of Names
Mariana   mar ē **ah** nah
Euching   ü **ching**

- You can send a letter.
- You can make a phone call.
- You can send a fax.
- You can send an e-mail. Good News!!

EXPRESS YOURSELF ▶ USE THE TELEPHONE

You want to order a school T-shirt. How can you do it?
Act out a phone call with a partner.

Example: 1. Euching: Hello, Mariana. This is Euching.
            Mariana: Hello, Euching.
            Euching: How can I get a school T-shirt?
            Mariana: Send a fax to the school.
            Euching: I don't have a fax machine.
            Mariana: Then just call on the phone.
            Euching: How much is a school T-shirt?
            Mariana: It is $15.00.
            Euching: Thanks.
            Mariana: You're welcome. Bye!
            Euching: See you tomorrow.

Language Development 47

UNIT 1 **LESSON 7**

LANGUAGE DEVELOPMENT: COMMUNICATION

OBJECTIVES

Functions: Use the Telephone; Express Social Courtesies

Concepts and Vocabulary:
🅣 Communication

Speaking: Role-Play

INTRODUCE

1. **Learn Words About Communication** Read the title. Point to each form of communication, name it, and read the caption. Check understanding: *If you want to talk to someone, what can you use?*

2. **Discuss Social Courtesies** Start a chart of courtesies people follow in phone communication. Explain different greetings for a friend, an adult you know well, and someone you don't know.

Greetings	Introducing Yourself on the Phone
Hi, what's up?	This is Vicente.
Hello, how are you?	My name is Kim Au.

PRACTICE & APPLY

3. **Conduct "Express Yourself"** Read the Example to model how to use the telephone. Read the part of Euching and have another person read the part of Mariana, if possible. If not, read both parts yourself, and have students follow along to see which character is speaking each line. Then have partners agree on a topic for a phone call and practice what they are going to say.

▶ **Language Practice Book** page 43

CLOSE AND ASSESS

Have partners act out their phone conversations in front of the class.

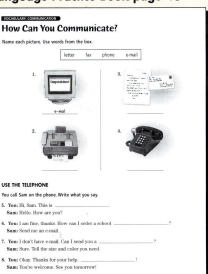

Language Practice Book page 43

Language Development **T47**

UNIT 1 **LESSON 8**

LANGUAGE AND LITERACY: THE BASICS BOOKSHELF

OBJECTIVES
Concepts and Vocabulary:
🅣 Communication Words
Listening: Listen to a Preview
Reading Strategies:
Activate Prior Knowledge; Preview
Learning to Read: Hold a Book and Turn Pages; Use Left-to-Right Directionality

BUILD LANGUAGE AND VOCABULARY

1. **Teach "Words to Know"** Have students look at pages 2–3. Say: *These pages show ways to communicate, or send a message. A message is an idea or information you want to tell someone.*

   Point to each photo, name the communication device, and explain how the message is sent: *This is a greeting card. You can put it in an envelope and send the card by mail.*

2. **Pantomime Communication** Point to the telephone on page 3. Act out dialing a telephone and having a conversation. Have partners pantomime sending and receiving messages using communication devices on these pages.

PREPARE TO READ

3. **Think About What You Know** Give an example of some good news you received and how you received it: *My cousin had a baby. She told me in an e-mail.* Ask students to describe some good news they have received and tell how it came. Have them identify the communication devices on pages 2 and 3 that they have used.

4. **Preview** Play the Audio Walk-Through for *Good News* on the **Selection Tape/CD** to give students the overall idea of the story.

   [Tape 1A / CD 1 Track 1]

CLOSE AND ASSESS

Have students draw a picture to show what the story will be about.

T48a Unit 1 | Glad to Meet You!

Good News
by Suzy Blackaby

Summary This realistic fiction shows how members of the Makki family share information. By letter, telephone, fax, and e-mail, they spread the good news: a cousin and aunt are moving to the United States. Simple text and photographs reinforce words about communication.

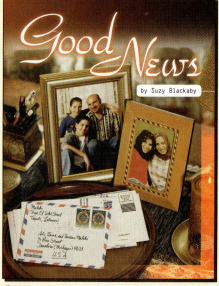

Cover

Pages 2–3

Multi-Level Strategies
LITERACY SUPPORT

PRELITERATE **Hold a Book and Turn Pages** Model holding the book correctly. Turn to pages 2–3. Point to the page numbers as you say: *This is page 2. This is page 3*. Repeat for pages 4–7. Then ask volunteers to turn to the remaining pages and identify the page numbers. Have partners practice holding the book correctly and turning the pages. Call out instructions for students to follow: *Turn to page 12.* Pause for students to find the corresponding page and hold up their books. Ask volunteers to take turns calling out page numbers for their classmates to find.

NON-ROMAN ALPHABET **Left-to-Right Directionality** Some languages, such as Farsi and Chinese, do not record text horizontally from left to right. To reinforce this English print convention, display pages 4–5 and model reading the text in left-to-right order. As you read, track the print with a finger and follow text from the left page to the right. Have students run a finger under the text in their copies as you read it.

Good News

Pronunciation of Names in *Good News*
Ali Makki	ah lē **mah** kē
Zeina Makki	zē nah **mah** kē
Hassan Makki	hah **sahn mah** kē
Layla	**lā** lah
Nour Gandour	nor gahn **dor**

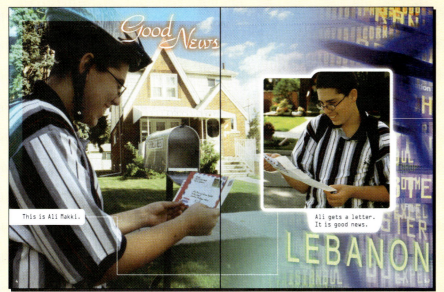

Pages 4–5

Pages 6–7

Strategies for Comprehensible Input

Page	Story Language	Strategy Options
4–5	This is Ali Makki.	**Point to the picture and explain:** The boy's name is Ali.
	letter	**Point to the picture.**
	good news	**Restate:** something that makes him happy
6–7	calls	**Demonstrate:** Pantomime making a phone call.
	phone	**Point to the picture.**
	This is Zeina Makki.	**Point to the picture and explain:** Zeina is Ali's mother.

Language and Literacy **T48b**

UNIT 1 **LESSON 8,** CONTINUED

LANGUAGE AND LITERACY: THE BASICS BOOKSHELF

OBJECTIVES

Function: Listen to a Book

Critical Thinking and Comprehension:
① Identify Sequence

Learning to Read:
Track Print; Identify Words

READ AND THINK TOGETHER

1 Read Aloud On your first reading of the book, use the "Strategies for Comprehensible Input" that appear at the bottom of pages T48b and T48d.

2 Read and Map: Identify Sequence Draw a sequence chain like the one below, but with empty boxes. Say: *A sequence chain shows the order, or sequence, in which things happen in a story.*

Read pages 4–5 aloud. Then think aloud as you model filling in the first box: *I will write* Ali *in box 1 because he gets the good news first. How did Ali get the message? He got a letter. I will write the word* letter *by Ali's name.*

Pause after reading each set of pages shown below and model completing the chain for the rest of the text.

3 Conduct Interactive Readings Choose from these options:

- **Read along and track print** Model pointing to each word with a finger as you read aloud. Then have students track the print as they read along with the recording of *Good News* on the **Selection Tape/CD**. *Tape 1A / CD 1 Track 2*

- **Read along and identify words** As you read, frame individual words and phrases such as *This is*. Ask students to identify these words. Continue reading as students track the print and identify other words they know.

CLOSE AND ASSESS

Have students tell their partners three sequential events from the story.

Pages 8–9

Pages 10–11

Sequence Chain for *Good News*

pages 4–5 → Ali – letter

pages 6–9 → Zeina – phone

pages 10–12 → Hassan – FAX

pages 13–15 → Makki family – e-mail

 Technology Support
See **Inspiration** Visual Learning software for support in creating the sequence chain.

T48c Unit 1 | Glad to Meet You!

Good News, CONTINUED

Pages 12–13

Pages 14–15

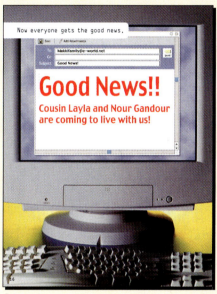

Page 16

Strategies for Comprehensible Input

Page	Story Language	Strategy Options
8–9	gets	**Explain:** Ali tells Zeina. She hears the good news.
	sends a fax	**Demonstrate:** Write a message on paper. Pantomime putting it in a machine and dailing a telephone number.
10–11	This is Hassan Makki	**Point to the picture and explain:** Hassan is Ali's father.
12–13	sends an e-mail	**Point to the picture and explain:** When you send an e-mail, you use the computer to send a message.
14–15	This is the Makki family.	**Point to the picture and explain:** These people are Ali's relatives. This is his grandmother and grandfather, his aunt, his uncle, and his cousin.
16	everyone gets	**Restate:** All the people in the family read the e-mail on their computers. They read about the good news.
	are coming to live with	**Summarize:** Point to the two women on the front cover. Then point to the photograph on the back cover and say: *Cousin Layla and Nour Gandour are moving to the United States. They will stay with Ali and his family.*

Language and Literacy **T48d**

UNIT 1 LESSON 9

LANGUAGE AND LITERACY: THE BASICS BOOKSHELF

OBJECTIVES

Function: Retell a Story
Learning Strategy: Use Graphic Organizers (sequence chain)
Critical Thinking and Comprehension: Identify Sequence

CHECK COMPREHENSION

1. **Make a Sequence Chain** Have students review *Good News* to identify important events for a sequence chain. Remind them that a sequence chain shows the order, or sequence, in which things happen.

   As you read aloud the directions for each step, pause for students to add information to the sections of their chains. Encourage students to review the story to clarify the order of events.

2. **Retell the Story** Have partners take turns using their sequence chains to tell the story in their own words. Then have partners compare their sequence chains to add and correct information.

CLOSE AND ASSESS

Ask students to complete this sentence:
A sequence chain shows _____.

COMPREHENSION: IDENTIFY SEQUENCE

Read and Think Together

Make a sequence chain for *Good News*.
Follow these steps.

1. Think about the story. Who got the good news first? Draw a box and write the name.

   [Ali]

2. How did he get the news? Write your answer in the box.

   [Ali – letter]

3. Draw boxes to show who got the news next. Tell how the news came: by e-mail, fax, or phone.

   [Ali – letter]
   ↓
   [Zeina — phone]
   ↓
   [Hassan — fax]
   ↓
   [The Makki family — e-mail]

4. Use your sequence chain to tell the story to a friend.

from *The Basics Bookshelf*

THEME BOOK

Learn how a family uses different forms of communication to share good news with each other.

48 Unit 1 | Glad to Meet You!

REACHING ALL STUDENTS

Language Development
USE THE TELEPHONE

Role-Play Turn to page 6 in *Good News*. Ask students what they think Ali said when he called his mother at work. Then look at page 8. Ask: *What do you think Zeina may have said when she heard the good news?* Invite partners to take the roles of Ali and Zeina. The partners will role-play the telephone conversation about the good news and share it with the class.

HIGH FREQUENCY WORDS
Words to Know

REVIEW WORDS YOU KNOW

Read the words aloud. Which word goes in the sentence?

soon	school	1. The girls are at _school_.
The	They	2. _They_ eat lunch.
has	help	3. She _has_ a lot of food.

LEARN TO READ

Learn new words.

from	I am **from** Russia.
home	My **home** is now in Detroit.
new	I have a **new** school, too.
go	I will **go** to school with my friend Rob.
there	My school schedule is **there** on the table.
many	I have **many** different classes!
first	**First** I have English class.
next	**Next** I have science class.
then	**Then** I have lunch.
one	I have only **one** class with Rob—math.

How to Learn a New Word
- Look at the word.
- Listen to the word.
- Listen to the word in a sentence. What does it mean?
- Say the word.
- Spell the word.
- Say the word again.

WORD WORK

Where does each new word fit in the chart? Say the word and spell it.

Example: 4. next / n-e-x-t

What to Look For	Word
4. starts with n	n e x t
5. ends with y	m a n y
6. starts with th	t h e r e
7. ends with n	t h e n
8. rhymes with no	g o

What to Look For	Word
9. starts with fr	f r o m
10. means "1"	o n e
11. is the opposite of old	n e w
12. is the opposite of last	f i r s t
13. means "where you live"	h o m e

Language and Literacy 49

Reading Practice Book page 38

HIGH FREQUENCY WORDS
Words to Know

READ AND WRITE

Read each word. Then write it.

1. new _____ 2. many _____ 3. one _____
4. from _____ 5. first _____ 6. then _____
7. go _____ 8. next _____ 9. there _____
10. home _____

WORD WORK

Read each sentence. Find the new words in the box.
Write the words on the lines.

11. These 2 words have 3 letters. ___new___ ___one___
12. These 2 words begin with **th**. _____
13. These 3 words have an **m**. _____
14. This word rhymes with **where**. _____
15. This word is the opposite of **stop**. _____
16. These 4 words have an **o**. _____
17. These 3 words tell "when." _____
18. These 5 words have 4 letters each. _____

Reading Fluency
RECOGNIZE HIGH FREQUENCY WORDS

To build automaticity with the new high frequency words:

- Have students make word cards to display on a classroom chart. Partners or groups can go to the chart to practice reading the words together or to test one another.

- Refer students to the list of new words on page 49. Give clues and have students point to and read each word. For example: *This word starts with* h. *It means "the place you live."*

UNIT 1 **LESSON 10**

LANGUAGE AND LITERACY: HIGH FREQUENCY WORDS

OBJECTIVES

Learning to Read:
- Recognize High Frequency Words

REVIEW WORDS

1 Review Known High Frequency Words Have the group read aloud the words in the green box. Listen for words students cannot read automatically and use the steps in the yellow box to reteach those words. Then have students look at the photo. Read each cloze sentence. Reread each sentence and pause for students to silently read the two words to the left of the sentence. Tell students to choose the word that goes in the sentence and tells about the picture.

INTRODUCE NEW WORDS

2 Learn High Frequency Words Use the High Frequency Word Script on page T312 to lead students through the steps in the yellow box.

PRACTICE

3 Conduct "Word Work" Use the Example to model how to use the clue to find the possible words in the list and then to use the number of letter blanks to choose the correct word or confirm it.

Have groups complete Items 5–13. Then discuss how the correct word matches the clue and number of blanks.

APPLY

4 Read Words in Context Students will apply the skill when they read high frequency words in context in the sentences on page 51 and the passage on page 52.

▶ **Reading Practice Book** page 38

CLOSE AND ASSESS

Call out the high frequency words one at a time. Have students point to them and spell the words as a group.

Language and Literacy **T49**

UNIT 1 **LESSON 11**

LANGUAGE AND LITERACY: PHONICS

OBJECTIVES

Learning to Read: Build Oral Vocabulary; Develop Phonemic Awareness; 🅣 Associate Sounds and Symbols: /a/ a; Blend Sounds to Decode Words

TEACH SHORT VOWELS: /a/ a

1 Build Oral Vocabulary Display Transparency 11. Talk through each picture to develop meaning for the words in the yellow boxes. For example, for Item 1, say:

• *Here is a* **man** (point). *He is wearing a* **hat** (point). *There are many kinds of* **hats** *to put on your head* (pantomime). *This* **hat** *protects him at work. It is yellow and hard.*

2 Develop Phonemic Awareness Remove the transparency and conduct the oral activities in Step 1 of the Script for Transparency 11.

3 Read Short *a* Words Display Transparency 11 again. Work through Steps 2 and 3 of the script.

CLOSE AND ASSESS

Display the words *hat, gas, mad,* and *lab.* Call on students to blend a word and identify the sound in the middle.

Transparency 11: ▶ Short *a*

▼ Script for Transparency 11

Words with Short *a*

1. Develop Phonemic Awareness
Isolate the Short *a* Sound Say: *Listen to the first sound in these words:* at, ax, an. *What is the sound?* (/a/) *Now listen for the sound /a/ in the middle of these words:* hat, sad, map. *Say the words with me. Now raise your hand each time you hear the sound /a/.* Say these words: fat, mad, made, cake, cat, hat, hate, rain, ran, past.

2. Associate Sounds and Symbols
Point to the map on **Transparency 11.** Say: *This is a map. It shows where places are. Say the word* map *with me.* Then point to the *a* in *map* and say: *The letter* a *makes the sound you hear in the middle of* map. *The sound in the middle is* /a/. *Say* /a/ *with me:* /aaa/. Point to the *a* and ask: *What's the letter? What's the sound?*

3. Blend Sounds to Read Words
Model/Teach Point to the letter *m* in *map* and say: *The sound for* m *is* /mmm/. *Repeat for* a: /aaa/. *As you slide your finger slowly from left to right below the letters* ma, *say: I can blend the two sounds:* /mmmaaa/. *Then point to the* p *and say: The sound for* p *is* /p/. *I can blend the three sounds together:* /mmmaaap/. *Now, I'm going to say the whole word:* map. Repeat the process, asking students to blend the sounds with you and then say the word.

Practice For Item 1, say: *Let's try that again. This picture shows a man with a hat, doesn't it? Read the words with me. Follow my finger as we blend the sounds* /haaat/, *and say the word:* hat. Repeat the process for the other words, calling special attention to the following:

• In Item 3, blend *last* with students and say: *When we read* last, *we blended the consonants* s *and* t *at the end.* Repeat for *fast* in Item 5.

• Read aloud the sentence in Item 6, pausing for students to decode *class* and *lab.* After you blend *class,* ask: *How many sounds do you hear?* (4) Then demonstrate again, blending the two consonants together at the beginning and saying only one sound for the two consonants at the end.

T50a Unit 1 | Glad to Meet You!

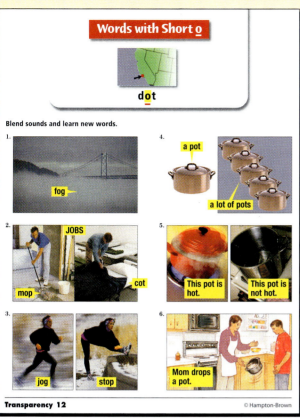

◀ **Transparency 12: Short o**

▼ **Script for Transparency 12**

Words with Short o

1. **Develop Phonemic Awareness**
   Isolate the Short o Sound Say: *Listen to the first sound in these words:* ox, on, octopus. *What is the sound?* (/o/) *Now listen for the sound /o/ in the middle of these words:* dot, box, job. *Say the words with me. Now signal "thumbs up" each time you hear the sound /o/. Say these words:* ox, jog, pat, note, on, up, rope.

2. **Associate Sounds and Symbols**
   Point to the dot on **Transparency 12**. Say: *This is a dot. It is shaped like a circle, and filled in. Say the word* dot *with me.* Then point to the *o* in *dot* and say: *The letter* o *makes the /o/ sound you hear in the middle of* dot. *Say /o/ with me: /ooo/.* Point to the *o* and ask: *What's the letter? What's the sound?*

3. **Blend Sounds to Read Words**
   Model/Teach Point to the letter *d* in *dot* and say: *The sound for* d *is: /d/.* Repeat for *o*: /ooo/. *As you slide your finger slowly from left to right below the letters* do, *say: I can blend the two sounds: /dooo/.* Then point to the *t* and say: *The sound for* t *is:* /t/. *I can blend the three sounds together as I move my finger below the word: /dooot/. Now, I'm going to say the whole word:* dot. Lead students in blending the sounds and then saying the word.

   Practice For Item 1, say: *Let's try that again. This picture shows a bridge in the fog. Read the word with me. Follow my finger as we blend the sounds /fffooog/, and say the word:* fog. Repeat the process for the other words, calling special attention to the following:

   • In Item 2, blend *jobs* with students and say: *When we read* jobs, *we blended the sounds* /b/ *and* /z/ *together at the end.* Repeat for *pots* in Item 4, with /t/ and /s/ at the end. Say: *Look at the picture. Does the word* pots *make sense?*

   • In Item 3, say *stop* with students and ask: *How many sounds do you hear?* (4) Then demonstrate blending the two consonants together at the beginning /stooop/, and then saying the word: *stop*.

OBJECTIVES

Learning to Read: Build Oral Vocabulary; Develop Phonemic Awareness; ⓣ Associate Sounds and Symbols: /o/ *o*; Blend Sounds to Decode Words

TEACH SHORT VOWELS: /o/ *o*

1. **Build Oral Vocabulary** Display Transparency 12. Play a game of "I Spy," giving a series of clues until students find the picture you're describing. For example, for Item 5, say:

   • *I spy a pot. You can cook soup in a pot. This pot is full. It's getting too hot!*

   When students find the boiling pot, say: *Yes,* **this pot is hot** (pantomime touching it and pulling back). Repeat the game to build context for the other words.

2. **Develop Phonemic Awareness** Remove the transparency and conduct the oral activities in Step 1 of the Script for Transparency 12.

3. **Read Short *o* Words** Display Transparency 12 again. Work through Steps 2 and 3 of the script.

CLOSE AND ASSESS

Display the words *mop, hot, fog,* and *pot*. Call on students to blend a word and identify the sound in the middle.

▶ **Reading Practice Book** page 39 (short *a* and short *o*)

Reading Practice Book page 39

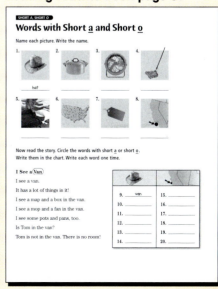

Language and Literacy **T50b**

UNIT 1 **LESSON 11,** CONTINUED

LANGUAGE AND LITERACY: PHONICS

OBJECTIVES
Learning to Read: Build Oral Vocabulary; Develop Phonemic Awareness; 🅣 Associate Sounds and Symbols: phonograms *-an, -ag, -at, -ad, -ap*; Blend Sounds to Decode Words

RECOGNIZE WORD FAMILIES

1. **Build Oral Vocabulary** Display Transparency 13. Use the pictures to develop the meaning of each word and use it in a sentence. For example, for Item 1, say:
   - *This is a **can**. Corn comes in a **can**. Just open the **can** and serve it.*

2. **Develop Phonemic Awareness** Remove the transparency and conduct the oral activities in Step 1 of the Script for Transparency 13.

3. **Read Words with Short *a* Phonograms** Display Transparency 13 again. Use the activity in Step 2 of the script to teach the word families.

4. **Build Words** Use Step 3 of the script to build words in the boxes on Transparency 13.

CLOSE AND ASSESS
Have one student build a word with letter tiles and read it. Ask other students to change the first letter to make a rhyming word and read it.

Transparency 13: Short *a* Phonograms

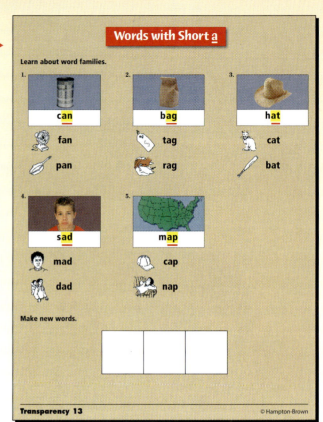

Materials
Letter tiles for:

a	b	c
d	f	g
l	m	n
r	s	t

▼ **Script for Transparency 13**

Words with Short *a* Phonograms

1. **Develop Phonemic Awareness**
   Listen for Rhyming Words/Blend Onset and Rime Say: *Listen to these two words:* man, van. *Say the words with me:* man, van. *These words rhyme—they end with the same sounds:* /an/. *Here are two more words; tell me if they rhyme:* pan, map. (no) *Continue with word pairs* map, cap; fan, bad; hat, pat; map, can; dad, bag. *Then give the onset and rime for several words in the list, for example:* /mmm/ - /ap/. *Have students blend them* /mmmap/ *and say the word:* map.

2. **Read Words with Short *a* Phonograms**
   Point to the first item on **Transparency 13.** Say: *Let's read the word that names this picture.* Slide a finger slowly under the letters to lead students in sounding out the word: /kaaannn/, can. Cover the letter *c* and explain: *The two letters* an *at the end stand for the last two sounds you hear in* can: /an/. *There are many words that end in* /an/ *and rhyme with* can, *like these two words below it.* (Point to *fan* and *pan*.) *Let's read these words, using what we know about their end sounds.* Have students sound out and blend the initial consonant with the phonogram *-an* to read the words. Repeat for the other phonograms.

3. **Build Words with Short *a* Phonograms**
   Teach Place letter tiles *c-a-n* in the boxes, read the word, and say: *The letters* an *spell the sounds* /an/ *at the end of* can. *Another word that rhymes with* can *is* man. *So I know the word* man *also ends with the letters* an. *To spell* man, *I have to change just the first letter. What sound do you hear at the beginning of* man? *Yes,* /m/, *and the letter* m *spells that sound.* Substitute letter tile *m* for *c* and confirm the word by blending the sounds to read *man*.

   Practice Have students build the other *-an* words on the transparency. Then repeat the process for the other phonograms. Add the following words to the word building activity after making sure students understand the meanings:

   -an: ran, tan   **-ag:** sag, wag   **-at:** mat, sat   **-ad:** pad, bad   **-ap:** lap, tap

T50c Unit 1 | Glad to Meet You!

◀ **Transparency 14: Short *o* Phonograms**

Materials
Letter tiles for:
a, c, d, f, g, h, j, l, m, n, o, p, p, t

▼ **Script for Transparency 14**

Words with Short *o* Phonograms

1. **Develop Phonemic Awareness**
   Listen for Rhyming Words/Blend Onset and Rime Say: *Listen to these two words:* dot, hot. *Say the words with me:* dot, hot. *These words rhyme—they end with the same sounds:* /ot/. *Here are two more words; tell me if they rhyme:* pot, fog. (no) *Continue with word pairs* fog, jog; cot, hop; dot, cot; mop, drop; top, jog. *Then give the onset and rime for several words in the list, for example:* /fff/-/og/. *Have students blend them* /fffog/ *and tell you the word:* fog.

2. **Read Words with Short *o* Phonograms**
   Point to the first item on **Transparency 14**. Say: *Let's read the word that names this picture.* Slide a finger slowly under the letters to lead students in sounding out the word: /dooot/, dot. Cover the letter *d* and explain: *The two letters* ot *at the end stand for the last two sounds you hear in* dot: /ot/. *There are many words that end in* /ot/ *and rhyme with* dot, *like these two words below it.* (Point to *cot* and *pot*.) *Let's read these words, using what we know about their end sounds.* Have students sound out and blend the initial consonant with the phonogram *-ot* to read the words. Repeat for the other phonograms.

3. **Build Words with Short *o* Phonograms**
   Teach Place letter tiles *d-o-t* in the boxes, read the word, and say: *The letters* ot *spell the sounds* /ot/ *at the end of* dot. *Another word that rhymes with* dot *is* hot. *So I know the word* hot *also ends with the letters* ot. *To spell* hot, *change just the first letter. What sound do you hear at the beginning of* hot? *Yes,* /h/, *and the letter* h *spells that sound.* Substitute letter tile *h* for *d* and confirm the word by blending the sounds to read *hot*.

   Practice Have students build the other *-ot* words on the transparency. Repeat for the other phonograms. Add these words, making sure students understand their meanings: **-ot:** got, not; **-op:** pop, lop; **-og:** hog, log.

   Then build words to contrast phonograms, such as *hot/hat* or *mop/map*.

OBJECTIVES

Learning to Read: Build Oral Vocabulary; Develop Phonemic Awareness; 🅣 Associate Sounds and Symbols: phonograms *-ot, -op, -og*; Blend Sounds to Decode Words

RECOGNIZE WORD FAMILIES

1 **Build Oral Vocabulary** Display Transparency 14. Use the pictures to develop meaning for each word. Use it in a sentence. For example, for Item 1, say:

• Look at this **dot**. The **dot** is on a map. What spot does the **dot** mark?

2 **Develop Phonemic Awareness** Remove the transparency and conduct the oral activities in Step 1 of the Script for Transparency 14.

3 **Read Words with Short *o* Phonograms** Display Transparency 14 again. Use the activity in Step 2 of the script to teach the word families.

4 **Build Words with Short *o* Phonograms** Use Step 3 of the script to build words in the boxes on Transparency 14.

CLOSE AND ASSESS

Have one student build a word with letter tiles and read it. Ask other students to change the first letter to make a rhyming word and read it.

▶ **Reading Practice Book** page 40 (short *a* and short *o* phonograms)

Reading Practice Book page 40

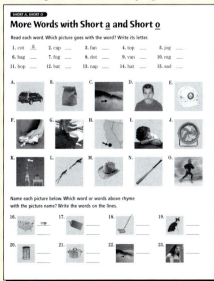

Language and Literacy **T50d**

UNIT 1 LESSON 12

LANGUAGE AND LITERACY: READING AND SPELLING

OBJECTIVES

Functions: Listen Actively; Repeat Spoken Language; Recite

Learning to Read: Develop Phonemic Awareness; ❶ Associate Sounds and Symbols: /a/ *a*, /o/ *o*; Blend Sounds to Decode Words

Spelling: ❶ Words with Short *a* and *o*

LISTEN AND LEARN

Tape 1A / CD 1 Track 3

1. **Sing a Song** Display Transparency 15 and play "On the Map" on the **Language Tape/CD**. After students have listened and learned the song, they can sing it, snapping their fingers each time they hear the word *snap*.

DEVELOP PHONEMIC AWARENESS

2. **Blend Onset and Rime/Segment Words into Sounds** Give the onset and rime for each word below, for example: /nnn/-/ap/. Have students blend the sounds and tell you the word: /nnnap/, *nap*.

nap	hat	pot	pop
cat	pan	jog	job
dad	rag	hop	log

Then lead students in segmenting several words in the lists into sounds: *Listen to this word and then say it with me: jog. Now let's say the sounds separately and count them:* /j/, /o/, /g/—three sounds.

CONNECT SOUNDS AND LETTERS

3. **Associate /a/ *a* and /o/ *o*** Identify the first picture and sound out its name: *This is a map, and here's the word. Let's point to each letter. Say the sound for each letter with me:* /mmm/, /aaa/, /p/. Repeat for the other pictures. Then read the question aloud: *What sound does each letter make?* Have a student call out the letters in a word while the group gives each letter's sound.

Afterwards, play the song again. Have students identify words with short *a* and *o*.

T50 Unit 1 | Glad to Meet You!

SHORT *A*, SHORT *O*

Reading and Spelling

LISTEN AND LEARN

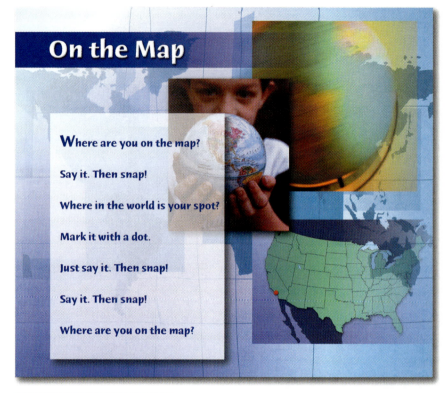

CONNECT SOUNDS AND LETTERS

What sound does each letter make?

m<u>a</u>p   b<u>a</u>g   j<u>o</u>g   d<u>o</u>t

50 Unit 1 | Glad to Meet You! ▶ Transparencies 11–1...

REACHING ALL STUDENTS

Multi-Level Strategies

LITERACY SUPPORT

INTERRUPTED SCHOOLING To anchor understanding of how to sound out words, set up letter tiles on an overhead projector. First blend words with two sounds, sliding the first tile over as you elongate the sound: /aaa/. Then add /t/ : /aaat/. Run your fingers slowly under the word and say: /aaat/, *at*. Then repeat with words having three sounds: /h/ - /aaat/, /haaat/, *hat*:

Good words for this activity are: *am, ham; at, sat; an, fan*.

PRELITERATE Copy the sentences in Items 7–12 of Reading and Spelling Practice onto sentence strips. Distribute the sentence strips and have students cut them apart into separate words. Have volunteers lead the group in reassembling each sentence by matching word order of the items on the page.

READING STRATEGY

Follow these steps to read a word.

1 Point to the first letter. Say the sound.

2 Point to the second letter. Say the sound.

3 Point to the last letter. Say the sound.

4 Now blend all the sounds together to say the word. Say the word again. What is it?

s + a + d = sad

I blend 3 sounds to say sad.

READING AND SPELLING PRACTICE

Blend the sounds to read these words.

1. job   2. at   3. gas   4. mom   5. mad   6. pot

Use what you learned to read the sentences.

7. What a bad day!
8. First I drop a new pot.
9. Then my mom is mad at me.
10. Next the van has no gas.
11. I go to my job.
12. At last, I go home!

13.–16. Now write the sentences that your teacher reads. *For dictation sentences, see Step 6 at right.*

WORD WORK

Look at the first picture. Then read the word. Use letter cards to make a new word for the next picture. Change just 1 letter each time.

Example:

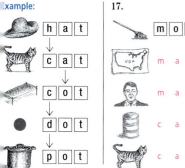

17.

m	o	p
m	a	p
m	a	n
c	a	n
c	a	t

18.

c	o	t
c	a	t
c	a	p
m	a	p
m	o	p

19.

f	a	n
c	a	n
c	a	b
c	a	t
c	o	t

Language and Literacy 51

Decodable Book

PRACTICE WITH SHORT *A* AND SHORT *O*

Decodable Book 1: *Not a Good Day!*

Assign **Decodable Book 1** for independent reading. The **Decodable Book** can be used in a variety of ways to help students become more fluent, automatic readers:

Discussion Circles Have students work in small groups to read aloud and discuss the book using the questions on the back cover. Encourage students to read aloud the text that supports their answers. Groups can also work together to complete the Word Work Activity.

Readers Theater Students can read aloud the stories in a class performance. Help them prepare by rereading the stories in daily rehearsals. Work with students to add narration or dialog. Encourage them to use natural phrasing and expression.

Rereading at Home Have students work with family members to reread the book at home. They can take turns reading aloud alternate pages, then rereading the book switching the pages each person reads.

LEARN A READING STRATEGY

4 Sound Out Words Write *sad* and model the blending strategy. Show how to hold the sounds as you point to the letters in sequence: /sssaaad/. Then say the whole word quickly: *sad*. Slide your finger under each letter again and ask students to say the sound with you, holding it until you point to the next letter. Then ask students to say the word.

Read steps 1–3 aloud to summarize the blending process you have demonstrated. For step 4, have students try out the strategy on their own. As they slide a finger under the letters, they should hold each sound without pausing. After blending the sounds in a stretched out manner, they should say the whole word quickly.

PRACTICE

5 Read Words and Sentences Sound out the words in Items 1–6 as a choral reading. Then distribute the Partner Prompts from page T311 to guide peers in reading the sentences in Items 7–12. Remind them to use the sound-out strategy to read words.

6 Write Sentences Dictate the following sentences for students to write. Read each sentence at normal speed once so students can listen, and then repeat it slowly word by word as they write:

13. I am at the lab.

14. The man can jog.

15. My cap is in the van.

16. The pot is not hot.

7 Conduct "Word Work" Read the directions and work through the Example. Then have partners complete Items 17–19. Check answers by working through the items as a group.

▶ **Reading Practice Book** pages 111–114 (Decodable Book 1)

CLOSE AND ASSESS

Across the board, write the first word from the sets in Word Work. Work through each set, saying each word. Students should come up to erase the letter that changes and write the new letter and read the word.

Language and Literacy **T51**

UNIT 1 LESSON 13

LANGUAGE AND LITERACY: INDEPENDENT READING

OBJECTIVES

Function: Read a Selection
Learning to Read:
- Recognize High Frequency Words;
- Decode Words (short *a* and short *o*)

Reading Strategies:
Predict; Set a Purpose for Reading; Retell
Critical Thinking and Comprehension:
- Identify Sequence

READ ON YOUR OWN

1. **Introduce Vocabulary** In "New at School" students apply phonics skills and read the high frequency words taught in Lessons 10–12. Introduce the following story words. Write each word, pronounce it, and spell it. Then give a definition and context sentence:

   - **Lupe, friends:** Lupe is a girl's name. Friends are people you know and like. *Lupe goes to the movies with her friends.*

   - **Lakeside:** the name of a school. *I go to Lakeside School.*

   - **science:** a subject at school. *We study science in the lab.*

2. **Make Predictions/Set Purposes** Point out the girl on the right in the photo, and say: *This is Lupe. She is a new student at school. Who do you think the other people are?* (students; new friends) *Read to find out what Lupe and her new friends do together at school.*

3. **Read and Think: Identify Sequence** Students should read the passage on their own, individually. After they read, have them use the sequence chain to retell the story to a partner.

4. **Build Reading Fluency** Use the **Language Tape/CD** with Reading Practice Book page 41 for fluency practice.

   ▶ **Reading Practice Book** page 41

CLOSE AND ASSESS

Have one student start and another continue until all the story events are retold.

T52 Unit 1 | Glad to Meet You!

COMPREHENSION: IDENTIFY SEQUENCE

Read on Your Own

New at School

Lupe is new at Lakeside School.
First she has science lab with Pat and Ron.
Pat helps Lupe.
Next they have P.E. class.
Pat and Lupe go fast. Ron does not go fast.
He has a cold and has to stop!
Then Pat, Lupe, and Ron go to lunch.
They have a lot of hot soup.
At last it is time to go home.
Lupe is glad to have 2 new friends!

CHECK YOUR UNDERSTANDING

Tell the story to your partner. Use the words and pictures.

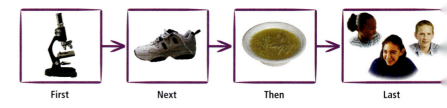

First   Next   Then   Last

Sample Response
Students retellings should include time-order words to make the sequence of events clear.

✓ **DECODING CHECK**
Give the Decoding Progress Check on page 1a of the Assessment Handbook.

52 Unit 1 | Glad to Meet You!

REACHING ALL STUDENTS

Reading Fluency
INTONATION PATTERNS/EXPRESSION

Read the title and introduction on **Reading Practice Book** page 41. Then read the explanations and go over the examples. Ask students to point to the period in one example and the exclamation mark in the other. Lead the group in a choral recitation of each sentence with expression.

Next, play "New at School" on the **Language Tape/CD**. Point out that the punctuation marks tell the reader how to say each sentence. Read the Practice and circulate among partners to check and support reading fluency.

Reading Practice Book page 41

STATEMENTS AND EXCLAMATIONS

She Likes School a Lot!

Some sentences tell something. Other sentences show a strong feeling.

This sentence tells something. It ends with a **period**.
> Pizza is a new food for Lupe**.**

This sentence shows a strong feeling. It ends with an **exclamation mark**.
> She likes it a lot**!**

All sentences start with a **capital letter**.
> **S**he wants to eat pizza every day.

STUDY SENTENCES

Look at the story on page 52. Answer these questions.

Example: 1. The first sentence ends with a period.

1. What does the first sentence end with? period
2. What does the last sentence end with? exclamation mark
3. How many words are in the fifth sentence? five
4. How many words are in the sixth sentence? five
5. Does each sentence start with a capital letter? yes

WRITE SENTENCES

Listen to the tape. Write these sentences correctly.

Example: 6. Lupe likes science lab.

6. Lupe likes science lab
7. she likes to study
8. the class has a test tomorrow
9. Lupe will do well
10. she also likes P.E. class
11. her teacher is Ms. Sampson
12. they run a lot
13. Lupe is fast
14. she likes soccer and football
15. Lupe likes school a lot

Answers:
6. Lupe likes science lab.
7. She likes to study.
8. The class has a test tomorrow.
9. Lupe will do well!
10. She also likes P.E. class.
11. Her teacher is Ms. Sampson.
12. They run a lot.
13. Lupe is fast!
14. She likes soccer and football.
15. Lupe likes school a lot!

Language and Literacy 53

Language Practice Book page 44

Multimodal Practice
WRITING SENTENCES

Visual Have students copy corrected Items 6–15 onto sentence strips and cut them apart to create word cards and end marks.

Kinesthetic This group can take the word cards made above and use the cards to rebuild the corrected sentences.

Auditory Students can replay the tape, pause after each sentence to repeat it, and practice correct intonation.

UNIT 1 **LESSON 14**

LANGUAGE AND LITERACY: STATEMENTS AND EXCLAMATIONS

OBJECTIVES

Function: Write
Patterns and Structures: Statements and Exclamations
Writing: Sentences with Correct Capitalization and End Marks

INTRODUCE

1 Learn About Statements and Exclamations Read the page title, and then the introduction, rules, and examples. Use exaggerated expression in reading the exclamation to help students distinguish it from a statement.

Point out the punctuation and initial capital letter in each example. Then call on volunteers to point out the exclamation mark, an initial capital letter, and a period.

PRACTICE

2 Study Sentences Read the directions aloud. Model reading Item 1 and looking at the first sentence in "New at School" to find the answer. Have partners do Items 2–5.

APPLY

3 Write Sentences Play the **Language Tape/CD**.
After each sentence, pause for students to write, using correct capitalization and punctuation.

For additional guided practice, read each sentence below with expression and guide the group in deciding if it is a statement or an exclamation:

- Rigo likes to write.
- He likes school a lot!
- Maya likes to run.
- She can run fast!

▶ **Language Practice Book** page 44

CLOSE AND ASSESS

Have volunteers write each corrected sentence on the board. Ask another student to point out the changes.

Language and Literacy **T53**

UNIT 1 **LESSON 15**

LANGUAGE ACROSS THE CURRICULUM: MATHEMATICS

OBJECTIVES
Function: Give Information
Concepts and Vocabulary: Numbers and Basic Operations
Critical Thinking: Solve Problems

LEARN ABOUT MATH PROBLEMS

1. **Study Basic Operations** Ask a volunteer to point out a math problem in the chart. Then, for each problem, identify the operation and read the labels. Model how to read the problem aloud. After modeling all four operations, call on volunteers to identify an operation, name its parts, and read it aloud.

SOLVE PROBLEMS

2. **Review Math Terms** Make a simple chart of math symbols and review how to say them. Review number vocabulary, as well.

plus	+
minus	−
times	×
divided by	÷ or ⟌
equals	=

3. **Read and Solve Problems** Call on a volunteer to read each problem: *Seven plus eight.* Others can repeat it chorally. Then have students solve the problem and reread it, this time with the answer.

4. **Do "Math in Action"** Copy the Math in Action problem on the board as students copy it on paper. Work through an example together.

CLOSE AND ASSESS
Discuss with students the Math in Action activity. Did it work? Have volunteers of different ages show their results.

T54 Unit 1 | Glad to Meet You!

SUCCESS IN MATHEMATICS

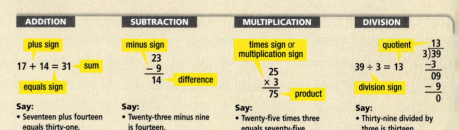

Learn About Math Problems

ADDITION
plus sign
$17 + 14 = 31$ — sum
equals sign

Say:
• Seventeen plus fourteen equals thirty-one.
• Seventeen and fourteen is thirty-one.

SUBTRACTION
minus sign
$\begin{array}{r} 23 \\ -\ 9 \\ \hline 14 \end{array}$ ← difference

Say:
• Twenty-three minus nine is fourteen.
• The difference between nine and twenty-three is fourteen.

MULTIPLICATION
times sign or multiplication sign
$\begin{array}{r} 25 \\ \times\ 3 \\ \hline 75 \end{array}$ ← product

Say:
• Twenty-five times three equals seventy-five.
• Twenty-five multiplied by three is seventy-five.

DIVISION
quotient $\begin{array}{r} 13 \\ 3\overline{)39} \\ -3 \\ \hline 09 \\ -\ 9 \\ \hline 0 \end{array}$
$39 \div 3 = 13$
division sign

Say:
• Thirty-nine divided by three is thirteen.
• Three into thirty-nine is thirteen.

Solve each problem. Then read it aloud.

Add, Subtract, Multiply, and Divide

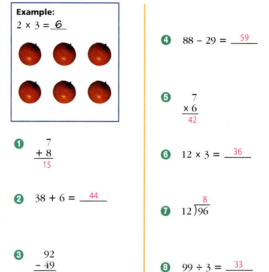

Example:
$2 \times 3 = \underline{6}$

1. $\begin{array}{r} 7 \\ +\ 8 \\ \hline 15 \end{array}$

2. $38 + 6 = \underline{44}$

3. $\begin{array}{r} 92 \\ -\ 49 \\ \hline 43 \end{array}$

4. $88 - 29 = \underline{59}$

5. $\begin{array}{r} 7 \\ \times\ 6 \\ \hline 42 \end{array}$

6. $12 \times 3 = \underline{36}$

7. $12\overline{)96}^{\,8}$

8. $99 \div 3 = \underline{33}$

Math in Action

Sample Response:

 Write your age.
$\times\ 7$

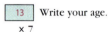 Find the product.
$\times\ 1443$

131313 Find the product. It is your age written 3 times.

54 Unit 1 | Glad to Meet You!

Mathematics Connection
ADD, SUBTRACT, MULTIPLY, DIVIDE

Group the class into two teams and have teams stand across from each other. Distribute flashcards with basic math problems, such as $8 + 2 =$, $9 - 7 =$, $3 \times 2 =$, and $6 \div 3 =$. Teams can take turns holding up a problem for members of the other team to read aloud and answer. Continue the game until everyone has a chance to read or solve a math problem.

Writing Project / POSTCARD

WRITING ASSESSMENT
Use the Writing Progress Checklist on page 51 of the Assessment Handbook to evaluate this writing project.

Make a postcard about yourself. Send the postcard to a friend or relative.

PLAN WHAT YOU WILL WRITE

Think about what you will write. Make some notes. Remember: there isn't much room on a postcard!

Pronunciation of Names
Jaime Santiago   hī mē sahn tē ah gō
Lupe   lü pe

WRITE YOUR POSTCARD

Include these parts on your postcard.

Tell about yourself. Use sentences like these:
- I am _____.
- We are _____.

Check Your Work
- Did you tell about yourself?
- Do your sentences start with a capital letter?
- Do your sentences end with the correct mark?

Make a picture of your home or town on the other side of the postcard.

SEND YOUR POSTCARD

Put a stamp on your postcard. Then put it in a mailbox!

Language Across the Curriculum 55

Language Practice Book page 45

Multi-Level Strategies

WRITING SUPPORT

LITERATE IN L1 For Spanish speakers, point out the following cognates to help students appreciate how many English words they already know.

November noviembre
Hello! ¡Hola!
message mensaje
stamp estampilla
apartment apartamento

UNIT 1 LESSON 16

LANGUAGE ACROSS THE CURRICULUM: WRITING

OBJECTIVES

Functions: Express Social Courtesies; Give Information; Write

Learning Strategies and Critical Thinking: Plan; Generate and Organize Ideas; Self-Assess

Writing: Postcard

CONDUCT THE WRITING PROJECT

1. **Explore Postcards** Share some postcards. Explain that the front side usually shows a picture of a place you are visiting or where you live. Next, preview the steps of the writing project and go over the postcard on the page, explaining the parts.

2. **Plan What You Will Write** Help students choose a topic that lends itself to a postcard, for example, a new place they visited.

3. **Write Your Postcard** For students who need additional support, provide a frame such as the one below.

```
_____ ____,
Dear _____
   Hello! How are you?
   I _____ _____.
   I like _____ _____.
              Your _____,
                 _____
```

When students finish writing their postcards, have them draw their town or their home on the other side.

4. **Send Your Postcard** Volunteers can read their cards to the class before stamping and mailing them.

▶ **Language Practice Book** page 45

CLOSE AND ASSESS

Have students look at their postcards. Say:
- *Show me a sentence about you.*
- *Show me a capital letter at the beginning of a sentence.*
- *Show me a mark at the end of a sentence. What does it mean?*

Language Across the Curriculum **T55**

Resources

For Success in Language and Literacy

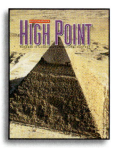

Student Book pages 56–69

For Language Skills Practice

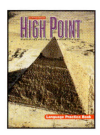

Language Practice Book pages 46–50

For Reading Skills Practice

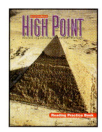

Reading Practice Book pages 42–45

For Vocabulary, Language Development, and Reading Fluency

Language Tape 1, Side B
Language CD 1, Tracks 6–9

For Reading Together

Theme Book *I Make Pictures Move!* from The Basics Bookshelf

For Audio Walk-Throughs and Selection Readings

Selection Tape 1B
Selection CD 1, Tracks 3–4

For Phonics Instruction

Transparencies 16–20

Transparency Scripts 16–20

Letter Tiles

For Comprehensive Assessment

Language Acquisition Assessment, Units 1–3 Test, Writing Assessment, Self-Assessment

For Planning and Instruction

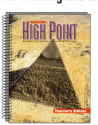

Teacher's Edition pages T56a–T69

T56a Unit Planner

UNIT 2
Set the Table

In This Unit

Vocabulary
- Colors, Shapes, and Sizes
- Foods and Food Groups

Language Functions
- Express Likes
- Describe

Patterns and Structures
- Adjectives
- Action Verbs
- Negative Sentences

Reading
- Phonics: Short *u*, Short *i*, Digraph *ch*, and *tch*
- Comprehension: Identify Steps in a Process (sequence chain)

Writing
- Sentences to Describe
- Sentences with *not*
- Exhibit Card

Content Area Connection
- Science (food pyramid)

UNIT 2

Activity and Assessment Planner

UNIT 2: Set the Table

LESSONS

1

UNIT 2 LAUNCH ▶ pages T56–T57

LESSON 1: INTRODUCE UNIT 2 pages T56–T57

Vocabulary
- T Colors, Shapes, Sizes
- T Foods

Viewing
Interpret a Visual Image

Learning Strategies
Preview

Build Background

Critical Thinking
Make Judgments

Generate Ideas

2–5

LANGUAGE DEVELOPMENT ▶ pages T58–T61

LESSON 2
ADJECTIVES
page T58

Functions
Express Likes

Describe

Patterns and Structures
- T Adjectives

LESSON 3
COLORS, SHAPES, AND SIZES
page T59

Function
Describe

Vocabulary
- T Colors, Shapes, Sizes

Patterns and Structures
- T Adjectives

Writing
- T Sentences

Vocabulary
- T Foods
- T Colors, Shapes, Sizes

Writing
Labels

LESSON 4
FOODS AND FOOD GROUPS
page T60

Function
Describe

Vocabulary
- T Foods

Food Groups

Patterns and Structures
- T Adjectives

Writing
List

LESSON 5
ACTION VERBS
page T61

Function
Describe Actions

Patterns and Structures
- T Present Tense Action Verbs

Writing
- T Sentences

6–12

LANGUAGE AND LITERACY ▶ pages T62a–T67

LESSON 6
BASICS BOOKSHELF
pages T62a–T62h

Function
Listen to a Book

Vocabulary
- T Foods
- T Colors, Shapes, Sizes

Reading Strategies
Activate Prior Knowledge

Preview

Learning to Read
Track Print
(directionality)

Critical Thinking and Comprehension
- T Identify Steps in a Process

LESSON 7
BASICS BOOKSHELF: COMPREHENSION
page T62

Function
Give Information

Learning Strategy
Use Graphic Organizers
(sequence chain)

Critical Thinking and Comprehension
- T Identify Steps in a Process

LESSON 8
HIGH FREQUENCY WORDS
page T63

Learning to Read
- T Recognize High Frequency Words

LESSON 9
PHONICS
pages T64a–T64d

Learning to Read
Build Oral Vocabulary

Develop Phonemic Awareness

- T Associate Sounds and Symbols: /i/ i; /u/ u;
/ch/ ch, tch;
phonograms -ig, -it,
-in, -ug, -un, -up

Blend Sounds to Decode Words

LESSON 10
READING AND SPELLING
pages T64–T65

Learning to Read
Develop Phonemic Awareness

- T Associate Sounds and Symbols: /i/ i, /u/ u,
/ch/ ch, tch

Blend Sounds to Decode Words

Spelling
- T Words with Short i,
Short u, ch, and tch

LESSON 11
INDEPENDENT READING
page T66

Function
Read a Selection

Learning to Read
- T Recognize High Frequency Words
- T Decode Words (short i,
short u, ch, and tch)

Reading Strategies
Set a Purpose for Reading

Retell

Critical Thinking and Comprehension
- T Identify Steps in a Process

LESSON 12
NEGATIVE SENTENCES
page T67

Functions
Describe

Write

Vocabulary
- T Foods
- T Colors, Shapes, Sizes

Patterns and Structures
- T Negative Sentences
- T Present Tense Verbs
(am, is, are)

Writing
- T Sentences

13–14

LANGUAGE ACROSS THE CURRICULUM ▶ pages T68–T69

LESSON 13
SCIENCE: FOOD GROUPS
page T68

Function
Follow Directions

Vocabulary
- T Foods

Food Groups

Research Skills and Learning Strategies
Gather Information

Use Graphic Organizers
(list)

Critical Thinking and Comprehension
Classify

Analyze Information

Draw Conclusions

LESSON 14
WRITING PROJECT: EXHIBIT CARD
page T69

Functions
Write

Describe

Learning Strategies and Critical Thinking
Plan

Generate and Organize Ideas

Self-Assess

Writing
- T Exhibit Card
(Description)

T56c Unit 2 | Set the Table

T = Objective Tested on Unit Test

ASSESSMENT OPTIONS

The **Teacher's Edition** and the **Assessment Handbook** include these comprehensive assessment tools:

▶ **Ongoing, Informal Assessment**
Check for understanding and achieve closure for every lesson with the targeted questions and activities in the **Close and Assess** boxes in your Teacher's Edition.

▶ **Decoding Progress Check**
These word lists for each unit provide a quick way to check on mastery of the phonics or word structure skills taught in the unit.

▶ **Language Acquisition Assessments**
To verify students' ability to use the language functions and grammar structures taught in Units 1–3, conduct these performance assessments.

▶ **Unit Test in Standardized Test Format**
This multiple-choice test measures students' cumulative understanding of the skills and language developed in Units 1–3.

▶ **Self-and Peer-Assessment**
Students use the Self-Assessment Form to evaluate their own work and develop learning strategies appropriate to their needs. Students offer feedback to their classmates with the Peer-Assessment Form.

▶ **Writing Assessment/Portfolio Opportunities**
You can evaluate students' writing in the Writing Projects using the Writing Progress Checklist. Then collaborate with students to choose work for their portfolios.

UNITS 1–3 ASSESSMENT OPPORTUNITIES

	Assessment Handbook Pages
Decoding Progress Check	1a
Language Acquisition Assessments	2
Units 1–3 Test	3–8
Self-Assessment Form	9
Peer-Assessment Form	50
Writing Progress Checklist	51
Portfolio Evaluation Form	52

RELATED RESOURCES

How My Parents Learned to Eat
by Ina R. Friedman
A Japanese-American girl tells how her parents met—and how each learned to use the eating utensils of the other's culture. (Houghton Mifflin)
Theme Book: Read Aloud

The Tortilla Factory
by Gary Paulsen
Poetic text tells how golden corn is ground into flour and made into perfectly round tortillas at a factory. (Available from Hampton-Brown)
Language Development: Adjectives

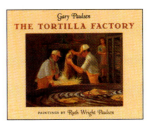

Start It Up!
by Bonita Ferraro
Patterned text about different kinds of boats. Each page ends with the refrain "Start it up. Let it run." (Available from Hampton-Brown)
Phonics Reinforcement: Short *u*

Growing Colors
by Bruce McMillan
Full-page photos of fruits and vegetables are labeled with the color of each plant. An appendix gives the names of the produce. (Available from Hampton-Brown)
Vocabulary: Colors

Ice Cream, Please
An interactive click-and-listen program that teaches over 50 nouns related to food. Available in Apple II or IBM diskette. (Edmark)
Multimedia: Disk Software

Unit Planner **T56d**

UNIT 2 **LESSON 1**

INTRODUCE UNIT 2: SET THE TABLE

> **OBJECTIVES**
>
> **Concepts and Vocabulary:**
> ⓣ Colors, Shapes, and Sizes; ⓣ Foods
> **Viewing:** Interpret a Visual Image
> **Learning Strategies:**
> Preview; Build Background
> **Critical Thinking:**
> Make Judgments; Generate Ideas
> **Speaking:** Describe

START WITH A COMMON EXPERIENCE

1. **Introduce "Set the Table"** Read the unit title. Explain that to "set the table" means to get a table ready for a meal. Show the meaning by displaying or sketching a place setting with a plate, bowl, cup, knife, fork, spoon, and napkin. Invite volunteers to add a self-stick label for each item.

2. **View the Illustration** Read the activity directions on page 57. Point out a few of the unusual food items in the art. (oversized apple, pickle hot dog, cookie pizza, etc.) To help partners talk about what is wrong with the picture, develop a vocabulary chart and model sentences: *The apple is too big.*

Food	Colors	Shapes	Sizes
apple	green	curvy	big
orange	purple	square	little

3. **Create and Describe a Funny Food** Have students draw and share their pictures. Refer students to the chart for help in stating what is wrong with each picture.

REACHING ALL STUDENTS

HOME CONNECTION

Family Foods Students can take home their "funny food" drawing to show their families. Then they can work with a family member to create another funny food. Suggest starting with a food from their home culture, and changing it to make it funny.

Encourage students to bring their new drawings back to class. Lead the group in describing what each food is usually like and how it is different in the drawing.

Set the Table

There are many things wrong with this picture! Tell your partner about them. Then draw a picture of another funny food. Ask the class to guess what is wrong with your picture.

In This Unit

Vocabulary
- Colors, Shapes, and Sizes
- Foods and Food Groups

Language Functions
- Express Likes
- Describe

Patterns and Structures
- Adjectives
- Action Verbs
- Negative Sentences

Reading
- Phonics: Short *u*, Short *i*, Digraph *ch*, and *tch*
- Comprehension: Identify Steps in a Process (sequence chain)

Writing
- Sentences to Describe
- Sentences with *not*
- Exhibit Card

Content Area Connection
- Science (food pyramid)

PREVIEW THE UNIT

4 Look for Activities and Information About Foods Leaf through the unit, previewing activities students will do, for example:

page 58—learning a chant about a tasty salad

page 59—describing colors and shapes of foods

page 62—listening to the Bookshelf book (Display a copy of the book.)

page 68—learning about the food pyramid

page 69—making art from food and then writing about it

Also ask students to look for ways to describe and categorize their favorite foods. For example, highlight the activity on page 59 and the creative project on page 69. Then sum up what the preview reveals: *Foods are fun to eat—and fun to be creative with.*

5 Set Your Goals Start a class mind map on foods. Use what students noted about the funny foods to focus on the characteristics of real foods. Prompt students for pictures or words to add, and have them describe other ideas for you to put into words. Talk together about what they want to learn about food in this unit.

CLOSE AND ASSESS

Ask students to tell or show you something they are interested in learning in this unit.

UNIT 2 Mind Map

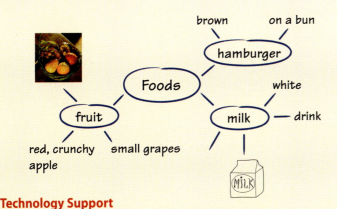

Technology Support

See **Inspiration** Visual Learning software for support in creating mind maps.

UNIT 2 **LESSON 2**

LANGUAGE DEVELOPMENT: ADJECTIVES

OBJECTIVES

Functions: Listen Actively; Repeat Spoken Language; Recite; Express Likes; Describe
Patterns and Structures: Adjectives
Concepts and Vocabulary: Foods; Colors, Shapes, and Sizes
Writing: Labels

INTRODUCE

1. **Listen and Chant** Play "Tasty Salad" on the **Language Tape/CD**. Students will listen and follow along with the words, then echo the lines, supply missing adjectives and nouns, and finally chime in on the entire chant.

2. **Learn About Adjectives** Read aloud the chart for adjectives and invite volunteers to find examples in the chant. To ensure understanding, ask questions such as *What adjectives tell about the lettuce?* (fresh, green) *What does the word* tasty *describe?* (salad)

PRACTICE

3. **Conduct "Express Yourself"** Model how to express likes and to describe what you like. Then have partners complete the activity.

> **How to Express Likes and Describe**
> • Name a food you like: *I like corn.*
> • Add words to tell more about the food: *I like fresh, yellow corn.*

APPLY

4. **Write Labels** Encourage students to trade pictures with a partner and use Partner Checklist 2 on page T310 to check the labels.

CLOSE AND ASSESS

Call on one student to name a food and have other students suggest adjectives to describe it.

T58 Unit 2 | Set the Table

ADJECTIVES

What Foods Do You Like?

Listen and chant.

Tasty Salad

Lettuce, lettuce,
Fresh, green lettuce.
Carrots, carrots,
Long, orange carrots.
Onions, onions,
Large, round onions.
Salad, salad,
Tasty salad.
What a treat!

Labels: little, red tomatoes; yellow corn; tiny green peas; purple cabbage; fresh, green lettuce; big, white cauliflower; long, orange carrot; large, round onion

Adjectives
An **adjective** describes a person, place, or thing.
long, orange carrot
large, round onions

EXPRESS YOURSELF ▶ EXPRESS LIKES; DESCRIBE

1.–6. Work with a partner. Tell your partner about 6 foods you like. Use an adjective to describe each food.

Example: **1.** I like yellow corn.

WRITE LABELS

7.–10. Draw 4 foods you like. Write a label for each picture. Use adjectives to describe each food.

Example: **7.** big, round bagel

58 Unit 2 | Set the Table

REACHING ALL STUDENTS

CULTURAL PERSPECTIVES

Home Culture: Foods Invite students to draw and label a fruit or vegetable that is popular in their home culture. Have them create couplets like those in the above chant:

Chile, chile.
Red, hot chile.

Bean sprouts, bean sprouts.
Fresh, long bean sprouts.

Then lead the class in a group chant, with students taking turns to display their drawings and say their lines.

VOCABULARY: COLORS, SHAPES, AND SIZES

What Is Red and Round? A Tomato!

Look at the picture. Read the words that name a color or shape.

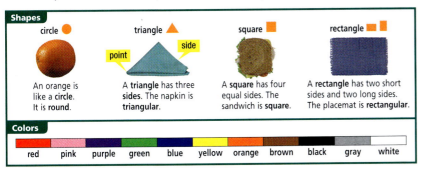

Shapes
- circle — An orange is like a **circle**. It is **round**.
- triangle — A **triangle** has three **sides**. The napkin is **triangular**. (point, side)
- square — A **square** has four equal sides. The sandwich is **square**.
- rectangle — A **rectangle** has two short sides and two long sides. The placemat is **rectangular**.

Colors
red | pink | purple | green | blue | yellow | orange | brown | black | gray | white

BUILD SENTENCES

Read each sentence below. Add words to tell the color, size, or shape. Say the new sentence.

Example: 1. A blueberry is round. It is also small.

Sample Responses:

1. A blueberry is <u>blue</u>. It is also <u>round</u>.

2. A pickle is <u>long</u>. It is also <u>green</u>.

3. A tomato is <u>round</u>. It is also <u>small</u>.

4. The cheese is <u>yellow</u>. It is <u>triangular</u>.

5. The candy bar is <u>brown</u>. It is <u>rectangular</u>.

6. The lettuce is <u>big</u>. It is also <u>green</u>.

7. The banana is <u>long</u>. It is also <u>yellow</u>.

8. The slice of bread is <u>square</u>. It is also <u>brown</u>.

WRITE SENTENCES

9.–16. Write a sentence for each picture above. Tell about the shape of the food.

Example: 9. A blueberry is like a circle.

Students' sentences should include the shape of each food.

Language Development 59

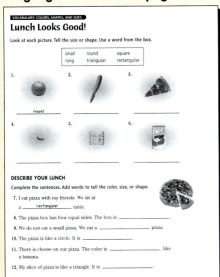

Language Practice Book page 46

Multi-Level Strategies

VOCABULARY: COLORS AND SHAPES

PRELITERATE Work with the group to create a matching game. Make a pair of cards for each color and shape in the chart. One card should show the color or shape; the other should have the word on it.

Have the group use the cards to play Concentration and/or Go Fish, taking turns to match the colors and shapes with the corresponding words.

UNIT 2 **LESSON 3**

LANGUAGE DEVELOPMENT: COLORS, SHAPES, AND SIZES

OBJECTIVES

Function: Describe
Concepts and Vocabulary:
- Colors, Shapes, and Sizes
Patterns and Structures: Adjectives
Writing: Sentences

INTRODUCE

1 Learn Words for Colors, Shapes, and Sizes Go over the chart together. Then ask students questions such as: *What shape is the napkin? How many sides does the sandwich have? What color is the placemat?*

2 Make a Sorting Chart Brainstorm words for color, shape, and size. Encourage students to use objects in the room to show concepts they cannot yet name. Group the adjectives into categories:

Color	Shape	Size
red	circle	small
blue	round	large
purple	square	long

PRACTICE

3 Build Sentences Encourage students to make up multiple sentences for each item; for example: *A blueberry is round. A blueberry is small. A blueberry is little. A blueberry is blue.*

APPLY

4 Write Sentences Expand on the example to encourage creativity: *A blueberry is small and round like a marble.* Students can work in small groups to do Items 9–16.

▶ Language Practice Book page 46

CLOSE AND ASSESS

Ask volunteers to read aloud a sentence they wrote in Items 9–16. Call on one student to identify each adjective and another to write it out.

Language Development **T59**

UNIT 2 LESSON 4
LANGUAGE DEVELOPMENT: FOODS AND FOOD GROUPS

OBJECTIVES
Functions: Listen Actively; Describe
Concepts and Vocabulary:
- Foods; Food Groups

Patterns and Structures: Adjectives
Speaking: Repeat Spoken Language
Writing: List

INTRODUCE

1. **Learn Words for Foods** Read the food labels aloud and have students echo them. Then call out food names and have students point to them in the illustration.

2. **Sort Foods** Work with students to categorize the foods in the picture:

Meats	Fruits/ Vegetables	Breads/ Grains
chicken steak	potato peach	rice roll

PRACTICE

3. **Conduct "Who's Talking?"** Play the **Language Tape/CD** to model how to name and describe foods. Have students listen, then pause the tape and replay it, if necessary, before students identify and describe the lunches.

Tape 1B
CD 1 Track 7

APPLY

4. **Write a List** Have small groups suggest adjectives to describe one another's food choices.

▶ Language Practice Book page 47

CLOSE AND ASSESS
Have volunteers read their lists. Discuss which foods and food groups are the most popular.

T60 Unit 2 | Set the Table

VOCABULARY: FOODS

What's for Lunch?

Look at the picture. Say the name of each food.

WHO'S TALKING? ▶ DESCRIBE

1.–3. Listen to each person talk about the lunch. Point to the correct lunch. Then describe it.

Answers:
1. the lunch with steak, corn, and peas
2. the lunch with potato and fish
3. the lunch with pasta, broccoli, and a roll

WRITE A LIST

4. What do you want for lunch? Write a list. Draw a picture of each food. Use adjectives to describe the food.

Example: 4.
TODAY'S LUNCH
a small, green salad
hot pizza
a tall glass of milk
red apple

60 Unit 2 | Set the Table

REACHING ALL STUDENTS

Vocabulary
FOOD GROUPS

Lunches Distribute a chart for planning lunches. Challenge groups to create as many lunches as they can in two minutes, writing a food in each column. View and discuss the menus together.

	Meats	Fruits/ Vegetables	Breads/ Grains
Lunch 1			
Lunch 2			

Language Practice Book page 47

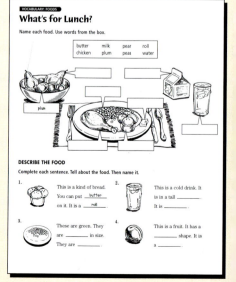

ACTION VERBS

How Do You Make a Fruit Drink?

An **action verb** tells what someone does.

I **make** great fruit drinks.
I **cut** bananas.
I **put** them in the blender.
I **add** ice.

BUILD SENTENCES

Tell how to make a fruit drink. Choose a verb from the box to complete each sentence. Say the new sentence.

Action Verbs		
put	open	cut
get	push	wash

Example: 1. I wash the strawberries.

1.
I <u>wash</u> the strawberries.

2.
I <u>cut</u> the strawberries.

3.
I <u>get</u> some ice.

4.
I <u>open</u> the yogurt.

5.
I <u>add</u> the yogurt in the blender.

6.
I <u>push</u> the button.

WRITE SENTENCES

7.–10. Write 4 sentences to tell how you make a sandwich. Write each sentence on a card. Mix up the cards. Have your partner put the sentences in order.

Example: 7.
I put jam on the bread.

Sample Responses:
7. I take 2 pieces of bread.
8. I put jam on one piece.
9. I put peanut butter on the other piece.
10. I put the 2 pieces together.

Language Development 61

Language Practice Book page 48

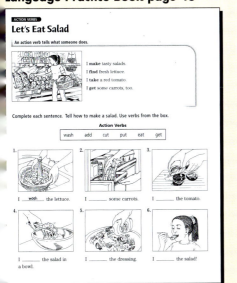

UNIT 2 **LESSON 5**

LANGUAGE DEVELOPMENT: ACTION VERBS

OBJECTIVES

Function: Describe Actions
Patterns and Structures:
🅣 Present Tense Action Verbs
Writing: 🅣 Sentences

INTRODUCE

1 **Learn About Action Verbs** Read the title, introduction, and examples. As you read aloud the second example, pantomime cutting bananas. Use gestures to convey the meanings for the remaining sentences. Then read the sentences again and pause for students to pantomime the action verbs.

PRACTICE

2 **Build Sentences** After students study each item, ask a volunteer to complete the sentence with an action verb from the box. Lead the group in repeating the sentence and pantomiming the action.

APPLY

3 **Write Sentences** Have students look back at pages 58–60 for foods to use in their sandwiches.

For students who need more support, provide a verb box and sentence frames:

get	eat	put	add

I _____ two slices of bread.
I _____ cheese on the bread.
I _____ some tomato.
I _____ the sandwich!

▶ **Language Practice Book** page 48

CLOSE AND ASSESS

Have students read their sentences. Ask volunteers to state the action verb in each sentence and to pantomime the action.

Language Development **T61**

UNIT 2 **LESSON 6**

LANGUAGE AND LITERACY: THE BASICS BOOKSHELF

OBJECTIVES
Concepts and Vocabulary:
🔵 Foods; 🔵 Colors, Shapes, and Sizes
Listening: Listen to a Preview
Reading Strategies:
Activate Prior Knowledge; Preview

BUILD LANGUAGE AND VOCABULARY

1. **Teach "Words to Know"** Have students look at page 2. Say: *This page shows many foods.* Read the names of the foods aloud. As you read, ask students to raise their hands to indicate foods they have tried.

   Then have students look at page 3. Say: *This page shows sizes, shapes, and colors.* Encourage students to copy your actions as you use gestures to show the different sizes. Then ask students to point to each shape and color as you say the words.

2. **Find a Match** Model size, shape, and color words to identify a food on page 2: *This fruit is small and red.* Students can guess the food (strawberry). Then invite volunteers to continue the activity with more foods.

PREPARE TO READ

3. **Think About What You Know** Ask students to describe the artist's actions on pages 8–9. Invite them to share their knowledge about drawing. Encourage students to do a quick drawing to share or have them tell about what they like to draw.

4. **Preview** Play the Audio Walk-Through for *I Make Pictures Move!* on the **Selection Tape/CD** to give students the overall idea of the story. *Tape 1B / CD 1 Track 3*

CLOSE AND ASSESS

Have students draw a picture of a favorite food and use size, shape, and color words to describe it to the class.

I Make Pictures Move!
by Daphne Liu

Summary This career sketch shows an animator at work. Andy Adams draws, scans, and colors while his animated dog builds and eats a larger-than-life sandwich. A flip book format lets students experience his animation. Simple text reinforces words about foods, colors, sizes, and shapes.

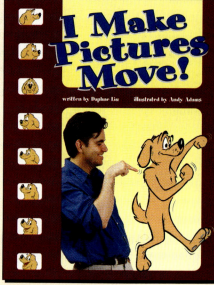
Cover

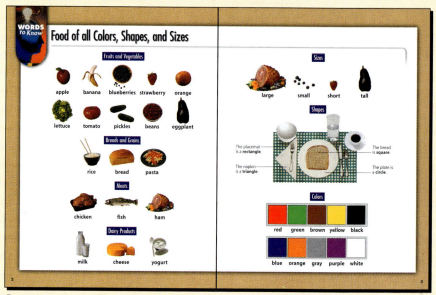
Pages 2–3

T62a Unit 2 | Set the Table

Pages 4–5

Pages 6–7

Strategies for Comprehensible Input

PAGE	STORY LANGUAGE	STRATEGY OPTIONS
4–5	Hi! My name is Andy.	**Point to the picture of Andy and explain:** This is Andy. He is telling the story. He says the words.
6–7	move	**Demonstrate:** Take a few steps as you say *move*. Then point to the first picture of the dog. Move your finger to the right, pausing at each picture as you say: *Andy draws pictures that show how the dog moves.*

Language and Literacy **T62b**

UNIT 2 **LESSON 6,** CONTINUED

LANGUAGE AND LITERACY: THE BASICS BOOKSHELF

OBJECTIVES
Function: Listen to a Book
Learning to Read: Use Picture Clues

READ AND THINK TOGETHER

1. **Read Aloud** On your first reading of the book, use the "Strategies for Comprehensible Input" that appear at the bottom of pages T62b, T62d, T62f, and T62h.

Pages 8–9

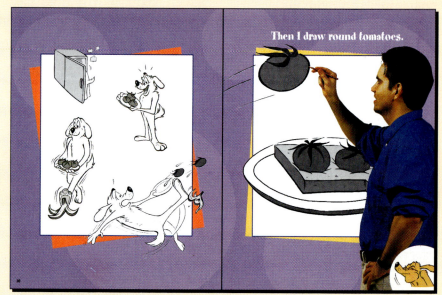

Pages 10–11

Multi-Level Strategies
LITERACY SUPPORT

PRELITERATE **Use Picture Clues** Turn to pages 4–5. Point to the photo of the animator in his studio. Say: *The pictures go with the words. The words tell about Andy. The picture shows how Andy looks. The words and pictures in this book explain how Andy does his job.* Next, point to the illustration of the dog at the top of page 4. Say: *This is Dingo. Andy draws the pictures of him. You will see a story about Dingo on the pages, too.*

Page through the book with students. Encourage them to point out the photos of Andy and the words on the page. Ask what Andy does on each page. Call on volunteers to predict what the words will tell about Andy. Then page through the book again and point out the large illustrations of Dingo (not in the circles at the bottom of the right-hand pages). Invite students to describe the dog's actions.

T62c Unit 2 | Set the Table

I Make Pictures Move!, CONTINUED

Pages 12–13

Pages 14–15

Strategies for Comprehensible Input

Page	Story Language	Strategy Options
8–9	draw	**Demonstrate:** Draw a square, circle, and triangle.
	sandwich	**Point to the picture.**
	square	**Point to the picture.** Use your finger to outline the shape of the square.
10–11	round	**Demonstrate:** Use your finger to trace a circle in the air.
	round tomatoes	**Point to the picture.** Repeat the gesture as you trace the tomatoes on the page.
12–13	I add	**Restate:** Next I draw
	ham, cheese	**Point to the pictures.**
14–15	pickles	**Point to the picture.**

Language and Literacy **T62d**

UNIT 2 **LESSON 6,** CONTINUED

LANGUAGE AND LITERACY: THE BASICS BOOKSHELF

> **OBJECTIVES**
>
> **Function:** Listen to a Book
> **Critical Thinking and Comprehension:**
> 🅣 Identify Steps in a Process

READ AND THINK TOGETHER, CONTINUED

2 Read and Map: Identify Steps in a Process Draw a sequence chain like the one below, but with empty boxes. Say: *A sequence chain shows the order, or sequence, in which things are done.*

Read pages 8–9 aloud. Then think aloud as you model completing the first box: *The words and pictures show Andy drawing a square piece of bread. In box 1, I will write* Andy draws bread.

Pause after reading each set of pages shown below and model completing the chain for the rest of the text.

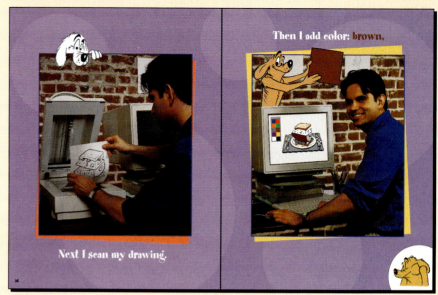

Pages 16–17

Pages 18–19

Sequence Chain for *I Make Pictures Move!*

pages 8–9	Andy draws bread.
pages 10–11	He draws tomatoes.
pages 12–15	He adds ham, cheese, and pickles.
page 16	He scans the drawing.
pages 17–21	He adds colors.

💿 **Technology Support**
See **Inspiration** Visual Learning software for support in creating the sequence chain.

T62e Unit 2 | Set the Table

I Make Pictures Move!, CONTINUED

Pages 20–21

Pages 22–23

Strategies for Comprehensible Input

PAGE	STORY LANGUAGE	STRATEGY OPTIONS
16–17	I scan my drawing.	**Point to the picture and explain:** A scanner is a machine that takes a picture of your work. Then you can see it and make changes on the computer.
	color	**Point to the picture.** Say the word *color* as you point to the color bar on the screen. Say *no color* as you point to the black and white sandwich.
	brown	**Point to the color tile in Dingo's hand.**
18–19	red, yellow	**Point to the color tiles in Dingo's hand.**
20–21	green, blue	**Point to the color tiles in Dingo's hand.**
22–23	Done!	**Restate:** The picture is finished.

Language and Literacy **T62f**

UNIT 2 **LESSON 6,** CONTINUED

LANGUAGE AND LITERACY: THE BASICS BOOKSHELF

OBJECTIVES

Functions: Listen to a Book; Repeat Spoken Language (choral reading)

Learning to Read: Track Print (directionality)

READ AND THINK TOGETHER, CONTINUED

3. **Conduct Interactive Readings** Choose from these options:

   - **Read along and track print** Have students point to each word as they read along with the recording of *I Make Pictures Move!* on the **Selection Tape/CD**.

   - **Echo reading** Use the text on page 8 to model echo reading. Read each sentence and have students repeat it after you. Continue with pages 11, 13, 14, 16–22, 28, 31, and 32. For less advanced students, work in a small group. Read one or two words at a time. Encourage students to point to the words as they echo read.

CLOSE AND ASSESS

Have students tell their partners three sequential steps in the way Andy makes pictures move.

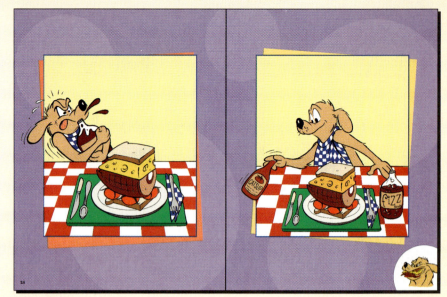

Pages 24–25

Pages 26–27

Multi-Level Strategies

LITERACY SUPPORT

LITERATE IN L1 **Read with a Partner/ Write Pattern Books** After students have participated in the interactive readings, encourage them to read the story with a partner. Distribute the Partner Prompts on page T311 to help partners work together to identify unfamiliar words and unlock their meanings, then read the text to each other. After the partner reading, have students make pattern books that express their preferences with the sentence frame: *I like _____.* Encourage them to add pictures and complete the sentence with adjectives and nouns: *I like pink flowers.* Have students read their books aloud.

INTERRUPTED SCHOOLING **Identify Steps in a Process** To anchor understanding of the skill, page through the book to identify the steps in the animation process. Point to pages 8–9 and say: *I think Andy drew bread first. On pages 8–9, the picture shows him drawing bread. I see the word* first *on page 8. Now I know I'm right.* Use sentence strips to copy each step. Then scramble the strips and ask volunteers to arrange them in the correct order.

T62g Unit 2 | Set the Table

I Make Pictures Move!, CONTINUED

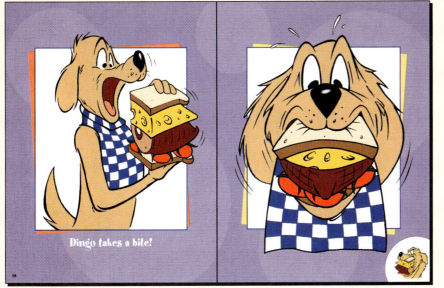

Pages 28–29

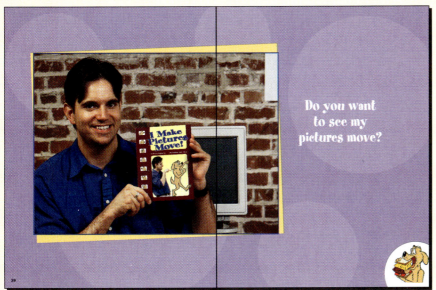

Pages 30–31

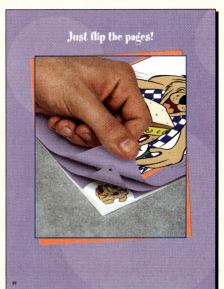

Page 32

Strategies for Comprehensible Input

Page	Story Language	Strategy Options
28–29	Dingo takes a bite	**Point to the picture and explain:** The name of the dog is Dingo. **Restate:** eats some of the sandwich
32	flip	**Demonstrate:** Flip the pages of the book from the back to the front.

Language and Literacy **T62h**

UNIT 2 **LESSON 7**

LANGUAGE AND LITERACY: THE BASICS BOOKSHELF

OBJECTIVES

Function: Give Information

Learning Strategy: Use Graphic Organizers (sequence chain)

Critical Thinking and Comprehension:
T Identify Steps in a Process

CHECK COMPREHENSION

1 **Make a Sequence Chain** Have students review *I Make Pictures Move!* to identify the steps in the process for a sequence chain. Remind them that a sequence chain shows the order, or sequence, in which things happen.

As you read aloud the directions for each step, pause for students to add information to the sections of their chains. Encourage students to review the story to clarify the steps in the process.

2 **Share Information from the Book** Have partners take turns using their sequence chains to describe the process in their own words. Then have partners compare their sequence chains to add and correct information.

CLOSE AND ASSESS

Ask students to complete this sentence: *A sequence chain shows _____.*

COMPREHENSION: IDENTIFY STEPS IN A PROCESS

Read and Think Together

Make a sequence chain to tell about *I Make Pictures Move!* Follow these steps.

1 Think about how Andy makes his drawing. Draw a box. In it, write what Andy does first.

> Andy draws bread.

2 Draw 4 more boxes. Tell what else Andy does.

> Andy draws bread.
> ↓
> He draws tomatoes.
> ↓
> He adds ham, cheese, and pickles.
> ↓
> He scans the drawing.
> ↓
> He adds colors.

3 Use your sequence chain to tell a partner how Andy makes his drawing. Then tell what Dingo does at the end of the story.

from
The Basics Bookshelf

THEME BOOK

First see how an artist draws a meal for his dog, and then flip the pages to watch the dog eat it!

62 **Unit 2** | Set the Table

REACHING ALL STUDENTS

Language Development
LISTEN ACTIVELY AND DESCRIBE

Directed Draw Choose a simple illustration from the book to describe. Give students verbal drawing instructions using color, shape, and size words: *Draw a large triangle. Color it yellow. Add circles.* (cheese wedge, page 19) When the drawings are finished, have students find the original illustration in the book. How close did they come to the original? Have partners take turns directing each other to draw items from the book or in the classroom.

T62 Unit 2 | Set the Table

HIGH FREQUENCY WORDS

Words to Know

REVIEW WORDS YOU KNOW

Read the words aloud. Which word goes in the sentence?

good	go
like	look
who	with

1. The lunch is **good**.
2. These kids **like** the food.
3. They eat **with** their hands.

LEARN TO READ

Learn new words.

something	I want **something** to eat.
make	I can **make** spaghetti!
long	First, I get a box of **long** noodles.
large	I put them in a **large** pot of hot water.
move	I **move** the pot to the back of the stove.
different	Then, I use a **different** pot for the sauce.
small	I cut an onion into **small** pieces.
open	I **open** a can of tomatoes.
same	I cook the onions and tomatoes in the **same** pot.
eat	At last, I **eat** my pasta!

How to Learn a New Word
- Look at the word.
- Listen to the word.
- Listen to the word in a sentence. What does it mean?
- Say the word.
- Spell the word.
- Say the word again.

WORD WORK

Write each new word on a card. Sort the cards into these groups:

4. These 2 words end in **t**.   different eat
5. These 3 words start with an **s**.   something small came
6. These 3 words tell about size.   long large small
7. These 4 words name actions.   make move open eat
8. This word is made up of 2 smaller words.   something

Read the words in each group aloud. Then make up new groups with a partner.

Example: 4.

different   eat

different
eat

Sample Groups
start with *m*: make, move.
are opposites: large, small; different, same

Language and Literacy 63

Reading Practice Book page 42

Reading Fluency
RECOGNIZE HIGH FREQUENCY WORDS

To build automaticity with the new high frequency words:

- Use letter tiles on the overhead to spell out words from the list. Pause after each letter to see if students can identify the word you are spelling. After a word is identified, ask a volunteer to complete it.
- Use the high frequency words to label classroom objects: *Open this door, long table, large desk,* etc. Then conduct a high frequency word hunt.

UNIT 2 **LESSON 8**

LANGUAGE AND LITERACY: HIGH FREQUENCY WORDS

OBJECTIVES

Learning to Read:
- Recognize High Frequency Words

REVIEW WORDS

1 **Review Known High Frequency Words** Have the group read aloud the words in the green box. Listen for words students cannot read automatically and use the steps in the yellow box to reteach those words. Then have students look at the photo. Read each cloze sentence. Reread each sentence and pause for students to silently read the two words to the left of the sentence. Tell students to choose the word that goes in the sentence and tells about the picture.

INTRODUCE NEW WORDS

2 **Learn High Frequency Words** Use the High Frequency Word Script on page T313 to lead students through the steps in the yellow box for each new word.

PRACTICE

3 **Conduct "Word Work"** For Item 4, model how to check each word card against the clue and make a group. After students complete Items 5–8, discuss why each word belongs in its group. Then encourage students to discover new groups, such as words that start with *l* or words with four letters.

APPLY

4 **Read Words in Context** Students will apply the skill when they read high frequency words in context in the sentences on page 65 and the passage on page 66.

▶ **Reading Practice Book** page 42

CLOSE AND ASSESS

Call out the high frequency words one at a time. Have students point to them and spell the words as a group.

Language and Literacy **T63**

UNIT 2 **LESSON 9**

LANGUAGE AND LITERACY: PHONICS

OBJECTIVES

Learning to Read: Build Oral Vocabulary; Develop Phonemic Awareness; ⓣ Associate Sounds and Symbols: /i/ i; Blend Sounds to Decode Words

TEACH SHORT VOWELS: /i/ i

1. **Build Oral Vocabulary** Display Transparency 16. Talk through each picture to develop meaning for the words in the yellow boxes. For example, for Item 1, say:

   • *The girl is playing tennis. She can* **hit** *the ball* (point and pantomime) *with the racquet. Then she can* **sit** (point and pantomime) *to rest.*

2. **Develop Phonemic Awareness** Remove the transparency and conduct the oral activities in Step 1 of the Script for Transparency 16.

3. **Read Short i Words** Display Transparency 16 again. Work through Steps 2 and 3 of the script.

CLOSE AND ASSESS

Display the words *hit, pig, fin,* and *six*. Call on students to blend a word and identify the sound in the middle.

Transparency 16: ▶ **Short** *i*

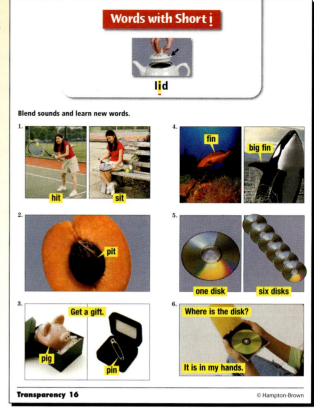

▼ **Script for Transparency 16**

Words with Short *i*

1. **Develop Phonemic Awareness**
   Isolate/Match Short *i* Say: *Listen to the first sound in these words:* it, ill, in. *What is the sound?* (/i/) *Now listen for the sound /i/ in the middle of these words:* sit, pin, lid. *Say the words with me. Now raise your hand each time you hear the sound* /i/. Say these words: *sip, wig, rain, bite, bit, tip, white, fine, fin, list.*

2. **Associate Sounds and Symbols**
   Point to the lid on **Transparency 16**. Say: *This is a lid. It covers a pot. Say the word* lid *with me.* Then point to the *i* in *lid* and say: *The letter* i *makes the sound you hear in the middle of* lid. *The sound in the middle is* /i/. *Say* /i/ *with me:* /iii/. Point to the *i* and ask: *What's the letter? What's the sound?*

3. **Blend Sounds to Read Words**
   Model/Teach Point to the letter *l* in *lid* and say: *The sound for* l *is:* /lll/. Repeat for *i*: /iii/. As you slide your finger slowly from left to right below the letters *li*, say: *I can blend the two sounds:* /lllii/. Then point to the *d* and say: *The sound for* d *is:* /d/. *I can blend the three sounds together:* /llliid/. *Now, I'm going to say the whole word:* lid. Lead students in blending the sounds and then saying the word.

   Practice For Item 1, say: *Let's try that again. This picture shows a girl hitting a tennis ball, doesn't it? Read the word with me. Follow my finger as we blend the sounds* /hiiit/, *and say the word:* hit. *Look at the picture. Does the word* hit *make sense?* Repeat for the other words, calling special attention to the following:

   • Read aloud the sentence in Item 3, pausing for students to decode *gift*. Repeat for Item 6, giving students time to decode *is, disk,* and *in*.

   • In Item 5, blend *disk* with students and say: *When we read* disk, *we blended the consonants* s *and* k *at the end.* Next read *six disks*. For *disks,* cover the final *s*, blend the root word, uncover the *s* and say the word with the ending. Explain: *The letter* s *at the end of a word can make the word mean "more than one."*

T64a Unit 2 | Set the Table

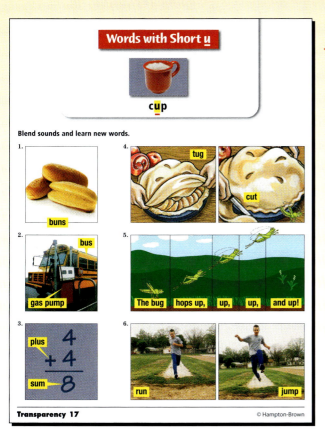

◀ Transparency 17: Short *u*

▼ Script for Transparency 17

Words with Short *u*

1. **Develop Phonemic Awareness**
   Isolate/Match Short *u* Say: *Listen to the first sound in these words:* up, us, under. *What is the sound?* (/u/) *Now listen for the sound* /u/ *in the middle of these words:* cup, bus, fun. *Say the words with me. Now raise your hand each time you hear the sound* /u/. *Say these words:* cut, tug, lid, run, rule, dust, June, dime, at, sun.

2. **Associate Sounds and Symbols**
   Point to the cup on **Transparency 17.** Say: *This is a cup. Say the word* cup *with me.* Then point to the *u* in *cup* and say: *The letter* u *makes the sound you hear in the middle of* cup. *The sound in the middle is* /u/. *Say* /u/ *with me:* /uuu/. Point to the *u* and ask: *What's the letter? What's the sound?*

3. **Blend Sounds to Read Words**
   Model/Teach Point to the letter *c* in *cup* and say: *The sound for* c *is:* /k/. Repeat for *u:* /uuu/. *As you slide your finger slowly from left to right below the letters cu,* say: *I can blend the two sounds:* /kuuu/. Then point to the *p* and say: *The sound for* p *is:* /p/. *I can blend the three sounds together:* /kuuup/. *Now, I'm going to say the whole word:* cup. Lead students in blending the sounds and then saying the words.

   Practice For Item 1, say: *Let's try that again. This picture shows some buns for hot dogs. Read the word with me. Follow my finger as we blend the sounds* /buuunnnzzz/, *and say the word:* buns. Ask: *What sound does* s *make at the end?* /z/ Repeat the blending process for the other words, calling special attention to the following:

   - In Item 2, blend *pump* with students and say: *When we read* pump, *we blended the consonants* m *and* p *at the end*. Repeat for the initial blend in *plus* in Item 3 and for the final blend in *jump* in Item 6.
   - Read aloud the sentence in Item 5, pausing for students to decode *bug* and *up*. Point out that *s* at the end of *hops* makes the sound /s/.

OBJECTIVES
Learning to Read: Build Oral Vocabulary; Develop Phonemic Awareness; ⓣ Associate Sounds and Symbols: /u/ *u*; Blend Sounds to Decode Words

TEACH SHORT VOWELS: /u/ *u*

1. **Build Oral Vocabulary** Display Transparency 17. Talk through each picture to develop meaning for the words in the yellow boxes. For example, for Item 4, say:
   - *When you make a pie, you* **tug** *the crust to stretch it over the top* (pantomime). *Then you* **cut** *the dough around the edges* (pantomime).

2. **Develop Phonemic Awareness** Remove the transparency and conduct the oral activities in Step 1 of the Script for Transparency 17.

3. **Read Short *u* Words** Display Transparency 17 again. Work through Steps 2 and 3 of the script.

CLOSE AND ASSESS
Display the words *run, sum, bug,* and *cut.* Call on students to blend a word and identify the sound in the middle.

▶ **Reading Practice Book** page 43 (short *i* and short *u*)

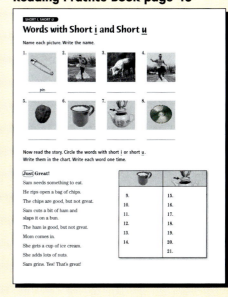

Reading Practice Book page 43

Language and Literacy **T64b**

UNIT 2 **LESSON 9,** CONTINUED

LANGUAGE AND LITERACY: PHONICS

OBJECTIVES

Learning to Read: Build Oral Vocabulary; Develop Phonemic Awareness; ⓣ Associate Sounds and Symbols: Phonograms -ig, -it, -in, -ug, -un, -up; Blend Sounds to Decode Words

RECOGNIZE WORD FAMILIES

1. **Build Oral Vocabulary** Display Transparency 18. Use the pictures to develop the meaning of each word and use it in a sentence. For example: *This is a **pig**. A **pig** is an animal.*

2. **Develop Phonemic Awareness** Remove the transparency and conduct the oral activities in Step 1 of the Script for Transparency 18.

3. **Read Words with Short *i* and Short *u* Phonograms** Display Transparency 18 again. Use the activities in Step 2 of the script to teach the word families.

4. **Build Words** Use Step 3 of the script to build words in the boxes on Transparency 18.

CLOSE AND ASSESS

Have one student build a word with letter tiles. Ask other students to change the first letter to make a rhyming word.

▶ **Reading Practice Book** page 44 (short *i* and short *u* phonograms)

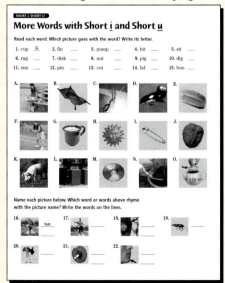

Transparency 18: ▶ **Short *i* and Short *u* Phonograms**

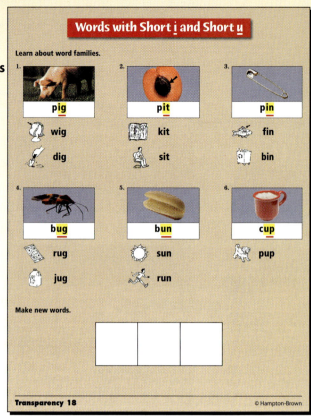

Materials
Letter tiles for:
b c d f g
i j k m n
p p r s t
u w

▼ **Script for Transparency 18**

Words with Short *i* and Short *u* Phonograms

1. **Develop Phonemic Awareness**
   Listen for Rhyming Words/Blend Onset and Rime Say: *Listen to these words: big, dig. Say them with me: big, dig. These words rhyme—they both end with /ig/. Do* wig *and* fin *rhyme?* (no) Continue with *sit, fit; pig, fin.* Then give the onset and rime for words in the list; for example: */sss/-/it/.* Have students blend them */sssit/,* and tell you the word: *sit.* Repeat for words with /u/, using *fun* and *sun,* and word pairs *jug, cup; bug, rug; fun, run.*

2. **Read Words with Short *i* and Short *u* Phonograms**
   Point to the first item on **Transparency 18**. Say: *Let's read the word that names this picture.* Slide a finger slowly under the letters to lead students in sounding out the word: */piiig/, pig.* Cover the letter *p* and explain: *The two letters* ig *at the end stand for the last two sounds you hear in* pig: /ig/. *There are many words that end in* /ig/ *and rhyme with* pig, *like these two words below it.* (Point out *wig* and *dig.*) *Let's read these words, using what we know about their end sounds.* Have students sound out and blend the initial consonant with the phonogram -*ig* to read the words. Repeat for the other phonograms.

3. **Build Words with Short *i* and Short *u* Phonograms**
   Teach Place letter tiles *p-i-g* in the boxes, read the word, and say: *The letters* ig *spell the sounds* /ig/ *at the end of* pig. Big *rhymes with* pig, *so I know* big *also ends with* ig. *To spell* big, *I change the first letter. What sound do you hear at the beginning of* big? *Yes,* /b/, *and* b *spells that sound.* Substitute letter tile *b* for *p,* and confirm the word by blending the sounds.

   Practice Have students build the other -*ig* words on the transparency. Repeat for the other phonograms. Add these words, after making sure students know the meanings:

   -ig: fig   **-it:** fit   **-in:** tin, win   **-ug:** mug, tug   **-un:** fun

   Then build words to contrast phonograms, such as *big/bug, pig/pin, fin/fun.*

T64c Unit 2 | Set the Table

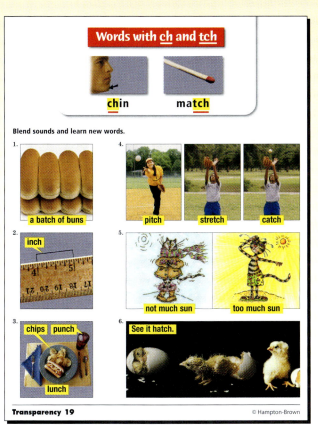

◀ Transparency 19: *ch* and *tch*

▼ Script for Transparency 19

Words with *ch* and *tch*

1. **Develop Phonemic Awareness**
   Isolate/Match /ch/ Say: *Listen to the first sound in these words:* chin, chop, check. *What is the sound?* (/ch/) *Now listen for the sound* /ch/ *at the end of these words:* catch, such, match. *Say the words with me. Now raise your hand each time you hear* /ch/: chat, jug, chip, pig, inch, bug, lunch, much, hat, catch.

2. **Associate Sounds and Symbols**
   Point to the chin on **Transparency 19.** Say: *This is a chin. Say the word* chin *with me.* Then point to the *ch* in *chin* and say: *The letters* ch *make the first sound you hear in* chin. *The first sound is* /ch/. *Say* /ch/ *with me:* /ch/. Point to *ch* and ask: *What are the letters? What sound do they make?* Repeat for *match*, pointing out that the three letters *tch* make the last sound in *match*.

3. **Blend Sounds to Read Words**
   Model/Teach Point to the letters *ch* in *chin* and say: *The sound for the letters* ch *is:* /ch/. *Repeat for* i: /iii/. *As you slide your finger below* chi, *say:* I can blend the two sounds: /chiii/. *Then point to the* n *and say:* The sound for n is: /nnn/. I can blend the three sounds together: /chiiinnn/. Now I'm going to say the whole word: chin. Repeat for *match*, reminding students that the letters *tch* make the sound /ch/. Lead students in blending the sounds and then saying the words *chin* and *match*.

   Practice For Item 1, say: *Let's try that again. This picture shows a batch of buns.* Read aloud the words, pausing for students to decode *batch* and *buns*. Then say: *Now let's read all the words again:* a batch of buns. Repeat for the other items, calling attention to the following:

   • In Item 2, blend *inch* with students and say: *In this word,* n *comes before* ch. *We blended* /n/ *with* /ch/: /iiinnnch/, inch. Repeat for *lunch* and *punch* in Item 3.

   • In Item 4, blend *stretch* with students and say: *When we read* stretch, *we blended three consonants,* s, t, *and* r, *at the beginning:* /str/.

OBJECTIVES

Learning to Read: Build Oral Vocabulary; Develop Phonemic Awareness; 🅣 Associate Sounds and Symbols: /ch/ *ch, tch;* Blend Sounds to Decode Words

TEACH *ch* AND *tch*

1. **Build Oral Vocabulary** Display Transparency 19. Talk through each picture to develop meaning for the words in the yellow boxes. For example, say:

   • Item 1: *Here is a* **bun** *(point to one). There are several* **buns** *in this* **batch**, *or group.*

   • Item 4: *This baseball player can* **pitch**, *or throw (pantomime pitching), the ball.*

2. **Develop Phonemic Awareness** Remove the transparency and conduct the oral activities in Step 1 of the Script for Transparency 19.

3. **Read Words with *ch* and *tch*** Display Transparency 19 again. Work through Steps 2 and 3 of the script.

CLOSE AND ASSESS

Display the words *inch, chin, pitch, catch,* and *much.* Call on students to blend a word and to identify the letters that spell the sound /ch/.

Language and Literacy **T64d**

UNIT 2 LESSON 10

LANGUAGE AND LITERACY: READING AND SPELLING

OBJECTIVES

Functions: Listen Actively; Repeat Spoken Language; Recite

Learning to Read:
Develop Phonemic Awareness;
🅣 Associate Sounds and Symbols: /i/ *i*, /u/ *u*, /ch/ *ch*, *tch*;
Blend Sounds to Decode Words

Spelling: 🅣 Words with Short *i*, Short *u*, *ch*, and *tch*

LISTEN AND LEARN

Tape 1B / CD 1 Track 8

1. **Sing a Song** Display Transparency 20 and play "Ice Cream" on the **Language Tape/CD.** After students have listened and learned the song, they can sing as they pantomime filling a cup with ice cream and wiping their chin.

DEVELOP PHONEMIC AWARENESS

2. **Blend Onset and Rime** Give the onset and rime for each word below, for example: /sss/-/it/. Have students blend and tell you the word: /sssiiit/, *sit*.

sit	fill	chin	catch
cup	big	punch	match
bus	nut	chick	pitch

CONNECT SOUNDS AND LETTERS

3. **Associate /i/ *i*, /u/ *u*, and /ch/ *ch*, *tch*** Identify the first picture and help students sound out its name. Say: *Find the cup, and look at the word. Let's point to each letter and say its sound:* /k/, /uuu/, /p/, *cup*. Repeat for the other pictures, pointing out that the two letters *ch* in *chin* make only one sound: /ch/. Then read the question aloud: *How many sounds does each word have?* Call on a student to read aloud each word and have the group count the number of sounds.

Afterwards, play the song again. Have students identify words with short *i*, short *u*, and /ch/.

T64 Unit 2 | Set the Table

WORDS WITH SHORT *I*, SHORT *U*, *CH*, AND *TCH*

Reading and Spelling

LISTEN AND LEARN 🎧

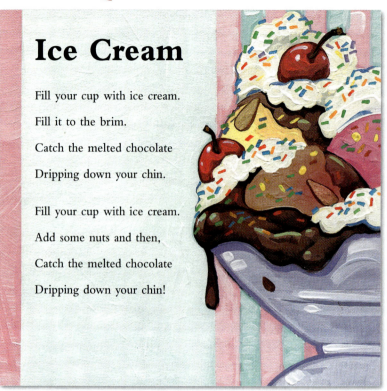

Ice Cream

Fill your cup with ice cream.
Fill it to the brim.
Catch the melted chocolate
Dripping down your chin.

Fill your cup with ice cream.
Add some nuts and then,
Catch the melted chocolate
Dripping down your chin!

CONNECT SOUNDS AND LETTERS

How many sounds does each word have?

three: /k/ /u/ /p/

c**u**p

three: /n/ /u/ /t/

n**u**t

three: /l/ /i/ /d/

l**i**d

three: /ch/ /i/ /n/

ch**i**n

64 Unit 2 | Set the Table ▶ Transparencies 16–2

REACHING ALL STUDENTS

Multi-Level Strategies

LITERACY SUPPORT

LITERATE IN L1 Students who read Chinese or another ideographic language look for the gestalt of the picture rather than blending sounds in a left-to-right sequence. Some languages, such as Arabic, are alphabetic with blendable sounds, but are read from right to left. In Thai, letters are not written from left to right; instead, vowels appear over, under, and around consonants. Students from these language groups need to establish the habit of saying sounds in left-to-right sequence. Provide practice exercises like these:

- Write words whose meanings are known on every other line of ruled paper. Have students put a dot under the first letter and then draw a loop to the next letter as they say the sounds in sequence.

- To encourage blending sounds to the end of the word, use letter tiles to set up minimal pairs of pictureable items on the overhead, for example: *pit* and *pin* or *bun* and *bug*. Have students blend the sounds and illustrate each word.

READING STRATEGY

Follow these steps to read a word.

① Point to the letters **ch**. Say the sound.

② Point to the next letter. Say the sound.

③ Point to the last letter. Say the sound.

④ Now blend all the sounds together to say the word. Say the word again. What is it?

ch + i + n = chin

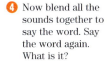

The letters **ch** make one sound. I blend 3 sounds to say **chin**.

READING AND SPELLING PRACTICE

Blend the sounds to read these words.

1. chin   2. cup   3. can   4. catch   5. jumps   6. bug

Use what you learned to read the sentences.

7. There is something in my cup.
8. I can see it move.
9. It is small and green.
10. It jumps up and lands on my hand.
11. Now the bug is on my chin!
12. Can I catch it? No!

13.–16. Now write the sentences that your teacher reads.   *For dictation sentences, see Step 6 at right.*

WORD WORK

Look at the first picture. Then read the word. Use letter cards to make a new word for the next picture.

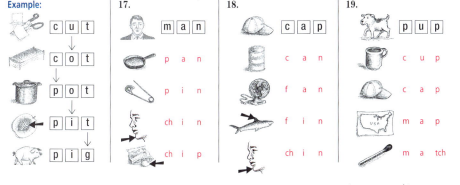

Language and Literacy 65

Decodable Book

PRACTICE WITH SHORT *I*, SHORT *U*, *CH*, AND *TCH*

Decodable Book 2: *Pop!*

Assign **Decodable Book 2** for independent reading. The **Decodable Book** can be used in a variety of ways to help students become more fluent, automatic readers:

Discussion Circles Have students work in small groups to read aloud and discuss the book using the questions on the back cover. Encourage students to read aloud the text that supports their answers. Groups can also work together to complete the Word Work Activity.

Readers Theater Students can read aloud the stories in a class performance. Help them prepare by rereading the stories in daily rehearsals. Work with students to add narration or dialog. Encourage them to use natural phrasing and expression.

Rereading at Home Have students work with family members to reread the book at home. They can take turns reading aloud alternate pages, then rereading the book switching the pages each person reads.

LEARN A READING STRATEGY

4 Sound Out Words Write *chin* and model the blending strategy. Show how to say one sound for *ch* and blend it with the other sounds: /chiiin/. Then say the whole word quickly: *chin*. Slide your finger under the letters again and ask students to say the sounds with you and then to say the whole word quickly.

Read steps 1–3 aloud to summarize the blending process you have shown. For step 4, have students try out the strategy on their own. As they slide a finger under the letters, they should hold each sound without pausing. After blending the sounds, they should say the whole word quickly.

PRACTICE

5 Read Words and Sentences Sound out the words in Items 1–6 as a choral reading. Then distribute the Partner Prompts from page T311 to guide peers in reading the sentences in Items 7–12. Remind them to read words using the sound-out strategy and to read words such as *there* and *something* as whole words.

6 Write Sentences Dictate the following sentences. Read each sentence at normal speed once so students can listen, and then repeat it slowly word by word as they write:

13. The lid is big.
14. The pup can run.
15. The chips are for lunch.
16. I can pitch and catch.

7 Conduct "Word Work" Read the directions and work through the Example. Then have partners complete Items 17–19. To help students check their answers, use letter tiles to build the words on an overhead projector.

▶ **Reading Practice Book** pages 115–118 (Decodable Book 2)

CLOSE AND ASSESS

Across the board, write the first word from each set in Word Work. Work through each set, saying the next picture name. Students should come up to erase the letter that changes and write the new letter.

Language and Literacy **T65**

UNIT 2 LESSON 11

LANGUAGE AND LITERACY: INDEPENDENT READING

OBJECTIVES

Function: Read a Selection

Learning to Read:
- Recognize High Frequency Words;
- Decode Words (short *i*, short *u*, *ch*, and *tch*)

Reading Strategies:
Set a Purpose for Reading; Retell

Critical Thinking and Comprehension:
Identify Steps in a Process

READ ON YOUR OWN

1. **Introduce Vocabulary** In the story, students apply the phonics skills and read high frequency words taught in Lessons 8–10. Introduce these story words. Write each word, say it, and spell it. Then give a definition and context sentence.

   - **cooks:** prepares food by heating it. *Dad cooks dinner every night.*
   - **onions, mustard:** An onion is a type of vegetable. Mustard is a yellow spread. *I like mustard and onions on my hot dogs.*
   - **pours:** tips a container to make a liquid flow into another container. *I pour milk from a carton into a glass.*

2. **Set Purposes** Point out the girl in the photo. Say: *This is Kim.* Ask: *What is Kim doing?* (eating with a friend) Say: *Read the story to find out what Kim makes for lunch.*

3. **Read and Think: Identify Steps in a Process** Students should read the passage on their own. Have them use the chain to retell the story to a partner.

4. **Build Reading Fluency** Use the **Language Tape/CD** with Reading Practice Book page 45 for fluency practice. *Tape 1B / CD 1 Track 9*

▶ **Reading Practice Book** page 45

CLOSE AND ASSESS

Students can retell the steps Kim took to make lunch and eat with her friend.

T66 Unit 2 | Set the Table

COMPREHENSION: IDENTIFY STEPS IN A PROCESS

Read on Your Own

Kim likes hot dogs for lunch.
She cooks a batch of hot dogs in a big pot.
Next Kim chops some small onions.
She opens a large bag of buns.
She fills the buns with hot dogs, mustard, and onions.
She opens a bag of chips, too.
She pours a cup of punch.
This is too much food to eat!
Kim calls Mitch.
Then they sit and eat a great lunch!

✓ **DECODING CHECK**
Give the Decoding Progress Check on page 1a of the Assessment Handbook.

CHECK YOUR UNDERSTANDING

Tell the story to your partner. Use the words and pictures.

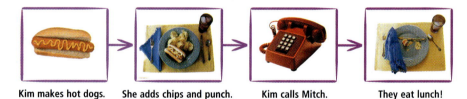

Kim makes hot dogs. → She adds chips and punch. → Kim calls Mitch. → They eat lunch!

66 Unit 2 | Set the Table

REACHING ALL STUDENTS

Reading Fluency
PHRASING

Read the introduction on **Reading Practice Book** page 45. Explain that the / in the examples shows where a reader pauses. Read the examples aloud, pausing at each /. Explain that the words between pauses go together as a group. Then lead the group in a choral reading of the two example sentences.

Next, play "Something Good for Lunch" on the **Language Tape/CD** and have students mark the sentences to show where the pauses occur. Check marks as a whole class before partners do the Practice section.

Reading Practice Book page 45

NEGATIVE SENTENCES
I Am Not a Cook!

A negative sentence has a negative word, like **not**.

The cake is **not** right.

The cookies are **not** good.

The kitchen is **not** clean.

I am **not** happy.

BUILD SENTENCES

Look at each picture below. Add a verb and the word *not* to complete each sentence. Say the new sentence.

Example: 1. The burrito is not green.

1.
The burrito _is_ _not_ green.

2.
The limes _are_ _not_ square.

3.
The watermelon _is_ _not_ thin.

4.
The crackers _are_ _not_ blue.

5.
The kiwi _is_ _not_ triangular.

6.
I _am_ _not_ a nurse.

WRITE SENTENCES

7.–12. Work with a partner. For each picture, write a new negative sentence. Use *is not* or *are not*.

Example: 7. The burrito is not purple.

Sample Responses
Students could use color, shape, and size words that do not describe each food in Items 1–5.
The limes are not triangular.
Students could use the name of another career for Item 6.
I am not a teacher.

Language and Literacy 67

Language Practice Book page 49

Language Development
NEGATIVE SENTENCES

Organize students for Think-Pair-Share (see Cooperative Learning Structures, page T337d). Write a list of false sentences about things in the room; for example:

  The teacher's desk is round.
  There are four windows in the room.
  Genya's sweater is blue.

Read a false sentence and model how to correct the statement by adding the word *not*: *The teacher's desk is not round.* Then have partners work together to correct the remaining sentences and read each resulting sentence aloud.

UNIT 2 **LESSON 12**

LANGUAGE AND LITERACY: NEGATIVE SENTENCES

OBJECTIVES

Function: Describe; Write
Concepts and Vocabulary:
T Foods; T Colors, Shapes, and Sizes
Patterns and Structures:
T Negative Sentences;
T Present Tense Verbs (*am, is, are*)
Writing: T Sentences

INTRODUCE

1 Learn About Negative Sentences
Read the title and introduction. Direct students' attention to the picture and read the examples aloud. Then ask each of the following questions and have students read or point to the example sentence that answers it: *Is the cake right? Are the cookies good?*

Reread each example. Have a volunteer say or point out the word that makes it a negative sentence. (*not*)

PRACTICE

2 Build Sentences Explain that students should add *am, is,* or *are,* and the word *not,* to complete each sentence. After modeling the Example, have partners do Items 2–6.

APPLY

3 Write Sentences Go over the Example and have volunteers suggest other negative sentences about the burrito. Write the sentences and call on students to underline the verb and circle the word *not* in each sentence.

Partners can work together to write sentences for Items 7–12. Encourage students to look back at the color and shape vocabulary on page 59 for adjectives to use in their sentences.

▶ **Language Practice Book** page 49

CLOSE AND ASSESS

Ask volunteers to read aloud a negative sentence. Write each sentence, replacing the verb and *not* with blanks. Then have students complete the sentences.

Language and Literacy **T67**

UNIT 2 **LESSON 13**

LANGUAGE ACROSS THE CURRICULUM: SCIENCE

OBJECTIVES

Function: Follow Directions
Concepts and Vocabulary:
- Foods; Food Groups

Research Skills and Learning Strategies:
Gather Information;
Use Graphic Organizers (list)

Critical Thinking and Comprehension:
Classify; Analyze Information;
Draw Conclusions

LEARN ABOUT FOOD GROUPS

1. **Explore Classifying** Read the introduction and have students sort objects such as writing tools and various fasteners. Discuss why the objects form a group, or category.

2. **Introduce Food Groups** Have students identify the foods in the photos. Then read the names of the food groups and the list of vegetables. Explain: *The chart shows one way to classify foods into groups. The list shows examples from the vegetable group.*

CONDUCT THE INVESTIGATION

3. **Gather Data** To help students calculate servings, display this chart and show samples of the cup and ounce measure:

```
1 serving = 1 slice of bread
            1 ounce of cereal
            1/2 cup rice or pasta
            1 cup vegetables
            1 apple or orange
            1 cup milk or yogurt
            2–3 ounces cooked meat
```

CHECK UNDERSTANDING

4. **Respond to "Think It Over"** Remind students to answer each question based on the results of the investigation.

CLOSE AND ASSESS

Have students complete the following sentence frames:

I eat many foods from the _____ group. I need to eat less food from the _____ group.

T68 Unit 2 | Set the Table

SUCCESS IN SCIENCE

Learn About Food Groups

CLASSIFICATION

When you **classify**, you put things in **categories**, or **groups**.

Study the food pyramid. Then do the activity.

What Kinds of Foods Do You Eat?

You will need: a notebook and a pencil

ACTIVITY STEPS

1. **Make a List**
Write all the foods you ate yesterday.

2. **Put the Foods in Groups**
Classify the foods on your list. Use the 6 food groups you learned about.

3. **Count the Servings**
Draw the food pyramid. Next to each group, write the number of servings you ate.
Use the chart at the left to help students calculate the number of servings they ate from each group.

THINK IT OVER

1. Look at the food pyramid you drew. From which food group did you eat the most servings?
2. Do you need to eat more from some groups? Which ones?
3. Do you need to eat less from some groups? Which ones?

Sample Responses for the Think It Over
Individual responses will vary. If the numbers of servings a student ate does not match the recommendations in the food pyramid, have the students identify foods to add or substitute in order to match the recommendations.

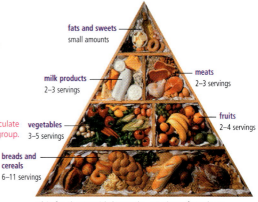

This food pyramid shows the number of servings you should eat each day. Eat more of the foods from the bottom of the pyramid. Eat fewer foods from the top.

68 Unit 2 | Set the Table

REACHING ALL STUDENTS

COMMUNITY CONNECTION

Special Foods Field Trip Visit local supermarkets or collect advertisement flyers from a variety of grocery stores and ethnic markets in your area. Have small groups draw pictures or cut out photographs of different foods. Affix the pictures to separate index cards with a label to identify each food.

Set up a bulletin board with a label for each of the six food categories. Encourage each small group to sort their food cards into the correct categories. Compare results and discuss any differences in classification.

Writing Project / Exhibit Card

✓ **WRITING ASSESSMENT** Use the Writing Progress Checklist on page 51 of the Assessment Handbook to evaluate this writing project.

Use food to make a piece of art. Write a card to tell how you make it. Then have an art show with your class!

CHOOSE YOUR DESIGN
Think of art you can make with food. Choose one.

- boat made of melon
- face made of fruits and vegetables
- octopus made of a banana

MAKE AND DESCRIBE YOUR ART

1. Get or draw the food you need. Build your piece of art.
2. Write your card. Tell how you make the art. Use adjectives to describe the foods. Check pages 310–311 of your Handbook for adjectives to use.
3. Work with a partner to check your work.

I pick a long yellow banana. I cut the peel into 8 long, thin strips. I add little black and white beans for eyes.

✓ Check Your Work
- Did you include all the steps?
- Did you use adjectives to describe the foods you used?
- Does each sentence begin with a capital letter and end in a period?

HAVE AN ART SHOW
Take a tour of the class art show. Read about your classmates' art. Tell which pieces you like the most.

Language Across the Curriculum **69**

Language Practice Book page 50

WRITING PROJECT: EXHIBIT CARD
Good Enough to Eat!
Tell your class how to make art with food. Draw a picture of the art you make. Then write a card. Follow these steps.

1. Draw a picture of your art.
2. Tell what your art is. Tell how you make it. Name each food. Describe the color, size, or shape. Tell the steps in order.

Picture

My art shows _____
I use _____
I cut _____
I add _____

Have a partner read your description. Did you tell all the steps? Show your art and your card to the class.

Multi-Level Strategies
WRITING SUPPORT

PRELITERATE Provide a writing frame to help students with their descriptions. Work with them to fill in the blanks.

My art shows ___(design)___.
I use ___(food)___ for ___(part)___.
Then I add ___(food)___ for ___(part)___.

Suggest adjectives students can add to describe each food, then help them copy the expanded descriptions onto a card for display with their art.

UNIT 2 LESSON 14

LANGUAGE ACROSS THE CURRICULUM: WRITING

OBJECTIVES
Functions: Write; Describe
Learning Strategies and Critical Thinking: Plan; Generate and Organize Ideas; Self-Assess
Writing: ❶ Exhibit Card (Description)

CONDUCT THE WRITING PROJECT

1. **Explore Food Art and How-To Directions** To help students understand the project, review the "funny food" activity on pages 56 and 57, and the how-to text on pages 61–63.

2. **Choose Your Design** Have students brainstorm different foods and what each food can represent. Chart the ideas:

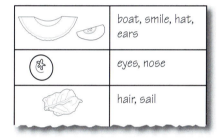

(melon)	boat, smile, hat, ears
(olive)	eyes, nose
(leaf)	hair, sail

3. **Make and Describe Your Art** After students make their art, go over the sample student description below the octopus as a model for students' writing.

4. **Have an Art Show** Display students' art with the cards, as in a museum exhibit. Have student judges present awards for creative art and thorough descriptions.

▶ **Language Practice Book** page 50

CLOSE AND ASSESS

Have students look at the descriptions they wrote. Say:
- *Show me the sentence that tells the first (last) step in your project.*
- *Read me some of the adjectives you used to describe your art.*
- *Show me a capital letter at the beginning of a sentence and a period at the end.*

Language Across the Curriculum **T69**

Resources

For Success in Language and Literacy

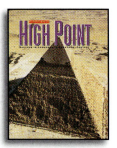

Student Book pages 70–83

For Language Skills Practice

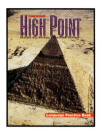

Language Practice Book pages 51–55

For Reading Skills Practice

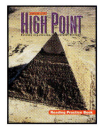

Reading Practice Book pages 46–49

For Vocabulary, Language Development, and Reading Fluency

Language Tape 2, Side A
Language CD 1, Tracks 10–13

For Reading Together

Theme Book *What Is It?* from The Basics Bookshelf

For Audio Walk-Throughs and Selection Readings

Selection Tape 2A
Selection CD 1, Tracks 5–6

For Phonics Instruction

Transparencies 21–25

Transparency Scripts 21–25

Letter Tiles

For Comprehensive Assessment

Language Acquisition Assessment, Units 1–3 Test, Writing Assessment, Self-Assessment

For Planning and Instruction

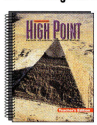

Teacher's Edition
pages T70a–T83

Unit Planner

UNIT 3

ON THE JOB

In This Unit

Vocabulary
- Actions
- Tools and Careers
- Science and Measurement Words

Language Functions
- Give Information
- Ask and Answer Questions

Patterns and Structures
- Present Tense Verbs
- Yes-or-No Questions
- Questions with *Who?*, *What?*, *Where?*, and *When?*

Reading
- Phonics: Short *e*, *sh*, *ck*, and Double Consonants
- Comprehension: Identify Details (concept web)

Writing
- Sentences
- Questions and Answers
- Job Handbook

Content Area Connection
- Science (scientific processes) and Mathematics (measurement)

UNIT 3

Activity and Assessment Planner

UNIT 3: On the Job

LESSONS

1

UNIT 3 LAUNCH
▶ *pages T70–T71*

LESSON 1: INTRODUCE UNIT 3 pages T70–T71

Vocabulary
T Careers; Tools

Viewing
Interpret a Visual Image

Learning Strategies
Preview

Build Background

Critical Thinking
Generate Ideas

2–5

LANGUAGE DEVELOPMENT
▶ *pages T72–T75*

LESSON 2
CAREERS AND ACTIONS
page T72

Function
Give Information

Vocabulary
T Careers; Actions

Patterns and Structures
T Present Tense Action Verbs

Writing
Labels

LESSON 3
PRESENT TENSE VERBS
page T73

Function
Give Information

Patterns and Structures
T Present Tense Action Verbs

Writing
T Sentences

LESSON 4
YES-OR-NO QUESTIONS
page T74

Function
Ask/Answer Questions

Patterns and Structures
T Yes-or-No Questions

T Pronouns

Writing
Questions

LESSON 5
TOOLS AND CAREERS
page T75

Functions
Ask/Answer Questions

Give Information

Vocabulary
T Careers; Tools

Patterns and Structures
T Yes-or-No Questions

Writing
Answers

6–12

LANGUAGE AND LITERACY
▶ *pages T76a–T81*

LESSON 6
BASICS BOOKSHELF
pages T76a–T76d

Function
Listen to a Book

Vocabulary
T Careers; Actions

Reading Strategies
Activate Prior Knowledge

Preview

Learning to Read
Track Print

Identify Capital Letters

Predict Words

Critical Thinking and Comprehension
T Identify Details

LESSON 7
BASICS BOOKSHELF: COMPREHENSION
page T76

Function
Retell a Story

Learning Strategy
Use Graphic Organizers (concept web)

Critical Thinking and Comprehension
T Identify Details

LESSON 8
HIGH FREQUENCY WORDS
page T77

Learning to Read
T Recognize High Frequency Words

LESSON 9
PHONICS
pages T78a–T78d

Learning to Read
Build Oral Vocabulary

Develop Phonemic Awareness

T Associate Sounds and Symbols: /e/ e; /l/ ll, /s/ ss, /z/ zz, /k/ ck; /sh/ sh; phonograms -et, -en, -ed

Blend Sounds to Decode Words

LESSON 10
READING AND SPELLING
pages T78–T79

Learning to Read
Develop Phonemic Awareness

T Associate Sounds and Symbols: /e/ e; /l/ ll, /s/ ss, /z/ zz, /k/ ck; /sh/ sh

Blend Sounds to Decode Words

Spelling
T Words with Short e, Final ll, ss, zz, ck, Digraph sh

LESSON 11
INDEPENDENT READING
page T80

Function
Read a Selection

Learning to Read
T Recognize High Frequency Words

T Decode Words (short e; final ll, ss, zz, ck; sh)

Reading Strategies
Predict

Set a Purpose for Reading

Retell

Critical Thinking and Comprehension
T Identify Details

LESSON 12
QUESTIONS
page T81

Functions
Ask and Answer Questions

Write

Patterns and Structures
Questions with *Who?*, *What?*, *Where?*, and *When?*

Writing
Questions and Answers

13–14

LANGUAGE ACROSS THE CURRICULUM
▶ *pages T82–T83*

LESSON 13
SCIENCE/MATH: MEASUREMENT
page T82

Functions
Describe

Give Information

Follow Directions

Vocabulary
Science Processes

Measurement Words

Research Skills and Learning Strategies
Make Observations

Gather Information

Use Graphic Organizers (observation log)

Critical Thinking and Comprehension
Make Comparisons

Classify

Analyze Information

Draw Conclusions

LESSON 14
WRITING PROJECT: JOB HANDBOOK
page T83

Functions
Ask and Answer Questions

Write

Listening and Speaking
Interview

Learning Strategies and Critical Thinking
Plan

Generate and Organize Ideas

Self-Assess

Research Skills
Conduct an Interview

Writing
Job Handbook

T70c Unit 3 | On the Job

T = Objective Tested on Unit Test

ASSESSMENT OPTIONS

The **Teacher's Edition** and the **Assessment Handbook** include these comprehensive assessment tools:

▶ **Ongoing, Informal Assessment**
Check for understanding and achieve closure for every lesson with the targeted questions and activities in the **Close and Assess** boxes in your Teacher's Edition.

▶ **Decoding Progress Check**
These word lists for each unit provide a quick way to check on mastery of the phonics or word structure skills taught in the unit.

▶ **Language Acquisition Assessments**
To verify students' ability to use the language functions and grammar structures taught in Units 1–3, conduct these performance assessments.

▶ **Unit Test in Standardized Test Format**
This multiple-choice test measures students' cumulative understanding of the skills and language developed in Units 1–3.

▶ **Self-and Peer-Assessment**
Students use the Self-Assessment Form to evaluate their own work and develop learning strategies appropriate to their needs. Students offer feedback to their classmates with the Peer-Assessment Form.

▶ **Writing Assessment/Portfolio Opportunities**
You can evaluate students' writing in the Writing Projects using the Writing Progress Checklist. Then collaborate with students to choose work for their portfolios.

UNITS 1–3 ASSESSMENT OPPORTUNITIES

	Assessment Handbook Pages
Decoding Progress Check	1a
Language Acquisition Assessments	2
Units 1–3 Test	3–8
Self-Assessment Form	9
Peer-Assessment Form	50
Writing Progress Checklist	51
Portfolio Evaluation Form	52

RELATED RESOURCES

How a House Is Built
by Gail Gibbons
Text and illustrations show the steps in building a house and describe the contributions of many different kinds of workers. (Holiday House)
Theme Book: Read Aloud

Tools
by Ann Morris
Photos from around the world show the many ways in which tools help us in our daily lives. (Available from Hampton-Brown)
Easy Reading;
Phonics Reinforcement: Short Vowels

Tools
by Ken Robbins
Color-tinted photos are labeled with the names of common tools such as *paintbrush, chisel, wrench, level,* and *trowel.* (Four Winds)
Vocabulary: Tools

An Auto Mechanic
by Douglas Florian
Describes the tools and duties of an auto mechanic in simple language. Part of a series that includes *A Fisher, A Chef,* and *A Carpenter.* (Greenwillow)
Language Development:
Present Tense Verbs

Tool Box
by Gail Gibbons
Simple text and illustrations identify different tools and the actions they perform. (Holiday)
Vocabulary: Tools and Actions

Unit Planner **T70d**

UNIT 3 LESSON 1

INTRODUCE UNIT 3: ON THE JOB

OBJECTIVES

Concepts and Vocabulary: Tools; T Careers
Viewing: Interpret a Visual Image
Learning Strategies: Preview; Build Background
Critical Thinking: Generate ideas
Representing: Illustrations

START WITH A COMMON EXPERIENCE

1. **Introduce "On the Job"** Read the unit title and say: *When people are on the job, they are at work.* Point out the man with the food cart and explain that his job is to sell food. Ask volunteers to name, describe, or pantomime other familiar jobs in the picture.

2. **Match Tools and Workers** Read the activity directions on page 71. Model drawing and naming one tool, such as a paint roller. Pantomime its use. Then have a volunteer point out the matching worker (painter, bottom left). Say: *The painter uses this tool.*

   Have partners draw several tools on separate index cards. Students can then exchange cards with another group and match the tool cards to the appropriate worker in the collage.

3. **Create a Chart** Invite volunteers to show their drawings. Help name each tool and worker. Label and display the cards on a chart.

Worker	Tool
police officer	radio
ballet dancer	dance shoes

Use the chart to build sentences with this pattern: *The _____ uses _____.* For example: The police officer uses a radio.

T70 Unit 3 | On the Job

REACHING ALL STUDENTS

HOME CONNECTION

Tool Cards Students can take home their drawings to share what they learned about workers and tools. Have students talk with family members about their jobs, and draw tools they use at work. Encourage students to bring the cards back to share with the class. As a group, name the tools and talk about the corresponding jobs.

ON THE JOB

Careers and Tools
Moving left to right and top to bottom, the careers in this picture are as follows. A tool (not always shown) is listed for each career:

clerk, cash register
artist, paint brush
plumber, wrench
business person, computer
emergency dispatcher, telephone
telemarketer, telephone
welder, face mask
telephone sales person, telephone
veterinarian, stethoscope
fire fighter, fire hose
doctor, stethoscope
bookstore sales clerk, books

camera operator, camera
stylist, hair dryer
chef, pan
baker, cooking pans
journalist, computer
computer designer, computer
fish market sales person, fish
postal worker, mail
caterer, plate of food
barber, scissors or clippers
seamstress, needle and thread

window cleaner, bucket
construction worker, drill
doorman, uniform
ballerina, ballet shoes
painter, roller
farmer, pitchfork
surveyor, surveying equipment
cab driver, taxi cab
construction worker, hard hat
hot dog vendor, cart
violinist, violin

Work with a partner. Look at the picture.
What workers do you see?
Draw tools they use. Trade drawings.
Match the drawings to the correct workers.

In This Unit

Vocabulary
- Actions
- Tools and Careers
- Science and Measurement Words

Language Functions
- Give Information
- Ask and Answer Questions

Patterns and Structures
- Present Tense Verbs
- Yes-or-No Questions
- Questions with *Who?*, *What?*, *Where?*, and *When?*

Reading
- Phonics: Short *e*, *sh*, *ck*, and Double Consonants
- Comprehension: Identify Details (concept web)

Writing
- Sentences
- Questions and Answers
- Job Handbook

Content Area Connection
- Science (scientific processes) and Mathematics (measurement)

71

PREVIEW THE UNIT

4 Look for Activities and Information About Careers Leaf through the unit, previewing activities students will do, for example:

page 72—learning a song about different jobs

pages 73–75—reading about different jobs and the tools that people use

page 76—listening to the Bookshelf book (Display a copy of the book.)

page 83—making a job handbook

Also ask students to look at the pictures in the unit to see some of the different jobs and tools. Help students name what they see in each picture. Then sum up what the preview reveals: *People have many different jobs and use many tools in their work.*

5 Set Your Goals Start a class mind map on workers, jobs, and tools, beginning with jobs at school. Prompt students for pictures or words to add, and have them act out and describe other ideas for you to put into words. Talk together about what they want to learn about jobs in this unit.

CLOSE AND ASSESS

Ask students to tell or show you something they are interested in learning in this unit.

UNIT 3 Mind Map

Worker	Job	Tools
teacher	teach, help students, grade papers	books, paper, pens, pencils, overhead projector
school nurse	help sick people at school	stethoscope, bandages

Technology Support
See **Inspiration** Visual Learning software for support in creating the mind maps.

Unit Launch **T71**

UNIT 3 LESSON 2
LANGUAGE DEVELOPMENT: CAREERS AND ACTIONS

OBJECTIVES
Functions: Listen Actively; Repeat Spoken Language; Recite; Give Information
Concepts and Vocabulary:
- Careers; Actions

Patterns and Structures:
- Present Tense Action Verbs

Writing: Labels

INTRODUCE

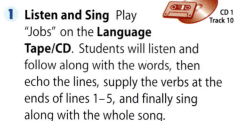

1. **Listen and Sing** Play "Jobs" on the **Language Tape/CD**. Students will listen and follow along with the words, then echo the lines, supply the verbs at the ends of lines 1–5, and finally sing along with the whole song.

2. **Learn About Action Words and Careers** Read aloud the chart of careers and actions and ask students to find examples in the song. To ensure understanding, have students find the pictures and labels that match the words in the chart.

PRACTICE

3. **Conduct "Express Yourself"** Model how to give information. Then have partners complete the activity.

> **How to Give Information**
> - Name some workers: *Artists*
> - Tell what actions the workers do: *Artists paint and draw.*

APPLY

4. **Write Labels** Encourage partners to share their drawings and check the labels they wrote. Distribute Partner Checklist 3 on page T310.

▶ **Language Practice Book** page 51

CLOSE AND ASSESS
Form two teams. One team names a worker and the other team tells what the worker does. Then teams switch roles. Students can use the chant and pictures for ideas, or name other careers and actions.

T72 Unit 3 | On the Job

VOCABULARY: ACTIONS/CAREERS

What Is the Job for Me?

Listen and sing.

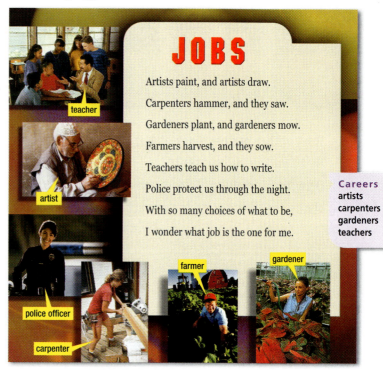

JOBS

Artists paint, and artists draw.
Carpenters hammer, and they saw.
Gardeners plant, and gardeners mow.
Farmers harvest, and they sow.
Teachers teach us how to write.
Police protect us through the night.
With so many choices of what to be,
I wonder what job is the one for me.

Careers	Actions
artists	draw
carpenters	build
gardeners	plant
teachers	teach

EXPRESS YOURSELF ▶ GIVE INFORMATION

1.–3. Work with a partner. Choose 3 jobs. Tell what the workers do.

Example: 1. Artists paint and draw.

WRITE LABELS

4. Draw a picture of a worker. Label your drawing.

Example: 4.

72 Unit 3 | On the Job

REACHING ALL STUDENTS

Vocabulary
ACTIONS, TOOLS, CAREERS

Charades Gather the labeled pictures of workers that students made and fan them out, face down. Have volunteers take a card and act it out for others to guess. Encourage students to guess the worker, what the worker does, and what tools the worker uses. Restate students' guesses as necessary, in sentences like the following: *You are a gardener. Gardeners plant seeds. Gardeners use hoses.*

Language Practice Book page 51

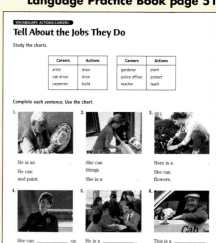

PRESENT TENSE VERBS

People in Action

To tell what another person or thing does, use a **verb** that ends in **-s**.

The carpenter **builds** a box.

He **uses** glue.

It **holds** the sides together.

His son **helps**.

BUILD SENTENCES

Say each sentence. Add the correct form of the action verb.   Example: 1. He mops the floor.

1. He <u>mops</u> the floor. (**mop**)

2.  She <u>waters</u> the plants. (**water**)

3.  She <u>sells</u> newspapers. (**sell**)

4.  It <u>cleans</u> the clothes. (**clean**)

5.  He <u>runs</u> . (**run**)

6.  She <u>reports</u> the news. (**report**)

WRITE SENTENCES ✎

7.–10. Think of a worker. Act out what the worker does. Have your partner guess the worker and write 4 sentences about his or her job.

Example: 7. The gardener pulls the weeds.

Language Development **73**

Language Practice Book page 52

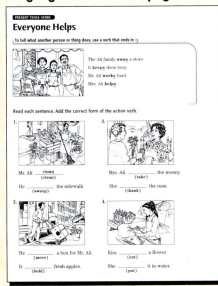

Multi-Level Strategies
LANGUAGE DEVELOPMENT

LITERATE IN L1 Speakers of Korean and Chinese, for example, may have difficulty with verbs in third person, which are not marked for person or number in their language. Sample errors: *He get book. She have chair.* Hindi speakers may use third person plural to show respect: *The teacher have pencil.*

Provide practice using verbs in third person by having students pantomime actions for others to describe: *They play golf. She rides a horse.*

UNIT 3 **LESSON 3**

LANGUAGE DEVELOPMENT: PRESENT TENSE VERBS

OBJECTIVES
Function: Give Information
Patterns and Structures:
🅣 Present Tense Action Verbs
Writing: 🅣 Sentences

INTRODUCE

1 **Learn About Present Tense Verbs** Read the page title and introduction. Use the photo to build meaning: *This man is a carpenter. His job is to build things. Here he builds a wooden box.*

Read the first example and point to the verb *builds*. Then have students point to the verbs in the other sentences as you read each one aloud. Summarize: *Each verb tells what one person or thing does, so the verb ends in the letter* s.

PRACTICE

2 **Build Sentences** Explain that Items 1–6 each tell what another person or thing does. Work through the Example, pointing out *s* at the end of *mops*. Then have partners complete Items 2–6. Go over the answers together and write the verb forms, underlining *s* in each one. Then have students work in an Inside-Outside Circle (see Cooperative Learning Structures, page T337d) to practice Items 1–6 orally again.

APPLY

3 **Write Sentences** Help students brainstorm a list of workers. Model selecting one worker and acting out four actions the worker does. List each base verb on the board, and invite volunteers to write sentences using the correct form of the verb.

▶ **Language Practice Book** page 52

CLOSE AND ASSESS

Ask students to dictate their sentences as you write on the board. Omit the verbs but give the base form. Ask a volunteer to fill in the correct verb form, and lead the class in reading the sentence.

Language Development **T73**

UNIT 3 LESSON 4
LANGUAGE DEVELOPMENT: YES-OR-NO QUESTIONS

OBJECTIVES
Function: Ask and Answer Questions
Patterns and Structures:
- Yes-or-No Questions; - Pronouns
Writing: Questions

INTRODUCE

1 Learn About Yes-or-No Questions
Read the skill explanation. Form two groups and lead a choral reading of the examples. First, group 1 asks the questions and group 2 answers, then groups reverse roles. For more work on choosing the correct pronoun for answers, display this chart and continue the choral recitations with new questions: *Is our school called [name of school]? Are [two students' names] in class now?*

If the question asks about:	In the answer, use the pronoun:
one thing	it
one boy or man	he
one girl or woman	she
more than one person or thing	they

PRACTICE

2 Answer Questions Work through the Example. For Items 2–6, organize students for Think-Pair-Share (see Cooperative Learning Structures, page T337d). Ask students to think about whether the answer to each question is *yes* or *no*. Then have pairs formulate their answers, using the pronoun chart above. Call on student A or B to share with the group.

APPLY

3 Write Questions Go over the Example, discussing why the question starts with *Is* and why the pronoun is *she*.

CLOSE AND ASSESS
Have volunteers read a question they wrote. Call on students to answer.

T74 Unit 3 | On the Job

YES-OR-NO QUESTIONS

Are They at Work?

Pronunciation of Names
Julia   hü lē ah
Miguel   mē gel

A question asks for information. It ends with a **question mark**.

You can answer some questions with *yes* or *no*.
    Is this the gym? Yes.

When you tell more in your answer, use the correct **pronoun**.
    Is this the gym? Yes, **it** is.
    Are the girls alone? No, **they** are not.
    Can Rob play? Yes, **he** can.

ANSWER QUESTIONS

Look at each picture below. Read the question. Answer it.   **Example:** 1. Yes, she can.

1.
Can the writer use the computer?   Yes, she can.

2.
Is the photographer in an office?   No, she is not.

3.
Are Linda and Brian carpenters?   No, they are not.

4.
Are Dave and Wendy pilots?   Yes, they are.

5.
Can the architect draw?   Yes, he can.

6.
Are Julia and Miguel dancers?   Yes, they are.

WRITE QUESTIONS

7.–12. Write a new question for each picture above. Start each question with *Is*, *Are*, or *Can*. Put a question mark at the end.   **Example:** 7. Is she a writer?

74 Unit 3 | On the Job

REACHING ALL STUDENTS

Multimodal Practice
PRESENT TENSE VERBS

Kinesthetic and Auditory
Ask students to pantomime an action on the page. The group names it: *She runs.* Other students listen for the action verb.

Visual Have this group identify the matching photo and write the action: *He mops the floor.*

VOCABULARY: TOOLS AND CAREERS

Tools of the Trade

Look at the pictures. Read the words.

The Beauty Shop: brush, scissors, stylist, hair dryer, customer

The Garage: tire, wrench, mechanic, mechanic, toolbox, screwdriver

WHO'S TALKING? ▶ ASK AND ANSWER QUESTIONS

1.–2. Listen.
Who is talking? Point to the correct person.
Then act out the scene with a partner.
Ask and answer questions.

Answers:
1. mechanics
2. stylist and customer

WRITE ANSWERS

Look at the pictures above. Ask a partner each question. Write your partner's answer.

Example: 3. Can the stylist cut hair?
Yes, she can.

In the Beauty Shop
3. Can the stylist cut hair? Yes, she can.
4. Is a customer in the chair? Yes, he is.
5. Is the hair dryer in her hand? No, it is not.
6. Are they in a cafeteria? No, they are not.

In the Garage
7. Are they in a garage? Yes, they are.
8. Is she a teacher? No, she is not.
9. Is the wrench in the toolbox? No, it is not.
10. Can they fix the car? Yes, they can.

Language Development 75

Language Practice Book page 53

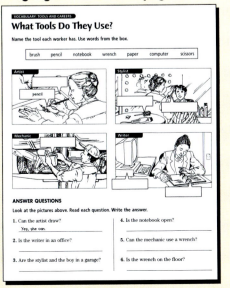

UNIT 3 LESSON 5

LANGUAGE DEVELOPMENT: TOOLS AND CAREERS

OBJECTIVES

Functions: Listen Actively; Ask and Answer Questions; Give Information
Concepts and Vocabulary: Tools; Careers
Patterns and Structures: Yes-or-No Questions
Speaking: Role-Play
Writing: Answers

INTRODUCE

1 Learn Words for Tools and Careers
Discuss each scene and the jobs people do. Explain each label: *A toolbox is a place to keep tools.* Then read the labels out of order and have students point to the correct picture.

2 Take a Quick Quiz Ask students yes-or-no questions using the vocabulary. For example, point to the stylist and ask: *Is she a mechanic?* Guide them in forming a complete answer: *No, she isn't.* Continue: *Is this a hair dryer? Are they mechanics? Can she fix a car?* Ask a mix of yes-or-no questions.

PRACTICE

3 Conduct "Who's Talking?"
Play "Who's Talking?" on the **Language Tape/CD**. Have students listen to a speaker, and then pause the tape and replay it, if necessary, for students to point to the correct person. Assign roles to volunteers and have them act out the scenes, asking and answering questions.

Tape 2A
CD 1 Track 11

APPLY

4 Write Answers Lead students in studying the Example. Remind them to start their written answers with *Yes* or *No*, and help them choose the correct pronouns, as necessary.

▶ **Language Practice Book** page 53

CLOSE AND ASSESS

Ask volunteers to pose an additional question about one of the pictures. Call on students to answer.

Language Development T75

UNIT 3 **LESSON 6**

LANGUAGE AND LITERACY: THE BASICS BOOKSHELF

OBJECTIVES

Concepts and Vocabulary:
🅣 Careers; Actions

Listening: Listen to a Preview

Reading Strategies:
Activate Prior Knowledge; Preview

Learning to Read:
Track Print; Identify Capital Letters

BUILD LANGUAGE AND VOCABULARY

1. **Teach "Words to Know"** Have students look at pages 2–3. Say: *These pages show people doing their jobs. They are all at work.*

    Point to the photos and give the name for each worker. Use description and pantomime to explain each job. For example, act out turning a steering wheel as you say: *A bus driver drives people from one place to another.*

2. **Play "Find the Worker"** Distribute slips of paper with one worker's name on each paper. Say: *This worker sweeps the floor. The worker keeps things clean. Who is it?* The student holding the paper with the word *custodian* should come forward and pantomime sweeping the floor. Then that student asks for another worker. Continue until all jobs have been described.

PREPARE TO READ

3. **Think About What You Know** Point to the astronaut on page 3 and ask students to share what they know about an astronaut's job. Mention the collection of moon rocks and discuss how scientists on Earth study them.

4. **Preview** Play the Audio Walk-Through for *What Is It?* on the **Selection Tape/CD** to give students the overall idea of the story.

   Tape 2A / CD 1 Track 5

CLOSE AND ASSESS

Have students draw a character from the story. Collect the drawings and post them on the wall.

What Is It?
by Shirleyann Costigan

Summary This humorous fantasy tells the adventures of a mysterious moon rock as it meets an astronaut, a scientist, a letter carrier, a museum director, students, teachers, and band members. In time, the moon rock is transformed into a rock star! Simple text reinforces career names and action words.

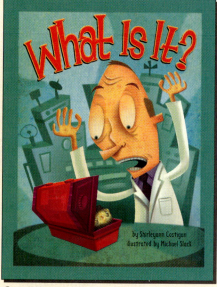
Cover

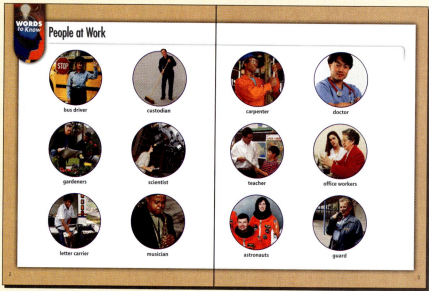
Pages 2–3

Multi-Level Strategies
LITERACY SUPPORT

PRELITERATE **Track Print** Model tracking print correctly. Turn to page 4. Put a finger under the word *The* as you read the word aloud. Point to each word as you continue to read aloud. Repeat for page 5. Then have students point to each word to track the text in their copies as you read the rest of the book aloud.

NON-ROMAN ALPHABET **Concepts of Print: Identify Capital Letters** Students who speak a language such as Chinese will need help understanding that a sentence starts with a capital letter. Display pages 4–5 and read the sentences aloud. Point out the capital *T* at the beginning of each sentence. Then point out the small *t* in the words *astronaut* and *it* to show the contrast. Have students identify the capital letters in the sentences on the rest of the pages. (*T, A, H, W*) For further reinforcement, have students work at the overhead to match letter tiles for these and other capital and lowercase letters.

T76a Unit 3 | On the Job

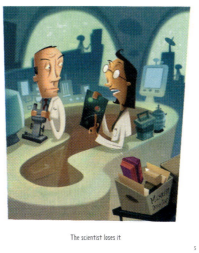

Pages 4–5

Pages 6–7

Strategies for Comprehensible Input

Page	Story Language	Strategy Options
4	astronaut	**Point to the picture and explain:** An astronaut goes into outer space.
	discovers it	**Explain:** She finds it for the first time. No one has seen it before.
5	scientist	**Point to the picture and explain:** A scientist studies things in our world.
	loses it	**Restate:** cannot find it
6	letter carrier	**Point to the picture and explain:** A letter carrier takes mail to different places.
	picks it up	**Demonstrate:** Pick up a book from a table or the floor.
7	drops it off	**Demonstrate:** Put the book down on a student's desk, then walk away.

Language and Literacy T76b

UNIT 3 **LESSON 6,** CONTINUED

LANGUAGE AND LITERACY: THE BASICS BOOKSHELF

OBJECTIVES
Function: Listen to a Book
Critical Thinking and Comprehension:
① Identify Details
Learning to Read:
Track Print; Predict Words

READ AND THINK TOGETHER

1. **Read Aloud** On your first reading of the book, use the "Strategies for Comprehensible Input" that appear at the bottom of page T76b and T76d.

2. **Read and Map: Identify Details** Draw a concept web like the one below, but with empty spaces at the end of each spoke. Say: *A concept web shows words that tell about a topic or answer a question.*

   Read aloud page 4. Then read the question in the center of the web. Think aloud as you model answering the question: *I will write the word* astronaut *because the astronaut is a person in the story.*

   Pause after reading each page shown below and model completing the web for the rest of the text.

3. **Conduct Interactive Readings** Choose from these options:

   - **Read along and track print** Have students work in pairs to read along with the recording of *What Is It?* on the **Selection Tape/CD**.

   - **Predict words** Read the text aloud, but omit a key word or phrase from each sentence. Have students supply the missing word. For example:

     page 4—The ____ discovers it. (astronaut)

     page 5—The ____ loses it. (scientist)

CLOSE AND ASSESS
Have students tell their partners two characters who were in the story.

T76c Unit 3 | On the Job

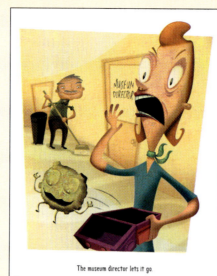
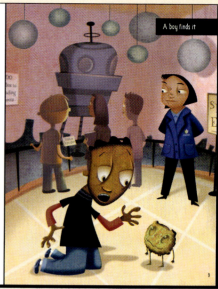

Pages 8–9

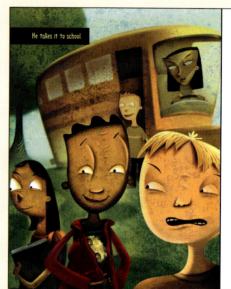

Pages 10–11

Concept Web for *What Is It?*

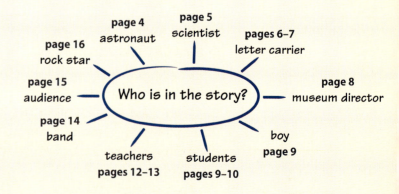

Technology Support
See **Inspiration** Visual Learning software for support in creating the concept web.

What Is It? CONTINUED

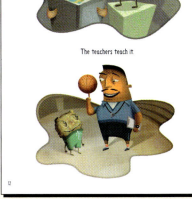

Pages 12–13

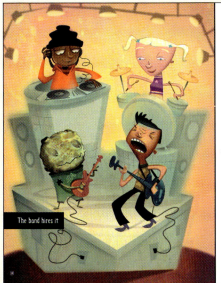

Pages 14–15

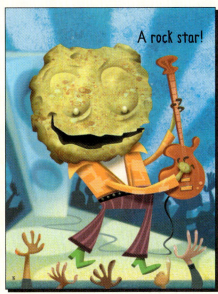

Page 16

Strategies for Comprehensible Input

Page	Story Language	Strategy Options
8–9	museum director	**Point to the picture and explain:** A museum director is in charge of a museum.
	lets it go	**Demonstrate:** Toss a small item from your hand. Use gestures to show that it goes away from you.
10–11	dress it	**Restate:** put clothes on it
12–13	teach it	**Point to the pictures and explain:** The teachers teach the rock reading, sports, science, and music.
14	band	**Point to the picture and explain:** People in a band make music together.
	hires it	**Explain:** They pay him money to work with them.
15	audience	**Point to the picture and explain:** The people who watch and listen to the band are called the audience.
	loves it	**Restate:** likes it very much
16	rock	**Demonstrate and explain:** Play or sing a few bars of rock and roll and say *Rock is a kind of music.*
	star	**Explain:** A star is someone famous or well-known. People know who a star is because they see the star act or sing, and they see the star's picture a lot.
	rock star	**Explain:** A rock star is someone who is famous for making rock-and-roll music.

Language and Literacy **T76d**

UNIT 3 LESSON 7

LANGUAGE AND LITERACY: THE BASICS BOOKSHELF

OBJECTIVES

Function: Retell a Story
Learning Strategy:
Use Graphic Organizers (concept web)
Critical Thinking and Comprehension:
❶ Identify Details

CHECK COMPREHENSION

1. **Make a Concept Web** Have students review *What Is It?* to identify the characters for the concept web. Remind them that a concept web can give information about details from a story. The center of the concept web can contain a question or a topic.

   As you read aloud the directions for each step, pause for students to add names of characters to their webs. Encourage students to review the story to make sure they have included all of the characters.

2. **Retell the Story** Have partners take turns using their concept webs to tell the story in their own words. Then have partners compare their concept webs to add and correct information.

CLOSE AND ASSESS

Ask students to raise their hands every time they hear you say the name of a character from the story. Include all characters, plus distractors such as *cook*, *writer*, and *firefighter*.

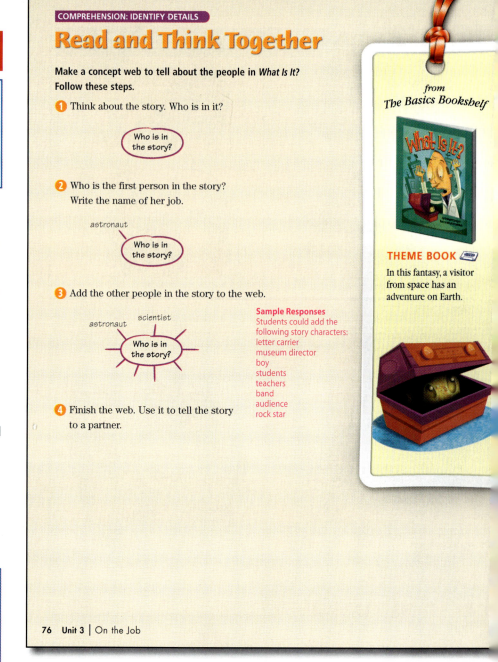

COMPREHENSION: IDENTIFY DETAILS

Read and Think Together

Make a concept web to tell about the people in *What Is It?* Follow these steps.

❶ Think about the story. Who is in it?

❷ Who is the first person in the story? Write the name of her job.

❸ Add the other people in the story to the web.

Sample Responses
Students could add the following story characters:
letter carrier
museum director
boy
students
teachers
band
audience
rock star

❹ Finish the web. Use it to tell the story to a partner.

from **The Basics Bookshelf**

THEME BOOK

In this fantasy, a visitor from space has an adventure on Earth.

76   Unit 3 | On the Job

REACHING ALL STUDENTS

Language Development
ASK AND ANSWER QUESTIONS

Interviews Have students work in pairs to search through the book for pictures of workers. Then ask them to think of questions to ask about the different jobs. Have each pair role-play an interview with a worker. One student will ask questions; the other student will answer as the worker. For example:

Interviewer: Ms. Scientist, what do you do at work?
Scientist: I study rocks and minerals.

T76   Unit 3 | On the Job

HIGH FREQUENCY WORDS
Words to Know

REVIEW WORDS YOU KNOW

Read the words aloud. Which word goes in the sentence?

what	work
many	you
There	Then

1. The photographers _work_ at the race.
2. They take _many_ pictures.
3. _There_ are 25 people in the race.

LEARN TO READ

Learn new words.

study	I **study** photography in school.
learn	I **learn** how to use a camera.
carry	I **carry** a camera in my backpack.
find	I always **find** something to photograph.
use	I **use** a lot of film.
love	I **love** to take pictures of my mom.
face	She always has a smile on her **face**.
when	My friends run **when** they see me.
want	They don't **want** to be photographed.
say	They **say**, "Don't take a picture of us!"

How to Learn a New Word
- Look at the word.
- Listen to the word.
- Listen to the word in a sentence. What does it mean?
- Say the word.
- Spell the word.
- Say the word again.

WORD WORK

4.–13. Work with a partner. Write each new word on a card. Mix your cards together for the game. Turn them so the words are down. Then:
- Turn over 2 cards.
- Spell the words. Are they the same?
- If so, keep them. If not, turn them over again.
- The player with more cards at the end wins.

Example:

s-t-u-d-y, s-t-u-d-y. These words are the same.

Language and Literacy **77**

Reading Practice Book page 46

Reading Fluency
RECOGNIZE HIGH FREQUENCY WORDS

To build automaticity with the new high frequency words:

- Have partners use the word cards they prepared in "Word Work" as flashcards. One student can hold up a card as the other reads the word and gives its meaning.

- Refer students to the list of new words on page 77. Give clues and have students point to and read each word. For example: *This word rhymes with* kind. *It means "to locate or discover something."*

UNIT 3 **LESSON 8**

LANGUAGE AND LITERACY: HIGH FREQUENCY WORDS

OBJECTIVES

Learning to Read:
- Recognize High Frequency Words

REVIEW WORDS

1 Review Known High Frequency Words Have the group read aloud the words in the green box. Listen for words students cannot read automatically and use the steps in the yellow box to reteach those words. Then have students look at the photo. Read each cloze sentence. Reread each sentence and pause for students to silently read the two words to the left of the sentence. Tell students to choose the word that goes in the sentence and tells about the picture.

INTRODUCE NEW WORDS

2 Learn High Frequency Words Use the High Frequency Word Script on page T314 to lead students through the steps in the yellow box for each new word. Explain that words that end in *se*, such as *use*, often have the /z/ sound.

PRACTICE

3 Conduct "Word Work" Guide pairs in making two sets of cards and setting up the game. Have partners take turns until they match all the pairs. Discuss the process students used to figure out the matches.

APPLY

4 Read Words in Context Students will apply the skill when they read high frequency words in context in the sentences on page 79 and the passage on page 80.

▶ **Reading Practice Book** page 46

CLOSE AND ASSESS

Call out the high frequency words one at a time. Have students point to them and spell the words as a group.

Language and Literacy **T77**

UNIT 3 LESSON 9

LANGUAGE AND LITERACY: PHONICS

OBJECTIVES

Learning to Read: Build Oral Vocabulary; Develop Phonemic Awareness; ❶ Associate Sounds and Symbols: /e/ e; Blend Sounds to Decode Words

TEACH SHORT VOWELS: /e/ e

1. **Build Oral Vocabulary** Display Transparency 21. Talk through each picture to develop meaning for the words in the yellow boxes. For example, for Item 6, say:

   • **Pets** are animals you take care of and keep at home. *Many people have **pets**. A **hen*** (point) *can be a **pet**. A lot of people get a **pup** or baby dog for a pet.*

2. **Develop Phonemic Awareness** Remove the transparency and conduct the oral activities in Step 1 of the Script for Transparency 21.

3. **Read Short e Words** Display Transparency 21 again. Work through Steps 2 and 3 of the script.

CLOSE AND ASSESS

Display the words *get, vet, jet,* and *hen.* Call on students to blend a word and identify the sound in the middle.

T78a Unit 3 | On the Job

Transparency 21: ▶
Short *e*

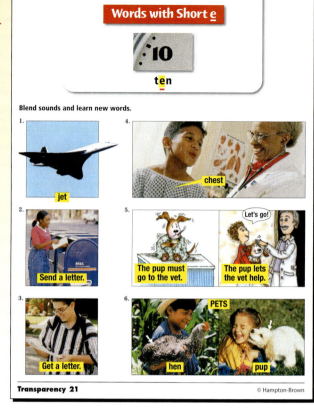

▼ Script for Transparency 21

Words With Short *e*

1. Develop Phonemic Awareness
Isolate/Match Short *e* Say: *Listen to the first sound in these words:* egg, Eddie, edge. *What is the sound?* (/e/) *Now listen for the sound* /e/ *in the middle of these words:* jet, web, hen. *Say the words with me. Raise your hand each time you hear the sound* /e/. *Say these words:* leg, bug, vet, pet, pat, chest, wet, chick.

2. Associate Sounds and Symbols
Point to the number ten on **Transparency 21**. Say: *This is the number ten. Say the word* ten *with me.* Then point to the *e* in *ten* and say: *The letter* e *makes the sound you hear in the middle of* ten. *The sound in the middle is* /e/. *Say* /e/ *with me:* /e/. Point to the letter e and ask: *What's the letter? What's the sound?*

3. Blend Sounds to Read Words
Model/Teach Point to the letter *t* in *ten.* Say: *The sound for* t *is* /t/. Repeat for *e:* /eee/. As you slide your finger slowly from left to right below the letters *te,* say: *I can blend the two sounds:* /teee/. Then point to the *n* and say: *The sound for* n *is:* /nnn/. *I can blend the three sounds together:* /teeennn/. *Now, I'm going to say the whole word:* ten.

Practice For Item 1, say: *Let's try that again. This picture shows a jet. Read the word with me. Follow my finger as we blend the sounds* /jeeet/, *and say the word:* jet. Repeat for the other words, calling attention to the following:

• For Items 2 and 3, point to the letter in each picture and say: *This is a letter.* Point to the word and read it aloud. Then have students blend *send* and read the rest of the sentence. Say: *Does* send *make sense?* Repeat for *get.*

• For item 5, read *Let's* in the speech balloon with students. Then write *let us* and say: Let's *is short for* let us. *This mark* (point) *is an apostrophe. It shows that the letter* u *has been left out.* Read the sentences aloud. Say: *Here is the word* lets *again, but this time it means that the pup won't stop the vet.*

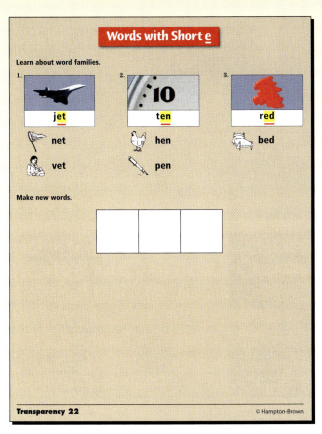

◀ **Transparency 22: Short e phonograms**

Materials
Letter tiles for:
b d e f h
j l m n p
r s t v w

▼ Script for Transparency 22

Words with Short *e* Phonograms

1. Develop Phonemic Awareness
Listen for Rhyming Words/Blend Onset and Rime Say: *Listen to these two words:* jet, let. *Say them with me:* jet, let. *These words rhyme; they end with the same sounds:* /et/. *Here are two more words; tell me if they rhyme:* met, pen. (no) Continue with word pairs *net, pet; ten, vet; led, fed; pen, den; bet, bed; jet, men; red, bed.* Then give the onset and rime for several words in the list, for example: /nnn/-/et/. Have students blend them /nnnet/, and say the word: *net.*

2. Read Words with Short *e* Phonograms
Point to the first item on **Transparency 22**. Say: *Let's read the word that names this picture.* Slide a finger slowly under the letters to lead students in sounding out the word: /jeeet/, *jet.* Cover the *j* and explain: *The two letters* et *at the end stand for the last two sounds you hear in* jet: /et/. *Many words that end in* /et/ *rhyme with* jet, *like these two words below it.* (Point out *net* and *vet.*) *Let's read these words, using what we know about their end sounds.* Have students sound out and blend the initial consonant with the phonogram -et to read the words. Repeat for the other phonograms.

3. Build Words with Short *e* Phonograms
Teach Place letter tiles *j-e-t* in the boxes, read the word, and say: *The letters* et *spell the sounds* /et/ *at the end of* jet. *Another word that rhymes with* jet *is* pet. *So I know the word* pet *also ends with the letters* et. *To spell* pet, *I have to change just the first letter. What sound do you hear at the beginning of* pet? *Yes,* /p/, *and the letter* p *spells that sound.* Substitute letter tile *p* for *j* and confirm the word by blending the sounds to read *pet.*

Practice Have students build the other -et words on the transparency. Then repeat the process for the other phonograms. Add the following words to the word building activity after making sure students understand the meanings:

-et: set, wet   -en: den, men   -ed: fed, led

OBJECTIVES

Learning to Read: Build Oral Vocabulary; Develop Phonemic Awareness; ❶ Associate Sounds and Symbols: phonograms -et, -en, -ed; Blend Sounds to Decode Words

RECOGNIZE WORD FAMILIES

1. **Build Oral Vocabulary** Display Transparency 22. Play a game of "I Spy." For example, for Item 1, say:

   • *I spy a jet. This jet flies fast.*

   When students find the jet, say: *Yes, the jet flies fast* (pantomime). Repeat to build context for the other words.

2. **Develop Phonemic Awareness** Remove the transparency and conduct the oral activities in Step 1 of the Script for Transparency 22.

3. **Read Words With Short *e* Phonograms** Display Transparency 22 again. Use the activity in Step 2 of the script to teach the word families.

4. **Build Words with Short *e* Phonograms** Use Step 3 of the script to build words in the boxes on Transparency 22.

CLOSE AND ASSESS

Have students build rhyming words with letter tiles.

▶ **Reading Practice Book** page 47 (short e and short e phonograms)

Reading Practice Book page 47

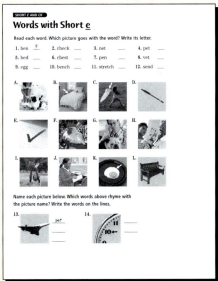

Language and Literacy **T78b**

UNIT 3 **LESSON 9,** CONTINUED

LANGUAGE AND LITERACY: PHONICS

OBJECTIVES

Learning to Read: Build Oral Vocabulary; Develop Phonemic Awareness;
T Associate Sounds and Symbols: /l/ ll, /s/ ss, /z/ zz, /k/ ck; Blend Sounds to Decode Words

TEACH SOUNDS FOR DOUBLE CONSONANTS AND *ck*

1 Build Oral Vocabulary Display Transparency 23. Talk through each picture to develop meaning for the words in the yellow boxes. For example, for Item 5, say:

• *This is a* **chick** (point). *The* **chick** *is* **sick** (pantomime). *Now the* **chick** *is* **well** (point and pantomime).

2 Develop Phonemic Awareness Remove the transparency and conduct the oral activities in Step 1 of the Script for Transparency 23.

3 Read Words That End in *ll, ss, zz, ck* Display Transparency 23 again. Work through Steps 2 and 3 of the script.

CLOSE AND ASSESS

Display the words *neck, jazz, well,* and *kiss.* Call on students to blend a word and identify the sound at the end.

▶ **Reading Practice Book** page 48 (final *ll, ss, zz, ck*)

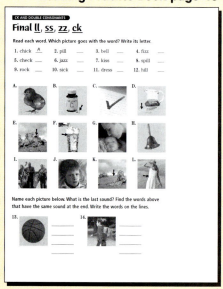

Transparency 23: ▶ Final *ll, ss, zz, ck*

▼ Script for Transparency 23

Words That End in *ll, ss, zz, ck*

1. Develop Phonemic Awareness
Isolate/Match Final Sounds Say: *Listen to the sound at the end of these words: bell, fill, tell. What is the sound?* (/l/) *Say the words with me: bell, fill, tell. Now raise your hand each time you hear two words that end with /l/. Say: hill, well; bed, fell; bell, will; sell, pill; fit, mill.* Repeat for final /s/ *ss,* /z/ *zz,* and /k/ *ck.*

2. Associate Sounds and Symbols
Point to the bell on **Transparency 23**. Say: *This is a bell. You can ring a bell. Say the word bell with me.* Then point to the *ll* in *bell* and say: *The letters ll make the sound you hear at the end of bell. The sound is /l/. You see two letters, but you say one sound. Say /l/ with me: /l/.* Follow a similar process for *kiss, fizz,* and *check.* Tell students that when they write words, they usually need to use the double consonants *ll, ss, ff,* and *zz* at the end of the words. For *check,* point out that the letters *ck* are different, but they still stand for one sound.

3. Blend Sounds to Read Words
Model/Teach Point to the letter *b* in *bell* and say: *The sound for b is /b/.* Repeat for *e:* /eee/. As you slide your finger slowly from left to right below the letters *be,* say: *I can blend the two sounds: /beee/.* Then point to the *ll* and say: *The sound for ll is /l/. I can blend the three sounds together: /beeel/. Now, I'm going to say the whole word: bell.* Repeat for *kiss, fizz,* and *check.* Lead students in sounding out each word.

Practice For Item 1, say: *Let's try that again. This picture shows some rocks by a hill. Read the words with me. Follow my finger as we blend the sounds /rrroook/, and say the word: rock.* Repeat for the other words, calling special attention to the following:

• For Item 3, blend *band* with students and say: *When we read* band, *we blended the consonants* n *and* d *at the end.* Repeat for the initial blends in *spill* in Item 4 and *black* and *dress* in Item 5.

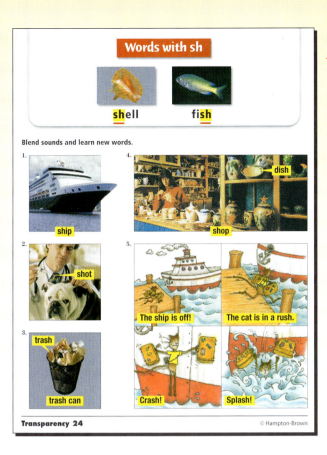

◀ **Transparency 24: Digraph *sh***

▼ **Script for Transparency 24**

Words with *sh*

1. Develop Phonemic Awareness
Isolate/Identify /sh/ Say: *Listen to the first sound in these words:* shell, ship, shop. *What is the sound?* (/sh/) *Now listen for the sound /sh/ at the end of these words:* rush, cash, dish. *Say the words with me. Now raise your hand each time you hear the sound /sh/:* shop, sock, shell, trash, jazz, shot, rush, last, share, wish.

2. Associate Sounds and Symbols
Point to the shell on **Transparency 24**. Say: *This is a shell. You can find shells by the sea. Say the word* shell *with me.* Then point to the *sh* in *shell* and say: *The letters* sh *make the first sound you hear in* shell. *The sound is* /sh/. *Say* /sh/ *with me:* /sh/. Point to *sh* and ask: *What are the letters? What sound do they make?* Repeat for *fish*, pointing out that /sh/ comes at the end of the word.

3. Blend Sounds to Read Words
Model/Teach Point to the letters *sh* in *shell* and say: *The sound for the letters* sh *is* /sh/. *Repeat for* e: /eee/. *As you slide your finger slowly from left to right below the letters* she, *say: I can blend the two sounds:* /sheee/. *Then point to the* ll *and say: The sound for* ll *is* /l/. *I can blend the three sounds together:* /sheeel/. *Now, I'm going to say the whole word:* shell. *Repeat for* fish. Lead students in sounding out *shell* and *fish*.

Practice For Item 1, say: *Let's try that again. This picture shows a ship. Follow my finger as we blend the sounds* /shiiip/, *and say the word:* ship. Repeat for the other words, calling attention to the following:

- In Item 3, blend *trash* with students and say: *When we read* trash, *we blended* t *and* r, *but we said just one sound for the letters* sh. Repeat for *crash* and *splash* in Item 5, pointing out that three consonants are blended in *splash*.

- For Item 5, point out that you say one sound for the two final consonants in *off*. Explain the meaning of the idioms *The ship is off* (The ship is leaving) and *in a rush* (in a hurry).

OBJECTIVES

Learning to Read: Build Oral Vocabulary; Develop Phonemic Awareness; ❶ Associate Sounds and Symbols: /sh/ *sh*; Blend Sounds to Decode Words

TEACH DIGRAPHS: /sh/ *sh*

1. **Build Oral Vocabulary** Display Transparency 24. Use the pictures to develop meaning for the words in yellow boxes. For example, for Item 2, say:

   - The vet gives the dog a **shot** (pantomime). There is medicine inside the needle. The **shot** will keep the dog healthy.

2. **Develop Phonemic Awareness** Remove the transparency and conduct the oral activities in Step 1 of the Script for Transparency 24.

3. **Read Words with *sh*** Display Transparency 24 again. Work through Steps 2 and 3 of the script.

CLOSE AND ASSESS

Display the words *shop, rush, ship,* and *trash*. Call on students to blend a word and identify the letters that spell the sound /sh/.

Language and Literacy **T78d**

UNIT 3 LESSON 10

LANGUAGE AND LITERACY: READING AND SPELLING

OBJECTIVES

Functions: Listen Actively; Repeat Spoken Language; Recite

Learning to Read: Develop Phonemic Awareness; ⓣ Associate Sounds and Symbols: /e/ e; /l/ ll, /s/ ss, /z/ zz, /k/ ck; /sh/ sh; Blend Sounds to Decode Words

Spelling: ⓣ Words with Short e, Final ll, ss, zz, ck, Digraph sh

LISTEN AND LEARN

Tape 2A / CD 1 Track 12

1. **Recite a Rap** Display Transparency 25 and play "Yes, Yes, Yes!" on the **Language Tape/CD**. After students have listened and learned the rap, they can recite it, saying each *yes* with increased enthusiasm.

DEVELOP PHONEMIC AWARENESS

2. **Blend Sounds to Form a Word** Say: *Can you guess the word I am trying to say? Listen to these sounds: /sh/ /e/ /l/. Now blend the sounds together to say the word: (/sheeel/). That's right:* shell. Continue with the following words: *bell, sick, jazz, hill, yes, dish, tell, fizz, ship, chick, jet, kiss.*

CONNECT SOUNDS AND LETTERS

3. **Associate /e/ *e*, /sh/ *sh*, /l/ *ll*, and /k/ *ck*** Identify the first picture and help students sound out its name. Say: *This is a jet, and here's the word. Let's point to each letter. Say the sound for each letter with me: /j/, /eee/, /t/. Now let's blend the sounds to say the word:* jet. Repeat for the other pictures, pointing out that *sh, ll, ch,* and *ck* each make one sound. Then read the question aloud: *How many sounds does each word have?* Have a student read each word while the group counts the number of sounds.

Afterwards, play the rap again. Have students identify words with short *e*, *sh*, or final *ck*.

T78 Unit 3 | On the Job

REACHING ALL STUDENTS

Multi-Level Strategies

LITERACY SUPPORT

LITERATE IN L1 Refer to the Phonics Transfer Chart on page T338 to identify English consonant sounds that may be unfamiliar to your students. (Bilingual aides and parent volunteers can help you identify the sounds for languages not represented in the chart.) After you select sounds for extended practice, read minimal pairs aloud and have students listen for the differences. For example, Vietnamese, Lao, Thai, Hmong, and Chinese use tones to convey differences in words. Therefore, for students from these groups, you might focus the activity on final consonant sounds, using these pairs of words: *cash, cast; rush, wish; sack, clock; will, win; fish, fill; him, hill; pill, tell; jazz, jam; fish, fizz; juice, jazz.* Students should tell if the two words end the same way and, if so, with what sound.

READING STRATEGY

Follow these steps to read a word.

1 Point to the first letter. Say the sound.

b**e**ll

2 Point to the second letter. Say the sound.

b**e**ll

3 Point to the last two letters. Say the sound.

b**e**ll

4 Now blend all the sounds together to say the word. Say the word again. What is it?

b + e + ll = **bell**

These two consonants are the same, so I say just one sound.

READING AND SPELLING PRACTICE

Blend the sounds to read these words.

1. shot   2. neck   3. vet   4. black   5. kiss   6. ten

Use what you learned to read the sentences.

7. My cat, Fuzz, is sick.
8. I carry him to the vet.
9. I kiss him on the neck.
10. The vet gives my cat a shot.
11. He gives me ten black pills for my cat.
12. Then I tell Fuzz, "Let's go home."

13.–16. Now write the sentences that your teacher reads.   *For dictation sentences, see Step 6 at right.*

WORD WORK

Name each picture. What letters are missing from the names?
Use letter cards to make the words.

Example: 17. j e t

17. j _e_ t
18. h _i_ ll
19. ro _c_ k
20. b _u_ s
21. v _a_ n
22. _s_ _h_ ell
23. ch _e_ ck
24. fi _s_ _h_
25. c _a_ p
26. p _o_ t
27. t _e_ n
28. c _u_ p

Language and Literacy **79**

Decodable Book

PRACTICE WITH SHORT E, SH, CK, AND DOUBLE CONSONANTS

Decodable Book 3: *Fred at Work*

Assign **Decodable Book 3** for independent reading. The **Decodable Book** can be used in a variety of ways to help students become more fluent, automatic readers:

Discussion Circles Have students work in small groups to read aloud and discuss the book using the questions on the back cover. Encourage students to read aloud the text that supports their answers. Groups can also work together to complete the Word Work Activity.

Readers Theater Students can read aloud the stories in a class performance. Help them prepare by rereading the stories in daily rehearsals. Work with students to add narration or dialog. Encourage them to use natural phrasing and expression.

Rereading at Home Have students work with family members to reread the book at home. They can take turns reading aloud alternate pages, then rereading the book switching the pages each person reads.

LEARN A READING STRATEGY

4 Sound Out Words Write *bell* and model the blending strategy. Demonstrate how to say the sound for each letter and then to say one sound for *ll* at the end of the word, blending the three sounds together: /beeel/. Then say the whole word quickly: *bell*. Slide your finger under the letters again and ask students to say the sounds with you and then to say the whole word quickly.

Read steps 1–3 aloud to summarize the blending process you have demonstrated. For step 4, have students try out the strategy on their own. As they slide a finger under the letters, they should hold each sound without pausing. After blending the sounds, they should say the whole word quickly.

PRACTICE

5 Read Words and Sentences Sound out the words in Items 1–6 as a choral reading. Then distribute the Partner Prompts from page T311 to guide peers in reading the sentences in Items 7–12.

6 Write Sentences Dictate the following sentences. Read each sentence at normal speed once so students can listen, and then repeat it slowly word by word as they write:

13. The men like jazz.

14. A red pen is in the trash can.

15. Fill the box with rocks and shells.

16. My black dress is wet.

7 Conduct "Word Work" Read the directions and work through the Example. Then have partners complete Items 18–28.

▶ **Reading Practice Book** pages 119–122 (Decodable Book 3)

CLOSE AND ASSESS

Write several of the incomplete words from Word Work. Say the name of each picture. Then say it sound by sound, asking a student to add the missing letter or letters. Sound out the completed word.

Language and Literacy **T79**

UNIT 3 LESSON 11

LANGUAGE AND LITERACY: INDEPENDENT READING

OBJECTIVES

Function: Read a Selection

Learning to Read: Recognize High Frequency Words; Decode Words (short *e*; final *ll*, *ss*, *zz*, *ck*; and digraph *sh*)

Reading Strategies: Predict; Set a Purpose for Reading; Retell

Critical Thinking and Comprehension: Identify Details

READ ON YOUR OWN

1 Introduce Vocabulary In "Let Ben Take It," students apply phonics skills and read high frequency words taught in Lessons 8–10. Introduce the story words. Write each word, pronounce it, and spell it. Then give a definition and context sentence:

- **bike:** a bicycle. *I ride my bike to school.*
- **messenger, letters:** A messenger is a person who carries something from one place to another. Letters are written messages or notes. *The messenger brings us some letters.*
- **flowers:** the blossoms on a plant. *My favorite flowers are red roses.*

2 Make Predictions/Set Purposes Point out the man on the bike and say: *This is Ben. He rides his bike around a city. What do you think Ben does?* (He's a bike messenger. He brings people letters and flowers.) *Read to find out about Ben's job.*

3 Read and Think: Identify Details Students should read the passage on their own. Then have them complete the web and use it to tell a partner about Ben's job.

4 Build Reading Fluency Tape 2A / CD 1 Track 13
Use the **Language Tape/CD** with Reading Practice Book page 49 for fluency practice.

▶ **Reading Practice Book** page 49

CLOSE AND ASSESS

Students can take turns telling a detail about Ben and his job until all the details on the map are mentioned.

T80 Unit 3 | On the Job

COMPREHENSION: IDENTIFY DETAILS

Read on Your Own

Let Ben Take It

Ben is a bike messenger.
Do you want to send something?
Ben can get it there fast.
Just tell him where it must go.
He gets his map.
He uses it to find a shop.
Then he hops on his bike and ... zip!
He is off like a jet.
Ben can carry a lot of different things:
food, pictures, letters, flowers.
They fit in the big bag on his back.
Ben loves his job.
When you want to send something,
let Ben take it!

✓ **DECODING CHECK**
Give the Decoding Progress Check on page 1a of the Assessment Handbook.

CHECK YOUR UNDERSTANDING

Copy and complete the map. Then tell a partner about Ben's job.

Sample Responses:

80 Unit 3 | On the Job

REACHING ALL STUDENTS

Reading Fluency
INTONATION PATTERNS/EXPRESSION

Read the title and introduction on **Reading Practice Book page 49**. Then read the explanation and go over the examples. Ask students to point to the word that starts each question. Lead the group in a choral recitation of each question with the proper intonation.

Next, play "Let Ben Take It" on the **Language Tape/CD**. Point out that the punctuation marks tell the reader how to say each sentence. Then read the Practice directions and circulate to check and support reading fluency.

Reading Practice Book page 49

QUESTIONS WITH *WHO?, WHAT?, WHERE?,* AND *WHEN?*

Questions About Work

You can use the words *Who, What, Where,* or *When* to start a question.

Use *Who* to ask about a person.
Who are you?

Use *What* to ask about a thing.
What is in your bag?

Use *Where* to ask about a place.
Where is the shop?

Use *When* to ask about a time.
When can you deliver the box?

MATCH QUESTIONS AND ANSWERS

Read each question. Find the sentence that answers it.
Read the questions and answers to a partner.

Example: **1.** Who is the bike messenger?
E. Ben is the bike messenger.

Questions
1. Who is the bike messenger?
2. What is in his bag?
3. Where is his helmet?
4. When is his next delivery?
5. Where is Ben?

Answers
A. His helmet is on his head.
B. A box is in his bag.
C. His next delivery is at 8:30.
D. Ben is in the city.
E. Ben is the bike messenger.

WRITE QUESTIONS AND ANSWERS

Make a question to go with each answer.
Then write the question and answer.

Example: **6.** What is in the bag? A box of candy is in the bag.

6. What _____? A box of candy is in the bag.
7. What _____? It is a birthday present for Mr. Lee.
8. Where _____? His office is in that tall building.
9. When _____? His birthday is tomorrow.
10. Who _____? Ben can deliver the box.
11. Where _____? Ben is near the tall building.
12. When _____? Ben is ready to deliver the box now!

Answers:
6. What is in the bag?
7. What is it?
8. Where is his office?
9. When is his birthday?
10. Who can deliver the box?
11. Where is Ben?
12. When is Ben ready to deliver the box?

Language and Literacy **81**

Language Practice Book page 54

COMMUNITY CONNECTION

Spotlight on Delivery Invite workers in delivery services to speak to the class about their jobs in the community. You might invite bike messengers, workers from other commercial delivery services, mail and parcel-post carriers, and delivery people from florists, restaurants, and other goods-based sources. Work with students to create questions to ask visitors, including:

Who are your customers?
What tools can you use?
Where is your company located?
When are you the busiest?

UNIT 3 **LESSON 12**

LANGUAGE AND LITERACY: QUESTIONS

OBJECTIVES

Functions:
Ask and Answer Questions; Write

Patterns and Structures: Questions with *Who?, What?, Where?,* and *When?*

Writing: Questions and Answers

INTRODUCE

1 Learn About Questions with *Who?, What?, Where?,* and *When?* Read the title and introduction, and then the first rule and question. Give another example: ***Who** is your teacher?* Read the other rules and questions, offering an additional example each time: ***What** is in my hand? **Where** is the door? **When** does class start?*

Write the examples and ask students to point out the word that asks about: a thing *(What)*; a time *(When)*; a place *(Where)*; and a person *(Who)*.

PRACTICE

2 Match Questions and Answers Use the Example to model matching the question and answer: *The question asks* who. *Look for an answer that tells about a person.* After students match answers to questions 2–5, have partners alternate asking and answering each question.

APPLY

3 Write Questions and Answers Read the directions and work through the Example. For students who need additional support, work through the items orally together before guiding them in writing the questions.

▶ **Language Practice Book** page 54

CLOSE AND ASSESS

Have students turn to page 75. Call on individuals to ask questions with *who, what, where,* and *when* about each scene. Have volunteers answer the questions.

Language and Literacy **T81**

UNIT 3 LESSON 13
LANGUAGE ACROSS THE CURRICULUM: SCIENCE/MATH

OBJECTIVES

Functions: Describe; Give Information; Follow Directions

Concepts and Vocabulary: Science Processes; Measurement Words

Research Skills and Learning Strategies: Make Observations; Gather Information; Use Graphic Organizers (observation log)

Critical Thinking and Comprehension: Make Comparisons; Classify; Analyze Information; Draw Conclusions

LEARN ABOUT MEASUREMENT

1. **Analyze Information** Introduce the vocabulary. Then read the headings aloud, restating as necessary:
   - **Observe:** *look and describe*
   - **Measure:** *find out size or weight*
   - **Compare:** *look for how things are alike and different*

   Then discuss each step and call out vocabulary, such as *big, heavy,* and *smooth.* Ask students to show you examples or pantomime actions to match the words.

OBSERVE AND REPORT

2. **Be a Scientist: Study Rocks** Guide students in relating Rock A in the photo to the data in the observation log: *What color is the rock? What size is the rock?*

3. **Do the Activity** If possible, provide enough rocks and scales for students to work in small groups. Otherwise, volunteers can perform the activity as the remaining students work in pairs to chart results.

CHECK UNDERSTANDING

4. **Respond to "Think It Over"** Help students use their observation logs to answer the questions.

CLOSE AND ASSESS

Have the class finish this sentence: *When we observe, we _____.* Repeat for *measure* and *compare.*

T82 Unit 3 | On the Job

SUCCESS IN SCIENCE AND MATHEMATICS

Learn About Measurement

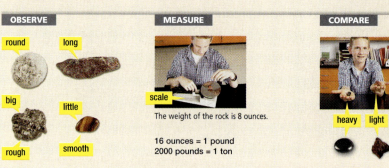

OBSERVE — round, long, big, little, rough, smooth

MEASURE — scale. The weight of the rock is 8 ounces.
16 ounces = 1 pound
2000 pounds = 1 ton

COMPARE — heavy, light

Read the instructions. Then do the activity.

Sample Responses for Think It Over
1. Some rocks, like lava rocks, can be large and quite light. Small rocks may be dense and quite heavy.
2. Answers will vary. Students may mention places such as rivers, oceans, mountains, cliffs, deserts, and volcanoes. Students might point out the differences in weight, texture, and appearance.

▶ Be a Scientist: Study Rocks

You will need: different kinds of rocks, a scale, a notebook, and a pencil

ACTIVITY STEPS

1. **Observe**
   Make an observation log. Assign each rock a letter to identify it. Study the rocks. Take notes in the log about how each rock looks and feels.

2. **Measure**
   Weigh each rock. Write the weights in your log.

3. **Compare**
   How are the rocks alike? How are they different? Find out which rocks are the lightest. Find out which are the heaviest.

4. **Sort**
   Put the rocks in groups, or categories. Is each rock heavy or light? Is it rough or smooth?

Rock	Color	Size	Shape	Weight
A	gray	big	round	10 oz.

THINK IT OVER
1. Is a big rock always heavier than a small one? Explain what you learned.
2. Where do you see different types of rocks in nature? How are they different?

82 Unit 3 | On the Job

REACHING ALL STUDENTS

Mathematics Connection
MEASUREMENT

Help students create measurement charts. Start by pointing out the weight equivalencies at the top of the page and model ways to include more information. For example:

16 ounces = 1 pound = 454 grams =

Provide, or help students find, sources for weight and other measurement equivalencies from math and science books and on the Web.

Writing Project / Job Handbook

Interview a worker about his or her job.
Make a job handbook to keep in your classroom.

✓ **WRITING ASSESSMENT**
Use the Writing Progress Checklist on page 51 of the Assessment Handbook to evaluate this writing project.

Pronunciation of Name
Varela   var **el** ah

INTERVIEW A WORKER

Think of a worker you want to interview. Plan a time you can talk with the person.

1 Think of questions.   **2** Ask your questions.   **3** Write the answers.

MAKE A JOB REPORT

Ask the worker for his or her picture.
Copy your questions and the answers.
At the top of the page, write the worker's job.

 Check Your Work
- Did you write all your questions?
- Did you end each question with a question mark?
- Did you write answers for all the questions?

MAKE A JOB HANDBOOK

Add your report and the picture to a class handbook.

Language Across the Curriculum **83**

Language Practice Book page 55

✓ **ASSESSMENT**

For opportunities to measure progress, see the Assessment Handbook:

- **Units 1–3 Test** evaluates basic vocabulary and the patterns and structures of English, mastery of phonics and high frequency words, reading comprehension, and writing.

- **The Language Acquisition Assessment** for Units 1–3 offers performance assessments for measuring growth through the stages of language acquisition.

- **Self- and Peer-Assessment** forms involve students in the assessment process.

UNIT 3 **LESSON 14**

LANGUAGE ACROSS THE CURRICULUM: WRITING

OBJECTIVES

Functions:
Ask and Answer Questions; Write

Listening and Speaking: Interview

Learning Strategies and Critical Thinking: Plan; Generate and Organize Ideas; Self-Assess

Research Skills: Conduct an Interview

Writing: Job Handbook

CONDUCT THE WRITING PROJECT

1 Learn About Interviews Say: *In an interview, two people talk. The interviewer asks questions and writes down what the other person says. An interview is a great way to gather information.* Play a tape of an interview, share an article in interview format, or role-play an interview.

2 Interview a Worker Brainstorm a list of workers to interview: school workers, family members and friends, workers who visit the classroom.

Help students prepare for the interviews by creating a class list of questions using *who, what, where,* and *when.* Remind students to leave space for answers. Then assign partners to conduct the interviews together, taking turns to ask questions and record answers.

3 Make a Job Report Students may add a photo or drawing of the worker to their interview.

4 Make a Job Handbook Place the job reports in a binder and add a table of contents. Use the handbook to develop vocabulary. For example, challenge students to find a job where someone works outdoors, or to name the tools a worker uses.

▶ **Language Practice Book** page 55

CLOSE AND ASSESS

Have students look at the job report they wrote. Say:
- *Show me a question and an answer.*
- *Show me a question mark.*

Language Across the Curriculum **T83**

Resources

For Success in Language and Literacy

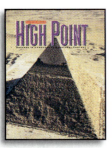

Student Book pages 84–97

For Language Skills Practice

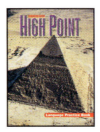

Language Practice Book pages 56–61

For Reading Skills Practice

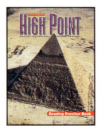

Reading Practice Book pages 50–53

For Vocabulary, Language Development, and Reading Fluency

Language Tape 2, Side B
Language CD 1, Tracks 14–17

For Reading Together

Theme Book *A Year Without Rain* from The Basics Bookshelf

For Audio Walk-Throughs and Selection Readings

Selection Tape 2B
Selection CD 1, Tracks 7–8

For Phonics Instruction

Transparencies 26–30

Transparency Scripts 26–30

Letter Tiles

For Comprehensive Assessment

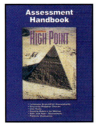

Language Acquisition Assessment, Units 4–6 Test, Writing Assessment, Self-Assessment

For Home-School Connections

High Point Newsletter 2 in seven languages

For Planning and Instruction

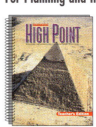

Teacher's Edition pages T84a–T97

T84a Unit Planner

UNIT 4

Numbers Count

In This Unit

Vocabulary
- Cardinal Numbers
- Ordinal Numbers
- Geography

Language Functions
- Ask Questions
- Give Information
- Express Needs

Patterns and Structures
- Questions with *Do* and *Does*
- Negative Sentences
- Contractions with *not*

Reading
- Phonics: Blends and Digraphs
- Comprehension: Identify Problems and Solutions (problem-and-solution chart); Identify Details

Writing
- Questions and Answers
- Sentences
- Fact Sheet

Content Area Connection
- Social Studies (geography/charts)

T84b

UNIT 4
Activity and Assessment Planner

UNIT 4: Numbers Count

LESSONS

1

UNIT 4 LAUNCH ▶ pages T84–T85

LESSON 1: INTRODUCE UNIT 4 pages T84–T85

Vocabulary
T Numbers

Viewing
Interpret a Visual Image

Learning Strategies
Preview

Build Background

Critical Thinking
Classify

Analyze Information

Make Observations

2–5

LANGUAGE DEVELOPMENT ▶ pages T86–T89

LESSON 2
QUESTIONS WITH DO AND DOES
page T86

Function
Ask Questions

Patterns and Structures
T Questions with Do and Does

Writing
Questions and Answers

LESSON 3
CARDINAL NUMBERS
page T87

Function
Give Information

Vocabulary
T Cardinal Numbers

Writing
T Sentences

LESSON 4
NEGATIVE SENTENCES
page T88

Function
Give Information

Patterns and Structures
T Negative Sentences

Writing
T Sentences

LESSON 5
ORDINAL NUMBERS
page T89

Functions
Express Needs

Ask and Answer Questions

Vocabulary
T Ordinal Numbers

Viewing
Respond to a Visual Image

Writing
T Sentences

6–12

LANGUAGE AND LITERACY ▶ pages T90a–T95

LESSON 6
BASICS BOOKSHELF
pages T90a–T90d

Function
Listen to a Book

Vocabulary
T Number Words

Reading Strategies
Activate Prior Knowledge

Preview

Learning to Read
Identify End Marks

Track Print

Recognize Statements and Questions

Critical Thinking and Comprehension
T Identify Problem and Solution

LESSON 7
BASICS BOOKSHELF: COMPREHENSION
page T90

Function
Retell a Story

Learning Strategy
Use Graphic Organizers (problem-and-solution chart)

Critical Thinking and Comprehension
T Identify Problem and Solution

LESSON 8
HIGH FREQUENCY WORDS
page T91

Learning to Read
T Recognize High Frequency Words

LESSON 9
PHONICS
pages T92a–T92d

Learning to Read
Build Oral Vocabulary

Develop Phonemic Awareness

T Associate Sounds and Symbols: Blends and Digraphs

Blend Sounds to Decode Words

LESSON 10
READING AND SPELLING
pages T92–T93

Learning to Read
Develop Phonemic Awareness

T Associate Sounds and Symbols: Blends and Digraphs

Blend Sounds to Decode Words

Spelling
T Words with Blends and Digraphs

LESSON 11
INDEPENDENT READING
page T94

Function
Read a Selection

Learning to Read
T Recognize High Frequency Words

T Decode Words with Blends and Digraphs

Reading Strategies
Predict

Set a Purpose for Reading

Retell

Critical Thinking and Comprehension
T Identify Details

LESSON 12
CONTRACTIONS WITH NOT
page T95

Functions
Write

Give Information

Patterns and Structures
T Negative Sentences

T Contractions with not

Writing
Sentences

13–14

LANGUAGE ACROSS THE CURRICULUM ▶ pages T96–T97

LESSON 13
SOCIAL STUDIES: GEOGRAPHY
page T96

Function
Listen to an Article

Vocabulary
Geography

Research Skills and Learning Strategies
Use Maps

Use Text Structures (charts)

Make Comparisons

Critical Thinking and Comprehension
Identify Cause and Effect

LESSON 14
WRITING PROJECT: FACT SHEET
page T97

Functions
Write

Ask Questions

Give Information

Learning Strategies and Critical Thinking
Plan

Generate and Organize Ideas

Self-Assess

Research Skills
Formulate Questions

Gather Information

Take Notes

Writing
Fact Sheet

T84c Unit 4 | Numbers Count

T = Objective Tested on Unit Test

ASSESSMENT OPTIONS

The **Teacher's Edition** and the **Assessment Handbook** include these comprehensive assessment tools:

▶ **Ongoing, Informal Assessment**
Check for understanding and achieve closure for every lesson with the targeted questions and activities in the **Close and Assess** boxes in your Teacher's Edition.

▶ **Decoding Progress Check**
These word lists for each unit provide a quick way to check on mastery of the phonics or word structure skills taught in the unit.

▶ **Language Acquisition Assessments**
To verify students' ability to use the language functions and grammar structures taught in Units 4–6, conduct these performance assessments.

▶ **Unit Test in Standardized Test Format**
This multiple-choice test measures students' cumulative understanding of the skills and language developed in Units 4–6.

▶ **Self- and Peer-Assessment**
Students use the Self-Assessment Form to evaluate their own work and develop learning strategies appropriate to their needs. Students offer feedback to their classmates with the Peer-Assessment Form.

▶ **Writing Assessment/Portfolio Opportunities**
You can evaluate students' writing in the Writing Projects using the Writing Progress Checklist. Then collaborate with students to choose work for their portfolios.

UNITS 4–6 ASSESSMENT OPPORTUNITIES	Assessment Handbook Pages
Decoding Progress Check	1a
Language Acquisition Assessments	10
Units 4–6 Test	11–16
Self-Assessment Form	17
Peer-Assessment Form	50
Writing Progress Checklist	51
Portfolio Evaluation Form	52

RELATED RESOURCES

Josefina
by Jeanette Winter
A biography of the Mexican folk artist Josefina Aguilar. Her painted clay figures are presented in numbered groups. (Harcourt Brace)
Theme Book: Read Aloud

Bring Me Your Horses
by Shirleyann Costigan
A horse trainer tells about the problems and challenges he faces in training a new horse with the fitting name "Pride." (Hampton-Brown)
Phonics Reinforcement: Blends

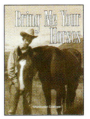

Seven Blind Mice
by Ed Young
This Indian fable, about seven blind mice working together to solve a riddle, also reinforces days of the week and colors. (Philomel Books)
Easy Reading

Hottest, Coldest, Highest, Deepest
by Steve Jenkins
Describes some of the natural wonders of the world, including the wettest place, which receives 463 inches of rain a year.
Vocabulary: Cardinal Numbers

Math Shop Deluxe
Offers thousands of math problems at five distinct levels. Based on NCTE standards; includes a classroom pack and teacher's edition. (Scholastic)
Multimedia: CD-ROM

Unit Planner **T84d**

UNIT 4 LESSON 1

INTRODUCE UNIT 4: NUMBERS COUNT

OBJECTIVES

Concepts and Vocabulary: 🅣 Numbers
Viewing: Interpret a Visual Image
Learning Strategies: Preview; Build Background
Critical Thinking: Classify; Analyze Information; Make Observations
Representing: Category Chart

START WITH A COMMON EXPERIENCE

1. **Introduce "Numbers Count"** Read the unit title and explain that it means "numbers matter," or "numbers are important." Direct students in interpreting the context of the numbers pictured on page 84:

   • *What numbers can you find at a store?* ($1.50 on cash register; 75% off on sale sign; $100 bill)

   • *What number tells who a person is?* (26 on jersey)

   • *Which numbers can you find in an office building?* (1–0 on telephone keypad, numbers on elevator buttons)

   Have partners discuss the other numbers, identifying what information the numbers give and where they can be found.

2. **Find More Numbers** Conduct a scavenger hunt. Small groups will chart numbers they can find around the school.

Number	Location
$1.99	cafeteria
555-4429	PTA flyer
831.21	library book

   Have groups share their charts and sort the numbers into categories such as phone numbers, prices, locations, dates, etc.

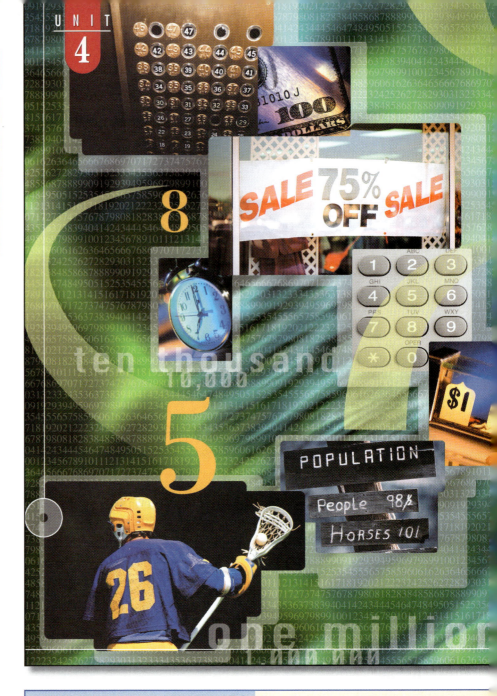

REACHING ALL STUDENTS

HOME CONNECTION

Numbers Everywhere! Send home a copy of *High Point Newsletter 2* in the **Teacher's Resource Book.** In the home activity, students and family list different uses of numbers around the house. Students bring in the lists to create a class chart of home number uses.

T84 Unit 4 | Numbers Count

Numbers Count

Look at the pictures.
What do they show?
Work with a partner to find
more numbers around you.

In This Unit

Vocabulary
- Cardinal Numbers
- Ordinal Numbers
- Geography

Language Functions
- Ask Questions
- Give Information
- Express Needs

Patterns and Structures
- Questions with *Do* and *Does*
- Negative Sentences
- Contractions with *not*

Reading
- Phonics: Blends and Digraphs
- Comprehension:
  Identify Problems and Solutions
  (problem-and-solution chart)
  Identify Details

Writing
- Questions and Answers
- Sentences
- Fact Sheet

Content Area Connection
- Social Studies (geography/charts)

PREVIEW THE UNIT

3 Look for Activities and Ways to Use Numbers Leaf through the unit, previewing activities students will do, for example:

page 86—learning a chant about numbers

page 87—using large numbers

page 89—learning about numbers that tell the order

page 90—listening to the Bookshelf book (Display a copy of the book.)

page 97—using numbers to write a geography fact sheet

Then sum up what the preview reveals: *Numbers give information about the world around us.*

4 Set Your Goals Start a class category chart showing the different things numbers can tell you. Prompt students for pictures or words to add, and have them act out and describe other ideas for you to put into words. Talk together about what they want to learn about numbers.

CLOSE AND ASSESS

Ask students to tell or show you something they are interested in learning in this unit.

UNIT 4 Mind Map

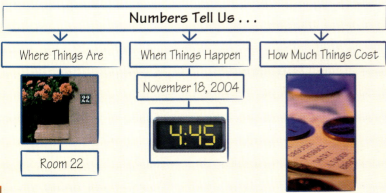

Technology Support
See **Inspiration** Visual Learning software for support in creating mind maps.

Unit Launch **T85**

UNIT 4 **LESSON 2**

LANGUAGE DEVELOPMENT: QUESTIONS WITH *DO* AND *DOES*

OBJECTIVES

Functions: Listen Actively; Repeat Spoken Language; Recite; Ask Questions

Patterns and Structures:
- Questions with *Do* and *Does*

Writing: Questions and Answers

INTRODUCE

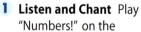

1. **Listen and Chant** Play "Numbers!" on the **Language Tape/CD.** Explain that to be *in a fix* means "to be in trouble," or "to have problems." Restate the stanza: *Without numbers, we would not know when the show starts.* Have students listen and follow along with the words. Then have them echo the lines, chime in softly, and chime in loudly.

2. **Learn About Questions with *Do* and *Does*** Read aloud the chart and model asking questions about the show: *Does the show start at four? Do we need to stand in line?*

PRACTICE

3. **Conduct "Express Yourself"** Model asking questions, then have partners complete the activity.

> **How to Ask Questions with *Do* and *Does***
> - Use *do* with the pronouns *I, you, we,* and *they.*
> - Use *does* with the pronouns *he, she,* and *it.*

APPLY

4. **Write Questions and Answers** Encourage partners to check their questions. Distribute Partner Checklist 4 on page T310.

▶ Language Practice Book page 56

CLOSE AND ASSESS

Display volunteers' questions. Circle *Do* or *Does* and underline the noun or pronoun.

T86 Unit 4 | Numbers Count

QUESTIONS WITH *DO* AND *DOES*

Numbers Everywhere!

Listen and chant.

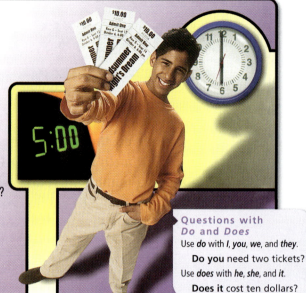

Numbers!

Does it cost ten dollars
To go to the show?
Without numbers
We wouldn't know.

Without numbers
We'd be in a fix.
Does the show start at five?
Or is it at six?

Do we need two tickets?
Or do we need three?
Without numbers,
Where would we be?

> **Questions with *Do* and *Does***
> Use *do* with *I, you, we,* and *they.*
> **Do** you need two tickets?
> Use *does* with *he, she,* and *it.*
> **Does** it cost ten dollars?

EXPRESS YOURSELF ▶ ASK QUESTIONS

1.–4. Work with a partner. Ask 4 questions. Choose words from each column.

Do you	have	five cookies?
Do they	see	two pencils?
Does he	need	seven backpacks?
Does she	want	three markers?

Example: 1. Do you need two pencils?
          2. Does she see five cookies?

WRITE QUESTIONS AND ANSWERS

5.–8. Write 4 questions on cards. Use *Do* or *Does.* Trade cards with a partner. Answer the questions you get.

Example: 5. Do you have a highlighter?
             No, I do not.

86 Unit 4 | Numbers Count

REACHING ALL STUDENTS

CULTURAL PERSPECTIVES

World Cultures: Numbers Every language has a system for naming and representing numbers. Work together to create a number chart that includes a row of numbers for each language represented in your classroom. Assign student "language experts" to add information about number symbols and number words from their primary languages. Then post the chart and use it to discuss similarities and differences between the languages.

Language Practice Book page 56

VOCABULARY: CARDINAL NUMBERS

From One to One Million

Number Words

0	zero	11	eleven	21	twenty-one	40	forty	100	one hundred
1	one	12	twelve	22	twenty-two	50	fifty	101	one hundred one
2	two	13	thirteen	23	twenty-three	60	sixty	500	five hundred
3	three	14	fourteen	24	twenty-four	70	seventy	550	five hundred fifty
4	four	15	fifteen	25	twenty-five	80	eighty	1,000	one thousand
5	five	16	sixteen	26	twenty-six	90	ninety	1,151	one thousand, one
6	six	17	seventeen	27	twenty-seven				hundred fifty-one
7	seven	18	eighteen	28	twenty-eight			5,000	five thousand
8	eight	19	nineteen	29	twenty-nine			10,000	ten thousand
9	nine	20	twenty	30	thirty			100,000	one hundred thousand
10	ten							500,000	five hundred thousand
								1,000,000	one million

Put commas after the millions place and the thousands place.

Beijing, China: population 13,800,000
thirteen million, eight hundred thousand

EXPRESS YOURSELF ▶ GIVE INFORMATION

Work with a partner. Read each fact about China in 2000.
Say a sentence with each fact. Begin your sentence with *China has.*

1. **65,650** kilometers of railways
2. **206** airports
3. **700,000,000** workers
4. **23,400,000** cellular phones
5. **3,240** television stations
6. **400,000,000** televisions

Example: 1. China has sixty-five thousand, six hundred fifty kilometers of railways.

Answers:
1. China has sixty-five thousand, six hundred fifty kilometers of railways.
2. China has two hundred six airports.
3. China has seven hundred million workers.
4. China has twenty-three million, four hundred thousand cellular phones.
5. China has three thousand, two hundred forty television stations.
6. China has four hundred million televisions.

WRITE SENTENCES

7.–10. Work with a partner to find numbers in your classroom. Write 4 sentences with the numbers you find. Write words for the numbers.

Example: 7. Our classroom has thirty-three desks.

Sample Responses
Students might notice numbers in the classroom on the clock, textbooks, notebooks, board, pencils, pens, rulers, calculators, backpacks, emergency plan, and so on.

Language Development **87**

Language Practice Book page 57

VOCABULARY: CARDINAL NUMBERS
Numbers Tell How Many

Read the number words. Write the numbers.

1. four thousand, five hundred forty — 4,540
2. nine hundred ninety-seven
3. three hundred ten thousand
4. two million, one hundred thousand
5. fifty-four thousand, one hundred one
6. eight hundred thirty-eight
7. five thousand, six hundred fourteen
8. seven hundred nineteen
9. thirty million, two hundred thousand
10. ten thousand, four hundred one

GIVE INFORMATION
Complete the facts about Fred's school. Use number words.

11. My school has three fields (3 fields)
12. My school _____ (12 classrooms)
13. My school _____ (24 computers)
14. My school _____ (347 students)

Vocabulary

CARDINAL NUMBERS

Number Match Create two card sets. In each set, half of the cards contain numerals and the other half contain the corresponding number words.

308	three hundred eight

Then distribute one set to each of two teams. The first team to match their cards wins. Afterwards, teams can hold up the numeral cards and challenge the other team to read the numbers aloud.

UNIT 4 **LESSON 3**

LANGUAGE DEVELOPMENT: CARDINAL NUMBERS

OBJECTIVES

Function: Give Information
Concepts and Vocabulary:
❶ Cardinal Numbers
Speaking: Give Information
Writing: ❶ Sentences

INTRODUCE

1 Learn Number Words Introduce number words as follows:

- **0–20** Model pronunciation and help students create simple sentences: *I have two cookies.*
- **21–99** Model how to form numbers. Then start out a series and have students continue: 30–39, 40–49, etc.
- **100–999** Model the cumulative formation of these numbers. Point out that you don't add *s* to *hundred: five hundred,* not *five hundreds.*
- **1,000–1,000,000** Introduce *thousand* and *million.* Explain that commas indicate a place to say one of these number words. Write the numeral 2,165,457 and read it aloud, pausing for students to supply the correct words: *two **million,** one hundred sixty-five **thousand,** four hundred fifty-seven.*

PRACTICE

2 Conduct "Express Yourself" Model how to give information and have partners do the activity.

> **How to Give Information**
> - Start with: *China has…*
> - Add a number fact: *China has two hundred six airports.*

APPLY

3 Write Sentences Encourage students to look for examples of large numbers: *This book has 344 pages.*

▶ **Language Practice Book** page 57

CLOSE AND ASSESS

Have volunteers write the numerals as students dictate their sentences.

Language Development **T87**

UNIT 4 LESSON 4
LANGUAGE DEVELOPMENT: NEGATIVE SENTENCES

OBJECTIVES
Function: Give Information
Patterns and Structures:
- Negative Sentences

Writing: Sentences

INTRODUCE

1 Learn About Negative Sentences Direct students' attention to the pictures and read the rules and the examples. Ask students to point to the words *am not*, *is not*, *don't*, and *does not* in the negative sentences.

PRACTICE

2 Build Negative Sentences As you work through the first Example, remind students to add the word *not* after *is* or *are*. Call on volunteers to build negative sentences orally for Items 2–4.

Read the second set of directions and the rule below Example 5. Then offer more examples: *The airport looks huge. It does not look small. The suitcase looks heavy. It does not look light.*

APPLY

3 Write Sentences Have partners proofread each other's sentences to make sure that they used the correct construction, depending on the verb, and that they took the *s* off the verb when building a negative sentence with *does not*.

▶ Language Practice Book page 58

CLOSE AND ASSESS

Write one positive and one negative sentence about your life: *I live in the library. I do not live in the library.* Read aloud both sentences and have the class vote on which sentence is true. Invite volunteers to say more sentence pairs.

T88 Unit 4 | Numbers Count

NEGATIVE SENTENCES

Flight 400 Is Not Late!

There are different ways to build negative sentences.

Add *not* after *am*, *is*, or *are*.

He is happy.
She is not happy.

Add *do not* or *does not* before other verbs.

She gets on the flight.
He does not get on the flight.

BUILD NEGATIVE SENTENCES

Read each sentence. Add *not* to make it a negative sentence. Say the new sentence.

1. We are on Flight 400.
2. It is 10:00.
3. We are late.
4. People are in a hurry.

Example: 1. We are on Flight 400.
We are not on Flight 400.

Answers:
1. We are not on Flight 400.
2. It is not 10:00.
3. We are not late.
4. People are not in a hurry.

Read each sentence. Add *do not* or *does not* to make it a negative sentence. Say the new sentence.

5. The plane leaves at 10:30.
6. We walk very fast.
7. We get to Gate 55.
8. A woman talks to us.
9. We miss the plane.
10. The plane leaves without us.

Example: 5. The plane *leaves* at 10:30.
The plane *does not leave* at 10:30.

When you use *does not*, take the *s* off the verb.

Answers:
5. The plane does not leave at 10:30.
6. We do not walk very fast.
7. We do not get to Gate 55.
8. A woman does not talk to us.
9. We do not miss the plane.
10. The plane does not leave without us.

WRITE SENTENCES

11.–20. Write the sentences you made in Items 1–10 above.

Example: 11. We are on Flight 400. We are not on Flight 400.

88 Unit 4 | Numbers Count

REACHING ALL STUDENTS

Language Practice Book page 58

CABULARY: ORDINAL NUMBERS

First, Second, Third...

Look at the picture. In what order are the people?

WHO'S TALKING? ▶ EXPRESS NEEDS

Listen. 🎧
Each person in line is talking?
Point to the correct person.
Say what the person needs.

Example: 1. This is the fifth person.
She needs a magazine.

Answers:
1. fifth—magazine
2. seventh—apple
3. second—newspaper
4. sixth—T-shirt
5. third—book
6. tenth—bear

WRITE SENTENCES ✏️

4. Write about 8 people in the line.
Say what each person needs.

Example: 7. The first person needs water.

Language Development 89

UNIT 4 **LESSON 5**

LANGUAGE DEVELOPMENT: ORDINAL NUMBERS

OBJECTIVES

Functions: Listen Actively; Express Needs; Ask and Answer Questions

Concepts and Vocabulary:
🅣 Ordinal Numbers

Viewing: Respond to a Visual Image

Writing: 🅣 Sentences

INTRODUCE

1 Learn About Ordinal Numbers
Read each ordinal number, and have students repeat it and point to the label in the picture. Give directions to check understanding: *Point to the third person. Point to the tenth person.*

2 Use Ordinal Numbers Write the ordinals *first* through *tenth* on the chalkboard. Line up ten students under the numbers. Then ask and answer questions about each person's location in line: *Where is Tri? He is ninth.* Invite volunteers to ask and answer questions using the same pattern.

PRACTICE

3 Conduct "Who's Talking?" Play "Who's Talking?" on the **Language Tape/CD**. Have students listen to each speaker. Then pause and replay, if necessary, for students to identify the speaker and what he or she needs.

Tape 2B
CD 1 Track 15

APPLY

4 Write Sentences Work with students to list the object each person needs. They can refer to the list as they write their sentences.

▶ **Language Practice Book** page 59

CLOSE AND ASSESS

Ask questions about the people in line: *Who is chewing gum?* Have students answer using ordinal numbers: *The fifth person is chewing gum.*

Language Practice Book page 59

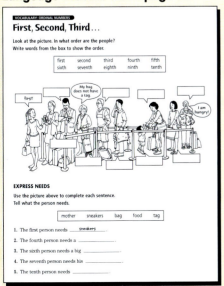

Multi-Level Strategies
VOCABULARY: ORDINAL NUMBERS

PRELITERATE Use an outdoor TPR activity to reinforce ordinal numbers. Divide students into teams and assign each member an ordinal number. Place an object an equal distance from each team and call out an ordinal number: *Ninth person, go!* The team member with the corresponding number will race to retrieve the object. The first one to reach the object wins and calls out the next ordinal number. When play is finished, give awards for first, second, third place.

Language Development **T89**

UNIT 4 **LESSON 6**

LANGUAGE AND LITERACY: THE BASICS BOOKSHELF

OBJECTIVES

Concepts and Vocabulary:
🅣 Number Words
Listening: Listen to a Preview
Reading Strategies:
Activate Prior Knowledge; Preview
Learning to Read: Identify End Marks

BUILD LANGUAGE AND VOCABULARY

1. **Teach "Words to Know"** Have students look at pages 2–3. Say: *These pages tell about numbers. Numbers can show how many things there are.* Point to each line on the chart. Indicate each number as you read the number word aloud.

   Then point to the illustration across the bottom of the pages and say: *These number words describe each person's place in line.* Say each word and point to the corresponding part of the illustration.

2. **Use Number Words** Line up several classroom items. Ask questions such as: *How many pencils are there? What color is the fourth ruler? Which thing is eighth in line?*

PREPARE TO READ

3. **Think About What You Know** Show the book cover and say: *This story tells about a drought. There is no rain. The ground is dry and the plants die.* Turn to pages 4–5, and invite students to identify more effects of a drought. (The crops are dead. The people and animals are hungry.)

4. **Preview** Play the Audio Walk-Through for *A Year Without Rain* on the **Selection Tape/CD** to give students the overall idea of the story.
   Tape 2B
   CD 1 Track 7

CLOSE AND ASSESS

Turn to pages 6–7, and call on volunteers to name the characters and explain how they helped during the drought.

A Year Without Rain
by Evelyn Stone

Summary This historical fiction is set during a drought in ancient China. Each child, monk, villager, merchant, and lord gives rice according to the person's station. The emperor donates one thousand jars of rice. The food is shared, and everyone eats. Patterned text reinforces number words.

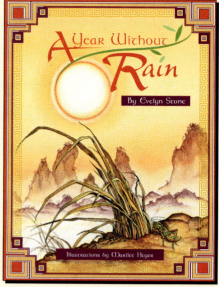
Cover

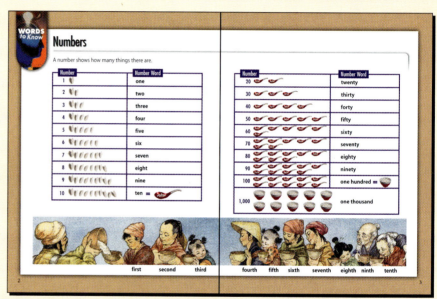
Pages 2–3

Multi-Level Strategies
LITERACY SUPPORT

PRELITERATE **Concepts of Print: Identify End Marks** Turn to page 8 and point to the period at the end of the first sentence. Say: *This is a period. It comes at the end of a sentence that tells something.* Then read the second sentence and point to the question mark. Say: *This is a question mark. It comes at the end of a sentence that asks a question. Listen to how these two types of sentences sound.* Read each sentence a few times with the correct intonation and ask students to echo what you say.

Leaf through pages 9–13 and have students point out the periods and question marks. Read each sentence with the correct intonation and invite students to chime in. On pages 14–15, point to each end mark and ask: *Is this a period or a question mark?*

T90a Unit 4 | Numbers Count

A Year Without Rain

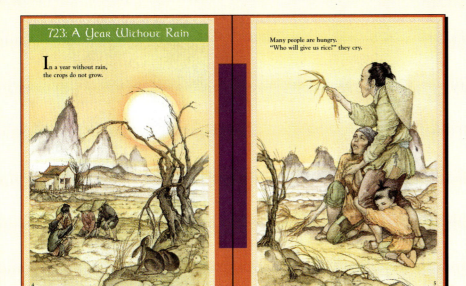

Pages 4–5

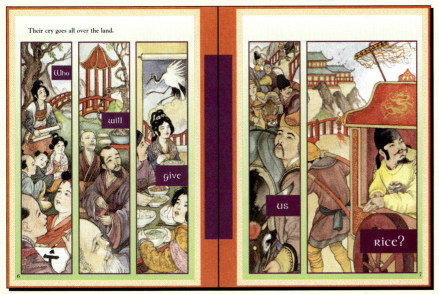

Pages 6–7

Strategies for Comprehensible Input

Page	Story Language	Strategy Options
4	a year without rain	**Restate:** In this year, it did not rain; There was no rain this year.
	crops	**Restate:** plants farmers grow for food
	grow	**Gesture:** Put your hand near the ground and gradually raise it.
5	are hungry	**Restate:** do not have food
	they cry	**Demonstrate:** Use a worried tone to say the sentence.
6–7	Their cry goes all over the land.	**Restate:** All the people in the country ask for rice. Everyone hears them.

Language and Literacy **T90b**

UNIT 4 **LESSON 6,** CONTINUED

LANGUAGE AND LITERACY: THE BASICS BOOKSHELF

OBJECTIVES
Function: Listen to a Book
Critical Thinking and Comprehension:
🅣 Identify Problem and Solution
Learning to Read: Track Print; Recognize Statements and Questions

READ AND THINK TOGETHER

1. **Read Aloud** On your first reading of the book, use the "Strategies for Comprehensible Input" at the bottom of pages T90b and T90d.

2. **Read and Map: Identify Problem and Solution** Draw a problem-and-solution chart like the one below, but write only the bold labels for each box. Say: *A problem-and-solution chart shows the problem, the steps to solve it, and the solution.*

   Review pages 4–7. Then think aloud as you fill in the first box: *What problem do the people need to solve? There is no rain. People are hungry. I'll write this in the box labeled* Problem.

   Pause after reading each set of pages shown below and model completing the chart for the rest of the text.

3. **Conduct Interactive Readings** Choose from these options:

   - **Read along and track print** Use page 8 to demonstrate tracking print. Have students practice as they read along with the recording of *A Year Without Rain* on the **Selection Tape/CD**. *(Tape 2B / CD 1 Track 8)*

   - **Read chorally** Model the intonation for a question and a statement. Then read the book together. On pages 8–15, have one group read the questions as the other reads the statements.

CLOSE AND ASSESS
Distribute slips of paper, each with one of these words or numbers: *problem, solution, 1, 2, 3, 4, 5, 6.* Have students retell their part of the story.

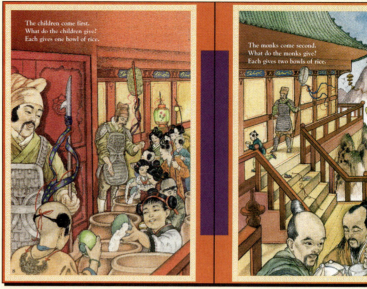
Pages 8–9

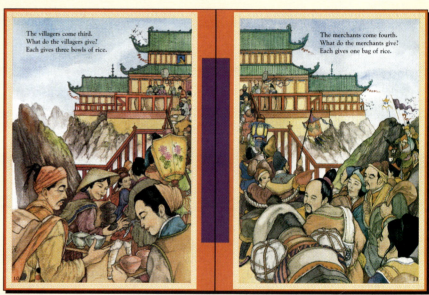
Pages 10–11

Problem-and-Solution Chart for *A Year Without Rain*

pages 4–7

Problem: There is no rain. People are hungry.

page 8	page 9	page 10
1. The children each give 1 bowl of rice.	2. The monks each give 2 bowls of rice.	3. The villagers each give 3 bowls of rice.
page 11	**pages 12–13**	**pages 14–15**
4. The merchants each give 1 bag of rice.	5. The lords each give 2 bags of rice.	6. The emperor gives 1,000 jars of rice.

page 16

Solution: Everyone shares, and everyone eats.

T90c Unit 4 | Numbers Count

A Year Without Rain, CONTINUED

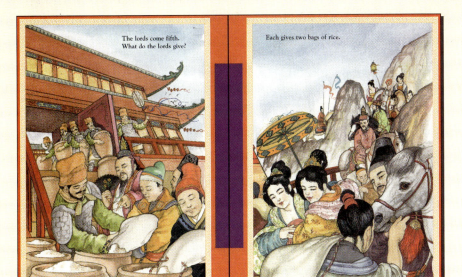

Pages 12–13

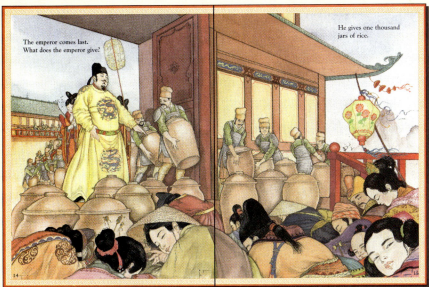

Pages 14–15

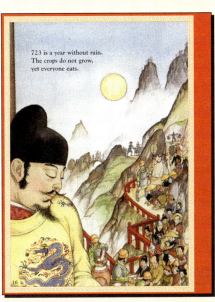

Page 16

Strategies for Comprehensible Input

Page	Story Language	Strategy Options
8	The children come first.	**Point to the children in the picture and explain:** The children are the first people to bring rice.
9	monks	**Explain:** Monks are religious teachers.
10	villagers	**Explain:** Villagers are people who live in a small town.
11	merchants	**Explain:** Merchants are people who have a business selling things.
	one bag	**Point to one bag in the picture.**
12	lords	**Explain:** Lords are people who own land that others live and work on.
13	two bags	**Demonstrate:** Hold up two fingers and count to two.
14	emperor	**Explain:** The emperor is the leader of the country.
	last	**Restate:** at the end (no one comes after him)
15	one thousand jars	**Point to the picture.**
16	everyone eats	**Explain:** There is enough rice for all the people.

Language and Literacy **T90d**

UNIT 4 LESSON 7

LANGUAGE AND LITERACY: THE BASICS BOOKSHELF

OBJECTIVES

Function: Retell a Story

Learning Strategy: Use Graphic Organizers (problem-and-solution chart)

Critical Thinking and Comprehension:
- Identify Problem and Solution

CHECK COMPREHENSION

1. **Make a Problem-and-Solution Chart** Remind students that a problem-and-solution chart identifies the problem, gives the steps to solve the problem in order, and tells the solution. Then have them review *A Year Without Rain* to record the problem, what each character gives, and the solution.

   As you read aloud the directions for each step, pause for students to add information to their charts. Encourage students to review the story to clarify important details.

2. **Retell the Story** Have partners compare charts to correct and add information. Then have each pair of students use their charts to tell the story to another pair.

CLOSE AND ASSESS

Ask students to complete this sentence: *A problem-and-solution chart shows _____.*

COMPREHENSION: IDENTIFY PROBLEMS AND SOLUTIONS

Read and Think Together

Make a problem-and-solution chart for *A Year Without Rain*. Follow these steps.

1. Think about the story. What is the main problem? Draw a box and write the problem.

   Problem: There is no rain. People are hungry.

2. What happens next? Add boxes. Write one event in each box.

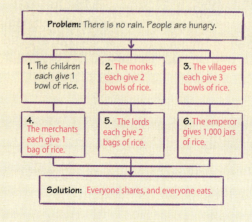

3. How is the problem solved? Write the solution in the box at the bottom of your chart.

4. Use your completed problem-and-solution chart to tell the story to a partner.

from **The Basics Bookshelf**

THEME BOOK
In a time without rain, crops do not grow, but people find a way to feed the hungry.

REACHING ALL STUDENTS

Language Development
ASK FOR AND GIVE PERMISSION

Role-Play Turn to page 16 in *A Year Without Rain*. Use these examples to model how to ask for and give permission:

Peasant to Guard: May I please take one bowl of rice from the jar?

Guard to Peasant: You may have three bowls of rice.

Collect other ways to ask for and give permission in a chart. Then have groups of three use the chart to role-play the scene on page 16.

How to Ask for Permission	How to Give Permission
May I _____?	Yes, you may _____.
Can I _____?	Yes, you can _____.
Do I have permission to _____?	You have my permission to _____.

HIGH FREQUENCY WORDS
Words to Know

REVIEW WORDS YOU KNOW

Read the words aloud. Which word goes in the sentence?

are	say
year	read
find	from

1. The people __are__ in an airport.
2. They __read__ the screens.
3. They __find__ their flight numbers.

LEARN TO READ

Learn new words.

leave	Stan and his friend **leave** in June for a vacation.
two	They go for **two** months: June and July.
out	They fly in and **out** of many airports.
three	China, Japan, and Laos are **three** Asian countries.
all	Stan likes them **all**.
says	Stan **says,** "Our first stop is in China."
second	"Our **second** stop is in Japan."
without	Stan never travels **without** his camera.
enough	He takes **enough** film to photograph everything.
more	He brings back **more** pictures of Japan than of China.

How to Learn a New Word
- Look at the word.
- Listen to the word.
- Listen to the word in a sentence. What does it mean?
- Say the word.
- Spell the word.
- Say the word again.

WORD WORK

Write each new word on a card. Sort the cards into these groups:

Example: 4.

second   enough

4. These 2 words have 6 letters.   second   enough
5. These 5 words have 3 or 4 letters.   two   out   all   says   more
6. This word is made up of 2 smaller words.   without
7. These 2 words name numbers.   two   three
8. These 2 words name actions.   leave   says

Read the words in each group aloud.
Make up new groups with a partner.

second
enough

Sample Groups:
These three words end in *e*:
leave   three   move
These three words have a long *e* sound:
leave   three   enough

Language and Literacy   91

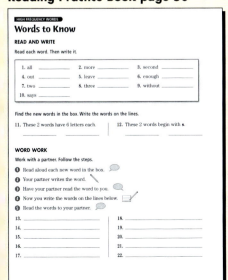

Reading Practice Book page 50

Reading Fluency
RECOGNIZE HIGH FREQUENCY WORDS

To build automaticity with the new high frequency words:

- Have students use their word cards as flashcards. Students can practice reading the cards together and have "flash reading contests," in which one student holds up a card and the others compete to name the word.

- Ask a volunteer to look at the classroom chart of words, choose a word, and begin spelling it slowly. The rest of the group tries to guess the word in as few letters as possible.

UNIT 4   **LESSON 8**

LANGUAGE AND LITERACY: HIGH FREQUENCY WORDS

OBJECTIVES

Learning to Read:
- Recognize High Frequency Words

REVIEW WORDS

1 **Review Known High Frequency Words** Have the group read aloud the words in the green box. Listen for words students cannot read automatically and use the steps in the yellow box to reteach those words. Then have students look at the photo. Read each cloze sentence. Reread each sentence and pause for students to silently read the two words to the left of the sentence. Tell students to choose the word that goes in the sentence and tells about the picture.

INTRODUCE NEW WORDS

2 **Learn High Frequency Words** Use the High Frequency Word Script on page T315 to lead students through the steps in the yellow box for each new word. Point out that *second* can mean "a unit of time—one sixtieth of a minute"—or "after first."

PRACTICE

3 **Conduct "Word Work"** Work through the Example with students, modeling how to use the first clue to sort the cards into a group.

Have partners complete Items 5–8. Review the groups and discuss why each word belongs in a group.

APPLY

4 **Read Words in Context** Students will read high frequency words in context in the sentences on page 93 and the passage on page 94.

▶ Reading Practice Book page 50

CLOSE AND ASSESS

Call out the high frequency words one at a time. Have students point to them and spell the words as a group.

Language and Literacy   **T91**

UNIT 4 LESSON 9

LANGUAGE AND LITERACY: PHONICS

OBJECTIVES

Learning to Read: Build Oral Vocabulary; Develop Phonemic Awareness; 🅣 Associate Sounds and Symbols: /ld/ ld, /lt/ lt, /nd/ nd, /nt/ nt, /nk/ nk, /ft/ ft, /mp/ mp, /st/ st, /sk/ sk; Blend Sounds to Decode Words

TEACH BLENDS

1. **Build Oral Vocabulary** Display Transparency 26. Talk through each picture to develop meaning for the words in the yellow boxes. For example, for Item 1, say:

   *Here is a **band** (point). People play music together in a **band**. One person in the **band** plays a horn (point and pantomime).*

2. **Develop Phonemic Awareness** Remove the transparency and conduct the oral activities in Step 1 of the Script for Transparency 26.

3. **Read Words with Blends** Display Transparency 26 again. Work through Steps 2 and 3 of the script.

CLOSE AND ASSESS

Display the words *nest, band, belt, camp, ant, disk, left,* and *bank.* Call on students to blend a word and identify the last two sounds.

Word Families

-EST AND -AMP

Materials: Letter Tiles

A large number of words can be generated from a few rhyming phonograms. Use letter tiles to build the word in dark type. Then change tiles to build other words in the *-est* and *-amp* families. Have students make a list of the words. Make sure students understand their meanings. Then ask them to read the word on their list and to identify the shared ending.

nest	rest	**stamp**	lamp
best	test	camp	ramp
chest	vest	champ	
pest	west	damp	

T92a Unit 4 | Numbers Count

Transparency 26: ▶ Blends

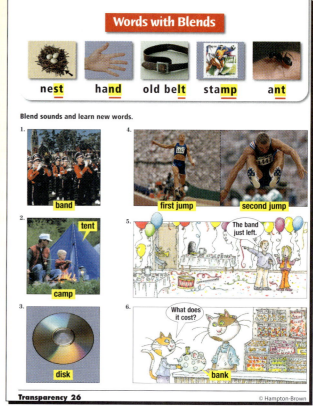

▼ Script for Transparency 26

Words with Blends

1. **Develop Phonemic Awareness**

   Isolate/Match the Blend Say: *Listen to the last two sounds in these words:* best, list, fast. *What are the sounds?* (/st/) *Say the words with me:* best, list, fast. *Now raise your hand each time you hear* /st/ *at the end of a word.* *Say these words:* past, band, just, hand, fist, camp, rest, lost, belt, dust. Repeat for other final blends: ld, lt, nd, nt, nk, ft, mp, sk.

2. **Associate Sounds and Symbols**

   Point to the nest on **Transparency 26**. Say: *This is a nest. Birds live in a nest. Say the word* nest *with me:* nest. Then point to the *st* in *nest* and say: *The letters* s *and* t *make the last two sounds you hear in* nest. *Blend* /s/ *and* /t/ *with me:* /st/. Repeat the process for the final blends in *hand, belt, stamp,* and *ant.*

3. **Blend Sounds to Read Words**

   Model/Teach Point to the letter *n* in *nest* and say: *The sound for* n *is* /nnn/. Repeat for *e:* /eee/. As you slide a finger slowly from left to right below the letters *ne,* say: *I can blend the two sounds:* /nnneee/. Then point to the *st* and say: *The sounds for the letters* st *are* /st/. *I can blend the four sounds together:* /nnneeest/. *Now, I'm going to say the whole word:* nest. Repeat for *hand, belt, stamp,* and *ant.* Lead students in sounding out the words.

   Practice For Item 1, say: *Let's try that again. This picture shows a band. A band plays music. Read the word with me. Follow my finger as we blend the sounds* /baaand/, *and say the word:* band. Repeat the process for the other words, calling special attention to the following:

   • Read aloud the phrases in Item 4, pausing for students to decode *jump.* Follow this process for the words *band, just, left,* and *cost* in Items 5 and 6. After students blend the words, say: *Say the sentence. Do the words make sense?*

◀ Transparency 27: Blends

▼ Script for Transparency 27

Words with Blends

1. **Develop Phonemic Awareness**
   Isolate/Match the Blend Say: *Listen to the first two sounds in these words:* free, frog, from. *What are the sounds?* (/fr/) *Say the words with me:* free, frog, from. *Now raise your hand each time you hear* /fr/ *at the beginning of a word.* Say these words: *slap, fruit, fry, friend, flag, snap, play, fresh, Friday, flower.* Repeat for other initial blends: *fl, sm, sn, sl.*

2. **Associate Sounds and Symbols**
   Point to the frog on **Transparency 27**. Say: *This is a frog. Say the word* frog *with me:* frog. Then point to the *fr* in *frog* and say: *The letters* fr *make the first two sounds you hear in* frog. *Blend* /f/ *and* /r/ *with me:* /fr/. Follow the process for the initial blends in *flag, smell, snap,* and *sled*.

3. **Blend Sounds to Read Words**
   Model/Teach Model how to read the word *frog*. Then invite students to blend the four sounds: /frooog/, and then say the whole word: *frog*. Repeat for *flag, smell, snap,* and *sled*.

   Practice Read aloud the first sentence in Item 1, pausing for students to decode *slams*. For *door*, say: *This word is* door (point to *door* and spell it). Repeat for the other sentences, calling special attention to the following:

   • In the second sentence of Item 1, blend *snack* with students and say: *A snack is a little bit to eat between meals.* In the fourth sentence, say *mmm* with students. Explain: *Mmm is a sound people make when something tastes good.*

   • Read aloud the sentences in Item 2, pausing for students to decode *frog, flip, slips, Smack,* and *flat*.

OBJECTIVES

Learning to Read: Build Oral Vocabulary; Develop Phonemic Awareness; 🅣 Associate Sounds and Symbols: /fr/ *fr*, /fl/ *fl*, /sm/ *sm*, /sn/ *sn*, /sl/ *sl*; Blend Sounds to Decode Words

TEACH BLENDS

1. **Build Oral Vocabulary** Display Transparency 27. Talk through each picture to develop meaning for the words in yellow boxes. For example, for the picture in Item 1, say:

   • *The man* **slams** *the door* (pantomime). *The door makes a loud sound. The taxi driver hears the door* **slam** (pantomime hearing door slam).

2. **Develop Phonemic Awareness** Remove the transparency and conduct the oral activities in Step 1 of the Script for Transparency 27.

3. **Read Words with Blends** Display Transparency 27 again. Work through Steps 2 and 3 of the script.

CLOSE AND ASSESS

Display the words *frog, smell, sled, snack,* and *flip*. Call on students to blend a word and identify the first two sounds.

Language and Literacy **T92b**

UNIT 4 LESSON 9, CONTINUED
LANGUAGE AND LITERACY: PHONICS

OBJECTIVES

Learning to Read: Build Oral Vocabulary; Develop Phonemic Awareness; 🅣 Associate Sounds and Symbols: /br/ *br*, /bl/ *bl*, /cr/ *cr*, /cl/ *cl*, /dr/ *dr*, /tr/ *tr*, /pl/ *pl*, /pr/ *pr*, /gr/ *gr*, /st/ *st*, /sp/ *sp*, /sw/ *sw*, /sk/ *sk*; Blend Sounds to Decode Words

TEACH BLENDS

1. **Build Oral Vocabulary** Display Transparency 28. Talk through each picture to develop meaning for the words. For example, for Item 1, say:

    Here is a **drop** *of water* (point). **Drops** *of water can drip from a faucet* (make a dripping sound). *People can also* **drop** *things* (pantomime).

2. **Develop Phonemic Awareness** Remove the transparency and work through Step 1 of the script.

3. **Read Words with Blends** Display Transparency 28 again. Work through Steps 2 and 3 of the script.

CLOSE AND ASSESS

Display *truck, plant, brush, spot, clap, swim, grin,* and *skunk*. Have students blend a word and name the first two sounds.

▶ **Reading Practice Book** page 51 (blends)

Transparency 28: ▶ Blends

▼ Script for Transparency 28

Words with Blends

1. **Develop Phonemic Awareness**
   Isolate/Match the Blend Say: *Listen to the first two sounds in these words:* clock, clap, clam. *What are the sounds?* (/kl/) *Say the words with me:* clock, clap, clam. *Now raise your hand each time you hear /kl/ at the beginning of a word.* Say these words: *clap, trip, drop, class, plum, clip, cloth, clock, crash, stop.* Repeat for other initial blends: *tr, st, pl, dr.*

2. **Associate Sounds and Symbols**
   Point to the clock on **Transparency 28**. Say: *This is a clock. You use a clock to tell time. Say the word* clock *with me.* Then point to the *cl* in *clock* and say: *The letters* c *and* l *make the first two sounds you hear in* clock. *Blend /k/ and /l/ with me:* /kl/. Repeat for the initial blends in the other words.

3. **Blend Sounds to Read Words**
   Model/Teach Model how to read the word *clock*. Then invite students to blend the four sounds together: /kloook/, and then say the whole word: *clock*. Repeat for the other words.

   Practice For Item 1, say: *Let's try that again. The first picture shows a drop of water. Read the word with me. Follow my finger as we blend the sounds* /drooop/, *and say the word:* drop. Repeat for the other words, calling special attention to the following:

   • In Item 2, blend *brush* with students and say: *When we read* brush, *the letters* s *and* h *at the end made one sound:* /sh/.

   • Read aloud the sentences in Item 3, pausing for students to decode *trick, class,* and *claps*. Follow this process for the other sentences.

Reading Practice Book page 51

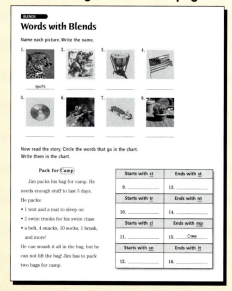

T92c Unit 4 | Numbers Count

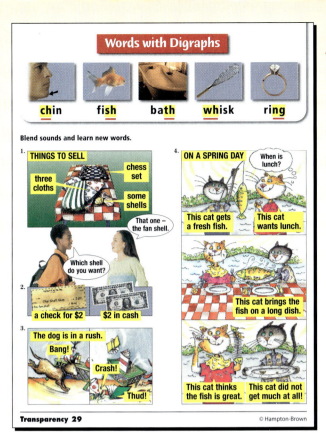

◀ Transparency 29: Digraphs

▼ Script for Transparency 29

Words with Digraphs

1. **Develop Phonemic Awareness**
   Isolate/Match Digraphs Say: *Listen to the first sound in these words:* chin, chest, chant. *What is the sound?* (/ch/) *Now listen for the sound /ch/ at the end of these words:* peach, rich, lunch. *Say the words:* peach, rich, lunch. *Now raise your hand each time you hear the sound /ch/:* shut, chip, ship, shop, chop, check, match. Repeat for /sh/, for /th/ and /TH/ *(bath, thin; this, that)* for /hw/, and for /ng/.

2. **Associate Sounds and Symbols**
   Point to the chin on **Transparency 29**. Say: *This is a chin. It is part of your face. Say the word* chin *with me.* Then point to the letters *ch* in *chin* and say: *The letters* c *and* h *make the first sound you hear in* chin. *The sound is /ch/. Say /ch/ with me: /ch/.* Repeat for the digraphs in *fish, bath, whisk,* and *ring.* Explain that the letters *th* can be pronounced /th/ or /TH/ with the vocal cords vibrating. Have students say the words *thin* and *this* while covering their ears to help them feel the difference between the voiced and unvoiced sounds of *th*.

3. **Blend Sounds to Read Words**
   Model/Teach Point to the letters *ch* in *chin* and say: *The sound for the letters* ch *is /ch/.* Repeat for *i: /iii/.* As you slide a finger slowly from left to right below *chi,* say: *I can blend the two sounds: /chiii/.* Then point to the *n* and say: *The sound for* n *is /n/. I can blend the three sounds together: /chiiinnn/. Now, I'm going to say the whole word:* chin. Repeat for *fish, bath, whisk,* and *ring.* Lead students in sounding out the words.

   Practice For Item 1, say: *This picture shows cloths, shells, and a chess set.* Read aloud the phrases and sentences on the page, pausing for students to decode the words with digraphs. Help students pronounce /th/ by showing them how to place their tongue between their front teeth and letting the air flow out.

OBJECTIVES

Learning to Read: Build Oral Vocabulary; Develop Phonemic Awareness; 🅣 Associate Sounds and Symbols: /ch/ *ch*, /sh/ *sh*, /th/ *th*, /TH/ *th*, /hw/ *wh*, /ng/ *ng*; Blend Sounds to Decode Words

TEACH DIGRAPHS

1. **Build Oral Vocabulary** Display Transparency 29. Use the pictures to develop the meaning of each word and use it in a sentence. For example, for Item 3, use your voice to mimic the sounds and say:

   • *The dog runs into the table. It makes the sound: Bang! The book falls off the table. Thud! The vase falls, too. Crash!*

2. **Develop Phonemic Awareness** Remove the transparency and conduct the oral activities in Step 1 of the Script for Transparency 29.

3. **Read Words with Digraphs** Display Transparency 29 again. Work through Steps 2 and 3 of the script.

CLOSE AND ASSESS

Display the words *bath, when, long, shop,* and *lunch.* Call on students to blend a word, identify the two letters that make one sound, and say the sound.

▶ **Reading Practice Book** page 52 (digraphs)

Reading Practice Book page 52

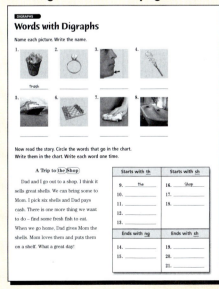

Language and Literacy **T92d**

UNIT 4 LESSON 10

LANGUAGE AND LITERACY: READING AND SPELLING

OBJECTIVES

Functions: Listen Actively; Repeat Spoken Language; Recite

Learning to Read: Develop Phonemic Awareness; 🅣 Associate Sounds and Symbols: Blends, Digraphs; Blend Sounds to Decode Words

Spelling: 🅣 Words with Blends and Digraphs

LISTEN AND LEARN

Tape 2B / CD 1 Track 16

1. **Sing a Song** Display Transparency 30 and play "Numbers All Around" on the **Language Tape/CD**.

DEVELOP PHONEMIC AWARENESS

2. **Blend Sounds to Form a Word** Say: *Listen to these sounds: /k/ /l/ /o/ /k/. Blend the sounds with me to say a word:* clock. Repeat for other words with blends *(nest, frog, flag, jump, hand)* and with digraphs *(fish, chin, ring, whisk, bath)*.

CONNECT SOUNDS AND LETTERS

3. **Associate Sounds and Symbols for Blends and Digraphs** For the first picture, say: *This is a clock, and here's the word. Let's point to the letters. Blend the sounds with me: /kloook/,* clock. Repeat for the other pictures, pointing out the two consonant sounds in *band, nest,* and *truck* that are blended together. For words with digraphs, point and say: *These two letters make one sound.* Then read the question aloud: *How many sounds does each word have?* (*clock, band, nest, truck* [4]; *fish, bath, check, ring* [3]) For each word, have a student tell whether each letter makes its own sound or whether two letters make one sound.

Afterwards, play the song again. Have students identify words with *cl, th, st, mp, sh, nk, tr,* and *pl*.

T92 Unit 4 | Numbers Count

BLENDS AND DIGRAPHS

Reading and Spelling

LISTEN AND LEARN

Numbers All Around

Clocks have them.
Stamps have them.
Buses, ships, and stores have them.
Months have them.
Banks have them.
Highways, trucks, and doors have them.
Two plus two. Ten plus four!
Do the math. Keep the score!

CONNECT SOUND AND LETTERS

How many sounds does each word have?

1. four: /k/ /l/ /o/ /k/ — **cl**o**ck**
   four: /b/ /a/ /n/ /d/ — b**and**

2. three: /f/ /i/ /sh/ — fi**sh**
   three: /b/ /a/ /th/ — ba**th**

four: /n/ /e/ /s/ /t/ — **n**e**st**
four: /t/ /r/ /u/ /k/ — **tr**u**ck**

three: /ch/ /e/ /k/ — **ch**e**ck**
three: /r/ /i/ /ng/ — ri**ng**

92 Unit 4 | Numbers Count

REACHING ALL STUDENTS

Multi-Level Strategies

LITERACY SUPPORT

INTERRUPTED SCHOOLING To anchor understanding of how to sound out words with blends and digraphs, use an overhead projector to display a covered word. Uncover the letter or letters that stand for each sound as you say it. After the whole word is revealed, slide a finger under the letters as you blend the sounds with students.

ch ☐   chi ☐   chin

PRELITERATE Display the picture banks on Transparencies 26–29, covering a word at a time. Say the word and guide students in spelling it letter by letter. Write the spellings as students suggest letters. Then uncover the word and have students check the spelling on the transparency.

READING STRATEGY

Follow these steps to read a word.

1. Sometimes 2 consonants stand for 1 sound. When you see **sh**, **ch**, **th**, **wh**, or **ng**, say 1 sound. Then blend all the sounds together to say the word.

   sho p   b a **th**

   sh + o + p = shop   b + a + th = bath

   Each word has 3 sounds.

2. When other consonants are together, each usually makes its own sound. Blend all the sounds together to say the word.

   dro p   w e **n**t

   d + r + o + p = drop   w + e + n + t = went

   Each word has 4 sounds.

READING AND SPELLING PRACTICE

Blend the sounds to read these words.

1. brush   2. bring   3. cash   4. class   5. costs   6. just

Use what you learned to read the sentences.

7. Beth needs a brush for art class this spring.
8. She has three dollars in cash.
9. That is enough for a small brush. It costs just $2.39.
10. A big, long brush costs $5.00.
11. Which brush does Beth bring home?

12.–15. Now write the sentences that your teacher reads. *For dictation sentences, see Step 6 at right.*

WORD WORK

16. Write each of these words on a card.

catch	chess	chin	inch	much
match	check	lunch	chat	chop

Say each word. Group the words that begin with the same sound.
Now group the words that end with the same sound.
Look at these words. What do you notice?

Example: 16.
Begin with /ch/:
chess
check
chin
chat
chop

End with /ch/:
catch
match
lunch
inch
much

Language and Literacy **93**

Decodable Book
PRACTICE WITH BLENDS AND DIGRAPHS

Decodable Book 4:
From Last to First

Assign **Decodable Book 4** for independent reading. The **Decodable Book** can be used in a variety of ways to help students become more fluent, automatic readers:

Discussion Circles Have students work in small groups to read aloud and discuss the book using the questions on the back cover. Encourage students to read aloud the text that supports their answers. Groups can also work together to complete the Word Work Activity.

Readers Theater Students can read aloud the stories in a class performance. Help them prepare by rereading the stories in daily rehearsals. Work with students to add narration or dialog. Encourage them to use natural phrasing and expression.

Rereading at Home Have students work with family members to reread the book at home. They can take turns reading aloud alternate pages, then rereading the book switching the pages each person reads.

LEARN A READING STRATEGY

4. **Sound Out Words** Work through the strategy with students, reading each step aloud and modeling the actions.

PRACTICE

5. **Read Words and Sentences** Sound out the words in Items 1–6 as a choral reading. Then distribute the Partner Prompts from page T311 to guide peers in reading the sentences in Items 7–11. Remind them to use the sound-out strategy to read words.

6. **Write Sentences** Dictate the following sentences for students to write. Read each sentence at normal speed once so students can listen, and then repeat it slowly word by word as they write:

   12. Fresh fish smells good.
   13. The frog jumps out of my hand.
   14. Which camp has a flag?
   15. How much does this belt cost?

   If students need extra support, guide them in spelling the decodable words. For example: *What is the first sound in fresh?* (/f/) *Write the letter that stands for /f/. Repeat for /r/ and /e/. For /sh/ prompt students to write the two letters that make the sound.*

7. **Conduct "Word Work"** Read the directions and work through the Example. Have partners complete the activity. Discuss what they learned about the ways to spell /ch/.

▶ **Reading Practice Book**
pages 123–126 (Decodable Book 4)

CLOSE AND ASSESS

Write *chin, drop, band, ring, nest,* and *shop.* Call on students to sound out the words, then tell which words have two letters that make one sound.

Language and Literacy **T93**

UNIT 4 LESSON 11

LANGUAGE AND LITERACY: INDEPENDENT READING

OBJECTIVES

Function: Read a Selection
Learning to Read: 🔵 Recognize High Frequency Words; 🔵 Decode Words with Blends and Digraphs
Reading Strategies: Predict; Set a Purpose for Reading; Retell
Critical Thinking and Comprehension: 🔵 Identify Details

READ ON YOUR OWN

1. **Introduce Vocabulary** In "Rush!," students apply phonics skills and read high frequency words taught in Lessons 8–10. Introduce these story words. Write each word, pronounce it, and spell it.

   - **plane:** an airplane. *Maria flew to Ecuador on a plane.*
   - **minutes:** 1 minute = 60 seconds. *Class begins in five minutes.*
   - **fall:** drop. *Apples fall from trees.*
   - **ticket:** a piece of paper that lets you do something, such as travel. *I bought a bus ticket to Miami.*

2. **Make Predictions/Set Purposes** Point out the man whose things are falling on the ground, and say: *This is Stan. He is in a big rush. Why do you think Stan is in a rush?* (He is going somewhere. He has to catch a plane.) *Read to find out why Stan is in a rush.*

3. **Read and Think: Identify Details** Students should read the passage on their own. Then have them complete the web and use it to retell the story to a partner.

4. **Build Reading Fluency** Tape 2B / CD 1 Track 17
   Use the **Language Tape/CD** with Reading Practice Book page 53 for fluency practice.

   ▶ Reading Practice Book page 53

CLOSE AND ASSESS

Have one student retell the beginning of the story and others continue until all the events and details are given.

T94 Unit 4 | Numbers Count

COMPREHENSION: IDENTIFY DETAILS

Read on Your Own

RUSH!

Stan is in a big rush. His plane leaves at 2:00 p.m. The clock says 1:57 p.m. Stan has three minutes to catch his plane. That is not very long! He jumps out of the cab and slams the door. Bang! He drops his bag. All of his things fall out of the bag. Then he drops his ticket! A man helps Stan. He picks up the ticket and asks, "When does your plane leave?"

Stan says, "I think it just left without me."

The man looks at Stan's ticket. He grins and tells Stan, "You have enough time. Your plane leaves tomorrow at two."

CHECK YOUR UNDERSTANDING

Copy the web. Then complete it. Tell the story to a partner.
Sample Responses

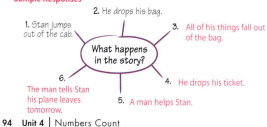

1. Stan jumps out of the cab.
2. He drops his bag.
3. All of his things fall out of the bag.
4. He drops his ticket.
5. A man helps Stan.
6. The man tells Stan his plane leaves tomorrow.

✓ **DECODING CHECK**
Give the Decoding Progress Check on page 1a of the Assessment Handbook.

REACHING ALL STUDENTS

Reading Fluency
PHRASING

Read the introduction on **Reading Practice Book** page 53. Explain that the / in the examples shows a short pause between groups of words and the // shows a longer pause between sentences. Model reading the examples and have students echo them.

Next, play "Rush!" on the **Language Tape/CD** and have students mark the sentences to show where the pauses occur. Check marks as a whole class before partners do the Practice section. Circulate during the Practice to check and support reading fluency.

Reading Practice Book page 53

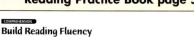

CONTRACTIONS WITH NOT

I Don't Want to Pay $10.00!

When you make a **contraction**, you join two words together.

| is + not = isn't | do + not = don't |
| are + not = aren't | does + not = doesn't |

no space — Write an apostrophe in place of the *o*.

Use these contractions in negative sentences.

The food at the airport **isn't** very good.
The cookies **aren't** big.
The cake **doesn't** have nuts.
I **don't** want anything to eat.

READ SENTENCES

Read the first sentence in each item. Then read the second sentence with the contraction. Listen to how the contraction sounds.

1. Stan does not want this food. Stan doesn't want this food.
2. The grapes are not green. The grapes aren't green.
3. The sandwich is not fresh. The sandwich isn't fresh.
4. The cookies do not have raisins. The cookies don't have raisins.

Read each sentence. Change the underlined words to a contraction. Then say the new sentence.

Example: 5. The salad does not have carrots.
The salad doesn't have carrots.

5. The salad does not have carrots.
6. The grapes do not taste sweet.
7. The cake is not chocolate.
8. The grapes are not cold.
9. The food is not cheap!
10. Stan is not hungry anymore.

Answers:
5. The salad doesn't have carrots.
6. The grapes don't taste sweet.
7. The cake isn't chocolate.
8. The grapes aren't cold.
9. The food isn't cheap!
10. Stan isn't hungry anymore.

WRITE SENTENCES

11.–14. Work with a partner. Write 4 new sentences to tell about the picture above. Use *isn't, aren't, don't,* and *doesn't*.

Example: 11. The salad isn't fresh.

Language and Literacy 95

Language Practice Book page 60

Multi-Level Strategies

WRITING SUPPORT

NON-ROMAN ALPHABET Focus on written contractions by playing "Contraction Concentration." First, students create pairs of cards for the contractions *isn't, aren't, don't, doesn't,* and the corresponding two-word phrases. Coach them on the mechanics of letter formation and left-to-right flow. Then shuffle the cards, lay them face down, and have students turn over two cards at a time to match contracted and uncontracted forms.

UNIT 4 **LESSON 12**

LANGUAGE AND LITERACY: CONTRACTIONS WITH NOT

OBJECTIVES
Function: Write; Give Information
Patterns and Structures: 🅣 Negative Sentences; 🅣 Contractions with *not*
Writing: Sentences

INTRODUCE

1 Learn About Contractions with *Not*
Read the page title and introduction. Explain: *In English, you can put together two words to make one word. The word that you make is called a* contraction.

Read the examples and point out where the apostrophe takes the place of a missing letter. Point out the vowel sound changes when you go from *do not* to *don't*. Then read the sentences aloud and have students repeat after you. Guide students in identifying the words each contraction stands for.

PRACTICE

2 Read Sentences Have students practice saying the contractions with Items 1–4. Then read the directions for Items 5–10. Form an Inside-Outside Circle (see Cooperative Learning Structures, page T337d), and have students in the inside circle read each item while students in the outside circle say the contracted form. Afterwards, have the circles switch roles and repeat.

APPLY

3 Write Sentences Encourage students to use the food prices in some of their sentences.

▶ **Language Practice Book** page 60

CLOSE AND ASSESS
Have volunteers say sentences with the contractions on this page. Call on students to replace the contraction with its two-word phrase.

Language and Literacy **T95**

UNIT 4 LESSON 13
LANGUAGE ACROSS THE CURRICULUM: SOCIAL STUDIES

OBJECTIVES
Function: Listen to an Article
Concepts and Vocabulary: Geography
Research Skills and Learning Strategies: Use Maps; Use Text Structures (charts); Make Comparisons
Critical Thinking and Comprehension: Identify Cause and Effect

LEARN ABOUT GEOGRAPHY

1 Use Geography Aids Read the title and the labels on the globe. Then have volunteers identify examples of the terms on a map or globe: *Africa is a continent. Canada is a country. The Arctic is an ocean.*

Turn to the chart, and go over the labels. Explain that *population* means how many people live in a place. Demonstrate using the chart to answer questions: *How many people live in China? Do more people live in China or Japan?*

READ AND THINK

2 Activate Prior Knowledge Read the title of the article and the focus question. Use a world map to locate Bolivia and Colombia. Point out topographical features such as mountains, lakes, and rivers.

3 Listen to the Article Restate and clarify vocabulary as necessary. Pause for students to view the photographs and chart, and discuss how they represent information from the article.

CHECK UNDERSTANDING

4 Answer the Review Questions Help students find information in the article and the chart.

CLOSE AND ASSESS

Use information from this page to pose questions about China, Japan, Bolivia, and Colombia. For example: *Which country has the greatest population? What is the area of Bolivia?*

T96 Unit 4 | Numbers Count

SUCCESS IN SOCIAL STUDIES
Learn About Geography

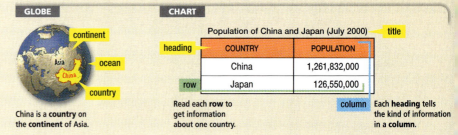

GLOBE — China is a **country** on the **continent** of Asia. (Labels: continent, ocean, country)

CHART — Population of China and Japan (July 2000) (title)

COUNTRY	POPULATION
China	1,261,832,000
Japan	126,550,000

Read each **row** to get information about one country.
Each **heading** tells the kind of information in a **column**.

Listen to the article and study the chart. Then do the Review.

Compare Populations
• Why do some places have a large population?

Answers for the Review:
1. The middle of the continent has many forests and mountains. This makes roads and towns difficult to build there. It is easier to build roads and towns on the coast.
2. South America
3. about 31 million

South America is a large **continent**. It has many different kinds of land.

Mountains

Rain Forest

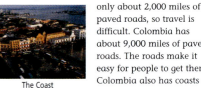
The Coast

Most people live near the coast. Not many people live in the middle of the continent because it has many forests and mountains. Roads and towns are difficult to build in places like that, and it is not easy to ship things.

Compare Colombia and Bolivia, for example. These **countries** are of similar size, but their populations are very different. One reason is the location of each country. Bolivia is an inland country with mountains and rain forests. It has only about 2,000 miles of paved roads, so travel is difficult. Colombia has about 9,000 miles of paved roads. The roads make it easy for people to get there. Colombia also has coasts on both the Caribbean Sea and Pacific Ocean. It is easy to ship things by land or sea. People like to live where it is easy to get the things they need.

Area and Population of Bolivia and Colombia (2000)

COUNTRY	AREA (in square miles)	POPULATION
Bolivia	424,164	8,153,000
Colombia	440,831	39,686,000

REVIEW
1. **Check Your Understanding** Why do most people in South America live near the coast?
2. **Vocabulary** In what continent are Colombia and Bolivia located?
3. **Use Charts** How many more people live in Colombia than in Bolivia?

96 Unit 4 | Numbers Count

REACHING ALL STUDENTS

Social Studies Connection
GATHER INFORMATION

Have students work in groups to research the area and population of a country of their choice. Encourage groups to use a variety of sources (such as almanacs, atlases, encyclopedias, and the Internet) to find information. Then collect each group's data onto a class area-and-population chart. Invite group members to present information about their country.

Writing Project / Fact Sheet

✓ **WRITING ASSESSMENT** Use the Writing Progress Checklist on page 51 of the Assessment Handbook to evaluate this writing project.

Find number facts about a country. Then write a fact sheet to share with the class.

FIND NUMBER FACTS

1. Choose a country to research. Make a list of questions like these.
2. Find answers. Get help from your teacher or librarian.
3. Take notes.

- How large is China?
- What is the population of China?
- What is the longest river?
- What is the population of the capital city?

The Yangtze River is almost 4,000 miles long!

- Size: over 3,700,000 square miles
- Population: 1,261,832,000 people
- Yangtze River is almost 4,000 miles long.
- The capital is Beijing. Its population is 13,800,000.

MAKE A FACT SHEET

Write the name of the country at the top of a piece of paper. Use your notes to write each question and answer.

 **Check Your Work**
Does each fact really answer the question?
Did you use commas in your numbers? Are they in the right place?
Did you write the names of places with a capital letter?

China
- How large is China? It is over 3,700,000 square miles.
- What is the population of China? The population of China is 1,261,832,000.
- What is the longest river in China? The Yangtze River is the longest. It is 4,000 miles long.
- What is the population of the capital city? The capital is Beijing. Its population is 13,800,000.

SHARE YOUR FACTS

Point to the country on a world map.
Share your facts with the class.

Language Across the Curriculum 97

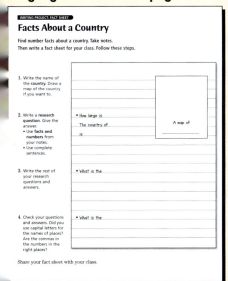

Language Practice Book page 61

Multi-Level Strategies

WRITING SUPPORT

PRELITERATE Pair up each preliterate student with a literate partner. Provide a fact-sheet frame for the partners to use as they gather information.

COUNTRY: _____
Q: What is the area?
A: _____
Q: What is the population?
A: _____
Q: What is the capital city?
A: _____

UNIT 4 **LESSON 14**

LANGUAGE ACROSS THE CURRICULUM: WRITING

OBJECTIVES

Functions: Write; Ask Questions; Give Information
Learning Strategies and Critical Thinking: Plan; Generate and Organize Ideas; Self-Assess
Research Skills: Formulate Questions; Gather Information; Take Notes; Use the Research Process
Writing: Fact Sheet

CONDUCT THE WRITING PROJECT

1. **Explore Countries** Read the introduction and look back at page 96 to review what students have learned about geography.

2. **Find Number Facts** Preview steps 1–3. Then model how to write questions and take notes on the answers. Using the article on page 96 as a basis, write out your questions as you think aloud: *I can research facts about Bolivia. I can ask:*
   - Where is Bolivia?
   - How large is the country?
   - How many people live there?
   - What landforms does it have?

   Review the article and model finding and recording each answer.

3. **Make a Fact Sheet** Use the fact sheet for China as a model for students' writing. Partners can use *Check Your Work* as part of the revision process.

4. **Share Your Facts** Have students take turns presenting the information in their fact sheets. Then collect the fact sheets into a class atlas. Alternately, students can start a writing portfolio, where they can keep their best writing projects.

▶ **Language Practice Book** page 61

CLOSE AND ASSESS

As students look at their fact sheets, say:
- *Show me a question and an answer.*
- *Point to the numbers in your facts. Read aloud the numbers.*
- *Did you write any contractions? If so, tell me what letter the apostrophe replaces.*

Language Across the Curriculum **T97**

Resources

For Success in Language and Literacy
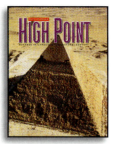
Student Book pages 98–113

For Language Skills Practice
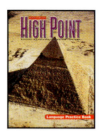
Language Practice Book pages 62–68

For Reading Skills Practice
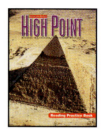
Reading Practice Book pages 54–57

For Vocabulary, Language Development, and Reading Fluency

Language Tape 3, Side A
Language CD 1, Tracks 18–21

For Reading Together

Theme Book *More Than a Meal* from The Basics Bookshelf

For Audio Walk-Throughs and Selection Readings

Selection Tape 3A
Selection CD 1, Tracks 9–10

For Phonics Instruction

Transparencies 31–35

Transparency Scripts 31–35

Letter Tiles

For Comprehensive Assessment
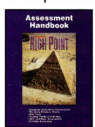
Language Acquisition Assessment, Units 4–6 Test, Writing Assessment, Self-Assessment

For Planning and Instruction
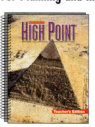
Teacher's Edition pages T98a–T113

T98a Unit Planner

UNIT 5

City Sights

In This Unit

Vocabulary
- Location Words
- Neighborhood
- Maps

Language Function
- Ask for and Give Information

Patterns and Structures
- Prepositions
- Regular Past Tense Verbs
- Statements with *There is* and *There are*
- Pronoun-Verb Contractions

Reading
- Word Patterns and Multisyllabic Words
- Comprehension: Identify Details (detail chart)

Writing
- Sentences
- Questions and Answers
- Journal Entry

Content Area Connection
- Social Studies (maps)

UNIT 5
Activity and Assessment Planner

UNIT 5: City Sights

LESSONS

1

UNIT 5 LAUNCH ▶ *pages T98–T99*

LESSON 1: INTRODUCE UNIT 5 pages T98–T99

Vocabulary
T Neighborhood

Viewing
Interpret a Visual Image

Learning Strategies
Preview

Build Background

Critical Thinking
Generate Ideas

Plan

2–7

LANGUAGE DEVELOPMENT ▶ *pages T100–T105*

LESSON 2
LOCATION WORDS
page T100

Function
Ask for and Give Information

Vocabulary
T Location Words

T Neighborhood

Writing
T Sentences

LESSON 3
NEIGHBORHOOD
page T101

Function
Ask for and Give Information

Vocabulary
T Neighborhood

Writing
Questions and Answers

LESSON 4
NEIGHBORHOOD
page T102

Functions
Ask for and Give Information

Role-Play

Vocabulary
T Neighborhood

T Location Words

Writing
Questions and Answers

LESSON 5
REGULAR PAST TENSE VERBS
page T103

Function
Give Information

Patterns and Structures
T Regular Past Tense Verbs

Writing
Sentences

LESSON 6
REGULAR PAST TENSE VERBS
page T104

Function
Give Information

Patterns and Structures
T Regular Past Tense Verbs

Writing
Sentences

LESSON 7
THERE IS/THERE ARE
page T105

Function
Give Information

Vocabulary
T Location Words

Patterns and Structures
T *There Is* and *There Are*

Writing
T Sentences

8–14

LANGUAGE AND LITERACY ▶ *pages T106a–T111*

LESSON 8
BASICS BOOKSHELF
pages T106a–T106f

Functions
Listen to a Book

Read Aloud a Story (choral reading)

Dramatize

Vocabulary
T Neighborhood

Reading Strategies
Activate Prior Knowledge

Preview

Learning to Read
Identify Where a Story Begins and Ends

Identify Capital Letters

Identify Words

Critical Thinking and Comprehension
T Identify Details

LESSON 9
BASICS BOOKSHELF: COMPREHENSION
page T106

Function
Retell a Story

Learning Strategy
Use Graphic Organizers (detail chart)

Critical Thinking and Comprehension
T Identify Details

LESSON 10
HIGH FREQUENCY WORDS
page T107

Learning to Read
T Recognize High Frequency Words

LESSON 11
PHONICS
pages T108a–T108d

Learning to Read
Build Oral Vocabulary

Develop Phonemic Awareness

Contrast Short and Long Vowel Sounds

Blend Sounds to Decode Words

T Use Word Patterns to Decode Words

T Divide Words into Syllables

T Decode Multisyllabic Words

LESSON 12
READING AND SPELLING
pages T108–T109

Learning to Read
Develop Phonemic Awareness

Contrast Short and Long Vowel Sounds

T Use Word Patterns to Decode Words

T Divide Words into Syllables

Spelling
T Short and Long Vowel Words

Multisyllabic Words

LESSON 13
INDEPENDENT READING
page T110

Function
Read a Selection

Learning to Read
T Recognize High Frequency Words

T Use Word Patterns

T Decode Multisyllabic Words

Reading Strategies
Activate Prior Knowledge

Build Background

Retell

Critical Thinking and Comprehension
T Identify Details

LESSON 14
CONTRACTIONS
page T111

Functions
Write

Give Information

Patterns and Structures
T Pronoun-Verb Contractions

Writing
Sentences

15–16

LANGUAGE ACROSS THE CURRICULUM ▶ *pages T112–T113*

LESSON 15 SOCIAL STUDIES: CITIES
page T112

Function
Listen to an Article

Vocabulary
Maps

Research Skills and Learning Strategies
Build Background

Use Text Structures (maps)

Critical Thinking and Comprehension
Identify Cause and Effect

T Identify Details

LESSON 16 WRITING PROJECT: JOURNAL ENTRY
page T113

Functions
Write

Give Information

Learning Strategies and Critical Thinking
Plan

Relate to Personal Experience

Generate and Organize Ideas

Self-Assess

Use Graphic Organizers (detail chart)

Relate Events in a Sequence

Writing
Journal Entry

T98c Unit 5 | City Sights

T = Objective Tested on Unit Test

ASSESSMENT OPTIONS

The **Teacher's Edition** and the **Assessment Handbook** include these comprehensive assessment tools:

▶ **Ongoing, Informal Assessment**
Check for understanding and achieve closure for every lesson with the targeted questions and activities in the **Close and Assess** boxes in your Teacher's Edition.

▶ **Decoding Progress Check**
These word lists for each unit provide a quick way to check on mastery of the phonics or word structure skills taught in the unit.

▶ **Language Acquisition Assessments**
To verify students' ability to use the language functions and grammar structures taught in Units 4–6, conduct these performance assessments.

▶ **Unit Test in Standardized Test Format**
This multiple-choice test measures students' cumulative understanding of the skills and language developed in Units 4–6.

▶ **Self- and Peer-Assessment**
Students use the Self-Assessment Form to evaluate their own work and develop learning strategies appropriate to their needs. Students offer feedback to their classmates with the Peer-Assessment Form.

▶ **Writing Assessment/Portfolio Opportunities**
You can evaluate students' writing in the Writing Projects using the Writing Progress Checklist. Then collaborate with students to choose work for their portfolios.

UNITS 4–6 ASSESSMENT OPPORTUNITIES	Assessment Handbook Pages
Decoding Progress Check	1a
Language Acquisition Assessments	10
Units 4–6 Test	11–16
Self-Assessment Form	17
Peer-Assessment Form	50
Writing Progress Checklist	51
Portfolio Evaluation Form	52

RELATED RESOURCES

Abuela
by Arthur Dorros
A whimsy about a young girl and her grandmother who get a bird's-eye view of New York City. Bilingual book, in English and Spanish.
(Available from Hampton-Brown)
Theme Book: Read Aloud

Round Trip
by Ann Jonas
Sparse text with black and white illustrations record the sights of an exciting trip to the city.
(Greenwillow)
Phonics Reinforcement: Word Patterns (CV, CVC)

Sing a Song of People
by Lois Lenski
A poetic evocation of city life: the crowds and unexpected moments of solitude in the city's parks, streets, and subways.
(Little, Brown)
Easy Reading

I Read Signs
by Tana Hoban
Engaging color photos of signs and symbols frequently seen on city streets.
(Available from Hampton-Brown)
Vocabulary: Neighborhood Signs

SimTown
Students build and manage the growth of a small town. (Edmark)
Multimedia: CD-ROM

Signs Around You
Point and click on one hundred signs around town. (Edmark)
Multimedia: Disk

Unit Planner **T98d**

UNIT 5 **LESSON 1**

INTRODUCE UNIT 5: CITY SIGHTS

OBJECTIVES

Concepts and Vocabulary:
🅣 Neighborhood
Viewing: Interpret a Visual Image
Learning Strategies: Preview; Build Background
Critical Thinking: Generate Ideas; Plan
Representing: Symbols; Signs

START WITH A COMMON EXPERIENCE

1. **Introduce "City Sights"** Explain that *city sights* are things you can see in a city. Point out that the pictures show things to see and do in the city of Miami, Florida.

2. **Study a City Sign** Read aloud the words on the sign: "Welcome to Miami." Ask: *Where might you see a sign like this?* (on the road as you drive into the city; at the airport; at a beach entrance) Then have students name the things they see on the sign. Ask: *What do these things tell you about the city?* (it has unusual animals, modern ships, interesting architecture, and lots of beaches)

3. **Create a City Sign** Read aloud the activity directions and have the class brainstorm sights to include on a sign for your city. Use a chart to categorize ideas:

Things to See	Things to Do	Places to Go
animals	sports	parks
plants	eat	museums
statues	sightsee	beach

Small groups can draw symbols or use images from magazines and brochures. Display the signs and discuss how the symbols represent your city.

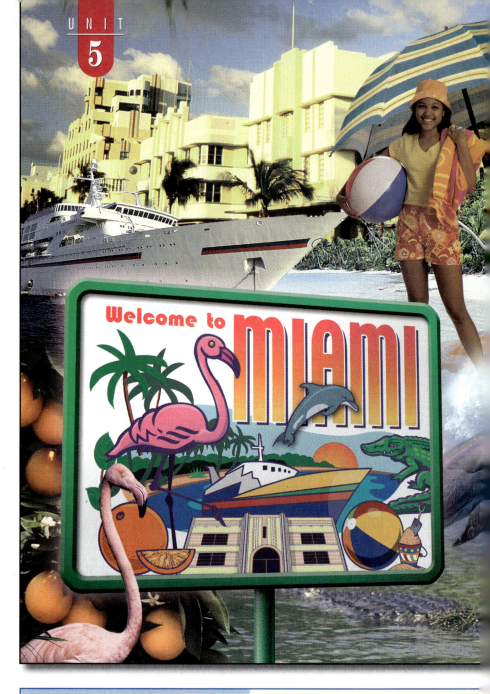

REACHING ALL STUDENTS

HOME CONNECTION

City-Sights Signs Have students take home a sketch of the sign they made in class to represent your city. Then they can work with a family member to create a sign for another city they have lived in or visited. Encourage them to use photographs or attach souvenirs from their time in the city. Ask them to bring the signs they create back to class to share with the group. Lead discussions about the symbols on the signs and what each city is like.

City Sights

Look at the sign. What does it tell you about this city? Work with a group to make a sign for your city. Describe your sign to the class.

In This Unit

Vocabulary
- Location Words
- Neighborhood
- Maps

Language Function
- Ask for and Give Information

Patterns and Structures
- Prepositions
- Regular Past Tense Verbs
- Statements with *There is* and *There are*
- Pronoun-Verb Contractions

Reading
- Word Patterns and Multisyllabic Words
- Comprehension: Identify Details (detail chart)

Writing
- Sentences
- Questions and Answers
- Journal Entry

Content Area Connection
- Social Studies (maps)

99

PREVIEW THE UNIT

4 Look for Activities and Ways to Learn about Places Leaf through the unit, previewing activities students will do, for example:

page 100—learning a song about locations in a city

pages 101 and 102—studying places in the neighborhood and at a mall

page 106—listening to the Bookshelf book (Display a copy of the book.)

page 111—writing a journal about things you have done in your city in the past week

Also ask students to look for the kinds of things people do around their city. Highlight the photos on pages 103–105 and the picture on page 111. Help students name the activities they see. Then sum up what the preview reveals: *There are lots of things to see and do wherever you live.*

5 Set Your Goals Start a class mind map on how to find out about your town or city. Prompt students for pictures or words to add, and have them act out and describe other ideas for you to put into words. Talk together about what they want to learn about city places and activities.

CLOSE AND ASSESS

Ask students to tell or show you something they are interested in learning in this unit.

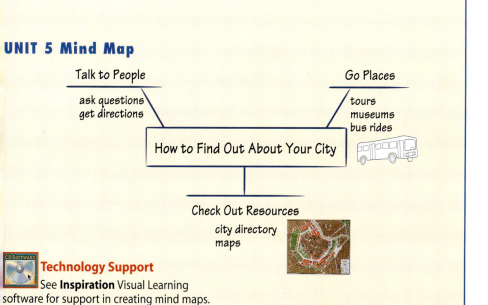

UNIT 5 Mind Map

Technology Support
See **Inspiration** Visual Learning software for support in creating mind maps.

Unit Launch **T99**

UNIT 5 **LESSON 2**

LANGUAGE DEVELOPMENT: LOCATION WORDS

OBJECTIVES

Functions: Listen Actively; Repeat Spoken Language; Recite; Ask For and Give Information

Concepts and Vocabulary:
- Location Words; - Neighborhood

Writing: - Sentences

INTRODUCE

Tape 3A
CD 1 Track 18

1. **Listen and Sing**
Play "My City" on the **Language Tape/CD**. Students listen and sing along, then echo the lines in the song, supply missing prepositions, and finally chime in on the entire song.

2. **Learn About Location Words** Read aloud the chart and find location words in "My City." Explain that *behind* and *in back of* are two ways to say the same location. Review the other word pairs. Then have students substitute the equivalent phrases in the song: *The park is in back of the school.*

PRACTICE

3. **Conduct "Express Yourself"** Model how to ask for and give information. Have partners complete the activity.

> **How to Ask For and Give Information**
> - Use *where* to ask for a location: **Where** is City Hall?
> - To answer, use a location word: It is **next to** the library.

APPLY

4. **Write Sentences** Encourage students to check their work with a partner. Distribute Partner Checklist 5 on page T310.

▶ **Language Practice Book** page 62

CLOSE AND ASSESS

Arrange nine students into three rows. Then ask the class to identify where each person is standing: *George is behind Ying Kit. He is in front of Yenny.*

T100 Unit 5 | City Sights

VOCABULARY: LOCATION WORDS

Out and About in the City

Listen and sing.

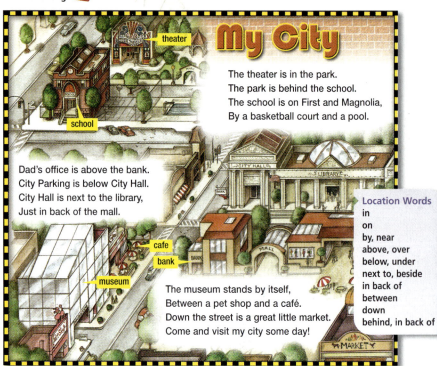

My City

The theater is in the park.
The park is behind the school.
The school is on First and Magnolia,
By a basketball court and a pool.

Dad's office is above the bank.
City Parking is below City Hall.
City Hall is next to the library,
Just in back of the mall.

The museum stands by itself,
Between a pet shop and a café.
Down the street is a great little market.
Come and visit my city some day!

Location Words
in
on
by, near
above, over
below, under
next to, beside
in back of
between
down
behind, in back of

EXPRESS YOURSELF ▶ Ask for and Give Information

Work with a partner. Ask each question about your school. Answer in a complete sentence. Use a location word.

Example: 1. Where is the library?
It is by the gym.

1. Where is the library?
2. Where is the parking lot?
3. Where is the main office?
4. Where is the cafeteria?
5. Where is the entrance?
6. Where is the gym?

WRITE SENTENCES

Sample Responses
Students' answers will reflect the location of things in your school.

7.–10. Choose 4 places in your school. Write sentences to tell where they are.

Example: 7. The gym is by the library.

100 Unit 5 | City Sights

REACHING ALL STUDENTS

Multi-Level Strategies

VOCABULARY: PREPOSITIONS

PRELITERATE Conduct a TPR activity. Give commands using location words: *Nico, please stand next to Tina. Tina, now move in front of Nico.* Then form small groups and invite individuals to take turns giving polite commands using the word *please* and location words. Afterwards, have a small group demonstrate a series of commands as you write out the location words to reinforce the written forms.

Language Practice Book page 62

VOCABULARY: NEIGHBORHOOD

What Happens Here?

Hardware Store — sign

Bus Station — bus

Hospital — ambulance

Post Office — flag

Library — fire engine
Fire Station — mailbox

Police Station — patrol car

Intersection — stop sign, crosswalk

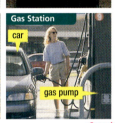
Gas Station — car, gas pump

Store — parking lot

Sample Responses:
bus stop: People wait for the bus.
hardware store: People buy tools.
hospital: Doctors help people.
library: People read books.
fire station: Fire fighters get fire engines ready to fight fires.
post office: People mail letters and packages.
police station: Police officers help people.
intersection: People walk across the street.
gas station: People get gas for their cars.
store: People buy food.

EXPRESS YOURSELF ▶ ASK FOR AND GIVE INFORMATION

1.–4. Work with a partner. Ask this question about 4 places in the neighborhood: *What happens at _____?* Answer your partner's questions.

Example: **1.** What happens at the bus station?
People wait for the bus.

WRITE QUESTIONS AND ANSWERS ✎

5.–14. Write a question and answer about each photo above.

Example: **5.** What happens at the hardware store?
People buy tools.

Sample Responses
Students could ask about what happens in each photo. They also could ask where things are (*Where is the gas pump? It's at the gas station*), who is in the picture (*Who is in front of the library? Children are in front of the library.*), what is in the picture (*What is in front of the post office? a flag and a mailbox*), and so on.

Language Development 101

UNIT 5 **LESSON 3**

LANGUAGE DEVELOPMENT: NEIGHBORHOOD

OBJECTIVES

Function: Ask for and Give Information
Concepts and Vocabulary:
🅣 Neighborhood
Speaking: Ask for and Give Information
Writing: Questions and Answers

INTRODUCE

1 Learn Neighborhood Words Go over the places and labels. Use the pictures to check understanding: *Point to the library. Where can you find a gas pump?*

2 Match Places and Events Make a chart of neighborhood locations and actions:

Locations	What Happens
gas station	pump gas, wash windows
post office	buy stamps

PRACTICE

3 Conduct "Express Yourself" Model how to ask for and give information. Partners can refer to the chart to find answers.

> **How to Ask for and Give Information**
>
> • Ask a question about a place: *What happens at the bus station?*
>
> • To answer, tell what people do there: *People wait for the bus.*

APPLY

4 Write Questions and Answers Remind students to put a question mark at the end of their questions.

▶ **Language Practice Book** page 63

CLOSE AND ASSESS

Play charades. Invite volunteers to pantomime actions while the class guesses where the action takes place.

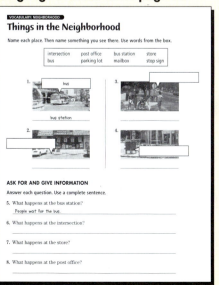

Language Practice Book page 63

Language Development **T101**

UNIT 5 **LESSON 4**

LANGUAGE DEVELOPMENT: NEIGHBORHOOD

> **OBJECTIVES**
>
> **Functions:** Listen Actively; Ask for and Give Information; Role-Play
>
> **Concepts and Vocabulary:**
> • Neighborhood; • Location Words
>
> **Speaking:** Ask for and Give Information; Role-Play
>
> **Writing:** Questions and Answers

INTRODUCE

1 Learn Neighborhood Words Read the title and go over the picture together, reading the labels. Compare the mall to a shopping center in your area.

2 Play "I Spy" Describe a location in the mall: *I spy a store on the second floor, next to a bookstore. It is above the jewelry store.* As students point to the correct store, read aloud the label: *pet shop.* Then invite volunteers to provide more sentences to describe the location: *Noah's Pets is next to Bookster.* Repeat the process to describe more locations.

PRACTICE

3 Conduct "Who's Talking?" Play "Who's Talking?" on the **Language Tape/CD** to model how to ask for and give information. Replay as necessary for students to identify the speakers. Then guide partners in role-playing each scene.

Tape 3A / CD 1 Track 19

APPLY

4 Write Questions and Answers Model, using the Example. Refer students to the location words on page 100 for help in writing answers.

> **CLOSE AND ASSESS**
>
> Have partners share their questions and answers with the larger group.

T102 Unit 5 | City Sights

VOCABULARY: NEIGHBORHOOD

At the Mall

WHO'S TALKING? ▶ Ask for and Give Information

1.–3. Listen to the people.
Where are they? Point to them in the picture.
Act out each scene with a partner. Ask for and give information.

Answers:
1. in the music store
2. at the information booth
3. in the jewelry store

WRITE QUESTIONS AND ANSWERS ✏

4.–8. Write 5 questions about the mall. Then trade papers with a partner and write the answers.

Example: 4. Where is the bench?
The bench is next to the information booth.

Sample Responses
Students should use different questions word
Who is on the escalator? What is in the pet shop
Where is the clothing store? Why do people go t
the restaurant? How do people get information
Encourage students to use the location word
they learned on page 100 in their answers.

102 Unit 5 | City Sights

REACHING ALL STUDENTS

Vocabulary
NEIGHBORHOOD WORDS

Word-O! Have each student prepare a bingo-style card in a 3 x 3 grid with neighborhood places from pages 101 and 102. Then call the words out randomly, and have students check them off on their cards. The winner is the first student who completes a line across, down, or diagonally, and reads the words back.

gas station	restaurant	music store
library	music store	parking lot
hospital	mall	toy store

REGULAR PAST TENSE VERBS

On My Street

A **verb** changes to show the past tense.

Fred **cleans** the car.   Fred **cleaned** the car.

BUILD SENTENCES

Look at each picture below. Choose the correct verb to go with each picture. Say the new sentence.

Example: 1. She plants the flowers.
She planted the flowers.

1. She plants the flowers. / She planted the flowers.

She ____(plants/planted)____ the flowers.

2. She pulls the weed. / She pulled the weed.

She ____(pulls/pulled)____ the weed.

3. They play basketball. / They played basketball.

They ____(play/played)____ basketball.

4. He pumps the tire. / He pumped the tire.

He ____(pumps/pumped)____ the tire.

WRITE SENTENCES

7–12. Write each sentence you made above.

Example: 7. She plants the flowers.

Language Development 103

Language Practice Book page 64

Language Development
PAST TENSE VERBS

Post these action verbs:

walk	laugh	paint
kick	talk	cook
jump	whisper	wash

Have the group sit in a circle. Then model saying a sentence with a present tense verb: *I walk to school.* The student to your right should change your sentence to past tense, adding a time word or phrase: *Yesterday, I walked to school.* The next student begins the pattern again with a sentence in the present tense. Continue, giving each student the opportunity to speak.

UNIT 5 **LESSON 5**

LANGUAGE DEVELOPMENT: REGULAR PAST TENSE VERBS

OBJECTIVES

Function: Give Information
Patterns and Structures:
- Regular Past Tense Verbs

Writing: Sentences

INTRODUCE

1 Learn About Regular Past Tense Verbs Read the examples and explain how the sentences differ. Say: *In the first picture, the verb* **cleans** *tells what Fred is doing now. In the second picture, Fred is finished. The verb in the sentence tells what happened before:* Fred **cleaned** the car. *In English, the verb endings change to show that the action happened in the past.*

Then point out the different verb forms. Explain: *The verb* cleans *goes with* Fred *so it has an* s *on the end. The verb changes to tell about the past. There is no* s *and the verb ends in* ed: cleaned.

Display pairs of sentences and note the changes in the verbs.

Present	Past
I clean my car.	I clean**ed** my car.
Sam cooks dinner.	Sam cook**ed** dinner.
They talk.	They talk**ed**.

PRACTICE

2 Build Sentences Go over the Example, then call on volunteers to do Items 2–4. Lead the group in saying each pair of sentences.

APPLY

3 Write Sentences Remind students to choose the correct present or past tense verb form.

▶ **Language Practice Book** page 64

CLOSE AND ASSESS

Have volunteers read a sentence. Ask a student to repeat it, changing the verb from present to past or past to present.

Language Development **T103**

UNIT 5 LESSON 6

LANGUAGE DEVELOPMENT: REGULAR PAST TENSE VERBS

OBJECTIVES

Function: Give Information
Patterns and Structures:
- Regular Past Tense Verbs

Writing: Sentences

INTRODUCE

1 Learn About Regular Past Tense Verbs Read the examples and establish that they tell about events that happened in the past. Point out the *-ed* ending on the three verbs.

Then have students listen to the last sound in each word as you say them aloud: *wanted, called, walked*. Point out that although all three end in *-ed*, the last sounds are pronounced /ed/, /d/, and /t/, respectively.

Display more verbs with the past tense ending *-ed* and lead students in pronouncing them and comparing the ending sounds.

Past Tense Verbs with *-ed*

/ed/	/d/	/t/
painted	yelled	talked
added	played	jumped
ended	learned	passed

PRACTICE & APPLY

2 Write About the Past Have students add *-ed* to each verb to make each sentence tell about the past.

3 Read Aloud Ask volunteers to read the sentences aloud. Guide them in the correct pronunciation of each past tense verb.

▶ Language Practice Book page 65

CLOSE AND ASSESS

Ask students to categorize the fifteen verbs from the exercises according to the sound of *-ed*.

T104 Unit 5 | City Sights

REGULAR PAST TENSE VERBS

Pronunciation of Name
Emilio e mē lē o

We Played Football in the Park

You can add *-ed* to many **verbs** to tell about things that happened in the past.

I **wanted** to play football on Saturday.

I **called** my friends.

We **walked** to the park.

WRITE ABOUT THE PAST

Write each sentence. Add the past tense of the word in dark type.

Example: 1. We enjoyed a fun day at the park.

1. **enjoy**   We _____ a fun day at the park. *enjoyed*
2. **play**   We _____ football on the grass. *played*
3. **miss**   I _____ the ball. *missed*
4. **roll**   It _____ by the picnic table. *rolled*
5. **turn**   Jessie _____ on the radio. *turned*
6. **pick**   She _____ a good station. *picked*
7. **enjoy**   I _____ it. *enjoyed*
8. **want**   Emilio _____ to hear his new CD. *wanted*
9. **ask**   Jessie _____ to hear it, too. *asked*
10. **listen** We _____ to the CD. *listened*
11. **jump**   Alvin _____ to the beat. *jumped*
12. **laugh** We all _____. *laughed*
13. **learn** Everyone _____ his funny dance. *learned*
14. **talk**   We _____ about school. *talked*
15. **pass**   The time _____ quickly. *passed*

READ ALOUD

16.–30. Work with your teacher. Read aloud each sentence you wrote.

104 Unit 5 | City Sights

REACHING ALL STUDENTS

Multimodal Practice

PAST TENSE VERBS

Have students complete the following activities for these verbs: *listen, laugh, paint, add, jump, tap*.

Kinesthetic Have students act out each action. Then have them use the past tense of the verb to tell what they did: *I laughed*.

Visual and Auditory Have students write the verbs on index cards. Make a card for the verb ending *-ed*. Then have students combine the cards to create past tense verbs and read them aloud.

Language Practice Book page 65

REGULAR PAST TENSE VERBS
We Visited the Zoo

You can add *-ed* to many verbs to tell about things that happened in the past.

We **wanted** to go to the city zoo.
I **asked** Mom to take us there.

Complete each sentence. Add the past tense of the verb in dark type.

1. We _walked_ around the zoo. (walk)
2. Sam _____ the young lions. (like)
3. They _____ so big! (look)
4. Tara _____ away from them! (stay)
5. I _____ to see the monkeys. (ask)
6. They _____ all around. (jump)
7. One monkey _____ a ball. (toss)
8. We _____ to them yell! (listen)
9. Mom _____. (laugh)
10. We all _____ our visit. (enjoy)

STATEMENTS WITH *THERE IS* AND *THERE ARE*

What Is in Our City?

You can start a sentence with *There is* or *There are*.

Use *There is* to talk about one person or thing.
 There is a bike trail near the park.

Use *There are* to talk about two or more persons or things.
 There are two girls on the trail.

BUILD SENTENCES

Say each sentence. Add *There is* or *There are*.

Example: 1. There are 2 lions.

1. _____ 2 lions.   *There are*
2. _____ a U.S. flag.   *There is*
3. _____ some steps.   *There are*
4. _____ a bus stop.   *There is*
5. _____ a trash can.   *There is*
6. _____ people.   *There are*

WRITE SENTENCES ✏️

7.–10. Work with a partner. Write 4 more sentences to tell about the photos above. Add location words.

Example: 7. There are 2 lions in front of the museum.

Sample Responses
Students can expand four of the sentences in Items 1–6 or create new sentences. Encourage them to use the location words they learned on page 100.

Language Development 105

Language Practice Book page 66

Multi-Level Strategies
LANGUAGE DEVELOPMENT

LITERATE IN L1 Portuguese, Japanese, and Vietnamese, along with other languages, have no expressions equivalent to the English phrases *there is* and *there are*. Sample errors: *In our class has fifteen students. The teacher says supplies for everyone.*

To address this, arrange sets of items around the room. Say sentences with *there is* and *there are*: *There are four books on the shelf. On the desk, there is a pencil.* Rearrange the number of items, then have partners practice the skill together.

UNIT 5 LESSON 7

LANGUAGE DEVELOPMENT:
THERE IS AND THERE ARE

OBJECTIVES

Function: Give Information
Concepts and Vocabulary:
 • Location Words
Patterns and Structures:
 • Statements with *There Is* and *There Are*
Writing: • Sentences

INTRODUCE

1 Learn About *There Is* and *There Are*
Read the first rule and example. Have students point to the trail in the photo. Ask: *How many trails do you see?* (one)

Next, read the second rule and example. Ask how many girls the sentence tells about (two). Restate the rules: *There is* tells about one person or thing. *There are* tells about more than one.

PRACTICE

2 Build Sentences Work through the Example, pointing out that *lions* are more than one thing, so you choose *There are*. Partners can complete Items 2–6 together.

APPLY

3 Write Sentences In the Example, point out that a new phrase has been added—*in front of the museum*—to tell the location of the lions. Review the location words on page 100 and have students work independently to write their sentences.

▶ **Language Practice Book** page 66

CLOSE AND ASSESS

Ask volunteers to place objects on their desks. Then ask students to tell about the objects using *there is* or *there are*: *There are two erasers on Ernesto's desk. There is one ruler on Yukiko's desk.*

Language Development T105

UNIT 5 **LESSON 8**

LANGUAGE AND LITERACY: THE BASICS BOOKSHELF

OBJECTIVES

Concepts and Vocabulary:
🅣 Neighborhood

Listening: Listen to a Preview

Reading Strategies:
Activate Prior Knowledge; Preview

Learning to Read: Identify Where a Story Begins and Ends; Identify Capital Letters

BUILD LANGUAGE AND VOCABULARY

1 Teach "Words to Know" Have students look at pages 2–3. Say: *These pages show buildings and signs in a neighborhood. A neighborhood is an area in a town where people live.*

Point to each sign on page 2. Explain where the sign is located and what it means. Then explain the purpose of each building as you point to the picture of the city: *You borrow books at the library. You go to the hospital when you are sick.*

2 Draw a Neighborhood Have students draw maps of a neighborhood. Encourage them to include signs and buildings from pages 2–3. Then invite them to describe their maps: *My neighborhood has a post office. It has four stop signs.*

PREPARE TO READ

3 Think About What You Know Brainstorm different people in the community who may need extra help, such as senior citizens or the disabled. List ways that a community can work together to help them.

4 Preview Play the Audio Walk-Through for *More Than a Meal* on the **Selection Tape/CD** to give students the overall idea of the story. *Tape 3A / CD 1 Track 9*

CLOSE AND ASSESS

Show students the cover of *More Than a Meal* and ask what Carlos does. Then have volunteers role-play a conversation between Carlos and another character.

More Than a Meal
by Suzy Blackaby

Summary This realistic fiction shows a teenager helping elderly and disabled neighbors. Every day, Carlos delivers meals and helps others, including the unfriendly Mr. Potter. One day, Mr. Potter is hurt and Carlos calls for help. Through the experience, Carlos and Mr. Potter become friends. Patterned text reinforces locations in the neighborhood.

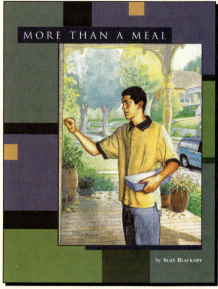
Cover

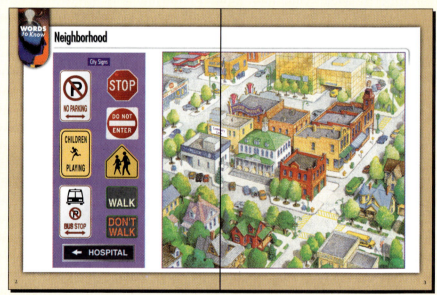
Pages 2–3

Multi-Level Strategies
LITERACY SUPPORT

PRELITERATE **Concepts of Print: Identify Where a Story Begins and Ends** Point out the text on page 4 and say: *The words of a story are called text. The story begins where the text starts. The story ends where all the text ends.* Have students identify where the story begins on page 4. Then leaf through the subsequent pages to identify where the story ends on page 24.

NON-ROMAN ALPHABET **Concepts of Print: Identify Capital Letters for Proper Nouns** Students fluent in ideographic languages such as Chinese, Japanese, or Korean will need instruction in using capital letters for proper nouns. Point out the words *Carlos* and *Community Center* on page 4. Tell students that names of people and special places begin with capital letters. On page 6, tell students that the names of days of the week and words such as *Mr.* begin with capital letters. Page through the book with students and have them identify other proper nouns. Record the words on a chart. Then have volunteers underline the capital letter in each word.

T106a Unit 5 | City Sights

Pronunciation of Names in *More Than a Meal*
Carlos   **car** lōs
Gonzales   gon **zahl** es

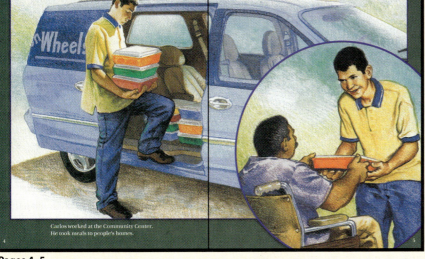

Pages 4–5

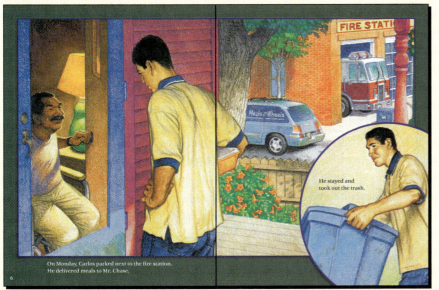

Pages 6–7

Strategies for Comprehensible Input

PAGE	STORY LANGUAGE	STRATEGY OPTIONS
4–5	Community Center	**Explain:** A Community Center is a place that helps people in the neighborhood.
	He took meals to people's homes.	**Restate:** Carlos carried food to people who could not drive or cook.
6	parked	**Restate:** left his car
	next to	**Point to the van in the picture and demonstrate:** Hold two objects side by side.
	delivered	**Restate:** took, carried
7	He stayed	**Explain:** He did not leave.
	took out the trash	**Point to the picture and explain:** Carlos carried the trash can to the street.

Language and Literacy **T106b**

UNIT 5 **LESSON 8,** CONTINUED

LANGUAGE AND LITERACY: THE BASICS BOOKSHELF

OBJECTIVES
Function: Listen to a Book
Critical Thinking and Comprehension:
🅣 Identify Details

READ AND THINK TOGETHER

1 Read Aloud On your first reading of the book, use the "Strategies for Comprehensible Input" that appear at the bottom of pages T106b, T106d, and T106f.

2 Read and Map: Identify Details
Draw a detail chart like the one below, listing the days of the week but leaving the second column blank. Say: *A detail chart shows the main events that happen in a story.*

Point to *Monday* on page 6 and say: *Here it says* Monday, *so I will read this section to find out what happened on Monday.* Then read pages 6–11 and think aloud as you model filling in the first section: *In the "Events" column I'll write* delivered meals, took out trash, *and* fixed a light *because that's what Carlos did on Monday.*

Pause after reading each set of pages shown below and model completing the chart.

Pages 8–9

Pages 10–11

Detail Chart for *More Than a Meal*

	Day	Events
pages 6–11	Monday	delivered meals, took out the trash, and fixed the light
pages 12–13	Tuesday	delivered meals, watered the plants, and washed the dishes
pages 14–19	Wednesday	delivered meals and called 9-1-1
pages 20–21	Thursday	visited Mr. Potter
pages 22–24	Friday	visited Mr. Potter and stayed

Technology Support
See **Inspiration** Visual Learning software for support in creating the detail chart.

T106c Unit 5 | City Sights

More Than a Meal, CONTINUED

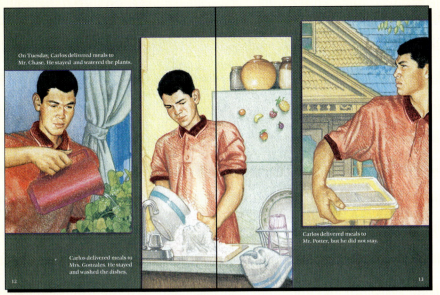

Pages 12–13

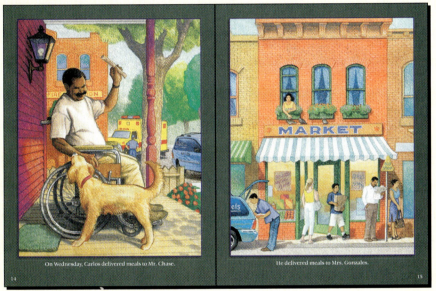

Pages 14–15

Strategies for Comprehensible Input

Page	Story Language	Strategy Options
8	in front of	**Point to the van in the picture and demonstrate:** Hold one object in front of another.
	market	**Restate:** store that sells food
9	fixed the light	**Explain:** The light was broken. He made the light work.
10	behind	**Point to the van in the picture and demonstrate:** Hold one object behind another.
11	he did not stay	**Explain:** Carlos went away. He did not spend more time with Mr. Potter.
12–13	watered the plants	**Point to the picture.**
	washed the dishes	**Point to the picture.**
15	Mrs. Gonzales	**Point to the picture of the woman in the window.**

Language and Literacy **T106d**

UNIT 5 **LESSON 8,** CONTINUED

LANGUAGE AND LITERACY: THE BASICS BOOKSHELF

OBJECTIVES

Functions: Listen to a Book; Read Aloud a Story (choral reading); Dramatize
Learning to Read: Identify Words

READ AND THINK TOGETHER, CONTINUED

3 Conduct Interactive Readings
Choose from these options:

- **Choral reading**
  Divide students into groups that represent a day of the week between Monday and Friday. Have each group read along with the corresponding day as you play the recording of *More Than a Meal* on the **Selection Tape/CD**.

  Tape 3A / CD 1 Track 10

- **Dramatize** Have small groups choose a portion of the text to dramatize. A narrator group can read the text, pausing for other students to act out the scene and add dialogue.

- **Read along and identify words**
  More Than a Meal contains many high frequency words that have been previously taught as follows:

an	home	not	the
and	how	of	this
are	I	on	time
at	in	school	to
feel	more	see	very
he	next	something	you

  As you read, frame individual words from the list and have students identify the words. Continue reading as students track the print and identify other words they know.

CLOSE AND ASSESS

Give each student a card with the name of a weekday. Have students tell what Carlos did on that day.

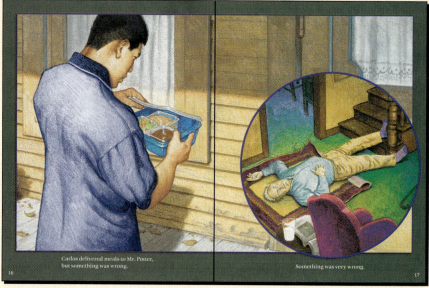
Pages 16–17

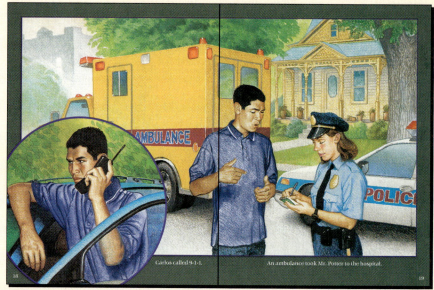
Pages 18–19

Multi-Level Strategies

LITERACY SUPPORT

LITERATE IN L1 **Read with a Partner/Write a Journal Entry** After students have participated in the interactive readings, encourage them to read the story with a partner. Distribute the Partner Prompts on page T311 to help partners work together to identify unfamiliar words and unlock their meanings, then read the text to each other. After the partner reading, have students write a page in Carlos' journal for one day of the week. Encourage them to use past tense verbs and location words. Provide sentence frames:

On _____, I visited _____.
I parked the van _____.
I stayed and _____.

INTERRUPTED SCHOOLING **Identify Details** To anchor understanding of the skill, ask questions about the story. On pages 6–7, ask: *What day is it? Whom does Carlos visit? How does Carlos help Mr. Chase?* Have students point to the text and illustration that answers the question.

T106e Unit 5 | City Sights

More Than a Meal, CONTINUED

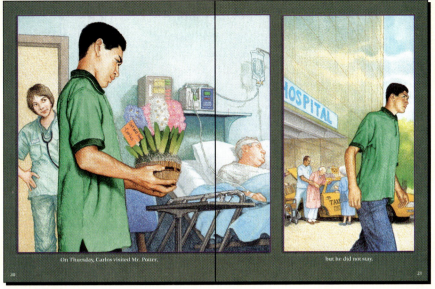

Pages 20–21

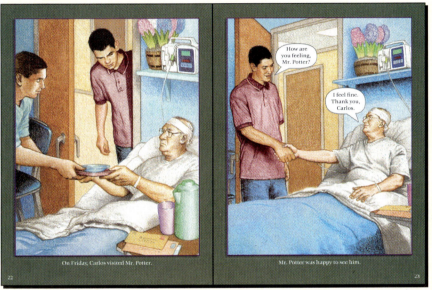

Pages 22–23

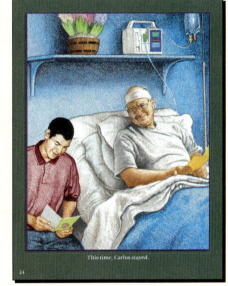

Page 24

Strategies for Comprehensible Input

Page	Story Language	Strategy Options
16–17	something was wrong	**Point to the picture and restate:** Mr. Potter needed help.
18	9-1-1	**Demonstrate and explain:** Pantomime dialing 9-1-1 on a telephone. Say: *In an emergency, dial 9-1-1 on the telephone.*
19	ambulance	**Point to the picture and explain:** An ambulance is a special van that carries sick people to the hospital.
	hospital	**Explain:** A hospital is a place where doctors and nurses help sick people.
20–21	visited	**Restate:** went to see
22–23	I feel fine.	**Restate:** I feel better now.
24	stayed	**Explain:** Carlos sat and talked with Mr. Potter.

Language and Literacy **T106f**

UNIT 5 LESSON 9
LANGUAGE AND LITERACY: THE BASICS BOOKSHELF

OBJECTIVES
Function: Retell a Story
Learning Strategy: Use Graphic Organizers (detail chart)
Critical Thinking and Comprehension: Identify Details

CHECK COMPREHENSION

Materials: index cards, one set with one day of the week per card (Monday through Friday) and another set with the events from the story for each day

1 Make a Detail Chart Have students review *More Than a Meal* to identify main events for a detail chart. Remind them that a detail chart can show the most important things that happened in the story, in the order in which they happened.

As you read aloud the directions for each step, pause for students to add information to the sections of their charts. Encourage students to review the story to clarify the main events.

2 Retell the Story Write the name of each weekday on a separate index card. On other cards, write one day's events. Distribute all cards. Have students match the days and events. Then start with students holding the cards for Monday and have them tell their day's events. Continue retelling through the set of cards for Friday.

CLOSE AND ASSESS
Ask students to complete this sentence:
A detail chart shows _____.

COMPREHENSION: IDENTIFY DETAILS

Read and Think Together

Make a detail chart to tell about *More Than a Meal*. Follow these steps.

1 Think about what Carlos did each day in the story. Draw a chart like the one below. Write what Carlos did on Monday.

Day	Events
Monday	delivered meals, took out trash, and fixed a light
Tuesday	delivered meals, watered plants, and washed the dishes
Wednesday	delivered meals and called 9-1-1
Thursday	visited Mr. Potter
Friday	visited Mr. Potter and stayed

2 What did Carlos do the rest of the week? Complete the chart with more details. Use words from the book.

3 Use your detail chart to tell the story to a friend.

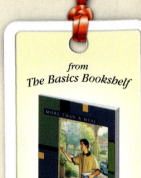

from The Basics Bookshelf

THEME BOOK
Meet Carlos in this story about city neighbors helping each other.

106 Unit 5 City Sights

REACHING ALL STUDENTS

Language Development
EXPRESS AND ACKNOWLEDGE GRATITUDE

Friendly Talk Turn to page 6 in *More Than a Meal*. Use these examples to model how Mr. Chase thanked Carlos, and how Carlos answered politely.

Mr. Chase: Thanks for the dinner, Carlos.

Carlos: You're welcome, Mr. Chase.

Collect other ways to express and acknowledge gratitude in a chart. Partners can then use the chart as they take the roles of Carlos and another character to role-play expressing and acknowledging gratitude.

Ways to Say "Thank You"	Ways to Say "You're Welcome"
Thanks!	Sure.
I appreciate it.	No problem.
That was a big help.	I'm glad to help.
Thanks for your help.	It was nothing.

T106 Unit 5 | City Sights

HIGH FREQUENCY WORDS
Words to Know

REVIEW WORDS YOU KNOW

Read the words aloud. Which word goes in the sentence?

Here	Have
where	want
take	things

1. _Here_ is the bus.
2. This is the bus they all _want_.
3. They _take_ this bus every day.

LEARN TO READ

Learn new words.

city	Padma lives in the **city** of Chicago.
above	She lives in an apartment high **above** the street.
by	It is on Belmont Street, **by** a Mexican restaurant.
sometimes	**Sometimes** she jogs to Lake Michigan.
her	**Her** dog, Bandit, likes to run, too.
come	Padma's mom says, "**Come** home before dinner."
animals	There is a park for dogs and other **animals**.
people	**People** call it "Bark Park."
down	Bandit runs up and **down** the hill there.
under	Then Padma and Bandit rest **under** a tree.

How to Learn a New Word
- Look at the word.
- Listen to the word.
- Listen to the word in a sentence. What does it mean?
- Say the word.
- Spell the word.
- Say the word again.

WORD WORK

Where does each new word fit in the chart? Say the word and spell it.

Example: 4. people p-e-o-p-l-e

What to Look For	Word
4. starts with p	p e o p l e
5. ends with y	c i t y
6. is the opposite of **over**	u n d e r
7. starts with a	a b o v e
8. ends with **er**	h e r

What to Look For	Word
9. has 3 syllables	a n i m a l s
10. means "next to"	b y
11. rhymes with **some**	c o m e
12. means the opposite of **up**	d o w n
13. has 2 smaller words in it	s o m e t i m e s

Language and Literacy 107

Reading Practice Book page 54

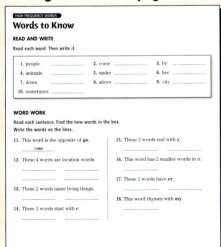

Reading Fluency
RECOGNIZE HIGH FREQUENCY WORDS

To build automaticity with the new high frequency words:

- Refer students to the list of new words on page 107 and have them cover the context sentences. Read the sentences aloud in random order, leaving out the high frequency word. Challenge students to name the missing word.

- Have students sort the words into these categories: words that tell about who, words that tell about where, words that have four letters each. Then invite students to create categories of their own and sort again.

UNIT 5 **LESSON 10**

LANGUAGE AND LITERACY: HIGH FREQUENCY WORDS

OBJECTIVES
Learning to Read:
- Recognize High Frequency Words

REVIEW WORDS

1 Review Known High Frequency Words Have the group read aloud the words in the green box. Listen for words students cannot read automatically and use the steps in the yellow box to reteach those words. Then have students look at the photo. Read each cloze sentence. Reread each sentence and pause for students to silently read the two words to the left of the sentence. Tell students to choose the word that goes in the sentence and tells about the picture.

INTRODUCE NEW WORDS

2 Learn High Frequency Words Use the High Frequency Word Script on page T316 to lead students through the steps in the yellow box for each new word.

PRACTICE

3 Conduct "Word Work" Model how to use the clue to find the possible words in the list and then to use the number of letter blanks to choose the correct word or confirm it.

Have small groups complete Items 5–13. Discuss how each correct word fits the clue and number of blanks.

APPLY

4 Read Words in Context Students will read high frequency words in context in the sentences on page 109 and the passage on page 110.

▶ **Reading Practice Book** page 54

CLOSE AND ASSESS

Call out the high frequency words one at a time. Have students point to them and spell the words as a group.

Language and Literacy T107

UNIT 5 LESSON 11

LANGUAGE AND LITERACY: PHONICS

OBJECTIVES

Learning to Read: Build Oral Vocabulary; Develop Phonemic Awareness; Contrast Short and Long Vowel Sounds /e/, /ē/; /o/, /ō/; /i/, /ī/; **T** Use Word Patterns to Decode Words; Blend Sounds to Decode Words

TEACH SHORT AND LONG VOWELS

1. **Build Oral Vocabulary** Display Transparency 31. Point and use dramatization to help explain word meanings. For example, for Item 4, say:

   • Meg (point) is **lost.** She doesn't know where she is (dramatize).

2. **Develop Phonemic Awareness** Remove the transparency and conduct the oral activities in Step 1 of the Script for Transparency 31.

3. **Contrast Short and Long Vowel Sounds** Display Transparency 31 again. Work through Step 2.

4. **Read Words with Short and Long Vowels** Work through Step 3.

CLOSE AND ASSESS

Display *be, hi, bed, hit, so, job,* and *sick.* Have students tell whether the vowel is long or short and blend the sounds to read the word.

Word Families

-UMP, -ICK, AND -ELL

Materials: Letter Tiles

A large number of words can be generated from a few rhyming phonograms. Use letter tiles to build the words in dark type. Then change tiles to build other words in the *-ump, -ick,* and *-ell* families. Have students make a list of the words. Make sure students understand their meanings. Then ask them to read the words on their list and to identify the shared ending.

pump	sick	well
bump	brick	bell
dump	kick	fell

T108a Unit 5 | City Sights

Transparency 31: ▶
Short and Long Vowels

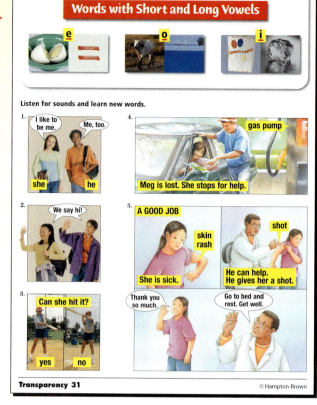

▼ Script for Transparency 31

Words with Short and Long Vowels

1. Develop Phonemic Awareness

Match Initial Sounds/Match Final Sounds Say: *Listen to these two words: egg, end. Say the words with me: egg, end. The first sound in these words is the same: /e/. Now listen: egg, equal. Is the first sound in each word the same?* (no) *Continue with ox, on; ox, open; ice, in; if, it; eat, easy; island, ice.* Then say: *Now listen to these two words: he, we. They end with the same sound: /ē/. Here are two more words: hi, he. Say the words with me: hi, he. Is the last sound in each word the same?* (no) *Continue with no, go; she, so; be, me; hi, he.*

2. Contrast Short and Long Vowel Sounds

Point to the letter *e* on **Transparency 31.** Say: *The letter e is a vowel. It has a short sound, /e/, and a long sound, /ē/. Say the names of the pictures with me: egg, equal.* Have students identify the vowel sound at the beginning of each word. Point to the *e* and ask: *What two sounds does the letter* e *have?* Repeat for *ox/ocean* and *invitation/ice.*

3. Use Word Patterns to Decode Words

Teach Point to the boy in Item 1 and say: *This boy talks about himself. Let's read this word* (point to *me*). *Point to the m in me and say: Say the sound for m with me: /mmm/.* Then point to the *e* and ask: *How many consonants come after the* e? (none) *When the vowel is at the end, it is long.* As you slide a finger under *me,* say: *Help me blend the two sounds: /m m m ē ē ē/. Now, let's say the whole word: me.* Then point to the word *Meg* in Item 4. Say: *A consonant comes after the* e*, so the* e *is short.* Blend *me/Meg* with students. Repeat for *hi/hit* in Items 2 and 3.

Practice For Item 1, say: *This picture* (point to the girl) *shows a girl. Read the word* (point to *she*) *with me. Remember, the vowel is at the end, so it is long. Let's blend the sounds* /s h ē ē ē/, *and say the word:* she. Read aloud the dialogue, pausing for students to decode *be* and *me.* Repeat for the other items. For the CVC words, remind students that a vowel followed by a consonant is short.

Transparency 32: Word Patterns

Words with Short and Long Vowels

hi	me	go
hit	met	got

All these words have long vowels.
- go
- he
- she
- hi

All these words have short vowels.
- got
- help
- shell
- hit

Find the pattern.
1. How many vowels are in each word? _____
2. Look at the words that end in a vowel. Is the vowel sound long or short? _____
3. Look at the words that end in one or more consonants. Is the vowel sound long or short? _____

Look for patterns in these words. Which word in each pair has a long vowel?

1. no	2. sock	3. hen	4. be
not	so	he	bell

Transparency 32 © Hampton-Brown

OBJECTIVES

Learning to Read: Build Oral Vocabulary; Develop Phonemic Awareness; ❶ Use Word Patterns to Decode Words

TEACH WORD PATTERNS

1 Build Oral Vocabulary Help students finish these sentences:
- *Another word for* hello *is* _____. (hi)
- *Get a bat and* _____ *the ball.* (hit)
- *When I talk about myself, I can say I or* _____. (me)
- *Let's* _____ *to the movies.* (go)
- *I see a* _____ *in the barn.* (hen)
- *Please ring the* _____. (bell)

2 Develop Phonemic Awareness and Contrast Vowel Sounds Conduct the oral activities in Step 1 of the Script for Transparency 32. Then display the transparency and do Step 2.

3 Use Word Patterns to Decode Words Work through Step 3 of the script.

CLOSE AND ASSESS

Display the words *he* and *hen*. Ask: *Why does* he *have a long vowel sound? Why does* hen *have a short vowel sound?*

▶ **Reading Practice Book** page 55 (word patterns: CV, CVC)

Script for Transparency 32

Words with Short and Long Vowels

1. Develop Phonemic Awareness
Isolate Long *e* and *o*/Match Final Sounds Say: *Listen to these words:* he, she, be. *What is the last sound in each word?* (/ē/) Say /ē/ *with me:* /ē ē ē/. *Now listen to these words:* we, wet. *Which word ends with* /ē/ *like* he? (we) Repeat for *bed, be; me, met.* Then repeat for /ō/, using: *no, not; go, got; so, sock.*

2. Teach Word Patterns
Say: *Look at the first card. Which letter is the consonant?* (h) *Which letter is the vowel?* (i) *Is there a consonant after the vowel?* (no) *Then the vowel* i *has a long sound:* /ī/. *Say* /ī/ *with me:* /ī ī ī/. As you slide a finger under *hi*, say: *Help me blend the two sounds* /h ī ī ī/, *and say the word:* hi. Have students look at the second card and name the two consonants in *hit*. (h, t) Say: *When a consonant comes after a vowel, the vowel is short. Say both words with me:* hi, hit. *Which word has the long sound for* i? (hi) *Which word has the short sound?* (hit) Repeat for *me/met* and *go/got*.

3. Use Word Patterns to Decode Words
Find the Pattern Read aloud each list of words, noting the long and short vowel sounds. Then use the questions in the box to explore the spelling patterns: *Look at* go *and* got. *How many vowels are in each word? Let's count them: one in* go *and one in* got. Repeat for the other pairs, and write the answer (one) on the first line in the box. Work through Items 2 and 3 and record the answers.

Summarize and Model the Strategy Say: *Look for patterns in words to help you read.* Point to the word *no* in Item 1 and say: *Here I see one vowel and it is at the end, so I will say the long vowel sound:* no. Point to *not* and say: *Here I see one vowel and then a consonant* t, *so I will say the short vowel sound:* not.

Practice Have students repeat the process for Items 2–4. First they should identify the word with the long vowel in each pair and then tell you how they figured out the vowel sound to blend each word.

Reading Practice Book page 55

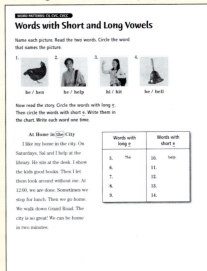

Language and Literacy **T108b**

UNIT 5 **LESSON 11,** CONTINUED

LANGUAGE AND LITERACY: WORD STRUCTURE

OBJECTIVES

Learning to Read: Build Oral Vocabulary; Develop Phonemic Awareness; ⓣ Divide Words into Syllables; ⓣ Decode Multisyllabic Words

TEACH SYLLABICATION RULES

1. **Build Oral Vocabulary** Display Transparency 33. Use the pictures to develop the meaning of each word and use it in a sentence. For example:
   - This is a **helmet**. A football player wears a **helmet**. A **helmet** is hard. It protects your head.

2. **Develop Phonemic Awareness** Remove the transparency and conduct the oral activities in Step 1 of the Script for Transparency 33.

3. **Decode Multisyllabic Words** Display Transparency 33 again. Work through Step 2 of the script.

CLOSE AND ASSESS

Display the words *tunnel* and *napkin*. Call on students to tell you where to divide each word. Have volunteers blend the parts to say the word.

Transparency 33: ▶ Multisyllabic Words

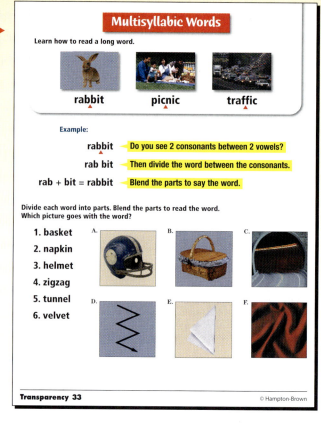

▼ Script for Transparency 33

Multisyllabic Words

1. Develop Phonemic Awareness
Count Syllables in Words Say: *Some words have one part, or syllable, such as* hat. *Clap the syllable with me as we say* hat: hat. (clap) *Some longer words have two parts, or syllables, such as* rabbit. *Clap the syllables with me as we say* rabbit: rab-bit. (clap, clap) Lead students in saying and clapping syllables for these words: *picnic, pin, truck, traffic, helmet, help*. Have students count the syllables as they clap. If students miscount, lead them in clapping the syllables again.

2. Decode Multisyllabic Words
Teach Say: *Now you are going to learn how to read a long word.* Point to the rabbit on **Transparency 33**. Say: *This animal is a rabbit.* Say rabbit *with me:* rabbit. *How many parts do you hear?* (2) *Now let's read the word and find out if we will also see two parts.*

Work through the Example below. First point to the *bb* in *rabbit* and say: *Do you see two consonants between two vowels? What are they?* (*bb*, between the vowels *a* and *i*) *Then divide the word between the consonants. How many parts do you see?* (2) *Blend the parts to say the word. Read the word with me.* Slide a finger slowly from left to right below the syllables as you say: /rrraaab/, /biiit/. *Now let's blend the parts together and read the word:* rab-bit, *rabbit*.

Repeat for *picnic* and *traffic*. Point out that the two consonants in the middle of *picnic* are different. Say: *Divide the word* picnic *between the two consonants, just as you divided* rabbit *between the two consonants.*

Practice Have students do Items 1–6. Ask a volunteer to show you where to divide each word. Write the parts on the chalkboard and lead the group in blending the parts to read the word. Then have the group identify the picture that goes with the word.

T108c Unit 5 | City Sights

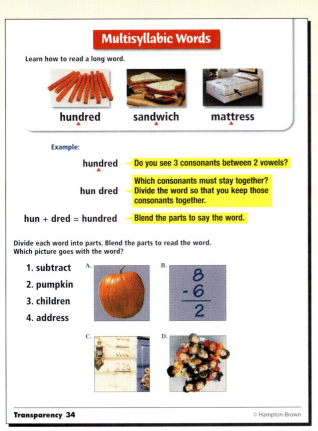

◀ Transparency 34: Multisyllabic Words

▼ Script for Transparency 34

Multisyllabic Words

1. **Develop Phonemic Awareness**
   Blend Syllables Say: *I'm going to say two word parts. Listen:* hun-dred. *Now blend the parts. Tell me the whole word.* (hundred) Repeat for *traffic, sandwich, helmet, tunnel, kitchen,* and *mattress.*

2. **Decode Multisyllabic Words**
   Teach Say: *Now you are going to learn how to read more long words.* Point to the picture of one hundred cubes on **Transparency 34**. Say: *There are one hundred cubes in this picture.* Say hundred *with me:* hundred. *How many parts do you hear?* (2) *Now let's read the word and find out if we will also see two parts.*

   Work through the Example below. First point to the letters *ndr* in *hundred* and say: *Do you see three consonants between two vowels? What are they?* (ndr, between the vowels *u* and *e*) *Which consonants must stay together?* (dr) *That's right, a consonant and r, like* dr, *usually stay together. Divide the word so that you keep those consonants together. Then blend the parts to say the word. Read the word with me.* Slide a finger slowly from left to right below the syllables as you say: /huuunnn/, /dreeed/. *Now let's blend the parts together and read the word:* hun-dred, hundred.

   Repeat for *sandwich* and *mattress.* Point out that two of the consonants in the middle of *mattress* are the same. Say: *Divide the word* mattress *between the two consonants* tt.

   Practice Have students do Items 1–4. Ask a volunteer to show you where to divide each word. Write the parts on the chalkboard and lead the group in blending the parts to read the word. Then have the group identify the picture that goes with the word.

OBJECTIVES

Learning to Read: Build Oral Vocabulary; Develop Phonemic Awareness;
① Divide Words into Syllables;
① Decode Multisyllabic Words

TEACH SYLLABICATION RULES

1 Build Oral Vocabulary Display Transparency 34. Play "I Spy." For example, for the second picture, say:

• *I spy a sandwich. A sandwich is something to eat.*

When students find the sandwich, say: *Yes,* **this is a sandwich** (pantomime eating). Repeat to build context for the other words.

2 Develop Phonemic Awareness Remove the transparency and work through Step 1 of the script.

3 Decode Multisyllabic Words Display Transparency 34 again. Work through Step 2 of the script.

CLOSE AND ASSESS

Display *children* and *address*. Have students tell you where to divide each word and blend the parts to say the word.

▶ **Reading Practice Book** page 56 (syllable division: VC/CV, VCCCV)

Reading Practice Book page 56

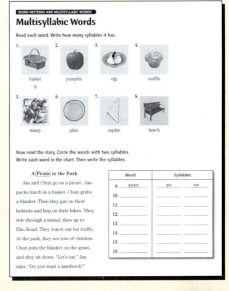

Language and Literacy **T108d**

UNIT 5 LESSON 12
LANGUAGE AND LITERACY: READING AND SPELLING

OBJECTIVES

Functions: Listen Actively; Repeat Spoken Language; Recite

Learning to Read:
Develop Phonemic Awareness; Contrast Short and Long Vowel Sounds /e/, /ē/; /o/, /ō/; /i/, /ī/;
- Use Word Patterns to Decode Words;
- Divide Words into Syllables

Spelling:
- Short and Long Vowel Words; Multisyllabic Words

LISTEN AND LEARN
Tape 3A / CD 1 Track 20

1 Recite a Chant Display Transparency 35 and play "New Friend" on the **Language Tape/CD**. After students have listened and learned the chant, have them recite it, waving on *Hi!* and *Hey!*, pointing to themselves on *I* and *me*, and to a classmate on *you*.

DEVELOP PHONEMIC AWARENESS

2 Segment Words into Sounds Say: *Listen to this word and say it with me: me. Now let's say each sound and count the sounds: /m/, /ē/—two sounds.* Follow this procedure with *melt*, pointing out that there are four sounds in *melt*. Continue the activity with *hi, him, web, we, go,* and *got*.

LOOK FOR WORD PATTERNS

3 CV, VC, CVC, and CVCC Word Patterns Read the first explanation, then point to *no* and say: *This word has only one vowel at the end, so the vowel is probably long. Read the word with me: no. Yes, the vowel o makes a long sound: /ō/.* Repeat for *hi* and *me*. For the second explanation, identify each short vowel sound in the examples and have students blend the sounds to read the words. Then write *so, if, sock,* and *met*. Have students identify the pattern and tell if it makes each vowel long or short.

Afterwards, play the chant again. Have students identify CV, VC, and CVC words.

T108 Unit 5 | City Sights

WORD PATTERNS AND MULTISYLLABIC WORDS
Reading and Spelling
LISTEN AND LEARN

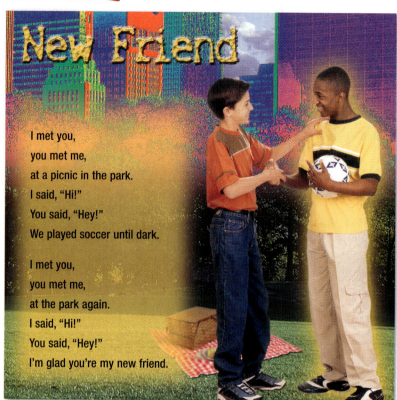

New Friend

I met you,
you met me,
at a picnic in the park.
I said, "Hi!"
You said, "Hey!"
We played soccer until dark.

I met you,
you met me,
at the park again.
I said, "Hi!"
You said, "Hey!"
I'm glad you're my new friend.

LOOK FOR WORD PATTERNS

Some words have only one vowel at the end. The vowel is usually long.	Some words have one vowel and then one or more consonants. The vowel is usually short.
n<u>o</u> h<u>i</u> m<u>e</u>	<u>o</u>n h<u>i</u>m m<u>e</u>lt

108 Unit 5 | City Sights   ▶ Transparencies 31–35

REACHING ALL STUDENTS

Multi-Level Strategies
LITERACY SUPPORT

INTERRUPTED SCHOOLING To anchor understanding of how to look for word patterns in multisyllabic words, write *rabbit* on the board. Divide the word into two parts, *rab|bit*. Then look for a pattern in each part, identifying the consonants and vowel. Say: *A consonant comes after the vowel in each part, so I know the vowel in each part is short.* Blend the sounds with students to read the word. Repeat for *basket, traffic, helmet, zigzag,* and *picnic*.

PRELITERATE Fold a sheet of paper into four parts and write *hit* on it, as shown. Explain that when the "door" (the part with *t*) closes next to the vowel *i*, the *i* is short. When the door is "open" (fold back the *t*) the vowel is long. Repeat for *me/met* and *go/got*.

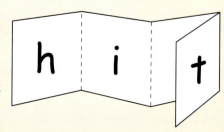

READING STRATEGY

Follow these steps to read a word.

1. Look for a pattern in the word. Find the vowel. How many consonants come after the vowel? Use the pattern to figure out the vowel sound.

go — The vowel **o** is at the end, so it is long.

got — A consonant comes after the vowel **o**, so the vowel is short.

Reading Help

Look for patterns in a long word, too.

First divide the word into parts. Then look for a pattern in each part.

basket   napkin
bas ket nap kin

What pattern do you see in each part? Is the vowel long or short?

2. Start at the beginning. Blend the sounds together to say the word.

go   g + o = go

got g + o + t = got

READING AND SPELLING PRACTICE

Use what you learned to read the sentences.

1. Meg is lost. She has to be in the city soon.
2. Meg stops to get gas. She asks for help.
3. A man by the pump gives her a map.
4. He tells her, "Take the tunnel at Elm Canyon."
5. "Then go down the hill to First Street, and go left."
6. "Thank you so much!" Meg answers.

7.–10. Now write the sentences that your teacher reads. *For dictation sentences, see Step 6 at right.*

WORD WORK

11.–18. Copy the chart. Then read these words:

| me | sock | be | bed |
| no | men | so | not |

go	got	we	web
11. no	13. sock	15. me	17. men
12. so	14. not	16. be	18. bed

Write each word in the chart. Put it under the word that has the same vowel sound.

Example: 11.

go
11. no

Language and Literacy 109

Decodable Book

PRACTICE WITH WORD PATTERNS AND MULTISYLLABIC WORDS

Decodable Book 5: *A City Food Festival*

Assign **Decodable Book 5** for independent reading. The **Decodable Book** can be used in a variety of ways to help students become more fluent, automatic readers:

Discussion Circles Have students work in small groups to read aloud and discuss the book using the questions on the back cover. Encourage students to read aloud the text that supports their answers. Groups can also work together to complete the Word Work Activity.

Readers Theater Students can read aloud the stories in a class performance. Help them prepare by rereading the stories in daily rehearsals. Work with students to add narration or dialog. Encourage them to use natural phrasing and expression.

Rereading at Home Have students work with family members to reread the book at home. They can take turns reading aloud alternate pages, then rereading the book switching the pages each person reads.

LEARN A READING STRATEGY

4. **Use Word Patterns** Work through the strategy with students, reading each step aloud and modeling the actions. Point out the Reading Help and read the explanation to students. Work through additional examples to help them apply the tip: *helmet, blanket, picnic, traffic*. For *helmet* and *blanket,* point out that the vowel sound changes slightly when the words are said quickly.

PRACTICE

5. **Read Sentences** Distribute the Partner Prompts from page T311 to guide peers in reading the sentences in Items 1–6. Remind them to use the word-pattern strategy to read words.

6. **Write Sentences** Dictate the following sentences for students to write. Read each sentence at normal speed once so students can listen, and then repeat it slowly word by word as they write:

   7. I go to the picnic with Tom and Ben.
   8. They have a big basket.
   9. We sit on a blanket.
   10. The traffic is very bad in the city.

   If students need extra support, guide them in saying each word aloud and clapping the number of syllables. Then ask them to read what they wrote and check that the word has the same number of syllables.

7. **Conduct "Word Work"** Read the directions and work through the Example. Then have partners complete Items 12–18. To help students check their answers, use letter tiles to build the words on an overhead projector.

▶ **Reading Practice Book** pages 127–130 (Decodable Book 5)

CLOSE AND ASSESS

Copy the completed chart from Word Work on the board. Point to each word. Have students identify the pattern in the word, tell you whether the vowel is long or short, and read the word aloud.

Language and Literacy **T109**

UNIT 5 **LESSON 13**

LANGUAGE AND LITERACY: INDEPENDENT READING

OBJECTIVES

Function: Read a Selection

Learning to Read: Recognize High Frequency Words; Use Word Patterns; Decode Multisyllabic Words

Reading Strategies: Activate Prior Knowledge; Build Background; Retell

Critical Thinking and Comprehension: Identify Details

READ ON YOUR OWN

1 Introduce Vocabulary In "Meet Jo," students apply phonics skills and read high frequency words. Introduce the story words. Write each word, pronounce it, and spell it.

- **hospital:** a place where doctors give medical care. *My cat got her shots at City Animal Hospital.*
- **special:** when something is different or important. *Puppies need to eat special food.*
- **bite:** to hold or cut something with teeth. *That dog might bite your leg.*

2 Activate Prior Knowledge/Build Background Ask students what the photos show. (an animal hospital) Ask: *Have you ever taken a pet to an animal hospital? What was it like? What happened?* Talk about how veterinarians in animal hospitals help different animals.

3 Read and Think: Identify Details Have students read the article and complete the chart. They can use the chart to tell a partner about Jo's job.

4 Build Reading Fluency Use the **Language Tape/CD** with Reading Practice Book page 57 for fluency practice. Tape 3A CD 1 Track 21

▶ **Reading Practice Book** page 57

CLOSE AND ASSESS

Have one student name an animal that Jo cares for, and then call on other students to retell what Jo does to help that animal. Repeat for each animal.

T110 Unit 5 | City Sights

COMPREHENSION: IDENTIFY DETAILS

Read on Your Own

DECODING CHECK Give the Decoding Progress Check on page 1a of the Assessment Handbook.

4D   The City Express   Tuesday, November 20, 2002

CITY PEOPLE
Tom Santos

Meet Jo

Jo works at the City Animal Hospital. I asked her to tell me about what she does at her job.

I have a great job. I love to help the animals. Look. This cat got hit in traffic. It is so sad when that happens. I had to make her a special bed.

This is Samson. Samson has a bad rash. He has this thing around his neck so he can't bite his skin. Sometimes we play catch. He needs to run a lot.

This rabbit is Velvet. I like to brush him. He is so soft! Velvet had to get his shots. He needs to rest for a day or two. Then he will go home.

So, that is my job. I help hundreds of animals. It is great to see them get well. I miss them when they go home.

CHECK YOUR UNDERSTANDING

Copy and complete the chart. Show what Jo does for each animal. Then tell a partner about Jo's job.

Wording may vary.

Animal	How Jo Helps
a cat that got hit	Jo makes a special bed.
a dog with a rash	Jo plays catch with him.
a rabbit that needed shots	Jo brushes him.

110   Unit 5   City Sights

REACHING ALL STUDENTS

Reading Fluency
INTONATION PATTERNS/EXPRESSION

Read the title and introduction on **Reading Practice Book** page 57. Then read the explanations and go over the examples.

Next, play "Meet Jo" on the **Language Tape/CD**. Point out that the punctuation marks tell the reader how to say each sentence. Then do the Practice and circulate among partners to check and support reading fluency.

Reading Practice Book page 57

PRONOUN-VERB CONTRACTIONS

They're at the Museum!

You can put a pronoun and a verb together to form a **contraction**.

Contraction	Example
I + am = I'm	I'm Mrs. Patch.
you + are = you're	You're at the Natural History Museum.
he + is = he's she + is = she's it + is = it's	Look at this bird. It's a falcon.
we + are = we're	We're happy to have birds like this.
they + are = they're	They're wonderful animals.

BUILD SENTENCES

Look at the underlined words in each sentence. Use a contraction in their place. Say the new sentence.

Example: 1. Mrs. Patch holds a falcon. It's a big bird.

1. Mrs. Patch holds a falcon. <u>It is</u> a big bird.
2. The children listen to Mrs. Patch. <u>They are</u> very interested.
3. One boy raises his hand. <u>He is</u> afraid of the bird.
4. "<u>You are</u> brave, Mrs. Patch. Does that falcon hurt people?"
5. <u>She is</u> happy to answer his question.
6. "No, falcons are afraid of humans. <u>We are</u> so big."

Answers:
1. It's a big bird.
2. They're very interested.
3. He's afraid of the bird.
4. You're brave, Mrs. Patch.
5. She's happy to answer his question.
6. We're so big.

WRITE SENTENCES

Replace the underlined words with pronouns. Then combine the pronoun and the word *is* or *are*. Write the new sentence.

Example: 7. She's helpful.

7. <u>Mrs. Patch</u> is helpful.
8. <u>The boy</u> is not afraid anymore.
9. <u>The visit</u> is over too soon.
10. <u>The students</u> are sad to go.
11. <u>A girl</u> is at the door.
12. <u>Her parents</u> are glad to see her.

Answers:
7. She's helpful.
8. He's not afraid anymore.
9. It's over too soon.
10. They're sad to go.
11. She's at the door.
12. They're glad to see her.

Language and Literacy 111

Language Practice Book page 67

UNIT 5 LESSON 15

LANGUAGE ACROSS THE CURRICULUM: SOCIAL STUDIES

OBJECTIVES

Function: Listen to an Article
Concepts and Vocabulary: Maps
Research Skills and Learning Strategies: Build Background; Use Text Structures (maps)
Critical Thinking and Comprehension: Identify Cause and Effect; Identify Details

LEARN ABOUT MAPS

1. **Study Map Features** Introduce the map features and have partners locate items identified in the legend or key. Model how to use the map scale to determine the approximate length of a highway or railroad.

LISTEN AND THINK

2. **Discuss Transportation** Explain that we use transportation to move people and things from one place to another. Use a chart to brainstorm vehicle names and where each vehicle travels.

Transportation

Vehicle	Places
boat	river, lake
car	road, highway, bridge
train	railroad, track

3. **Listen to the Article** Have students preview the maps. Then read the article, pausing to identify how the maps show what is described in the reading.

CHECK UNDERSTANDING

4. **Answer the Review Questions** Encourage partners to take turns reading and answering the questions orally before writing them.

CLOSE AND ASSESS

Have partners create a question about St. Louis, based on the article, for the group to answer.

T112 Unit 5 | City Sights

SUCCESS IN SOCIAL STUDIES

Learn About Cities

MAP

Use the scale to measure the distance between places on a map.

12 inches = 1 foot
3 feet = 1 yard
1,760 yards = 1 mile

Answers for the Review:
1. Boats could easily travel to St. Louis on the Missi and Missouri Rivers.
2. Some highways that go into St. Louis: 61, 44, 64, 7
3. The dot symbol marks where the city of St. Louis

Listen to the article and study the maps. Then do the Review.

Saint Louis, Gateway to the West

• How and why has St. Louis changed over the years?

Saint Louis, Missouri, is located near where the Mississippi and Missouri Rivers meet. Fur traders settled in the area in 1764 because boats could easily travel there. Soon the town became the starting point for explorers, fur trappers, and settlers traveling west.

Rivers Connected to the Mississippi

In the 1850s, the railroads joined St. Louis with other large cities like Chicago. Companies could easily ship goods in and out of the city. From 1840 to 1870, St. Louis' population increased by almost 300,000 people!

St. Louis Highways

Highways and bridges across the Mississippi River made it even easier to get to St. Louis. Today St. Louis is one of the leading railway and trucking centers in the United States.

REVIEW

1. **Check Your Understanding** Why did the fur traders choose to settle in the St. Louis area?
2. **Vocabulary** Name some highways that go to St. Louis.
3. **Use Maps** What does the dot symbol on the map of rivers mean?

112 Unit 5 | City Sights

REACHING ALL STUDENTS

CULTURAL PERSPECTIVES

Home Culture: Maps Provide small groups with maps of students' countries of origin. Have each group create a chart to list specific information taken from the maps. Model how to use a scale to measure distances between cities or length of rivers or roads. Then encourage volunteers to present the information they found to the larger group.

Facts About Puerto Rico

cities	San Juan Aguadilla
rivers	Río Grande de Añasco Río Grande de Manatí
airports	Luis Muñoz Marín Airport Fajardo Airport
roads	Las Américas Expressway

Writing Project / Journal Entry

WRITING ASSESSMENT Use the Writing Progress Checklist on page 51 of the Assessment Handbook to evaluate this writing project.

Write a journal entry for each day last week. Tell what you did each day.

THINK ABOUT LAST WEEK

Make a detail chart. Tell what you did last week and where you did it.

Day	Events	Place
Monday	walked the dog	in the park
Tuesday	played basketball	on the court at the Youth Center
Wednesday	skated	behind the school
Thursday	walked	near the library
Friday	cooked soup	in the kitchen
Saturday	washed cars	at the gas station
Sunday	painted a picture	in my bedroom

WRITE YOUR JOURNAL ENTRY

Use your detail chart to write your journal entry. Check pages 314–319 in your Handbook for verbs to use. Check and correct your work.

✓ Check Your Work
- Does your journal entry explain what you did last week?
- Did you use the correct past tense verbs?
- Do all your sentences start with a capital letter and end with the correct mark?

Write your journal entry on a clean sheet of paper. Add drawings or photos.

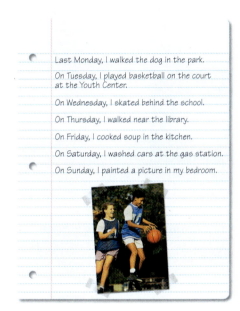

Last Monday, I walked the dog in the park.
On Tuesday, I played basketball on the court at the Youth Center.
On Wednesday, I skated behind the school.
On Thursday, I walked near the library.
On Friday, I cooked soup in the kitchen.
On Saturday, I washed cars at the gas station.
On Sunday, I painted a picture in my bedroom.

Language Across the Curriculum **113**

UNIT 5 LESSON 16

LANGUAGE ACROSS THE CURRICULUM: WRITING

OBJECTIVES

Functions: Write; Give Information

Learning Strategies and Critical Thinking: Plan; Relate to Personal Experience; Generate and Organize Ideas; Self-Assess; Use Graphic Organizers (detail chart); Relate Events in a Sequence

Writing: Journal Entry

CONDUCT THE WRITING PROJECT

1. **Explore Journals** Read the introduction, and explain that people all over the world write about their lives in journals or diaries. Share excerpts from a published work, such as *The Diary of Anne Frank* or *Zlata's Diary*.

2. **Plan What You Will Write** Explain that, although most journals are private, students will share the information they write for this project. Then brainstorm events students might share in their journal entries, including activities from the school week.

3. **Think About Last Week** Refer students to pages 100, 103, and 104 for help with past tense verbs and location words.

4. **Write Your Journal Entry** Go over the model and use it to develop this sentence frame for students to use:

   On ___(day)___, I ___(did what)___ ___(where)___.

   Have students share their completed journal entries with the class.

▶ **Language Practice Book** page 68

CLOSE AND ASSESS

As students read their journals, say:
- *Show me the word for the day of the week.*
- *Point to a verb with an -ed ending. Read the verb aloud.*
- *Show me a sentence that starts with a capital letter. What does it end with?*

Language Practice Book page 68

Multi-Level Strategies
WRITING SUPPORT

PRELITERATE Encourage students to draw pictures that show the events they want to record in their journals. Then use a language-experience approach by encouraging students to dictate events to you or a partner. Recast their sentences to add the day of the week, the correct past tense forms of verbs, and location words, as necessary. You might ask students to name the first letter of words they dictate, to practice letter/sound learning. Then coach them in reading back their finished entries.

Language Across the Curriculum **T113**

Resources

For Success in Language and Literacy

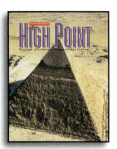

Student Book pages 114–127

For Language Skills Practice

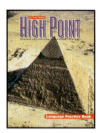

Language Practice Book pages 69–73

For Reading Skills Practice

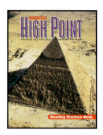

Reading Practice Book pages 58–61

For Vocabulary, Language Development, and Reading Fluency

Language Tape 3, Side B
Language CD 1, Tracks 22–25

For Reading Together

Theme Book *Families* from The Basics Bookshelf

For Audio Walk-Throughs and Selection Readings

Selection Tape 3B
Selection CD 1, Tracks 11–12

For Phonics Instruction

Transparencies 36–40

Transparency Scripts 36–40

Letter Tiles

For Comprehensive Assessment

Language Acquisition Assessment,
Units 4–6 Test, Writing Assessment,
Self-Assessment

For Planning and Instruction

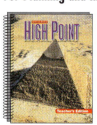

Teacher's Edition
pages T114a–T127

T114a Unit Planner

UNIT 6

Welcome Home!

In This Unit

Vocabulary
- Family
- Rooms in a House
- Household Objects
- Mathematics

Language Functions
- Give Information
- Ask and Answer Questions

Patterns and Structures
- Present Tense Verbs *(have, has)*
- Plural Nouns

Reading
- Phonics: Long Vowels
- Comprehension: Relate Main Idea and Details (main-idea diagram)

Writing
- Sentences
- Questions and Answers
- Family Album

Content Area Connection
- Mathematics (fractions, decimals, and percents)

T114b

UNIT 6
Activity and Assessment Planner

UNIT 6: Welcome Home!

LESSONS

1

UNIT 6 LAUNCH			▶ *pages T114–T115*

LESSON 1: INTRODUCE UNIT 6 pages T114–T115

Vocabulary **T** Family **T** Rooms in a House	**Viewing** Respond to a Visual Image	**Learning Strategies** Relate to Personal Experience Preview Build Background	**Critical Thinking** Make Inferences Generate Ideas

2–5

LANGUAGE DEVELOPMENT			▶ *pages T116–T119*

LESSON 2 **FAMILY** page T116 **Function** Give Information **Vocabulary** **T** Family **Writing** Labels for a Family Tree	**LESSON 3** **PRESENT TENSE VERBS** page T117 **Function** Give Information **Vocabulary** **T** Family	**Patterns and Structures** **T** Present Tense Verbs *(has, have)* **Writing** Sentences	**LESSON 4** **ROOMS IN A HOUSE** page T118 **Function** Give Information **Vocabulary** **T** Rooms in a House **T** Household Objects **Writing** **T** Sentences	**LESSON 5** **HOUSEHOLD OBJECTS** page T119 **Function** Ask/Answer Questions **Vocabulary** **T** Rooms in a House **T** Household Objects	**Patterns and Structures** Questions and Answers **T** Present Tense Verbs *(has, have)* **Writing** **T** Sentences

6–12

LANGUAGE AND LITERACY					▶ *pages T120a–T125*

LESSON 6 **BASICS BOOKSHELF** pages T120a–T120j **Function** Listen to a Book **Vocabulary** **T** Family **Reading Strategies** Activate Prior Knowledge Preview **Learning to Read** Identify Title and Author Predict Words Identify Words **Critical Thinking and Comprehension** Identify Details that Support a Main Idea	**LESSON 7** **BASICS BOOKSHELF: COMPREHENSION** page T120 **Function** Give Information **Learning Strategy** Use Graphic Organizers (main idea diagram) **Critical Thinking and Comprehension** Identify Details that Support a Main Idea	**LESSON 8** **HIGH FREQUENCY WORDS** page T121 **Learning to Read** **T** Recognize High Frequency Words **LESSON 9** **PHONICS** pages T122a–T122d **Learning to Read** Build Oral Vocabulary Develop Phonemic Awareness **T** Use Word Patterns to Decode Words **T** Identify Plural Endings *(-s, -es)* Decode Words with Endings	**LESSON 10** **READING AND SPELLING** pages T122–T123 **Learning to Read** Develop Phonemic Awareness **T** Use Word Patterns to Decode Words **T** Identify Plural Endings *(-s, -es)* Decode Words with Endings **Spelling** **T** Long Vowel Words	**LESSON 11** **INDEPENDENT READING** page T124 **Function** Read a Selection **Learning to Read** **T** Recognize High Frequency Words **T** Use Word Patterns to Decode Words *(CVC, CVCe)* Plurals **Reading Strategies** Preview Make Predictions Retell **Critical Thinking and Comprehension** Relate Main Idea and Details	**LESSON 12** **PLURAL NOUNS** page T125 **Functions** Write Ask Questions **Patterns and Structures** **T** Plural Nouns **Writing** Questions

13–14

LANGUAGE ACROSS THE CURRICULUM			▶ *pages T126–T127*

LESSON 13 **MATHEMATICS: FRACTIONS, DECIMALS, AND PERCENTS** page T126 **Function** Give Information	**Vocabulary** Mathematics (fractions, decimals, and percents)	**Critical Thinking and Comprehension** Solve Problems	**LESSON 14** **WRITING PROJECT: FAMILY ALBUM** page T127 **Functions** Give Information Write	**Learning Strategies and Critical Thinking** Plan Generate and Organize Ideas Self-Assess	**Representing** Use Graphic Organizers (chart) **Writing** Family Album

T114c Unit 6 | Welcome Home!

T = Objective Tested on Unit Test

ASSESSMENT OPTIONS

The **Teacher's Edition** and the **Assessment Handbook** include these comprehensive assessment tools:

▶ **Ongoing, Informal Assessment**
Check for understanding and achieve closure for every lesson with the targeted questions and activities in the **Close and Assess** boxes in your Teacher's Edition.

▶ **Decoding Progress Check**
These word lists for each unit provide a quick way to check on mastery of the phonics or word structure skills taught in the unit.

▶ **Language Acquisition Assessments**
To verify students' ability to use the language functions and grammar structures taught in Units 4–6, conduct these performance assessments.

▶ **Unit Test in Standardized Test Format**
This multiple-choice test measures students' cumulative understanding of the skills and language developed in Units 4–6.

▶ **Self- and Peer-Assessment**
Students use the Self-Assessment Form to evaluate their own work and develop learning strategies appropriate to their needs. Students offer feedback to their classmates with the Peer-Assessment Form.

▶ **Writing Assessment/Portfolio Opportunities**
You can evaluate students' writing in the Writing Projects using the Writing Progress Checklist. Then collaborate with students to choose work for their portfolios.

UNITS 4–6 ASSESSMENT OPPORTUNITIES

	Assessment Handbook Pages
Decoding Progress Check	1a
Language Acquisition Assessments	10
Units 4–6 Test	11–16
Self-Assessment Form	17
Peer-Assessment Form	50
Writing Progress Checklist	51
Portfolio Evaluation Form	52

RELATED RESOURCES

In My Family
by Carmen Lomas Garza
Vignettes of family life in an Hispanic community in Texas. Bilingual book in English and Spanish.
(Children's Book Press)
Theme Book: Read Aloud

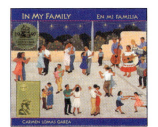

This Is My House
by Arthur Dorros
Children around the world tell about their homes. The refrain "This is my house," is repeated throughout in the local language. (Scholastic)
**Phonics Reinforcement:
Long Vowels in CVCe Pattern**

Houses and Homes
by Ann Morris
Simple text and photos show different kinds of houses around the world and what makes them homes.
(Lothrop, Lee & Shepard)
Easy Reading

Homes Are for Living
by Ina Cumpiano
Animals and humans live in many different kinds of homes. This book explores those homes through pictures, photos, diagrams, and explanatory text. (Hampton-Brown)
**Language Development:
Present Tense Verbs**

Knock Knock
A 3-week science unit that explores the concept of "house"—for people as well as for animals and household objects. (Demco)
Multimedia: CD-ROM

Unit Planner **T114d**

UNIT 6 LESSON 1

INTRODUCE UNIT 6: WELCOME HOME!

OBJECTIVES

Concepts and Vocabulary:
🅣 Family; 🅣 Rooms in a House
Viewing: Respond to a Visual Image
Learning Strategies: Relate to Personal Experience; Preview; Build Background
Critical Thinking: Make Inferences; Generate Ideas
Speaking: Role-Play

START WITH A COMMON EXPERIENCE

1. **Introduce "Welcome Home!"** Read the unit title. Explain that people say this when family members return home from being away. Talk about special occasions that draw family members back home from far away. (weddings, births, funerals, traditional holidays, birthdays, etc.)

2. **Meet the Family** Have students study the painting. Ask where and when the scene takes place. (in a kitchen, preparing for a celebration) Encourage students to point out and explain clues that support these conclusions.

3. **Role-Play the Scene** Assign roles to volunteers. To help students prepare for the role-play, display these sentence frames and guide students in completing them for their characters:

    I am the <u>(character)</u>.
    Today, I will <u>(action)</u>.

    Have characters take their places, to match the picture. Then begin by suggesting something for one of the characters to say.

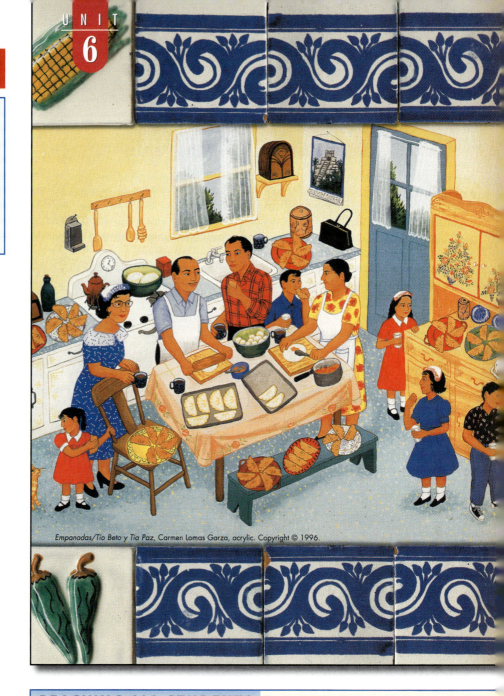

Empanadas/Tío Beto y Tía Paz, Carmen Lomas Garza, acrylic. Copyright © 1996.

REACHING ALL STUDENTS

HOME CONNECTION

Family Gathering Invite students to show family members the painting on page 114. Have students and family illustrate a scene showing their own family gathering. Encourage students to share their artwork and tell about the occasion.

T114 Unit 6 | Welcome Home!

Welcome Home!

Look at the picture. What does each person say? What does each person do? Act out the scene with a partner or a group.

In This Unit

Vocabulary
- Family
- Rooms in a House
- Household Objects
- Mathematics

Language Functions
- Give Information
- Ask and Answer Questions

Patterns and Structures
- Present Tense Verbs (*have, has*)
- Plural Nouns

Reading
- Phonics: Long Vowels
- Comprehension: Relate Main Idea and Details (main-idea diagram)

Writing
- Sentences
- Questions and Answers
- Family Album

Content Area Connection
- Mathematics (fractions, decimals, and percents)

115

PREVIEW THE UNIT

4 Look for Activities About Families
Leaf through the unit, previewing activities students will do, for example:

page 116—learning a song about the members of a family

pages 118–119—learning about rooms and objects in a house

page 120—listening to the Bookshelf book (Display a copy of the book.)

page 127—making a family album

Highlight the family tree on page 116 and the family album on 127. Then sum up what the preview reveals: *Families share special times and memories.*

5 Set Your Goals Start a mind map about different aspects of family life. Prompt students for pictures or words to add, and have them act out and describe other ideas for you to put into words.

CLOSE AND ASSESS

Ask students to tell or show you something they are interested in learning in this unit.

UNIT 6 Mind Map

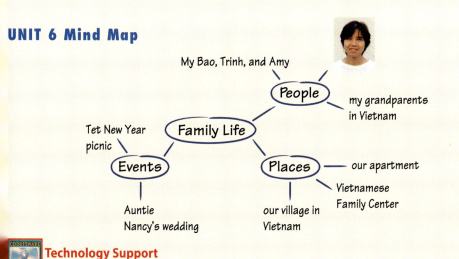

Technology Support
See **Inspiration** Visual Learning software for support in creating mind maps.

Unit Launch **T115**

UNIT 6 **LESSON 2**

LANGUAGE DEVELOPMENT: FAMILY

OBJECTIVES

Functions: Listen Actively; Repeat Spoken Language; Recite; Give Information
Concepts and Vocabulary: Family
Writing: Labels for a Family Tree

INTRODUCE

Tape 3B
CD 1 Track 22

1. **Listen and Sing** Play "My Family Tree" on the **Language Tape/CD**. Students will listen and read along with the words, echo the lines, supply words, and chime in on the entire chant.

2. **Learn About Family Words** Create a list of family words from the song and chart. Add family members such as *grandson, niece, stepmother*. Suggest different words that can be used for the same person, such as *mom, momma*, and *mommy*.

PRACTICE

3. **Conduct "Express Yourself"** Model how to give information. Have partners complete the activity.

   How to Give Information
   - First, I think about a family.
   - Next, I list the family members: *One aunt, two cousins,…*
   - Finally, I change the song to tell about the family.

APPLY

4. **Write Labels for a Family Tree** Encourage students to check their answers with a partner. Distribute Partner Checklist 6 on page T310.

▶ **Language Practice Book** page 69

CLOSE AND ASSESS

Have volunteers display their family trees and identify family members.

T116 Unit 6 | Welcome Home!

VOCABULARY: FAMILY

Meet My Family

Listen and sing.

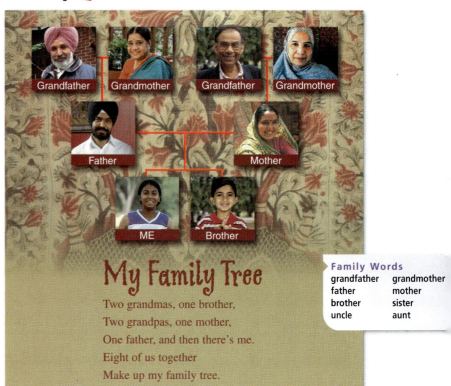

My Family Tree

Two grandmas, one brother,
Two grandpas, one mother,
One father, and then there's me.
Eight of us together
Make up my family tree.

Family Words
grandfather	grandmother
father	mother
brother	sister
uncle	aunt

EXPRESS YOURSELF ▶ GIVE INFORMATION

1. Change the song to tell about another family. Sing it to a partner.

WRITE LABELS FOR A FAMILY TREE

2.–3. Cut pictures of people out of magazines. Use them to make a family tree. Trade papers with a partner. Write labels for the family tree.

Example: 1. One grandma, two brothers,
One sister, one mother,
One uncle, and then there's me.
Seven of us together
Make up our family tree.

Sample Responses
Students should use the family tree in the chant poster as a model for creating their family tree. Then their partner should label each family member. Student responses should be reasonable, based on the age and gender of the person depicted in each picture.

116 Unit 6 | Welcome Home!

REACHING ALL STUDENTS

Vocabulary

FAMILY WORDS

Post a student's family tree, with the labels covered by self-stick notes. Have some students take turns calling out family-member words, while other students point to the correct pictures. Remove the notes to reveal the correct answers. Then invite volunteers to role-play a family member and have students introduce themselves: *I am the father.*

Language Practice Book page 69

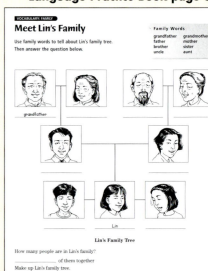

PRESENT TENSE VERBS: *HAVE* AND *HAS*

I Have a Great Family

Use *have* with *I*, *you*, *we*, and *they*. Use *has* with *he*, *she*, or *it*.

Hi, I'm Robert. I **have** a sister. I **don't have** any brothers. We **have** a big house. It **has** four bedrooms. My dad **has** an office in our house.

BUILD SENTENCES

Read each sentence. Add *have* or *has*. Then say the sentence.

Example: 1. She has a brother.

She _has_ a brother.

They _have_ two children.

He _has_ an aunt.

"I _have_ a wonderful grandmother!"

The house _has_ two bedrooms.

The sisters _have_ a new brother.

WRITE SENTENCES

7–10. Write 4 sentences about people in your family. Use *have* or *has*.

Example: 7. I have a brother.

Language Development 117

Language Practice Book page 70

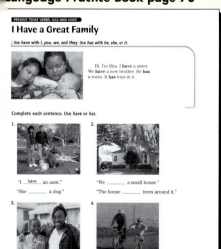

UNIT 6 **LESSON 3**

LANGUAGE DEVELOPMENT: PRESENT TENSE VERBS

OBJECTIVES

Function: Give Information
Concepts and Vocabulary: ❶ Family
Patterns and Structures:
❶ Present Tense Verbs (*has*, *have*)
Writing: Sentences

INTRODUCE

1 Learn About Verbs Read aloud the introduction and sample paragraph. Then read each sentence again and lead students in repeating the subject-verb phrase with *has* or *have* after each example: *I **have** a sister… I **have**.*

Offer more examples: *I **have** an uncle. He **has** a soccer team. They **have** a good record. His team **has** games on Saturday.* Again, have students echo the subject-verb phrases with *has* or *have*.

PRACTICE

2 Build Sentences Remind students to choose *has* or *have* based on the subject of the sentence. Refer them to the top of the page for the list of subjects that go with each verb form. Have partners read the completed sentences to each other.

APPLY

3 Write Sentences Encourage students to write sentences with singular and plural subjects.

▶ **Language Practice Book** page 70

CLOSE AND ASSESS

Invite volunteers to write their sentences on the board, leaving a blank in place of the verb *has* or *have*. Then have other students fill in the correct verbs and read the completed sentences aloud.

Language Development **T117**

UNIT 6 LESSON 4

LANGUAGE DEVELOPMENT: ROOMS IN A HOUSE

OBJECTIVES
Functions:
Listen Actively; Give Information
Concepts and Vocabulary:
- Rooms in a House;
- Household Objects

Writing: Sentences

INTRODUCE

1 Learn About the Rooms in a House
Have students point to the photos as you read aloud the room names and other labels. Then check understanding: *Point to the bathroom. Find a closet. Where can you find a pot and a spoon?*

PRACTICE

2 Conduct "Who's Talking?" Play "Who's Talking?" on the **Language Tape/CD**. The first time through, have students listen only. Then replay, pausing after each speaker so students can point to the correct person and identify the room.

Tape 3B CD 1 Track 23

APPLY

3 Write Sentences Work with students to create sentences about the people, rooms, and features shown in the house. Model how to give information: *The mother is in the living room. She has a vacuum cleaner.* Then provide sentence frames for students to use:

```
The _____ is in the _____.
_____ has _____.
```

CLOSE AND ASSESS
Conduct a call-and-response activity based on what's shown in the house. Say: *I see a mirror.* The group responds: *You are in the bathroom.* Continue with: *I have a guitar; I have a vacuum cleaner; I have a pot and a spoon.*

T118 Unit 6 | Welcome Home!

VOCABULARY: ROOMS IN A HOUSE

Let Me Show You My House!

Pronunciation of Name
Pablo   **pah** blō

WHO'S TALKING?   ▶ GIVE INFORMATION

1.–3. Listen.
Who is talking? Point to the correct person.
Then tell where each person is in the house.

Answers:
1. The girl is in the bedroom.
2. The man is in the kitchen.
3. The woman is in the living room.

WRITE SENTENCES ✏️

4.–7. Work in a group of 4. Each person acts out a scene from above. Tell where each person is and what each person has. Then write the sentences.

Example: 4. Pablo is in the bedroom. He has a guitar.

Sample Responses:
4. [Student's name] is in the bedroom. He/she has a guitar.
5. [Student's name] is in the bathroom. He/she has a toothbrush.
6. [Student's name] is in the kitchen. He/she has a spoon.
7. [Student's name] is in the living room. He/she has a vacuum cleaner.
Be sure that students use the correct pronoun when they tell about each pers

118 Unit 6 | Welcome Home!

REACHING ALL STUDENTS

Multi-Level Strategies
WRITING SUPPORT

PRELITERATE Make sets of index cards that list family members: *The daughter, The son, The mother, The father.* Add cards that list the rooms in a house: *living room, bedroom, bathroom, kitchen,* and the phrase *is in the.* Have partners create sentences that match the pictures on the page: *The daughter is in the bedroom.* Then ask them to create new sentences with the word cards: *The daughter is in the kitchen.* Have students copy the completed sentences. Coach them on the shaping of the letters and note the left-to-right flow.

VOCABULARY: HOUSEHOLD OBJECTS

What Is in Each Room?

EXPRESS YOURSELF ▶ Ask and Answer Questions

Work with a partner. Ask each question. Answer in a complete sentence.

Example: 1. Where is the bed? The bed is in the bedroom.

1. Where is the bed? bedroom
2. Where is the refrigerator? kitchen
3. Where is the shower? bathroom
4. Where is the table? living room
5. Where are the curtains? kitchen
6. Where is the sofa? living room

WRITE SENTENCES ✏️

7.–10. What kind of house do you want? Draw it. Then write 4 sentences to tell about your house.

Example: 7. My house has three bedrooms.

Sample Responses
Students might tell about the furniture or other household objects they have in their dream houses. Encourage students to be specific: *It has three refrigerators in the kitchen.*

Language Development 119

UNIT 6 **LESSON 5**

LANGUAGE DEVELOPMENT: HOUSEHOLD OBJECTS

OBJECTIVES

Function: Ask and Answer Questions
Concepts and Vocabulary:
● Rooms in a House;
● Household Objects
Patterns and Structures: Questions and Answers; ● Present Tense Verbs *(has, have)*
Writing: ● Sentences

INTRODUCE

1 Learn Words for Household Objects
Have students view the photos as you read the labels. Use questions to check understanding: *Where can I sleep? Where can I find a book?*

2 Make a Chart of Household Objects
List the objects labeled in the photograph, then add objects that are commonly found in each room.

Living Room	Kitchen	Bedroom
sofa	sink	bed
television	toaster	mirror
telephone	sponge	stereo

PRACTICE

3 Conduct "Express Yourself" Model how to ask and answer questions. Have partners do the activity.

> **How to Ask and Answer Questions**
> • To ask a question, I start with a question word like *where* or *what*: **Where** *is the bed?*
> • To answer a question, I think about the information needed: *The bed is in the bedroom.*

APPLY

4 Write Sentences Students can use the Example as a model.

▶ **Language Practice Book** page 71

CLOSE AND ASSESS

Have volunteers give "walking tours" of their illustrated dream homes, describing the objects in each room.

Language Practice Book page 71

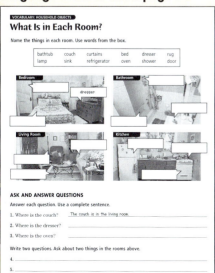

Vocabulary
HOUSEHOLD OBJECTS

Dream-House Design Have students work in groups to design a "dream home." Each member will draw one room in the house, complete with household objects. Then have the group combine the pictures onto a large posterboard and work together to label each room and object. Encourage students to use their creativity as they personalize their rooms. Then have group members take turns describing the rooms in their dream house.

Language Development T119

UNIT 6 **LESSON 6**

LANGUAGE AND LITERACY: THE BASICS BOOKSHELF

OBJECTIVES

Concepts and Vocabulary:
- Family

BUILD LANGUAGE AND VOCABULARY

Materials: family pictures; index cards, each with a family word on it; magazines with pictures of people

1. **Teach "Words to Know"** Have students look at page 2. Say: *This page shows names for people in families.*

   Point to the girl in the center photo and say: *This page shows the people in the girl's family. They are her relatives.* Point to each photo and name the family member in relation to the girl: *This man is the girl's grandfather. She calls him Grandpa.* On page 3, use the photo to point out the parents, brothers, sisters, sons, and daughters.

2. **Introduce Families and Form Family Groups** Have students show photos or drawings of their families and introduce each person: *This is my mother. This is my brother.*

   Then distribute cards with a name of one family member on each card. Have small groups arrange the cards into a family group. They can then name the people in their fictitious families and cut out magazine pictures to add to their cards.

T120a Unit 6 | Welcome Home!

Families
by Ann Morris

Summary This photo essay shows families from all over the world as they care for and help each other, work and play together, and celebrate. The essay presents different family arrangements, including children living with grandparents or a foster family, and offers opportunities to reinforce names for family members.

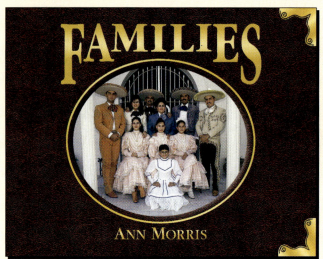

Cover

The Basics Bookshelf
Families

Pages 2–3

Pages 4–5

Pages 6–7

Language and Literacy **T120b**

UNIT 6 **LESSON 6,** CONTINUED

LANGUAGE AND LITERACY: THE BASICS BOOKSHELF

OBJECTIVES

Listening: Listen to a Preview

Reading Strategies:
Activate Prior Knowledge; Preview

Learning to Read: Identify Title and Author; Represent English Sounds in Print

PREPARE TO READ

3 Think About What You Know Invite students to share what they know about families. Encourage them to talk about homes and family customs in their native countries.

4 Preview Play the Audio Walk-Through for *Families* on the **Selection Tape/CD** to give students the overall idea of the story.

Tape 3B

CD 1 Track 11

CLOSE AND ASSESS

Divide the class into small groups and invite each group member to name one activity that families do together.

Multi-Level Strategies
LITERACY SUPPORT

PRELITERATE **Concepts of Print: Identify Title and Author** Point to the word *Families* on the cover of the book as you read it aloud. Say: *This is the title. It is the name of the book.* Then point to the author's name. Say: *This is the name of the author. Ann Morris wrote this book. Her first name is* Ann. *Her last name is* Morris. Open to the title page and have students point to the title and the author's name. Ask: *What does the title tell us? What did the author do?*

NON-ROMAN ALPHABET **Represent English Sounds in Print** Ask students to draw pictures of their favorite family activities. Then ask volunteers to dictate sentences for you to record on chart paper. Say each word aloud as you write it: *My family likes to hike. We have picnics and catch fish.* Use the stories to point out words with common sounds: *"Have" and "hike" both begin with /h/. "Picnics" and "fish" have the short /i/ sound.* Have small groups categorize words that share sounds. See the Phonics Transfer Chart on page T338 to determine the sounds that are most important to target for the language groups represented in your class.

T120c Unit 6 | Welcome Home!

Families, CONTINUED

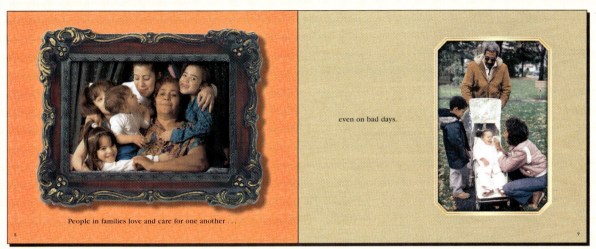

Pages 8–9

Pages 10–11

Pages 12–13

Language and Literacy **T120d**

UNIT 6 **LESSON 6,** CONTINUED

**LANGUAGE AND LITERACY:
THE BASICS BOOKSHELF**

OBJECTIVES

Function: Listen to a Book

READ AND THINK TOGETHER

1 Read Aloud On your first reading of the book, use the "Strategies for Comprehensible Input" that appear on this page.

Strategies for Comprehensible Input

PAGE	STORY LANGUAGE	STRATEGY OPTIONS
4–5	Everyone	**Gesture:** Stretch your hands out to all the students.
	everywhere	**Gesture:** Use a wide, sweeping movement around a globe or a map.
6–7	is part of	**Restate:** belongs to
8–9	love	**Gesture:** Clasp your hands over your heart.
	care for one another	**Restate:** help each other
	bad days	**Restate:** days when you are upset or don't feel well
10–11	one another	**Point to one of the pairs in the picture.**
12–13	work together	**Restate:** do a job with each other
14–15	play together	**Point to the pictures and restate:** have fun with each other
16–17	cook	**Restate:** They make something to eat.
	eat	**Gesture:** Pretend to eat something.
18–19	celebrate	**Restate:** have fun on special days
20–21	Families come in all sizes.	**Restate:** Families can be large or small.
	children, brothers, sisters	**Point to the people in the first picture.**
	none	**Point to the child in the second picture and restate:** no brothers or sisters
	lots, fewer	**Demonstrate:** Show one hand with several small items and the other hand with fewer.
22–23	mothers and fathers	**Point to the parents in the pictures.**
	stepparents	**Explain:** A stepparent is someone who married one of your parents after you were born.
24–25	foster family	**Explain:** A foster family cares for a child when the child's parents cannot.
	adopted	**Explain:** An adopted child becomes a part of new family.
26–27	lands near or far	**Restate:** this country or other countries
28–29	sharing	**Demonstrate:** Hold two pencils, then give one to a student.
	wherever you are	**Restate:** everywhere you go; anywhere you go

T120e Unit 6 | Welcome Home!

The Basics Bookshelf
Families, CONTINUED

Pages 14–15

Pages 16–17

Pages 18–19

Language and Literacy **T120f**

UNIT 6 **LESSON 6,** CONTINUED

LANGUAGE AND LITERACY: THE BASICS BOOKSHELF

OBJECTIVES

Function: Listen to a Book
Critical Thinking and Comprehension: Identify Details that Support a Main Idea

READ AND THINK TOGETHER, *CONTINUED*

2 **Read and Map: Identify Details that Support a Main Idea** Draw a main idea diagram like the one below, but with empty rows. Say: *A main idea diagram tells an important idea. It also gives details that tell more about the main idea.*

Invite students to leaf through pages 4–19. Say: *These pages show that families do many things together. I will write that as my main idea.* Flip through the pages and point out the photo and text on page 8. Say: *Families love and care for one another. That is something families do. I will write it in the next row.*

Pause after reading each set of pages shown by the graphic organizers and model completing each diagram.

CLOSE AND ASSESS

Say one of the main ideas from *Families.* Ask volunteers for pictures or words that support each main idea.

Main Idea Diagram for *Families,* pages 4–19

	Families do a lot of things together.
pages 8–9	They love and care for one another.
pages 10–11	They help one another.
pages 12–13	They work.
pages 14–15	They play.
pages 16–19	They cook, eat, and celebrate.

Main Idea Diagram for *Families,* pages 20–25

	Children live in many kinds of families.
page 20	Some have brothers and sisters, and some do not.
page 21	Some have a lot of relatives, and some do not.
page 22	Some live with their mothers and fathers.
page 23	Some have stepparents or live with just one parent.
page 24	Some live with a grandparent or a foster family.
page 25	Some are adopted.

Technology Support
See **Inspiration** Visual Learning software for support in creating the main idea diagrams.

T120g Unit 6 | Welcome Home!

The Basics Bookshelf

Families, CONTINUED

Pages 20–21

Pages 22–23

Pages 24–25

Language and Literacy **T120h**

UNIT 6 **LESSON 6,** CONTINUED

LANGUAGE AND LITERACY: THE BASICS BOOKSHELF

OBJECTIVES

Function: Listen to a Book
Learning to Read: Predict Words; Identify Words

READ AND THINK TOGETHER, CONTINUED

3 **Conduct Interactive Readings** Choose from these options:

- **Predict words** Play the recording of *Families* on the **Selection Tape/CD**. Pause the tape to have students supply these words:

  page 7—family

  page 11—another

  page 14—together

  page 16—cook

  page 17—eat

  page 20—sisters

  page 22—fathers

  page 26—families

- **Read along and identify words**
  Families contains many high frequency words that have been previously taught, as follows:

a	for	on	there
all	go	one	they
and	have	people	to
are	help	play	who
by	in	small	with
come	is	some	work
day	love	them	you
eat	of		

  As you read, frame individual words from the list and have volunteers identify the words. Continue reading as students track the print and identify other words they know.

CLOSE AND ASSESS

Have students describe one type of family and one family activity to a partner.

Multi-Level Strategies

LITERACY SUPPORT

LITERATE IN L1 **Read with a Partner/ Write Family Stories** After students have participated in the interactive readings, encourage them to read the story with a partner. Distribute the Partner Prompts on page T311 to help partners work together to identify unfamiliar words and unlock their meanings, then read the text to each other. After the partner reading, have students write and illustrate short stories about their families. Provide sentence frames if necessary:

My family likes to _____.

The people in my family _____.

Students may enjoy tape recording their stories and inviting other students to listen as they read along with the text.

INTERRUPTED SCHOOLING **Identify Details that Support a Main Idea** To anchor understanding of the skill, write the main idea for each diagram. Distribute sentence strips with one detail per strip. Invite volunteers to read aloud their sentence strip. Then ask: *Does this tell something families do, or tell something about a kind of family?* As students respond, have them put their strip under the corresponding main idea. Then have the group read aloud the main idea and details.

Families, CONTINUED

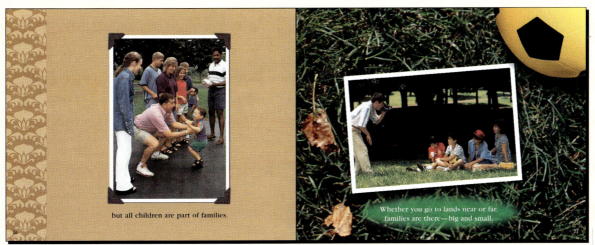

Pages 26–27

Pages 28–29

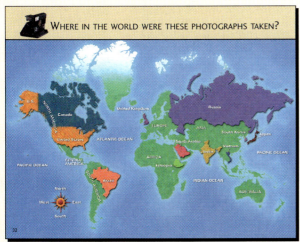

Page 32

Language and Literacy **T120j**

UNIT 6 **LESSON 7**

LANGUAGE AND LITERACY: THE BASICS BOOKSHELF

OBJECTIVES

Function: Give Information
Learning Strategy: Use Graphic Organizers (main idea diagram)
Critical Thinking and Comprehension: Identify Details that Support a Main Idea

CHECK COMPREHENSION

1. **Make a Main Idea Diagram** Have students review *Families* to identify details that support the two main ideas. Remind them that a main idea diagram shows the most important idea and details that support it.

   As you read aloud the directions for each step, pause for students to add information to the sections of their diagrams. Then have one group of students check the details for pages 4–19 while another group checks the details for pages 20–26. Invite groups to share their information.

2. **Share Information from the Book** Have small groups use their main idea diagrams to tell about the book. Group members can say the main idea together, and then take turns giving the details.

CLOSE AND ASSESS

Ask students to complete this sentence: *A main idea diagram shows _____.*

T120 Unit 6 | Welcome Home!

COMPREHENSION: RELATE MAIN IDEA AND DETAILS

Read and Think Together

Make two diagrams to tell about the main ideas of *Families*. Follow these steps.

① Think about pages 4–19 in the book. What are the pages mainly about? Write a sentence in a box.

| Families do a lot of things together. |

② Think of details from the book that tell about this main idea. Add them to your diagram.

| Families do a lot of things together. |

Sample Responses
- They love and care for one another.
- They help one another.
- They work together.
- They play together.
- They cook, eat, and celebrate together.

③ Make a new main idea diagram for pages 20–26 of the book.

| Children live in many kinds of families. |

- Some have brothers and sisters, and some do not.
- Families come in all sizes.
- Some children have lots of aunts, uncles, cousins.
- Some children live with their mothers and fathers.
- Others live with just one parent.
- Some children live with a grandparent.

④ Use your main idea diagrams to tell a partner about *Families*.

120 Unit 6 | Welcome Home!

from *The Basics Bookshelf*

THEME BOOK
This photo essay shows how family members everywhere love and care for each other.

REACHING ALL STUDENTS

Language Development

GIVE OR EXPRESS PRAISE/ GIVE OR ACCEPT COMPLIMENTS

Compliment Time Use photos from the book to introduce praise and compliments. On page 11, the father might say: *Good job, Joon! You play the violin well.* The child might say: *Thanks for helping me practice, Dad.*

Create a chart to show ways to give praise and accept compliments. Have partners role-play a scene from the book in which two family members give and accept praise or compliments. Encourage students to present their dialogues to the class.

How to Give Praise	How to Accept Compliments
Good work!	Thank you.
You did a great job!	Thanks.
I like what you did.	I'm glad that you liked it.

Words to Know

REVIEW WORDS YOU KNOW

Read the words aloud. Which word goes in the sentence?

down	day
small	same
city	see

1. It's a good <u>day</u> to ride bikes.
2. The boy rides a <u>small</u> bike.
3. They can <u>see</u> a bridge.

LEARN TO READ

Learn new words.

family	There are six people in my **family**.
together	We ride bicycles **together**.
other	We like to do **other** things, too.
really	We **really** like to hike in the woods.
father	My **father** carries a heavy backpack.
mother	My **mother** walks fast. Everyone follows her.
our	She is **our** leader!
watch	We sometimes stop to **watch** the birds.
eyes	Once I saw an eagle with my own **eyes**.
head	It was flying in circles over my **head**!

How to Learn a New Word
- Look at the word.
- Listen to the word.
- Listen to the word in a sentence. What does it mean?
- Say the word.
- Spell the word.
- Say the word again.

WORD WORK

4.–13. Work with a partner. Write each new word on a card. Mix your cards together for the game. Turn them so the words are down. Then:

- Turn over 2 cards.
- Spell the words. Are they the same?
- If so, keep them. If not, turn them over again.
- The player with more cards at the end wins.

Example:

f-a-m-i-l-y
f-a-m-i-l-y
These words are the same.

Language and Literacy **121**

Reading Fluency
RECOGNIZE HIGH FREQUENCY WORDS

To build automaticity with the new high frequency words:

- Have students display their word cards from Step 3 on a classroom chart. Partners can use the chart to practice reading the words together or test each other by spelling a word for the other to guess.

- Refer students to the list of new words on page 121. Give clues and have students identify and read the word. For example: *This word starts with w. It means "to look at."*

UNIT 6 **LESSON 8**

LANGUAGE AND LITERACY: HIGH FREQUENCY WORDS

OBJECTIVES

Learning to Read:
- Recognize High Frequency Words

REVIEW WORDS

1 Review Known High Frequency Words Have the group read aloud the words in the green box. Listen for words students cannot read automatically and use the steps in the yellow box to reteach those words. Then have students look at the photo. Read each cloze sentence. Reread each sentence and pause for students to silently read the two words to the left of the sentence. Tell students to choose the word that goes in the sentence and tells about the picture.

INTRODUCE NEW WORDS

2 Learn High Frequency Words Use the High Frequency Word Script on page T317 to lead students through the steps in the yellow box. Explain that *watch* can mean "to look at" or "a small clock you wear on your wrist."

PRACTICE

3 Conduct "Word Work" Guide pairs in making two sets of cards and setting up the game. Have partners take turns until they match all the pairs. Discuss the process students used to figure out the matches.

Students can switch partners and play again for additional practice.

APPLY

4 Read Words in Context Students will read high frequency words in context in the sentences on page 123 and the passage on page 124.

▶ **Reading Practice Book** page 58

CLOSE AND ASSESS

Call out the high frequency words one at a time. Have students point to them and spell the words as a group.

Language and Literacy **T121**

UNIT 6 **LESSON 9**

LANGUAGE AND LITERACY: PHONICS

OBJECTIVES

Learning to Read: Build Oral Vocabulary; Develop Phonemic Awareness; ⊤ Use Word Patterns to Decode Words

TEACH WORD PATTERNS

1 **Build Oral Vocabulary** Display Transparency 36. Play "I Spy. For example, for the first scene, say:

- *I spy a* **cake**. *A* **cake** *is something good to eat. A* **cake** *tastes sweet.*

When students find the cake, say: *Yes,* **this is a cake** (point and pantomime eating). Repeat the game to build context for the other words.

2 **Develop Phonemic Awareness and Contrast Vowel Sounds** Remove the transparency and work through Steps 1 and 2 of the script.

3 **Use Word Patterns to Decode Words** Display Transparency 36 again. Work through Step 3 of the script.

CLOSE AND ASSESS

Display the words *hope* and *hop*. Ask: *Why does* hop *have a short vowel sound? Why does* hope *have a long vowel sound?*

Word Families

-AME AND -AKE

Materials: Letter Tiles

A large number of words can be generated from a few rhyming phonograms. Use letter tiles to build the words in dark type. Then change tiles to build other words in the -*ame* and -*ake* families. Have students make a list of the words. Make sure students understand their meanings. Then ask them to read the word on their list and to identify the shared ending.

name	**cake**
same	bake
game	take

T122a Unit 6 | Welcome Home!

Transparency 36: ▶
Word Patterns

Words with Long a and Long o

cap   cape   rod   rode

Study the words in the pictures below.

home
name
cake
robe
stove
cane

Find the pattern.

1. How many vowels are in each word? _____
2. Where is the e? _____
3. Does the e have a sound? _____
4. Is the vowel sound long or short? _____

Look for patterns in these words. Which word in each pair has a long vowel?

1. not	2. tape	3. back	4. same	5. mad	6. stop
note	tap	bake	Sam	made	stove

Transparency 36   © Hampton-Brown

▼ **Script for Transparency 36**

Words with Long *a* and Long *o*

1. Develop Phonemic Awareness
Isolate/Match Initial and Medial Vowel Sounds Say: *Listen to this word:* ate. *What is its first sound?* (/ā/) *Say* /ā/ *with me:* /ā ā ā/. *Now listen to these words:* cake, late. *Where do you hear* /ā/? (in the middle) Then say: *Tell me which sound,* /ā/ *or* /ō/, *is in these words:* name, home, rose, tape.

2. Contrast Short and Long Vowels
Say: *The letter* a *is a vowel. It has a short sound,* /a/, *and a long sound,* /ā/. *Say the names of the pictures with me:* cap, cape. *What sound do you hear in the middle of* cap? (/a/) *Say* /a/ *with me:* /a/. *The short sound of the letter* a *is* /a/. *What sound do you hear in the middle of* cape? (/ā/) *Say* /ā/ *with me:* /ā/. *The long sound of the letter* a *is* /ā/. Point to the *a* and ask: *What two sounds does the letter* a *have?* (/a/ and /ā/) Repeat to teach the short and long sounds for *o*.

3. Use Word Patterns to Decode Words
Find the Pattern Read the words in the scenes, noting the long vowel sounds. Then use the questions in the box to explore the spelling pattern: *How many vowels are in each word? Let's count them: two in* name, *two in* cake, *etc.* Write the answer. (two) Next ask: *Where is the* e? (at the end of each word) *Does the* e *have a sound?* (no) *Is the vowel sound long or short?* (long) Record the answers. Then have students look at the words *cap/cape* and *rod/rode* in the top box, tell you how their patterns are different, and explain how the pattern affects the vowel sound.

Summarize and Model the Strategy Say: *Look for patterns in words to help you read.* Point to *not* in Item 1, say: *Here I see one vowel and then the consonant* t, *so I'll say the short sound for* o: not. Point to *note* and say: *Here I see one vowel, the consonant* t, *and an* e *at the end, so I'll say the long sound for* o: note.

Practice Have students do items 2–6. They should identify for each pair the word with the long vowel and then tell you how they figured out the vowel sound in each word.

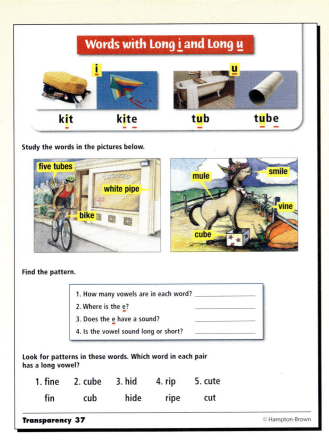

▼ Script for Transparency 37

Words with Long *i* and Long *u*

1. **Develop Phonemic Awareness**
   Isolate/Match Initial and Medial Vowel Sounds Say: *Listen to this word:* ice. *What is the first sound?* (/ī/) *Say /ī/ with me:* /ī ī ī/. *Now listen to these words:* bike, fine. *Where do you hear /ī/?* (in the middle) Then say: *Tell me which sound, /ī/ or /ū/, is in these words:* rule, mile, tune, kite, June, bike.

2. **Contrast Short and Long Vowels**
   Say: *The letter* i *is a vowel. It has a short sound, /i/, and a long sound, /ī/. Say the names of the pictures with me:* kit, kite. *What sound do you hear in the middle of* kit? (/i/) *Say /i/ with me: /i/. The short sound of the letter* i *is /i/. What sound do you hear in the middle of* kite? (/ī/) *Say /ī/ with me: /ī/. The long sound of the letter* i *is /ī/. Point to the* i *and ask: What two sounds does the letter* i *have?* (/i/ and /ī/) Repeat to teach the short and long sounds for *u*.

3. **Use Word Patterns to Decode Words**
   Find the Pattern Read the words in the scenes, noting the long vowel sounds. Point out that in *mule* and *cube* long *u* sounds like /yōō/. Then ask the questions in the box: *How many vowels are in each word? Let's count them: two in* five, *etc.* Write the answer. (two) Next ask: *Where is the* e? (next to last in *tubes*; at the end of the other words) *Does the* e *have a sound?* (no) *Is the vowel sound long or short?* (long) Record the answers. Then have students look at *kit/kite* and *tub/tube* in the top box, tell you how their patterns are different, and explain how the pattern affects the vowel sound.

   Summarize and Model the Strategy Say: *Look for patterns in words.* Point to *fine* in Item 1 and say: *I see one vowel, the consonant* n, *and an* e, *so I'll say the long sound for* i: fine. Point to *fin* and say: *I see one vowel and the consonant* n, *so I'll say the short sound for* i: fin.

   Practice Have students do Items 2–5. They should identify for each pair the word with the long vowel and then tell you how they figured out the vowel sound in each word.

OBJECTIVES

Learning to Read: Build Oral Vocabulary; Develop Phonemic Awareness;
🅣 Use Word Patterns to Decode Words

TEACH WORD PATTERNS

1. **Build Oral Vocabulary** Display Transparency 37. Use the pictures to develop the meaning of each word and use it in a sentence. For example, for *bike* in the first scene, say:

   • *Look at the bike. You can ride a bike. Someone is riding this bike. The bike has two wheels.*

2. **Develop Phonemic Awareness and Contrast Vowel Sounds** Remove the transparency and conduct the oral activities in Steps 1 and 2 of the Script for Transparency 37.

3. **Use Word Patterns to Decode Words** Display Transparency 37 again. Work through Step 3 of the script.

CLOSE AND ASSESS

Display the words *cut* and *cute*. Ask: *Why does* cut *have a short vowel sound? Why does* cute *have a long vowel sound?* Repeat the process with *kit* and *kite*.

▶ **Reading Practice Book** page 59 (long vowels: *a, o, i, u*)

Reading Practice Book page 59

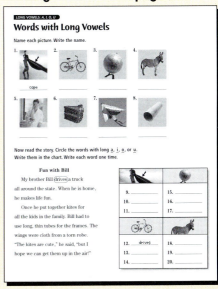

Language and Literacy **T122b**

UNIT 6 LESSON 9, CONTINUED

LANGUAGE AND LITERACY: PHONICS

OBJECTIVES

Learning to Read: Build Oral Vocabulary; Develop Phonemic Awareness; ❶ Use Word Patterns to Decode Words

TEACH WORD PATTERNS

1. **Build Oral Vocabulary** Help students finish these sentences:
   - *You can buy some food in a ____.* (can)
   - *The man walks with a ____.* (cane)
   - *Rabbits jump and ____.* (hop)
   - *If you wish for something, you ____ for it.* (hope)
   - *Doctors carry supplies in a ____.* (kit)
   - *On windy days, I fly my ____.* (kite)

2. **Develop Phonemic Awareness and Contrast Vowel Sounds** Work through Steps 1 and 2 of the script.

3. **Use Word Patterns to Decode Words** Display the transparency and work through Step 3 of the script.

CLOSE AND ASSESS

Display the words *hope* and *hop*. Ask: *Why does* hope *have a long vowel sound? Why does* hop *have a short vowel sound?*

▶ **Reading Practice Book** page 60 (word patterns: CVC, CVCe)

Transparency 38: ▶
Word Patterns

Words with Short and Long Vowels

| can | hop | kit | tub |
| cane | hope | kite | tube |

All these words have short vowels.	All these words have long vowels.
tap	tape
not	note
hid	hide
cut	cute

Find the pattern.

1. Look at the first list of words.
   How many vowels are in each word? _____
   What kind of letter comes after the vowel? _____
   Is the vowel sound long or short? _____
2. Look at the second list of words.
   How many vowels are in each word? _____
   Where is the *e*? It does not have a sound. _____
   Is the vowel sound long or short? _____

Look for patterns in these words. Which word in each pair has a <u>short</u> vowel? Which word in each pair has a <u>long</u> vowel?

| 1. made | 2. rip | 3. hope | 4. cap | 5. cute | 6. rob |
| mad | ripe | hop | cape | cut | robe |

Transparency 38 © Hampton-Brown

▼ **Script for Transparency 38**

Words with Short and Long Vowels

1. Develop Phonemic Awareness

Discriminate Between Vowel Sounds Say: *Listen. Which two words have the same vowel sound:* cap, can, cane? *(cap, can) What is the sound? (/a/) Now listen again. Which two words have the same vowel sound:* cane, tape, map? *(cane, tape) What is the sound? (/ā/) Repeat for short and long o with these sets of words:* mop, home, dot; rose, box, bone.

2. Contrast Short and Long Vowel Sounds

Say: *The vowel* a *has a short sound: /a/. Say /a/ with me: /aaa/. The vowel* a *also has a long sound: /ā/. Say /ā/ with me: /ā ā ā/. Now listen to these words:* can, cane. *Say them with me:* can, cane. *Which word has the long sound for the letter* a? *(cane) Which word has the short sound? (can) Repeat the process for* hop/hope, kit/kite, *and* tub/tube.

3. Use Word Patterns to Decode Words

Find the Pattern Read aloud each list of words, noting the short and long vowel sounds. Then use the questions in the box to explore the spelling pattern in each list: *Look at the word* tap. *How many vowels are in* tap? *(one) What kind of letter comes after the vowel? (a consonant) Is the vowel long or short? (short)* Repeat for the other words in the first list and record the answers. Then work through the second set of questions.

Summarize and Model the Strategy Say: *Look for patterns in words to help you read.* Point to *made* in Item 1 and say: *Here I see two vowels. The* e *is silent, so I will say the long sound for* a: */m m m ā ā ā d/,* made. Point to *mad* and say: *Here I see one vowel and the consonant* d, *so I will say the short vowel sound: /mmmaaad/,* mad.

Practice Have students repeat the process for Items 2–6. First they should identify the word with the short vowel and then tell you how they figured out the vowel sound to read each word.

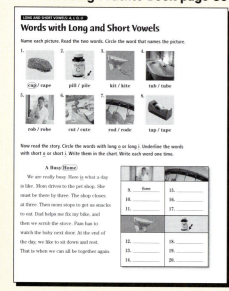

Reading Practice Book page 60

T122c Unit 6 | Welcome Home!

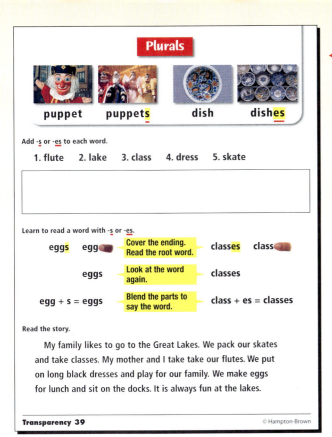

◀ Transparency 39: Plurals

▼ Script for Transparency 39

Plurals

1. Develop Phonemic Awareness
Contrast Final Sounds Say: *Listen to these two words: cat, cats. Listen again: I have a cat. My friend has three cats. Are the words* cat *and* cats *the same?* Repeat: *cat, cats.* (no) Explain: *The second word,* cats, *has an extra sound at the end. What is it?* (/s/) Repeat for *pen* and *pens,* using these sentences: *I have one blue pen. Joon has two blue pens.* (The extra sound is /z/.) Then repeat for *bench* and *benches: I sat on the green bench. The blue benches were wet.* (The two extra sounds are /ez/.) Then repeat for *lunch* and *lunches: We took our lunch to the park. I put our lunches on a bench.* (The two extra sounds are /ez/.)

2. Learn to Spell Plurals
Point to *puppet* on **Transparency 39**. Say: *I see one puppet.* Then point to *puppets* and say: *Here are many puppets.* Explain: *You can hear a difference between* puppet *and* puppets, *and you can see a difference, too.* Cover the *s* in *puppets,* and say: *Here is the root word* puppet. *For* puppet *and most other words, you add an* s *(uncover the* s*) to tell about the plural, or more than one.* Repeat for *dish* and *dishes,* explaining that you add *-es* to words that end in *x, ch, sh, ss,* or *zz* to make them plural. Then use letter tiles to spell and model the pronunciation of the plural forms of the nouns in Items 1–5.

3. Learn to Read Plurals
Teach Work through the Examples below. Point to *eggs* and say: *This word ends with -s. To read the word, cover the -s. Look for a pattern in the root word. Do you see a vowel followed by one or more consonants? If so, the vowel in the root word is short. Sound it out: /eeeg/,* egg. *Then uncover the ending and read the whole word:* eggs. Repeat for *classes.*

Practice Read the story. Pause before each plural word ending in *-s* or *-es.* Ask students to read the word. If they need help, have them cover the *-s* or *-es* and apply the strategy.

OBJECTIVES
Learning to Read: Build Oral Vocabulary; Develop Phonemic Awareness; ⓣ Identify Plural Endings (*-s, -es*); Decode Words with Endings

TEACH PLURALS: *-s, -es*

1 Build Oral Vocabulary Tell students that *plural* means "more than one." Then use pictures, definitions, and props to convey the singular and plural meanings of the nouns on Transparency 39. For example:

- **puppet:** Say: *Here is one puppet.* Point to the picture. Then point to the picture of the puppets and say: *This picture shows many puppets.*

- **flute:** Show or draw a flute. Say: *This is one flute.* Adapt for *flutes.*

2 Develop Phonemic Awareness Conduct the oral activities in Step 1 of the Script for Transparency 39.

3 Learn to Spell and Read Plurals Display Transparency 39 again. Work through Steps 2 and 3 of the script.

CLOSE AND ASSESS
Write the nouns *dish, egg, skate,* and *class.* Have groups write the plural of each noun and read it to the class.

Language and Literacy **T122d**

UNIT 6 LESSON 10

LANGUAGE AND LITERACY: READING AND SPELLING

OBJECTIVES

Functions: Listen Actively; Repeat Spoken Language; Recite

Learning to Read: Develop Phonemic Awareness; 🅣 Use Word Patterns to Decode Words; 🅣 Identify Plural Endings (*-s*, *-es*); Decode Words with Endings

Spelling: 🅣 Long Vowels Words

LISTEN AND LEARN

1 Recite a Chant
Display Transparency 40 and play "Family Gifts" on the **Language Tape/CD**.

Tape 3B CD 1 Track 24

DEVELOP PHONEMIC AWARENESS

2 Segment Words into Sounds Say: *Listen to this word and say it with me:* cake. *Now let's say the sounds separately and count them:* /k/, /ā/, /k/ —*three sounds.* Follow the same procedure with *back, bike, cap, cape, plate,* and *globe.* Point out that there are four sounds in *plate* and *globe.*

LOOK FOR WORD PATTERNS

3 Long Vowels: *a, i, o, u* Point to the cake and say: *This is a cake, and here's the word.* Point to the letters as you say: *I see one vowel, followed by a consonant and an* e *at the end. The* e *is silent, and the* a *has the long sound:* /kāāāk/, cake. Repeat for the other pictures, covering the *-s* in *flutes* and modeling how to blend the root word and then add /s/. Then read the questions aloud: *How are the words alike? Is the vowel sound short or long?* (Each word has a vowel, a consonant, and a silent *e*. The vowel sound in each word is long.) Have students read the words aloud.

Afterwards, play the chant again. Students can identify words with long *a, i,* and *o.*

LONG VOWELS: A, I, O, U

Reading and Spelling

LISTEN AND LEARN

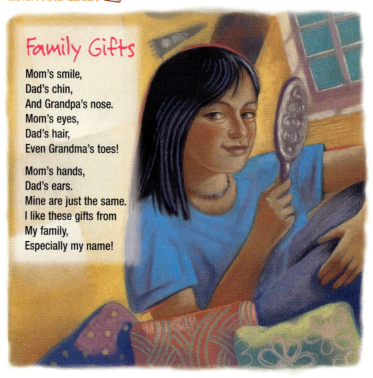

Family Gifts

Mom's smile,
Dad's chin,
And Grandpa's nose.
Mom's eyes,
Dad's hair,
Even Grandma's toes!

Mom's hands,
Dad's ears.
Mine are just the same.
I like these gifts from
My family,
Especially my name!

LOOK FOR WORD PATTERNS

How are the words alike? Is the vowel sound short or long?

All the words have silent e *at the end. The vowel sounds are all long.*

c**a**k**e**   b**i**k**e**   gl**o**b**e**   fl**u**t**e**s

122 Unit 6 | Welcome Home!   ▶ Transparencies 36–40

REACHING ALL STUDENTS

Multi-Level Strategies
LITERACY SUPPORT

NON-ROMAN ALPHABET To build understanding of how to represent English sounds in print, identify the letters on letter tiles and then use the tiles to build words sound by sound. Start by building the word *cap.* Then build *cape,* pointing out that the *e* after the *p* makes the *a* long: /ā/. Say: *The* e *at the end is silent, but it makes the vowel* a *say its name.*

Good words for this activity are *cub, cube; tap, tape; kit, kite.*

PRELITERATE Copy the sentences in Items 1–5 of Reading and Spelling Practice onto sentence strips. Distribute the sentence strips and have students cut them apart into separate words. Have volunteers lead the group in reassembling each sentence by matching the word order of the items on the page.

READING STRATEGY

Follow these steps to read a word.

❶ Look for a pattern. The **e** makes the other vowel say its name: **a**.

l **a** k **e**

Reading Help

A few words that end in **e** do <u>not</u> have a long vowel sound.

    give   some   have

❷ Start at the beginning. Blend the sounds together in your head. Then say the word.

l **a** k **e**   l + a + k + ~~e~~ = lake

*The **e** at the end of a word has no sound. It tells me that the **a** is long.*

READING AND SPELLING PRACTICE

Use what you learned to read the sentences.

1. My mother likes to make cakes.
2. She says to use pure butter.
3. She melts the butter on the stove.
4. I taste the cake mix. Yum!
5. It's fun to bake a cake at home!

6.–9. Now write the sentences that your teacher reads.   For dictation sentences, see Step 6 at right.

WORD WORK

10.–21. Copy the chart. Then read these words:

back	can	made	mad
hop	robe	cane	rob
note	hope	not	bake

map	cake	dot	rope
10. back	13. made	16. hop	19. note
11. can	14. cane	17. not	20. robe
12. mad	15. bake	18. rob	21. hope

Write each word in the chart. Put it under the word that has the same vowel sound.

Example: 10.

Language and Literacy   123

Decodable Book

PRACTICE WITH LONG VOWELS: A, I, O, U

Decodable Book 6:
At Home

Assign **Decodable Book 6** for independent reading. The **Decodable Book** can be used in a variety of ways to help students become more fluent, automatic readers:

Discussion Circles Have students work in small groups to read aloud and discuss the book using the questions on the back cover. Encourage students to read aloud the text that supports their answers. Groups can also work together to complete the Word Work Activity.

Readers Theater Students can read aloud the stories in a class performance. Help them prepare by rereading the stories in daily rehearsals. Work with students to add narration or dialog. Encourage them to use natural phrasing and expression.

Rereading at Home Have students work with family members to reread the book at home. They can take turns reading aloud alternate pages, then rereading the book switching the pages each person reads.

LEARN A READING STRATEGY

4 Use Word Patterns Work through the strategy with students, reading each step aloud and modeling the actions shown on the page.

For step 2, to help students internalize the blending process, ask them to blend *lake* silently in their heads and then say the word. Model by quietly saying each sound and waiting for students to say the whole word. Point out the Reading Help and read the explanation to students.

Remind students that these are words they know and should be read as a whole, without sounding them out. Work through additional examples to help them apply the tip: *come, move, love.*

PRACTICE

5 Read Sentences Distribute the Partner Prompts from page T311 to guide peers in reading the sentences in Items 1–5. Remind them to use the word-pattern strategy to read words.

6 Write Sentences Dictate the following sentences for students to write. Read each sentence at normal speed once so students can listen, and then repeat it slowly word by word as they write:

6. I made a cake with five eggs.

7. Wipe the cups and dishes.

8. We can tape our boxes shut.

9. I hope the robe is really cute.

7 Conduct "Word Work" Read the directions and work through the Example. Then have partners complete Items 11–21. Check answers by working through the items as a group.

▶ **Reading Practice Book** pages 131–134 (Decodable Book 6)

CLOSE AND ASSESS

Copy the chart from Word Work on the board. Have volunteers read a word from the lists and write it in the chart in the correct column. Then have students identify the vowel sound and tell whether it is short or long.

Language and Literacy   **T123**

UNIT 6 LESSON 11
LANGUAGE AND LITERACY: INDEPENDENT READING

OBJECTIVES

Function: Read a Selection
Learning to Read: Recognize High Frequency Words; Use Word Patterns to Decode Words (CVC, CVCe); Plurals
Reading Strategies: Preview; Make Predictions; Retell
Critical Thinking and Comprehension: Relate Main Idea and Details

READ ON YOUR OWN

1. **Introduce Vocabulary** In the story, students apply phonics skills and read high frequency words. Introduce the story words. Write each word, pronounce it, and spell it.

   - **paper:** material you write on and wrap gifts in. *Write on the paper.*
   - **arms:** Point to your arms and say *These are my arms.*
   - **parade:** lines of people who march in the street to celebrate something. *Our town has parades on holidays.*
   - **piñatas:** figures filled with candy. *Break the piñatas to get treats.*

2. **Preview/Make Predictions** Point out the boy in the photo and say: *This is Pablo. He's using paper to make something. What do you think he's making? Read to find out.*

3. **Read and Think: Relate Main Idea and Details** Have students read the story on their own. They can use the diagram to tell a partner how Pablo made a puppet.

4. **Build Reading Fluency** Use the Language Tape/CD with Reading Practice Book page 61 for fluency practice. (Tape 3B, CD 1 Track 25)

   ▶ **Reading Practice Book** page 61

CLOSE AND ASSESS

Ask: *What is La Gigantona? How did the Soto family make it?* Have groups use their main-idea diagrams to answer the questions.

T124 Unit 6 | Welcome Home!

COMPREHENSION: RELATE MAIN IDEA AND DETAILS

Read on Your Own

Pronunciation of Names
Pablo Soto — pah blō sō tō
Sandra — sahn drah
La Gigantona — lah hē gahn tō nah

When We Came to Wisconsin

La Gigantona can come in different colors and shapes. Here is one in a parade.

Hi. My name is Pablo Soto. My mother's name is Sandra. We are from Nicaragua.

In Nicaragua, my family made big puppets to sell. The name of one puppet that we made is *La Gigantona*. We made the head of this puppet with paper and paste. We made the eyes of the puppet really big, with long, thick lashes. We made the arms from long tubes. They swing from side to side. We put a white robe and a cute hat on the puppet. People like to watch this big puppet in parades.

My mother and I left Nicaragua and came to Wisconsin. Here, we make piñatas. We make a piñata with paper and paste, just like we made the head of *La Gigantona*. One day, a man came to our store. He asked us to make a big puppet for a parade in Wisconsin. At last, *La Gigantona* is back in our family!

CHECK YOUR UNDERSTANDING

Copy and complete this diagram. Add details that support the main idea. Then tell your partner how the family made the big puppet.

Sample Responses

We made a big puppet.
We made the head with paper and paste.
— We made the eyes really big, with long, thick lashes.
— We made the arms from long tubes.
— We put a white robe and cute hat on the puppet.

✓ **DECODING CHECK** Give the Decoding Progress Check on page 51 of the Assessment Handbook.

124 Unit 6 Welcome Home!

REACHING ALL STUDENTS

Reading Fluency
PHRASING

Read the introduction on **Reading Practice Book** page 61. Explain that the / in the examples shows a short pause between groups of words and the // shows a longer pause between sentences. Model reading the examples and have students echo them.

Next, play "When We Came to Wisconsin" on the **Language Tape/CD** and have students mark the sentences to show where the pauses occur. Check marks as a whole class before partners do the Practice section. Circulate during the Practice to check and support reading fluency.

Reading Practice Book page 61

COMPREHENSION
Build Reading Fluency
When you read, pause between groups of words that go together.

In Nicaragua, / my family made / big puppets to sell. //
We made the arms / from long tubes. //

LISTEN AND LEARN TO READ
Listen to the story. When you hear a short pause, write a /.
When you hear a long pause, write //.
Example: We made the arms / from long tubes. //

When We Came to Wisconsin

Hi. My name is Pablo Soto. My mother's name is Sandra. We are from Nicaragua.
In Nicaragua, my family made big puppets to sell. The name of one puppet that we made is *La Gigantona*. We made the head of this puppet with paper and paste. We made the eyes of the puppet really big, with long, thick lashes. We made the arms from long tubes. They swing from side to side. We put a white robe and a cute hat on the puppet. People like to watch this big puppet in parades.

PRACTICE
Now read the story to a partner. Use the marks you made to read groups of words together.

PLURAL NOUNS

Boxes and Boxes—We're Moving!

A **noun** names a person, place, or thing.

A **singular noun** names one thing.

box

A **plural noun** names more than one thing.

boxes

Study these rules for forming plurals.

To make most nouns plural, just add -s.	boy boys	girl girls	book books	truck trucks
If the noun ends in *x, ch, sh, s,* or *z*, add *-es*.	box boxes	dish dishes	glass glasses	lunch lunches
Some nouns change in different ways to show the plural.	man men	woman women	child children	foot feet

BUILD SENTENCES

Say each sentence. Use the plural form of the missing words.

Example: 1. The women drink from glasses.

1.  The women drink from glasses.

2. The children read on the sofa.

3.  The men eat sandwiches.

4.  The boys pack books.

5.  The movers carry the boxes.

6.  Their friends wave good-bye.

WRITE QUESTIONS

7.–10. Choose 4 pictures from above. Write a question about each picture. Ask a partner your questions.

Example: 7. What do the men eat?

Sample Responses
Students should use different question words: *Who drinks from glasses? What do the boys pack? Where are the children?* and so on.

Language and Literacy 125

UNIT 6 **LESSON 12**

LANGUAGE AND LITERACY: PLURAL NOUNS

OBJECTIVES
Functions: Write; Ask Questions
Patterns and Structures: ❶ Plural Nouns
Writing: Questions

INTRODUCE

1 Learn About Plural Nouns Read the introduction and discuss the difference between the two photos: *The first picture shows only one box. The second picture shows many boxes. Repeat with me:* one box, many boxes.

Then read the first rule for forming plurals, and lead students in saying the word pairs. Point out that the *-s* ending can sound like /s/, as in *books* and *trucks,* or like /z/, as in *boys*.

Read the second rule and have students repeat the word pairs. Note that the *-es* ending adds a syllable.

Read about irregular plurals and note the examples. Use each example in a context sentence, to be sure that students understand the concept.

PRACTICE

2 Build Sentences Work through the Example. Then have volunteers complete each sentence using the rules in the rule box.

APPLY

3 Write Questions Remind students to start each question with a question word, such as *What* or *When,* and to put a question mark at the end.

▶ **Language Practice Book** page 72

CLOSE AND ASSESS

Have volunteers read their sentences aloud. Then call on students to write the plural nouns on the board.

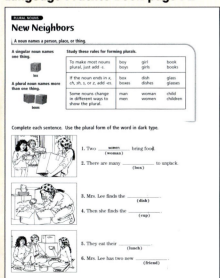

Language Practice Book page 72

Multi-Level Strategies

WRITING SUPPORT

LITERATE IN L1 The rules for forming plurals vary across different languages. In Korean and Chinese, there is no plural form for nouns that follow a number. In Haitian-Creole, the plural form can be omitted.

To practice this skill, write a list of singular nouns and ask volunteers to write the plural forms. Then have groups copy the pairs on word cards, lay them face down, and play "Concentration," revealing two cards at a time to find matching pairs.

Language and Literacy T125

UNIT 6 LESSON 13
LANGUAGE ACROSS THE CURRICULUM: MATHEMATICS

OBJECTIVES
Function: Give Information
Concepts and Vocabulary: Mathematics (fractions, decimals, and percents)
Critical Thinking and Comprehension: Solve Problems

LEARN ABOUT FRACTIONS, DECIMALS, AND PERCENTS

1 Explore the Concepts Ask a volunteer to read the list of family members. Ask how many people there are in the family, and how many people are children. (5, 3) Then point out the fraction in the first column and read the explanation. Relate the 3 and 5 in the fraction to the three children and five total people.

Go over the example and explanation of a decimal and a percent. Summarize by saying that the three number types all compare the number of children to the total number of people in the family.

READ AND THINK

2 Family Math Work through the three steps to show how fractions, decimals, and percents are related. Provide an additional example of a family with ten total members and five kids. Work through the steps to get:

5/10 or 1/2 = 0.5 = 50%

3 Complete the Exercises Ask students to count the total number of slices of pizza, and how many Sabina ate. (8, 2) Have partners work through the numbered steps to find the answers. Then repeat the process to identify what percentage of the candles on the birthday cake are blue.

CLOSE AND ASSESS
Write the six answers (from the two problems) on index cards, one number per card. Then have volunteers read aloud each number.

SUCCESS IN MATHEMATICS

Learn About Fractions, Decimals, and Percents

Pronunciation of Names
Sabina   sah bē nah

My Family
1. Mama
2. Grandma
3. Sabina, my sister
4. Alex, my brother
5. Tom—me!

FRACTION	DECIMAL	PERCENT
numerator $\frac{3}{5}$ denominator	0.6 (decimal point)	60% (percent symbol)
Say: three-fifths	**Say:** six-tenths	**Say:** sixty percent
Example: Three-fifths of my family are kids.	**Example:** Six-tenths of my family are kids.	**Example:** Sixty percent of my family are kids.

Study the lesson. Then do the Exercises.

Family Math

Think and Discuss
You can use fractions, decimals, or percents to describe the family in the picture.

1 Write a fraction:
Ask yourself how many of the people are kids. This is the numerator. How many people are there in the whole family? This is the denominator.

kids $\frac{3}{5}$ whole family

2 Write a decimal:
Divide the numerator by the denominator.

$5 \overline{)3.0}$ = 0.6   — Show the decimal point in the answer.
— Add a decimal point and a zero.

3 Write a percent:
Multiply the decimal by 100. Add the percent symbol.

$0.6 \times 100 = 60$
60% — percent symbol

Three-fifths of my family are kids. Six-tenths of my family are kids. Sixty percent of my family are kids.

Exercises

Answers:
1. 6/8 or 3/4   0.75   75%
2. 6/10 or 3/5   0.6   60%

Write a fraction, a decimal, and a percent for each answer.

1 Sabina ate 2 slices of pizza. How much of the pizza is left?

2 How many candles are red?

126 Unit 6 | Welcome Home!

REACHING ALL STUDENTS

Mathematics Connection
FRACTIONS, DECIMALS, PERCENTS

Have students write one example each of a fraction, a decimal, and a percent, on three separate index cards. Then form an Inside-Outside Circle (see Cooperative Learning Structures, page T337d) and have partners randomly display one of their cards to each other to read aloud. When the circle rotates, new cards are displayed to new partners.

Writing Project  FAMILY ALBUM

✓ **WRITING ASSESSMENT**
Use the Writing Checklist in the Assessment Handbook to evaluate this writing project.

Make an album with information about the people in your family.

PLAN YOUR FAMILY ALBUM

What will you show for each person: a photo, an object, or a drawing? What will you say? Make a chart.

Who?	What the Person Likes	What the Person Has	Where?
sister	fish	fish bowl	in her bedroom
mother	flowers	flower press	in the kitchen

MAKE AND SHARE YOUR FAMILY ALBUM

Write 2 sentences to go with each photo, object, or drawing. Then check and correct your work.

✓ **Check Your Work**
Did you show something for each person in your family?
Did you use the correct plural forms?
Do all your sentences start with a capital letter and end with the correct mark?

Put your photos, objects, and drawings into a book. Copy your sentences. Display the book in your classroom.

My Family by Mikhail

 My mother likes flowers. She has a flower press in the kitchen.

 My brother has a lot of video games. He plays them in the living room.

 My sister likes fish. She has a fish bowl in her bedroom.

Language Across the Curriculum 127

Language Practice Book page 73

WRITING PROJECT: FAMILY ALBUM
My Family
Tell your class about your family. Make a chart. Then make a page for a family album. Follow these steps.

1. Write a title and your name.
2. Choose a person from your chart. Write two sentences about the person. Use plural nouns.
3. Draw a picture to show something the person likes or has.
4. Tell about another person in your family. Add another drawing.

Make more pages about other people in your family. Display your family album in your classroom.

✓ **ASSESSMENT**

For opportunities to measure progress, see the Assessment Handbook:

- **Units 4–6 Test** evaluates basic vocabulary and the patterns and structures of English, mastery of phonics and high frequency words, reading comprehension, and writing.

- **The Language Acquisition Assessment** for Units 4–6 offers performance assessments for measuring growth through the stages of language acquisition.

- **Self- and Peer-Assessment** forms involve students in the assessment process.

UNIT 6 LESSON 14

LANGUAGE ACROSS THE CURRICULUM: WRITING

OBJECTIVES

Functions: Give Information; Write
Learning Strategies and Critical Thinking: Plan; Generate and Organize Ideas; Self-Assess
Representing: Use Graphic Organizers (chart)
Writing: Family Album

CONDUCT THE WRITING PROJECT

1. **Explore Family Albums** Explain that people create albums to honor family and friends, to record important events, and to share memories. If possible, share an album of photos and mementos.

APPLY

2. **Plan the Family Album** Read the directions and help students make their charts. (Some students may be uncomfortable focusing on their own families. Invite them to create an album of extended family or friends.)

3. **Make and Share the Family Album** Provide sentence frames for students to use:

   (Name) likes ____.
   (He/She/They) (has/have) ____.
   (He/She) (verb) in (place).

Students may start individual albums with these pages, or combine their pages for a class book.

▶ **Language Practice Book** page 73

CLOSE AND ASSESS

As students look at their albums, say:
- *Show me the item you included for each person.*
- *Point to a plural form in your writing.*
- *Point to a capital letter that starts a sentence.*

Language Across the Curriculum **T127**

Resources

For Success in Language and Literacy
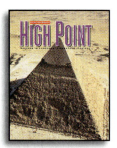
Student Book pages 128–141

For Language Skills Practice
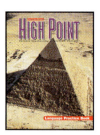
Language Practice Book pages 74–79

For Reading Skills Practice
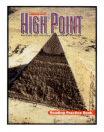
Reading Practice Book pages 62–66

For Vocabulary, Language Development, and Reading Fluency

Language Tape 4, Side A
Language CD 2, Tracks 1–5

For Reading Together

Theme Book *Explore!* from The Basics Bookshelf

For Audio Walk-Throughs and Selection Readings

Selection Tape 4A
Selection CD 2, Tracks 1–2

For Phonics Instruction

Transparencies 41–45

Transparency Scripts 41–45

Letter Tiles

For Comprehensive Assessment
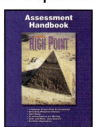
Language Acquisition Assessment, Units 7–9 Test, Writing Assessment, Self-Assessment

For Home-School Connections

High Point Newsletter 3 in seven languages

For Planning and Instruction
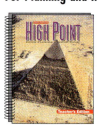
Teacher's Edition pages T128a–T141

T128a Unit Planner

UNIT 7
PACK YOUR BAGS!

In This Unit

Vocabulary
- Landforms and Transportation
- Weather and Clothing
- Diagrams

Language Functions
- Give and Carry Out Commands
- Describe Places
- Give Information

Patterns and Structures
- Commands
- Verbs *(can)*
- Proper Nouns

Reading
- Phonics: Long Vowels (ai, ay; ee, ea; oa, ow)
- Comprehension: Classify (concept map)

Writing
- Sentences
- Postcard
- Class Travel Book

Content Area Connection
- Science (water cycle)

UNIT 7

Activity and Assessment Planner

UNIT 7: Pack Your Bags!

LESSONS

1

UNIT 7 LAUNCH ▶ pages T128–T129

LESSON 1: INTRODUCE UNIT 7 pages T128–T129

Vocabulary	Viewing	Learning Strategies	Critical Thinking
T Landforms	Respond to a Visual Image	Preview	Draw Conclusions
T Weather		Build Background	Classify

2–5

LANGUAGE DEVELOPMENT ▶ pages T130–T133

LESSON 2
COMMANDS
page T130

Function
Give/Carry out Commands

Patterns and Structures
T Commands

Writing
Commands

LESSON 3
LANDFORMS AND TRANSPORTATION
page T131

Functions
Describe Places

Give Information

Writing
Postcard

Vocabulary
T Landforms

T Transportation

LESSON 4
WEATHER/CLOTHING
page T132

Function
Give Information

Vocabulary
T Weather

T Clothing

Writing
T Sentences

LESSON 5
VERBS (CAN)
page T133

Functions
Give Information

Describe

Patterns and Structures
T Verbs (can)

Writing
Sentences

6–12

LANGUAGE AND LITERACY ▶ pages T134a–T139

LESSON 6
BASICS BOOKSHELF
pages T134a–T134d

Function
Listen to a Book

Vocabulary
T Weather

T Habitats

Reading Strategies
Activate Prior Knowledge

Preview

Learning to Read
Use Text Features (photos, captions, and labels)

Identify Exclamations and Statements

Critical Thinking and Comprehension
T Classify Information

LESSON 7
BASICS BOOKSHELF: COMPREHENSION
page T134

Function
Give Information

Learning Strategy
Use Graphic Organizers (concept map)

Critical Thinking and Comprehension
T Classify Information

LESSON 8
HIGH FREQUENCY WORDS
page T135

Learning to Read
T Recognize High Frequency Words

LESSON 9
PHONICS
pages T136a–T136d

Learning to Read
Build Oral Vocabulary

Develop Phonemic Awareness

T Associate Sounds and Symbols: Long Vowels

Blend Sounds to Decode Words

T Use Word Patterns to Decode Words

Divide Words into Syllables

Decode Multisyllabic Words

LESSON 10
READING AND SPELLING
pages T136–T137

Learning to Read
Develop Phonemic Awareness

T Associate Sounds and Symbols: /ā/ ai, ay; /ē/ ee, ea; /ō/ oa, ow

T Use Word Patterns to Decode Words

Divide Words into Syllables (compound words)

Spelling
T Long Vowels: ai, ay; ee, ea; oa, ow

Compound Words

LESSON 11
INDEPENDENT READING
page T138

Function
Read a Selection

Learning to Read
T Recognize High Frequency Words

T Decode Long Vowel Words (ai, ay; ee, ea; oa, ow)

Recognize Compound Words

Reading Strategies
Set a Purpose for Reading

Retell

Critical Thinking and Comprehension
T Classify

LESSON 12
PROPER NOUNS
page T139

Functions
Write

Give Information

Patterns and Structures
T Proper Nouns

Writing
Sentences

13–14

LANGUAGE ACROSS THE CURRICULUM ▶ pages T140–T141

LESSON 13 SCIENCE: CYCLES
page T140

Functions
Listen to an Article

Give Information

Vocabulary
Diagrams; Cycles

Research Skills and Learning Strategies
Build Background

Use Text Structures (diagrams)

Critical Thinking and Comprehension
Steps in a Process

Generate Ideas

Summarize

LESSON 14 WRITING PROJECT: CLASS TRAVEL BOOK
page T141

Functions
Give Information

Describe

Write

Learning Strategies and Critical Thinking
Plan

Generate/Organize Ideas

Self-Assess

Writing
Class Travel Book

T128c Unit 7 | Pack Your Bags!

T = Objective Tested on Unit Test

ASSESSMENT OPTIONS

The **Teacher's Edition** and the **Assessment Handbook** include these comprehensive assessment tools:

▶ **Ongoing, Informal Assessment**
Check for understanding and achieve closure for every lesson with the targeted questions and activities in the **Close and Assess** boxes in your Teacher's Edition.

▶ **Decoding Progress Check**
These word lists for each unit provide a quick way to check on mastery of the phonics or word structure skills taught in the unit.

▶ **Language Acquisition Assessments**
To verify students' ability to use the language functions and grammar structures taught in Units 7–9, conduct these performance assessments.

▶ **Unit Test in Standardized Test Format**
This multiple-choice test measures students' cumulative understanding of the skills and language developed in Units 7–9.

▶ **Self- and Peer-Assessment**
Students use the Self-Assessment Form to evaluate their own work and develop learning strategies appropriate to their needs. Students offer feedback to their classmates with the Peer-Assessment Form.

▶ **Writing Assessment/Portfolio Opportunities**
You can evaluate students' writing in the Writing Projects using the Writing Progress Checklist. Then collaborate with students to choose work for their portfolios.

UNITS 7–9 ASSESSMENT OPPORTUNITIES	Assessment Handbook Pages
Decoding Progress Check	1a
Language Acquisition Assessments	18
Units 7–9 Test	19–24
Self-Assessment Form	25
Peer-Assessment Form	50
Writing Progress Checklist	51
Portfolio Evaluation Form	52

RELATED RESOURCES

Deserts
by Gail Gibbons
An introduction to the habitats and inhabitants of the desert. Also includes information on how deserts are formed. (Holiday)
Theme Book: Read Aloud

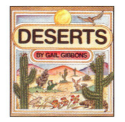

Hide and Seek
by Evelyn Stone
A photo-essay about underwater life. The text challenges the reader to find the creatures hiding, peeking, and seeking. (Hampton-Brown)
Phonics Reinforcement: Vowel Teams

Weather Words and What They Mean
by Gail Gibbons
An introduction to basic weather terms and concepts. Also includes fun weather facts from around the world. (Holiday)
Vocabulary: Weather

On the Go
by Ann Morris
A photo essay about the many different modes of transportation around the world, from camels and donkeys to high-speed trains.
(Available from Hampton-Brown)
Vocabulary: Transportation

Road Adventures USA
Students work on geography, math, and problem-solving skills as they experience a virtual road trip across the country. (The Learning Company)
Multimedia: CD-ROM

UNIT 7 **LESSON 1**

INTRODUCE UNIT 7: PACK YOUR BAGS!

> **OBJECTIVES**
> **Function:** Listen Actively; Write
> **Concepts and Vocabulary:**
> ⓣ Landforms; ⓣ Weather
> **Viewing:** Respond to a Visual Image
> **Learning Strategies:**
> Preview; Build Background
> **Critical Thinking:**
> Draw Conclusions; Classify

START WITH A COMMON EXPERIENCE

1. **Introduce "Pack Your Bags!"** Read the unit title and explain: *When you "pack your bags," you get ready for a trip or a journey. You pack the clothes, maps, and other things you will need to bring.*

2. **Identify Rain-Forest Sounds** Play the **Language Tape/CD**. Students will listen to sounds from four different habitats to identify the sounds that match the illustration. (number 3)

   Tape 4A / CD 2 Track 1

3. **Study Rain-Forest Creatures** Discuss the illustration. Create a chart of animals that students recognize. Use this opportunity to introduce new animal vocabulary:

Tree Animals	Land Animals	Water Animals
bird	jaguar	fish
bat	porcupine	snake
monkey	armadillo	frog

4. **Write About Rain-Forest Animals** Have partners use the chart to complete the following paragraph frame:

> There are many animals to see in the rain forest. You can see _____ in the sky and trees. You can find _____ on the ground. There are many kinds of _____ in the water.

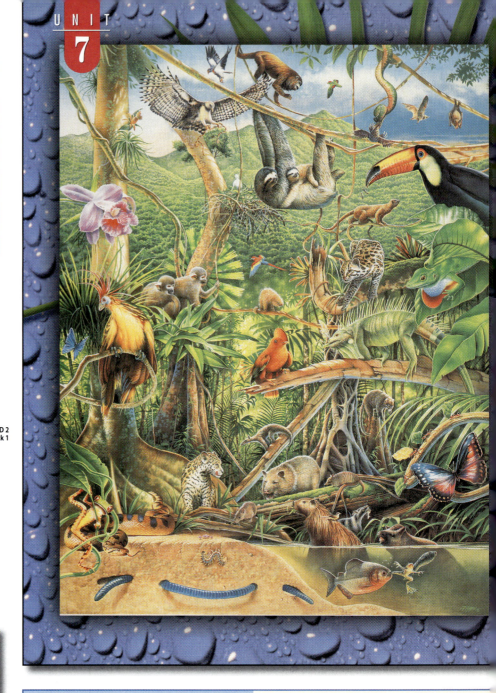

REACHING ALL STUDENTS

HOME CONNECTION

Habitat Poster Send home a copy of *High Point Newsletter 3* in the **Teacher's Resource Book**. In the home activity, students work with their family to create a poster about a specific habitat in their home country. Family members will use text and art to present information about plants and animals.

T128 Unit 7 | Pack Your Bags!

PACK YOUR BAGS!

Look at the picture of the rain forest.
What do you see? Listen to the tape.
What sounds do you hear?

In This Unit

Vocabulary
- Landforms and Transportation
- Weather and Clothing
- Diagrams

Language Functions
- Give and Carry Out Commands
- Describe Places
- Give Information

Patterns and Structures
- Commands
- Verbs (can)
- Proper Nouns

Reading
- Phonics: Long Vowels (ai, ay; ee, ea; oa, ow)
- Comprehension: Classify (concept map)

Writing
- Sentences
- Postcard
- Class Travel Book

Content Area Connection
- Science (water cycle)

UNIT 7 Mind Map

Pack Your Bags — for the Rain Forest!

Plants	Animals	Landforms	What to Pack
trees ferns vines	monkeys cockatiels	waterfall river rocks	rain gear insect repellent

Technology Support
See **Inspiration** Visual Learning software for support in creating mind maps.

PREVIEW THE UNIT

5 Look for Activities and Information on Travel Leaf through the unit, previewing activities students will do, for example:

page 130—learning a chant about traveling

pages 131–132—exploring landforms, transportation, and weather

page 134—listening to the Bookshelf book (Display a copy of the book.)

page 136—listening to a song about the beach

page 141—writing a page for a class travel book

Ask students to identify some of the habitats they will explore in this unit. Highlight the photos on page 131, for example. Then sum up what the preview reveals: *There are many exciting places to explore.*

6 Set Your Goals Start a class mind map of the concepts and vocabulary associated with the rain forest. Prompt students for pictures or words to add, and have them act out and describe other ideas for you to put into words. As you read, create mind maps for the different habitats.

CLOSE AND ASSESS

Ask students to tell or show you something they are interested in learning in this unit.

Unit Launch **T129**

UNIT 7 LESSON 2
LANGUAGE DEVELOPMENT: COMMANDS

> **OBJECTIVES**
> **Functions:** Listen Actively; Repeat Spoken Language; Recite; Give and Carry out Commands
> **Patterns and Structures:** 🅣 Commands
> **Writing:** Commands

INTRODUCE

Tape 4A
CD 2 Track 2

1. **Listen and Chant** Play "Let's Go!" on the **Language Tape/CD**. Students will listen and follow along with the words, then echo every two lines, chime in with a soft voice, and then again in a loud voice.

2. **Learn About Commands** Read aloud the chart for commands and find more examples in the chant. To ensure understanding, give a few classroom commands and have students respond through TPR: *Open your books. Don't raise your hand. Raise your hand now.*

PRACTICE

3. **Conduct "Express Yourself"** Model how to give and carry out commands. Have partners complete the activity.

   > **How to Give and Carry Out Commands**
   > • To give a command, tell someone to do an action: *Pack your bags.*
   > • To carry out a command, do what another person tells you.

APPLY

4. **Write Commands** Encourage students to check their answers with a partner. Distribute Partner Checklist 7 on page T310.

   ▶ Language Practice Book page 74

> **CLOSE AND ASSESS**
> Have partners demonstrate giving and carrying out commands such as: *Walk around the room. Wave good-bye.*

T130 Unit 7 | Pack Your Bags!

COMMANDS
Come Along!

Listen and chant.

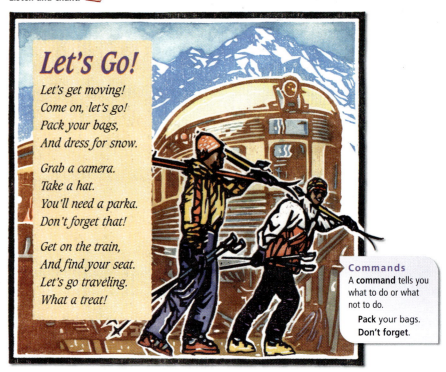

Let's Go!

Let's get moving!
Come on, let's go!
Pack your bags,
And dress for snow.

Grab a camera.
Take a hat.
You'll need a parka.
Don't forget that!

Get on the train,
And find your seat.
Let's go traveling.
What a treat!

> **Commands**
> A **command** tells you what to do or what not to do.
> **Pack** your bags.
> **Don't forget.**

EXPRESS YOURSELF ▶ GIVE AND CARRY OUT COMMANDS

Work with a partner. Read the commands from the chant. Act them out.

1. Pack your bags.   3. Dress for snow.   5. Get on the train.
2. Grab a camera.   4. Take a hat.   6. Find your seat.

WRITE COMMANDS ✏️

7.–10. Your partner wants to take a trip. Write 4 commands to tell your partner what to do on the trip.

Example: 7. Dress for rain.

Sample Responses
Students' responses should be brief commands dealing with travel, for example: Dress for rain. Take a jacket. Pack your lunch. Get in the car.

130   Unit 7 | Pack Your Bags!

REACHING ALL STUDENTS

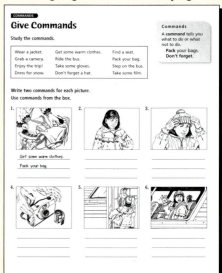

Language Practice Book page 74

VOCABULARY: LANDFORMS AND TRANSPORTATION

What Places Can You Explore?

Pronunciation of Name
Lin Yang — lin yang
Sanjana — **sahn** jahn ah

The Mountains: mountain, forest, valley, lake, raft

The Seashore: airplane, beach, island, ocean, sailboat

The Canyon: canyon, river

The Desert: cactus, bicycle, sand

EXPRESS YOURSELF ▶ DESCRIBE PLACES

1.–4. Work with a partner. Describe each picture above. Use adjectives.

Example: 1. There are tall trees in the green forest. The blue lake is large. The raft is slow.

Adjectives

blue	tiny	slow	short	hot
green	small	fast	tall	cold
brown	big		long	wet
white	large			dry

WRITE A POSTCARD

5. Choose a place to explore. Describe it in a postcard.

Example: 5.

Dear Lin,
I am in the mountains. There is a big lake here. A lot of tall trees grow around the lake.
Your friend,
Sanjana

Lin Yang
8362 Hoover Street
New York, NY 10165

Sample Responses for Express Yourself
Students' descriptions should consist of a sentence or sentences containing adjectives appropriate to each setting, for example:
Mountains: tall trees; green forest; blue lake; slow raft.
Seashore: long island; small sailboat; hot beach; cold, blue ocean.
Desert: tall, green cactus; hot sand.
Canyon: fast river; large, brown canyon.

Sample Responses for Write a Postcard
Students should choose a place from the pictures above. They should use adjectives in their descriptions. Remind them to include a greeting, closing, and address in their postcards.

Language Development 131

UNIT 7 LESSON 3
LANGUAGE DEVELOPMENT: LANDFORMS; TRANSPORTATION

OBJECTIVES

Functions:
Describe Places; Give Information

Concepts and Vocabulary:
• Landforms; • Transportation

Writing: Postcard

INTRODUCE

1 Learn Words for Landforms and Transportation Introduce the four habitats pictured. Then read aloud each label and have students point out the landform.

Note that three of the photos include modes of transportation. Brainstorm a list of vehicles and how they travel.

Transportation

by land	by water	by air
bike	boat	plane
jeep	raft	helicopter
train	canoe	hang glider

PRACTICE

2 Conduct "Express Yourself" Read the adjectives in the word box and point out that they are arranged to show color, size, speed, and how something feels. Model how to describe. Then have partners complete the activity.

How to Describe

• Name a place or a thing: *the lake*.

• Add an adjective before the noun: *a **large** lake*.

• Or, use the adjective after the verb *is* or *are*: *The lake is **large***.

APPLY

3 Write a Postcard Use the Example to model how to write a postcard.

▶ Language Practice Book page 75

CLOSE AND ASSESS

Name a landform (for example, *lake*) and have volunteers respond by adding an adjective: *blue lake* or *The lake is blue*.

Language Practice Book page 75

VOCABULARY: LANDFORMS AND TRANSPORTATION
What Do You See?
Name the places and things in the picture. Use words from the box.

| ocean | sailboat | beach |
| forest | airplane | island |

DESCRIBE A PLACE
Complete each sentence. Describe the picture above. Use adjectives from the box.

| small | tall | hot | dry | fast |

1. The island has a forest with ___tall___ trees.
2. A _____ airplane flies over the island.
3. A _____ sailboat sails on the ocean.
4. The _____ sun shines on the beach.
5. It makes the sand hot and _____.

Multi-Level Strategies

VOCABULARY: LANDFORMS

LITERATE IN L1 For Spanish speakers, point out the following cognates to help students appreciate how many English words they already know.

mountains montañas
valley valle
lake lago
island isla
canyon cañón
desert desierto
bicycle bicicleta

Language Development T131

UNIT 7 LESSON 4
LANGUAGE DEVELOPMENT: WEATHER AND CLOTHING

OBJECTIVES
Functions:
Listen Actively; Give Information
Concepts and Vocabulary:
 Weather; Clothing
Writing: Sentences

INTRODUCE

1 Learn Words for Weather Use the icons and labels to introduce the weather words. Then use gestures and pantomime to represent each of the weather types. For example, shade your eyes and fan your face. Have students call out the weather term. (sunny and warm) Repeat the process for the remaining terms.

2 Learn Clothing Words Explain: *We wear different clothes for different kinds of weather.* Point to the four photos and read the captions to identify the locations and weather. Read aloud each clothing label and discuss why the clothes are appropriate in each scene.

PRACTICE

3 Conduct "Who's Talking?" Play "Who's Talking?" on the **Language Tape/CD** to model how to give information. Replay the tape, if necessary, before students point to the person and tell about the weather.

APPLY

4 Write About the Weather Remind students to use the weather symbols, photos, and captions to complete Items 4–8.

▶ Language Practice Book page 76

CLOSE AND ASSESS
Invite volunteers to present weather reports that include advice about what to wear: *It is cold. Wear a scarf and gloves.*

T132 Unit 7 | Pack Your Bags!

VOCABULARY: WEATHER AND CLOTHING

It is **sunny and warm** at the seashore.

It is **cold** in the mountains.

It is **windy** in the city.

WHO'S TALKING? ▶ GIVE INFORMATION

1.–3. Listen.
Which person is talking? Point to the correct picture. Tell what the weather is like there.

Answers:
1. woman at the seashore
2. woman in the city
3. girl in the mountains

It is **rainy** in the forest.

WRITE ABOUT THE WEATHER 🖍

Write each sentence. Add words to tell about the weather.

Example: 4. I wear a parka when it is cold.

4. I wear a parka when it is ___cold___.
5. I wear sandals when it is ___sunny___ and ___warm___.
6. I wear a coat when it is ___windy___.
7. I wear a raincoat when it is ___rainy___.
8. I wear gloves when it is ___cold___.

132 Unit 7 | Pack Your Bags!

REACHING ALL STUDENTS

Vocabulary
WEATHER

Work together to create a national weather report. Have students study national weather reports from newspapers, news reports, or the Internet to find the weather for five major cities in the United States. Create cards with weather symbols and labels. Then have volunteers say the weather reports aloud: *In Boston, the weather is cloudy and cold.* Ask volunteers to affix the correct weather labels onto a U.S. map.

Language Practice Book page 76

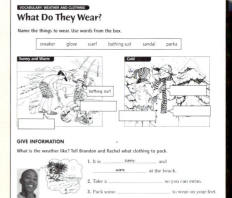

VERBS: CAN

We Can Explore All Year Long

Use **can** before another **verb** to tell what people are able to do.

can + hike = can hike

In this park, we **can hike** up the mountain.

I **can see** some pretty trees.

My friend **can take** a lot of pictures.

Never add *-s* to *can*.

BUILD SENTENCES

Look at each picture below. Make a sentence to go with the picture. Choose words from each column. Say the sentence.

Sample Responses
Students' sentences should go with their pictures and should include an element from each column.

In the winter,	I can	sail a boat.
In the spring,	you can	hike.
In the summer,	he can	ride a bike.
In the fall,	she can	ice-skate.
	we can	
	they can	

Example: 1. In the winter, you can ice-skate.

 1. winter
 2. spring
 3. summer
 4. fall

WRITE SENTENCES

5.–8. Draw a picture for each season. Show what people can do then. Write a sentence to go with the picture. Use words from the box.

swim in a lake	plant a garden
ski in the mountains	eat outside
play soccer	read a book

Example: 5. In the spring, we can swim in a lake.

Sample Responses
Students' sentences should go with their pictures and should describe activities appropriate to each season.

Language Development 133

Language Practice Book page 77

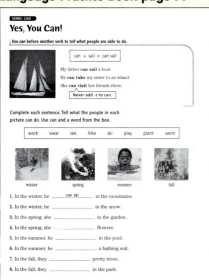

UNIT 7 **LESSON 5**

LANGUAGE DEVELOPMENT: VERBS (CAN)

OBJECTIVES

Functions: Give Information; Describe
Patterns and Structures: Verbs (can)
Writing: Sentences

INTRODUCE

1 Learn About Verbs Read the title and introduction. Then direct students' attention to the picture and read aloud the first example. Explain that *hike* means "walk to enjoy nature." Then read the other examples, and the rule against adding *-s* to *can*. Offer this pair of examples to illustrate the latter: *He hikes all day. He can hike all day.*

PRACTICE

2 Build Sentences Demonstrate how to build a sentence by choosing a phrase from each column. Then have partners complete the exercise.

APPLY

3 Write Sentences Use the Example to show how to put together a sentence. Remind students to choose activities that match the weather for each season.

▶ **Language Practice Book** page 77

CLOSE AND ASSESS

Have volunteers display their pictures and sentences. Call on students to read the sentences aloud.

Vocabulary

WEATHER AND CLOTHING

Word Webbing Have groups use team word webbing (see Cooperative Learning Structures, page T337d) to categorize weather, clothing, and activities for a season. Rotate until each team has studied each season.

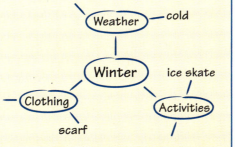

UNIT 7 **LESSON 6**

LANGUAGE AND LITERACY: THE BASICS BOOKSHELF

OBJECTIVES
Concepts and Vocabulary:
- Weather; - Habitats

Listening: Listen to a Preview

Reading Strategies:
Activate Prior Knowledge; Preview; Use Text Features (photos, captions, labels)

BUILD LANGUAGE AND VOCABULARY

1. **Teach "Words to Know"** Have students look at pages 2–3. Say: *These pictures show habitats from around the world. A habitat is a place where animals and plants live.* Read aloud the habitat labels as you point to each photograph.

   Indicate the weather icons at the top of page 3. Say: *These words and symbols tell about the weather.* Have students identify the weather icons for each habitat. Explain that some habitats can have more than one weather pattern.

2. **Give a Weather Report** Invite volunteers to present a weather report that includes a habitat and the type of weather. Model for students: *I am in the desert. It is very hot.*

PREPARE TO READ

3. **Think About What You Know** Invite students to tell about trips they have taken. Ask: *How did you get there? What was the weather like? What kinds of things did you do there?* Use a world map to mark countries where students have visited or lived.

4. **Preview** Play the Audio Walk-Through for *Explore!* on the **Selection Tape/CD** to give students the overall idea of the story.   *Tape 4A CD 2 Track 1*

CLOSE AND ASSESS
Have students draw or find a magazine picture to show a habitat they will study in the book. Have them label the habitat and draw a symbol to show the weather.

Explore!
by Janine Wheeler

Summary This photo essay features six habitats from around the world, including a forest, an island, a rain forest, a desert, an ocean, and the mountains. Photo insets show weather icons and explain appropriate clothes for each habitat. Simple text reinforces the use of commands and the pattern *You can _____.*

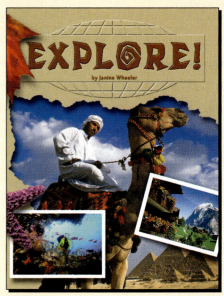
Cover

Pages 2–3

Multi-Level Strategies
LITERACY SUPPORT

PRELITERATE Use Text Features: Photos, Captions, and Labels
Turn to pages 4–5. Point to the first photo at the bottom of page 4. Explain what the picture shows: *This picture shows trees with colorful leaves.* Then point to the caption below the photo and read the sentence aloud. Say: *This sentence is called a* caption. *It gives information about the picture.* Read the next two captions and think aloud as you explain how the pictures and captions correspond.

Next, call students' attention to the photo inset on page 5. Point to the clothing labels and say: *These words are called* labels. *They give information about the parts of a picture. The labels in this picture tell what the girl is wearing.* Read the words as you point to each article of clothing. On subsequent pages, ask students to take turns showing you captions and labels. Then read them aloud.

T134a Unit 7 | Pack Your Bags!

Pages 4–5

Pages 6–7

Strategies for Comprehensible Input

Page	Story Language	Strategy Options
4	EXPLORE	**Explain:** When you explore, you go to a new place to learn about it.
	FOREST	**Explain:** A forest is a place with many trees.
	look at, listen to, search for	**Demonstrate:** Pantomime these actions.
5	Dress for	**Restate:** Wear clothes that are right for
	cool weather	**Explain:** When the weather is cool, it is a little cold.
6	ISLAND	**Explain:** An island is land that has water on all sides.
	count, fly, watch	**Demonstrate:** Pantomime these actions.
7	warm weather	**Explain:** When the weather is warm, it is a little hot.

Language and Literacy **T134b**

UNIT 7 **LESSON 6,** CONTINUED

LANGUAGE AND LITERACY: THE BASICS BOOKSHELF

OBJECTIVES

Function: Listen to a Book

Critical Thinking and Comprehension:
T Classify Information

Learning to Read:
Identify Exclamations and Statements

READ AND THINK TOGETHER

1. **Read Aloud** On your first reading of the book, use the "Strategies for Comprehensible Input" that appear at the bottom of pages T134b and T134d.

2. **Read and Map: Classify Information** Set up a concept map like the one below, with empty sections, except for the center. Say: *A concept map shows how to put information in groups, or categories.*

    Read pages 4–5 aloud. Think aloud as you fill in the first section: *I will write* Forest *because the forest is a place to explore. Then I'll add things you can find in the forest:* wolves, leaves, *and* birds. *These details go at the ends of the short lines.*

    Pause after reading each set of pages shown below and model completing the concept map.

3. **Conduct Interactive Readings** Have students do the following:

    - **Read with expression** Point to the exclamation marks on pages 4–5. Model reading each exclamation with enthusiasm, then have students echo the sentences. Encourage students to listen for the difference between exclamations and statements as they read along with *Explore!* on the **Selection Tape/CD**.

CLOSE AND ASSESS

Have students name one habitat, the weather, and one item of clothing to wear there.

Pages 8–9

Pages 10–11

Concept Map for *Explore!*

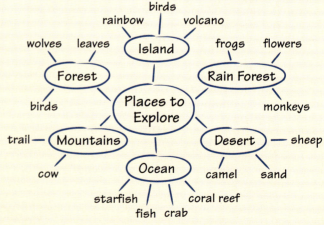

Technology Support
See **Inspiration** Visual Learning software for support in creating the concept map.

T134c Unit 7 | Pack Your Bags!

Explore!, CONTINUED

Pages 12–13

Pages 14–15

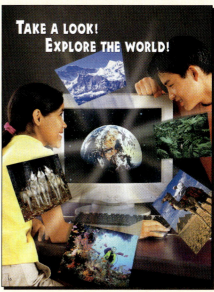

Page 16

Strategies for Comprehensible Input

Page	Story Language	Strategy Options
8	RAIN FOREST	**Explain:** A rain forest is a place that is covered with trees and gets a lot of rain.
9	smell	**Demonstrate:** Pantomime smelling a flower.
10	DESERT	**Explain:** A desert is a larger place that is hot and dry.
11	spot	**Demonstrate:** Pantomime these actions.
12	OCEAN	**Point to a map and explain:** An ocean is a part of the earth that is covered with water.
	swim	**Demonstrate:** Pantomime swimming.
13	discover	**Explain:** When you discover something, you see or learn about it for the first time.
14	MOUNTAINS	**Explain:** A mountain is a tall piece of land.
15	take a picture, hike, greet	**Demonstrate:** Pantomime these actions.
	snow	**Point to the picture.**
16	TAKE A LOOK!	**Restate:** See what you can find.

Language and Literacy **T134d**

UNIT 7 LESSON 7

LANGUAGE AND LITERACY: THE BASICS BOOKSHELF

OBJECTIVES
Function: Give Information
Learning Strategy:
Use Graphic Organizers (concept map)
Critical Thinking and Comprehension:
🅣 Classify Information

CHECK COMPREHENSION

1. **Make a Concept Map** Have students review *Explore!* to identify habitats and things found in each habitat. Remind them that a concept map is a way to group, or categorize, information.

   As you read aloud the directions for each step, pause for students to add information to the sections of their concept maps. Encourage students to review the book, using the inset photos to find the items that pertain to each habitat. They may also view the large photos and find more details on their own.

2. **Share Information from the Book** Have partners take turns using their concept maps to tell about the habitats in the book. Then give the partners a slip of paper containing the name of one habitat. Invite students to tell the class about that habitat.

CLOSE AND ASSESS
Ask students to complete this sentence:
A concept map shows _____.

T134 Unit 7 | Pack Your Bags!

COMPREHENSION: CLASSIFY

Read and Think Together

Make a concept map to tell about *Explore!*
Follow these steps.

1. Think about the book. What is it mainly about?

   (Places to Explore)

2. What places does the book describe? Add sections to the map. Write the name of a place inside each section.

   (Forest) — (Places to Explore)

3. Write words around each place. Tell what you can find there.

   leaves wolves
              birds
   (Forest) — (Places to Explore)

4. Use your completed map to tell a partner about the book.

   Sample Responses
   Students' concept maps should show the following places and things to see:

Island	**Desert**	**Mountains**
rainbow	sheep	snow
birds	sand	trails
volcano	camel	cow

Rain Forest	**Ocean**
frog	starfish
flowers	fish
monkeys	crab
	coral reef

134 Unit 7 | Pack Your Bags!

from The Basics Bookshelf

THEME BOOK
Enjoy sights around the world as you read this book about travel.

REACHING ALL STUDENTS

Social Studies Connection
CREATE TRAVEL GUIDES

World Travel Divide the class into six groups to study the habitats on pages 2 and 3. Model using a world map to locate four specific examples of the habitat. For example, the group studying islands may locate Hawaii, Japan, Australia, and Madagascar.

Then have each group create a travel poster that presents the four locations, using pictures, photos, and captions. Display the travel posters and take a world tour. At each location, stop for the tour guides to present information.

HIGH FREQUENCY WORDS

Words to Know

REVIEW WORDS YOU KNOW

Read the words aloud. Which word goes in the sentence?

family	first
says	she
letters	learn

1. The _family_ hikes together.
2. Father _says_ the names of plants.
3. The children _learn_ about trees.

LEARN TO READ

Learn new words.

places	Jean likes to explore unusual **places**.
important	Travel is very **important** to her.
world	She travels all around the **world**.
always	She **always** plans her trips carefully.
or	She travels either by plane **or** by boat.
river	She sails up the Amazon **River** in a boat.
through	She hikes **through** the Amazon rain forest, too.
once	She goes to Tahiti not **once**, but twice a year.
water	She loves swimming in the clear **water**.
below	She can see hundreds of fish **below** her!

How to Learn a New Word

- Look at the word.
- Listen to the word.
- Listen to the word in a sentence. What does it mean?
- Say the word.
- Spell the word.
- Say the word again.

WORD WORK

Work with a partner. Answer each question.
Then use each word in a sentence.

Example: **4.** important

My family is important to me.

4. Which word has 9 letters?   important
5. Which word begins with 3 consonants?   through
6. Which words have 1 syllable?   world or through once
7. Which words have 2 syllables?   places always river water below
8. Which word means "one time"?   once
9. Which word means "all the time"?   always

Language and Literacy   **135**

Reading Practice Book page 62

HIGH FREQUENCY WORDS
Words to Know

READ AND WRITE
Read each word. Then write it.

1. once ____	2. world ____	3. below ____
4. or ____	5. river ____	6. water ____
7. places ____	8. always ____	9. through ____
10. important ____		

Find the new words. Write the words on the lines.

11. These 4 words have a **w**.	12. These 4 words have 1 syllable.
____ ____	____ ____
____ ____	____ ____

WORD WORK
Work with a partner. Follow the steps.
1. Read aloud each new word in the box.
2. Your partner writes the words.
3. Have your partner read the words to you.
4. Now you write the words on the lines below.
5. Read the words to your partner.

13. ____	18. ____
14. ____	19. ____
15. ____	20. ____
16. ____	21. ____
17. ____	22. ____

Reading Fluency
RECOGNIZE HIGH FREQUENCY WORDS

To build automaticity with the new high frequency words:

- Have students make word cards, cut the letters apart, and scramble the letters for each word. Students can compete in small groups to see who can reassemble the words the fastest.

- Invite students to reorder the words in different ways. For example, students can list the words in alphabetical order, in reverse alphabetical order, and from shortest to longest.

UNIT 7 **LESSON 8**

LANGUAGE AND LITERACY: HIGH FREQUENCY WORDS

OBJECTIVES

Learning to Read:
🅣 Recognize High Frequency Words

REVIEW WORDS

1 **Review Known High Frequency Words** Have the group read aloud the words in the green box. Listen for words students cannot read automatically and use the steps in the yellow box to reteach those words. Then, have students look at the photo. Read each cloze sentence. Reread each sentence and pause for students to silently read the two words to the left of the sentence. Tell students to choose the word that goes in the sentence and tells about the picture.

INTRODUCE NEW WORDS

2 **Learn High Frequency Words** Use the High Frequency Word Script on page T318 to lead students through the steps in the yellow box.

PRACTICE

3 **Conduct "Word Work"** Model using the clue in Item 1 to find the word and then read the sentence for it.

Have partners complete Items 5–9. Afterwards, have students discuss how they answered each question. Invite them to create new questions, for example: *Which words mean the same as "under"? Which words have a* w?

APPLY

4 **Read Words in Context** Students will read high frequency words in context in the sentences on page 137 and the passage on page 138.

▶ **Reading Practice Book** page 62

CLOSE AND ASSESS

Call out the high frequency words one at a time. Have students point to them and spell the words as a group.

Language and Literacy   **T135**

UNIT 7 **LESSON 9**

LANGUAGE AND LITERACY: PHONICS

OBJECTIVES

Learning to Read: Build Oral Vocabulary; Develop Phonemic Awareness; 🅣 Associate Sounds and Symbols /ā/ ai, ay; Blend Sounds to Decode Words

TEACH LONG VOWELS: /ā/ ai, ay

1. **Build Oral Vocabulary** Display Transparency 41. Talk through each picture to develop meaning for the words in the yellow boxes. For example, for Item 1, say:

   • Here are some people on a *trail* (trace the trail with a finger). *One girl holds the* **rail** (point and pantomime). *The boy wants his friends to* **wait** (pantomime waiting).

2. **Develop Phonemic Awareness** Remove the transparency and conduct the oral activities in Step 1 of the Script for Transparency 41.

3. **Read Long *a* Words** Display Transparency 41 again. Work through Steps 2 and 3 of the script.

CLOSE AND ASSESS

Display the words *play, train, day,* and *rain.* Call on students to read the words and identify the letters that make the long *a* sound.

Word Families

-AIL, -AIN, AND -AY

Materials: Letter Tiles

A large number of words can be generated from a few rhyming phonograms. Use letter tiles to build the words in dark type. Then change tiles to build other words in the -ail, -ain, and -ay families.

sail	train	tray
mail	chain	day
pail	drain	gray
rail	main	May
tail	pain	play

T136a Unit 7 | Pack Your Bags!

Transparency 41: ▶
Long a (ai, ay)

▼ **Script for Transparency 41**

Words with Long *a*

1. Develop Phonemic Awareness
Isolate Final/Medial Long *a* Say: *What is the last sound in the words* day *and* stay? *(/ā/) Listen for the sound /ā/ in the middle of these words:* rain, pain. *I am going to say words with the sound /ā/. Raise your hand each time you hear /ā/ in the middle of a word:* day, paid, rain, tray, say, wait.

2. Associate Sounds and Symbols
Point to the sail on **Transparency 41.** Say: *This is a sail on a boat. Say the word* sail *with me:* sail. *Point to the* ai *and say: The letters* ai *make the sound you hear in the middle of* sail. *The sound in the middle is /ā/. Say /ā/ with me: /ā ā ā/. Point to* ai *and ask: What are the letters? What's the sound?* Repeat for *tray,* explaining that the letters *ay* spell the /ā/ sound at the end of words.

3. Blend Sounds to Read Words
Model/Teach Point to the letter *s* in *sail* and say: *The sound for* s *is* /s/. *Repeat for* ai: /ā ā ā/. *As you slide a finger below the letters* sai, *say: I can blend the two sounds: /s ā ā ā/. Then point to the* l *and say: The sound for* l *is* /l/. *I can blend the three sounds together: /s ā ā ā l/. Now, I'm going to say the whole word:* sail. Repeat for *train, tray,* and *gray,* pointing out that *train* has four sounds. Have students sound out the words with you.

Practice For Item 1, say: *Let's try that again. This picture shows children on a* trail *standing by a* rail. *Read the words with me. Follow my finger as we blend the sounds* /t r ā ā ā l/, *and say the word:* trail. Repeat for the other words, calling attention to the following:

• Read aloud the sentence in Item 1, pausing for students to decode *Wait* and *us.* Repeat for other sentences.

• To read *cattails* in Item 1, cover *tails* and read *cat* with students. Then cover *cat* and read *tails.* Uncover the whole word and blend the parts to read *cattails.* Repeat for *Sunday* and *inside* in Item 3.

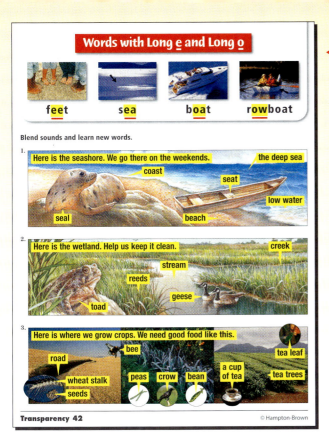

◀ Transparency 42:
Long e *(ee, ea)* and
Long o *(oa, ow)*

▼ Script for Transparency 42

Words with Long *e* and Long *o*

1. **Develop Phonemic Awareness**
   Match Medial Long *e* and Long *o* Say: *Listen for the sound /ē/ in the middle of these words:* feet, seat, bean. *Say the words with me:* feet, seat, bean. *Now raise your hand each time you hear the sound /ē/.* Say: seal, sell, bed, beach, den, deep. Repeat for the long *o* sound in *boat, road,* and *goal.* Have students raise their hands when they hear /ō/ in these words: rod, road, boat, goat, got.

2. **Associate Sounds and Symbols**
   Point to the feet on **Transparency 42**. Say: *These are feet. You walk on your feet. Say the word* feet *with me:* feet. Then point to the *ee* in *feet* and say: *The letters* ee *make the sound you hear in the middle of* feet. *The sound is /ē/. Say /ē/ with me:* /ē ē ē/. Point to *ee* and ask: *What are the letters? What's the sound?* Repeat for the vowel teams in *sea, boat,* and *rowboat.* Use *crow* in Item 3 to explain that the letters *ow* spell the /ō/ sound at the end of words.

3. **Blend Sounds to Read Words**
   Model/Teach Point to the *f* in *feet* and say: *The sound for f is /f/.* Repeat for *ee:* /ē ē ē/. As you slide a finger below the letters *fee,* say: *I can blend the two sounds: /f ē ē ē/.* Then point to the *t* and say: *The sound for t is /t/. I can blend the three sounds together: /f ē ē ē t/. Now I'm going to say the whole word:* feet. Repeat for *sea* and *boat,* pointing out that *sea* has two sounds. To read *rowboat,* cover *boat* and read *row.* Then cover *row* and read *boat.* Uncover the whole word and blend the parts to read *rowboat.* Lead students in sounding out *feet, sea,* and *boat.*

   Practice For Item 1, say: *Let's try that again. The deep sea is part of this picture. Follow my finger to blend these words* (point to *deep* and *sea*). Repeat for the other words with long *e* and long *o.* Call special attention to the following:

   • To read the compound words in Items 1 and 2, follow the process used for *rowboat* in Model/Teach.

   • In Item 3, read and define *stalk* for students.

OBJECTIVES

Learning to Read: Build Oral Vocabulary; Develop Phonemic Awareness; 🅣 Associate Sounds and Symbols /ē/ ee, ea; /ō/ oa, ow; Blend Sounds to Decode Words

TEACH LONG VOWELS:
/ē/ ee, ea; /ō/ oa, ow

1 Build Oral Vocabulary Display Transparency 42. Play a game of "I Spy." For Item 1, say:

• *I spy a seat. The seat is in the rowboat. You sit* (demonstrate) *on a seat.*

When students find the seat in the rowboat, say: *Yes,* **this is a seat** (point to the seat). Repeat the game to build context for the other words.

2 Develop Phonemic Awareness Remove the transparency and work through Step 1 of the script.

3 Read Long *e* and Long *o* Words Display Transparency 42 again. Work through Steps 2 and 3 of the script.

CLOSE AND ASSESS

Display *low, road, trees,* and *leaf.* Have students read a word, identify the vowel sound, and name the letters that make the sound.

▶ **Reading Practice Book** page 63 (vowel teams: *ai, ay; oa, ow; ee, ea*)

Reading Practice Book page 63

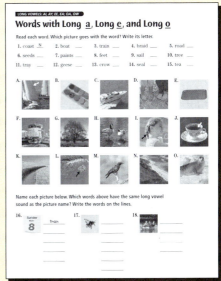

Language and Literacy **T136b**

UNIT 7 LESSON 9, CONTINUED

LANGUAGE AND LITERACY: PHONICS

OBJECTIVES

Learning to Read: Build Oral Vocabulary; Develop Phonemic Awareness; ① Use Word Patterns to Decode Words

TEACH WORD PATTERNS

1 Build Oral Vocabulary Work with students to finish these sentences:
- *I _____ an A on my math test!* (got)
- *A _____ is a farm animal.* (goat)
- *Jeans and chinos are _____.* (pants)
- *Painters use colorful _____.* (paints)
- *Five plus five is _____.* (ten)
- *A short way to say teenager is _____.* (teen)

2 Develop Phonemic Awareness and Contrast Vowel Sounds Work through Step 1 of the script. Then display the transparency and do Step 2.

3 Use Word Patterns to Decode Words Work through Step 3 of the script.

CLOSE AND ASSESS

Display the words *coat* and *cot*. Ask: *Why does* coat *have a long vowel sound? Why does* cot *have a short vowel sound?*

▶ **Reading Practice Book** page 64 (word patterns: CVC, CVVC)

Transparency 43: ▶ **Word Patterns**

Words with Short and Long Vowels

| got | pants | ten | set |
| goat | paints | teen | seat |

All these words have short vowels.
ran
met
sell
cost

All these words have long vowels.
rain
meet
seal
coast

Find the pattern.

1. Look at the first list of words.
   How many vowels are in each word? _____
   What kind of letters come after the vowel? _____
   Is the vowel sound long or short? _____
2. Look at the second list of words.
   How many vowels are in each word? _____
   Is the vowel sound long or short? _____
   Which vowel does not have a sound? _____

Look for patterns in these words. Which word in each pair has a <u>short</u> vowel? Which word in each pair has a <u>long</u> vowel?

| 1. rod | 2. pens | 3. fell | 4. paid | 5. cot |
| road | peas | feel | pad | coat |

Transparency 43 © Hampton-Brown

▼ **Script for Transparency 43**

Words with Short and Long Vowels

1. Develop Phonemic Awareness
Discriminate Between Vowel Sounds Say: *Listen. Which two words have the same vowel sound:* got, box, boat? (got, box) *What is the sound?* (/o/) *Now listen again. Which two words have the same vowel sound:* boat, road, pot? (boat, road) *What is the sound?* (/ō/) *Repeat for short and long* a *and* e *with these sets of words:* rain, ran, cat; train, wait, pan; men, teen, tent; seat, meet, let.

2. Contrast Short and Long Vowel Sounds
Say: *The vowel* o *has a short sound:* /o/. *Say* /o/ *with me:* /ooo/. *The vowel* o *also has a long sound:* /ō/. *Say* /ō/ *with me:* /ō ō ō/. *Now listen to these words:* got, goat. *Say them with me:* got, goat. *Which word has the long sound for the letter* o? (goat) *Which word has the short sound?* (got) *Repeat the process for* pants, paints; ten, teen; *and* set, seat.

3. Use Word Patterns to Decode Words
Find the Pattern Read aloud each list of words, noting the short and long vowel sounds. Use the questions in the box to explore the spelling pattern in each list: *Look at the first list of words. How many vowels are in each word? Let's count them: one in* ran. Repeat for the other words. Write the answer (one) on the first line in the box. Work through the remaining questions for Items 1 and 2 in the box and record the answers. In the second list of words, explain that the second vowel in each pair is silent and the first vowel is long.

Summarize and Model the Strategy Say: *Look for patterns in words to help you read.* Point to the word *rod* in Item 1 and say: *Here I see one vowel and then the consonant* d, *so I'll say the short vowel sound for* o: rod. Point to *road* and say: *Here are two vowels together, so I'll say the long vowel sound for the first vowel:* road.

Practice Have students repeat the process for Items 2–5. First they should identify the word with the short vowel sound and then tell you how they figured out the vowel sound in each word.

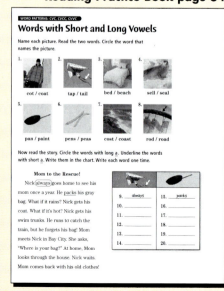

Reading Practice Book page 64

T136c Unit 7 | Pack Your Bags!

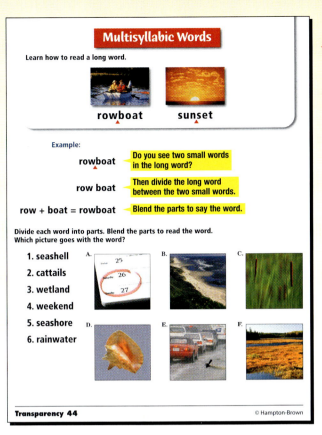

◀ Transparency 44: Multisyllabic Words

OBJECTIVES

Learning to Read: Build Oral Vocabulary; Develop Phonemic Awareness; Divide Words into Syllables; Decode Multisyllabic Words

TEACH COMPOUND WORDS

1 Build Oral Vocabulary Display Transparency 44. Use the pictures to develop the meaning of each word and use it in a sentence. For example:

• *This is a* **wetland**. *A* **wetland** *is a low, wet place. Many plants and animals live in a* **wetland**.

2 Develop Phonemic Awareness Remove the transparency and conduct the oral activities in Step 1 of the Script for Transparency 44.

3 Decode Compound Words Display Transparency 44 again. Work through Step 2 of the script.

CLOSE AND ASSESS

Display the words *seashell* and *weekend*. Call on students to tell you where to divide each word. Have volunteers blend the parts to read the word.

▶ **Reading Practice Book** page 65 (syllable division: compound words)

▼ Script for Transparency 44

Multisyllabic Words

1. Develop Phonemic Awareness

Count Syllables in Words Say: *Some words have one part, or syllable, such as* boat. *Clap the syllable with me as we say* boat: boat. (clap) *Some longer words have two parts, or syllables, such as* rowboat. *Clap the syllables as we say* rowboat: row-boat. (clap, clap) *Lead students in saying and clapping syllables for* set, sunset, weekend, week, shell, seashell. *Then have students say the words after you and count the syllables on their own.*

2. Decode Compound Words

Teach Say: *You are going to learn to read a long word.* Point to the rowboat on **Transparency 44**. Say: *This is a rowboat. Say* rowboat *with me:* rowboat. *How many parts do you hear?* (2) *Let's read the word and find out if we will also see two parts.* Explain that *rowboat* is a compound word, a word made up of two smaller words. Tell students that all the words on the transparency are compound words.

Work through the Example. Point to *rowboat* and say: *This long word is made up of two small words. Divide the long word between the two small words. How many parts do you see?* (2) *Blend the first part with me.* Slide a finger slowly from left to right below the syllable as you say: /r r r ō ō ō/. Then have students blend the second syllable as you slide your finger and say: /b ō ō ō t/. *Now let's blend the parts together and read the word:* row-boat, rowboat. Repeat for *sunset*.

Practice Have volunteers show you where to divide each word in Items 1–6. Write the parts and lead the group in blending them to read the word. Call attention to the following:

• For *rainwater* in Item 6, tell students that the second small word is *water*. Have them sound out *rain* and read *water* as a whole word. Ask: *How many syllables did you hear in* rainwater? (3) Point out that the words that make up a compound word sometimes have more than one syllable.

Reading Practice Book page 65

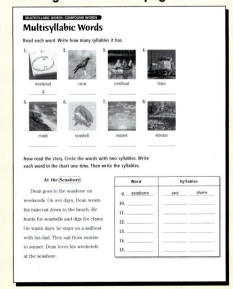

Language and Literacy **T136d**

UNIT 7 LESSON 10
LANGUAGE AND LITERACY: READING AND SPELLING

OBJECTIVES

Functions: Listen Actively; Repeat Spoken Language; Recite

Learning to Read: Develop Phonemic Awareness;
🅣 Associate Sounds and Symbols: /ā/ ai, ay; /ē/ ee, ea; /ō/ oa, ow;
🅣 Use Word Patterns to Decode Words; Divide Words into Syllables (compound words)

Spelling: 🅣 Long Vowels: ai, ay; ee, ea; oa, ow; Compound Words

LISTEN AND LEARN

1 Sing a Song Display Transparency 45 and play "On the Beach" on the **Language Tape/CD**. *(Tape 4A, CD 2 Track 4)*

DEVELOP PHONEMIC AWARENESS

2 Segment Words into Sounds
Say: *Listen to this word and then say it with me:* sail. *Now let's say the sounds separately and count them:* /s/, /ā/, /l/—*three sounds.* Repeat with *sat, seat, feet, boat, trap, tray,* and *row*.

LOOK FOR WORD PATTERNS

3 Long Vowels: *ai, ay; ee, ea; oa, ow*
Identify the first picture. Say: *This is a sail, and here's the word. Let's point to the letters. Say the sounds for the letters with me:* /s s s ā ā ā l l l/. Repeat for the other pictures, pointing out that *ay, ee, ea, oa,* and *ow* work together to make one long vowel sound. Then read the questions aloud: *How are the words alike?* (Two vowels make one long vowel sound.) *Are the vowel sounds long or short?* (long) Then tell students: *When you see two vowels together in a word, the first is usually long, and the second is silent.* Have students name the two letters in each word or syllable that make the long vowel sound.

Afterwards, play the song again. Have students identify words with long *a, e,* and *o*.

T136 Unit 7 | Pack Your Bags!

LONG VOWELS: AI, AY; EE, EA; OA, OW

Reading and Spelling

LISTEN AND LEARN

On the Beach

Sailboats sail along the bay
As the sunset ends the day.
Little crabs and starfish play
In the pools along the shore.
Seaweed gathers on the beach.
As the seagulls dive and soar,
Endless waves will sweep the sand
With a whisper or a roar.
The high tide and the low tide
Bring sea gifts to my door.

LOOK FOR WORD PATTERNS

How are the words alike? Are the vowel sounds long or short?

All the words have two vowels together. The vowel sounds are long.

1. s**ai**l
2. f**ee**t
3. b**oa**t

 t**r**a**y**
 s**ea**
 ro**wb**o**a**t

136 Unit 7 | Pack Your Bags!   ▶ Transparencies 41–45

REACHING ALL STUDENTS

Multi-Level Strategies
LITERACY SUPPORT

LITERATE IN L1 Study the errors students make in the sentence dictation in Items 7–10 and compare them to the Phonics Transfer Chart on page T338. Students may incorrectly encode sounds because they do not exist in their native languages (e.g., there is no long *o* sound in Hmong) or, they may use a spelling that stands for the sound in the native language (e.g., Spanish speakers may use *i* or *y* to represent long *e*). For errors that reflect transfer issues, such as these, conduct minimal pair activities:

- For sound recognition, say three words such as *cot, coat, coat*. Have students hold up cards with the numbers 1, 2, and 3 to indicate which words are the same. Some minimal pairs for vowel teams are: *bean, bin; lead, lid; sheep, ship; feel, fill; ran, rain; blue, blow*.

- For oral production, have students repeat sentences with minimal pairs: *I put my coat on the cot.* Then students can write the sentences and read them back.

READING STRATEGY

Follow these steps to read a word.

❶ Look for a pattern. Do you see two vowels together?

 dream   *The two vowels in each word are a team. They make one **long vowel** sound.*   play

❷ Start at the beginning of the word. Blend the sounds in your head. Then say the word.

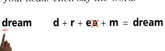
dream   d + r + e~~a~~ + m = dream   play   p + l + a~~y~~ = play

Reading Help
Some long words are made up of two small words.

day + dream = daydream
sail + boat = sailboat
sea + shell = seashell

To read these words, find the two small words. Then sound them out and say the two words together.

READING AND SPELLING PRACTICE

Use what you learned to read the sentences.

1. Joan and her family spend weekends at the seashore.
2. They keep a rowboat by the beach.
3. Joan likes to swim in the water or row the boat.
4. When it rains, she always stays inside.
5. A good book and hot tea are all she needs.
6. She just sits and reads all day!

7.–10. Now write the sentences that your teacher reads. *For dictation sentences, see Step 6 at right.*

Answers for Word Work

long a	long e	long o
rain	beach	coast
sail	leaf	road
paint	read	boat
stay	bee	snow
play	deep	show
	sweet	grow

WORD WORK

11. Write each word on a card.

rain	coast	sail	leaf	play	paint
stay	snow	deep	show	grow	road
beach	bee	sweet	read	feet	boat

Then say each word. Sort the words by vowel sound. Make 3 groups.

12. Now make 6 new groups. Put the words with the same vowel sound *and* spelling together. What do you notice?

Example: 12.

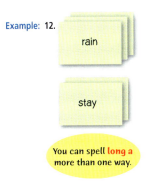

*You can spell **long a** more than one way.*

Language and Literacy 137

Decodable Book
PRACTICE WITH LONG VOWELS
AI, AY; EE, EA; OA, OW

 Decodable Book 7: *On the River*

Assign **Decodable Book 7** for independent reading. The **Decodable Book** can be used in a variety of ways to help students become more fluent, automatic readers:

Discussion Circles Have students work in small groups to read aloud and discuss the book using the questions on the back cover. Encourage students to read aloud the text that supports their answers. Groups can also work together to complete the Word Work Activity.

Readers Theater Students can read aloud the stories in a class performance. Help them prepare by rereading the stories in daily rehearsals. Work with students to add narration or dialog. Encourage them to use natural phrasing and expression.

Rereading at Home Have students work with family members to reread the book at home. They can take turns reading aloud alternate pages, then rereading the book switching the pages each person reads.

LEARN A READING STRATEGY

4 Use Word Patterns Work through the strategy with students, reading each step aloud and modeling the actions shown on the page. Point out the Reading Help and read the explanation to students. Work through additional examples to help them apply the tip: *snowman, seaweed, rainbow, speedboat.*

PRACTICE

5 Read Sentences Distribute the Partner Prompts from page T311 to guide peers in reading the sentences in Items 1–6. Remind them to use the word-pattern strategy to read words and to blend the words silently.

6 Write Sentences Dictate the following sentences for students to write. Read each sentence at normal speed once so students can listen, and then repeat it slowly word by word as they write:

7. This boat can sail on the deep sea.
8. We play in the water at the seashore.
9. Plant the seeds and watch them grow!
10. I have to read two books this weekend.

If students need extra support, guide them in spelling the compound words syllable by syllable. For example: *How many parts do you hear in* weekend? (2) *Let's spell the first part. Write the first sound you hear in* week. Repeat for the second syllable.

7 Conduct "Word Work" Read the directions for Item 11. After students complete the first sort, read the second set of directions and work through the Example. Have partners complete the activity. Check answers as a group.

▶ **Reading Practice Book** pages 135–138 (Decodable Book 7)

CLOSE AND ASSESS

Ask students what letters spell /ē/. Then ask how /ā/ is spelled in the middle of a word. Ask how it is spelled at the end of a word. Repeat for long *o*.

Language and Literacy T137

UNIT 7 LESSON 11
LANGUAGE AND LITERACY: INDEPENDENT READING

OBJECTIVES

Function: Read a Selection

Learning to Read: 🅣 Recognize High Frequency Words; 🅣 Decode Long Vowel Words (ai, ay; ee, ea; oa, ow); Recognize Compound Words

Reading Strategies: Set a Purpose for Reading; Retell

Critical Thinking and Comprehension: 🅣 Classify

READ ON YOUR OWN

1. **Introduce Vocabulary** In "Explore a Wetland," students apply phonics skills and read high frequency words. Introduce the story words. Write each word, pronounce it, and spell it.

   - **welcome:** something you say to greet people when they first arrive. *Welcome to your new school!*
   - **afternoon:** part of the day from noon to evening. *After lunch, I work all afternoon.*
   - **guide:** a person who shows the way. *We followed a guide up the hill.*
   - **geese:** large birds with webbed feet and long necks. *Geese fly in flocks.*

2. **Set Purposes** Read the title, point out the visuals, and say: *You are going to read about* Black Creek Wetland *in Canada. Read to find out what the wetland is like.*

3. **Read and Think: Classify** Have students complete the map and use it to tell a partner what they learned about the wetland.

4. **Build Reading Fluency** Use the **Language Tape/CD** with Reading Practice Book page 66 for fluency practice.

   ▶ **Reading Practice Book** page 66

CLOSE AND ASSESS

Go around the group to describe Black Creek Wetland. Have students name the different plants and animals.

T138 Unit 7 | Pack Your Bags!

COMPREHENSION: CLASSIFY

Read on Your Own

DECODING CHECK
Give the Decoding Progress Check on page 1a of the Assessment Handbook.

Welcome to Black Creek Wetland. What a great way to spend a Sunday afternoon! My name is Jean Clay. I am your guide. Step into the rowboat. Stay in your seat while we move through the water.

Canada has many wetlands. Black Creek Wetland is one of them. A wetland is a low, wet place. Rainwater and many streams keep it wet. Black Creek is on the shore of Lake Ontario. Plants such as reeds and cattails grow here. This is an important place for animals, too. Ducks and geese lay their eggs here in May.

Sometimes, people drain the water from wetlands. Then they use the land to grow wheat or other crops. Not here. We plan to keep this wetland for the ducks, geese, and other animals.

CHECK YOUR UNDERSTANDING

Copy and complete the map. Tell a partner what you learned about Black Creek Wetland.

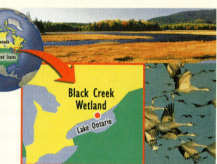

138 Unit 7 Pack Your Bags!

REACHING ALL STUDENTS

Reading Fluency
PHRASING

Read the introduction on **Reading Practice Book** page 66. Explain that the / in the examples shows a short pause between groups of words and the // shows a longer pause between sentences. Model reading the examples and have students echo them.

Next, play "Explore a Wetland" on the **Language Tape/CD** and have students mark the paragraphs to show where the pauses occur. Check marks as a whole class before partners do the Practice section. Circulate during the Practice to check and support reading fluency.

Reading Practice Book page 66

CAPITALIZATION: PROPER NOUNS
Special Places, Special People

Pronunciation of Names
Jorge — hor hā
El Yunque — el yün kā
San Juan — san hwahn
Hsu — shü

A **proper noun** names one particular person, place, or thing.

A proper noun begins with a **capital letter**.

name of a person	**Jorge** is a scientist.
name of a special place, a city, or a country	He will go to **El Yunque** near **San Juan**, **Puerto Rico**, to study the birds.
name of a month or a day	He will leave **Monday**, **July** 15.

STUDY CAPITALIZATION

Look at the story on page 138. Answer these questions. *Students' additional responses will vary.*

Example: 1. Jean Clay is the name of a person. Joyce Hsu is another person's name.

1. Which 2 words are the name of a person? Tell another person's name. *Jean Clay*
2. Which word names a country? Name another country. *Canada*
3. Which word names a month? Name another month. *May*
4. Which word names a day of the week? Name another day of the week. *Sunday*
5. Which words name a special place? Name another special place. *Black Creek Wetland*

WRITE SENTENCES

Write each sentence correctly. Add the capital letters. *Underscores indicate letters that should be capitalized.*

Example: 6. Jorge will take a trip to Puerto Rico.

6. Jorge will take a trip to puerto rico.
7. On Monday, july 15, he flies into San Juan.
8. On tuesday, July 16, Jorge takes a bus to the rain forest.
9. The rain forest is called el yunque.
10. It is 40 kilometers from san juan.
11. He will stay there until thursday, july 18.
12. On Sunday, July 21, Jorge flies back to the united states.
13. He goes to his home in miami, Florida.

Jorge studies the birds in the rain forest.

Language and Literacy 139

Language Practice Book page 78

Multi-Level Strategies
LANGUAGE DEVELOPMENT

LITERATE IN L1 Rules for capitalization vary widely from language to language. Some, such as Farsi and Japanese, do not use capital letters at all. Students learning English capitalization for the first time may experience "negative transference."

Remind students that, in English, capital letters normally appear only at the beginning of a word. Then use capital and lowercase letter tiles to create proper nouns for students to copy.

UNIT 7 LESSON 12

LANGUAGE AND LITERACY: PROPER NOUNS

OBJECTIVES

Functions: Write; Give Information
Patterns and Structures: 🅣 Proper Nouns
Writing: Sentences

INTRODUCE

1 Learn About Proper Nouns Read the title and introduction. Then go over the kinds of proper nouns and the examples. Summarize by saying: *Capitalize the names of specific people, places, months, and days.*

Write a student's name with correct capitalization. Next, ask for a person's birthdate, and write it. Finally, ask for a city, state, and country, and write these. Go through the words and phrases you wrote and have students name each of the capital letters.

PRACTICE

2 Study Capitalization Read aloud Item 1 and demonstrate how to find the answer in the story on page 138. Give your own name as an example of an answer to the second part. Have partners alternate answering the first or second part of each item. Encourage them to use a map or a calendar if they need help thinking of more words.

APPLY

3 Write Sentences In the Example, point out that *Puerto Rico* is the name of a country, so each word begins with a capital letter. Have students write Items 6–13 and then trade papers with a partner for peer review.

▶ **Language Practice Book** page 78

CLOSE AND ASSESS

Call on volunteers to write the sentences, displaying the corrections they made. Discuss the reasons for the capitalization of each proper noun.

Language and Literacy **T139**

UNIT 7 LESSON 13

LANGUAGE ACROSS THE CURRICULUM: SCIENCE

OBJECTIVES

Functions:
Listen to an Article; Give Information

Concepts and Vocabulary:
Diagrams; Cycles

Research Skills and Learning Strategies:
Build Background; Use Text Structures (diagrams)

Critical Thinking and Comprehension:
Identify Steps in a Process; Generate Ideas; Summarize

Representing: Diagram

LEARN ABOUT CYCLES

1 Explore Diagrams and Cycles
Explain that a diagram often shows the steps in a process. Say: *A label can name something or show how it works. These labels show the stages in the life cycle of a beetle.*

Explain that a *cycle* is a process that repeats over and over again. Read each label aloud and have students point to the part of the diagram that it goes with. Note that the eggs the adult beetle lays make new larvae, and the cycle starts over again.

READ AND THINK

2 Build Background Soak a paper towel in water, then place it in front of a fan or near a heater. Ask: *Where does the water go when the paper towel dries up?* (It goes into the air.)

3 Listen to the Article Explain that the water cycle shows how water changes as it moves through the environment. Then read the article and go over the diagram, using the title, labels, and caption to give information about the steps of the cycle.

CHECK UNDERSTANDING

4 Answer the Review Questions Help students answer each question based on the diagram and the text.

CLOSE AND ASSESS

Ask students to explain the water cycle to a partner in their own words.

T140 Unit 7 | Pack Your Bags!

SUCCESS IN SCIENCE

Learn About Cycles

DIAGRAMS

A **cycle** is a series of events that happen again and again.

A **diagram** is a drawing. It can show how a cycle works.

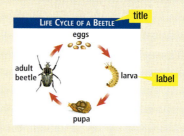

LIFE CYCLE OF A BEETLE — title
eggs
adult beetle
larva — label
pupa

Sample Responses for the Review:
1. The sun heats water on the Earth. The water becomes water vapor. The water vapor cools in the air and forms clouds. Water falls from the clouds and becomes part of the water on Earth. The cycle repeats.
2. Possible cycles include: life cycle of a plant or animal; recycling and reuse of an aluminum can.
3. Students should include arrows, labels, and a title in their diagrams.

Study the diagram and listen to the article. Then do the Review.

Earth's Amazing Water Cycle

• How does the water cycle work?

The Earth's water can take many forms. It can be a **liquid**, like rainwater, or a **solid**, like ice.

rain

ice

THE WATER CYCLE
Sun, Clouds, Rain, Evaporation, Lake, River flow, Ocean

It can even take the form of **vapor**. You cannot see vapor. When water boils, it turns to water vapor.

The Earth's water is recycled. Heat from the sun turns water on the Earth into water vapor. This process is called **evaporation**. The water vapor is carried up by the air. Air that is full of water vapor can cool off. When this happens, clouds form and the water vapor turns into water again. The water falls from the clouds as rain or snow, for example, and becomes part of the water on Earth. Some of this water—in rivers and lakes, for example—evaporates, and the cycle begins again.

REVIEW

1. **Check Your Understanding** Tell in your own words how the water cycle works. Use the diagram.
2. **Vocabulary** Give an example of another cycle.
3. **Use Diagrams** Draw a diagram to show how another cycle works.

140 Unit 7 | Pack Your Bags!

REACHING ALL STUDENTS

Science Connection
WEATHER AND LANDFORMS

Help students create an expanded diagram of the water cycle that includes landforms and bodies of water. Then use index cards to create labels for weather, landforms, and the stages of the water cycle. Invite students to arrange the cards on the diagram. Call on volunteers to use the diagram to describe the water cycle.

Writing Project / CLASS TRAVEL BOOK

WRITING ASSESSMENT
Use the Writing Progress Checklist on page 51 of the Assessment Handbook to evaluate this writing project.

Create a travel book like *Explore!* Each person can make one page. Describe where you want to go. Tell how you can get there. Tell what you can see and do.

CHOOSE A PLACE

1. Where do you want to go? Look in books, magazines, or newspapers for information. Take notes. Start a concept map.

2. Collect or draw pictures.

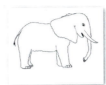

PLAN YOUR PAGE

What will you show on your page? Use your notes to complete these sentences:
1. Take ____.
2. Explore ____.
3. You can ____. You can ____.

MAKE AND SHARE YOUR PAGE

Put your pictures on construction paper.
Write your sentences on another piece of paper.
Check and correct your work.

> ✓ **Check Your Work**
> Does your page describe a place and how to get there?
> Did you tell what you can see and do?
> Did you use capital letters correctly?

Then put your sentences on the construction paper. Put everyone's pages together to make a class travel book. Read the book aloud.

Language Across the Curriculum 141

UNIT 7 LESSON 14

LANGUAGE ACROSS THE CURRICULUM: WRITING

OBJECTIVES

Functions:
Give Information; Describe; Write

Learning Strategies and Critical Thinking: Plan; Generate and Organize Ideas; Self-Assess

Writing: Class Travel Book

CONDUCT THE WRITING PROJECT

1. **Explore New Places** Read the introduction. Then page through the *Explore!* book to review how it uses text, pictures, and captions to describe places to explore.

2. **Choose a Place** Preview Steps 1 and 2 with students. To help them select a location, provide travel magazines, tourist brochures, or atlases. After students have chosen their subjects, encourage them to find information about the location in encyclopedias, atlases, or the Internet.

3. **Plan Your Page** Use the example page on India to model how to complete the sentence frames and add picture support.

4. **Make and Share Your Page** Invite students to share their work with the class. Then have them take turns taking the class travel book home to share with their families.

▶ **Language Practice Book** page 79

CLOSE AND ASSESS

As students look at a page, say:
- *Show me where you tell how to get there.*
- *Look at the place names—did you use capitalization correctly?*
- *Point to a caption that says what you can see and do.*

Language Practice Book page 79

Multi-Level Strategies

WRITING SUPPORT

PRELITERATE Support students by using the Language Experience Approach. Invite small groups to use photographs and drawings to show their ideas about a location. Then ask questions about the pictures and have the group members take turns dictating their ideas for you to record. As you write, pause and ask students to spell high frequency words. Then have the group copy the sentences and arrange the pictures to complete the page.

Language Across the Curriculum T141

Resources

For Success in Language and Literacy

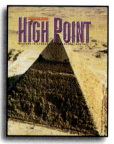

Student Book pages 142–155

For Language Skills Practice

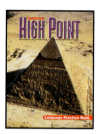

Language Practice Book pages 80–85

For Reading Skills Practice

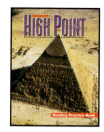

Reading Practice Book pages 67–70

For Vocabulary, Language Development, and Reading Fluency

Language Tape 4, Side B
Language CD 2, Tracks 6–9

For Reading Together

Theme Book *Friends Are Like That* from The Basics Bookshelf

For Audio Walk-Throughs and Selection Readings

Selection Tape 4B
Selection CD 2, Tracks 3–4

For Phonics Instruction

Transparencies 46–50

Transparency Scripts 46–50

Letter Tiles

For Comprehensive Assessment

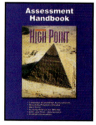

Language Acquisition Assessment, Units 7–9 Test, Writing Assessment, Self-Assessment

For Planning and Instruction

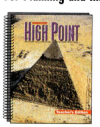

Teacher's Edition pages T142a–T155

UNIT 8

In This Unit

Vocabulary
- Feelings
- Graphs

Language Functions
- Describe Actions
- Express Feelings

Patterns and Structures
- Regular Past Tense Verbs
- Irregular Past Tense Verbs (was, were)
- Negative Sentences and Contractions with *not*
- Possessive Nouns

Reading
- Verb Ending: -ed
- Comprehension: Identify Cause and Effect (cause-and-effect chart)

Writing
- Sentences
- Friendship Book

Content Area Connection
- Mathematics (bar graphs)

T142b

UNIT 8

Activity and Assessment Planner

UNIT 8: Friend to Friend

LESSONS

1

UNIT 8 LAUNCH	▶ *pages T142–T143*

LESSON 1: INTRODUCE UNIT 8 pages T142–T143

Vocabulary
T Feelings

Viewing
Interpret a Visual Image

Learning Strategies
Preview

Build Background

Critical Thinking and Speaking
Make Inferences

Generate Ideas

Role-Play

2–5

LANGUAGE DEVELOPMENT	▶ *pages T144–T147*

**LESSON 2
REGULAR PAST TENSE VERBS**
page T144

Function
Describe Actions

Patterns and Structures
Regular Past Tense Verbs

Writing
Sentences

**LESSON 3
FEELINGS**
page T145

Functions
Express Feelings

Demonstrate Non-Verbal Communication

Vocabulary
T Feelings

Writing
T Sentences

**LESSON 4
IRREGULAR PAST TENSE VERBS**
page T146

Function
Describe Actions

Patterns and Structures
T Irregular Past Tense Verbs *(was, were)*

Writing
Sentences

**LESSON 5
NEGATIVE SENTENCES**
page T147

Function
Describe Actions

Patterns and Structures
T Negative Sentences

T Contractions with *not*

Writing
T Sentences

6–12

LANGUAGE AND LITERACY	▶ *pages T148a–T153*

**LESSON 6
BASICS BOOKSHELF**
pages T148a–T148f

Functions
Listen to a Book

Role-Play

Read Aloud a Story (choral reading)

Vocabulary
T Feelings

Reading Strategies
Activate Prior Knowledge

Preview

Learning to Read
Identify Dialogue

Critical Thinking and Comprehension
Identify Cause and Effect

**LESSON 7
BASICS BOOKSHELF: COMPREHENSION**
page T148

Function
Retell a Story

Learning Strategy
Use Graphic Organizers (cause-and-effect chart)

Critical Thinking and Comprehension
Identify Cause and Effect

**LESSON 8
HIGH FREQUENCY WORDS**
page T149

Learning to Read
T Recognize High Frequency Words

**LESSON 9
PHONICS**
pages T150a–T150d

Learning to Read
Build Oral Vocabulary

Develop Phonemic Awareness

Associate Sounds and Symbols: Verb Endings

Blend Sounds to Decode Words

Identify Verb Endings *(-ed)*

T Decode Words with Endings

**LESSON 10
READING AND SPELLING**
pages T150–T151

Learning to Read
Develop Phonemic Awareness

Associate Sounds and Symbols: /d/ -ed; /t/ -ed; /ed/ -ed

Listen for the Sound of -ed

Identify Verb Endings *(-ed)*

T Decode Words with Endings

Spelling
T Verb Ending -ed

**LESSON 11
INDEPENDENT READING**
page T152

Function
Read a Selection

Learning to Read
T Recognize High Frequency Words

T Decode Words with Endings

Reading Strategies
Preview

Predict

Retell

Critical Thinking and Comprehension
Identify Cause and Effect

**LESSON 12
POSSESSIVE NOUNS**
page T153

Function
Write

Patterns and Structures
T Possessive Nouns

Writing
Sentences

13–14

LANGUAGE ACROSS THE CURRICULUM	▶ *pages T154–T155*

**LESSON 13
MATHEMATICS: BAR GRAPHS**
page T154

Function
Give Information

Vocabulary
Graphs

Research Skills and Learning Strategies
Conduct a Survey

Use Text Structures (bar graphs)

Critical Thinking and Comprehension
Make Comparisons

Analyze Information

Draw Conclusions

**LESSON 14
WRITING PROJECT: FRIENDSHIP BOOK**
page T155

Functions
Describe Actions

Express Feelings

Write

Learning Strategies and Critical Thinking
Plan

Relate to Personal Experience

Generate and Organize Ideas

Self-Assess

Writing
Friendship Book

T142c Unit 8 | Friend to Friend

T = Objective Tested on Unit Test

ASSESSMENT OPTIONS

The **Teacher's Edition** and the **Assessment Handbook** include these comprehensive assessment tools:

▶ **Ongoing, Informal Assessment**
Check for understanding and achieve closure for every lesson with the targeted questions and activities in the **Close and Assess** boxes in your Teacher's Edition.

▶ **Decoding Progress Check**
These word lists for each unit provide a quick way to check on mastery of the phonics or word structure skills taught in the unit.

▶ **Language Acquisition Assessments**
To verify students' ability to use the language functions and grammar structures taught in Units 7–9, conduct these performance assessments.

▶ **Unit Test in Standardized Test Format**
This multiple-choice test measures students' cumulative understanding of the skills and language developed in Units 7–9.

▶ **Self- and Peer-Assessment**
Students use the Self-Assessment Form to evaluate their own work and develop learning strategies appropriate to their needs. Students offer feedback to their classmates with the Peer-Assessment Form.

▶ **Writing Assessment/Portfolio Opportunities**
You can evaluate students' writing in the Writing Projects using the Writing Progress Checklist. Then collaborate with students to choose work for their portfolios.

UNITS 7–9 ASSESSMENT OPPORTUNITIES	Assessment Handbook Pages
Decoding Progress Check	1a
Language Acquisition Assessments	18
Units 7–9 Test	19–24
Self-Assessment Form	25
Peer-Assessment Form	50
Writing Progress Checklist	51
Portfolio Evaluation Form	52

RELATED RESOURCES

The Bracelet
by Yoshiko Uchida
When Emi and her family are sent to an internment camp during World War II, Emi's best friend gives her a bracelet to remember her by. (Philomel Books)
Theme Book: Read Aloud

The Leaving Morning
by Angela Johnson
A young boy and his sister prepare to say good-bye to their friends, cousins, and neighbors on the day their family moves. (Orchard)
Phonics Reinforcement: -ed

Voices of the Heart
by Ed Young
Cut-paper collages of Chinese characters for the words *joy, sorrow, worry,* and twenty-three other emotions. (Scholastic)
Vocabulary: Feelings

The Giving Tree
by Shel Silverstein
A poignant story about the friendship between a man and a tree with a very big heart. (HarperCollins)
Language Development: Past Tense Verbs

The Journey of Natty Gann
A charming story of friendship between a young girl searching for her father, a wild dog, and a kind young drifter. Set during the Depression.
Multimedia: Film/Video

UNIT 8 **LESSON 1**

INTRODUCE UNIT 8: FRIEND TO FRIEND

OBJECTIVES

Concepts and Vocabulary: 🅣 Feelings
Viewing: Interpret a Visual Image
Learning Strategies: Preview; Build Background
Critical Thinking: Make Inferences; Generate Ideas
Speaking: Role-Play

START WITH A COMMON EXPERIENCE

1. **Introduce "Friend to Friend"** Read the unit title aloud and explain that when you say something from "friend to friend," you talk honestly to a friend you trust.

2. **Meet Two Friends** Direct attention to the photos and tell students that the pictures tell a story about two friends named Miguel (on the left in the picture at top left) and Len (on the right). Ask students to view the photos to find out what the boys are doing. (making a pizza)

3. **Study the Scenes** Starting with the upper left photo, ask students to describe each boy's actions. Encourage them to study the boys' facial expressions and gestures to interpret what they might say and feel. Chart students' ideas for each scene.

Scene 1

Doing	Feeling	Saying
Miguel: rolling dough for a pizza crust	Miguel: happy, confident	Miguel: "Great! Now we just roll it out with this."

4. **Role-Play Miguel and Len** Read the activity directions on page 143. Have partners choose their roles and then role-play each scene. Afterwards, call on different pairs to act out the scenes for the group.

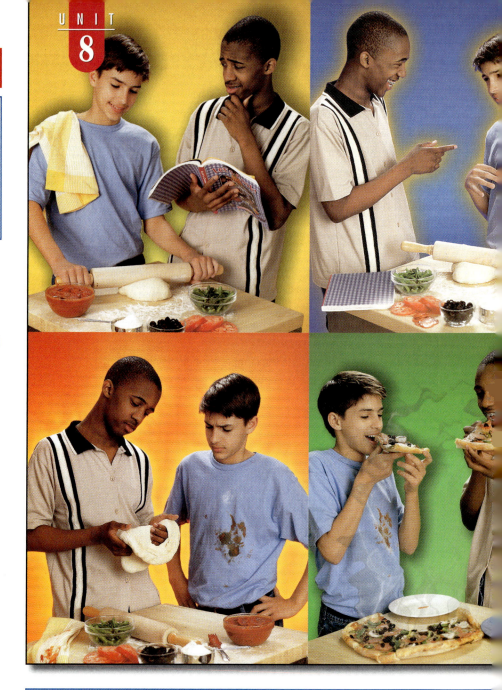

REACHING ALL STUDENTS

HOME CONNECTION

Family Recipes Invite volunteers to tell about cooking at home. Ask: *Who cooks in your house? Do family members ever cook together? Do you use a cookbook? What are your favorite family recipes?* Then encourage students to cook a dish or meal with a family member. Back in class, invite volunteers to discuss their experiences.

Look at the pictures.

Act out the scenes with a partner.

Talk about how each character feels.

Sample Responses
Students should notice that, in the first scene, one boy is happy and confident while the other is confused. In the second scene, one is amused while the other is embarrassed and surprised. In the third scene, they are frustrated and discouraged. In the fourth scene, they are both happy, excited, and proud.

In This Unit

Vocabulary
- Feelings
- Graphs

Language Functions
- Describe Actions
- Express Feelings

Patterns and Structures
- Regular Past Tense Verbs
- Irregular Past Tense Verbs *(was, were)*
- Negative Sentences and Contractions with *not*
- Possessive Nouns

Reading
- Verb Ending: -ed
- Comprehension: Identify Cause and Effect (cause-and-effect chart)

Writing
- Sentences
- Friendship Book

Content Area Connection
- Mathematics (bar graphs)

143

PREVIEW THE UNIT

5 Look for Activities About Friends and Friendship Leaf through the unit, noting that students will meet several friends who appear throughout the unit. Preview activities students will do, for example:

page 144—learning a song about friendship

page 148—listening to the Bookshelf book (Display a copy of the book.)

page 150—reading a chant about two best friends

page 155—making a friendship book

Ask students to notice how the characters express feelings. Then sum up what the preview reveals: *Friends share good and bad times. They share their feelings with each other.*

6 Set Your Goals Start a class mind map about friends and friendship. Prompt students for pictures or words to add, and have them act out and describe other ideas for you to put into words. Have students talk about friendship and what friendship means to them.

CLOSE AND ASSESS

Ask students to tell or show you something they are interested in learning in this unit.

UNIT 8 Mind Map

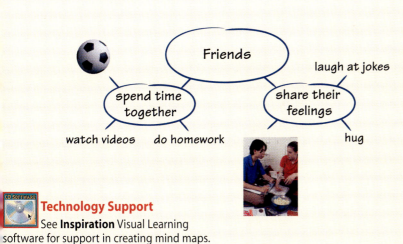

Technology Support
See **Inspiration** Visual Learning software for support in creating mind maps.

Unit Launch **T143**

UNIT 8 LESSON 2

LANGUAGE DEVELOPMENT: REGULAR PAST TENSE VERBS

OBJECTIVES

Functions: Listen Actively; Repeat Spoken Language; Recite; Describe Actions
Patterns and Structures: Regular Past Tense Verbs
Writing: Sentences

INTRODUCE

Tape 4B
CD 2 Track 6

1. **Listen and Sing** Play "Through the Years" on the **Language Tape/CD**. Students will listen and read along, then echo the lines, supply missing verbs and phrases, and finally chime in on the entire song.

2. **Learn About Past Tense Verbs** Read aloud the chart for past tense verbs and point out the -ed ending for each word. Introduce and practice the three different pronunciations for -ed: /d/ as in *learned*, /ed/ as in *started*, and /t/ as in *talked*.

PRACTICE

3. **Conduct "Express Yourself"** Model how to use past tense verbs to describe actions. Then have partners complete the activity.

> **How to Describe Actions in the Past**
> • Use a past tense verb to tell what you or someone else did in the past:
> I **finished** the race. My friends **yelled**.

APPLY

4. **Write Sentences** To spark ideas for students' sentences, ask volunteers to tell about a time they did something silly, funny, or exciting.

Distribute Partner Checklist 8 on page T310 and encourage partners to check their sentences.

▶ **Language Practice Book** page 80

CLOSE AND ASSESS

Divide students into small groups. The group members will take turns reading their sentences aloud while the rest of the group pantomimes the action.

T144 Unit 8 | Friend to Friend

REGULAR PAST TENSE VERBS

Together We Dreamed

Listen and sing.

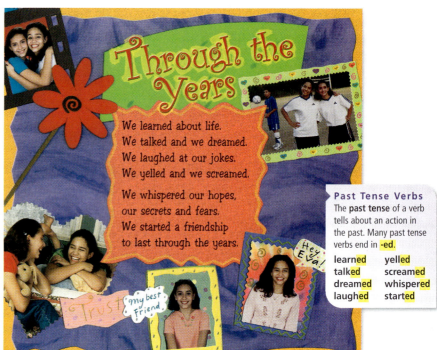

Through the Years

We learned about life.
We talked and we dreamed.
We laughed at our jokes.
We yelled and we screamed.

We whispered our hopes,
our secrets and fears.
We started a friendship
to last through the years.

Past Tense Verbs
The **past tense** of a verb tells about an action in the past. Many past tense verbs end in **-ed**.

learned	yelled
talked	screamed
dreamed	whispered
laughed	started

EXPRESS YOURSELF ▶ DESCRIBE ACTIONS

Complete each sentence. Tell what your friends did.
You can use a verb from the box above.

Example: 1. I finished the race. My friends yelled.
Sample Responses:

1. I finished the race. My friends _yelled_.
2. I danced a funny dance. My friends ____. *laughed*
3. I learned a sport. My friends _learned_ it, too.
4. I shared my dreams. My friends ____, too. *dreamed*

WRITE SENTENCES

5.–8. Write about 4 things you did. Then tell what your friends did.

Example: 5. I talked about my idea. My friends listened.
Sample Responses
Students' responses should include past tense verbs.

144 Unit 8 | Friend to Friend

REACHING ALL STUDENTS

Multi-Level Strategies

LANGUAGE DEVELOPMENT

▶ **LITERATE IN L1** Several languages, such as Chinese and Hmong, do not inflect verbs for tense. Instead, they rely on time words and phrases to give context for the past tense. A sample error might be: *I go to the store yesterday.*

To practice using past tense verbs, have a volunteer demonstrate an action and give a sentence in the present tense: *I walk to the door.* Ask another student to describe the action in the past tense: *Farida walked to the door.*

Language Practice Book page 80

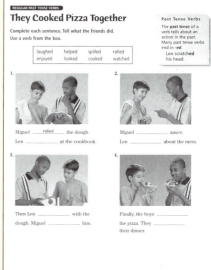

VOCABULARY: FEELINGS

How Do the Friends Feel?

Pronunciation of Names
Eva — ē vah
Sofia — sō fē ah
Miguel — mē gel

Len has lots of friends. Like all people, Len and his friends feel different at different times.

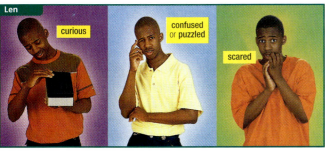

WHO'S TALKING? ▶ EXPRESS FEELINGS

1.–4. Listen.
Who is talking? Point to the correct person. Act out the scene. Tell how you feel. Use your face and body to show your feelings, too.

Answers:
1. Veronica
2. Eva
3. Eddie
4. Miguel

WRITE ABOUT FEELINGS

5.–8. Work in a group of 4. Write each feeling word on a card. Mix up the cards. Each person chooses a card and acts out the feeling. Write a sentence to tell how each person feels.

Example: 5. Nora is bored.

Language Development **145**

Language Practice Book page 81

Vocabulary
FEELING WORDS

Snapshot Poster Create a class picture dictionary by inviting students to pose for close-up shots of themselves showing one clear emotion. Arrange the photos in a grid on posterboard and invite students to label their own photo with the appropriate feeling word.

excited

UNIT 8 **LESSON 3**

LANGUAGE DEVELOPMENT: FEELINGS

OBJECTIVES
Functions: Listen Actively; Express Feelings; Demonstrate Non-Verbal Communication
Concepts and Vocabulary: 🅣 Feelings
Writing: 🅣 Sentences

INTRODUCE

1 Learn Words for Feelings Read the introduction, then point to each photo and say a sentence that uses a character's name and a feeling: *Len looks scared here. Eva feels bored.*

2 Role-Play Feeling Words Use the photos to discuss how body language, facial expressions, and gestures help express feelings. For example, point to the picture of Eva and say: *Eva's head is tilted and she is playing with her hair. She looks bored.* Then invite volunteers to pantomime a feeling word, while the other students guess which feeling is being portrayed.

PRACTICE

3 Conduct "Who's Talking?" Play "Who's Talking?" on the **Language Tape/CD**. Replay, if necessary, for students to identify each speaker. Then call on volunteers to act out each scene with dialogue and nonverbal communication.

Tape 4B
CD 2 Track 7

APPLY

4 Write About Feelings Provide sentence frames for students who need extra support:

(Name) is (feeling word).
(Name) feels (feeling word).

▶ **Language Practice Book** page 81

CLOSE AND ASSESS

Suggest common events such as receiving a letter, getting a graded test, or going to a new school. Have volunteers pantomime different responses.

Language Development **T145**

UNIT 8 **LESSON 4**

LANGUAGE DEVELOPMENT: IRREGULAR PAST TENSE VERBS

OBJECTIVES

Functions:
Describe Actions

Patterns and Structures:
- Irregular Past Tense Verbs (*was, were*)

Writing: Sentences

INTRODUCE

1 Learn About Irregular Past Tense Verbs Read the title and introduction. Explain that some verbs do not use *-ed* to form the past tense. Direct students' attention to the photo, and go over the skill box. Explain that *was* is the past tense form of *am* or *is,* and that *were* is the past tense form of *are.* Use the example sentences to introduce the constructions *there was* and *there were.*

PRACTICE

2 Build Sentences Direct students' attention to the photo and explain that Items 1–9 describe the scene with present tense verbs. Work through the Example to model changing a sentence to past tense. Then have partners work together to revise and say the sentences.

APPLY

3 Write Sentences Remind students to use the skill box and verb chart for help in choosing the correct verb.

▶ Language Practice Book page 82

CLOSE AND ASSESS

Provide cards with *was* and *were* on different sides. Read aloud a sentence from Items 1–9. Have students hold up their cards to display the correct past tense form. Then lead the group in saying the past tense sentence.

T146 Unit 8 | Friend to Friend

IRREGULAR PAST TENSE VERBS: *WAS* AND *WERE*

Were the Friends Happy?

Use *was* and *were* to tell about the past.

Pronoun	Verb	Example
I	was	I **was** happy.
you	were	You **were** excited.
he, she, it	was	He **was** proud.
we	were	We **were** the winning team!
they	were	They **were** good losers, though.

Use *There was* for one person or thing.
Use *There were* for two or more.

There was one girl on their team.
There were two girls on our team.

BUILD SENTENCES

Read each sentence. Change the <u>underlined</u> verb to the past tense. Say the new sentence.

Example: 1. We were at my house.

Present	Past
is	was
are	were

1. We <u>are</u> at my house.   were
2. We <u>are</u> on the sofa.   were
3. The sofa <u>is</u> too small for all of us.   was
4. Len <u>is</u> on the floor.   was
5. Veronica <u>is</u> on the floor, too.   was
6. There <u>are</u> no pillows to sit on.   were
7. Len and Veronica <u>are</u> mad.   were
8. Finally, there <u>is</u> food to eat!   was
9. We <u>are</u> all happy again.   were

WRITE SENTENCES

10.–14. Write 5 sentences about the past. Tell about a day with your friends. Use *was* and *were.*

Example: 10. Yesterday I was at the library.
11. A lot of my friends were there, too.

146 Unit 8 | Friend to Friend

REACHING ALL STUDENTS

Language Practice Book page 82

NEGATIVE SENTENCES AND CONTRACTIONS WITH *NOT*

The Friends Didn't Scare Len!

There are different ways to build negative sentences in the past tense.

Add the word *not* after *was* and *were*.
  Len **was not** scared.
  Eddie and Miguel **were not** happy.

With other verbs, add *did not* before the verb.
  The trick work~~ed~~. (did not inserted before "worked")

> When you add *did not* to a sentence, take the *-ed* off the main verb.

BUILD SENTENCES

Read the sentences in number 1. Then answer the questions in number 2. Say your answer in a complete sentence. Use *did not*, *was not*, or *were not*.

Example: **2.** They did not trick Sofia.

1. The friends tricked Veronica.
   They were proud!
   The snake jumped out.
   Veronica was afraid.
   She screamed.

2. Did the friends trick Sofia?
   Were they proud?
   Did the snake jump out?
   Was Sofia afraid?
   Did she scream?

Answers:
2. They did not trick Sofia.
   They were not proud.
   The snake did not jump out.
   Sofia was not afraid.
   She did not scream.

WRITE SENTENCES

3.–7. Write each sentence you made above. Then write it again. Use contractions to replace *did not*, *was not*, and *were not*.

Example: **3.** They did not trick Sofia.
         They didn't trick Sofia.

Answers:
Students' sentences should include the following contractions:
3. didn't   5. didn't   7. didn't
4. weren't 6. wasn't

Contractions
did + not = didn't
was + not = wasn't
were + not = weren't

Language Development 147

Language Practice Book page 83

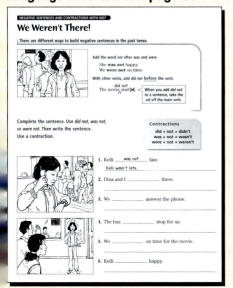

Multi-Level Strategies
LANGUAGE DEVELOPMENT

LITERATE IN L1 Most languages place negative markers consistently either before or after the verb. It is rare for a language to vary the placement in different constructions. To reinforce this basic English skill, turn to page 145 and have students make word cards for each character's name, each feeling, and the words *and*, *was*, *were*, *did*, *not*, *didn't*, *wasn't*, and *weren't*. Partners can use the cards to create sentences: *Eva was not proud. Eva and Sofia weren't excited. Sofia didn't like the joke.*

UNIT 8 **LESSON 5**

LANGUAGE DEVELOPMENT: NEGATIVE SENTENCES

OBJECTIVES

Functions:
Describe Actions

Patterns and Structures: 🅣 Negative Sentences; 🅣 Contractions with *not*

Writing: 🅣 Sentences

INTRODUCE

1 Learn About Negative Sentences and Contractions with *Not* Discuss the photo and explain that Len is holding a "trick" or "joke" can: when someone opens it, a toy snake pops out to surprise the person.

Then read the rules and examples aloud, pausing to point out the position of the word *not* in each sentence. Use additional sample sentences to reinforce the skill:

> did not
> The boys ^ laugh~~ed~~.
>
>   not
> The joke was ^ funny.

PRACTICE

2 Build Sentences Point to the first picture and read about what happened when the boys tricked Veronica. Then point to the second picture and explain that the trick did not work on Sofia. Work through the Example and have students complete the sentences.

APPLY

3 Write Sentences Point out the process for forming contractions. Model the Example and have partners write their sentence pairs.

▶ **Language Practice Book** page 83

CLOSE AND ASSESS

Display the sentences from the skills box. Call on students to rewrite each sentence using a contraction.

Language Development **T147**

UNIT 8 **LESSON 6**

LANGUAGE AND LITERACY: THE BASICS BOOKSHELF

OBJECTIVES
Concepts and Vocabulary: 🅣 Feelings
Listening: Listen to a Preview
Reading Strategies: Activate Prior Knowledge; Preview
Learning to Read: Identify Dialogue

BUILD LANGUAGE AND VOCABULARY

1. **Teach "Words to Know"** Have students study the photos on pages 2–3. Say: *These pages show words about feelings. Everyone has feelings.*

   Use the pictures to describe each feeling word on pages 2–3. For example, point to the first photo and say: *The girl is angry. The boy broke her glasses. The boy is sorry. He does not want his friend to be angry.*

2. **Role-Play Feelings** Model how to express feelings by using gestures, facial expressions, and sentences that contain the verbs *was* and *felt*. For example, frown as you say *I felt sad when my aunt left.* Ask students to role-play more feelings using non-verbal communication and these patterns: *I felt ___ when ___. I was ___ when ___.*

PREPARE TO READ

3. **Think About What You Know** Invite students to discuss friendship. Then ask what they would do if they were upset about something a friend said or did.

4. **Preview** Play the Audio Walk-Through for *Friends Are Like That* on the **Selection Tape/CD** to give students the overall idea of the story.

CLOSE AND ASSESS
Have volunteers take the roles of Eddie, Veronica, and Eva and role-play or tell how each character felt about events in the story.

T148a Unit 8 | Friend to Friend

Friends Are Like That
by Daphne Liu

Summary This fictional journal focuses on friendship and communication. Veronica's life is perfect until she suspects her best friend, Eva, of liking the boy she likes. The two girls talk and Veronica discovers that Eva and Eddie were planning her birthday surprise. Simple text reinforces feeling words.

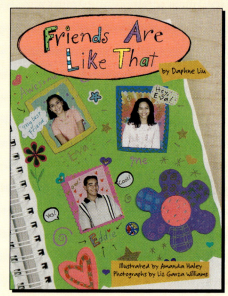
Cover

Pages 2–3

Multi-Level Strategies
LITERACY SUPPORT

PRELITERATE **Concepts of Print: Identify Dialogue** Read the book through page 14. On page 15, trace the outline of the speech balloon as you say: *This is a speech balloon. The end of the balloon points to the picture of Eva. The words inside tell what Eva says to Veronica.* On pages 16–23, ask volunteers to identify the dialogue in the speech balloons, then tell who is talking and to whom.

Point out to the quotation marks on page 24. Say: *Quotation marks are another way to show what someone says. The first quotation mark shows when someone starts talking. The last quotation mark shows when the person stops talking. The words in between are the words the person says.*

Have trios take the roles of Veronica, Eva, and Eddie. Invite them to echo read the dialogue in the book as you read the narration aloud.

Friends Are Like That

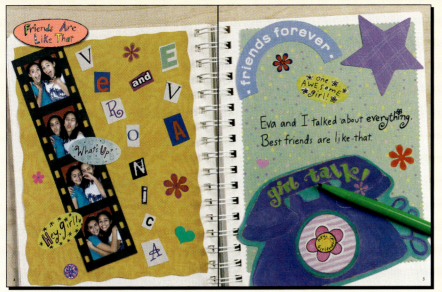

Pages 4–5

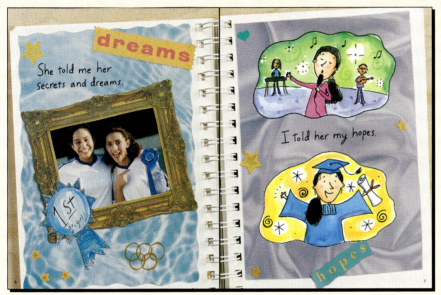

Pages 6–7

Strategies for Comprehensible Input

Page	Story Language	Strategy Options
4–5	Best friends are like that.	**Restate:** Good friends talk about everything.
6–7	secrets	**Explain:** Secrets are ideas or thoughts you don't want many people to know.
	dreams	**Restate:** the things she wants to do in the future
	my hopes	**Restate:** the things I want to do

Language and Literacy T148b

UNIT 8 **LESSON 6,** CONTINUED

LANGUAGE AND LITERACY: THE BASICS BOOKSHELF

OBJECTIVES

Function: Listen to a Book
Critical Thinking and Comprehension: Identify Cause and Effect

READ AND THINK TOGETHER

1 Read Aloud On your first reading of the book, use the "Strategies for Comprehensible Input" that appear at the bottom of pages T148b, T148d, and T148f.

2 Read and Map: Identify Cause and Effect Draw a cause-and-effect chart like the one below, but with the cause-and-effect columns empty. Say: *A cause-and-effect chart shows what happens and why it happens.*

Read pages 4–9 aloud. Then think aloud to model connecting ideas in the story: *In this part of the story, I learn that Eva and Veronica talk a lot and share their dreams. They do that because they are best friends.* Then model filling in the first row: *Under* Cause, *I will write* Eva and Veronica are best friends. *What happens because of their friendship? In the* Effects *column I will write* They talk a lot. *That is what happens because they are best friends.*

Pause after reading each set of pages shown below and model completing the cause-and-effect chart for the rest of the text.

Pages 8–9

Pages 10–11

Cause-and-Effect Chart for *Friends Are Like That*

	Cause	Effect
pages 4–9	Eva and Veronica are best friends.	They talk about everything.
pages 10–13	Veronica saw Eva walking with Eddie.	Veronica felt betrayed and jealous. She didn't talk to Eva.
pages 14–21	Eva asked Veronica to tell her what was wrong.	They talked about friendship and trust.
pages 22–24	Veronica found out that Eva had helped Eddie choose her gift.	Veronica felt foolish. She apologized.

Technology Support
See **Inspiration** Visual Learning software for support in creating the cause-and-effect chart.

T148c Unit 8 | Friend to Friend

Friends Are Like That, CONTINUED

Pages 12–13

Pages 14–15

Strategies for Comprehensible Input

Page	Story Language	Strategy Options
8–9	cute	**Restate:** good-looking
	Life was perfect.	**Restate:** My life was just the way I wanted it.
10–11	betrayed	**Explain:** When a friend does something to hurt you or make you upset, you feel betrayed.
	jealous	**Explain:** When you are jealous, you think your friend likes someone else more than you.
	didn't	**Explain:** *Didn't* is a short way to say *Did not*.
12–13	birthday	**Explain:** Your birthday is the day you were born.
14–15	house	**Point to the picture.**
	Tell me what is wrong.	**Restate:** Tell me why you are mad.

Language and Literacy T148d

UNIT 8 **LESSON 6,** CONTINUED

LANGUAGE AND LITERACY: THE BASICS BOOKSHELF

OBJECTIVES

Functions: Listen to a Book; Role-Play; Read Aloud a Story (choral reading)

READ AND THINK TOGETHER, CONTINUED

3. **Conduct Interactive Readings**
   Choose from these options:

   - **Role-Play** Ask three volunteers to play the characters in the story. Have the characters pantomime the scenes as the rest of the class reads along with the recording of *Friends Are Like That* on the **Selection Tape/CD**.

   Tape 4B
   CD 2 Track 4

   - **Choral reading** Divide the class into two groups. As you read the narration aloud, have one group read Eva's dialogue while the other group reads Veronica's dialogue.

CLOSE AND ASSESS

Divide the class into small groups. Have them retell the story to the class in a round-robin format. The first student tells something from the beginning of the story, the second student tells the next event, and so forth. Continue until the entire story is completed.

Pages 16–17

Pages 18–19

Multi-Level Strategies

LITERACY SUPPORT

LITERATE IN L1 **Read with a Partner/ Write a Class Thank-You Note**
After students have participated in the interactive readings, encourage them to read the story with a partner. Distribute the Partner Prompts on page T311 to help partners work together to identify unfamiliar words and unlock their meanings, then read the text to each other. After the partner reading, work with students to write a thank-you note from Veronica to Eva or Eddie. Prepare a large chart paper with the greeting *Dear* _____, and the closing *Sincerely, Veronica.* Encourage students to include Veronica's thoughts and feelings. As students dictate the letter, pause to ask them how to spell words they have previously learned.

INTERRUPTED SCHOOLING **Identify Cause and Effect** To anchor understanding of the skill, use chart paper to list cause-and-effect pairs. For example: *Veronica was angry with Eva. Veronica did not talk to Eva for days.* Read the sentence pairs aloud. Then ask volunteers to label each sentence as a *cause* or an *effect*.

T148e Unit 8 | Friend to Friend

Friends Are Like That, CONTINUED

Pages 20–21

Pages 22–23

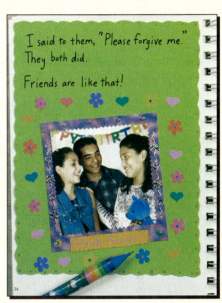

Page 24

Strategies for Comprehensible Input

Page	Story Language	Strategy Options
20–21	hours	**Demonstrate:** Show the hour indicators on a clock.
22–23	I promised not to tell.	**Restate:** I said that I would not let you know; I said I would keep it a secret.
	foolish	**Explain:** When you feel foolish, you feel silly and embarrassed.
24	Please forgive me.	**Explain:** When you ask someone to forgive you, you say that you are sorry for doing something wrong.

Language and Literacy **T148f**

UNIT 8 LESSON 7

LANGUAGE AND LITERACY: THE BASICS BOOKSHELF

OBJECTIVES

Function: Retell a Story
Learning Strategy: Use Graphic Organizers (cause-and-effect chart)
Critical Thinking and Comprehension: Identify Cause and Effect

CHECK COMPREHENSION

1 Make a Cause-and-Effect Chart
Have students review *Friends Are Like That* to identify causes and effects. Remind them that a cause-and-effect chart shows things that happen and why they happen.

After you read aloud the directions for Step 1, pause for students to add the effects to the chart. To identify the effect, encourage students to ask themselves: *What happened?*

2 Retell the Story Write each cause and effect on a separate index card. Distribute all cards. Have students match the causes and effects. Then start with students holding the first cause and effect cards and have the class retell the story in order.

CLOSE AND ASSESS

Ask students to complete this sentence:
A cause-and-effect chart shows _____.

COMPREHENSION: IDENTIFY CAUSE AND EFFECT

Read and Think Together

Make a cause-and-effect chart for *Friends Are Like That*. Follow these steps.

1 Copy the following cause-and-effect chart. Think about the story. Write the effect next to each cause.

Wording may vary.

Cause	Effect
Eva and Veronica are best friends.	They talk about everything.
Veronica saw Eva walking with Eddie.	Veronica felt betrayed and jealous. She didn't talk to Eva.
Eva asked Veronica to tell her what was wrong.	They talked about friendship and trust.
Veronica found out that Eva had helped Eddie choose her gift.	Veronica felt foolish. She apologized.

2 Use your completed chart to retell the story to a partner.

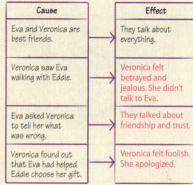

from The Basics Bookshelf

THEME BOOK
Veronica invites you to read her diary. Find out how she learned to trust her best friend.

148 Unit 8 | Friend to Friend

REACHING ALL STUDENTS

Language Development
MAKE AND ACCEPT AN APOLOGY

Role-Play Reread page 24 and explain that when Veronica says, "Please forgive me," she is making an apology. Model how to make and accept an apology:

Veronica: I'm sorry I didn't trust you, Eva. I apologize.

Eva: That's okay. I accept your apology.

Use the chart to present other suitable language. Then invite students to role-play the conversation in which Veronica apologizes and Eddie or Eva accepts the apology. Encourage students to use non-verbal communication as they perform.

Make an Apology	Accept an Apology
I'm sorry.	That's okay.
I apologize.	I accept your apology.
Please forgive me.	I forgive you.
I really didn't mean it.	I know. We can be friends again.

HIGH FREQUENCY WORDS

Words to Know

REVIEW WORDS YOU KNOW

Read the words aloud. Which word goes in the sentence?

which	watch
around	always
Sometimes	Something

1. The boys will <u>watch</u> a movie.
2. They <u>always</u> buy popcorn at the movies.
3. _____ they get cold drinks, too.   Sometimes

LEARN TO READ

Learn new words.

saw	Last week I **saw** a movie.
was	I **was** sitting in the first row.
were	A lot of kids from school **were** there.
their	Some kids came with **their** mothers and fathers.
said	"Look, there's Sofia," I **said** to my dad.
began	They shut off the lights, and the movie **began**.
about	The movie was **about** some kids in the 1950s.
dance	I watched them **dance** to old music.
thought	My dad **thought** the music was great.
again	We want to see that movie **again** next week.

How to Learn a New Word
- Look at the word.
- Listen to the word.
- Listen to the word in a sentence. What does it mean?
- Say the word.
- Spell the word.
- Say the word again.

WORD WORK

Write each sentence. Add the missing word.   Example: 4. My friends were at school the next day.

4. My friends <u>w e r e</u> at school the next day.
5. I asked them what they <u>t h o u g h t</u> of the movie.
6. "It <u>w a s</u> good!" Sofia <u>s a i d</u>. "My mom and dad can <u>d a n c e</u> like that."
7. "All <u>t h e i r</u> friends dance like that, too."
8. Math class <u>b e g a n</u>, and we sat down.
9. Then Ms. Jong said something <u>a b o u t</u> the movie.
10. She said, "I <u>s a w</u> that movie when I was in sixth grade!"
11. "It will be fun to see it <u>a g a i n</u> with my children!"

Pronunciation of Name
Jong   jong

Language and Literacy   149

Reading Practice Book page 67

HIGH FREQUENCY WORDS
Words to Know
READ AND WRITE
Read each word. Then write it.

1. saw   2. was   3. again
4. their 5. were   6. about
7. said   8. began 9. dance
10. thought

WORD WORK
Write the answer to each question. Find the new words in the box. Write the words on the lines.

11. Which 2 words start with **a**?
    again _about_
12. Which 2 words have 3 letters?
13. Which word rhymes with **red**?
14. Which word rhymes with **her**?
15. Which word means "started"?
16. Which word is the past tense of **think**?
17. Which word is the past tense of **see**?
18. Which 5 words have 5 letters each?
19. Which word means "once more"?
20. Which 3 words have 2 syllables?

Reading Fluency
RECOGNIZE HIGH FREQUENCY WORDS

To build automaticity with the new high frequency words:

- Ask volunteers to look at the classroom chart of words, choose a word on it, and begin spelling it. The rest of the group should try to guess the word in as few letters as possible.
- Have partners or small groups challenge one another to find high frequency words in classroom books, including *Friends Are Like That*.

UNIT 8 LESSON 8

LANGUAGE AND LITERACY: HIGH FREQUENCY WORDS

OBJECTIVES
Learning to Read:
① Recognize High Frequency Words

REVIEW WORDS

1 Review Known High Frequency Words Have the group read aloud the words in the green box. Listen for words students cannot read automatically and use the steps in the yellow box to reteach those words. Then have students look at the photo. Read each cloze sentence. Reread each sentence and pause for students to silently read the two words to the left of the sentence. Tell students to choose the word that goes in the sentence and tells about the picture.

INTRODUCE NEW WORDS

2 Learn High Frequency Words Use the High Frequency Word Script on page T319 to lead students through the steps in the yellow box.

Review the homonyms *their*, *there*, and *they're*.

PRACTICE

3 Conduct "Word Work" Model how to use sentence context to find words in the list that make sense, and then use the number of letter blanks to choose the correct word or confirm it.

Have groups complete Items 5–11. Then discuss how the correct word matches the context and number of blanks.

APPLY

4 Read Words in Context Students will read high frequency words in context in the sentences on page 151 and the passage on page 152.

▶ **Reading Practice Book** page 67

CLOSE AND ASSESS

Call out the high frequency words one at a time. Have students point to them and spell the words as a group.

Language and Literacy **T149**

UNIT 8 LESSON 9

LANGUAGE AND LITERACY: PHONICS

OBJECTIVES

Learning to Read: Build Oral Vocabulary; Develop Phonemic Awareness; Associate Sounds and Symbols /d/ -ed; /t/ -ed; /ed/ -ed; Listen for the Sound of -ed; Blend Sounds to Decode Words

TEACH SOUNDS FOR -ed

1. **Build Oral Vocabulary** Display Transparency 46. Talk through each picture to develop meaning for the words ending in -ed. For example, for Item 2, say:

   • *This boy* (point) **ripped** *his sleeve* (dramatize). *When something rips, it tears* (demonstrate with paper). *I wonder how the boy* **ripped** *his sleeve.*

2. **Develop Phonemic Awareness** Remove the transparency and conduct the oral activities in Step 1 of the Script for Transparency 46.

3. **Listen to and Read Words with -ed** Display Transparency 46 again. Work through Steps 2 and 3 of the script.

CLOSE AND ASSESS

Say the words *ripped, planned, picked,* and *waited.* Call on students to count the syllables in each word and to identify the sound(s) they hear at the end of the word.

Transparency 46: ▶
Sounds for -ed

▼ Script for Transparency 46

Verbs with -ed

1. Develop Phonemic Awareness
Count Syllables in Words Say: *You can tell how many syllables, or parts, a word has by the number of vowel sounds. Listen to this word:* rubbed. *Clap the syllable with me as we say* rubbed: rubbed. *(clap) Now listen to this word:* planted. *Clap the two syllables with me as we say* planted: plant-ed. *(clap, clap) Lead students in saying and clapping syllables for these words:* picked, ripped, waited, flipped, landed, lifted. *Then have students count the syllables in the words. If students miscount, lead them in clapping the syllables again.*

2. Associate Sounds and Symbols/Listen for the Sound of -ed
Point to the first picture on **Transparency 46.** Say: *This cat rubbed* (pantomime) *the boy's leg with its body. Say the word* rubbed *with me.* Then point to the -ed in *rubbed* and say: *We add the letters* -ed *to words to tell about something that happened in the past. In this word, the letters* -ed *make the sound* /d/: rubbed. Have students repeat the word, emphasizing the final sound. Repeat for *picked,* pointing out that the letters -ed make the sound /t/. For *planted,* point out that the letters -ed make two sounds: /ed/, and that *planted* has two syllables, *plant* and -ed.

3. Blend Sounds to Read Words
Teach Point to *planted* and read the word, noting that the letters -ed make the sounds /ed/. Then lead students in blending the sounds of the root word and adding /ed/ to say the whole word. Repeat for *picked* with -ed as /t/ and *rubbed* with -ed as /d/.

Practice For Item 1, say: *Let's try that again. This picture shows a boy and girl. The girl tapped his shoulder* (act out and read the sentence): *She tapped me.* Then read *tapped* again, noting that the letters -ed make the sound /t/. Lead students in blending the root word and adding /t/ to say the whole word. Repeat the process for the other verbs with -ed.

T150a Unit 8 | Friend to Friend

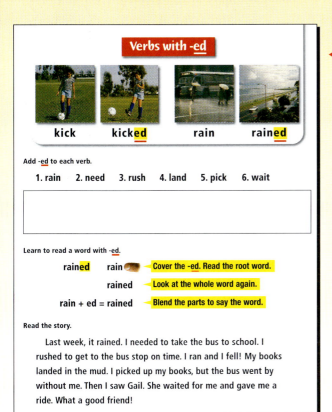

◀ Transparency 47: Verb Endings

▼ Script for Transparency 47

Verbs with -ed

1. **Develop Phonemic Awareness**
   Contrast/Isolate Final Sounds Say: *Listen to these two words:* kick, kicked. *Listen again: I kick the ball every day. I kicked the ball yesterday. Are the words* kick *and* kicked *the same?* Repeat: *kick, kicked.* (no) Explain: *The second word,* kicked, *has an extra sound at the end. What is it?* (/t/) Repeat for *play* and *played,* using these sentences: *We play soccer after school. Yesterday we played two games.* (The extra sound is /d/.) Then repeat for *need* and *needed: I need some paper. Yesterday I needed a pen.* (The two extra sounds are /ed/.)

2. **Learn to Spell Past Tense Verbs**
   Point to *kick* on **Transparency 47**. Say: *Look at her kick the ball!* Then point to *kicked* and say: *She kicked the ball away.* Explain: *You can hear a difference between* kick *and* kicked, *and you can see a difference, too.* Cover the *-ed* in *kicked,* and say: *Here is the root word* kick. *It has one vowel and then two consonants,* ck. Uncover *-ed.* Say: *For words like* kick *that end in two consonants, you just add* -ed *to the root.* Follow a similar process for *rain,* pointing out that the ending *-ed* is added directly to words that have two vowels and then a consonant. Then use letter tiles to spell and model the pronunciation of the past tense of the verbs in Items 1–6.

3. **Learn to Read Past Tense Verbs**
   Teach Point to *rained* in the Example and say: *This word ends with* -ed. *To read the word, cover the* -ed. *Read the root word:* rain. *Look at the whole word again. Blend the parts to say the word. I'll say* /d/ *at the end:* /r ā n d/, *rained. That sounds right.*

   Practice Read the story. Pause before each word ending in *-ed.* Ask students to read the word. If they need help, have them cover the *-ed* and apply the strategy. After students read each word ending in *-ed,* ask them to check that the word makes sense in the sentence.

OBJECTIVES

Learning to Read: Build Oral Vocabulary; Develop Phonemic Awareness; Identify Verb Endings (-ed); ❶ Decode Words with Endings

TEACH VERB ENDINGS

1. **Build Oral Vocabulary** Pantomime or restate the meanings of each verb on Transparency 47. For example:
   - **kick:** Say: *I can kick.* Then kick your leg three times and say: *I kicked three times.*
   - **rain:** Point to the last picture and say: *It rained in the morning. Now everything is wet.*

2. **Develop Phonemic Awareness** Conduct the oral activities in Step 1 of the Script for Transparency 47.

3. **Learn to Spell and Read Past Tense Verbs** Display Transparency 47 again. Work through Steps 2 and 3 of the script.

CLOSE AND ASSESS

Display the verbs *rush, rain, pick,* and *need.* Have groups each write the past tense of one verb and read it to the class.

▶ **Reading Practice Book** page 68 (Verb Ending *-ed:* no root change)

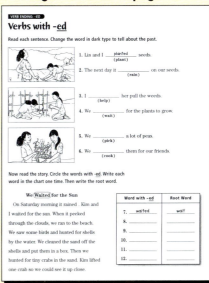

Reading Practice Book page 68

Language and Literacy **T150b**

UNIT 8 **LESSON 9,** CONTINUED

LANGUAGE AND LITERACY: WORD STRUCTURE

OBJECTIVES
Learning to Read: Build Oral Vocabulary; Develop Phonemic Awareness; Identify Verb Endings (-ed); 🅣 Decode Words with Endings

TEACH VERB ENDINGS

1 Build Oral Vocabulary Pantomime or restate the meaning of each verb on Transparency 48. For example:

- **hop:** Say: *I will hop.* Then hop a few times and say: *I hopped.*

- **grab:** As you grab a pencil, say: *I am grabbing a pencil.* Hold the pencil and say: *I grabbed the pencil.*

2 Develop Phonemic Awareness Conduct the oral activities in Step 1 of the Script for Transparency 48.

3 Learn to Spell and Read Past Tense Verbs Display Transparency 48 again. Work through Steps 2 and 3 of the script.

CLOSE AND ASSESS
Display the verbs *hop, slip, grab,* and *clap.* Have groups each write the past tense of one verb and read it to the class.

Transparency 48: ▶
Verb Endings

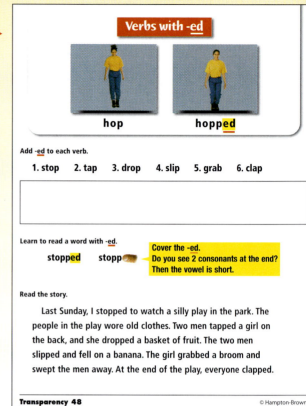

Materials
Letter tiles for:

a	b	b	c
d	d	e	g
i	l	o	p
p	r	s	t

▼ **Script for Transparency 48**

Verbs with -ed

1. Develop Phonemic Awareness
Contrast/Isolate Final Sounds Say: *Listen to these two words:* walk, walked. *Listen again:* I walk to school every day. I walked to the park yesterday. *Are the words* walk *and* walked *the same?* Repeat: walk, walked. (no) Explain: *The second word,* walked, *has an extra sound at the end. What is it?* (/t/) Repeat for *jog* and *jogged,* using these sentences: *We jog to school. Yesterday we jogged to school together.* (The extra sound is /d/.) Then repeat for *pat* and *patted. We pat our dog a lot. Yesterday we patted the dog before we left.* (The two extra sounds are /ed/.)

2. Learn to Spell Past Tense Verbs
Point to *hop* **on Transparency 48.** Say: *Look at her hop!* Then point to *hopped* and say: *She hopped up in the air and came back down.* Explain: *You can hear a difference between* hop *and* hopped, *and you can see a difference, too.* Cover the *ped* in *hopped,* and say: *Here is the root word* hop. *It has one vowel and then one consonant, the* p. *For a word like* hop, *you need to repeat the last consonant before you add* -ed. Uncover *ped.* Point to the second *p* in *hopped.* Then use letter tiles to spell and model the pronunciation of the past tense of the verbs in Items 1–6.

3. Learn to Read Past Tense Verbs
Teach Point to *stopped* in the Example and say: *This word ends with* -ed. *To read the word, cover the* -ed. *Look at the letters just before the* -ed. *Do you see two consonants, like the* pp *here? If so, the vowel in the root word is short. Sound it out:* /stooop/, stop. *Then uncover the ending and blend it with* stop *to read the whole word:* stopped. Explain that when you read the word, you say the sound /p/ only one time.

Practice Read the story. Pause before each word ending in -ed. Ask students to read the word. If they need help, have them cover the -ed and apply the strategy. After students read each word ending in -ed, ask them to check that the word makes sense in the sentence.

T150c Unit 8 | Friend to Friend

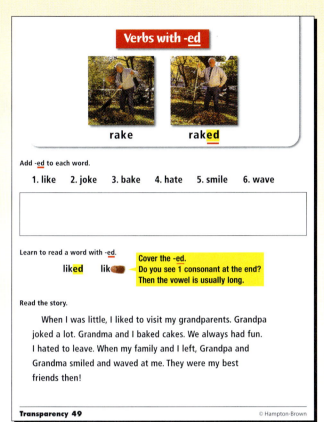

◀ Transparency 49: Verb Endings

Materials
Letter tiles for: a b d e h i j k l m o s t v w

▼ Script for Transparency 49

Verbs with -ed

1. Develop Phonemic Awareness
Contrast/Isolate Final Sounds Say: *Listen to these two words:* rake, raked. *Listen again:* I rake leaves every week. Yesterday I raked the leaves into a big pile. *Are the words* rake *and* raked *the same? Repeat:* rake, raked. (no) Explain: *The second word,* raked, *has an extra sound at the end. What is it?* (/t/) Repeat for *smile* and *smiled*, using these sentences: *I smile a lot. Yesterday I smiled at everyone.* (The extra sound is /d/.) Then repeat for *hate* and *hated*: *I hate cold weather. Yesterday I hated the cold wind.* (The two extra sounds are /ed/.)

2. Learn to Spell Past Tense Verbs
Point to *rake* on **Transparency 49**. Say: *Look at him rake the leaves!* Then point to *raked* and say: *He raked the leaves into a big pile.* Explain: *You can hear a difference between* rake *and* raked, *and you can see a difference, too.* Point to *rake* and say: *The word* rake *has one long vowel followed by a consonant and an* e *at the end.* Cover the *-ed* in *raked*, and say: *Here is what happens to the root word* rake *when the ending* -ed *is added to it. The final* e *is dropped before the ending* -ed *is added to the root.* Uncover the *-ed*, and say: *For words like* rake *that have a long vowel sound and a silent* e, *you need to drop the final* e *before you add the ending* -ed *to the root.* Then use letter tiles to spell and model the pronunciation of the past tense of the verbs in Items 1–6.

3. Learn to Read Past Tense Verbs
Teach Point to *liked* in the Example and say: *This word ends with* -ed. *To read the word, cover the* -ed. *Look at the letters just before the* -ed. *Do you see one consonant at the end? Then the vowel is usually long. Sound it out:* /l ī ī ī k/. *Then uncover the ending and blend it with* like *to read the whole word:* liked.

Practice Read the story. Pause before each word ending in *-ed*. Ask students to read the word. If they need help, have them cover the *-ed* and apply the strategy. After students read each word ending in *-ed*, ask them to check that the word makes sense in the sentence.

OBJECTIVES
Learning to Read: Build Oral Vocabulary; Develop Phonemic Awareness; Identify Verb Endings (*-ed*); ⓣ Decode Words with Endings

TEACH VERB ENDINGS

1 Build Oral Vocabulary Pantomime or restate the meaning of each verb on Transparency 49. For example:

- **rake:** Say: *I rake the leaves.* Then pantomime raking leaves, stop, and say: *I raked the leaves.*
- **wave:** Say: *I wave at my friends.* Pantomime waving, then stop and say: *I waved at my friends.*

2 Develop Phonemic Awareness Conduct the oral activities in Step 1 of the Script for Transparency 49.

3 Learn to Spell and Read Past Tense Verbs Display Transparency 49 again. Work through Steps 2 and 3 of the script.

CLOSE AND ASSESS
Display the verbs *like, joke, smile,* and *wave*. Have groups each write the past tense of one verb and read it to the class.

▶ **Reading Practice Book** page 69 (Verb Ending *-ed*: double consonant, drop final *e*)

Reading Practice Book page 69

Language and Literacy **T150d**

UNIT 8 LESSON 10

LANGUAGE AND LITERACY: READING AND SPELLING

OBJECTIVES

Functions: Listen Actively; Repeat Spoken Language; Recite

Learning to Read: Develop Phonemic Awareness; Associate Sounds and Symbols /d/ -ed; /t/ -ed; /ed/ -ed; Listen for the Sound of -ed; Identify Verb Endings (-ed); ❶ Decode Words with Endings

Spelling: ❶ Verb Ending -ed

LISTEN AND LEARN

Tape 4B / CD 2 Track 8

1. **Recite a Chant** Display Transparency 50 and play "Best Friends" on the **Language Tape/CD**.

DEVELOP PHONEMIC AWARENESS

2. **Isolate Final Sounds** Say: *Listen to this word:* hugged. *What sound do you hear at the end of* hugged? (/d/) Follow the same procedure with *picked.* (/t/) Continue the activity with the words *ripped, rubbed, planned, rained, kicked,* and *liked.* Then say: *What two sounds do you hear at the end of* needed? (/e/ + /d/) Repeat for *planted, landed,* and *waited.*

STUDY VERB ENDINGS

3. **Verb Ending: -ed** Say: *For some verbs you just add* -ed *to the root word to tell about the past. Read these words with me.* Point to each part as you go through the equation: Wish *plus* ed *equals* wished. Repeat for *need.* Follow a similar process for *smile* and *hug.* Remind students that verbs with a long vowel that end in silent *e* drop the *e* before adding -ed, and that verbs that end in a short vowel and one consonant double the final consonant before adding -ed.

Afterwards, play the chant again. Have students identify words with -ed. Discuss the spelling patterns.

T150 Unit 8 | Friend to Friend

VERB ENDING: -ED

Reading and Spelling

LISTEN AND LEARN

Best Friends

My best friend had a bracelet.
I wanted a bracelet, too.
I wished,
I hoped,
I waited,
But my wish did not come true.

My friend gave me a bracelet.
I didn't know she knew!
I smiled,
She laughed,
We hugged.
That's just
what best friends do.

STUDY VERB ENDINGS

For some verbs, you can just add **-ed**.	This verb ends in silent **e**.	This verb ends in one vowel and one consonant.
wish + ed = wished	smile	hug
need + ed = needed	When you add **-ed**, drop the e.	When you add **-ed**, double the consonant.
	smil~~e~~ + ed = smiled	hug**g**ed

150 Unit 8 | Friend to Friend ▶ Transparencies 46–50

REACHING ALL STUDENTS

Multi-Level Strategies

LITERACY SUPPORT

INTERRUPTED SCHOOLING To anchor understanding of the different pronunciations of the ending *-ed*, distribute index cards with verbs ending in *-ed* such as *used, liked, ended*. Across the board, write the headings: *Sound* d; *Sound* t; *Sounds* ed. Call on students to read the word on their card, identify its end sound or sounds, and place it in the correct category.

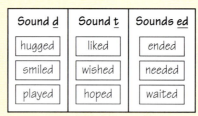

Sound d	Sound t	Sounds ed
hugged	liked	ended
smiled	wished	needed
played	hoped	waited

READING STRATEGY

Follow these steps to read a word with -ed.

1. Look for the ending you know. Cover it.

   lift**ed**

   lift

2. Look for vowel and consonant patterns to sound out the root word.

   lift   l + i + f + t = lift

   I see two consonants after the vowel i, so the i is short.

3. Look at the entire word again. Blend the root word and the ending to read the word.

   lift + ed = lifted

   Blend lift and ed to say the word lifted.

Reading Help

There are three different sounds for **-ed**.

1. The sound for *d*

   waved   hugged
   smiled   rained

2. The sound for *t*

   picked   liked
   wished   hoped

3. The sound for *ed*

   waited   ended
   needed   melted

Say each word. Which group has words with two syllables?

READING AND SPELLING PRACTICE

Use what you learned to read the sentences.

1. Eddie hated to be sick. He was so bored!
2. He needed something to do.
3. He picked a book to read and flipped through it.
4. Just then, Eddie saw Len at his window.
5. Eddie waved. "I'm so glad you stopped by!" he said.

6.–9. Now write the sentences that your teacher reads. For dictation sentences, see Step 6 at right.

WORD WORK

10.–15. Read these words. Then write each word on a card. Match the 6 pairs that go together. What do you notice?

waited	need	wait
rub	hope	liked
hoped	like	needed
rip	rubbed	ripped

Example:

10. rub   rubbed

I double the b when I add -ed.

Answers:
10. rub   rubbed
11. rip   ripped
When a verb ends in one consonant and one vowel, the consonant doubles.

12. hope   hoped
13. like   liked
When a verb ends in silent **e**, you drop the e and then add **-ed**.

14. need   needed
15. wait   waited
For some verbs, you just add **-ed**.

Language and Literacy 151

Decodable Book
PRACTICE WITH VERB ENDING -ED

Decodable Book 8: *About Duke*

Assign **Decodable Book 8** for independent reading. The **Decodable Book** can be used in a variety of ways to help students become more fluent, automatic readers:

Discussion Circles Have students work in small groups to read aloud and discuss the book using the questions on the back cover. Encourage students to read aloud the text that supports their answers. Groups can also work together to complete the Word Work Activity.

Readers Theater Students can read aloud the stories in a class performance. Help them prepare by rereading the stories in daily rehearsals. Work with students to add narration or dialogue. Encourage them to use natural phrasing and expression.

Rereading at Home Have students work with family members to reread the book at home. They can take turns reading aloud alternate pages, then rereading the book switching the pages each person reads.

LEARN A READING STRATEGY

4 Recognize Word Endings Work through the strategy with students, reading each step aloud and modeling the actions. Point out the Reading Help and read the explanation. Work through additional examples with students: /d/ *rubbed, peeled, grabbed;* /t/ *flipped, dropped, raked;* /ed/ *planted, lifted, heated.*

PRACTICE

5 Read Sentences Distribute the Partner Prompts from page T311 to guide peers in reading the sentences in Items 1–5. Remind them to use the recognize-word-parts strategy to read words and to blend the words silently in their head.

6 Write Sentences Dictate the following sentences for students to write. Read each sentence at normal speed once so students can listen, and then repeat it slowly word by word as they write:

6. It rained, so I baked cupcakes.

7. I slipped and dropped the pan.

8. Ted rushed in and smiled.

9. The pan landed in his hands!

If students need extra support, guide them in spelling the past tense verbs by first spelling the root, and then making any necessary changes before adding the letters *-ed*. For example: *What is the root word in* baked? *Write the word. Does it have a final* e? *Drop the* e *before you add* -ed.

7 Conduct "Word Work" Read the directions and work through the Example. Point out the thought balloon and discuss the rule: *I double the* b *when I add* -ed. Have partners complete the remaining items. Check answers as a group.

▶ **Reading Practice Book** pages 139–142 (Decodable Book 8)

CLOSE AND ASSESS

Have students write on the board the pairs of words from Word Work. Call on students to explain the rules for adding *-ed* to a root word.

Language and Literacy **T151**

UNIT 8 LESSON 11

LANGUAGE AND LITERACY: INDEPENDENT READING

OBJECTIVES

Function: Read a Selection
Learning to Read: ❶ Recognize High Frequency Words; ❶ Decode Words with Endings
Reading Strategies: Preview; Predict; Retell
Critical Thinking and Comprehension: Identify Cause and Effect

READ ON YOUR OWN

1. **Introduce Vocabulary** In "Eva's Lesson," students apply phonics skills and read high frequency words taught in Lessons 8–10. Introduce the story words. Write each word, pronounce it, and spell it out. Give a definition and a context sentence:

   - **Eva, Veronica:** Eva and Veronica are girls' names. *Eva dances with her friend Veronica.*
   - **foot:** Point to your foot and say: *This is my foot. I kick the ball with my foot.*
   - **high:** up above the ground. Show and say: *I reach low. I reach high.*

2. **Preview/Make Predictions** Read the title, point out the girl in the top illustration, and say: *This is Eva. She is waiting for her friend Veronica. She looks mad.* (Point to the bottom picture.) Ask: *Who do you think is helping Eva?* (Veronica) *What lesson do you think Eva learns?*

3. **Read and Think: Identify Cause and Effect** Have students complete the chart and use it to retell the story to a partner.

4. **Build Reading Fluency** Use the **Language Tape/CD** with Reading Practice Book page 70 for fluency practice. Tape 4B / CD 2 Track 9

▶ Reading Practice Book page 70

CLOSE AND ASSESS

Have a group retell the story: one student gives a cause and another gives its effect. The pattern repeats until the entire story is retold.

T152 Unit 8 | Friend to Friend

COMPREHENSION: IDENTIFY CAUSE AND EFFECT

Read on Your Own

DECODING CHECK
Give the Decoding Progress Check on page 1a of the Assessment Handbook.

Eva's Lesson

Eva was mad. She tapped her foot. She looked at the clock above the stove. "Veronica has ten more seconds to get here," she said. Eva waited and waited. Veronica was always late. They had planned to work on their dance for the school show. Eva thought Veronica was not very good. She thought Veronica needed a lot of help.

While she waited, Eva played the CD for their dance. She clapped her hands an kicked to the beat. She began to sing. She kicked again. This time, she kicked too high. She slipped and landed on the rug! Just then, Veronica peeked in the kitchen window. She saw Eva and rushed to help her. Eva smiled and rubbed her leg. "Now I know I was the one who needed help," she joked.

CHECK YOUR UNDERSTANDING

Copy and complete this chart. Write what happened as a result of each cause. Use the finished chart to tell the story to your partner.

Wording may vary.

Cause	Effect
Veronica and Eva wanted to dance in the school show.	They needed to practice.
Veronica was late.	Eva was mad. She started to practice.
Eva kicked too high.	She slipped and landed on the rug.
Veronica helped Eva.	Eva joked that she needed help.

152 Unit 8 Friend to Friend

REACHING ALL STUDENTS

Reading Fluency
PHRASING

Read the introduction on **Reading Practice Book** page 70. Explain that the **/** in the examples shows a short pause between groups of words and the **//** shows a longer pause between sentences. Model reading the examples and have students echo them.

Next, play "Eva's Lesson" on the **Language Tape/CD** and have students mark the paragraphs to show where the pauses occur. Check marks as a whole class before partners do the Practice section. Circulate during the Practice to check and support reading fluency.

Reading Practice Book page 70

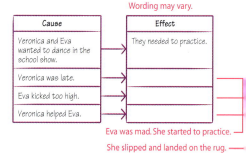

POSSESSIVE NOUNS

Eddie's Friends Do Well

Some nouns show ownership. They end in **'s**.

Eva and Veronica picked costumes for their show. Eva**'s** costume was purple and green. Veronica**'s** costume was red and blue. Sofia**'s** mom gave them matching caps to wear.

BUILD SENTENCES

Say each sentence. Add **'s** to the word in dark print.

Example: 1. Eva's mom and dad came to the show.

Eva	___ mom and dad came to the show.	Eva's
Veronica	___ mom came, too.	Veronica's
friend	She borrowed her ___ camera to record the show.	friend's
show	Eva and Veronica were the ___ final act.	show's
crowd	The ___ cheers made them feel good.	crowd's
Eddie	Veronica was very proud when she saw ___ big smile.	Eddie's

WRITE SENTENCES

7–9. Work with a partner. Look at the picture. Write 3 sentences about the picture. Use possessive nouns.

Example: 7. Miguel's shirt is orange.

Language and Literacy 153

UNIT 8 **LESSON 12**

LANGUAGE AND LITERACY: POSSESSIVE NOUNS

OBJECTIVES

Function: Write
Patterns and Structures:
🅣 Possessive Nouns
Writing: Sentences

INTRODUCE

1 Learn About Possessive Nouns
Read the title and view the photo together. Then read the rule and paragraph. Explain that the apostrophe here does not take the place of any letter, as it does in a contraction.

Ask: *Who owns the red and blue costume?* (Veronica) Then restate: *The red and blue costume is Veronica's.* Write *Veronica's* on the board and underline *'s*. Follow a similar procedure for the other sentences with possessive nouns.

PRACTICE

2 Build Sentences Explain that Items 1–6 tell more about the show. Work through the Example and have volunteers complete the sentences.

APPLY

3 Write Sentences Go over the Example, and have students work with partners to write their sentences. Then ask them to trade papers with new partners and check for *'s* on the nouns that show ownership in each sentence.

▶ **Language Practice Book** page 84

CLOSE AND ASSESS

Have volunteers write out their sentences on the board. Call on students to underline the noun that shows ownership in each sentence.

Language Practice Book page 84

Multi-Level Strategies

LANGUAGE DEVELOPMENT

LITERATE IN L1 Different languages indicate possession in different ways. Spanish, French, and Vietnamese do it through syntax; for example: *the book of Diego*. In Polish, a vowel is added to the noun.

To reinforce possessive nouns in English, hold up items and ask: *Whose backpack is this?* Students answer: *That is Zhenya's backpack.* For written practice, have students create labels on self-stick notes: *Zhenya's backpack, teacher's desk*.

Language and Literacy **T153**

UNIT 8 LESSON 13

LANGUAGE ACROSS THE CURRICULUM: MATHEMATICS

OBJECTIVES

Function: Give Information

Concepts and Vocabulary: Graphs

Research Skills and Learning Strategies: Conduct a Survey; Use Text Structures (bar graphs)

Critical Thinking and Comprehension: Make Comparisons; Analyze Information; Draw Conclusions

Representing: Bar Graph

LEARN ABOUT BAR GRAPHS

1. **Explore Bar Graphs** Read aloud the introduction and demonstrate how to find information on the bar graph. Point to the first column and say: *This bar shows information for the month of January.* Explain: *The top of the bar reaches the number 3. This means that three students have birthdays in January.* Use the graph to ask questions: *How many students were born in April? What month has the most birthdays?*

MAKE A SURVEY AND GRAPH THE RESULTS

2. **Learn About Surveys** Say: *A survey is a way to gather information. First, you ask many people the same question. Then you study the results.* Discuss how to gather and chart information in Step 1.

3. **Complete the Activity** Have students conduct their interviews. Then help groups complete Steps 2 and 3.

CHECK UNDERSTANDING

4. **Respond to "Think It Over"** Post a few bar graphs. Then lead a discussion comparing the information, before answering Items 1–3.

CLOSE AND ASSESS

Have partners create a new topic for a survey that can be displayed in a bar graph. Have them conduct the new survey and plot the results.

T154 Unit 8 | Friend to Friend

SUCCESS IN MATHEMATICS

Learn About Bar Graphs

BAR GRAPHS

A **bar graph** compares numbers. It is a good way to see information quickly.

This bar graph shows how many students have birthdays in January, February, March, and April.

Sample Responses for
1. Students' responses sh trends or patterns sho data.
2. Students will have diff responses such as pec allowed to talk longer on the phone as they get older; or, kids may questions from homework as they get older.
3. A bar graph is a good way to compare numbers because you can results quickly.

Read the instructions. Then do the activity.

▶ Make a Survey and Graph the Results

You will need: a data chart, a calculator, graph paper

ACTIVITY STEPS

1 Make a Survey
Interview three students in each age group. Ask: "How many minutes do you talk on the phone each day?" Record the results in a chart.

2 Find Averages
- Add the minutes for each age group. Write the total.
- Divide each total by 3 to get the average number of minutes on the phone.

3 Make a Bar Graph
- Label the bottom line of your graph: **Ages**.
- Label the scale: **Minutes on the Phone**.
- Draw the bars to make the graph.
- Write a title.

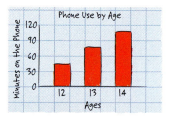

THINK IT OVER

1. Look at your chart. What do the numbers tell you?
2. Why might there be differences among age groups?
3. Why is a bar graph a good way to see the results of your survey?

154 Unit 8 Friend to Friend

REACHING ALL STUDENTS

Mathematics Connection

BAR GRAPHS

Create a class profile. Have students answer questions like the ones shown at right. Then have small groups graph the results of one question. Display the series of bar graphs to create your class profile.

Group Survey
- How old are you?
- What country are you from?
- What languages do you speak?
- How long have you been in the U.S.?

Writing Project — FRIENDSHIP BOOK

Make a page for a friendship book. Tell about a day with a good friend. Tell how you felt.

WRITING ASSESSMENT Use the Writing Progress Checklist on page 51 of the Assessment Handbook to evaluate this writing project.

Pronunciation of Names
Rosa Arias   rō sah   ah rē ahs

THINK ABOUT A SPECIAL TIME

Make a chart like this. What do you remember? Add your notes to the chart.

What We Did	Where	My Feelings
shopped	at the mall	excited
talked and laughed	at the mall	happy
had ice cream	at a restaurant	happy
watched a movie	in the theater	surprised

PLAN YOUR PAGE

What will you show? Draw pictures or use photographs. What words will you use? Check page 312 of your Handbook for feeling words.

MAKE AND SHARE YOUR PAGE

Write sentences for your book. Use your notes. Check and correct your work.

✓ Check Your Work
- Did you tell about a day with a friend?
- Did you tell your feelings?
- Do your verbs tell about the past?

Copy your sentences. Put them and your artwork on construction paper. Add your page to a class friendship book.

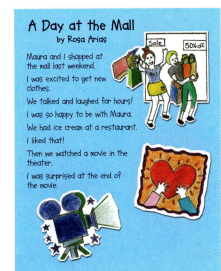

A Day at the Mall
by Rosa Arias

Maura and I shopped at the mall last weekend.
I was excited to get new clothes.
We talked and laughed for hours!
I was so happy to be with Maura.
We had ice cream at a restaurant.
I liked that!
Then we watched a movie in the theater.
I was surprised at the end of the movie.

Language Across the Curriculum 155

Language Practice Book page 85

WRITING PROJECT: FRIENDSHIP BOOK
A Special Time with Friends

Write a page for a friendship book. Make a chart to plan your page. Then write about a day with a friend. Follow these steps.

1. Write a **title** and your name.
2. Tell the **names** of your friends in the first sentence.
3. Tell what you did. Use verbs in the **past tense**. Tell how you felt. Use **feeling words**.
4. Add pictures. Tell about each picture.

Put your page on construction paper. Add it to a class friendship book.

Multi-Level Strategies

WRITING SUPPORT

PRELITERATE Some students may have difficulty converting the chart into sentences. Supply writing frames and take dictation, as necessary:

My friend's name is _____.
One special day was _____.
We went to _____.
First we _____.
I felt _____.
Then we _____.
We were _____.

UNIT 8 **LESSON 14**

LANGUAGE ACROSS THE CURRICULUM: WRITING

OBJECTIVES

Functions: Describe Actions; Express Feelings; Write

Learning Strategies and Critical Thinking: Plan; Relate to Personal Experience; Generate and Organize Ideas; Self-Assess

Writing: Friendship Book

CONDUCT THE WRITING PROJECT

1. **Explore Memory Books** Explain that many people have scrapbooks or albums where they keep photos and things that will help them remember a friend or an event. Then read the introduction aloud. Explain that the students will create a friendship book, with special memories about a good friend.

2. **Think and Plan** Have students copy and complete the chart for their special memories. Encourage them to include feeling words (see page 145). Then look through *Friends Are Like That* for inspiration and have students plan what photographs, illustrations, and mementos to include.

3. **Make and Share Your Page** Invite students to share their pages with the class. After they read, ask them to tell about the photos, illustrations, and mementos they included.

▶ **Language Practice Book** page 85

CLOSE AND ASSESS

Have students look at the friendship-book pages they made. Say:
- *Show me a sentence that tells what you did with your friend.*
- *What feelings do you tell about?*
- *Point to a verb in the past tense.*

Language Across the Curriculum **T155**

Resources

For Success in Language and Literacy

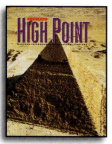

Student Book pages 156–169

For Language Skills Practice

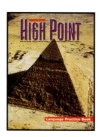

Language Practice Book
pages 86–90

For Reading Skills Practice

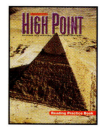

Reading Practice Book
pages 71–73

For Vocabulary, Language Development, and Reading Fluency

Language Tape 5, Side A
Language CD 2, Tracks 10–13

For Reading Together

Theme Book *Let's Dance!*
from The Basics Bookshelf

For Audio Walk-Throughs and Selection Readings

Selection Tape 5A
Selection CD 2, Tracks 5–6

For Phonics Instruction

Transparencies 51–53

Transparency Scripts 51–53

Letter Tiles

For Comprehensive Assessment

Language Acquisition Assessment,
Units 7–9 Test, Writing Assessment,
Self-Assessment

For Planning and Instruction

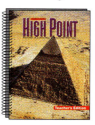

Teacher's Edition
pages T156a–T169

T156a Unit Planner

UNIT 9

Let's Celebrate!

In This Unit

Vocabulary
- Actions
- Country Words
- Geography

Language Functions
- Ask and Answer Questions
- Describe People

Patterns and Structures
- Adverbs
- Present Progressive Verbs
- Phrases with *like to* and *want to*

Reading
- Verb Ending: *-ing*
- Comprehension: Classify (concept map); Identify Details

Writing
- Sentences
- Description
- Celebration Poster

Content Area Connection
- Social Studies (maps)

T156b

UNIT 9

Activity and Assessment Planner

UNIT 9: Let's Celebrate!

LESSONS

1

UNIT 9 LAUNCH ▶ *pages T156–T157*

LESSON 1: INTRODUCE UNIT 9 pages T156–T157

Vocabulary
Actions

Viewing
Interpret a Visual Image

Learning Strategies
Preview

Build Background

Critical Thinking and Writing
Generate Ideas

Relate Events in a Sequence

Write Captions

2–5

LANGUAGE DEVELOPMENT ▶ *pages T158–T161*

LESSON 2
ADVERBS
page T158

Function
Ask and Answer Questions

Patterns and Structures
🅣 Adverbs

Writing
Answers to Questions

LESSON 3
PRESENT PROGRESSIVE VERBS
page T159

Function
Describe People

Patterns and Structures
🅣 Present Progressive Verbs

🅣 Adverbs

Writing
🅣 Sentences

LESSON 4
COUNTRY WORDS
page T160

Functions
Describe People

Ask/Answer Questions

Vocabulary
🅣 Country Words

Speaking
Conduct an Interview

Writing
Description

LESSON 5
LIKE TO* AND *WANT TO
page T161

Function
Describe People

Vocabulary
🅣 Country Words

Patterns and Structures
🅣 Phrases with *like to* and *want to*

Writing
Sentences

6–11

LANGUAGE AND LITERACY ▶ *pages T162a–T167*

LESSON 6
BASICS BOOKSHELF
pages T162a–T162h

Function
Listen to a Book

Vocabulary
Actions

Patterns and Structures
🅣 Action Verbs/Adverbs

Reading Strategies
Activate Prior Knowledge

Preview

Learning to Read
Track Print

Identify Words

Critical Thinking and Comprehension
🅣 Classify Information

LESSON 7
BASICS BOOKSHELF: COMPREHENSION
page T162

Function
Give Information

Learning Strategy
Use Graphic Organizers (concept web)

Critical Thinking and Comprehension
🅣 Classify Information

LESSON 8
HIGH FREQUENCY WORDS
page T163

Learning to Read
🅣 Recognize High Frequency Words

LESSON 9
WORD STRUCTURE
pages T164a–T164b

Learning to Read
Build Oral Vocabulary

Develop Phonemic Awareness

🅣 Identify Verb Endings (*-ing*)

🅣 Decode Words with Endings

LESSON 10
READING AND SPELLING
pages T164–T165

Learning to Read
Develop Phonemic Awareness

Identify Verb Endings (*-ing*)

🅣 Decode Words with Endings

Spelling
🅣 Verb Ending: *-ing*

LESSON 11
INDEPENDENT READING
pages T166–T167

Functions
Read a Selection

Describe

Learning to Read
🅣 Recognize High Frequency Words

🅣 Decode Words with Endings

Reading Strategies
Activate Prior Knowledge

Set a Purpose for Reading

Visualize

Critical Thinking and Comprehension
🅣 Identify Details

Writing
Description

12–13

LANGUAGE ACROSS THE CURRICULUM ▶ *pages T168–T169*

LESSON 12 SOCIAL STUDIES: MAPS
page T168

Function
Listen to a Selection

Vocabulary
Country Words

Geography

Research Skills and Learning Strategies
Use Text Structures (maps)

Locate Information

Critical Thinking and Comprehension
🅣 Identify Details

LESSON 13 WRITING PROJECT: CELEBRATION POSTER
page T169

Functions
Ask Questions

Describe

Write

Speaking/Listening
Interview

Learning Strategies and Critical Thinking
Plan

Formulate Questions

Organize Ideas

Self-Assess

Research Skills
Gather Information

Take Notes

Conduct an Interview

Representing/Writing
Celebration Poster

T156c Unit 9 | Let's Celebrate!

🅣 = Objective Tested on Unit Test

ASSESSMENT OPTIONS

The **Teacher's Edition** and the **Assessment Handbook** include these comprehensive assessment tools:

▶ **Ongoing, Informal Assessment**
Check for understanding and achieve closure for every lesson with the targeted questions and activities in the **Close and Assess** boxes in your Teacher's Edition.

▶ **Decoding Progress Check**
These word lists for each unit provide a quick way to check on mastery of the phonics or word structure skills taught in the unit.

▶ **Language Acquisition Assessments**
To verify students' ability to use the language functions and grammar structures taught in Units 7–9, conduct these performance assessments.

▶ **Unit Test in Standardized Test Format**
This multiple-choice test measures students' cumulative understanding of the skills and language developed in Units 7–9.

▶ **Self- and Peer-Assessment**
Students use the Self-Assessment Form to evaluate their own work and develop learning strategies appropriate to their needs. Students offer feedback to their classmates with the Peer-Assessment Form.

▶ **Writing Assessment/Portfolio Opportunities**
You can evaluate students' writing in the Writing Projects using the Writing Progress Checklist. Then collaborate with students to choose work for their portfolios.

UNITS 7–9 ASSESSMENT OPPORTUNITIES	Assessment Handbook Pages
Decoding Progress Check	1a
Language Acquisition Assessments	18
Units 7–9 Test	19–24
Self-Assessment Form	25
Peer-Assessment Form	50
Writing Progress Checklist	51
Portfolio Evaluation Form	52

RELATED RESOURCES

Celebrations of Light
by Nancy Luenn
Short essays about festivals of light in various countries. There are twelve essays, one for each month of the year. With illustrations. (Atheneum)
Theme Book: Read Aloud

Dance
by Bill T. Jones and Susan Kuklin
Color photos of a dancer are accompanied by simple text that tells of the dancer's thoughts and feelings. (Hyperion)
Phonics Reinforcement: -ing

Ayu and the Perfect Moon
by David Cox
An old woman in Bali tells three girls about her participation in a traditional village dance when she herself was very young. (Hampton-Brown)
Easy Reading

Nine O'Clock Lullaby
by Marilyn Singer
Ten P.M. in Puerto Rico is 10 A.M. in China. Text and pictures show what is going on at the same time around the world. (Available from Hampton-Brown)
Vocabulary: Country Words

Up, Up and Away
by Ruth Heller
A colorful grammar lesson which introduces the use and formation of adverbs. Examples are given throughout—all in rhyming verse. (Grosset)
Language Development: Adverbs

UNIT 9 **LESSON 1**

INTRODUCE UNIT 9: LET'S CELEBRATE!

OBJECTIVES
Concepts and Vocabulary: Actions
Viewing: Interpret a Visual Image
Learning Strategies: Preview; Build Background
Critical Thinking: Generate Ideas; Relate Events in a Sequence
Writing: Captions

START WITH A COMMON EXPERIENCE

1. **Introduce "Let's Celebrate!"** Read the unit title and explain that *Let's Celebrate!* means "Let's do something special to show our joy." Describe dance as one way to celebrate, and ask about other ways, such as special meals, ceremonies, parties, and gifts.

2. **Learn the Dance** Explain that a dance is made up of many steps. View the photographs together, and read the captions aloud to teach each step. Then call out the captions as you lead volunteers in performing the actions.

   Play the **Language Tape/CD**, and have students point to the correct photos as they read along. Then have them echo the reading once, and finally chime in as the music plays. When students are familiar with the music and actions, call on volunteers to perform the dance. (There is a music-only rendition for students to perform the dance.)

   Tape 5A CD 2 Track 10

3. **Create a New Dance** Encourage small groups to create their own dances. Begin by having students sketch out a series of actions, with a caption below each picture. Provide time for groups to practice, then invite them to perform before the class. One group member can lead the dance by calling out instructions for the group to follow.

REACHING ALL STUDENTS

HOME CONNECTION

Family Dances Have students take home the dance they created on paper to teach a family member. Encourage them to interview a family member about a traditional or modern dance. Students can learn the dance, record the steps, then bring the new dances to class to share with others.

T156 Unit 9 | Let's Celebrate!

Let's Celebrate!

Learn the dance. Try it!
Then use some of the moves to
make up a new dance.

In This Unit

Vocabulary
- Actions
- Country Words
- Geography

Language Functions
- Ask and Answer Questions
- Describe People

Patterns and Structures
- Adverbs
- Present Progressive Verbs
- Phrases with *like to* and *want to*

Reading
- Verb Ending: *-ing*
- Comprehension:
  Classify (concept map)
  Identify Details

Writing
- Sentences
- Description
- Celebration Poster

Content Area Connection
- Social Studies (maps)

PREVIEW THE UNIT

4 Look for Activities and Celebrations
Leaf through the unit, previewing activities students will do, for example:

page 158—learning a chant about dancing

page 160—learning about celebrations around the world

page 162—listening to the Bookshelf book (Display a copy of the book.)

page 169—making a celebration poster

Also ask students to look for ways people like to celebrate. Highlight the dances on pages 160–161 and the parade on page 163, for example. Then sum up what the preview reveals: *All over the world, people celebrate in many ways.*

5 Set Your Goals Start a class mind map on celebrations. Prompt students for pictures or words to add, and have them act out and describe other ideas for you to put into words. Talk together about what they want to learn about celebrations in this unit.

CLOSE AND ASSESS

Ask students to tell or show you something they are interested in learning in this unit.

UNIT 9 Mind Map

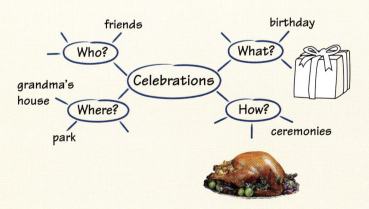

UNIT 9 LESSON 2
LANGUAGE DEVELOPMENT: ADVERBS

OBJECTIVES

Functions: Listen Actively; Repeat Spoken Language; Recite; Ask and Answer Questions

Patterns and Structures: 🅣 Adverbs

Writing: Answers to Questions

INTRODUCE

1. **Listen and Chant** Play the three renditions of "You Can Dance!" on the **Language Tape/CD**. Students will listen and follow along with the words, echo the lines, and then supply the answers to the questions in the chant. *(Tape 5A, CD 2 Track 11)*

2. **Learn About Adverbs** Read aloud the chart for adverbs. Then have two volunteers demonstrate the same action with two different adverbs: *Jump low. Jump high.* Call out more commands for the group to follow: *Step forward. Jump back.*

PRACTICE

3. **Conduct "Express Yourself"** Model how to ask and answer questions, and then have partners do Items 1–6.

   How to Ask and Answer Questions
   - Some questions start with *Can*. Use *yes* or *no* in your answer. *Can you dance? No, I can't dance.*
   - Some questions start with *How*. Add information in your answer. *How do you dance? I dance fast.*

APPLY

4. **Write Answers to Questions** Encourage students to check their answers with a partner. Distribute Partner Checklist 9 on page T310.
   ▶ **Language Practice Book** page 86

CLOSE AND ASSESS

Call on one student to ask a question about an action: *How do you walk?* Have other students give responses with adverbs: *I walk quickly. I walk forward.*

T158 Unit 9 | Let's Celebrate!

ADVERBS

How Do You Dance?

Listen and chant.

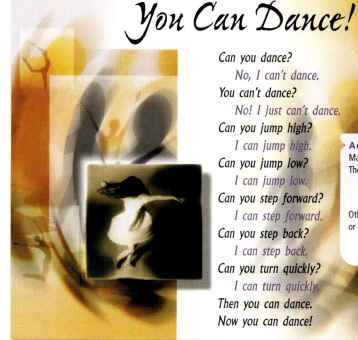

You Can Dance!

Can you dance?
  No, I can't dance.
You can't dance?
  No! I just can't dance.
Can you jump high?
  I can jump high.
Can you jump low?
  I can jump low.
Can you step forward?
  I can step forward.
Can you step back?
  I can step back.
Can you turn quickly?
  I can turn quickly.
Then you can dance.
Now you can dance!

Adverbs
Many **adverbs** end in **-ly**. They tell how:
  turn quick**ly**
  dance wild**ly**

Other adverbs tell when or where:
  dance **now**
  step **back**

EXPRESS YOURSELF ▶ ASK AND ANSWER QUESTIONS

Work with a partner. Ask these questions. Answer in a complete sentence. Then act it out.

1. Can you jump high?
2. Can you jump low?
3. Can you step forward?
4. How do you jump?
5. Where do you step?
6. How do you turn?

Example: 1. Can you jump high?
Yes, I can jump high.

Sample Responses Students should answer questions 1–3 with *or no*. Answers to questions 4–6 should have an adverb (*quickly, low, forward, back,* and so on.)

WRITE ANSWERS TO QUESTIONS ✏️

7.–10. How do you dance? Write 4 sentences to answer the question. Use adverbs to tell how you dance.

Example: 7. I dance fast.

158 Unit 9 | Let's Celebrate!

REACHING ALL STUDENTS

Multimodal Practice
QUESTIONS AND ANSWERS

Visual Lead the group in finding questions and answers in the chant. Then have students copy the chant to make posters, using one color to write the questions and another color for the answers.

Auditory Form two groups to recite the chant. One group chants the questions, and the other responds with the answers.

Kinesthetic Encourage partners to create their own dramatic (physical) presentations of the chant.

Language Practice Book page 86

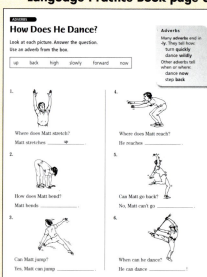

PRESENT PROGRESSIVE VERBS

What Are They Doing?

These **verbs** tell what is happening now.

The man **is jumping**.

The women **are standing**.

They **are dancing**.

BUILD SENTENCES

Look at the pictures below. Say sentences to go with each picture. Choose words from each column.

Sample Responses
Students' responses should go with the picture and include an item from each column.

The boy The girl The people He She They	is are	jumping. playing the drums. turning around. kicking. dancing. marching.

Example: 1. The girl is turning around.

1.
2.
3.
4.

WRITE SENTENCES

5.–8. Write 2 sentences for each picture. Tell how the people are moving. Use an adverb in each sentence.

Example: 5. The girl is turning around quickly.
She is dancing happily.

Adverbs
high   up
carefully   quickly
happily   slowly
loudly   wildly

Language Development 159

Language Practice Book page 87

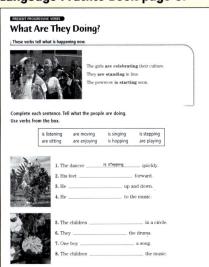

Language Development
PRESENT PROGRESSIVE/ADVERBS

Play a game of pantomime and description, using adverbs and verbs in present progressive form. First, display a list of phrases:

dancing happily	jumping back
stepping forward	reaching high
turning quickly	playing wildly

Have volunteers pantomime an action for the others to guess.

UNIT 9 **LESSON 3**

LANGUAGE DEVELOPMENT: PRESENT PROGRESSIVE VERBS

OBJECTIVES
Function: Describe People
Patterns and Structures:
• Present Progressive Verbs; • Adverbs
Writing: • Sentences

INTRODUCE

1 Learn About Present Progressive Verbs Read the title and explain that the question asks about an action that is happening now. Present the examples and ask students to point to the part of the photo that goes with each sentence. Explain: *To tell about something while it is happening, use* is *or* are *and a verb with the ending* -ing.

PRACTICE

2 Build Sentences Remind students to use *is* to tell about one person or thing and *are* to tell about more than one person or thing. Then discuss what the people are doing in each picture. Go over the Example and model using the columns to create another sentence for the same picture: *She is dancing.* Have students build sentences for each picture and say them aloud for the group.

APPLY

3 Write Sentences Read the adverbs in the word box and point out that many adverbs end in *-ly*. Explain that this ending turns a word like *quick* into a new word that tells how something is done: *quickly*.

Go over the Example and discuss how the adverb adds information. Say: *Use an adverb to tell more about an action.* Have partners write two sentences for each picture.

▶ **Language Practice Book** page 87

CLOSE AND ASSESS

Call on partners to share their sentence pairs. Then ask other students to point out the picture they describe.

Language Development **T159**

UNIT 9 LESSON 4
LANGUAGE DEVELOPMENT: COUNTRY WORDS

OBJECTIVES
Functions: Listen Actively; Describe People; Ask and Answer Questions
Concepts and Vocabulary:
- Country Words

Speaking: Conduct an Interview
Writing: Description

INTRODUCE

1. **Learn Country Words** Go over the maps, photos, and captions aloud. Ask questions to check understanding: *Which photo shows a Mexican dance? Do the Chinese dancers have costumes?*

2. **Make a Nationalities Chart** Go over the proper adjectives and point out the three main endings for nationalities: *-ese, -an, -ish.* Then sort the words and add more examples.

China/Chin**ese**	Mexico/Mexic**an**	England/Engl**ish**
Taiwan/Taiwan**ese**	Chile/Chile**an**	Finland/Finn**ish**
Sudan/Sudan**ese**	Bosnia/Bosni**an**	Spain/Span**ish**

PRACTICE

3. **Conduct "Who's Talking?"** Play "Who's Talking?" on the **Language Tape/CD** to model how to describe people. Have volunteers describe the dancers.

Tape 5A / CD 2 Track 12

APPLY

4. **Write a Description** Provide questions for students to use in their interviews:
   - What country are you from?
   - What are people from your country called?

▶ **Language Practice Book** page 88

CLOSE AND ASSESS
Conduct a call-and-response activity with country names and nationalities. Call: *I am from (Cuba).* Response: *You are (Cuban).*

T160 Unit 9 | Let's Celebrate!

VOCABULARY: COUNTRY WORDS

People Celebrate Around the World

Look at the pictures. Read about the people.

This dragon dance is from **China.** People do the dragon dance to celebrate the **Chinese** New Year.

These dancers are from **Mexico.** They are doing a **Mexican** dance.

These dancers are **English.** They are doing an old dance from **England.**

WHO'S TALKING? ▶ DESCRIBE PEOPLE

1.–3. Listen.
Who is talking? Point to the correct picture.
Then describe the dancers.
Tell what they look like. Tell what they are doing.

Sample Responses
1. Mexican woman with red dress
2. Chinese man holding the dragon head
3. first English dancer

Students' descriptions should include details about how the dancers look and what they are doing.

WRITE A DESCRIPTION

4.–8. Interview 5 people from different countries. Write 2 sentences to describe each person.

Example: 4. Juan is from Cuba.
He is Cuban.

Sample Responses
Students sentences should include each person's name, country, and nationality.

Country	A Person from the Country
India	Indian
Mongolia	Mongolian
Japan	Japanese
Vietnam	Vietnamese
Cuba	Cuban
Guatemala	Guatemalan
Nicaragua	Nicaraguan
Ireland	Irish

160 Unit 9 | Let's Celebrate!

REACHING ALL STUDENTS

Multi-Level Strategies
LANGUAGE DEVELOPMENT

PRELITERATE Have students create a pattern book with information from their interviews. Prepare pages with sentence frames for students to use, as shown below. Then each student draws a picture of each person he or she interviews, and fills in the sentence frames.

This is Flor.
She is from Guatemala.
She is Guatemalan.

Language Practice Book page 88

VOCABULARY: COUNTRY WORDS
Dancers Around the World
Look at each picture. Complete the sentences. Use words from the box.

Scotland | Scottish | Cambodia | Cambodian

1. This dancer is from ___Scotland___.
She is ___.

2. These dancers are ___.
They are doing a dance from ___.

DESCRIBE PEOPLE
Describe the dancers. Tell what they look like. Tell what they are doing. Complete the sentences.
3. The Scottish dancer is from ___Scotland___.
4. She wears a ___.
5. The dancer is ___.
6. The ___ dancers are sitting.
7. They have ___.
8. These dancers are ___.

PHRASES WITH *LIKE TO* AND *WANT TO*

Everyone Likes to Dance

Use a verb to complete a phrase with *like to* or *want to*.

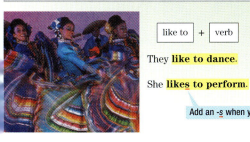

like to	+	verb

They **like to dance**.
She **likes to perform**.

want to	+	verb

They **want to celebrate**.
She **wants to keep** a tradition.

Add an *-s* when you use *he*, *she*, or *it*.

BUILD SENTENCES

Read each sentence. Add the correct form of *like to* or *want to*. Say the new sentence.

Example: 1. The dancers like to march.

Students will add *want(s) to* or *like(s) to* to each sentence.

1. China
The dancers ____ march.

2. Mexico
He ____ perform.

3. England
The men ____ jump.

4. Turkey
The dancers ____ move.

5. Korea
She ____ turn.

6. Japan
She ____ celebrate.

WRITE SENTENCES

7.–12. Write 2 sentences for each picture above. Use *like to* or *want to* and a country word.

Example: 7. The dancers from China want to celebrate.
The Chinese dancers like to march.

Language Development 161

UNIT 9 LESSON 5

LANGUAGE DEVELOPMENT: *LIKE TO* AND *WANT TO*

OBJECTIVES

Function: Describe People

Concepts and Vocabulary:
- Country Words

Patterns and Structures:
- Phrases with *like to* and *want to*

Writing: Sentences

INTRODUCE

1 Learn About Phrases with *Like to* and *Want to* Read the title and introduction. As you read aloud each sentence, have students point to the phrase *like to* or *want to*. Explain that these phrases are usually followed by a verb.

Then read the rule for adding *-s* to the verbs *like* or *want* and point out that the verbs that follow do not change. Ask volunteers to suggest other statements with *like to* or *want to* to describe the photo: *The dancers like to turn quickly. She wants to dance at the festival.*

PRACTICE

2 Build Sentences Read the directions and work through the Example. Have partners build sentences for each picture.

APPLY

3 Write Sentences Read the directions and work through the Example, pointing out the two ways to add a country word. Encourage students to use the chart on page 160 to find more examples of country words.

▶ **Language Practice Book** page 89

CLOSE AND ASSESS

Have partners work together. One partner pantomimes an action while the other partner describes the action with *likes to* or *wants to*: *Shinji wants to play basketball. He likes to shoot baskets.*

Language Development **T161**

Language Practice Book page 89

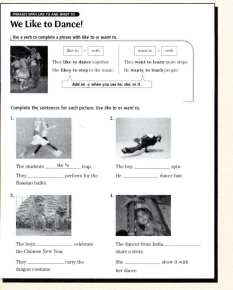

UNIT 9 **LESSON 6**

LANGUAGE AND LITERACY: THE BASICS BOOKSHELF

OBJECTIVES
Concepts and Vocabulary: Actions
Patterns and Structures:
🔵 Action Verbs; 🔵 Adverbs
Listening: Listen to a Preview
Reading Strategies:
Activate Prior Knowledge; Preview
Learning to Read: Track Print

BUILD LANGUAGE AND VOCABULARY

1. **Teach "Words to Know"** Have students look at pages 2–3. Say: *These pages show actions, or ways to move.* Point to each action in the book, demonstrate it, and then have students perform the action.

2. **Create a Dance** Model how to create a simple dance that uses three or four basic actions from pages 2–3. Describe each action: *First, I reach up. Next, I step forward. Then I turn around and around.* Have students work in small groups to create new dances. Invite them to perform their dances. Ask other class members to name each action as it is performed.

PREPARE TO READ

3. **Think About What You Know** Invite students to show pictures, demonstrate, or describe dances from their native countries.

4. **Preview** Play the Audio Walk-Through for *Let's Dance!* on the **Selection Tape/CD** to give students the overall idea of the story.

Tape 5A
CD 2 Track 5

CLOSE AND ASSESS
Play "Simon says." Call out actions for students to perform: *Simon says turn around.* Students should only perform the action if they hear "Simon says." After you model the process, ask volunteers to give directions.

Let's Dance!
by George Ancona

Summary This colorful photo essay introduces students to dances from many cultures. Photos and captions feature traditional dances from such places as the Congo, Scotland, China, Afghanistan, England, Spain, India, and Mexico. Many types of dances are portrayed as well: contra dancing, break dancing, wheelchair dancing, ballet, etc. Pictures provide support for the simple text and can prompt the use of verbs and adverbs.

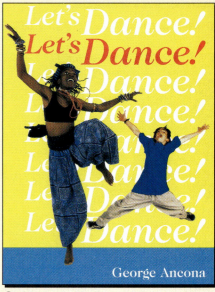
Cover

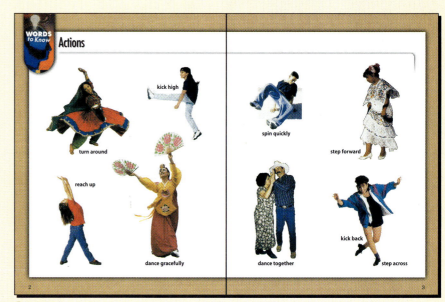
Pages 2–3

Multi-Level Strategies
LITERACY SUPPORT

PRELITERATE / NON-ROMAN ALPHABET **Track Print** Review how to find and track print on a page. Turn to pages 30 and 31 to show that text can appear at the top or the bottom of the page. Have partners work together to leaf through the book and find more examples of text on the top and bottom of the page.

Use pages 4 and 5 to model reading text that is broken up on the page. Demonstrate tracking print from left to right for the first three lines, sweeping from the end of each line to the beginning of the next. Then model reading the remaining text from left to right and from top to bottom on each page. On page 4, use a finger to track print along the top row, then sweep across to the first word on the bottom row. At the end of the page, sweep again to the top of page 5 and repeat the process. Have students track print as you read the text aloud.

T162a Unit 9 | Let's Celebrate!

Pages 4–5

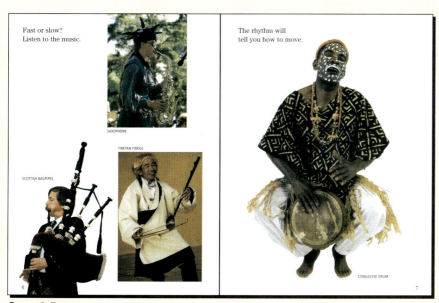

Pages 6–7

Strategies for Comprehensible Input

PAGE	STORY LANGUAGE	STRATEGY OPTIONS
4–5	speak, sing, walk, dance	**Demonstrate the actions.**
	All you have to do is	**Explain:** You can dance if you can do the movements shown on these pages.
6–7	Fast or slow?	**Demonstrate:** Play a few bars of a fast tune and say: *This is fast music.* Repeat for slow music.
	rhythm	**Demonstrate:** Clap out a rhythm.

Language and Literacy **T162b**

UNIT 9 **LESSON 6,** CONTINUED

LANGUAGE AND LITERACY: THE BASICS BOOKSHELF

OBJECTIVES

Function: Listen to a Book

READ AND THINK TOGETHER

1. **Read Aloud** On your first reading of the book, use the "Strategies for Comprehensible Input" that appear at the bottom of pages T162b, T162d, T162f, and T162h.

Pages 8–9

Pages 10–11

Multi-Level Strategies

LITERACY SUPPORT

PRELITERATE **Concepts of Print: Using Captions** Turn to pages 8–9 and point to the text at the bottom of each page. Say: *These words tell about the dances.* Then point to the caption box on page 8. Say: *The words in this box tell about the dance in the photograph.* Have students locate more caption boxes in the book.

Next have students name an event that their families celebrate. Ask students to draw pictures of their own family celebrations. Take dictation as students tell you a caption for their drawing.

T162c Unit 9 | Let's Celebrate!

Let's Dance!, CONTINUED

Dancing is a way of celebrating.

Pages 12–13

There are dances that celebrate the seasons.

Pages 14–15

Strategies for Comprehensible Input

PAGE	STORY LANGUAGE	STRATEGY OPTIONS
8–9	alone	**Restate:** by yourself
	with a friend	**Point to the picture.**
10–11	a whole bunch of people	**Restate:** many people
12–13	celebrating	**Restate:** having fun on a special day
14–15	the seasons	**Explain:** The seasons are four times of the year. The four seasons are summer, fall, winter, and spring.

Language and Literacy **T162d**

UNIT 9 **LESSON 6,** CONTINUED

LANGUAGE AND LITERACY: THE BASICS BOOKSHELF

OBJECTIVES

Function: Listen to a Book
Critical Thinking and Comprehension:
🅣 Classify Information

READ AND THINK TOGETHER, CONTINUED

2 Read and Map: Classify Information
Draw a concept web like the one below, but with only the label in the center. Say: *A concept map gives details or answers questions about the topic.*

Show students the cover and page through the book. Think aloud as you model filling in the web: *I want to add what I learned about dancing. I will write* Who? *in the first section. Then I'll read through the book to find examples of people who dance. I see that men, women, and children dance. I will write these words around the word* Who?*. Repeat this procedure with the question words* why, where, *and* how*. Sample responses are shown in the web below. Other answers are possible, based on the text and pictures in the book.

Dances from the old countries   were brought to the New World.

Pages 16–17

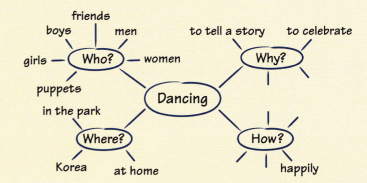

Pages 18–19

Concept Web for *Let's Dance!*

```
        friends
   boys        men      to tell a story   to celebrate
girls — Who? — women          Why?
   puppets
   in the park         Dancing
              Where?          How?
        Korea    at home           happily
```

Technology Support
See **Inspiration** Visual Learning software for support in creating the concept web.

T162e Unit 9 | Let's Celebrate!

Let's Dance!, CONTINUED

Pages 20–21

Pages 22–23

Strategies for Comprehensible Input

PAGE	STORY LANGUAGE	STRATEGY OPTIONS
16–17	the old countries	**Point to a map and explain:** The countries in Europe are called the old countries.
	the New World	**Point to a map and explain:** North and South America are called the New World.
18–19	traditional clothes	**Explain:** clothes that have been worn in a country for many years
20–21	in their parents' footsteps	**Restate:** the way their parents do it
	Over time	**Restate:** As the years go by
22–23	men, women	**Point to the pictures and explain:** *Men* means more than one *man*, and *women* means more than one *woman*.

Language and Literacy **T162f**

UNIT 9 **LESSON 6,** CONTINUED

LANGUAGE AND LITERACY: THE BASICS BOOKSHELF

OBJECTIVES
Function: Listen to a Book
Learning to Read: Track Print (directionality); Identify Words

READ AND THINK TOGETHER, *CONTINUED*

3 Conduct Interactive Readings
Choose from these options:

- **Read along and track print** Point out that the text can appear at the top of a page (pages 6–7) and sometimes at the bottom (page 8–9). Review how to track text from left to right, sweeping from one line to the next. Then play the recording of *Let's Dance!* on the **Selection Tape/CD**.

  Tape 5A
  CD 2 Track 6

- **Read along and identify words**
  Let's Dance! contains many high frequency words that have been previously taught, as follows:

a	city	move	their
all	dance	new	there
and	do	of	time
animals	for	old	to
are	from	on	together
around	have	or	were
can	how	people	will
celebrate	in	some	with
change	is	that	world
children	most	the	you

  As you read, frame individual words from the list and have students identify the words. Continue reading as students track the print and identify other words they know.

CLOSE AND ASSESS
Have students tell three things they learned about dances or dancing.

Animals dance.

TIBETAN YAK DANCE. The noble yak provides milk, clothing, and transportation for Tibetans. Two men wear a yak costume and dance to poke fun at humans.

24

Puppets dance.

MEXICAN PUPPETS are carried by little boys who dance for the entertainment of children at birthday parties. The puppets are made by the town's piñata maker.

25

Pages 24–25

There are country dances and city dances.

CONTRA DANCING was called country dancing in England. Dancers switch partners as they move up and down the line. Families gather at BARN DANCES to dance the Texas two-step.

26

BREAK DANCING began on the streets and playgrounds of the inner cities. Young men try to outdo each other with acrobatic movements to hip-hop music.

27

Pages 26–27

Multi-Level Strategies

LITERACY SUPPORT

LITERATE IN L1 **Read with a Partner/Create a Class Book** After students have participated in the interactive readings, encourage them to read the book with a partner. Distribute the Partner Prompts on page T311 to help partners work together to identify unfamiliar words and unlock their meanings, then read the text to each other. Then have students draw themselves performing a dance from the book. Encourage them to add captions with the sentence frames: *I am ____. I am wearing ____. I dance with ____. We are celebrating ____.* Combine the pages into a class book.

INTERRUPTED SCHOOLING **Classify Information** To anchor understanding of the skill, review question words. Say: *The word* who *tells about people. The word* why *gives reasons. The word* where *tells a place. The word* when *tells a time.* Set up the concept map with the word *Dancing* and the question words in place. Distribute self-stick notes containing the words from the web, one word per note. Help students affix the notes to the concept web.

T162g Unit 9 | Let's Celebrate!

Let's Dance!, CONTINUED

Pages 28–29

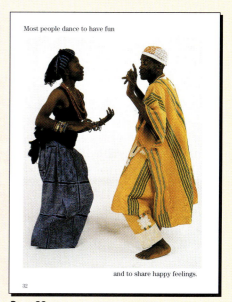

Pages 30–31   Page 32

Strategies for Comprehensible Input

Page	Story Language	Strategy Options
28–29	tell stories	**Explain:** As the dancers move, they act out a story.
30–31	performed on stage	**Point to the pictures.**
32	happy feelings	**Gesture:** Smile and clap.

Language and Literacy **T162h**

UNIT 9 LESSON 7

LANGUAGE AND LITERACY: THE BASICS BOOKSHELF

OBJECTIVES

Function: Give Information
Learning Strategy:
Use Graphic Organizers (concept web)
Critical Thinking and Comprehension:
T Classify Information

CHECK COMPREHENSION

1. **Make a Concept Web** Remind students that a concept web answers questions or gives information about the selection.

   As you read aloud the directions for each step, pause for students to add information to the sections of their concept webs. Have them review *Let's Dance!* to help them find the information they need.

2. **Share Information from the Book** Have partners compare their concept webs and check them for accuracy. Then they can take turns sharing information related to one section of the web at a time.

CLOSE AND ASSESS

Ask students to complete this sentence:
A concept web shows _____.

COMPREHENSION: CLASSIFY

Read and Think Together

Make a concept map to tell about *Let's Dance!* Follow these steps.

1. Think about the book. What is it mostly about?

2. Who dances? Add a section to the map. Write **Who?** inside. Write the people who dance.

3. What else does the book tell you? Add more sections with **Why?**, **How?**, and **Where?**

4. Add a few words from the book for each section. Then use your map to tell a partner about the book.
   Possible Responses

from
The Basics Bookshelf

THEME BOOK
This photo essay shows how people around the world celebrate through dance.

162 Unit 9 Let's Celebrate!

REACHING ALL STUDENTS

Language Development

EXTEND AND ACCEPT AN INVITATION; EXPRESS REGRETS

Role-Play Explain that the phrase "Let's Dance!" is an invitation. Model how to extend an invitation and accept it or express regrets:

Will you please dance with me?
Yes, thanks, I will.

Would you like to join our group?
No thank you. I already have a group.

Use the chart to present suitable language. Then have students page through the book and role-play conversations in which characters ask each other to dance.

Extend an Invitation	Accept an Invitation	Express Regrets
Would you like to…?	I would like that. Thanks.	No, I can't.
Do you want to…?	Yes, thanks!	No, thanks.
You're invited to…	I'll do it. Thanks for inviting me.	I don't think that I can come.

T162 Unit 9 | Let's Celebrate!

HIGH FREQUENCY WORDS
Words to Know

REVIEW WORDS YOU KNOW

Read the words aloud. Which word goes in the sentence?

enough	through
really	world
above	on

1. The parade goes _through_ the streets.
2. The floats are _really_ big.
3. This parade is _on_ Thanksgiving Day.

LEARN TO READ

Learn new words.

celebrate	We like to **celebrate**. Today is my sister's birthday.
most	**Most** of her friends are here, but not all of them.
young	Her friends are **young** kids from school.
children	There are about 10 **children** in our yard.
started	The party **started** at 3:00.
beginning	It is now 4:00, and it is **beginning** to rain.
change	My mother says, "We need to **change** our plans!"
another	"Let's move the party to **another** place!"
only	The house is the **only** place to go.
following	The kids are quickly **following** me inside. This is fun!

How to Learn a New Word
- Look at the word.
- Listen to the word.
- Listen to the word in a sentence. What does it mean?
- Say the word.
- Spell the word.
- Say the word again.

WORD WORK

Write each sentence. Add the missing word. Example: 4. In my family, we dance when we celebrate.

4. In my family, we dance when we _c e l e b r a t e_.
5. I learned the waltz when I was very _y o u n g_.
6. I _s t a r t e d_ to learn it when I was five.
7. The basic dance steps never _c h a n g e_.
8. The waltz is not the _o n l y_ dance I know.
9. My father is teaching me _a n o t h e r_ dance called the cha-cha.
10. He wants all his _c h i l d r e n_ to know how to dance.
11. My house is _b e g i n n i n g_ to look like a dance club!

Language and Literacy 163

Reading Practice Book page 71

HIGH FREQUENCY WORDS
Words to Know
READ AND WRITE
Read each word. Then write it.
1. celebrate 2. most 3. young
4. following 5. change 6. started
7. children 8. only 9. another
10. beginning

WORD WORK
Read each clue. Find the new words in the box.
Write the words on the lines.
11. This word starts with f.
    Following
12. These 2 words begin with ch.
13. These 2 words have 4 letters each.
14. This word ends with e.
15. These 2 words have st.
16. These 2 words end with -ing.
17. This word has the word other in it.
18. This word means "more than one child."
19. This word is the opposite of old.
20. This word is the opposite of ended.

Reading Fluency
RECOGNIZE HIGH FREQUENCY WORDS

To build automaticity with the new high frequency words:

- Ask students to make a card for each word, putting the meaning on the back. Show how to use the cards for practice "in both directions:" look at the meaning and name the word, or read the word and give the meaning.
- Display pictures of families, dances, and celebrations. Small groups can use new and review words from the classroom word chart to create sentences about the pictures.

UNIT 9 **LESSON 8**

LANGUAGE AND LITERACY: HIGH FREQUENCY WORDS

OBJECTIVES

Learning to Read:
- Recognize High Frequency Words

REVIEW WORDS

1 Review Known High Frequency Words Have the group read aloud the words in the green box. Listen for words students cannot read automatically and use the steps in the yellow box to reteach those words. Then have students look at the photo. Read each cloze sentence. Reread each sentence and pause for students to silently read the two words to the left of the sentence. Tell students to choose the word that goes in the sentence and tells about the picture.

INTRODUCE NEW WORDS

2 Learn High Frequency Words Use the High Frequency Word Script on page T320 to lead students through the steps in the yellow box for each new word.

PRACTICE

3 Conduct "Word Work" Use item 4 to model how to use context to find possible words in the list and then to use the number of letter blanks to confirm the selected word.

Have partners complete Items 5–11. Discuss how each correct word fits the meaning and number of blanks.

APPLY

4 Read Words in Context Students will read high frequency words in context in the sentences on page 165 and the passages on page 166.

▶ **Reading Practice Book** page 71

CLOSE AND ASSESS

Call out the high frequency words one at a time. Have students point to them and spell the words as a group.

Language and Literacy **T163**

UNIT 9 **LESSON 9**

LANGUAGE AND LITERACY: WORD STRUCTURE

OBJECTIVES

Learning to Read: Build Oral Vocabulary;
Develop Phonemic Awareness;
🅣 Identify Verb Endings *(-ing)*;
🅣 Decode Words with Endings

TEACH VERB ENDINGS

1 **Build Oral Vocabulary** Pantomime or restate the meaning of each verb on Transparency 51. For example:

- **lift:** Say: *I can lift the chair.* Lift a chair, saying: *I am lifting the chair.*

- **reach:** Pantomime reaching for a book and say: *I can reach for the book. I am reaching for the book.*

2 **Develop Phonemic Awareness** Conduct the oral activities in Step 1 of the Script for Transparency 51.

3 **Learn to Spell and Read Verbs with** *-ing* Display Transparency 51 again. Work through Steps 2 and 3 of the script.

CLOSE AND ASSESS

Display the verbs *help, lift, greet,* and *scream.* Have groups each write the present progressive form of one verb and read it to the class.

T164a Unit 9 | Let's Celebrate!

Transparency 51: ▶
Verb Endings

Verbs with -ing

lift + ing = lift**ing**   reach + ing = reac**hing**

Add -ing to each verb.

1. help   2. lift   3. greet   4. play   5. reach   6. scream

Learn to read a word with -ing.

help**ing**   help ⬤ — Cover the -ing. Read the root word.

helping — Look at the whole word again.

help + ing = helping — Blend the parts to say the word.

Read the story.

I am helping my mother at a party. I am lifting some boxes of glasses. She is greeting people at the door. We do not see my little brother. He is playing with the tablecloth. He is reaching for the cake. People are screaming. All the food is about to fall!

Transparency 51   © Hampton-Brown

Materials
Letter tiles for:

a	c	e	e	f
g	g	h	i	i
l	m	n	p	r
s	t	u	y	

▼ **Script for Transparency 51**

Verbs with -*ing*

1. Develop Phonemic Awareness
Count Syllables in Words/Contrast Final Sounds Say: *Some words have one part, or syllable, such as* teach. *Clap the syllable with me as we say* teach: teach. (clap) *Some longer words have two parts, or syllables, such as* teaching. Have students repeat *teaching* and practice saying /ing/ several times. Say: *Now clap the syllables with me for* teaching: teach-ing. (clap, clap) Then lead students in saying and clapping syllables for: *lifting, lift, reach, reaching, greet, scream, greeting, screaming.* Have students count the syllables in the words. If they miscount, lead them in clapping the syllables again. Next, have students contrast final sounds. Say: *Listen to these two words:* teach, teaching. *Are the words* teach *and* teaching *the same?* Repeat: *teach, teaching.* (no) Explain: *The second word,* teaching, *has two extra sounds at the end:* /ing/. *Let's say these two sounds together:* /ing/.

2. Associate Sounds and Symbols/Learn to Spell Verbs with -*ing*
Point to the picture of the dancer lifting the man on **Transparency 51**. Say: *The dancer is lifting the man. Say* lifting *with me.* Then point to the -*ing* in *lifting* and say: *The letters* -ing *make the sounds* /ing/: lifting. Have students repeat *lifting,* emphasizing the final sounds. Then point to *lift* and say: Lift *has one vowel and then two consonants. For a word like* lift, *you can just add* -ing. Repeat for *reaching,* pointing out that *reach* has two vowels followed by a consonant. Then use letter tiles to spell the -*ing* form of the verbs in Items 1–6.

3. Learn to Read Verbs with -*ing*
Teach Point to *helping* in the Example and say: *This word ends with* -ing. *To read the word, cover the ending* -ing. *What you see is the root word. This is a word you know. Read it with me:* help. *Now blend the parts to say the word:* help-ing, helping.

Practice Read the story. Pause and have students read each word ending in -*ing.* If they need help, have them cover the -*ing* and apply the strategy.

◀ Transparency 52: Verb Endings

Materials
Letter tiles for: a, c, e, g, g, h, i, i, k, m, n, o, p, p, s, t, t, v, w

▼ Script for Transparency 52

Verbs with -ing

1. **Develop Phonemic Awareness**
   Contrast Long and Short Vowel Sounds Say: *Listen to these two words:* hopping, hoping. *Listen again:* He is hopping on one foot. He is hoping he will break a world record. *The word* hopping *has the short* o *sound:* /o/. *Hoping has the long* o *sound:* /ō/. Repeat for *tapping, taping; jogging, joking; matching, making*.

2. **Learn to Spell Verbs with -ing**
   Point to the picture of the person skating on **Transparency 52**. Say: *Look at this person skate! This person is skating.* Explain: *You can hear a difference between* skate *and* skating, *and you can see a difference, too.* Point to *skating* and say: *The word* skate *has a long vowel followed by one consonant and silent* e. *For a word like* skate, *you need to drop the silent e before you add* -ing. Follow a similar process for *skipping*. Point out that for words that end in a short vowel and one consonant, such as *skip,* the final consonant needs to be repeated before -*ing* is added. Then use letter tiles to spell the -*ing* form of the verbs in Items 1–6.

3. **Learn to Read Verbs with -ing**
   Teach Point to *getting* in the Example and say: *This word ends with* -ing. *To read the word, cover the* -ing. *Look at the letters just before the* -ing. *Do you see two consonants? If so, the vowel in the root word is short. Blend the word silently in your head and then say it.* Allow time for students to silently blend the word and say *get*. Then uncover the ending and read the whole word: *getting*. Next, point to *taking* and say: *This word ends with* -ing. *To read the word, cover the* -ing. *Look at the letters just before the* -ing. *Do you see one consonant? If so, the vowel is usually long. Sound it out in your head and then say it.* Wait a few seconds and ask students to say the word aloud: *take*. Then uncover the ending and read the whole word: *taking*.

   Practice Read the story. Pause before each word ending in -*ing*. Ask students to read the word. If they need help, have them cover the -*ing* and apply the strategy.

OBJECTIVES

Learning to Read: Build Oral Vocabulary; Develop Phonemic Awareness; Identify Verb Endings (*-ing*); ❶ Decode Words with Endings

TEACH VERB ENDINGS

1 Build Oral Vocabulary Pantomime or restate the meaning of each verb on Transparency 52. For example:

- **get:** Say: *I can get a dictionary.* Then lift out a dictionary, saying: *I am getting a dictionary.*

- **take:** Offer an eraser, saying: *Please take an eraser.* Pick up an eraser yourself, and say: *I am taking an eraser.*

2 Develop Phonemic Awareness Conduct the oral activities in Step 1 of the Script for Transparency 52.

3 Learn to Spell and Read Verbs with -ing Display Transparency 52 again. Work through Steps 2 and 3 of the script.

CLOSE AND ASSESS

Display the verbs *get, wave, hop,* and *smile*. Have groups each write the present progressive form of one verb and read it to the class.

▶ **Reading Practice Book** page 72 (Verb Ending *-ing*)

Reading Practice Book page 72

Language and Literacy **T164b**

UNIT 9 LESSON 10

LANGUAGE AND LITERACY: READING AND SPELLING

OBJECTIVES

Functions: Listen Actively; Repeat Spoken Language; Recite

Learning to Read: Develop Phonemic Awareness; Identify Verb Endings (-ing); **T** Decode Words with Endings

Spelling: **T** Verb Ending: -ing

LISTEN AND LEARN

Tape 5A / CD 2 Track 13

1. **Recite a Chant** Display Transparency 53 and play "Invitation" on the **Language Tape/CD**.

DEVELOP PHONEMIC AWARENESS

2. **Manipulate Words—Delete Final Sounds** Say: *Listen to this word:* tapping. *Listen again:* tapping. *Now say* tapping *for me without* /ing/. (tap) Repeat the procedure with *shaking, jumping, hopping, leaping,* and *waving*.

STUDY VERB ENDINGS

3. **Verb Ending: -ing** Read aloud each rule and work through the examples in the box. Point out the two vowels together in *leap* and the single vowel plus two final consonants in *jump*. Say: *For words like* leap *and* jump, *you can just add* -ing. Follow a similar process to teach the other rules. Then show students these words and ask them to tell you which rule applies: *meet, ask, hop, hope*.

Afterwards, play the chant again. Have students identify verbs ending with *-ing*. Discuss the spelling patterns.

T164 Unit 9 | Let's Celebrate!

VERB ENDING: -ING

Reading and Spelling

LISTEN AND LEARN

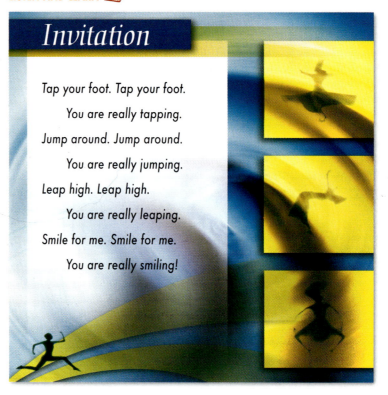

Invitation

Tap your foot. Tap your foot.
    You are really tapping.
Jump around. Jump around.
    You are really jumping.
Leap high. Leap high.
    You are really leaping.
Smile for me. Smile for me.
    You are really smiling!

STUDY VERB ENDINGS

For some verbs, you can just add -ing.	This verb ends in silent e.	This verb ends in one vowel and one consonant.
leap + ing = leaping jump + ing = jumping	smile When you add -ing, drop the e. smil~~e~~ + ing = smiling	tap When you add -ing, double the consonant. tap**p**ing

164 Unit 9 | Let's Celebrate!

▶ Transparencies 51–53

REACHING ALL STUDENTS

Multi-Level Strategies

LITERACY SUPPORT

LITERATE IN L1 Link English concepts to skills that exist in students' native language. For example, Spanish speakers will be familiar with the concept of adding an ending (*-ando* and *-iendo*) to verbs to create the progressive form. Clarify for them that *-ing* is the English equivalent. Then have students use letter tiles or letter cards to build verbs with the ending *-ing* to reinforce concepts that are new in English, such as doubling the final consonant or dropping the *e*.

PRELITERATE Copy the sentences in Items 1–5 of the Reading and Spelling Practice onto sentence strips. Distribute the sentence strips and have students cut them apart into separate words. Have volunteers lead the group in reassembling each sentence by matching the text in the items on the page. Then read each sentence in phrases for students to echo. Repeat, reading the entire sentence. Point to each word as you say it.

READING STRATEGY

Follow these steps to read a word with *-ing*.

1 Look for the ending you know. Cover it.

leap**ing**

leap

Reading Help

Some words end in silent **e**. They have a long vowel sound.

shake

Look at this word and cover the *-ing*.

shaking

You do not see the **e** in the root word, but the vowel is still long.

2 Look for vowel and consonant patterns to sound out the root word.

leap

l + ea + p = leap

*Remember that **ea** makes one vowel sound. Blend three sounds to say **leap**.*

3 Uncover the ending. Blend the syllables to read the entire word.

leap + ing = leaping

*Blend **leap** and **ing** to say the word **leaping**.*

READING AND SPELLING PRACTICE

Use what you learned to read the sentences.

1. The first grade class is getting ready for a show.
2. I am helping with the costumes and taking care of the children.
3. Most of the children are running around. Some are screaming!
4. The music is playing. The show is beginning.
5. Two kids are waving at me. They dance very well!
6.–9. Now write the sentences that your teacher reads. *For dictation sentences, see Step 6 at right.*

WORD WORK

10.–15. Read these words. Then write each word on a card.
Match the 6 pairs that go together. What do you notice?

jumping	reach	jump
hop	smile	waving
smiling	wave	reaching
make	hopping	making

Answers: Drop *e*, add *-ing*:
10. wave waving
11. smile smiling
12. make making

Add *-ing*:
13. jump jumping
14. reach reaching

Double consonant, add *-ing*:
15. hop hopping

Example:
10.
wave   waving

*I drop the **e** when I add **-ing**.*

Language and Literacy 165

Decodable Book
PRACTICE WITH VERB ENDING *-ING*

Decodable Book 9: *Celebrate the Past*

Assign **Decodable Book 9** for independent reading. The **Decodable Book** can be used in a variety of ways to help students become more fluent, automatic readers:

Discussion Circles Have students work in small groups to read aloud and discuss the book using the questions on the back cover. Encourage students to read aloud the text that supports their answers. Groups can also work together to complete the Word Work Activity.

Readers Theater Students can read aloud the stories in a class performance. Help them prepare by rereading the stories in daily rehearsals. Work with students to add narration or dialogue. Encourage them to use natural phrasing and expression.

Rereading at Home Have students work with family members to reread the book at home. They can take turns reading aloud alternate pages, then rereading the book switching the pages each person reads.

LEARN A READING STRATEGY

4 Recognize Word Endings Work through the strategy with students, reading each step aloud and modeling the actions shown on the page. Point out the Reading Help and read the explanation to students. Work through additional examples to help them apply the tip: *hoping, naming, making, taking, waving, saving, hiding, riding.*

PRACTICE

5 Read Sentences Distribute the Partner Prompts from page T311 to guide peers in reading the sentences in Items 1–5. Remind them to use the word-ending strategy to read words and to blend the words silently.

6 Write Sentences Dictate the following sentences for students to write. Read each sentence at normal speed once so students can listen, and then repeat it slowly word by word as they write:

6. I am helping Dad.

7. My sister is running on the beach.

8. The boys are smiling and waving.

9. They are waiting for her to stop.

7 Conduct "Word Work" Read the directions and work through the Example. Point out the thought balloon and discuss the rule: *I drop the e when I add -ing.* Then have partners complete the remaining items. Check answers by working through the items as a group.

▶ **Reading Practice Book** pages 143–146 (Decodable Book 9)

CLOSE AND ASSESS

Call on students to display the pairs of words from Word Work that go together. Have them read the words aloud and explain the rule for adding *-ing* to the root word.

Language and Literacy **T165**

UNIT 9 LESSON 11

LANGUAGE AND LITERACY: INDEPENDENT READING

OBJECTIVES

Function: Read a Selection; Describe
Learning to Read: ❶ Recognize High Frequency Words; ❶ Decode Words with Endings
Reading Strategies: Activate Prior Knowledge; Set a Purpose for Reading; Visualize
Critical Thinking and Comprehension: ❶ Identify Details
Writing: Description

READ ON YOUR OWN

1. **Introduce Vocabulary** In "Dance to Celebrate!" students will apply the phonics skills and read high frequency words taught in Lessons 8–10. Introduce the following story words. Write each word, pronounce it, and spell it. Then give a definition and a context sentence:

   - **holiday:** day of celebration. *New Year's Day is a holiday.*
   - **Chinese:** describes someone or something from China. *The Chinese New Year celebration is very exciting.*
   - **dragon:** an imaginary animal. *A dragon is long like a snake. It has a big head.*
   - **special:** something that is not usual. *People do a special dance to celebrate the New Year.*

2. **Activate Prior Knowledge/Set Purposes** View the photos and discuss what students already know about the celebrations. Then model setting a purpose: *I'll read these paragraphs to find out how people celebrate.* Encourage volunteers to state their purposes for reading.

3. **Read and Think: Visualize** Students should read the passage on their own, individually. Suggest that as they read, they make a movie in their mind of the celebrations. Prompt the action: *How do the people move? What sounds do you hear?*

T166 Unit 9 | Let's Celebrate!

COMPREHENSION: IDENTIFY DETAILS

Read on Your Own

DECODING CHECK
Give the Decoding Progress Check on page 1a of the Assessment Handbook.

Dance to Celebrate!

Chinese New Year

People dance to celebrate a holiday. These people are beginning the Chinese New Year with a dance. They are greeting the Chinese dragon, which brings good luck. Nine men inside the costume are lifting the dragon with long poles. Another man is beating a drum. He is following the dragon.

Jewish Wedding

People dance to celebrate an important day in the family. This bride is having fun at her wedding. Three men are lifting her in her seat while her husband watches. The family is dancing around them. They are smiling and clapping.

English Maypole Dance

People dance to celebrate the seasons. May Day is the time to welcome spring. These children are skipping around a maypole. They are weaving ribbons over and under, making a braid around the maypole.

All around the world, people dance to celebrate the special times in their lives!

166 Unit 9 Let's Celebrate!

REACHING ALL STUDENTS

CULTURAL PERSPECTIVES

Home Culture: Dances Discuss the occasions for dancing on page 166. (to celebrate the new year, a wedding, the beginning of spring) Ask students to think about occasions for dancing in their home cultures, similar to these: holiday dances, important days in the life of a person or a family, seasonal celebrations. Ask volunteers to describe or demonstrate dances they know, and to teach others the dances. If students are interested, consider planning a school dance festival.

CHECK YOUR UNDERSTANDING

Write each sentence. Label it *T* for *True* or *F* for *False*.
If it is false, write the sentence again to make it true.

Example: **1.** There are six men inside the dragon costume. **F**
There are nine men inside the dragon costume.

Chinese New Year

1. There are six men inside the dragon costume.
2. People dance to celebrate a holiday.
3. The Chinese dragon brings bad luck.

Jewish Wedding

4. A wedding is an important day.
5. The bride is standing.
6. The bride is sad.
7. The family is dancing.

English Maypole Dance

8. The children are skipping around the maypole.
9. The children are celebrating summer.
10. The children are weaving ribbons.

Answers:
1. F There are nine men inside the dragon costume
2. T
3. F The Chinese dragon brings good luck.
4. T
5. F The bride is sitting.
6. F The bride is happy.
7. T
8. T
9. F The children are celebrating spring.
10. T

EXPAND YOUR VOCABULARY

11.–13. Tell about each picture on page 166. Use some of these words and phrases.

| wedding | bride | around the maypole | May | dancing |
| spring | dragon | having fun | costume | in the family |

Example: **11.** People are lifting the dragon. **Sample Response**
They are inside the costume. Students' responses should go with each picture.

WRITE ABOUT CELEBRATIONS ✏

14. Choose a celebration from page 166. Write sentences to describe it.

Example: **14.** Children are dancing around a maypole.
They are celebrating spring.

Sample Response
Students should write at least two sentences describing one of the celebrations on page 166.

Language and Literacy **167**

CHECK YOUR UNDERSTANDING

4 **Comprehension: Identify Details**
Explain the meanings of *true* and *false:* True *means "correct." A sentence is true if all the information in the sentence is correct.* False *means "not correct." If just one detail in a sentence is wrong, the sentence is false.* Then show students how to use the information in the paragraph to tell if item 1 is true or false. Say: *Item 1 says, "There are six men inside the dragon costume." The fourth sentence in the passage says that there are nine men inside the costume, so we mark this* F *for False. Then we write the sentence to make it true,* by changing *six* to *nine.*

EXPAND YOUR VOCABULARY

5 **Describe Pictures** Read the directions and go over the vocabulary in the green box. Use the Example to model describing the first photo on page 166. Point out the details in the picture that go with the description. Then encourage volunteers to use other words and phrases from the vocabulary box to describe the other photos.

WRITE

6 **Describe Celebrations** Point out that the Example describes the last photo on page 166. Then ask students to choose a photo to describe. Students who choose the same photo can work in pairs or small groups to write their descriptions together.

For students who need additional support in writing, provide sentence frames and help students choose present progressive verbs to complete them:

> People are _____.
> They are _____.
> One person is _____.

▶ **Reading Practice Book** page 73

CLOSE AND ASSESS

Have students take turns giving a sentence that describes a detail in one of the pictures. The others should tell which picture the sentence describes.

Language and Literacy **T167**

Reading Practice Book page 73

COMPREHENSION
Build Reading Fluency

Read the article. Stop when the timer goes off. Mark your score. Then try it again two more times on different days.

Celebrate the 4th of July

America's birthday is the 4th of July. It is a time to celebrate. You can have a picnic in the park or watch a parade. Hundreds of people stand on the street and wait for the parade to begin. The school bands are first. You can feel the drums. Next are the fire trucks with wailing sirens. Then the floats pass by. Boys and girls clap and yell. They wave red, white, and blue flags.

Celebrating brings people together. They all come to have a good time. Old people and young children dance in the streets. Kids eat hot dogs and corn on the cob. They smile as their dads take pictures. This is the best way to celebrate the 4th of July!

	Day 1	Day 2	Day 3
Total Words Read in One Minute			
Minus Words Missed			
Words Read Correctly in One Minute			

Reading Fluency
TIMED READINGS

Read the directions on **Practice Book** page 73. Set the timer and have a student read the passage to you. Use the script on page T320 to mark words the student misses and to note the last word read in one minute. Have students graph their performance and set a goal for improving in subsequent timed readings. Plan for two additional timed readings and encourage partners to practice reading the passage to each other between the timed readings.

UNIT 9 LESSON 12

LANGUAGE ACROSS THE CURRICULUM: SOCIAL STUDIES

OBJECTIVES
Function: Listen to a Selection
Concepts and Vocabulary: Country Words; Geography
Research Skills and Learning Strategies: Use Text Structures (maps); Locate Information
Critical Thinking and Comprehension:
• Identify Details

LEARN ABOUT MAPS

1 Explore Maps Use the maps, labels, and captions at the top of the page to introduce the geography terms and map symbols. Then have students find other examples of countries, cities, capitals, and borders on the large map.

READ AND THINK

2 Activate Prior Knowledge Read aloud the title of the article and the focus question. Go over when and how the New Year is celebrated in the U.S., and ask volunteers to describe New Year celebrations they know about. Point to the map and explain: *This article is about New Year celebrations in two of the countries on the map.*

3 Listen to the Article Use a large world map to show students Southeast Asia. As you read, restate ideas and clarify vocabulary to aid students' comprehension. Pause for students to locate on the map the countries and cities mentioned in the article.

CHECK UNDERSTANDING

4 Answer the Review Questions Encourage students to refer to the text of the article and to the map as they complete the Review.

CLOSE AND ASSESS
Have partners create a new question based on information from the map: *What is the capital of Laos? What is one country that borders Myanmar?* Have another pair answer the question.

T168 Unit 9 | Let's Celebrate!

SUCCESS IN SOCIAL STUDIES

Learn About Maps

Answers for the Review:
1. Vietnam: People celebrate for a week in January or February. They put small fruit trees full of orange-colored fruit in their homes. Thailand: People celebrate in April. They splash water on each other to wash away bad luck.
2. Cambodia, Laos, or Myanmar
3. Rangoon, Vientiane, Hanoi, Phnom Penh, Bangkok

MAPS

Thailand is a **country**.

On a map, a dot shows a **city**.

A star on a map shows the **capital**. The government of a country is located in the capital city.

A **border** divides one country from another. The black lines on this map show borders.

Listen to the article and study the map below. Then do the Review.

New Year Celebrations in Southeast Asia
• How do people in Southeast Asia celebrate the new year?

People in Southeast Asia celebrate the new year at different times and in different ways. Some countries celebrate in winter after the shortest day of the year. In Vietnam, people celebrate for an entire week in January or early February. During this time, the Vietnamese people of Ho Chi Minh City decorate their homes with small fruit trees full of orange-colored fruit.

Other countries celebrate the new year at the beginning of spring. In Thailand, people celebrate the new year from April 13 to April 15. All over Thailand, especially in the city of Chiang Mai, people splash water on each other to wash away bad luck.

REVIEW
1. **Check Your Understanding** How do people in Thailand and Vietnam celebrate the new year?
2. **Vocabulary** Name a country that has a border with Thailand.
3. **Use Maps** List the capitals shown on the map.

168 Unit 9 | Let's Celebrate!

REACHING ALL STUDENTS

Social Studies Connection
MAPS

Apply the map vocabulary in a sorting game. Prepare index cards with the name of a country, a non-capital city, or a capital from page 168 on each. Distribute the cards. Have students read a card aloud and put it in the correct category according to the maps and geography symbols on page 168. Encourage students to make and sort cards with more countries, cities, and capitals they know.

Countries	Non-Capital Cities	Capitals
Thailand	Chiang Mai	Bangkok
Vietnam	Ho Chi Minh City	Hanoi

Writing Project / CELEBRATION POSTER

WRITING ASSESSMENT
Use the Writing Progress Checklist on page 51 of the Assessment Handbook to evaluate this writing project.

Make a poster about a family celebration. Describe the celebration. Tell what you do. Tell what you wear and what you eat.

INTERVIEW SOMEONE IN YOUR FAMILY

1 Brainstorm questions.   **2** Ask your questions.   **3** Take notes.

PLAN YOUR POSTER

What will you show? Draw or find pictures. What words will you use? Be sure to spell them correctly.

MAKE AND SHARE YOUR POSTER

Put your pictures on your poster. Write sentences on another piece of paper. Tell what is happening in your pictures. Then check and correct your work.

Check Your Work
Do your sentences describe the picture?
Did you use a verb with -ing to tell what is happening?
Did you use capital letters correctly?

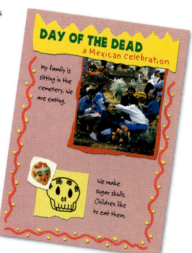

Write your sentences on the poster.
Read your sentences aloud.
Tell your class about your poster.

Language Across the Curriculum **169**

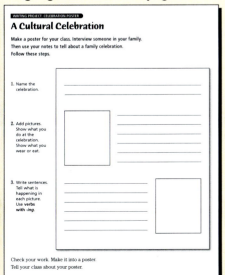

Language Practice Book page 90

ASSESSMENT

For opportunities to measure progress, see the Assessment Handbook:

- **Units 7–9 Test** evaluates basic vocabulary and the patterns and structures of English, mastery of phonics and high frequency words, reading comprehension, and writing.

- **The Language Acquisition Assessment** for Units 7–9 offers performance assessments for measuring growth through the stages of language acquisition.

- **Self- and Peer-Assessment** forms involve students in the assessment process.

UNIT 9 LESSON 13

LANGUAGE ACROSS THE CURRICULUM: WRITING

OBJECTIVES

Functions: Ask Questions; Describe; Write
Speaking and Listening: Interview
Learning Strategies and Critical Thinking: Plan; Formulate Questions; Organize Ideas; Self-Assess
Research Skills: Gather Information; Take Notes; Conduct an Interview; Locate Resources
Representing and Writing: Celebration Poster

CONDUCT THE WRITING PROJECT

1 Explore Cultural Celebrations Review the cultural celebrations on pages 160–161, 163, 166–168, and the book *Let's Dance!* Work together to identify country origins and customs for a few celebrations. Display these in a chart or web.

2 Choose a Topic Read aloud the page title and directions. Encourage students to choose a favorite cultural celebration. Students from the same country may collaborate on one poster, using resources from the library.

3 Interview Someone in Your Family Help students write interview questions, and demonstrate how to take notes by recording important words and phrases.

4 Plan Your Poster Help students plan what images and text they will show on their poster, and how they will arrange them for best effect.

5 Make and Share Your Poster Display the cultural posters, by region, around the room. Then call on students to share their work.

▶ **Language Practice Book** page 90

CLOSE AND ASSESS

Have groups look at the posters. Say:
- *Show me a sentence that describes a picture.*
- *Point to the name of a country, written with a capital letter.*
- *Find a verb that tells what is happening now. Does it end with -ing?*

Language Across the Curriculum **T169**

Resources

For Success in Language and Literacy

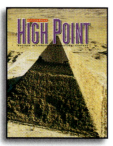

Student Book pages 170–183

For Language Skills Practice

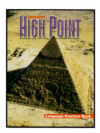

Language Practice Book pages 91–95

For Reading Skills Practice

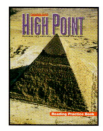

Reading Practice Book pages 74–76

For Vocabulary, Language Development, and Reading Fluency

Language Tape 5, Side B
Language CD 2, Tracks 14–16

For Reading Together

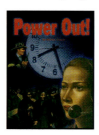

Theme Book *Power Out!* from The Basics Bookshelf

For Audio Walk-Throughs and Selection Readings

Selection Tape 5B
Selection CD 2, Tracks 7–8

For Phonics Instruction

Transparencies 54–56

Transparency Scripts 54–56

Letter Tiles

For Comprehensive Assessment

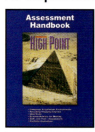

Language Acquisition Assessment, Units 10–12 Test, Writing Assessment, Self-Assessment

For Home-School Connections

High Point Newsletter 4 in seven languages

For Planning and Instruction

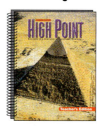

Teacher's Edition pages T170a–T183

T170a Unit Planner

UNIT 10

Here to Help

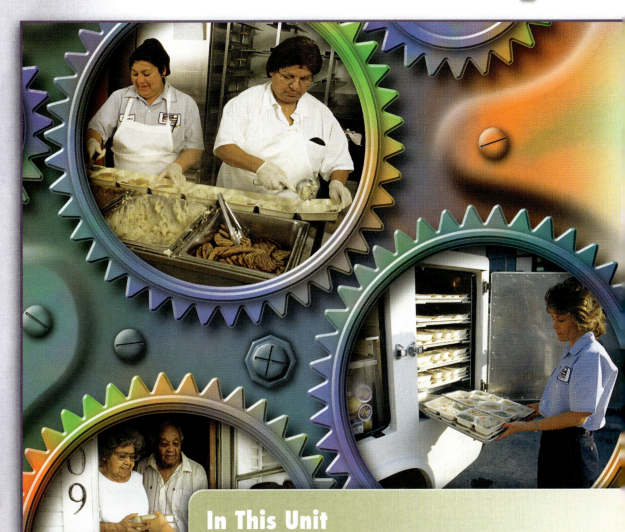

In This Unit

Vocabulary
- Time
- Local Government

Language Function
- Tell What May Happen

Patterns and Structures
- Verbs (*may, might, could*)
- Phrases with *have to* and *need to*
- Possessive Pronouns

Reading
- Long Vowels: *ie, igh; ui, ue*
- Comprehension: Identify Cause and Effect (cause-and-effect chart)

Writing
- Sentences
- Captions
- Job Advertisement

Content Area Connection
- Social Studies (local government)

T170b

UNIT 10

Activity and Assessment Planner

UNIT 10: Here to Help

LESSONS

1

UNIT 10 LAUNCH
▶ *pages T170–T171*

LESSON 1: INTRODUCE UNIT 10 pages T170–T171

Vocabulary
Community Workers

Viewing
Interpret a Visual Image

Learning Strategies
Preview

Build Background

Critical Thinking and Representing
Generate Ideas

Create Illustrations

2–5

LANGUAGE DEVELOPMENT
▶ *pages T172–T175*

LESSON 2
MAY, MIGHT, COULD
page T172

Function
Express Possibility or Probability

Patterns and Structures
🅣 Verbs (*may, might, could*)

Writing
🅣 Sentences

LESSON 3
TIME
page T173

Function
Express Possibility or Probability

Vocabulary
🅣 Time

Writing
🅣 Sentences

LESSON 4
HAVE TO AND ***NEED TO***
page T174

Functions
Express Intentions

Describe Actions

Patterns and Structures
🅣 Phrases with *have to* and *need to*

Writing
🅣 Sentences

LESSON 5
POSSESSIVE PRONOUNS
page T175

Function
Give Information

Patterns and Structures
🅣 Possessive Pronouns

Writing
Captions

6–11

LANGUAGE AND LITERACY
▶ *pages T176a–T181*

LESSON 6
BASICS BOOKSHELF
pages T176a–T176d

Function
Listen to a Book

Vocabulary
Community Workers

Reading Strategies
Activate Prior Knowledge

Preview

Analyze Story Elements (characters)

Critical Thinking and Comprehension
🅣 Identify Cause and Effect

LESSON 7
BASICS BOOKSHELF: COMPREHENSION
page T176

Function
Retell a Story

Learning Strategy
Use Graphic Organizers (cause-and-effect chart)

Critical Thinking and Comprehension
🅣 Identify Cause and Effect

LESSON 8
HIGH FREQUENCY WORDS
page T177

Learning to Read
🅣 Recognize High Frequency Words

LESSON 9
PHONICS
pages T178a–T178b

Learning to Read
Build Oral Vocabulary

Develop Phonemic Awareness

🅣 Associate Sounds and Symbols: /ī/ *ie, igh;* /ū/ *ui, ue;* /yōo/ *ue*

Blend Sounds to Decode Words

LESSON 10
READING AND SPELLING
pages T178–T179

Learning to Read
Develop Phonemic Awareness

🅣 Associate Sounds and Symbols: /ī/ *ie, igh;* /ū/ *ui, ue;* /yōo/ *ue*

Blend Sounds to Decode Words

Spelling
🅣 Words with Long Vowels: *ie, igh; ui, ue*

LESSON 11
INDEPENDENT READING
pages T180–T181

Functions
Read a Selection

Describe

Learning to Read
🅣 Recognize High Frequency Words

🅣 Decode Words (*ie, igh* and *ui, ue*)

Reading Strategies
Activate Prior Knowledge

Set a Purpose for Reading

Ask Questions

Clarify

Critical Thinking and Comprehension
🅣 Identify Cause and Effect

Writing
Clues

12–13

LANGUAGE ACROSS THE CURRICULUM
▶ *pages T182–T183*

LESSON 12
SOCIAL STUDIES: LOCAL GOVERNMENT
page T182

Function
Listen to a Selection

Vocabulary
Local Government

Learning Strategies
Build Background

Set a Purpose for Reading

Critical Thinking and Comprehension
Identify Details

Analyze Information

LESSON 13
WRITING PROJECT: JOB ADVERTISEMENT
page T183

Functions
Ask and Answer Questions

Write

Learning Strategies and Critical Thinking
Plan

Formulate Questions

Generate and Organize Ideas

Self-Assess

Writing
Job Advertisement

T170c Unit 10 | Here to Help

🅣 = Objective Tested on Unit Test

ASSESSMENT OPTIONS

The **Teacher's Edition** and the **Assessment Handbook** include these comprehensive assessment tools:

▶ **Ongoing, Informal Assessment**
Check for understanding and achieve closure for every lesson with the targeted questions and activities in the **Close and Assess** boxes in your Teacher's Edition.

▶ **Decoding Progress Check**
These word lists for each unit provide a quick way to check on mastery of the phonics or word structure skills taught in the unit.

▶ **Language Acquisition Assessments**
To verify students' ability to use the language functions and grammar structures taught in Units 10–12, conduct these performance assessments.

▶ **Unit Test in Standardized Test Format**
This multiple-choice test measures students' cumulative understanding of the skills and language developed in Units 10–12.

▶ **Self- and Peer-Assessment**
Students use the Self-Assessment Form to evaluate their own work and develop learning strategies appropriate to their needs. Students offer feedback to their classmates with the Peer-Assessment Form.

▶ **Writing Assessment/Portfolio Opportunities**
You can evaluate students' writing in the Writing Projects using the Writing Progress Checklist. Then collaborate with students to choose work for their portfolios.

UNITS 10–12 ASSESSMENT OPPORTUNITIES

	Assessment Handbook Pages
Decoding Progress Check	1a
Language Acquisition Assessments	18
Units 10–12 Test	19–24
Self-Assessment Form	25
Peer-Assessment Form	50
Writing Progress Checklist	51
Portfolio Evaluation Form	52

RELATED RESOURCES

Emergency!
by Gail Gibbons
Illustrations and simple text tell about the professionals and vehicles that come to the scene of accidents, fires, crimes, and other emergencies. (Holiday)
Theme Book: Read Aloud

Make a Tune
by Lada Kratky
In Kenya, people like to make music. This book tells about Kenyan instruments and the sounds they make.
(Hampton-Brown)
Phonics Reinforcement: Long *u*

A Road Might Lead to Anywhere
by Rachel Field
A road might lead around the corner or all the way to Mexico. Cut-paper collages give this reverie a nostalgic atmosphere. (Little, Brown)
Language Development: *might*

Nine O'Clock Lullaby
by Marilyn Singer
Ten P.M. in Puerto Rico is 10 A.M. in China. Text and pictures show what is going on at the same time around the world. (Available from Hampton-Brown)
Vocabulary: Time

Coaches
by Katie Bagley
Photos and straightforward text tell about coaches and their importance to the community. Part of the "Community Helpers" series.
(Bridgestone Books)
Easy Reading

UNIT 10 **LESSON 1**

INTRODUCE UNIT 10: HERE TO HELP

OBJECTIVES

Concepts and Vocabulary:
Community Workers
Viewing: Interpret a Visual Image
Learning Strategies:
Preview; Build Background
Critical Thinking: Generate Ideas
Representing: Illustrations

START WITH A COMMON EXPERIENCE

1. **Introduce "Here to Help"** Study the images together and discuss how each worker helps the worker in the next gear: *This person is making a meal. Look for the meal in another picture. How does the meal get to the people?* (delivery person)

2. **Explore Interdependence** Start a chart of interdependent jobs. Write a job description in one cell of each row and have students add more entries.

technician makes heart monitor	delivery people take it to the hospital	hospital workers use it for patients
factory worker makes chalk	school worker orders supplies	teacher uses chalk in classroom
phone workers lay phone lines	911 operator takes call	police go to accident scene
trucker delivers wood	carpenter builds plant nursery	nursery workers care for the plants

Next, conduct the launch activity. After viewing students' art, add their job chains to the chart. Challenge students to build on the chains you charted earlier.

REACHING ALL STUDENTS

HOME CONNECTION

Community Workers Send home a copy of *High Point Newsletter 4* in the **Teacher's Resource Book**. In the home activity, students talk with a family member about a community worker and how the community depends on his or her job. Together the student and the family member draw a picture and write a description of the job. Encourage students to share their work with the class and add their job descriptions to a class book.

T170 Unit 10 | Here to Help

Look at the pictures. These women work as a team to get people what they need. Tell what is happening in each picture. Then work in a small group. Think of 3 other workers who depend on one another to get people what they need. Draw a picture to show how they work together.

Sample Responses:
This is a series of people who help with Meals on Wheels. The people are preparing the meal trays, loading the trays into the van, and delivering a meal. Students should think of other interdependent jobs in the community. Students' pictures should illustrate how the jobs depend on one another.

In This Unit

Vocabulary
- Time
- Local Government

Language Function
- Tell What May Happen

Patterns and Structures
- Verbs (*may*, *might*, *could*)
- Phrases with *have to* and *need to*
- Possessive Pronouns

Reading
- Long Vowels: *ie*, *igh*; *ui*, *ue*
- Comprehension: Identify Cause and Effect (cause-and-effect chart)

Writing
- Sentences
- Captions
- Job Advertisement

Content Area Connection
- Social Studies (local government)

171

PREVIEW THE UNIT

3 Look for Activities and Ways to Learn About Community Workers Leaf through the unit, previewing activities students will do, for example:

page 172—learning a limerick about a girl who wants to be a paramedic

pages 173–175—reading about community workers

page 176—listening to the Bookshelf book (Display a copy of the book.)

page 182—reading about local government

page 183—writing a job ad

Also ask students to look for people who work together to help others. Then sum up what the preview reveals: *Many workers help take care of our communities.*

4 Set Your Goals Start a class mind map on how people in the community rely on one another. Write the worker or job words on large self-stick notes and connect the notes together with lines or arrows if they relate to one another in some way. Prompt students for pictures or words to add, and have them act out and describe other ideas for you to put into words.

CLOSE AND ASSESS

Ask students to tell or show you something they are interested in learning in this unit.

UNIT 10 Mind Map

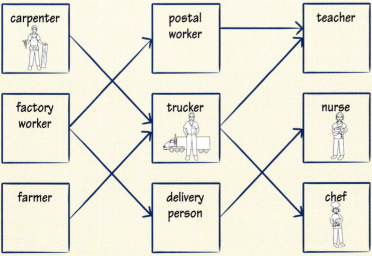

Unit Launch **T171**

UNIT 10 LESSON 2

LANGUAGE DEVELOPMENT: MAY, MIGHT, COULD

OBJECTIVES

Functions: Listen Actively; Repeat Spoken Language; Recite; Express Possibility or Probability

Patterns and Structures:
- Verbs (may, might, could)

Writing: Sentences

INTRODUCE

1. **Listen and Chant** Play "I Could Be a Paramedic" on the **Language Tape/CD**. Students will listen and follow along, then echo the lines, supply phrases with *may*, *might*, and *could*, and finally chime in on the entire limerick.

   Tape 5B / CD 2 Track 14

2. **Learn About Verbs (may, might, could)** Read aloud the verb chart. Ask questions and have students answer in full sentences, based on the limerick. For example:
   - *What could the girl be?* (She could be a paramedic.)
   - *Who might call?* (A man might call.)

PRACTICE

3. **Conduct "Express Yourself"** Model how to tell about what may happen. Have partners complete the activity.

   How to Tell What May Happen
   - If I want to tell about something I'm not sure will happen, I can start with: *I may, I might,* or *I could* . . .
   - Then I add another verb: *I may go to Mexico next year.*

APPLY

4. **Write Sentences** Encourage partners to check their sentences. Distribute Partner Checklist 10 on page T310.

   ▶ Language Practice Book page 91

CLOSE AND ASSESS

Take dictation as students read their sentences aloud. Ask volunteers to circle the words *may, might,* or *could* and underline the verb that follows.

T172 Unit 10 | Here to Help

VERBS: MAY, MIGHT, COULD

I Could Help

Listen and chant.

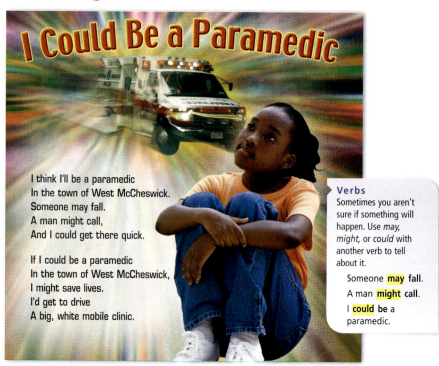

I Could Be a Paramedic

I think I'll be a paramedic
In the town of West McCheswick.
Someone may fall.
A man might call,
And I could get there quick.

If I could be a paramedic
In the town of West McCheswick,
I might save lives.
I'd get to drive
A big, white mobile clinic.

Verbs
Sometimes you aren't sure if something will happen. Use *may, might,* or *could* with another verb to tell about it.

Someone **may** fall.
A man **might** call.
I **could** be a paramedic.

EXPRESS YOURSELF ▶ TELL WHAT MAY HAPPEN

Work with a partner. Read each question. Answer with *may, might,* or *could*.

Example: 1. What kind of job could you have?
I could be a police officer.

1. What kind of job could you have?
2. What might you do in your work?
3. Where might you work?
4. How may you help your community?

WRITE SENTENCES

5.–7. Interview a partner. What might he or she be? Write 3 sentences about what you learn. Use *may, might,* and *could*.

Example: 5. Jasmine may be a firefighter

172 Unit 10 | Here to Help

REACHING ALL STUDENTS

COMMUNITY CONNECTION

Team Up Invite a team of workers to speak to the class about how they help and depend upon one another in their jobs. Some possible teams to invite: emergency-room personnel, firefighters, law-enforcement groups, construction workers, lab researchers, news teams. Work with students to create questions to ask visitors, including:

- How are your jobs related?
- What might happen if you didn't do your job?
- How could you help one another more?

Language Practice Book page 91

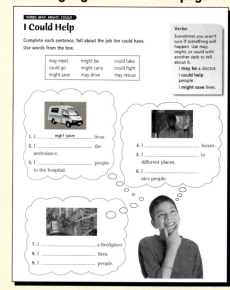

VOCABULARY: TIME

They All Work in Our City

7:00 a.m.
It's seven o'clock.

9:30 a.m.
It's nine thirty.
It's half past nine.

12:00 p.m.
It's noon.
It's twelve o'clock.

4:15 p.m.
It's four fifteen.
It's a quarter after four.
It's fifteen after four.

5:50 p.m.
It's five fifty.
It's ten to six.
It's ten of six.

12:00 a.m.
It's midnight.
It's twelve o'clock.

WHO'S TALKING? ▶ TELL WHAT MAY HAPPEN

1.–3. Listen.
Who is talking? Point to the correct person.
Say what time it is. Tell what the person may do.

WRITE SENTENCES

Read each clock. Write a sentence. Tell something that you might do at that time.

Answers:
1. Female police officer. Midnight. She may find a lost cat and take it back to its owner.
2. Woman raking leaves. Seven o'clock. She may rake a lot of leaves and not finish until after dark.
3. Hot-dog vendor. Noon. She may make an extra batch of hot dogs.

Example: **4.** At seven thirty, I may call you.

4. 	5.	6.	7.	8.	9.
(a.m.)	(p.m.)	(p.m.)	(p.m.)	(a.m.)	(a.m.)

Language Development 173

Language Practice Book page 92

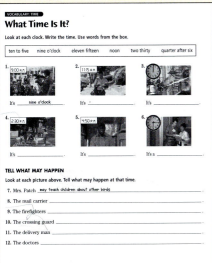

Multi-Level Strategies
VOCABULARY: TIME

PRELITERATE Have students make clock faces with paper plates, tagboard, metal fasteners, and markers. Then call out a time and ask students to show it on their clocks. After a few examples, pairs can take turns, one partner stating a time and the other showing it on the clock. Work together to write the times in numbers and in words, and lead the group in reading the phrases aloud.

UNIT 10 **LESSON 3**

LANGUAGE DEVELOPMENT: TIME

OBJECTIVES

Functions: Listen Actively; Express Possibility or Probability
Concepts and Vocabulary: 🅣 Time
Writing: 🅣 Sentences

INTRODUCE

1 Learn About Words for Time Read the time above each picture. Explain A.M. and P.M. using a diagram of a 24-hour day.

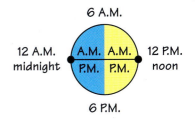

2 Use Time Words Read the captions and explain the rules for telling time:

- Say *o'clock* at the exact hour.
- Say the hour and the minutes: *9:18*
- Use *after* and *past* for times before the half hour: *twenty after four*
- Use *of*, *to*, or *till* for times after the half hour: *ten till six*
- Use *quarter* and *half* for fifteen minute intervals: *quarter past one*

PRACTICE

3 Conduct "Who's Talking?" Play "Who's Talking?" on the **Language Tape/CD**. Replay for students to identify the speakers.

Tape 5B
CD 2 Track 15

APPLY

4 Write Sentences Encourage students to use *morning, afternoon, evening,* and *night* in place of A.M. and P.M.

▶ Language Practice Book page 92

CLOSE AND ASSESS

Have teams list as many ways as possible to read the times shown in Items 4–9.

Language Development **T173**

UNIT 10 **LESSON 4**

LANGUAGE DEVELOPMENT: *HAVE TO* AND *NEED TO*

OBJECTIVES

Functions:
Express Intentions; Describe Actions
Patterns and Structures:
• Phrases with *have to* and *need to*
Writing: • Sentences

INTRODUCE

1 **Learn About Phrases with *Have to* and *Need to*** Read the title and introduction. Then read aloud the examples and have students identify the phrases in bold print.

PRACTICE

2 **Build Sentences** Post a chart to help students use the correct verb forms:

For Sentences with . . .	Use a Phrase with . . .
I, you, we, they	need to have to
he, she, it	needs to has to

Use the sentence frames in Items 1–6 to point out that the second verb in each phrase does not change form.

APPLY

3 **Write About Jobs** Use the Example to model with a volunteer: pantomime being a bus driver until the volunteer guesses the job. Then have partners complete the activity.

▶ Language Practice Book page 93

CLOSE AND ASSESS

Ask volunteers to role-play a worker in Items 1–6 and say a sentence with *have to* or *need to*: *I have to work at the hospital. I need to take your pulse.* The rest of the class guesses the worker. (doctor)

T174 Unit 10 | Here to Help

PHRASES WITH *HAVE TO* AND *NEED TO*

We Have to Help!

Use a verb to complete a **phrase** with *have to* or *need to*.

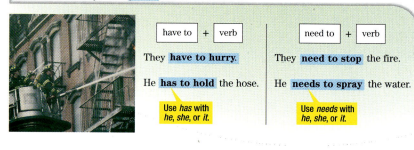

have to + verb
They **have to hurry**.
He **has to hold** the hose.
Use *has* with *he, she,* or *it.*

need to + verb
They **need to stop** the fire.
He **needs to spray** the water.
Use *needs* with *he, she,* or *it.*

BUILD SENTENCES

Look at each picture. Read the sentence. Add the correct form of *have to* or *need to*. Say the new sentence.

Example: 1. He needs to recycle the trash.

1.
He _____ recycle the trash.
has to / needs to

2.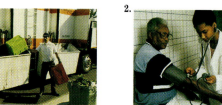
She _____ help the sick.
has to / needs to

3.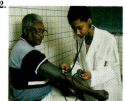
They _____ fight the fire.
have to / need to

4.
They _____ fix the road.
have to / need to

5.
They _____ work on the wires.
have to / need to

6.
He _____ deliver the mail.
has to / needs to

WRITE ABOUT JOBS ✏️

7.–9. Work with a partner. Act out 3 jobs. Your partner guesses what you *need to* or *have to* do. Write the sentence.

Example: 7. You need to drive the bus.

174 Unit 10 | Here to Help

REACHING ALL STUDENTS

Language Development
HAVE TO, NEED TO/MAY, MIGHT, COULD

Set up three-step interviews (see Cooperative Learning Structures, page T337d) to help students practice using phrases with *have to* and *need to,* and the modals *may, might,* and *could.* Partners will interview each other about what jobs they might do in the future, and what they must to do in order to accomplish their goals. Then they will report back to the larger group on what they found out from their partner: *Eduardo might become a lawyer like his father. He needs to go to law school. He has to study hard.*

Language Practice Book page 93

POSSESSIVE PRONOUNS

What Is Your Job?

These **pronouns** tell who or what owns something.

Pronoun	Example
my	I am in this picture. **My** hand is on Malcolm's chin.
your	You can see Mark. He is on **your** left.
his	He has **his** hand on Malcolm's shoulder.
her	Sally's lifting Malcolm's legs on **her** shoulder.
its	The ocean is rough. **Its** waves almost knocked us down.
our	We are practicing **our** rescue plan.
your	Did your team practice **your** rescue plan, too?
their	Our supervisors are watching from **their** towers on the beach.

BUILD SENTENCES

Read each sentence. Add the missing pronoun. Say the new sentence.

Example: 1. This young man fell and hurt his arm.

1. This young man fell and hurt ___(**his**/your)___ arm.
2. We called his parents. They are waiting for ___(its/**their**)___ son at the hospital.
3. We need to get this man into ___(**our**/its)___ ambulance.
4. I have tightened all the straps around ___(his/**her**)___ body.
5. Are you ready to lift the stretcher, Tom? Are you holding ___(their/**your**)___ side?
6. Is Joanne ready? Does she have ___(his/**her**)___ equipment?
7. One, two, three lift! Do you all still have ___(**your**/my)___ sides of the stretcher?
8. OK. The ambulance is ready to go. It has ___(my/**its**)___ sirens on. Everything will be all right!

WRITE CAPTIONS

9.–12. Talk with a group. List some things people own. Draw 4 things and write captions. Use the correct pronoun.

Example: 9.

his flashlight

Language Development 175

Language Practice Book page 94

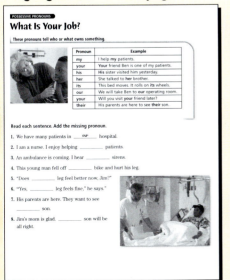

UNIT 10 LESSON 5

LANGUAGE DEVELOPMENT: POSSESSIVE PRONOUNS

OBJECTIVES
Function: Give Information
Patterns and Structures:
- Possessive Pronouns

Writing: Captions

INTRODUCE

1 Learn About Possessive Pronouns
Read the introduction. Then view the photo, and have students identify the people as you read the Examples.

Post a chart to show how subject pronouns and possessive pronouns relate.

Subject Pronouns		Possessive Pronouns
I	→	my
you	→	your
he	→	his
she	→	her
it	→	its
we	→	our
they	→	their

Then go over the examples again, relating each possessive pronoun to the corresponding subject pronoun.

PRACTICE

2 Build Sentences Encourage students to use the chart to choose possessive pronouns. Then have volunteers role-play the scene.

APPLY

3 Write Captions Suggest that groups include a few objects that are owned by more than one person.

▶ **Language Practice Book** page 94

CLOSE AND ASSESS

Have individuals and pairs hold up objects. Call on students to identify the object(s) with the correct possessive pronoun: *This is Leah's pen. This is **her** pen.*

Language Development **T175**

UNIT 10 **LESSON 6**

LANGUAGE AND LITERACY: THE BASICS BOOKSHELF

OBJECTIVES
Concepts and Vocabulary: Community Workers
Listening: Listen to a Preview
Reading Strategies: Activate Prior Knowledge; Preview; Analyze Story Elements (characters)

BUILD LANGUAGE AND VOCABULARY

1. **Teach "Words to Know"** Have students look at pages 2–3. Say: *These pages show workers who help the community. Some workers drive special vehicles such as cars and trucks.*

   As you point to each photo, read the name of the worker and the worker's vehicle. Use simple sentences to describe the job: *A trash collector drives a trash truck. The trash collector takes garbage from our homes and drives it to the dump.*

2. **Play "What's Your Job?"** Choose a community worker on pages 2–3. Invite students to ask questions to discover the worker's identity. Model using yes-or-no questions: *Does the worker drive a vehicle? Does the worker drive people from one place to another?* Have students take turns choosing and guessing other workers.

PREPARE TO READ

3. **Think About What You Know** Make a class list of machines that require electricity. Then talk about what problems might occur if the electricity went out in your area.

4. **Preview** Play the Audio Walk-Through for *Power Out!* on the **Selection Tape/CD** to give students the overall idea of the story.   *Tape 5B / CD 2 Track 7*

CLOSE AND ASSESS

Have students draw two pictures. The first shows the city with the power on and the second shows the same scene with the power out.

T176a Unit 10 | Here to Help

Power Out!
by Sherilin Chanek

Summary This realistic fiction shows how a community pulls together during a power out. Emergency operators direct calls, police officers direct traffic and rescue subway commuters, firefighters help trapped workers, and ordinary citizens help each other. Simple text reinforces words for community workers.

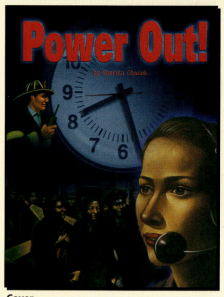
Cover

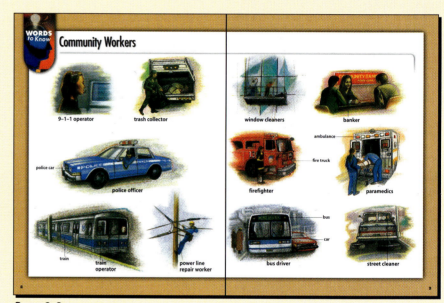
Pages 2–3

Multi-Level Strategies
LITERACY SUPPORT

PRELITERATE **Analyze Story Elements: Characters** Explain that characters are the people in the story. Turn to page 6 and point to the picture of the police officer. Say: *This man is a police officer. He is a character in the story.* Call on volunteers to identify more characters by reading their names and showing pictures from the text. List the characters on a large chart paper as students dictate.

Work with students to brainstorm more community workers such as paramedics, teachers, and lawyers. Have students write new episodes for *Power Out!* using the text on page 8 as a model: *10:51 A.M. The cook can't make the soup. The stove does not work.* Provide sentence frames:

_____ A.M. / P.M.
The _____ can't _____.
The _____ does not work.

Power Out!

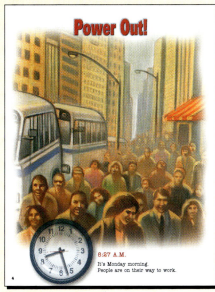
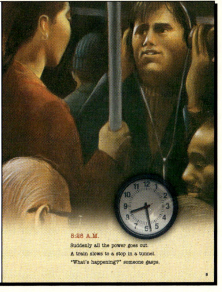

Pages 4–5

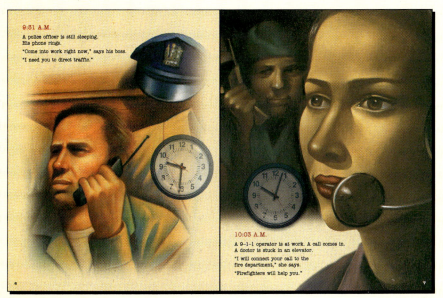

Pages 6–7

Strategies for Comprehensible Input

Page	Story Language	Strategy Options
4	A.M.	**Restate:** in the morning
	People are on their way to work.	**Restate:** People are going to work.
5	Suddenly all the power goes out.	**Restate:** Without warning all the machines stop working.
	slows to a stop	**Demonstrate:** Pantomime how an object gradually comes to a stop.
	"What's happening?"	**Restate:** "What is going on?"
	gasps	**Demonstrate:** gasp
6	boss	**Explain:** The boss tells the police officer what to do for his job.
	direct traffic	**Demonstrate:** Pantomime directing traffic.
7	9-1-1 operator	**Explain:** When you dial 9-1-1 on the phone, an operator sends help.
	A call comes in.	**Restate:** The phone rings.
	stuck in an elevator	**Explain:** The elevator can't move. The doctor can't get out.
	"I will connect your call to the fire department."	**Restate:** "I will let you talk to the fire department."

Language and Literacy **T176b**

UNIT 10 **LESSON 6,** CONTINUED

LANGUAGE AND LITERACY: THE BASICS BOOKSHELF

OBJECTIVES

Functions: Listen to a Book; Repeat Spoken Language (echo reading)

Critical Thinking and Comprehension:
🅣 Identify Cause and Effect

READ AND THINK TOGETHER

1. **Read Aloud** On your first reading of the book, use the "Strategies for Comprehensible Input" that appear at the bottom of pages T176b and T176d.

2. **Read and Map: Identify Cause and Effect** Draw a cause-and-effect chart like the one below, but with only the labels for *Cause* and *Effect* filled in. Say: *A cause-and-effect chart tells what happens and why it happens.*

    Read aloud pages 4–5. Then think aloud to model connecting ideas in the story: *On these pages, I learn that a train stops in a tunnel. It stops because the power goes out. For* **Cause,** *I will write* The power goes out. *What happens after the power goes out? Under* **Effect 1,** *I will write* The train stops in a tunnel. *That happens because the power goes out.*

    Pause after reading the pages shown below and model completing the cause-and-effect chart for the rest of the text. Then read pages 14–16 to complete the book.

3. **Conduct an Interactive Reading** Have the students do the following:

    - **Read along and echo read** Play the recording of *Power Out!* on the **Selection Tape/CD**. Pause the tape after each page and have students echo the text.

CLOSE AND ASSESS

Divide students into groups of four. Ask each group member to tell one effect of the power outage.

T176c Unit 10 | Here to Help

Pages 8–9

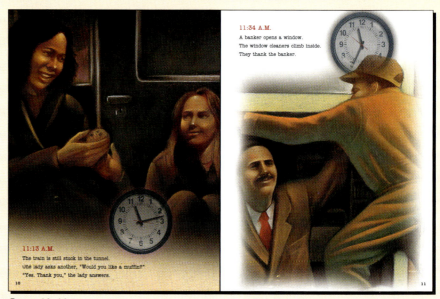
Pages 10–11

Cause-and-Effect Chart for *Power Out!*

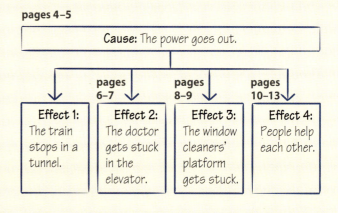

Technology Support
See **Inspiration** Visual Learning software for support in creating the cause-and-effect chart.

Power Out!, CONTINUED

Pages 12–13

Pages 14–15

Page 16

Strategies for Comprehensible Input

Page	Story Language	Strategy Options
8–9	Their platform is stuck	**Point to the picture and explain:** It won't go up or down.
10	muffin	**Point to the picture and explain:** A muffin is like sweet bread.
11	banker	**Explain:** A bank is a building where people keep their money. A banker works in the bank.
12–13	walk out of the tunnel	**Explain:** The people walk up stairs to the street.
	Everyone is safe.	**Restate:** No one is hurt.
14–15	P.M.	**Restate:** in the afternoon
	power line repair workers	**Point to the picture on page 2.**
	comes back on	**Restate:** works again
16	The scare is over.	**Restate:** Now the people are not worried or afraid.

Language and Literacy **T176d**

UNIT 10 LESSON 7

LANGUAGE AND LITERACY: THE BASICS BOOKSHELF

OBJECTIVES

Function: Retell a Story
Learning Strategy: Use Graphic Organizers (cause-and-effect chart)
Critical Thinking and Comprehension:
❶ Identify Cause and Effect

CHECK COMPREHENSION

1. **Make a Cause-and-Effect Chart**
   Have students review *Power Out!* and identify causes and effects. Remind them that a cause-and-effect chart shows things that happen and the reasons why they happen.

   As you read aloud the directions for each step, pause for students to add information to the sections of their cause-and-effect charts. Encourage students to ask themselves: *What happened? Why did it happen?*

2. **Retell the Story** Have small groups take turns using their cause-and-effect charts to tell the story in their own words. Then have group members compare their charts to add and correct information.

CLOSE AND ASSESS

Ask students to complete this sentence:
A cause-and-effect chart shows _____.

COMPREHENSION: IDENTIFY CAUSE AND EFFECT

Read and Think Together

Make a cause-and-effect chart for *Power Out!* Follow these steps.

❶ Draw a box like the one below. What important event happens in the beginning of the story? Write it in the box.

> **Cause:** The power goes out.

❷ What happens because the power goes out? Draw 4 boxes. Draw a picture of the effect in each box. Write about it, too.

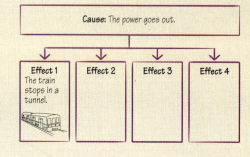

❸ Compare your chart with a partner. Did you choose the same effects?

❹ Use your finished chart to retell the story to your partner.

Sample Responses:
Students may illustrate the following effects:
• The doctor gets stuck in the elevator.
• The window cleaners' platform gets stuck.
• People help each other.

from **The Basics Bookshelf**

THEME BOOK
Learn how people help each other get through an emergency in a big city.

176 Unit 10 | Here to Help

REACHING ALL STUDENTS

Language Development
EXPRESS CERTAINTY

Role-Play Turn to page 6 and role-play several sentences that the police officer is sure of: *I am a police officer. I am sure this will be a busy day. I know that the power will work, soon.*

Use the chart to present other suitable language. Then have students role-play other characters in the story, giving statements that express certainty.

How to Express Certainty
I am sure that _____.
I know for sure that _____.
It's a fact that _____.
I am positive that _____.

HIGH FREQUENCY WORDS
Words to Know

REVIEW WORDS YOU KNOW

Read the words aloud. Which word goes in the sentence?

river	picture
only	important
were	water

1. The _____ is rising fast.   river
2. It is _____ to work together.   important
3. The sandbags will hold back the _____.   water

LEARN TO READ

Learn new words.

been	Mina has **been** in India since 1992.
four	**Four** years ago, there was an earthquake.
sound	Mina heard a loud **sound**.
caused	The earthquake **caused** her house to fall down.
between	Mina was trapped **between** a wall and a table.
could	She **could** not move.
almost	She **almost** didn't get out, but she did.
life	A rescue team saved her **life**.
often	Mina **often** tells that story.
never	We **never** get tired of hearing it.

How to Learn a New Word
- Look at the word.
- Listen to the word.
- Listen to the word in a sentence. What does it mean?
- Say the word.
- Spell the word.
- Say the word again.

WORD WORK

Where does each new word fit in the chart? Say the word and spell it.

Example: 4. caused c-a-u-s-e-d

What to Look For	Word
4. ends in **ed**	c a u s e d
5. ends in **nd**	s o u n d
6. is a number	f o u r
7. begins with **al**	a l m o s t
8. means "many times"	o f t e n

What to Look For	Word
9. has one syllable and **ee**	b e e n
10. has **tw**	b e t w e e n
11. has a long **i** sound	l i f e
12. rhymes with **good**	c o u l d
13. is the opposite of **always**	n e v e r

Language and Literacy 177

Reading Practice Book page 74

HIGH FREQUENCY WORDS
Words to Know
READ AND WRITE
Read each word. Then write it.
1. life _____ 2. been _____ 3. sound _____
4. four _____ 5. almost _____ 6. caused _____
7. often _____ 8. never _____ 9. could _____
10. between _____

Answer each question.
11. Which words start with c? _____
12. Which words have the letters ee together? _____

WORD WORK
Read each sentence. Choose a word from the box above.
Then write it in the sentence.
13. My little brother is four years old.
14. Kento has been lost only once in his _____.
15. He _____ always holds Mom's hand.
16. One day Mom said he _____ walk without her.
17. He has always _____ fast, and he ran from her.
18. A clerk heard a _____.
19. She _____ helps lost children.
20. Kento _____ Mom a lot of worry.
21. He _____ runs from her now.
22. He stays _____ Mom and me!

Reading Fluency
RECOGNIZE HIGH FREQUENCY WORDS

To build automaticity with the new high frequency words:

- Have pairs make two sets of word cards and play a matching game. Partners lay the cards face down and take turns turning two cards over in random order to try to make a matching pair. Have students read each word aloud and spell it to confirm the match.

- Partners can display one set of word cards on a classroom chart, then go to the chart with the other set and match their cards. Encourage students to spell the words after they match them.

UNIT 10   **LESSON 8**

LANGUAGE AND LITERACY: HIGH FREQUENCY WORDS

OBJECTIVES
Learning to Read:
- Recognize High Frequency Words

REVIEW WORDS

1 Review Known High Frequency Words Have the group read aloud the words in the green box. Listen for words students cannot read automatically and use the steps in the yellow box to reteach those words. Then have students look at the photo. Read each cloze sentence. Reread each sentence and pause for students to silently read the two words to the left of the sentence. Tell students to choose the word that goes in the sentence and tells about the picture.

INTRODUCE NEW WORDS

2 Learn High Frequency Words Use the High Frequency Word Script on page T321 to lead students through the steps in the yellow box.

PRACTICE

3 Conduct "Word Work" Use the Example to model how to use the clue to find the possible words in the list and then to use the number of letter blanks to choose the correct word or confirm it.

Have groups complete Items 5–13. Then discuss how the correct word matches the clue and number of blanks.

APPLY

4 Read Words in Context Students will apply the skill when they read high frequency words in context in the sentences on page 179 and the passage on page 180.

▶ **Reading Practice Book** page 74

CLOSE AND ASSESS

Call out the high frequency words one at a time. Have students point to them and spell the words as a group.

Language and Literacy   **T177**

UNIT 10 LESSON 9

LANGUAGE AND LITERACY: PHONICS

OBJECTIVES

Learning to Read: Build Oral Vocabulary; Develop Phonemic Awareness; ⓣ Associate Sounds and Symbols /ī/ *ie, igh*; Blend Sounds to Decode Words

TEACH LONG VOWELS: /ī/ *ie, igh*

1. **Build Oral Vocabulary** Display Transparency 54. Talk through each picture to develop meaning for the words in the yellow boxes. For example, for Item 1, say:

   • *Here are some city lights* (point). *The lights shine brightly at night. The lights* (point) *are bright.*

2. **Develop Phonemic Awareness** Remove the transparency and conduct the oral activities in Step 1 of the Script for Transparency 54.

3. **Read Long *i* Words** Display Transparency 54 again. Work through Steps 2 and 3 of the script.

CLOSE AND ASSESS

Display the words *night, tie, right,* and *tried.* Call on students to read each word and identify the letters that make the vowel sound.

Word Families

-IE AND -IGHT

Materials: Letter Tiles

A large number of words can be generated from a few rhyming phonograms. Use letter tiles to build the words in dark type. Then change tiles to build other words in the *-ie* and *-ight* families. Have students make a list of the words. Make sure students understand their meanings. Then ask them to read the words on their list and to identify the shared ending.

tie	night
die	bright
lie	right
pie	fright
	tight

T178a Unit 10 | Here to Help

Transparency 54: ▶
Long *i* (*ie, igh*)

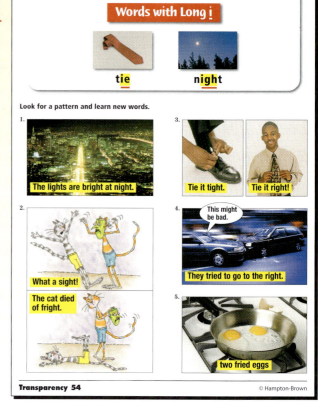

Transparency 54   © Hampton-Brown

▼ Script for Transparency 54

Words with Long *i*

1. **Develop Phonemic Awareness**
   Isolate/Match Final and Medial Long *i* Say: *Listen to the last sound in these words:* tie, pie, lie. *What is the sound?* (/ī/) *Now listen for the sound* /ī/ *in the middle of these words:* ties, right, night. *Say the words with me. Now raise your hand each time you hear the sound* /ī/. *Say these words:* pin, pie, fight, fit, tin, tight, tie, tip.

2. **Associate Sounds and Symbols**
   Point to the tie on **Transparency 54**. Say: *This is a tie. A man wears a tie around his neck.* Say the word *tie* with me. Then point to the *ie* in *tie* and say: *The letters* ie *make the sound you hear at the end of* tie. *The sound is* /ī/. *Say* /ī/ *with me:* /ī ī ī/. Point to *ie* and ask: *What are the letters? What's the sound?* Repeat for *night,* pointing out that the letters *igh* make the long *i* sound in the middle of *night.*

3. **Blend Sounds to Read Words**
   Model/Teach Point to the letter *t* in *tie* and say: *The sound for* t *is* /t/. Repeat for *ie:* /ī ī ī/. *As you slide a finger slowly from left to right below the letters* tie, say: *I can blend the two sounds:* /t ī ī ī/. *Now, I'm going to say the whole word:* tie. Repeat for *night,* pointing out that the letters *igh* make the sound /ī/. Have students sound out the words *tie* and *night* with you.

   Practice For Item 1, say: *Let's try that again. This picture shows lights at night, doesn't it? Read this word with me* (point to *lights*). *Follow my finger as we blend the sounds* /l ī ī ī t s/, *and say the word:* lights. Read aloud the sentence, pausing for students to decode *lights, bright, at* and *night.* Repeat for the other sentences, calling special attention to the following:

   • In Items 3 and 4, point out the two meanings of *right.* In Item 3, *right* means "correctly." In Item 4, *right* means "a direction" (demonstrate).

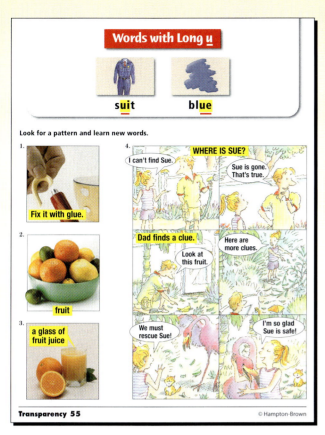

◀ Transparency 55: Long u (ui, ue)

▼ Script for Transparency 55

Words with Long u

1. **Develop Phonemic Awareness**
   Isolate/Match Final and Medial Long u Say: *Listen to the last sound in these words:* blue, true, glue. *What is the sound?* (/ū/) *Now listen for the sound* /ū/ *in the middle of these words:* suit, juice. *Say the words with me. Now raise your hand each time you hear the sound* /ū/. *Say these words:* clue, cup, suit, jug, juice, true.

2. **Associate Sounds and Symbols**
   Point to the suit on **Transparency 55**. Say: *This is a suit. Say the word* suit *with me.* Then point to the *ui* in *suit* and say: *The letters* ui *make the sound you hear in the middle of* suit. *The sound is* /ū/. *Say* /ū/ *with me:* /ū ū ū/. Point to *ui* and ask: *What are the letters? What's the sound?* Repeat for *blue*, pointing out that the letters *ue* make the sound /ū/ at the end of the word *blue*. Then point to *ue* in *rescue* in Item 4. Say: *The letters* ue *can also make the sound you hear at the end of* rescue: /yōō/. Explain that the letters *ue* can make /ū/ (as in *blue*) or /yōō/ (as in *rescue*).

3. **Blend Sounds to Read Words**
   Model/Teach Point to the letter *s* in *suit* and say: *The sound for* s *is* /s/. Repeat for *ui*: /ū ū ū/. As you slide a finger below the letters *sui*, say: *I can blend the two sounds:* /s ū ū ū/. Then point to the *t* and say: *The sound for* t *is* /t/. *I can blend the three sounds together:* /s ū ū ū t/. *Now, I'm going to say the whole word:* suit. Repeat for *blue*. Have students sound out the words *suit* and *blue* with you.

   Practice For Item 1, say: *Let's try that again. This picture shows some glue, doesn't it?* Point to the sentence and say: *Follow my finger to blend the sounds and then say these words* (point to *Fix, it, with,* and *glue*). Repeat for the other words, calling attention to the following:

   • In Item 3, read aloud the word *juice* for students.

   • In Item 4, help students read *rescue* by dividing it between the consonants *sc* and blending the two syllables. Remind students: *The letters* ue *make the sound* /yōō/ *in rescue.*

OBJECTIVES

Learning to Read: Build Oral Vocabulary; Develop Phonemic Awareness; ⓣ Associate Sounds and Symbols /ū/ *ui, ue;* /yōō/ *ue;* Blend Sounds to Decode Words

TEACH LONG VOWELS: /ū/ui, ue; /yōō/ue

1. **Build Oral Vocabulary** Display Transparency 55. Talk through each picture to develop meaning for the words in the yellow boxes. For example, for Item 1, say:

   • *Here is some* **glue** (point). **Glue** *is sticky* (pantomime with fingers). *When things break, you can use* **glue** *to put them back together.*

2. **Develop Phonemic Awareness** Remove the transparency and conduct the oral activities in Step 1 of the Script for Transparency 55.

3. **Read Long *u* Words** Display Transparency 55 again. Work through Steps 2 and 3 of the script.

CLOSE AND ASSESS

Display the words *suit, blue, fruit,* and *clue*. Call on students to read each word and identify the letters that make the sound /ū/.

▶ **Reading Practice Book** page 75 (long i: *ie, igh* and long u: *ui, ue*)

Reading Practice Book page 75

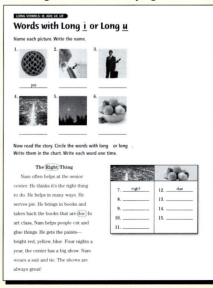

Language and Literacy **T178b**

UNIT 10 LESSON 10

LANGUAGE AND LITERACY: READING AND SPELLING

OBJECTIVES

Functions: Listen Actively; Repeat Spoken Language; Recite

Learning to Read: Develop Phonemic Awareness; 🅣 Associate Sounds and Symbols: /ī/ *ie, igh*; /ū/ *ui, ue*; /yōō/ *ue*; Blend Sounds to Decode Words

Spelling: 🅣 Words with Long Vowels: *ie, igh; ui, ue*

LISTEN AND LEARN

Tape 5B
CD 2 Track 16

1. **Sing a Song** Display Transparency 56 and play "Night Watch" on the **Language Tape/CD**.

DEVELOP PHONEMIC AWARENESS

2. **Isolate Final and Medial Sounds**
Say: *Listen to these words. Where do you hear /ī/ in each word?* Say: *high, tie, sigh.* (at the end) *Now, where do you hear /ī/ in these words?* Say: *right, light, night.* (in the middle) Repeat for /ū/, using *blue, glue, clue; suit, juice.*

CONNECT SOUNDS AND LETTERS

3. **Associate /ī/ *ie, igh* and /ū/ *ui, ue*** Identify the first picture and sound out its name. Say: *This is a tie, and here's the word. Let's point to the letters and say the sounds together:* /t/, /ī ī ī/, tie. Point to the letters *ie* and remind students that when two vowels are together, the first is usually long and the second is silent. Contrast the word *tie* with the word *tip*. Write *tip* and ask students to sound it out. Point out that when a word has one vowel and then a consonant, the vowel is short.

Help students sound out the other words, pointing out that three letters make one sound in *night*. Read the question aloud: *What letters stand for the vowel sound in each word?* (*ie* and *igh* for /ī/ in *tie* and *night; ui* and *ue* for /ū/ in *suit* and *blue*) Have a student name the letters that make /ī/ or /ū/ in each word. Explain that *ue* spells the /ū/ sound at the end of words.

T178 Unit 10 | Here to Help

LONG VOWELS: *IE, IGH; UI, UE*

Reading and Spelling

LISTEN AND LEARN

Night Watch

The night watchman at the museum
wears a suit of blue,
a bright red tie, a badge, a belt,
and shiny leather shoes.

The night watchman at the museum
works the whole night through.
He checks the lights, the doors, the locks,
each painting, and the statues.

CONNECT SOUNDS AND LETTERS

What letters stand for the vowel sound in each word?

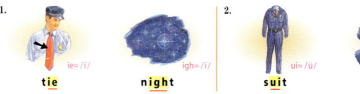

1. **t**<u>ie</u>   ie=/ī/   **n**<u>igh</u>**t**   igh=/ī/
2. **s**<u>ui</u>**t**   ui=/ū/   **bl**<u>ue</u>   ue=/ū/

178 Unit 10 | Here to Help   ▶ Transparencies 54–56

REACHING ALL STUDENTS

Multi-Level Strategies

LITERACY SUPPORT

NON-ROMAN ALPHABET To anchor understanding of how to represent English sounds in print and blend sounds to decode words, have students use letter cards to build the following words: *tie, lie, glue, clue, true, night, sight, light, suit, fruit*. Use letter tiles on the overhead projector to model how to build each word, sound by sound.

t → i e

PRELITERATE Cover target words on Transparencies 54 and 55. Point to the picture for *night,* for example, and say the name. Have students spell *night* sound by sound: *What is the first sound in* night? (/n/) *Write the letter that stands for* n. Continue through *night,* guiding students to write three letters for /ī/. Reveal the word and have students check their work.

READING STRATEGY

Follow these steps to read a word.

❶ Look for a pattern of letters.

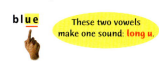
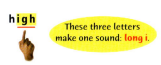

❷ Start at the beginning. Blend the sounds in your head. Then say the word.

 b + l + u~~e~~ = blue   h + igh = high

READING AND SPELLING PRACTICE

Look for a pattern to read these words.

1. lights   2. suit   3. blue   4. tie   5. Sue   6. high

Use what you learned to read the sentences.

7. Sue fixes street lights between 6 and 9 at night.
8. One night she did not tie her safety belt.
9. The belt opened. Sue almost fell from a high pole!
10. Her blue suit got stuck on the pole. That saved her life.
11. "I might die if I don't tie my belt right," Sue said.
12.–16. Now write the sentences that your teacher reads.

For dictation sentences, see Step 6 at right.

WORD WORK

17. Write each of these words on a card.

| tie | high | true | sight | fried | right | clue |
| pie | fruit | blue | die | sigh | suit | glue |

Say each word. Sort the words by vowel sound. Make 2 groups.

18. Then put the words with the same vowel sound *and* spelling together. Make 4 groups. What do you notice?

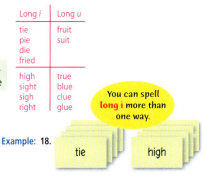

Long i	Long u
tie	fruit
pie	suit
die	
fried	
high	true
sight	blue
sigh	clue
right	glue

You can spell long i more than one way.

Example: 18. tie   high

Language and Literacy 179

Decodable Book

PRACTICE WITH LONG VOWELS IE, IGH; UI, UE

Decodable Book 10: *Rescue at the Beach*

Assign **Decodable Book 10** for independent reading. The **Decodable Book** can be used in a variety of ways to help students become more fluent, automatic readers:

Discussion Circles Have students work in small groups to read aloud and discuss the book using the questions on the back cover. Encourage students to read aloud the text that supports their answers. Groups can also work together to complete the Word Work Activity.

Readers Theater Students can read aloud the stories in a class performance. Help them prepare by rereading the stories in daily rehearsals. Work with students to add narration or dialog. Encourage them to use natural phrasing and expression.

Rereading at Home Have students work with family members to reread the book at home. They can take turns reading aloud alternate pages, then rereading the book switching the pages each person reads.

LEARN A READING STRATEGY

4 Sound Out Words Work through the strategy with students, reading each step aloud and modeling the actions shown on the page. For the X'ed out *e*, remind students that when two vowels are together, the first is usually long and the second vowel is silent.

PRACTICE

5 Read Words and Sentences Have students look for a pattern and sound out the words in Items 1–6 as a choral reading. Then distribute the Partner Prompts from page T311 to guide peers in reading the sentences in Items 7–11. Remind them to use the sound-out strategy to read words.

6 Write Sentences Dictate the following sentences for students to write. Read each sentence at normal speed once so students can listen, and then repeat it slowly word by word as they write:

12. I want a blue suit and a red tie.

13. This glue can fix that cup.

14. The lights are bright at night.

15. The fruit is sweet.

16. Fried eggs taste good, too.

If students need support spelling words with long *u*, suggest that they think about whether long *u* is in the middle or at the end of a word.

7 Conduct "Word Work" Read the directions and work through the Example. Then have partners complete the activity. Discuss what students discovered about the ways to spell long *i* and long *u*.

▶ **Reading Practice Book** pages 147–150 (Decodable Book 10)

CLOSE AND ASSESS

Write *fried, high, right, glue, night, fruit,* and *pie*. Call on students to read the words and then tell two ways to spell long *i* and two ways to spell long *u*.

Language and Literacy T179

UNIT 10 **LESSON 11**

LANGUAGE AND LITERACY: INDEPENDENT READING

OBJECTIVES

Functions: Read a Selection; Describe

Learning to Read: ❶ Recognize High Frequency Words; ❶ Decode Words (with long *i* spelled *ie, igh* and long *u* spelled *ui, ue*)

Reading Strategies: Activate Prior Knowledge; Set a Purpose for Reading; Ask Questions; Clarify

Critical Thinking and Comprehension: ❶ Identify Cause and Effect

Writing: Clues

READ ON YOUR OWN

1. **Introduce Vocabulary** In "Hot Crumbs Cause Fire," students apply phonics skills and read high frequency words taught in Lessons 8–10. Introduce the story words. Write each word, pronounce it, and spell it. Then give a definition and a context sentence:

   - **burned:** hurt by fire or heat. *The flame burned his fingers.*
   - **paramedics:** emergency medical workers. *Paramedics put the injured man on a stretcher.*
   - **firefighters/fire station:** people who put out fires are called firefighters; they work at a fire station. *The firefighters from the Seaside Fire Station put out the fire.*
   - **tempura, crumbs:** Tempura is a food covered in batter and deep-fried in oil. Crumbs are small pieces of food. *The crumbs from the tempura are very hot.*

2. **Activate Prior Knowledge/Set Purposes** View the photos and discuss what students know about fires. Model setting a purpose: *I'll read this article to find out how this fire started.* Encourage volunteers to state their purposes for reading.

3. **Read and Think: Ask Questions/Clarify** Students should read the passage on their own. Suggest that they ask themselves questions for clarification as they read, then reread or read on to find the answers.

T180 Unit 10 | Here to Help

COMPREHENSION: IDENTIFY CAUSE AND EFFECT

Read on Your Own

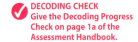
DECODING CHECK
Give the Decoding Progress Check on page 1a of the Assessment Handbook.

Friday, June 2, 1999   THE TIMES   5A

Hot Crumbs Cause Fire

TOKYO, JAPAN — A fire woke Kenji Yamada at 4 a.m. last night. He called the fire station. Fire trucks soon came to the rescue.

"The flames were so high and so bright!" Yamada said. "It's true! I almost died!" When he tried to throw water on the fire, he burned his right hand. Paramedics treated him.

Firefighters asked what caused the fire. At first, Yamada didn't have a clue. He said he went to bed. Then he smelled smoke. It came from his kitchen. "I think it was something in my trash," he sighed.

Yamada had some fruit at 9 p.m. At 9:30 he made tempura. He put the fried crumbs in his trash can.

When you cook tempura, the oil gets very hot.

Those crumbs can be as hot as 100°C. After a while, the crumbs might start a fire. They did last night at Yamada's home. In fact, hot crumbs caused six fires in Tokyo this year.

180 Unit 10 | Here to Help

REACHING ALL STUDENTS

COMMUNITY CONNECTION

Emergency Workers Point out that in the article on page 180, Kenji Yamada called the fire station when he noticed the fire. Invite a representative from the fire or police department to tell how emergency calls are handled and how help is provided. Later, students can role-play a 911 operator and someone reporting an emergency, then the 911 operator and a paramedic, then the paramedic and the person who reported the emergency.

CHECK YOUR UNDERSTANDING

Write sentences that tell what happened in the article. Use a sentence starter from column 1 and a sentence ending from column 2.

Example: 1. Yamada made tempura, and the crumbs caused a fire.

Column 1
1. Yamada made tempura, C
2. Yamada called the fire station D
3. The fire trucks came B
4. Yamada burned his hand E
5. Hot crumbs caused A

Column 2
A. six fires in Tokyo this year.
B. after Yamada called the fire station.
C. and the crumbs caused a fire.
D. because he smelled smoke.
E. when he tried to throw water on the fire.

EXPAND YOUR VOCABULARY

6. Copy the concept map. Work with a group to add community workers. Add words to tell what each worker does.

Sample Responses:

Use the concept map to tell your group about community workers who help in emergencies.

Example: Firefighters are community workers. They put out fires.

WRITE ABOUT COMMUNITY WORKERS

7. Write 3 clues about a community worker and then ask, "Who is it?" Trade clues with a partner. Try to guess your partner's community worker.

Example: 7. He uses a ladder.
He rescues people.
He puts out fires.
Who is it?

Reading Practice Book page 76

Build Reading Fluency

Read the article. Stop when the timer goes off. Mark your score. Then try it again two more times on different days.

First-Aid Class

I went to a first-aid class at school. I learned the right way to treat cuts and sprains and other injuries. I thought the class was a lot of fun.

Then, last week, Tom and I went bike riding. Tom fell off his bike and got a cut over his eye. He sprained his right foot, too. The first thing I did was call his mom. I asked her to bring some ice. Then I got the first-aid kit from my backpack. I cleaned up Tom's cut and put a band-aid over it. His foot started to swell. I wrapped it with a strip of elastic bandage, but made sure it wasn't too tight!

Tom was very impressed. "You should be a doctor!" he said.

The first-aid class was fun, but I never dreamed it was so important. Some things are really good to know.

	Day 1	Day 2	Day 3
Total Words Read in One Minute			
Minus Words Missed			
Words Read Correctly in One Minute			

Reading Fluency
TIMED READINGS

Read the directions on **Reading Practice Book** page 76. Set the timer and have a student read the passage to you. Use a copy of the page to mark words the student misses and to note the last word read in one minute. Have students graph their performance and set a goal for improving in subsequent timed readings. Plan for two additional timed readings, and encourage partners to practice reading the passage to each other between the timed readings.

CHECK YOUR UNDERSTANDING

4 Comprehension: Identify Cause and Effect Tell students to write a sentence about an event described in the article by matching a sentence starter in Column 1 with a sentence ending in Column 2. Say: *Item 1 in Column 1 says, "Yamada made tempura." I have to read the items in Column 2 to find the sentence ending that makes sense and tells about something in the article. After reading the items in Column 2, I realize that Item C is the right answer.*

EXPAND YOUR VOCABULARY

5 List Community Workers and Their Jobs Read the directions and go over the vocabulary in the map. Students can work in a group to think of other community workers to add to the map and to tell what they do. Go over the second set of directions with students, and use the Example to model telling about emergency workers.

WRITE

6 Write Clues About Community Workers Read aloud the Example and have students guess the community worker the clues describe. (a firefighter) Then ask each student to choose a community worker and write three clues to describe the worker. When students finish, they can swap clues with a partner and try to guess each other's community worker.

For students who need additional support in writing, provide sentence frames and help students choose present-tense verbs and nouns to complete them:

> She uses ____.
> She ____.
> She ____.
> Who is it?

▶ **Reading Practice Book** page 76

CLOSE AND ASSESS

Have a student retell the beginning of the article and others continue until all the key events are mentioned.

UNIT 10 LESSON 12

LANGUAGE ACROSS THE CURRICULUM: SOCIAL STUDIES

OBJECTIVES

Function: Listen to a Selection

Concepts and Vocabulary:
Local Government

Learning Strategies: Build Background; Set a Purpose for Reading

Critical Thinking and Comprehension: Identify Details; Analyze Information

LEARN ABOUT LOCAL GOVERNMENT

1. **Build Background** Go over the photos and captions at the top of the page. As you read the first caption aloud, have students point to the names of the state, county, and city on the map.

   Next, read about the mayor and city council. Explain that these leaders are elected to represent the citizens.

   Read the section about taxes, budget, and services. Explain that the article will tell how the mayor and council help the city provide for its services.

LISTEN AND THINK

2. **Set a Purpose for Reading** Read the article title and the focus question. Ask: *What will you learn about in this article?* (how the mayor and city council help the city)

3. **Read the Article Aloud** Restate ideas and clarify vocabulary as necessary. As you read, have students take notes about the duties of the mayor and city council.

CHECK UNDERSTANDING

4. **Answer the Review Questions** Encourage students to review the article and their notes in order to complete the items.

CLOSE AND ASSESS

Invite groups to find photos and stories in local newspapers showing the people or services they have learned about.

T182 Unit 10 | Here to Help

SUCCESS IN SOCIAL STUDIES

Learn About Local Government

LOCAL GOVERNMENT

A **city** is usually part of a **county**. There are many counties in a **state**.

Many cities have a **mayor** and a **city council**. Together, they **govern** the city.

People pay **taxes** to the city where they live. The city makes a **budget**, or plan, for how to spend the money.

The budget provides for important **services** such as fire protection.

Listen to the article. Then do the Review.

Answers to the Review:
1. Helps decide how to spend the city's money; makes a budget; hires city workers; represents the city at special meetings and events; runs the meetings of the city council; helps make important decisions that meet the needs of people in the city.
2. buses, roads, fire and rescue, police, trash collection, library
3. state, county, city

Your Local Government in Action

• How do the mayor and city council help the city?

City governments can be organized in different ways. Some cities have a mayor and a city council. They are elected by the voters to govern the city.

The mayor and the city council run the city. They decide how to spend the city's money. They make a budget to pay for important services like these:

 buses   roads   fire and rescue

police   trash collection   library

The mayor may hire city workers such as the Fire Chief or Police Chief. The mayor represents the city at special meetings and events.

The mayor runs the meetings of the city council. The mayor and the council work together to make important decisions that meet the needs of people in their city. For example, they may decide to spend money on a new park. They may have to set limits on how much water people use. Their leadership can affect the lives of the people in the city for many years.

REVIEW

1. **Check Your Understanding** Tell three things the mayor does.
2. **Vocabulary** Name three services that might be in a city's budget.
3. **Vocabulary** Order the following from largest to smallest: county, city, state.

182 Unit 10 | Here to Help

REACHING ALL STUDENTS

Social Studies Connection

LOCAL GOVERNMENT

Set up a mock council to discuss how to distribute the class budget. Elect representatives and list items they need to discuss, such as: *art supplies, sports equipment, field trips, party food/supplies.*

Explain that the council meeting will discuss what percentage of the class budget should go to each activity. As the mayor presides, the council will listen to class members' opinions. Then the mayor and council will vote on how to divide the budget.

Writing Project — JOB ADVERTISEMENT

WRITING ASSESSMENT
Use the Writing Progress Checklist on page 51 of the Assessment Handbook to evaluate this writing project.

You depend on many community services. Think of a service you would like to have at your school. Work with a partner and write an ad for the job.

CHOOSE A JOB

1 Brainstorm jobs. They can be real or funny jobs. Check page 305 of your Handbook for job names.

2 Write questions.

- What is the job?
- Where is the job?
- When does the worker need to work?
- What does the worker have to do?

3 Answer the questions.

- What is the job? The job is for a computer game teacher.
- Where is the job? at Lakeside School
- When does the worker need to work? from 8:30 to noon
- What does the worker have to do? The worker has to teach fun games and help kids.

PLAN YOUR AD

What words will you use? Use your notes.

MAKE AND SHARE YOUR AD

Use poster paper. Make drawings or find magazine pictures for the poster. Write your sentences. Check and correct your work.

Check Your Work
- Does your ad describe the job?
- Did you write what the worker has to do?
- Did you check your spelling?

Display your job ad in the classroom. Read the ads that your classmates made. Can you suggest someone for one of the jobs?

Language Across the Curriculum **183**

UNIT 10 LESSON 13
LANGUAGE ACROSS THE CURRICULUM: WRITING

OBJECTIVES

Functions:
Ask and Answer Questions; Write

Learning Strategies and Critical Thinking:
Plan; Formulate Questions; Generate and Organize Ideas; Self-Assess

Writing: Job Ad

CONDUCT THE WRITING PROJECT

1 Explore Job Ads Show job ads from the classified section of a newspaper. Note key features that appear in most ads, such as: headline, job description, location, work hours, etc.

Next, read the introduction to the writing project and tell students they will be writing their own job ads.

2 Choose a Job Work as a class to brainstorm jobs in Step 1. Partners can then select jobs from the list and complete Steps 2 and 3.

3 Plan Your Ad Work with students to create catchy headlines. Have them study published ads, and brainstorm phrases to get a reader's attention.

Headlines
Be Our _____!
Do You Love _____?
Kids Need You for _____!
Who Wants to Be a _____?

4 Make and Share Your Ad Help students include necessary information such as job description, location, and hours. Ask students if they would like to include their job ad in their **Portfolio**.

▶ **Language Practice Book** page 95

CLOSE AND ASSESS

Have students look at their ads. Say:
- *How did you describe the work?*
- *Show me a sentence that tells what the worker has to do.*
- *Are there any words you think may be misspelled?*

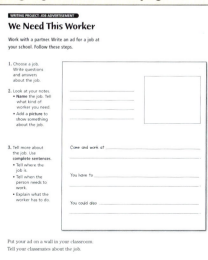

Language Practice Book page 95

Multi-Level Strategies

WRITING SUPPORT

PRELITERATE Use a language experience approach, having students dictate or fill in entries in this frame:

The job is _____.
The person has to _____.
Hours: _____ a.m. to _____ p.m.
Days (circle): Monday Tuesday Wednesday Thursday Friday
Where: _____.

As students dictate, encourage them to spell words they already know.

Language Across the Curriculum **T183**

Resources

For Success in Language and Literacy

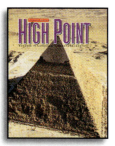

Student Book pages 184–197

For Language Skills Practice

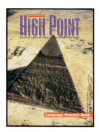

Language Practice Book pages 96–100

For Reading Skills Practice

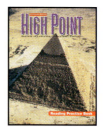

Reading Practice Book pages 77–80

For Vocabulary, Language Development, and Reading Fluency

Language Tape 6, Side A
Language CD 2, Tracks 17–19

For Reading Together

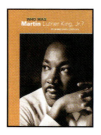

Theme Book *Who Was Martin Luther King, Jr.,?* from The Basics Bookshelf

For Audio Walk-Throughs and Selection Readings

Selection Tape 6A
Selection CD 2, Tracks 9–10

For Phonics Instruction

Transparencies 57–61

Transparency Scripts 57–61

Letter Tiles

For Comprehensive Assessment

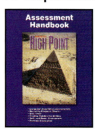

Language Acquisition Assessment, Units 10–12 Test, Writing Assessment, Self-Assessment

For Planning and Instruction

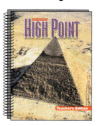

Teacher's Edition pages T184a–T197

T184a Unit Planner

UNIT 11
Make a Difference!

In This Unit

Vocabulary
- Direction Words
- Civil Rights
- Data Displays

Language Functions
- Give Information
- Give Directions
- Express Wants and Feelings

Patterns and Structures
- Irregular Past Tense Verbs
- Prepositions

Reading
- R-Controlled Vowels
- Comprehension: Identify Sequence (time line); Classify Information

Writing
- Directions
- Charts
- Personal Narrative in a Mandala

Content Area Connection
- Mathematics (chart, table, and circle graph)

T184b

UNIT 11

Activity and Assessment Planner

UNIT 11: Make a Difference!

LESSONS

1

UNIT 11 LAUNCH ▶ *pages T184–T185*

LESSON 1: INTRODUCE UNIT 11 pages T184–T185

Vocabulary
Helping Others

Viewing
Interpret Visual Images

Learning Strategies
Preview

Build Background

Plan and Set Goals

Critical Thinking and Representing
Relate Steps in a Process

Generate Ideas

Create Illustrations

2–5

LANGUAGE DEVELOPMENT ▶ *pages T186–T189*

LESSON 2
IRREGULAR PAST TENSE VERBS
page T186

Function
Give Information

Patterns and Structures
T Irregular Past Tense Verbs

Writing
Sentences

LESSON 3
DIRECTION WORDS
page T187

Function
Give Directions

Vocabulary
T Direction Words

Viewing
Identify Visual Symbols

Writing
T Directions

LESSON 4
CIVIL RIGHTS
page T188

Function
Express Wants and Feelings

Vocabulary
T Civil Rights

Writing
Chart

LESSON 5
IRREGULAR PAST TENSE VERBS
page T189

Function
Give Information

Patterns and Structures
T Irregular Past Tense Verbs

Writing
T Sentences

6–11

LANGUAGE AND LITERACY ▶ *pages T190a–T195*

LESSON 6
BASICS BOOKSHELF
pages T190a–T190f

Functions
Listen to a Book

Read Aloud a Book

Vocabulary
T Civil Rights

Reading Strategies
Activate Prior Knowledge

Preview

Use Text Features (captions)

Learning to Read
Use Captions

Track Print

Critical Thinking and Comprehension
T Identify Sequence

LESSON 7
BASICS BOOKSHELF: COMPREHENSION
page T190

Function
Give Information

Learning Strategy
Use Graphic Organizers (time line)

Critical Thinking and Comprehension
T Identify Sequence

LESSON 8
HIGH FREQUENCY WORDS
page T191

Learning to Read
T Recognize High Frequency Words

LESSON 9
PHONICS
pages T192a–T192d

Learning to Read
Build Oral Vocabulary

Develop Phonemic Awareness

T Associate Sounds and Symbols: R-Controlled Vowels

Blend Sounds to Decode Words

LESSON 10
READING AND SPELLING
pages T192–T193

Learning to Read
Develop Phonemic Awareness

T Associate Sounds and Symbols: R-Controlled Vowels

Blend Sounds to Decode Words

Spelling
T R-Controlled Vowels

LESSON 11
INDEPENDENT READING
pages T194–T195

Functions
Read a Selection

Give Information

Learning to Read
T Recognize High Frequency Words

T Decode Words with R-Controlled Vowels

Reading Strategies
Activate Prior Knowledge

Set a Purpose for Reading

Use Visuals

Critical Thinking and Comprehension
T Classify Information

Writing
Information About People

12–13

LANGUAGE ACROSS THE CURRICULUM ▶ *pages T196–T197*

LESSON 12
MATHEMATICS: REPRESENT DATA
page T196

Functions
Listen to an Article

Give Information

Vocabulary
Data Displays

Research Skills and Learning Strategies
Build Background

Use Text Structures (table, circle graph)

Critical Thinking and Comprehension
Identify Details

Make Judgments

Make Comparisons

LESSON 13
WRITING PROJECT: MANDALA
page T197

Functions
Express Feelings

Give Information

Write

Learning Strategies and Critical Thinking
Plan

Generate/Organize Ideas

Self-Assess

Use Graphic Organizers

Representing and Writing
Personal Narrative in a Mandala

T184c Unit 11 | Make a Difference!

T = Objective Tested on Unit Test

ASSESSMENT OPTIONS

The **Teacher's Edition** and the **Assessment Handbook** include these comprehensive assessment tools:

▶ **Ongoing, Informal Assessment**
Check for understanding and achieve closure for every lesson with the targeted questions and activities in the **Close and Assess** boxes in your Teacher's Edition.

▶ **Decoding Progress Check**
These word lists for each unit provide a quick way to check on mastery of the phonics or word structure skills taught in the unit.

▶ **Language Acquisition Assessments**
To verify students' ability to use the language functions and grammar structures taught in Units 10–12, conduct these performance assessments.

▶ **Unit Test in Standardized Test Format**
This multiple-choice test measures students' cumulative understanding of the skills and language developed in Units 10–12.

▶ **Self- and Peer-Assessment**
Students use the Self-Assessment Form to evaluate their own work and develop learning strategies appropriate to their needs. Students offer feedback to their classmates with the Peer-Assessment Form.

▶ **Writing Assessment/Portfolio Opportunities**
You can evaluate students' writing in the Writing Projects using the Writing Progress Checklist. Then collaborate with students to choose work for their portfolios.

UNITS 10–12 ASSESSMENT OPPORTUNITIES	Assessment Handbook Pages
Decoding Progress Check	1a
Language Acquisition Assessments	26
Units 10–12 Test	27–32
Self-Assessment Form	33
Peer-Assessment Form	50
Writing Progress Checklist	51
Portfolio Evaluation Form	52

RELATED RESOURCES

I Am Rosa Parks
by Rosa Parks with Jim Haskins
Ms. Parks tells the story of her life, her involvement in the Civil Rights movement, and her hopes for the future. (Puffin)
Theme Book: Read Aloud

Happy Birthday, Martin Luther King
by Jean Marzollo
More about the life and work of the great Civil Rights leader. Illustrated by Brian Pinkney. (Scholastic)
Phonics Reinforcement:
***R*-Controlled Vowels**

Behind the Mask
by Ruth Heller
Explores through rhyming text the subject of prepositions and how they are used. (Grosset & Dunlap)
Language Development: Prepositions

Oh, Freedom!
by Casey King and Linda Barrett Osborne
Kids interview adults about their involvement in the Civil Rights movement. Includes photos with explanatory captions and information text. (Knopf)
Vocabulary: Civil Rights

Dear Dr. King
edited by Jan Colbert and Ann McMillan Harms
Letters from today's children to a great leader from the past. Includes historical photos of the Civil Rights era. (Hyperion)
Easy Reading

UNIT 11 LESSON 1

INTRODUCE UNIT 11: MAKE A DIFFERENCE!

OBJECTIVES
Concepts and Vocabulary: Helping Others
Viewing: Interpret Visual Images
Learning Strategies: Preview; Build Background; Plan and Set Goals
Critical Thinking: Relate Steps in a Process; Generate Ideas
Representing: Illustrations
Writing: Plan

START WITH A COMMON EXPERIENCE

1 Introduce "Make a Difference!" Read the unit title and say: *When people make a difference, they try to make the world a better place.*

2 View the Photo Have students discuss what the young people are doing in the photo. Read the photo caption to confirm. Then read the introduction and guide students in brainstorming ways that they can make a difference at home, at school, in the community, or in the environment. Students can use these ideas to draw their pictures.

After students finish their drawings, have them mingle to find others with similar ideas or pictures.

3 Make It Happen Model how to make a step-by-step action plan:

How We'll Make a Difference: Volunteer for the After-School Program
Steps:
1. Find out more about the program.
2. Figure out when we can be there.
3. Call to volunteer.
4. Explain how we can help: tutor kids who don't speak English, teach crafts, coach sports.
5. Find more volunteers to help.

After groups create their own plans, discuss the steps and invite the class to suggest additions and modifications. Encourage interested students to carry out their plans.

T184 Unit 11 | Make a Difference!

UNIT 11

These kids are working together to make their community look better.

REACHING ALL STUDENTS

HOME CONNECTION

Family Discussion Have students take home their action plans. They can share their ideas with a family member and discuss how they might also help a relative, a neighbor, or a friend. In class, volunteers can share their new ideas. Use the opportunity to discuss how we can make a difference starting with those closest to us.

Make a Difference!

How can you make the world a better place? Draw a picture to show your idea. Get into a group with students who have ideas like yours. Make a list of the steps you can take to make your idea happen.

In This Unit

Vocabulary
- Direction Words
- Civil Rights
- Data Displays

Language Functions
- Give Information
- Give Directions
- Express Wants and Feelings

Patterns and Structures
- Irregular Past Tense Verbs
- Prepositions

Reading
- R-Controlled Vowels
- Comprehension:
  Identify Sequence (time line)
  Classify Information

Writing
- Directions
- Charts
- Personal Narrative in a Mandala

Content Area Connection
- Mathematics (table and circle graph)

185

PREVIEW THE UNIT

4 **Look for Activities and Ways to Help Others** Leaf through the unit, previewing activities students will do, for example:

page 186—learning a song about helping someone new at school

page 188–189—reading about how civil rights can make a difference

page 190—listening to the Bookshelf book (Display a copy of the book.)

page 194—reading about real kids who help other kids

page 195—creating a mandala showing a time they helped someone

Also ask students to look for stories and pictures of people who make a difference in the world. Then sum up what the preview reveals: *There are many ways we can make a difference in our own lives and in the lives of others.*

5 **Set Your Goals** Start a class mind map about how students can make a difference. Prompt students for pictures or words to add, and have them act out and describe other ideas for you to put into words. Talk together about what they want to learn about ways to help the world.

CLOSE AND ASSESS

Ask students to tell or show you something they are interested in learning in this unit.

UNIT 11 Mind Map

In the Environment

recycle

For People in Need
make sack lunches for the homeless

Make a Difference

For Friends and Family
help grandma shop, baby-sit my cousin

In the Community
clean up graffiti, volunteer at the community center

Unit Launch **T185**

UNIT 11 LESSON 2
LANGUAGE DEVELOPMENT: IRREGULAR PAST TENSE VERBS

OBJECTIVES
Functions: Listen Actively, Repeat Spoken Language, Recite; Give Information
Patterns and Structures:
- Irregular Past Tense Verbs

Writing: Sentences

INTRODUCE

1. **Listen and Sing** Play "A Better Place" on the **Language Tape/CD.** Students will listen and follow along, and then echo the lines before singing along, first in a soft voice and then in a loud voice.

   Tape 6A / CD 2 Track 17

2. **Learn About Irregular Past Tense Verbs** Review adding *-ed* to regular past tense verbs, by displaying word pairs such as *look, looked; walk, walked; paint, painted.* Then read the chart to present irregular past tense verbs. Say: *Some past tense verbs do not end in -ed. They are called irregular past tense verbs.* Have students find the irregular verbs in the song.

PRACTICE

3. **Conduct "Express Yourself"** Model how to give information. Then have partners complete the activity.

   #### How to Give Information
   - Use a past tense verb to tell whom you met: *I met Monica.*
   - Tell about how you felt or what you did: *I felt more comfortable. She made me smile.*

APPLY

4. **Write Sentences** Encourage partners to check their answers. Distribute Partner Checklist 11 on page T310.
   ▶ **Language Practice Book** page 96

CLOSE AND ASSESS

Have volunteers share their sentences about the first day of school. As they read, have the class identify the irregular past tense verbs.

T186 Unit 11 | Make a Difference!

IRREGULAR PAST TENSE VERBS

You Made a Difference!

Listen and sing.

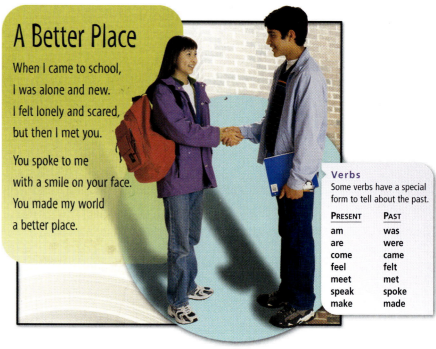

A Better Place

When I came to school,
I was alone and new.
I felt lonely and scared,
but then I met you.

You spoke to me
with a smile on your face.
You made my world
a better place.

Verbs
Some verbs have a special form to tell about the past.

PRESENT	PAST
am	was
are	were
come	came
feel	felt
meet	met
speak	spoke
make	made

EXPRESS YOURSELF ▶ GIVE INFORMATION

1. Work with a partner. Talk about someone who made a difference your first day at school. Use some of the past tense verbs that you learned.

Example: 1. I met Sokha. She made me feel happy at my new school.

WRITE SENTENCES

Write each sentence. Change the underlined verb to the past tense.   Example: 2. I came to my new sch

2. I come to my new school.   came
3. I feel worried and nervous.   felt
4. I meet my new teacher.   met
5. I am curious about my classmates.   was
6. The students are friendly.   were
7. I make a new friend.   made

186 Unit 11 | Make a Difference!

REACHING ALL STUDENTS

Language Practice Book page 96

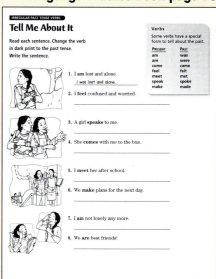

VOCABULARY: DIRECTION WORDS

How Do Kids Help at the Senior Center?

Luisa pushes Mrs. Adams **around** the pond.

Lee and Mr. Roberts walk **into** the room.

Shabbir goes **up** the ladder.

Jared and his grandfather walk **down** the ramp.

Jim and his grandfather go **across** the bridge.

EXPRESS YOURSELF ▶ GIVE DIRECTIONS

Work with a partner. Give directions to get:
1. from the rose bushes to the couch
2. from the piano to the bridge
3. from the television to the bench
4. from the fish pond to the card table
5. from the card table to the bench

Example: 1. Go around the fish pond. Go up the ramp. Go into the room. There is the couch!

Sample Responses
Students' directions should use the prepositions they have just learned. Accept all reasonable answers.

WRITE DIRECTIONS ✎

6. Choose two places in your school. Write directions from one place to the other. Then help your partner follow the directions.

Example: 6. Start in our classroom. Go into the hallway. Turn right. Go down the stairs. Walk across the hallway to the first door. Open the door. Go into the room. You are in the band room!

Language Development **187**

UNIT 11 LESSON 3

LANGUAGE DEVELOPMENT: DIRECTION WORDS

OBJECTIVES

Function: Give Directions
Concepts and Vocabulary:
🅣 Direction Words
Viewing: Identify Visual Symbols
Writing: 🅣 Directions

INTRODUCE

1 View the Images Read aloud the sentences and invite volunteers to identify the correct person in the illustration. After the class has found the correct image, model using a finger to trace the path indicated by the direction word.

2 Demonstrate Direction Words As you read each direction word, perform an action and have students imitate it in a total-physical-response activity. For example, walk *around* a desk or pantomime walking *up* and *down* stairs. Demonstrate *turn right* and *turn left* and have students act out each phrase as you call it out.

PRACTICE

3 Conduct "Express Yourself" Model the Example by tracing the route with a finger as you read the directions. Remind partners to use the illustration and the direction words to complete Items 2–5.

APPLY

4 Write Directions Review the Example and then give another example in your classroom that includes the phrases *turn right* and *turn left*. Read the directions slowly and invite volunteers to find the correct destination. Then help students as they complete the activity.

▶ **Language Practice Book** page 97

CLOSE AND ASSESS

Have partners exchange their directions with another pair. See if the new partners can follow the directions to the destination.

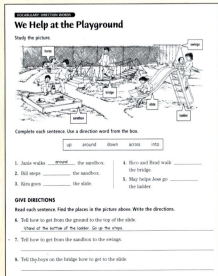

Language Practice Book page 97

Language Development
DIRECTION WORDS

Conduct a "treasure hunt" in which students give oral directions to find a hidden prize. Set up an obstacle course. Then tell one partner where the item is hidden. That partner gives directions to lead the other partner around the obstacles and to the hidden item. Coach by suggesting direction words and by pointing out missed obstacles. The object you hide can be the prize.

Language Development **T187**

UNIT 11 LESSON 4
LANGUAGE DEVELOPMENT: CIVIL RIGHTS

OBJECTIVES
Functions: Listen Actively; Express Wants and Feelings
Concepts and Vocabulary:
- Civil Rights

Writing: Chart

INTRODUCE

1. **Activate Prior Knowledge** Explain that civil rights are rights that all people should have. Say: *As students, you have the right to go to school. You have the right to ask questions and share ideas.* Brainstorm more rights of students and teachers. Then expand the discussion to include the rights granted to people who live in the United States.

2. **Learn Words for Civil Rights** Explain that many civil rights allow people to show their opinions. Read aloud the label, call-outs, and caption for each photo. Then discuss how the people use letters, articles, signs, speeches, and votes to share their ideas.

PRACTICE

3. **Conduct "Who's Talking?"** Play "Who's Talking?" on the **Language Tape/CD** to model expressing wants and feelings. Replay as necessary for students to point to the correct picture and identify what each person wants and feels.

Tape 6A / CD 2 Track 18

APPLY

4. **Write About Something You Want to Change** Go over the Example. Then copy the chart headings and brainstorm entries with the group.

▶ **Language Practice Book** page 98

CLOSE AND ASSESS
Ask students to tell you about a right that is important to them. Encourage them to share how they feel about it.

T188 Unit 11 | Make a Difference!

VOCABULARY: CIVIL RIGHTS

Use Your Rights to Change the World

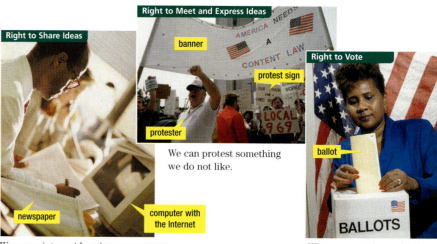

Right to Share Ideas — newspaper
We can print our ideas in a newspaper or publish them over the Internet.

Right to Meet and Express Ideas — banner, protest sign, protester, computer with the Internet
We can protest something we do not like.

Right to Vote — ballot
When we vote in an election, we choose our leaders.

WHO'S TALKING? ▶ EXPRESS WANTS AND FEELINGS

1.–3. Listen.
Who is talking? Point to the correct picture.
Talk to a partner about what each person wants and feels.

Answers:
1. Protester. He wants more pay. He feels tired of wai
2. Man at the computer. He wants to inform people. feels good about his job.
3. Woman voting. She wants Deborah Vasquez to be elected Senator. She is proud to make a difference

WRITE ABOUT SOMETHING YOU WANT TO CHANGE

4. What do you want to change at your school? How can you make those changes? Work with your class to make a chart like this.

Example: 4.

What to Change	Who Makes the Decision	What Strategies to Use
have art class for everyone	school board	go to school board meetings, write letters

188 Unit 11 | Make a Difference!

REACHING ALL STUDENTS

Vocabulary
CIVIL RIGHTS

Class Election Hold a class *election* to model the democratic process. Introduce and develop the vocabulary highlighted below. Start by creating a list of class officers, such as: *president, party planner, vice president, flag-salute leader.*

To hold the election, have the class *nominate candidates* for each position, and assign groups to prepare *signs, banners,* and *speeches.* On *election day,* pass out *ballots* and assign volunteers to count the *votes.*

Language Practice Book page 98

VOCABULARY: CIVIL RIGHTS
Work for Change
These people want to save an old house. What can they do?
Complete the sentences. Use words from the box.

banner   ballot   letters   vote   protest   print   sign   Internet

1. The people can ___protest___.
2. They can use a ___ or a ___.
3. Adults can ___.
4. They can use a ___ in an election.
5. People can write ___.
6. They can ___ their ideas in a newspaper.
7. They can publish ideas over the ___, too.

EXPRESS WANTS AND FEELINGS
Answer each question. Write a complete sentence.
8. How do the people feel about the house? ___
9. What do the protesters want others to do? ___

IRREGULAR PAST TENSE VERBS

Some People Who Led America

These verbs have special forms to tell about the past.

Present	Past	Example
think	thought	Susan B. Anthony and Elizabeth Cady Stanton **thought** women should have the right to vote.
lead	led	Together, they **led** a movement to get more rights for women.
go	went	They **went** to cities around the country.
give	gave	They **gave** speeches to try to change the law.
speak	spoke	They **spoke** at many meetings.
see	saw	Many people **saw** them. In 1920, Congress passed a law that gave women the right to vote.

BUILD SENTENCES

Read each sentence. Change the underlined verb to tell about the past.
Say the new sentence to a partner.

Example: 1. In 1965, César Chávez led a protest to get better treatment for farmworkers.

1. In 1965, César Chávez <u>leads</u> a protest to get better treatment for farmworkers.
2. He <u>goes</u> to farms throughout California.
3. He <u>speaks</u> to many farmworkers. By 1970, many growers agreed to fair treatment for the farmworkers.

4. Martin Luther King, Jr., <u>thinks</u> African Americans should have equal rights.
5. He <u>gives</u> many speeches.
6. Thousands of people <u>see</u> him. A new law was passed in 1964 to give all Americans equal rights.

Answers:
1. led   2. went   3. spoke

4. thought   5. gave   6. saw

WRITE ABOUT EVENTS IN YOUR HISTORY

7.–10. Write 4 sentences to tell about when you came to the United States. What did you think? What did you do?

Example: 7. I thought everyone looked so different.

Language Development   189

UNIT 11 LESSON 5

LANGUAGE DEVELOPMENT: IRREGULAR PAST TENSE VERBS

OBJECTIVES

Function: Give Information
Patterns and Structures:
🅣 Irregular Past Tense Verbs
Writing: 🅣 Sentences

INTRODUCE

1 Learn About Irregular Past Tense Verbs Read the introduction and point out the chart of present and past tense verb forms. Say: *Remember that for regular verbs we add the ending -ed to show past tense. Irregular verbs do not add -ed; look at the special past tense forms of these verbs.* Go over the verb pairs and read the examples aloud. Ask students to point out each past tense verb.

PRACTICE

2 Build Sentences Explain that Items 1–6 tell about the work of two more civil rights leaders in the United States. Work through the Example. Then have partners revise and read the sentences. Remind them to use the verb chart at the top of the page for help.

APPLY

3 Write About Events in Your History In the Example, point out that the same sentence can include regular and irregular past tense verbs. Have students consult page 318 in their Handbook for other irregular verbs.

▶ **Language Practice Book** page 99

CLOSE AND ASSESS

Ask students to read their sentences aloud while volunteers list regular and irregular past tense verbs.

Language Practice Book page 99

Vocabulary

IRREGULAR VERBS

Flash Cards Have partners or groups turn to Handbook page 318 and look together at the irregular verbs listed. Explain that the only way to learn irregular verbs is to memorize them. Then have students create flash cards with the present tense form of a verb on one side and the past tense form on the other. Partners or groups can use the flash cards to practice and learn irregular verbs.

Language Development   T189

UNIT 11 **LESSON 6**

LANGUAGE AND LITERACY: THE BASICS BOOKSHELF

OBJECTIVES

Concepts and Vocabulary:
🅣 Words About Civil Rights

Listening: Listen to a Preview

Reading Strategies:
Activate Prior Knowledge; Preview; Use Text Features (captions)

BUILD LANGUAGE AND VOCABULARY

1. **Teach "Words to Know"** Use the photos on pages 2–3 to present the vocabulary words. Develop definitions like the ones below:

   - **Civil rights** are the rights that all people should have.
   - A **leader** is someone who shows others how to do something.
   - A **march** is when people walk together.
   - You **protest** when you say that something is wrong. In a **peaceful protest,** people say what they think, but no one gets hurt.
   - With **free speech,** you can say what you want.
   - When you **speak out,** you say what you think.
   - You **vote** to choose a leader.
   - A **ballot box** is a place to collect everyone's votes.

PREPARE TO READ

2. **Think About What You Know** Invite students to share ideas about the word *freedom*. Organize their ideas and examples in a word web.

3. **Preview** Play the Audio Walk-Through for *Who Was Martin Luther King, Jr.?* on the **Selection Tape/CD** to give students the overall idea of the story.

   Tape 6A / CD 2 Track 9

CLOSE AND ASSESS

Have students work in small groups to list the important things they learned about Martin Luther King, Jr., and other things they know about him.

T190a Unit 11 | Make a Difference!

Who Was Martin Luther King, Jr.?
by Shirleyann Costigan

Summary This photographic biography presents the life and work of Martin Luther King, Jr. The key events in Dr. King's life are set against the backdrop of the American civil rights movement. Simple text reinforces irregular past tense verbs and words about civil rights.

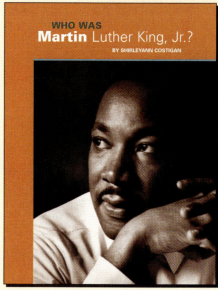

Cover

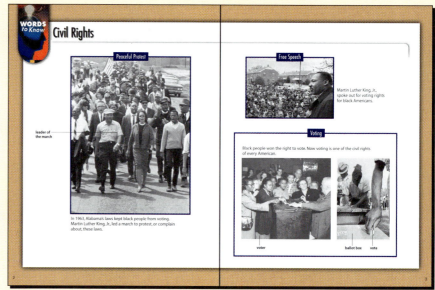

Pages 2–3

Multi-Level Strategies
LITERACY SUPPORT

PRELITERATE Use Text Structures: Captions Point out the caption on page 4 and say: *These words tell about the picture.* Have students page through the book to find the other captions. Then encourage them to echo read as you read aloud each caption.

Encourage small groups to create captions for the uncaptioned photos in the book. Assist with questions such as *Who is in the picture? What is happening?* Take dictation and write the captions on self-stick notes. Affix the notes to the photos in a book. Then read aloud the new captions with the entire group.

As a review, remove the captions. Read each one aloud and have students find the picture that is being described.

Who Was Martin Luther King, Jr.?

Pages 4–5

Pages 6–7

Strategies for Comprehensible Input

PAGE	STORY LANGUAGE	STRATEGY OPTIONS
4	Altanta, Georgia, the South	**Show the places on a United States map.**
5	neighborhoods	**Explain:** A neighborhood is part of a city where people live.
6	restaurants	**Explain:** At a restaurant you can buy food and sit there to eat it.
7	attend	**Restate:** go to study in

Language and Literacy **T190b**

UNIT 11 **LESSON 6,** CONTINUED

LANGUAGE AND LITERACY: THE BASICS BOOKSHELF

OBJECTIVES

Function: Listen to a Book
Critical Thinking and Comprehension:
 Identify Sequence

READ AND THINK TOGETHER

1. **Read Aloud** On your first reading of the book, use the "Strategies for Comprehensible Input" that appear at the bottom of pages T190b, T190d, and T190f.

2. **Read and Map: Identify Sequence** Draw a time line like the one below, but without dates and sentences. Say: *A time line shows events in the order in which they happen. Some time lines are vertical, or go down a page. For these time lines, the earliest event is at the top. Later events are in order under it. A time line usually has dates and descriptions.*

   Read page 4 aloud. Then think aloud as you model filling in the first section: *I will write the date* 1929 *and the sentence* Martin was born in Atlanta, Georgia. *This is the first thing that happened in the book. Now I will add more important dates and events from the rest of the book.*

   As you read the book, use sentence strips to record the dates and key events shown below. Next put the strips in order by date and time. Then model how to complete the time line.

Pages 8–9

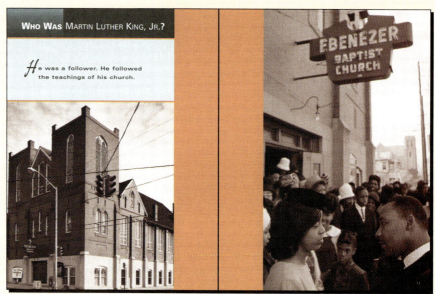
Pages 10–11

Time Line for *Who Was Martin Luther King, Jr.?*

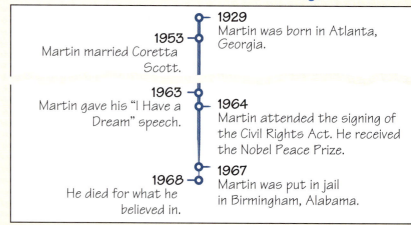

Technology Support
See **Inspiration** Visual Learning software for support in creating the time line.

T190c Unit 11 | Make a Difference!

Who Was Martin Luther King, Jr.?,
CONTINUED

Pages 12–13

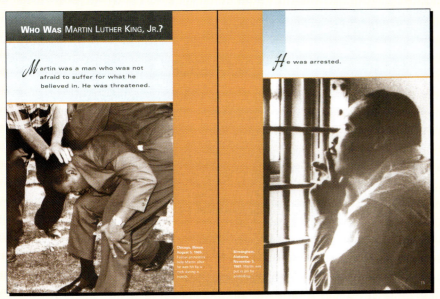

Pages 14–15

Strategies for Comprehensible Input

PAGE	STORY LANGUAGE	STRATEGY OPTIONS
8	minister	**Explain:** A minister is a person who leads a church.
10	He was a follower.	**Explain:** He did what he was taught to do in church.
12	leader	**Explain:** A leader tells or shows other people what to do.
	civil rights	**Explain:** Civil rights are things the law says everyone should be able to do.
13	a better future	**Restate:** a better time in later years
14	suffer for what he believed in	**Restate:** be punished or hurt because of what he thought
	He was threatened.	**Explain:** People said they would try to stop him or hurt him.
15	arrested	**Point to the picture and restate:** put in jail

Language and Literacy T190d

UNIT 11 **LESSON 6,** CONTINUED

LANGUAGE AND LITERACY: THE BASICS BOOKSHELF

OBJECTIVES

Functions: Listen to a Book; Read Aloud a Book (choral reading)
Learning to Read: Track Print

READ AND THINK TOGETHER, CONTINUED

3 Conduct Interactive Readings
Choose from these options:

- **Read along and track print** Students can read along and point to the words as you play the recording of *Who Was Martin Luther King, Jr.?* on the **Selection Tape/CD**.

  Tape 6A
  CD 2 Track 10

- **Choral reading** Have one student read the question at the top of pages 4, 8, 10, 14, and 18. Partners or small groups can take turns reading the rest of the text.

CLOSE AND ASSESS

Arrange students into six groups. Assign each group one date from the book and have them describe the event for that date. Start with 1929 and work in order.

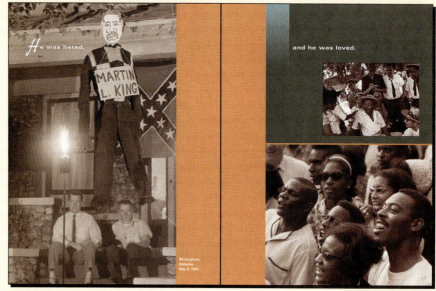
Pages 16–17

Pages 18–19

Multi-Level Strategies
LITERACY SUPPORT

LITERATE IN L1 **Read with a Partner/ Make a Wall of Fame** After students have participated in the interactive readings, encourage them to read the story with a partner. Distribute the Partner Prompts on page T311 to help partners work together to identify unfamiliar words and unlock their meanings, then read the text to each other. After the partner reading, assign groups to study civil rights leaders such as Gandhi, Nelson Mandela, Annie Clemenc, or César Chávez. Then have each group illustrate a scene from the leader's life. Add a caption: *Who was César Chávez? César Chávez was a leader. He led migrant farmworkers in California.*

INTERRUPTED SCHOOLING **Identify Sequence** To anchor understanding of the skill, have students page through the book to find the dates. As they find each date, ask: *What happened on this date?* Have students record each date and list the event on an index card. Draw a vertical time line with the dots marked. Have students attach the index cards by the appropriate dates.

T190e Unit 11 | Make a Difference!

Who Was Martin Luther King, Jr.?, CONTINUED

Pages 20–21

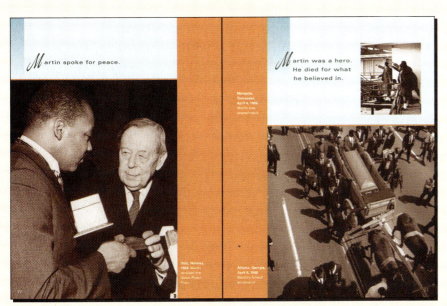

Pages 22–23

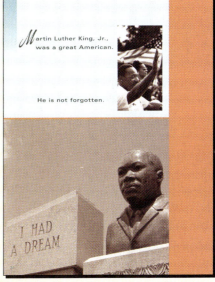

Page 24

Strategies for Comprehensible Input

PAGE	STORY LANGUAGE	STRATEGY OPTIONS
16	hated	**Restate:** not liked
17	loved	**Gesture:** Place your hands over your heart.
18	a great speaker	**Restate:** Someone who said his ideas well
19	He spoke out against hate and violence.	**Restate:** He said that people should not hate or hurt others.
20	his hopes and dreams	**Restate:** the things he wanted to have happen
	nation	**Restate:** country
	judged by the color of their skin	**Restate:** liked or disliked because they are black or white
21	by the content of their character	**Restate:** by what they are like
22	peace	**Restate:** a time when people live together happily
23	hero	**Explain:** A hero does brave things to help others.
	He died for what he believed in	**Explain:** He was killed because of what he said and did.
24	He is not forgotten.	**Explain:** People still think and talk about him.

Language and Literacy **T190f**

UNIT 11 LESSON 7

LANGUAGE AND LITERACY: THE BASICS BOOKSHELF

OBJECTIVES

Function: Give Information
Learning Strategy:
Use Graphic Organizers (time line)
Critical Thinking and Comprehension:
🅣 Identify Sequence

CHECK COMPREHENSION

Materials: index cards

1. **Make a Time Line** Remind students that a time line shows the dates of events in the order in which they happened. It also includes information about the events.

   Have students work in small groups. The group should first collect dates and key events from *Who was Martin Luther King, Jr.?* on index cards. Then students should put the cards in order.

   As you read aloud the directions for each step, pause for the group to start their time line or add information to it. Students can complete their time line using Team Word-Webbing (see Cooperative Learning Structures, page T337d).

2. **Share Information from the Book** Have students pass the time line around the group. Each member reads the event for a point on the time line and tells additional information about the event.

CLOSE AND ASSESS

Ask students to complete this sentence:
A time line shows _____ .

T190 Unit 11 | Make a Difference!

COMPREHENSION: IDENTIFY SEQUENCE

Work with a group to make a time line for *Who Was Martin Luther King, Jr.?* Follow these steps.

❶ What happened first? Draw a dot. Write the year that Martin was born. Then write a sentence that tells what happened in that year.

• 1929
Martin was born in Atlanta, Georgia.

❷ What happened next? Draw a line. Add another dot for each important date and event. Tell what happened. Use words from the story to write the sentence.

1929
Martin was born in Atlanta, Georgia.

1953
Martin married Coretta Scott.

❸ Use your finished time line to tell the class about the life of Martin Luther King, Jr. Each student in your group can tell about one of the events.

Sample Responses:
(Each year should appear next to a point on the time line.)
1963   He gave his "I Have a Dream" speech.
1964   He attended the signing of the Civil Rights Act. He received the Nobel Peace Prize.
1967   He was put in jail in Birmingham, Alabama.
1968   He died for what he believed in.

190 Unit 11 | Make a Difference!

from
The Basics Bookshelf

THEME BOOK
Read this biography of Martin Luther King, Jr., to learn why he was one of America's great leaders.

REACHING ALL STUDENTS

Language Development
STATE A GOAL

Role-Play Turn to page 21 and read aloud the quote from the famous "I Have a Dream" speech. Work with students to identify King's goals: *My children will not be judged by the color of their skin. My children will be judged by the content of their character.* Model stating personal goals: *My students will be treated fairly. My students will not fail.* Then use the chart to provide sentence frames for students to state their own goals. Invite students to take the role of a famous person and state a goal, or state a goal for themselves.

How to State a Goal
My ____ will ____ .
My ____ will not ____ .
I dream that ____ .
I hope that someday ____ .

HIGH FREQUENCY WORDS
Words to Know

REVIEW WORDS YOU KNOW

Read the words aloud. Which word goes in the sentence?

play	places
their	to
of	other

1. This woman goes to different <u>places</u>.
2. She teaches people <u>to</u> read.
3. A lot <u>of</u> people thank her.

LEARN TO READ

Learn new words.

country	Indra was born in a **country** in Asia.
called	The country is **called** Indonesia.
lived	He **lived** there as a child.
house	He grew up in a **house** built on long posts.
now	Indra came to the U.S. **Now** he lives in California.
American	Last year, Indra became an **American** citizen.
would	He **would** like to help people in Indonesia.
know	He **knows** how they could grow more food.
should	He thinks they **should** plant different crops each year.
also	Indra **also** wants to help the farmers sell their crops.

How to Learn a New Word
- Look at the word.
- Listen to the word.
- Listen to the word in a sentence. What does it mean?
- Say the word.
- Spell the word.
- Say the word again.

WORD WORK

4.–13. Make a map for each new word. Write the word in the center. Complete the other boxes. Then use the word in a sentence of your own.

Example: 4.

- 5 — number of letters
- house
- or — I go **out** of the house. — How can you remember it?
- My house in China was by a river.

Language and Literacy **191**

Reading Practice Book page 77

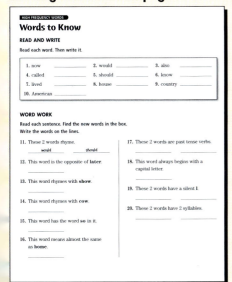

Reading Fluency
RECOGNIZE HIGH FREQUENCY WORDS

To build automaticity with the new high frequency words:

- Have students make word cards to display on a classroom chart. Partners or groups can go to the chart to practice reading the words together or to test one another.

- Have students sort the words into these categories: words that end with *-ed*, words that tell about a person or a place, words that have three or four letters each, words that rhyme. Then invite students to create categories of their own and sort again.

UNIT 11 **LESSON 8**

LANGUAGE AND LITERACY: HIGH FREQUENCY WORDS

OBJECTIVES

Learning to Read:
- Recognize High Frequency Words

REVIEW WORDS

1 Review Known High Frequency Words Have the group read aloud the words in the green box. Listen for words students cannot read automatically and use the steps in the yellow box to reteach those words. Then have students look at the photo. Read each cloze sentence. Reread each sentence and pause for students to silently read the two words to the left of the sentence. Tell students to choose the word that goes in the sentence and tells about the picture.

INTRODUCE NEW WORDS

2 Learn High Frequency Words Use the High Frequency Word Script on page T322 to lead students through the steps in the yellow box.

PRACTICE

3 Conduct "Word Work" Use the Example to model how to make a word map. In the last box, point out how the letters *ou* in *out* are a clue to the spelling of *house*.

Have groups complete Items 5–13. Then have volunteers share their memory aids and sentences.

APPLY

4 Read Words in Context Students will read high frequency words in context in the sentences on page 193 and the passage on page 194.

▶ **Reading Practice Book** page 77

CLOSE AND ASSESS

Call out the high frequency words one at a time. Have students point to them and spell the words as a group.

Language and Literacy **T191**

UNIT 11 LESSON 9
LANGUAGE AND LITERACY: PHONICS

OBJECTIVES
Learning to Read: Build Oral Vocabulary; Develop Phonemic Awareness; ⓣ Associate Sounds and Symbols /är/ ar, /ôr/ or; Blend Sounds to Decode Words

TEACH R-CONTROLLED VOWELS: /är/ar, /ôr/or

1 Build Oral Vocabulary Display Transparency 57. Talk through each picture to develop meaning for the words in the yellow boxes. Present the two different meanings of the words in Items 1–3. For example, for Item 1, say:

- Look. The people **form**, or make, a star (trace the star with a finger). Here (point to the second picture) is another meaning of **form**. The picture shows three **forms**, or kinds, of art.

2 Develop Phonemic Awareness Remove the transparency and work through Step 1 of the script.

3 Read Words with ar, or Display Transparency 57 again. Work through Steps 2 and 3 of the script.

CLOSE AND ASSESS
Display the words *hard, porch, storm,* and *park*. Call on students to read each word and identify the two letters that make the vowel sound /är/ or /ôr/.

Word Families
-ORN AND -ART

Materials: Letter Tiles

A large number of words can be generated from a few rhyming phonograms. Use letter tiles to build the words in dark type. Then change tiles to build other words in the -orn and -art families. Have students make a list of the words. Make sure students understand their meanings. Then ask them to read the words on their list and to identify the shared ending.

horn	part
born	art
corn	cart
torn	chart
thorn	part

T192a Unit 11 | Make a Difference!

Transparency 57: ▶
R-Controlled Vowels

▼ Script for Transparency 57

Words with R-Controlled Vowels

1. Develop Phonemic Awareness
Isolate/Match /är/ and /ôr/ Say: *Listen to the last sound in these words:* car, far, jar. *What is the sound?* (/är/) *Now listen for the sound* /är/ *in the middle of these words:* park, hard, mark. *Now raise your hand each time you hear the sound* /är/. *Say these words:* car, tall, star, stand, far, barn, back, park. Repeat the process for /ôr/, using the words *for, fat, storm, not, horn, home, log, porch, stone, sport.*

2. Associate Sounds and Symbols
Point to the star on **Transparency 57**. Say: *This is a star. You can see a star in the sky. Say the word* star *with me.* Then point to the *ar* in *star* and say: *The letters* ar *make the sound you hear at the end of* star. *The sound is* /är/. *Say* /är/ *with me:* /är/. Point to *ar* and ask: *What are the letters? What's the sound?* Repeat for *horn,* pointing out that the letter *o* followed by *r* makes one vowel sound: /ôr/.

3. Blend Sounds to Read Words
Model/Teach Point to the word *star* and say: *This word has three sounds.* As you slide a finger slowly from left to right below *star*, say: *I can blend the three sounds:* /s t ä r/. *Now, I'm going to say the whole word:* star. Repeat for *horn,* pointing out that the letters *or* make the vowel sound /ôr/. Have students sound out the words *star* and *horn* with you.

Practice For Item 1, say: *Let's try that again. In these pictures people form a star and we see three forms of art.* Read aloud the sentences with students, pausing for students to decode *form, star, forms,* and *art*. Then discuss the different meanings of *form* ("to make" and "kind or type of") and point out the multiple-meaning words *park* in Item 2 and *hard* in Item 3. Call special attention to the following:

- In Item 4, help students use the strategy for compound words to read *farmhouse*.

- In Item 5, help students cover the ending -ed, read the root word, and blend it with the sounds /ed/ to read *started* and *painted*.

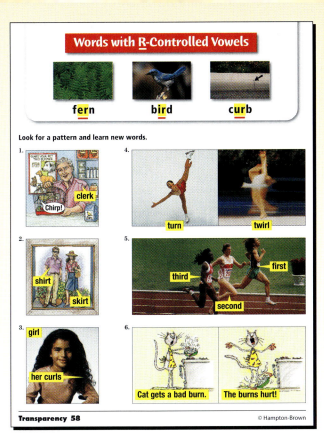

◀ Transparency 58: *R*-Controlled Vowels

▼ Script for Transparency 58

Words with R-Controlled Vowels

1. **Develop Phonemic Awareness**
   Isolate/Match /ûr/ Say: *Listen to the sound in the middle of these words:* turn, bird, hurt. *What is the sound?* (/ûr/) *Say the words with me. Now raise your hand each time you hear the sound /ûr/. Say these words:* turn, top, first, fit, school, skirt, burns, beds, third, this.

2. **Associate Sounds and Symbols**
   Point to the fern on **Transparency 58**. Say: *This is a fern. A fern is a kind of plant. Say the word* fern *with me*. Then point to the *er* in *fern* and say: *The letters* er *make the sound you hear in the middle of* fern. *The sound is /ûr/. Say /ûr/ with me: /ûr/.* Point to *er* and ask: *What are the letters? What's the sound?* Repeat for *bird* and *curb*, pointing out that the letters *ir* and *ur* also make the vowel sound /ûr/.

3. **Blend Sounds to Read Words**
   Model/Teach Point to the letter *f* in *fern* and say: *The sound for f is: /f/*. Repeat for the letters *er* and then for *n*. As you slide a finger under *fern*, say: *I can blend the three sounds: /f û r n/. Now, I'm going to say the whole word:* fern. Repeat the process for *bird* and *curb*. Have students sound out the three words with you.

   Practice For Item 1, say: *Let's try that again. This picture shows a clerk holding a bird cage. The bird says* chirp, *doesn't it? Read the words with me. Follow my finger as we blend the sounds /klûrk/, /chûrp/ and say the words:* clerk, chirp. Repeat for the other words, calling special attention to the following:

   • After you read *shirt* with students in Item 2, ask: *How many sounds do you hear in* shirt? (3) Point out that the letters *sh* make one sound: /sh/. Then blend *skirt* with students. Say: *When we read* skirt, *we blended the consonants* s *and* k *at the beginning*. Repeat for the consonants *tw* in *twirl* in Item 4.

   • In Item 5, blend *first* with students and point out that you blended the consonants *s* and *t* at the end of the word. After you read *third* with students, point out that the letters *th* make one sound: /th/.

OBJECTIVES

Learning to Read: Build Oral Vocabulary; Develop Phonemic Awareness; 🅣 Associate Sounds and Symbols /ûr/ *er, ir, ur*; Blend Sounds to Decode Words

TEACH *R*-CONTROLLED VOWELS: /ûr/*er, ir, ur*

1 **Build Oral Vocabulary** Display Transparency 58. Use the pictures to develop the meaning of each word and use it in a sentence. For example:

   • *This is a* **clerk** *(point). A* **clerk** *helps customers in a store* (dramatize with a volunteer). *In a pet store, a* **clerk** *helps people buy pets and the things pets need.*

2 **Develop Phonemic Awareness** Remove the transparency and work through Step 1 of the script.

3 **Read Words with *er, ir, ur*** Display Transparency 58 again. Work through Steps 2 and 3 of the script.

CLOSE AND ASSESS

Display the words *clerk, shirt, turn,* and *first*. Call on students to read each word and identify the two letters that make the vowel sound /ûr/.

▶ **Reading Practice Book** page 78 (*r*-controlled: *ar, or, er, ir, ur*)

Reading Practice Book page 78

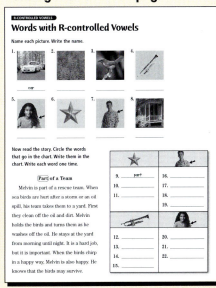

Language and Literacy **T192b**

UNIT 11 **LESSON 9**, CONTINUED

LANGUAGE AND LITERACY: PHONICS

OBJECTIVES
Learning to Read: Build Oral Vocabulary; Develop Phonemic Awareness; **T** Associate Sounds and Symbols /âr/ *air, ear*; Blend Sounds to Decode Words

TEACH *R*-CONTROLLED VOWELS: /âr/ *air, ear*

1. **Build Oral Vocabulary** Display Transparency 59. Play "I Spy." For example, for Item 5, say:
   - *I spy a lair. A lair is a place where animals rest or live. Two bears are in this lair.*

   When students find the lair, say: *Yes, this is the lair* (point). Repeat to build context for other words.

2. **Develop Phonemic Awareness** Remove the transparency and conduct the oral activities in Step 1 of the Script for Transparency 59.

3. **Read Words with *air, ear*** Display Transparency 59 again. Work through Steps 2 and 3 of the script.

CLOSE AND ASSESS
Display the words *hair, stair, wears,* and *tear*. Call on students to read each word and identify the three letters that make the /âr/ vowel sound.

Word Families
-AIR AND -EAR

Materials: Letter Tiles

A large number of words can be generated from a few rhyming phonograms. Use letter tiles to build the words in dark type. Then change tiles to build other words in the *-air* and *-ear* families. Have students make a list of the words. Make sure students understand their meanings. Then ask them to read the words on their list and to identify the shared ending.

chair	**bear**
hair	pear
pair	tear
stair	wear

T192c Unit 11 | Make a Difference!

Transparency 59: ▶
***R*-Controlled Vowels**

Transparency 59

▼ **Script for Transparency 59**

Words with *R*-Controlled Vowels

1. **Develop Phonemic Awareness**
   Isolate/Match /âr/ Say: *Listen to the last sound in these words:* hair, pear, chair. *What is the sound?* (/âr/) *Now raise your hand each time you hear the sound /âr/. Say these words:* chain, chair, cheer, wear, when, star, stair, burn, bear.

2. **Associate Sounds and Symbols**
   Point to the chair on **Transparency 59**. Say: *This is a chair. You sit in a chair. Say the word* chair *with me.* Then point to the *air* in *chair* and say: *The three letters* air *make the sound you hear at the end of* chair. *The sound is /âr/. Say /âr/ with me:* /âr/. Point to *air* and ask: *What are the letters? What's the sound?* Repeat for *bear*, pointing out that the three letters *ear* make the sound /âr/ in *bear*.

3. **Blend Sounds to Read Words**
   Model/Teach Point to the letters *ch* in *chair* and say: *The sound for the letters* ch *is /ch/. Repeat for the letters* air: /âr/. *As you slide a finger under* chair, *say: I can blend the two sounds:* /châr/. *Now, I'm going to say the whole word:* chair. Repeat for *bear*, pointing out that in *bear*, the letters *ear* make the sound /âr/. Have students sound out *chair* and *bear* with you.

   Practice For Item 1, say: *Let's try that again. This picture shows a girl with long hair, doesn't it? Read the word with me. Follow my finger as we blend the sounds /hâr/, and say the word:* hair. Repeat for the other words, calling special attention to the following:

   - In Item 2, use the picture to help explain the phrase *on the air*: *The radio station broadcasts a show right now. The woman is on the air.*
   - In Item 4, explain that when things are *fair*, everyone is treated the same way. When things are *not fair*, some people get special treatment.
   - In Item 5, explain that *fair* also means "a place where people buy and sell things and where there are rides, games, and good things to eat." Also explain that *pair* means "two of something."

◀ Transparency 60:
R-Controlled Vowels

▼ Script for Transparency 60

Words with R-Controlled Vowels

1. **Develop Phonemic Awareness**
   Isolate/Match /îr/ Say: *Listen to the last sound in these words: fear, deer, tear. What is the sound?* (/îr/) *Say the words with me. Now raise your hand each time you hear the sound /îr/. Say these words: year, bear, near, bird, dear, dirt, cheers, chair.*

2. **Associate Sounds and Symbols**
   Point to the tear on **Transparency 60**. Say: *This is a tear. When you cry, your eyes make tears. Say the word* tear *with me.* Then point to the letters *ear* in *tear* and say: *The letters* ear *make the sound you hear at the end of* tear. *The sound is* /îr/. *Say* /îr/ *with me:* /îr/. Point to *ear* and ask: *What are the letters? What's the sound?* Repeat for *deer,* pointing out that the letters *eer* also make the vowel sound /îr/.

3. **Blend Sounds to Read Words**
   Model/Teach Point to the letter *t* in *tear* and say: *The sound for* t *is* /t/. Repeat for the letters *ear:* /îr/. As you slide your finger under *tear,* say: *I can blend the two sounds:* /tîr/. *Now, I'm going to say the whole word:* tear. Repeat the process for *deer.* Have students sound out *tear* and *deer* with you.

   Practice For Item 1, say: *Let's try that again. This picture shows a man driving, doesn't it? The man steers a cart.* As you read the sentences with students, call special attention to the following:

   • In item 1 blend *steers* with students. Then say: *When we read* steers, *we blended the consonants* s *and* t *at the beginning.*

   • After you read *cheer* in item 2, point out that the *s* and *t* in *steers* make two sounds, but that *c* and *h* make one sound: /ch/. Blend *team* with students and say: *What two vowels do you see together in* team? (ea) *The vowels* ea *in* team *work together to make one sound:* /ē/. Then compare *ea* in *team* to *ear* in *year* in Item 3. Explain: *The* r *changes the vowel sound from* /ē/ *to* /îr/.

OBJECTIVES

Learning to Read: Build Oral Vocabulary; Develop Phonemic Awareness; 🅣 Associate Sounds and Symbols /îr/ *ear, eer;* Blend Sounds to Decode Words

TEACH R-CONTROLLED VOWELS: /îr/ ear, eer

1 **Build Oral Vocabulary** Display Transparency 60. Talk through each picture to develop meaning for the words in the yellow boxes. For example, for Item 1, say:

   • *This man* (point) **steers** *the cart. He turns the steering wheel* (pantomime). *You also* **steer** *cars and boats* (pantomime again).

2 **Develop Phonemic Awareness** Remove the transparency and conduct the oral activities in Step 1 of the Script for Transparency 60.

3 **Read Words with *ear, eer*** Display Transparency 60 again. Work through Steps 2 and 3 of the script.

CLOSE AND ASSESS

Display the words *steers, deer, year,* and *near.* Call on students to read each word and identify the three letters that make the vowel sound /îr/.

▶ **Reading Practice Book** page 79
(r-controlled: /âr/ *air, ear;* /îr/ *ear, eer*)

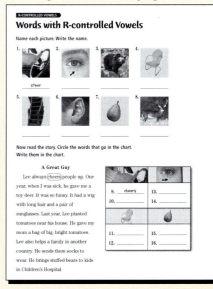

Reading Practice Book page 79

Language and Literacy **T192d**

UNIT 11 LESSON 10
LANGUAGE AND LITERACY: READING AND SPELLING

OBJECTIVES
Functions: Listen Actively; Repeat Spoken Language; Recite

Learning to Read: Develop Phonemic Awareness; 🅣 Associate Sounds and Symbols: /är/ ar; /ôr/ or; /ûr/ er, ir, ur; /âr/ air, ear; /îr/ ear, eer; Blend Sounds to Decode Words

Spelling: 🅣 R-Controlled Vowels

LISTEN AND LEARN
Tape 6A CD 2 Track 19

1 **Recite a Poem** Display Transparency 61 and play "Let Hope Burn Bright" on the **Language Tape/CD**.

DEVELOP PHONEMIC AWARENESS

2 **Blend Sounds to Form a Word** Say: *Listen to these three sounds: /s/ /t/ /är/. Say the sounds with me: /s/ /t/ /är/. Now blend the sounds together and say the word: /ssstär/, star.* Follow the same procedure with /f/ /ûr/ /n/ *fern*, /h/ /ôr/ /n/ *horn*, and /t/ /îr/ *tear*. Continue the activity with: /ch/ /âr/ *chair*, /y/ /îr/ *year*, /b/ /ûr/ /d/ *bird*, and /k/ /är/ *car*.

CONNECT SOUNDS AND LETTERS

3 **Associate Sounds and Symbols for R-Controlled Vowels** Identify the picture in Item 1 and sound out its name, pointing as you say: *This is a star, and here's the word. I see the vowel a followed by r. A* **vowel + r** *makes one vowel sound. Now blend the sounds and read the word with me: /s/, /t/, /är/, star.* Follow a similar process for Items 2–5. For Item 3, point out that the sound /ûr/ can be spelled three ways: *er, ir, ur*. For Items 4 and 5, point out that *ear* can be pronounced /âr/ or /îr/. Then read the question aloud: *What is the vowel sound in each word?* (1. /är/, 2. /ôr/, 3. /ûr/, 4. /âr/, 5. /îr/) Call on students to answer.

Afterwards, play the poem again. Have students identify words with the vowel sounds they have been learning.

T192 Unit 11 | Make a Difference!

R-CONTROLLED VOWELS
Reading and Spelling

LISTEN AND LEARN

Let Hope Burn Bright

Let hope burn bright,
bright as a star,
for everyone.

Let hope sing sweet,
sweet as a song,
for everyone.

Let hope fly high,
high as a bird,
for everyone.

Let hope be strong,
strong as a bear,
for everyone.

CONNECT SOUNDS AND LETTERS
What is the vowel sound in each word?

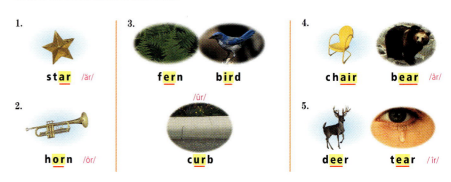

1. st**ar** /är/
2. h**or**n /ôr/
3. f**er**n   b**ir**d   /ûr/
   c**ur**b
4. ch**air**   b**ear** /âr/
5. d**ee**r   t**ear** /îr/

192 Unit 11 | Make a Difference!   ▶ Transparencies page 57–6

REACHING ALL STUDENTS

Multi-Level Strategies
LITERACY SUPPORT

LITERATE IN L1 The English sound /r/ is difficult for many students. See the Phonics Transfer Chart on page T338. Build recognition of /r/ and r-controlled vowels and then involve students in producing the sound:

- For recognition activities, have students tell you which word begins with /r/. Then read minimal pairs such as *road, load; rag, bag; right, light; read, lead*.
- Repeat for *r*-controlled vowels, asking students to say which words rhyme: *star, car; fur, for; bird, bark; corn, torn; cut, curb; hair, chair*.
- For oral production activities, have students repeat sentences with minimal pairs: *The corn is in the barn*.

PRELITERATE Use letter tiles to build and blend words with *r*-controlled vowels on the overhead. After blending the sounds in a word, have students say the vowel sound and point to the letters that make the sound. Good words to use are: *burn, star, horn, fern, bird, curb, chair, bear, fear*, and *deer*.

READING STRATEGY

Follow these steps to read a word.

❶ Look for a pattern in the word. Do you see a **vowel + r**?

y**ar**d   b**ir**d

❷ Start at the beginning. Blend the sounds in your head. Then say the word.

y**ar**d   y + ar + d = yard   b**ir**d   b + ir + d = bird

  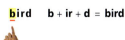

A **vowel + r** makes one sound.

READING AND SPELLING PRACTICE

Blend the sounds to read these words.

1. hair   2. skirts   3. forms   4. art   5. wear   6. year

Use what you learned to read the sentences.

7. Carmen is part of a group that helps women in Latin America.
8. The women make shirts and skirts to wear.
9. They also make hair clips and other crafts to sell.
10. Carmen thinks that these crafts are forms of art.
11. Next year, the group would like to sell the crafts in the U.S.

12.–16. Now write the sentences that your teacher reads.   For dictation sentences, see Step 6 at right.

WORD WORK

17.–24. Read these words. Then write each word on a card. Match the two words that start with the same sound. What do you notice about the vowel sound?

cat	porch	jar	bun	deep	car
deer	heat	fat	hear	pond	jam
burn	chirp	chip	far		

Example:

17.

The **r** changes the vowel sound in a word.

Answers:
7. cat   car
8. deer deep
9. burn bun
10. porch pond
21. heat hear
22. chirp chip
23. jar   jam
24. fat   far

The *r* changes the vowel sound in a word.

Language and Literacy **193**

Decodable Book
PRACTICE WITH R-CONTROLLED VOWELS

Decodable Book 11:
Community Bulletin Board

Assign **Decodable Book 11** for independent reading. The **Decodable Book** can be used in a variety of ways to help students become more fluent, automatic readers:

Discussion Circles Have students work in small groups to read aloud and discuss the book using the questions on the back cover. Encourage students to read aloud the text that supports their answers. Groups can also work together to complete the Word Work Activity.

Readers Theater Students can read aloud the stories in a class performance. Help them prepare by rereading the stories in daily rehearsals. Work with students to add narration or dialog. Encourage them to use natural phrasing and expression.

Rereading at Home Have students work with family members to reread the book at home. They can take turns reading aloud alternate pages, then rereading the book switching the pages each person reads.

LEARN A READING STRATEGY

4 Sound Out Words Work through the strategy with students, reading each step aloud and modeling the actions shown on the page.

PRACTICE

5 Read Words and Sentences Sound out the words in Items 1–6 as a choral reading. Then distribute the Partner Prompts from page T311 to guide peers in reading the sentences in Items 7–11. Remind them to use the sound-out strategy to blend the words silently.

6 Write Sentences Dictate the following sentences for students to write. Read each sentence at normal speed once so students can listen, and then repeat it slowly word by word as they write:

12. She has dark hair.
13. Her skirt twirls when she turns.
14. There is a chair on the porch.
15. There are deer and bears in the park.
16. Now you can hear the birds chirp.

7 Conduct "Word Work" Read the directions and work through the Example. Then have partners complete the activity. Have students read aloud each matched pair and explain how the *r* changes the vowel sound.

▶ **Reading Practice Book** pages 151–154 (Decodable Book 11)

CLOSE AND ASSESS

Write the words *deep, deer, heat, far, burn, jam, porch,* and *hear*. Ask volunteers to read each word and to underline the letter or letters that make the vowel sound.

Language and Literacy **T193**

UNIT 11 LESSON 11

LANGUAGE AND LITERACY: INDEPENDENT READING

OBJECTIVES

Functions:
Read a Selection; Give Information

Learning to Read: ▶ Recognize High Frequency Words; ▶ Decode Words with *R*-Controlled Vowels

Reading Strategies: Activate Prior Knowledge; Set a Purpose for Reading; Use Visuals

Critical Thinking and Comprehension: Classify Information

Writing: Information About People

READ ON YOUR OWN

1 Introduce Vocabulary In the article, students apply the phonics skills and read high frequency words they have learned. Introduce the story words. Write each word, pronounce it, and spell it.

- **ethnic group:** people with the same race and culture. *Many ethnic groups live in my neighborhood: Koreans, Mexicans, Haitians, Russians.*

- **war:** fighting that kills and injures many people. *During the war, people had to hide in their homes.*

- **radio:** heard on a radio. *He listens to radio shows that play folk music.*

- **courage:** bravery. *It takes courage to rescue people from fires.*

- **women:** grown girls. *There are three women in my family: my mother, my aunt, my grandmother.*

Note: The acronym KIND stands for Kudirat Initiative for Democracy. Kudirat was the name of Hafsat's mother, killed in 1996.

2 Activate Prior Knowledge/Set Purposes View the photos and map and discuss what students know about the countries shown. Then model setting a purpose based on the title: *I'll read to find out how the kids in the pictures are helping other kids.*

3 Read and Think: Use Visuals Suggest that students look at the map as they read to better understand where each person works or is from.

T194 Unit 11 | Make a Difference!

COMPREHENSION: CLASSIFY INFORMATION

Read on Your Own

Pronunciation of Names
Nadja Halilbegovich — nahd jah hahl il be gō vich
Hafsat Abiola — hahf saht ah bē ō lah

Nadja Halilbegovich is from Bosnia.

Hafsat Abiola is from Nigeria.

Kids Are Helping Kids

Kids can help other kids in important ways. Nadja, Hafsat, and Craig show us how.

Nadja helped kids in Bosnia. When Nadja was a girl, ethnic groups in Bosnia started a war. Kids lived in fear. A lot of them were hurt. Nadja started a radio show. She sang on the air to give children courage. She also published two books. They tell how hard it is to live through a war. She hopes her books will help end fighting in the world.

Hafsat helps kids in Nigeria. She formed a group called KIND. The group teaches children their rights. It shows kids how to be leaders. KIND also helps women and children get fair treatment.

Craig was 12 years old when he read that many kids were made to work in hard jobs for no pay. People treated them very badly. He had to help these kids. He formed a group called Free the Children. Now, his group speaks out for children's rights in 27 countries.

Craig Kielburger is from Canada.

✓ **DECODING CHECK**
Give the Decoding Progress Check on page 1a of the Assessment Handbook.

194 Unit 11 | Make a Difference!

REACHING ALL STUDENTS

COMMUNITY CONNECTION

Virtual Visit Have students use the Internet to find programs for kids started by young people in their community, or programs for kids run by local agencies. Ask students to suggest key words to use in a search, such as *<name of city or town>* "teenagers who help other people," *<name of city or town> children assistance,* or the names of agencies they have heard of. Students can "visit" the programs or agencies via the Internet and share what they learn with one another.

CHECK YOUR UNDERSTANDING

1.–3. Copy the chart and then complete it.

Who Helped Others?	Where?	What Group of People Did He or She Help?	How?
1. Nadja Halilbegovich	Bosnia	children	She published two books. She started a radio show.
2. Hafsat Abiola	Nigeria	kids, women	She started a group. It teaches children their rights. It shows them how to be leaders. It helps them get fair treatment.
3. Craig Kielburger	27 countries	children	He formed a group. It speaks out for children's rights.

EXPAND YOUR VOCABULARY

4.–6. Tell a partner about each person on page 194. Use information from your chart and some of these words and phrases.

brings hope	fair treatment	hard jobs
sang on the air	rights	formed a group
war	published	Free the Children

Example: **4.** Nadja published two books.
The books tell about the war in Bosnia.

WRITE ABOUT PEOPLE 🖊

7. Choose one of the kids from page 194 or another person you know. Tell how the person makes a difference.

Example: **7.** Craig helps kids who were made to work in hard jobs.
He formed a group called Free the Children.

Language and Literacy **195**

Reading Practice Book page 80

COMPREHENSION
Build Reading Fluency

Read the article. Stop when the timer goes off. Mark your score.
Then try it again two more times on different days.

Another Kid Helps Kids

Kimmie Weeks started making a difference when he was 10. The year was 1991. His country, Liberia, was at war. Many homes and schools were destroyed. Hundreds of children had no food. Many were sick. The fighting was so bad, children were trained to be soldiers. No one seemed to know what to do. Kimmie felt he had to help.

He and other kids started cleaning the streets. They picked up bricks, stones, and other trash left after the fighting. Then he started speaking on the radio. He said that children should not fight in war. His speeches helped. In 1996, Liberia stopped training children to fight.

Kimmie is now a young man. He is still helping the children of his country. He raises money to open more schools. Today, many children have better lives thanks to Kimmie Weeks.

	Day 1	Day 2	Day 3
Total Words Read in One Minute			
Minus Words Missed			
Words Read Correctly in One Minute			

CHECK YOUR UNDERSTANDING

4 **Comprehension: Classify Information** Copy the chart and read the directions aloud. Use the sample answers to model completing the chart with information from the passage. Say: *First, I'll read the question at the top of the first column: "Who Helped Others?" The first person in the article is Nadja, so I'll write her name in the first row. I'll write the name of another person in each of these spaces* (point to the second and third rows in column 1). Continue for the remaining columns.

EXPAND YOUR VOCABULARY

5 **Give Information** Read the directions and go over the vocabulary in the green box. Use the Example to model giving information about Nadja using the word *published* and information in the chart. Encourage volunteers to use other words and phrases from the vocabulary box as well as their charts to give more information about Nadja and about Hafsat and Craig.

WRITE

6 **Write About People** Point out that the Example gives information about how Craig helped others. Then ask students to give information about a person in the passage or about someone they know who helps others.

For students who need additional support in writing, provide these question prompts:

• *Who helps other people?*
• *Where does the person help?*
• *What does the person do to help?*

▶ **Reading Practice Book** page 80

CLOSE AND ASSESS

Have students take turns giving information about the passage by answering the questions: *who? where? what?* and *how?*

Reading Fluency
TIMED READINGS

Read the title and introduction on **Reading Practice Book** page 80. Set the timer and have a student read the passage to you. Use the script on page T322 to mark words the student misses and to note the last word read in one minute. Have students graph their performance and set a goal for improving in subsequent timed readings. Plan for two additional timed readings, and encourage partners to practice reading the passage to each other between the timed readings.

Language and Literacy **T195**

UNIT 11 **LESSON 12**

LANGUAGE ACROSS THE CURRICULUM: MATHEMATICS

OBJECTIVES

Functions:
Listen to an Article; Give Information

Concepts and Vocabulary: Data Displays

Research Skills and Learning Strategies:
Build Background; Use Text Structures (table, circle graph)

Critical Thinking and Comprehension:
Identify Details; Make Judgments; Make Comparisons

LEARN HOW TO REPRESENT DATA

1 Explore Data Displays Read the introduction and labels for the table and circle graph. Explain that both organizers show the same data, but in different ways. Then present the vocabulary and model how to use each organizer to find information.

READ AND THINK

2 Build Background Read the title of the article and the focus question. Explain that U.S. citizens vote for leaders such as the mayor of a city, the governor of a state, and the president of the country. Explain: *This article tells about the history of voting in the U.S. It tells how people changed the laws over time to allow more citizens to vote.*

3 Read the Article Aloud Restate and clarify information as necessary as you read the article. Go over the information in the graphic, incorporating the vocabulary *circle graph*, *section*, and *key*.

CHECK UNDERSTANDING

4 Answer the Review Questions Help students use the information they have learned to answer Items 1–3.

CLOSE AND ASSESS

Ask students to use data from the circle graphs to give information about the two elections: *In the 2000 election, 51.2% of the people voted.*

T196 Unit 11 | Make a Difference!

SUCCESS IN MATHEMATICS

Learn How to Represent Data

TABLES AND CIRCLE GRAPHS

Data is information. You can **represent**, or show, data in different ways.

Voter Participation for 2000 U.S. Election

	Number	Percent
People who were old enough to vote, but did not vote	100,441,000	48.8%
People who voted	105,381,000	51.2%

table

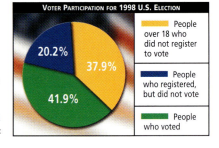

circle graph — Voter Participation for 2000 U.S. Election — 48.8% / 51.2% — *section*

key
- People who were old enough to vote, but did not vote
- People who voted

Answers for the Review:
1. American citizens 18 years or older register can vote. Student opinions to whether Americans use their right
2. A circle graph clearly represents the proportions of the total number.
3. 2000. The corresponding section of and the given percentage is larger f election than for the 1998 election.

Listen to the article. Study the circle graph below. Then do the Review.

Voting Patterns in U.S. Elections

• Do Americans make good use of their right to vote?

In the United States today, you can vote if you are a citizen and if you are 18 years old or older. You also have to register, or sign a paper saying that you want to vote.

It hasn't always been so easy to vote. In the Revolutionary War of 1776, Americans fought the British for the right to vote. For almost a hundred years after the war, only white men could vote. Over the years, several amendments to the United States Constitution have expanded the right to vote:
- In 1870, after the Civil War, the 15th Amendment gave all men of any race the right to vote.
- In 1920, the 19th Amendment gave women the right to vote.
- In 1971, the 26th Amendment lowered the voting age to 18.

Some citizens who are 18 or older do not take the time to register to vote. Others register, but do not vote. Study the circle graph to see data for a typical year.

VOTER PARTICIPATION FOR 1998 U.S. ELECTION
- 20.2% — People over 18 who did not register to vote
- 37.9% — People who registered, but did not vote
- 41.9% — People who voted

REVIEW

1. **Check Your Understanding** Who can vote in the United States today? Do Americans use their right to vote? Explain your answer.
2. **Vocabulary** How does a circle graph help you to compare data?
3. **Use Circle Graphs** Compare the data for the 1998 election and the 2000 election. In which year did a higher percentage of people vote? How can you tell?

196 Unit 11 Make a Difference!

REACHING ALL STUDENTS

Social Studies Connection
CIVIL RIGHTS AND RESPONSIBILITIES

Use a classroom example to discuss the balance between individual rights and responsibilities: *I have the right to say what I think, but I have the responsibility to respect your feelings when I talk.* Then review the rights shown on page 188 and discuss how these civil rights also require personal responsibility. For example, the right to protest needs to be balanced by the responsibility to protest peacefully and without hurting others.

Writing Project / MANDALA

✓ **WRITING ASSESSMENT**
Use the Writing Progress Checklist on page 51 of the Assessment Handbook to evaluate this writing project.

When did you make a difference in the world? Make a mandala to show your class what you did. A mandala is a design in the shape of a circle. You can use it to tell a story with pictures.

GATHER YOUR IDEAS

Think of ways you have helped. Maybe you helped someone at school, someone younger than you, or even a stranger. Maybe you helped a little. Maybe you helped a lot. Gather your ideas in a chart like this. Then choose an idea.

What I Saw	What I Did and How I Felt
My sister didn't know math.	I taught her subtraction. I felt proud.
Mom wanted to speak to the clerk at the grocery store. She didn't know the English words to use.	I spoke to the clerk for my mom. I felt happy to help.

MAKE YOUR MANDALA

Draw a circle. Think about your idea. In the top half of the circle, draw what you saw. In the bottom half of the circle, draw what you did. Write a sentence about each picture.

✓ **Check Your Work**
Did you tell how you helped someone?
Did you describe how you felt?
Did you use the correct form of each verb?

Write your sentences next to each picture on the mandala. Decorate the mandala. Display it in your classroom.

Language Across the Curriculum 197

Language Practice Book page 100

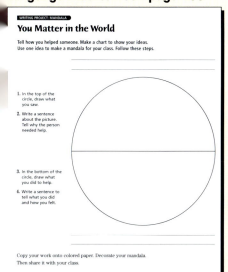

Multi-Level Strategies

WRITING SUPPORT

PRELITERATE Some students may need extra support in recording information onto their mandalas. Encourage them to create a sketch of the two pictures they want to include. As students dictate their sentences for you to write, pause to review the spelling of regular and irregular past tense verbs. Students can then copy the sentences onto their final projects.

UNIT 11 **LESSON 13**

LANGUAGE ACROSS THE CURRICULUM: WRITING

OBJECTIVES

Functions:
Express Feelings; Give Information; Write

Learning Strategies and Critical Thinking:
Plan; Generate and Organize Ideas; Self-Assess; Use Graphic Organizers (chart)

Representing and Writing:
Personal Narrative in a Mandala

CONDUCT THE WRITING PROJECT

1 **Explore Mandalas** Read aloud the introduction and preview the activity steps. Use the sample mandala and the chart to help students brainstorm their own ideas.

2 **Make Your Mandala** Provide a circle diagram to illustrate the directions:

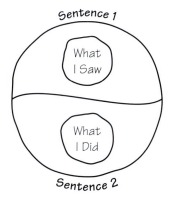

Have students sketch their ideas and proofread their sentences before creating the final product. Students may decide to use photographs, magazine pictures, or symbols to represent their ideas.

3 **Display the Mandalas** Have students present their mandalas before displaying them around the room.

▶ Language Practice Book page 100

CLOSE AND ASSESS

Have students look at the mandalas they made. Say:
- *Show me a sentence that tells how you helped someone.*
- *Point to words that tell your feelings.*
- *Show me the past tense form of a verb. Is it regular or irregular? How do you know?*

Language Across the Curriculum **T197**

Resources

For Success in Language and Literacy

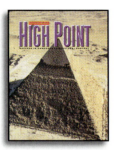

Student Book pages 198–211

For Language Skills Practice

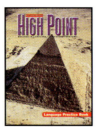

Language Practice Book
pages 101–105

For Reading Skills Practice

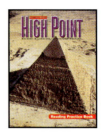

Reading Practice Book
pages 81–83

For Vocabulary, Language Development, and Reading Fluency

Language Tape 6, Side B
Language CD 2, Tracks 20–22

For Reading Together

Theme Book *Rachel Carson*
from The Basics Bookshelf

For Audio Walk-Throughs and Selection Readings

Selection Tape 6B
Selection CD 2, Tracks 11–12

For Phonics Instruction

Transparencies 62–64

Transparency Scripts 62–64

Letter Tiles

For Comprehensive Assessment

Language Acquisition Assessment,
Units 10–12 Test, Writing Assessment,
Self-Assessment

For Planning and Instruction

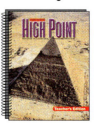

Teacher's Edition
pages T198a–T211

UNIT 12

Our Living Planet

In This Unit

Vocabulary
- Opinion Words
- Animals, Plants, and Habitats
- Graphs

Language Functions
- Give Opinions
- Describe Places
- Make a Suggestion

Patterns and Structures
- Sensory Adjectives
- Verbs (*must, should*)

Reading
- Multisyllabic Words
- Comprehension: Identify Sequence (data chart, time line); Identify Details, Cause and Effect

Writing
- Opinions
- Description
- Fact-and-Opinion Poster

Content Area Connection
- Science and Mathematics (line graphs)

T198b

UNIT 12

Activity and Assessment Planner

UNIT 12: Our Living Planet

LESSONS

1 — UNIT 12 LAUNCH ▶ pages T198–T199

LESSON 1: INTRODUCE UNIT 12 pages T198–T199

Vocabulary
Animals

Habitats

Viewing
Respond to a Visual Image

Learning Strategies
Preview

Build Background

Use Graphic Organizers (chart)

Critical Thinking and Writing
Make Comparisons

Generate Ideas

Classify

🅣 Write Sentences

2–5 — LANGUAGE DEVELOPMENT ▶ pages T200–T203

LESSON 2
OPINION WORDS
page T200

Function
Give Opinions

Vocabulary
Opinion Words

Patterns and Structures
🅣 Modals (must, should)

Writing
Opinions

LESSON 3
ANIMALS AND HABITATS
page T201

Function
Describe Places

Vocabulary
🅣 Animals and Habitats

Viewing
Interpret a Visual Image

Writing
Description

LESSON 4
PLANTS AND HABITATS
page T202

Functions
Make a Suggestion

Give Opinions

Vocabulary
🅣 Plants and Habitats

Writing
Suggestions

LESSON 5
SENSORY ADJECTIVES
page T203

Function
Describe Places

Patterns and Structures
🅣 Sensory Adjectives

Writing
Description

6–11 — LANGUAGE AND LITERACY ▶ pages T204a–T209

LESSON 6
BASICS BOOKSHELF
pages T204a–T204h

Function
Listen to a Book

Vocabulary
🅣 Habitats, Plants, and Animals

Reading Strategies
Activate Prior Knowledge

Preview

Learning to Read
Identify Words

Use Text Features (labels)

Critical Thinking and Comprehension
🅣 Identify Sequence

LESSON 7
BASICS BOOKSHELF: COMPREHENSION
page T204

Function
Give Information

Learning Strategy
Use Graphic Organizers (data chart, time line)

Critical Thinking and Comprehension
🅣 Identify Sequence

LESSON 8
HIGH FREQUENCY WORDS
page T205

Learning to Read
🅣 Recognize High Frequency Words

LESSON 9
PHONICS
pages T206a–T206b

Learning to Read
Build Oral Vocabulary

Develop Phonemic Awareness

🅣 Recognize Syllable Types (r-controlled)

Decode Multisyllabic Words

LESSON 10
READING AND SPELLING
pages T206–T207

Learning to Read
Develop Phonemic Awareness

🅣 Recognize Syllable Types

Decode Multisyllabic Words

Spelling
Syllable Types

LESSON 11
INDEPENDENT READING
pages T208–T209

Functions
Read a Selection

Describe

Learning to Read
🅣 Recognize High Frequency Words

🅣 Recognize Syllable Types to Decode Multisyllabic Words

Reading Strategies
Activate Prior Knowledge

Set a Purpose for Reading

Visualize

Critical Thinking and Comprehension
Identify Details

🅣 Identify Cause and Effect

Writing
Description

12–13 — LANGUAGE ACROSS THE CURRICULUM ▶ pages T210–T211

LESSON 12 SCIENCE AND MATH: LINE GRAPHS
page T210

Function
Listen to a Selection

Vocabulary
Graphs

🅣 Animals/Habitats

Research Skills and Learning Strategies
Build Background

Use Text Structures (line graphs)

Critical Thinking and Comprehension
🅣 Identify Cause and Effect

LESSON 13 WRITING PROJECT: FACT-AND-OPINION POSTER
page T211

Functions
Give Opinions

Write

Learning Strategies and Critical Thinking
Plan

Generate/Organize Ideas

Self-Assess

Research Skills
Gather Information

Critical Thinking and Comprehension
Distinguish Between Facts and Opinions

Writing
Fact-and-Opinion Poster

T198c Unit 12 | Our Living Planet

🅣 = Objective Tested on Unit Test

ASSESSMENT OPTIONS

The **Teacher's Edition** and the **Assessment Handbook** include these comprehensive assessment tools:

▶ **Ongoing, Informal Assessment**
Check for understanding and achieve closure for every lesson with the targeted questions and activities in the **Close and Assess** boxes in your Teacher's Edition.

▶ **Decoding Progress Check**
These word lists for each unit provide a quick way to check on mastery of the phonics or word structure skills taught in the unit.

▶ **Language Acquisition Assessments**
To verify students' ability to use the language functions and grammar structures taught in Units 10–12, conduct these performance assessments.

▶ **Unit Test in Standardized Test Format**
This multiple-choice test measures students' cumulative understanding of the skills and language developed in Units 10–12.

▶ **Self- and Peer-Assessment**
Students use the Self-Assessment Form to evaluate their own work and develop learning strategies appropriate to their needs. Students offer feedback to their classmates with the Peer-Assessment Form.

▶ **Writing Assessment/Portfolio Opportunities**
You can evaluate students' writing in the Writing Projects using the Writing Progress Checklist. Then collaborate with students to choose work for their portfolios.

UNITS 10–12 ASSESSMENT OPPORTUNITIES

	Assessment Handbook Pages
Decoding Progress Check	1a
Language Acquisition Assessments	26
Units 10–12 Test	27–32
Self-Assessment Form	33
Peer-Assessment Form	50
Writing Progress Checklist	51
Portfolio Evaluation Form	52

RELATED RESOURCES

Common Ground: The Water, Earth, and Air We Share
by Molly Bang
An essay that presents a persuasive argument for working together to preserve our natural resources. (Available from Hampton-Brown)
Theme Book: Read Aloud

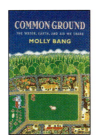

Where the Forest Meets the Sea
by Jeannie Baker
A boy visits an Australian reef with his father and imagines what it was like a hundred million years ago. (Greenwillow)
Easy Reading

Hairy, Scary, Ordinary
by Brian P. Cleary
Rhyming text and comical characters present numerous examples of adjectives. (Carolrhoda)
Language Development: Adjectives

Beast Feast
by Douglas Florian
A collection of humorous poems about all kinds of mammals, reptiles, insects, and fish. A companion to *In the Swim*. (Harcourt)
Phonics: Multisyllabic Words

The World of Nature
Presents a wealth of information on plants, animals, insects, the environment, and different ecosystems. (Queue)
Multimedia: CD-ROM

Unit Planner **T198d**

UNIT 12 LESSON 1

INTRODUCE UNIT 12: OUR LIVING PLANET

OBJECTIVES

Concepts and Vocabulary: Animals; Habitats
Viewing: Respond to a Visual Image
Learning Strategies: Preview; Build Background; Use Graphic Organizers (chart)
Critical Thinking: Make Comparisons; Generate Ideas; Classify
Writing: 🅣 Sentences

START WITH A COMMON EXPERIENCE

1. **Introduce "Our Living Planet"**
   Read the unit title and say: *The planet Earth is home to many living plants, animals, and people.*

   Then view the animal pictures with students and read the names aloud. Model how to find similarities between the animals on the page. For example, point to the tiger in the center and say: *A tiger has stripes. What other animals have stripes?* (zebra, butterfly) Brainstorm a chart to show ways that animals can be categorized:

habitat	ability	diet
forest	swim	meat
desert	fly	plants
ocean	run	insects

2. **Play the Game** Read the game directions and invite two volunteers to model the game as the class observes. Then have partners play the game on their own. Encourage students to use the chart as they look for similarities between animal pairs.

3. **Write About Animals** Provide sentence frames to help students write about two animals:

   The ____ and the ____ are alike.
   They both are ____.
   They both have ____.
   They both can ____.

UNIT 12

REACHING ALL STUDENTS

HOME CONNECTION

Interview Have students interview a family member about wild animals, asking such questions as: *What is your favorite wild animal? Why is it your favorite? Where does it live? What other animal is it like?* Students can draw the animal on one side of a card and write facts about the animal on the other side. Encourage students to trade their cards and learn more about animals around the world.

T198 Unit 12 | Our Living Planet

Our Living Planet

Play this game with a partner. Toss two coins onto the page at left. Make them land on two different animals. Tell one way the animals are the same. Your partner should tell another way the animals are alike. See who can think of the most ways.

Sample Responses
Students should notice similarities such as color, size, fur/no fur, stripes, number of legs, ears/no ears, and so on.

In This Unit

Vocabulary
- Opinion Words
- Animals, Plants, and Habitats
- Graphs

Language Functions
- Give Opinions
- Describe Places
- Make a Suggestion

Patterns and Structures
- Sensory Adjectives
- Verbs (*must, should*)

Reading
- Multisyllabic Words
- Comprehension:
  Identify Sequence (data chart, time line)
  Identify Details, Cause and Effect

Writing
- Opinions
- Description
- Fact-and-Opinion Poster

Content Area Connection
- Science and Mathematics (line graphs)

199

PREVIEW THE UNIT

4 Look for Activities and Ways to Learn About Animals Leaf through the unit, previewing activities students will do, for example:

page 200—learning a song about protecting the Earth for animals

page 201—learning about life in different habitats

page 204—listening to the Bookshelf book (Display a copy of the book.)

page 210—reading about an endangered animal

page 211—making a fact-and-opinion poster about an animal

Also ask students to look for ways to describe places or to give information. Highlight the writing activity on page 201 and the use of graphs on page 210. Then sum up what the preview reveals: *The Earth is home to many plants, animals, and people. We must protect our planet.*

5 Set Your Goals Start a class mind map on ways to help animals. Prompt students for pictures or words to add, and have them act out and describe other ideas for you to put into words.

CLOSE AND ASSESS
Ask students to tell or show you something they are interested in learning in this unit.

UNIT 12 Mind Map

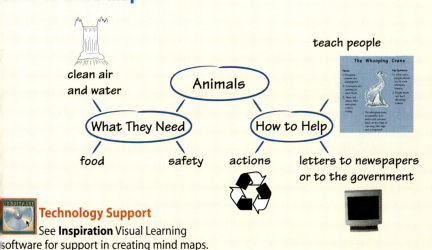

Technology Support
See **Inspiration** Visual Learning software for support in creating mind maps.

Unit Launch **T199**

UNIT 12 LESSON 2
LANGUAGE DEVELOPMENT: OPINION WORDS

OBJECTIVES
Functions: Listen Actively; Repeat Spoken Language; Recite; Give Opinions
Concepts and Vocabulary: Opinion Words
Patterns and Structures:
🔊 Modals (*must, should*)
Writing: Opinions

INTRODUCE

1 Listen and Sing *Tape 6B · CD 2 Track 20*
Play "Our Earth" on the **Language Tape/CD**. Students will listen and follow along with the words, and then echo the lines before chiming in on the entire song.

2 Learn About Opinion Words Read aloud the chart for opinion words and find examples in the song. To ensure understanding, ask questions such as: *What does the writer think we must do? What does the writer believe? What is this writer's opinion about pollution?*

PRACTICE

3 Conduct "Express Yourself" Model how to give opinions. Then have partners complete the activity.

How to Give Opinions
- Use opinion words to tell what you think: *I **believe** it's important to keep the environment clean.*
- Then give reasons for your opinion: *A clean environment is best for people and animals.*

APPLY

4 Write Opinions Encourage students to check their answers with a partner. Distribute Partner Checklist 12 on page T310.

▶ Language Practice Book page 101

CLOSE AND ASSESS
Have volunteers share the opinions they wrote. Call on students to identify the opinion word used.

T200 Unit 12 | Our Living Planet

VOCABULARY: OPINION WORDS

We Must Care for Our Earth!

Listen and sing.

Our Earth
We must keep the air clean
for the eagle to fly.
We must clean up our oceans
so the whales can swim by.
I think we should fight
for our water and sky.
We must help our Earth.
I believe we must try!

Opinion Words
People use these words to give an opinion.
| must | should |
| think | believe |

EXPRESS YOURSELF ▶ GIVE YOUR OPINION

How should we protect plants and animals? Work with your class to think of ideas. Finish each sentence below.

Example: 1. We should pick up trash.

1. We should ____.
2. We must ____.
3. I believe that ____.
4. I think that ____.

WRITE OPINIONS ✏️

5.–8. What should we do to help the Earth? Work with a group to write 4 ideas. Use opinion words.

Example: 5. We should keep the rivers clean.

200 Unit 12 | Our Living Planet

REACHING ALL STUDENTS

Language Development
OPINIONS

Invite partners or small groups to create posters that show their opinions about the environment. Use the song "Our Earth" as an example, reviewing how the text and the images strongly state an opinion. Then encourage students to work with the sentences they wrote or to create new ones. Students can illustrate their posters with their own art or create collages from magazines and news photos. Display the posters in the classroom or in a public area at school.

Language Practice Book page 101

VOCABULARY: OPINION WORDS
What Is Your Opinion?
Read the opinion. Then write your own opinion. Use words from the box.

Opinion Words
People use these words to give an opinion.
must should
think believe

1. Everyone should care for the Earth.
   My Opinion: *I believe that everyone should care for the Earth.*
2. We must clean up our water.
   My Opinion: ____
3. You should pick up trash.
   My Opinion: ____
4. We should stop air pollution.
   My Opinion: ____
5. We must protect the forest.
   My Opinion: ____

VOCABULARY: ANIMALS AND HABITATS

What Lives Around the Water?

EXPRESS YOURSELF ▶ DESCRIBE PLACES

1.–2. Work with a group. Describe each place. Tell what you can see there.

Sample Responses
Students' descriptions should include some of the vocabulary they have just learned.

Example: 1. There are big waves at the seashore.
There is white sand.

WRITE A DESCRIPTION

3.–8. Write 3 sentences about each picture above. Use adjectives to describe the animals you see.

Example: 3. I see a brown beaver and a very big frog at the pond.

Adjectives	
green	large
brown	small
orange	big
white	little

Sample Responses
Students' sentences should include adjectives supported by the illustrations above.

Language Development 201

Language Practice Book page 102

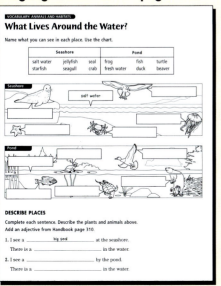

UNIT 12 **LESSON 3**

LANGUAGE DEVELOPMENT: ANIMALS AND HABITATS

OBJECTIVES

Function: Describe Places
Concepts and Vocabulary:
🅣 Animals; 🅣 Habitats
Viewing: Interpret a Visual Image
Writing: Description

INTRODUCE

1 Activate Prior Knowledge Direct students to pages 128, 136, and 138 of Unit 7 to review habitats they have already studied. (rain forest, beach, wetland) Say: *Each habitat is a special place where certain plants and animals live.* Ask questions to link animals with their habitats: *What animals live in a rain forest?* (monkey, toucan, etc.) *Where can you find a seagull?* (beach)

2 Learn Words for Animals and Habitats Direct attention to the illustrations on page 201 and have students follow along as you name the plants, animals, and features found in each habitat.

PRACTICE

3 Conduct "Express Yourself" Model the Example for students. Provide the sentence starters below for students who need them. Then have small groups complete the activity.

In the _____ habitat,
I see _____.
There is/are _____
at the _____.

APPLY

4 Write a Description Read the list of adjectives and model the Example. Point out the adjectives *brown* and *big* and the words they describe (beaver and frog, respectively). Then have students complete the activity.

▶ **Language Practice Book** page 102

CLOSE AND ASSESS

Have volunteers read their sentences while everyone listens with eyes closed to visualize the descriptions.

Language Development **T201**

UNIT 12 **LESSON 4**

LANGUAGE DEVELOPMENT: PLANTS AND HABITATS

OBJECTIVES
Functions: Listen Actively; Make a Suggestion; Give Opinions
Concepts and Vocabulary:
🅣 Plants; 🅣 Habitats
Writing: Suggestions

INTRODUCE

1 Learn Words for Plants and Habitats Have students study the photos and point to the items as you read aloud the labels. If possible, bring in real or artificial plants for students to label.

Then, if plants, flowers, and trees are accessible near your classroom, take a walk with your class and have partners make labeled sketches. Have students present their work. Then combine the pictures into a "field guide" of neighborhood plants.

PRACTICE

2 Conduct "Who's Talking?" Play "Who's Talking?" on the **Language Tape/CD** to model how to make a suggestion. Pause and replay as necessary for students to point to the correct speaker. Have pairs of volunteers act out the scene.

APPLY

3 Write Suggestions Explain that a suggestion is an idea or a plan that you try to get other people to do. Go over the instructions and have students use the sentence starters provided to write their own suggestions.

▶ Language Practice Book page 103

CLOSE AND ASSESS

Have volunteers read their suggestions aloud. Call on students to make the same suggestion in a different way.

T202 Unit 12 | Our Living Planet

SENSORY ADJECTIVES
Describe the Earth

Adjectives can tell what something is like.

An adjective can tell how something looks.
　　The tree is **tall**.

An adjective can tell how something sounds.
　　A **loud** bird lives in the tree.

An adjective can tell how something feels.
　　The tree trunk feels **rough**.

BUILD SENTENCES

Look at each picture below. Add an adjective to tell how each thing looks, sounds, or feels. See Handbook pages 310–311. Say each sentence.

Sample responses are given. Others are possible.

Example: 1. The desert is hot and dry.

1. The desert is ____. hot
2. A ____ cactus grows there. tall
3. The snake makes a ____ sound. rattling

4. The mountain is ____. beautiful
5. A ____ deer lives there. brown
6. The squirrel makes a ____ sound. noisy

WRITE A DESCRIPTION

7. Draw a picture of a scene in nature. Write a description of your drawing. Use adjectives.

Example: 7. The brown owl is in the tall tree. The forest is quiet and cool.

Language Development 203

Language Practice Book page 104

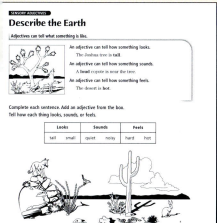

Multi-Level Strategies
LANGUAGE DEVELOPMENT

LITERATE IN L1 The use of adjectives varies greatly across languages. For example, in languages such as Hmong, Portuguese, Spanish, and Vietnamese, adjectives can follow nouns. Speakers of these languages may say: *the book red, my class favorite*. In many languages, such as Spanish and Arabic, adjectives reflect gender and number: *the reds books*.

To reinforce the use of adjectives in English, have partners label magazine pictures with adjective-noun phrases such as *cool lake, tall boy*.

UNIT 12 **LESSON 5**

LANGUAGE DEVELOPMENT: SENSORY ADJECTIVES

OBJECTIVES
Function: Describe Places
Patterns and Structures:
🅣 Sensory Adjectives
Writing: Description

INTRODUCE

1 Learn About Sensory Adjectives
Read the title and introduction. Go over the examples and relate them to the photo. Then provide items or experiences that can be described with sensory adjectives; for example: a **loud** whistle; a **thin**, **red** leaf; a **rough** rock; a **tiny** flower; a **soft** voice. Write the adjectives on a chart like the one below and ask students to add more examples for each category.

Sensory Adjectives

Looks	Sounds	Feels
tiny	loud	rough
red	soft	soft
thin		thin

PRACTICE

2 Build Sentences Locate the list of adjectives on Handbook pages 310–311. Then go over the Example, providing several possible adjectives to complete Item 1.

APPLY

3 Write a Description Discuss the Example. Encourage students to look at habitats on earlier pages for ideas. Remind them that adjectives can be placed before a noun or after a verb: *The **quiet** seashore is **sandy** and **cool**.*

▶ **Language Practice Book** page 104

CLOSE AND ASSESS

Have students set up a gallery of their artwork and take turns reading their sentences aloud. Ask volunteers to tell if the adjectives tell about something they can see, hear, or feel.

Language Development **T203**

UNIT 12 **LESSON 6**

LANGUAGE AND LITERACY: THE BASICS BOOKSHELF

OBJECTIVES
Concepts and Vocabulary:
🅣 Habitats; 🅣 Plants; 🅣 Animals
Listening: Listen to a Preview
Reading Strategies:
Activate Prior Knowledge; Preview

BUILD LANGUAGE AND VOCABULARY

Materials: bingo cards with 9 blank spaces; small objects for place markers

1. **Teach "Words to Know"** Describe the habitats on pages 2–5: *A forest is a large area where many trees grow. A pond is a small body of water. A seashore is sandy land near the ocean. A farm is a place where crops are grown and animals are raised.* Then point to the illustrations and read the labels. Ask students if the drawing shows a plant or an animal.

2. **Play Bingo** Have partners draw one animal from pages 2–5 in each cell of a bingo card. To play the game, describe an animal: *This animal lives in the forest. It is big and has brown fur.* Partners who have drawn a bear should cover the corresponding cell. The first team to get a bingo gives the next set of clues.

PREPARE TO READ

3. **Think About What You Know** Lead students on a brief outdoor walking tour. When you return, make a class chart of the plants and animals you observed. Ask students to add sketches and illustrations.

4. **Preview** Play the Audio Walk-Through for *Rachel Carson* on the **Selection Tape/CD** to give students the overall idea of the story. *Tape 6B / CD 2 Track 11*

CLOSE AND ASSESS
Conduct a Think-Pair-Share (See Cooperative Learning Structures, page T337d) about the book. For the Share step, ask partners to tell you one fact about Rachel's life.

Rachel Carson
by William Accorsi

Summary This biography describes the life of noted environmentalist Rachel Carson and her work to protect the environment from pesticides. A sketchbook format combines the events of Carson's life with historical photos. Detailed sketches present four habitats with vocabulary for plants and animals.

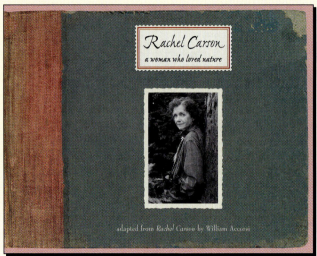

Cover

Rachel Carson

Plants and Animals

Pages 2–3

Plants and Animals

Pages 4–5

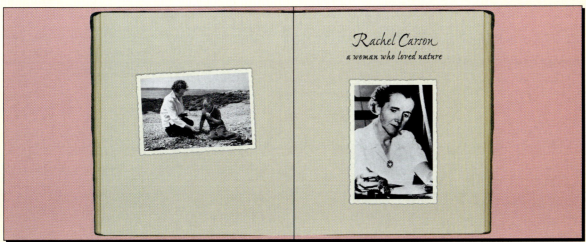

Pages 6–7

Language and Literacy **T204b**

UNIT 12 LESSON 6, CONTINUED

LANGUAGE AND LITERACY: THE BASICS BOOKSHELF

OBJECTIVES

Function: Listen to a Book

READ AND THINK TOGETHER

1 **Read Aloud** On your first reading of the book, use the "Strategies for Comprehensible Input" that appear on this page.

Strategies for Comprehensible Input

PAGE	STORY LANGUAGE	STRATEGY OPTIONS
8–9	nature	**Restate:** birds, plants, and other living things
	Pennsylvania	**Point to the map of Pennsylvania.**
10–11	college	**Explain:** After high school, you can study more at college.
	plants, animals	**Point to the pictures.**
12–13	became interested in	**Restate:** wanted to know more about
	huge success	**Explain:** Many people read and liked the book.
14–15	letters	**Point to the picture.**
	poisons	**Explain:** A poison is something that can hurt or kill you if you eat or breathe it.
	insects	**Point to the picture.**
16–17	was in danger	**Restate:** might get sick or hurt
18–19	*Silent Spring*	**Explain:** The book is about how plants and animals died. The spring was full of life. When the animals were gone, it was all quiet.
	angry	**Restate:** mad; unhappy
20–21	television	**Point to the picture.**
	President of the United States	**Point to the picture and explain:** The president is the leader of the country.
22–23	protect	**Restate:** take care of
	environment	**Explain:** The environment is the air, land, and water around us.

T204c Unit 12 | Our Living Planet

Rachel Carson, CONTINUED

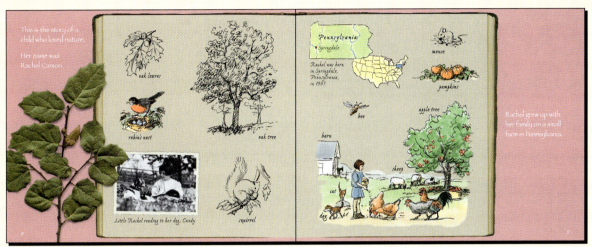

Pages 8–9

Pages 10–11

Pages 12–13

Language and Literacy **T204d**

UNIT 12 **LESSON 6,** CONTINUED

LANGUAGE AND LITERACY: THE BASICS BOOKSHELF

OBJECTIVES
Function: Listen to a Book
Critical Thinking and Comprehension:
🅣 Identify Sequence

READ AND THINK TOGETHER, CONTINUED

2 Read and Map: Identify Sequence
Set up a data chart with page numbers in place, but with columns 2–4 blank:

Page	Event	Date	Words
9	Rachel was born.	1907	baby
11	She went to college.	1927	20 years old
13	She wrote a book.	1939	32 years old
14	She moved to Maine.	1952	45 years old
22	Rachel died.	1964	57 years old

As you read pages 8–23, record the main events of Rachel Carson's life.

On page 11, model how to calculate dates. Say: *The caption says that Rachel was in college when she was 20 years old. To find the date, I'll add 20 to 1907, the year she was born. Rachel entered college in 1927.* Turn to page 13 and have students calculate the date when Rachel wrote her first book. [birthdate (1907) plus age (32) = 1939]

On page 14 show students how to calculate Rachel's age. Say: *Rachel moved to Maine in 1952. To find out her age, I'll subtract 1907 from 1952. Rachel was 45 when she moved to Maine.* Turn to page 22 and have students calculate Rachel's age when she died. (57 years old)

After reading, use the data in the chart to make a time line like the one shown. Remind students that a time line shows events in the order in which they happen.

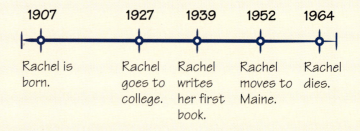

Time Line for *Rachel Carson*

1907	1927	1939	1952	1964
Rachel is born.	Rachel goes to college.	Rachel writes her first book.	Rachel moves to Maine.	Rachel dies.

Technology Support
See **Inspiration** Visual Learning software for support in creating the time line.

Rachel Carson, CONTINUED

Pages 14–15

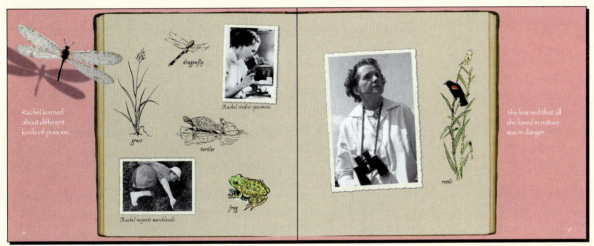

Pages 16–17

Pages 18–19

Language and Literacy T204f

UNIT 12 **LESSON 6,** CONTINUED

LANGUAGE AND LITERACY: THE BASICS BOOKSHELF

OBJECTIVES
Function: Listen to a Book
Learning to Read: Identify Words
Reading Strategies:
Use Text Features (labels)

READ AND THINK TOGETHER, CONTINUED

3 Conduct Interactive Readings
Choose from these options:

- **Read along** Play the recording of *Rachel Carson* on the **Selection Tape/CD**.

CD 2 Track 12

- **Identify words** *Rachel Carson* contains many high frequency words that have been previously taught, as follows:

a	her	over	together
about	important	people	under
all	in	said	was
and	is	she	we
animals	it	small	were
another	know	some	what
around	letters	story	when
book	many	take	who
called	more	that	with
different	name	the	work
does	now	they	world
family	of	think	write
find	old	this	years
first	on	thought	
help	other	to	

As you read, frame individual words from the list and have students identify the words.

CLOSE AND ASSESS
Have students tell about one event in Rachel Carson's life.

Multi-Level Strategies
LITERACY SUPPORT

PRELITERATE **Read Dates and Ages** Have students write the numbers 0–9 onto cards, one number per card. Turn to page 9 and point out the date, *1907,* in the caption. Use number cards to model forming the number as you read the date aloud: *You can say* nineteen hundred seven *or* nineteen-o-seven. Call out more dates from the biography (see pages 13 and 22), have partners form the dates with their number cards, and read them aloud.

Next, turn to page 11 and point out the age, *20 years old*. On page 13, point out the word *thirty-two*. Explain that these are two ways to write a person's age. Have volunteers call out more ages from the book as the rest of the class forms the numbers with number cards and reads them. You can also add the ages to Carson's birth year to obtain more dates to form and read.

NON-ROMAN ALPHABET **Use Text Features: Labels** Explain that labels can be used to identify pictures. Turn to pages 4–5, and read aloud the labels *clam* and *fruit trees* as you point to the illustrations. Use a finger to trace the line from each of these labels to the picture as you say: *Some labels have lines that point to the picture.* Then call attention to several other labels as you explain that labels can appear above, below, or to the sides of an illustration. Then have partners work together to search the book for more labels. One partner should read aloud the label. The other partner should point to the corresponding illustration that is closest to the label.

LITERATE IN L1 **Read with a Partner/Create Opinion Posters** After students have participated in the interactive readings, encourage them to read the story with a partner. Distribute the Partner Prompts on page T311 to help partners work together to identify unfamiliar words and unlock their meanings, then read the text to each other. After the partner reading, have students make posters that state their opinions about saving the environment. Provide sentence frames that reinforce opinion words:

I think we should _____.
I believe _____ hurts _____.
We must _____.

Encourage students to illustrate and display their posters on a classroom bulletin board.

T204g Unit 12 | Our Living Planet

Rachel Carson, CONTINUED

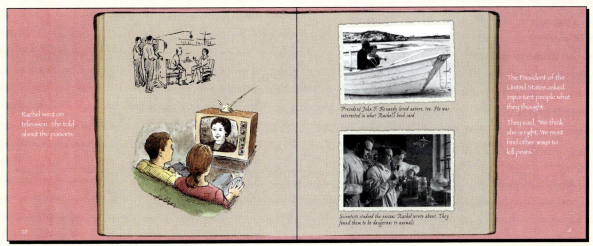

Pages 20–21

Pages 22–23

Language and Literacy **T204h**

UNIT 12 LESSON 7

LANGUAGE AND LITERACY: THE BASICS BOOKSHELF

OBJECTIVES
Function: Give Information
Learning Strategy: Use Graphic Organizers (data chart, time line)
Critical Thinking and Comprehension:
- Identify Sequence

CHECK COMPREHENSION

1. **Make a Data Chart** Have students copy the chart in Step 1, then review *Rachel Carson* to identify the main events and dates. Remind students how to add Rachel's age to her birthdate in order to calculate the dates. (See page T204e.)

2. **Make a Time Line** Remind students that a time line shows events in the order in which they happen. Explain that it can be vertical like the one they made for the life of Martin Luther King, Jr., or it can be horizontal like this one. Read aloud the directions for each step and pause for students to construct their time lines.

3. **Share Information from the Book** Have small groups use their time lines to tell about Rachel Carson's life in their own words. Have each group member tell about one or more events. Remind students to retell the events in the correct time order.

CLOSE AND ASSESS
Ask students to complete this sentence: *A time line shows _____.*

T204 Unit 12 | Our Living Planet

COMPREHENSION: IDENTIFY SEQUENCE

Read and Think Together

Make a data chart and time line for *Rachel Carson*. Follow these steps.

1. Copy the chart below. Read the book again. Collect these facts about Rachel's life.

Page	Event	Year	Age
9	Rachel was born.	1907	baby
11	She went to college.	1927	20 years old
13	She wrote a book.	1939	32 years old
14	She moved to Maine.	1952	45 years old
22	Rachel died.	1964	57 years old

2. Use the data chart to make a time line. Draw the line. Add a dot for the first event. Write the year above the dot. Below the dot, write a sentence to tell what happened in that year.

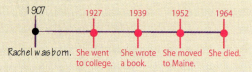

3. Finish the time line. Add 4 more dots, each with a date and a sentence.

4. Use your finished time line to tell a group about Rachel Carson's life.

204 Unit 12 | Our Living Planet

from **The Basics Bookshelf**

THEME BOOK
This biography tells how Rachel Carson changed the way people treat our natural world.

REACHING ALL STUDENTS

Language Development
MAKE A SUGGESTION; MAKE A DENIAL

Role-Play Use the scene on page 19 to model how to make a suggestion and a denial:

Farmer: I think that you should not write about the poisons. You might want to talk to more farmers first.

Rachel: I disagree. Plants and animals are in danger. I want people to stop using poisons!

Have partners use the chart to role-play another conversation between Rachel and a farmer.

How to Make a Suggestion	How to Make a Denial
You might want to _____.	I disagree.
It may be helpful to _____.	I don't think you're right.
I think that you should _____.	I think that you're wrong.

HIGH FREQUENCY WORDS

Words to Know

REVIEW WORDS YOU KNOW

Read the words aloud. Which word goes in the sentence?

house	head
other	Answer
new	Now

1. One person holds the bird's _____.   head
2. _____ person holds its body.   Another
3. _____ they can help the bird.   Now

LEARN TO READ

Learn new words.

mountains	Alaska has beautiful beaches and tall **mountains**.
oil	In 1989, a ship spilled **oil** into a bay in Alaska.
found	People **found** sick birds on the beach.
because	The birds got sick **because** they ate the oil when they cleaned their feathers.
few	Many people, not just a **few**, came to help.
try	The people wanted to **try** to save the birds.
over	When their work was **over**, many birds were saved.
away	The people went **away**, but they did not forget.
why	Everyone asked **why** the spill happened.
story	Newspapers around the world told the **story**.

How to Learn a New Word
- Look at the word.
- Listen to the word.
- Listen to the word in a sentence. What does it mean?
- Say the word.
- Spell the word.
- Say the word again.

WORD WORK

Write each sentence. Add the missing word.   Example: 1. Why did the oil spill happen?

w h y did the oil spill happen?
It happened b e c a u s e the ship ran aground.
The ship started to leak o i l.
In just a f e w days, the oil was everywhere.
Before the spill was o v e r, the oil had coated 1,300 miles of the Alaska shoreline.
Ten years later, people still f o u n d oil on the beaches.
The s t o r y of the Alaska oil spill is a sad one.

Language and Literacy **205**

Reading Practice Book page 81

Reading Fluency
RECOGNIZE HIGH FREQUENCY WORDS

To build automaticity with the new high frequency words:

- Have students make up their own sentences using letter blanks for the new high frequency words. Partners can complete each other's sentences.
- Have small groups sort words into groups: words that name things; words that name actions; words with three letters, words with two syllables. Encourage students to think of more groups. Then have students read their lists.

UNIT 12 **LESSON 8**

LANGUAGE AND LITERACY: HIGH FREQUENCY WORDS

OBJECTIVES

Learning to Read:
- Recognize High Frequency Words

REVIEW WORDS

1 Review Known High Frequency Words Have the group read aloud the words in the green box. Listen for words students cannot read automatically and use the steps in the yellow box to reteach those words. Then have students look at the photo. Read each cloze sentence. Reread each sentence and pause for students to silently read the two words to the left of the sentence. Tell students to choose the word that goes in the sentence and tells about the picture.

INTRODUCE NEW WORDS

2 Learn High Frequency Words Use the High Frequency Word Script on page T323 to lead students through the steps in the yellow box. Discuss the new meaning of *over*. ("completed or finished")

PRACTICE

3 Conduct "Word Work" Use the Example to model how to use context to find possible words in the list and then to use the number of letter blanks to confirm the word.

Have partners complete Items 5–10. Discuss how each correct word fits the context and the number of blanks.

APPLY

4 Read Words in Context Students will read high frequency words in context in the sentences on page 207 and the passage on page 208.

▶ **Reading Practice Book** page 81

CLOSE AND ASSESS

Call out the high frequency words one at a time. Have students point to them and spell the words as a group.

Language and Literacy **T205**

UNIT 12 LESSON 9

LANGUAGE AND LITERACY: PHONICS

OBJECTIVES

Learning to Read: Build Oral Vocabulary; Develop Phonemic Awareness; ⓣ Recognize Syllable Types (*r*-controlled); Decode Multisyllabic Words

TEACH SYLLABLE TYPES

1 Build Oral Vocabulary Display Transparency 62. Play a game of "I Spy," giving a series of clues until students find the picture you're describing. For example, for Item 1, say:

• *I spy a **garter snake**. The **garter snake** is in a garden. A sunny rock is a nice place for a **garter snake**.*

When students find the garter snake, say: *Yes, **this is a garter snake*** (point). Repeat the game to build context for the other words.

2 Develop Phonemic Awareness Remove the transparency and conduct the oral activities in Step 1 of the Script for Transparency 62.

3 Use Syllable Types to Decode Words Display Transparency 62 again. Work through Step 2 of the script.

CLOSE AND ASSESS

Display *under, summer, timber, burrow,* and *forest*. Call on students to read each word and identify the two syllables.

Transparency 62: Syllable Types

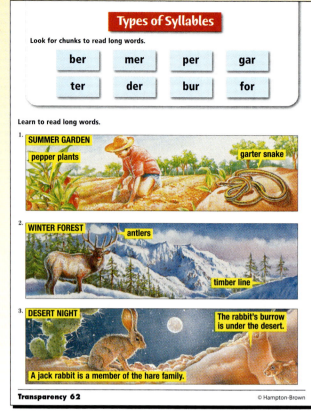

▼ Script for Transparency 62

Types of Syllables

1. Develop Phonemic Awareness

Identify/Match Syllables Say: *Some words have more than one syllable, or part, like the word* number. *Clap out the parts with me:* num-ber. (clap, clap) *Where do you hear the syllable* ber? (at the end) *Which of these words also ends with* ber *like* number: winter, member? (member) *Repeat for word pairs* timber, paper; wonder, lumber. *Then say: Here is another syllable that you often hear in words:* mer. *Listen to these words and tell me if you hear* mer *in the first or last syllable:* summer (last), mermaid (first), hammer (last), merchant (first).

2. Decode Multisyllabic Words

Teach Point to the word chunks at the top of **Transparency 62**. Say: *These chunks often appear as syllables in long words.* Read *ber* and the other chunks with students. Then say: *Look for chunks you know at the beginning and at the end of long words.*

Point to the illustration in Item 1. Say: *This picture shows a woman in a garden, doesn't it?* Point to *summer* and say: *Take a look at this word. To read it, look for a chunk you know.* Run your finger under *mer* in *summer,* and say: *I know this chunk,* mer. *Next, divide the word* (indicate a division between the two *m*'s). *Keep the chunk together.* Then point to *sum,* and say: *Here is the first syllable.* Point to *mer,* and say: *Here is the syllable* mer. *Blend the syllables to say the word.* Slide a finger under *sum* and *mer,* blending the parts /sssuuummm/-mer, sum-mer, and saying the word: *summer.*

Practice Point to the word *garden* in Item 1, and say: *Let's try that again. I see a chunk I know:* gar. *Let's divide the word* (indicate a division between *r* and *d*), *keeping the chunk together. Now let's blend the syllables to say the word:* gar-/deeennn/, gar-den, garden. Follow a similar procedure with students to read the other words with *r*-controlled syllables. In Item 2, point out the chunk *lers* in *antlers.* In Item 3, point to the word *desert,* frame the letters *des,* and tell students that it is the first syllable. Also point out that *hare* has the vowel sound /âr/.

T206a Unit 12 | Our Living Planet

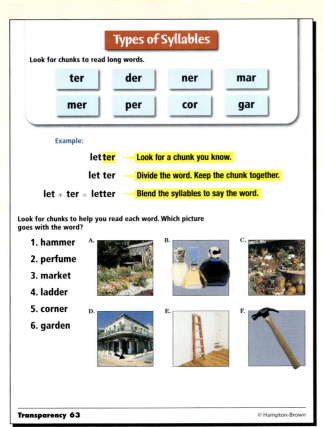

◀ Transparency 63: Syllable Types

▼ Script for Transparency 63

Types of Syllables

1. **Develop Phonemic Awareness**
   Identify Syllables Say: *Some words have more than one syllable, or part, like the word* corner. *Clap out the parts with me:* (cor-ner.) *(clap, clap) Where do you hear the syllable* ner? *(at the end) Which of these words also ends with* ner *like* corner: number, winner? *(winner) Repeat for word pairs* runner, winter; market, partner. Then say: *Here is another syllable that you hear in many words:* per. *Listen to these words and tell me if you hear* per *in the first or last syllable:* person (first), paper (last), supper (last), perfume (first).

2. **Decode Multisyllabic Words**
   Teach Point to the word chunks at the top of **Transparency 63**. Say: *These chunks often appear as syllables in long words.* Read the first chunk: ter. Then say: *Look for chunks you know at the beginning and at the end of long words.*

   Work through the Example to model the strategy. Point to *letter*, and say: *Take a look at this word. To read it, look for a chunk you know.* Run your finger under *ter* in *letter*, and say: *I know this chunk,* ter. *Next, divide the word. Keep the chunk together.* Point to the separated parts and say: *Here are the two syllables:* let-ter. Then continue: *Now blend the syllables to say the word.* Run a finger under *let* and *ter*, blending the parts /llleeet/-ter, let-ter, and saying the word: *letter*.

   Practice Have students do Items 1–6. Ask a volunteer to point out a familiar chunk and divide the word, keeping the chunk together. Write the syllables on the board and lead the group in blending them to read the word. In Item 2, after students have identified *per* as a familiar chunk, have them apply their knowledge of the CVCe pattern to recognize that the *u* in *fume* is long. In Item 5, point out that *corner* has two familiar chunks, *cor* and *ner*.

OBJECTIVES

Learning to Read: Build Oral Vocabulary; Develop Phonemic Awareness; 🅣 Recognize Syllable Types (*r*-controlled); Decode Multisyllabic Words

TEACH SYLLABLE TYPES

1. **Build Oral Vocabulary** Display Transparency 63. Play a game of "I Spy," giving a series of clues until students find the picture you're describing. For example, for Item E, say:

   • *I spy a **ladder**. You climb a **ladder**. This **ladder** is leaning against a wall.*

   When students find the ladder, say: *Yes, **this is a ladder*** (point and pantomime climbing a ladder). Repeat the game to build context for the other words.

2. **Develop Phonemic Awareness** Remove the transparency and conduct the oral activities in Step 1 of the Script for Transparency 63.

3. **Use Syllable Types to Decode Words** Display Transparency 63 again. Work through Step 2 of the script.

CLOSE AND ASSESS

Display *hammer*, *market*, *corner* and *garden*. Call on students to identify a chunk they know in each word and to tell you where to divide the word. Have volunteers blend the syllables to read the word.

▶ **Reading Practice Book** page 82 (syllable types: *r*-controlled)

Reading Practice Book page 82

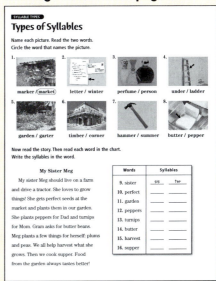

Language and Literacy **T206b**

UNIT 12 LESSON 10

LANGUAGE AND LITERACY: READING AND SPELLING

OBJECTIVES

Functions: Listen Actively; Repeat Spoken Language; Recite
Learning to Read: Develop Phonemic Awareness; ❶ Recognize Syllable Types; Decode Multisyllabic Words
Spelling: Syllable Types

LISTEN AND LEARN

Tape 6B / CD 2 Track 22

1 Recite a Poem Display Transparency 64 and play "Under the Moon" on the **Language Tape/CD**.

DEVELOP PHONEMIC AWARENESS

2 Blend Syllables to Form a Word
Say: *Listen to these two syllables:* whis, per. *Say the syllables with me:* whis, per. *Now blend the syllables to say the word:* whis-per, whisper. Repeat for *per, son* (person). Then say *whisper* and *person* and ask students where they hear *per* in each word. (last syllable in *whisper,* first in *person*) Continue asking students where they hear the *r*-controlled syllable in these pairs: *spider, under; supper, perfume; letter, butter.*

LOOK FOR SYLLABLES IN LONG WORDS

3 Recognize Syllables Read the directions aloud and say: *Look at the words in the first column. Which syllable is the same in these words?* (ter) Guide students in dividing each word into syllables and blending the syllables to read the word. Repeat for columns 2 and 3.

Afterwards, play the poem again. Have students identify words with two syllables that contain familiar chunks.

T206 Unit 12 | Our Living Planet

SYLLABLE TYPES

Reading and Spelling

LISTEN AND LEARN

Under the Moon

The silent spider
spins her web.
See the fine silver thread,
under the moon.

The silent turtle
swims in the sea.
Feel the swish of flippers,
under the moon.

The silent owl
hunts his supper.
Hear the whisper of wings,
under the moon.

Listen!

LOOK FOR SYLLABLES IN LONG WORDS

Read the words in each group. Which syllable is the same?

1.		2.		3.	
	butter		person		ladder
	sister		flipper		under
	letter		supper		spider

206 Unit 12 | Our Living Planet   ▶ Transparencies 62–64

REACHING ALL STUDENTS

Multi-Level Strategies

LITERACY SUPPORT

INTERRUPTED SCHOOLING To anchor understanding of how to read long words, use letter tiles to model reading *silver*. First point out the syllable *ver*. Then divide the word, keeping the chunk intact. Blend the sounds to read each syllable, then blend the two parts: /sssiiilll/-ver, sil-ver, *silver*.

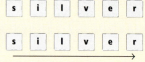

Repeat with *sister, spider, under, flipper, supper, person,* and *whisper*.

PRELITERATE Copy the words at the bottom of page 206 onto separate strips. Distribute the strips and guide students in cutting them into syllables. Have volunteers lead the group in reassembling each word to match the word on the page.

READING STRATEGY

Follow these steps to read a word.

1 In a long word, look for a syllable you know.

 garden   af**ter**

Reading Help

Look for these syllables in long words:

mar	cor	ber	mer
gar	nor	ter	der
par	tor	ner	per

2 Divide the word. Keep the syllable together.

gar den   af **ter**

3 Blend the two syllables together to read the word.

gar + **den** = **garden**   **af** + **ter** = **after**

READING AND SPELLING PRACTICE

Use what you learned to read the sentences.

1. Garter snakes are small members of the reptile family.
2. In summer, garters can be found in forests, farms, and open lands.
3. A few may make a home in wet corners of a garden.
4. In winter, garters may be hard to find because they stay under the ground.
5. Garters don't bite, so some people keep them as pets!

6.–10. Now write the sentences that your teacher reads. *For dictation sentences, see Step 6 at right.*

WORD WORK

11.–18. Copy the chart. Then read these words:

| hammer | winter | sister | ladder |
| pepper | under | perfume | summer |

Write each word in the chart. Put it under the word that has the same syllable.

merchant	person	letter	spider
11. hammer	13. pepper	15. winter	17. under
12. summer	14. perfume	16. sister	18. ladder

Example: 11.

Language and Literacy **207**

Decodable Book
PRACTICE WITH SYLLABLE TYPES

Decodable Book 12:
The Perfect Moose

Assign **Decodable Book 12** for independent reading. The **Decodable Book** can be used in a variety of ways to help students become more fluent, automatic readers:

Discussion Circles Have students work in small groups to read aloud and discuss the book using the questions on the back cover. Encourage students to read aloud the text that supports their answers. Groups can also work together to complete the Word Work Activity.

Readers Theater Students can read aloud the stories in a class performance. Help them prepare by rereading the stories in daily rehearsals. Work with students to add narration or dialog. Encourage them to use natural phrasing and expression.

Rereading at Home Have students work with family members to reread the book at home. They can take turns reading aloud alternate pages, then rereading the book switching the pages each person reads.

LEARN A READING STRATEGY

4 **Recognize Syllable Types** Work through the strategy with students, reading each step aloud and modeling the actions. Point out the Reading Help and read the explanation to students. Work through these words to help them apply the tip: *actor, garden, winter, thunder, slipper, summer, number, perfect, market, correct, northern.*

PRACTICE

5 **Read Sentences** Distribute the Partner Prompts from page T311 to guide peers in reading the sentences in Items 1–5. Remind them to use the recognize-syllable-types strategy to read words and to blend the words silently in their heads.

6 **Write Sentences** Dictate the following sentences for students to write. Read each sentence at normal speed once so students can listen, and then repeat it slowly word by word as they write:

  6. A few pepper plants grow in the garden.
  7. A rabbit burrow is in the corner.
  8. I found the hammer by the ladder.
  9. He cuts timber in the forest.
  10. The perfume is from the market.

If students need extra support, guide them in spelling the words with *r*-controlled syllables. For example: *What chunk do you know in* pepper? (per) *What syllable comes before* per? (pep) *Let's start with* pep. *Write the letter that stands for* /p/. Continue through the remaining sounds.

7 **Conduct "Word Work"** Display the completed chart from Word Work. Point to each word. Have students identify the shared *r*-controlled syllable and read the word aloud.

▶ **Reading Practice Book**
pages 155–158 (Decodable Book 12)

CLOSE AND ASSESS

Ask students to add words to the completed Word Work chart on the board.

Language and Literacy **T207**

UNIT 12 LESSON 11
LANGUAGE AND LITERACY: INDEPENDENT READING

OBJECTIVES
Functions: Read a Selection; Describe
Learning to Read:
- Recognize High Frequency Words;
- Recognize Syllable Types to Decode Multisyllabic Words

Reading Strategies:
Activate Prior Knowledge; Set a Purpose for Reading; Visualize

Critical Thinking and Comprehension:
Identify Details, Identify Cause and Effect

Writing: Description

READ ON YOUR OWN

1. **Introduce Vocabulary** In "Animals in the Wild," students apply the phonics skills and read high frequency words they have learned. Introduce the story words. Write each word, pronounce it, and spell it. Then give a definition and a context sentence:

   - **wild:** land not changed by people. *The bear lives in a zoo. It doesn't live in the wild.*
   - **coyote:** an animal that looks like a wolf. *The coyote has large pointy ears and a bushy tail.*
   - **desert:** a sandy region with little rain and no trees. *It is hard to find water in the desert.*
   - **howl:** to cry with a long, sad sound. *I hear dogs howl at night.*

2. **Activate Prior Knowledge/Set Purposes** View the photos and discuss what students already know about these or similar animals. Then model setting a purpose: *I'll read to find out where these animals live.* Encourage volunteers to state their purposes for reading.

3. **Read and Think: Visualize** Students should read the passage on their own. Suggest that as they read, they make a movie in their minds of each animal. Prompt the action: *Where does the animal live? What does this area look like? What does the animal look like?*

T208 Unit 12 | Our Living Planet

COMPREHENSION: IDENTIFY DETAILS, CAUSE AND EFFECT
Read on Your Own

DECODING CHECK
Give the Decoding Progress Check on page 1a of the Assessment Handbook.

Animals in the Wild

Bighorn Sheep

The bighorn sheep is a mountain animal. It is also found in the desert. It can live above the timberline, where trees don't grow. Bighorn sheep have large, curled horns and a short tail. They can go up steep trails. Because they have thick fur, they can live through winter storms.

White-Tailed Deer

The white-tailed deer is a forest animal with a short tail. It has brown fur in the summer. In the winter, when there is snow, it has gray-white fur. That is why it is so hard to see a white-tailed deer.

The male deer has antlers that drop off in the winter and grow again in the spring. These new antlers soon grow hard and sharp.

Coyote

The coyote is a desert animal. It is also found in mountains and on flat plains. It has long fur and a long tail. The coyote is a member of the dog family. It hunts after dark. At night, you may hear a few coyotes howl. From far away, their sound is like a sad song.

208 Unit 12 | Our Living Planet

REACHING ALL STUDENTS

Science Connection
ANIMALS AND THEIR HABITATS

Have students make a poster featuring a wild animal and its habitat. Students can use encyclopedias, nonfiction books, and Internet resources to gather details about the animal and where it lives. Encourage students to include a labeled drawing or picture of their animal, a map that shows where it lives, and labeled illustrations of its habitat. Guide students as necessary to include captions that describe the animal and its surroundings.

CHECK YOUR UNDERSTANDING

Write the correct answer to each item.

Example: **1.** The bighorn sheep has large, curled horns.

1. The bighorn sheep has _____.
   A. a long tail
   B. short, sharp antlers
   C. large, curled horns

2. The bighorn sheep can live through winter storms because it has _____.
   F. thick fur
   G. gray-white fur
   H. large, curled horns

3. The deer's antlers grow again in the _____.
   A. spring
   B. winter
   C. summer

4. Why is it hard to see the white-tailed deer in the winter?
   F. It stays in its burrow.
   G. Its fur turns gray-white.
   H. There are a lot of winter storms.

5. The coyote and the _____ are in the same family.
   A. deer
   B. dog
   C. bear

6. What does the coyote do at night?
   F. It howls.
   G. It sleeps.
   H. It turns gray-white.

EXPAND YOUR VOCABULARY

7. Work with a partner. Copy this chart. Put a ✓ in the correct box.

Animal	Has fur	Howls at night	Has a short tail
Bighorn Sheep	✓		✓
White-Tailed deer	✓		✓
Coyote	✓	✓	

Use the chart and the article on page 208 to tell your partner about the animals.

Example: **7.** All the animals have fur. The bighorn sheep and the white-tailed deer have short tails.

WRITE ABOUT ANIMALS ✎

8. Choose a wild animal. Write sentences to describe it.

Example: **8.** The coyote looks like a dog. It hunts at night.

Language and Literacy **209**

Reading Practice Book page 83

READING FLUENCY
Build Reading Fluency

Read the article. Stop when the timer goes off. Mark your score.
Then try it again two more times on different days.

A Robin's Nest

The American robin is the biggest member of the thrush family. It is not hard to spot a robin. It is gray with a black head. The throat is white with black streaks. The chest is an orange-red.

After winter, most birds make new nests. Many birds use twigs and leaves to make their nests. A robin uses twigs, leaves, spring grasses, and mud. They use the mud to make the nest strong. Then they line the nest with grass. The grass makes the nest soft and warm for the eggs. A robin lays four or five eggs each spring. The eggs are light blue without any spots.

Robins are quite at home living near people, so you may find their nests in parks or gardens. Look for them in spring!

	Day 1	Day 2	Day 3
Total Words Read in One Minute			
Minus Words Missed			
Words Read Correctly in One Minute			

Reading Fluency
TIMED READINGS

Read the title and introduction on **Reading Practice Book** page 83. Set the timer and have a student read the passage to you. Use the script on page T323 to mark words the student misses and to note the last word read in one minute. Have students graph their performance and set a goal for improving in subsequent timed readings. Plan for two additional timed readings, and encourage partners to practice reading the passage to each other between the timed readings.

CHECK YOUR UNDERSTANDING

4 **Comprehension: Identify Details, Cause and Effect** Read the directions aloud and work through the Example with students. Say: *I need to complete the sentence in Item 1: "The bighorn sheep has _____." I can choose an answer from the choices listed in A–C.* Read the choices, and then say: *The paragraph about the bighorn sheep says it has large, curled horns, so I know that C is the correct choice.* Then point out Items 4 and 6. Say: *These are questions. Just look at the choices and write the correct answer.*

EXPAND YOUR VOCABULARY

5 **Complete a Details Chart** Read the directions and model how to read a chart, using its horizontal and vertical coordinates. Say: *I need to put a checkmark in the box for each detail that describes an animal.* Point to the first row and say: *This is the row for bighorn sheep. I read that bighorn sheep have thick fur, so I will put a checkmark in the "Has fur" column.* Tell students that after they finish the chart, they can use it and the article to tell a partner about the animals.

WRITE

6 **Describe an Animal** Point out that the Example describes the coyote. Ask students to choose an animal to describe. Students who choose the same animal can work in pairs or small groups to write their descriptions together.

For students who need support in writing, provide sentence frames and help students choose nouns and adjectives to complete them:

> The __(animal)__ lives in the _____.
> It has _____.
> It also has _____.

▶ **Reading Practice Book** page 83

CLOSE AND ASSESS

Have students take turns giving a sentence with a clue about one of the animals. The others should tell which animal the sentence describes.

Language and Literacy **T209**

UNIT 12 LESSON 12

LANGUAGE ACROSS THE CURRICULUM: SCIENCE/MATH

OBJECTIVES

Function: Listen to a Selection

Concepts and Vocabulary:
Graphs; ⓣ Animals; ⓣ Habitats

Research Skills and Learning Strategies:
Build Background; Use Graphic Organizers (line graphs)

Critical Thinking and Comprehension:
ⓣ Identify Cause and Effect

LEARN ABOUT LINE GRAPHS

1 Explore Line Graphs Have students locate the parts of a line graph as you read the labels aloud. Explain: *This graph shows how the number of whooping cranes—a type of bird—changed over time.* Model how to find data for a specific year by putting a finger on a date, tracing a line up to the point, and moving left to find the number on the y-axis.

READ AND THINK

2 Build Background Read the article title and the focus question. Write the word *endangered,* underline *danger* within it, and define the word: *Endangered means "in danger of dying out completely." An endangered animal could become* extinct: *all the animals could die, without even one remaining."*

3 Listen to the Article As you read, restate ideas and clarify vocabulary to aid students' comprehension. Pause for students to locate the data for 1940 and 2000 on the line graph to track the whooping-crane population increase.

CHECK UNDERSTANDING

4 Answer the Review Questions Have students work with partners to complete the items. As they work, circulate to help them review the article and the line graph for the information they need.

CLOSE AND ASSESS

Copy the line graph onto the board. Ask students to label the parts.

SUCCESS IN SCIENCE AND MATHEMATICS

Learn About Line Graphs

Answers for the Review:
1. They were hunted. The wetlands where they lived were drained and turned into farms.
2. y-axis, x-axis, scale, labels, title, points
3. 25; 200; 1980

LINE GRAPH

A line graph shows how something changes over time.

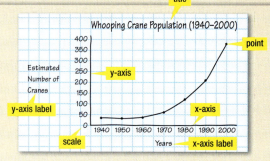

Listen to the article. Study the picture and the graph below. Then do the Review.

The Whooping Crane: An Endangered Bird

• Can the whooping crane be saved?

In the 1800s, there were hundreds of whooping cranes in North America. Then the cranes became endangered. Many were hunted. Many of the wetlands where they lived were drained and turned into farms. By the 1940s, only a few whooping cranes were left.

Scientists are working hard to save these cranes. Each spring, whooping cranes lay two eggs and raise only one chick. Some scientists take the extra egg and hatch the chick. Then they release the chick into the wild. This work has helped increase the number of whooping cranes. By 2000, there were about 400 whooping cranes in North America.

The whooping crane is beautiful. It is white with red and black on its head. It has long, thin legs and a long beak.

REVIEW

1. **Check Your Understanding** Why did whooping cranes become endangered?
2. **Vocabulary** Name the parts of a line graph.
3. **Use Line Graphs** About how many whooping cranes were counted in 1950? In 1990? In what year were there about 125 whooping cranes?

210 Unit 12 | Our Living Planet

REACHING ALL STUDENTS

Science and Mathematics Connection

THE CALIFORNIA CONDOR

The California condor is an endangered animal that has benefited from a captive-breeding program at the San Diego Wild Animal Park and the Los Angeles Zoo. Download photographs and information about this project from Internet Web sites such as:

www.sandiegozoo.org

www.lazoo.org/cfacts.htm

Then post this chart and have students use the data to construct a line graph showing the changing population of the California condor.

Saving the California Condor

Year	Approximate Number of California Condors
1960	55
1970	30
1980	25
1990	40
2000	150

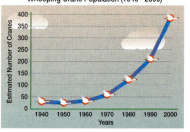

Writing Project — Fact-and-Opinion Poster

Make a poster to give facts and opinions about an animal. Then share your poster with the class.

RESEARCH AN ANIMAL

1. Choose an animal. Find out information about it. Ask your teacher or librarian for help. Write facts about the animal in a chart.

2. What do you think or believe about the animal? Add your opinions to the chart.

Facts About Whooping Cranes	My Opinions
1. They are white with red and black on their heads.	1. I think more people should try to save the whooping cranes.
2. They are endangered.	2. People must not hunt whooping cranes.
3. Scientists are helping them.	
4. There are about 400 today.	

MAKE AND SHARE YOUR POSTER

Draw or find a picture of the animal. Write a caption to describe your animal. Check pages 310–311 of your Handbook for adjectives you can use. Write your facts and opinions. Work with a partner to check your work.

Check Your Work
- Did you write facts and opinions about the animal?
- Did you use adjectives to describe the animal?
- Did you use opinion words like *think* or *should*?

Use heavy paper. Fold it into 3 sections. Put your picture and caption in the middle section. Write your sentences on the outside sections.

Present your poster to the class. Look at the other posters. Talk about what you learned.

The Whooping Crane

Facts:
1. Whooping cranes are endangered.
2. Scientists are working to save them.
3. There are about 400 whooping cranes today.

My Opinions:
1. I think more people should try to save whooping cranes.
2. People must not hunt whooping cranes.

The whooping crane is beautiful. It is white with red and black on its head. It has long, thin legs and a long beak.

Language Across the Curriculum 211

WRITING ASSESSMENT
Use the Writing Progress Checklist on page 51 of the Assessment Handbook to evaluate this writing project.

UNIT 12 LESSON 13
LANGUAGE ACROSS THE CURRICULUM: WRITING

OBJECTIVES

Functions: Give Opinions; Write
Learning Strategies and Critical Thinking: Plan; Generate and Organize Ideas; Self-Assess
Research Skills: Gather Information
Writing: Fact-and-Opinion Poster
Comprehension: Distinguish Between Facts and Opinions

CONDUCT THE WRITING PROJECT

1. **Explore Fact-and-Opinion Posters** Preview the steps of the writing project and go over the sample. Explain that the poster shows both *facts* (scientific information about the animal) and *opinions* (the writer's ideas and feelings).

2. **Research an Animal** Brainstorm a list of animals students may study. You may suggest some endangered species, such as: San Joaquin kit fox, West Indian manatee, jaguar, blue whale or humpback whale, yellow-shouldered blackbird, American crocodile, Houston toad, Puerto Rican boa. Encourage students to take notes as they look for facts about the animal.

   Then have students develop the two-column chart suggested in the text.

3. **Make and Share Your Poster** Use the sample poster as a model for placing facts, opinions, and students' illustrations. Remind students to use adjectives to describe their animals. Students may also wish to include line graphs and tables in their posters.

4. **Display the Posters** Invite other classes to learn about animals. Student "scientists" may stand by their work to give more information.

▶ **Language Practice Book** page 105

CLOSE AND ASSESS

Have students look at their posters. Say:
- *Point to one fact and one opinion.*
- *Show me an adjective that describes your animal.*
- *Read some opinion words you used.*

Language Across the Curriculum T211

Language Practice Book page 105

WRITING PROJECT: FACT-AND-OPINION POSTER
We Must Protect This Animal

Find facts about an animal. Write the facts and your opinions in a chart. Use your notes to make a poster for your class. Follow these steps.

1. Start in the middle section. Name the animal. Draw a picture of it.
2. Write a caption for your picture. Use **adjectives** to describe the animal.

Facts: / My Opinions:

The ___
is ___
It ___

3. Write **facts** about the animal in this section. Put your work on heavy paper. Share your poster with the class.
4. Write your opinions about the animal in this section. Use **opinion words** like *think* or *should*.

ASSESSMENT

For opportunities to measure progress, see the Assessment Handbook:

- **Units 10–12 Test** evaluates basic vocabulary and the patterns and structures of English, mastery of phonics and high frequency words, reading comprehension, and writing.

- **The Language Acquisition Assessment** for Units 10–12 offers performance assessments for measuring growth through the stages of language acquisition.

- **Self- and Peer-Assessment** Forms involve students in the assessment process.

Resources

For Success in Language and Literacy

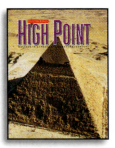

Student Book pages 212–227

For Language Skills Practice

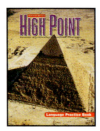

Language Practice Book
pages 106–110

For Reading Skills Practice

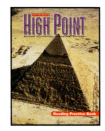

Reading Practice Book
pages 84–87

For Vocabulary, Language Development, and Reading Fluency

Language Tape 7, Side A
Language CD 3, Tracks 1–3

For Reading Together

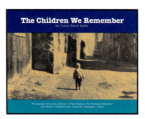

Theme Book
The Children We Remember
from The Basics Bookshelf

For Audio Walk-Throughs and Selection Readings

Selection Tape 7A
Selection CD 3, Tracks 1–2

For Phonics Instruction

Transparencies 65–67

Transparency Scripts 65–67

Letter Tiles

For Comprehensive Assessment

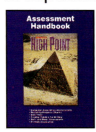

Language Acquisition Assessment,
Units 13–15 Test, Writing Assessment,
Self-Assessment

For Home-School Connections

High Point Newsletter 5
in seven languages

For Planning and Instruction

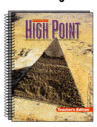

Teacher's Edition
pages T212a–T227

UNIT 13
PAST AND PRESENT

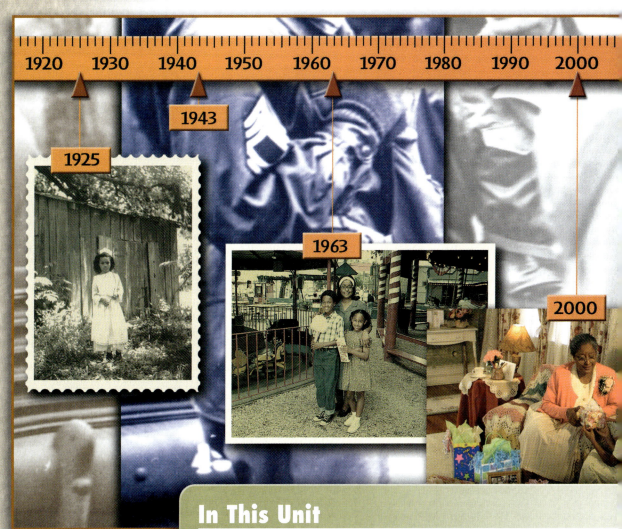

In This Unit

Vocabulary
- History and Historical Records
- U.S. Government

Language Functions
- Have a Discussion
- Make Comparisons

Patterns and Structures
- Nouns
- Present and Past Tense Verbs
- Object Pronouns

Reading
- Phonics: Words with y
- Comprehension: Make Comparisons (comparison chart)

Writing
- Comparisons
- Letter
- Comparison Poster

Content Area Connection
- Social Studies (U.S. government)

UNIT 13

Activity and Assessment Planner

UNIT 13: Past and Present

LESSONS

1

UNIT 13 LAUNCH
▶ *pages T212–T213*

LESSON 1: INTRODUCE UNIT 13 pages T212–T213

Vocabulary	**Learning Strategies**	**Critical Thinking, Representing and Writing**	
T History	Preview	Make Inferences	Relate Events in a Sequence
Viewing	Build Background	Relate to Personal	
Interpret a Visual Image	Use Visuals	Experience	Create a Time Line

2–7

LANGUAGE DEVELOPMENT
▶ *pages T214–T219*

LESSON 2 HISTORY page T214	**LESSON 3 HISTORICAL RECORDS** page T215	**LESSON 4 NOUNS** page T216	**LESSON 5 PRESENT AND PAST TENSE** page T217	**LESSON 6 OBJECT PRONOUNS** page T218	**LESSON 7 OBJECT PRONOUNS** page T219
Function Have a Discussion	**Function** Make Comparisons	**Function** Give Information	**Function** Give Information	**Function** Give Information	**Function** Give Information
Vocabulary **T** History	**Vocabulary** **T** History	**Vocabulary** **T** History	**Patterns and Structures** **T** Present and Past Tense Verbs	**Patterns and Structures** **T** Object Pronouns	**Patterns and Structures** **T** Object Pronouns
Writing Sentences	**Writing** Comparisons	**Patterns and Structures** Nouns	**Writing** **T** Sentences	**Writing** Paragraph	**Writing** Letter
		Writing Paragraph			

8–13

LANGUAGE AND LITERACY
▶ *pages T220a–T225*

LESSON 8 BASICS BOOKSHELF pages T220a–T220h	**LESSON 9 BASICS BOOKSHELF: COMPREHENSION** page T220	**LESSON 10 HIGH FREQUENCY WORDS** page T221	**LESSON 12 READING AND SPELLING** pages T222–T223	**LESSON 13 INDEPENDENT READING** pages T224–T225	
Functions Listen to a Book	**Function** Give Information	**Learning to Read** **T** Recognize High Frequency Words	**Learning to Read** Develop Phonemic Awareness	**Functions** Read a Selection	**Critical Thinking and Comprehension** Make Comparisons
Read Aloud a Book (choral reading)	**Learning Strategy** Use Graphic Organizers (comparison chart)	**LESSON 11 PHONICS** pages T222a–T222b	**T** Associate Sounds and Symbols: /y/ y, /ī/ y, /ē/ y	Make Comparisons	**Writing** Comparisons
Vocabulary World War II Words	**Critical Thinking and Comprehension** Make Comparisons	**Learning to Read** Build Oral Vocabulary	Identify Noun Endings (-s, -ies)	Have a Discussion	
Reading Strategies Build Background		Develop Phonemic Awareness	Blend Sounds to Decode Words	**Learning to Read** **T** Recognize High Frequency Words	
Activate Prior Knowledge		**T** Associate Sounds and Symbols: /y/, /ī/, /ē/ y	**Spelling** **T** Words with y	**T** Decode Words with y	
Preview		Identify Noun Endings		**Reading Strategies** Activate Prior Knowledge	
Learning to Read Predict Words		Blend Sounds to Decode Words		Set a Purpose for Reading	
Track Print		Decode Words with Endings		Paraphrase	
Critical Thinking and Comprehension Make Comparisons					
Form Opinions					

14–15

LANGUAGE ACROSS THE CURRICULUM
▶ *pages T226–T227*

LESSON 14 SOCIAL STUDIES: U.S. GOVERNMENT page T226		**LESSON 15 WRITING PROJECT: COMPARISON POSTER** page T227			
Function Listen to a Selection	**Learning Strategy** Build Background	**Functions** Make Comparisons	**Learning Strategies and Critical Thinking** Relate to Personal Experience	Use Graphic Organizers (chart)	Generate and Organize Ideas
Vocabulary U.S. Government	**Comprehension** Identify Details	Write	Plan	Make Comparisons	Self-Assess
					Writing Comparison Poster

T212c Unit 13 | Past and Present

T = Objective Tested on Unit Test

ASSESSMENT OPTIONS

The **Teacher's Edition** and the **Assessment Handbook** include these comprehensive assessment tools:

▶ **Ongoing, Informal Assessment**
Check for understanding and achieve closure for every lesson with the targeted questions and activities in the **Close and Assess** boxes in your Teacher's Edition.

▶ **Decoding Progress Check**
These word lists for each unit provide a quick way to check on mastery of the phonics or word structure skills taught in the unit.

▶ **Language Acquisition Assessments**
To verify students' ability to use the language functions and grammar structures taught in Units 13–15, conduct these performance assessments.

▶ **Unit Test in Standardized Test Format**
This multiple-choice test measures students' cumulative understanding of the skills and language developed in Units 13–15.

▶ **Self- and Peer-Assessment**
Students use the Self-Assessment Form to evaluate their own work and develop learning strategies appropriate to their needs. Students offer feedback to their classmates with the Peer-Assessment Form.

▶ **Writing Assessment/Portfolio Opportunities**
You can evaluate students' writing in the Writing Projects using the Writing Progress Checklist. Then collaborate with students to choose work for their portfolios.

UNITS 13–15 ASSESSMENT OPPORTUNITIES

	Assessment Handbook Pages
Decoding Progress Check	1a
Language Acquisition Assessments	34
Units 13–15 Test	35–40
Self-Assessment Form	41
Peer-Assessment Form	50
Writing Progress Checklist	51
Portfolio Evaluation Form	52

RELATED RESOURCES

Baseball Saved Us
by Ken Mochizuki
A young boy tells how baseball gave him and other prisoners in a Japanese internment camp a way to endure their injustice. (Scholastic)
Theme Book: Read Aloud

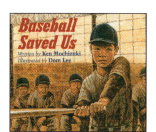

The Flag We Love
by Pam Muñoz Ryan
A history of our flag and what it means to the people who made it, fought for it, and pledge allegiance to it.
(Available from Hampton-Brown)
Language Development: Present and Past Tense Verbs

The Butterfly
by Patricia Polacco
During the Nazi occupation of France, Monique is surprised to find out that her mother has been hiding a Jewish family in their home. (Philomel)
Phonics Reinforcement: Words with *y*

My Fellow Americans
by Alice Provensen
An illustrated album of notable Americans, from colonial times to the more recent past. (Harcourt)
Vocabulary: U.S. History

The Bicycle Man
by Allen Say
Two U.S. soldiers entertain a group of school children in occupied Japan with their antics on an old bicycle.
(Houghton Mifflin)
Easy Reading

Unit Planner **T212d**

UNIT 13 **LESSON 1**

INTRODUCE UNIT 13: PAST AND PRESENT

OBJECTIVES

Concepts and Vocabulary: 🅣 History
Viewing: Interpret a Visual Image
Learning Strategies: Preview; Build Background; Use Visuals
Critical Thinking: Make Inferences; Relate to Personal Experience; Relate Events in a Sequence
Representing and Writing: Time Line

START WITH A COMMON EXPERIENCE

1. **Introduce "Past and Present"** Point to the time line and explain that the pictures show what one woman did at different times in her life. Then read aloud the unit title and say: *A time line is one way to tell about someone's past and present. It's a good way to tell the story of someone's life.*

2. **Study the Pictures** Lead a discussion about the time line: *Who are some important people in the woman's life?* (her family, her children) *What is an important event in her life?* (being in the army) *What can you learn about this woman from the time line?* (she is brave, she was born a long time ago)

3. **Create a Personal Time Line** Model creating a time line for important dates and events in a student's life.

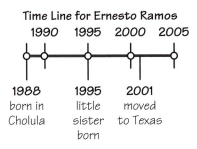

Help students create their own time lines with words, drawings, and photos. Encourage volunteers to display their finished time lines and to tell about their past and present.

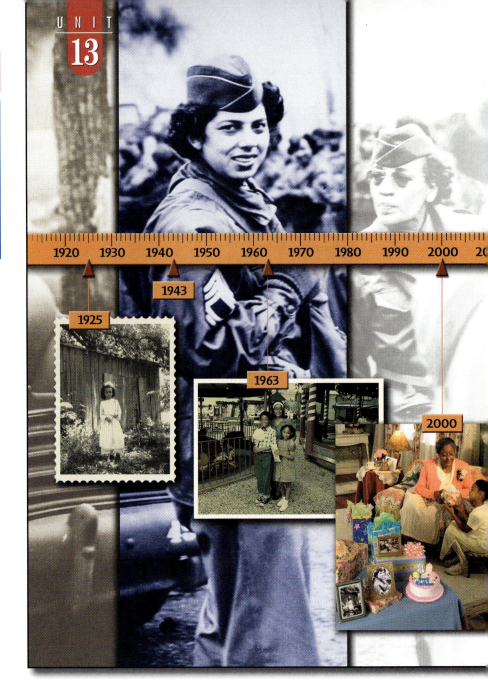

REACHING ALL STUDENTS

HOME CONNECTION

Family Time Lines Send home a copy of *High Point Newsletter 5* in the **Teacher's Resource Book**. In the home activity, each student creates a time line for a family member, using his or her own time line as a model. Then they discuss how life in the family member's past was the same as now, and how it was different. Have students share with the class the time line they created.

PAST AND PRESENT

Look at the time line of this woman's life.
What can you tell about her?
Make a time line of your life.
Draw pictures to show important events.
Label the years. Tell the class about
your past and present.

In This Unit

Vocabulary
- History and Historical Records
- U.S. Government

Language Functions
- Have a Discussion
- Make Comparisons

Patterns and Structures
- Nouns
- Present and Past Tense Verbs
- Object Pronouns

Reading
- Phonics: Words with y
- Comprehension:
  Make Comparisons (comparison chart)

Writing
- Comparisons
- Letter
- Comparison Poster

Content Area Connection
- Social Studies (U.S. government)

213

PREVIEW THE UNIT

4 Look for Activities and Information About the Past Leaf through the unit, previewing activities students will do, for example:

page 214—learning a song about how to study history

page 219—writing a letter from the point of view of a person in the past

page 220—listening to the Bookshelf book (Display a copy of the book.)

page 224—reading on the Internet about how kids can make history

page 227—making a poster that compares the present with the past

Also ask students to look for information on the past. Highlight the historical records on page 215 and the photos on pages 216–221, for example. Then sum up what the preview reveals: *History tells us about the past and helps us understand the present.*

5 Set Your Goals Start a class mind map about the different ways in which students can learn about history. Explain that in this unit students will learn about many historic events in the 1940s. Prompt students for pictures or words to put on the mind map, based on what they've seen so far, and have them act out and describe other ideas for you to put into words.

CLOSE AND ASSESS

Ask students to tell or show you something they are interested in learning in this unit.

UNIT 13 Mind Map

movies

TV

Internet

books — How Can We Learn About the Past? — newspapers and magazines

World War II

diaries and journals

photos

The Diary of Anne Frank

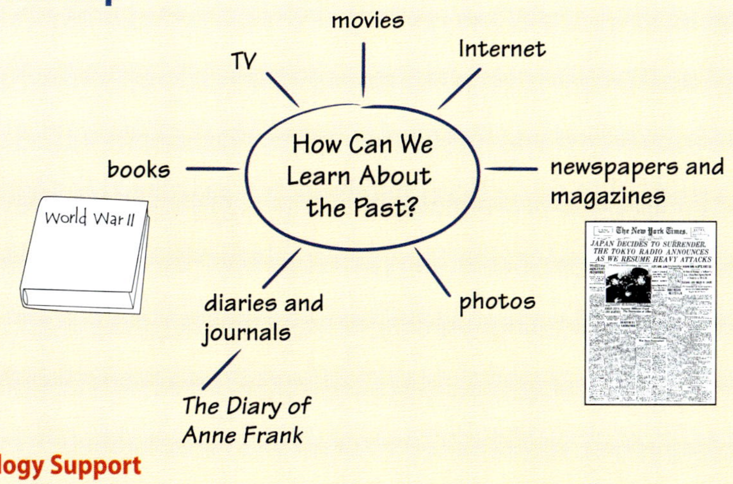

Technology Support
See **Inspiration** Visual Learning Software for support in creating the mind map.

Unit Launch **T213**

UNIT 13 **LESSON 2**

LANGUAGE DEVELOPMENT: HISTORY

> **OBJECTIVES**
>
> **Functions:** Listen Actively; Repeat Spoken Language; Recite; Have a Discussion
> **Concepts and Vocabulary:** 🟠 History
> **Writing:** Sentences

INTRODUCE

Tape 7A
CD 3 Track 1

1. **Listen and Sing** Play "History's No Mystery" on the **Language Tape/CD**. Students will listen and follow along with the words, then echo the lines, and finally chime in on the entire song.

2. **Learn About History** Show examples of each resource and talk about how it presents information: *How can photos help us find out about history?* (they show what life looked like in the past) *Where else can you learn about the past?* (newspapers, museums, family, Internet, etc.)

PRACTICE

3. **Conduct "Express Yourself"**
Explain: *When you have a discussion, you talk with other people. You share your thoughts, feelings, and ideas about a topic.* Help small groups complete the activity.

> **How to Engage in a Discussion**
>
> • Wait for your turn to make comments and ask questions.
> • Listen while others speak.
> • Pay attention to the topic.
> • Respect others' opinions.

APPLY

4. **Write Sentences** Encourage partners to check their sentences. Distribute Partner Checklist 13 on page T310.

> **CLOSE AND ASSESS**
>
> Ask students to respond orally to the title of the page: *What is history?*

T214 Unit 13 | Past and Present

VOCABULARY: HISTORY

What Is History?

Listen and sing.

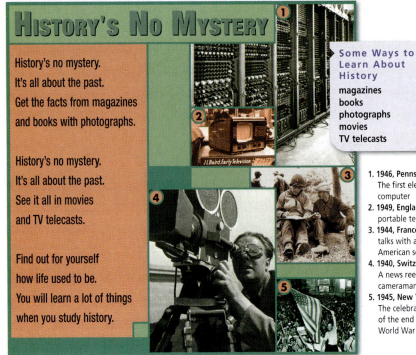

EXPRESS YOURSELF ▶ HAVE A DISCUSSION

Meet with a group. Use the questions below to start a discussion.

Example: 1. I like to read books to learn about the past.

1. How do you like to learn about the past?
2. Why is it important to learn about history?
3. Have you seen a movie about the past? Tell about it. What did you learn from the movie?

WRITE SENTENCES ✏️

4. Write a sentence. Tell one important thing you learned in the discussion.

Example: 4. You can get movies about the past at the library.

214 Unit 13 | Past and Present

REACHING ALL STUDENTS

Multi-Level Strategies
VOCABULARY: HISTORY

PRELITERATE Reproduce and distribute this word-search puzzle. Have students find and circle these words from the song: *history, past, facts, magazines, books, photographs, movies, TV telecasts.* Explain that words can run forward or down, and that letters in some words overlap. Model locating a word. (To make the task simpler, highlight the starting letter for each word.)

P	H	O	T	O	G	R	A	P	H	S	X
O	R	H	I	S	T	O	R	Y	E	S	R
Z	N	G	R	U	M	K	Z	M	P	I	J
M	T	S	I	X	S	M	B	O	O	K	S
P	O	F	B	R	B	N	T	V	O	D	A
A	U	A	M	A	G	A	Z	I	N	E	S
S	M	C	C	X	F	E	B	E	T	Z	T
T	V	T	E	L	E	C	A	S	T	S	R
S	T	S	D	R	G	X	F	O	L	P	P

VOCABULARY: HISTORICAL RECORDS

How We Learn About the Past

We call the early 1940s "The War Years" because the U.S. fought in World War II from 1941–1945. Here are some ways you can learn about the 1940s.

diary

newspaper
photograph

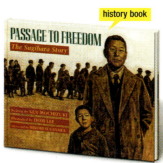
history book

Some people wrote about their lives in **diaries** or **journals**. You can read them to see what people's lives were like in the past.

You can read old **newspapers**. They reported the daily events as they happened. **Photographs** made the news come alive.

Look in books written later by **historians**. A historian reads many **sources** and tells the story of the past.

WHO'S TALKING? ▶ MAKE COMPARISONS

1.–3. Listen.
Three students are talking about their research. Which record of history is each student talking about? Point to the correct picture. Then work with a partner. Compare two of the records shown above.

Answers:
1. diary or journal
2. history book
3. newspaper

WRITE COMPARISONS

4.–6. Write 3 comparisons. In each, compare 2 other kinds of records, like movies or magazines. Use words from the box.

Example: **4.** A magazine and a movie both give us information. A magazine tells about the past with words and pictures, but a movie shows action with pictures that move.

Words That Compare
alike   unalike
same   different
and   but
both

Language Development 215

Language Practice Book page 106

Language Development
MAKE COMPARISONS

Use a feature-analysis chart to show how historical records compare. Model how to check boxes that apply to each record, deciding what is usually the case and what exceptions might exist.

Historical Records

	photos	drawings	private	public	tells feelings	tells facts
diary/journal		X	X		X	X
TV telecasts	X			X		X
newspaper	X	X		X		X

UNIT 13 **LESSON 3**

LANGUAGE DEVELOPMENT: HISTORICAL RECORDS

OBJECTIVES
Functions:
Listen Actively; Make Comparisons
Concepts and Vocabulary: 🅣 History
Writing: Comparisons

INTRODUCE

1 Learn Words for Historical Records Explain that two of the ways in which people record historical events are writing and photographs. Then read the title and introduction. Have students study the pictures as you read the captions and labels.

PRACTICE

Tape 7A
CD 3 Track 2

2 Conduct "Who's Talking?" Play "Who's Talking?" on the **Language Tape/CD**. Replay as necessary. Then model making comparisons before partners complete the activity:

> **How to Make Comparisons**
> - Choose two things to compare: for example, a journal and a newspaper.
> - Tell how they are alike, using signal words like *and, both,* and *same*: Journals **and** newspapers **both** tell about things that just happened.
> - Tell how they are different, using signal words like *but* and *different*: Journals don't have photos, **but** newspapers do.

APPLY

3 Write Comparisons Review the signal words in the chart and go over the Example. Students can look back at page 214 to choose records to compare.

▶ **Language Practice Book** page 106

CLOSE AND ASSESS

Have students read a sentence from their comparisons. Ask the class: *Which words did she/he use to compare? What's another way these records are alike or different?*

UNIT 13 **LESSON 4**

LANGUAGE DEVELOPMENT: NOUNS

OBJECTIVES

Function: Give Information
Concepts and Vocabulary: 🅣 History
Patterns and Structures: Nouns
Writing: Paragraph

INTRODUCE

1 Learn About Nouns Read the page title and introduction. Then go over the example sentences together. Pause after the first sentence to point out that *World War II* is a proper noun, so the words are capitalized.

Have students identify the nouns in the following sentence and tell whether each noun names a person, a place, or a thing:

> The <u>photographer</u> traveled to
>   person
> <u>Europe</u> in an <u>airplane</u>.
> place   thing

PRACTICE

2 Read Sentences Explain that Items 1–6 tell about two more people who recorded the history of the war. Work through the Example. Then have volunteers read the sentences and identify the types of nouns.

APPLY

3 Write a Paragraph As students complete the paragraph, have them consider whether they need to add a person, a place, or a thing to complete each sentence.

▶ Language Practice Book page 107

CLOSE AND ASSESS

Have volunteers read aloud the sentences in the paragraph. For each noun, call on students to tell whether it names a person, a place, or a thing.

T216 Unit 13 | Past and Present

NOUNS

The 1940s: Who? What? Where?

A <u>noun</u> names a person, place, or thing.

<u>World War II</u> began in 1939.
   thing

<u>Margaret Bourke-White</u> took <u>photographs</u> of the <u>war</u> in <u>Europe</u>.
   person   things   thing   place

<u>Magazines</u> printed her amazing <u>pictures</u>.
  things   things

<u>Americans</u> could see what their <u>soldiers</u> were doing.
  people   people

Margaret Bourke-White

READ SENTENCES

Say each sentence. Tell if each <u>underlined</u> noun is a person, a place, or a thing.

Example: 1. Bill Mauldin is the name of a person.

1. <u>Bill Mauldin</u> also recorded the <u>events</u> of <u>World War II</u>.
2. While he was in the <u>army</u> in <u>Italy</u>, he drew <u>cartoons</u> of American <u>soldiers</u>.
3. His <u>pictures</u> were often published in the <u>newspaper</u> *Stars and Stripes*.

Bill Mauldin

Answers:
1. person, things, thing
2. thing, place, things, persons
3. things, thing

4. Ollie Stewart was a <u>reporter</u>.
5. He was the first <u>journalist</u> from the <u>newspaper</u> *Afro-American* to go to the frontline in <u>North Africa</u>.
6. He was also in <u>France</u> when the <u>war</u> ended there.

Ollie Stewart

4. person
5. person, thing, place
6. place, thing

WRITE A PARAGRAPH ✏️

Write the paragraph.
Add the missing words.

| award | newspapers | soldiers |
| Japan | photographs | |

The photographer Joe Rosenthal took ___(7)___ during World War II. He was on an island in ___(8)___ when he took a famous picture of six American ___(9)___ lifting a flag. Many magazines and ___(10)___ printed the picture. Joe won an ___(11)___ for the picture.

Answers:
7. photographs
8. Japan
9. soldiers
10. newspapers
11. award

Joe Rosenthal took this photo in Iwo J Japan, in 1945.

216 Unit 13 | Past and Present

REACHING ALL STUDENTS

Language Practice Book page 107

NOUNS
Person, Place, or Thing?

A noun names a person, place, or thing.

<u>Rosie the Riveter</u> stood for all the <u>women</u> who worked in
   person   people
<u>factories</u> in <u>America</u> during <u>World War II</u>.
 thing   place   thing

Rosie the Riveter

Read each sentence. Tell if the underlined word is a person, place, or thing.

1. During <u>World War II</u>, many American men had to go to war.   thing
2. They went to <u>Europe</u>, Africa, and Asia. ___
3. They had to leave their jobs in the <u>factories</u>. ___
4. Soon <u>women</u> went to work in the factories. ___
5. They wanted to help <u>America</u> win the war. ___
6. Some workers helped build <u>airplanes</u>. ___
7. Other women helped build <u>ships</u>. ___
8. The American <u>soldiers</u> were thankful for their work. ___
9. The <u>workers</u> were proud to help their country. ___
10. They proved that women can do any <u>job</u>. ___

American women helped build ships and airplanes.

PRESENT AND PAST TENSE VERBS

The 1940s: What We Did

A **verb** changes to show when an action happens.

Use a present tense verb to tell what happens now.
Today we **listen** to songs on the radio.

Use a past tense verb to tell what happened in the past. To form the past tense, you usually add *-ed*.
In the 1940s, families **listened** to war news on the radio.

Study the verbs in the box. They have a special form to show the past tense.

Present	Past
are	were
build	built
eat	ate
is	was
leave	left
say	said
wear	wore

BUILD SENTENCES

Say each sentence. Add the past tense of the verb in dark type.

Example: 1. In the United States, people's lives changed a lot during World War II.

1. **change** — In the United States, people's lives ___ a lot during World War II. *changed*
2. **are** — There ___ not many things to buy. *were*
3. **print** — The government ___ special stamps. *printed*
4. **use** — Everyone ___ the stamps to get things like sugar and cheese. *used*
5. **plant** — Families ___ gardens to grow food. *planted*
6. **wear** — Women ___ simple dresses and shoes. *wore*
7. **collect** — Children ___ old rubber, paper, and aluminum. *collected*
8. **build** — Factories ___ bombs and airplanes from them. *built*
9. **eat** — People ___ food like powdered eggs and potatoes. *ate*
10. **is** — There ___ not much gasoline either. *was*
11. **say** — Everyone ___ that life was hard. *said*
12. **leave** — The hardest part was when someone ___ to go to war. *left*

People used ration stamps like these.

WRITE SENTENCES

13.–15. Choose 3 present tense verbs from the box at the top of the page. Write a sentence for each verb. Trade papers with a partner. Write the sentences again. Put the verb in the past tense.

Example: 13. Factories build airplanes.
Factories built airplanes.

Women worked in airplane factories for the first time during World War II.

Language Development 217

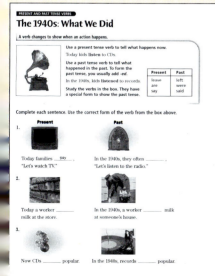

Language Practice Book page 108

Multimodal Practice
PRESENT AND PAST TENSE VERBS

Have students work through the following activity for these verbs: *build, eat, march, study, leave, bake, wear, report, sit, listen, see.*

Kinesthetic Act out a verb for everyone to guess, then write the present tense form on the board.

Visual Rewrite the verb with the correct past tense form.

Auditory Pronounce the verbs, noting the correct sound for *-ed,* if appropriate.

UNIT 13 **LESSON 5**

LANGUAGE DEVELOPMENT: PRESENT AND PAST TENSE

OBJECTIVES

Function: Give Information
Patterns and Structures:
• Present and Past Tense Verbs
Writing: • Sentences

INTRODUCE

1 Learn About Present and Past Tense Verbs Read the introduction, then go over the first rule and example. Point out the word *Today* as you explain how to use the present tense.

Then read the second rule and point to the photo as you explain: *This picture was taken many years ago. It shows a family from the past.* Read the example and point out the words *In the 1940s*.

Finally, go over the chart for irregular past tense verbs and give sample sentences: *Today girls often **wear** pants. In the 1940s, girls almost always **wore** dresses.*

PRACTICE

2 Build Sentences Work through the Example. Remind students to refer to the chart to see if the verb has a special form for the past. Then have partners complete and say the sentences. Check answers as a group.

APPLY

3 Write Sentences Go over the Example and have students refer to the chart at the top of the page.

▶ **Language Practice Book** page 108

CLOSE AND ASSESS

Call on students to read a present tense sentence they wrote. Ask a volunteer to say the sentence in the past tense.

Language Development **T217**

UNIT 13 LESSON 6

LANGUAGE DEVELOPMENT: OBJECT PRONOUNS

OBJECTIVES
Function: Give Information
Patterns and Structures:
- Object Pronouns
Writing: Paragraph

INTRODUCE

1 Learn About Object Pronouns Read the general rule for object pronouns and go over each particular case and example in the chart.

Remind students that we can use pronouns instead of saying the noun again. Model with two sentences:

> Hitler was a leader.
> The Nazi soldiers followed ~~Hitler~~ him.

Have students complete these sentences:

- **Mark** is here.
  Give the book to _____. (him)

- This **book** is great!
  You should read _____. (it)

- **Anne Frank** was smart.
  I admire _____. (her)

PRACTICE

2 Build Sentences Explain that Items 1–5 tell about Anne Frank. Think aloud as you model the Example: *An office is a thing. I will use the pronoun it.* Have partners complete Items 2–5.

APPLY

3 Write a Paragraph Remind students to identify the noun before choosing the correct pronoun. In the Example, point out that *it* refers to *Anne's diary* in the previous sentence. Have students complete the paragraph.

CLOSE AND ASSESS

Call out a common or proper noun, for example, *Anne Frank*. Students respond with the correct object pronoun: *her*. Invite volunteers to call out more nouns.

T218 Unit 13 | Past and Present

OBJECT PRONOUNS

World War II: A Tragic Time

A **pronoun** can refer to a **noun**.

Anne Frank was a teenager in 1940.

Use these pronouns after an action verb and after words like *to*, *in*, or *with*.

Pronoun	Use for:	Examples
him	a boy or a man	**Adolf Hitler** was Germany's leader in World War II. The Nazi Party was loyal to **him**.
her	a girl or a woman	**Anne Frank** was Jewish. The Nazis made **her** wear a yellow star.
it	a thing	Anne wrote about her life in a **diary**. You can read **it** today.
them	two or more people or things	The **Franks** had to hide during the war. A few friends helped **them**.

BUILD SENTENCES

Look at the **noun** in the first sentence. Say both sentences. Add the pronoun that refers to, or goes with, the noun.

Example: 1. Otto Frank, Anne's father, had an office. The family hid above it.

1. Otto Frank, Anne's father, had an **office**. The family hid above __it__.
2. A **boy** named Peter also hid there. Anne became good friends with __him__.
3. One horrible morning, the Nazis found the **family**. The soldiers took __them or it__ to prison camps.
4. Anne left her **diary** in the hiding place. A friend found __it__.
5. **Anne** died in the prison camps. After the war Mr. Frank published her diary. He wanted people to remember __her__.

WRITE A PARAGRAPH ✏️

Work with a partner. Write this paragraph. Add the word *him*, *her*, *it*, or *them* in each blank.

Example: 6. Many people have read it.

You can read Anne's diary in many languages. Many people have read __(6)__. Nelson Mandela, a leader in South Africa, said the story encouraged __(7)__. Several writers have been interested in Anne. They wrote books about __(8)__. Many people feel Anne's diary helped __(9)__ to understand what happened in World War II.

Answers:
6. it   8. her
7. him   9. them

218 Unit 13 | Past and Present

REACHING ALL STUDENTS

CULTURAL PERSPECTIVES

World Cultures: Celebrating Courage
As a class, research an observance held in spring or summer that commemorates courage in times of adversity. The list at right presents some possibilities.

April
  Jewish Heritage Week (final week)
May
  5 Cinco de Mayo (Mexican holiday)
  25 African Freedom Day
June
  10 Race Unity Day
  16 Soweto Day (South African Solidarity)
  18 International Peace Day
July
  4 U.S. Independence Day
August
  10 Hiroshima Day/Peace Festival
  26 Women's Equality Day

OBJECT PRONOUNS

Things Changed for Us

When you use a **pronoun,** be sure to tell about the right person.

Use these pronouns after an action verb and after words like *to, in,* or *with.*

Pronoun	Use:	Example
me	for yourself	My sister sent this photo to **me** in 1942.
you	to talk to another person or persons	"I will write to **you** every day," she promised.
us	for yourself and another person	My sister sent letters to **us** from all over the world.
him, her, it, or them	to tell about other people or things	We still read **them** often.

BUILD SENTENCES

Read each sentence. Choose the correct pronoun. Say the complete sentence.

Example: 1. During the war, things changed for us.

1. During the war, things changed for _____(us)/ it_____.
2. Dad planted a garden. I helped _____(him)/ us_____ take care of it.
3. Mom asked _____(me)/ you_____ to put up some special curtains.
4. We called _____(it)/ them_____ "blackout curtains."
5. At night, airplanes couldn't see _____(us)/ him_____ or our lights through the curtains.
6. I wanted new shoes. Dad said, "We can't buy shoes for _____them /(you)_____ now."
7. There wasn't much rubber. Factories used _____(it)/ us_____ for the war.
8. We missed my sister. We talked about _____(her)/ him_____ a lot.
9. She wrote some letters just to _____(me)/ her_____.
10. I still have all of _____you /(them)_____.

WRITE A LETTER ✏️

11. Imagine that you are the boy above. Write a letter to your sister. Tell what you are doing. Use *me, you, him, her, it, us,* and *them.*

Example: 11.

May 1944

Dear Sister,
Dad planted a garden. I help him water it and pull the weeds. We grew tomatoes. I wish you could be with us, but we are so proud of you!

Love,
Jim

Language Development 219

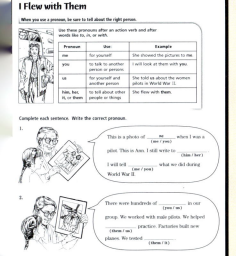

UNIT 13 **LESSON 8**

LANGUAGE AND LITERACY: THE BASICS BOOKSHELF

> **OBJECTIVES**
>
> **Concepts and Vocabulary:**
> Words About World War II
>
> **Reading Strategies:** Build Background; Activate Prior Knowledge; Preview

BUILD LANGUAGE AND VOCABULARY

1 **Teach "Words to Know"** Introduce page 2: *This page tells about World War II. Many countries fought this war from 1939 until 1945.*

Then use simple sentences to explain key words and concepts for each panel of the time line. Point to the first panel and say: **Adolf Hitler** *was a* **dictator.** *He led Germany in the war. He hated the* **Jews** *because they believed in a religion called Judaism.*

Indicate the second panel as you say: *The* **Nazis** *followed Hitler. Nazi armies took over many countries. They made millions of Jews leave their homes. They sent the Jews to* **prison camps.** *Many Jews died in the camps.*

For panel three, say: *In 1945, Germany lost the war. The Jewish prisoners were set free.*

PREPARE TO READ

2 **Think About What You Know** Create a class T-chart to record facts and a few opinions about World War II.

3 **Preview** Play the Audio Walk-Through for *The Children We Remember* on the **Selection Tape/CD** to give students the overall idea of the story.

Tape 7A
CD 3
Track 1

> **CLOSE AND ASSESS**
>
> Show students the cover of *The Children We Remember* and then have partners tell each other one fact about the children in the book.

The Children We Remember
by Chana Byers Abells

Summary This historical account sensitively explains Hitler's campaign against the Jews during World War II. Easy to read text reinforces words about the escalating world conflict by depicting its effects on the lives of Jewish children in Europe. Photos show the children's lives before, during, and after the Nazi regime.

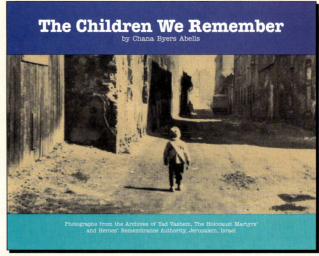

Cover

T220a Unit 13 | Past and Present

The Basics Bookshelf
The Children We Remember

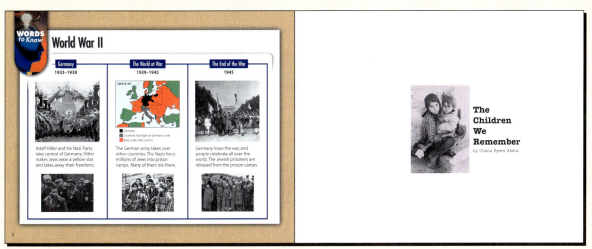

Pages 2–3

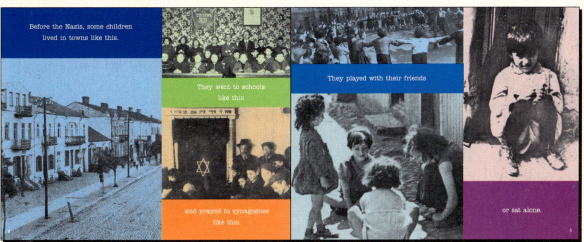

Pages 4–5

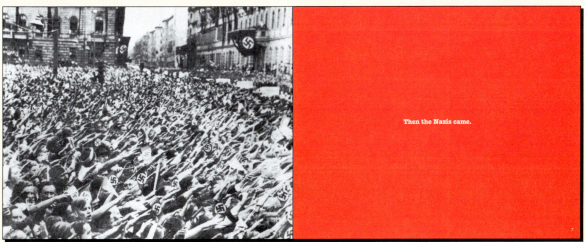

Pages 6–7

Language and Literacy T220b

UNIT 13 **LESSON 8,** CONTINUED

LANGUAGE AND LITERACY: THE BASICS BOOKSHELF

OBJECTIVES
Function: Listen to a Book

READ AND THINK TOGETHER

1 Read Aloud On your first reading of the book, use the "Strategies for Comprehensible Input" that appear on this page.

Strategies for Comprehensible Input

PAGE	STORY LANGUAGE	STRATEGY OPTIONS
4–5	Nazis	**Explain:** The Nazis were a group in Germany who tried to get rid of people they didn't like.
	synagogues	**Point to the picture and restate:** buildings where Jewish people pray
	alone	**Point to the picture and explain:** No one is with her. She is by herself.
6–7	Then the Nazis came.	**Restate:** Then the Nazis took over; Then the Nazis got the power.
8–9	sew patches	**Point to the pictures and demonstrate:** Pretend to sew.
	closed Jewish stores and schools	**Restate:** did not let the Jews have businesses or go to schools
	burned synagogues	**Point to the picture and restate:** set Jewish religious buildings on fire
10–11	took away homes	**Explain:** The Nazis made people leave their homes.
	were forced to	**Restate:** had to
12–13	cold	**Gesture:** Pantomime shivering.
	wrapped themselves in rags	**Gesture:** Wrap an imaginary scarf around your neck.
	hungry	**Explain:** You feel hungry when you do not have food to eat.
	shared the little they had	**Explain:** They did not have much food, but they gave some of it to others.
14–15	the old, the sick, and and each other	**Point to the pictures.**
16–17	hated	**Restate:** did not like
	took them away	**Demonstrate:** Line up three small items and then take one of them.
	far	**Gesture:** Stretch and extend arm outward.
18–19	put children to death	**Restate:** killed the children
20–21	survived	**Restate:** stayed alive; lived
	escaped	**Restate:** safely got away
	rescued	**Restate:** helped
22–23	pretended to be non-Jews	**Explain:** They hid by acting as if they were not Jewish.
24	just like the children we remember	**Summarize:** Turn back to pages 4-5, read the text, point to the pictures, and say: *Sometimes when we see children now, it helps us think about the children who died.*

T220c Unit 13 | Past and Present

The Basics Bookshelf
The Children We Remember,
CONTINUED

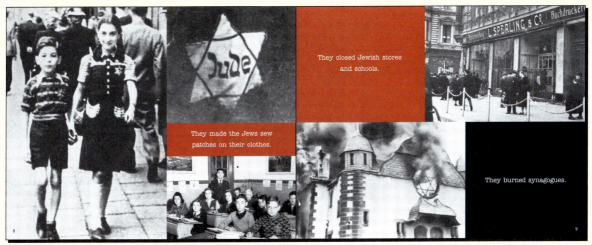
Pages 8–9

Pages 10–11

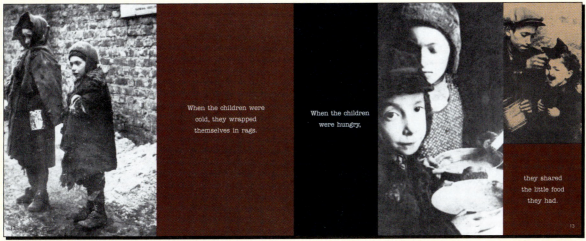
Pages 12–13

Language and Literacy T220d

UNIT 13 **LESSON 8,** CONTINUED

LANGUAGE AND LITERACY: THE BASICS BOOKSHELF

OBJECTIVES

Function: Listen to a Book

Critical Thinking and Comprehension:
Make Comparisons; Form Opinions

Listening and Speaking:
Participate in a Discussion

READ AND THINK TOGETHER, CONTINUED

2 Read and Map: Make Comparisons
Draw a comparison chart like the one here but with only the headings. Say: *A comparison chart shows how things are the same or different.*

Read pages 4–11 aloud. Then think aloud as you model filling in the first row: *The first column tells about life before the Nazis. Page 4 says the Jewish children lived in towns. I'll write that in column one. Next I'll look for what happened to the homes after the Nazis came. On page 10, I see that the Nazis took away homes. On page 11, I see people living in the streets. I'll put this information in the "After" column.*

Repeat the process to complete the last row of the comparison chart.

3 Discuss World War II Explain that a discussion is a way to share ideas. Participants support their opinions with facts. Post these guidelines:

• Let each person talk and listen.
• Respect everyone's ideas.
• Talk about one topic at a time.

Have three volunteers model a discussion about World War II.

• **Student 1:** In my opinion, World War II was a sad time.
• **Student 2:** I agree because many people died.
• **Student 3:** I think it was good that some Jews survived.

Provide sentence frames:

In my opinion _____.
I think _____.
I agree because _____.
I do not agree because _____.

Comparison Chart for *The Children We Remember*

	Before the Nazis	After the Nazis
pages 4–11	Some Jewish children lived in towns.	The Nazis took away their homes. They lived on the streets.
pages 4–11	Children went to school.	The Nazis closed the schools.
pages 4–11	The children prayed in synagogues.	The Nazis burned synagogues.
pages 5–17	The children played with friends or sat alone.	The Nazis sent the children away.

Technology Support
See **Inspiration** Visual Learning software for support in creating the comparison chart.

T220e Unit 13 | Past and Present

THE BASICS BOOKSHELF
The Children We Remember,
CONTINUED

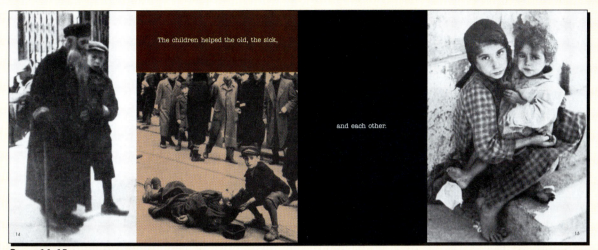

Pages 14–15

Pages 16–17

Pages 18–19

Language and Literacy **T220f**

UNIT 13 **LESSON 8,** CONTINUED

LANGUAGE AND LITERACY: THE BASICS BOOKSHELF

OBJECTIVES

Functions: Listen to a Book; Read Aloud a Book (choral reading)

Learning to Read: Predict Words; Track Print

READ AND THINK TOGETHER, *CONTINUED*

4 Conduct Interactive Readings
Choose from these options:

- **Predict words** Have students follow along with the recording of *The Children We Remember* on the **Selection Tape/CD.** Pause the tape on the following pages for students to supply these words:

Tape 7A
CD 3 Track 2

page 5	friends
page 8	clothes
page 9	schools
page 10	homes
page 11	streets
page 12	rags
page 17	far from home
page 20	survived

- **Choral reading** Divide the class into three groups to read the book aloud. Have Group 1 read aloud pages 4–5 and 20–24. For pages 6–19, have Group 2 read aloud the even numbered pages while Group 3 reads the odd numbered pages. Invite one volunteer from each group to lead and "conduct" the reading of the correct sections.

CLOSE AND ASSESS

Have partners work together to retell the events in the book. One partner tells what happened before the Nazis came, and the other tells what happened afterward.

Multi-Level Strategies
LITERACY SUPPORT

PRELITERATE **Concepts of Print: Track Print** Explain that text can appear at different positions on a page, and can be broken up into separate chunks on the same page. Read aloud the first sentence on page 4 as you sweep the words with a finger. Show students how the second sentence begins under one photo and ends under another. Then explain that when text is broken into chunks, it should be read from the top left of the page to the bottom right of the page. Have students follow along as you track the sentences from pages 5–13.

On pages 14–15, point out that a sentence can start on one page and finish on another. Then have students work with a partner to track the remaining sentences on pages 16–24 as you read.

LITERATE IN L1 **Read with a Partner/ Write Summary Sentences** After students have participated in the interactive readings, encourage them to read the story with a partner. Distribute the Partner Prompts on page T311 to help partners work together to identify unfamiliar words and unlock their meanings, then read the text to each other. After the partner reading, have students write summary sentences about events in the book: *The Nazis hated Jews. They put Jews in prison camps.*

INTERRUPTED SCHOOLING **Make Comparisons** To anchor understanding of the skill, work with students to find key words that compare life for the Jews before and after the Nazis. Point out the word "before" on page 4. Say: *The Nazis were not there yet.* Turn to page 7 and say: *The word* then *shows that things changed. The next pages tell what happened after the Nazis came.* Go back to page 4 and point out the first picture and sentence. Say: *Now I want to find out how the children lived after the Nazis came. I'll look for photos of homes or the words* homes *and* lived. *I see these on pages 10–11.* Continue the process, using the key words *school* and *synagogues* on pages 4 and 9. For pages 5 and 17, say: *When the children played, they were with their families. What happened after the Nazis came?*

T220g Unit 13 | Past and Present

THE BASICS BOOKSHELF
The Children We Remember,
CONTINUED

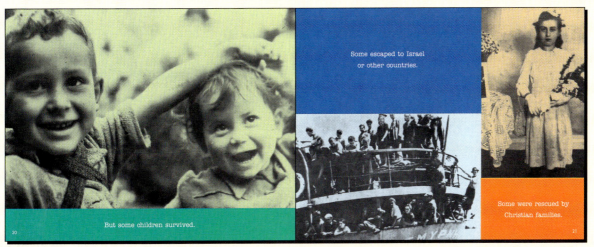
Pages 20–21

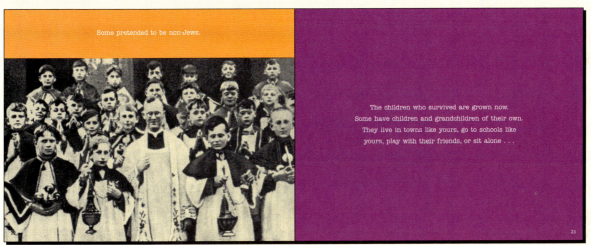
Pages 22–23

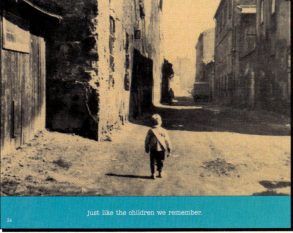
Page 24

Language and Literacy T220h

UNIT 13 LESSON 9

LANGUAGE AND LITERACY: THE BASICS BOOKSHELF

OBJECTIVES

Function: Give Information

Learning Strategy: Use Graphic Organizers (comparison chart)

Critical Thinking and Comprehension: Make Comparisons

CHECK COMPREHENSION

1 Make a Comparison Chart Have students review *The Children We Remember* to compare the children's lives before and after the Nazis. Remind them that a comparison chart shows how things are the same or different.

As you read aloud the directions for each step, pause for students to add information to the sections of their charts. Remind them that they should compare the same things at two different times.

2 Share Information from the Book Have students work in an Inside-Outside Circle (see Cooperative Learning Structures, page T337d) to make comparisons based on the book. Students in the outer circle tell one thing about the children's lives before the Nazis came. Students in the inner circle compare this with life after the Nazis. Then students rotate to create new partnerships.

CLOSE AND ASSESS

Ask students to complete this sentence: *A comparison chart shows _____.*

T220 Unit 13 | Past and Present

COMPREHENSION: MAKE COMPARISONS

Read and Think Together

Make a comparison chart to tell about *The Children We Remember.* Follow these steps.

1 Think about the story. What was life like for Jewish children before the Nazis took control? What was life like for them after the Nazis took control?

2 Show the changes in a chart. In the first column, write details about what things were like before the Nazis came. Use pages 4–5 from the book.

Wording may vary.

Before the Nazis	After the Nazis
Some Jewish children lived in towns.	The Nazis took away their homes
Children went to school.	The Nazis closed the schools.
The children prayed in synagogues.	The Nazis burned the synagogues.
The children played with friends or sat alone.	The Nazis sent the children away.

3 Read pages 7–18 again. Tell how life changed after the Nazis came. Write the information in the second column.

Before the Nazis	After the Nazis
Some Jewish children lived in towns.	The Nazis took away their homes.

4 Work with a partner. Compare the children's lives before and after the Nazis. Use your completed chart.

220   Unit 13 | Past and Present

---

from
The Basics Bookshelf

The Children We Remember

THEME BOOK

This historical account tells what happened to many Jewish children during World War II.

REACHING ALL STUDENTS

Social Studies Connection

STUDY WORLD WAR II

Use Research Materials Use the map on page 2 of *The Children We Remember* to introduce European countries involved in World War II. Explain: *Countries that joined Hitler were called* Axis Powers. *Countries that fought against him were called* Allied Powers. Assign six groups to study the war's principal combatants. Help them use atlases and encyclopedias to find information about the country's name, leader, and position in the war. Have the groups present their information.

Country	Leader	Position
Germany	Hitler	Axis
Great Britain	Churchill	Allied
Italy	Mussolini	Axis
Japan	Hideki	Axis
Soviet Union	Stalin	Allied
United States	Roosevelt	Allied

IGH FREQUENCY WORDS

Words to Know

EVIEW WORDS YOU KNOW

ead the words aloud. **Which word goes in the sentence?**

ome	come
elebrate	country
hildren	American

1. Where did all these people _come_ from?
2. They _____ the end of the war.   celebrate
3. They wave the _____ flag.   American

1945, New York City People were happy when Germany surrendered.

ARN TO READ

arn new words.

news	People here shout the great **news**: The war is over!
words	I cannot find the **words** to say how happy I am.
much	There is so **much** excitement everywhere.
along	I am an army nurse. I work **along** with 10 other nurses.
question	We all have the same **question**: When can we go home?
before	I hope to be home **before** the end of May.
miss	I will **miss** the nurses in my group.
example	Our group is a good **example** of a successful team.
ever	These nurses are the best friends I **ever** had.
back	Still, it will be so good to get **back** to my family.

How to Learn a New Word

- Look at the word.
- Listen to the word.
- Listen to the word in a sentence. What does it mean?
- Say the word.
- Spell the word.
- Say the word again.

ORD WORK

13. Work with a partner. Write each new word
 a card. Mix your cards together for the game.
rn them so the words are down. Then:

Turn over 2 cards.
Spell the words. Are they the same?
If so, use the words in a sentence and
keep the cards. If not, turn them over again.
The player with more cards at the end wins.

Example:

m-u-c-h
m-u-c-h
I am learning so much
about World War II.

much

much

Language and Literacy   **221**

Reading Practice Book page 84

HIGH FREQUENCY WORDS
Words to Know

READ AND WRITE

Read each word. Then write it.

1. words _____	2. back _____	3. example _____
4. ever _____	5. miss _____	6. along _____
7. much _____	8. news _____	9. before _____
10. question _____		

WORD WORK

Read the clue. Write the word in the chart.
Then write the word again in the sentence.

What to Look For	Word	Sentence
11. ends with ss	m i s s	I _miss_ my friend.
12. has a v	_ _ _ _	He's the best friend I _____ had.
13. means "a lot"	_ _ _ _	I like him so _____.
14. has an x	_ _ _ _ _ _ _	Ted is an _____ of a true friend.
15. tells when	_ _ _ _ _ _	He left _____ summer.
16. ends with ng	_ _ _ _ _	I went _____ to say good-bye.
17. has ew	_ _ _ _	Now I send Ted my _____.
18. begins with w	_ _ _ _ _	I write lots of _____.
19. ends with tion	_ _ _ _ _ _ _ _	I ask him one _____.
20. ends with ck	_ _ _ _	When will you come _____?

Reading Fluency
RECOGNIZE HIGH FREQUENCY WORDS

To build automaticity with the new high frequency words:

- Have students work independently to sort their cards into groups: words with 4 letters, words with 5 letters, and words with 6 or more letters. After sorting on their own, students can check their groupings with a partner.

- Challenge students to spell the words without looking. Have partners take turns reading a word without showing it, and checking the other's oral or written spelling.

UNIT 13 **LESSON 10**

LANGUAGE AND LITERACY: HIGH FREQUENCY WORDS

OBJECTIVES

Learning to Read:
T Recognize High Frequency Words

REVIEW WORDS

1 **Review Known High Frequency Words** Have the group read aloud the words in the green box. Listen for words students cannot read automatically and use the steps in the yellow box to reteach those words. Then have students look at the photo. Read each cloze sentence. Reread each sentence and pause for students to silently read the two words to the left of the sentence. Tell students to choose the word that goes in the sentence and tells about the picture.

INTRODUCE NEW WORDS

2 **Learn High Frequency Words** Use the High Frequency Word Script on page T324 to lead students through the steps in the yellow box. Point out the new meaning of *along*: "together." Explain that in the last sentence *back* means "to a place from the past." Remind students that they learned *back* as "a part of the body."

PRACTICE

3 **Conduct "Word Work"** Guide pairs in making two sets of cards and setting up the game. Have partners take turns until they match all the pairs. Discuss how students figured out the matches.

APPLY

4 **Read Words in Context** Students will read high frequency words in context in the sentences on page 223 and the passage on page 224.

▶ **Reading Practice Book** page 84

CLOSE AND ASSESS

Call out the high frequency words one at a time. Have students point to them and spell the words as a group.

Language and Literacy **T221**

UNIT 13 LESSON 11
LANGUAGE AND LITERACY: PHONICS

OBJECTIVES
Learning to Read: Build Oral Vocabulary; Develop Phonemic Awareness; ⓣ Associate Sounds and Symbols /y/ y, /ī/ y, /ē/ y; Blend Sounds to Decode Words

TEACH WORDS WITH y

1 Build Oral Vocabulary Display Transparency 65. Talk through each picture to develop meaning for the words. For example, for Item 1, say:

- *This boy reads a book about* **history** (point). **History** *means "the important events of the past." When you* **study** *history, you read to learn about things that happened in the past.*

2 Develop Phonemic Awareness Remove the transparency and conduct the oral activities in Step 1 of the Script for Transparency 65.

3 Read Words with y Display Transparency 65 again. Work through Steps 2 and 3 of the script.

CLOSE AND ASSESS
Display the words *year, try, study, fly,* and *lucky*. Call on students to read each word and identify the sound made by the letter *y*.

▶ **Reading Practice Book** page 85 (words with *y*)

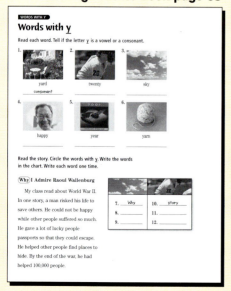

Reading Practice Book page 85

T222a Unit 13 | Past and Present

Transparency 65: ▶ Words with *y*

▼ Script for Transparency 65

Words with y

1. Develop Phonemic Awareness
Isolate/Match Final Sounds for *y* Say: *Listen to the sound at the end of these words: my, fly, try. What is the sound?* (/ī/) *Say the words with me. Now raise your hand each time you hear the sound /ī/: by, we, shy, try, no, why, say. Now listen to the sound at the end of these words: happy, study, funny. What is the sound?* (/ē/) *Say the words with me. Now raise your hand each time you hear the sound /ē/: lucky, cry, candy, fry, sticky, sky, easy.*

2. Associate Sounds and Symbols
Point to *year* on **Transparency 65**. Say: *A calendar shows each month of the year. Say* year *with me.* Point to the *y* and say: *The* y *makes the sound you hear at the beginning of* year. *The sound is /y/. Say /y/ with me: /y/. When* y *comes at the beginning of a word, it is a consonant and makes the sound /y/.* Repeat for *sky* and *happy*. Explain: *When* y *comes at the end of a word, it is a vowel. If it is the only vowel,* y *makes the sound /ī/. Say /ī/ with me: /ī/. If there is another vowel in the word and* y *follows a consonant, it makes the sound /ē/. Say /ē/ with me: /ē/.*

3. Blend Sounds to Read Words
Teach Point to the *y* in *year* and say: *Say the sound for* y *with me: /y/.* Repeat, pointing to the letters *ear:* /îr/. As you slide a finger below the letters, say: *Help me blend the two sounds /yîr/, and say the word:* year. Repeat for *sky*, asking what sound *y* makes (/ī/) and blending the three sounds. For *happy*, help students divide the word into syllables. Ask what vowel sound *y* makes (/ē/) and blend the syllables with students to read the word.

Practice To read the sentence in Item 1, say: *This word is* study (point) *and this word is* history (point). *Follow my finger to blend the other words in the sentence.* Read aloud the other sentences, pausing for students to decode the words with *y*. As they read each word, ask them if it makes sense in the sentence. In Item 5, read *Charles Lindbergh* for students.

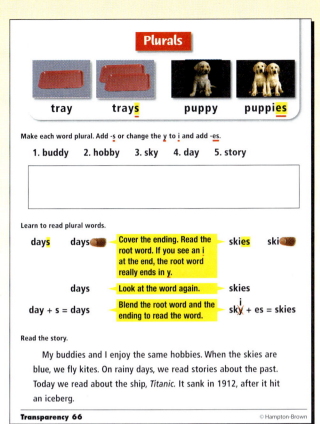

◀ Transparency 66: Plurals with *y*

▼ Script for Transparency 66

Plurals

1. Develop Phonemic Awareness
Contrast/Identify Final Sounds Say: *Listen to these two words:* tray, trays. *Listen again:* I put food on a tray. I see five trays on the table. *Are the words* tray *and* trays *the same?* (no) *The second word,* trays, *has an extra sound at the end. What is it?* (/z/) Repeat for *puppy* and *puppies*: *Mira has a new puppy. Dragan's dog had four puppies.* (The extra sound is /z/.) Then repeat for *story* and *stories*: *Read me another story. I already read three stories!* (The extra sound is /z/.)

2. Learn to Spell Plurals
Point to *tray* on **Transparency 66**. Say: *Here is one tray*. Then point to *trays* and say: *Here are two trays*. Explain: *Use* trays *to name more than one tray. You can hear a difference between* tray *and* trays, *and you can see a difference, too*. Cover the *s* in *trays*, and say: *Here is the root word* tray. *The word ends in the vowel* a *plus* y. *You can add an* s (uncover the *s*) *to the end of a word that ends in a vowel plus* y *to make it plural*. Point to *puppy*. Say: *Puppy* ends in a consonant plus y. Cover the *-es* in *puppies* and say: *Puppy* ends with y, *but when you make a word like* puppy *plural, you have to change the* y *to* i. Uncover the *-es,* and say: *Then you add* -es *to the end of the word*. Use letter tiles to spell the plurals of Items 1–5.

3. Learn to Read Plural Words
Teach Point to *days* and say: *This word ends with* -s. *To read the word, cover the* -s. *Read the root word. Then uncover the* s *and read the entire word*. Point to *skies* and say: *This word ends in* -es. *To read the word, cover the* -es. *Look at the root word. If you see an* i *at the end, you know the root word ends in* y. *To read it, blend the root word and the sound of the ending that means "more than one":* /s k ī z/, *skies*.

Practice Read the story. Pause before each word ending in *-s* or *-ies*. Ask students to read the word. If they need help, have them cover the *-s* or *-es* and apply the strategy. Point out that the plural form has the same vowel sound for *y* as the root word. Remind students to look for letter patterns to divide long words into syllables and blend the two syllables.

OBJECTIVES

Learning to Read: Build Oral Vocabulary; Develop Phonemic Awareness; Identify Noun Endings (*-s, -ies*); Decode Words with Endings

TEACH PLURALS:
y + *s*; *y* to *i* + *es*

1 Build Oral Vocabulary Help students finish these sentences:
- *Another word for* friend *is* _____. (buddy)
- *Stamp collecting is one kind of* _____. (hobby)
- *The sun shines in the* _____. (sky)
- *The opposite of night is* _____. (day)
- *The child said, "Read me a* _____." (story)

2 Develop Phonemic Awareness Conduct the oral activities in Step 1 of the Script for Transparency 66.

3 Learn to Spell and Read Plurals with *y* Display Transparency 66 again. Work through Steps 2 and 3 of the script.

CLOSE AND ASSESS

Display the nouns *day, hobby, story,* and *tray*. Have groups each write the plural form of one noun and read it to the class.

▶ **Reading Practice Book** page 86 (plurals: *y* + *s*; *y* to *i* + *es*)

Reading Practice Book page 86

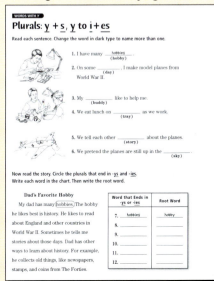

Language and Literacy **T222b**

UNIT 13 **LESSON 12**

LANGUAGE AND LITERACY: READING AND SPELLING

OBJECTIVES

Functions: Listen Actively; Repeat Spoken Language; Recite

Learning to Read: Develop Phonemic Awareness; 🅣 Associate Sounds and Symbols: /y/ y, /ī/ y, /ē/ y; Identify Noun Endings (-s, -ies); Blend Sounds to Decode Words

Spelling: 🅣 Words with y

LISTEN AND LEARN

Tape 7A · CD 3 Track 3

1 **Recite a Rap** Display Transparency 67 and play "Take a Look at Today" on the **Language Tape/CD**.

DEVELOP PHONEMIC AWARENESS

2 **Isolate Final Sounds** Say: *Listen to this word:* sky. *What is the last sound you hear?* Repeat: /s k ī ī ī/ (ī) Repeat for *happy*. Then continue with *buddy, candy, fly, story, try, my,* and *fry*.

CONNECT SOUNDS AND LETTERS

3 **Associate /y/ y, /ī/ y, and /ē/ y** Discuss the first picture and sound out *year: A calendar shows the twelve months of the year. Let's point to the letters in* year *and sound them out:* /y î r/, year. Say: *When y comes at the beginning of a word, it is a consonant. It makes the sound* /y/. Repeat for *sky,* pointing out that *y* is a vowel when it comes at the end of a word. Explain: *The letter* y *has the sound* /ī/ *when it is the only vowel.* For *happy,* lead students in dividing the word between the two *p*s and blending the syllables to read the word. Explain that *y* has the sound /ē/ when there is more than one vowel and the *y* comes after a consonant.

Afterwards, play the rap again. Have students identify words with the three sounds of *y.*

T222 Unit 13 | Past and Present

WORDS WITH Y

Reading and Spelling

LISTEN AND LEARN

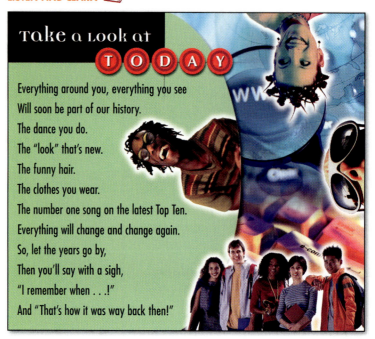

take a Look at TODAY

Everything around you, everything you see
Will soon be part of our history.
The dance you do.
The "look" that's new.
The funny hair.
The clothes you wear.
The number one song on the latest Top Ten.
Everything will change and change again.
So, let the years go by,
Then you'll say with a sigh,
"I remember when . . . !"
And "That's how it was way back then!"

CONNECT SOUNDS AND LETTERS

The letter *y* can have 3 sounds.

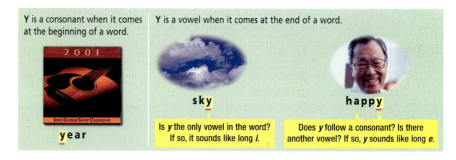

Y is a consonant when it comes at the beginning of a word.

year

Y is a vowel when it comes at the end of a word.

sky — Is *y* the only vowel in the word? If so, it sounds like long *i*.

happy — Does *y* follow a consonant? Is there another vowel? If so, *y* sounds like long *e*.

222 Unit 13 | Past and Present   ▶ Transparencies 65–67

REACHING ALL STUDENTS

Multi-Level Strategies

LITERACY SUPPORT

LITERATE IN L1 In some languages, such as Spanish, a sound is frequently represented consistently by the same symbol. In English a sound can often be represented by several different spellings. Have students categorize words to help them pay attention to the position of letters in words as well as to word and letter patterns that cue the sound:

- Provide simple reading material such as familiar books from The Basics Bookshelf, newspaper advertising inserts, or easy news stories. Have students find words with *y* and write them on index cards.

- Highlight each *y* in one color. Highlight the vowels in another color. Pronounce each word for students and have them echo it.

- Students place the cards into groups according to the sound for *y* and study the highlights to tell how the position and letter patterns cue the sound.

READING STRATEGY

Follow these steps to read words that end in *y*.

1 Does the word have one vowel or more than one vowel?

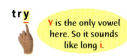

Y is the only vowel here. So it sounds like long i.

I see two vowels, e and y. So the y sounds like long e.

2 If there is one vowel, start at the beginning of the word and blend the sounds.

If there are two vowels, divide the word into syllables. Blend the syllables. Say the long **e** sound for the **y** at the end.

READING AND SPELLING PRACTICE

1. In fifty years, people can look back at your life today.
2. Just make a time capsule that tells your story. Try it!
3. Get a box. On top, write "My Year 2002," for example.
4. Put in your school yearbook, along with things from your hobbies or sports.
5. Include funny things, like an old pair of dirty sneakers.
6. Write words that explain what each thing means to you.

7.–11. Now write the sentences that your teacher reads. *For dictation sentences, see Step 6 at right.*

Spelling Help

For words that end in a **consonant + y**, change the **y** to **i** and add **-es** to form the plural.

sky	skies
penny	pennies

WORD WORK

12. Read these words. Then write each word on a card.

puppy	penny	why
sky	candy	funny
twenty	by	sticky
fly	try	my

Put the words with the long *i* sound in one group.
Put the words with the long *e* sound in another group.
What do you notice?

Example: 12.

These words have 2 syllables.

Long *i*	Long *e*
sky	puppy
fly	twenty
by	penny
try	candy
why	funny
my	sticky

Language and Literacy   223

Decodable Book
PRACTICE WITH WORDS WITH y

Decodable Book 13:
Kathy's Diary

Assign **Decodable Book 13** for independent reading. The **Decodable Book** can be used in a variety of ways to help students become more fluent, automatic readers:

Discussion Circles Have students work in small groups to read aloud and discuss the book using the questions on the back cover. Encourage students to read aloud the text that supports their answers. Groups can also work together to complete the Word Work Activity.

Readers Theater Students can read aloud the stories in a class performance. Help them prepare by rereading the stories in daily rehearsals. Work with students to add narration or dialog. Encourage them to use natural phrasing and expression.

Rereading at Home Have students work with family members to reread the book at home. They can take turns reading aloud alternate pages, then rereading the book switching the pages each person reads.

LEARN A READING STRATEGY

4 Sound Out Words Work through the strategy with students, reading each step aloud and modeling the actions.

PRACTICE

5 Read Sentences Distribute the Partner Prompts from page T311 to guide peers in reading the sentences in Items 1–6. Remind them to use the sound-out strategy to read words and to blend the words silently.

6 Write Sentences Point out the Spelling Help and read the explanation. Work through additional examples to help students apply the tip: *spy, spies; city, cities; cherry, cherries; bunny, bunnies; fly, flies.* Then dictate the following sentences for students to write. Read each sentence at normal speed once so students can listen, and then repeat it slowly word by word as they write:

   7. Randy is my buddy.
   8. We read stories on rainy days.
   9. We fly kites on windy days.
   10. Last year his dog had puppies.
   11. I got the puppy with yellow fur.

If students need extra support, guide them in spelling the two-syllable words, syllable by syllable. For example, say: *What are the two syllables you hear in* windy? (win-dy). *The first syllable is* win. *Write the letter for each sound you hear in* win. *Now write the letters that make the sounds in the second syllable:* dy. *What letter spells /ē/ at the end of words?* (y)

7 Conduct "Word Work" Read the directions and work through the Example. Then have partners complete the activity. Discuss what students noticed about the sound of *y* at the end of two-syllable words and at the end of one-syllable words.

▶ **Reading Practice Book** pages 159–162 (Decodable Book 13)

CLOSE AND ASSESS

Write these words from Word Work: *funny, try, twenty, why, candy, by.* Call on students to tell how many syllables each word has and to identify the sound of *y*.

Language and Literacy   **T223**

UNIT 13 **LESSON 13**

LANGUAGE AND LITERACY: INDEPENDENT READING

OBJECTIVES

Functions: Read a Selection; Make Comparisons; Have a Discussion

Learning to Read: 🔵 Recognize High Frequency Words; 🔵 Decode Words with *y*

Reading Strategies: Activate Prior Knowledge; Set a Purpose for Reading; Paraphrase

Critical Thinking and Comprehension: Make Comparisons

Writing: Comparisons

READ ON YOUR OWN

1. **Introduce Vocabulary** In "Kidworks for Peace," students apply phonics skills and read high frequency words taught in Lessons 10–12. Introduce the following story words. Write each word, pronounce it, and spell it. Then give a definition and a context sentence:

   - **peace:** no fighting; harmony. *When countries do not have wars, there is peace.*
   - **radio:** sent by radio, or electric waves. *My favorite radio station plays music by the band Loud Mouth.*
   - **government:** the system for ruling a country or smaller area. *We vote in elections to choose people in the government.*

2. **Activate Prior Knowledge/Set Purposes** Read the question in the title and view the photos and the on-line chat page. Discuss what students know about the Internet and on-line chat. Then model setting a purpose: *I'll read to find out what these people think about the question, "Can Kids Make History?"* Encourage volunteers to state their purposes for reading.

3. **Read and Think: Paraphrase** Students should read the passage on their own. To help them better understand each person's message, suggest that they stop after each paragraph and silently repeat the information in their own words.

T224 Unit 13 | Past and Present

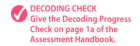

COMPREHENSION: MAKE COMPARISONS

Read on Your Own

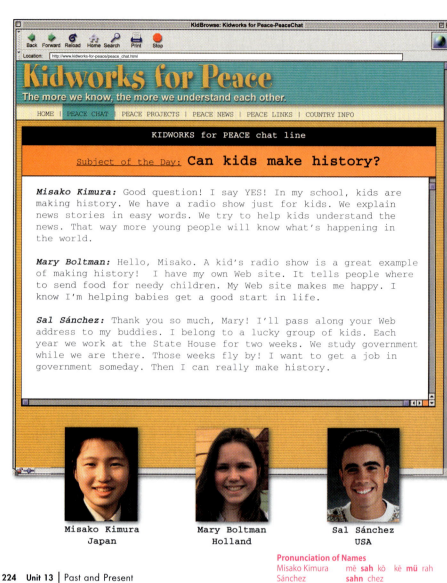

224 Unit 13 | Past and Present

REACHING ALL STUDENTS

CULTURAL PERSPECTIVES

World Culture: Internet "Chat" Discuss the range of on-line chat: people all over the world can talk to one another in "real time." Invite students who have participated in on-line chat to share experiences. Discuss common rules, or protocols, of chat behavior, such as:

- Be polite.
- Don't interrupt other people.
- Read comments to see what is being discussed before sharing your thoughts.
- Don't insult people.

Encourage students to compare chat-room protocols and other features of chat with "in-person" discussions.

CHECK YOUR UNDERSTANDING

Answer each question.

Example: **1.** Misako tries to help kids understand the news.

2. Misako, Mary, and Sal all have goals. What are they? Finish these sentences:
   Misako tries to ____. *help kids understand the news*
   Mary wants to help ____. *babies get a good start in life*
   Sal wants to get ____. *a job in the government someday*

3. How are their goals alike? How are they different? Finish this sentence:
   Both Misako and *Mary* want to help *kids*, but Sal wants to find a *job in the government*.

4. Do Misako, Mary, and Sal all like what they do? How do you know? *Yes; They all are enthusiastic about what they are doing and are sharing it with other kids.*

5. Work with your class to complete this chart. Then compare ideas. Which ones do you agree with?

Can kids make history?	
Yes	**No**
My friend Olga sings. She made an album and is famous now.	Kids are too young to make history.

EXPAND YOUR VOCABULARY

Sample Responses to Expand Your Vocabulary
• American Revolution 1776–1783
• Mexican Revolution 1910–1920
Students may choose any historical event.

6. Copy this word map. Work with a group to complete it.

```
            An event in history
    ┌──────────┬──────────┬──────────┬──────────┐
World War II  Space Station Mir
1939–1945     1986–2001
```

7. Choose two events from the map. Tell your group about them. Tell how they are alike or different. Use words from the green box.

alike	and	but
same	both	different

Example: World War II was a horrible time when countries fought each other, but countries worked together on Space Station Mir.

WRITE ABOUT KIDS AND HISTORY ✏️

8. Pretend you are part of the on-line chat on page 224. Write an e-mail to say what you think: Can kids make history?

Example: **6.** Yes! My class painted a mural at school. It will be there for a long time!

Language and Literacy **225**

CHECK YOUR UNDERSTANDING

4 Comprehension: Make Comparisons Read aloud the directions, and tell students that in this activity they will make comparisons. Explain that when you make comparisons, you tell how two or more people or things are alike or different. Then read Item 1 and use the Example to model how to find information in the selection to finish the sentences. Say: *To finish the first three sentences, I have to tell what Misako's, Mary's, and Sal's goals are. I can look at the selection to find the answers. In the first paragraph, Misako says that she has a radio show, and that she tries to help kids understand the news. I will complete the sentence "Misako tries to" with "help kids understand the news."* For Item 4, guide the discussion, pointing out similarities and differences among students' ideas.

EXPAND YOUR VOCABULARY

5 Compare Historic Events Read the directions for the word map. Read the second set of directions and go over the words in the green box. Use the Example to model how to use a word from the box to compare two events. Encourage students to use a different word in each comparison statement.

WRITE

6 Contribute to a Discussion Explain that the Example shows another student's e-mail message for the on-line chat discussion on page 224. Encourage students to write an e-mail that tells what they think about the topic, *Can Kids Make History?*

For students who need support in writing, provide sentence frames:

> I think kids ____ make history.
> They ____ and ____.

▶ **Reading Practice Book** page 87

CLOSE AND ASSESS

Have students take turns comparing the goals of two chat participants on page 224, and explaining whether they think their goals really will make history.

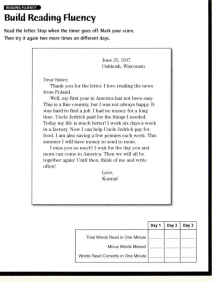
Reading Practice Book page 87

Reading Fluency
TIMED READINGS

Read the title and introduction on **Reading Practice Book** page 87. Set the timer and have a student read the passage to you. Use the script on page T324 to mark words the student misses and to note the last word read in one minute. Have students graph their performance and set a goal for improving in subsequent timed readings. Plan for two additional timed readings, and encourage partners to practice reading the passage to each other between the timed readings.

Language and Literacy **T225**

UNIT 13 **LESSON 14**

LANGUAGE ACROSS THE CURRICULUM: SOCIAL STUDIES

OBJECTIVES

Function: Listen to a Selection
Concepts and Vocabulary: U.S. Government
Learning Strategies: Build Background
Comprehension: Identify Details

LEARN ABOUT THE U.S. GOVERNMENT

1. **Explore the U.S. Government** Read the page title and the main heading. Explain that the U.S. government is divided into three parts called *branches*. Each branch has its own responsibilities. Then study the photos, captions, and labels.

READ AND THINK

2. **Gather Information** Point to the Web page and read the introduction. Explain that the Internet is a good source of information about government and history. Read the introduction for *Kidworks* and explain that this Web page tells what the three government branches do. Have students locate the chart for each branch.

3. **Listen to the Web Page** Restate ideas and clarify vocabulary as necessary; for example: *A term is how long a leader's job lasts.* Pause for students to match each branch of government shown in the photos at the top of the page, with the information presented in the Web site.

CHECK UNDERSTANDING

4. **Answer the Review Questions** Help students analyze the charts to find the needed information.

CLOSE AND ASSESS

Have groups create three questions about the U.S. government, based on information on the Web page. Have groups take turns asking and answering questions.

T226 Unit 13 | Past and Present

SUCCESS IN SOCIAL STUDIES

Learn About the U.S. Government

THE THREE BRANCHES OF THE U.S. GOVERNMENT

LEGISLATIVE BRANCH: CONGRESS
Senate
House of Representatives

EXECUTIVE BRANCH
President — Vice President
cabinet members

Franklin D. Roosevelt was President during World War II.

JUDICIAL BRANCH
Supreme Court
Chief Justice

Answers to the Review:
1. The Executive Branch carries out the laws. Legislative Branch makes the laws. The Judicial Branch listens to legal cases and interprets.
2. Representatives are elected every 2 years. President and Vice President are elected every 4 years. Senators are elected every 6 years.

KIDWORKS for PEACE created a Web page to explain the kinds of governments in each country. Read their page. Then do the Review.

KidBrowse: Kidworks for Peace-Country Info
Location: http://www.kidworks-for-peace/country-info/usa.html

Kidworks for Peace
The more we know, the more we understand each other.

HOME | PEACE CHAT | PEACE PROJECTS | PEACE NEWS | PEACE LINKS | COUNTRY INFO

The United States 🇺🇸

The structure of the U.S. government has not changed very much since it was established in 1789. The U.S. government is a democracy. That means the people choose the leaders. There are three branches in the U.S. government:

The Executive Branch carries out laws.

President and Vice President	Cabinet
• The President and Vice President are elected by the people. • Term: 4 years	• The President appoints the members of the cabinet. Members include the Secretary of State and the Attorney General.

The Judicial Branch listens to legal cases and interprets laws.

Supreme Court
• The nine Justices of the Supreme Court are appointed by the President and approved by the Senate. One is the Chief Justice. • Term: lifetime

The Legislative Branch is the Congress. It makes laws.

Senate	House of Representatives
• The people of each state elect two Senators. • Term: 6 years	• The number of Representatives from each state depends on its population. • Term: 2 years

REVIEW
1. **Check Your Understanding** Name the three branches of the U.S. government. What is the role of each branch?
2. **Vocabulary** Who is elected every 2 years? Every 4 years? Every 6 years?

226 Unit 13 | Past and Present

REACHING ALL STUDENTS

Social Studies Connection

U.S. GOVERNMENT

Apply the U.S. government vocabulary in a sorting game. Ask students to review page 226 to locate the groups, offices, and positions associated with each branch of government, and to make a word card for each. Then make a three-column chart with the branches as headings. Distribute the cards and have students read each one aloud and put it in the correct column. Lead students in reading the cards in each column of the finished chart.

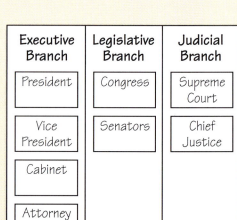

Writing Project COMPARISON POSTER

WRITING ASSESSMENT Use the Writing Progress Checklist on page 51 of the Assessment Handbook to evaluate this writing project.

How was life different in the past? Compare your own life to life in the 1940s. Then make a poster with the information.

COLLECT INFORMATION

What do you know about the 1940s? Get more information from books or an interview. Make a chart to compare life in the 1940s with your life today.

1940s	Today
People needed special stamps to buy things.	We can just use money.
Lots of people had gardens for food.	Some people grow gardens for food.
People collected old paper and aluminum.	We recycle paper and aluminum.
People ate powdered eggs and potatoes.	We eat some powdered food, but not eggs.

MAKE AND SHARE YOUR POSTER

What will you show? Find or draw pictures. Write sentences to explain how life is the same or different. Check and correct your work.

> **Check Your Work**
> Do your sentences make comparisons?
> Did you use the correct forms of the past tense?
> Did you use the correct pronouns?

Put your pictures on a poster. Copy your sentences below the pictures. Tell the class about your poster.

In some ways, life in the 1940s and life today is the same. In other ways, it is different. In the 1940s, people had to use special stamps to buy things, but today we just use money. In the 1940s, a lot of people had gardens to grow their food. Today most people grow food in a garden just for fun. In the 1940s, people collected old paper and aluminum, and people still do that today.

Language Across the Curriculum 227

UNIT 13 LESSON 15

LANGUAGE ACROSS THE CURRICULUM: WRITING

OBJECTIVES

Functions: Make Comparisons; Write
Learning Strategies and Critical Thinking: Relate to Personal Experience; Plan; Use Graphic Organizers (chart); Make Comparisons; Generate and Organize Ideas; Self-Assess
Writing: Comparison Poster

CONDUCT THE WRITING PROJECT

1 Explore Comparisons Read the introduction and remind students that a comparison chart shows how two things are the same or how they are different.

2 Collect Information Guide students in reviewing the unit to learn about what life was like in the 1940s. Have them write notes in the left column of a comparison chart. Then help them go over each item and write how things are the same or different today.

3 Make and Share Your Poster Provide a list of signal words for students to use in writing comparison sentences.

Signal Words

For Similarities	For Differences
and	but
like	unlike
same	different
too	not

Create a poster gallery and have volunteers present their work.

▶ **Language Practice Book** page 110

CLOSE AND ASSESS

As students look at their posters, say:
- *Read a sentence that makes a comparison. What two things does it compare?*
- *Point to a verb in the past tense. Is that the correct form for that verb?*
- *Show me a pronoun you wrote. What noun does it go with?*

Language Practice Book page 110

WRITING PROJECT: COMPARISON POSTER
Then and Now

Make a comparison poster for your class. Use your chart to compare life in the 1940s with your life today.

The 1940s and Today

1. Find or draw pictures of life in the 1940s and today.
2. Write sentences to explain how life is the same or different. Tell about what people did and how they do it today.
   - Use **present** and **past tense** verbs in your sentences.
   - Use the correct **pronouns**.
   - Use **words that compare**.

Put your work on a poster. Read your poster to the class.

Multi-Level Strategies

WRITING SUPPORT

PRELITERATE Provide two sentence frames: one about how life in the 1940s differed from today, and one about how it's the same. Talk over students' ideas, and have them dictate the sentence completions.

> In the 1940s, people _____, but today they _____.
>
> In the 1940s, people _____, and today they do, too.

Language Across the Curriculum **T227**

Resources

For Success in Language and Literacy
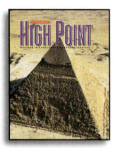
Student Book pages 228–241

For Language Skills Practice
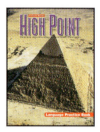
Language Practice Book pages 111–115

For Reading Skills Practice
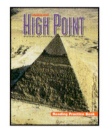
Reading Practice Book pages 88–91

For Vocabulary, Language Development, and Reading Fluency

Language Tape 7, Side B
Language CD 3, Tracks 4–6

For Reading Together

Theme Book *The Eagle and the Moon Gold* from The Basics Bookshelf

For Audio Walk-Throughs and Selection Readings

Selection Tape 7B
Selection CD 3, Tracks 3–4

For Phonics Instruction

Transparencies 68–72

Transparency Scripts 68–72

Letter Tiles

For Comprehensive Assessment
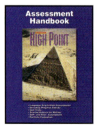
Language Acquisition Assessment, Units 13–15 Test, Writing Assessment, Self-Assessment

For Planning and Instruction
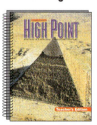
Teacher's Edition pages T228a–T241

T228a Unit Planner

UNIT 14

Tell Me More

In This Unit

Vocabulary
- Story Elements
- Opposites
- Phrases for Times and Places

Language Functions
- Ask for and Give Advice
- Ask for and Accept a Favor
- Describe Actions

Patterns and Structures
- Prepositions
- Commands

Reading
- Diphthongs and Variant Vowels
- Comprehension: Story Elements— Characters (character map), Setting, Plot

Writing
- Notes
- Commands
- Story Endings

Content Area Connection
- Language Arts (myths)

UNIT 14 Activity and Assessment Planner

UNIT 14: Tell Me More

LESSONS

1

UNIT 14 LAUNCH ▶ pages T228–T229

LESSON 1: INTRODUCE UNIT 14 pages T228–T229

Vocabulary	**Viewing**	**Learning Strategies**	**Critical Thinking and Speaking**
T Story Elements	Interpret a Visual Image	Preview Build Background	Make Inferences Generate Ideas Role-Play

2–5

LANGUAGE DEVELOPMENT ▶ pages T230–T233

LESSON 2 STORY ELEMENTS page T230

Function
Ask for and Give Advice

Vocabulary
T Story Elements

Writing
T Sentences with Advice

LESSON 3 OPPOSITES page T231

Function
Ask for and Accept a Favor

Vocabulary
T Opposites

Writing
Note

LESSON 4 TIMES AND PLACES page T232

Function
Describe Actions

Vocabulary
T Times and Places

Patterns and Structures
Prepositions

Writing
Description

LESSON 5 COMMANDS page T233

Function
Give and Carry Out Commands

Patterns and Structures
T Commands

Writing
Commands

6–11

LANGUAGE AND LITERACY ▶ pages T234a–T239

LESSON 6 BASICS BOOKSHELF pages T234a–T234f

Functions
Listen to a Book

Dramatize

Vocabulary
T Opposites

Reading Strategies
Activate Prior Knowledge

Preview

Learning to Read
Identify Quotation Marks

Identify Indentation of Paragraphs

Identify Words

Critical Thinking and Comprehension
T Identify Character Traits

LESSON 7 BASICS BOOKSHELF: COMPREHENSION page T234

Function
Retell a Story

Learning Strategy
Use Graphic Organizers (character map)

Critical Thinking and Comprehension
T Identify Character Traits

LESSON 8 HIGH FREQUENCY WORDS page T235

Learning to Read
T Recognize High Frequency Words

LESSON 9 PHONICS pages T236a–T236d

Learning to Read
Build Oral Vocabulary

Develop Phonemic Awareness

T Associate Sounds and Symbols: Diphthongs, Variant Vowels

Blend Sounds to Decode Words

LESSON 10 READING AND SPELLING pages T236–T237

Learning to Read
Develop Phonemic Awareness

T Associate Sounds and Symbols: Diphthongs, Variant Vowels

Blend Sounds to Decode Words

Spelling
T Words with Diphthongs and Variant Vowels

LESSON 11 INDEPENDENT READING pages T238–T239

Functions
Read a Selection

Describe a Character

Learning to Read
T Recognize High Frequency Words

T Decode Words (diphthongs and variant vowels)

Reading Strategies
Set a Purpose for Reading

Make, Confirm, and Revise Predictions

Critical Thinking and Comprehension
T Analyze Story Elements

Writing
Description

12–13

LANGUAGE ACROSS THE CURRICULUM ▶ pages T240–T241

LESSON 12 LANGUAGE ARTS: MYTHS page T240

Function
Listen to a Selection

Vocabulary
Myths

T Story Elements

Research Skills and Learning Strategies
Build Background

Critical Thinking and Comprehension
T Analyze Story Elements

LESSON 13 WRITING PROJECT: NEW STORY ENDING page T241

Functions
Describe Actions

Write

Vocabulary
T Story Elements

T Times and Places

Learning Strategies and Critical Thinking
Plan

Generate and Organize Ideas

Use Graphic Organizers (storyboard)

Writing
Story Ending

T228c Unit 14 | Tell Me More

T = Objective Tested on Unit Test

ASSESSMENT OPTIONS

The **Teacher's Edition** and the **Assessment Handbook** include these comprehensive assessment tools:

▶ **Ongoing, Informal Assessment**
Check for understanding and achieve closure for every lesson with the targeted questions and activities in the **Close and Assess** boxes in your Teacher's Edition.

▶ **Decoding Progress Check**
These word lists for each unit provide a quick way to check on mastery of the phonics or word structure skills taught in the unit.

▶ **Language Acquisition Assessments**
To verify students' ability to use the language functions and grammar structures taught in Units 13–15, conduct these performance assessments.

▶ **Unit Test in Standardized Test Format**
This multiple-choice test measures students' cumulative understanding of the skills and language developed in Units 13–15.

▶ **Self- and Peer-Assessment**
Students use the Self-Assessment Form to evaluate their own work and develop learning strategies appropriate to their needs. Students offer feedback to their classmates with the Peer-Assessment Form.

▶ **Writing Assessment/Portfolio Opportunities**
You can evaluate students' writing in the Writing Projects using the Writing Progress Checklist. Then collaborate with students to choose work for their portfolios.

UNITS 13–15 ASSESSMENT OPPORTUNITIES

	Assessment Handbook Pages
Decoding Progress Check	1a
Language Acquisition Assessments	34
Units 13–15 Test	35–40
Self-Assessment Form	41
Peer-Assessment Form	50
Writing Progress Checklist	51
Portfolio Evaluation Form	52

RELATED RESOURCES

Cinder-Elly
by Frances Minters
A rap version of the Cinderella story, in which Prince Charming is a basketball star in search of an adoring fan. (Hampton-Brown)
Theme Book: Read Aloud

Seven Blind Mice
by Ed Young
An Indian fable about seven blind mice who each have a different view of the strange Something by their pond. A Caldecott winner.
(Available from Hampton-Brown)
Easy Reading

Hoop Dancers
by Shirley Frederick
A photo-essay about the traditional hoop dance performed by the Lakota of South Dakota. (Hampton-Brown)
Phonics Reinforcement: *oo* and *ew*

The Fox in the Moon
by Juan Quintana and Michael Ryall
In this retelling of a Peruvian folktale, Fox concocts a plan for getting to the moon, and persuades Mole to come with him. (Hampton-Brown)
Vocabulary: Phrases for Times and Places

The Princess and the Pea
This interactive program allows students to create alternative endings to the fairy tale about a finicky princess.
(Bradford)
Multimedia: Diskette

UNIT 14 **LESSON 1**

INTRODUCE UNIT 14: TELL ME MORE

> **OBJECTIVES**
>
> **Concepts and Vocabulary:** 🅣 Story Elements
> **Viewing:** Interpret a Visual Image
> **Speaking:** Role-Play
> **Learning Strategies:** Preview; Build Background
> **Critical Thinking:** Make Inferences; Generate Ideas

START WITH A COMMON EXPERIENCE

1. **Introduce "Tell Me More"** Read the unit title and explain: *People say "tell me more" when they want to hear what happens next in a story.* Demonstrate this by giving a brief story starter: *It is a dark night. Two friends see a bright light in the sky. The light moves closer . . .* Call on a student to continue the story: *Paola, tell me more.*

2. **Analyze the Action** Have students view the photo and follow along as you read the directions. Explain that the actors are acting out a story on a stage. Discuss what the story could be about:
   - Who are the people in the story?
   - Where and when does it take place?
   - What are the people saying?
   - What happened right before this?
   - What will happen next?

3. **Role-Play the Scene** Organize groups to talk about what the scene is about. Provide time to practice, then invite the groups to role-play their versions. Afterward, discuss the direction each group took the story. Talk about the similarities and the differences among the groups' stories.

UNIT 14

REACHING ALL STUDENTS

HOME CONNECTION

Family Stories Many families pass on favorite stories. Students can ask a family member to tell one of these. Encourage them to take notes and to record or remember as much as possible about the special words, voices, expressions, or actions the family member uses in telling the story. Encourage volunteers to share their stories with the class.

Tell Me More

What is happening in this play? What are the people saying? What will happen next? Discuss your ideas with your classmates. Then act out the scene together.

In This Unit

Vocabulary
- Story Elements
- Opposites
- Phrases for Times and Places

Language Functions
- Ask for and Give Advice
- Ask for and Accept a Favor
- Describe Actions

Patterns and Structures
- Prepositions
- Commands

Reading
- Diphthongs and Variant Vowels
- Comprehension:
  Story Elements—Characters (character map), Setting, Plot

Writing
- Notes
- Commands
- Story Endings

Content Area Connection
- Language Arts (myths)

229

PREVIEW THE UNIT

4 Look for Activities and Stories Leaf through the unit, previewing activities students will do, for example:

page 230—learning a chant about how to create a story

pages 232–233—reading about Paul Bunyan and Aladdin

page 234—listening to the Bookshelf book (Display a copy of the book.)

page 238—reading a scary story

page 241—writing a new story ending

Also ask students to look for information about the important elements, or parts, that make a good story. Then sum up what the preview reveals: *People love hearing and telling stories.*

5 Set Your Goals Start a class mind map on stories. Prompt students for pictures or words to add, and have them act out and describe other ideas for you to put into words.

CLOSE AND ASSESS

Ask students to tell or show you something they are interested in learning in this unit.

UNIT 14 Mind Map

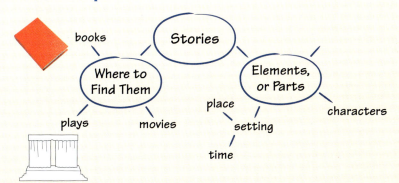

Technology Support
See **Inspiration** Visual Learning Software for support in creating mind maps.

Unit Launch **T229**

UNIT 14 LESSON 2

LANGUAGE DEVELOPMENT: STORY ELEMENTS

> **OBJECTIVES**
>
> **Functions:** Listen Actively; Repeat Spoken Language; Recite; Ask for and Give Advice
> **Concepts and Vocabulary:** 🅣 Story Elements
> **Writing:** 🅣 Sentences with Advice

INTRODUCE

1. **Listen and Chant** Play "Recipe for a Story" on the **Language Tape/CD**. Students will listen and read along, then echo the lines, fill in the story elements, and chime in on the entire chant. *(Tape 7B / CD 3 Track 4)*

2. **Learn About Story Elements** Read aloud the "What's in a Story?" chart and use the terms to discuss the story suggested by the illustration: *Who are the characters? Where are they? What are two things that are happening? What problem does the woman have?*

PRACTICE

3. **Conduct "Express Yourself"** Model how to ask for and give advice. Then have partners complete the activity.

   > **How to Ask for and Give Advice**
   >
   > • To ask for advice, ask for help with a problem: *How should I get away?*
   >
   > • To give advice, say what you think the person should do. Use opinion words like *should, must,* and *have to: You have to climb the cliff.*

APPLY

4. **Write Sentences with Advice** Point to the monster and talk about what it wants. Encourage students to check their sentences with a partner. Distribute Partner Checklist 14 on page T310.

   ▶ **Language Practice Book** page 111

> **CLOSE AND ASSESS**
>
> Have students share the advice they wrote. Discuss how it might affect the plot.

T230 Unit 14 | Tell Me More

VOCABULARY: STORY ELEMENTS

How to Make a Story

Listen and chant. 🎧

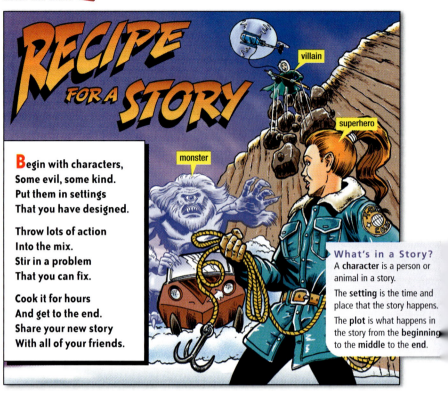

Begin with characters,
Some evil, some kind.
Put them in settings
That you have designed.

Throw lots of action
Into the mix.
Stir in a problem
That you can fix.

Cook it for hours
And get to the end.
Share your new story
With all of your friends.

> **What's in a Story?**
> A **character** is a person or animal in a story.
> The **setting** is the time and place that the story happens.
> The **plot** is what happens in the story from the **beginning** to the **middle** to the **end**.

EXPRESS YOURSELF ▶ Ask for and Give Advice

1.–2. Imagine that you are the superhero in the picture. Ask a partner: *What should I do to get away?* Your partner gives you advice. Then change roles.

Example: 1. What should I do to get away? You should use your rope and climb the mountain.

WRITE SENTENCES WITH ADVICE ✏️

3.–6. Talk with a partner. What advice would you give the monster in the picture? Write 4 sentences.

Example: 3. You should drive toward the mountain.

230 Unit 14 | Tell Me More

REACHING ALL STUDENTS

Language Practice Book page 111

CABULARY: OPPOSITES

Two Sides of the Story

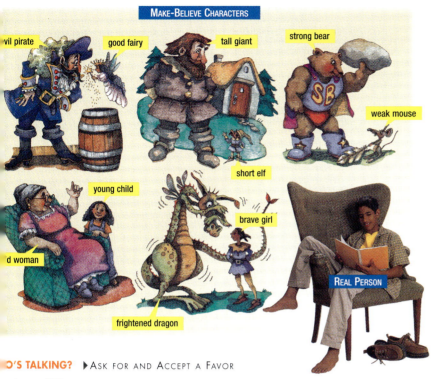

MAKE-BELIEVE CHARACTERS
- vil pirate
- good fairy
- tall giant
- strong bear
- weak mouse
- short elf
- young child
- brave girl
- frightened dragon
- d woman
- REAL PERSON

O'S TALKING? ▶ ASK FOR AND ACCEPT A FAVOR

Listen.

h two characters are talking? Point to them.
ut each scene with a partner. Ask for a favor.

Answers:
1. evil pirate and good fairy
2. frightened dragon and brave girl
3. strong bear and weak mouse
4. old woman and young child

TE A NOTE

rite a note to one of the characters above.
or a favor. Read your note to the class.

Example: 5.
> Dear Elf,
> I dropped my pencil under the steps. I'm too tall to get it. You are short. Can you help me?
> Thank you,
> Oscar

Language Development **231**

Language Practice Book page 112

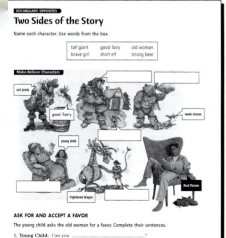

Vocabulary
OPPOSITES

Word Match Play "Concentration," with opposite pairs from the chart you made at right. Have students make up word cards, with one word per card. After shuffling and laying the cards face down, a student selects two cards to try to match opposites. If all agree they're a match, the student keeps the pair. Students take turns; the student with the most pairs at the end is the winner.

UNIT 14 **LESSON 3**

LANGUAGE DEVELOPMENT: OPPOSITES

OBJECTIVES

Functions: Listen Actively; Ask for and Accept a Favor
Concepts and Vocabulary: 🅣 Opposites
Writing: Note

INTRODUCE

1 Learn Words for Opposites Explain that two words are *opposites* when they have completely different meanings. Direct attention to the illustrations and read the labels. Say: *Each pair of characters has completely different traits. The words that describe them are opposites.*

2 Listen for Opposites Say word pairs and have students raise their hands when they hear a pair of opposites: *tall/short* (yes), *short/old* (no). Create a chart of opposite pairs.

Opposites	
tall/short	young/old
evil/good	weak/strong
frightened/brave	hot/cold

PRACTICE

3 Conduct "Who's Talking?" Explain that when you ask for a favor, you ask someone to help you. Play "Who's Talking?" on the **Language Tape/CD** to model how to ask for and accept a favor. Volunteers can perform the scenes for the group.

Tape 7B
CD 3
Track 5

APPLY

4 Write a Note Model using the characters' traits to determine what they may need: *The elf is short. He may ask the giant to help him reach something high.*

▶ **Language Practice Book** page 112

CLOSE AND ASSESS

Have students find opposites in the room: *The eraser is short. The ruler is long.*

Language Development **T231**

UNIT 14 LESSON 4

LANGUAGE DEVELOPMENT: TIMES AND PLACES

OBJECTIVES
Function: Describe Actions
Concepts and Vocabulary:
- Phrases for Times and Places

Patterns and Structures: Prepositions
Writing: Description

INTRODUCE

1 Learn Phrases for Times and Places
Read aloud the title. Explain that the time and place of a story is called the *setting*. Then go over the pictures and sentences and identify the phrases that tell the time or the place. Show them on a chart.

Setting

Times	Places
in the morning	Eagle Mountain
after his walk	home

PRACTICE

2 Conduct "Express Yourself" Model how to describe actions. Then have partners complete the activity.

How to Describe Actions
- First I think about what happened: *Paul went somewhere.*
- I tell when: *At 7:00 a.m.*
- I tell where: *up the mountain.*
- Finally, I put the ideas together: *At 7:00 a.m., Paul went up the mountain.*

APPLY

3 Write a Description Encourage students to include details of time and place in their pictures and writing.

▶ Language Practice Book page 113

CLOSE AND ASSESS
Ask questions about students' work: *What is the setting you show in your picture? What happens?*

T232 Unit 14 | Tell Me More

VOCABULARY: PHRASES FOR TIMES AND PLACES

A Time and a Place for Everything

Read the story. Look for phrases that tell **when** and **where** things happen.

In the morning, Paul went up Eagle Mountain. After his walk, he went back home.

During breakfast, Paul sat beside the other men. He ate 275 pancakes.

At 12:00, Paul began to plant trees near his home. He worked from noon to 3:00 and made the North Woods!

Before dinner, Paul walked across Minnesota. He walked until 6:00. His footsteps made 10,000 lakes.

EXPRESS YOURSELF ▶ DESCRIBE ACTIONS

1.–4. Make up settings for 4 new stories about Paul Bunyan.
Use words from each column to make a sentence that tells the setting.

At 7:00 a.m.		around the lake.
During lunch	Paul went	into the river.
In the afternoon		up the mountain.
Before dinner		through the forest.

Example: 1. At 7:00 a.m., Paul went up the mountain.

WRITE A DESCRIPTION

5. Choose a setting you made above. Draw a picture to show it. Then describe the action. Tell the class what happened next.

Example: 5. At 7 a.m., Paul went up the mountain. He walked up the mountain with just three steps.

232 Unit 14 | Tell Me More

REACHING ALL STUDENTS

Language Practice Book page 113

COMMANDS

A Genie at Your Command

A command tells someone to do something.

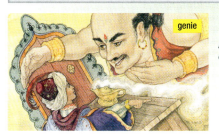

genie

A command can end with a **period** or an **exclamation mark**.

Listen to my wish**.**
Go to the kitchen**.**
Make something for me to eat**!**

BUILD SENTENCES

Aladdin gave the genie a new command every day. Choose the correct word to complete each command. Then say the command.

Example: 1. Get some slippers for me.

1. " (**Get**/Paint) some slippers for me."
2. " (**Put**/Build) a gold ring on my finger."
3. " (Swim/**Bring**) gold and jewels to me."
4. " (Put/**Sing**) me a song."
5. " (**Build**/Put) a new castle for me."
6. " (**Take**/Paint) me to the princess."

WRITE COMMANDS

7.–12. Imagine you have your own genie. Work with a partner to write 6 commands for the genie. Put a period or an exclamation mark at the end of each command.

Example: 7. Do my homework.

Sample Responses
Encourage students to use different verbs in their commands. Remind them to use an exclamation point when they are giving a command with a lot of emotion.

Language Development 233

Language Practice Book page 114

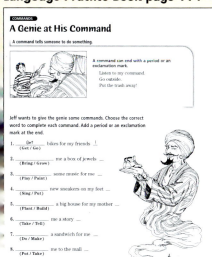

Multi-Level Strategies

LANGUAGE DEVELOPMENT

LITERATE IN L1 Different languages form commands in different ways. In Vietnamese and Hmong, the adverb *now* is added after the verb to be emphasized. In Russian and Arabic, commands are inflected for type and person. In most cases, languages rely on tone to indicate commands.

To practice commands in English, model giving commands to students: *Walk three steps. Turn around.* Call on volunteers to give more commands, using the correct intonation.

UNIT 14 **LESSON 5**

LANGUAGE DEVELOPMENT: COMMANDS

OBJECTIVES
Function: Give and Carry Out Commands
Patterns and Structures: 🅣 Commands
Writing: Commands

INTRODUCE

1 Learn About Commands Remind students that on page 231 they learned how to ask for a favor. Explain the difference between a favor and a command: *When you ask for a favor, you ask someone for help. When you give a command, you tell someone what to do.*

Next, ask students if they know the story of Aladdin and the magic lamp. Develop a basic familiarity with the characters and action of this classic tale, as necessary. Then discuss the illustration in the skill box and read the rule and examples. Confirm understanding by asking students to choose which of these two sentences is a command:

   I want a nice sandwich.
   Bring me a nice sandwich!

PRACTICE

2 Build Sentences Explain that commands often begin with a verb. Read the directions and go over the Example. Point out that *Get* makes sense in the command and *Paint* does not. Have partners work together to complete and say the commands.

APPLY

3 Write Commands Explain that students can use exclamation marks to give special emphasis to a command, but that this is not necessary.

▶ **Language Practice Book** page 114

CLOSE AND ASSESS

Have volunteers write a command on the board. Have the group read the command, and note whether it ends in a period or an exclamation mark.

Language Development **T233**

UNIT 14 **LESSON 6**

LANGUAGE AND LITERACY: THE BASICS BOOKSHELF

OBJECTIVES
Concepts and Vocabulary: ⓣ Opposites
Listening: Listen to a Preview
Reading Strategies: Activate Prior Knowledge; Preview
Learning to Read: Identify Quotation Marks; Identify Indentation of Paragraphs

BUILD LANGUAGE AND VOCABULARY

1 **Teach "Words to Know"** Have students look at pages 2–3. Say: *These pages show words that are opposites. When two words are opposites, they have completely different meanings.*

Point to the words *poor* and *rich* on page 2 and say: *The words* poor *and* rich *are opposites. One man is poor. He has a small house. His clothes are old. The other man is rich. He has a big house. His clothes are fancy.* Then introduce the other opposites.

2 **Play Concentration** Copy the vocabulary on index cards, one word per card. Scramble the cards and lay them face down. Then have partners take turns revealing two cards in order to find a pair of opposites. When a match occurs, have the team use words, pictures, or objects to show the opposites: *A watch is small, but a clock is large.*

PREPARE TO READ

3 **Think About What You Know** Invite students to share fables from other countries.

4 **Preview** Play the Audio Walk-Through for *The Eagle and the Moon Gold* on the **Selection Tape/CD** to give students the overall idea of the story.

Tape 7B
CD 3
Track 3

CLOSE AND ASSESS
Have volunteers tell what happened each time the eagle went to the moon.

The Eagle and the Moon Gold
Adapted by Yeemay Chan

Summary This Hmong fable uses opposites to teach a moral about the danger of greed. When a magical eagle takes kindhearted Yaoh to the moon, the boy is content with taking a few pieces of moon gold. When the eagle offers Gwa the same opportunity, the greedy man tries to take all of the gold, but the rising sun melts him and his gold.

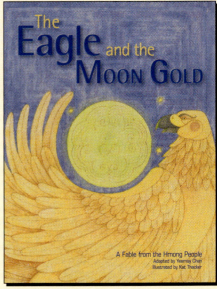
Cover

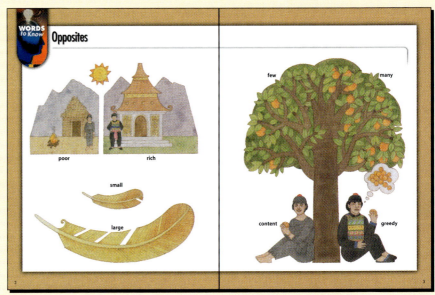
Pages 2–3

Multi-Level Strategies
LITERACY SUPPORT

PRELITERATE **Concepts of Print: Identify Quotation Marks** Point to the quotation marks on page 5 and say: *Quotation marks come at the beginning and end of the words a character says.* Read aloud the eagle's words. Students can then find the quotation marks on pages 6 and 7 as you read aloud the dialogue. Point out that speaker words can come before the dialogue (page 7), after the dialogue (page 15), or in the middle (page 6).

NON-ROMAN ALPHABET **Concepts of Print: Identify Indentation of Paragraphs** Introduce the conventions of English paragraph structure. Turn to page 18 and say: *These sentences make a paragraph.* Point to the indentation and explain: *The first word of each paragraph is indented. This space shows where a new paragraph begins.* Have students page through the book to point out other paragraphs.

T234a Unit 14 | Tell Me More

Pages 4–5

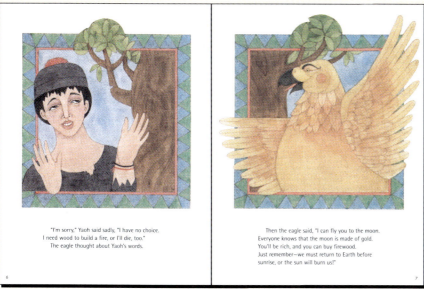

Pages 6–7

Strategies for Comprehensible Input

Page	Story Language	Strategy Options
4	poor boy	**Explain:** A poor boy does not have much money.
	chop down	**Demonstrate:** Make a chopping motion with your hands.
5	babies	**Point to the picture.**
6–7	I have no choice.	**Restate:** There is nothing else I can do.
	return	**Restate:** come back
	sunrise	**Explain:** Sunrise is early in the morning when you can see the sun first come up in the sky.

Language and Literacy

UNIT 14 **LESSON 6,** CONTINUED

LANGUAGE AND LITERACY: THE BASICS BOOKSHELF

OBJECTIVES

Function: Listen to a Book
Critical Thinking and Comprehension:
Identify Character Traits

READ AND THINK TOGETHER

1. **Read Aloud** On your first reading of the book, use the "Strategies for Comprehensible Input" that appear at the bottom of pages T234b, T234d, and T234f.

2. **Read and Map: Identify Character Traits** Draw a character map like the one below, but with only the bold headings for each column. Say: *A character map shows what a character is like. It tells what the character does.*

   Read pages 4–6 aloud. Then think aloud as you model filling in the first row: *Yaoh is the first character in the story. I will write his name in column 1. I think that Yaoh is hard-working. The pictures and words show that Yaoh chops wood to stay warm. I will write this information about Yaoh in column 2. Chopping wood is hard work and Yaoh does it all by himself, so I will write* hard-working *in column 3.*

   Pause after reading each set of pages shown below and model completing the character map for the rest of the story.

Pages 8–9

Pages 10–11

Character Map for *The Eagle and the Moon Gold*

	Character	What Character Does	What Character is Like
pages 4–6	Yaoh	He chops wood to stay warm.	hard-working
pages 7–13		He takes only a few pieces of gold.	content
pages 14–17	the eagle	She asks the men to save her nest.	protective
pages 18–21		She flies the men to the moon.	strong
pages 22–24	Gwa	He takes too much gold.	greedy

Technology Support
See **Inspiration** Visual Learning software for support in creating the character map.

Unit 14 | Tell Me More

The Eagle and the Moon Gold,
CONTINUED

Pages 12–13

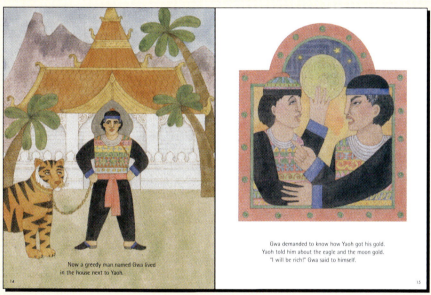

Pages 14–15

Strategies for Comprehensible Input

Page	Story Language	Strategy Options
8–9	flew	**Demonstrate:** Make a flying motion with your hands.
10–11	content	**Restate:** happy; satisfied
12–13	never	**Restate:** not one time; not ever again
	chop wood	**Demonstrate:** Make a chopping motion with your hands.
14	greedy man	**Explain:** A greedy man always wants more and more money.
	next to	**Demonstrate:** Put two items next to each other.
15	demanded to know	**Restate:** forced Yaoh to tell him

Language and Literacy T2

UNIT 14 LESSON 6, CONTINUED

LANGUAGE AND LITERACY: THE BASICS BOOKSHELF

OBJECTIVES
Functions: Listen to a Book; Dramatize
Learning to Read: Identify Words

READ AND THINK TOGETHER, CONTINUED

Tape 7B
CD 3 Track 4

3 **Conduct Interactive Readings** Choose from these options:

- **Dramatize** Explain that words can represent sounds. Point out the words *Ter! Ter! Ter!* on pages 4 and 16, and *Shu! Shu! Shu!* on pages 9 and 21. Invite volunteers to add sound effects as you read aloud the story.

- **Read along and identify words** The fable contains many high frequency words that have been taught, as follows:

a	home	next	then
about	house	no	this
again	how	not	thought
all	I	now	to
an	in	of	too
and	into	one	was
before	is	or	we
boy	it	people	what
can	know	put	will
day	large	said	with
down	many	same	words
few	more	small	you
from	my	started	
have	need	that	
he	never	the	

As you read, have students identify words from the list. Continue reading as students track the print.

CLOSE AND ASSESS
Divide students into groups of three. Have each student take the role of one character and tell that part of the story.

Pages 16–17

Pages 18–19

Multi-Level Strategies

LITERACY SUPPORT

LITERATE IN L1 **Read with a Partner/Write a Moral** After students have participated in the interactive readings, encourage them to read the story with a partner. Distribute the Partner Prompts on page T311 to help partners work together to identify unfamiliar words and unlock their meanings, then read the text to each other. After the partner reading, turn to page 24 and read aloud the moral. Say: *A moral is a lesson that a story teaches.* Have students create additional morals. For example: *Be content with what you have. Don't be jealous.*

INTERRUPTED SCHOOLING **Identify Character Traits and Motives** To anchor understanding of the skill, have partners write a few important actions that each character does in the story: *Yaoh chops the tree. Yaoh helps the eagle.* Then help students explain what the action tells about the character's personality. *Yaoh chops his own firewood, so he is hard-working.*

Unit 14 | Tell Me More

The Eagle and the Moon Gold,
CONTINUED

Pages 20–21

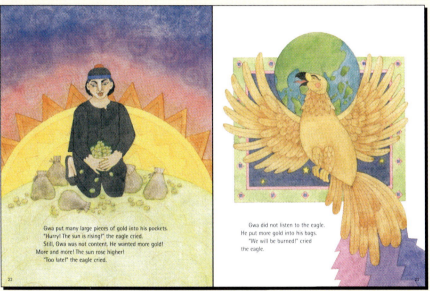

Pages 22–23

Page 24

Strategies for Comprehensible Input

Page	Story Language	Strategy Options
16–17	lied	**Restate:** did not tell the truth
18–19	the sun will burn us	**Explain:** When the sun comes up, it will get too hot. They will die if they stay after sunrise.
20–21	flew	**Point to the picture.**
22–23	Hurry!	**Restate:** Move faster!
	The sun is rising!	**Demonstrate and restate:** Move your hands upward as you say: *The sun is coming up.*
	rose higher	**Gesture:** Bring your hands up to above your head.
24	melted	**Explain:** When something melts it turns into a liquid.
	moral	**Explain:** A moral is a lesson that you learn.

Language and Literacy T23

UNIT 14 **LESSON 7**

LANGUAGE AND LITERACY: THE BASICS BOOKSHELF

OBJECTIVES

Function: Retell a Story
Learning Strategy: Use Graphic Organizers (character map)
Critical Thinking and Comprehension:
🅣 Identify Character Traits

CHECK COMPREHENSION

1. **Make a Character Map** Have students review *The Eagle and the Moon Gold* to identify the characters and their traits. Remind them that a character map shows who is in the story and what the characters are like.

   As you read aloud the directions for each step, pause for students to add information to the rows of their maps. Encourage students to review the story to find words that tell what the characters are like as well as what they do.

2. **Retell the Story** Have students work in groups of three. One student says a riddle describing a character's trait or actions from their character map: *I took too much gold. Who am I?* (Gwa) Other students guess the answer and take turns giving more riddles. The group then retells the story: one member tells the parts involving Yaoh, another tells what the eagle does, and the last tells the parts involving Gwa.

CLOSE AND ASSESS

Ask students to complete this sentence: *A character map shows _____.*

Unit 14 | Tell Me More

COMPREHENSION: CHARACTERS

Read and Think Together

Make a character map for the characters in *The Eagle and the Moon Gold*. Follow these steps.

❶ Draw a character map like this.

Character	What the Character Does	What the Character Is Like
Yaoh		
the eagle		
Gwa		

❷ Read the story again. Think about Yaoh's actions. List them in the second column. What do Yaoh's actions show about his character? Write words to describe Yaoh in the third column.

Character	What the Character Does	What the Character Is Like
Yaoh	He chops wood to stay warm.	hard-working

❸ Now think about the eagle and Gwa. Complete the character map for each character.

❹ Use your finished map to tell a partner about the three characters in the story.

Character	What the Character Does	What the Character is Like
Yaoh	He chops wood to stay warm. He takes only a few pieces of gold.	hard-working content
Eagle	She asks the men to save her nest. She flies the men to the moon.	protective strong
Gwa	He takes too much gold.	greedy

234 Unit 14 | Tell Me More

from **The Basics Bookshelf**

THEME BOOK

This Hmong fable has a lesson about the cost of greed.

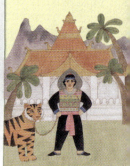

Pronunciation of Names in *The Eagle and the Moon Gold:*
Yaoh   ya ō
Gwa   guwah

REACHING ALL STUDENTS

Language Development
DRAMATIZE

Role-Play Have groups of four take the parts of the eagle, Gwa, Yaoh, and the narrator. The group can make setting cards to describe prepositions from the story: *at the eagle's tree, to the moon, on the moon,* etc. The narrator reads and displays each card as the setting changes. The other actors read aloud dialogue from the book as they act out the scenes.

HIGH FREQUENCY WORDS
Words to Know

REVIEW WORDS YOU KNOW
Read the words aloud. Which word goes in each sentence?

study	story
our	over
before	because

1. He tells a _story_.
2. It was first told by _our_ grandfathers.
3. They told the story _before_ we were born.

LEARN TO READ
Learn new words.

as	Listen carefully **as** I tell you a story.
sentence	Pay attention to every **sentence** I say.
idea	I got the **idea** for this story from my grandfather.
plants	A frog lived in the garden among the tall **plants**.
into	One day, it jumped and fell **into** a pail of cream.
until	The frog swam and swam **until** its legs got tired.
but	The frog was tired, **but** it did not stop swimming.
seemed	Then the cream **seemed** a little thicker.
each	With **each** kick, the cream got thicker and thicker.
made	In a few minutes, the frog **made** a pail of butter!

How to Learn a New Word
- Look at the word.
- Listen to the word.
- Listen to the word in a sentence. What does it mean?
- Say the word.
- Spell the word.
- Say the word again.

WORD WORK
Write each sentence. Add the missing word. Example: 4. The children listen as the man tells a story.

4. The children listen _a s_ the man tells a story.
5. The first _s e n t e n c e_ in the story starts with "A frog lived…".
6. The frog came out of the tall _p l a n t s_ where it lived.
7. The frog fell _i n t o_ a pail of cream.
8. The frog got tired, _b u t_ it did not stop swimming.
9. _E a c h_ time it kicked, the frog _m a d e_ the cream thicker.
10. The frog kicked _u n t i l_ the cream turned to butter.
11. The children laughed. They _s e e m e d_ to like the story.

Language and Literacy 235

Reading Practice Book page 88

Reading Fluency
RECOGNIZE HIGH FREQUENCY WORDS

To build automaticity with the new high frequency words:

- Invite volunteers to start writing one of the new words slowly on the board, one letter at a time, until someone guesses it. The person who guesses the word then goes to the board to finish writing it.
- Have small groups make word cards and use them to test how many words each person can read aloud correctly in ten seconds. One student can use the second hand on a watch or clock to keep time.

UNIT 14 **LESSON 8**

LANGUAGE AND LITERACY: HIGH FREQUENCY WORDS

OBJECTIVES
Learning to Read:
- Recognize High Frequency Words

REVIEW WORDS

1 Review Known High Frequency Words Have the group read aloud the words in the green box. Listen for words students cannot read automatically and use the steps in the yellow box to reteach those words. Then have students look at the photo. Read each cloze sentence. Reread each sentence and pause for students to silently read the two words to the left of the sentence. Tell students to choose the word that goes in the sentence and tells about the picture.

INTRODUCE NEW WORDS

2 Learn High Frequency Words Use the High Frequency Word Script on page T325 to lead students through the steps in the yellow box for each new word.

PRACTICE

3 Conduct "Word Work" Use the Example to model how to use context to find possible words in the list and then to use the number of letter blanks to confirm the word.

Have partners complete Items 5–11. Discuss how each correct word fits the context and the number of blanks.

APPLY

4 Read Words in Context Students will apply the skill when they read high frequency words in context in the sentences on page 237 and the passage on page 238.

▶ **Reading Practice Book** page 88

CLOSE AND ASSESS

Call out the high frequency words one at a time. Have students point to them and spell the words as a group.

Language and Literacy **T235**

UNIT 14 LESSON 9

LANGUAGE AND LITERACY: PHONICS

OBJECTIVES

Learning to Read: Build Oral Vocabulary; Develop Phonemic Awareness; 🅣 Associate Sounds and Symbols /oi/ *oi, oy*; Blend Sounds to Decode Words

TEACH DIPHTHONGS: /oi/ *oi, oy*

1 Build Oral Vocabulary Display Transparency 68. Talk through each picture to develop meaning for the words in the yellow boxes. For example, for Item 1, say:

- *This person uses a pointer to* **point to,** *or show something. When you* **point** (pantomime) *to an object, you show someone where the object is.*

2 Develop Phonemic Awareness Remove the transparency and conduct the oral activities in Step 1 of the Script for Transparency 68.

3 Read Words with Diphthongs *oi, oy* Display Transparency 68 again. Work through Steps 2 and 3 of the script.

CLOSE AND ASSESS

Display the words *boil, point, joy,* and *toys.* Call on students to read each word and identify the two letters that make the vowel sound /oi/.

Word Families

-OY AND -OIL

Materials: Letter Tiles

A large number of words can be generated from a few rhyming phonograms. Use letter tiles to build the words in dark type. Then change tiles to build other words in the *-oy* and *-oil* families. Have students make a list of the words. Make sure students understand their meanings. Then ask them to read the words on their list and to identify the shared ending.

boy	boil
joy	oil
soy	soil
toy	spoil
enjoy	foil

T236a Unit 14 | Tell Me More

Transparency 68: ▶ Diphthongs

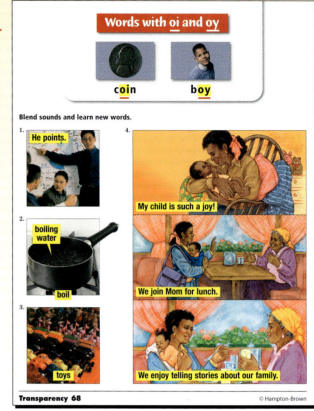

▼ Script for Transparency 68

Words with *oi* and *oy*

1. Develop Phonemic Awareness
Isolate/Match Final and Medial Sounds Say: *Listen to the sound at the end of these words:* boy, joy, toy. *What is the sound?* (/oi/) *Now listen for the sound /oi/ in the middle of these words:* boil, coin, foil. *Say the words with me. Now raise your hand each time you hear the sound* /oi/. *Say these words:* coin, curb, boil, enjoy, paint, point, pot, jam, join, say, boy.

2. Associate Sounds and Symbols
Point to the coin on **Transparency 68**. Say: *This is a coin. It is a type of money. Say the word* coin *with me.* Then point to the *oi* in *coin* and say: *The letters* oi *make the vowel sound you hear in the middle of* coin. *The sound is* /oi/. *Say* /oi/ *with me:* /oi/. Repeat for *boy,* pointing out that the letters *oy* make the vowel sound /oi/ at the end of *boy.*

3. Blend Sounds to Read Words
Model/Teach Point to *coin* and say: *The word* coin *has three sounds.* As you slide a finger slowly from left to right below *coin,* say: *I can blend the three sounds together:* /koinnn/. *Now, I'm going to say the whole word:* coin. Adapt for *boy* (two sounds). Lead students in sounding out the words with you.

Practice For Item 1, say: *Let's try that again. In this picture, a person points to something. Read the words with me. Follow my finger as we blend the sounds.* Point to each word in the sentence and have students blend the sounds and then say the word. Model blending the sounds to read the other words, calling special attention to the following:

- In Item 3, after you read *toys* with students, point out that *s* has the sound /z/.

- In Item 4, remind students to divide *enjoy* between the two consonants and help them blend the two syllables to read the word. After reading *stories* with students, ask them to identify the root word. (*story*) Review how to form the plural of words ending with a consonant plus *y*. (change *y* to *i* and add *-es*)

◀ **Transparency 69: Diphthongs**

12 Mistakes in Item 5: upside down rainbow; upside down *A* on flag; people eating on roof; flowers in chimney; cloud with stripes and polka dots; bike missing front tire; backward horse; pig in baby carriage; boy ice-skating on sidewalk; cow in window; numbers on clock out of order; rowboat in street

▼ **Script for Transparency 69**

Words with *ou* and *ow*

1. **Develop Phonemic Awareness**
   Isolate/Match Beginning and Medial Sounds Say: *Listen to the first sound in these words: owl, out, ouch. What is the sound? (/ou/) Now listen for /ou/ in the middle of these words: loud, town, down. Say the words with me. Now raise your hand each time you hear /ou/:* pound, coin, clown, shout, show, crowd, cloud, town, toy, count, dot.

2. **Associate Sounds and Symbols**
   Point to the cloud on **Transparency 69**. Say: *This is a cloud. You see clouds in the sky. Say* cloud *with me.* Point to the *ou* and say: *The letters* ou *make the vowel sound you hear in* cloud. *The sound is /ou/. Say /ou/ with me: /ou/.* Repeat for *crown*, explaining that the letters *ow* also make the sound /ou/.

3. **Blend Sounds to Read Words**
   Model/Teach Point to *cloud* and say: *The word* cloud *has four sounds.* As you slide a finger slowly below *cloud*, say: *I can blend the four sounds: /kloud/, and say the whole word:* cloud. Repeat for *crown*. Then lead students in sounding out the words with you.

   Practice For Item 1, say: *Let's try that again. This picture shows a sad clown. He has a frown.* To read *frown* and the phrase with students, say: *Read the words with me. Follow my finger as we blend the sounds.* Point to each word and have students blend the sounds and then say the word. Repeat for the other items, calling attention to the following:

   • In Item 3, cover the *-er* in *louder* and ask students to read the root word. Then uncover the *-er* and tell them to blend the two syllables to say the word. Explain that *louder* means "more loud."

   • For *mistakes* in Item 5, review how to read a long word with two consonants between two vowels. Have students divide the word into syllables, look for familiar patterns to read each syllable, and then blend the syllables together to read the word.

OBJECTIVES

Learning to Read: Build Oral Vocabulary; Develop Phonemic Awareness; ❶ Associate Sounds and Symbols /ou/ *ou, ow*; Blend Sounds to Decode Words

TEACH DIPHTHONGS: /ou/ *ou, ow*

1. **Build Oral Vocabulary** Display Transparency 69. Talk through each picture to develop meaning for the words in the yellow boxes. For example, for Item 3, say:

   • *This cat* (point) **pounds** *some drums* (pantomime). *The drums make a* **loud sound** (press ears). *Now the cat pounds these drums* (point to second picture). *The sound gets* **louder** (press ears harder).

2. **Develop Phonemic Awareness** Remove the transparency and conduct the oral activities in Step 1 of the Script for Transparency 69.

3. **Read Words with Diphthongs** *ou, ow* Display Transparency 69 again. Work through Steps 2 and 3 of the script.

CLOSE AND ASSESS

Display the words *crowd, loud, sound,* and *town*. Call on students to read each word and identify the two letters that make the vowel sound /ou/.

▶ **Reading Practice Book** page 89 (diphthongs: *oi, oy; ou, ow*)

Reading Practice Book page 89

Language and Literacy **T236b**

UNIT 14 **LESSON 9**, CONTINUED

LANGUAGE AND LITERACY: PHONICS

OBJECTIVES

Learning to Read: Build Oral Vocabulary; Develop Phonemic Awareness; ⓣ Associate Sounds and Symbols /o͞o/ oo, ew; Blend Sounds to Decode Words

TEACH VARIANT VOWELS: /o͞o/ oo, ew

1 Build Oral Vocabulary Display Transparency 70. Play "I Spy." For example, for Item 5, say:

- *I spy some* **bamboo.** **Bamboo** *is a plant.* **Bamboo** *plants grow tall.*

When students find the bamboo, say: *Yes,* **this is bamboo** (point). Repeat to build context for the other words.

2 Develop Phonemic Awareness Remove the transparency and conduct the oral activities in Step 1 of the Script for Transparency 70.

3 Read Words with Variant Vowels oo, ew Display Transparency 70 again. Work through Steps 2 and 3 of the script.

CLOSE AND ASSESS

Display the words *broom, cool, grew,* and *screw.* Call on students to read each word and identify the two letters that make the vowel sound /o͞o/.

Word Families

-EW AND -OOM

Materials: Letter Tiles

A large number of words can be generated from a few rhyming phonograms. Use letter tiles to build the words in dark type. Then change tiles to build other words in the *-ew* and *-oom* families. Have students make a list of the words. Make sure students understand their meanings. Then ask them to read the words on their list and to identify the shared ending.

stew	**room**
chew	boom
few	broom
grew	groom
new	zoom

T236c Unit 14 | Tell Me More

Transparency 70: ▶ **Variant Vowels (oo, ew)**

▼ **Script for Transparency 70**

Words with oo and ew

1. Develop Phonemic Awareness
Isolate/Match Final and Medial Sounds Say: *Listen to the sound at the end of these words:* too, new, grew. *What is the sound?* (/o͞o/) *Now listen for the sound /o͞o/ in the middle of these words:* boot, moon, chews. *Say the words with me. Now raise your hand each time you hear the sound /o͞o/. Say these words:* pool, pet, foot, chew, men, moon, room, rub, new, store, stew.

2. Associate Sounds and Symbols
Point to the moon on **Transparency 70.** Say: *This picture shows the moon. Say the word* moon *with me.* Then point to the *oo* in *moon* and say: *The letters* oo *make the vowel sound you hear in* moon. *The sound is* /o͞o/. *Say* /o͞o/ *with me:* /o͞o/. Repeat for *screw,* explaining that the letters *ew* make the vowel sound /o͞o/ at the end of *screw.*

3. Blend Sounds to Read Words
Model/Teach Point to the word *moon* and say: *The word* moon *has three sounds.* As you slide a finger slowly from left to right below *moon,* say: *I can blend the three sounds together:* /mo͞on/. *Now, I'm going to say the whole word:* moon. Adapt the process for *screw* (four sounds). Then lead the students in sounding out the words with you.

Practice For Item 1, say: *Let's try that again. This picture shows a broom in a room, doesn't it? Read the words with me. Follow my finger as we blend the sounds* /bro͞om/, *and say the word:* broom. Repeat for the other words, calling special attention to the following:

- In Item 2, explain that when something is *cool,* it is very popular, or in style. In Item 4, explain that *cool* also means "a little bit cold."

- Also in Item 4, point out the ending *-er,* and explain that *cooler* means "more cool."

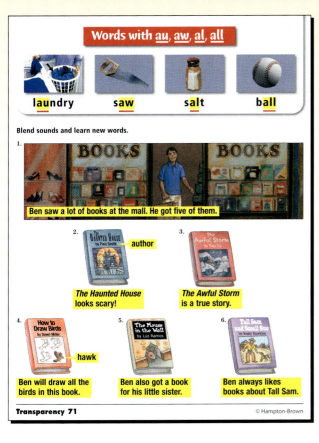

▼ Script for Transparency 71

Words with *au*, *aw*, *al*, *all*

1. **Develop Phonemic Awareness**
   Isolate/Match Final and Medial Sounds Say: *Listen to the sound at the end of these words:* saw, draw. *What is the sound?* (/ô/) *Now listen for /ô/ in the middle of these words:* yawn, sauce, dawn. *Say the words with me. Now raise your hand each time you hear /ô/:* lawn, sand, sauce, draw, laundry, city. *Repeat for /ôl/, using these words:* wall, salt, sat, ball, back, can, call, sand.

2. **Associate Sounds and Symbols**
   Point to the picture of laundry on **Transparency 71**. Say: *This laundry is in a basket. Laundry is clothing and other things you wash in a machine. Say* laundry *with me.* Then point to the *au* in *laundry* and say: *The letters* au *make the first vowel sound you hear in* laundry. *The sound is /ô/. Say /ô/ with me.* Repeat for *saw, salt,* and *ball.* Explain that the letters *aw* also make the vowel sound /ô/, and that the letters *al* and *all* make the sounds /ôl/.

3. **Blend Sounds to Read Words**
   Model/Teach Point to *laundry* and say: *Laundry has two vowel sounds, so it has two syllables. Let's divide the word and blend the first syllable.* As you slide a finger below the letters *laun,* say: *I can blend the three sounds together: /lôn/. Now, I can blend the second syllable. When a word has two vowel sounds and the vowel* y *follows a consonant, the* y *usually has a long* e *sound: /d r ē/. I'm going to blend the two parts* laun-dry, *and say the word:* laundry. Model blending the sounds in the one-syllable words *saw* (two sounds), *salt* (four sounds), and *ball* (three sounds). Lead students in sounding out the words with you.

   Practice For Item 1, say: *Let's read the first sentence together.* Read aloud the sentence, pausing for students to decode *saw* and *mall.* Repeat for the other sentences, calling attention to the following:

   • In Item 2, read *scary* for students and spell it: s-c-a-r-y. Write *scare,* erase the *e,* and add *y.* Explain: *I added* y *to the root word* scare. *The* y *is pronounced /ē/.*

OBJECTIVES

Learning to Read: Build Oral Vocabulary; Develop Phonemic Awareness; 🅣 Associate Sounds and Symbols /ô/ *au, aw;* /ôl/ *al, all;* Blend Sounds to Decode Words

TEACH VARIANT VOWELS: /ô/ *au, aw;* /ôl/ *al, all*

1. **Build Oral Vocabulary** Display Transparency 71. Talk through each picture to develop meaning for the words in the yellow boxes. For example, for Item 1, say:
   • *Here is a boy at a* **mall** (point). *There are lots of stores in a* **mall**. *The boy bought some books at this store in the* **mall**.

2. **Develop Phonemic Awareness** Remove the transparency and conduct the oral activities in Step 1 of the Script for Transparency 71.

3. **Read Words with Variant Vowels** *au, aw, al, all* Display Transparency 71 again. Work through Steps 2 and 3 of the script.

CLOSE AND ASSESS

Display *laundry, draw, salt,* and *mall.* Call on students to read each word and identify the letters that make the sound /ô/ or the sounds /ôl/.

▶ **Reading Practice Book** page 90 (variant vowels: *oo, ew; au, aw; al, all*)

Reading Practice Book page 90

Language and Literacy **T236d**

UNIT 14 **LESSON 10**

LANGUAGE AND LITERACY: READING AND SPELLING

OBJECTIVES

Functions: Listen Actively; Repeat Spoken Language; Recite

Learning to Read: Develop Phonemic Awareness; 🅣 Associate Sounds and Symbols: /oi/ oi, oy; /ou/ ou, ow; /o͞o/ oo, ew; /ô/ au, aw; /ôl/ al, all; Blend Sounds to Decode Words

Spelling: 🅣 Words with Diphthongs and Variant Vowels

LISTEN AND LEARN

1 **Sing a Song** Display Transparency 72 and play "Tell Me a Tale" on the **Language Tape/CD**.

Tape 7B
CD 3 Track 6

DEVELOP PHONEMIC AWARENESS

2 **Manipulate Words: Delete the Initial Sound** Say: *Listen to this word: boil. Say boil with me: boil. Now let's take away the first sound /b/ in boil. Say boil without the /b/.* (oil) Repeat, deleting the first sound in *tall, fan, fall, soil, cat, call,* and *shout*.

CONNECT SOUNDS AND LETTERS

3 **Associate Sounds and Symbols for Diphthongs and Variant Vowels**
Point to the pictures in Item 1 and say: *This is a coin, and here's the word. Let's point to the letters as we say the sounds: /k/, /oi/, /n/*. Repeat for *boy*. Then say: *Two pairs of letters make the vowel sound /oi/: oi and oy.* Repeat for Items 2–5, pointing out in Item 4 that two (*al*) or three letters (*all*) can make the sounds /ôl/. Then read the directions and question aloud: *Read the words. How do you spell each vowel sound?* Have students read each word, repeat the vowel sounds, and identify the letters that stand for the sounds (/oi/ oi, oy; /ou/ ou, ow; /ô/ au, aw; /ē/ y; /ôl/ al, all; /o͞o/ oo, ew).

Afterwards, play the song again. Have students identify words with the sounds they have been learning.

T236 Unit 14 | Tell Me More

DIPHTHONGS AND VARIANT VOWELS

Reading and Spelling

LISTEN AND LEARN

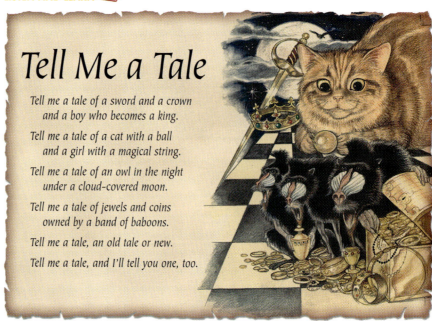

Tell Me a Tale

Tell me a tale of a sword and a crown
 and a boy who becomes a king.
Tell me a tale of a cat with a ball
 and a girl with a magical string.
Tell me a tale of an owl in the night
 under a cloud-covered moon.
Tell me a tale of jewels and coins
 owned by a band of baboons.
Tell me a tale, an old tale or new.
Tell me a tale, and I'll tell you one, too.

CONNECT SOUNDS AND LETTERS
Read the words. How do you spell each vowel sound?

1. oi, oy — c**oi**n, b**oy**
2. ou, ow — cl**ou**d, cr**ow**n
3. au, aw — l**au**ndry, s**aw**
4. al, all — s**al**t, b**all**
5. oo, ew — m**oo**n, scr**ew**

236 Unit 14 | Tell Me More ▶ Transparencies 68

REACHING ALL STUDENTS

Multi-Level Strategies
LITERACY SUPPORT

LITERATE IN L1 Study the errors students make in the sentence dictation in Items 7–11 and compare them to the Phonics Transfer Chart on page T338. Students may incorrectly encode sounds because they do not exist in their native languages (e.g., /oi/ does not exist as a sound in Hmong), or they may use a spelling that stands for the sound in the native language (e.g., *au* is a spelling for /ou/ in Spanish). For these errors, conduct minimal pair activities:

- For sound recognition, say three words such as *boil, boil, ball*. Have students hold up cards with the numbers 1, 2, and 3 to indicate which words are the same. Minimal pairs for variant vowels are *down, dawn; tan, town; oil, owl*.

- For oral production, have students repeat sentences with the minimal pairs: *Do not boil a soccer ball!* Dictate sentences for students to write and read back.

PRELITERATE Use Transparencies 68–71. Choose a word, such as *coin*, and point to each letter as you slowly spell *coin*, and then read it aloud. Repeat, having students use letter cards or tiles to spell the word with you.

READING STRATEGY

Follow these steps to read a word.

❶ Look for pairs of letters that make a vowel sound.

 t<u>oy</u>   When **o** and **y** are next to each other, they combine to make a new sound, like the **oy** in b**oy**.

 m<u>oo</u>n   When **o** and **o** are next to each other, they combine to make a new sound. Here they sound like long **u**.

❷ Start at the beginning. Blend the sounds in your head. Then say the word.

 t<u>oy</u>   t + oy = toy

 m<u>oo</u>n   m + oo + n = moon

READING AND SPELLING PRACTICE

Use what you learned to read the sentences.

1. My mother is an author. She writes stories for teens.
2. She also draws pictures to go with each story.
3. I enjoy all of Mom's stories. They are very cool.
4. When she needs a new idea for a story, she goes out.
5. Sometimes I join her. We go to the mall or into town.
6. Mom jots down notes as she watches the crowd.

7.–11. Now write the sentences that your teacher reads.   *For dictation sentences, see Step 6 at right.*

WORD WORK

12. Write each of these words on a card.

coin	now	joy	boil	oil
town	toy	moist	count	point
out	loud	owl	clown	boy

Then say each word. Sort the words by vowel sound. Make 2 groups. What do you notice about each group?

13. Now make 4 new groups. Put the words with the same vowel sound *and* spelling together.

oi/oy	ou/ow
coin	out
moist	loud
boil	count
oil	
point	
toy	town
joy	now
boy	owl
	clown

Use **oy** to spell the sound at the end of a word. Use **oi** in the middle.

Example: 13.

Language and Literacy **237**

LEARN A READING STRATEGY

4 Sound Out Words Work through the strategy with students, reading each step aloud and modeling the actions shown on the page.

PRACTICE

5 Read Sentences Distribute the Partner Prompts from page T311 to guide peers in reading the sentences in Items 1–6. Remind them to use the sound-out strategy to read words and to blend the words silently in their head.

6 Write Sentences Dictate the following sentences for students to write. Read each sentence at normal speed once so students can listen, and then repeat it slowly word by word as they write:

 7. Sam has a new toy drum.
 8. I saw a cloud by the moon.
 9. Wait until the water boils.
 10. There are three malls in this town.
 11. Is this all the laundry?

If students need extra support, guide them in spelling the words with diphthongs and variant vowels. Have them write the two different spellings for a vowel sound, such as /ou/ in *town,* and decide which looks right.

7 Conduct "Word Work" Read the directions and work through the Example. Then have partners complete the activity. Discuss what students learned about the different ways to spell /oi/ and /ou/.

▶ **Reading Practice Book** pages 163–166 (Decodable Book 14)

CLOSE AND ASSESS

Across the board, write the words from Word Work. Have students read the words, tell where the vowel sound /oi/ or /ou/ appears in each word, and tell how it is spelled.

Decodable Book

PRACTICE WITH DIPHTHONGS AND VARIANT VOWELS

 Decodable Book 14: *A Pinch of Salt*

Assign **Decodable Book 14** for independent reading. The **Decodable Book** can be used in a variety of ways to help students become more fluent, automatic readers:

Discussion Circles Have students work in small groups to read aloud and discuss the book using the questions on the back cover. Encourage students to read aloud the text that supports their answers. Groups can also work together to complete the Word Work Activity.

Readers Theater Students can read aloud the stories in a class performance. Help them prepare by rereading the stories in daily rehearsals. Work with students to add narration or dialog. Encourage them to use natural phrasing and expression.

Rereading at Home Have students work with family members to reread the book at home. They can take turns reading aloud alternate pages, then rereading the book switching the pages each person reads.

Language and Literacy **T237**

UNIT 14 **LESSON 11**

LANGUAGE AND LITERACY: INDEPENDENT READING

OBJECTIVES

Functions:
Read a Selection; Describe a Character

Learning to Read: ⓣ Recognize High Frequency Words; ⓣ Decode Words (diphthongs and variant vowels)

Reading Strategies: Set a Purpose for Reading; Make, Confirm, and Revise Predictions

Critical Thinking and Comprehension: ⓣ Analyze Story Elements

Writing: Description

READ ON YOUR OWN

1. **Introduce Vocabulary** In "A Chill in the Air," students apply phonics skills and read high frequency words taught in Lessons 8–10. Introduce the following story words. Write each word, pronounce it, and spell it. Then give a definition and a context sentence:

   - **welcome:** a friendly greeting. *When someone new comes to our school, we say, "Welcome to (name of your school)!"*
   - **tonight:** this night. *They have to study tonight after dinner.*
   - **listened:** heard. *We listened to songs on the radio.*
   - **scared:** frightened, afraid. *The movie about bats scared me.*

2. **Set Purposes** Discuss the mood created by the the illustrations and the story title. Ask students if they think the story is about something scary that happens in the house. Model setting a purpose: *I'll read this story to find out if something scary happens in this house.* Encourage volunteers to state their purposes for reading.

3. **Read and Think: Make, Confirm, and Revise Predictions** Students should read the passage on their own. Encourage them to predict what is making the noise, revise as they read, and confirm their prediction after reading.

T238 Unit 14 | Tell Me More

COMPREHENSION: STORY ELEMENTS

Read on Your Own

DECODING CHECK
Give the Decoding Progress Check on page 1a of the Assessment Handbook.

A Chill in the Air

"Welcome to your new home, Paul!" Mr. Brown handed Paul a story on tape and a set of keys to his room.

"Thank you! I love stories on tape," said Paul. "Come in and join me for tea."

"I can't tonight," said Mr. Brown. "I hope you enjoy the tape. It's a great story."

Paul nodded. He knew the author. He liked all of her stories.

Paul waited until 9:00. He made himself a cup of tea and put the tape into his tape deck. The story was about a small boy who lived in a haunted house. Each time the boy saw an owl, someone died.

As Paul listened, something started to pound on the pipes inside his walls. The sound seemed to grow louder and louder as the room grew cooler. Paul was so scared that he called Mr. Brown.

"There is something awful inside the walls!" he cried.

"It's just me," said Mr. Brown. "I was working on the pipes. I had to turn off the heat to fix them. I hope you don't mind."

238 Unit 14 | Tell Me More

REACHING ALL STUDENTS

CULTURAL PERSPECTIVES

World Cultures: Legends Start a discussion about scary stories and legends from different cultures. Afterward, suggest that students interview family members and use Internet and library resources to learn more about these or other tales. Working individually or in pairs or small groups, students can learn a tale, practice reciting it, and present it during a storyteller's hour.

CHECK YOUR UNDERSTANDING

Copy and complete the story map. Tell what happens in the beginning, in the middle, and at the end of the story on page 238.

Beginning

1. Paul moved into his new <u>new home.</u>
2. Mr. Brown gave Paul <u>a story</u> on tape and a set of keys.
3. Paul asked Mr. Brown <u>to come</u> in and have tea.

Middle

4. Paul listened to <u>the tape.</u>
5. It was about <u>a small</u> boy in a haunted house.
6. Each time the boy saw an owl, <u>someone</u> died.

End

7. Something started to pound on ____. <u>the pipes in the walls.</u>
8. Paul felt <u>scared.</u>
9. The sound was caused by ____. <u>Mr. Brown working on the pipes.</u>

Example:

> **Beginning**
> 1. Paul moved into his new home.
> Students should put sentences 1–3 in this box.
>
> **Middle**
> Students should put sentences 4–6 in this box.
>
> **End**
> Students should put sentences 7–9 in this box.

EXPAND YOUR VOCABULARY

Read the sentences.

10. The story was about a <u>small</u> boy.
11. Paul was so <u>scared</u>.
12. "There is something <u>awful</u> inside the walls!" he cried.

Work with a group to think of other words that mean *small*, *scared*, and *awful*. Make a list. Then say each sentence with a new word.

Sample Responses

small — young, little, tiny
scared — afraid, frightening, fearful
awful — terrible, horrible, unpleasant, bad

WRITE ABOUT CHARACTERS

13. Choose a character from a story you know. Write sentences to describe the character.

Example: 13. Yaoh was a poor boy. He was wise to listen to the eagle. He was content with a few coins.

Language and Literacy 239

Reading Practice Book page 91

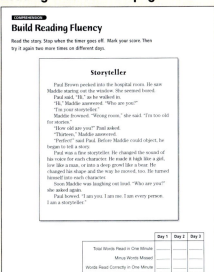

Reading Fluency
TIMED READINGS

Read the title and introduction on **Reading Practice Book** page 91. Set the timer and have a student read the passage to you. Use the script on page T325 to mark words the student misses and to note the last word read in one minute. Have students graph their performance and set a goal for improving in subsequent timed readings. Plan for two additional timed readings, and encourage partners to practice reading the passage to each other between the timed readings.

CHECK YOUR UNDERSTANDING

4 Comprehension: Story Elements Copy the story map (without the sentence), and read aloud the directions, pointing to *Beginning*, *Middle*, and *End* on the map. Explain that a story map shows the events of a story in order. Say: *On this map, you'll write what happens in the beginning, in the middle, and at the end.* Read Item 1 aloud, complete it in the Beginning box, and say: *This is the first event in the story, so I wrote it under "Beginning." Now complete Item 2 and write it under the first sentence to show what happened next.* Have students continue in this way.

EXPAND YOUR VOCABULARY

5 List Synonyms Read the directions and sentences with students. Use the examples to explain that synonyms are words that mean nearly the same thing, such as *small* and *young*. Have students list additional synonyms to use in place of the underlined words in Items 10–12.

WRITE

6 Describe Characters Point out that the Example describes Yaoh, a character in *The Eagle and the Moon Gold*. Then ask students to describe another story character in three or four sentences.

For students who need additional support in writing, provide a character map. Help them use the adjectives and actions they list to write sentences about the character.

Character _____

What the Character Does	What the Character Is Like
1.	1.
2.	2.
3.	3.

▶ **Reading Practice Book** page 91

CLOSE AND ASSESS

Call on students to identify the characters and tell the main events in the beginning, middle, and end of the story.

Language and Literacy T239

UNIT 14 **LESSON 12**

LANGUAGE ACROSS THE CURRICULUM: LANGUAGE ARTS

OBJECTIVES

Function: Listen to a Selection
Concepts and Vocabulary: Myths;
• Story Elements
Research Skills and Learning Strategies: Build Background
Critical Thinking and Comprehension:
• Analyze Story Elements

LEARN ABOUT MYTHS

1. **Explore Myths** Read the definition of *myth* and go over the story elements. Use the definitions for *character*, *setting*, and *plot* (from page 230) as you identify the specific examples on this page.

   Then point to the diagram under *Plot* and explain: *A story map shows important parts of a story. This story map shows a problem the characters have, the events in the* plot *of the story, and how the problem is solved.*

LISTEN AND THINK

2. **Build Background** Read aloud the title of the story and help students locate Athens on the map of ancient Greece. Explain: *Many myths were made up long ago in the country of Greece.* Point to the illustrations of Poseidon and Athena and say: *Ancient Greek myths have characters with special powers. They are called* gods *and* goddesses. *This myth tells how the gods named the city of Athens.*

3. **Read Aloud the Story** As you read, restate ideas and clarify difficult vocabulary, as necessary.

CHECK UNDERSTANDING

4. **Answer "Check Your Understanding"** Remind students to review the myth and the diagrams at the top of the page to find the necessary information.

CLOSE AND ASSESS

Ask students to share about characters that appear in myths from Greece or from any other part of the world.

T240 Unit 14 | Tell Me More

SUCCESS IN LANGUAGE ARTS

Learn About Myths

Pronunciation of Names
Poseidon   pō **sī** dun
Athena   ah **thē** nah

CHARACTERS   **SETTING**   **PLOT**

A myth is a story that was made up long ago. Often it explains something people could not understand.

god / goddess

ANCIENT GREECE
Delphi, Thebes, Olympia, Corinth, Athens, Sparta

time: thousands of years ago
place: Athens, Greece

beginning
Problem: Athena and Poseidon both want the same city.

middle
Events: They agree to each give a gift to the city. The one who gives the best gift wins. Poseidon's gift is a river of salt water. Athena's gift is an olive tree.

Solution: The people choose Athena.
end

Like all stories, a myth has **characters**, a **setting**, and a **plot**.

Listen to the myth. Then answer the questions.

Answers for Check Your Understanding:
1. Poseidon and Athena
2. thousands of years ago in ancient Greece
3. The first paragraph tells the problem. Poseidon and Athena have a co[ntest]. They give gifts to the city. The myth ends when the city chooses Athe[na].

THE BEGINNING OF ATHENS

Thousands of years ago, the gods were dividing up the land. Poseidon, the god of the sea, found a city that he liked. He wanted it for his own. Athena, the goddess of wisdom, saw the same city. She wanted it, too.

Poseidon and Athena agreed to a contest. They decided to each give a gift to the city and let the people choose the best gift. The winner could have the city.

Poseidon touched the rocky mountainside. A river gushed out. Athena touched the dark earth. An olive tree sprang up.

The people looked at the gifts. They tasted the water. It was salty, like the sea. It was of no use to them.

Then they studied the tree. They saw that they could eat the fat olives or make oil from them.

Poseidon's gift is a river of salt water. Athena's gift is an olive tree.

They knew that they could use the tree's wood to build things. They chose Athena.

Athena named the city Athens. The people built a large building to honor her, but they never forgot Poseidon. For many years, a salty pond and an olive tree remained near the building to remind people of the contest.

CHECK YOUR UNDERSTANDING

1. Who are the two main characters in this myth?
2. What is the setting of this story?
3. Which paragraph tells about the problem in the myth? What happens next? How does the myth end?

240 Unit 14 | Tell Me More

REACHING ALL STUDENTS

COMMUNITY CONNECTION

Myth Share Organize a day for community members to share their favorite cultural myths with the class. Before the visitors arrive, form small groups to serve as the readers' hosts. Each group will be responsible for introducing the storyteller and completing a problem-and-solution chart for the storyteller's myth. Debrief by sharing the charts and finding story elements that are common in many myths.

Problem-and-Solution Chart
Title: _____
Characters: _____
Setting: _____

Problem:

↓

Events:

↓

Solution:

Writing Project / NEW STORY ENDING

Write a different ending for *The Eagle and the Moon Gold*. Then share it with the class.

WRITING ASSESSMENT
Use the Writing Progress Checklist on page 51 of the Assessment Handbook to evaluate this writing project.

CHOOSE AN IDEA

Think about different endings for *The Eagle and the Moon Gold*. Choose one.

> Gwa gets a ride home from a passing rocket.
> ✓ Eagle and Yaoh return to save Gwa.
> Yaoh goes with the eagle to the stars.

WRITE THE NEW ENDING

Draw pictures on a storyboard to plan your ending.
Write a sentence under each picture to tell what happens.
Work with a partner to check your work.

Before sunrise, Yaoh rides to the moon.

Gwa and Yaoh ride back to Earth. They get home in the morning.

Gwa gives Yaoh a tiger. He thanks Yaoh for his help.

Gwa changes from an evil man to a good man.

✓ Check Your Work
- Is your ending different from the one in the book?
- Did you describe the characters' actions?
- Did you use words that tell the time and place?

TELL YOUR STORY

Read aloud your new ending. Listen to the endings that your classmates wrote. Tell which endings you like the most.

Language Across the Curriculum **241**

UNIT 14 **LESSON 13**

LANGUAGE ACROSS THE CURRICULUM: WRITING

OBJECTIVES

Functions: Describe Actions; Write
Concepts and Vocabulary: 🅣 Story Elements; 🅣 Phrases for Times and Places
Learning Strategies and Critical Thinking: Plan; Generate and Organize Ideas; Use Graphic Organizers (storyboard)
Writing: Story Ending

CONDUCT THE WRITING PROJECT

1 Explore Story Endings Reread the first two paragraphs of "The Beginning of Athens" on page 240 and brainstorm different gifts that Poseidon could have given the city. Discuss each possibility, and suggest how a different gift may have changed the ending of the myth.

2 Choose an Idea and Write the New Ending Go over the steps of the writing project. Invite students to brainstorm new endings for *The Eagle and the Moon Gold*. Have each student choose an ending and create a storyboard. Remind students to arrange the events in the correct order, and to include time and place words to show the setting and the sequence of events.

Then help students convert their storyboards into a story in standard running text. Encourage them to use *The Eagle and the Moon Gold* and the Greek myth on page 240 as models. Students can include dialogue and a new moral for the fable.

3 Tell Your Story Have students vote for the best stories. Then form groups to dramatize the new endings. Ask students to decide if they will keep this story in their **Portfolio**.

▶ **Language Practice Book** page 115

CLOSE AND ASSESS

As students look at their work, say:
- *Tell me how your ending is different from the one in the book.*
- *Name a character and tell one action that the character did.*
- *Point to words that show time and place.*

Language Across the Curriculum **T241**

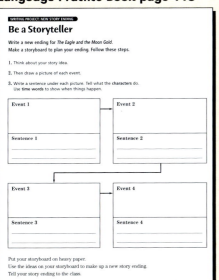

Language Practice Book page 115

Multi-Level Strategies

WRITING SUPPORT

PRELITERATE Provide support for this group by having them dictate captions for their illustrations. Describe sound-letter relationships as you write: *When I write the word tiger, I hear /t/ in the beginning, so I know it starts with the letter* t.

When you have finished writing the sentences, have students pick out words they recognize and trace over them in a different color or copy them on a separate sheet of paper.

Resources

For Success in Language and Literacy

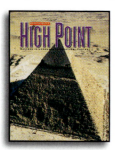

Student Book pages 242–255

For Language Skills Practice

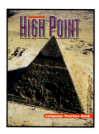

Language Practice Book pages 116–120

For Reading Skills Practice

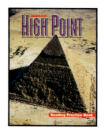

Reading Practice Book pages 92–95

For Vocabulary, Language Development, and Reading Fluency

Language Tape 8, Side A
Language CD 3, Tracks 7–9

For Reading Together

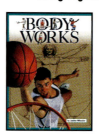

Theme Book *Body Works* from The Basics Bookshelf

For Audio Walk-Throughs and Selection Readings

Selection Tape 8A
Selection CD 3, Tracks 5–6

For Phonics Instruction

Transparencies 73–77

Transparency Scripts 73–77

Letter Tiles

For Comprehensive Assessment

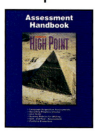

Language Acquisition Assessment, Units 13–15 Test, Writing Assessment, Self-Assessment

For Planning and Instruction

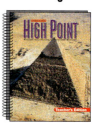

Teacher's Edition pages T242a–T255

T242a Unit Planner

UNIT 15

Personal Best

In This Unit

Vocabulary
- The Body
- Sports

Language Functions
- Ask for and Give Information
- Express Thanks

Patterns and Structures
- Present Tense Verbs
- Pronouns

Reading
- Phonics: Variant Vowels and Consonants
- Comprehension: Relate Main Idea and Details (main-idea diagram)

Writing
- Facts
- Thank-You Speech
- Paragraph for a

Content Area
- Language
  paragraph

UNIT 15

Activity and Assessment Planner

UNIT 15: Personal Best

LESSONS

1

UNIT 15 LAUNCH ▶ *pages T242–T243*

LESSON 1: INTRODUCE UNIT 15 pages T242–T243

Vocabulary
- **T** The Body
- **T** Sports

Viewing
Interpret a Visual Image

Learning Strategies
Preview

Build Background

Use Graphic Organizers (graph)

Research Skills and Critical Thinking
Conduct an Experiment

Analyze Information

Draw Conclusions

2–5

LANGUAGE DEVELOPMENT ▶ *pages T244–T247*

LESSON 2
THE BODY
page T244

Function
Ask for and Give Information

Vocabulary
- **T** The Body

Writing
- **T** Facts

LESSON 3
PRESENT TENSE VERBS
page T245

Function
Give Information

Patterns and Structures
- **T** Present Tense Verbs

Writing
Sentences

LESSON 4
SPORTS
page T246

Function
Express Thanks

Vocabulary
- **T** Sports

Speaking
Express Thanks

Writing
Thank-You Speech

LESSON 5
PRONOUNS
page T247

Function
Give Information

Vocabulary
- **T** Sports

Patterns and Structures
- **T** Pronouns

Writing
- **T** Sentences

6–11

LANGUAGE AND LITERACY ▶ *pages T248a–T253*

LESSON 6
BASICS BOOKSHELF
pages T248a–T248f

Function
Listen to a Book

Vocabulary
- **T** The Body

Reading Strategies
Activate Prior Knowledge

Preview

Learning to Read
Predict Words

Critical Thinking and Comprehension
- **T** Relate Main Ideas and Details

LESSON 7
BASICS BOOKSHELF: COMPREHENSION
page T248

Function
Give Information

Learning Strategy
Use Graphic Organizers (main idea and detail diagram)

Critical Thinking and Comprehension
- **T** Identify Main Idea and Details

LESSON 8
HIGH FREQUENCY WORDS
page T249

Learning to Read
- **T** Recognize High Frequency Words

LESSON 9
PHONICS
pages T250a–T250d

Learning to Read
Build Oral Vocabulary

Develop Phonemic Awareness

- **T** Associate Sounds and Symbols: Variant Vowels and Consonants

- **T** Use Letter Patterns to Decode Words

Blend Sounds to Decode Words

LESSON 10
READING AND SPELLING
pages T250–T251

Learning to Read
Develop Phonemic Awareness

- **T** Associate Sounds and Symbols: Variant Vowels and Consonants

- **T** Use Letter Patterns to Decode Words

Spelling
- **T** Words with Variant Vowels and Consonants

LESSON 11
INDEPENDENT READING
pages T252–T253

Functions
Read a Selection

Give Information

Learning to Read
- **T** Recognize High Frequency Words

- **T** Decode Words (variant vowels and consonants)

Reading Strategies
Activate Prior Knowledge

Set a Purpose for Reading

Relate to Personal Experience

Critical Thinking and Comprehension
- **T** Relate Main Idea and Details

Writing
Giving Information

12–13

LANGUAGE ACROSS THE CURRICULUM ▶ *pages T254–T255*

LESSON 12
LANGUAGE ARTS: PARAGRAPHS
page T254

Functions
Give Information

Write

Vocabulary
Paragraphs

Research Skills and Learning Strategies
Use Graphic Organizers (main-idea diagram)

Critical Thinking and Comprehension
- **T** Relate Main Idea and Details

Writing
Paragraph

LESSON 13
WRITING PROJECT: CLASS BOOK ON HEALTHY HABITS
page T255

Functions
Give Information

Write

Vocabulary
- **T** Sports
- **T** The Body

Learning Strategies and Critical Thinking
Relate to Personal Experience

Plan

Generate and Organize Ideas

Writing
Paragraph for a Healthy-Habits Book

Use Graphic Organizers (main-idea diagram)

- **T** Relate Main Idea and Details

Self-Assess

I Personal Best

T = Objective Tested on Unit Test

ASSESSMENT OPTIONS

The **Teacher's Edition** and the **Assessment Handbook** include these comprehensive assessment tools:

▶ **Ongoing, Informal Assessment**
Check for understanding and achieve closure for every lesson with the targeted questions and activities in the **Close and Assess** boxes in your Teacher's Edition.

▶ **Decoding Progress Check**
These word lists for each unit provide a quick way to check on mastery of the phonics or word structure skills taught in the unit.

▶ **Language Acquisition Assessments**
To verify students' ability to use the language functions and grammar structures taught in Units 13–15, conduct these performance assessments.

▶ **Unit Test in Standardized Test Format**
This multiple-choice test measures students' cumulative understanding of the skills and language developed in Units 13–15.

▶ **Self- and Peer-Assessment**
Students use the Self-Assessment Form to evaluate their own work and develop learning strategies appropriate to their needs. Students offer feedback to their classmates with the Peer-Assessment Form.

▶ **Writing Assessment/Portfolio Opportunities**
You can evaluate students' writing in the Writing Projects using the Writing Progress Checklist. Then collaborate with students to choose work for their portfolios.

UNITS 13–15 ASSESSMENT OPPORTUNITIES

	Assessment Handbook Pages
Decoding Progress Check	1a
Language Acquisition Assessments	34
Units 13–15 Test	35–40
Self-Assessment Form	41
Peer-Assessment Form	50
Writing Progress Checklist	51
Portfolio Evaluation Form	52

RELATED RESOURCES

Wilma Unlimited
by Kathleen Krull
The life story of Wilma Rudolph, who overcame polio as a child and won three gold medals in the 1960 Summer Olympics. (Harcourt)
Theme Book: Read Aloud

For the Love of the Game
by Eloise Greenfield
Poetic text conveys how basketball legend Michael Jordan inspires two young children to reach for their dreams. (HarperCollins)
Language Development: Present Tense Verbs

Sports
by Tim Hammond
Labeled photographs define the clothing, equipment, players, and rules of many different team, target, and court sports. (Knopf)
Vocabulary: Sports

My Soccer Book
by Gail Gibbons
Summarizes a soccer game, with diagrams showing the playing field and players. (HarperCollins)
Easy Reading

100 Unforgettable Moments in the Summer Olympics
by Bob Italia
Articles about the trials and triumphs of the Summer Olympics' greatest stars, such as Wilma Rudolph and Greg Louganis. (ABDO)
Language Development: Subject and Object Pronouns

UNIT 15 **LESSON 1**

INTRODUCE UNIT 15: PERSONAL BEST

OBJECTIVES

Concepts and Vocabulary:
🅣 The Body; 🅣 Sports
Viewing: Interpret a Visual Image
Learning Strategies: Preview; Build Background; Use Graphic Organizers (graph)
Research Skills: Conduct an Experiment
Representing: Graph
Critical Thinking:
Analyze Information; Draw Conclusions

START WITH A COMMON EXPERIENCE

1. **Introduce "Personal Best"** Read the unit title. Explain that it means "the best you have ever done," and is often said about sports. A runner's personal best is his or her fastest time in a race; a gymnast's personal best might be winning a competition. Ask volunteers to share personal bests they have reached.

2. **Take Your Pulse** Read the activity directions. Explain: *Your pulse is the beat of your heart as it pushes blood through your body. You can feel the beats at your neck or your wrist.*

   Model taking your pulse by holding two fingers at a wrist and counting the beats aloud for one minute. Then help students complete the activity. Provide sentence frames:

   > At rest, my heart rate is _____ beats per minute.
   >
   > After exercise, my heart rate is _____ beats per minute.

3. **Study a Data Chart** Go over the heart-rate chart and discuss how it reflects students' observations: *Exercise makes the heart beat faster.*

   Conduct an experiment to see how different exercises affect the heart rate. Have a few volunteers do activities such as walking, running in place, and push-ups. Then display the results on a line graph, with a different color for each person. Discuss the results.

REACHING ALL STUDENTS

HOME CONNECTION

Family Fitness Survey Work with the class to brainstorm a list of activities people do to stay physically fit. (walking, biking, sports, etc.) Then have them survey a few family members to discuss their fitness habits. Students can take notes and share the information with the class: *My cousin lifts weights every night for 20 minutes. My sister plays softball at the park every Saturday.* Discuss how exercise helps keep the body healthy.

T242 Unit 15 | Personal Best

Surfers and other athletes work hard.
Their hearts beat fast. How is your heart?
Sit in a chair and take your pulse.
Hop on one foot for 20 seconds.
Then take your pulse again.
What do you notice?

In This Unit

Vocabulary
- The Body
- Sports

Language Functions
- Ask for and Give Information
- Express Thanks

Patterns and Structures
- Present Tense Verbs
- Pronouns

Reading
- Phonics: Variant Vowels and Consonants
- Comprehension: Relate Main Idea and Details (main-idea diagram)

Writing
- Facts
- Thank-You Speech
- Paragraph for a Healthy-Habits Book

Content Area Connection
- Language Arts (how to build a paragraph)

243

PREVIEW THE UNIT

4 Look for Activities and Information on Sports and the Body Leaf through the unit, previewing activities students will do, for example:

page 244—learning a chant about the different systems that make the body work

page 248—listening to the Bookshelf book (Display a copy of the book.)

page 252—reading about a Special Olympics state competition

page 255—writing a healthy-habits book

Also ask students to look for information on sports and the body. Point out the photos and illustrations on pages 244–248 and page 252, for example. Discuss how people work toward their personal best in sports. Then sum up what the preview reveals: *Sports are one way to keep healthy. You have to practice to reach your "personal best."*

5 Set Your Goals Start a class mind map on the different areas in which students can strive for a "personal best." Suggest a few categories and give examples. Then prompt students for pictures or words to add, and have them act out and describe other ideas for you to write. Talk together about what different measures might set a personal best in each case.

CLOSE AND ASSESS

Ask students to tell or show you something they are interested in learning in this unit.

UNIT 15 Mind Map

School
1st place in science fair

Character
being responsible
helping others
setting goals

Personal Best

Sports
winning the basketball championship
running a mile in 10 minutes

Other Activities
piano
painting

Technology Support
See **Inspiration** Visual Learning software for support in creating mind maps.

Unit Launch **T243**

UNIT 15 LESSON 2
LANGUAGE DEVELOPMENT: THE BODY

OBJECTIVES

Functions: Listen Actively; Repeat Spoken Language; Recite; Ask for and Give Information
Concepts and Vocabulary: 🅣 The Body
Writing: 🅣 Facts

INTRODUCE

1. **Listen and Chant** Play "Busy Body" on the **Language Tape/CD**. Students will listen and follow along with the words, echo the lines, then chime in using first a soft and then a loud voice. *(Tape 8A, CD 3 Track 7)*

2. **Learn Words for the Body** Read the vocabulary chart for "The Body" and have students match the words to the correct illustrations. Ask questions to check understanding: *What do your lungs do? What helps you move? Where is your stomach?*

PRACTICE

3. **Conduct "Express Yourself"** Model how to ask for and give information. Have partners complete the activity.

   How to Ask for and Give Information
   - Use a question word to ask for information: *What do the lungs do?*
   - To answer, think about or look up the information needed. Then give your answer: *The lungs help you breathe.*

APPLY

4. **Write Facts About the Body** Encourage students to check their answers with a partner. Distribute Partner Checklist 15 on page T310.
   ▶ Language Practice Book page 116

CLOSE AND ASSESS

Write the names of body parts on separate slips of paper. Distribute the slips and ask questions about the body: *What body part senses feelings?* (nerves) The student with the correct answer holds up the slip and responds.

T244 Unit 15 | Personal Best

VOCABULARY: THE BODY
Body Basics

Listen and chant.

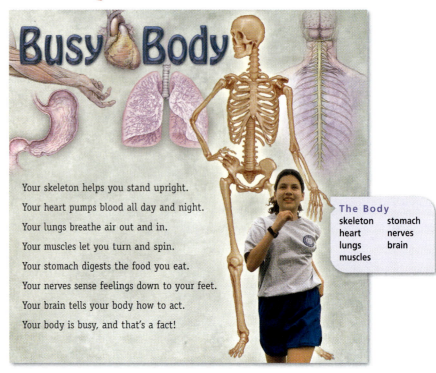

Your skeleton helps you stand upright.
Your heart pumps blood all day and night.
Your lungs breathe air out and in.
Your muscles let you turn and spin.
Your stomach digests the food you eat.
Your nerves sense feelings down to your feet.
Your brain tells your body how to act.
Your body is busy, and that's a fact!

The Body
skeleton   stomach
heart   nerves
lungs   brain
muscles

EXPRESS YOURSELF ▶ Ask for and Give Information

Ask a partner a question about each of these parts of the body. Answer your partner's questions in complete sentences.

1. skeleton   3. lungs   5. stomach
2. heart   4. muscles   6. brain

Example: 1. What does the skeleton do?
It supports your body and protects the heart and lungs.

Sample Responses
Students should use information they know and information from the chant to complete this exercise.

WRITE FACTS ABOUT THE BODY ✏️

7.–10. Write 4 facts about the body.   Example: 7. Muscles help you move.

244 Unit 15 | Personal Best

REACHING ALL STUDENTS

Language Development
ASK FOR INFORMATION

Provide practice writing questions. Have small groups write a line from "Busy Body" on a sentence strip; for example: *Your skeleton helps you stand upright.* Cut the strip into word cards, then add cards for these words and phrases: *How does, How do, What does, What do, does, do, help, you,* and a question mark. Help students rearrange the word cards to write as many questions as they can: *What does the skeleton do? How does your skeleton help you? How do you stand upright?*

Language Practice Book page 116

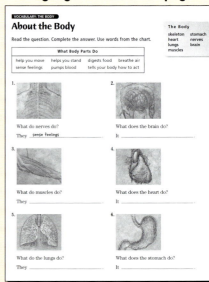

PRESENT TENSE VERBS

Our Workout Routine

Use **present tense verbs** to tell what happens all the time.

We always **exercise** to stay healthy.

Every morning we **run** two miles.

We **stretch** before every run.

Every day we **make** our bodies strong.

BUILD SENTENCES

Say a sentence for each picture below. Choose words from each column.

Each Every	day morning afternoon Saturday week month	I the boys the girls the people the athletes they	bike. exercise. play. practice. run. swim.

Example: **1.** Every afternoon the girls practice.

1.
2.
3.
4.

WRITE SENTENCES

5.–8. Tell a partner about some sport or exercise you do all the time. Work together to write 4 sentences about it.

Example: **5.** Every day I play basketball.

Sample Responses
Students should use present tense in their responses.

Language Development **245**

Language Practice Book page 117

UNIT 15 **LESSON 3**

LANGUAGE DEVELOPMENT: PRESENT TENSE VERBS

OBJECTIVES

Function: Give Information
Patterns and Structures:
• Present Tense Verbs
Writing: Sentences

INTRODUCE

1 Learn About Present Tense Verbs
Read the page title and introduction. Direct students' attention to the photo, and read the example sentences. Ask students to identify the time word or phrase in each sentence that means "all the time." (always, Every morning, every run, Every day)

Encourage volunteers to describe exercises they do regularly. Display the sentences and have students identify the present tense verbs.

• I **exercise** every morning.
• We always **run** laps on Fridays.

PRACTICE

2 Build Sentences Use the Example to model building the sentence by using a word or phrase from each column. Then call on students to say sentences for each photo.

APPLY

3 Write Sentences In the Example, point out that the phrase *Every day* signals that the action happens all the time. Remind students to use time words and present tense verbs in each sentence.

▶ **Language Practice Book** page 117

CLOSE AND ASSESS

Have volunteers read a sentence they wrote. The group repeats the sentence and names the present tense verb.

Language Development **T245**

UNIT 15 **LESSON 4**

LANGUAGE DEVELOPMENT: SPORTS

OBJECTIVES

Functions: Listen Actively; Express Thanks
Concepts and Vocabulary: 🅣 Sports
Speaking: Express Thanks
Writing: Thank-You Speech

INTRODUCE

1. **Learn Sports Words** Read the title and explain: *People who play sports are called* athletes. *These photos show different athletes.* Go over the captions and labels together.

2. **Chart Sports Words** Work with students to sort the words. Add terms as necessary to complete the chart.

Sport	Players Wear	Players Use
football	uniforms, helmets	football
tennis	shorts, head bands	rackets, tennis balls

PRACTICE

3. **Conduct "Who's Talking?"** Play "Who's Talking?" on the **Language Tape/CD** to model how to express thanks. Replay as necessary. Ask volunteers to identify the athletes who are talking and to role-play the scenes.

Tape 8A
CD 3
Track 5

APPLY

4. **Write a Thank-You Speech** Explain that people give thank-you speeches when they win awards or contests. Have students choose a sport to represent. Then invite them to give their speeches at an "awards banquet."

▶ **Language Practice Book** page 118

CLOSE AND ASSESS

Ask students to choose a sport and tell what they know about it. Add the information to the chart above.

T246 Unit 15 | Personal Best

VOCABULARY: SPORTS

Meet the Athletes

She **bowls**.

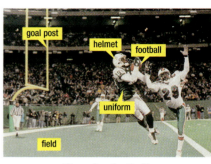

They play **football**.

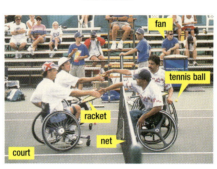

They play **tennis**.

She plays **basketball**.

WHO'S TALKING? ▶ EXPRESS THANKS

1.–3. Listen.
Who is talking? Point to the correct athlete. Act out the roles you hear on the tape. Thank your teammate, coach, or another player.

Answers:
1. the bowler
2. the woman who plays tennis
3. the tennis player without a hat

WRITE A THANK-YOU SPEECH

4. You are a champion athlete and just won an award. Write a thank-you speech. Tell who helped you play the sport so well.

Example: 4. Thank you for the basketball trophy. My coach helped me a lot. I also want to thank my teammates. We have the best basketball team in the city!

246 Unit 15 | Personal Best

REACHING ALL STUDENTS

Vocabulary

SPORTS

Word Search Provide small groups with highlighters, newspaper sports pages, and sports magazines. Challenge them to find and highlight as many sports words as they can within a time limit. Then have students read their words, as you chart them by sport. Volunteers can explain or pantomime meanings as necessary.

Language Practice Book page 118

PRONOUNS
Watch Them Play

Pronunciation of Names
Farnez — far **nez**
Hari Amrit — har **ē** **ahm** rit

Use the correct **pronoun** when you talk about a person, place, or thing.

goalie

Use these pronouns to tell who does the action.

| I | you | he | she | it | we | they |

He kicked the ball.

Use these pronouns after an action verb or after a word like *to*, *for*, or *with*.

| me | you | him | her | it | us | them |

- The goalie missed **it**.
- The goalie kicks the ball to **her**.

BUILD SENTENCES

Say each sentence. Add the correct pronoun.

Example: 1. Our coach talked to us at half time. She gave us a plan.

1. Our coach talked to us at half time. ___(**She**/Her)___ gave us a plan.
2. Randy got ready. I passed the ball to ___(he/**him**)___.
3. ___(**He**/Him)___ missed the ball!
4. The other team got the ball. ___(**They**/Them)___ raced away.
5. We chased ___(they/**them**)___.
6. Our goalie got the ball. She kicked it to ___(**I**/me)___.
7. I saw Farnez. I shouted to ___(she/**her**)___.
8. Another player knocked ___(she/**her**)___ down!
9. I had no choice. ___(**I**/me)___ shot at the goal.
10. We scored! The crowd cheered for ___(we/**us**)___.

WRITE SENTENCES

1.–15. Write 5 sentences. Tell about a sport you like to watch. Use at least 3 pronouns.

Sample Responses
Check that students use the appropriate form of the appropriate pronoun in each sentence.

Example: 11. I watch hockey with Hari Amrit.
12. She likes the team from San Jose.

Language Development 247

Language Practice Book page 119

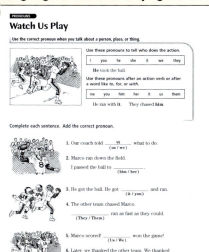

Multi-Level Strategies
LANGUAGE DEVELOPMENT

LITERATE IN L1 Subject and object pronouns can be problematic for English language learners. For example, Korean does not distinguish between subject and object pronouns. Chinese, Hmong, and other languages do not indicate gender for third person singular.

To practice pronouns, provide sentence strips and have students replace the nouns with pronouns; for example: **Melissa** kicks **the ball** to **José**. (**She** kicks **it** to **him**.)

UNIT 15 LESSON 5
LANGUAGE DEVELOPMENT: PRONOUNS

OBJECTIVES
Function: Give Information
Concepts and Vocabulary: ⊤ Sports
Patterns and Structures: ⊤ Pronouns
Writing: ⊤ Sentences

INTRODUCE

1. **Learn About Pronouns** Read the title and introduction. Remind students that pronouns take the place of nouns. For students who are ready, you can introduce the terms *subject pronouns* and *object pronouns*. Then use a chart to show the difference:

Subject Pronouns	Object Pronouns
I	me
you	you
he	him
she	her
it	it
we	us
they	them

PRACTICE

2. **Build Sentences** Work through the Example, modeling how to look back at the skills box or chart to determine the correct pronoun.

APPLY

3. **Write Sentences** Read the example sentences and have volunteers list the pronouns they recognize. Then help students write their own sentences.

▶ **Language Practice Book** page 119

CLOSE AND ASSESS

Have volunteers read their sentences. Ask students to identify the pronouns.

Language Development T247

UNIT 15 **LESSON 6**

LANGUAGE AND LITERACY: THE BASICS BOOKSHELF

OBJECTIVES
Concepts and Vocabulary: 🅣 The Body
Listening: Listen to a Preview
Reading Strategies:
Activate Prior Knowledge; Preview

BUILD LANGUAGE AND VOCABULARY

1. **Teach "Words to Know"** Treat page 2 as a review of the body parts introduced in Lakeside School (see pages T28–T29). Call out the name of a body part and have students show you the label.

   If you are introducing body parts, identify the picture, then point to the body part on your own body and give a sentence: *This is my arm.*

   Introduce the body systems on page 3. Explain: *These pictures show the inside of the body.* Refer to pages 10 and 14 so students can see where the heart and lungs are located.

2. **Play "I Spy"** Give a clue, such as: *I spy something that is part of the foot. What is it?* (toe) Have students point to the picture. Then invite volunteers to call out more clues.

PREPARE TO READ

3. **Think About What You Know** Provide an outline of the body. Take dictation as students identify the body parts.

4. **Preview** Play the Audio Walk-Through for *Body Works* on the **Selection Tape/CD** to give students the overall idea of the story.

   Tape 8A / CD 3 Track 5

CLOSE AND ASSESS

Have partners write ten body parts on separate self-stick notes. Then have them page through the book and label the photographs of athletes.

T248a Unit 15 | Personal Best

Body Works
by Janine Wheeler

Summary This science essay uses simple text, photos, and diagrams to introduce basic systems and organs of the human body including: the skeleton, muscles, heart, blood, lungs, nervous system, brain, and the senses. Additional information focuses on the importance of developing healthy habits at an early age.

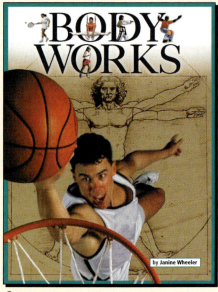
Cover

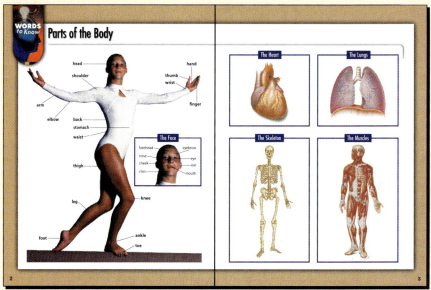
Pages 2–3

Multi-Level Strategies
LITERACY SUPPORT

PRELITERATE **Concepts of Print: Use the Table of Contents and Glossary**
Point to page 5 and say: *The table of contents shows what is in the book. It lists the topics and the pages where you can find them.* Point out the entry for the lungs and its location on page 14. Then have the class turn to page 14 as you point out the corresponding heading and page number. Ask questions to make sure students can use the table of contents: *Where can you read about the brain?* (page 18) *What subject is covered on page 12?* (blood)

Have students turn to the glossary on page 24. Say: *A glossary tells what words mean.* Explain how to use alphabetical order to find a word. Then read aloud the definition for *exercise*. Point out the sentence in italic type that shows how the word is used. Check to make sure students can use the glossary: *Show me the entry for* oxygen. *Show me the definition. Show me the sample sentence.*

Body Works

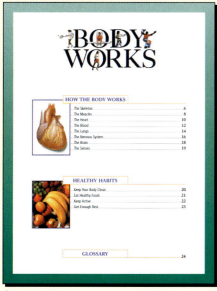

Page 5

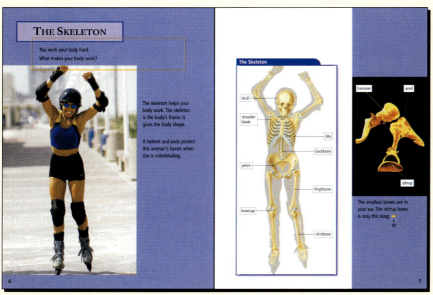

Pages 6–7

Strategies for Comprehensible Input

PAGE	STORY LANGUAGE	STRATEGY OPTIONS
6	You work your body hard.	**Explain:** You make your body work hard every day.
	What makes your body work?	**Restate:** How does your body move?
	helmet, pads	**Point to the pictures.**
	protect this woman's bones	**Restate:** keep her bones from getting hurt.
7	ear	**Gesture:** Point to your ear.

Language and Literacy **T248b**

UNIT 15 **LESSON 6,** CONTINUED

LANGUAGE AND LITERACY: THE BASICS BOOKSHELF

OBJECTIVES

Function: Listen to a Book

Critical Thinking and Comprehension:
T Relate Main Ideas and Details

READ AND THINK TOGETHER

1. **Read Aloud** On your first reading of the book, use the "Strategies for Comprehensible Input" that appear at the bottom of pages T248b, T248d, and T248f.

2. **Read and Map: Identify Main Idea and Details** Set up a diagram like the one below, but with only the bold labels in each box. Say: *The* main idea *is the most important idea in a section of the book. The* details *give more information about the main idea.*

   Read pages 6–7 aloud. Then think aloud as you model filling in the first section: *Page 6 says that the skeleton helps your body work. This is the main idea of the section. I'll write it in the top box. Next, I'll look for details that tell about the skeleton. I will write the details in the small boxes.*

   A sample diagram appears below for The Skeleton section on pages 6–7. As you continue to read through the book, pause to make diagrams for these sections:

   • pages 8–9: The Muscles
   • pages 12–13: The Blood
   • pages 14–15: The Lungs

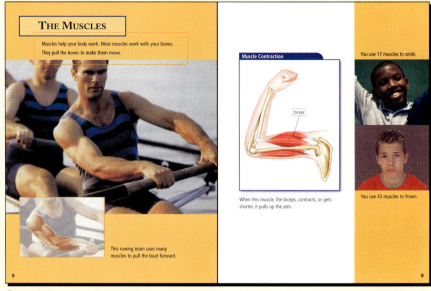
Pages 8–9

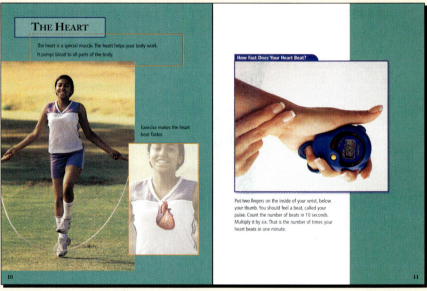
Pages 10–11

Main Idea and Detail Diagram for *Body Works*

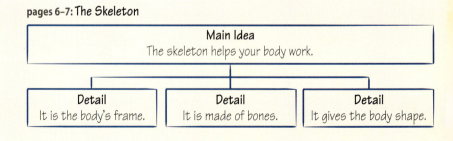

Technology Support
See **Inspiration** Visual Learning software for support in creating main idea and detail diagram.

T248c Unit 15 | Personal Best

THE BASICS BOOKSHELF

Body Works, CONTINUED

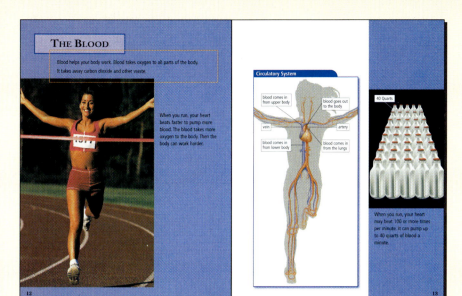

Pages 12–13

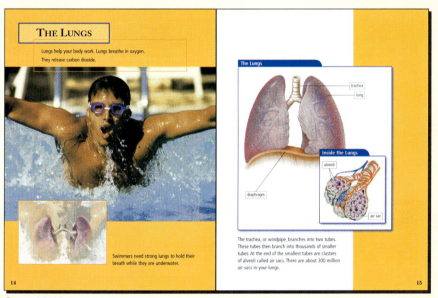

Pages 14–15

Strategies for Comprehensible Input

PAGE	STORY LANGUAGE	STRATEGY OPTIONS
8	forward	**Demonstrate:** Hold your hand in front of you and point forward.
9	smile, frown	**Demonstrate the expressions.**
11	pulse	**Demonstrate:** Find your pulse at your wrist or neck.
	count	**Demonstrate:** Count the beats aloud.
	multiply	**Demonstrate:** Do the multiplication on the board.
13	40 quarts	**Point to the picture.**
14	breathe, release	**Demonstrate:** Take a few slow breaths. As you breathe in, move your hand toward your nose and down. As you breathe out, reverse the motion.
15	branches into	**Restate:** divides into; becomes

Language and Literacy T248d

UNIT 15 **LESSON 6,** CONTINUED

LANGUAGE AND LITERACY: THE BASICS BOOKSHELF

OBJECTIVES
Functions: Listen to a Book; Repeat Spoken Language (echo reading)
Learning to Read: Predict Words

READ AND THINK TOGETHER, CONTINUED

3 Conduct Interactive Readings
Choose from these options:

- **Echo reading** Play the recording of *Body Works* on the **Selection Tape/CD**. Pause the tape after the introduction to each section and have students echo it. *(Tape 8A / CD 3 Track 6)*

- **Predict words** As you read aloud the book, pause before key words and phrases. Ask students to supply missing words such as:

page 6	work
page 8	bones
page 9	arm
page 10	blood
page 12	waste
page 14	oxygen
page 16	brain
page 18	body systems
page 19	touch
page 21	vitamins
page 22	muscles

CLOSE AND ASSESS
Distribute cards with one main idea or detail per card. Have students holding main idea cards find the corresponding detail card holders. Then have the group read their cards to the class.

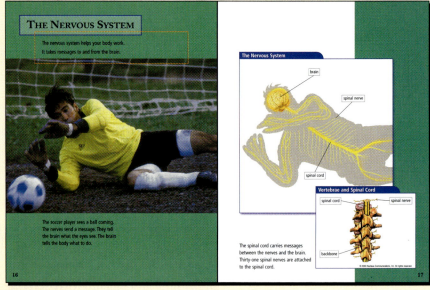
Pages 16–17

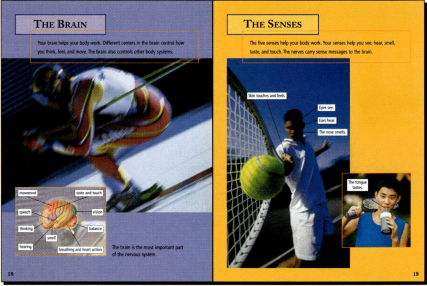
Pages 18–19

Multi-Level Strategies
LITERACY SUPPORT

LITERATE IN L1 **Read with a Partner/ Make a Healthy Habits Poster**
After students have participated in the interactive readings, encourage them to read the story with a partner. Distribute the Partner Prompts on page T311 to help partners work together to identify unfamiliar words and unlock their meanings, then read the text to each other. After the partner reading, ask students to draw themselves doing a healthy activity. Provide a sentence frame: *I _____ because it is healthy.*

INTERRUPTED SCHOOLING **Identify Main Idea and Details** To anchor understanding of the skill, explain that the main idea is often found near the beginning of the page. Point out the main idea sentence on page 6: *The skeleton helps your body work.* To help students find details, ask: *How does the skeleton help your body work?* Point out main ideas in a few other sections and ask questions to help students locate the details. Then ask students to find the main idea and details in additional sections.

T248e Unit 15 | Personal Best

Body Works, CONTINUED

Pages 20–21

Pages 22–23

Page 24

Strategies for Comprehensible Input

Page	Story Language	Strategy Options
16	It takes messages to and from the brain.	**Restate:** It tells the brain what you need.
17	spinal cord	**Point to the picture.**
19	see, hear, smell, taste, and touch	**Demonstrate:** Demonstrate using each of the senses.
20	healthy habits	**Explain:** A habit is something you do all the time. A healthy habit is something you do to help your body.
21	bottom, top	**Point to the bottom and top of the picture.**
22	strengthens	**Explain:** When you strengthen something, you make it stronger.
23	quiet	**Demonstrate:** Put your finger to your lips and say *shhh*.

Language and Literacy T248f

UNIT 15 LESSON 7

LANGUAGE AND LITERACY: THE BASICS BOOKSHELF

OBJECTIVES
Function: Give Information
Learning Strategy: Use Graphic Organizers (main idea and detail diagram)
Critical Thinking and Comprehension:
🎯 Identify Main Idea and Details

CHECK COMPREHENSION

1 Make a Main Idea and Detail Diagram Remind students that a main idea and detail diagram gives information about the most important ideas in a section of the book.

Have students review pages 6–7. Then read aloud the directions for Steps 1 and 2, pausing for students to add information to their diagrams.

Then form at least three small groups. Have each group work together to make diagrams for the other sections noted in Step 3.

2 Share Information from the Book Write the main idea of each section on chart paper, one main idea per page. Post the four pages around the room. Assign a group to each section. Have them add the supporting details to the chart and then tell the class what they learned from their section about the body.

CLOSE AND ASSESS

Ask students to complete this sentence: *A main idea and detail diagram shows _____.*

COMPREHENSION: RELATE MAIN IDEA AND DETAILS

Read and Think Together

Work in a group. Make diagrams to show the main ideas and details in *Body Works*. Follow these steps.

1 Read pages 6–7 of *Body Works*. What is the most important idea in this section? Write it inside a box, like this:

> **Main Idea**
> The skeleton helps your body work.

2 What details in these pages help to support, or explain, the main idea? Write them in boxes connected to your main-idea box, like this:

> **Main Idea**
> The skeleton helps your body work.
>
> **Detail** – It is the body's frame.
> **Detail** – It is made of bones.
> **Detail** – It gives the body shape.

3 Make diagrams for more sections of *Body Works* to show the main idea and details.
   The Muscles   pages 8–9
   The Blood   pages 12–13
   The Lungs   pages 14–15

4 Use your completed diagrams to tell the class what you learned about the body.

Sample Responses

Main Idea for the Muscles:
Muscles help your body work.
Details:
Most muscles work with your bones. They pull bones to make them move.

Main Idea for the Blood:
Blood helps your body work.
Details:
Blood takes oxygen to all parts of the body.
It takes away carbon dioxide and other waste.
When you exercise, your heart pumps more blood to take more oxygen to your body.
Blood travels in veins and arteries.
Your heart can pump up to 40 quarts of blood a minute.

Main Idea for the Lungs:
Lungs help your body wor[k]
Details:
Lungs breathe in oxygen.
They release carbon dioxi[de]
The lungs have about 300 million air sacs.

248 Unit 15 | Personal Best

---

from **The Basics Bookshelf**

THEME BOOK

Learn about parts of the body and how to keep your body in good shape.

REACHING ALL STUDENTS

Language Development
MAKE AND SUBSTANTIATE AN EXCUSE

Role-Play Turn to page 23 in *Body Works*. Use this example to model how to make and substantiate an excuse:
I can't go to gym class today because I hurt my foot.

Use the chart to present other suitable language. Then pose scenarios and have students make and substantiate an excuse:

- You planned a basketball game, but you must go to a wedding.
- You agreed to jog with a friend, but you have to babysit.

How to Make and Substantiate an Excuse

I cannot _____ because I _____.

I'm sorry, but I can't _____.
I have to _____.

I won't be able to _____ because I must _____.

I would like to _____, but I need to _____ instead.

T248 Unit 15 | Personal Best

HIGH FREQUENCY WORDS

Words to Know

REVIEW WORDS YOU KNOW

Read the words aloud. Which word goes in each sentence?

along	also
into	again
any	very

1. They walk _along_ the trail.
2. It goes _into_ the mountains.
3. Their packs are _very_ big.

LEARN TO READ

Learn new words.

friends	My **friends** and I love to hike.
asked	"Will you help me put on my pack?" **asked** Celia.
walked	We **walked** to the start of the trail.
trees	We passed pines, oaks, and other **trees**.
air	We breathed the crisp mountain **air**.
talked	We **talked** about the hike.
if	"**If** you feel tired, stop and rest," I said.
even	"Drink water **even** if you're not thirsty."
while	We drank water **while** we walked.
such	I have **such** a good time when I hike!

How to Learn a New Word
- Look at the word.
- Listen to the word.
- Listen to the word in a sentence. What does it mean?
- Say the word.
- Spell the word.
- Say the word again.

WORD WORK

4.–13. Make a map for each new word. Write the word in the center. Complete the other boxes.

Example: 4.

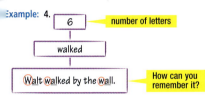

Language and Literacy **249**

Reading Practice Book page 92

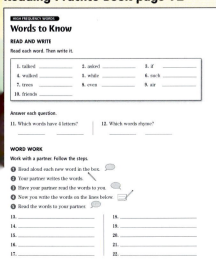

Reading Fluency

RECOGNIZE HIGH FREQUENCY WORDS

To build automaticity with the new high frequency words:

- Have small groups make word cards and lay them face down in a row. Students turn over two cards at random and then try to use those words in a sentence; for example: *I walked under the trees.* Students can replace a card if they can't create a sentence from the original pair.

- Students can cut the letters of their word cards apart and scramble them. Encourage groups to compete to see who can reassemble the words the fastest.

UNIT 15 LESSON 8

LANGUAGE AND LITERACY: HIGH FREQUENCY WORDS

OBJECTIVES

Learning to Read:
- Recognize High Frequency Words

REVIEW WORDS

1 Review Known High Frequency Words Have the group read aloud the words in the green box. Listen for words students cannot read automatically and use the steps in the yellow box to reteach those words. Then have students look at the photo. Read each cloze sentence. Reread each sentence and pause for students to silently read the two words to the left of the sentence. Tell students to choose the word that goes in the sentence and tells about the picture.

INTRODUCE NEW WORDS

2 Learn High Frequency Words Use the High Frequency Word Script on page T326 to lead students through the steps in the yellow box.

PRACTICE

3 Conduct "Word Work" Use the Example to model how to make a word map. Point out that the letters *wal* in the words in the last box are clues to the spelling of *walked*. As another memory aid, students can visualize a crosswalk sign they have seen on the street and draw a sign with the word *Walk* inside. Have groups complete Items 4–13. Ask volunteers to share their maps.

APPLY

4 Read Words in Context Students will read high frequency words in context in the sentences on page 251 and the passage on page 252.

▶ **Reading Practice Book** page 92

CLOSE AND ASSESS

Call out the high frequency words one at a time. Have students point to them and spell the words as a group.

Language and Literacy **T249**

UNIT 15 LESSON 9

LANGUAGE AND LITERACY: PHONICS

OBJECTIVES
Learning to Read: Build Oral Vocabulary; Develop Phonemic Awareness; T Use Letter Patterns to Decode Words

TEACH HARD AND SOFT c

1. **Build Oral Vocabulary** Display Transparency 73. Work through these sentences with students:
   - *He lives in a big ____.* (city)
   - *Who won the ____?* (contest)
   - *The rock ____ was great.* (concert)
   - *Stand in the middle, or ____, of the room.* (center)
   - *We race around the orange traffic ____ in the gym.* (cones)

2. **Develop Phonemic Awareness and Contrast the Sounds of c** Remove the transparency and conduct the oral activities in Steps 1 and 2 of the script.

3. **Use Letter Patterns to Decode Words** Display Transparency 73 again. Work through Step 3 of the script.

CLOSE AND ASSESS
Display the words *contest* and *city*. Ask: Why does *contest* have a hard c sound? Why does *city* have a soft c sound?

Word Families
-AP AND -ICE

Materials: Letter Tiles

A large number of words can be generated from a few rhyming phonograms. Use letter tiles to build the words in dark type. Then change tiles to build other words in the -ap, and -ice families. Have students make a list of the words. Make sure students understand their meanings. Then ask them to read the words on their list and to identify the shared ending.

cap	**nice**
tap	mice
map	rice
clap	price
wrap	slice

T250a Unit 15 | Personal Best

Transparency 73: Hard and Soft c

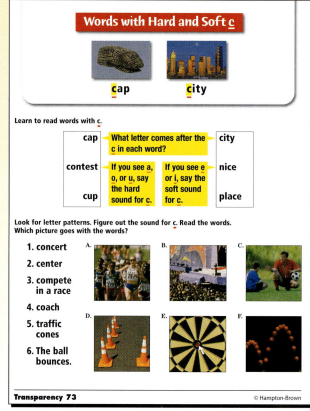

▼ Script for Transparency 73

Words with Hard and Soft c

1. Develop Phonemic Awareness
Isolate Beginning Sounds/Identify Sounds Say: *Listen to this word:* cap. *What is its first sound?* (/k/) *Now listen to this word:* city. *What is its first sound?* (/s/) *Tell me which sound, /k/ or /s/, you hear in these words:* cent, cup, coach, center, car.

2. Contrast Hard c and Soft c
Say: *The letter c is a consonant. It has a hard sound, /k/, and a soft sound, /s/. Say the names of the pictures with me:* cap, city. *What is the first sound you hear in* cap? (/k/) *Say /k/ with me. The hard sound of the letter c is /k/. What is the first sound you hear in* city? (/s/) *Say /s/ with me. The soft sound of the letter c is /s/.*

3. Use Letter Patterns to Decode Words
Look for Patterns Read the words in the column on the left, noting the hard *c* sound: /k/. Then use the question in the box to explore the spelling pattern: *What letter comes after the c in each word? Let's look: a comes after the c in* cap; *o comes after the c in* contest; *u comes after the c in* cup. *If you see a, o, or u after c, say the hard sound for c: /k/.* Then read the words on the right; note the soft *c* sound: /s/. Use the question again to explore the spelling pattern, pointing out that the letter i or e comes after the *c* in each word. Say: *If you see e or i after c, say the soft sound for c: /s/.* Ask: *What letter spells /k/ before e or i?* (k)

Summarize and Model the Strategy Say: *Look for patterns with c to help you read.* For Item 1, say: *This word has two consonants in between two vowels. I'll divide it into syllables between the n and c. I see a c in each syllable. The letter o comes after the first c, so I'll say the hard sound for c: /kon/. I see an e after the c in the second syllable, so that means the c is soft: /sûrt/. Blend the syllables* con-cert, *and say the word:* concert. *Then identify the picture that goes with* concert.

Have students do Items 2–6. Students should tell how they figured out the sound for c in each word, then read the word. For Item 5, tell students that the *c* in *traffic* has the hard sound /k/.

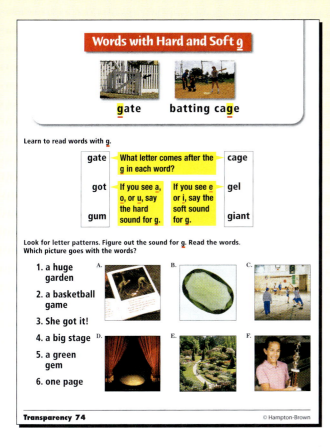

◀ Transparency 74: Hard and Soft g

▼ Script for Transparency 74

Words with Hard and Soft g

1. **Develop Phonemic Awareness**
   Isolate Beginning Sounds/Identify Sounds Say: *Listen to this word:* gate. *What is its first sound?* (/g/) *Say /g/ with me:* /g/. *Now listen to this word:* gentle. *What is its first sound?* (/j/) Then say: *Tell me which sound, /g/ or /j/, is in these words:* girl, gate, germ, gum, giant, goal, gentle, game, page, garden.

2. **Contrast Hard g and Soft g**
   Say: *The letter* g *is a consonant. It has a hard sound,* /g/, *and a soft sound,* /j/. *Say the names of the pictures with me:* gate, batting cage. *What is the first sound you hear in* gate? (/g/) *Say /g/ with me. The hard sound of the letter* g *is* /g/. *What is the last sound in* cage? (/j/) *Say /j/ with me. The soft sound of the letter* g *is* /j/.

3. **Use Letter Patterns to Decode Words**
   Look for Patterns Read the words in the column on the left, noting the hard g sound /g/. Then use the question in the box to explore the spelling pattern: *What letter comes after the* g *in each word? Let's look:* a *comes after the* g *in* gate; o *comes after the* g *in* got; u *comes after the* g *in* gum. *If you see* a, o, *or* u *after* g, *say the hard sound for* g: /g/. Then read the words in the column on the right; note the soft g sound /j/. Use the question again to explore the spelling pattern, pointing out that the letter e or i comes after the g in each word. Say: *If you see* e *or* i *after* g, *say the soft sound for* g: /j/.

   Summarize and Model the Strategy Say: *Look for patterns with* g *to help you read.* For huge in Item 1, say: *I see a* g *followed by the letter* e, *so I'll say the soft sound for* g: /hyōoj/, huge. For game in Item 2, say: *I see a* g *followed by* a, *so I'll say the hard sound for* g: /g ā m/, game.

   Practice Have students do Items 3–6. Students should tell how they figured out the sound for g in each word, then read the word.

OBJECTIVES
Learning to Read: Build Oral Vocabulary; Develop Phonemic Awareness; ❶ Use Letter Patterns to Decode Words

TEACH HARD AND SOFT g

1. **Build Oral Vocabulary** Display Transparency 74. Play a game of "I Spy," giving a series of clues until students find the picture you're describing. For example, for Item D say:

   • *I spy a big* **stage**. *People give plays and concerts on a* **stage**. *Right now, no one is on the big* **stage** *I see.*

   When students find the big stage, say: *Yes,* **this is a big stage** (point). Repeat to build context for the other words.

2. **Develop Phonemic Awareness and Contrast the Sounds of g** Remove the transparency and conduct the oral activities in Steps 1 and 2 of the script.

3. **Use Letter Patterns to Decode Words** Display Transparency 74 again. Work through Step 3 of the script.

CLOSE AND ASSESS
Display the words *games* and *stage*. Ask: *Why does* games *have a hard* g *sound? Why does* stage *have a soft* g *sound?*

▶ **Reading Practice Book** page 93 (hard and soft c and g)

Reading Practice Book page 93

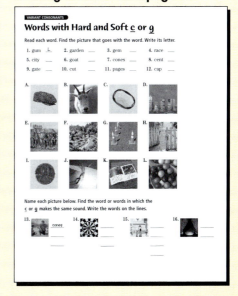

Language and Literacy **T250b**

UNIT 15 **LESSON 9,** CONTINUED

LANGUAGE AND LITERACY: PHONICS

OBJECTIVES

Learning to Read: Build Oral Vocabulary; Develop Phonemic Awareness; **T** Associate Sounds and Symbols /o͞o/ oo; Blend Sounds to Decode Words

TEACH VARIANT VOWELS: /o͝o/ oo

1 Build Oral Vocabulary Display Transparency 75. Talk through each picture to develop meaning for the words in the yellow boxes. For example, for Item 3, sit down and say:

- *These fans* (point) **stood up** (stand up) *at the game. They stood up* (repeat sitting and standing) *to clap for their team.*

2 Develop Phonemic Awareness Remove the transparency and conduct the oral activities in Step 1 of the Script for Transparency 75.

3 Read Words with /o͝o/ oo Display Transparency 75 again. Work through Steps 2 and 3 of the script.

CLOSE AND ASSESS

Display *good, stood, shook,* and *cook*. Call on students to read each word and identify the two letters that make the vowel sound /o͝o/.

Word Families

-OOK AND -OOD

Materials: Letter Tiles

A large number of words can be generated from a few rhyming phonograms. Use letter tiles to build the words in dark type. Then change tiles to build other words in the -*ook* and -*ood* families. Have students make a list of the words. Make sure students understand their meanings. Then ask them to read the words on their list and to identify the shared ending.

book	good
cook	hood
hook	stood
look	wood
took	

T250c Unit 15 | Personal Best

Transparency 75: ▶ **Variant Vowels** (*oo*)

▼ **Script for Transparency 75**

Words with oo

1. Develop Phonemic Awareness
Isolate/Match Medial /o͝o/ Say: *Listen to the sound in the middle of these words:* book, good, cook. *What is the sound?* (/o͝o/) *Say the words with me:* book, good, cook. *Now raise your hand each time you hear the sound* /o͝o/. *Say these words:* hot, good, boot, book, lock, look, hook, luck, cookie.

2. Associate Sounds and Symbols
Point to the book on **Transparency 75**. Say: *This is a book. Say the word* book *with me.* Then point to the *oo* in *book* and say: *The letters* oo *make the vowel sound you hear in* book. *Say* /o͝o/ *with me:* /o͝o/.

3. Blend Sounds to Read Words
Model/Teach Model how to read the word *book*. Then have students blend the sounds with you. As you slide a finger slowly from left to right below *book*, say: *Let's blend the sounds together:* /bo͝ok/. *Now, let's say the whole word:* book.

Practice For Item 1, say: *Let's try that again. In this picture, there is a football and a hook, isn't there? Read the words with me.* (Point to the word *football*.) *You can see that this word is made up of two smaller words. Let's read the first word. Follow my finger as we blend the sounds:* /ffo͝ot/, *and say the word:* foot. *Now let's blend the sounds to read the second word:* /bôl/, ball. *Let's blend the two small words together* foot-ball, *and say the word:* football. Model blending the three sounds in *hook*. Then repeat for the other words, calling special attention to the following:

- For *clapped* in Item 3, remind students to cover the -*ed*, read the root word, and then blend the parts to read the word. Remind them that -*ed* can have three different sounds. Ask: *What is the sound of* -ed *in* clapped? (/t/)

- In Item 5, point to *sister*. Remind students to look for chunks they know to read long words. Have them divide the word, keeping the chunks *ter* together. Then have them blend the syllables and say the word. Repeat for *party*.

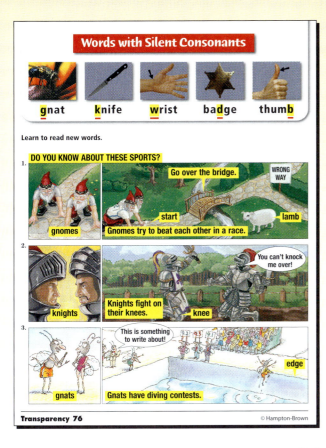

◀ **Transparency 76: Silent Consonants**

▼ **Script for Transparency 76**

Words with Silent Consonants

1. **Develop Phonemic Awareness**
   Isolate Beginning and Final Sounds Say: *Listen to the first sound in these words:* knife, gnome, new. *What is the sound?* (/n/) *Listen for the first sound in these words:* rest, write, wrong. *What is the sound?* (/r/) *Now listen for the last sound in these words:* judge, edge, bridge. *What is the sound?* (/j/) *What sound do you hear at the end of these words:* him, lamb, thumb? (/m/)

2. **Associate Sounds and Symbols**
   Point to the gnat on **Transparency 76**. Say: *This is a gnat. A gnat is a kind of bug, or insect. Say the word* gnat *with me.* Then point to the *gn* in *gnat* and say: *The letters* gn *make the sound* /n/ *you hear at the beginning of* gnat. *The consonant* g *is silent. Say* /n/ *with me:* /nnn/. Follow a similar procedure for *knife, wrist, badge,* and *thumb,* pointing out the silent consonant in each word.

3. **Blend Sounds to Read Words**
   Model/Teach Model how to read the word *gnat*. Then have students blend the sounds with you. Point to the letters *gn* in *gnat* and say: *Say the sound for* gn *with me:* /n/. Repeat for *a:* /a/. As you slide a finger below the letters *gna,* say: *Help me blend the two sounds:* /na/. Then point to the *t* and say: *Say the sound for* t *with me:* /t/. *Now let's blend the three sounds together* /nat/, *and say the word:* gnat. Follow a similar procedure for *wrist* and *thumb*. Before blending *knife,* point out the final *e* and ask students what sound the *i* makes. (/ī/). For *badge,* point out that the letters *dge* make the soft g, or /j/ sound, and the vowel sound is short *a*. Contrast the spelling of /j/ at the end of *badge* with its spelling at the end of *cage*. Explain the spelling rule: Use *ge* after a long vowel and *dge* after a short vowel.

   Practice Read aloud the question above Item 1, pausing for students to decode *know*. Ask: *How many sounds did you hear?* (2) *How many letters do you see?* (4) Emphasize that although the word has four letters, it has only two sounds: the letters *kn* make the sound /n/ and the letters *ow* make the vowel sound /ō/. Follow this procedure for other sentences.

OBJECTIVES

Learning to Read: Build Oral Vocabulary; Develop Phonemic Awareness; 🅣 Associate Sounds and Symbols /n/ gn, kn; /r/ wr; /j/ dge; /m/ mb; Blend Sounds to Decode Words

TEACH SILENT CONSONANTS

1. **Build Oral Vocabulary** Display Transparency 76. Talk through each picture to develop meaning for the words in the yellow boxes. For example, for Item 3, say:
   - *Here is the **edge** (point). The **edge** of something is the part where it begins or ends.*

2. **Develop Phonemic Awareness** Remove the transparency and conduct the oral activities in Step 1 of the Script for Transparency 76.

3. **Read Words with Silent Consonants** Display Transparency 76 again. Work through Steps 2 and 3 of the script.

CLOSE AND ASSESS

Display the words *gnat, knee, write, bridge,* and *lamb*. Call on students to read each word and identify the silent consonant.

▶ **Reading Practice Book** page 94 (variant vowels: *oo;* silent consonants)

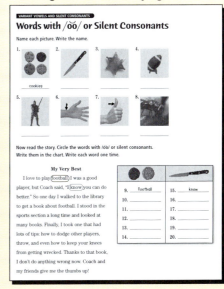

Reading Practice Book page 94

Language and Literacy **T250d**

UNIT 15 LESSON 10
LANGUAGE AND LITERACY: READING AND SPELLING

OBJECTIVES

Functions: Listen Actively; Repeat Spoken Language; Recite

Learning to Read: Develop Phonemic Awareness; 🅣 Associate Sounds and Symbols: /ŏŏ/ *oo*; /n/ *gn, kn*; /r/ *wr*; /j/ *dge*; /m/ *mb*; hard and soft *c* and *g*; 🅣 Use Letter Patterns to Decode Words

Spelling: 🅣 Words with Variant Vowels and Consonants

LISTEN AND LEARN
Tape 8A / CD 3 Track 9

1 Sing a Song Display Transparency 77 and play "Good Advice" on the **Language Tape/CD**. After students have listened and learned the song, they can sing it, pantomiming eating when they hear *eat* and running when they hear *run*.

DEVELOP PHONEMIC AWARENESS

2 Blend Sounds to Form a Word Say: *Listen to these sounds: /k/, /ā/, /j/. Say them with me: /k/, /ā/, /j/. Now blend them together. What word do they make?* (cage) Follow the same procedure with /s/, /i/, /t/, /ē/ (city). Continue with: /g/, /ŏŏ/, /d/ (good); /g/, /o/, /t/ (got); /k/, /ŏŏ/, /k/ (cook); /f/, /ā/, /s/ (face).

LOOK FOR LETTER PATTERNS

3 Identify the Vowel to Determine Hard or Soft *c* and *g* Sounds Read the rules and examples aloud. Then write these words on the board: *gum, cup, cent, age, cot, city, place, gel, camp*. Call on students to read the words and tell how they decided whether the word has a hard or soft *c* or *g* sound.

Afterwards, play the song again. Have students identify words with hard and soft *c* or *g*.

VARIANT VOWELS AND CONSONANTS

Reading and Spelling

LISTEN AND LEARN

Good Advice

If you want to feel great,
Here's my advice:
Eat healthy food
Such as corn, meat, and rice.

With ice cream and cake
Or too many snacks,
You'll be dragging your heels
As you run down the track.

LOOK FOR LETTER PATTERNS

When **c** comes before **a, o,** or **u**, it makes a hard sound.
Joe has a new baseball **c**ap.

When **g** comes before **a, o,** or **u**, it makes a hard sound.
He **g**ot it!

When **c** comes before **e** or **i**, it makes a soft sound.
Look at Dawn's fa**c**e mask.

When **g** comes before **e** or **i**, it usually makes a soft sound.
Dawn swings the bat in the batting ca**g**e.

250 Unit 15 | Personal Best ▶ Transparencies 73–77

REACHING ALL STUDENTS

Multi-Level Strategies
LITERACY SUPPORT

NON-ROMAN ALPHABET To anchor understanding of how to represent sounds in print, help students build words with soft and hard *c* or *g*. Display letter tiles *ca, ce, ci, ga, ge* on the overhead. Dictate each of the following words and ask students to supply the missing letters to build the word: **cap**, ni**ce**, **ci**ty, **ga**te, a**ge**.

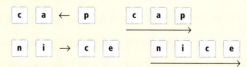

PRELITERATE Use Transparencies 73–76. Cover a word at the top, such as *book*. Point to the picture and say the name. Then have students spell it sound by sound. Say: *What is the first sound in book?* (/b/) *Write the letter that stands for /b/.* Repeat for the remaining sounds. Then uncover the word so that students can check the spelling.

READING STRATEGY

Follow these steps to read words with *c* and *g*.

① When you see the consonant **c** or **g** in a word, look at the vowel that comes next. It will tell you how to say the consonant.

 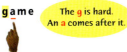

Reading Help

Look for these letter patterns in words:

wr   kn   gn
dge mb

One consonant is silent.

write   writ~~e~~
knife   ~~k~~nife
gnat   ~~g~~nat
badge   bad~~g~~e
thumb   thum~~b~~

② Start at the beginning. Blend the sounds in your head. Then say the word.

r a c e   r + a + c + ~~e~~ = race   g a m e   g + a + m + ~~e~~ = game

READING AND SPELLING PRACTICE

Use what you learned to read the sentences.

1. Ginny stood in the center of the huge diving board.
2. She walked to the edge of the board and bounced twice.
3. She took a deep breath. Then she jumped.
4. Below her, the water looked like blue glass.
5. She cut through the water like a knife!
6. Her friends had never seen such a good dive.

7.–11. Now write the sentences that your teacher reads. *For dictation sentences, see Step 6 at right.*

WORD WORK

12.–23. Copy the chart. Then read the words in this box:

catch   page   golf   good   age   gel
center place contest cup   ice   gate

Write each word in the chart. Put it under the word that has the same sound for *c* or *g*.

Example: 12.

cap	race	game	huge
12. catch	15. center	18. golf	21. page
13. contest	16. place	19. good	22. age
14. cup	17. ice	20. gate	23. gel

Language and Literacy 251

Decodable Book

PRACTICE WITH VARIANT VOWELS AND CONSONANTS

Decodable Book 15: *A Good Game*

Assign **Decodable Book 15** for independent reading. The **Decodable Book** can be used in a variety of ways to help students become more fluent, automatic readers:

Discussion Circles Have students work in small groups to read aloud and discuss the book using the questions on the back cover. Encourage students to read aloud the text that supports their answers. Groups can also work together to complete the Word Work Activity.

Readers Theater Students can read aloud the stories in a class performance. Help them prepare by rereading the stories in daily rehearsals. Work with students to add narration or dialog. Encourage them to use natural phrasing and expression.

Rereading at Home Have students work with family members to reread the book at home. They can take turns reading aloud alternate pages, then rereading the book switching the pages each person reads.

LEARN A READING STRATEGY

4 Sound Out Words Work through the strategy with students, reading each step aloud and modeling the actions. Point out the Reading Help and read the explanation to students. Work through these additional examples to help them apply the tip: *wrong, wrist, knock, knot, gnaw, bridge, ledge, lamb.*

PRACTICE

5 Read Sentences Distribute the Partner Prompts from page T311 to guide peers in reading the sentences in Items 1–6. Remind them to use the sound-out strategy to read words and to blend the words silently.

6 Write Sentences Dictate the following sentences for students to write. Read each sentence at normal speed once so students can listen, and then repeat it slowly word by word as they write:

7. A lamb stood by the gate.
8. I hurt my wrist and knee.
9. The coach can bounce the ball high.
10. Gnats flew around the hedge.
11. Turn the page and look at the picture.

If students need extra support, guide them in spelling the words with /o͞o/ and silent consonants. For example, ask: *Does a silent* b *follow the* m *in* lamb? *What two letters make the vowel sound* /o͞o/ *in* stood?

7 Conduct "Word Work" Read the directions and work through the Example. Then have partners complete Items 13–23. Check answers by working through the items as a group.

▶ **Reading Practice Book** page 167–170 (Decodable Book 15)

CLOSE AND ASSESS

Copy the completed chart from Word Work onto the board. Point to the *c* or *g* in each word. Have students explain why the *c* or *g* is hard or soft, and then read the word aloud.

Language and Literacy T251

UNIT 15 LESSON 11

LANGUAGE AND LITERACY: INDEPENDENT READING

OBJECTIVES

Functions: Read a Selection; Give Information

Learning to Read: 🅣 Recognize High Frequency Words; 🅣 Decode Words (variant vowels, silent consonants, hard and soft *c* and *g*)

Reading Strategies: Activate Prior Knowledge; Set a Purpose for Reading; Relate to Personal Experience

Critical Thinking and Comprehension: 🅣 Relate Main Idea and Details

Writing: Giving Information

READ ON YOUR OWN

1 Introduce Vocabulary In the article, students apply phonics skills and read high frequency words taught in Lessons 8–10. Introduce the story words. Write each word, pronounce it, and spell it. Then give a definition and a context sentence:

- **Special Olympics:** sports competition for people with disabilities. *Athletes in wheelchairs compete in the Special Olympics.*

- **volunteers:** workers who don't get paid. *We are volunteers. Once a year, we help clean the beach.*

- **field:** grassy area where sports are played. *We play soccer on this field.*

- **won:** came in first, was the winner. *Stella won the race and got first prize.*

- **in training:** exercising and eating right to prepare for a sports event. *I am in training: I eat healthy food, practice my sport, and get plenty of sleep.*

2 Activate Prior Knowledge/Set Purposes Discuss what students know about the Special Olympics. Then model setting a purpose: *I'll read the article to find out why the games were a big hit, or very popular.*

3 Read and Think: Relate to Personal Experience Students should read the article on their own. Suggest that they compare what they read with their own experiences as athletes or as spectators at a sports event.

T252 Unit 15 | Personal Best

COMPREHENSION: RELATE MAIN IDEA AND DETAILS

Read on Your Own

DECODING CHECK
Give the Decoding Progress Check on page 1a of the Assessment Handbook.

4A   Monday, August 4, 2002

Summer Games Are a Big Hit

Athletes try for gold at Bridge Park on Saturday.

GARDEN CITY— The Special Olympics State Summer Games were a big hit this weekend at Bridge Park. About 3,000 athletes, coaches, and volunteers came from around the state. Tents were set up in a football field by the park to make an Olympic Village.

The rock band Thumbs Up gave a concert at the edge of the park to open the games. A huge crowd came to see the band. Some lucky fans even got to go on stage and sing with the band.

The next day, athletes competed in different sports. They rode bikes, ran, threw a softball, and raced in wheelchairs. Cindy Collins, a 20-year-old from Garden City, won the wheelchair race.

"My next goal is to win at the World Games," Cindy said. "I'm in training now. I move my wrists to make them strong. I also race around traffic cones. If I knock a cone over, I try again."

"I met so many nice people while I was here," Sam Wong, another winner, said. "We're all good friends now!"

252 Unit 15 | Personal Best

REACHING ALL STUDENTS

CULTURAL PERSPECTIVES

World Cultures: Special Olympics
Tell students that the Special Olympics is an international program, but that it was started in the United States by Eunice Kennedy Shriver in 1968. Encourage students to learn more about the history of the Special Olympics and what the organization does. Students can gather information from newspaper articles, encyclopedia articles, and the Internet. Invite them to share their findings by giving an oral report and showing photos they clipped or downloaded.

CHECK YOUR UNDERSTANDING

Copy the paragraph. Add the missing words or phrases to tell the main idea and important details in the news story.

Example: 1.–2. The article is about the Special Olympics State Summer Games in Garden City.

The article is about the ___(1)___ ___(2)___ State Summer Games in Garden City. About 3,000 athletes, ___(3)___, and volunteers came for the games. They stayed in tents in the Olympic ___(4)___. On opening day, a band gave a ___(5)___ in the park. The next day, the athletes competed. They rode bikes, ran, threw a softball, and ___(6)___ in wheelchairs. The winner of the wheelchair race was ___(7)___ ___(8)___.

Answers:
1. Special
2. Olympics
3. coaches
4. Village
5. concert
6. raced
7. Cindy
8. Collins

EXPAND YOUR VOCABULARY

Read the sentences.

9. The runners <u>race</u> around the track.
10. Crowds of people watch them and <u>cheer</u>.
11. Everyone has a <u>good</u> time.

Work with a group to think of other words that mean *race*, *cheer*, and *good*. Make a list. Then say each sentence with a new word.

race — run, move, hurry, fly
cheer — clap, yell, shout, scream
good — wonderful, great, excellent, pleasant

WRITE ABOUT SPORTS

12. Choose a sport. Give information about it.

Example: 12. You need two teams to play softball.
You use a bat. You use a ball. You use mitts.
One team is at bat.
The other team is in the field.
Players hit the ball and run around the bases.

Language and Literacy 253

Reading Practice Book page 95

Reading Fluency
TIMED READINGS

Read the title and introduction on **Reading Practice Book** page 95. Set the timer and have a student read the passage to you. Use the script on page T326 to mark words the student misses and to note the last word read in one minute. Have students graph their performance and set a goal for improving in subsequent timed readings. Plan for two additional timed readings, and encourage partners to practice reading the passage to each other between the timed readings.

CHECK YOUR UNDERSTANDING

4 Comprehension: Relate Main Idea and Details Read aloud the directions, then use the Example to model how to use information from the article to complete Items 1 and 2 in the paragraph. Read aloud the first incomplete sentence, and say: *In the article, I find the answer to Items 1 and 2: "The Special Olympics State Summer Games were a big hit this weekend at Bridge Park." I write* Special *for Item 1 and* Olympics *for Item 2.*

EXPAND YOUR VOCABULARY

5 List Synonyms Read the directions and sentences. Use the examples to model how to list synonyms for *race*, *cheer*, and *good*. Then have groups list synonyms to use in place of the underlined words in sentences 9–11:

- **race:** hurry, gallop, dash, fly, zoom, rush, sprint, zip
- **cheer:** shout, hoot, holler, root, applaud, scream
- **good:** fantastic, terrific, fine, excellent, enjoyable, lovely, nice

WRITE

6 Give Information Point out that the Example uses present tense verbs to give information about softball. Then ask students to choose a team sport to write about. Remind students to use present tense verbs in their sentences.

For students who need support in writing, provide a paragraph frame and help students complete it.

Indent here. **Write your topic sentence here.**

> You need ___ teams to play ___. You use a ___. You use a ___. One team ___. The other team ___. Players ___ and ___.

Write important details here.

▶ **Reading Practice Book** page 95

CLOSE AND ASSESS

Have students take turns telling the main idea and important details in each paragraph of the article.

Language and Literacy T253

UNIT 15 LESSON 12
LANGUAGE ACROSS THE CURRICULUM: LANGUAGE ARTS

OBJECTIVES
Functions: Give Information; Write
Concepts and Vocabulary: Paragraphs
Research Skills and Learning Strategies: Use Graphic Organizers (main-idea diagram)
Critical Thinking and Comprehension:
T Relate Main Idea and Details
Writing: Paragraph

LEARN ABOUT PARAGRAPHS
1 Explore Paragraphs Read the title and explanation, and then read the paragraph through once. Next, have students follow along as you read the label for each part. Have them point to each part as you reread the paragraph.

PRACTICE YOUR PARAGRAPHS
2 Think and Discuss Guide students through Steps 1–4. Read through the diagram and explain that it shows the main idea and details for the paragraph above. Say: *The writer used the main idea to write a topic sentence. The supporting details are used to write the next three sentences. They all give more information about the main idea.*

EXERCISE
3 Write a Paragraph Explain that students will use the new diagram to write a new paragraph about Brigitte McMahon, a triathlon athlete. Remind students to indent the first line of their paragraph and to be sure to include a topic sentence and sentences with supporting details.

CLOSE AND ASSESS
Have students show you their paragraphs. Ask them to point out the indent, the topic sentence, and the sentences that give supporting details.

T254 Unit 15 | Personal Best

SUCCESS IN LANGUAGE ARTS
Learn About Paragraphs

PARAGRAPHS

A **paragraph** is a group of sentences. All the sentences tell about one main idea.

> indent → **A triathlon is a race that includes three different sports.** Athletes start with a swim race. Next they hop onto bicycles for a bike race. The last part of a triathlon is a running race.

The **topic sentence** tells the main idea.

The other sentences give **supporting** details. They tell more about the main idea.

Study the lesson. Then do the Exercise.

Practice Your Paragraphs

Think and Discuss
Follow these steps to write a paragraph.

1 Think about your main idea. What details support it? Make a diagram.

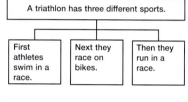

A triathlon has three different sports.
- First athletes swim in a race.
- Next they race on bikes.
- Then they run in a race.

2 Write a topic sentence to tell the main idea. Be sure to indent it.

3 Add the detail sentences.

4 Read your paragraph. Make sure all the sentences tell about one main idea.

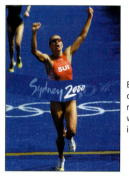

Brigitte McMahon, of Switzerland, races in the women's triathlon in Sydney, Australia.

Exercise
Write a paragraph. Use ideas in this diagram.

In 2000, Brigitte McMahon won the first triathlon at the Olympic Games.
- First she swam 1500 meters.
- Next she rode a bike for 40 kilometers.
- Then she ran for 10 kilometers.

254 Unit 15 | Personal Best

Sample Responses for the Exercise
Students should use the main idea in their topic sentence. The detail sentences should include the 3 details above.

REACHING ALL STUDENTS

COMMUNITY CONNECTION

Support Your Local Team Research a sports team from a local high school or college. Organize a trip to watch the team in action, or show clips from a videotaped game. Have students look for newspaper articles about the team, and consider inviting some players to speak to the class about their team and sport. Then assign small groups to write paragraphs about individual athletes, sports rules, or specific games. Encourage them to use main-idea diagrams to organize their ideas before writing.

Writing Project — Class Book on Healthy Habits

What are some of your healthy habits? Write a paragraph about something that you do to take care of your body. Draw a picture. Then add your page to a class book.

✓ **WRITING ASSESSMENT** Use the Writing Progress Checklist on page 51 of the Assessment Handbook to evaluate this writing project.

CHOOSE A HEALTHY ACTIVITY

List the healthy things you do each day. Choose one to write about.

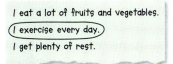

PLAN AND WRITE A PARAGRAPH

Make a diagram to show your main idea and details:

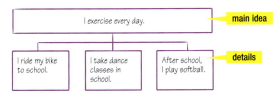

Then follow the steps on page 254 to write your paragraph.

Work with a partner to check your paragraph. Look in *Body Works* if you need to check a word.

✓ **Check Your Work**
- Does your topic sentence tell the main idea?
- Does your paragraph have at least three supporting details?
- Do the details tell more about the main idea?

MAKE A CLASS BOOK

Copy your paragraph or type it on a computer. Make a drawing or add a photo. Put your page together with your classmates' pages to make a "Healthy Habits" book.

I exercise every day to keep my body strong and healthy. I ride my bike to school. I take special dance classes in school. After school, I get to play softball with my friends.

Language Across the Curriculum 255

Language Practice Book page 120

✓ ASSESSMENT

For opportunities to measure progress, see the Assessment Handbook:

- **Units 13–15 Test** evaluates basic vocabulary and the patterns and structures of English, mastery of phonics and high frequency words, reading comprehension, and writing.

- **The Language Acquisition Assessment** for Units 13–15 offers performance assessments for measuring growth through the stages of language acquisition.

- **Self- and Peer-Assessment** forms involve students in the assessment process.

UNIT 15 **LESSON 13**

LANGUAGE ACROSS THE CURRICULUM: WRITING

OBJECTIVES

Functions: Give Information; Write

Concepts and Vocabulary:
🅣 Sports; 🅣 The Body

Learning Strategies and Critical Thinking: Relate to Personal Experience; Plan; Generate and Organize Ideas; Use Graphic Organizers (main-idea diagram); 🅣 Relate Main Idea and Details; Self-Assess

Writing: Paragraph for a Healthy-Habits Book

CONDUCT THE WRITING PROJECT

1 Explore Healthy Habits Explain that a *healthy habit* is something that you do regularly to keep your body strong and well. Review pages 20–23 in *Body Works* to show examples of a few healthy habits. Then read the title, introduction, and first step of the project. Help students brainstorm a list of healthy activities that they do regularly.

2 Plan and Write a Paragraph Go over the main-idea diagram. Have students refer to the annotated paragraph at the top of page 254 to review how to organize the information to write their paragraph:

- Write the topic sentence first, giving the main idea. Be sure to indent.
- Then write at least three sentences that give details to support the main idea.

3 Make a Class Book Help students put together the class book. You can make a copy of the book for students to take home and share with family members.

▶ **Language Practice Book** page 120

CLOSE AND ASSESS

As students review their work, say:
- *Point to the paragraph indent.*
- *Read me your topic sentence.*
- *Show me the supporting details.*

Language Across the Curriculum T255

Resources

For Success in Language and Literacy

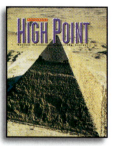

Student Book pages 256–269

For Language Skills Practice

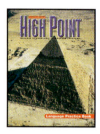

Language Practice Book pages 121–125

For Reading Skills Practice

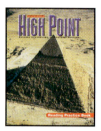

Reading Practice Book pages 96–99

For Vocabulary, Language Development, and Reading Fluency

Language Tape 8, Side B
Language CD 3, Tracks 10–13

For Reading Together

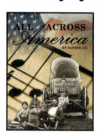

Theme Book *All Across America* from The Basics Bookshelf

For Audio Walk-Throughs and Selection Readings

Selection Tape 8B
Selection CD 3, Tracks 7–8

For Phonics Instruction

Transparencies 78–82

Transparency Scripts 78–82

Letter Tiles

For Comprehensive Assessment

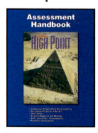

Language Acquisition Assessment, Units 16–18 Test, Writing Assessment, Self-Assessment

For Home-School Connections

High Point Newsletter 6 in seven languages

For Planning and Instruction

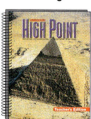

Teacher's Edition pages T256a–T269

T256a Unit Planner

UNIT 16
This Land Is Our Land

In This Unit

Vocabulary
- American History
- Landforms and Bodies of Water
- Geography

Language Functions
- Ask and Answer Questions
- Give Directions

Patterns and Structures
- Questions with *How?* and *Why?*
- Capitalization: Proper Nouns (geographical names)

Reading
- Multisyllabic Words
- Comprehension: Classify (category chart, concept map)

Writing
- Questions and Answers
- Directions
- Biographical Sketch

Content Area Connection
- Social Studies (regions of the U.S.)

T256b

UNIT 16 — Activity and Assessment Planner

UNIT 16: This Land Is Our Land

LESSONS

1 — UNIT 16 LAUNCH
▶ *pages T256–T257*

LESSON 1: INTRODUCE UNIT 16 pages T256–T257

Vocabulary
Geography

Viewing
Interpret a Visual Image

Learning Strategies
Preview

Build Background

Critical Thinking
Generate Ideas

2–5 — LANGUAGE DEVELOPMENT
▶ *pages T258–T261*

LESSON 2
AMERICAN HISTORY
page T258

Function
Ask and Answer Questions

Vocabulary
🅣 American History

Patterns and Structures
Questions with *Who?, What?, When?,* and *Where?*

Writing
Questions

LESSON 3
HOW? AND WHY?
page T259

Function
Ask and Answer Questions

Patterns and Structures
🅣 Questions with *How?* and *Why?*

Writing
Answers

LESSON 4
LANDFORMS/WATER
page T260

Function
Give Directions

Vocabulary
🅣 Landforms

🅣 Bodies of Water

Geography

Writing
Directions

LESSON 5
CAPITALIZATION—PROPER NOUNS
page T261

Function
Give Information

Patterns and Structures
🅣 Capitalization of Proper Nouns and Initials in Proper Names

Writing
Sentences

6–11 — LANGUAGE AND LITERACY
▶ *pages T262a–T267*

LESSON 6
BASICS BOOKSHELF
pages T262a–T262f

Function
Listen to a Book

Vocabulary
People Words

Landforms

Reading Strategies
Activate Prior Knowledge

Preview

Use Text Structures (maps)

Learning to Read
Track Print

Identify Words

Critical Thinking and Comprehension
Classify

LESSON 7
BASICS BOOKSHELF: COMPREHENSION
page T262

Function
Give Information

Learning Strategy
Use Graphic Organizers (category chart)

Critical Thinking and Comprehension
Classify

LESSON 8
HIGH FREQUENCY WORDS
page T263

Learning to Read
🅣 Recognize High Frequency Words

LESSON 9
PHONICS
pages T264a–T264d

Learning to Read
Build Oral Vocabulary

Develop Phonemic Awareness

🅣 Divide Words into Syllables

Decode Multisyllabic Words

Decode Multisyllabic Words with /ə/ *a*

LESSON 10
READING AND SPELLING
pages T264–T265

Learning to Read
Develop Phonemic Awareness

Associate Sounds and Symbols /ə/ *a*

🅣 Divide Words into Syllables

Decode Multisyllabic Words

Spelling
🅣 Multisyllabic Words

LESSON 11
INDEPENDENT READING
pages T266–T267

Functions
Read a Selection

Answer Questions

Learning to Read
🅣 Recognize High Frequency Words

🅣 Divide Words into Syllables to Decode Multisyllabic Words

Reading Strategies
Set a Purpose for Reading

Adjust Reading Rate

Critical Thinking and Comprehension
Classify

Writing
Postcard

12–13 — LANGUAGE ACROSS THE CURRICULUM
▶ *pages T268–T269*

LESSON 12
SOCIAL STUDIES: REGIONS
page T268

Function
Listen to an Article

Vocabulary
Geography

🅣 Landforms

🅣 Bodies of Water

Research Skills and Learning Strategies
Preview

Use Text Structures and Features (maps, symbols, photographs)

Critical Thinking and Comprehension
Identify Details

Summarize

Relate to Personal Experience

LESSON 13
WRITING PROJECT: BIOGRAPHICAL SKETCH
page T269

Functions
Ask and Answer Questions

Give Information

Write

Learning Strategies and Critical Thinking
Plan

Generate and Organize Ideas

Self-Assess

Research Skills
Gather Information

Take Notes

Locate Resources

Writing
🅣 Paragraph (biographical sketch)

T256c Unit 16 | This Land Is Our Land

🅣 = Objective Tested on Unit Test

ASSESSMENT OPTIONS

The **Teacher's Edition** and the **Assessment Handbook** include these comprehensive assessment tools:

▶ **Ongoing, Informal Assessment**
Check for understanding and achieve closure for every lesson with the targeted questions and activities in the **Close and Assess** boxes in your Teacher's Edition.

▶ **Decoding Progress Check**
These word lists for each unit provide a quick way to check on mastery of the phonics or word structure skills taught in the unit.

▶ **Language Acquisition Assessments**
To verify students' ability to use the language functions and grammar structures taught in Units 16–18, conduct these performance assessments.

▶ **Unit Test in Standardized Test Format**
This multiple-choice test measures students' cumulative understanding of the skills and language developed in Units 1–3.

▶ **Self-and Peer-Assessment**
Students use the Self-Assessment Form to evaluate their own work and develop learning strategies appropriate to their needs. Students offer feedback to their classmates with the Peer-Assessment Form.

▶ **Writing Assessment/Portfolio Opportunities**
You can evaluate students' writing in the Writing Projects using the Writing Progress Checklist. Then collaborate with students to choose work for their portfolios.

UNITS 1–3 ASSESSMENT OPPORTUNITIES	Assessment Handbook Pages
Decoding Progress Check	1a
Language Acquisition Assessments	42
Units 16–18 Test	43–48
Self-Assessment Form	49
Peer-Assessment Form	50
Writing Progress Checklist	51
Portfolio Evaluation Form	52

RELATED RESOURCES

Grandfather's Journey
by Allen Say
The author tells about his grandfather's journey across the United States, and his bicultural identity.
(Available from Hampton-Brown)
Theme Book: Read Aloud

My Fellow Americans
by Alice Provensen
An illustrated album of notable Americans. Categories include "Pilgrims and Puritans," "Expatriates," and "Writers."
(Harcourt)
Phonics: Multisyllabic Words

Geography From A to Z
by Jack Knowlton
An illustrated glossary of geographic terms. The index serves as a guide to other terms highlighted in the explanatory text. (HarperCollins)
Vocabulary: Geography

America the Beautiful
by Katharine Lee Bates
An illustrated edition of the popular song. A guide in the back gives information about fourteen national parks, monuments, and regions. (Atheneum)
Language Development: Capitalization of Proper Nouns

Honest Abe
by Edith Kunhardt
The life story of our sixteenth president, from his birth in a log cabin to his assassination. Illustrated with folk-art paintings. (Hampton-Brown)
Easy Reading

Unit Planner **T256d**

UNIT 16 **LESSON 1**

INTRODUCE UNIT 16: THIS LAND IS OUR LAND

OBJECTIVES

Concepts and Vocabulary: Geography
Function: Listen Actively
Viewing: Interpret a Visual Image
Learning Strategies: Preview; Build Background
Critical Thinking: Generate Ideas

START WITH A COMMON EXPERIENCE

1 **Introduce "This Land Is Our Land"**
Point out the photos and explain that they show people playing different types of music that you can hear in the U.S. Read the unit title and explain that it means that the beauty and history of the U.S. belongs to everyone who lives here.

2 **Listen to the Music** Tape 8B CD 3 Track 10
Read the directions and then play "This Land Is Our Land" on the **Language Tape/CD**. Have students point to the region on the map as you read aloud each label. Display a U.S. map and help students locate the each state. Then, using the map, share information about geography, cities, and famous places of each region. For example:

Region	Geography	Places to See
Northeast	Appalachian Mountains	Statue of Liberty in New York
Southeast	Florida Everglades	French Quarter in New Orleans
Midwest	Great Lakes	Gateway Arch in St. Louis
Southwest	Grand Canyon	Johnson Space Center in Houston
West	Yellowstone	Golden Gate Bridge in San Francisco

3 **Tell What You Know About the U.S.**
Have students use the map to point out places and tell facts they know about the U.S.

T256 Unit 16 | This Land Is Our Land

MIDWEST/Wisconsin
MIDWEST/Illinois
NORTHEAST/New York
SOUTHEAST/Kentucky
WEST/California
SOUTHWEST/Arizona
WEST/Hawaii
SOUTHEAST/Georgia

REACHING ALL STUDENTS

HOME CONNECTION

Family Travel Map Send home a copy of *High Point Newsletter 6* in the **Teacher's Resource Book**. In the home activity, students and family use a map of the U.S. to label places where family members have visited or lived. Then they add sentences to describe each location. Students can bring their maps back to class and tell about their own family histories in the United States.

This Land Is Our Land

There are many kinds of music played in the United States. Listen to some. Which music do you like the most? On a map, find the place where it is played.

In This Unit

Vocabulary
- American History
- Landforms and Bodies of Water
- Geography

Language Functions
- Ask and Answer Questions
- Give Directions

Patterns and Structures
- Questions with *How?* and *Why?*
- Capitalization: Proper Nouns (geographical names)

Reading
- Multisyllabic Words
- Comprehension: Classify (category chart, concept map)

Writing
- Questions and Answers
- Directions
- Biographical Sketch

Content Area Connection
- Social Studies (regions of the U.S.)

PREVIEW THE UNIT

4 Look for Activities and Special People and Places Leaf through the unit, previewing activities students will do, for example:

page 258—learning a chant about people in American History

page 262—listening to the Bookshelf book (Display a copy of the book.)

page 268—reading about the Southwest region of the United States

page 269—writing a biographical sketch of a famous American

Also ask students to look for information about the people and places that make up the United States. Highlight the information about people on pages 258, 259, and 261, and the article about the Grand Canyon on page 266, for example. Then sum up what the preview reveals: *The United States is rich in people, rich in culture, and rich in natural wonders.*

5 Set Your Goals Create a mind map to record what students know about the United States. Add categories as suggested by the students. Prompt students for pictures or words to add.

CLOSE AND ASSESS
Ask students to tell or show you something they are interested in learning in this unit.

UNIT 16 Mind Map

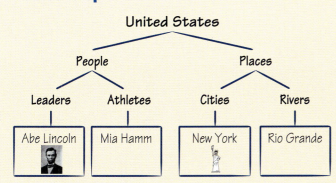

Technology Support
See **Inspiration** Visual Learning software for support in creating mind maps.

UNIT 16 LESSON 2

LANGUAGE DEVELOPMENT: AMERICAN HISTORY

OBJECTIVES

Functions: Listen Actively; Repeat Spoken Language; Recite; Ask and Answer Questions

Concepts and Vocabulary:
- American History

Patterns and Structures: Questions with *Who?*, *What?*, *When?*, and *Where?*

Writing: Questions

INTRODUCE

1. **Listen and Chant** Play "The Builders of Our Nation" on the **Language Tape/CD**. Students will listen and read along, then echo the lines, and chime in using first a soft and then a loud voice. *(Tape 8B, CD 3 Track 11)*

2. **Learn Words in American History** Explain that this page shows *nation builders* who made the country what it is today. Use each term to build background on American history.

PRACTICE

3. **Conduct "Express Yourself"** Review how to ask and answer questions. Have partners complete the activity.

How to Ask and Answer Questions

- Use *who* to ask about a person: **Who** built new towns?
- Use *what* to ask about a thing: **What** did immigrants want to find?
- Use *when* to ask about a time: **When** did pilgrims cross the sea?
- Use *where* to ask about a place: **Where** did pioneers travel?

APPLY

4. **Write Questions** Have partners check each other's work. Distribute Partner Checklist 16 on page T310.

▶ **Language Practice Book** page 121

CLOSE AND ASSESS

Ask volunteers to read their questions. Call on students to answer them.

T258 Unit 16 | This Land Is Our Land

VOCABULARY: AMERICAN HISTORY

Who Built America?

Listen and chant.

The Builders of Our Nation

The Pilgrims sailed across the sea
To practice their religion in Plymouth Colony.

Colonists built new American towns.
They won their liberty from the British crown.

Explorers traveled across the land
So our growing nation could expand.

To reach the Pacific, in long wagon trains,
The pioneers traveled from the golden plains.

Immigrants escaped from hunger and strife
To seek work, education, and a better life.

All of us here in our nation today
Are the many faces of the U.S. of A.

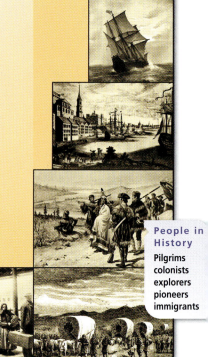

People in History
Pilgrims
colonists
explorers
pioneers
immigrants

EXPRESS YOURSELF ▶ ASK AND ANSWER QUESTIONS

1.–6. Work with a partner. Ask each other 6 questions about the chant. Then answer your partner's questions.

Example: 1. Who sailed across the sea? The Pilgrims sailed across the sea.

Question Words
who   when
what where

WRITE QUESTIONS

7.–12. Write the questions you made above.

Example: 7. Where did the Pilgrims practice their religion?

258 Unit 16 | This Land Is Our Land

REACHING ALL STUDENTS

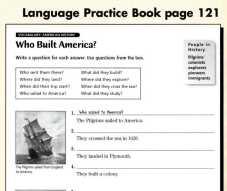

Language Practice Book page 121

QUESTIONS WITH *HOW?* AND *WHY?*
People of America

You can use the word **how** or **why** to ask a question.

Sample Responses for Build Questions
1. How do scientists do experiments?
   Why do they experiment carefully?
2. How do soldiers fight? Why do soldiers fight bravely?
3. How do most cowboys ride? Why do most cowboys ride well?
4. How do farmers harvest their crops?
   Why do farmers use machines to harvest?

Use *how* to ask about the way people do something.
How did the pioneers travel?
They traveled in wagons.

Use *why* to ask for a reason.
Why did the pioneers travel west?
They traveled west **because** they wanted land to farm.

You can use *because* to answer a question with *why*.

BUILD QUESTIONS

Read each answer. Then ask 2 questions to go with the answer: How ____? Why ____?

Example: 1. How do scientists do experiments?
Why do they do experiments carefully?

1. Scientists do experiments carefully because they want to get correct results.

2. Soldiers fight bravely because they want to protect their country.

3.  Most cowboys ride horses very well because they spend a lot of time on horseback.

4.  Farmers use machines to harvest their crops because machines work quickly.

WRITE ANSWERS

Work with a partner. Use the chant on page 258 to find the answer to each question below. Write your answer as a complete sentence. Use the word *because*.

5. Why did the Pilgrims leave home?
6. Why did explorers travel across the land?
7. Why did immigrants come to the United States?
8. Why did pioneers leave the plains?

Example: 5. The Pilgrims left home because they wanted to practice their religion.

Answers:
5. The Pilgrims left home because they wanted to practice their religion.
6. Explorers traveled because they wanted to find more land for our nation.
7. The immigrants came to the U.S. because they wanted work, education, and a better life.
8. The pioneers left the plains because they wanted to reach the Pacific.

Language Development 259

Language Practice Book page 122

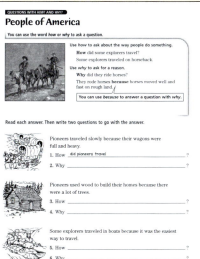

Language Development
QUESTIONS

Use the chant on page 258 to play a game of questions and answers. Create a game board with a column for each people group and a row for each of these question words: *who, what, when, where, why,* and *how.* Divide the class into two teams and call on a player from each side. Toss a game piece to select a people group and a question word. The first player to write a properly punctuated question with the question word gets a point.

UNIT 16 **LESSON 3**

LANGUAGE DEVELOPMENT: *HOW?* AND *WHY?*

OBJECTIVES
Function: Ask and Answer Questions
Patterns and Structures:
❶ Questions with *How?* and *Why?*
Writing: Answers

INTRODUCE

1 Learn About Questions with *How?* and *Why?* Read aloud the title and introduction. Then go over the first rule and sample sentences. Provide a sentence starter for the answer: *They traveled ____.* Complete several answers based on the pictures: *They traveled with horses. They traveled in groups. They traveled across rocky ground.*

Then read the second rule, including the rule for using *because.* Pose a question based on the picture: *Why was travel difficult for pioneers?* Brainstorm possible answers: *It was difficult because there were no roads. It was difficult because some people walked.*

PRACTICE

2 Build Questions Go over the Example and suggest more questions students can ask: *How do scientists learn new things? Why do scientists do experiments?* Have partners work together to complete Items 1–4.

APPLY

3 Write Answers Model how to use words from the question and the word *because* to form a complete sentence:

Why did Pilgrims leave home?
Pilgrims left home because ____.

▶ Language Practice Book page 122

CLOSE AND ASSESS

Have volunteers read a question and the answer they wrote, and point out the information in the chant.

Language Development **T259**

UNIT 16 LESSON 4
LANGUAGE DEVELOPMENT: LANDFORMS/WATER

OBJECTIVES

Functions: Listen Actively; Give Directions
Concepts and Vocabulary: 🅣 Landforms; 🅣 Bodies of Water; Geography
Writing: Directions

INTRODUCE

1 Learn Words for Landforms and Bodies of Water Go over the map and labels, discussing landforms and bodies of water, and noting examples of each. Then ask students to locate and name two mountain ranges, two lakes, and two rivers.

Discuss the historic trails and explain that settlers and pioneers followed these trails as they moved west. Have students trace the trails on the map and discuss where each leads.

2 Learn Direction Words Explain that a compass rose shows the directions *north, south, east,* and *west.* Lead students in reading each direction word and indicating the direction on the map. Ask questions using landforms and direction words; for example: *What mountain range is east of the Great Salt Lake?* (the Rockies) *What ocean is west of the United States?* (Pacific)

PRACTICE

3 Conduct **"Who's Talking?"** Play "Who's Talking?" on the **Language Tape/CD** to model how to give directions. Replay as necessary for students to identify the routes.

Tape 8B / CD 3 Track 12

APPLY

4 Write Directions Students can use the map and compass rose to create their maps and directions.

▶ **Language Practice Book** page 123

CLOSE AND ASSESS

Ask volunteers to read aloud their directions as the group traces the route to find the destination.

T260 Unit 16 | This Land Is Our Land

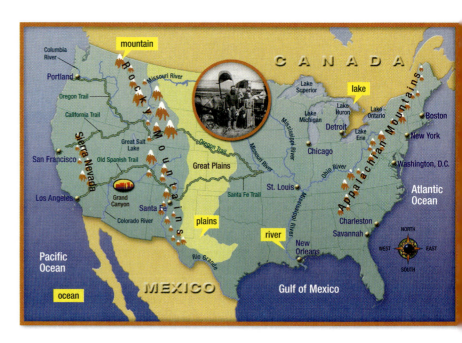

VOCABULARY: LANDFORMS AND BODIES OF WATER

Our Natural Treasures

WHO'S TALKING? ▶ GIVE DIRECTIONS

1.–2. Listen.

Two students are giving directions to the pioneers.
What route is each student describing? Trace it on the map.

Answers:
1. Start in St. Louis; north on the Mississippi River; we on the Missouri River; west on the Santa Fe Trail; a the Colorado River; west on the Old Spanish Trail Los Angeles; north along the coast to San Francisco
2. Start in St. Louis; north on the Mississippi River; we the Missouri River; west on the Oregon Trail; acros Rocky Mountains; south on the California Trail thre the Sierra Nevada; west to San Francisco.

WRITE DIRECTIONS

3. Work with a partner. Draw the outline of the United States. Mark where you are now. Where do you want to go? Label the landforms and cities along the way. Then write directions to get there.

Example: 3. How to go to Washington, D.C., in the northeastern part of the country:
- Start in New Orleans. Go north along the Mississippi River.
- Follow the Ohio River east. Keep going east until you get to Washington, D.C.

Sample Responses:
Students' directions should include direction words (*north, south, east,* and *west*) as well as the names of cities, landforms, trails, and bodies of water.

260 Unit 16 | This Land Is Our Land

REACHING ALL STUDENTS

Vocabulary
GEOGRAPHY/MAP TERMS

Map Search Divide the class into groups and provide a different state map for each group. Then call out instructions using geography and map terms and have groups answer with information about their states.

Instruction: *Name two mountains in your state.*

Answer: *Two mountains in California are Mount Shasta and Mount Whitney.*

Instruction: *Name a city on the eastern side of your state.*

Answer: *Philadelphia is a city on the eastern side of Pennsylvania.*

Language Practice Book page 123

CAPITALIZATION: PROPER NOUNS

Americans from Other Lands

A **proper noun** names a particular person, place, or thing.

Capitalize the proper names of:	Examples
countries, cities, and states	John Muir was born in **Scotland** in 1838. He moved to **Portage, Wisconsin,** when he was 11 years old.
bodies of water	Muir walked 1,000 miles to the **Gulf of Mexico.**
landforms	Muir studied the plants and animals of the **Yosemite Valley.**

STUDY SENTENCES

Say the sentences. Look at the underlined words. Do they need capital letters? If so, tell why.

A red underscore indicates the letter should be a capital.

Example: 1. *Guangzhou* needs a capital letter. It is the name of a city.

1. I. M. Pei was born in guangzhou, China. *city*
2. In 1935, he came to massachusetts to study architecture. *state*
3. One of the buildings he designed is at the foot of the rocky mountains. ⎤
4. Another is next to boston harbor. ⎦
5. He designed other buildings across the country. *common noun*

           ⎣ landform
           ⎣ body of water

6. Alexandra Nechita was born in romania. *country*
7. Now the young artist lives in Los Angeles, California, near the pacific ocean. *body of water*
8. In 2000, she designed a giant angel sculpture in the city. *common noun*
9. Her other artwork is in galleries from hawaii to new york. *states*
10. When she was 12 years old, she met the Emperor of japan. *country*

WRITE SENTENCES ✏

1.–20. Write the sentences above with the correct capitalization.

Example: 11. I. M. Pei was born in Guangzhou, China.

Language Development **261**

Language Practice Book page 124

Language Development
ABBREVIATIONS: PROPER NAMES

Call attention to the name I. M. Pei in Item 1. Write the full name (Ieoh Ming Pei) on the board and show how you can take just the first letter of the first and middle name and write a period after each. Explain that sometimes people write just the *initial*, or first letter, of a name. Emphasize that these initials are also capitalized.

Write the full names of some well-known people on the board and have students abbreviate them. Then have students write their own names using initials.

UNIT 16 **LESSON 5**

LANGUAGE DEVELOPMENT: CAPITALIZATION—PROPER NOUNS

OBJECTIVES

Function: Give Information
Patterns and Structures:
🅣 Capitalization of Proper Nouns; Capitalization of Initials in Proper Names
Writing: Sentences

INTRODUCE

1 Learn About Capitalization Read the title and introduction, then go over the chart of rules and sample sentences. Brainstorm more examples of proper nouns for each category. Point out the name *John Muir* in the first sentence, and remind students that people's names are proper nouns and should be capitalized as well.

Confirm understanding by having volunteers use proper nouns to complete the following paragraph about themselves:

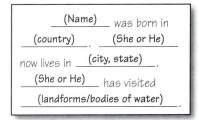

PRACTICE

2 Study Sentences Work through the Example, pointing out that it tells which word needs a capital letter, and why. Then assign the sentences to volunteers.

APPLY

3 Write Sentences Review the Example and explain that now students will write the sentences you discussed above.

▶ **Language Practice Book** page 124

CLOSE AND ASSESS

Have volunteers copy one of their sentences on the board. The class can check the sentence and discuss why it is correctly or incorrectly capitalized.

Language Development **T261**

UNIT 16 **LESSON 6**

LANGUAGE AND LITERACY: THE BASICS BOOKSHELF

OBJECTIVES
Concepts and Vocabulary:
People Words; Landforms
Listening: Listen to a Preview
Reading Strategies:
Activate Prior Knowledge; Preview; Use Text Structures (maps)

BUILD LANGUAGE AND VOCABULARY

1. **Teach "Words to Know"** Have students look at pages 2–3. Say: *These pages show words about important people in the United States.*

   Give the names of the specific people shown: explorer, Hernando DeSoto; inventor, Thomas Edison; leader, Martin Luther King, Jr.; artist, Lulu Delacre. Have students suggest more names for each group.

2. **Sing About Landforms** Use gestures to introduce landforms on pages 4–5: *mountains:* touch index finger tips in an inverted "V"; *plains:* place hands flat, with palms down; *streams:* make a rippling motion with fingers. Teach the song refrain and invite students to sing along with hand motions.

PREPARE TO READ

3. **Think About What You Know** Invite students to share about important people around the world. Use a world map to show where each person lived.

4. **Preview** Play the Audio Walk-Through for *All Across America* on the **Selection Tape/CD** to give students the overall idea of the story.

   Tape 8B
   CD 3 Track 7

CLOSE AND ASSESS
Show students the cover of *All Across America* and have them name the groups of people in the book.

All Across America
by Daphne Liu

Summary This lively song highlights the many faces of the United States. Simple lyrics introduce people groups such as explorers, pioneers, cowboys, inventors, immigrants, soldiers, leaders, and artists. Captions, historical photos, and illustrations give information about famous people from our country's past and present.

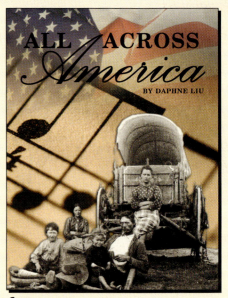
Cover

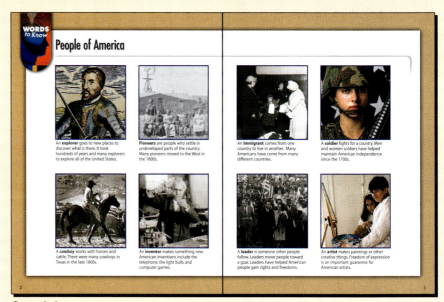
Pages 2–3

Multi-Level Strategies
LITERACY SUPPORT

PRELITERATE Use Text Structures: Maps Show a topographical map of the United States. Point out landforms such as oceans, lakes, rivers, canyons, and deserts. Then use the compass rose to teach *north, south, east,* and *west*. Place your finger on the center of the map. As you say each word, move a finger across the map in the corresponding direction. Then give directions to the class: *Point to the Grand Canyon. Move your finger north. Where are you?* (Rocky Mountains)

Have one partner give directions using the pattern:

   Point to _____.
   Move your finger _____.
   Where are you?

The other partner traces the route, saying:

   I am in _____.

T262a Unit 16 | This Land Is Our Land

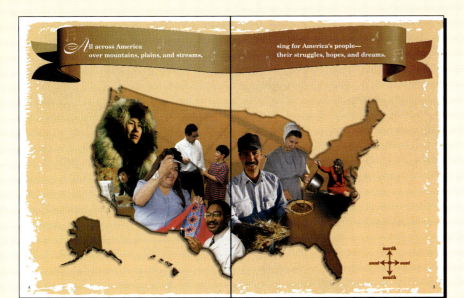

Pages 4–5

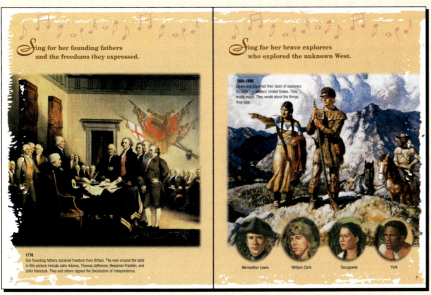

Pages 6–7

Strategies for Comprehensible Input

Page	Story Language	Strategy Options
4	mountains, plains, streams	**Point to these features on a topographical map.**
5	struggles	**Explain:** Struggles are the hard times people go through.
	hopes, and dreams	**Restate:** things they wanted to happen in the future
	her	**Explain:** Some people use the words *her* or *she* in place of the United States.
6	founding fathers	**Point to the picture and explain:** The founding fathers are the men who created the first government for the United States of America.
	expressed	**Restate:** talked and wrote about
7	explorers	**Explain:** An explorer is someone who goes to a place to see and learn new things.
	West	**Point to the Western United States on a map.**

Language and Literacy

UNIT 16 **LESSON 6,** CONTINUED

LANGUAGE AND LITERACY: THE BASICS BOOKSHELF

OBJECTIVES

Function: Listen to a Book
Critical Thinking and Comprehension: Classify

READ AND THINK TOGETHER

1. **Read Aloud** On your first reading of the book, use the "Strategies for Comprehensible Input" that appear at the bottom of pages T262b, T262d, and T262f.

2. **Read and Map: Classify** Set up a chart like the one below with empty spaces for the examples in column 2. In column 1, list categories from pages 2–3. Then say: *A category chart shows how to classify, or group, information. The words in the first column are the categories, or groups. In the second column, I will write examples, or the names of people who belong in each group.*

   Read pages 4–11 and model how to fill in examples. On page 11, for example, say: *The caption says John Wesley Powell explored the Rocky Mountains, so I'll list him by "Explorers."* Talk about names that may fall under more than one category, such as Benjamin Franklin (founding father, inventor) or Laura Ingalls Wilder (pioneer, artist). Provide background information as necessary.

   Then read pages 12–17 and 18–24. Pause after each set of pages and model how to categorize more names in the chart.

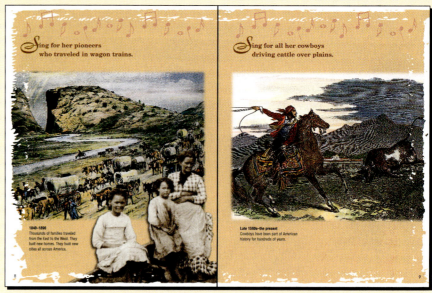

Pages 8–9

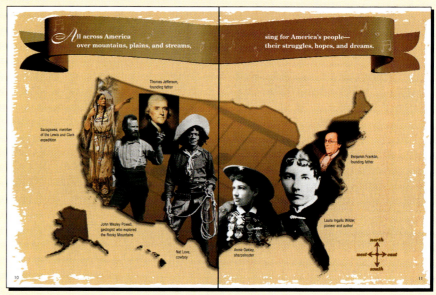

Pages 10–11

Category Chart for *All Across America*

Category	Examples
Explorers	Meriwether Lewis, William Clark, Sacagawea, York, John Wesley Powell, Sally Ride
Pioneers	Laura Ingalls Wilder
Cowboys	Nat Love, Annie Oakley
Inventors	Benjamin Franklin, Wright Brothers, Henry Ford, George Washington Carver, Jonas Salk, Stephen Wozniak, Stephanie Louise Kwolek

Technology Support
See **Inspiration** Visual Learning software for support in creating the category chart.

T262c Unit 16 | This Land Is Our Land

All Across America, CONTINUED

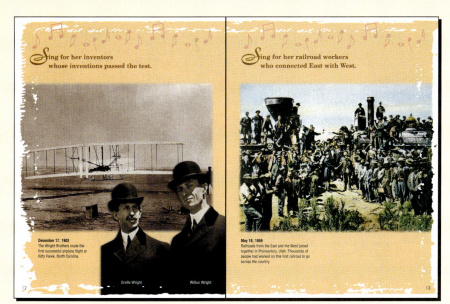

Pages 12–13

Pages 14–15

Strategies for Comprehensible Input

Page	Story Language	Strategy Options
8	pioneers	**Explain:** A pioneer is one of the first people to move to a place.
	wagon trains	**Point to the picture.**
9	driving	**Restate:** moving
	cattle	**Point to the picture and explain:** Cattle means many cows.
12	inventors, inventions	**Explain:** Inventors are people who think of new ideas. They make new things called inventions.
	passed the test	**Restate:** worked very well
13	railroad workers	**Explain:** Railroad workers built train tracks.
	connected	**Demonstrate and restate:** Put two fists together as you say *put together*.
	East	**Point to the Eastern United States on a map.**
14	immigrants	**Explain:** An immigrant is someone who moves to a new country.
	crossed	**Restate:** traveled across
15	in search of liberty	**Restate:** looking for freedom

Language and Literacy **T262d**

UNIT 16 **LESSON 6,** CONTINUED

LANGUAGE AND LITERACY: THE BASICS BOOKSHELF

OBJECTIVES

Function: Listen to a Book
Learning to Read:
Track Print; Identify Words

READ AND THINK TOGETHER, *CONTINUED*

3 **Conduct Interactive Readings**
Choose from these options:

- **Read along and track print** Play the recording of *All Across America* on the **Selection Tape/CD**. Invite students to sing along with the refrain as they track print in the song lyrics. *(Tape 8B, CD 3 Track 8)*

- **Identify words** *All Across America* contains many high frequency words that have been previously taught, as follows:

all	have	of	they
and	her	on	this
both	in	over	to
country	made	people	were
for	mountains	the	who
go	not	their	with

As you read, frame individual words from the list and have volunteers identify the words. Continue reading as students track the print and identify other words they know.

CLOSE AND ASSESS

Have students work with partners. One partner names a group from the song. The other partner gives one example from the book.

Pages 16–17

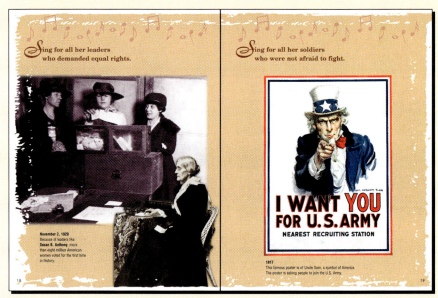
Pages 18–19

Multi-Level Strategies

LITERACY SUPPORT

LITERATE IN L1 **Read with a Partner/Compose a Class Song** After students have participated in the interactive readings, encourage them to read the story with a partner. Distribute the Partner Prompts on page T311 to help partners work together to identify unfamiliar words and unlock their meanings, then read the text to each other.

Then have students create new lines for the song: *Sing for Kwan who sailed across the sea*. Combine the new verses.

INTERRUPTED SCHOOLING **Classify** To anchor understanding of the skill, first explain the concept of categories. Say: *Things in a category are the same in some way*. On page 2, read aloud the definition of *explorer*. Show students how to look for *explorers* as a key word on page 7 to find names for the category. On pages 10 and 20, model how to look for related words, such as *expedition* and *explore* on page 10. On page 20, say: *Sally Ride is an astronaut. She **explores** outer space*. Have students look for key words to find examples for other categories.

T262e Unit 16 | This Land Is Our Land

All Across America, CONTINUED

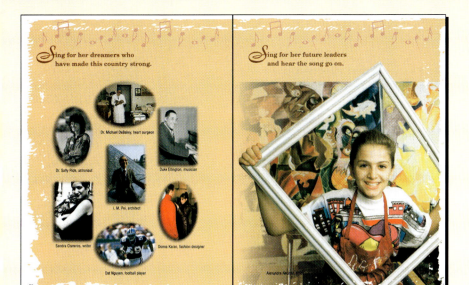

Pages 20–21

Pages 22–23

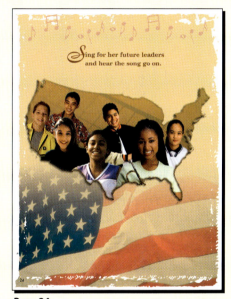

Page 24

Strategies for Comprehensible Input

PAGE	STORY LANGUAGE	STRATEGY OPTIONS
18	leaders	**Explain:** Leaders are people who tell or show other people what to do.
	equal rights	**Explain:** When you have equal rights, you have the same rights as anyone else has.
19	soldiers	**Explain:** Soldiers are men and women who fight for their country.
20–21	future	**Explain:** The future is the time that comes in later years.

Language and Literacy **T262f**

UNIT 16 LESSON 7

LANGUAGE AND LITERACY: THE BASICS BOOKSHELF

OBJECTIVES
Function: Give Information
Learning Strategy: Use Graphic Organizers (category chart)
Critical Thinking and Comprehension: Classify

CHECK COMPREHENSION

1. **Make a Category Chart** Have students form small groups. Read aloud Step 1 and have the group set up their category chart. Say: *A category chart shows how to classify, or group, information. What will you write in column 2 of the chart?* (the names of people who fit each category)

   Read aloud Step 2 and encourage students to reread each refrain and look again at the illustrations to find examples for each category.

2. **Share Information from the Book** Read aloud the directions in Steps 3 and 4. After students have compared and updated their charts, regroup them according to the category that most interests them. Encourage students to share information about the people in that category.

CLOSE AND ASSESS
Ask students to complete this sentence:
A category chart shows _____.

COMPREHENSION: CLASSIFY

Read and Think Together

Make a category chart about the people in *All Across America*. Follow these steps.

1. Draw a chart with two columns, like the one below. In column 1, write the categories of people from pages 2–3 of *All Across America*.

Category	Examples
explorers	
pioneers	
cowboys	
inventors	

2. Read the book again. As you read, put the name of each person you read about in the correct category. (Some people may belong in more than one category.)

Category	Examples
explorers	Meriwether Lewis, William Clark, Sacagawea, York, John Wesley Powell, Sally Ride

3. Compare your finished category chart with a classmate's chart. Did you list the same people? Talk about the people you included in the chart.

Sample Responses

Explorers	Meriwether Lewis, William Clark, Sacagawea, York, John Wesley Powell, Sally Ride
Pioneers	Laura Ingalls Wilder
Cowboys	Nat Love
Inventors	Thomas Jefferson, Benjamin Franklin, Wright Brothers, Henry Ford, George Washington Carver, Jonas Salk, Stephen Wozniak, Stephanie Louise Kwolek

262 Unit 16 | This Land Is Our Land

from The Basics Bookshelf

THEME BOOK

This song about America tells about the many different people who built this nation.

REACHING ALL STUDENTS

Social Studies Connection
DISCUSS FAMOUS AMERICANS

Engage in Discussion Arrange students into groups of four to ask and answer questions about individuals in the book. Two students will ask questions using the question words *how*, *when*, and *where*. The other two will search the book for the answers. Then have pairs switch roles.

> Q: Where did Lewis and Clark explore?
> A: They explored the western United States.

HIGH FREQUENCY WORDS
Words to Know

REVIEW WORDS YOU KNOW

Read the words aloud. Which word goes in the sentence?

lives	life
my	by
no	knows

1. This girl __lives__ in Alaska.
2. Her home is __by__ a frozen lake.
3. She __knows__ how to keep warm.

LEARN TO READ

Learn new words.

state	Alaska is the largest **state** in the United States.
than	It is much bigger **than** Texas.
high	Alaska has very **high** mountains.
million	It has about 51 **million** acres of parks.
form	The Aleutian Islands **form** a long chain of islands.
sea	They stretch far out into the **sea**.
near	Little Diomede Island in Alaska is **near** Russia.
miles	It is only 2.5 **miles** away!
explore	To **explore** Juneau, the capital city, go in summer.
earth	Alaska is one of the coldest places on **earth**.

How to Learn a New Word
- Look at the word.
- Listen to the word.
- Listen to the word in a sentence. What does it mean?
- Say the word.
- Spell the word.
- Say the word again.

WORD WORK

4.–13. Work with a partner. Write each new word on a card. Mix your cards together for the game. Turn them so the words are down. Then:

- Turn over 2 cards.
- Spell the words. Are they the same?
- If so, use the word in a sentence and keep the cards. If not, turn them over.
- The player with more cards at the end wins.

Example:

s-t-a-t-e
s-t-a-t-e
I live in the state of Texas.

Language and Literacy 263

Reading Practice Book page 96

Reading Fluency
RECOGNIZE HIGH FREQUENCY WORDS

To build automaticity with the new high frequency words:

- Partners can use their cards from "Word Work" to play a spelling game. Students take turns secretly selecting a card and spelling the word slowly. The partner holds up the correct card from his or her set after guessing the word. Then that student reads the word aloud and spells it.

- Refer students to the list of new words on page 263. Give clues and have students identify and then read each word. For example: *This word rhymes with tear and means "close to."*

UNIT 16 **LESSON 8**

LANGUAGE AND LITERACY: HIGH FREQUENCY WORDS

OBJECTIVES
Learning to Read:
- Recognize High Frequency Words

REVIEW WORDS

1 Review Known High Frequency Words Have the group read aloud the words in the green box. Listen for words students cannot read automatically and use the steps in the yellow box to reteach those words. Then have students look at the photo. Read each cloze sentence. Reread each sentence and pause for students to silently read the two words to the left of the sentence. Tell students to choose the word that goes in the sentence and tells about the picture.

INTRODUCE NEW WORDS

2 Learn High Frequency Words Use the High Frequency Word Script on page T327 to lead students through the steps in the yellow box for each new word.

PRACTICE

3 Conduct "Word Work" Guide pairs in making two sets of cards, setting up the game, and reading the rules. Have partners take turns until they match all the pairs. Discuss the process students used to figure out the matches.

APPLY

4 Read Words in Context Students will read high frequency words in context in the sentences on page 265 and the passage on page 266.

▶ **Reading Practice Book** page 96

CLOSE AND ASSESS

Call out the high frequency words one at a time. Have students point to them and spell the words as a group.

Language and Literacy **T263**

UNIT 16 **LESSON 9**

LANGUAGE AND LITERACY: WORD STRUCTURE

OBJECTIVES

Learning to Read: Build Oral Vocabulary; Develop Phonemic Awareness; ⓣ Divide Words into Syllables; Decode Multisyllabic Words

TEACH SYLLABICATION RULES

1. **Build Oral Vocabulary** Display Transparency 78. Talk through each picture to develop meaning for the words in the yellow boxes. For example, for Item 1, say:

   • *There is a **river** (point) at the **bottom** of the **canyon** (indicate). A river can cut through a canyon and make steep cliff walls* (demonstrate, using the picture).

2. **Develop Phonemic Awareness** Remove the transparency and conduct the oral activities in Step 1 of the Script for Transparency 78.

3. **Decode Multisyllabic Words** Display Transparency 78 again. Work through Step 2 of the script.

CLOSE AND ASSESS

Display the words *visit, bottom, hundred,* and *open*. Call on students to divide each word into syllables and to blend the syllables to read the word.

Transparency 78: ▶ Multisyllabic Words

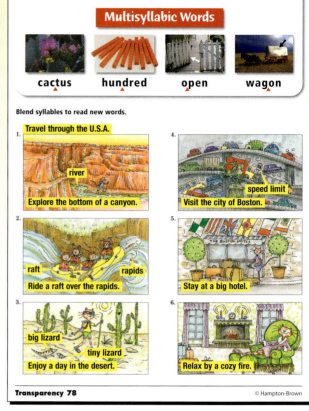

▼ Script for Transparency 78

Multisyllabic Words

1. **Develop Phonemic Awareness**
   Blend Syllables Say: *Listen to the two parts I say:* bot-tom. *Now say the whole word.* (bottom) Repeat for *can-yon, cit-y, ho-tel, sun-ny, o-pen,* and *mu-sic*.

2. **Decode Multisyllabic Words**
   Teach Point to the cactus on **Transparency 78**. Say: *This plant is a cactus. I'm going to divide this word into syllables and read it.* Put your finger between the letters *c* and *t* in *cactus* and say: *I see two consonants between two vowels, so I'll divide the word between the two consonants and blend each part:* /kaaak/-/tuuusss/. *Now I'll blend the parts together and say the word:* cac-tus, cactus. Repeat for *hundred*, pointing out the three consonants (*ndr*) between the vowels *u* and *e*. Remind students that the letters *dr* stay together.

   Then point to the open gate and say: *This gate is open.* Point to the *p* in *open* and say: *Do you see one consonant between two vowels?* (yes) *First, divide the word before the consonant and see if that works. Read the word with me.* Slide a finger slowly from left to right below the syllables as you say: /ō ō ō/-/p e e e n n n/. *Now let's blend the parts together and read the word:* o-pen, open. *Yes, that sounds right with the long o sound.*

   Repeat for *wagon*. First, divide *wagon* before the *g* and say: *The first syllable ends in a vowel, so I'll say the long a sound:* wā-gon, wāgon. *No, that doesn't sound right. I'll try dividing the word after the g.* Place a finger between the *g* and the *o* and blend the syllables to read *wagon* for students. Point out that the vowel sound in the first syllable is short *a* because the syllable ends in a consonant. Then ask students to blend the syllables to read *wagon* with you.

   Practice Read the words and sentences on the transparency with students. In the label above item 1, point to *U.S.A.* and tell students that the letters *U.S.A.* stand for *United States of America,* and that they should say the name of each letter. Remind them to try a long vowel sound in the first syllable of words with one consonant between two vowels, and then ask themselves if the word sounds right.

T264a Unit 16 | This Land Is Our Land

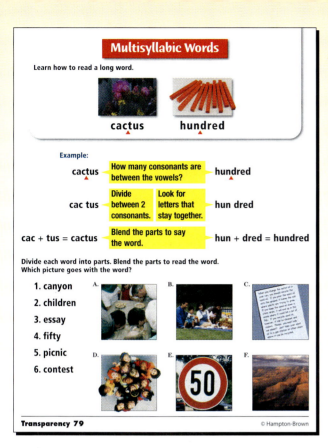

◀ Transparency 79: Multisyllabic Words

▼ Script for Transparency 79

Multisyllabic Words

1. Develop Phonemic Awareness
Count Syllables in Words Say: *Some words have one part, or syllable, such as* can. *Clap the syllable with me as we say* can: can. (clap) *Some longer words have two parts, or syllables, such as* canyon. *Clap the syllables with me as we say* canyon: can-yon. (clap, clap) Lead students in saying and clapping syllables for these words: *hundred, hand, children, check, picnic, pick, contest, crush*. Then have students repeat each word and count the syllables.

2. Decode Multisyllabic Words
Teach Say: *Now you are going to read words with a pattern you know.* Point to the cactus on **Transparency 79**. Ask: *What is the name of this plant?* (cactus). *Say* cactus *with me:* cactus. *How many parts do you hear?* (2) *Now let's study the word and find the two parts.*

Work through the Example. Point to the *ct* in *cactus* and say: *How many consonants are between the vowels?* (2) *The consonants* c *and* t *are between the vowels* a *and* u. *Where should you divide the word?* (between the consonants). Say: *Follow my finger as we blend each part:* /kaaak/-/tuuusss/. *Now let's blend the parts together and read the word:* cac-tus, cactus. Point out that when you blended the syllables and said the word, the first syllable was stressed and the vowel sound in the second syllable changed slightly.

Repeat for *hundred*, pointing out that there are three consonants between the vowels. Say: *If you see 3 consonants, look for a blend, or letters that stay together at the beginning of a syllable. What blend do you see in* hundred? (dr) *Right,* dr. *Keep the* d *and* r *together in the same syllable. Blend the syllables to say the word.*

Practice Have students do Items 1–6. Ask a volunteer to show you where to divide each word. Write the parts on the chalkboard and lead the group in blending the parts to read the word. Then have the group identify the picture that goes with the word.

OBJECTIVES

Learning to Read: Build Oral Vocabulary; Develop Phonemic Awareness; ❶ Divide Words into Syllables; Decode Multisyllabic Words

TEACH SYLLABICATION RULES

1 Build Oral Vocabulary Display Transparency 79. Play "I Spy," giving a series of clues until students find the picture. For example, for Item D, say:

- *I spy **children**. A group of boys and girls are all together. The **children** are looking up.*

When students find the children, say: *Yes, **these are children*** (point). Repeat to build context for the other words.

2 Develop Phonemic Awareness Remove the transparency and conduct the oral activities in Step 1 of the Script for Transparency 79.

3 Decode Multisyllabic Words Display Transparency 79 again. Work through Step 2 of the script.

CLOSE AND ASSESS

Display the words *canyon, fifty, hundred,* and *children*. Call on students to tell you where to divide each word. Have volunteers blend the parts to read the word.

▶ **Reading Practice Book** page 97 (syllable division: VC/CV, VCCCV)

Reading Practice Book page 97

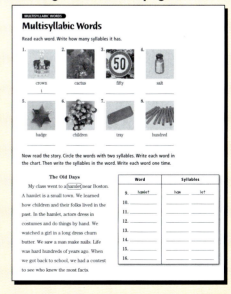

Language and Literacy **T264b**

UNIT 16 **LESSON 9,** CONTINUED

LANGUAGE AND LITERACY: WORD STRUCTURE

OBJECTIVES

Learning to Read: Build Oral Vocabulary; Develop Phonemic Awareness; 🅣 Divide Words into Syllables; Decode Multisyllabic Words

TEACH SYLLABICATION RULES

1 Build Oral Vocabulary Display Transparency 80. Play "I Spy." For example, for Item C, say:

• *I spy the* **bottom level** *of a parking lot. People park their cars in a parking lot. The* **bottom level** *is the lowest level.*

When students find the bottom level, say: *Yes,* **this is the bottom level** (point). Repeat the game to build context for the other words.

2 Develop Phonemic Awareness Remove the transparency and conduct the oral activities in Step 1 of the Script for Transparency 80.

3 Decode Multisyllabic Words Display Transparency 80 again. Work through Step 2 of the script.

CLOSE AND ASSESS

Display the words *planet* and *student.* Call on students to tell you where to divide each word. Have volunteers blend the parts to read the word.

Transparency 80: ▶ **Multisyllabic Words**

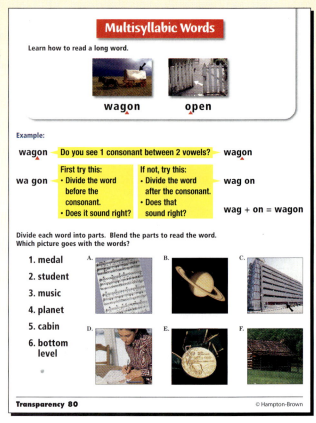

▼ Script for Transparency 80

Multisyllabic Words

1. Develop Phonemic Awareness

Contrast/Match Long and Short Vowel Sounds Say: *Some two-syllable words have a long vowel sound in the first syllable. Listen:* baby, spider, robot. *Other two-syllable words have a short vowel sound in the first syllable. Listen:* cabin, river, closet. *I'm going to say three words. Tell me which two words have the same vowel sound in the first syllable:* visit, river, pilot (visit, river); music, hundred, student (music, student); baby, magic, planet (magic, planet); pilot, visit, silent (pilot, silent). *If students cannot identify the pairs with the same vowel sound, have them repeat each word in the group.*

2. Decode Multisyllabic Words

Teach Say: *Now you are going to learn how to read a long word.* Point to the wagon on **Transparency 80**. Say: *This is a wagon. Many years ago people traveled across the country in wagons. Horses pulled the wagons. Say* wagon *with me:* wagon. *How many parts do you hear?* (2) *Now let's read the word and find out if we will also see two parts.*

Work through the Example below. First point to the *g* in *wagon* and say: *Do you see one consonant between two vowels?* (yes) *The consonant* g *is between the vowels* a *and* o. *First, try this: Divide the word before the consonant. Say the long sound for the first vowel when you read the word:* wā-gon, wāgon. *Does the word sound right?* (no) *When the word does not sound right, try this: Divide the word after the consonant. Say the short sound for the first vowel:* wag-on, wagon. *Does the word sound right now?* (yes) Repeat for *open,* pointing out that the word sounds right when it is divided before the consonant and the *o* has the long vowel sound.

Practice Have students do Items 1–6. Ask a volunteer to show you where to divide each word. Write the parts and lead the group in blending them to read the word. Decide whether the word sounds right. If not, have the volunteer divide the word again and repeat the blending. Then have the group identify the picture that goes with the word.

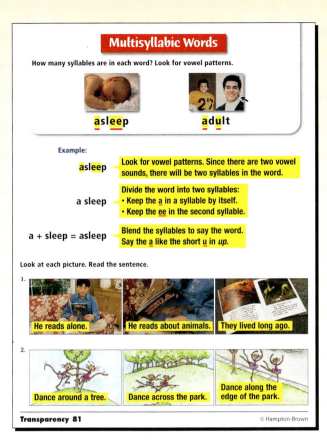

◀ Transparency 81: Multisyllabic Words

▼ Script for Transparency 81

Multisyllabic Words

1. Develop Phonemic Awareness
Listen for the Stressed Syllable/Identify Schwa Say: *In some two-syllable words, you say the second syllable longer and louder than the first syllable.* Say the following words, stressing the second syllable: *asleep, around, alone, about. What is the first syllable you hear in these words?* (/ə/). *Yes, the first syllable is a sound like the short u in up.* Lead students in saying these words, clapping on the second, stressed syllable: *asleep, around, alone, about, adult, ago, across, along.*

2. Decode Multisyllabic Words
Teach Say: *Now you are going to learn how to use vowel patterns to figure out how many syllables a word has.* Point to the sleeping baby on **Transparency 81**. Say: *This baby is asleep.* Say *asleep* with me: *asleep. How many parts do you hear?* (2) *Now let's read the word and find out if we will also see two parts.*

Work through the Example below. First point to *asleep* and say: *Look for vowel patterns. The* a (point) *makes one vowel sound. In this word* a *makes the sound* /u/. *The two vowels* ee (point) *work together to make one vowel sound:* /ē/. *Since there are two vowel sounds, there will be two syllables in the word.* Then point to *asleep* and say: *To read this word, divide the word into two syllables. Keep the* a *in a syllable by itself. Keep the* ee *together in the second syllable. Blend the syllables to say the word. Say the* a *like the short* u *in up:* /ə/-/s l ē ē ē p/, a-sleep, asleep. Repeat the process for *adult.* Explain that the word *adult* can also be pronounced ad-ult with the stress on the first syllable and the short *a* sound.

Practice Have students read Items 1–2. Ask a volunteer to show you where to divide each two-syllable word that begins with *a*. Write the parts on the board and lead the group in blending the parts to read the word. Then read the entire sentence together.

OBJECTIVES
Learning to Read: Build Oral Vocabulary; Develop Phonemic Awareness; ⓣ Divide Words into Syllables; Decode Multisyllabic Words with /ə/ *a*

TEACH SYLLABICATION RULES

1. **Build Oral Vocabulary** Display Transparency 81. Talk through each picture to develop meaning for the words. For example, for Item 1, say:
   - *This student reads a book **alone*** (point), *or by himself. He is the only one reading the book.*

2. **Develop Phonemic Awareness** Remove the transparency and conduct the oral activities in Step 1 of the Script for Transparency 81.

3. **Decode Multisyllabic Words** Display Transparency 81 again. Work through Step 2 of the script.

CLOSE AND ASSESS
Display the words *ago* and *about*. Call on students to tell you where to divide each word. Have volunteers blend the parts to read the word.

▶ **Reading Practice Book** page 98 (multisyllabic words)

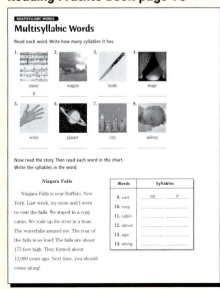

Reading Practice Book page 98

Language and Literacy **T264d**

UNIT 16 **LESSON 10**

LANGUAGE AND LITERACY: READING AND SPELLING

OBJECTIVES

Functions: Listen Actively; Repeat Spoken Language; Recite

Learning to Read: Develop Phonemic Awareness; Associate Sounds and Symbols /ə/ *a*; **T** Divide Words into Syllables; Decode Multisyllabic Words

Spelling: **T** Multisyllabic Words

LISTEN AND LEARN

Tape 8B / CD 3 Track 13

1. **Recite a Poem** Display Transparency 82 and play "Town in the Desert" on the **Language Tape/CD**.

DEVELOP PHONEMIC AWARENESS

2. **Manipulate Words—Delete the Initial or Final Syllable** Say: *Listen to this word:* canyon. *Say* canyon *without* yon. (can) Continue with *cabin without* in (cab); *away without a* (way); *contest without* con (test); *open without o* (pen); *wagon without on* (wag).

STUDY LONG WORDS

3. **Identify Syllables** For Item 1, say: *This is a cactus. Here's the word. I see 2 consonants between 2 vowels, so I divide the word between the consonants. Then I blend the parts to read the word:* cac-tus. Repeat for Items 2–5. For Item 2, point out the 3 consonants between 2 vowels. Note that the blend *dr* should be kept together when dividing *hundred*. For Items 3 and 4, identify 1 consonant between 2 vowels and say: *Divide the word before the consonant. Say the long sound for the first vowel. If that doesn't sound right, divide the word after the consonant, and say the short sound for the first vowel.* For Item 5, say: *The* a *makes the vowel sound* /u/ *and the letters* ee *make the sound* /ē/. Then read the question and have students identify the pattern in each word.

Afterwards, play the poem again. Have students identify words with more than one syllable.

T264 Unit 16 | This Land Is Our Land

MULTISYLLABIC WORDS

Reading and Spelling

LISTEN AND LEARN

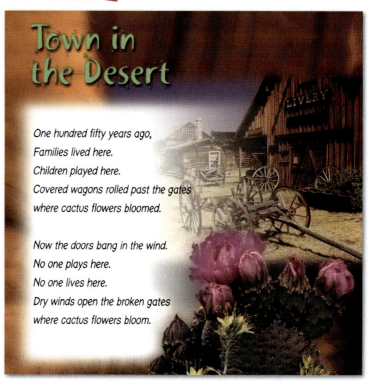

Town in the Desert

One hundred fifty years ago,
Families lived here.
Children played here.
Covered wagons rolled past the gates
where cactus flowers bloomed.

Now the doors bang in the wind.
No one plays here.
No one lives here.
Dry winds open the broken gates
where cactus flowers bloom.

STUDY LONG WORDS

How should you divide each word into syllables? Look for the pattern.

1. cactus
2. hundred
3. open gate
4. wagon
5. asleep

264 Unit 16 | This Land Is Our Land ▶ Transparencies 78–81

REACHING ALL STUDENTS

Multi-Level Strategies

LITERACY SUPPORT

INTERRUPTED SCHOOLING To anchor understanding of how to divide words into syllables, write these words: *canyon, hundred, open, planet, alone*. First, mark the pattern of consonants and vowels as shown. Use the pattern to determine how to divide the word into syllables. Then blend the syllables together to read each word. For practice, have students divide these words: *fifty, children, hotel, cabin,* and *alone*.

c(a)n y(o)n	can‚yon
h(u)ndr(e)d	hund‚red
(o)p(e)n	o‚pen
pl(a)n(e)t	plan‚et
(a)l(o)ne	a‚lone

PRELITERATE One at a time, display the picture banks from Transparencies 78–81 on an overhead projector, covering the words with a strip of paper. As you say each word, guide students in spelling it letter by letter. Then remove the strip and have students check their work.

READING STRATEGY

Follow these steps to read long words.

Pronunciation of Name
Chen Lu   chen lü

1. Look for the pattern of vowels and consonants in the middle of the word.

   canyon — *There are two consonants between two vowels.*

   music — *There are one consonants between two vowels.*

2. Blend the syllables together to read the word.

   canyon
   can + yon = canyon

   You can break words like music either way. See which way sounds right

   mu**s**ic or mu**s**ic

   mu + sic = music

   This one sounds right. The u is long.

READING AND SPELLING PRACTICE

Use what you learned to read the sentences.

1. About one hundred fifty years ago, California became the thirty-first state.
2. Adults and children traveled over 2,000 miles to build homes there.
3. They built cabins in the high mountains and in the low deserts.
4. They built farms all across the open lands.
5. They built cities near the lakes, the rivers, and along the coast.
6. Today, millions of people enjoy living in this sunny state.

7.–11. Now write the sentences that your teacher reads. *For dictation sentences, see Step 6 at right.*

WORD WORK

12.–20. Read the newspaper article. Find all the words with two syllables. Copy the chart. Write each word under the word that has the same pattern.

Boy Wins Essay Contest

Chen Lu is on his way to Boston! He won first place in an essay contest called "This Land is Our Land." The contest was open to all students in grades 5 through 8. Chen won a medal and a visit to Boston. Chen's essay, "The Broken Wagon," was based on a book he read.

canyon	event	cabin
12. essay	15. open	18. medal
13. contest	16. students	19. visit
14. Boston	17. broken	20. wagon

Example: 12. essay

Language and Literacy 265

Decodable Book

PRACTICE WITH MULTISYLLABIC WORDS

Decodable Book 16: *Postcards from Deven*

Assign **Decodable Book 16** for independent reading. The **Decodable Book** can be used in a variety of ways to help students become more fluent, automatic readers:

Discussion Circles Have students work in small groups to read aloud and discuss the book using the questions on the back cover. Encourage students to read aloud the text that supports their answers. Groups can also work together to complete the Word Work Activity.

Readers Theater Students can read aloud the stories in a class performance. Help them prepare by rereading the stories in daily rehearsals. Work with students to add narration or dialog. Encourage them to use natural phrasing and expression.

Rereading at Home Have students work with family members to reread the book at home. They can take turns reading aloud alternate pages, then rereading the book switching the pages each person reads.

LEARN A READING STRATEGY

4. **Divide Words into Syllables** Work through the strategy with students, reading each step aloud and modeling the actions. To contrast the two possible ways to divide *music*, have students divide the word before the *s*, with the long *u* sound. Then have them divide it after *s* and say the short sound for the first vowel. Then write these words: *about, along, around, across, alone, agree, asleep, away.* Explain that in some two-syllable words, you say the second syllable longer and louder (demonstrate). When these words begin with *a*, the *a* has a sound like short *u* in *up*.

PRACTICE

5. **Read Sentences** Distribute the Partner Prompts from page T311 to guide peers in reading the sentences in Items 1–6. Remind them to use the recognize-word-patterns strategy to read words and to blend the words silently.

6. **Write Sentences** Dictate the following sentences for students to write. Read each sentence at normal speed once so students can listen, and then repeat it slowly word by word as they write:

   7. There are fifty children at the picnic.
   8. There are about one hundred adults.
   9. We hike along a river in the canyon.
   10. The old cabin is sunny and warm.
   11. A cactus grows in the desert.

7. **Conduct "Word Work"** Read the directions and work through the Example. Then have partners complete Items 13–20. Check answers by working through the items as a group.

▶ **Reading Practice Book** pages 171–174 (Decodable Book 16)

CLOSE AND ASSESS

Write the following words: *enjoy, broken, students, wagon, along.* Call on students to identify the pattern in each word, divide it into syllables, and read the word.

Language and Literacy **T265**

UNIT 16 LESSON 11

LANGUAGE AND LITERACY: INDEPENDENT READING

OBJECTIVES

Functions:
Read a Selection; Answer Questions

Learning to Read: ❶ Recognize High Frequency Words; ❶ Divide Words into Syllables to Decode Multisyllabic Words

Reading Strategies: Set a Purpose for Reading; Adjust Reading Rate

Critical Thinking and Comprehension: Classify

Writing: Postcard

READ ON YOUR OWN

1. **Introduce Vocabulary** In "Deep Canyon," students apply phonics skills and read high frequency words taught in Lessons 8–10. Introduce the following story words. Write each word, pronounce it, and spell it. Then give a definition and a context sentence. Use the postcard on page 267 to help teach *layers* and *rapids*:

   - **Colorado:** the name of a river and a state, from the Spanish word *colorado*, meaning "colored red." *The Colorado River flows through Colorado and many other states.*

   - **layers:** levels or sections that lie one on top of the other. *The cake has two layers with chocolate frosting in between.*

   - **rapids:** rushing water of a river. *The rapids tipped the boat over.*

   - **relax:** to have fun; to take it easy. *After school I relax. I play basketball or talk to my friends.*

2. **Set Purposes** View the photo and the map. Then model setting a purpose: *I'll read to find out what the Grand Canyon is like.*

3. **Read and Think: Adjust Reading Rate** Students should read the passage on their own. Suggest that they read paragraph 1 slowly to understand the scientific information. They can speed up for paragraph 2.

T266 Unit 16 | This Land Is Our Land

COMPREHENSION: CLASSIFY

Read on Your Own

DEEP CANYON

Would you like to go back millions of years in time? A visit to the Grand Canyon will take you there. It took the Colorado River millions of years to cut through the land that is now the Grand Canyon. The river cut so deep into the earth that you can see nine thick layers of rock. These layers sit one on top of the other, like pancakes. The bottom layer is the oldest. At this level, you may see some of the oldest rocks on Earth.

There is a lot to do in the Grand Canyon. Take a boat ride where the Colorado River runs slow. Take a raft across rapids where the river runs fast. Enjoy a picnic near a waterfall. Explore 400 miles of trails. Look for tiny birds. At the end of the day, relax in a cabin or a tent. There is no limit to what you can see and do in the Grand Canyon!

The Grand Canyon is located in the northwestern corner of Arizona.

✓ **DECODING CHECK**
Give the Decoding Progress Check on page 1a of the Assessment Handbook.

266 Unit 16 | This Land Is Our Land

REACHING ALL STUDENTS

World Cultures: Natural Sights Point out that the photo on page 266 shows the Grand Canyon, which was formed by the Colorado River. Tell students that the Grand Canyon is one of the most spectacular canyons in the world, and that it is a popular tourist spot in the United States. Then invite volunteers to tell about spectacular natural sights in other parts of the world that they have seen or read about. Students can work together to locate rivers, waterfalls, or landforms on maps. After they gather information in the library or on the Internet, they can create travel brochures for tourists.

CHECK YOUR UNDERSTANDING

Pronunciation of Name
Kashmir Komanapali   kash **mear**   kō mahn ah **pahl** ē

<u>1</u>. Copy this concept map. Work with a partner to add other details. Use the finished map to discuss what you learned about the Grand Canyon.

Sample Responses

EXPAND YOUR VOCABULARY

Work with a partner. Read each sentence aloud. Add different words. Make as many new sentences as you can.

Example: 2. The Grand Canyon is very old. The Grand Canyon has a river and waterfalls.

2. The Grand Canyon _____.
3. The Colorado River _____.
4. There is a lot to do at the Grand Canyon. You can _____.
5. It is fun to be outdoors, where you can see _____.

WRITE ABOUT A VISIT TO THE GRAND CANYON

<u>6</u>. Imagine you are at the Grand Canyon. Write a postcard to a friend. Tell what you see and do there.

Example: 6.

> Dear Kashmir,
>
> I am in the Grand Canyon! The rocks are beautiful. Yesterday, I hiked on a trail. I took a lot of photos. Some day, I want to take a raft down the river.
>
> Your friend,
> Alex

Kashmir Komanapali
300 S. Orange Street
Miami, FL 33109

Language and Literacy 267

CHECK YOUR UNDERSTANDING

4 Comprehension: Classify Read aloud the directions. Tell students that they will add details to the map by answering the questions in the two smaller ovals. Say: *To answer the question "What can you see there?" I will write the things people can see at the Grand Canyon.* Then model looking for a detail in the passage (for example, "layers of rock"). Next, say: *To answer "What can you do there?" I will look in the second paragraph and write the things you can do at the Grand Canyon.* Model again looking for a detail (for example, "take a boat ride"). After students finish, encourage them to use their maps to tell what they learned about the Grand Canyon.

EXPAND YOUR VOCABULARY

5 Describe Places Read the directions and use the Example to model how to use details from the passage to write different sentences for Item 2. Tell students to make as many sentences as they can for each item.

WRITE

6 Describe the Grand Canyon Point out that the Example shows a postcard from the Grand Canyon. Ask students to name things they can see and do there. Then invite them to write their own postcard from the Grand Canyon.

For students who need support in writing, provide a postcard frame:

> Dear _____,
> I am in _____
> _____
> _____
> _____
> Your friend,
> _____

▶ Reading Practice Book page 99

CLOSE AND ASSESS

Have students take turns giving sentences about something they can see and do at the Grand Canyon.

Reading Practice Book page 99

COMPREHENSION
Build Reading Fluency

Read the article. Stop when the timer goes off. Mark your score. Then try it again two more times on different days.

The Pony Express Trail

Before 1860, it took three weeks to carry mail across the United States. It traveled slowly by boat and by stage coach. Then the U.S. started a new mail service. It was called the Pony Express. Many boys worked for the Pony Express. They rode fast ponies between the state of Missouri and the California coast. Each rider rode about 75 miles, changing ponies along the way. After 75 miles, another rider would take the mailbag. The riders rode day and night. They rode through heat, rain, and snow. They traveled 1,966 miles across plains, deserts, and high mountains. The entire trip took ten days. The riders were paid $100 to $150 a month. That was a lot of money in 1860, and the riders earned every penny of it.

	Day 1	Day 2	Day 3
Total Words Read in One Minute			
Minus Words Missed			
Words Read Correctly in One Minute			

Reading Fluency
TIMED READINGS

Read the title and introduction on **Reading Practice Book** page 99. Set the timer and have a student read the passage to you. Use the script on page T327 to mark words the student misses and to note the last word read in one minute. Have students graph their performance and set a goal for improving in subsequent timed readings. Plan for two additional timed readings, and encourage partners to practice reading the passage to each other between the timed readings.

Language and Literacy **T267**

UNIT 16 LESSON 12
LANGUAGE ACROSS THE CURRICULUM: SOCIAL STUDIES

OBJECTIVES
Function: Listen to an Article
Concepts and Vocabulary:
Geography; 🔊 Landforms; 🔊 Bodies of Water
Research Skills and Learning Strategies:
Preview; Use Text Structures and Features (maps, symbols, photographs)
Critical Thinking and Comprehension:
Identify Details; Summarize; Relate to Personal Experience

LEARN ABOUT REGIONS

1 Explore Regions Read aloud the introductory text, then point out the map within the article in the lower part of the page and explain that the U.S. can be divided into five regions.

Point to the map at the top of the page and explain: *This map shows just the Southwest region. This region includes the states of Arizona, New Mexico, Texas, and Oklahoma.* Point out that the map gives information about some of the region's products and where each is found. Finally, go over the discussion of climate.

READ AND THINK

2 Preview/Use Visuals Read the article title and the focus question. Then point out the photos and read their captions. Remind students that photos can be used to understand the text.

3 Read the Article Aloud Restate ideas and clarify vocabulary as necessary. Refer to the photos at relevant points in the text.

CHECK UNDERSTANDING

4 Answer the Review Questions Remind students to refer to the informational map at the top of the page, as well as to the article, as they answer Items 1–3.

CLOSE AND ASSESS
Have partners create questions about the maps or the article. Lead the group in checking the page for the answers.

T268 Unit 16 | This Land Is Our Land

SUCCESS IN SOCIAL STUDIES

Learn About Regions of the U.S.

THE SOUTHWEST

A **region** is a part of a country.

The **geography** of a region includes its physical features, like mountains, rivers, forests, or deserts.

The **climate** of a region is what the weather is usually like there. In the Southwest the weather is usually hot and dry in the summer.

Answers for the Review
1. Students' answers sho[uld] summarize the information in the arti[cle].
2. Arizona: cattle, copper, and cotton. Texas: cattl[e], cotton, natural gas, an[d] oil.
3. West, Midwest, Northe[ast], and Southeast. Help students name the reg[ion] in which you live.

Listen to the article. Then do the Review.

The Southwest: A Region of Richness
• What is the southwestern region of the United States like?

The southwestern region of the United States is made up of Arizona, New Mexico, Texas, and Oklahoma. It covers over 572,300 square miles.

Most of the region has a warm and dry climate in the summer. For example, it is about 83°F in Houston, Texas, in July. Only 3.3 inches of rain fall there at that time.

You can see interesting landforms in the region. One of the most famous is the Grand Canyon. Flat-topped hills called **mesas** are in Arizona and New Mexico. Texas has many dry plains.

Mesa

The Southwest produces useful products. There is a lot of oil and natural gas throughout the region. Many people raise cattle, too. Cotton and copper are two other important products from the region.

Oil Well

The Southwest was once part of Mexico. Cities, rivers, and other places still have Spanish names. Mexican celebrations are important in the culture of the region. Many Mexican Americans live in the Southwest.

Most people who live in the Southwest live near the major cities. For example, more than 1,992,000 people live in the Houston, Texas, area.

The Southwest is a region of richness from its geography to its products.

REVIEW
1. **Check Your Understanding** What is the Southwest like?
2. **Use Product Maps** What does Arizona produce? What does Texas produce?
3. **Vocabulary** Name the other regions in the United States. In which region do you live?

268 Unit 16 | This Land Is Our Land

REACHING ALL STUDENTS

Social Studies Connection
STATES, GEOGRAPHY, PRODUCTS

Provide blank maps of your region, then assign small groups to research one of the following topics:

• landforms and bodies of water
• products and natural resources
• cities and state capitals

Help students use encyclopedias, atlases, and the Internet to find information and use symbols to label the maps. Combine the maps to form an informational atlas of your region.

Writing Project / Biographical Sketch

WRITING ASSESSMENT Use the Writing Progress Checklist on page 51 of the Assessment Handbook to evaluate this writing project.

A biography tells about a person's life. Write a paragraph to give the biography of a famous American. What makes the person special?

FIND INFORMATION

1. Choose a person to study. Look through *All Across America*, or ask your teacher or a librarian for help.

2. Brainstorm questions. Put each question on a card. Then find the answers. Ask a teacher, look in a book, or use the Internet.

PLAN AND WRITE YOUR PARAGRAPH

Use the information you learned to write your paragraph. First write a **topic sentence**. Tell the person's name and what he or she did. Then give the **details**:
- Tell when and where the person lived.
- Tell why the person is famous.
- Tell how the person helped the United States.

Check Your Work
- Does your biography give facts about a famous American?
- Does your paragraph follow the plan above?
- Did you capitalize the names of people and places?

Dr. Sally Ride

Dr. Sally Ride is a scientist and astronaut. She was born on May 26, 1951, and lives in California. She was the first American woman in outer space. She was a mission specialist in space. Later she wrote three books about space. Now she is a physics teacher at a university in San Diego.

SHARE YOUR BIOGRAPHY

Copy your paragraph or type it on a computer. Add illustrations, if you like. Read your paragraph to the class. Then display it on a bulletin board.

Language Across the Curriculum **269**

UNIT 16 LESSON 13

LANGUAGE ACROSS THE CURRICULUM: WRITING

OBJECTIVES
Functions: Ask and Answer Questions; Give Information; Write

Learning Strategies and Critical Thinking: Plan; Generate and Organize Ideas; Self-Assess

Research Skills: Gather Information; Take Notes; Locate Resources

Writing: ❶ Paragraph (biographical sketch)

CONDUCT THE WRITING PROJECT

1 Explore Biographical Sketches Remind students that *All Across America* describes Americans who are famous for their contributions in different areas. Explain that a short article about a person's life is called a *biographical sketch*.

2 Find Information Preview the numbered steps. Once students have chosen a person to study, guide them in preparing questions using the question words they learned on pages 258–259. Help them conduct research in print or electronic encyclopedias, history textbooks, or the Internet.

3 Plan and Write Your Paragraph Go over the directions and the sample sketch. Then have students organize their index cards. Offer assistance in formulating a topic sentence, then have students write their paragraphs independently. Remind them to indent the first line.

4 Share Your Biography Encourage students to add a drawing or photo. Ask students if they would like to include their biographies in their **Portfolio**.

▶ **Language Practice Book** page 125

CLOSE AND ASSESS
As students look at their work, say:
- *What famous American did you write about? Read me one fact about him or her.*
- *Read aloud your topic sentence. Point to the paragraph indent.*
- *Show me the people and place names in your writing. Are they capitalized?*

Language Practice Book page 125

WRITING PROJECT: BIOGRAPHICAL SKETCH
A Famous American
Write a paragraph about a famous American. Use your notes to tell what makes the person special. Follow these steps.

1. Write a title.
2. Write a **topic sentence**. Tell the person's name and what he or she did.
3. Add the **details**.
   - Tell **when** and **where** the person lived.
   - Tell **why** the person is famous.
   - Tell **how** the person helped the United States.

Type or copy your paragraph on a clean sheet of paper. Add illustrations, if you like. Read your paragraph to the class.

Multi-Level Strategies
WRITING SUPPORT
PRELITERATE Provide a paragraph frame for students to complete. Model how to make word choices that reflect the correct tense for verbs and the correct gender for pronouns. Take dictation as needed.

Famous Person: _____
_____ is/was a famous _____.
She/He lives/lived in _____.
She/He is famous because _____.
She/He helped the United States by _____.

Language Across the Curriculum **T269**

Resources

For Success in Language and Literacy

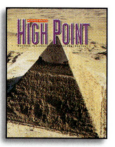

Student Book pages 270–283

For Language Skills Practice

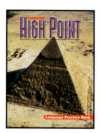

Language Practice Book pages 126–130

For Reading Skills Practice

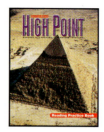

Reading Practice Book pages 100–104

For Vocabulary, Language Development, and Reading Fluency

Language Tape 9, Side A
Language CD 3, Tracks 14–16

For Reading Together

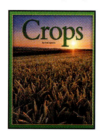

Theme Book *Crops*
from The Basics Bookshelf

For Audio Walk-Throughs and Selection Readings

Selection Tape 9A
Selection CD 3, Tracks 9–10

For Phonics Instruction

Transparencies 83–87

Transparency Scripts 83–87

Letter Tiles

For Comprehensive Assessment

Language Acquisition Assessment,
Units 16–18 Test, Writing Assessment,
Self-Assessment

For Planning and Instruction

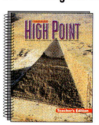

Teacher's Edition
pages T270a–T283

T270a Unit Planner

UNIT 17
Harvest Time

In This Unit

Vocabulary
- Farming
- At the Restaurant
- Plants

Language Functions
- Buy or Sell an Item
- Give Information
- Order an Item

Patterns and Structures
- Questions with *How many?* and *How much?*
- Sensory Adjectives

Reading
- Suffixes: -ly, -y, -less, -ful
- Prefixes: un-, re-
- Comprehension: Make Comparisons (comparison chart, concept map)

Writing
- Questions and Answers
- Descriptions
- Crop Comparison Report

Content Area Connection
- Science (plants)

T270b

UNIT 17 Activity and Assessment Planner

UNIT 17: Harvest Time

LESSONS

1

UNIT 17 LAUNCH ▶ *pages T270–T271*

LESSON 1: INTRODUCE UNIT 17 pages T270–T271

Vocabulary
T Farming

Viewing
Interpret a Visual Image

Learning Strategies
Preview

Build Background

Critical Thinking
Relate Steps in a Process

2–5

LANGUAGE DEVELOPMENT ▶ *pages T272–T275*

LESSON 2
HOW MANY? HOW MUCH?
page T272

Function
Buy or Sell an Item

Patterns and Structures
T Questions with *How Many?* and *How Much?*

Writing
Questions

LESSON 3
FARMING
page T273

Function
Give Information

Vocabulary
T Farming

Writing
Questions and Answers

LESSON 4
AT THE RESTAURANT
page T274

Function
Order an Item

Vocabulary
T Restaurant Words

Writing
Restaurant Order

LESSON 5
SENSORY ADJECTIVES
page T275

Function
Describe

Patterns and Structures
T Sensory Adjectives

Writing
Description

6–11

LANGUAGE AND LITERACY ▶ *pages T276a–T281*

LESSON 6
BASICS BOOKSHELF
pages T276a–T276f

Function
Listen to a Book

Vocabulary
T Crops

Reading Strategies
Activate Prior Knowledge

Preview

Use Text Structures (maps, charts)

Learning to Read
Predict Words

Critical Thinking and Comprehension
T Make Comparisons

LESSON 7
BASICS BOOKSHELF: COMPREHENSION
page T276

Function
Give Information

Learning Strategy
Use Graphic Organizers (comparison chart)

Critical Thinking and Comprehension
T Make Comparisons

LESSON 8
HIGH FREQUENCY WORDS
page T277

Learning to Read
T Recognize High Frequency Words

LESSON 9
PHONICS
pages T278a–T278d

Learning to Read
Build Oral Vocabulary

Develop Phonemic Awareness

T Decode Words with Suffixes (*-ly, -y, -less, -ful*)

T Decode Words with Prefixes (*un-, re-*)

LESSON 10
READING AND SPELLING
pages T278–T279

Learning to Read
Develop Phonemic Awareness

T Decode Words with Prefixes and Suffixes (*un-, re-, -ly, -y, -less, -ful*)

Spelling
T Words with Prefixes and Suffixes

LESSON 11
INDEPENDENT READING
pages T280–T281

Functions
Read a Selection

Make Comparisons

Learning to Read
T Recognize High Frequency Words

T Decode Words with Prefixes and Suffixes (*un-, re-, -ly, -y, -less, -ful*)

Reading Strategies
Activate Prior Knowledge

Set a Purpose for Reading

Compare Texts

Critical Thinking and Comprehension
T Make Comparisons

Writing
Crop Comparisons

12–13

LANGUAGE ACROSS THE CURRICULUM ▶ *pages T282–T283*

LESSON 12
SCIENCE: PLANTS
page T282

Function
Listen to an Article

Vocabulary
Plants

T Farming

Research Skills and Learning Strategies
Build Background

Activate Prior Knowledge

Critical Thinking and Comprehension
Identify Steps in a Process

Summarize

LESSON 13
WRITING PROJECT: CROP REPORT
page T283

Functions
Make Comparisons

Write

Vocabulary
T Farming

Plants

Learning Strategies and Critical Thinking
Plan

Generate and Organize Ideas

T Make Comparisons

Self-Assess

Research Skills
Gather Information

Take Notes

Locate Resources

Use the Research Process

Representing
Venn Diagram

Writing
Report

T270c Unit 17 | Harvest Time

T = Objective Tested on Unit Test

ASSESSMENT OPTIONS

The **Teacher's Edition** and the **Assessment Handbook** include these comprehensive assessment tools:

▶ **Ongoing, Informal Assessment**
Check for understanding and achieve closure for every lesson with the targeted questions and activities in the **Close and Assess** boxes in your Teacher's Edition.

▶ **Decoding Progress Check**
These word lists for each unit provide a quick way to check on mastery of the phonics or word structure skills taught in the unit.

▶ **Language Acquisition Assessments**
To verify students' ability to use the language functions and grammar structures taught in Units 1–3, conduct these performance assessments.

▶ **Unit Test in Standardized Test Format**
This multiple-choice test measures students' cumulative understanding of the skills and language developed in Units 1–3.

▶ **Self-and Peer-Assessment**
Students use the Self-Assessment Form to evaluate their own work and develop learning strategies appropriate to their needs. Students offer feedback to their classmates with the Peer-Assessment Form.

▶ **Writing Assessment/Portfolio Opportunities**
You can evaluate students' writing in the Writing Projects using the Writing Progress Checklist. Then collaborate with students to choose work for their portfolios.

UNITS 1–3 ASSESSMENT OPPORTUNITIES	Assessment Handbook Pages
Decoding Progress Check	1a
Language Acquisition Assessments	42
Units 16–18 Test	43–48
Self-Assessment Form	49
Peer-Assessment Form	50
Writing Progress Checklist	51
Portfolio Evaluation Form	52

RELATED RESOURCES

Farms
by Sylvia Madrigal
A photo-essay about food production on a variety of different farms, including a dairy farm and a wheat farm.
(Hampton-Brown)
Theme Book: Read Aloud

Farming
by Gail Gibbons
Simple text, labels, and captions introduce different kinds of farms and the work done on them from season to season. (Available from Hampton-Brown)
Vocabulary: Farming

Corn
by Pam Robson
A photo-essay about the cultivation and processing of corn. Part of a series called *What's for Lunch?* (Children's Press)
Phonics Reinforcement:
Suffixes *-ly, -y, -ful*

Apples
by Gail Gibbons
Text and illustrations explain how apples were brought to North America, how they are grown, and their cultural significance. (Holiday)
Easy Reading

The Milk Makers
This episode from the popular TV reading series shows the route that milk takes from dairy farm to supermarket. (Reading Rainbow)
Multimedia: Videocassette

Unit Planner **T270d**

UNIT 17 **LESSON 1**

INTRODUCE UNIT 17: HARVEST TIME

OBJECTIVES
Concepts and Vocabulary: ⓣ Farming
Viewing: Interpret a Visual Image
Learning Strategies:
Preview; Build Background
Critical Thinking:
Relate Steps in a Process

START WITH A COMMON EXPERIENCE

1 **Introduce "Harvest Time"** Read the unit title and point to the photo labeled "Harvest." Explain that "harvest time" comes when the fruits or vegetables that a farmer is growing are ready to be picked.

2 **Learn About Farming** Explain that each picture shows one step in the process of growing food and getting it to market. Post a sentence frame:

    The farmers _____ the _____.

Then work as a class to complete the sentence for each picture: *The farmers water the plants. The farmers plant the seedlings.* Discuss each step in the process to be sure that students understand. Have partners copy each sentence on a separate self-stick note.

3 **Place Steps in Order** Read the activity directions, and think aloud as you model identifying the first step: *The first thing farmers do is plow the field. They get the ground ready for the seedlings. I'll put this sentence first.* Have partners organize the remaining steps by sequencing the sentences on the self-stick notes.

Provide a list of time order words, such as: *First, Then, Next, After that,* and *Finally.* Then have pairs take turns describing the farming process in order: *First, the farmers plow the field.*

REACHING ALL STUDENTS

HOME CONNECTION

Interview Have students interview a family member who has experience in raising plants. Students can use what they learned about farming to ask questions: *How do you get the ground ready for the plants? Do you sell your plants?* Have students take notes and illustrate each step of the process. Then invite volunteers to share their information and their illustrations with the class.

T270 Unit 17 | Harvest Time

HARVEST TIME

Work with a partner.
What is the correct order for the pictures?
Use the pictures to tell how broccoli comes from the farm to your table.

Answers:
The correct order is: plow, plant, water, harvest, transport, sell and buy.

In This Unit

Vocabulary
- Farming
- At the Restaurant
- Plants

Language Functions
- Buy or Sell an Item
- Give Information
- Order an Item

Patterns and Structures
- Questions with *How many?* and *How much?*
- Sensory Adjectives

Reading
- Suffixes: -ly, -y, -less, -ful
- Prefixes: un-, re-
- Comprehension: Make Comparisons (comparison chart, concept map)

Writing
- Questions and Answers
- Descriptions
- Crop Comparison Report

Content Area Connection
- Science (plants)

271

PREVIEW THE UNIT

4 Look for Activities and Information About Farming Leaf through the unit, previewing activities students will do, for example:

page 272—learning a song about selling apples in a market

page 273—learning words about farming

page 276—listening to the Bookshelf book (Display a copy of the book.)

page 278—learning a poem about planting corn

page 283—writing a report comparing crops

Also ask students to look for information about buying, selling, or ordering crops. Highlight the farmers' market on page 272 and the menu on page 274, for example. Then sum up what the preview reveals: *There's a lot to know about food, including: how it's grown, how it's sold,* and *how it's served.*

5 Set Your Goals Start a class mind map about growing, selling, and serving food. Prompt students for pictures or words to add, and have them act out and describe other ideas for you to put into words.

CLOSE AND ASSESS

Ask students to tell or show you something they are interested in learning in this unit.

UNIT 17 Mind Map

```
              Food Production
              and Marketing
       /           |            \
     Farm        Market       Restaurant
```

Farm
plow field
plant seeds
water plants
harvest crop
transport crop

Market
sell food
buy food

Restaurant
choose from a menu
take an order
cook food
serve food
eat!

Technology Support
See **Inspiration** Visual Learning software for support in creating mind maps.

Unit Launch **T271**

UNIT 17 LESSON 2
LANGUAGE DEVELOPMENT: HOW MANY? HOW MUCH?

OBJECTIVES
Functions: Listen Actively; Repeat Spoken Language; Recite; Buy or Sell an Item
Patterns and Structures: 🅣 Questions with *How Many?* and *How Much?*
Writing: Questions

INTRODUCE

1 Listen and Sing Play "At the Farmers' Market" on the **Language Tape/CD**. Students will read along, echo the lines, and chime in on the entire song. *(Tape 9A / CD 3 Track 14)*

2 Learn About *How Many?* and *How Much?* Read the Questions chart, then ask: *Which questions in the song ask about things you can count? Which questions ask about price?*

PRACTICE

3 Conduct "Express Yourself" Model how to buy and sell an item. Then have partners complete the activity.

How to Buy and Sell an Item
- Use *how many* to ask about a number: *How many apples are in a bag?*
- Use *how much* to ask what something costs: *How much are the apples?*
- To sell an item, tell about your products and answer questions: *There are 6 apples in a bag. Each bag costs $3.00.*

APPLY

4 Write Questions Encourage students to check their work with a partner. Distribute Partner Checklist 17 on page T310.

▶ **Language Practice Book** page 126

CLOSE AND ASSESS
Have volunteers share their questions. Ask students if the question asks about cost or about things you can count.

T272 Unit 17 | Harvest Time

QUESTIONS: HOW MANY? HOW MUCH?

The Market Price

Listen and sing.

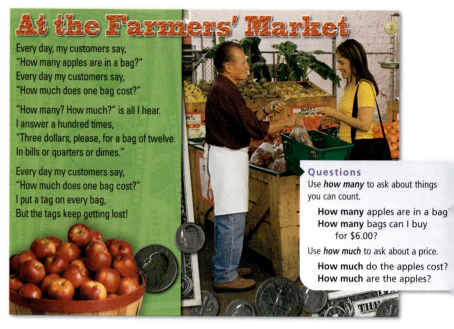

At the Farmers' Market

Every day, my customers say,
"How many apples are in a bag?"
Every day my customers say,
"How much does one bag cost?"

"How many? How much?" is all I hear.
I answer a hundred times,
"Three dollars, please, for a bag of twelve.
In bills or quarters or dimes."

Every day my customers say,
"How much does one bag cost?"
I put a tag on every bag,
But the tags keep getting lost!

Questions
Use *how many* to ask about things you can count.
   How many apples are in a bag
   How many bags can I buy for $6.00?
Use *how much* to ask about a price.
   How much do the apples cost?
   How much are the apples?

EXPRESS YOURSELF ▶ Buy or Sell an Item

Work with a partner. Act out a scene at a farmers' market. Buy and sell the food shown below.

Example: 1. Buyer: How much are the apple
Seller: They are $3.00 a bag.

1.
apples
$3.00 for a bag

2.
green peppers
3 for $1.00

3.
carrots
50¢ per pound

4.
lettuce
$1.00 each

WRITE QUESTIONS

5.–8. Write 4 of the questions you made above on index cards. Trade cards with a partner. Write answers to your partner's questions.

Example: 5. How much are the
They are $3.00 a b

272 Unit 17 | Harvest Time

REACHING ALL STUDENTS

COMMUNITY CONNECTION

Go to Market Arrange a class trip to a farmers' market in your community. Or visit a local produce market or the fresh-produce section of a supermarket. Provide a grocery list of fruits and vegetables for partners to locate. Ask them to complete a chart for their items:

Produce	Price	Amount
Fuji apples	$1.99 for a pound	3 apples per pound
carrots	$1.50 per bunch	8 carrots in a bunch

Language Practice Book page 126

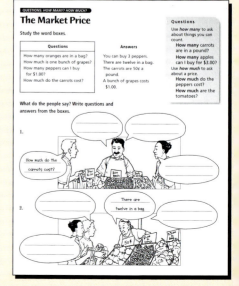

VOCABULARY: FARMING

Down on the Farm

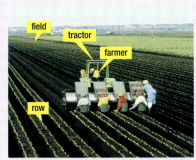

The farmer plows the field and plants the lettuce.

The farmer waters the field.

The farmer gets help to harvest the crop.

EXPRESS YOURSELF ▶ GIVE INFORMATION

1.–3. Work with a partner. Use farming words to tell about each picture.

Example: 1. The farmer drives a tractor. The tractor makes rows in the field.

WRITE QUESTIONS AND ANSWERS ✏️

4.–6. Write 3 questions about farmers' work. Trade papers with a partner. Write answers to your partner's questions.

Example: 4. What does a farmer do first?
The farmer plows the field.

Sample Answers:
1. The farmer drives the tractor. The tractor makes rows in the field. The farmer plants the lettuce.
2. The farmer waters the seedlings in the soil.
3. People help the farmer harvest the crop. They put the food in crates.

Language Development 273

UNIT 17 **LESSON 3**

LANGUAGE DEVELOPMENT: FARMING

OBJECTIVES

Function: Give Information
Concepts and Vocabulary: 🅣 Farming
Writing: Questions and Answers

INTRODUCE

1 Learn Words About Farming Read the captions and labels for each scene. Develop the meaning of each term by pointing out the picture support and using the word in context. Then check understanding: *What does a farmer use to plow?* (a tractor) *What are new plants called?* (seedlings)

PRACTICE

2 Conduct "Express Yourself" Model how to give information. Then have partners complete the activity. They may wish to use the caption as the first sentence, and use the labels to add information about each scene.

> **How to Give Information**
>
> • Use farming words to tell about the picture: *The man is a farmer. He drives a tractor.*
>
> • Add details that tell more: *The farmer drives a tractor to plow rows in the field.*

APPLY

3 Write Questions and Answers Go over the Example. Students can view the pictures here or on pages 270–271 for ideas.

▶ **Language Practice Book** page 127

CLOSE AND ASSESS

Write the farming words on separate slips of paper. Invite volunteers to select a slip, and have the class ask yes-or-no questions to guess the word: *Is it a machine? Is it used to harvest crops?*

Language Practice Book page 127

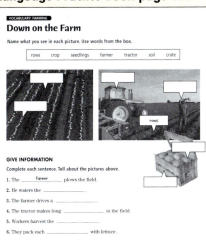

Vocabulary
WORDS FOR FARMING

Farm Mural Divide the class into six groups to study the steps of the farming process on page 270. Find information in books or Web sites, such as:

www.kidsfarm.com/crops.htm
www.usda.gov/news/usdakids
www.cyberspaceag.com

Have each group illustrate the step on chart paper, using self-stick notes to label farming words. Create a class mural, and have groups lead the class through the farming process.

Language Development T273

UNIT 17 LESSON 4
LANGUAGE DEVELOPMENT: AT THE RESTAURANT

OBJECTIVES

Functions: Listen Actively; Order an Item
Concepts and Vocabulary:
 🅣 Restaurant Words
Writing: Restaurant Order

INTRODUCE

1 Learn Restaurant Words Point to the scene and explain that it takes place in a restaurant. Go over the labels and discuss the action. Then review the menu, explaining the categories and asking questions to build meaning: *How much does a pizza cost? What beverages does this restaurant serve?*

2 Build Background Brainstorm phrases that customers and servers say in a restaurant:

Servers	Customers
May I take your order?	I'm ready to order.
What would you like to eat?	I'd like to have _____.
Can I get you anything else?	May I have a refill, please?

PRACTICE

3 Conduct "Who's Talking?" Play "Who's Talking?" on the **Language Tape/CD** to model how to order at a restaurant. Replay as necessary and have students identify the speakers. Then assign roles for students to act out.

Tape 9A
CD 3
Track 15

APPLY

4 Write an Order Explain that the server writes down the items the customer wants. Then the server adds the prices from the menu.

▶ Language Practice Book page 128

CLOSE AND ASSESS

Play the role of server and have students place an order with you.

T274 Unit 17 | Harvest Time

VOCABULARY: AT THE RESTAURANT

Place Your Order

WHO'S TALKING? ▶ ORDER AN ITEM

1.–3. Listen.
Who is talking? Point to the correct person.
Then work in a group of four. Act out the scene. One person is the server. Three people are customers. Order items from the menu.

Answers:
1. server
2. girl ordering
3. boy looking at menu

I want some chicken salad and milk, please.

WRITE AN ORDER

4. Work with a partner. Order some food. Your partner writes down the order. Then change roles.

Example: 4.

102 Guest Check	
date April 18 waiter David	
1. 1 chicken salad	$4.50
2. 1 milk	$1.00
3.	
4.	
TOTAL	$5.50
Thank You!	$5.50

274 Unit 17 | Harvest Time

REACHING ALL STUDENTS

Language Practice Book page 128

SENSORY ADJECTIVES
Describe the Food!

An **adjective** can tell how something looks, feels, smells, sounds, or tastes.

These nachos smell **delicious**. The cheese is **soft** and **warm**. The peppers are **green** and **shiny**. The chips taste **salty**. They sound **loud** and **crunchy**, too!

BUILD SENTENCES

Look at the pictures below. Study the sensory adjectives on pages 310–311 of your Handbook. Use them to describe these foods.

Sample Responses:

Example: 1. The cinnamon rolls are sticky, sweet, and warm.

1.
cinnamon rolls
sticky, sweet, warm

2.
noodles
yellow, long, sticky

3. grapefruit
round, pink, juicy, sour

4.
chili
hot, spicy, delicious

5.
vegetables
crunchy, fresh

6. banana split
sweet, delicious

7.
hamburger
juicy, delicious

8.
orange juice
orange, sweet

9. corn
long, yellow, bumpy

WRITE A DESCRIPTION

10. Write a description of your favorite food. Share the description with a group. Make a chart of all the sensory adjectives your group used.

Example: 10. Chili tastes spicy and delicious. It is hot. It smells really good.

Language Development 275

Language Practice Book page 129

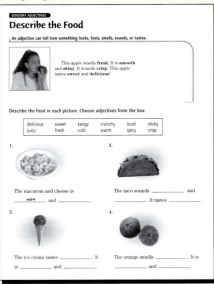

Multi-Level Strategies
LANGUAGE DEVELOPMENT

LITERATE IN L1 In languages such as Chinese, some nouns and adjectives can share the same form. Students who speak these languages may confuse noun and adjective forms and say "She wanted very much to be independence."

Reinforce related nouns and adjectives by having partners write adjectives on one color of card and nouns on another. Have partners draw a card of each color to make a phrase.

UNIT 17 **LESSON 5**

LANGUAGE DEVELOPMENT: SENSORY ADJECTIVES

OBJECTIVES
Function: Describe
Patterns and Structures:
• Sensory Adjectives
Writing: Description

INTRODUCE

1 Learn About Sensory Adjectives Read the title, introduction, and example. Then have volunteers identify sensory adjectives and what they describe: *The word* delicious *tells how the nachos taste. The word* soft *describes how the cheese feels.*

PRACTICE

2 Build Sentences Turn to Handbook pages 310–311 and have students study the sensory adjectives. Develop meaning for some of the entries, as necessary. Then have students refer to these lists (or think of other adjectives) as they complete Items 2–9.

APPLY

3 Write a Description Encourage students to include their favorite ethnic foods. They then can read aloud their descriptions to share their experiences: *Miso soup looks cloudy. Some types of miso are salty. Others are sweet.*

▶ **Language Practice Book** page 129

CLOSE AND ASSESS

Have volunteers read their descriptions. Call on students to choose an adjective from a description and tell what sense it goes with.

UNIT 17 **LESSON 6**

LANGUAGE AND LITERACY: THE BASICS BOOKSHELF

OBJECTIVES

Concepts and Vocabulary: 🅣 Crops
Listening: Listen to a Preview
Reading Strategies: Activate Prior Knowledge; Preview; Use Text Structures (maps, charts)

BUILD LANGUAGE AND VOCABULARY

Materials: supermarket advertisement flyers

1. **Teach "Words to Know"** Turn to pages 2–5 and say: *A crop is a plant that a farmer grows to eat, use, or sell.*

   Describe each crop as you point to the photo. For example: *Rice is a grain. It grows in fields.* Ask students to raise their hands when they see a crop with which they are familiar.

2. **Sort Crops** Have students use supermarket advertisements to cut out pictures of fruits, vegetables, and grains. Invite them to draw and label pictures of more items from their own culture. Then have students sort the crops into a class chart.

Fruits	Vegetables	Grains
apple	broccoli	rice
banana	carrot	wheat

PREPARE TO READ

3. **Think About What You Know** Invite students to draw pictures showing farms. Ask them to share what they know about crops and farming.

4. **Preview** Play the Audio Walk-Through for *Crops* on the **Selection Tape/CD** to give students the overall idea of the story.

   Tape 9A
   CD 3 Track 9

CLOSE AND ASSESS

Draw a large picture of a farm. Have students draw crops in the fields.

Crops
by Fred Ignacio

Summary This informative book features six crops that are produced in the United States, including: cranberries, wheat, cotton, potatoes, oranges, and sugarcane. Text, photos, and illustrations outline the farming process; maps and charts show farm regions in the country.

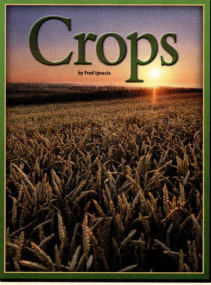

Cover

Pages 2–3

Multi-Level Strategies
LITERACY SUPPORT

PRELITERATE **Use Text Structures: Maps and Charts** Explain that maps and charts are good ways to picture information. Point to the map of the United States on page 6 and say: *This map shows the states where cranberry crops grow best. Look for states that are dark green. The map shows each state's name and location.* Then read aloud the state names: *Cranberries grow in states like Washington, Oregon, Wisconsin, Massachusetts, and New Jersey.* Have partners look at the maps on pages 8, 12, 16, 19, and 22 and tell where each crop is grown.

Next model reading the chart on page 11. Point to the title and ask: *What is the chart about?* Read the headings and say: *The chart tells what farmers were paid for their wheat.* Read across the first row to get information about the first state. Ask: *How much were farmers paid in Kansas in 1998? Which state paid a higher price for wheat in 1997?* Show students how to read down column 2 to compare the prices for the year. Then turn to page 14 and read the chart with students. Ask questions to clarify understanding: *Which states are shown on the chart? Which state grows the most cotton?*

T276a Unit 17 | Harvest Time

Crops

Pages 4–5

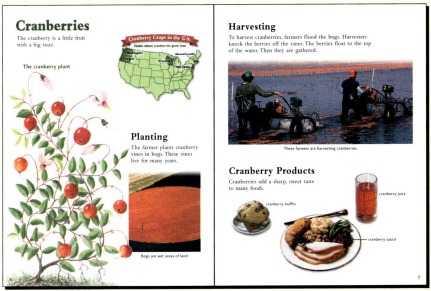

Pages 6–7

Strategies for Comprehensible Input

Page	Story Language	Strategy Options
4–5	different, alike	**Demonstrate:** Show a pencil and a book. Say: *These are different; they are not the same.* Show two pencils. Say: *These are alike or the same.*
6	Planting	**Demonstrate:** Pantomime digging a hole and putting in a plant.
	vines, bogs	**Point to the pictures.**
7	harvest	**Restate:** pick; collect
	gathered	**Explain:** When you gather something, you pick it up.
	Cranberry Products	**Restate:** Things Made From Cranberries

Language and Literacy **T276b**

UNIT 17 **LESSON 6,** CONTINUED

LANGUAGE AND LITERACY: THE BASICS BOOKSHELF

OBJECTIVES
Function: Listen to a Book
Critical Thinking and Comprehension:
T Make Comparisons

READ AND THINK TOGETHER

1. **Read Aloud** On your first reading of the book, point out the six crops on pages 4–5 and turn to the first page noted for each crop. For example, turn to page 6, point out the head *Cranberries,* and say: *This is a main head. It shows where the section on cranberries starts.* Point to *Planting* and say: *This is a subhead. It lets me know that this part of the section will be about planting.* Continue to point out the other sections. Then use the "Strategies for Comprehensible Input" that appear at the bottom of pages T276b, T276d, and T276f.

2. **Read and Map: Make Comparisons** Draw a comparison chart like the one below, but show only the bold headings. Say: *A comparison chart shows how things are the same and different.*

   Read pages 6–7 aloud. Then think aloud as you model filling in the first row: *These pages tell about cranberries. I will write the word* cranberries *as the name of the crop.* Read aloud the remaining headings and model finding information from the text and captions.

   Pause after reading each set of pages shown below and model completing the chart for the rest of the text.

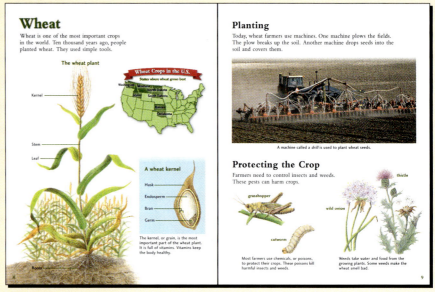

Pages 8–9

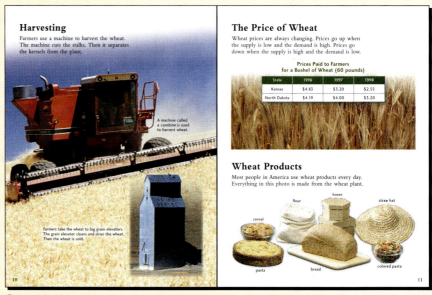

Pages 10–11

Comparison Chart for *Crops*

	Crop	Planting	Harvesting	Products
pages 6–7	cranberries	in bogs	by machine	juice, sauce
pages 8–11	wheat	in fields	by machine	bread, flour
pages 12–15	cotton	in raised beds of soil	by hand or machine	cloth, oil, soap
pages 16–18	potatoes	in rows in fields	by machine	food
pages 19–21	oranges	in groves	by hand	food, juice
pages 22–23	sugarcane	in fields	by hand or machine	sugar, molasses

Technology Support
See **Inspiration** Visual Learning software for support in creating the comparison chart.

Pages 12–13

Pages 14–15

Strategies for Comprehensible Input

Page	Story Language	Strategy Options
8	tools	**Explain:** People use tools to dig or cut.
9	Protecting the Crop	**Restate:** Taking Care of the Crop
	pests	**Explain:** Pests are bugs or insects that eat plants.
	harm	**Restate:** hurt
10	separates	**Demonstrate:** Put your hands together and then move them apart.
11	supply	**Explain:** the amount of wheat there is to sell
	demand	**Explain:** the number of people who want to buy the wheat
12	Almost everyone	**Restate:** Most people
13	raised	**Demonstrate:** Raise your hand six inches from the floor.
	beds	**Explain:** Some crops are planted in lines called beds.
15	is useful	**Restate:** can be used

Language and Literacy T276d

UNIT 17 **LESSON 6,** CONTINUED

LANGUAGE AND LITERACY: THE BASICS BOOKSHELF

OBJECTIVES

Functions: Listen to a Book; Repeat Spoken Language (echo reading)
Learning to Read: Predict Words

READ AND THINK TOGETHER, CONTINUED

3 Conduct Interactive Readings
Choose from these options:

- **Echo reading** Play the recording of *Crops* on the **Selection Tape/CD**. Pause the tape after a sentence on each page and have the group echo the sentence. *(Tape 9A / CD 3 Track 10)*

- **Predict words** As you read aloud the book, pause before key words. Ask students to supply missing phrases such as:

page 6	a big taste in bogs
page 8	most important crops in the world
page 9	use machines harm crops
page 10	harvest the wheat
page 11	from the wheat plant
page 13	raised beds of soil
page 14	by hand use machines
page 15	all these products
page 16	favorite vegetable
page 17	six rows of potatoes at a time
page 18	harvest the crop
page 20	in groves like this
page 21	by hand
page 23	cut by hand or harvested by machine

CLOSE AND ASSESS

Use a small object to play a review game. Name a crop, then pass the object to a student. Have the student say one fact about the crop before naming a new crop and passing the object. Continue until each crop in the book has been reviewed.

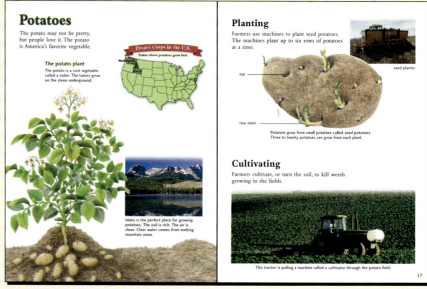

Pages 16–17

Pages 18–19

Multi-Level Strategies

LITERACY SUPPORT

LITERATE IN L1 **Read with a Partner/Make a Poster** After students have participated in the interactive readings, encourage them to read the story with a partner. Distribute the Partner Prompts on page T311 to help partners work together to identify unfamiliar words and unlock their meanings, then read the text to each other. After the partner reading, have partners make a poster advertising the products of one crop. Encourage them to use illustrations and make up a slogan such as: *Cranberries taste sharp and sweet. Cranberries are good to eat!* Display the posters in the classroom.

INTERRUPTED SCHOOLING **Make Comparisons** To anchor understanding of the skill, model finding information on the comparison chart. Point to the title and say: *This chart compares crops.* Read the headings and say: *The chart tells how crops are planted, how they are harvested, and the products that are made from them.* Read across the first row to get information about the first crop. Say: *Cranberries are planted in bogs.* Then read down column 2 to compare the crops. Ask: *How many crops are planted in fields?* Ask more questions using the rest of the chart.

T276e Unit 17 | Harvest Time

Crops, CONTINUED

Pages 20–21

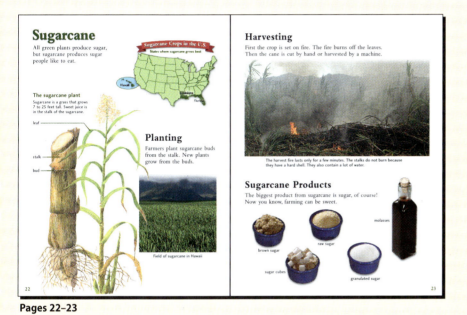

Pages 22–23

Page 24

Strategies for Comprehensible Input

PAGE	STORY LANGUAGE	STRATEGY OPTIONS
16–17	America's favorite vegetable	**Restate:** a vegetable that many people in the United States like to eat
	rows	**Explain:** Some farmers plant their crops in straight lines called rows.
18–19	digs	**Gesture:** Make a digging motion.
	loads	**Demonstrate:** Pantomime putting potatoes on a truck
20–21	groves	**Point to the picture and explain:** A grove is a large group of trees.
22–23	produce	**Restate:** make

Language and Literacy **T276f**

UNIT 17 LESSON 7

LANGUAGE AND LITERACY: THE BASICS BOOKSHELF

OBJECTIVES

Function: Give Information

Learning Strategy: Use Graphic Organizers (comparison chart)

Critical Thinking and Comprehension:
- Make Comparisons

CHECK COMPREHENSION

1. **Make a Comparison Chart** Remind students that a comparison chart shows how things are the same and different.

   Have students work with partners. Read Step 1. Partners should refer to pages 4–5 to set up the crops in column 1.

   Read aloud the directions for Steps 2 and 3. Pause for partners to review the topic for each crop and gather information to add to their charts.

2. **Share Information from the Book** Have small groups use information from their charts to create a rap about one crop and present it to the class. Provide the frame:

   > _____ is a crop.
   > It's planted in _____.
   > It's harvested by _____.
   > _____ and _____ are made from _____.

CLOSE AND ASSESS

Ask students to complete this sentence: *A comparison chart shows _____.*

COMPREHENSION: MAKE COMPARISONS

Read and Think Together

Work with a partner. Make a comparison chart for *Crops*. Follow these steps.

1. Set up a chart like the one below.

Crop	Planting	Harvesting	Products
cranberries			
wheat			
cotton			
potatoes			
oranges			
sugar cane			

2. Read the book again. As you read, fill in the rest of the chart. Tell how farmers plant and harvest each crop. Tell what products are made from the crops.

Crop	Planting	Harvesting	Products
cranberries	in bogs	by machine	juice, sauce
wheat			

3. Use your completed chart to compare the crops. Talk to a partner. Discuss how some of the crops are alike. Discuss how they are different. Use words like these:

   alike   same   but
   and   both   different

Crop	Planting	Harvesting	Products
cranberries	in bogs	by machine	juice, sauce, muffins
wheat	in fields	by machine	bread, flour, cereal, pasta, boxes, hats
cotton	in raised beds	by hand or machine	cloth, oil, soap, thread, cotton balls, yarn, dressing
potatoes	in rows	by machine	food
oranges	in groves	by hand	food, juice, marmalade, perfume, cookies, candies
sugar cane	in fields	by hand or machine	sugar, molasses

276 Unit 17 | Harvest Time

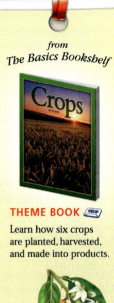

from *The Basics Bookshelf*

THEME BOOK

Learn how six crops are planted, harvested, and made into products.

REACHING ALL STUDENTS

Language Development
MAKE COMPARISONS

Compare Information Use a Venn diagram to compare how crops are harvested. Model how to add information to the diagram, listing similarities in the center section and differences in the outer sections. Then help students complete the diagram and use the information to make comparisons: *Cranberries, wheat, cotton, and potatoes are harvested by machine.*

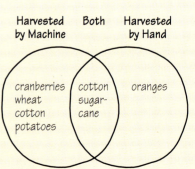

T276 Unit 17 | Harvest Time

HIGH FREQUENCY WORDS
Words to Know

REVIEW WORDS YOU KNOW
Read the words aloud. Which word goes with the sentence?

too	good	1. She takes <u>good</u> care of the garden.
way	why	2. This is the <u>way</u> she does it.
each	earth	3. She gives <u>each</u> plant what it needs.

LEARN TO READ
Learn new words.

weigh	Ana buys tomatoes that **weigh** over 2 pounds.
beautiful	The **beautiful** tomatoes are firm and bright red.
special	They come from a **special** market across town.
own	"I want to grow my **own** tomatoes," Ana thought.
any	She did not have **any** seeds, so she bought some.
indoors	She planted them **indoors**, by her kitchen window.
warm	It was winter, but her kitchen was **warm** and sunny.
healthy	Soon, she had strong and **healthy** seedlings.
cold	By the end of April, the **cold** weather was over.
outdoors	It was time to put her plants **outdoors** in the yard.

How to Learn a New Word
- Look at the word.
- Listen to the word.
- Listen to the word in a sentence. What does it mean?
- Say the word.
- Spell the word.
- Say the word again.

WORD WORK
Write each sentence. Add the missing word. **Example:** 4. You can grow your own flowers at home.

4. You can grow your <u>o w n</u> flowers at home.
5. Sunflower seeds can be planted <u>o u t d o o r s</u> in the garden at the start of spring.
6. Sunflowers are big. The flowers can <u>w e i g h</u> more than a pound!
7. Other seeds must be planted inside the house. The pots stay <u>i n d o o r s</u> for a few weeks.
8. In the summer when it gets <u>w a r m</u> outside, you can put the young plants in your garden.
9. Plant many colorful flowers. They will make your garden look <u>b e a u t i f u l</u>!

10.–13. Find the 4 words you didn't use. Write sentences with those words.

Example: 10. It is too cold to grow vegetables in the winter.
Answers: The words not used are **cold**, **special**, **any**, **healthy**. Students' sentences should show they understand their meaning.

Language and Literacy 277

UNIT 17 LESSON 8
LANGUAGE AND LITERACY: HIGH FREQUENCY WORDS

OBJECTIVES
Learning to Read:
- Recognize High Frequency Words

REVIEW WORDS

1 Review Known High Frequency Words Have the group read aloud the words in the green box. Listen for words students cannot read automatically and use the steps in the yellow box to reteach those words. Then have students look at the photo. Read each cloze sentence. Reread each sentence and pause for students to silently read the two words to the left of the sentence. Tell students to choose the word that goes in the sentence and tells about the picture.

INTRODUCE NEW WORDS

2 Learn High Frequency Words Use the High Frequency Word Script on page T328 to lead students through the steps in the yellow box for each new word.

PRACTICE

3 Conduct "Word Work" Use the Example to model how to use context to find possible words in the list and then to use the number of letter blanks to confirm the selected word.

Have small groups complete Items 5–9. Discuss how each word fits the context and number of blanks. Groups can work together again to write sentences with the other four words.

APPLY

4 Read Words in Context Students will read high frequency words in context in the sentences on page 279 and the passage on page 280.

▶ Reading Practice Book page 100

CLOSE AND ASSESS

Call out the high frequency words one at a time. Have students point to them and spell the words as a group.

Language and Literacy T277

UNIT 17 **LESSON 9**

LANGUAGE AND LITERACY: WORD STRUCTURE

OBJECTIVES

Learning to Read: Build Oral Vocabulary; Develop Phonemic Awareness; ❶ Decode Words with Suffixes (*-ly*)

TEACH SUFFIXES

1 **Build Oral Vocabulary** Display Transparency 83. Talk through each picture to develop meaning for the words in the yellow boxes. For example, for Item 1, say:

• *This person* (point) *is carrying the American flag and walking* **proudly**. *When you walk* **proudly** (demonstrate), *you walk in a way that shows you feel good about yourself and your actions.*

2 **Develop Phonemic Awareness** Remove the transparency and conduct the oral activities in Step 1 of the Script for Transparency 83.

3 **Decode Words with Suffixes** Display Transparency 83 again. Work through Step 2 of the script.

CLOSE AND ASSESS

Display *loudly, suddenly, quickly,* and *safely.* Call on students to identify the root word and the suffix, then blend the two together to read the word.

Transparency 83: ▶
Suffixes

Materials
Letter tiles for:

b	d	l	l
o	s	w	y

Word Parts: Suffix -ly

Learn how to read a word with a suffix.

She runs quickly.

Example:

quick**ly**   quick   *Cover the suffix. Read the root word.*

quickly   *Look at the whole word again.*

quick + ly = quickly   *Blend the parts to say the word.*

Read the words. Look for word parts you know.

1. walk proudly
2. happen suddenly
3. ride safely
4. think deeply
5. shine brightly
6. play loudly

Add **-ly** to each word.

slow
bold

Transparency 83   © Hampton-Brown

▼ **Script for Transparency 83**

Word Parts: Suffix -*ly*

1. Develop Phonemic Awareness

Blend Word Parts Say: *Listen to these word parts:* quick, ly. *Say them with me:* quick, ly. *Now let's blend the two parts to say a new word:* quick-ly, quickly. *Repeat the process with the following word parts:* loud, ly (loudly), bright, ly (brightly); safe, ly (safely); slow, ly (slowly).

2. Decode Words with Suffixes

Teach Say: *Now you are going to learn how to read a word with a suffix. A suffix is a word part that is added at the end of a word.* Frame the root word *quick* in the sentence at the top of **Transparency 83**. Say: *This is the word* quick. *Say it with me:* quick. Explain: *The girl in the picture runs. She is quick.* Point to the suffix *-ly* in *quickly* and say: *I can add this suffix to the word* quick *and change it from an adjective that describes the girl to an adverb that tells how she runs. You can add the suffix -ly to the word* quick *to make the word* quickly. *It means "in a quick way."* Ask: *How does the girl run?* Then read the sentence with students: *She runs quickly.*

Work through the Example to model how to read a word with a suffix. Point to *quickly* and say: *This word has a suffix. To read the word, first cover the suffix. Then read the root word:* quick. Point to *quickly* on the next line and say: *Now look at the whole word again.* Point to the last line and say: *Let's blend the parts to read the word:* quick-ly, quickly.

Practice Have students do Items 1–6. Ask a volunteer to cover the suffix. Have the group read the root word. Then lead the group in blending the parts to read the entire word. At the bottom of the transparency, spell the root words *slow* and *bold* with letter tiles. Have students add the suffix *-ly* to make new words. *(slowly, boldly)* Help students use each word in a sentence.

T278a Unit 17 | Harvest Time

◀ Transparency 84: Suffixes

OBJECTIVES

Learning to Read: Build Oral Vocabulary; Develop Phonemic Awareness;
ⓣ Decode Words with Suffixes *(-y)*

TEACH SUFFIXES

1 Build Oral Vocabulary Display **Transparency 84.** Talk through each picture to develop meaning for the words in the yellow boxes. For example, for Item 6, say:

- This is a **rocky** beach. It is covered with rocks. It can be hard to walk on a **rocky** beach (pantomime).

2 Develop Phonemic Awareness Remove the transparency and conduct the oral activities in Step 1 of the Script for Transparency 84.

3 Decode Words with Suffixes Display Transparency 84 again. Work through Step 2 of the script.

CLOSE AND ASSESS

Display *dirty, sticky, sleepy,* and *windy*. Call on students to identify the root word and the suffix, then blend the two together to read the word.

▶ **Reading Practice Book** page 101 (suffixes: *-ly, -y*)

▼ Script for Transparency 84

Word Parts: Suffix -y

1. Develop Phonemic Awareness
Match/Delete Word Parts Say: *Listen to these words:* dirty, messy. *What part is the same in these words?* (final /ē/) Repeat for *sandy, sticky* (final /ē/); *windy, sleepy* (final /ē/); *rocky, sandy* (final /ē/). Repeat each word and ask students to say it without the final /ē/.

2. Decode Words with Suffixes
Teach Say: *Now you are going to learn how to read new words with a suffix. Remember that a suffix is a word part that is added at the end of a word.* Frame the root word *dirt* in the sentence at the top of **Transparency 84.** Say: *This is the word* dirt. *Say it with me:* dirt. Explain: *The shirt in the picture is not clean. It is dirty.* Point to the suffix *-y* in *dirty* and say: *I can add this suffix to the word* dirt *and change it from a noun that names something you see on the shirt to an adjective that describes the shirt. You can add the suffix* -y *to the word* dirt *to make the word* dirty. *It means "not clean."* Then read the sentence with students: *I'll clean the dirty shirt.*

Work through the Example to model how to read a word with a suffix. Point to *dirty* and say: *This word has a suffix. To read the word, first cover the suffix. Then read the root word:* dirt. Point to *dirty* on the next line and say: *Now look at the whole word again.* Point to the last line and say: *Let's blend the parts to read the word:* dirt-y, dirty.

Practice Have students do Items 1–6. Ask a volunteer to cover the suffix. Have the group read the root word. Then lead the group in blending the parts to read the word. At the bottom of the transparency, spell the root words *sand* and *wind* with letter tiles. Have students add the suffix *-y* to make new words. *(sandy, windy)* Help students use each word in a sentence.

Reading Practice Book page 101

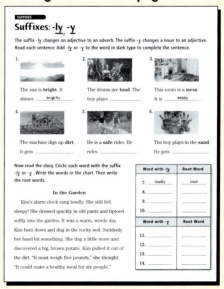

Language and Literacy **T278b**

UNIT 17 **LESSON 9,** CONTINUED

LANGUAGE AND LITERACY: WORD STRUCTURE

OBJECTIVES

Learning to Read: Build Oral Vocabulary; Develop Phonemic Awareness; 🅣 Decode Words with Suffixes (-less, -ful)

TEACH SUFFIXES

1. **Build Oral Vocabulary** Display Transparency 85. Use the pictures to develop meaning for each word with *-less* or *-ful*. Use the word in a sentence. For example, for Item 4, say:

   • The **graceful** ballerina is not clumsy. She moves smoothly across the floor. Her movements are **graceful**.

2. **Develop Phonemic Awareness** Remove the transparency and conduct the oral activities in Step 1 of the Script for Transparency 85.

3. **Decode Words with Suffixes** Display Transparency 85 again. Work through Step 2 of the script.

CLOSE AND ASSESS

Display *harmless, peaceful, graceful,* and *fearless.* Call on students to identify the suffix and the root word, then blend the two together to read the word.

▶ **Reading Practice Book** page 102 (suffixes: *-less, -ful*)

Transparency 85: ▶ **Suffixes**

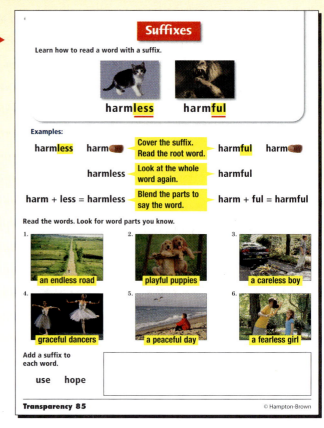

Materials
Letter tiles for:

e	e	f	h
l	o	p	s
s	s	u	u

▼ **Script for Transparency 85**

Suffixes

1. Develop Phonemic Awareness
Blend Word Parts Say: *Listen to these word parts:* harm, less. *Say them with me:* harm, less. *Now let's blend the two parts to say a new word:* harm-less, harmless. Repeat the process for the following word parts: *end, less* (endless); *grace, ful* (graceful); *peace, ful* (peaceful); *use, ful* (useful); *care, less* (careless); *hope, less* (hopeless); *fear, less* (fearless).

2. Decode Words with Suffixes
Teach Say: *Now you are going to learn how to read new words with a suffix. When you read, where do you look for a suffix?* (at the end of a word). Point to *harmless* on **Transparency 85**. Say: *This is the word* harmless. *Say it with me:* harmless. Explain: *The kitten in the picture is not dangerous. It will not hurt, or harm, anyone.* Point to the suffix *-less* in *harmless* and say: *I can add the suffix* -less *to a word and change its meaning. The suffix* -less *often means "without." Someone who feels* hopeless *is "without hope."*

Work through the left side of the Example to model how to read a word with the suffix *-less*. Point to *harmless* and say: *This word has a suffix. To read the word, first cover the suffix. Then read the root word:* harm. Point to *harmless* on the next line and say: *Now look at the whole word again.* Point to the last line and say: *Let's blend the parts to read the word:* harm-less, harmless.

Use the picture for *harmful* to introduce the suffix *-ful*. Say: *The suffix* -ful *(point) often means "full of." The word* harmful *means "full of harm."* Work through the right side of the Example to model how to read a word with the suffix *-ful*.

Practice Have students do Items 1–6. Ask a volunteer to cover the suffix. Have the group read the root word. Then lead the group in blending the parts to read the word. At the bottom of the transparency, spell the root words *use* and *hope* with letter tiles. Have students add the suffixes *-less* and *-ful* to make new words. (*useless, hopeless, useful, hopeful*) Help students use each word in a sentence.

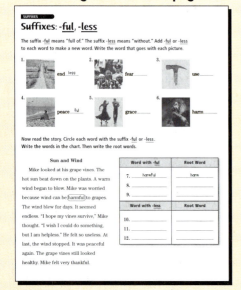

Reading Practice Book page 102

T278c Unit 17 | Harvest Time

◀ Transparency 86: Prefixes

▼ Script for Transparency 86

Prefixes

1. **Develop Phonemic Awareness**
   Match Word Parts Say: *Listen to these words:* unhappy, untied. *What part is the same in these words?* (un) Repeat for *replay, retell* (re); *unlock, undo* (un); *redo, refill* (re), *unwrap, untie* (un).

2. **Decode Words with Prefixes**
   Teach Say: *Now you are going to learn how to read a word with a prefix. A prefix is a word part that is added at the beginning of a word.* Point to *happy* on **Transparency 86**. Say: *This is the word* happy. *Say it with me:* happy. Explain: *The boy in the picture has a big smile. He is happy.* Point to the prefix *un-* in *unhappy* and say: *I can add the prefix* un *to the word* happy *and change the word's meaning. Now the word is* unhappy. *It means "not happy." Let's check the picture. Is the boy happy? No, he is unhappy. The prefix* un- *often means "not," so it changes the meaning of* happy *to "not happy."*

   Work through the Example to model how to read a word with a prefix. Point to *unhappy* and say: *This word has a prefix. To read the word, first cover the prefix. Then read the root word:* happy. Point to *unhappy* on the next line and say: *Now look at the whole word again.* Point to the last line and say: *Let's blend the parts to read the word:* un-happy, unhappy.

   Use the pictures for *build* and *rebuild* to introduce the prefix *re-:* Re- *can mean "again." When I add* re- *to* build, *I get the word* rebuild. *It means "to build again."* Then use the word *rebuild* below the picture to demonstrate the strategy again.

   Practice Have students do Items 1–6. Ask a volunteer to cover the prefix. Have the group read the root word. Then lead the group in blending the parts to read the word. At the bottom of the transparency, spell the root words *safe* and *tell* with letter tiles. Have students add the prefix *un-* or *re-* to make new words. (*unsafe, retell*) Help students use each word in a sentence.

OBJECTIVES

Learning to Read: Build Oral Vocabulary; Develop Phonemic Awareness;
🅣 Decode Words with Prefixes (*un-, re-*)

TEACH PREFIXES

1. **Build Oral Vocabulary** Display Transparency 86. Use the pictures to develop meaning for each word with *un-* or *re-*. Use the word in a sentence. For example, for Item 1, say:
   - *You can use a key to **unlock** a lock. You can use a key to **unlock** a door, too. When you **unlock** something, you open it.*

2. **Develop Phonemic Awareness** Remove the transparency and conduct the oral activities in Step 1 of the Script for Transparency 86.

3. **Decode Words with Prefixes** Display Transparency 86 again. Work through Step 2 of the script.

CLOSE AND ASSESS

Display the words *unlock, untie, replace* and *rewrite*. Call on students to identify the prefix and the root word, then blend the two together to read the word.

▶ **Reading Practice Book** page 103 (prefixes: *un-, re-*)

Reading Practice Book page 103

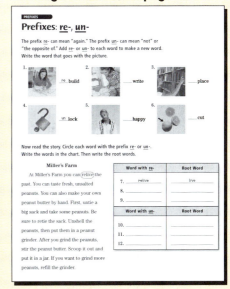

Language and Literacy **T278d**

UNIT 17 LESSON 10

LANGUAGE AND LITERACY: READING AND SPELLING

OBJECTIVES

Functions: Listen Actively; Repeat Spoken Language; Recite

Learning to Read: Develop Phonemic Awareness; ❶ Decode Words with Prefixes and Suffixes (un-, re-, -ly, -y, -less, -ful)

Spelling: ❶ Words with Prefixes and Suffixes

LISTEN AND LEARN
Tape 9A / CD 3 Track 16

1 Recite a Poem Display Transparency 87 and play "Young Corn" on the **Language Tape/CD**. After students have listened and learned the poem, they can pantomime pushing into the earth in the first verse and stretching toward the sky in the second.

DEVELOP PHONEMIC AWARENESS

2 Segment Words into Syllables Say: *Listen to this word:* quickly. *Say the two parts you hear in* quickly. (quick, ly) Follow the same procedure with *unlock.* Continue the activity with *proudly, replant, unseen, repay, graceful, endless,* and *sleepy.*

STUDY WORD PARTS

3 Prefixes and Suffixes Work through each example in the charts. Say: *You can add a prefix to the beginning of a word to make a new word. The prefix* un- *can mean "not." When you add* un- *to the beginning of the root word* seen, *you make a new word:* unseen. Unseen *means "not seen."* Follow a similar procedure for the remaining prefixes and suffixes. Then, on the board, write *unlike, unmade, untie, redo, replay, slowly, sleepy, sleepless,* and *playful.* Call on students to read each word, identify the prefix or suffix, and tell what each word means.

Afterwards, play the poem again. Have students identify words with prefixes or suffixes.

T278 Unit 17 | Harvest Time

PREFIXES AND SUFFIXES
Reading and Spelling

LISTEN AND LEARN

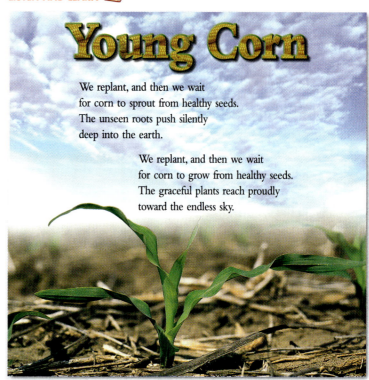

Young Corn

We replant, and then we wait
for corn to sprout from healthy seeds.
The unseen roots push silently
deep into the earth.

We replant, and then we wait
for corn to grow from healthy seeds.
The graceful plants reach proudly
toward the endless sky.

STUDY WORD PARTS

You can add a **prefix** to the beginning of a word.

Prefix	Meaning	Example
un-	not	unseen
	the opposite of	unlock
re-	again	replant
	back	repay

You can add a **suffix** to the end of a word.

Suffix	Meaning	Example
-ly	in a certain way	proudly
-y	full of	healthy
-less	without	endless
-ful	full of	graceful

278 Unit 17 | Harvest Time ▶ Transparencies 83–8?

REACHING ALL STUDENTS

Multi-Level Strategies
LITERACY SUPPORT

INTERRUPTED SCHOOLING To anchor understanding of how to recognize word parts, write *unlock* on the board. Demonstrate how to read the word. First identify the prefix *un-*. Cover it. Then read the root word *lock*. Uncover the prefix, and blend the syllables to read the word: *un-lock, unlock*. Follow a similar procedure to read the word *slowly*, first identifying the suffix. Then call on students to demonstrate how to read the following words: *untie, replace, brightly, dirty, careless, careful, peaceful*.

PRELITERATE Copy the following words and word parts onto index cards: *loud, slow, sleep, stick, care, fear, lock, place, tie, ly, y, less, ful, un,* and *re*. Write the following words on the board: *loudly, slowly, sleepy, sticky, careless, fearless, sleepless, careful, fearful, unlock, replace, untie, retie*. Have students combine two index cards to form each word.

READING STRATEGY

Follow these steps to read a word with a prefix or suffix.

❶ Look for a prefix or a suffix. Cover it. Then read the root word.

untie tie — *When I cover the prefix **un**–, I see a word I know: **tie**.*

Reading Help
Sometimes the letters **re** and **ly** are not prefixes or suffixes. To find out, cover **re** or **ly** and see if you are left with a word. For example:

real   silly
al   sil

❷ Uncover the prefix or the suffix. Blend the syllables to read the entire word.

un + tie = **un**tie — *Untie means "the opposite of tie."*

READING AND SPELLING PRACTICE

Use what you learned to read the sentences.

1. Insects are killing the healthy plants in Matt's garden.
2. He will not use insect sprays. They are messy and unsafe.
3. So he buys ladybugs that eat the harmful insects.
4. When he replants each spring, he fills his garden with these wonderful red bugs.
5. In a few months, Matt will proudly show you his garden.
6. It will be full of vegetables and harmless red bugs!

7.–11. Now write the sentences that your teacher reads.   *For dictation sentences, see Step 6 at right.*

WORD WORK

12.–16. Read the newspaper article. Find words with the prefix *un*-. Copy the chart. Write each word next to its meaning.

The Top Tomato

Tomato lovers from all over the county unpacked crates of big, juicy tomatoes for the Tomato Festival on Sunday.

Fernando Robles, of Oak Park, grew a tomato unlike any other. It weighed 6.4 pounds! Pat Tanaka, also of Oak Park, was unhappy. Her 5.1 pound tomato won second place. Fernando remains unbeaten three years in a row.

"My secret is to find the best tomato on the vine, and then take off the unwanted ones," says Fernando.

Words with un-	Meaning
12. unpacked	emptied
13. unbeaten	not beaten
14. unwanted	not wanted
15. unhappy	sad
16. unlike	different from

Example: 12. unpacked

Language and Literacy **279**

Decodable Book
PRACTICE WITH PREFIXES AND SUFFIXES

Decodable Book 17:
The Orchard

Assign **Decodable Book 17** for independent reading. The **Decodable Book** can be used in a variety of ways to help students become more fluent, automatic readers:

Discussion Circles Have students work in small groups to read aloud and discuss the book using the questions on the back cover. Encourage students to read aloud the text that supports their answers. Groups can also work together to complete the Word Work Activity.

Readers Theater Students can read aloud the stories in a class performance. Help them prepare by rereading the stories in daily rehearsals. Work with students to add narration or dialog. Encourage them to use natural phrasing and expression.

Rereading at Home Have students work with family members to reread the book at home. They can take turns reading aloud alternate pages, then rereading the book switching the pages each person reads.

LEARN A READING STRATEGY

4 Recognize Word Parts Work through the strategy with students, reading each step aloud and modeling the actions shown on the page. Point out the Reading Help and read the explanation to students. Work through additional examples to help them apply the tip: r*ead*y, f*ly*, *re*nt, *re*ar, *re*scue, tro*ly*

PRACTICE

5 Read Sentences Distribute the Partner Prompts from page T311 to guide peers in reading the sentences in Items 1–6. Remind them to use the recognize-word-parts strategy to read words and to blend the words silently.

6 Write Sentences Dictate the following sentences for students to write. Read each sentence at normal speed once so students can listen, and then repeat it slowly word by word as they write:

7. This harmful bug has sticky wings.
8. The peaceful day seemed endless.
9. Please rewrite this messy paper.
10. Unlock the gate quickly!
11. The sleepy children eat slowly.

If students need extra support, guide them in spelling the words with prefixes and suffixes. For example: *What suffix do you hear in* careless? (-less) *Write the word* care. *Then add the suffix* -less.

7 Conduct "Word Work" Read the directions and work through the Example. Then have partners complete Items 13–16. Check answers as a group.

▶ **Reading Practice Book** pages 175–178 (Decodable Book 17)

CLOSE AND ASSESS

Write these words: *unhappy, messy, harmful, proudly, replant, harmless, unlock,* and *repay*. Call on students to identify the prefix or suffix in each word, read the word, and give its meaning.

Language and Literacy **T279**

UNIT 17 LESSON 11
LANGUAGE AND LITERACY: INDEPENDENT READING

OBJECTIVES

Functions:
Read a Selection; Make Comparisons

Learning to Read: ⓣ Recognize High Frequency Words; ⓣ Decode Words with Prefixes and Suffixes (un-, re-, -ly, -y, -less, -ful)

Reading Strategies: Activate Prior Knowledge; Set a Purpose for Reading; Compare Texts

Critical Thinking and Comprehension:
ⓣ Make Comparisons

Writing: Crop Comparisons

READ ON YOUR OWN

1. **Introduce Vocabulary** In "Many Places to Plant a Plant," students apply phonics skills and read high frequency words taught in Lessons 8–10. Introduce the story words. Write each word, pronounce it, and spell it. Then give a definition and a context sentence:

   - **fields:** pieces of land used for growing crops. *The farmers plant corn in the fields.*
   - **shelters:** safe places, away from cold, heat, and wind. *A porch is a good shelter in the summer heat.*
   - **protect:** to keep safe. *Wear a helmet when you ride a bike. It will protect your head.*
   - **diseases:** illnesses, sicknesses. *Cancer and malaria are diseases.*
   - **buy:** to pay money to own something. *I have ten dollars to buy a new cap.*

2. **Activate Prior Knowledge/Set Purposes** View the photos, read the title, and discuss what students already know about the topic. Then model setting a purpose: *I'll read to find out where people grow plants.*

3. **Read and Think: Compare Texts** Students should read the passage on their own. Suggest that as they read, they compare the information to the information in *Crops*. In the book, where are the crops planted? Why are they planted there?

T280 Unit 17 | Harvest Time

COMPREHENSION: MAKE COMPARISONS
Read on Your Own

DECODING CHECK
Give the Decoding Progress Check on page 1a of the Assessment Handbook.

Many Places to Plant a Plant

Farmers plant on a big scale! They fill huge fields with millions of seeds. Plants grow well in these open fields, but not all plants are grown there. Many plants are first grown indoors, in greenhouses and in nurseries. Unlike open fields, these shelters protect plants from too much heat or cold. They also protect young plants from harmful diseases, insects, and weeds.

Greenhouses have glass walls that let the sunshine in. Plants that like heat grow well inside the warm, sunny space. On really cold days, steam pipes heat and reheat the greenhouse to keep the plants healthy. Summer crops, such as peppers and eggplant, can be grown year-round in greenhouses.

A nursery is another place where plants grow in a sheltered place. Some nurseries grow priceless plants and collect their seeds. They sell some of the seeds and use others to grow more plants.

Some nurseries are huge, with a shop that sells plants and gardening tools. After people buy plants from the nursery, they replant them outdoors in gardens at home. Visit a nursery! Get a daisy plant and some roses. Buy a rake. You'll be ready to start a garden of your own.

280 Unit 17 | Harvest Time

REACHING ALL STUDENTS

HOME CONNECTION

Personal Gardens Point out that the photos on page 280 show three places where plants are grown: a field, a greenhouse, a nursery. Then invite students to tell about places at home where they grow plants (for example, a back yard, container garden on a patio or balcony, windowbox, greenhouse). Encourage students to bring photos, samples, or plant cuttings to class to share and discuss.

CHECK YOUR UNDERSTANDING

1. Copy the concept map. Work with a partner to add details to it. Use your finished map to compare places to grow plants.

Example: 1. A greenhouse has glass walls, but an open field is unprotected. Both places are often sunny and warm.

Sample Responses:

EXPAND YOUR VOCABULARY

2. Work with a group to collect words and phrases related to plants. Put the word or phrase and a picture on each card. Put the cards in groups and store them in a file.

WRITE MORE COMPARISONS

3.–8. Choose cards from your word file. Find things to compare. Write 6 comparisons. Use the words in the box to tell how the things are alike or different.

both	alike	different
and	same	but

Example: 3. Peppers and carrots are both vegetable crops. Carrots taste sweet, but peppers are hot and spicy.

Language and Literacy 281

Reading Practice Book page 104

Reading Fluency
TIMED READINGS

Read the title and introduction on **Reading Practice Book** page 104. Set the timer and have a student read the passage to you. Use the script on page T328 to mark words the student misses and to note the last word read in one minute. Have students graph their performance and set a goal for improving in subsequent timed readings. Plan for two additional timed readings, and encourage partners to practice reading the passage to each other between the timed readings.

CHECK YOUR UNDERSTANDING

4 Comprehension: Make Comparisons Copy the incomplete map, and use the examples to model how to complete it. Say: *The selection said that fields are "huge," so I will write* huge *at the end of this ray* (point). Repeat the process for the remaining examples. Then have partners copy and complete the map and use it to compare places to grow plants. Explain that when you compare two or more things, you tell how they are different and alike. To illustrate, work through the Example with students pointing out the signal words *but* and *both*.

EXPAND YOUR VOCABULARY

5 Make Plant Cards Read aloud the directions and point out the groups of cards. Make sure students understand that each card has a word or phrase related to plants and an illustration, and that the cards are then arranged according to different categories. Invite students to make as many cards as they can.

WRITE

6 Compare and Contrast Crops Read aloud the directions and the Example. Point out that the Example tells how peppers and carrots are alike and different. Then read the words in the Word Box. Tell students to use them to make comparisons.

For students who need additional support in writing, provide sentence frames for them to complete.

____ and ____ are both ____.
____ are ____, but ____ are ____.

▶ **Reading Practice Book** page 104

CLOSE AND ASSESS

Have students take turns giving a sentence that compares two places where plants are grown. Students should tell one thing that is the same and one thing that is different about the two places.

Language and Literacy T281

UNIT 17 **LESSON 12**

LANGUAGE ACROSS THE CURRICULUM: SCIENCE

> **OBJECTIVES**
>
> **Function:** Listen to an Article
>
> **Concepts and Vocabulary:**
> Plants; 🅣 Farming
>
> **Research Skills and Learning Strategies:**
> Build Background; Activate Prior Knowledge
>
> **Critical Thinking and Comprehension:**
> Identify Steps in a Process; Summarize

LEARN ABOUT PLANTS

1. **Explore Plants** Read the title and go over the visuals, reading captions and labels. Make sure students understand that the photos represent stages in the life of a sunflower. Explain that the seeds that come from the flower start the cycle all over again.

READ AND THINK

2. **Activate Prior Knowledge** Read the title of the article and the focus question. Review the pictures on pages 270 and 273. Then ask volunteers to predict how oranges are grown. As you read, have students check their predictions.

3. **Read the Article Aloud** Restate ideas and clarify vocabulary as necessary. Use the photos to develop meaning. For the final two paragraphs, use page 21 of *Crops* to show how oranges are harvested by hand and how they can be used to make a variety of products.

CHECK UNDERSTANDING

4. **Answer the Review Questions** Remind students to refer to the article and the photos as they answer the questions.

> **CLOSE AND ASSESS**
>
> Ask students to tell one thing they learned about oranges from listening to the article.

T282 Unit 17 | Harvest Time

SUCCESS IN SCIENCE

Learn About Plants

LIFE CYCLE OF A PLANT

The **seed** sprouts. It grows into a **plant**.

The **plant** forms a **bud**.

The **bud** blooms into a **flower**.

The **flower** has the **seeds** that start the cycle over again.

Answers for the Review:
1. Grafted orange trees are stronger and produce better fruit than ungrafted trees.
2. orange juice, perfumes, oils, jams, candies, and as fruit to eat
3. Students' diagrams should show a complete mature sunflower plant with the three labels placed in the correct places.

Listen to the article. Then do the Review.

Oranges: From Tree to Market

• How are oranges grown?

Although farmers start some crops with seeds, farmers grow orange crops in a different way. Growers start by planting young **grafted** trees.

A grafted tree is made of two trees. The farmer takes a part of one young tree and attaches it to the roots of another young tree. The trees grow together to make a stronger tree. A grafted tree also produces fruit that is better than the fruit of an ungrafted tree. The grafted trees start producing oranges after about 2 years.

When the oranges are ripe, farmers harvest the fruit. Most farmers pick oranges by hand. Then they take the oranges to a storage area.

Farmers sell almost half of the harvested oranges to people who make orange juice. They also sell oranges to people who make perfumes, oils, jams, and candies. Some oranges go directly to a market where you can buy them.

Development of an Orange Tree

A grafted tree ready to be planted

A young orange tree

A mature orange tree

REVIEW

1. **Check Your Understanding** Why do farmers graft orange trees?
2. **Check Your Understanding** What are some of the ways that people use oranges?
3. **Vocabulary** Draw a diagram of a sunflower. Add these labels: *stem, leaf,* and *flower*.

282 Unit 17 | Harvest Time

REACHING ALL STUDENTS

Science Connection
COOPERATIVE DIAGRAMS

Provide resources—such as encyclopedias, gardening magazines, garden reference books, or the Internet—where students can find pictures of different kinds of fruit trees. Have each student draw a picture of a fruit tree and identify the tree. Then partners exchange pictures and each one labels the picture he or she gets with as many of the following labels as apply: *branch, roots, bud, leaf, blossom, fruit, trunk*. Display the finished diagrams around the room or gather them into a class reference resource.

Writing Project / CROP REPORT

✓ **WRITING ASSESSMENT** Use the Writing Progress Checklist on page 51 of the Assessment Handbook to evaluate this writing project.

Use a Venn diagram to compare two crops. Then write a report.

RESEARCH TWO CROPS
Choose two crops to compare. Use *Crops* or ask a librarian to help you find another book.

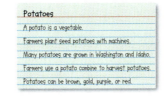

PLAN YOUR REPORT
Use a Venn diagram to compare the two crops.

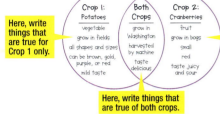

WRITE AND SHARE YOUR REPORT
Use your completed Venn diagram to write the report. Tell how the crops are alike. Tell how they are different. Use sensory adjectives to describe how the crops look and taste. See pages 310–311 of your Handbook. Then work with a partner. Check and correct your work.

✓ **Check Your Work**
Did you tell how the crops are alike and different?
Did you use signal words like *both*, *but*, and *and*?
Did you use sensory adjectives?

Copy your report or type it on a computer. Add pictures. Read your report and put your it on a bulletin board.

Language Across the Curriculum **283**

Language Practice Book page 130

WRITING PROJECT: CROP REPORT
Comparing Crops

Write a crop report for your class. Use a Venn diagram to compare two crops. Then follow these steps.

1. Write a title. Name the two crops you want to compare.
2. Write a topic sentence. Name the two crops again.
3. Turn the ideas in your Venn diagram into sentences.
   - Tell how the crops are alike. Use the words *both* and *and*.
   - Tell how the crops are different. Use the word *but*.
   - Tell how the crops look and taste. Use sensory adjectives like *small*, *red*, or *sour*. Get more ideas from pages 310–311 of your Handbook.

Copy your report or type it on a computer. You may want to add pictures. Read your report to the class.

Multi-Level Strategies
WRITING SUPPORT

PRELITERATE Provide sentence frames for students who need support in writing about similarities and differences.

To tell how the crops are the same:
- (Crop 1) and (Crop 2) are alike because they both _____.
- Both crops _____.

To tell how the crops are different:
- (Crop 1) is _____, but (Crop 2) is _____.

UNIT 17 LESSON 13

LANGUAGE ACROSS THE CURRICULUM: WRITING

OBJECTIVES

Functions: Make Comparisons; Write
Concepts and Vocabulary:
T Farming; Plants
Learning Strategies and Critical Thinking: Plan; Generate and Organize Ideas; T Make Comparisons; Self-Assess
Research Skills: Gather Information; Take Notes; Locate Resources; Use the Research Process
Representing: Venn Diagram
Writing: Report

CONDUCT THE WRITING PROJECT

1. **Explore Reports** Explain: *A report is a way to share information.* Read the introduction; tell students they will write a report that compares two crops.

2. **Research Two Crops** Brainstorm a list of crops, including produce from students' native lands. Help them choose two crops to compare. Then look for information in encyclopedias, agriculture books, or Web sites such as:
   www.cyberspaceag.com
   www.mda.state.mi.us/kids

3. **Plan Your Report** Go over the labels and content of the Venn diagram. Explain how to fill in the three sections of the diagram. Then encourage students to answer questions like these:
   - Are the crops fruits or vegetables?
   - How are they planted and harvested?
   - Where are the crops grown?

4. **Write and Share Your Report** Go over the sample Crop Report. Point out how signal words such as *and*, *both*, and *unlike* help the reader understand the similarities and differences between the two crops.

▶ **Language Practice Book** page 130

CLOSE AND ASSESS

Have students look at their reports. Say:
- *Read how the crops are different.*
- *Read me a sentence that tells about both crops. What signal words did you use?*
- *Read some sensory adjectives you used.*

Language Across the Curriculum **T283**

Resources

For Success in Language and Literacy

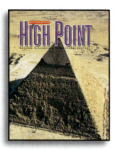

Student Book pages 284–297

For Language Skills Practice

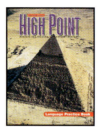

Language Practice Book pages 131–136

For Reading Skills Practice

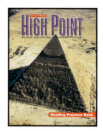

Reading Practice Book pages 105–109

For Vocabulary, Language Development, and Reading Fluency

Language Tape 9, Side B
Language CD 3, Tracks 17–18

For Reading Together

Theme Book *Sunny and Moonshine* from The Basics Bookshelf

For Audio Walk-Throughs and Selection Readings

Selection Tape 9B
Selection CD 3, Tracks 11–12

For Phonics Instruction

Transparencies 88–92

Transparency Scripts 88–92

Letter Tiles

For Comprehensive Assessment

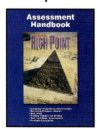

Language Acquisition Assessment, Units 16–18 Test, Writing Assessment, Self-Assessment

For Planning and Instruction

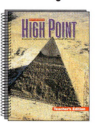

Teacher's Edition pages T284a–T297

T284a Unit Planner

UNIT 18

Superstars

In This Unit

Vocabulary
- Idioms
- Space

Language Functions
- Agree and Disagree
- Give Information

Patterns and Structures
- Future Tense Verbs
- Verb Tense Review (present, past, future)
- Contractions

Reading
- Multisyllabic Words
- Comprehension: Relate Goal and Outcome (goal-and-outcome map)

Writing
- Opinions
- Description
- Diamante Poem

Content Area Connection
- Science (outer space)

UNIT 18

Activity and Assessment Planner

UNIT 18: Superstars

LESSONS

1

UNIT 18 LAUNCH
▶ *pages T284–T285*

LESSON 1: INTRODUCE UNIT 18 pages T284–T285

Vocabulary
Stars

Viewing
Respond to Visual Images

Learning Strategies
Preview

Build Background

Critical Thinking, Representing and Writing
Generate Ideas

Create Captioned Drawings

2–5

LANGUAGE DEVELOPMENT
▶ *pages T286–T289*

LESSON 2
IDIOMS
page T286

Function
Agree and Disagree

Vocabulary
🅣 Idioms

Writing
Opinions

LESSON 3
FUTURE TENSE/CONTRACTIONS
page T287

Function
Give Information

Patterns and Structures
🅣 Future Tense Verbs
🅣 Contractions with *will*

Writing
🅣 Sentences

LESSON 4
SPACE
page T288

Function
Give Information

Vocabulary
🅣 Space

Writing
🅣 Sentences

LESSON 5
VERB TENSES
page T289

Functions
Give Information

Describe

Patterns and Structures
🅣 Verb Tenses

Writing
Description

6–11

LANGUAGE AND LITERACY
▶ *pages T290a–T295*

LESSON 6
BASICS BOOKSHELF
pages T290a–T290f

Functions
Listen to a Book

Read Aloud a Book (choral reading)

Vocabulary
🅣 The Solar System

Reading Strategies
Activate Prior Knowledge

Preview

Use Text Structures (diagrams)

Learning to Read
Identify Words

Critical Thinking and Comprehension
🅣 Relate Goal and Outcome

LESSON 7
BASICS BOOKSHELF: COMPREHENSION
page T290

Function
Retell a Story

Learning Strategy
Use Graphic Organizers (goal-and-outcome map)

Critical Thinking and Comprehension
🅣 Relate Goal and Outcome

LESSON 8
HIGH FREQUENCY WORDS
page T291

Learning to Read
🅣 Recognize High Frequency Words

LESSON 9
WORD STRUCTURE
pages T292a–T292d

Learning to Read
Build Oral Vocabulary

Develop Phonemic Awareness

Identify Syllable Types (consonant + *le;* vowel team; vowel-silent *e*)

🅣 Divide Words into Syllables

Decode Multisyllabic Words (2 and 3 syllables)

LESSON 10
READING AND SPELLING
pages T292–T293

Learning to Read
Develop Phonemic Awareness

Identify Syllable Types (consonant + *le;* vowel team; vowel-silent *e*)

🅣 Divide Words into Syllables

Decode Multisyllabic Words (2 and 3 syllables)

Spelling
🅣 Multisyllabic Words

LESSON 11
INDEPENDENT READING
pages T294–T295

Functions
Read a Selection

Give Information

Learning to Read
🅣 Recognize High Frequency Words

🅣 Divide Words into Syllables to Decode Multisyllabic Words

Reading Strategies
Activate Prior Knowledge

Set a Purpose for Reading

Visualize

Critical Thinking and Comprehension
🅣 Relate Goal and Outcome

Writing
Give Information

12–13

LANGUAGE ACROSS THE CURRICULUM
▶ *pages T296–T297*

LESSON 12
SCIENCE: OUTER SPACE
page T296

Function
Listen to an Article

Vocabulary
🅣 Space

Learning Strategy
Build Background

Critical Thinking and Comprehension
Identify Details

LESSON 13
WRITING PROJECT: DIAMANTE POEM
page T297

Functions
Give Information

Write

Learning Strategies and Critical Thinking
Plan

Generate and Organize Ideas

🅣 Make Comparisons

Self-Assess

Research Skills
Gather Information

Use the Research Process

Writing
Diamante Poem

T284c Unit 18 | Superstars

🅣 = Objective Tested on Unit Test

ASSESSMENT OPTIONS

The **Teacher's Edition** and the **Assessment Handbook** include these comprehensive assessment tools:

▶ **Ongoing, Informal Assessment**
Check for understanding and achieve closure for every lesson with the targeted questions and activities in the **Close and Assess** boxes in your Teacher's Edition.

▶ **Decoding Progress Check**
These word lists for each unit provide a quick way to check on mastery of the phonics or word structure skills taught in the unit.

▶ **Language Acquisition Assessments**
To verify students' ability to use the language functions and grammar structures taught in Units 1–3, conduct these performance assessments.

▶ **Unit Test in Standardized Test Format**
This multiple-choice test measures students' cumulative understanding of the skills and language developed in Units 16–18.

▶ **Self-and Peer-Assessment**
Students use the Self-Assessment Form to evaluate their own work and develop learning strategies appropriate to their needs. Students offer feedback to their classmates with the Peer-Assessment Form.

▶ **Writing Assessment/Portfolio Opportunities**
You can evaluate students' writing in the Writing Projects using the Writing Progress Checklist. Then collaborate with students to choose work for their portfolios.

UNITS 1–3 ASSESSMENT OPPORTUNITIES	Assessment Handbook Pages
Decoding Progress Check	1a
Language Acquisition Assessments	42
Units 1–3 Test	43–48
Self-Assessment Form	49
Peer-Assessment Form	50
Writing Progress Checklist	51
Portfolio Evaluation Form	52

RELATED RESOURCES

The Lost Children
by Paul Goble
A Blackfoot legend about six brothers who travel to the heavens and become the constellation of the "Lost Children," or Pleiades. (Bradbury)
Theme Book: Read Aloud

The Planets
by Gail Gibbons
Diagrams, captions, and explanatory text discuss the movement and characteristics of the nine planets in our solar system. (Available from Hampton-Brown)
Phonics Reinforcement: Multisyllabic Words

Postcards from Pluto
by Loreen Leedy
Dr. Quasar takes a group of kids on a field trip through the solar system, from Mercury to Pluto. (Holiday House)
Vocabulary: Space

The International Space Station
by Franklyn M. Branley
Illustrations and text tell about the project to build an international space station, which began in 1998 and is still underway. (HarperCollins)
Language Development: Present, Past, and Future Tense Verbs

My Place in Space
by Robin and Sally Hirst
A boy gives a bus driver overly detailed directions to his house by giving its precise location in the universe. (Available from Hampton-Brown)
Easy Reading

UNIT 18 LESSON 1

INTRODUCE UNIT 18: SUPERSTARS

OBJECTIVES

Concepts and Vocabulary: Stars
Viewing: Respond to Visual Images
Learning Strategies: Preview; Build Background
Critical Thinking: Generate Ideas
Representing and Writing: Captioned Drawing

START WITH A COMMON EXPERIENCE

1. **Introduce "Superstars"** Read the unit title and explain: *A superstar is a famous person that everyone knows. Many superstars are actors, entertainers, or athletes.* Ask students to name current superstars and what they do.

2. **See Stars and More Stars** Explain that the common meaning of *star* is a shining light in the night sky, but that the idea, shape, and image of a star can be used to describe people and things.

   Work together to identify each image and ask volunteers to explain how each item relates to a star. Encourage both creativity and reasoning. For example: *A starfish is a fish that is shaped like a star.*

3. **Draw a Star** Read the activity directions. Then have students use photographs, drawings, clip art, or objects to show their stars. Provide sentence frames for students to use as they describe their work to the class:

   > The star I like is _____.
   > You'll find my star in _____.
   > I like this star because _____.

   Combine the objects to create a class star collage.

REACHING ALL STUDENTS

HOME CONNECTION

Star Search Review the photographs and brainstorm more examples of stars, such as: stars on the U.S. flag, all-star sports teams, star students, etc. Have students conduct a survey in which they ask family members to complete this sentence:

> When I hear the word "star," I think of _____.

Use the results to make a class bar graph to identify popular responses.

T284 Unit 18 | Superstars

Superstars

There are all kinds of stars! Work with a group. Draw a star you like. Describe your star to the class.

In This Unit

Vocabulary
- Idioms
- Space

Language Functions
- Agree and Disagree
- Give Information

Patterns and Structures
- Future Tense Verbs
- Verb Tense Review (present, past, future)
- Contractions

Reading
- Multisyllabic Words
- Comprehension: Relate Goal and Outcome (goal-and-outcome map)

Writing
- Opinions
- Description
- Diamante Poem

Content Area Connection
- Science (outer space)

PREVIEW THE UNIT

4 Look for Activities with Different Kinds of Stars Leaf through the unit, previewing activities students will do, for example:

page 286—learning a chant about three friends discussing the music of some rock stars

page 290—listening to the Bookshelf book (Display a copy of the book.)

page 294—reading a Native American story about the Sun and the seasons

page 297—writing a diamante poem

Also ask students to look for information about all kinds of stars. Highlight the activities about people on pages 286–287 and the solar system on pages 288–289, for example. Then sum up what the preview reveals: *There are many kinds of stars. Some stars are in outer space. Other stars are right here on Earth.*

5 Set Your Goals Start a class mind map about stars. Prompt students for pictures or words to add, and have them act out and describe other ideas for you to put into words.

CLOSE AND ASSESS

Ask students to tell or show you something they are interested in learning in this unit.

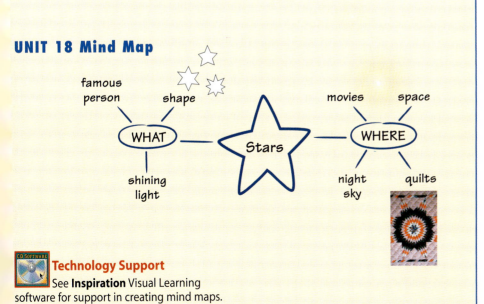

UNIT 18 Mind Map

Technology Support
See **Inspiration** Visual Learning software for support in creating mind maps.

UNIT 18 LESSON 2
LANGUAGE DEVELOPMENT: IDIOMS

OBJECTIVES

Functions: Listen Actively; Repeat Spoken Language; Recite; Agree and Disagree
Concepts and Vocabulary: 🅣 Idioms
Writing: Opinions

INTRODUCE

1. **Listen and Chant** Play "What Do You Think?" on the **Language Tape/CD**. Students will listen and read along before echoing the lines and finally chiming in on the entire chant. Point out that each typeface signals a different speaker. *Tape 9B / CD 3 Track 17*

2. **Learn About Idioms** Explain that an idiom is a phrase with a meaning that is different from the meaning of its words. Read the idioms in the chant and restate the meanings: *No way!* means *I disagree.*

PRACTICE

3. **Conduct "Express Yourself"** Brainstorm formal and informal ways to agree and disagree. Have partners use the chart to complete the activity.

To Agree	To Disagree
You are right.	You're wrong.
That is correct.	That is not true.

How to Agree and Disagree

- If I agree or disagree, I can say so and then tell more:

  Yes, I agree! I think you're right! I disagree! That isn't true!

APPLY

4. **Write Opinions** Have students check answers with partners. Distribute Partner Checklist 18 on page T310.

   ▶ **Language Practice Book** page 131

CLOSE AND ASSESS

Give an opinion about music. Call on students to agree or disagree.

T286 Unit 18 | Superstars

VOCABULARY: IDIOMS
Music Stars

Listen and chant.

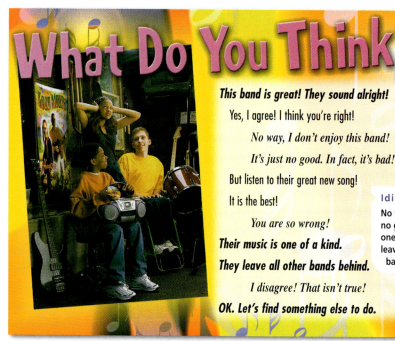

What Do You Think?

This band is great! They sound alright!
Yes, I agree! I think you're right!
No way, I don't enjoy this band!
It's just no good. In fact, it's bad!
But listen to their great new song!
It is the best!
You are so wrong!
Their music is one of a kind.
They leave all other bands behind.
I disagree! That isn't true!
OK. Let's find something else to do.

Idioms
No way!
no good
one of a kind
leave all other bands behind

EXPRESS YOURSELF ▶ AGREE AND DISAGREE

Read each opinion. Say if you agree or disagree.

Example: 1. I agree. Jazz music is great. I disagree. I don't like jazz music.

1. Jazz music is great.
2. CDs are better than tapes.
3. All kids like the same music.
4. Music videos are beautiful.

WRITE OPINIONS

6.–8. Work with 2 partners. Each of you writes an opinion about rock stars. Then one partner writes a statement that agrees with your opinion. The other partner writes a statement that disagrees with it.

Example: 6. Rock stars have a hard life.
I agree because they are never alone.
I disagree. They have a lot of money.

286 Unit 18 | Superstars

REACHING ALL STUDENTS

Language Practice Book page 131

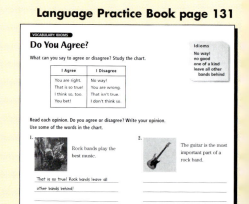

FUTURE TENSE VERBS AND CONTRACTIONS

You Will Be a Star Some Day!

A verb in the future tense tells what will happen later, or in the future.

Here are some ways to show the future tense.

will + verb	Our band **will play** at the park next week.
am are + going to + verb is	I **am going to play** the guitar. You **are going to sing**. The concert **is going to be** great!
we'll + verb	We will practice tonight. **We'll practice** tonight. *The contraction for we will is we'll.*
won't + verb	We will not stop until we know every song. We **won't stop** until we know every song! *The contraction for will not is won't.*

BUILD SENTENCES

Change each sentence to tell about the future. Say each sentence 2 different ways.

1. We practice at Ana's house.
2. You and Ana learn a new song.
3. It sounds great.
4. Many people hear our music at the park.
5. We become superstars!

Example: 1. We will practice at Ana's house.
We are going to practice at Ana's house.

Answers:
1. We will (we'll) practice/are going to practice at Ana's house.
2. You and Ana will learn/are going to learn a new song.
3. It will (it'll) sound/is going to sound great.
4. Many people will hear/are going to hear our music at the park.
5. We will (We'll) become/are going to become super stars!

Use the contraction *won't* to make each sentence negative. Say the new sentence.

6. I will sing.
7. You will play the guitar.
8. Ana will get worried.
9. We will forget the songs.
10. The audience will want to leave.

Example: 6. I won't sing.

Answers:
6. I won't sing.
7. You won't play the guitar.
8. Ana won't get worried.
9. We won't forget the songs.
10. The audience won't want to leave.

WRITE ABOUT YOUR FUTURE ✏️

11. You, too, can become a superstar! Maybe you'll be a star in music, maybe in math. Write what you will do to become a superstar.

Sample Responses
Students' sentences should be in future tense.

Example: 11. I am going to learn to write computer games.
I'll write every day.
I will make a popular game.

Language Development **287**

Language Practice Book page 132

Language Development
FUTURE TENSE/CONTRACTIONS

Have the group sit in a circle. Then model saying a sentence in the future tense: *I will paint my portrait.* The student to your right should use the word *won't* to make the sentence negative, then say a new future tense sentence: *I won't paint my portrait. I am going to write a story.* Continue until each student has had the opportunity to say an affirmative and a negative sentence.

UNIT 18 **LESSON 3**

LANGUAGE DEVELOPMENT: FUTURE TENSE/CONTRACTIONS

OBJECTIVES

Function: Give Information
Patterns and Structures: 🅣 Future Tense Verbs; 🅣 Contractions with *will*
Writing: 🅣 Sentences

INTRODUCE

1 Learn About Future Tense Read the title and introduction, then go over the first two rows in the skills box. Explain that both *will* and *going to* show future tense. Have students restate each sentence using the other construction: *Our band is going to play at the park next week. I will play the guitar.*

Read the last two rows in the skills box and explain that the contractions take the place of the underlined words. Point out that in contractions with *will* the apostrophe usually takes the place of the letters *w-i*. Explain that *won't* is a special case or an exception.

PRACTICE

2 Build Sentences Read Example 1 and model how to choose the correct verb to match the subject. Then go over Example 6 and model how to replace the verb *will* with the contraction *won't*.

APPLY

3 Write About Your Future Provide sentence frames for students who need support:

> In the future, I am going to _____.
> I will _____.
> I won't ever _____.

▶ **Language Practice Book** page 132

CLOSE AND ASSESS

Ask students to read one of their sentences. Have a volunteer repeat the sentence using another way to express the future tense.

Language Development **T287**

UNIT 18 LESSON 4

LANGUAGE DEVELOPMENT: SPACE

OBJECTIVES
Function: Give Information
Concepts and Vocabulary: 🅣 Space
Writing: 🅣 Sentences

INTRODUCE

1 Learn Words About Space Have students point to the pictures as you read aloud the labels. Then check understanding: *Name two planets that are next to Earth.* (Venus, Mars) *How many planets are in our solar system?* (nine)

PRACTICE

2 Conduct "Express Yourself" Model how to give information about the objects in the pictures. Then have partners complete the activity.

How to Give Information
- I can tell what I know about the objects in the picture: *The moon is in the sky.*
- I can add details to tell how the objects look and where they are: *The moon is bright. It is above the horizon.*

APPLY

3 Write About a Trip into Space Partners can use the new words to complete these sentence frames, if necessary:

> I will travel to _____.
> I am going to _____.
> I won't _____.

▶ Language Practice Book page 133

CLOSE AND ASSESS

One partner can read the sentences aloud while the other points out objects on the illustration at the top of the page, if appropriate.

T288 Unit 18 | Superstars

VOCABULARY: SPACE

Stars in the Sky

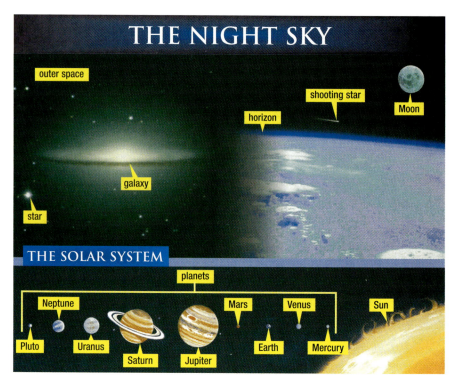

EXPRESS YOURSELF ▶ GIVE INFORMATION

1.–6. Study the pictures. Tell a partner 3 facts about the night sky and 3 facts about the solar system.

Example: 1. Earth is the third planet from the Sun.

Sample Responses
Students can tell about the colors, shapes, or sizes of the things in the photo. They could where the things are in the sky and in relatic to one another.

WRITE ABOUT A TRIP INTO SPACE ✏️

7. Work with a partner. Write about a trip to outer space. Use future tense. Describe what you will see on your trip.

Example: 7. I will go to outer space.
I'll see many stars.
I will fly by Venus and Mars.

288 Unit 18 | Superstars

REACHING ALL STUDENTS

Multi-Level Strategies
VOCABULARY: SPACE

PRELITERATE Have small groups create unlabeled posters of outer space and the solar system, using the illustrations on page 288 as models. Guide them in making word cards for all labels on the page, then shuffle the cards. As the groups rotate among the posters, have students draw a card and affix it to what it names on the poster. After all labels have been affixed, have teams check whether their poster was labeled correctly.

Language Practice Book page 133

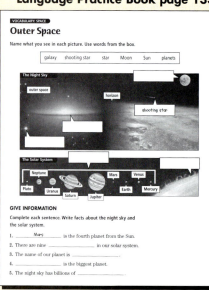

VERB TENSES

Star Power

The tense of a **verb** shows when the action happens.

Tense	Tells	Example
Past	what happened earlier	The star Antares **formed** millions of years ago.
Present	what is happening now	It now **shines** with a bright orange light.
Future	what will happen later	Some day Antares **is going to explode**. It **will turn** into a supernova, or exploding star.

BUILD SENTENCES

1.–9. Read the words below. Choose words from each column to make a sentence. Use each verb correctly.

	traveled revolved moved		in the past.
Mars	travels revolves moves	in outer space around the Sun	today.
	will travel is going to revolve will move		in the future.

Sample Responses
- Past tense verbs should be used with **in the past**.
- Present tense verbs should be used with **today**.
- Future tense verbs should be used with **in the future**.

Example: 1. Mars moved around the Sun in the past.

WRITE A DESCRIPTION

10.–15. Work with a partner. Write 2 sentences to describe the Moon in the picture. Then write 2 sentences to describe the Moon last night. What will the Moon look like tomorrow night? Write 2 more sentences to describe it.

Example: 10. The Moon is big and bright.

Sample Responses
Students' first 2 sentences should use present tense. Their second 2 sentences should use past tense. Their last 2 sentences should use future tense.

Language Development 289

Language Practice Book page 134   **Language Practice Book page 135**

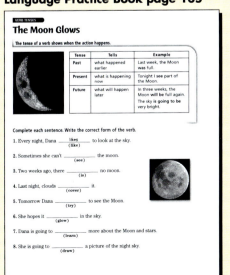

UNIT 18 **LESSON 5**

LANGUAGE DEVELOPMENT: VERB TENSES

OBJECTIVES
Functions: Give Information; Describe
Patterns and Structures: Verb Tenses
Writing: Description

INTRODUCE

1 Learn About Verb Tenses Go over the chart, using the time words and phrases to cue the tense of the verb. Review how to form the past tense and the future tense of verbs.

Read aloud these sentences and have students identify the verb tense:

- *My class **learns** about space.* (present)
- *Last week, we **studied** the stars.* (past)
- *Later, we **are going to see** a film.* (future)
- *We **are learning** a lot of facts.* (present)
- *Next month, we **will visit** the space museum.* (future)

PRACTICE

2 Build Sentences Work through the Example to model how to build a sentence with an entry from each column. Remind students to match the verb tense in column 2 with the time words and phrases in column 4. Then have partners complete the activity.

APPLY

3 Write a Description For additional support, provide sentence frames:

The moon was _____ last night.
The moon is _____ tonight.
The moon will be/is going to be _____ tomorrow night.

▶ **Language Practice Book** pages 134 and 135

CLOSE AND ASSESS
Ask students to tell something they did in the past, something they do now, and something they plan to do in the future.

Language Development **T289**

UNIT 18 **LESSON 6**

LANGUAGE AND LITERACY: THE BASICS BOOKSHELF

OBJECTIVES

Concepts and Vocabulary:
- The Solar System

Listening: Listen to a Preview

Reading Strategies:
Activate Prior Knowledge; Preview; Use Text Structures (diagrams)

BUILD LANGUAGE AND VOCABULARY

1. **Teach "Words to Know"** Have students look at pages 2–3. Say: *These pages show the Sun, the Moon, Earth, and other planets. They are all part of the Solar System.*

   Read the captions under the Earth and the Sun on page 2. As you point out the remaining illustrations, read aloud the captions and have students identify the Sun and Earth.

   On page 3, use gestures to explain Earth's orbit around the Sun and the Moon's orbit around Earth.

2. **Discuss the Planets** Model how to ask questions with *where*: *Where is Earth?* Use sentences with prepositions to give information about each planet: *Earth is between Venus and Mars.* Have partners ask for and give information about the planets using the illustration at the bottom of page 3.

PREPARE TO READ

3. **Think About What You Know** Invite each student to tell one thing he or she knows about the Solar System. Chart the responses.

4. **Preview** Play the Audio Walk-Through for *Sunny and Moonshine* on the **Selection Tape/CD** to give students the overall idea of the story.

   Tape 9B CD 3 Track 11

CLOSE AND ASSESS

Have small groups discuss how the story characters relate to the information about the Solar System.

Sunny and Moonshine
by Shirleyann Costigan

Summary This fantasy uses a love story to teach about a solar eclipse. Moonshine falls in love with a rock star named Sunny, but her Earth Mother stands in the way of their meeting. Each day, Moonshine gets closer and closer to Sunny until she finally blocks her Earth Mother and gives him a kiss. The couple drifts apart and returns again at each solar eclipse.

Cover

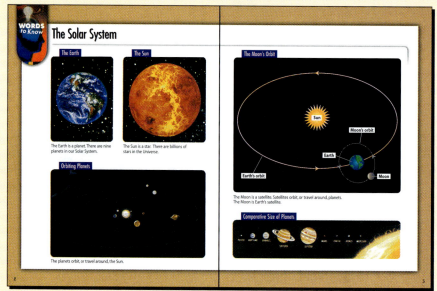
Pages 2–3

Multi-Level Strategies
LITERACY SUPPORT

PRELITERATE **Use Text Structures: Diagrams** Show the diagrams on pages 2, 3, and 24 to explain orbits and eclipses. Explain the movement of Earth, the Moon, and the Sun by using gestures and prepositions. For example, as you trace the lines of the Moon's orbit, say: *The Moon travels around Earth.*

Next write the prepositions *around, between,* and *across.* Have students work in pairs to use the prepositions and the diagrams to give information about the Solar System: *In a solar eclipse, the Moon's shadow falls across Earth.*

Pages 4–5

Pages 6–7

Strategies for Comprehensible Input

Page	Story Language	Strategy Options
4	pale	**Restate:** white
	lit up the night	**Restate:** made the night sky bright
5	They were very close.	**Explain:** They loved each other very much.
6–7	famous	**Explain:** When you are famous, a lot of people know who you are.
	put on a show	**Restate:** played music for many people to hear and see
	Sky Dome	**Point to the picture and explain:** The band plays music in a place called the Sky Dome.

Language and Literacy **T290b**

UNIT 18 **LESSON 6,** CONTINUED

LANGUAGE AND LITERACY: THE BASICS BOOKSHELF

OBJECTIVES
Function: Listen to a Book
Critical Thinking and Comprehension:
- Relate Goal and Outcome

READ AND THINK TOGETHER

1. **Read Aloud** On your first reading of the book, use the "Strategies for Comprehensible Input" that appear at the bottom of pages T290b, T290d, and T290f.

2. **Read and Map: Relate Goal and Outcome** Set up a map like the one below, but with only the words *Goal, Event,* and *Outcome* shown. Explain that the *goal* tells what a character wants to do or have. The *events* tell what happens, and the *outcome* tells if the goal is reached.

   Read pages 4–8 aloud. Then think aloud as you model filling in the goal: *Moonshine wants to meet Sunny. That is her goal. Now I'll keep reading to see what happens, and to find out if she does meet Sunny.*

   Pause after reading each set of pages shown below and model completing the map for the rest of the text.

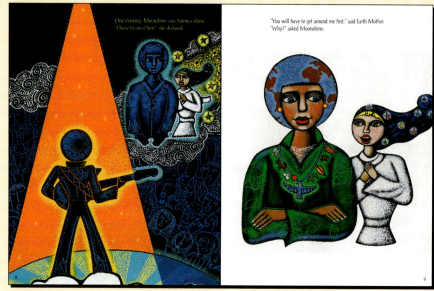

Pages 8–9

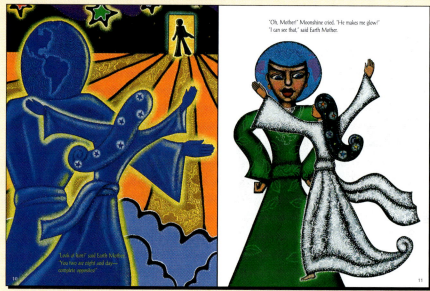

Pages 10–11

Goal-and-Outcome Map for *Sunny and Moonshine*

pages 4–8

Goal
Moonshine wants to meet Sunny.

pages 9–12 — **Event 1** Moonshine goes to Sunny's shows.

pages 13–15 — **Event 2** Earth Mother lets Moonshine meet Sunny.

pages 16–19 — **Event 3** Moonshine runs onto the stage and gives Sunny a kiss.

pages 20–23

Outcome
Moonshine and Sunny got to meet. Then they drifted apart and only saw each other once in a while.

T290c Unit 18 | Superstars

Sunny and Moonshine, CONTINUED

Pages 12–13

Pages 14–15

Strategies for Comprehensible Input

Page	Story Language	Strategy Options
8	declared	**Restate:** said
9	get around me	**Explain:** This is a saying that means, "I don't want you to do this."
10	complete opposites	**Explain:** Two things are opposite when they are very different.
11	glow	**Restate:** feel happy and bright
12–13	arrived	**Restate:** went
	stood in the way	**Demonstrate:** Stand between two students.
14	Finally	**Restate:** At last; After a long time.
15	begged	**Restate:** asked
	Okay	**Restate:** Yes, you may.

Language and Literacy T290d

UNIT 18 **LESSON 6,** CONTINUED

LANGUAGE AND LITERACY: THE BASICS BOOKSHELF

OBJECTIVES
Functions: Listen to a Book; Read Aloud a Book (choral reading)
Learning to Read: Identify Words

READ AND THINK TOGETHER, CONTINUED

3 Conduct Interactive Readings
Choose from these options:

- **Choral reading**
  Have small groups take the roles of Sunny, Moonshine, and Earth Mother. As you play the recording of *Sunny and Moonshine* on the **Selection Tape/CD**, have the groups read the dialogue for their characters.

  Tape 9B / CD 3 Track 12

- **Read along and identify words**
  Sunny and Moonshine contains many high frequency words that have been previously taught, as follows:

a	first	night	then
again	for	no	they
all	get	now	time
always	have	on	to
and	he	once	together
are	her	one	two
around	I	out	very
asked	in	put	was
at	is	really	were
been	lived	said	what
began	look	saw	while
between	love	see	why
but	makes	she	will
by	many	show	with
can	me	small	years
day	mother	story	you
each	my	that	your
few	name	the	

As you read, frame individual words from the list and have students identify the words.

CLOSE AND ASSESS
Have a student begin retelling the story. Others follow until the entire story has been retold.

Pages 16–17

Pages 18–19

Multi-Level Strategies
LITERACY SUPPORT

LITERATE IN L1 **Read with a Partner/Write Friendly Letters** After students have participated in the interactive readings, encourage them to read the story with a partner. Distribute the Partner Prompts on page T311 to help partners work together to identify unfamiliar words and unlock their meanings, then read the text to each other. After the partner reading, have partners take the roles of Sunny and Moonshine and write letters to each other. Partners can answer the letters.

INTERRUPTED SCHOOLING **Relate Goal and Outcome** To anchor understanding of the skill, have students answer questions about the goal, events, and outcome of the story. Show students how to find the page in the book that answers the question: *What does Moonshine want to do? Where does she go? What does Earth Mother finally let her do? What does Moonshine do then? What happens after Moonshine meets Sunny?* Then work with students to fill in the goal-and-outcome map.

T290e Unit 18 | Superstars

Sunny and Moonshine, CONTINUED

Pages 20–21

Pages 22–23

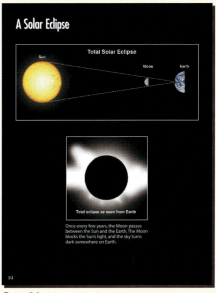

Page 24

Strategies for Comprehensible Input

Page	Story Language	Strategy Options
16–17	all the lights blew out	**Explain:** The lights went out. It got dark.
18–19	no longer in the dark	**Restate:** light; not in the dark anymore
	became a big hit	**Restate:** was liked by many people
20–21	went together	**Restate:** stayed together; spent time together
	drift apart	**Demonstrate:** Put your hands together, then gradually move them apart.
	like night and day	**Explain:** This is a saying that means "very different."
22–23	Once in a while	**Restate:** Sometimes; Now and then

Language and Literacy **T290f**

UNIT 18 LESSON 7

LANGUAGE AND LITERACY: THE BASICS BOOKSHELF

OBJECTIVES

Function: Retell a Story
Learning Strategy: Use Graphic Organizers (goal-and-outcome map)
Critical Thinking and Comprehension:
❶ Relate Goal and Outcome

CHECK COMPREHENSION

1 Make a Goal-and-Outcome Map
Have students review *Sunny and Moonshine* to identify the goal, events, and outcome. Remind them that a goal is what the character wants to do, the events are things that happen, and the outcome tells whether or not the character achieves the goal.

As you read aloud the directions for Steps 1–3, pause for students to make their maps and add information to its sections. Encourage students to review the story to check for accuracy.

2 Retell the Story Have groups look at each other's maps to add or correct information. Then partners can use their goal-and-outcome maps to retell the story to each other.

CLOSE AND ASSESS

Ask students to complete this sentence:
A goal-and-outcome map shows _____.

COMPREHENSION: RELATE GOAL AND OUTCOME

Read and Think Together

What does Moonshine want? Make a goal-and-outcome map for *Sunny and Moonshine*. Follow these steps.

❶ Draw a map like the one below.

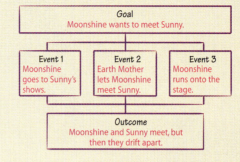

❷ Read pages 4–8 of *Sunny and Moonshine* again. Write Moonshine's goal in the top box.

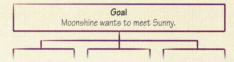

❸ Read the rest of the book again. What happens when Moonshine tries to reach her goal? Write an event in each of the small boxes. Write what happens at the end of the story in the last box.

❹ Use your completed goal-and-outcome map to retell the story to a partner.

290 Unit 18 | Superstars

from The Basics Bookshelf

THEME BOOK
This fantasy tells about a meeting between the Sun and the Moon.

REACHING ALL STUDENTS

Language Development
MAKE A PROMISE

Role-Play Use the scene on page 15 to model how Moonshine might make a promise to Earth Mother: *I promise that I'll come back soon. You have my word that I won't stay away too long.*

Use the chart to present other suitable language for making a promise. Then turn to pages 22 and 23 and have partners use the chart to role-play how Sunny and Moonshine might promise to meet at the next solar eclipse.

How to Make a Promise
I promise that I'll _____.
I will _____.
You have my word that I'll _____.
I promise that I won't _____.
I will never _____.

T290 Unit 18 | Superstars

HIGH FREQUENCY WORDS
Words to Know

REVIEW WORDS YOU KNOW

Read the words aloud. Which word goes in each sentence?

great	large	1. I think this band plays _great_ music.
Do	Does	2. _Do_ you like it, too?
most	might	3. They _might_ play a song for you!

LEARN TO READ

Some words have more than one meaning. Read each sentence. Think about the meaning of the word in dark type.

show	verb	Let me **show** you my new guitar.
show	noun	I am going to play it in the **show** tonight.
right	adverb	I need to practice to play the songs **right**.
right	adjective	I strum the strings with my **right** hand.
close	adverb	I keep the music book **close** to me while I play.
close	verb	**Close** it now and see if I can play the song.
watch	verb	Many people will come to **watch** us perform.
watch	noun	I have to check my **watch** so I won't be late.
kind	noun	I wonder what **kind** of music people will like.
kind	adjective	I hope the audience will be **kind** and won't shout "Boo!"

WORD WORK

Write each sentence. Add the missing word.   **Example:** 4. The show will start at 7:30.

4. The s h o w will start at 7:30.
5. Come at 7:00 so you can sit c l o s e to the stage.
6. My w a t c h broke. I don't know what time it is.
7. I can't wait to s h o w you how well we play.
8. Sometimes I c l o s e my eyes while I play.
9. I hope I sing all the r i g h t words to the songs.
10. Look for me on the r i g h t side of the stage.

Language and Literacy 291

Reading Practice Book page 105

Reading Fluency
RECOGNIZE HIGH FREQUENCY WORDS

To build automaticity with the high frequency words:

- Have teams write a pair of new sentences for each word. Challenge them to write a sentence for each meaning of the word, such as *Please show me where the theater is. The show has three dance acts.* Have teams trade sentences and take turns reading them aloud.

- Invite students to sort the words in different ways. For example, students can write the words in alphabetical order, sort them by vowel sound, or sort them by part of speech.

UNIT 18 LESSON 8

LANGUAGE AND LITERACY: HIGH FREQUENCY WORDS

OBJECTIVES
Learning to Read:
T Recognize High Frequency Words

REVIEW WORDS

1 **Review Known High Frequency Words** Have the group read aloud the words in the green box. Listen for words students cannot read automatically and use the steps in the yellow box to reteach those words. Then have students look at the photo. Read each cloze sentence. Reread each sentence and pause for students to silently read the two words to the left of the sentence. Tell students to choose the word that goes in the sentence and tells about the picture.

INTRODUCE NEW WORDS

2 **Learn High Frequency Words** Use the High Frequency Word Script on page T329 to lead students through the steps for learning *right* and *kind* and to reinforce the multiple meanings of the other words. For *close,* point out the adverb ends in /s/, and the verb in /z/.

PRACTICE

3 **Conduct "Word Work"** Model how to use context to find possible words in the list and then to use the number of letter blanks to confirm the word.

Have groups complete Items 5–10. Ask students to read aloud Items 5 and 8, saying *close* correctly.

APPLY

4 **Read Words in Context** Students will read high frequency words in context in the sentences on page 293 and the passage on page 294.

▶ **Reading Practice Book** page 105

CLOSE AND ASSESS
Call out the high frequency words one at a time. Have students point to them and spell the words as a group.

Language and Literacy T291

UNIT 18 **LESSON 9**

LANGUAGE AND LITERACY: WORD STRUCTURE

OBJECTIVES

Learning to Read: Build Oral Vocabulary; Develop Phonemic Awareness; Identify Syllable Types (consonant + le); ❶ Divide Words into Syllables; Decode Multisyllabic Words

TEACH SYLLABLE TYPES

1 Build Oral Vocabulary Display Transparency 88. Talk through each picture to develop meaning for the words. For example, for Item E, say:

• *These stars* (point) **twinkle**, *or shine. They are bright and* **twinkle** *(make twinkling motions with fingers) like diamonds.*

2 Develop Phonemic Awareness Remove the transparency and conduct the oral activities in Step 1 of the Script for Transparency 88.

3 Decode Multisyllabic Words Display Transparency 88 again. Work through Step 2 of the script.

CLOSE AND ASSESS

Display *circle, candle, gentle,* and *able*. Call on students to identify a chunk they know in each word and to read the word.

▶ **Reading Practice Book** page 106 (syllable type: consonant + *le*)

Transparency 88: ▶ Syllable Types

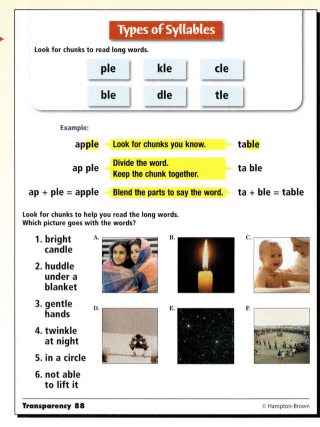

▼ Script for Transparency 88

Types of Syllables

1. Develop Phonemic Awareness
Identify the Final Syllable Say: *Some two-syllable words end in /pəl/ like apple, people, staple. Say /pəl/ with me. Now say /təl/ with me. You hear /təl/ at the end of words like* gentle, little, *and* title. Repeat the process using the words *circle, cycle, uncle* to model the pronunciation of /kəl/. Then say the following words, and ask students to say the last syllable they hear in each word: *middle* (dle), *apple* (ple), *circle* (cle), *table* (ble), *little* (tle).

2. Decode Multisyllabic Words
Teach Point to the word chunks at the top of **Transparency 88**. Say: *These chunks often appear as syllables in long words.* As you point to each chunk, read it aloud with students. Point to each chunk again and ask students to read it aloud on their own. Then say: *Look for chunks you know in long words.*

Work through the Example to model the strategy. Point to *apple,* and say: *Look at this word. To read it, look for a chunk you know.* Run your finger under *ple* in *apple,* and say: *I know this chunk,* ple /pəl/. *Next, divide the word. Keep the chunk together.* Point to the two parts and say: *Here are the two syllables. Now let's blend the parts to say the word.* Run a finger under *ap* and *ple,* blending the parts ap-ple, and saying the word: *apple.* Point out that when you blended the syllables and said the word quickly, you pronounced only one *p*. Repeat the procedure to read *table,* pointing out that the first syllable ends in a vowel, which means that the *a* has the long sound /ā/.

Practice Have students do Items 1–6. Ask a volunteer to point out a familiar chunk and divide the word keeping the chunk together. Write the syllables on the board and lead the group in blending them to read the word.

Reading Practice Book page 106

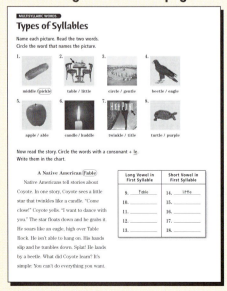

T292a Unit 18 | Superstars

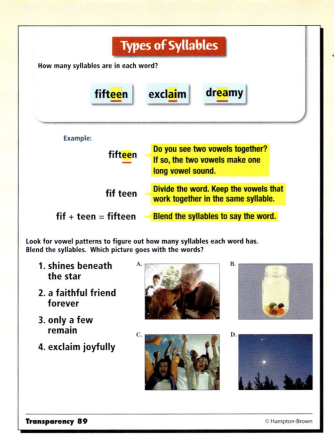

◀ Transparency 89: Syllable Types

▼ Script for Transparency 89

Types of Syllables

1. **Develop Phonemic Awareness**
   Blend Syllables to Form a Word/Identify Vowel Sounds Say: *I'm going to say the two parts in a word and I want you to guess what the word is. Let's try one:* fif-teen. *Blend the parts to say the whole word:* fifteen. Repeat with the following syllables: be-neath, six-teen, may-be, rain-y, re-pay, be-tween. After students blend the syllables to say each word, ask them to identify the two vowel sounds they hear in the word.

2. **Decode Multisyllabic Words**
   Teach Point to the word *fifteen* at the top of **Transparency 89**. Say: *How many syllables are in this word? The number of syllables is the same as the number of vowel sounds. Look for the vowel patterns to help you figure out how many syllables are in the word.*

   Work through the Example to model the strategy. Say: *How many vowels do you see?* (3) *Do you see two vowels together?* (yes, two e's) *Yes, there are two e's together* (point to ee). *These two vowels are a team. They work together to make one sound:* /ē/. *The first vowel is long. The second vowel is silent. Now divide the word. Keep the vowels that are a team in the same syllable.* Point to the two parts and say: *Here are the two syllables.* Then continue: *Now blend the syllables to say the word.* Run a finger under *fif* and *teen*, blending the parts fif-teen, and saying the word: *fifteen*. Follow a similar procedure to read *exclaim* and *dreamy*, pointing out the vowel team *ai* in *exclaim* and *ea* in *dreamy*.

   Practice Have students do Items 1–4. Ask a volunteer to identify the vowels in the words with two syllables and to divide the words keeping the vowel teams together. Write the syllables on the board and lead the group in blending them to read the words. In Item 1, remind students that the *e* in *shines* is silent, and the *i* is long. In Item 4, help students work from the end of the word *joyfully* to identify and cover the suffixes -ly and -ful. Then help them blend the three syllables in sequence to read the word: joy-ful-ly, *joyfully*.

OBJECTIVES

Learning to Read: Build Oral Vocabulary; Develop Phonemic Awareness; Identify Syllable Types (vowel team);
❶ Divide Words into Syllables; Decode Multisyllabic Words (2 and 3 syllables)

TEACH SYLLABLE TYPES

1. **Build Oral Vocabulary** Display Transparency 89. Talk through each picture to develop meaning for the words in Items 1–4. For example, for Item A, say:
   - *Here is a dog* (point) *with its owner. A dog is a **faithful friend** because it stays with you. A dog is a faithful friend **forever**, or always.*

2. **Develop Phonemic Awareness** Remove the transparency and conduct the oral activities in Step 1 of the Script for Transparency 89.

3. **Decode Multisyllabic Words** Display Transparency 89 again. Work through Step 2 of the script.

CLOSE AND ASSESS

Display *exclaim, faithful, beneath,* and *remain*. Call on students to identify the vowel team in each word, tell you where to divide the word, and read it.

Language and Literacy **T292b**

UNIT 18 **LESSON 9,** CONTINUED

LANGUAGE AND LITERACY: WORD STRUCTURE

OBJECTIVES

Learning to Read: Build Oral Vocabulary; Develop Phonemic Awareness; Identify Syllable Types (vowel-silent e); 🅣 Divide Words into Syllables; Decode Multisyllabic Words (2 and 3 syllables)

TEACH SYLLABLE TYPES

1 Build Oral Vocabulary Display Transparency 90. Talk through each picture to develop meaning for the words. For example, for Item A, say:

- *This girl* (point) *waves to a friend.* (pantomime waving) *She **recognizes**, or knows, her.*

2 Develop Phonemic Awareness Remove the transparency and conduct the oral activities in Step 1 of the Script for Transparency 90.

3 Decode Multisyllabic Words Display Transparency 90 again. Work through Step 2 of the script.

CLOSE AND ASSESS

Display *reptile, recognize, alone,* and *celebrate*. Call on students to identify the vowel sounds in each word. Have volunteers read the words.

▶ **Reading Practice Book** page 107 (syllable types: vowel team, vowel-silent *e*)

Reading Practice Book page 107

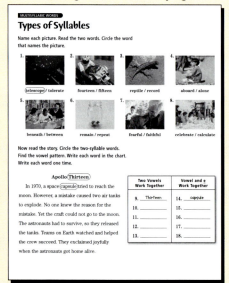

Transparency 90: ▶ **Syllable Types**

▼ **Script for Transparency 90**

Types of Syllables

1. Develop Phonemic Awareness
Count Syllables/Segment Words into Syllables Say: *Some words have two syllables, or parts, such as* hopeful. *Clap out the parts with me:* hope-ful. *(clap, clap) Other words have three syllables, such as* hopefully. *Clap the syllables with me:* hope-ful-ly *(clap, clap, clap). Lead students in saying and clapping each syllable in* beside (be-side), *recognize* (rec-og-nize), *alone* (a-lone), *celebrate* (cel-e-brate), *joyfully* (joy-ful-ly), *suddenly* (sud-den-ly).

2. Decode Multisyllabic Words
Teach Point to the word *reptile* at the top of **Transparency 90**. Say: *How many syllables are in this word? Look for the vowel patterns to help you figure out how many syllables it has. Each syllable has a vowel sound. I see three vowels:* (point to the vowels) *an* e, *an* i, *and a final* e.

Work through the Example to model the strategy. Say: *Do you see a vowel and then a consonant and an* e? (yes) Point to *tile,* saying: *When there is a vowel and then a consonant and an* e, *the vowel and the* e *work together to make one vowel sound. The first vowel is long* (point to the *i*). *The* e *is silent. Now divide the word. Keep the* i *and the* e *in the same syllable.* Point to the two parts and say: *Here are the two syllables.* Then continue: *Now blend the syllables to say the word.* Run a finger under *rep* and *tile,* blending the parts: rep-tile, and saying the word: *reptile.*

Practice Have students do Items 1–4. Ask a volunteer to identify the vowel sounds in each multisyllabic word and divide the word keeping the vowel-consonant-silent *e* together in the same syllable. Write the syllables on the board and lead the group in blending them to read the words. For Items 2 and 4, remind them to use the strategy for dividing words with one consonant between two vowels. Also remind them that the letters *br* in *celebrate* stay together. For Item 3, remind students that the *a* in *alone* has the /ə/ sound.

T292c Unit 18 | Superstars

Multisyllabic Words

suddenly   visible   reappear

HOW TO READ LONG WORDS
- Look for familiar parts and cover them.
- Divide the root word.
- Blend all the syllables to say the word.
- Ask yourself if it sounds right.

Read the article silently. Then read it aloud to a partner.

In the year 2061, something wonderful will suddenly appear in our night sky. It will look like a fuzzy star with a long tail. It will be visible for a few nights, then disappear. This visitor from space is Halley's Comet.

Most comets are visible only through a telescope, but not Halley's. People are able to see it without a telescope. Halley's Comet is special for another reason, too. It keeps coming back!

The Chinese wrote about this comet in 240 B.C. After that, people saw a bright comet every seventy-six years or so. In 1682, a man named Halley figured it out. He predicted that the comet would reappear in 1720, and it did! Halley's Comet will be back in 2061. So mark your calendars!

Transparency 91   © Hampton-Brown

◀ Transparency 91: Multisyllabic Words

▼ Script for Transparency 91

Multisyllabic Words

1. Develop Phonemic Awareness

Blend Syllables to Form a Word/Segment Words into Syllables Say: *Some long words have three parts. I'm going to say the three parts of a word and I want you to guess the word. Let's try one:* won-der-ful. *Blend the parts to guess the word:* wonderful. *Now tell me the three parts you hear in the word* wonderful (won-der-ful). Repeat with students blending the following syllables to form a word and then segmenting the word into syllables: sud-den-ly, dis-ap-pear, tel-e-scope, cal-en-dar, hope-ful-ly, cel-e-brate.

2. Decode Multisyllabic Words

Model Remind students that they have learned different strategies to help them read long words. Point to the word *suddenly* on **Transparency 91** and say: *Some of you may already know this word, but I don't want you to say it. I'm going to show you how you could figure it out while you were reading if you didn't recognize it. First I'll look for any prefixes or suffixes. I'll also look to see if the word is made of two smaller words. I see the suffix* -ly (point), *so I'll cover the* -ly *and look at the root word.* Cover *-ly. Now I'll look for patterns to help me divide the root word into syllables. I see the vowel* u (point) *followed by the two consonants* dd (point) *and then the vowel* e (point). *I'll break the word into syllables between the two consonants. Now I'll blend the sounds in each syllable and say the word.* Run a finger from left to right below the letters as you blend the sounds and read the word: sud-den-ly, *suddenly*. Read the list of strategies at the top of the page and point out the ones you used to read the word *suddenly*. Model how to use these strategies to figure out the words *visible* and *reappear*.

Practice Have students read the passage silently before reading it aloud to a partner. Then partners can choose three new words from the passage and use the list of strategies to tell each other which strategies they used to figure out each new word.

OBJECTIVES

Learning to Read: Build Oral Vocabulary; Develop Phonemic Awareness; ❶ Divide Words into Syllables; Decode Multisyllabic Words (2 and 3 syllalbes)

REVIEW READING STRATEGIES

1 Build Oral Vocabulary Display Transparency 91. Introduce these words:

- **visible:** something is **visible** if you can see it.
- **disappear, reappear:** to go away; to come back
- **telescope:** an instrument for making objects in the sky look closer
- **predicted:** guessed that something would happen

2 Develop Phonemic Awareness Remove the transparency and conduct the oral activities in Step 1 of the Script for Transparency 91.

3 Decode Multisyllabic Words Display Transparency 91 again. Work through Step 2 of the script.

CLOSE AND ASSESS

Display *another, visible, reappear, reason, recognize,* and *telescope.* Ask students to read each word aloud and tell which strategies they used to figure out the word.

▶ **Reading Practice Book** page 108 (syllable division: 2- and 3-syllable words)

Reading Practice Book page 108

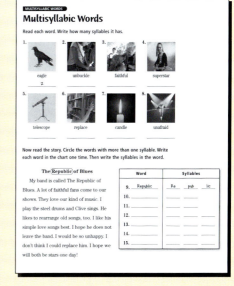

Language and Literacy **T292d**

UNIT 18 LESSON 10
LANGUAGE AND LITERACY: READING AND SPELLING

OBJECTIVES
Functions: Listen Actively; Repeat Spoken Language; Recite

Learning to Read: Develop Phonemic Awareness; Identify Syllable Types (consonant + *le*, vowel team, vowel-silent *e*); ⓣ Divide Words into Syllables; Decode Multisyllabic Words (2 and 3 syllables)

Spelling: ⓣ Multisyllabic Words

LISTEN AND LEARN
Tape 9B / CD 3 Track 18

1. **Sing a Song** Display Transparency 92 and play "Starship Earth" on the **Language Tape/CD**.

DEVELOP PHONEMIC AWARENESS

2. **Blend Syllables to Form a Word** Say: *Listen to these word parts:* cir, cle. *Blend them together to say the word.* (cir-cle, *circle*) Continue with these word parts: gen, tle; can, dle; si, lent, ly; ea, gle; grace, ful, ly; com, plete, ly; re, ap, pear; hap, pi, ly.

STUDY LONG WORDS

3. **Identify/Count Syllables** Point to the first picture and say: *This is an eagle, and here is the word. I recognize the word part* gle, *and I know that it stays together as one syllable* (put your finger on the triangle). *Now let's blend the syllables to read the word* (slide your finger from left to right): ea-gle, *eagle*. Repeat the procedure for the remaining words. For *fifteen* and *telescope,* point out the vowel team and the vowel-silent *e* patterns. For *carefully,* point out the suffixes *ful* and *ly*. Then read the question aloud and call on students to answer it. (*eagle,* 2; *fifteen,* 2; *telescope,* 3; *hold,* 1; *carefully,* 3)

Afterwards, play the song again. Have students identify letter patterns and word parts that helped them read the multisyllabic words.

T292 Unit 18 | Superstars

MULTISYLLABIC WORDS
Reading and Spelling

LISTEN AND LEARN

Starship Earth

Safely,
And silently,
Earth goes around the Sun.
And each time our Earth circles that Sun
Another year is done.

Gracefully,
Silently,
Earth spins while she rings the Sun.
And each time our Earth has completely spun
Another day is done.

STUDY LONG WORDS

How many syllables are in each word? Look for letter patterns and word parts.

2 syllables	2 syllables	3 syllables	1 syllable/3 syllables
eagle	fifteen	telescope	hold carefully

292 Unit 18 | Superstars ▶ Transparencies 88–9

REACHING ALL STUDENTS

Multi-Level Strategies
LITERACY SUPPORT

LITERATE IN L1 Students who read Chinese or another ideographic language are used to looking for the gestalt of the picture to read. Reading long words in English, however, requires identifying word parts and blending syllables.

Use hands-on word-building activities to help students pay attention to the parts of long words. For example, provide word cards with *un, safe, ly, less, care, hope,* and *ful*. Students can manipulate the cards to build and read *unsafe, careless, careful, carelessly, carefully, hopeful, hopefully*.

Speakers of Romance languages, such as Spanish or Portuguese, will transfer their knowledge of affixes and the concept of syllabication even though syllabication rules may vary. Also encourage these students to use cognates such as the Spanish word *completamente* and the English word *completely* to unlock long words in English.

READING STRATEGIES

There are several ways to read a long word.

1 Look for familiar parts—prefixes, suffixes, or endings like *-ed* or *-ly*. Cover them.

completely   complete

2 Figure out how to divide the root word.

complete

com   plete

I can look for a letter pattern. I see a vowel, three consonants, and another vowel.

complete

com   plete

Or, I can look for a vowel pattern. I need to keep the vowel, consonant, and final e *together.*

3 Blend the syllables to say the root word. Then uncover the suffix and read the entire word.

com + plete   com + plete + ly = completely

READING AND SPELLING PRACTICE

Use what you learned to read the sentences.

1. Chan waited on the rooftop beneath the night sky.
2. He carefully checked his watch. It was close to midnight.
3. The North Star twinkled in the middle of the night sky.
4. Chan was able to see Venus. Then he saw a flash of light!
5. Was it a rocket launch? No! It was just lightning.
6.–10. Now write the sentences that your teacher reads.   For dictation sentences, see Step 6 at right.

WORD WORK

11.–16. Read the newspaper article. Find the words with 3 syllables. List them. Divide them into syllables.

Example: 11. important   im por tant

A Star in Space

Here is some news for fans of Kim Mills. The film star will go to Houston to train for an important space flight with NASA. She will hopefully blast off sometime in June.

"I have to prepare for the flight." Ms. Mills said with excitement.

The star plans to act in two different films this fall: *A Terrible Surprise* and a remake of *The Forbidden*.

Answers:
11. important   im por tant
12. hopefully   hope ful ly
13. excitement ex cite ment
14. different   dif fer ent
15. terrible   ter ri ble
16. forbidden   for bid den

Language and Literacy **293**

Decodable Book
PRACTICE WITH MULTISYLLABIC WORDS

Decodable Book 18:
Meteor Shower

Assign **Decodable Book 18** for independent reading. The **Decodable Book** can be used in a variety of ways to help students become more fluent, automatic readers:

Discussion Circles Have students work in small groups to read aloud and discuss the book using the questions on the back cover. Encourage students to read aloud the text that supports their answers. Groups can also work together to complete the Word Work Activity.

Readers Theater Students can read aloud the stories in a class performance. Help them prepare by rereading the stories in daily rehearsals. Work with students to add narration or dialog. Encourage them to use natural phrasing and expression.

Rereading at Home Have students work with family members to reread the book at home. They can take turns reading aloud alternate pages, then rereading the book switching the pages each person reads.

REVIEW READING STRATEGIES

4 Divide Words into Syllables Work through the strategies with students, reading each step aloud and modeling the actions shown on the page. Make sure students understand that they can use different strategies to help them divide long words into manageable, recognizable chunks.

PRACTICE

5 Read Sentences Distribute the Partner Prompts from page T311 to guide peers in reading the sentences in Items 1–6. Remind them to use all the strategies they have learned to divide long words and to blend the words silently as they read.

6 Write Sentences Dictate the following sentences for students to write. Read each sentence at normal speed once so students can listen, and then repeat it slowly, word by word as they write:

  7. She sits alone at the table.
  8. Suddenly she sees fifteen candles.
  9. Her faithful friends baked a cake!
  10. They want to celebrate her birthday.
  11. She carefully cuts the cake.

If students need extra support, guide them in repeating each word after you and clapping out the syllables. Then they should read aloud what they wrote, making sure they have written the correct number of syllables.

7 Conduct "Word Work" Read the directions and work through the Example. Then have partners complete the activity. Discuss the strategies students used to divide the words into syllables.

▶ **Reading Practice Book** pages 179–182 (Decodable Book 18)

CLOSE AND ASSESS

Write *surprise, silently, different, middle* and *carefully*. Ask students to divide the words into syllables. Have them blend the syllables to read the words.

Language and Literacy **T293**

UNIT 18 **LESSON 11**

LANGUAGE AND LITERACY: INDEPENDENT READING

OBJECTIVES

Functions:
Read a Selection; Give Information

Learning to Read: Recognize High Frequency Words; Divide Words into Syllables to Decode Multisyllabic Words

Reading Strategies: Activate Prior Knowledge; Set a Purpose for Reading; Visualize

Critical Thinking and Comprehension: Relate Goal and Outcome

Writing: Give Information

READ ON YOUR OWN

1. **Introduce Vocabulary** In "Fifth Moon's Story," students apply phonics skills and read high frequency words taught in Lessons 8–10. Introduce the following story words. Write each word, pronounce it, and spell it. Then give a definition and a context sentence:

   - **Native American:** describes the people who were originally in the Americas; American Indian. *The Navajo and the Hopi are Native American groups.*

   - **fields:** open spaces with few trees. *Wildflowers grow in sunny fields.*

2. **Activate Prior Knowledge/Set Purposes** Read the title and the first two sentences of the story. Discuss what students know about myths or fables about the seasons. Then model setting a purpose: *I'll read this story to find out what happens to Winter.* Encourage volunteers to state their purposes for reading.

3. **Read and Think: Visualize** Students should read the story on their own. Suggest that as they read, they make a movie in their minds. Prompt the action: *What do Winter and Sun do? Where are they? What do they look like? How do they change?*

T294 Unit 18 | Superstars

COMPREHENSION: RELATE GOAL AND OUTCOME

Read on Your Own

Many Native American calendars divide the year into thirteen moons. Each moon has its own story. Read this one about the Fifth Moon.

✓ **DECODING CHECK** Give the Decoding Progress Check on page 1a of the Assessment Handbook.

Fifth Moon's Story

In the Old Time, Winter stayed on Earth forever. Rain and snow fell on the land. Fields and rivers were covered with snow. The Earth Children asked the kind Sun for help, "Please send Winter away!"

Sun went to Winter's house. Winter sat all alone. He was huddled close to a cold fire. He recognized Sun. "Go away!" Winter shouted.

"No!" Sun exclaimed. "It is you who must go. Leave the Land of the Earth Children, now!"

Winter frowned. He blasted Sun with icy rain, but he was not able to make Sun leave.

Thirteen moons on Turtle's back

Sun just watched and smiled happily. He kept shining and shining. At last, Winter began to melt away. He grew smaller and smaller until he became the size of a snowflake. Sun then called to Owl. Owl flew into the room. Sun said, "Take Winter to the snows in the far north. He will remain there a long time." Owl did as Sun asked.

Suddenly the Land of the Earth Children began to grow warm. Green leaves reappeared on the trees.

The people came together to celebrate. They danced joyfully as gentle Spring came back into their land.

294 Unit 18 | Superstars

REACHING ALL STUDENTS

CULTURAL PERSPECTIVES

World Cultures: Compare Oral Traditions Point out that many Native American stories were passed orally from one generation to the next. Invite students to learn more about oral traditions in Native American and other cultures and to share some of the stories, songs, and sayings they discover. Encourage students whose families have a strong oral tradition to share information about that aspect of their culture.

CHECK YOUR UNDERSTANDING

1. Copy this goal-and-outcome map and complete it. Use the completed map to retell "Fifth Moon's Story" to a partner.

Sample Responses
- **Event 1:** Earth Children ask Sun for help.
- **Event 2:** Sun visits Winter. Winter melts.
- **Event 3:** Owl takes Winter away.
- **Outcome:** Spring arrives.

EXPAND YOUR VOCABULARY

2. Copy the chart. Work with a group to add words. Tell about the weather and what you do in each season.

Sample Responses

Season	Weather	Activities
winter	cold, snowy, icy	ice skate, eat soup
spring	warm, rainy	hike, plant a garden
summer	hot, dry	swim, eat outdoors
fall	cool, windy	ride bikes, fly a kite

WRITE ABOUT THE SUN

3. Talk with a partner about how the Sun helps people. Can the Sun be bad for people, too? Write sentences to tell about the Sun.

Example: 3. The Sun helps people grow crops.
The Sun is bad for your skin when you stay out too long.

Language and Literacy 295

Reading Practice Book page 109

Build Reading Fluency

Read the myth. Stop when the timer goes off. Mark your score. Then try it again two more times on different days.

A Tale from Greece

When the sun is very hot, the people of Greece remember an old tale. It is about an inventor named Daedalus. The king was angry with Daedalus because he helped destroy the king's monster bull. The king punished him by locking him and his son Icarus inside a high tower.

Daedalus planned a clever escape. He plucked feathers from birds that visited the tower. He used candle wax to glue the feathers onto wooden frames. In this way, he made two pairs of wings.

When they put on the wings, Daedalus told Icarus, "Promise me you will not fly too high. If you do, the sun will melt the wax."

Icarus nodded, but when he flew into the sky, the boy forgot his promise. He flew higher and higher. Daedalus called out, but his cry came too late. The boy's wings melted, and he fell into the sea.

	Day 1	Day 2	Day 3
Total Words Read in One Minute			
Minus Words Missed			
Words Read Correctly in One Minute			

Reading Fluency
TIMED READINGS

Read the title and introduction on **Reading Practice Book** page 109. Set the timer and have a student read the passage to you. Use the script on page T329 to mark words the student misses and to note the last word read in one minute. Have students graph their performance and set a goal for improving in subsequent timed readings. Plan for two additional timed readings, and encourage partners to practice reading the passage to each other between the timed readings.

CHECK YOUR UNDERSTANDING

4 Comprehension: Relate Goal and Outcome Explain the meanings of *goal* and *outcome*: Goal *means "something you want to get or do."* Outcome *means "the result or what happened in the end." Often it takes several steps, or events, to reach a goal.* Then show students how to use information in the story to complete the goal-and-outcome map. Say: *The goal in this story is that Earth Children want Winter to go away, so I will write that under* Goal. Point to the remaining boxes as you say: *Then I'll write the events that helped them reach their goal and the outcome.*

EXPAND YOUR VOCABULARY

5 Describe Seasons Read the directions and the headings in the chart. Use the sample answers in row 1 to model describing winter weather and winter activities. Encourage students to work in groups to tell about the other seasons.

WRITE

6 Give Information About the Sun Point out that the Example describes one helpful thing the Sun does and one way in which the Sun harms people. Have partners work together to write similar pairs of sentences.

For students who need additional support in writing, provide sentence frames. Help students choose present tense verbs to complete them:

> The sun helps people _____.
> The sun is bad for people because _____.

▶ **Reading Practice Book** page 109

CLOSE AND ASSESS

Have partners take turns telling each other the goal, main events, and outcome in *Fifth Moon's Story*.

Language and Literacy **T295**

UNIT 18 **LESSON 12**

LANGUAGE ACROSS THE CURRICULUM: SCIENCE

OBJECTIVES

Function: Listen to an Article
Concepts and Vocabulary: 🔊 Space
Learning Strategies: Build Background
Critical Thinking and Comprehension: Identify Details

LEARN ABOUT OUTER SPACE

1. **Explore Outer Space** Read the title. Then read aloud the labels and captions for each photo. Point out that Earth has mountains, plains, and even craters, just like the Moon.

READ AND THINK

2. **Take Notes** Read aloud the article title and the focus question. Begin a chart to take organized notes of what the students are learning about the Moon and the stars.

Moon	Stars
The bright places on the Moon are mountains.	A star can form from dust and gas in space.

3. **Read the Article Aloud** As you read, restate ideas and clarify vocabulary, as needed. Pause after the second paragraph to go over the photographs and captions. Have students continue adding to their charts as they listen to the article.

CHECK UNDERSTANDING

4. **Answer the Review Questions** Encourage students to refer to the pictures and the text to complete Items 1–2.

CLOSE AND ASSESS

As a class, summarize what students have learned about the moon and the stars from the article. Write down other questions students have that they might want to research through further reading.

T296 Unit 18 | Superstars

SUCCESS IN SCIENCE

Learn About Outer Space

THE MOON AND STARS

The **surface**, or outside, of the Moon looks like this:

The bright places on the Moon are areas of **mountains**. The dark places are flat **plains**. Both have a lot of **craters**.

The **soil** and **rocks** on the Moon are made of minerals also found on Earth.

This is how a star is born:

A **nebula** is a cloud of dust and gas. If enough of the dust and gas come together, a **star** will form in the nebula.

Listen to the article. Then do the Review.

Answers for the Review:
1. The rocks on the Moon have aluminum, silica, iron, other minerals, and some gases in them. Much of the Moon's soil is made up of small pieces of glass. Stars are made of hot gases.
2. There are mountains, plains, craters, soil, and rocks on the surface of the Moon.

The Moon and the Stars

• What are the Moon and the stars made of?

Since the beginning of time, people have had questions about outer space. What is the Moon made of? Why do stars glow? Scientists on Earth are now answering some of the questions.

Astronauts have walked through the Moon's plains. They collected rocks and soil and brought them back to Earth. Here, scientists found that the rocks from the Moon have aluminum, silica, iron, and other minerals in them. There are also some gases trapped in the rocks. Scientists found that much of the Moon's soil is made up of small pieces of glass.

Scientists use telescopes and other special tools to study the stars. They learned that stars are huge balls of hot gases. They are not solid like the Moon or the Earth. The gases in the stars give off both heat and light.

We still have questions about the Moon and stars. Scientists are learning more about outer space every day.

The minerals in rocks from the Moon are also found on Earth.

We use **aluminum** in cans. Glass is made of **silica**. This pan is made of **iron**.

REVIEW

1. **Check Your Understanding** What did the scientists find out about the rocks and soil on the Moon? What are the stars made of?
2. **Vocabulary** What is on the surface of the Moon?

296 Unit 18 | Superstars

REACHING ALL STUDENTS

COMMUNITY CONNECTION

Studies in Space Organize a class trip to a local planetarium, space museum, or science museum. Or, invite a scientist or astronomer to your class. Before the scientist arrives, brainstorm a list of questions about space and have the class make predictions about the answers. Encourage students to confirm or revise their predictions as the scientist speaks. If possible, invite the scientist to lead the class in a nighttime stargazing tour.

Writing Project / Diamante Poem

WRITING ASSESSMENT
Use the Writing Progress Checklist on page 51 of the Assessment Handbook to evaluate this writing project.

Write a poem about two things in outer space.

WRITE A DIAMANTE POEM

1 Draw 9 lines in a diamond pattern. At the top and bottom, write the names of two different things from outer space.

2 Then finish your poem like this:

- Write 2 adjectives that describe the noun above.
- Write 2 adjectives that describe the noun below.
- Write 3 verbs that end in *-ing*. The verbs must tell about both nouns.

```
        sun
    hot     bright
shining  glowing  gleaming
    round    cold
        moon
```

MAKE AND SHARE YOUR STAR

Find interesting facts about the things at the top and bottom of your diamante. Look in the book *Sunny and Moonshine*, or ask your teacher or a librarian for help. Your facts can be about the past, present, or future.

✓ **Check Your Work**
Does your poem tell about two opposite, or different, things?
Did you put the right kind of word on each line?
Did you include facts about both things in your poem?

Cut a star shape out of card stock or heavy paper. Copy your diamante on one side of the star. On the other side, write your facts. Decorate your star. Read your poem to the class and share your facts. Then hang your stars from the ceiling to create a classroom poetry constellation.

Language Across the Curriculum **297**

Language Practice Book page 136

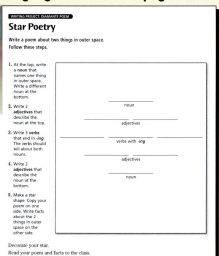

✓ ASSESSMENT

For opportunities to measure progress, see the Assessment Handbook:

- **Units 16–18 Test** evaluates basic vocabulary and the patterns and structures of English, mastery of phonics and high frequency words, reading comprehension, and writing.

- **The Language Acquisition Assessment** for Units 16–18 offers performance assessments for measuring growth through the stages of language acquisition.

- **Self- and Peer-Assessment** forms involve students in the assessment process.

UNIT 18 **LESSON 13**

LANGUAGE ACROSS THE CURRICULUM: WRITING

OBJECTIVES

Functions: Give Information; Write
Learning Strategies and Critical Thinking: Plan; Generate and Organize Ideas; ⓣ Make Comparisons; Self-Assess
Research Skills: Gather Information; Use the Research Process
Writing: Diamante Poem

CONDUCT THE WRITING PROJECT

1 Explore Diamante Poems Point to the sample poem and explain that a diamante poem follows a pattern to tell about two different objects. The words form a diamond shape.

2 Write a Diamante Poem Follow the text in the book to explain the structure of a diamante poem. To get students started on their own poems, brainstorm a list of noun pairs that they can use for the top and bottom lines:

space/Earth	Sun/Earth
star/Moon	Moon/Earth
crater/mountain	night/sky

3 Make and Share Your Star Guide students in finding facts about the two subjects of their poems. Plan a read-aloud of the diamante poems. Then use thread to suspend the star poems.

▶ **Language Practice Book** page 136

CLOSE AND ASSESS

Have students look at their poems. Say:
- *Tell me the two things you wrote your poem about.*
- *Point to the verbs that tell about both of the things.*
- *Read me a fact about each thing.*

Language Across the Curriculum **T297**

High Point Handbook

This Handbook is especially designed for beginning English learners. Students can use the Handbook independently as a resource for learning as they participate in the language arts and content area activities in each unit. You may also want to use appropriate sections to teach or reinforce skills and strategies developed in the program.

HIGH POINT
Handbook

▶ **Handbook Contents**

Strategies for Learning Language	300
Sentences	302
Nouns	304
▶ **Word Files:** Nouns That Name People	305
Nouns That Name Places	306
Pronouns	307
Adjectives	309
▶ **Word Files:** Sensory Adjectives	310
Feelings	312
Numbers	313
Verbs	314
▶ **Word Files:** Action Verbs	315
Irregular Verbs	318
Capital Letters	319
Paragraphs	320

Handbook: Strategies for Learning/Sentences

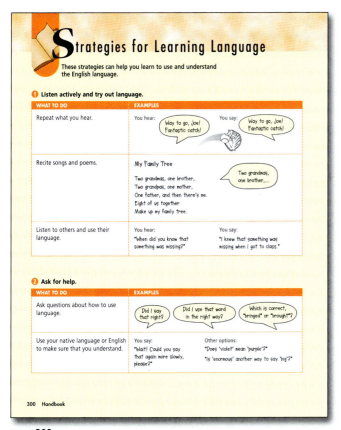
page 300

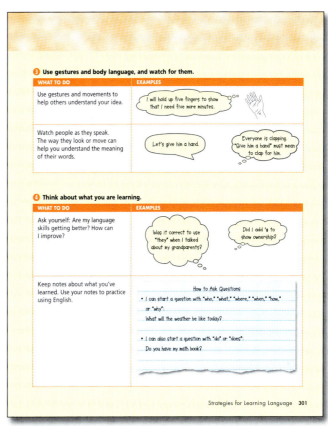
page 301

page 302

page 303

Handbook: Nouns/Pronouns

page 304

page 305

page 306

page 307

T300 Handbook: Nouns/Pronouns

Handbook: Pronouns/Adjectives

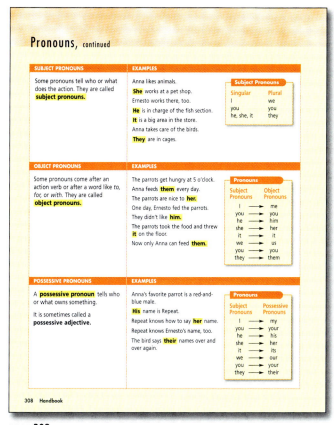

page 308

page 309

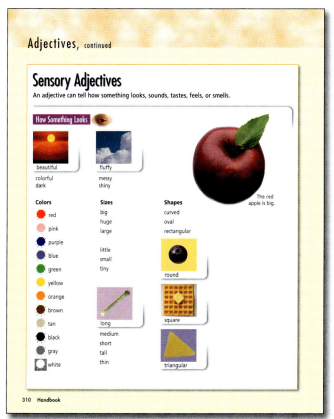

page 310

page 311

Handbook: Pronouns/Adjectives **T301**

Handbook: Adjectives/Verbs

page 312

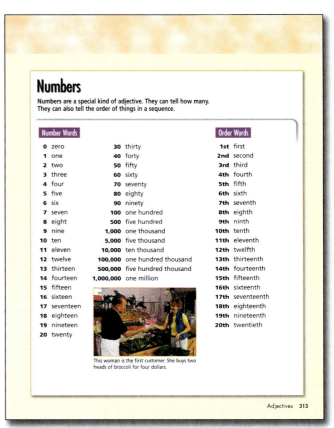

page 313

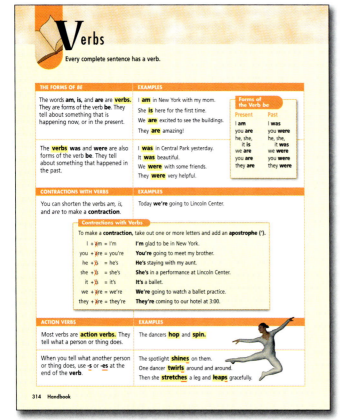

page 314

page 315

T302 Handbook: Adjectives/Verbs

Handbook: Verbs/Capital Letters

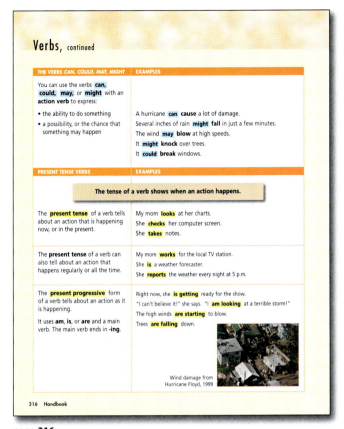

page 316

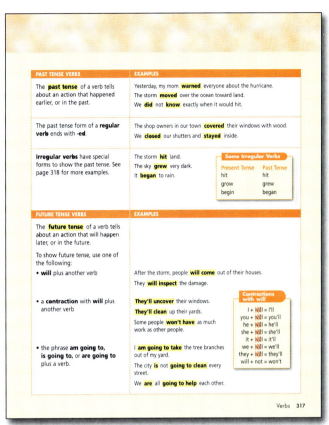

page 317

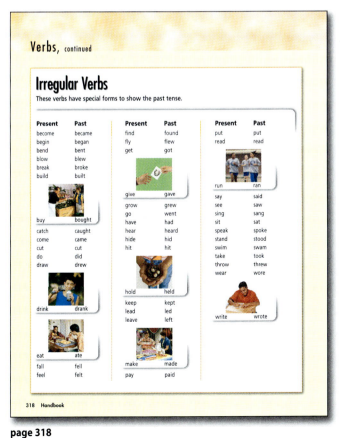

page 318

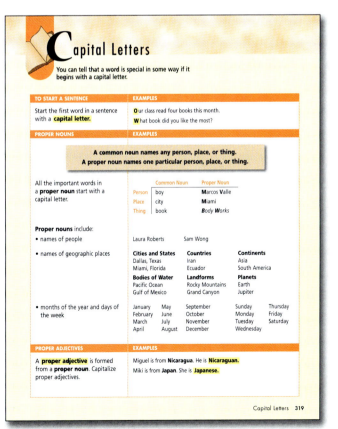

page 319

Handbook: Verbs/Capital Letters **T303**

Handbook: Paragraphs

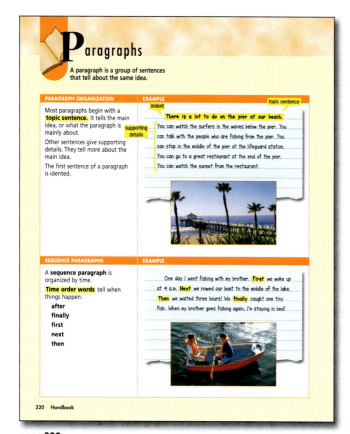

page 320

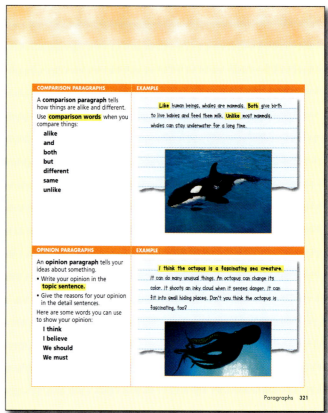

page 321

Bibliography of Related Literacy Research

Adams, M. J. 1990. Phonological prerequisites: Becoming aware of spoken words, syllables, and phonemes. *Beginning to read: thinking and learning about print.* Cambridge, MA: MIT Press.

Adams, M. J., B. R. Foorman, I. Lundberg, and T. Beeler. 1997. *Phonemic awareness in young children: A classroom curriculum.* Baltimore, MD: Brookes.

Atwell, N. 1987. *In the middle: Writing, reading, and learning with adolescents.* Portsmouth, NH: Heinemann.

Baker, S. K., D. C. Simmons, and E. J. Kameenui. 1998. Vocabulary acquisition: Instructional and curricular basics and implications. In D. C. Simmons and E. J. Kameenui (eds.), *What reading research tells us about children with diverse learning needs: Bases and basics.* Mahwah, NJ: Erlbaum.

Baker, S. K., D. C. Simmons, and E. J. Kameenui. 1998. Vocabulary acquisition: Research bases. In D. C. Simmons and E. J. Kameenui (eds.), *What reading research tells us about children with diverse learning needs: Bases and basics.* Mahwah, NJ: Erlbaum.

Bear, D. R., M. Invernizzi, S. Templeton, and F. Johnston. 2000. *Words their way: Word study for phonics, vocabulary, and spelling instruction* (2nd ed.). Upper Saddle River, NJ: Prentice-Hall.

Bernhardt, E. B. and M. Kamil. 1995. Interpreting relationships between L1 and L2 reading: Consolidating the linguistic threshold and the linguistic interdependence hypotheses. *Applied linguistics* 16, pp. 15–34.

Biemiller, A. 1999. *Language and reading success.* Cambridge, MA: Brookline Books.

Blachowicz, C., and P. Fisher. 1996. *Teaching vocabulary in all classrooms.* Upper Saddle River, NJ: Prentice-Hall.

California State Board of Education. 1999. *Reading/language arts framework for California public schools: Kindergarten through grade twelve.* Sacramento: California Department of Education.

Carnine, D. W., J. Silbert, and E. J. Kameenui. 1997. *Direct instruction reading* (3rd ed.). Upper Saddle River, NJ: Prentice Hall.

Chall, J. S., and H. M. Popp. 1996. *Teaching and assessing phonics: A guide for teachers.* Cambridge, MA: Educators Publishing Service.

Chard, D. J., D. C. Simmons, and E. J. Kameenui. 1998. Word recognition: Research bases. In D. C. Simmons and E. J. Kameenui (eds.), *What reading research tells us about children with diverse learning needs: Bases and basics.* Mahwah, NJ: Erlbaum.

Dickson, S. V., D. C. Simmons, and E. J. Kameenui. 1998. Text organization: Research bases. In D. C. Simmons and E. J. Kameenui (eds.), *What reading research tells us about children with diverse learning needs: Bases and basics.* Mahwah, NJ: Erlbaum.

Dowhower, S. 1994. Repeated reading revisited: Research into practice. *Reading and Writing Quarterly* 10.

Dowhower, S. 1991. Speaking of prosody: Fluency's unattended bedfellow. *Theory Into Practice*, 30 (3).

Ehri, L. C., and S. McCormick. 1998. Phases of word learning: Implications for instruction with delayed and disabled readers. *Reading and Writing Quarterly* 14, pp. 135–163.

El-Dinary, P. B., R. Brown, and P. Van Meter. 1995. Strategy instruction for improving writing. In E. Wood, V. E. Woloshyn, and T. Willoughby (eds.), *Cognitive strategy instruction for middle and high schools.* Cambridge, MA: Brookline Books.

Good, R. H., D. C. Simmons, and S. B. Smith. 1998. Effective academic interventions in the United States: Evaluating and enhancing the acquisition of early reading skills. *Educational and Child Psychology* 15 (1).

Hadaway, N. L., S. M. Vardell, and T. A. Young. 2001. Scaffolding oral language development through poetry for students learning English. *The Reading Teacher* 54 (8).

Hasbrouck, J. E. and G. Tindal. 1992. Curriculum-based oral reading fluency norms for students in grades 2 through 5. *Teaching Exceptional Children* (Spring), pp. 41–44.

Henry, M. 1990. *Words: integrated decoding and spelling instruction based on word origin and word structures.* Austin, TX: PRO-ED.

Honig, B., L. Diamond, and L. Gutlohn. 2000. *CORE teaching reading sourcebook for kindergarten through eighth grade.* Novato, CA: Arena Press.

Irvin, J. L. 1998. Comprehending text. *Reading and the middle school student: Strategies to enhance literacy* (2nd ed.). Needham Heights, MA: Allyn & Bacon.

Irvin, J. L. 1998. Prior Knowledge. *Reading and the middle school student: Strategies to enhance literacy* (2nd ed.). Needham Heights, MA: Allyn & Bacon.

Bibliography of Related Literacy Research, continued

Irvin, J. L. 1998. Vocabulary knowledge. *Reading and the middle school student: Strategies to enhance literacy* (2nd ed.). Needham Heights, MA: Allyn & Bacon.

Juel, C., and C. Minden-Cupp. 1999. *Learning to read words: Linguistic units and strategies*. Ann Arbor, MI: Center for the Improvement of Early Reading Achievement. CIERA Report #1-008.

Koskinen, P., L. Gambrell, B. Kapinus, and B. Heathington. 1988. Retelling: A strategy for enhancing students' reading comprehension. *The Reading Teacher* (Spring) 41 (9).

Lapp, D., J. Flood, and R. P. Hoffman. 1996. Using concept mapping as an effective strategy in content area instruction. In D. Lapp, J. Flood, and N. Farnan (eds.), *Content area reading and learning: Instructional strategies* (2nd ed.). Needham Heights, MA: Allyn & Bacon.

Moats, L. C. 2000. *Speech to print: Language essentials for teachers*. Baltimore, MD: Brookes Publishing.

Moats, L. C. 1998. Teaching Decoding. *American Educator* (Spring/Summer).

Myers, M. 1995. Using cognitive strategies to enhance second language learning. In E. Wood, V. E. Woloshyn, and T. Willoughby (eds.), *Cognitive strategy instruction for middle and high schools*. Cambridge, MA: Brookline Books.

Nagy, W. E. 1998. *Teaching vocabulary to improve reading comprehension*. Newark, DE: International Reading Association.

National Institute of Child Health and Human Development. Fluency. 2000. In *Report of the national reading panel: Teaching children to read, reports of the subgroups.*

National Institute of Child Health and Human Development. 2000. Phonemic awareness instruction. In *Report of the national reading panel: Teaching children to read, reports of the subgroups*. NIH Pub. No. 00-4754.

National Institute of Child Health and Human Development. 2000. Phonics instruction. In *Report of the national reading panel: Teaching children to read, reports of the subgroups*. NIH Pub. No. 00-4754.

National Institute of Child Health and Human Development. 2000. Text comprehension instruction. In *Report of the national reading panel: Teaching children to read, reports of the subgroups*. NIH Pub. No. 00-4754.

Olson, C. B. (ed.). 1996. *Practical ideas for teaching writing as a process at the elementary school and middle school levels*. Sacramento, CA: California Department of Education.

Pressley, M., S. Symons, J. McGoldrick, and B. Snyder. 1995. Reading comprehension strategies. In M. Pressley and V. Woloshyn (eds.), *Cognitive strategy instruction that really improves children's academic performance*. Brookline, MA: Brookline Books.

Rasinski, T. V. 1994. Developing syntactic sensitivity in reading through phrase-cued texts. *Intervention in school and clinic* 29 (3).

Smith, S. B., D. C. Simmons, and E. J. Kameenui. 1998. Phonological awareness: Research bases. In D. C. Simmons and E. J. Kameenui (eds.), *What reading research tells us about children with diverse learning needs: Bases and basics*. Mahwah, NJ: Erlbaum.

Spandel, V. 1998. *Seeing with new eyes: A guidebook on teaching and assessing beginning writers* (4th ed.). Portland, OR: Northwest Regional Educational Laboratory.

Stahl, S. A. 1999. *Vocabulary development*. Cambridge, MA: Brookline Books.

Stahl, S., G. Richek, and R. Vandevier. 1991. Learning word meanings through listening: A sixth-grade replication. In J. Zutell & S. McCormick (eds.), *Learning factors/teacher factors: Issues in literacy research*. Chicago: Fortieth Yearbook of the National Reading Conference.

Symons, S., C. Richards, and C. Green. 1995. Cognitive strategies for reading comprehension. In E. Wood, V. E. Woloshyn, and T. Willoughby (eds.), *Cognitive strategy instruction for middle and high schools*. Cambridge, MA: Brookline Books.

Templeton, S. 1997. Diversity and multiculturalism in the integrated classroom community. *Teaching the integrated language arts* (2nd ed.). Boston, MA: Houghton Mifflin.

Torgesen, J. K. and P. Mathes. 2001. What every teacher should know about phonological awareness. *CORE reading research anthology* (2nd ed.). Novato, CA: Arena Press.

Wallace Gillet, J., and C. Temple. 1994. Adolescent students with reading problems. *Understanding reading problems: Assessment and instruction* (4th ed.). New York, NY: HarperCollins.

Decoding Skills Sequence in The Basics

UNITS AND SKILLS

LAKESIDE SCHOOL: LETTERS AND SOUNDS
Letters and Sounds: *Mm, Ss, Ff, Hh, Tt, Aa*
Blend Words with Short *a*
Letters and Sounds: *Nn, Ll, Pp, Gg, Ii*
Blend Words with Short *i*
Letters and Sounds: *Rr, Dd, Cc, Vv, Oo*
Blend Words with Short *o*
Letters and Sounds: *Jj, Bb, Ww, Kk, Ee*
Blend Words with Short *e*
Letters and Sounds: *Zz, Yy, Qq, Xx, Uu*
Blend Words with Short *u*

UNIT 1: SHORT VOWELS
Short *a*
Short *o*
Short *a* Phonograms: *-at, -an, -ad, -ag, -ap*
Short *o* Phonograms: *-og, -op, -ot*

UNIT 2: SHORT VOWELS AND DIGRAPHS
Short *i*
Short *u*
Short *i* Phonograms: *-ig, -it, -in*
Short *u* Phonograms: *-un, -ug, -up*
Digraph *ch; tch*

UNIT 3: SHORT VOWELS, DIGRAPHS, AND DOUBLE CONSONANTS
Short *e*
Short *e* Phonograms: *-et, -en, -ed*
Final Double Consonants: *ll, ss, zz, ck*
Digraph *ck*
Digraph *sh*

UNIT 4: BLENDS AND DIGRAPHS
Blends: *ld, lt, nd, nt, nk, ft, mp, st, sk*
Blends: *fr, fl, sm, sn, sl*
Blends: *br, bl, cr, cl, dr, tr, pl, pr, gr, st, sp, sw, sk*
Digraphs: *ch, sh, th, wh, ng*

UNIT 5: WORD PATTERNS AND MULTISYLLABIC WORDS
Short and Long Vowels in CVC (*wet*) and CV (*we*) Word Patterns
Multisyllabic Words: Two Consonants Between Two Vowels (*bas/ket, kit/ten*)
Multisyllabic Words: Three Consonants Between Two Vowels (*hun/dred*)

UNIT 6: LONG VOWELS AND WORD PATTERNS
Long *a* (*cape*) and Long *o* (*globe*)
Long *i* (*bike*) and Long *u* (*mule, flute*)
Short and Long Vowels in CVC (*cap*) and CVCe (*cape*) Word Patterns
Plurals: *-s, -es*

UNIT 7: LONG VOWELS AND WORD PATTERNS
Long *a*: *ai* (*sail*), *ay* (*tray*)
Long *e*: *ee* (*feet*), *ea* (*sea*)
Long *o*: *oa* (*boat*), *ow* (*blow*)
Short and Long Vowels in CVC (*got*) and CVVC (*goat*) Word Patterns
Multisyllabic Words: compound words

UNITS AND SKILLS

UNIT 8: INFLECTIONS
Sounds for *-ed*: /ed/, /t/, /d/
Add *-ed* to Verbs: no change to root
Add *-ed* to Verbs: double final consonant
Add *-ed* to Verbs: drop final *e*

UNIT 9: INFLECTIONS
Add *-ing* to Verbs: no change to root
Add *-ing* to Verbs: double final consonant
Add *-ing* to Verbs: drop final *e*

UNIT 10: LONG VOWELS
Long *i*: *ie* (*tie*), *igh* (*night*)
Long *u*: *ui* (*suit*), *ue* (*blue*)

UNIT 11: *R*-CONTROLLED VOWELS
R-controlled Vowels: /är/ *ar* (*star*)
R-controlled Vowels: ôr/ *or* (*horn*)
R-controlled Vowels: /ûr/ *er* (*fern*), *ir* (*bird*), *ur* (*curb*)
R-controlled Vowels: /âr/ *air* (*chair*), *ear* (*bear*)
R-controlled Vowels: /îr/ *ear* (*tear*), *eer* (*deer*)

UNIT 12: MULTISYLLABIC WORDS
Types of Syllables: *R*-controlled

UNIT 13: WORDS WITH Y
Y as a Consonant (*yellow*)
Y as Long *i* (*sky*) and as Long *e* (*happy*)
Plurals with *y*

UNIT 14: DIPHTHONGS AND VARIANT VOWELS
Diphthongs: *oi* (*coin*), *oy* (*boy*)
Diphthongs: *ou* (*cloud*), *ow* (*crown*)
Variant Vowels: /ü/ *oo* (*moon*), *ew* (*screw*)
Variant Vowels: /ô/ *au* (*laundry*), *aw* (*saw*); /ôl/ *al* (*salt*), *all* (*ball*)

UNIT 15: VARIANT VOWELS AND CONSONANTS
Hard and Soft *c*
Hard and Soft *g*
Variant Vowels: /ú/ *oo* (*book*)
Silent Consonants: /n/ *gn* (*gnat*), *kn* (*knife*); /r/ *wr* (*wrist*);
/j/ *dge* (*badge*); /m/ *mb* (*lamb*)

UNIT 16: MULTISYLLABIC WORDS
Multisyllabic Words: Two Consonants Between Two Vowels (*bas/ket, kit/ten*)
Multisyllabic Words: Three Consonants Between Two Vowels (*hun/dred*)
Multisyllabic Words: One Consonant Between Two Vowels (*mu/sic, cab/in*)
Multisyllabic Words: Schwa *a* in the First Syllable (*a/bout*)

UNIT 17: MULTISYLLABIC WORDS (SUFFIXES AND PREFIXES)
Suffixes: *-ly, -y, -less, -ful*
Prefixes: *un-, re-*

UNIT 18: MULTISYLLABIC WORDS
Types of Syllables: Consonant + *le*
Types of Syllables: Vowel Team
Types of Syllables: Vowel-silent *e*
Multisyllabic Words: All Syllable Types and Syllabication Rules

Decoding Skills Sequence **T307**

High Frequency Words in *The Basics*

LAKESIDE SCHOOL HIGH FREQUENCY WORDS

Lakeside School high frequency words are available as **Word Tiles**. Two tiles are available for the asterisked words, one with the initial letter as a capital and one with all letters lowercase.

a	good	no*	things
am	great	not	think
an	group	number	this*
and	has	of	those*
answer	have	old	time
are*	he*	on	to
around	help	picture	tomorrow
at	here*	play	too
book	how*	point*	very
both	I	put*	we*
boy	in	read*	what*
call	is*	school	where*
can*	it*	see*	which*
day	later	she*	who*
do*	letters	show*	will*
does*	like	some*	with
don't	little	soon	work
feel	look*	take*	write*
food	me	that*	year
for	my*	the*	yes*
get	name	them	you*
girl	need	these*	your*
give	night	they*	

UNITS 1–18 HIGH FREQUENCY WORDS

Unit 1: first, from, go, home, many, new, next, one, then, there

Unit 2: different, eat, large, long, make, move, open, same, small, something

Unit 3: carry, face, find, learn, love, say, study, use, want, when

Unit 4: all, enough, leave, more, out, says, second, three, two, without

Unit 5: above, animals, by, city, come, down, her, people, sometimes, under

Unit 6: eyes, family, father, head, mother, other, our, really, together, watch

Unit 7: always, below, important, once, or, places, river, through, water, world

Unit 8: about, again, began, dance, said, saw, their, thought, was, were

Unit 9: another, beginning, celebrate, change, children, following, most, only, started, young

Unit 10: almost, been, between, caused, could, four, life, never, often, sound

Unit 11: also, American, called, country, house, know, lived, now, should, would

Unit 12: away, because, few, found, mountains, oil, over, story, try, why

Unit 13: along, back, before, ever, example, miss, much, news, question, words

Unit 14: as, but, each, idea, into, made, plants, seemed, sentence, until

Unit 15: air, asked, even, friends, if, such, talked, trees, walked, while

Unit 16: earth, explore, form, high, miles, million, near, sea, state, than

Unit 17: any, beautiful, cold, healthy, indoors, outdoors, own, special, warm, weigh

Unit 18: close, kind, right, show, watch

HIGH FREQUENCY WORD CUMULATIVE LIST

a
about
above
again
air
all
almost
along
also
always
am
American
an
and
animals
another
answer
any
are
around
as
asked
at
away
back
beautiful
been
because
before
began
beginning
below
between
book
both
boy
but
by
call
called
can
carry
caused
celebrate
change
children
city
close
cold
come
could
country
dance

day
different
do
does
don't
down
each
earth
eat
enough
even
ever
example
explore
eyes
face
family
father
feel
few
find
first
following
food
for
form
found
four
friends
from
get
girl
give
go
good
great
group
has
have
he
head
healthy
help
her
here
high
home
house
how
I
idea
if
important

in
indoors
into
is
it
kind
know
large
later
learn
leave
letters
life
like
little
lived
long
look
love
made
make
many
me
miles
million
miss
more
most
mother
mountains
move
much
my
name
near
need
never
new
news
next
night
no
not
now
number
of
often
oil
old
on
once
one
only

open
or
other
our
out
outdoors
over
own
people
picture
places
plants
play
point
put
question
read
really
right
river
said
same
saw
say
says
school
sea
second
see
seemed
sentence
she
should
show
small
some
something
sometimes
soon
sound
special
started
state
story
study
such
take
talked
than
that
the
their
them

then
there
these
they
things
think
this
those
three
thought
through
time
to
together
tomorrow
too
trees
try
two
under
until
use
very
walked
want
was
warm
watch
water
we
weigh
were
what
when
where
which
while
who
why
will
with
without
words
work
world
would
write
year(s)
yes
you
young
your

High Frequency Word Lists **T309**

Partner Checklists

These Partner Checklists allow students to monitor and evaluate their work as they carry out a writing assignment. Use them with the writing activities on the pages indicated.

Partner Checklist 1 page T42
- ✓ Sentences about yourself start with *I*.
- ✓ Sentences about your partner start with *You*.
- ✓ Sentences about both of you start with *We*.

Partner Checklist 7 page T130
- ✓ The commands tell the person what to do or what not to do.
- ✓ Each command ends with a period or an exclamation mark.

Partner Checklist 13 page T214
- ✓ The sentence begins with a capital letter and ends with a period.
- ✓ It tells an important idea from the discussion.

Partner Checklist 2 page T58
- ✓ Each sentence starts with "I like" and ends with a period.
- ✓ Each label names a food.
- ✓ Each label has an adjective that tells about the food.

Partner Checklist 8 page T144
- ✓ One sentence tells what you did. Another tells what your friends did.
- ✓ Sentences that describe actions in the past have past tense verbs.

Partner Checklist 14 page T230
- ✓ Sentences give advice about what to do or how to do something.
- ✓ Sentences include words like *should*, *must*, and *have to*.

Partner Checklist 3 page T72
- ✓ The drawing shows a worker.
- ✓ The label names the worker.

Partner Checklist 9 page T158
- ✓ Each sentence starts with *I*.
- ✓ There is an action verb.
- ✓ There is an adverb.
- ✓ The sentence ends with a period.

Partner Checklist 15 page T244
- ✓ Sentences tell facts about the body.
- ✓ Spelling of words for the parts of the body is correct.

Partner Checklist 4 page T86
- ✓ Questions start with *Do* or *Does*.
- ✓ *Do* or *does* goes with the correct pronoun.
- ✓ Questions end with a question mark.

Partner Checklist 10 page T172
- ✓ Sentences tell about something that may happen in the future.
- ✓ Sentences include *may, might,* or *could* and another verb.

Partner Checklist 16 page T258
- ✓ Questions start with *Who, What, When,* or *Where*.
- ✓ Questions ask about people or places in the chant.
- ✓ Questions end with a question mark.

Partner Checklist 5 page T100
- ✓ Sentences tell about places in the school.
- ✓ Sentences use location words to tell where places are.
- ✓ Sentences begin with a capital letter and end with a period.

Partner Checklist 11 page T186
- ✓ Sentences use correct past tense form of the irregular verb.
- ✓ Sentences begin with a capital letter and end with a period.

Partner Checklist 17 page T272
- ✓ Questions about number use *how many*.
- ✓ Questions about price use *how much*.
- ✓ Answers give information asked for in the questions.

Partner Checklist 6 page T116
- ✓ Each label names a family member.
- ✓ Labels show how people are related.
- ✓ The family-member words are spelled correctly.

Partner Checklist 12 page T200
- ✓ Sentences tell ways to help the Earth.
- ✓ Each sentence uses an opinion word such as *must, think, should* or *believe*.

Partner Checklist 18 page T286
- ✓ Each sentence starts with a phrase that means *I agree* or with a phrase that means *I disagree*.
- ✓ After *I agree* or *I disagree*, the statements tell more about the writer's opinion.

Partner Prompts

PARTNER PROMPTS FOR READING AND SPELLING PRACTICE SENTENCES

The Partner Prompts are designed to support students' decoding and comprehension skills through peer-assisted learning. The prompts lead students to work cooperatively to read the text, summarize, formulate questions, and clarify what they have read. Read the prompts with students and model how to use them to work through a set of practice sentences. Then pair students with reading partners and distribute the prompts. Circulate among the groups to monitor their work.

Be a Pal

Work with a partner.

1. Read the sentences silently.
2. Take turns reading each sentence aloud. Point to each word as you say it.
3. If your partner needs help with a word, you might say:

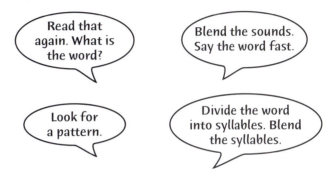

- Read that again. What is the word?
- Blend the sounds. Say the word fast.
- Look for a pattern.
- Divide the word into syllables. Blend the syllables.

4. Choose a role: reteller or listener.

   Reteller: Tell what the sentences are about in your own words.

   Listener: Tell if you agree or disagree. Add other important ideas.

   Both: Is there anything you don't understand? Ask questions and read that part again.

   Switch roles the next time you read with your partner.

PARTNER PROMPTS FOR READING BOOKS IN *THE BASICS BOOKSHELF*

The Partner Prompts are designed to support students' decoding and comprehension skills and enhance their enjoyment of the literature through peer-assisted learning. The prompts lead students to work cooperatively to read sections of the text, formulate questions, clarify, and summarize what they read. Read the prompts with students and model how to use them to work through one section of a book in *The Basics Bookshelf*. Then pair students with reading partners and distribute the prompts. Circulate among the groups to monitor their work.

Be a Pal

Work with a partner.

1. First both of you read a few pages of the book silently.
2. If your partner needs help with a word:
   - Read the word aloud.
   - Tell your partner what you think it means. Use the other words in the sentence to help you.
3. After you read, ask each other questions about the pages. <u>Only ask about important ideas.</u> Answer your partner's questions.
4. Tell what the pages are about in your own words. Make sure you and your partner agree.
5. Read a few more pages. Repeat the steps until you finish the entire book.

Audio Scripts

Unit 1

SCRIPT FOR WHO'S TALKING? (page 46)

ITEM 1

Tell students:

Turn to page 46 in your book. Look at the pictures. One person is talking. Listen.

Take the role of Lupe Valle, who filled out the order form on the right, and say:

I live in Chicago. My house is on Maple Street. My phone number is 773-555-9664. I want a cap. It costs eight dollars.

Then ask students:

Who is talking? Point to the right order form. Say the name of the person.

ITEM 2

Tell students:

Another person is talking. Listen.

Take the role of Maylin Yee, who filled out the order form on the left, and say:

I live in Chicago, too. I live on Culver Street. I want to buy a blue Lakeside T-shirt. I will order a medium size.

Then ask students:

Who is talking? Point to the right order form. Say the name of the person.

SCRIPT FOR HIGH FREQUENCY WORDS (page 48)

Tell students:

Turn to page 49 in your book. Follow along in your book and listen. We are going to learn new words.

Look at the first word: *from.*

Listen to the word: *from.*

Listen to the word in a sentence: *I am from Russia.* You say you are *from* Russia if you lived in that country. You say it if you were born in Russia.

Say the word with me: *from, from.* Now you say it.

Spell the word with me: *from, f-r-o-m.* Now you spell it.

Say the word again: *from, from.*

Repeat the process to present the other words. Use the following context sentences and elaborated meanings.

For *home:*

Listen to the word in a sentence: *My home is now in Detroit.* That means I live in Detroit now.

For *new:*

Listen to the word in a sentence: *I have a new school, too.* If you are in a place for the first time, it is *new.*

For *go:*

Listen to the word in a sentence: *I will go to school with my friend Rob.* When you *go* somewhere, you move from one place to another.

For *there:*

Listen to the word in a sentence: *My school schedule is there on the table.* You use the word *there* to talk about a place that is not right where you are.

For *many:*

Listen to the word in a sentence: *I have many different classes! Many* means the same thing as *a lot.* You can say *I have many different classes* or *I have a lot of different classes!*

For *first:*

Listen to the word in a sentence: *First I have English class.* That means I have English class before all my other classes.

For *next:*

Listen to the word in a sentence: *Next I have science class. Next* means the same thing as *after that.* You can say *Next I have science class* or *After that I have science class.*

For *then:*

Listen to the word in a sentence: *Then I have lunch.* That means I have lunch after English class and after science class.

For *one:*

Listen to the word in a sentence: *I have only one class with Rob—math.* A math class is *one* class. A math class and a science class are two classes.

T312 Audio Scripts

Unit 2

SCRIPT FOR WHO'S TALKING? (page 60)

ITEM 1

Tell students:
> Turn to page 60 in your book. Look at the picture. One person is talking. Listen.

Take the role of the person eating steak, on the lower left-hand side of the picture, and say:
> I have a large steak and lots of small, green peas on my plate. I also have yellow corn on the cob.

Then ask students:
> Who is talking? Point to the correct lunch.

ITEM 2

Tell students:
> Another person is talking. Listen.

Take the role of the person eating baked potato, on the lower right-hand side of the picture, and say:
> I have a big potato on my plate. I have some fresh fish, too. I have a glass of cold milk to drink.

Then ask students:
> Who is talking? Point to the correct lunch.

ITEM 3

Tell students:
> Another person is talking. Listen.

Take the role of the person eating pasta and a roll, on the upper right-hand side of the picture, and say:
> I am hungry! I have lots of delicious pasta on my plate. I also have some green broccoli. I have a brown roll and a tall glass of juice to drink.

Then ask students:
> Who is talking? Point to the correct lunch.

SCRIPT FOR HIGH FREQUENCY WORDS (page 63)

Tell students:
> Turn to page 63 in your book. Follow along in your book and listen. We are going to learn new words.
>
> Look at the first word: *something*.
>
> Listen to the word: *something*.
>
> Listen to the word in a sentence: *I want something to eat.* When you say *something*, you don't name the thing. For example, *something* to eat could be an apple, a sandwich, or a cookie.
>
> Say the word with me: *something, something*. Now you say it.
>
> Spell the word with me: *something, s-o-m-e-t-h-i-n-g*. Now you spell it.
>
> Say the word again: *something, something*.

Repeat the process to present the other words. Use the following context sentences and elaborated meanings.

For *make:*
> Listen to the word in a sentence: *I can make spaghetti!* When you cook something or build something, you *make* it.

For *long:*
> Listen to the word in a sentence: *First, I get a box of long noodles. Long* means the opposite of *short.* Spaghetti noodles are long and thin.

For *large:*
> Listen to the word in a sentence: *I put them in a large pot of hot water. Large* means the same as *big.*

For *move:*
> Listen to the word in a sentence: *I move the pot to the back of the stove.* That means I take the pot from one place and put it in another place.

For *different:*
> Listen to the word in a sentence: *Then, I use a different pot for the sauce.* That means I don't use the same pot. I use a new pot for the sauce.

For *small:*
> Listen to the word in a sentence: *I cut an onion into small pieces. Small* means the same thing as *little.* You can say *I cut an onion into small pieces* or *I cut an onion into little pieces.*

For *open:*
> Listen to the word in a sentence: *I open a can of tomatoes.* That means I take the top off the can to pour out the tomatoes.

For *same:*
> Listen to the word in a sentence: *I cook the onions and tomatoes in the same pot.* That means I don't cook the onions and the tomatoes in two different pots. I cook them together in one pot.

For *eat:*
> Listen to the word in a sentence: *At last, I eat my pasta!* People *eat* lots of different foods, like pizza, chicken, bananas, and cake.

Audio Scripts **T313**

Audio Scripts, continued

Unit 3

SCRIPT FOR WHO'S TALKING? (page 75)

ITEM 1

Tell students:

Turn to page 75 in your book. Look at the pictures. Two people are talking. Listen.

Take the roles of the mechanics in the second picture and say:

FEMALE MECHANIC:	Ernesto, can you help me change this tire?
MALE MECHANIC:	Yes, I can. Can you pass me a wrench? I need one.
FEMALE MECHANIC:	Is this the correct wrench?
MALE MECHANIC:	No, I need a different wrench.

Then ask students:

What two people are talking? Point to the correct picture.

ITEM 2

Tell students:

Two more people are talking. Listen.

Take the roles of the hair stylist and customer in the first picture and say:

CUSTOMER:	Can you cut my hair a little shorter on top?
STYLIST:	Yes, I can. Is this the way you like it?
CUSTOMER:	Yes, thank you. Can you wash my hair, too?
STYLIST:	Yes, I will wash it. Then I will dry it with the hair dryer.

Then ask students:

What two people are talking? Point to the correct picture.

SCRIPT FOR HIGH FREQUENCY WORDS (page 77)

Tell students:

Turn to page 77 in your book. Follow along in your book and listen. We are going to learn new words.

Look at the first word: *study*.

Listen to the word: *study*.

Listen to the word in a sentence: *I study photography in school*. When you *study*, you read and find out about something.

Say the word with me: *study, study*. Now you say it.

Spell the word with me: *study, s-t-u-d-y*. Now you spell it.

Say the word again: *study, study*.

Repeat the process to present the other words. Use the following context sentences and elaborated meanings.

For *learn*:

Listen to the word in a sentence: *I learn how to use a camera*. You *learn* something when you figure out how to do it.

For *carry*:

Listen to the word in a sentence: *I carry a camera in my backpack*. That means I put the camera in my backpack. I take it with me.

For *find*:

Listen to the word in a sentence: *I always find something to photograph*. When you *find* something, you discover it or see it for the first time.

For *use*:

Listen to the word in a sentence: *I use a lot of film*. When you *use* something, you do things with it.

For *love*:

Listen to the word in a sentence: *I love to take pictures of my mom*. *Love* means the same thing as *really like*. You can say *I love to take pictures* or *I really like to take pictures*.

For *face*:

Listen to the word in a sentence: *She always has a smile on her face*. The *face* is the part of the head with the eyes, nose, and mouth.

For *when*:

Listen to the word in a sentence: *My friends run when they see me*. That means the moment my friends see me, they run away from me.

For *want*:

Listen to the word in a sentence: *They don't want to be photographed*. When you *want* something, you like it to happen. When you don't want it, you don't want it to happen.

For *say*:

Listen to the word in a sentence: *They say, "Don't take a picture of us!"* When you say something, you talk; you tell someone what you think.

Unit 4

SCRIPT FOR WHO'S TALKING? (page 89)

ITEM 1

Tell students:
> Turn to page 89 in your book. Look at the picture. One person is talking. Listen.

Take the role of the fifth person in line and say:
> This magazine is great. It has good pictures in it. I need it for my trip!

Then ask students:
> Who is talking? Point to the correct person. Where in line is the person? What does the person need?

ITEM 2

Tell students:
> Another person is talking. Listen.

Take the role of the seventh person in line and say:
> I need something to eat! This apple will be great.

Then ask students:
> Who is talking? Point to the correct person. Where in line is the person? What does the person need?

ITEMS 3–6

Repeat the script for Item 2 above, modifying it for different persons in line.

For the second person in line, say:
> I like to read something before I get on the airplane. I need a newspaper. This one has all the latest news.

For the sixth person in line, say:
> I need a gift for Mai. I will buy this t-shirt for her. I think she will like it.

For the role of the third person in line, say:
> My trip is 4 hours. I need something to read on the plane. Here's a good book.

For the role of the tenth person in line, say:
> I need to get a present. It's for my new grandson! I will get this cute brown bear.

SCRIPT FOR HIGH FREQUENCY WORDS (page 91)

Tell students:
> Turn to page 91 in your book. Follow along in your book and listen. We are going to learn new words.
>
> Look at the first word: *leave.*
>
> Listen to the word: *leave.*
>
> Listen to the word in a sentence: *Stan and his friend leave in June for a vacation.* When you *leave*, you go away.
>
> Say the word with me: *leave, leave.* Now you say it.
>
> Spell the word with me: *leave, l-e-a-v-e.* Now you spell it.
>
> Say the word again: *leave, leave.*

Repeat the process to present the other words. Use the following context sentences and elaborated meanings.

For *two:*
> Listen to the word in a sentence: *They go for two months: June and July. Two* means the number 2. [Write the numeral and hold up two fingers.]

For *out:*
> Listen to the word in a sentence: *They fly in and out of many airports.* When you go *out*, you go away from a place. The planes fly to the airport. Then they fly away.

For *three:*
> Listen to the word in a sentence: *China, Japan, and Laos are three Asian countries. Three* means the number 3. [Write the numeral and hold up three fingers.]

For *all:*
> Listen to the word in a sentence: *Stan likes them all.* That means Stan likes every country.

For *says:*
> Listen to the word in a sentence: *Stan says, "Our first stop is in China."* When someone *says* something, the person speaks, tells what he or she is thinking.

For *second:*
> Listen to the word in a sentence: *"Our second stop is in Japan."* When something is *second*, it comes after the first one. First, Stan visits China. Then he goes to Japan.

For *without:*
> Listen to the word in a sentence: *Stan never travels without his camera.* When you are *without* something, you don't have it. Stan always has his camera with him.

For *enough:*
> Listen to the word in a sentence: *He takes enough film to photograph everything.* When you have *enough*, you have all that you need.

For *more:*
> Listen to the word in a sentence: *He brings back more pictures of Japan than of China.* That means that the number of pictures of Japan is higher than the number of pictures of China.

Audio Scripts **T315**

Audio Scripts, continued

Unit 5

SCRIPT FOR WHO'S TALKING? (page 102)

ITEM 1

Tell students:

Turn to page 102 in your book. Look at the picture. Two people are talking. Listen.

Take the roles of the salesperson and customer at the music store and say:

CUSTOMER: I want to buy a jazz CD for my mom's birthday present. Do you sell them at this music store?

SALESPERSON: Yes, we sell them. All jazz CDs are next to the classical music section on this wall. I'll show you.

CUSTOMER: Thank you, I want this to be the best birthday present ever.

Then ask students:

Where are the people who are talking? Point to them in the picture.

ITEM 2

Tell students:

Another two people are talking. Listen.

Take the roles of the man in the information booth and the girl asking him a question and say:

GIRL: Excuse me, is this the information booth?

MAN: Yes, it is.

GIRL: Where can I find a bookstore?

MAN: There is a bookstore on the second floor. It's next to the Cool Duds clothing store.

GIRL: Thank you! I think I can find it!

Then ask students:

Where are the people who are talking? Point to them in the picture.

ITEM 3

Tell students:

Another two people are talking. Listen.

Take the roles of the salesperson and customer in the jewelry store and say:

SALESPERSON: Hello, welcome to Jim's Jewels. Can I help you find something?

CUSTOMER: Yes, please. Today is my sister's birthday and I want to buy her some earrings.

SALESPERSON: Our store has many pairs of earrings. Follow me and I will show you where they are. Would she like silver or gold earrings?

CUSTOMER: I think she would like gold.

Then ask students:

Where are the people who are talking? Point to them in the picture.

SCRIPT FOR HIGH FREQUENCY WORDS (page 107)

Tell students:

Turn to page 107 in your book. Follow along in your book and listen. We are going to learn new words.

Look at the first word: *city*.

Listen to the word: *city*.

Listen to the word in a sentence: *Padma lives in the city of Chicago*. A *city* is a place with many people and buildings. Chicago is the name of a large city.

Say the word with me: *city, city*. Now you say it.

Spell the word with me: *city, c-i-t-y*. Now you spell it.

Say the word again: *city, city*.

Repeat the process to present the other words. Use the following context sentences and elaborated meanings.

For *above*:

Listen to the word in a sentence: *She lives in an apartment high above the street. Above* means the same thing as *over* or *on top of*. The building is tall. The apartment is high over the street.

For *by*:

Listen to the word in a sentence: *It is on Belmont Street, by a Mexican restaurant. By* means *next to* or *near*. The apartment is near a restaurant.

For *sometimes*:

Listen to the word in a sentence: *Sometimes she jogs to Lake Michigan*. That means Padma doesn't jog all the time. She does it once in a while.

For *her*:

Listen to the word in a sentence: *Her dog, Bandit, likes to run, too*. The dog belongs to Padma, so you can say it is *her* dog.

For *come*:

Listen to the word in a sentence: *Padma's mom says, "Come home before dinner."* That means Padma's mother wants her to go back to her house before it is time to eat.

For *animals*:

Listen to the word in a sentence: *There is a park for dogs and other animals*. Dogs, cats, and horses are *animals*.

For *people*:

Listen to the word in a sentence: *People call it "Bark Park."* People are men, women, boys, and girls.

For *down*:

Listen to the word in a sentence: *Bandit runs up and down the hill there*. When you go *down*, you go from a high place to a lower place.

For *under*:

Listen to the word in a sentence: *Then Padma and Bandit rest under a tree. Under* means the same as *below*. Padma and the dog sit below a tree to rest.

T316 Audio Scripts

Unit 6

SCRIPT FOR WHO'S TALKING? (page 118)

ITEM 1

Tell students:

> Turn to page 118 in your book. Look at the pictures. One person is talking. Listen.

Take the role of the young woman in the bedroom playing the guitar and say:

> I am in my bedroom. I am sitting on the bed. I like to play my guitar.

Then ask students:

> Who is talking? Point to the correct person. What room is the person in?

ITEM 2

Tell students:

> Another person is talking. Listen.

Take the role of the man cooking in the kitchen and say:

> I am in the kitchen. I like to cook. I have some soup in the pot. Dinner will be ready soon.

Then ask students:

> Who is talking? Point to the correct person. What room is the person in?

ITEM 3

Tell students:

> Another person is talking. Listen.

Take the role of the woman vacuuming the rug in the living room and say:

> I am in the living room. I need to clean the rug. I use the vacuum cleaner to clean it.

Then ask students:

> Who is talking? Point to the correct person. What room is the person in?

SCRIPT FOR HIGH FREQUENCY WORDS (page 121)

Tell students:

> Turn to page 121 in your book. Follow along in your book and listen. We are going to learn new words.
>
> Look at the first word: *family*.
>
> Listen to the word: *family*.
>
> Listen to the word in a sentence: *There are six people in my family*. People like your father, mother, sister, brother, grandmother, and uncle make up your *family*.
>
> Say the word with me: *family, family*. Now you say it.
>
> Spell the word with me: *family, f-a-m-i-l-y*. Now you spell it.
>
> Say the word again: *family, family*.

Repeat the process to present the other words. Use the following context sentences and elaborated meanings.

For *together*:

> Listen to the word in a sentence: *We ride bicycles together*. When you do something with another person, you do it *together*.

For *other*:

> Listen to the word in a sentence: *We like to do other things, too. Other* things means *more* things, *different* things.

For *really*:

> Listen to the word in a sentence: *We really like to hike in the woods. Really* means *very much* or *a lot*. When you really like something, you like it very much.

For *father*:

> Listen to the word in a sentence: *My father carries a heavy backpack*. A *father* is a man who has one or more children.

For *mother*:

> Listen to the word in a sentence: *My mother walks fast. Everyone follows her*. A *mother* is a woman who has one or more children.

For *our*:

> Listen to the word in a sentence: *She is our leader!* That means she is the leader of all the family.

For *watch*:

> Listen to the word in a sentence: *We sometimes stop to watch the birds*. When you *watch* something, you look at it. You can watch birds to see what they do.

For *eyes*:

> Listen to the word in a sentence: *Once I saw an eagle with my own eyes*. Your *eyes* help you see. Some people have brown eyes. Others have blue eyes.

For *head*:

> Listen to the word in a sentence: *It was flying in circles over my head!* Your *head* is on top of your body. Your eyes, ears, and mouth are on your head.

Audio Scripts **T317**

Audio Scripts, continued

Unit 7

SCRIPT FOR WHO'S TALKING? (page 132)

ITEM 1

Tell students:

> Turn to page 132 in your book. Look at the pictures. One person is talking. Listen.

Take the role of the woman in the first photo and say:

> It is a great day! It is sunny and warm. There are no clouds in the sky. When it's hot outside, like today, we like to go to the beach.

Then ask students:

> Which person is talking? Point to the correct picture.

ITEM 2

Tell students:

> Another person is talking. Listen.

Take the role of the woman in the long coat, in the third photo, and say:

> I am in the city. It is very windy today! I am glad that I have my long black coat.

Then ask students:

> Which person is talking? Point to the correct picture.

ITEM 3

Tell students:

> Another person is talking. Listen.

Take the role of the girl in the second photo and say:

> It is cold in the mountains! My parka and gloves keep me warm. I have my scarf wrapped around my neck. My hat keeps my head warm, too.

Then ask students:

> Which person is talking? Point to the correct picture.

SCRIPT FOR HIGH FREQUENCY WORDS (page 135)

Tell students:

> Turn to page 135 in your book. Follow along in your book and listen. We are going to learn new words.

> Look at the first word: *places*.

> Listen to the word: *places*.

> Listen to the word in a sentence: *Jean likes to explore unusual places*. That means she likes to explore unusual cities, towns, forests, mountains, fields, etc.

> Say the word with me: *places, places*. Now you say it.

> Spell the word with me: *places, p-l-a-c-e-s*. Now you spell it.

> Say the word again: *places, places*.

Repeat the process to present the other words. Use the following context sentences and elaborated meanings.

For *important*:

> Listen to the word in a sentence: *Travel is very important to her*. When something is *important*, you care about it. Jean cares about traveling. She thinks a lot about going to new places.

For *world*:

> Listen to the word in a sentence: *She travels around the world*. That means she travels all over the planet, all over the Earth.

For *always*:

> Listen to the word in a sentence: *She always plans her trips carefully. Always* means *every time*. Every time Jean goes on a trip, she makes careful plans.

For *or*:

> Listen to the word in a sentence: *She travels either by plane or by boat*. That means Jean has a choice. She can fly in a plane, *or* she can ride in a boat.

For *river*:

> Listen to the word in a sentence: *She sails up the Amazon River in a boat*. A *river* is a stream of water that keeps moving. Rivers go to lakes or oceans.

For *through*:

> Listen to the word in a sentence: *She hikes through the Amazon rain forest, too*. When you go *through* something, you go from one side to the other.

For *once*:

> Listen to the word in a sentence: *She goes to Tahiti not once, but twice a year. Once* means *one time*. Jean does not go one time. She goes two times a year.

For *water*:

> Listen to the word in a sentence: *She loves swimming in the clear water. Water* is clear and wet. You can drink water and swim in it.

For *below*:

> Listen to the word in a sentence: *She can see hundreds of fish below her! Below* means the same as *under*. When Jean swims, she can see fish when she looks down.

Unit 8

SCRIPT FOR WHO'S TALKING? (page 145)

ITEM 1

Tell students:

> Turn to page 145 in your book. Look at the pictures. One person is talking. Listen.

Take the role of Veronica and say:

> This is the best day ever! I have great friends. I am so happy!

Then ask students:

> Who is talking? Point to the correct person. How is that person feeling? Use your face and body to show the feeling.

ITEM 2

Tell students:

> Another person is talking. Listen.

Take the role of Eva and say:

> I am wasting my time here. There is nothing fun to do. I am very bored!

Then ask students:

> Who is talking? Point to the correct person. How is that person feeling? Use your face and body to show the feeling.

ITEM 3

Tell students:

> Another person is talking. Listen.

Take the role of Eddie and say:

> My best friend is moving to another school. I will miss her very much. It is going to be so hard to keep in touch. I'm so sad.

Then ask students:

> Who is talking? Point to the correct person. How is that person feeling? Use your face and body to show the feeling.

ITEM 4

Tell students:

> Another person is talking. Listen.

Take the role of Miguel and say:

> All right! My project won first place at the Science Fair! My parents will be really happy, and so will my teacher. I am really proud!

Then ask students:

> Who is talking? Point to the correct person. How is that person feeling? Use your face and body to show the feeling.

SCRIPT FOR HIGH FREQUENCY WORDS (page 149)

Tell students:

> Turn to page 149 in your book. Follow along in your book and listen. We are going to learn new words.
>
> Look at the first word: *saw*.
>
> Listen to the word: *saw*.
>
> Listen to the word in a sentence: *Last week I saw a movie. Saw* means the same thing as *watched.* You can say *Last week I saw a movie* or *Last week I watched a movie.*
>
> Say the word with me: *saw, saw.* Now you say it.
>
> Spell the word with me: *saw, s-a-w.* Now you spell it.
>
> Say the word again: *saw, saw.*

Repeat the process to present the other words. Use the following context sentences and elaborated meanings.

For *was:*

> Listen to the word in a sentence: *I was sitting in the first row.* You can use *was* to tell about the past. *Yesterday I was in the first row. Today I am in another row.*

For *were:*

> Listen to the word in a sentence: *A lot of kids from school were there. Were* tells about the past, too. Use *were* to tell about more than one person or thing.

For *their:*

> Listen to the word in a sentence: *Some kids came with their mothers and fathers.* One kid brings *his* or *her* mother and father. Many kids bring *their* mothers and fathers.

For *said:*

> Listen to the word in a sentence: *"Look, there's Sofia," I said to my dad. Said* means the same thing as *told.* I talked to my father. I told him about Sofia.

For *began:*

> Listen to the word in a sentence: *They shut off the lights, and the movie began. Began* means the same thing as *started.* You can say *The movie began* or *The movie started.*

For *about:*

> Listen to the word in a sentence: *The movie was about some kids in the 1950s.* That means the movie described the kids. I showed what they were like. It told what they did.

For *dance:*

> Listen to the word in a sentence: *I watched them dance to old music.* When you *dance*, you move your body to the sound of music.

For *thought:*

> Listen to the word in a sentence: *My dad thought the music was great.* In the present, you say *My dad thinks the music is great.* In the past, you use *thought.*

For *again:*

> Listen to the word in a sentence: *We want to see that movie again next week. Again* means *one more time.*

Audio Scripts **T319**

Audio Scripts, continued

Unit 9

SCRIPT FOR WHO'S TALKING? (page 160)

ITEM 1

Tell students:

Turn to page 160 in your book. Look at the pictures. One person is talking. Listen.

Take the role of the female dancer in the red and white dress in the second photo and say:

I am from Mexico. My friend and I are doing a Mexican dance at a celebration. I am wearing a red-and-white dress. I have a red bow in my hair.

Then ask students:

Who is talking? Point to the picture of the person.

ITEM 2

Tell students:

Another person is talking. Listen.

Take the role of the first man, holding the head of the dragon, in the first photograph and say:

I come from China. I am carrying the head of the dragon. My friends and I are doing a Chinese dance. We are celebrating the Chinese New Year!

Then ask students:

Who is talking? Point to the picture of the person.

ITEM 3

Tell students:

Another person is talking. Listen.

Take the role of the first dancer in the last photograph and say:

I live in England. I am doing an English dance with my friends. We are wearing white shirts and black pants. We are waving white cloths in the air. I am the first dancer you see in the photo.

Then ask students:

Who is talking? Point to the picture of the person.

SCRIPT FOR HIGH FREQUENCY WORDS (page 163)

Tell students:

Turn to page 163 in your book. Follow along in your book and listen. We are going to learn new words.

Look at the first word: *celebrate*.

Listen to the word: *celebrate*.

Listen to the word in a sentence: *We like to celebrate. Today is my sister's birthday*. When we *celebrate*, we do something special. We show that we are happy. When we celebrate a birthday, we give gifts and eat cake.

Say the word with me: *celebrate, celebrate*. Now you say it.

Spell it with me: *celebrate, c-e-l-e-b-r-a-t-e*. Now you spell it.

Say the word again: *celebrate, celebrate*.

Repeat the process to present the other words. Use the following context sentences and elaborated meanings.

For *most*:

Listen to the word in a sentence: *Most of her friends are here, but not all of them*. That means that many of her friends are here. A few friends are missing.

For *young*:

Listen to the word in a sentence: *Her friends are young kids from school*. Her friends are not old. They are boys and girls.

For *children*:

Listen to the word in a sentence: *There are about 10 children in our yard*. Boys and girls are *children*. Do you see a word you know in the word *children*? Yes, it's the word *child*.

For *started*:

Listen to the word in a sentence: *The party started at 3:00. Started* means the same as *began*. At 3:00, the party began.

For *beginning*:

Listen to the word in a sentence: *It is now 4:00, and it is beginning to rain. Beginning* means the same as *starting*. You can say *It is beginning to rain* or *It is starting to rain*.

For *change*:

Listen to the word in a sentence: *My mother says, "We need to change our plans!"* When you *change* something, you do something different. You stop and do a new thing.

For *another*:

Listen to the word in a sentence: *"Let's move the party to another place!" Another* means *different*. When you go to another place, you go somewhere else. Do you see a word you know in the word *another*? It's the word *other*.

For *only*:

Listen to the word in a sentence: *The house is the only place to go*. That means there is nowhere else to go. There is just one place.

For *following*:

Listen to the word in a sentence: *The kids are quickly following me inside. This is fun!* When someone is *following* you, they are walking behind you. They are going where you go.

Unit 10

SCRIPT FOR WHO'S TALKING? (page 173)

ITEM 1

Tell students:

> Turn to page 173 in your book. Look at the pictures. A person is talking. Listen.

Take the role of the police officer holding a flashlight in the last picture and say:

> I walk around the park at night. I need to make sure that everything is quiet and safe. Tonight I may find a lost cat. We might have to take it back to its owner.

Then ask students:

> Who is talking? Point to the correct picture. What time is it in the picture?

ITEM 2

Tell students:

> Another person is talking. Listen.

Take the role of the woman raking leaves in the first picture and say:

> I keep the park neat and clean. I rake the leaves that fall on the ground. I may rake a lot of leaves today—it's windy. I might not finish until after dark!

Then ask students:

> Who is talking? Point to the correct picture. What time is it in the picture?

ITEM 3

Tell students:

> Another person is talking. Listen.

Take the role of the woman selling hot dogs in the picture at top right and say:

> I sell food and drinks on a corner of the park. At lunchtime, I sell hot dogs and soda. I could use some help today. Everyone seems to be hungry. I might have to make an extra batch of hot dogs.

Then ask students:

> Who is talking? Point to the correct picture. What time is it in the picture?

SCRIPT FOR HIGH FREQUENCY WORDS (page 177)

Tell students:

> Turn to page 177 in your book. Follow along in your book and listen. We are going to learn new words.

> Look at the first word: *been*.

> Listen to the word: *been*.

> Listen to the word in a sentence: *Mina has been in India since 1992*. That means Mina has lived in India since 1992. She has stayed there since then.

> Say the word with me: *been, been*. Now you say it.

> Spell the word with me: *been, b-e-e-n*. Now you spell it.

> Say the word again: *been, been*.

Repeat the process to present the other words. Use the following context sentences and elaborated meanings.

For *four:*

> Listen to the word in a sentence: *Four years ago, there was an earthquake. Four* means the number 4. [Write the numeral and hold up four fingers.]

For *sound:*

> Listen to the word in a sentence: *Mina heard a loud sound*. A *sound* is a *noise*. Mina heard a loud noise.

For *caused:*

> Listen to the word in a sentence: *The earthquake caused her house to fall down*. That means the earthquake made her house fall. It fell down because of the earthquake.

For *between:*

> Listen to the word in a sentence: *Mina was trapped between a wall and a table. Between* means *in the middle of two things*. The wall was on one side. The table was on the other.

For *could:*

> Listen to the word in a sentence: *She could not move*. That means she was not able to move.

For *almost:*

> Listen to the word in a sentence: *She almost didn't get out, but she did. Almost* means *very close to*.

For *life:*

> Listen to the word in a sentence: *The rescue team saved her life*. That means the rescue workers helped Mina. She would have died without their help.

For *often:*

> Listen to the word in a sentence: *Mina often tells that story. Often* means *a lot* or *many times*. Mina tells that story a lot. She tells it over and over again.

For *never:*

> Listen to the word in a sentence: *We never get tired of hearing it. Never* means *not ever*. We always like to hear Mina's story. We do not ever get tired of it.

Audio Scripts **T321**

Audio Scripts, continued

Unit 11

SCRIPT FOR WHO'S TALKING? (page 188)

ITEM 1

Tell students:

> Turn to page 188 in your book. Look at the pictures. One person is talking. Listen.

Take the role of the protester in the foreground in the center photo and say:

> We work hard at our factory, and we want more pay! We are tired of waiting. This protest will continue until we get what we want!

Then ask students:

> Who is talking? Point to the correct picture. What does the person want? How does the person feel?

ITEM 2

Tell students:

> Another person is talking. Listen.

Take the role of the reporter in the photo at left and say:

> I love my job! I get to report the news. I feel good when I can publish my news reports on the Internet. I want to write more so that people will be informed.

Then ask students:

> Who is talking? Point to the correct picture. What does the person want? How does the person feel?

ITEM 3

Tell students:

> Another person is talking. Listen.

Take the role of the voter in the photo at right and say:

> I want Deborah Vasquez to be elected Senator. She understands what matters to us. That's why I am voting. I am proud to make a difference.

Then ask students:

> Who is talking? Point to the correct picture. What does the person want? How does the person feel?

SCRIPT FOR HIGH FREQUENCY WORDS (page 191)

Tell students:

> Turn to page 191 in your book. Follow along in your book and listen. We are going to learn new words.
>
> Look at the first word: *country.*
>
> Listen to the word: *country.*
>
> Listen to the word in a sentence: *Indra was born in a country in Asia.* China, Japan, and Vietnam are all *countries* in Asia. There are many cities, buildings, and people in a country.
>
> Say the word with me: *country, country.* Now you say it.
>
> Spell the word with me: *country, c-o-u-n-t-r-y.* Now you spell it.
>
> Say the word again: *country, country.*

Repeat the process to present the other words. Use the following context sentences and elaborated meanings.

For *called:*

> Listen to the word in a sentence: *The country is called Indonesia.* That means the name of the country is Indonesia.

For *lived:*

> Listen to the word in a sentence: *He lived there as a child. Lived* means *stayed.* He stayed there when he was young. It was his home.

For *house:*

> Listen to the word in a sentence: *He grew up in a house built on long posts.* A *house* is a building where people live.

For *now:*

> Listen to the word in a sentence: *Indra came to the U.S. Now he lives in California. Now* means *at this time.* Two years ago, Indra lived in Indonesia. Today, he lives in California.

For *American:*

> Listen to the word in a sentence: *Last year, Indra became an American citizen.* People who live in the United States are called *Americans.* Last year, Indra became a citizen of the U.S.

For *would:*

> Listen to the word in a sentence: *He would like to help people in Indonesia.* When you *would like to do something,* you want to do it in the future. Indra wants to help people in his old country.

For *know:*

> Listen to the word in a sentence: *He knows how they could grow more food.* When you *know* something, you understand it. Indra has ideas about how to grow food.

For *should:*

> Listen to the word in a sentence: *He thinks they should plant different crops each year.* He thinks it would be good to plant different crops.

For *also:*

> Listen to the word in a sentence: *Indra also wants to help the farmers sell their crops. Also* means *too.* He wants to help them sell their crops, too.

Unit 12

SCRIPT FOR WHO'S TALKING? (page 202)

ITEM 1

Tell students:

> Turn to page 202 in your book. Look at the picture of the two girls. They are talking. Listen.

Take the roles of the two girls in the picture and say:

GIRL AT RIGHT:	This trail is beautiful. Oh, but look at this mess! Someone left trash by the trail. Let's clean it up. We have to keep the forest clean.
GIRL AT LEFT:	That is not my trash. I won't pick it up.
GIRL AT RIGHT:	Will you at least help me then? Please just hold the bag and I'll put the trash in it, okay? I'll carry the bag in my backpack.
GIRL AT LEFT:	Okay. I will do that.

Then ask students:

> Who made the suggestions? Point to the correct person.

SCRIPT FOR HIGH FREQUENCY WORDS (page 205)

Tell students:

> Turn to page 205 in your book. Follow along in your book and listen. We are going to learn new words.
>
> Look at the first word: *mountains.*
>
> Listen to the word: *mountains.*
>
> Listen to the word in a sentence: *Alaska has beautiful beaches and tall mountains. Mountains* are very high hills. The Rockies and the Alps are *mountains.*
>
> Say the word with me: *mountains, mountains.* Now you say it.
>
> Spell the word with me: *mountains, m-o-u-n-t-a-i-n-s.* Now you spell it.
>
> Say the word again: *mountains, mountains.*

Repeat the process to present the other words. Use the following context sentences and elaborated meanings.

For *oil:*

> Listen to the word in a sentence: *In 1989, a ship spilled oil into a bay in Alaska. Oil* is petroleum, a dark, thick liquid that comes out of the ground. Gasoline is made from oil.

For *found:*

> Listen to the word in a sentence: *People found sick birds on the beach.* People looked and saw sick birds on the beach.

For *because:*

> Listen to the word in a sentence: *The birds got sick because they ate the oil when they cleaned their feathers.* That means the oil made the birds sick. They got sick after eating the oil.

For *few:*

> Listen to the word in a sentence: *Many people, not just a few, came to help.* A *few* people is a small group of people.

For *try:*

> Listen to the word in a sentence: *The people wanted to try to save the birds.* When you *try* something, you do what you can to make it work.

For *over:*

> Listen to the word in a sentence: *When their work was over, many birds were saved. Over* means the same as *finished* or *done.*

For *away:*

> Listen to the word in a sentence: *The people went away, but they did not forget.* When you go *away,* you do not stay in the same place. You go somewhere else.

For *why:*

> Listen to the word in a sentence: *Everyone asked why the spill happened.* When you ask *why,* you want to know what made something happen, you want to know the reason.

For *story:*

> Listen to the word in a sentence: *Newspapers around the world told the story.* That means the newspapers told what happened in Alaska.

Audio Scripts **T323**

Audio Scripts, continued

Unit 13

SCRIPT FOR WHO'S TALKING? (page 215)

ITEM 1

Tell students:

> Turn to page 215 in your book. Look at the pictures. One student is talking. Listen.

Take the role of a student describing the diary in the first photograph and say:

> This is very interesting. It's a notebook filled with handwriting. In it, a young girl tells about her life during World War II. She describes what is happening to her every day and how she feels about it.

Then ask students:

> What record of history is this student talking about? Point to the correct picture.

ITEM 2

Tell students:

> Another student is talking. Listen.

Take the role of a student describing the history book in the third photograph and say:

> This book was written many years after the war ended. A historian at the university did a lot of research for it. It tells about events that happened during the war.

Then ask students:

> What record of history is this student talking about? Point to the correct picture.

ITEM 3

Tell students:

> Another student is talking. Listen.

Take the role of a student describing the newspaper in the second photograph and say:

> A newspaper is a good way to learn about the daily events that happened in the past. You can read about events that were happening on a specific day. You can find out what people thought about the events. I just read about how the First World War ended in Europe.

Then ask students:

> What record of history is this student talking about? Point to the correct picture.

SCRIPT FOR HIGH FREQUENCY WORDS (page 221)

Tell students:

> Turn to page 221 in your book. Follow along in your book and listen. We are going to learn new words.
>
> Look at the first word: *news.*
>
> Listen to the word: *news.*
>
> Listen to the word in a sentence: *People here shout the great news: The war is over!* When you hear *news*, you find out what is happening.
>
> Say the word with me: *news, news.* Now you say it.
>
> Spell the word with me: *news, n-e-w-s.* Now you spell it.
>
> Say the word again: *news, news.*

Repeat the process to present the other words. Use the following context sentences and elaborated meanings.

For *words:*

> Listen to the word in a sentence: *I cannot find the words to say how happy I am.* You use words to make sentences and tell your ideas.

For *much:*

> Listen to the word in a sentence: *There is so much excitement everywhere. Much* means *a lot of.* There is a lot of excitement wherever we go.

For *along:*

> Listen to the word in a sentence: *I am an army nurse. I work along with 10 other nurses. Along* means *next to* or *together with.*

For *question:*

> Listen to the word in a sentence: *We all have the same question: When can we go home?* You ask a *question* when you want to know something.

For *before:*

> Listen to the word in a sentence: *I hope to be home before the end of May. Before* means *sooner than.* I hope to be home *sooner* than May.

For *miss:*

> Listen to the word in a sentence: *I will miss the nurses in my group.* When you *miss* people, you feel sad because they are not with you.

For *example:*

> Listen to the word in a sentence: *Our group is a good example of a successful team.* An *example* shows how something should look. You can learn by watching a good example.

For *ever:*

> Listen to the word in a sentence: *These nurses are the best friends I ever had.* The nurses are better friends than anyone I knew before.

For *back:*

> Listen to the word in a sentence: *Still, it will be good to get back to my family.* When you get *back* to a place, you return to it.

Unit 14

SCRIPT FOR WHO'S TALKING? (page 231)

ITEM 1

Tell students:

Turn to page 231 in your book. Look at the pictures. Two characters are talking. Listen.

Take the roles of the evil pirate and the good fairy at top left and say:

FAIRY: Excuse me, Pirate, can I ask you for a favor?

PIRATE: What do you want, Ms. Fairy? You're about to be food for the sharks!

FAIRY: Could you please hand me that wand?

PIRATE: Here it is. That's the last favor I'll do for you.

FAIRY: Thank you. Now I can get free! Good-bye!

Then ask students:

Which characters are talking? Point to them.

ITEM 2

Tell students:

Another two characters are talking. Listen.

Take the roles of the frightened dragon and the brave girl at bottom and say:

DRAGON: Help! Some kids have been making fun of me. They are calling me names. I am scared of them! Can anyone help me, please?

GIRL: I will help you. I'm not scared of anyone. Here, take my hand.

DRAGON: Thank you! You are so brave!

Then ask students:

Which characters are talking? Point to them.

ITEMS 3–4

Repeat the script for Item 2 above, modifying it for different characters.

For the strong bear and the weak mouse at top right, say:

MOUSE: You are so strong, Strong Bear. Can you help me lift this feather? I want to take it my house, but I cannot lift it. It is too heavy!

BEAR: I will help you, Mouse. You can count on me.

MOUSE: Thank you, Strong Bear.

BEAR: You're welcome. That's what friends are for!

For the old woman and young child at bottom left, say:

CHILD: I am having trouble sleeping. I always fall asleep faster when you tell me a story. Could you please tell me a story so I can fall asleep, Grandma?

WOMAN: Sure. I know just the story to tell you.

CHILD: Thank you, Grandmother. You are the best.

SCRIPT FOR HIGH FREQUENCY WORDS (page 235)

Tell students:

Turn to page 235 in your book. Follow along in your book and listen. We are going to learn new words.

Look at the first word: *as.*

Listen to the word: *as.*

Listen to the word in a sentence: *Listen carefully as I tell you a story. As* means *while.* You can say *Listen as I tell you a story* or *Listen while I tell you a story.*

Say the word with me: *as, as.* Now you say it.

Spell the word with me: *as, a-s.* Now you spell it.

Say the word again: *as, as.*

Repeat the process to present the other words. Use the following context sentences and elaborated meanings.

For *sentence:*

Listen to the word in a sentence: *Pay attention to every sentence I say.* A *sentence* is a group of words. You can write or say a sentence to tell what you think.

For *idea:*

Listen to the word in a sentence: *I got the idea for this story from my grandfather.* An *idea* is something you think of. It can be a thought or a plan.

For *plants:*

Listen to the word in a sentence: *A frog lived in the garden among the tall plants.* Trees, flowers, and grass are *plants.*

For *into:*

Listen to the word in a sentence: *One day, it jumped and fell into a pail of cream. Into* means the same as *inside.* You can say *It fell into a pail* or *It fell inside a pail.*

For *until:*

Listen to the word in a sentence: *The frog swam and swam until its legs got tired.* The frog kept swimming so much that his legs got tired.

For *but:*

Listen to the word in a sentence: *The frog was tired, but it did not stop swimming.* Even though the frog was tired, it did not stop swimming.

For *seemed:*

Listen to the word in a sentence: *Then the cream seemed a little thicker. Seemed* means *looked.* You can say *The cream seemed thicker* or *The cream looked thicker.*

For *each:*

Listen to the word in a sentence: *With each kick, the cream got thicker and thicker. Each* means the same as *every.* Every time the frog kicked, the cream got thicker.

For *made:*

Listen to the word in a sentence: *In a few minutes, the frog made a pail of butter!* The frog's work turned the cream to butter.

Audio Scripts **T325**

Audio Scripts, continued

Unit 15

SCRIPT FOR WHO'S TALKING? (page 246)

ITEM 1

Tell students:
> Turn to page 246 in your book. Look at the pictures. One person is talking. Listen.

Take the role of the girl with the bowling trophy and say:
> Thank you for the beautiful trophy. I am very happy I won the tournament. Thanks to my parents and to the other bowlers. They bowled well, too.

Then ask students:
> Who is talking? Point to the correct athlete.

ITEM 2

Tell students:
> Another person is talking. Listen.

Take the role of the female tennis player in the wheelchair and say:
> Hey, guys, thanks for a great match! You had us rolling all over the court. We went so fast that I lost my hat. You play a great game of tennis. Thanks a lot!

Then ask students:
> Who is talking? Point to the correct athlete.

ITEM 3

Tell students:
> Another person is talking. Listen.

Take the role of the football player catching the ball and say:
> My coach showed me how to jump up high like this to catch the football. I'm very grateful to him for that. Now I can score more touchdowns. I appreciate your help, Coach. Thanks a lot!

Then ask students:
> Who is talking? Point to the correct athlete.

SCRIPT FOR HIGH FREQUENCY WORDS (page 249)

Tell students:
> Turn to page 249 in your book. Follow along in your book and listen. We are going to learn new words.
>
> Look at the first word: *friends.*
>
> Listen to the word: *friends.*
>
> Listen to the word in a sentence: *My friends and I love to hike. Friends* are people who like each other. They do things together.
>
> Say the word with me: *friends, friends.* Now you say it.
>
> Spell the word with me: *friends, f-r-i-e-n-d-s.* Now you spell it.
>
> Say the word again: *friends, friends.*

Repeat the process to present the other words. Use the following context sentences and elaborated meanings.

For *asked:*
> Listen to the word in a sentence: *"Will you help me put on my pack?"* asked Celia. When you *ask* something, you say a question.

For *walked:*
> Listen to the word in a sentence: *We walked to the start of the trail.* We went on foot to the beginning of the trail.

For *trees:*
> Listen to the word in a sentence: *We passed pines, oaks, and other trees. Trees* are tall plants that have leaves and branches.

For *air:*
> Listen to the word in a sentence: *We breathed the crisp mountain air.* People and animals need *air* to live. We breathe air in and out of our bodies.

For *talked:*
> Listen to the word in a sentence: *We talked about the hike.* We told each other about the hike.

For *if:*
> Listen to the word in a sentence: *"If you feel tired, stop and rest," I said.* When you are not sure that something will happen, you can say *if.*

For *even:*
> Listen to the word in a sentence: *Drink water even if you're not thirsty.* You may not feel thirsty, but you should still drink water.

For *while:*
> Listen to the word in a sentence: *We drank water while we walked. While* means at the *same time.* We drank water and walked at the same time.

For *such:*
> Listen to the word in a sentence: *I have such a good time when I hike!* You can use *such* to mean *very.* I have a very good time when I hike!

Unit 16

SCRIPT FOR WHO'S TALKING? (page 260)

ITEM 1

Tell students:

> Turn to page 260 in your book. Look at the picture. Some pioneers are in St. Louis and want to go to San Francisco. Listen to this student tell how they should go. Trace the route on the map.

Take the role of a student proposing a route and say:

> I think the pioneers should go this way: Start in St. Louis. Go north on the Mississippi River, and then west on the Missouri River until you meet the Santa Fe Trail. Then continue west on the Santa Fe Trail. Go across the Colorado River and follow the Old Spanish Trail west to Los Angeles. Go north along the coast until you reach San Francisco.

ITEM 2

Tell students

> Now another student is talking. Listen. Trace the route this student describes.

Take the role of a a different student proposing a route and say:

> I think the pioneers can go a better route: Start in St. Louis. Go north on the Mississippi River, and then west on the Missouri River until you meet the Oregon Trail. Then continue west on the Oregon Trail across the Rocky Mountains until you reach the California Trail. Follow the California Trail south through the Sierra Nevada. Go west to San Francisco.

Then ask students:

> Which route do you think is best? Trace the routes on the map again and explain why.

SCRIPT FOR HIGH FREQUENCY WORDS (page 263)

Tell students:

> Turn to page 263 in your book. Follow along in your book and listen. We are going to learn new words.
>
> Look at the first word: *state.*
>
> Listen to the word: *state.*
>
> Listen to the word in a sentence: *Alaska is the largest state in the United States.* The United States has 50 areas called states. Each *state* has its own laws and leaders.
>
> Say the word with me: *state, state.* Now you say it.
>
> Spell the word with me: *state, s-t-a-t-e.* Now you spell it.
>
> Say the word again: *state, state.*

Repeat the process to present the other words. Use the following context sentences and elaborated meanings.

For *than:*

> Listen to the word in a sentence: *It is much bigger than Texas.* Use the word *than* to compare two things. Texas is big, but Alaska is bigger than Texas.

For *high:*

> Listen to the word in a sentence: *Alaska has very high mountains. High* means the same as *tall.* You can say *The mountains are high* or *The mountains are tall.*

For *million:*

> Listen to the word in a sentence: *It has about 51 million acres of parks.* A *million* is the number 1 followed by six zeroes.

For *form:*

> Listen to the word in a sentence: *The Aleutian Islands form a long chain of islands.* When you *form* something, you put something together to make a shape.

For *sea:*

> Listen to the word in a sentence: *They stretch far out into the sea.* The sea is the ocean, a large body of salty water.

For *near:*

> Listen to the word in a sentence: *Little Diomede Island in Alaska, is near Russia. Near* means the same as close to. You can say the island is *near* Russia or *close to* Russia. *Near* is the opposite of *far.*

For *miles:*

> Listen to the word in a sentence: *It is only 2.5 miles away!* A *mile* is a unit of measurement; it is about 1.6 kilometers.

For *explore:*

> Listen to the word in a sentence: *To explore Juneau, the capital city, go in summer.* When you *explore* a place, you travel around and see what it is like.

For *earth:*

> Listen to the word in a sentence: *Alaska is one of the coldest places on earth.* Our planet is called the Earth. It is the world we live on.

Audio Scripts **T327**

Audio Scripts, continued

Unit 17

SCRIPT FOR WHO'S TALKING? (page 274)

ITEM 1

Tell students:

> Turn to page 274 in your book. Look at the picture. Some people are at a restaurant. Listen.

Take the role of the server in the photograph and say:

> Hello. My name is Mike. Welcome to our restaurant. I will be your server today. May I take your order?

Then ask students:

> Who is talking? Point to the correct person?

ITEM 2

Tell students:

> Another person is talking. Listen.

Take the role of the female customer and say:

> I would like a pizza and a soda, please. We would like to have some nachos as an appetizer.

Then ask students:

> Who is talking? Point to the correct person?

ITEM 3

Tell students:

> Another person is talking. Listen.

Take the role of the boy looking at the menu and say:

> Um, I don't really know what I want yet. Could you come back and take my order in a few minutes. I need to look at this menu some more.

Then ask students:

> Who is talking? Point to the correct person?

SCRIPT FOR HIGH FREQUENCY WORDS (page 277)

Tell students:

> Turn to page 277 in your book. Follow along in your book and listen. We are going to learn new words.
>
> Look at the first word: *weigh.*
>
> Listen to the word: *weigh.*
>
> Listen to the word in a sentence: *Ana buys tomatoes that weigh over 2 pounds.* That's how heavy each tomato is: two pounds.
>
> Say the word with me: *weigh, weigh.* Now you say it.
>
> Spell the word with me: *weigh, w-e-i-g-h.* Now you spell it.
>
> Say the word again: *weigh, weigh.*

Repeat the process to present the other words. Use the following context sentences and elaborated meanings.

For *beautiful:*

> Listen to the word in a sentence: *The beautiful tomatoes are firm and bright red.* When something is *beautiful* it is nice to look at. It is very pretty.

For *special:*

> Listen to the word in a sentence: *They come from a special market across town.* Something is *special* when there aren't very many things like it.

For *own:*

> Listen to the word in a sentence: *"I want to grow my own tomatoes," Ana thought.* When something belongs to you, you call it your *own.*

For *any:*

> Listen to the word in a sentence: *She did not have any seeds, so she bought some.* She had no seeds, so she bought some.

For *indoors:*

> Listen to the word in a sentence: *She planted them indoors, by her kitchen window. Indoors* means *inside the house.*

For *warm:*

> Listen to the word in a sentence: *It was winter, but her kitchen was warm and sunny.* Something is *warm* if it is not too hot and not too cold.

For *healthy:*

> Listen to the word in a sentence: *Soon, she had strong and healthy seedlings. Healthy* means *strong* and *well.* Something that is healthy is not sick or weak.

For *cold:*

> Listen to the word in a sentence: *By the end of April, the cold weather was over.* In winter, the weather is cold. *Cold* is the opposite of *hot.*

For *outdoors:*

> Listen to the word in a sentence: *It was time to put her plants outdoors in the yard. Outdoors* means *outside the house.* It is the opposite of *indoors.*

T328 Audio Scripts

Unit 18

SCRIPT FOR HIGH FREQUENCY WORDS (page 291)

Tell students:

Turn to page 291 in your book. Follow along in your book and listen. We are going to learn words that can mean more than one thing.

Look at the first word: *show.*

Listen to the word: *show.*

Show **can have different meanings. Sometimes it can mean** *let someone see something.* **It has that meaning in this sentence:** *Let me show you my new guitar.* **Other times, it can mean a performance, something that people go to see, such as a concert or a circus. It has that meaning in this sentence:** *I am going to play it in the show tonight.*

Say the word with me: *show, show.* **Now you say it.**

Spell the word with me: *show, s-h-o-w.* **Now you spell it.**

Say the word again: *show, show.*

Repeat the process to present the other words. Use the following context sentences and elaborated meanings.

For *right:*

Sometimes *right* **can mean** *correctly, the way it's supposed to be.* **It has that meaning in this sentence:** *I need to practice to play the songs right.* **Other times, it can mean the opposite of** *left.* **It has that meaning in this sentence:** *I strum the strings with my right hand.*

For *close:*

Sometimes *close* **can mean** *next to, nearby.* **It has that meaning in this sentence:** *I keep the music book close to me while I play.* **Other times, it can mean the same as** *shut;* **the opposite of** *open.* **It has that meaning in this sentence:** *Close it now and see if I can play the song.*

For *watch:*

Sometimes *watch* **can mean** *look at.* **It has that meaning in this sentence:** *Many people will come to watch us perform.* **Other times, it can mean the thing that you wear on your wrist to tell time. It has that meaning in this sentence:** *I have to check my watch so I won't be late.*

For *kind:*

Sometimes *kind* **can mean the same as** *type* **or** *sort.* **It has that meaning in this sentence:** *I wonder what kind of music people will like.* **Other times, it can mean** *helpful, friendly, nice.* **It has that meaning in this sentence:** *I hope the audience will be kind and won't shout "Boo!"*

High Point Scope and Sequence

Language Development and Communication

SOCIAL AND ACADEMIC LANGUAGE FUNCTIONS	THE BASICS	A	B	C
Listen actively	•	•	•	•
Repeat spoken language	•			
Express social courtesies	•	•		
Ask and answer questions	•	•	•	
Use the telephone	•	•		
Conduct a transaction	•	•		
Demonstrate non-verbal communication	•	•	•	•
Adjust communication to the occasion or audience (formal/informal)		•	•	•
Express likes and dislikes	•	•	•	•
Express feelings, needs, opinions, intentions	•	•	•	•
Give and carry out commands	•	•	•	
Describe people, places, things, events	•	•	•	•
Listen to a preview of a selection	•	•	•	
Listen to a selection	•	•	•	•
Recite	•	•	•	•
Read a selection	•	•	•	•
Give/Follow directions	•	•	•	•
Role-play	•	•	•	•
Dramatize	•	•	•	•
Ask for/Give information	•	•	•	•
Make comparisons	•	•	•	•
Engage in discussion	•	•	•	•
Persuade		•	•	•
Retell a story	•	•	•	•
Tell an original story		•	•	•
Define and explain		•	•	•
Clarify		•	•	•
Verify or confirm information		•	•	•
Justify		•	•	•
Elaborate		•	•	•
Negotiate		•	•	•
Write	•	•	•	•

LANGUAGE PATTERNS AND STRUCTURES	THE BASICS	A	B	C
Statements	•	•		
Statements with *There is/are/was/were* and *Here is/are/was/were*	•	•		
Statements with infinitives	•	•		
Questions/Exclamations/Commands	•	•	•	
Negative sentences	•	•	•	
Complete sentences		•	•	•
Compound sentences		•	•	•
Complex sentences		•	•	•
Relative clauses			•	•
Compound-complex sentences				•
Conditional sentences			•	•
Pronouns and pronoun agreement	•	•	•	

LANGUAGE PATTERNS AND STRUCTURES, continued	THE BASICS	A	B	C
Demonstrative pronouns	•	•		
Indefinite pronouns			•	•
Adjectives	•	•	•	•
Adjectives that compare		•	•	•
Modals (*can, could, would, might, must,* etc.)	•	•	•	•
Present tense verbs	•	•	•	•
Past tense verbs	•	•	•	•
Future tense verbs	•	•	•	•
Present perfect tense verbs		•	•	•
Past perfect tense verbs			•	•
Future perfect tense verbs			•	•
Progressive forms of verbs	•	•	•	•
Two-word verbs		•	•	•
Active/passive voice			•	•
Gerunds			•	•
Contractions	•	•	•	•
Adverbs	•	•	•	•
Adverbs that compare		•	•	•
Prepositions	•	•	•	•

Concepts and Vocabulary

EVERYDAY CONCEPTS AND VOCABULARY	THE BASICS	A	B	C
Greetings and other social courtesies	•	•		
Personal information (name, address, etc.)	•	•		
Categories: Clothing, Food, School, etc.	•	•		

ACADEMIC CONCEPTS AND VOCABULARY	THE BASICS	A	B	C
In Language Arts and Literature	•	•	•	•
In Science, Social Studies, Mathematics	•	•	•	•
In Fine Arts: Music, Art, Drama		•	•	•

VOCABULARY STRATEGIES	THE BASICS	A	B	C
Relate words	•	•	•	•
Structural clues	•	•	•	•
Compound words	•			
Prefixes and suffixes	•	•	•	•
Latin and Greek roots			•	•
Context clues	•	•	•	•
Multiple-meaning words	•	•	•	•
Idioms	•	•	•	•
Figurative language			•	•
Analogies			•	•
Denotation and connotation			•	•
Locate and use definitions		•	•	•
Locate word origins			•	•

Reading

LEARNING TO READ	THE BASICS	A	B	C
Use concepts of print (directionality, etc.)	•			
Recognize high-frequency words	•	•		
Develop phonemic awareness	•			
Associate sounds and symbols	•			
Blend sounds to decode words	•			
Recognize word families	•	•	•	•
Use word patterns to decode words	•			
Use letter patterns to decode words	•			
Identify root words and inflectional endings	•	•	•	
Identify root words and affixes	•	•	•	•
Recognize Greek and Latin roots			•	•
Divide words into syllables	•			
Identify syllable types	•			
Read multisyllabic words	•	•	•	•
Build reading fluency	•	•	•	•

READING STRATEGIES	THE BASICS	A	B	C
Pre-Reading Strategies	•	•	•	•
Activate prior knowledge/Relate to personal experience	•	•	•	•
Preview	•	•	•	•
Build background	•	•	•	•
Predict	•	•	•	•
Set a purpose for reading	•	•	•	•
Relate reading rate to purpose		•	•	•
Skim		•	•	•
Scan			•	•
Use graphic organizers to prepare for reading	•	•	•	•
Self-Monitoring Strategies	•	•	•	•
Ask questions	•	•	•	•
Clarify	•	•	•	•
Visualize	•	•	•	•
Paraphrase	•	•	•	•
Use visuals	•	•	•	•
Relate to personal knowledge or experience	•	•	•	•
Compare selection to other texts with similar theme, genres, or text structures	•	•	•	•
Make, confirm, and revise predictions	•	•	•	•
Adjust purposes for reading		•	•	•
Confirm word meaning	•	•	•	•
Use punctuation clues	•	•		
Use signal words	•	•		
Corrective Strategies	•	•	•	•
Reread	•	•	•	•
Read on	•	•	•	•
Search for new clues		•	•	•
Adjust reading rate	•	•	•	•
Reduce the amount of text read at one time		•	•	•
Use reference aids (glossary, dictionary, etc.)		•	•	•

READING STRATEGIES, continued	THE BASICS	A	B	C
Comprehension Strategies (See also Comprehension)	•	•	•	•
Review	•	•	•	•
Connect new information to known	•	•	•	•
Use text structures	•	•	•	•
Use text and graphic features	•	•	•	•
Use graphic organizers to relate ideas	•	•	•	•
Retell	•	•	•	•
Use SQ3R			•	•
Summarize	•	•	•	•

COMPREHENSION	THE BASICS	A	B	C
Follow directions	•	•	•	•
Identify details	•	•	•	•
Classify	•	•	•	•
Identify character's traits, feelings, point of view, motive	•	•	•	•
Identify sequence	•	•	•	•
Identify steps in a process	•	•	•	
Identify or relate cause and effect	•	•	•	•
Identify or relate main idea and details	•	•	•	•
Identify or relate problem and solution	•	•	•	•
Identify or relate goal and outcome	•	•	•	•
Make comparisons	•	•	•	•
Make an inference	•	•	•	•
Draw conclusions	•	•	•	•
Summarize	•	•	•	•
Form generalizations			•	•
Identify author's purpose		•	•	•
Identify author's biases and point of view		•	•	•
Identify author's assumptions and beliefs			•	•
Analyze story elements	•	•	•	•
Analyze information	•	•	•	•
Distinguish between facts and opinions	•	•	•	•
Recognize missing information				•
Identify fallacies of logic				•
Identify multiple levels of meaning			•	•
Distinguish between fantasy and reality	•	•	•	•
Distinguish between relevant and irrelevant information			•	•
Distinguish between important and unimportant information		•	•	•
Distinguish between apparent message and hidden agenda			•	•
Form opinions	•	•	•	•
Make judgments or decisions	•	•	•	•
Support judgments	•	•	•	•
Identify propaganda		•	•	•
Evaluate information		•	•	•
Synthesize information			•	•
Recognize how personal background and viewpoint influence interpretation of a selection		•	•	•

Scope and Sequence **T331**

Literary Analysis and Appreciation

RECOGNIZE GENRES

	THE BASICS	A	B	C
Article	•	•	•	•
Autobiography		•	•	•
Biographical fiction			•	•
Biography	•	•	•	•
Character Sketch		•	•	•
Description	•	•	•	•
Diary/Journal	•	•	•	•
Documentary				•
Drama		•	•	•
Essay	•	•	•	•
Fable		•	•	•
Family portrait/Self-portrait		•	•	
Fantasy		•	•	•
Fiction	•	•	•	•
Folk tale/Legend	•	•	•	•
Historical account	•			•
Historical fiction	•	•	•	•
How-to article	•	•	•	•
Interview	•	•	•	•
Memoir/Personal narrative	•	•	•	•
Myth	•	•	•	•
Nonfiction	•	•	•	•
News article/Newscast	•	•	•	•
Persuasive essay		•	•	•
Photo or art essay	•	•	•	•
Play		•	•	•
Poetry	•	•	•	•
Rhymed verse	•	•	•	•
Free verse	•	•	•	•
Proverb/Saying		•	•	•
Quotation		•	•	•
Realistic fiction	•	•	•	•
Report	•	•	•	•
Science article	•	•	•	•
Science fiction		•	•	•
Song/Chant	•	•	•	•
Speech			•	•
Short Story			•	•
Tall tale	•	•		

RECOGNIZE LITERARY DEVICES

	THE BASICS	A	B	C
Alliteration		•	•	•
Allusion				•
Analogy				•
Assonance and consonance			•	•
Characterization	•	•	•	•
Compressed language				•
Description		•	•	•

RECOGNIZE LITERARY DEVICES, continued

	THE BASICS	A	B	C
Dialect				•
Dialogue		•	•	•
Figurative language		•	•	•
Hyperbole/Exaggeration		•	•	•
Imagery/Sensory language		•	•	•
Simile		•	•	•
Metaphor		•	•	•
Personification			•	•
Irony				•
Mood and tone		•	•	•
Narrator's Point of view		•	•	•
Onomatopoeia			•	•
Plot development	•	•	•	•
Goal and outcome or Problem and solution	•	•	•	•
Conflict/Complications/Climax/Resolution		•	•	•
Rising and falling action			•	•
Flashback			•	•
Foreshadowing			•	•
Suspense			•	•
Repetition		•	•	•
Rhyme	•	•	•	•
Rhyme scheme			•	•
Rhythm/meter		•	•	•
Setting	•	•	•	•
Style		•	•	•
Symbolism			•	•
Theme		•	•	•
Word choice		•	•	•

RESPOND TO LITERATURE

	THE BASICS	A	B	C
Interpret literature	•	•	•	•
Apply literature to personal life	•	•	•	•
Identify questions of personal importance and answer them through literature	•	•	•	•
Develop personal preferences in reading	•	•	•	•
Recognize how literature expands and enriches personal viewpoints and experiences	•	•	•	•
Recognize that literature may elicit a variety of valid responses	•	•	•	•

EVALUATE LITERATURE

	THE BASICS	A	B	C
Evaluate the impact of literary devices, medium, or genre on meaning or quality		•	•	•
Evaluate the impact of the author's background, qualifications, biases, or point of view on meaning		•	•	•
Evaluate the impact of culture, time period, customs, or outlooks on meaning		•	•	•
Evaluate the literary quality of a selection		•	•	•
Compare literature on a variety of points (theme, genre, point of view, etc.)		•	•	•
Recognize the defining characteristics of classical literature (timelessness, universality of themes, etc.)			•	•

Cognitive Academic Skills

LEARNING STRATEGIES	THE BASICS	A	B	C
Strategies for Language Learning	•	•	•	•
Listen to and imitate others	•	•	•	•
Recite songs and poems	•	•	•	•
Use gestures and mime to get across an idea	•	•	•	•
Explore alternate ways of saying things	•	•	•	•
Test hypotheses about language	•	•	•	•
Ask for help, feedback, and clarification	•	•	•	•
Use visuals to construct meaning	•	•	•	•
Compare nonverbal and verbal cues	•	•	•	•
Compare and contrast elements of language and identify patterns in language		•	•	•
Incorporate language "chunks"	•	•	•	•
Use reference aids to verify language/spelling		•	•	•
Practice new language (repeating, etc.)	•	•	•	•
Analyze situations to determine appropriate language use (formal/informal)		•	•	•
Self-monitor language use and self-assess	•	•	•	•
Strategies for Reading *See page T331*	•	•	•	•
Strategies for Listening, Speaking, Viewing, Representing, Writing	•	•	•	•
Activate prior knowledge	•	•	•	•
Relate to personal knowledge or experience	•	•	•	•
Predict	•	•	•	•
Ask questions	•	•	•	•
Clarify		•	•	•
Visualize		•	•	•
Paraphrase		•	•	•
Connect new information to known	•	•	•	•
Review		•	•	•
Make comparisons	•	•	•	•
Use graphic organizers	•	•	•	•
Interact with peers	•	•	•	•
Plan and set goals	•	•	•	•
Brainstorm	•	•	•	•
Generate and organize ideas	•	•	•	•
Gather information	•	•	•	•
Make observations	•	•	•	•
Take notes	•	•	•	•
Outline		•	•	•
Summarize	•	•	•	•
Self-monitor and self-assess	•	•	•	•

STRATEGIES FOR TAKING TESTS	THE BASICS	A	B	C
Read directions carefully		•	•	•
Plan time for each item/section		•	•	•
Clarify vocabulary in passages/questions		•	•	•
Use typographic clues to meaning		•	•	•
Reread passages to clarify information		•	•	•
Note test format and select appropriate strategies		•	•	•
Mark answers and check for legibility		•	•	•

CRITICAL THINKING	THE BASICS	A	B	C
Classify	•	•	•	•
Relate events in a sequence	•	•	•	•
Relate steps in a process	•	•	•	•
Relate cause and effect	•	•	•	•
Relate main ideas and details	•	•	•	•
Relate problem and solution	•	•	•	•
Relate goal and outcome	•	•	•	•
Formulate questions	•	•	•	•
Formulate hypotheses			•	•
Clarify information		•	•	•
Make comparisons	•	•	•	•
Make inferences	•	•	•	•
Draw conclusions	•	•	•	•
Summarize	•	•	•	•
Form generalizations			•	•
Analyze information	•	•	•	•
Form opinions	•	•	•	•
Make judgments or decisions	•	•	•	•
Evaluate information		•	•	•
Synthesize information			•	•
Generate ideas	•	•	•	•
Solve problems	•	•	•	•

RESEARCH SKILLS	THE BASICS	A	B	C
Use the research process	•	•	•	•
Locate resources (library, computerized card catalog, *Reader's Guide*, etc.)	•	•	•	•
Gather information	•	•	•	•
Use alphabetical order		•		
Survey/Skim and scan/Look up key words		•	•	•
Use print resources	•	•	•	•
almanac			•	•
atlas, globe	•	•	•	•
books	•	•	•	•
dictionary			•	•
thesaurus			•	•
encyclopedia			•	•
magazines and newspapers		•	•	•
Use electronic resources: CD-ROM, electronic encyclopedia, the Internet		•	•	•
Use audio-visual resources	•	•	•	•
Use graphic aids (charts, time line, etc.)	•	•	•	•
Conduct observations, surveys, experiments, and interviews	•	•	•	•
Take notes	•	•	•	•
Organize and synthesize information from multiple sources		•	•	•
Generate new research questions			•	•
Write a research report		•	•	•
Cite sources			•	•

Scope and Sequence **T333**

Listening, Speaking, Viewing, and Representing

LEVELS	THE BASICS	A	B	C
LISTENING AND SPEAKING				
Listen actively	•	•	•	•
Listen for information	•	•	•	•
Listen critically to determine purpose and message		•	•	•
Listen to a poem or song	•	•	•	•
Listen to a selection	•	•	•	•
Listen and speak effectively in a discussion	•	•	•	•
Listen and speak effectively in a peer conference		•	•	•
Listen and speak effectively to work with a partner or on a team	•	•	•	•
Speak at an appropriate rate and volume		•	•	•
Make eye contact		•	•	•
Use language and tone appropriate to the audience, purpose, and occasion		•	•	•
Give and follow directions or commands	•	•	•	•
Express feelings, needs, ideas, and opinions	•	•	•	•
Describe	•	•	•	•
Ask and answer questions	•	•	•	•
Conduct an interview	•	•	•	•
Recite	•	•	•	•
Read aloud	•	•	•	•
Role-play or dramatize	•	•	•	•
Retell a story	•	•	•	•
Tell a story		•	•	•
Inform or explain	•	•	•	•
Give an oral report		•	•	•
Give a speech		•	•	•
Persuade		•	•	•
Participate in a debate		•	•	•
Demonstrate non-verbal communication	•	•	•	•
REPRESENTING IDEAS AND INFORMATION				
Create graphic organizers	•	•	•	•
Create illustrations or photographs	•	•	•	•
Create posters and other visual displays	•	•	•	•
Create a map	•	•	•	•
Create a multimedia presentation		•	•	•
VIEWING				
Respond to a visual image	•	•	•	•
Interpret a visual image	•	•	•	•
Identify visual symbols	•	•	•	•
View critically to determine purpose and message		•	•	•
Recognize various types of mass media		•	•	•
Compare and evaluate media		•	•	•

Writing

LEVELS	THE BASICS	A	B	C
HANDWRITING				
Letter formation and spacing	•			
Left-to-right directionality	•			
WRITING PURPOSES, MODES, AND FORMS				
Write for a variety of purposes and audiences	•	•	•	•
Choose the mode and form of writing that works best for the topic, audience, and purpose		•	•	•
Write in a variety of modes	•	•	•	•
Narrative	•	•	•	•
Expository	•	•	•	•
Descriptive	•	•	•	•
Expressive	•	•	•	•
Persuasive		•	•	•
Write in a variety of forms	•	•	•	•
Biography	•	•	•	•
Character sketch		•	•	•
Critique		•	•	•
Description	•	•	•	•
Diary/Journal entry	•	•	•	•
E-mail/ Internet page		•	•	•
Essay		•	•	•
Fact sheet	•	•	•	•
Letter	•	•	•	•
Magazine/News article/Newscast		•	•	•
Myth			•	
Paragraph	•	•	•	•
Personal narrative/ Self-portrait/ Memoir	•	•	•	•
Persuasive essay		•	•	•
Play				•
Poem/Rhyme/Song	•	•	•	•
Poster	•	•	•	•
Quickwrite		•	•	•
Report		•	•	•
Sentences	•	•	•	•
Speech		•	•	•
Story		•	•	•
Summary		•	•	•
WRITING PROCESS				
Prewriting	•	•	•	•
Analyze published and student models		•	•	•
Brainstorm and collect ideas	•	•	•	•
Choose a topic	•	•	•	•
Plan writing with an FATP Chart (**F**orm, **A**udience, **T**opic, **P**urpose)		•	•	•
Organize ideas	•	•	•	•

Writing, continued

LEVELS	THE BASICS	A	B	C
WRITING PROCESS, continued				
Drafting	●	●	●	●
Write to communicate ideas	●	●	●	●
Use writing techniques appropriate to the purpose, audience, and form		●	●	●
Use appropriate organizing structures	●	●	●	●
logical order	●	●	●	●
sequential order	●	●	●	●
spatial order		●	●	●
to make comparisons	●	●	●	●
to show causes and effects		●	●	●
to show goals and outcomes	●	●	●	●
to show problems and solutions	●	●	●	●
to show thesis and supporting arguments		●	●	●
Revising	●	●	●	●
Evaluate the draft	●	●	●	●
Participate in peer-conferencing		●	●	●
Add, elaborate, delete, combine, and rearrange the text to improve the draft	●	●	●	●
Editing and Proofreading	●	●	●	●
Check the revised copy for correct conventions of written English and make corrections	●	●	●	●
Use reference materials (dictionary, etc.)		●	●	●
Publishing	●	●	●	●
Create the final version of the work and prepare it for publication, using visuals or multimedia to complement or extend meaning	●	●	●	●
Reflect and Evaluate		●	●	●
Use rubrics to evaluate the work		●	●	●
Use evaluations to set goals as a writer		●	●	●
WRITER'S CRAFT				
Introductions that catch the reader's interest		●	●	●
Effective conclusions		●	●	●
Word choice: colorful, specific, precise words; vocabulary appropriate for the audience, etc.	●	●	●	●
Effective sentences		●	●	●
Combine sentences		●	●	●
Break up run-on sentences		●	●	●
Sentence variety		●	●	●
Effective paragraphs	●	●	●	●
Topic sentence and supporting details	●	●	●	●
Transition words			●	●
Consistent verb tense and point of view			●	●
Show, don't tell		●	●	●
Include important or interesting information		●	●	●
Exclude unnecessary details		●	●	●
Elaborate		●	●	●
Use visual and organizational aids	●	●	●	●
Develop a personal voice or style			●	●
Constantly evaluate the writing		●	●	●
Keep a writing portfolio	●	●	●	●

Grammar, Usage, Mechanics, Spelling

LEVELS	THE BASICS	A	B	C
SENTENCES				
Sentence types	●	●	●	●
Negative sentences	●	●	●	●
Conditional sentences			●	●
Sentence structures	●	●	●	●
Phrases		●	●	●
Clauses		●	●	●
Simple sentences	●	●	●	●
Compound sentences		●	●	●
Complex sentences		●	●	●
Compound-complex sentences				●
Properly placed clauses and modifiers			●	●
Subjects and predicates		●	●	●
Complete subject		●	●	●
Simple subject		●	●	●
Understood subject (*you*)		●	●	●
It as the subject (*It* is raining)		●	●	●
Compound subject			●	●
Complete predicate		●	●	●
Simple predicate (verb)		●	●	●
Compound predicate			●	●
Complete sentences/Fragments		●	●	●
Subject–verb agreement	●	●	●	●
PARTS OF SPEECH				
Nouns	●	●	●	●
Common and proper	●	●	●	●
Count and noncount	●	●	●	●
Plurals	●	●	●	●
Possessive	●	●	●	●
Articles		●	●	●
Pronouns	●	●	●	●
Subject	●	●	●	●
Object	●	●	●	●
Possessive	●	●	●	●
Reflexive		●	●	●
Indefinite		●	●	●
Demonstrative	●	●	●	●
Relative			●	●
Adjectives	●	●	●	●
Adjectives that compare		●	●	●
Verbs	●	●	●	●
Action	●	●	●	●
Linking	●	●	●	●
Modals (*can, could, would, might, must,* etc.)	●	●	●	●
Helping	●	●	●	●
Transitive and intransitive verbs			●	●

Grammar, Usage, Mechanics, Spelling, continued

LEVELS	THE BASICS	A	B	C
PARTS OF SPEECH, continued				
Verb tenses	●	●	●	●
Present tense	●	●	●	
Habitual present tense	●	●	●	●
Past tense (regular and irregular)	●	●	●	●
Future tense	●	●	●	
Present perfect tense		●	●	●
Past perfect tense			●	●
Future perfect tense			●	●
Progressive forms of verbs	●	●	●	●
Two-word verbs		●	●	
Active/passive verbs			●	●
Gerunds				●
Participial phrases				●
Contractions		●	●	●
Adverbs	●	●	●	●
Adverbs that compare		●	●	●
Prepositions and prepositional phrases	●	●	●	●
Conjunctions		●	●	●
Interjections		●	●	●
CAPITALIZATION				
First word of a sentence	●	●		
Pronoun I	●			
Proper nouns	●	●	●	●
Abbreviations of proper nouns	●	●	●	●
Proper adjectives	●	●	●	●
In letters		●	●	●
In titles		●	●	●
In direct quotations		●	●	●
PUNCTUATION				
Period	●	●	●	●
Question mark	●	●	●	●
Exclamation mark	●	●	●	●
Comma		●	●	●
Apostrophe	●	●	●	●
Quotation marks		●		
Colon			●	●
Semicolon			●	●
Dash			●	●
Hyphen			●	●
Italics			●	
Underline			●	●
Parentheses			●	●
SPELLING				
Use spelling strategies	●	●	●	●
Memorize reliable rules	●	●	●	●

Technology/Media

LEVELS	THE BASICS	A	B	C
TECHNOLOGICAL LITERACY				
Identify forms, purposes and functions of technology		●	●	●
Operate a computer		●	●	●
Operate audio and visual recording devices		●	●	●
USING TECHNOLOGY				
Use e-mail		●	●	●
Use audio, video, and electronic media to generate ideas, gather information, conduct interviews, etc., during the writing process	●	●	●	●
Use word-processing software		●	●	●
Use desktop publishing or multiple media to publish work		●	●	●
Use the Internet and other technology to locate resources		●	●	●
Evaluate quality and reliability of information from electronic resources		●	●	●
Make databases and spreadsheets			●	●
MEDIA STUDY AND MULTIMEDIA PRESENTATIONS				
Evaluate and select media for presentations (based on message, purpose, audience)		●	●	●
Design and create multimedia presentations		●	●	●
Compare print, visual, and electronic media			●	●
Explain how the use of different media affects the message			●	●

Cultural Perspectives

LEVELS	THE BASICS	A	B	C
MULTICULTURAL AWARENESS AND APPRECIATION				
Connect personal experiences and ideas with those of others	●	●	●	●
Compare oral traditions, folk tales, and literature across regions and cultures	●	●	●	●
Read and conduct research to increase knowledge of many cultures		●	●	●
Understand that language and literature are the primary means by which culture is transmitted			●	●
Recognize universal themes that cross cultures		●	●	●
Appreciate the diversity of cultures and generations	●	●	●	●
Appreciate and share aspects of the home, U.S., and world culture	●	●	●	●
History	●	●	●	●
Language	●	●	●	●
Folklore and literature	●	●	●	●
Symbols	●	●	●	●
Holidays, customs, and traditions	●	●	●	●
Political systems and government	●	●	●	●
Media		●	●	●

Staff Development: Teaching English Learners

Meeting the Multi-Level Challenge

English learners entering middle school come from a variety of backgrounds. Some bring a solid educational foundation from their native country. In their home language, they have developed academic skills that are on a par with their native English-speaking peers. Some of these students may be literate in languages such as Arabic, Russian, Chinese, or in other non-Roman alphabet scripts. Even with the challenge of a new written code to crack, these students already bring many of the skills and experiences that will help them succeed in a structured academic setting. They will be able to build on their academic foundation and draw upon an established repertoire of learning strategies as they approach the challenge of learning English and new academic content in English.

Other English learners come with a patchwork of academic and life experiences. War, epidemics, natural disasters, or economic conditions may have caused students and their families to relocate within their home country or in other countries even before arriving in the U.S. School attendance may have been sporadic, with acquisition of skills and content more random than systematic. Such students may also be affected by the emotional aftermath of violence or trauma. Limited academic experiences and the lack of formal literacy skills create special challenges for these students and their teachers. However, the depth of their life experiences can also enrich learning for both peers and teachers.

Between these ends of the spectrum are English learners with every possible constellation of academic and life experiences. The goal of **High Point** is to ensure that each of these students succeeds in becoming a fluent speaker of English and moves into the academic mainstream at a level comparable to fluent English-speaking peers. How is it possible to meet this range of diverse needs?

One key part of the solution is to use standards-based instruction as the medium for learning English. The language arts, mathematics, science, and social studies content of **High Point** is aligned to national and state curriculum standards, ensuring that students gain important experience with key grade-level concepts, vocabulary, and themes as they progress towards fluency in English.

Another key part of ensuring success for all English learners is to tailor the instruction to students' stages of language acquisition. Language acquisition is a process that moves learners through predictable stages of language development on the path toward native-like fluency. However, the way individuals progress through these stages varies widely depending on many factors, including academic background, life experiences, learning styles, and other aspects of individual development. Progress along the pathway toward fluency is not always signalled by forward movement alone. Rather, a student who shows a growth spurt in acquiring new vocabulary, for example, may exhibit less control in using it grammatically. Such spurts and lags in language development are highly individual, and are a normal part of the language acquisition process. For this reason, it is important to identify where each student stands on the language acquisition continuum, and to then use the instructional strategies and techniques that will be most effective in creating continuing language growth and development.

The first level of **High Point**, **The Basics**, is designed specifically for newcomer students and English learners in the beginning stages of language acquisition. Instructional strategies in the **Teacher's Edition** focus on the needs of preliterate students with no formal schooling, students literate in another primary language, students literate in non-Roman alphabets, and students with interrupted schooling.

At Levels A-C, **High Point** offers differentiated instruction for students across the stages of language acquisition. These differentiated instructional strategies and techniques are embedded through-out the **Teacher's Edition** (see the Multi-Level Strategies features), and are summarized on page T337a to help you target individual students with the most effective language development strategies for their stages of English acquisition.

> *High Point* offers standards-based instruction with specialized strategies for English learners.

The Stages of Language Acquisition

High Point *incorporates instructional strategies and techniques to help English learners move through the stages of language development.*

STAGES AND BEHAVIORS

BEGINNING

Students with limited formal schooling:
- have a language acquisition profile that is similar to Early Beginning students
- need lots of age-appropriate oral-to-print and emergent literacy experiences
- understand new concepts best when they are previewed in their home language

Early Beginning students:
- need to gain familiarity with the sounds, rhythm, and patterns of English
- understand simple messages presented with contextual support (gestures, role-play, etc.)
- respond non-verbally by pointing, gesturing, nodding, or drawing
- begin to respond with yes/no or one- or two-word answers
- read simple language that has already been experienced orally
- write labels, patterned sentences, one- or two-word responses

Advanced Beginning students:
- understand "chunks" or gist of language, and the gist of group reading by relying on picture clues, titles, and summaries
- repeat and recite memorable language; use routine expressions independently
- respond with phrases, fragments, and simple subject/verb-based structures
- respond to literature with structured support
- read familiar, patterned text; read Language Experience texts
- write patterned text, short captions; complete simple cloze sentences

INTERMEDIATE

Early Intermediate students:
- understand more details in spoken English
- respond using longer phrases or sentences with increasing grammatical accuracy
- respond using newly-acquired receptive vocabulary to form messages in English
- read material independently following oral previews or experiences with print
- respond to literature by explaining, describing, comparing, and retelling
- write from models for a variety of purposes

Advanced Intermediate students:
- participate more fully in discussions, including those with academic content
- understand and respond with increasing levels of accuracy and correctness
- respond with connected discourse, using more extensive vocabulary
- respond with higher-order language (persuade, evaluate, etc.)
- read and comprehend a wider range of narrative genre and content texts
- read, write, and discuss content-area concepts in greater depth
- write connected narrative and expository texts

ADVANCED

Early Advanced students:
- understand non-literal, idiomatic, everyday, and academic language
- respond with connected discourse, extensive vocabulary, and decreasing grammatical errors
- read a wider range of narrative and expository texts with increasing comprehension, including self-selected material
- write using more standard forms with increased depth and breadth of topics and purposes and more creative and analytical writing

Advanced/Transitioning students:
- respond using varied grammatical structures and vocabulary comparable to native English speakers of the same age
- read and write a range of grade-level texts in a variety of subjects
- use a repertoire of language-learning strategies to self-monitor, correct, and further develop English language skills

TEACHING STRATEGIES

BEGINNING

Students with limited formal schooling benefit when teachers:
- implement an intensive individualized or small-group emergent literacy program
- include them in group activities by using strategies for Beginning students
- pair students with a "buddy" with the same home language

Beginning students benefit when teachers:
- provide abundant opportunities for active listening, utilizing props, visuals, and real objects
- avoid forcing students to speak before they are ready
- model memorable language with songs, raps, and poems
- pair or group students with more proficient learners
- activate prior knowledge, build background, and use visuals before reading activities
- ask yes/no, either/or, and Who? What? Where? questions; have students complete sentences with one- or two-word responses
- expose students to a variety of understandable texts
- have students label/manipulate pictures and real objects
- provide writing frames and models

INTERMEDIATE

Intermediate students benefit when teachers:
- have students describe personal experiences, objects, etc.
- structure group discussion
- structure research projects and guide use of reference material for research
- provide opportunities to create oral and written narratives
- focus on communication in meaningful contexts where students express themselves in speech and print for a wide range of purposes and audiences
- ask open-ended questions; model, expand, restate, and enrich student language
- use graphic organizers or storyboards for retelling or role-plays
- provide content-area texts, trade books, newspapers, magazines, etc., to promote conceptual development
- respond genuinely to student writing and hold conferences that highlight student strengths and progress

ADVANCED

Advanced students benefit when teachers:
- structure group discussion
- guide use of reference material for research
- facilitate more advanced literature studies
- provide for meaningful writing experiences in a variety of modes and forms (fiction, research, penpals, etc.)
- publish student-authored stories, newsletters, bulletins, etc.
- encourage drama, art, music, and other forms of creative expression to represent meaning and increase students' sense of aesthetics
- continue on-going language development through integrated language arts and content-area activities

Good Teaching Practices for English Learners

*The **High Point** Teacher's Editions incorporate these instructional strategies to address the varying needs of English learners and to maximize growth in language and concept development.*

SET STUDENTS UP FOR SUCCESS!

In **High Point** students acquire English as they learn key grade-level curriculum. To allow students to maximize language learning while processing complex and abstract ideas, each unit begins in a way that sets students up for success:

- **Hands-On Experiences** Each unit is launched with a quick experiential activity that makes the theme of the unit concrete and explicit. For example, in a Community unit, individual students view a visual and list elements that they observe, then repeat the process with a group. This illustrates the powerful dynamics of a community, and the benefits and challenges of working together.

- **Unit Mind Map** As students debrief the Unit Launch activity, they begin to generate key vocabulary that is recycled and developed as the unit progresses. The Unit Mind Map provides an open-ended structure for collecting unit vocabulary, empowering students to take ownership of their learning while providing a structure to facilitate the processing of higher-order vocabulary.

- **Guiding Questions** Each unit in Levels A-C explores two related themes. Guiding questions introduced at the outset of each theme establish some of the key ideas to explore through literature, language arts, and content activities. These questions give students an overview of the exploration they are about to undertake and serve as touchstones while the unit progresses. This process helps make learning objectives—and their mastery—visible to students, further empowering them as learners.

The **High Point** program is structured so that key ideas, vocabulary, and content are reviewed, revisited, and expanded at various points within and across courses. This spiraling helps students connect new learning to familiar material and provides an expanding contextual base to help students assimilate new language and concepts with increasing facility.

BUILD BACKGROUND AND ACTIVATE PRIOR KNOWLEDGE

All English learners—even those with limited or no formal schooling—have enough life experience and knowledge to acquire the complex concepts appropriate for middle school students. However, many students do not have a strong enough command of English to rely on spoken or written language alone to grasp new concepts. Here are two crucial strategies that build context for new concepts:

- **Activate Prior Knowledge** Before you introduce new concepts, review familiar, related concepts that help build context. When you invite students to share their experiences, it helps build a common knowledge base. For newly-arrived students, a quick preview in the home language is often the most effective way to ensure that students grasp a complex new concept. If you cannot provide this support, enlist the help of students, volunteers, or bilingual instructional assistants.

- **Build Background** When students have no prior experience with new concepts, common experiential activities, such as the Unit Launch experiences, will help build the concepts and vocabulary that allow students to grasp complex new concepts.

MAKE IT MEANINGFUL!

Imagine listening to a radio newscast in an unfamiliar language. How much do you think you would really comprehend? Help your students get as much meaning as possible from the language they experience:

- **Use Visuals** A picture is worth a thousand words—in any language! In addition to the visuals included in **High Point**, you may wish to begin a picture file with images from magazines, Internet downloads, and content-area books. Although you may not consider yourself artistic, you'll be pleasantly surprised to see how much a simple sketch on the chalkboard can convey to your students! Real objects that students can hold and manipulate also help anchor new vocabulary and concepts in memory.

- **Use Graphic Organizers** Graphic organizers are concrete visuals that help students see the relationship between words and ideas. Quick sketches added to graphic organizers enhance the comprehensibility of these visuals for Beginners.

- **Body Language** Get creative with facial expressions, gestures, pantomime, and role-plays and see how much information you can convey!

Staff Development: Teaching English Learners **T337b**

- **Restate, Repeat, Reduce Speed** Once you become aware of these simple modifications, you can make your language more comprehensible and build new vocabulary. Incorporate familiar vocabulary and structures into your speech. After using a familiar word, pause and restate using a new expression. This paraphrasing helps link the meaning of new vocabulary to familiar terms. You should also be aware of the length, speed, and complexity of your speech, and modify it to fit your students' needs.

ENCOURAGE INTERACTION

When students learn through an interactive approach, lessons become more memorable and meaningful. Vocabulary and language patterns become anchored in memory, especially for kinesthetic learners.

- **Cooperative Learning** Cooperative learning activities provide a structure that allows students with varying levels of proficiency to participate meaningfully in group projects. These projects offer authentic communication for a wide range of meaningful purposes—from dealing with the logistics of choosing roles, to identifying resources and gathering information, to presenting findings. (See "Cooperative Learning Strategies" on page T337d for detailed descriptions.)

> In an interactive approach, lessons are more memorable and meaningful.

CREATE MIXED GROUPINGS

If your class includes students at various levels of English proficiency, use heterogeneous groupings to turn this challenge to your advantage. When students at differing proficiency levels work together, they all must stretch their communication skills in order to accomplish their goals. This also builds a positive, cooperative learning environment.

LOOK AT LEARNING STRATEGIES

When students understand the strategies that help build language, they can support their own learning process. In addition to the *High Point* lessons in learning strategies, try these techniques:

- **Build Metacognitive Awareness** Be sure to familiarize students with the "Strategies for Learning Language" in the Handbook (see page T299). Encourage students to identify and share strategies they use successfully.

- **Tailor Instruction to Address Language Transfer Issues** See the Phonics and Language Structure Transfer Charts on pages T338–349 or seek help from bilingual parents and aides to acquaint yourself with points of positive and negative transfer between your students' home languages and English. This information will help you know which skills to reinforce and how to address error correction.

- **Capitalize on Cognates** Students' home languages can provide helpful information for building context and meaning. As you preview literature, encourage students to look for home-language cognates, and to see how much they already know! Cognates are noted in some Multi-Level Strategies to facilitate their use of this strategy.

SEND LEARNING HOME

The *High Point Newsletters* (available in seven languages; see the **Teacher's Resource Book**) allow you to extend learning into students' homes, where families can participate in exploring unit themes in their home language.

CONNECT TO CULTURE

High Point reflects a wide range of cultural traditions. Extend this inclusive approach in your classroom by welcoming students' contributions about the cultural traditions they know best. When students respect each others' linguistic and cultural backgrounds, they will all feel more secure as they learn the language and culture of the United States. A comfortable, non-threatening classroom environment helps all learners achieve at optimum levels.

T337c Staff Development: Teaching English Learners

Cooperative Learning Strategies

High Point's cooperative learning activities involve students of varying language proficiencies in content-rich activities. These four structures are introduced in The Basics and six others are added in Levels A–C.

STRUCTURE & GRAPHIC	DESCRIPTION	BENEFITS & PURPOSES
INSIDE-OUTSIDE CIRCLE	• Students stand in concentric circles facing each other. • Students in the outside circle ask questions; those inside answer. • On a signal, students rotate to create new partnerships. • On another signal, students trade inside/outside roles.	• Talking one-on-one with a variety of partners gives risk-free practice in speaking skills. • Interactions can be structured to focus on specific speaking skills. • Students practice both speaking and active listening.
TEAM WORD WEBBING	• Provide each team with a single large piece of paper. Give each student a different colored marker. • Teacher assigns a topic for a word web. • Each student adds to the part of the web nearest to him/her. • On a signal, students rotate the paper and each student adds to the nearest part again.	• Individual input to a group product ensures participation by all students. • Shifting points of view support both broad and in-depth understanding of concepts.
THINK, PAIR, SHARE	• Students think about a topic suggested by the teacher. • Pairs discuss the topic. • Students individually share information with the class.	• The opportunity for self-talk during individual think time allows the student to formulate thoughts before speaking. • Discussion with a partner reduces performance anxiety and enhances understanding.
THREE-STEP INTERVIEW	• Students form pairs. • Student A interviews student B about a topic. • Partners reverse roles. • Student A shares with the class information from student B; then B shares information from student A.	• Interviewing supports language acquisition by providing scripts for expression. • Responding provides opportunities for structured self-expression.

Cooperative Learning Strategies **T337d**

Language Transfer Issues

English learners arrive at the doors of our schools from many different countries and every walk of life. With them, they bring a wealth of linguistic and cultural diversity which transforms the simplest classroom into a unique cultural experience.

Regardless of their previous educational experiences, second-language learners have a developed sense of how language operates. Through home language experiences, they understand how sounds combine to form words and how words combine to convey meaning, sense, and ideas. Students' understanding of their first language serves sometimes to accelerate and other times to detour their acquisition of similar skills in English.

When you learn to identify and capitalize on students' existing language skills, you can accelerate their progress. For example, you can use explicit instruction to develop pronunciation skills by explaining how sounds are the same or approximate. Once you know which grammatical structures transfer negatively to standard English conventions, you can adjust instruction to provide maximum reinforcement for skills lessons on these structures.

The charts on the following pages address language transfer items between English and six of the most common languages spoken by English learners in U.S. schools.

- The **Phonics Transfer Chart** compares the sounds of English to those of six other languages. As you work with students to teach phonics or develop pronunciation skills, use the chart to identify which sounds students may already know and which are new. In your instruction, devote particular practice to sounds that do not exist, or exist with different symbols, in students' primary languages. Take time to explain and demonstrate the mouth and tongue positions noted in the chart on pages T342–T345. Provide mirrors so that students can watch themselves as they try out the sounds of English.

> **Students' understanding of their first language serves sometimes to accelerate and other times to detour English acquisition.**

- The **Language Structure Transfer Chart** explains grammar differences between English and six other languages to identify points of negative transfer. Compare students' errors to the transfer errors in the chart. This will help you understand why the error is occurring so that you can design appropriate instruction. You may also wish to encourage students to identify and share ways in which English parallels or differs from their own home languages.

For languages other than those shown in the charts, make use of the resources in your district (including community volunteers, district language translators, and in-class primary language support) to identify the points of positive and negative transfer for your students.

Also take advantage of the Multi Level Strategies in this Teacher's Edition that address transfer items for students literate in the primary languages noted in the charts and other languages, such as Arabic, Farsi, Japanese, Polish, Portuguese, and Russian.

Hampton-Brown recognizes that more than 150 languages are spoken by English learners in our schools. We hope these charts, though they address just six of those languages, are a good start on the transfer issues involved in the education of our English learners.

T337e Staff Development: Teaching English Learners

Transfer Charts

The following charts are designed to help teachers locate potential transfer issues in a simple, practical way. Hampton-Brown recognizes that language structures and pronunciation can vary based upon multiple factors including region, dialect, and even sociological issues. For this reason, we have enlisted the aid of the following language consultants, educators, linguists, and phonologists to compile and review information about each of the six target languages. We gratefully acknowledge their assistance and appreciate the contributions they made to the compilation of the Transfer Charts. We especially acknowledge the assistance of OMA Graphics, Inc., in Fremont, California, in locating language consultants throughout the United States.

In a few cases, the language consultants were unable to reach a consensus on specific items. The resulting charts show our best attempt to reconcile the information in a clear and consistent fashion. We welcome additional input and suggestions that will assist us in updating this information and in adding information for other languages in future publications.

Cantonese Language Consultants

Dr. John Whelpton
English Instructor
Baptist Lui Ming Choi Secondary School
Shatin, Hong Kong, PRC

Jihua Zhou
Cantonese Professor
Defense Language Institute
Monterey, California

Haitian-Creole Language Consultants

Dr. Jean-Robert Cadely
Associate Professor
Florida International University
Miami, Florida

Hmong Language Consultants

Max Leyang
ELL Community Specialist
St. Paul Public School District
St. Paul, Minnesota

Brian McKibben
Author, *English-White Hmong Dictionary*, 1992
Bridgeport, West Virginia

Korean Language Consultants

Koong-Ja Lauridsen
Assistant Principal and Education Technology Consultant
Alexandria Avenue Elementary School
Los Angeles, California

Jewel H. Lee
Assistant Professor
Defense Language Institute
Monterey, California

Saekyun Harry Lee
Assistant Professor
Defense Language Institute
Monterey, California

Spanish Language Consultants

Guadalupe López
Senior Editor
Hampton-Brown
Carmel, California

Vietnamese Language Consultants

Le Ba Nhon
Associate Professor
Defense Language Institute Foreign Language Center
Monterey, California

Mai Tran
Translator for Asian Pacific and Other Languages Offices
Los Angeles Unified School District
Los Angeles, California

Phonics Transfer Chart

ENGLISH			SPANISH		CANTONESE		VIETNAMESE	
Phoneme	Grapheme	Key Word	Sound Transfer?	Sound-Symbol Match?	Sound Transfer?	Sound-Symbol Match?	Sound Transfer?	Sound-Symbol Match?
Consonants								
/b/	b	book	yes	yes	approx.	no	approx.	yes
/k/	c	carrot	yes	yes	yes	no	yes	yes
	k	key	yes	yes	yes	no	yes	yes
	ck	check	yes	no	yes	no	yes	no
/d/	d	desk	approx.	yes	approx.	no	approx.	yes
/f/	f	fish	yes	yes	yes	no	yes	no
/g/	g	girl	yes	yes	approx.	no	yes	yes
/h/	h	hand	yes	no	yes	no	yes	yes
/j/	j	jacket	no	no	approx.	no	approx.	no
	g	cage	no	no	approx.	no	approx.	no
	dge	badge	no	no	approx	no	approx.	no
/l/	l	lamp	yes	yes	yes	no	yes	yes
/m/	m	map	yes	yes	yes	no	yes	yes
/n/	n	newspaper	yes	yes	yes	no	yes	yes
/p/	p	pizza	yes	yes	yes	no	yes	yes
/kw/	qu	quarter	yes	no	approx.	no	yes	yes
/r/	r	red	approx.	approx.	no	no	no	no
/s/	s	seed	yes	yes	yes	no	yes	yes
	c	city	yes	yes	yes	no	yes	yes
/t/	t	ten	yes	yes	yes	no	approx.	yes
/v/	v	van	yes	yes	no	no	yes	yes
/w/	w	window	yes	yes	yes	no	no	no
/ks/	x	six	yes	yes	no	no	no	no
/y/	y	yellow	yes	yes	yes	no	no	no
/z/	z	zero	no	no	no	no	yes	no
Digraphs								
/ch/	ch	chin	yes	yes	approx.	no	no	no
	tch	match	yes	no	approx.	no	no	no
/sh/	sh	shell	no	no	no	no	yes	no
/hw/	wh	whisk	no	no	no	no	no	no
/th/	th	bath	approx.	no	no	no	approx.	yes
/TH/	th	this	approx.	no	no	no	no	no
/ng/	ng	ring	yes	yes	yes	no	yes	yes
Short Vowels								
/a/	a	map	approx.	no	no	no	approx.	yes
/e/	e	ten	yes	yes	approx.	no	approx.	yes
/i/	i	lid	approx.	no	approx.	no	no	no
/o/	o	dot	approx.	no	approx.	no	approx.	yes
/u/	u	cup	approx.	no	approx.	no	yes	no

T338 Staff Development: Teaching English Learners

TEACHER'S CORNER

ENGLISH			HMONG		KOREAN		HAITIAN CREOLE	
Phoneme	Grapheme	Key Word	Sound Transfer?	Sound-Symbol Match?	Sound Transfer?	Sound-Symbol Match?	Sound Transfer?	Sound-Symbol Match?
Consonants								
/b/	b	book	approx.	no	approx.	no	yes	yes
/k/	c	carrot	yes	no	yes	no	yes	yes
	k	key	yes	yes	yes	no	yes	yes
	ck	check	yes	no	yes	no	yes	yes
/d/	d	desk	yes	yes	approx.	no	yes	yes
/f/	f	fish	yes	yes	no	no	yes	yes
/g/	g	girl	approx.	no	approx.	no	yes	yes
/h/	h	hand	yes	yes	yes	no	approx.	yes
/j/	j	jacket	no	no	approx.	no	yes	yes
	g	cage	no	no	approx.	no	yes	yes
	dge	badge	no	no	approx.	no	yes	yes
/l/	l	lamp	yes	yes	yes	no	yes	yes
/m/	m	map	yes	yes	yes	no	yes	yes
/n/	n	newspaper	yes	yes	yes	no	yes	yes
/p/	p	pizza	approx.	yes	yes	no	yes	yes
/kw/	qu	quarter	no	no	yes	no	yes	yes
/r/	r	red	no	no	no	no	yes	yes
/s/	s	seed	yes	no	yes	no	approx.	approx.
	c	city	yes	no	yes	no	approx.	approx.
/t/	t	ten	approx.	yes	yes	no	yes	yes
/v/	v	van	yes	yes	no	no	yes	yes
/w/	w	window	no	no	yes	no	yes	yes
/ks/	x	six	no	no	yes	no	yes	yes
/y/	y	yellow	yes	yes	yes	no	yes	yes
/z/	z	zero	no	no	no	no	yes	yes
Digraphs								
/ch/	ch	chin	yes	no	yes	no	yes	yes
	tch	match	yes	no	yes	no	yes	yes
/sh/	sh	shell	yes	no	yes	no	yes	yes
/hw/	wh	whisk	no	no	yes	no	yes	yes
/th/	th	bath	no	no	no	no	yes	yes
/TH/	th	this	no	no	no	no	yes	yes
/ng/	ng	ring	yes	no	yes	no	approx.	approx.
Short Vowels								
/a/	a	map	yes	yes	yes	no	yes	yes
/e/	e	ten	no	no	yes	no	no	no
/i/	i	lid	no	no	yes	no	yes	yes
/o/	o	dot	approx.	yes	approx.	no	yes	yes
/u/	u	cup	no	no	yes	no	no	no

Phonics Transfer Chart **T339**

Phonics Transfer Chart, continued

ENGLISH			SPANISH		CANTONESE		VIETNAMESE	
Phoneme	Grapheme	Key Word	Sound Transfer?	Sound-Symbol Match?	Sound Transfer?	Sound-Symbol Match?	Sound Transfer?	Sound-Symbol Match?
Long Vowels								
/ā/	a_e	cake	yes	no	approx.	no	approx.	no
	ai	sail	yes	no	approx.	no	approx.	no
	ay	tray	yes	no	approx.	no	approx.	no
/ē/	ee	feet	yes	no	approx.	no	yes	no
	ea	sea	yes	no	approx.	no	yes	no
	y	happy	yes	no	approx.	no	yes	no
/ī/	i_e	bike	yes	no	approx.	no	yes	no
	ie	tie	yes	no	approx.	no	yes	no
	igh	night	yes	no	approx.	no	yes	no
	y	sky	yes	no	approx.	no	yes	no
/ō/	o_e	globe	yes	no	approx.	no	approx.	no
	oa	boat	yes	no	approx.	no	approx.	no
	ow	rowboat	yes	no	approx.	no	approx.	no
/ū/	u_e	flutes	yes	no	approx.	no	yes	yes
	ui	suit	yes	no	approx.	no	yes	no
	ue	blue	yes	no	approx.	no	yes	no
/yōō/	u_e	mule	yes	no	approx.	no	no	no
	ue	rescue	yes	no	approx.	no	no	no
R-Controlled Vowels								
/är/	ar	star	approx.	yes	approx.	no	no	no
/ôr/	or	horn	approx.	yes	approx.	no	no	no
/ûr/	er	fern	approx.	yes	approx.	no	no	no
	ir	bird	approx.	no	approx.	no	no	no
	ur	curb	approx.	no	approx.	no	no	no
/âr/	air	chair	no	no	no	no	no	no
	ear	bear	no	no	no	no	no	no
/îr/	eer	deer	no	no	no	no	no	no
	ear	tear	no	no	no	no	no	no
Variant Vowels								
/oi/	oi	coin	yes	yes	approx.	no	approx.	yes
	oy	boy	yes	yes	approx.	no	approx.	no
/ou/	ou	cloud	yes	no	approx.	no	yes	no
	ow	crown	yes	no	approx.	no	yes	no
/ô/	aw	saw	approx.	no	yes	no	yes	no
	au	laundry	approx.	no	approx.	no	yes	no
/ôl/	al	salt	approx.	yes	approx.	no	no	no
	all	ball	approx.	no	approx.	no	no	no
/ōō/	oo	moon	yes	no	approx.	no	approx.	no
	ew	screw	yes	no	approx.	no	approx.	no
/ŏŏ/	oo	book	no	no	approx.	no	approx.	no
/ə/	a (initial syllable)	asleep	no	no	no	no	approx.	no

T340 Staff Development: Teaching English Learners

TEACHER'S CORNER

ENGLISH			HMONG		KOREAN		HAITIAN CREOLE	
Phoneme	Grapheme	Key Word	Sound Transfer?	Sound-Symbol Match?	Sound Transfer?	Sound-Symbol Match?	Sound Transfer?	Sound-Symbol Match?
Long Vowels								
/ā/	a_e	cake	approx.	no	yes	no	yes	yes
	ai	sail	approx.	no	yes	no	yes	no
	ay	tray	approx.	no	yes	no	yes	no
/ē/	ee	feet	yes	no	yes	no	yes	yes
	ea	sea	yes	no	yes	no	yes	no
	y	happy	yes	no	yes	no	yes	no
/ī/	i_e	bike	yes	no	yes	no	yes	yes
	ie	tie	yes	no	yes	no	yes	yes
	igh	night	yes	no	yes	no	yes	yes
	y	sky	yes	no	yes	no	yes	yes
/ō/	o_e	globe	no	no	yes	no	yes	yes
	oa	boat	no	no	yes	no	yes	yes
	ow	rowboat	no	no	yes	no	yes	yes
/ū/	u_e	flutes	yes	yes	yes	no	yes	yes
	ui	suit	yes	no	yes	no	yes	yes
	ue	blue	yes	no	yes	no	yes	no
/yōō/	u_e	mule	no	no	yes	no	no	no
	ue	rescue	no	no	yes	no	no	no
R-Controlled Vowels								
/är/	ar	star	no	no	no	no	no	no
/ôr/	or	horn	no	no	no	no	no	no
/ûr/	er	fern	no	no	no	no	no	no
	ir	bird	no	no	no	no	no	no
	ur	curb	no	no	no	no	no	no
/âr/	air	chair	no	no	no	no	no	no
	ear	bear	no	no	no	no	no	no
/îr/	eer	deer	no	no	no	no	no	no
	ear	tear	no	no	no	no	no	no
Variant Vowels								
/oi/	oi	coin	no	no	yes	no	yes	yes
	oy	boy	no	no	yes	no	yes	yes
/ou/	ou	cloud	approx.	no	yes	no	yes	yes
	ow	crown	approx.	no	yes	no	yes	no
/ô/	aw	saw	approx.	no	approx.	no	yes	no
	au	laundry	approx.	no	approx.	no	yes	yes
/ôl/	al	salt	no	no	approx.	no	yes	yes
	all	ball	no	no	approx.	no	yes	yes
/ōō/	oo	moon	yes	no	yes	no	yes	yes
	ew	screw	yes	no	yes	no	yes	yes
/ŏŏ/	oo	book	no	no	approx.	no	no	no
/ə/	a (initial syllable)	asleep	no	no	yes	no	yes	yes

Phonics Transfer Chart **T341**

Articulation of English Consonant and Vowel Sounds

WHAT ARE THE CLASSIFICATIONS OF CONSONANT PHONEMES?

Consonant phonemes may be classified according to place of articulation, manner of articulation, and whether they are voiced or unvoiced. They can be further classified as either continuous or stop sounds. To produce a consonant phoneme the air flow is cut off either partially or completely.

CONSONANT PHONEME CLASSIFICATIONS

Place of Articulation
Where in the mouth is the sound produced?
- Lips (bilabial)
- Lips and teeth (labiodental)
- Tongue between teeth (dental)
- Tongue behind teeth (alveolar)
- Roof of mouth (palatal)
- Back of mouth (velar)
- Throat

Manner of Articulation
How is the sound produced?
- PLOSIVES: formed by closing or blocking off the air flow and then exploding a puff of air; for example, /b/ as in box.
- NASALS: formed when the mouth is closed forcing air through the nose; for example, /m/ as in man.
- FRICATIVES: formed by narrowing the air channel and then forcing air through it, creating friction in the mouth; for example, /v/ as in voice.

Manner of Articulation (continued)
- AFFRICATIVES: formed by a stop followed by a fricative; for example, /ch/ as in chip.
- GLIDES: formed in similar ways as vowels; for example, /y/ as in yes.
- LIQUIDS: formed by interrupting the air flow slightly, but no friction results; for example, /l/ as in line.

Voiced or Unvoiced
- VOICED: the vocal cords vibrate; for example, /z/ as in zoo.
- UNVOICED: the vocal cords do not vibrate; for example, /s/ as in sit.

Continuous or Stop
- CONTINUOUS: a sound that can be pronounced for several seconds without distorting the sound; for example, /s/ as in sun.
- STOP: a sound that can be pronounced for only an instant; for example, /p/ as in pop.

CONSONANT PHONEME ARTICULATION (Boldface phoneme indicates voiced sound.)

Manner ▶ ▼ Place	Plosives	Nasals	Fricatives	Affricatives	Glides	Liquids
Lips	**/b/** /p/	**/m/**			**/w/** /hw/	
Lips and teeth			**/v/** /f/			
Tongue between teeth			**/TH/** /th/			
Tongue behind teeth	**/d/** /t/	**/n/**	**/z/** /s/			**/l/**
Roof of mouth			**/zh/** /sh/	**/j/** /ch/	**/y/**	**/r/**
Back of mouth	**/g/** /k/	**/ng/**				
Throat					/h/	

CONSONANT PHONEMES

Continuous Sounds
/f/, /l/, /m/, /n/, /r/, /s/, /v/, /w/, /y/, /z/

Stop Sounds
/b/, /d/, /g/, /h/, /j/, /k/, /p/, /kw/qu/, /t/, /ks/x/

T342 Staff Development: Teaching English Learners

Some students may need extra practice in producing consonant sounds that do not transfer from their primary languages. Use the scripts and information below as a model for discussing the English consonant sounds.

/m/

Place of Articulation: Lips
Manner of Articulation: Nasal
Voiced

When I ask you to say /m/, what part of your mouth moves? (the lips) How? (They come together.) Does any air come out? (yes) Try holding your nose. Can you still say /m/? (no) That is because the air comes out through your nose.

/p/

Place of Articulation: Lips
Manner of Articulation: Stop
Unvoiced

Your lips help make /p/ also. Do they stay together? (no) They start out closed and then they open. Does any air come out? (a lot!) This sound stops the air for a moment, and then the air rushes out. Put your hand in front of your mouth and feel the air when you say /p/.

/t/

Place of Articulation: Tongue behind teeth
Manner of Articulation: Stop
Unvoiced

Now say the sound /t/. Do you feel a lot of air coming out? (yes) Try to close your lips and say /t/. Can you do it? (no) Another part of your mouth makes /t/. Can you feel what part? (the tongue) Where does it stop the air? (on the hard ridge behind your upper teeth)

/b/

Place of Articulation: Lips
Manner of Articulation: Stop
Voiced

Do you remember when we practiced making /p/? What stopped the air? (the lips) Could you feel a lot of air come out? (yes) Now I want you to use your mouth in the same way, but use your voice also. This sound is /b/. Do you think you really use your voice? Cover your ears and say /p/ and /b/. Which one sounds louder? (/b/) That is because you are using your voice. Say big, pig. When you change the sound, you change the meaning.

/k/

Place of Articulation: Back of mouth
Manner of Articulation: Stop
Unvoiced

Try making /k/. Does a lot of air come out? (yes) Let's find out what stops the air. Do your lips move? (no) Do you put your tongue up behind your top teeth? (no) Where is your tongue? (The front is low because the back of the tongue stops the air.) Where? (in the back of the mouth)

/n/

Place of Articulation: Tongue behind teeth
Manner of Articulation: Nasal
Voiced

Say the sound /n/. Keep making the sound and put your hand in front of your mouth. Do you feel any air come out? (no) Hold your nose. Can you still make the sound? (no) In what other sound did air come out through the nose? (/m/) Make that sound now. What did you have to move? (your lips) We don't use our lips for the /n/ sound. Make /m/, then /n/. Where did your tongue go? Say map, nap. The tongue is in a different place even though the air comes out the nose.

/d/

Place of Articulation: Tongue behind teeth
Manner of Articulation: Stop
Voiced

Try making /d/. Does a lot of air come out? (yes) How do you know that? (by putting your hand in front of your mouth) Cover your ears when you make /d/. Do you use your voice in making this sound? (yes) Say /d/, /t/, /d/, /t/. How are these sounds different? (We use our voice for /d/ but not for /t/.)

/g/

Place of Articulation: Back of mouth
Manner of Articulation: Stop
Voiced

Look at me as I say the sound /g/. Can you see any part of my face move? (no) (If someone notices your throat, you should recognize the good observation and come back to it in a moment.) Now you make the sound and see if a lot of air comes out. (yes) If you didn't put your hand up to check, you were only guessing. Do you use your voice? How can you be sure? (cover your ears) Notice where your tongue stops the air when you start to make the sound. (Start to make the sound and then stop.) Is it the front of your mouth or the back? (the back) Now say /g/, /k/, /g/, /k/. We make these sounds in the same place, but we use our voice for one. Which one? (/g/)

/l/

Place of Articulation: Tongue behind teeth
Manner of Articulation: Liquid
Voiced

Make the sound /l/. Does a lot of air come out? (no) If you said yes, try putting your hand in front of your mouth and saying /l/, /t/, /l/, /t/, or melt. The air is not stopped for /l/, so you don't feel a puff of air when you make this sound. Make /l/ and hold it. Can you make /t/ and hold it? (no) The air has to stop on /t/ and then rush out. For /l/, it comes out at the sides of the tongue. Can you tell where the tip of the tongue is? (on the upper ridge behind the front teeth)

Articulation of English Sounds

/f/

Place of Articulation: Lips and teeth **Manner of Articulation: Fricative** **Unvoiced**	*Try making /f/. Can you make this sound and hold it?* (yes) *Watch me make the sound /f/. What part of my mouth moved?* (Children will probably say lips.) *Look again closely. Do both lips move?* (no, just one) *Which?* (the lower one) *Make the sound /f/ yourself. The lower lip comes up close to your upper teeth and makes the air sound noisy. Hold the /f/ and hear how noisy the air is.*

/h/

Place of Articulation: Throat **Manner of Articulation: Glide** **Unvoiced**	*Try saying /h/, /h/, /h/. Can you feel a puff of air?* (yes) *Keep your hand in front of your mouth and say* e-e-e. *Now say* he, he, he. *Did you feel a difference from when you said* e-e-e? (yes) *Now try* o-o-o, ho, ho, ho. *When we put a quiet puff of air before another sound, it is the /h/ sound. Say* i, hi, *or* eat, heat. *Does the /h/ sound make a difference in the meaning?* (yes)

/r/

Place of Articulation: Roof of mouth **Manner of Articulation: Liquid** **Voiced**	*Make the sound /r/. Can you hold this sound for a long time?* (yes) */r/ does not stop the air. Stop making /r/, but keep your tongue ready to say the sound. Now take a deep breath. The part of your tongue that feels cool is the part that helps to make this sound. It is the under part of the tip of your tongue. This part comes close to a part of your mouth. What part of your mouth does the tongue come close to?* (the roof of the mouth) *Say* at. *Now put the /r/ first and say* rat. *Do* at *and* rat *mean different things?* (Yes, the /r/ makes a difference in meaning.)

/w/

Place of Articulation: Lips **Manner of Articulation: Glide** **Voiced**	*I am going to get my mouth ready to say this next sound, but I won't say it. See if you can guess what it is.* (Round your lips to pronounce /w/, but do not say it.) *Can you tell me what sound I was going to make?* (/w/) *Now everyone make the /w/ sound. What part of your mouth moves?* (your lips) *What do they do?* (get round and tight) *Do you use your voice to say the /w/ sound?* (yes) *Say* itch, *then* witch. *Does the /w/ sound make a difference in meaning?* (yes)

/sh/

Place of Articulation: Roof of mouth **Manner of Articulation: Fricative** **Unvoiced**	*Now we are going to make another sound where the lips are round but not as tight. Try /sh/. Can you hold this sound?* (yes) (Have a child stand in the corner of the room and make the /sh/.) *Could everyone hear (child's name) make the /sh/?* (yes) *The air is very noisy. Remember, the air gets noisy when it rushes past a close or narrow place. The lips help make this place. So does the top of the front part of the tongue. It comes close to part of your upper mouth.*

/s/

Place of Articulation: Tongue behind teeth **Manner of Articulation: Fricative** **Unvoiced**	*Watch me change from /sh/ to this sound, /s/. How do my lips change?* (They are no longer rounded.) *Does the air make a lot of noise in /s/?* (yes) *Are your teeth close together or far apart?* (close) *The top of your tongue makes this sound also, but it has moved from the ridge to come close to another part of your mouth. Can you tell where?* (It comes close behind your teeth.) *Say* she, see, *or* shock, sock. *Does /s/ make a difference in meaning?* (yes)

SOURCE

From the *CORE Teaching Reading Sourcebook* (pp. 3.6–3.9) by Bill Honig, Linda Diamond, and Linda Gutlohn. Reprinted with permission of Arena Press, Novato, CA. Copyright 2000 by CORE. All rights reserved. This material was adapted from *Phonological Awareness Training for Reading* (pp. 7, 32, 33–34) by Joseph K. Torgesen and Bryan R. Bryant, 1994. Austin, TX: PRO-ED. Copyright © 1994 by PRO-ED, Inc. Adapted with permission.

Teacher's Corner

WHAT ARE THE CLASSIFICATIONS OF VOWEL PHONEMES?

To produce a consonant phoneme, the air flow is cut off either partially or completely; in order to produce a vowel phoneme, the air flow is unobstructed, or continuous. Vowel phonemes are classified as continuous sounds. They are further classified according to tongue and mouth position.

VOWEL PHONEME CLASSIFICATIONS

Tongue Position
1. Is the tongue high, mid, or low in the mouth?
2. Is the tongue near the front, central, or back of the mouth?

Mouth Position
1. How rounded are the lips?
2. How tense are the mouth and jaw muscles?

In the chart below, the most common English spellings are listed under each vowel sound. Notice that to pronounce the /ē/ sound in the word *three*, the mouth position is wide and smiling; the jaw muscles are tense. To pronounce the /o/ sound in the word *hot*, the mouth position is round and wide open; the jaw muscles are relaxed. To pronounce the /o͞o/ sound in the word *moon*, the mouth position is round and partially open; the jaw muscles are tense.

VOWEL PHONEMES BY MOUTH POSITION

/ē/	/i/	/ā/	/e/	/a/	/ī/	/ə/	/o/	/u/	/aw/	/ō/	/o͝o/	/o͞o/
three	hit	cake	met	hat	lime	table	hot	but	saw	poke	book	moon
these	been	sail	lead	have	tie	about	sock	blood	ball	toe	put	cube
me	gym	tray	said	plaid	sight	soda	talk	rough	water	coat	would	suit
eat		they	says	laugh	sky	apron	father	does	cause	show		chew
key		eight			rifle		broad	cover		open		ruby
sunny		vein			buy			among		old		
thief		great										
either												

/oi/ /oy/ coil, toy, lawyer

/ou/ /ow/ how, loud

/ûr/ bird, her, fur

/är/ far

/ôr/ four, or

Articulation of English Sounds **T345**

Language Structure Transfer Chart

ENGLISH STRUCTURE	LANGUAGE TRANSFER ISSUE	LANGUAGES	SAMPLE TRANSFER ERRORS IN ENGLISH
Articles	no indefinite articles	**Chinese** **Hmong** **Korean** **Vietnamese**	He goes to one class on Wednesdays. = He goes to a class on Wednesdays. I bought one cake from bakery. = I bought a cake from a bakery.
	definite article can be omitted	**Hmong** **Spanish**	Do you have book? = Do you have the book? Do you have a book?
	indefinite article is not used before a profession	**Chinese** **Haitian Creole** (article is optional if the predicate contains the verb "to be") **Korean** **Spanish** **Vietnamese**	He is teacher. = He is a teacher. My sister is famous doctor. = My sister is a famous doctor.
	definite article can be used with a profession	**Spanish**	The Professor Ruiz is helpful. = Professor Ruiz is helpful.
	singular and plural definite articles are added at the end of nouns	**Haitian Creole** **Example:** zanmi an = friend (the) zanmi yo = friends (the)	*Students may place definite articles incorrectly.*
Nouns	no plural form for nouns (plurals can be expressed through an adjective quantifier)	**Chinese** **Hmong** **Korean** (plurals are usually used for "people" nouns, such as "my friends," and other nouns) **Vietnamese**	I have many good idea. = I have many good ideas. The paper has several problem. = The paper has several problems.
	no plural form after a number	**Chinese** **Haitian Creole** (plural form is often omitted) **Hmong** **Korean** **Vietnamese**	There are three new student. = There are three new students. Vacation is four week. = Vacation is four weeks.
	plural is formed by placing a plural marker after the noun	**Haitian Creole** (indefinite plurals are unmarked) **Korean**	*Students may add an additional word rather than adding -s to the noun.*

T346 Staff Development: Teaching English Learners

Teacher's Corner

ENGLISH STRUCTURE	LANGUAGE TRANSFER ISSUE	LANGUAGES	SAMPLE TRANSFER ERRORS IN ENGLISH
Nouns (continued)	In English, *-es* is added only after the consonants *s, x, ch, sh, ss*. Also, *y* is changed to *i* before adding *-es*. In other languages, *-es* is added to nouns that end in *y* or any consonant to form the plural.	**Spanish**	*walles* = walls *rayes* = rays
	English contains noncount nouns that do not have a plural form (for example: *fishing, money, bread, honesty, water,* and *snow*). Other languages do not distinguish between count and noncount nouns.	**Chinese** **Haitian Creole** **Hmong** **Korean** **Vietnamese**	I like dancings. = I like dancing. She wears jewelrys. = She wears jewelry. I eat cereals for breakfast. = I eat cereal for breakfast.
	proper names can be listed last-name first **Chinese Example:** Chan Fu Kwan is written last-name first without a comma. **Vietnamese Example:** Tran My Bao is written last, middle, first.	**Chinese** (always last-name first) **Hmong** (in Asia) **Korean** **Vietnamese**	Teachers and students may confuse first and last names.
	a first name is preferred when repeating a person's name	**Hmong** **Vietnamese**	Mr. Kou Xiong is a teacher. Mr. Kou (first name) speaks many languages.
	possessive nouns are formed with an *of* phrase	**Haitian Creole** (Southern Haiti only) **Spanish** **Vietnamese**	This is the chair of Jamie. = This is Jamie's chair.
Pronouns	no distinction between subject and object pronouns	**Chinese** **Haitian Creole** **Hmong** **Spanish** **Vietnamese**	I gave the forms to she. = I gave the forms to her. Him helped I. = He helped me.
	no gender difference for third person singular pronouns	**Chinese** (spoken language only) **Haitian Creole** **Hmong** (uses the pronoun *it*) **Vietnamese** (uses familiar form of third person singular)	The boy carried her bag. = The boy carried his bag. Talk to the girl and give it advice. = Talk to the girl and give her advice.
	no distinction between simple, compound, subject, object, and reflexive pronouns	**Hmong**	The book is I. = The book is mine. She is I sister. = She is my sister. I go I. = I go by myself.

Language Structure Transfer Chart **T347**

Language Structure Transfer Chart, continued

ENGLISH STRUCTURE	LANGUAGE TRANSFER ISSUE	LANGUAGES	SAMPLE TRANSFER ERRORS IN ENGLISH
Pronouns (continued)	no relative pronouns	**Korean** (modifying clause can function as a relative clause) **Vietnamese**	Look at the backpack is on the floor. = Look at the backpack which is on the floor.
	can omit the pronoun *it* as a subject	**Chinese** **Hmong** **Korean** **Vietnamese**	What time? = What time is it? Three o'clock already. = It is three o'clock already.
	definite articles can be used in place of some possessive pronouns	**Spanish** (definite article used for parts of the body)	Cindy broke the leg. = Cindy broke her leg.
	possessive pronoun is formed by placing a separate word or character before the pronoun	**Vietnamese**	This car is (of) him. = This car is his.
	possessive pronoun is formed by placing a separate word, character, or article between the pronoun and the noun	**Chinese** (suffix may be omitted in some cases) **Hmong**	he (possessive character) book = his book
	possessive pronoun is placed after the noun	**Haitian Creole**	That book is (for) me. = That is my book.
	possessive pronouns are omitted when the association is clear	**Korean** **Vietnamese**	He raised hand. = He raised his hand.
	no distinction between personal pronouns and possessive pronouns	**Vietnamese**	It is book I. = It is my book.
Verbs	the verb *to be* can be omitted with adjectives and prepositional phrases	**Chinese** **Haitian Creole** **Hmong** **Korean** **Vietnamese**	We always cheerful. = We are always cheerful. I hungry. = I am hungry. You at home. = You are at home.
	the verb *to be* is not used for adjectives or places	**Hmong** **Vietnamese**	She beautiful. = She is beautiful. The book on the table. = The book is on the table.
	no tense inflections (tense is usually indicated through context, or by adding an expression of time)	**Chinese** **Hmong** (infinitive form of the verb is used with an expression of time) **Vietnamese**	When I am small, I ask many questions. = When I was small, I asked many questions. She teach math next semester. = She will teach math next semester.

T348 Staff Development: Teaching English Learners

ENGLISH STRUCTURE	LANGUAGE TRANSFER ISSUE	LANGUAGES	SAMPLE TRANSFER ERRORS IN ENGLISH
Verbs (continued)	verb is not inflected for person and number	**Chinese** **Haitian Creole** **Hmong** **Korean** (verbs are inflected to reflect age or status) **Vietnamese**	That house have a big door. = That house has a big door. Everyone like you. = Everyone likes you.
	several verbs can be used together with no words or punctuation to separate them	**Hmong** **Vietnamese**	I cook eat at home. = I cook and eat at home.
	no gerund form (*-ing*) and/or no distinction between gerunds and infinitives	**Chinese** (no form to show that an action is ongoing) **Haitian Creole** **Hmong** **Korean** **Spanish** **Vietnamese**	She hates to read. = She hates reading. She kept to talk. = She kept talking.
	verb tense does not change within the same sentence	**Haitian Creole** **Hmong**	When we finish, we leave. = When we finish, we will leave.
	present perfect tense can be used in place of past tense	**Haitian Creole**	I have seen Mary yesterday. = I saw Mary yesterday.
	the verb *to be* can be used in place of *have*	**Korean**	I am car. = I have one car.
	infinitives are not used to indicate purpose	**Haitian Creole**	I want learn English. = I want to learn English. I go to the library for study. = I go to the library to study.
	a *that* clause is used rather than an infinitive	**Hmong** **Spanish**	I want that they try harder. = I want them to try harder.
	have is used in place of *there is, there are,* or *there were*	**Hmong** **Vietnamese**	In the library have many books. = In the library, there are many books.
	present tense can be used in place of future and present perfect tenses	**Haitian Creole** **Hmong** **Spanish**	I finish it tomorrow. = I will finish it tomorrow.
	the verb *have* is used to express states of being (such as age or hunger)	**Spanish**	She has ten years. = She is ten years old. I have hunger. = I am hungry.

Language Structure Transfer Chart **T349**

Language Structure Transfer Chart, continued

ENGLISH STRUCTURE	LANGUAGE TRANSFER ISSUE	LANGUAGES	SAMPLE TRANSFER ERRORS IN ENGLISH
Adverbs	adverbs are not used (two verbs can take the place of a verb and adverb)	**Hmong**	I run fast fast. = I run really fast. I run run to school. = I run quickly to school.
Adjectives	adjectives can reflect number and gender	**Spanish**	I have kinds parents. = I have kind parents.
	adjectives follow the nouns they modify	**Hmong** **Spanish** (the position of the adjective can also indicate meaning) **Vietnamese**	They have a house big. = They have a big house. We live in a village Laotian. = We live in a Laotian village.
	some nouns and adjectives share the same form	**Chinese**	*Students may have difficulty choosing between noun and adjective forms.* She wants to be independence. =She wants to be independent.
	comparative adjectives do not change form	**Hmong** (add adverbs after the adjective) **Korean** **Spanish**	She is more pretty than you. = She is prettier than you. She runs fast more. = She runs faster.
Word Order	verb precedes subject	**Spanish**	Arrived the teacher late. = The teacher arrived late.
	verbs are placed last in a sentence	**Korean**	The teacher the assignment gives. = The teacher gives the assignment.
	subject and verb order is rarely changed	**Chinese** **Haitian Creole** **Korean**	She is content and so I am. = She is content and so am I.
	subject pronoun can be omitted when the subject is understood	**Chinese** **Korean** (can omit the subject pronoun *you*) **Spanish**	Is crowded. = It is crowded. Am hungry. = I am hungry.
	direct object precedes an indirect object (when the indirect object is a pronoun)	**Chinese** (Cantonese only)	I gave an apple him. = I gave him an apple.
	adverbs and adverbial phrases can precede verbs	**Chinese** **Korean**	I hard study. = I study hard. He by train goes to school. = He goes to school by train.
Questions	can be formed by adding an element to the end of a declarative statement	**Chinese** **Hmong** **Korean** **Vietnamese** (statement followed by phrase "or not")	The book is interesting, yes? = Is the book interesting? You like that color, no? = Do you like that color?

T350 Staff Development: Teaching English Learners

ENGLISH STRUCTURE	LANGUAGE TRANSFER ISSUE	LANGUAGES	SAMPLE TRANSFER ERRORS IN ENGLISH
Questions (continued)	can be formed by adding a verb followed by its negative within a statement	**Chinese** **Vietnamese**	You want/not want watch movie? = Do you want to watch a movie or not? She is/is not teacher? = Is she a teacher or not?
	can be formed by adding the question word between the pronoun and the verb	**Hmong**	You (question word) like the school? = Do you like the school?
	question words are placed according to the position of the answer (for example, if the answer functions as an object, the question words are placed in the regular object position)	**Chinese** **Korean**	He told you what? = What did he tell you? Tell me he is where? = Tell me where he is.
	the answers "yes" and "no" vary depending upon the verb used in the question	**Hmong**	Students may substitute a verb for a yes-or-no answer. Do you speak English? Speak. = Do you speak English? Yes. Do you speak English? No speak. = Do you speak English? No.
Commands	can be formed by adding an adverb after verbs to be emphasized	**Hmong** (add the adverb *now*) **Vietnamese** (add the adverb *right now*)	Do now. = Do it!
	can be formed by adding a time indicator after the verbs to be emphasized	**Hmong**	Fix the car at 3:00. = Fix the car.
	can be formed by adding the verb *go* for emphasis at the end of the sentence	**Vietnamese**	Buy my groceries, go! = Buy my groceries.
	formed by changing the verb ending	**Korean**	Bring(ing) it over here. = Bring it over here.
Negatives	double negatives are routinely used	**Haitian Creole** **Spanish**	They don't like nothing. = They don't like anything.
	negative marker goes before the verb phrase	**Korean** (especially in informal situations) **Spanish**	Joey not has finished the homework. = Joey has not finished the homework.

Language Structure Transfer Chart **T351**

Index

Program Features and Resources

ASSESSMENT 14–19, T10e, T40k, T55, T56d, T69, T70d, T83, T84d, T97, T98d, T113, T114d, T127, T128d, T141, T142d, T155, T156d, T169, T170d, T183, T184d, T197, T198d, T211, T212d, T227, T228d, T241, T242d, T255, T256d, T269, T270d, T283, T284d, T297

AUDIO SCRIPTS T312–T329

AUDIO WALK-THROUGHS T48a, T62a, T76a, T90a, T106a, T120c, T134a, T148a, T162a, T176a, T190a, T204a, T220a, T234a, T248a, T262a, T276a, T290a

BASICS BOOKSHELF, THE T48a–d, T48, T62a–h, T62, T76a–d, T76, T90a–d, T90, T106a–f, T106, T120a–j, T120, T134a–d, T134, T148a–f, T148, T162a–h, T162, T176a–d, T176, T190a–f, T190, T204a–h, T204, T220a–h, T220, T234a–f, T234, T248a–f, T248, T262a–f, T262, T276a–f, T276, T290a–f, T290

BIBLIOGRAPHY OF RELATED LITERACY RESEARCH T305–T306

COMMUNITY CONNECTIONS T22, T68, T81, T172, T180, T194, T240, T254, T272, T296

CONTENT AREA CONNECTIONS T54, T68, T82, T96, T112, T126, T134, T140, T154, T168, T182, T196, T208, T210, T220, T226, T240, T254, T262, T268, T282, T296

COOPERATIVE LEARNING T337c–d
  Inside-outside circle T13, T17, T42, T73, T95, T126, T220
  3-Step interviews T174
  Team word webbing T133
  Think, pair, share T30, T33, T67, T74

CULTURAL PERSPECTIVES T15, T34, T44, T58, T86, T112, T166, T218, T224, T238, T252, T266, T294

DECODABLE BOOKS T51, T65, T79, T93, T109, T123, T137, T151, T165, T179, T193, T207, T223, T237, T251, T265, T279, T293

DECODING SKILLS SEQUENCE T307

HANDBOOK
  Strategies for learning language T299
  Sentences T299
  Nouns T300
  Pronouns T300–T301
  Adjectives T301–T302
  Verbs T302–T303
  Capital letters T303
  Paragraphs T304

HIGH FREQUENCY WORD LIST T308–T309

HOME CONNECTIONS T10, T19, T26, T38, T40, T56, T70, T84, T98, T114, T128, T142, T156, T170, T184, T198, T212, T228, T242, T256, T270, T280, T284

LANGUAGE STRUCTURE TRANSFER CHART T346–T351

LESSON PLANS T10b–d, T40j, T56c, T70c, T84c, T98c, T114c, T128c, T142c, T156c, T170c, T184c, T198c, T212c, T228c, T242c, T256c, T270c, T284c

MULTI-LEVEL STRATEGIES
  Preliterate T13b, T48a, T50, T59, T62c, T69, T76a, T89–T90a, T92, T97, T100, T106a, T108, T113, T118, T120c, T122, T134a, T141, T148a, T155, T160, T162a, T162c, T164, T173, T176a, T178, T183, T190a, T192, T197, T204g, T206, T214, T220g, T227, T234a, T236, T241, T248a, T250, T262a, T264, T269, T276a, T278, T283, T288, T290a

Literate in L1 T37b, T39b, T43, T45, T55, T62g, T64, T73, T78, T105, T106e, T120i, T125, T131, T136, T139, T144, T147, T148e, T153, T162g, T164, T190e, T192, T203, T204g, T220g, T222, T233, T234e, T236, T247, T248e, T262e, T275, T276e, T290e, T292

Non-Roman alphabet T31b, T48a, T76a, T95, T106a, T111, T120c, T122, T162a, T178, T204g, T234a, T250

Interrupted schooling T50, T62g, T92, T106e, T108, T120i, T148e, T150, T162g, T190e, T206, T220g, T234e, T248e, T262e, T264, T276e, T278, T290e

PACING OPTIONS 42–43, T10e

PARTNER CHECKLIST T310

PARTNER PROMPTS T311

PHONICS TRANSFER CHART T338–T341

PHONICS TRANSPARENCIES *See* **Transparencies**.

PROGRAM GUIDE FOR ASSESSMENT AND INSTRUCTION 15–43

SCOPE AND SEQUENCE T307, T330–T336

STAFF DEVELOPMENT T337–T351

STANDARDS-BASED INSTRUCTION 12–13, 17, T330–T337f

TEACHER SCRIPTS T15b, T17b, T19b, T21b, T23b, T25b, T27b, T29b, T33b, T35b, T50a–d, T64a–d, T78a–d, T92a–d, T108a–d, T122a–d, T136a–d, T150a–d, T164a–b, T178a–b, T192a–d, T206a–b, T222a–b, T236a–d, T250a–d, T264a–d, T278a–d, T292a–T292d

TECHNOLOGY T41, T48c, T57, T62e, T71, T76c, T85, T99, T106c, T115, T120g, T129, T134c, T143, T148c, T162e, T176c, T190c, T199, T204e, T213, T220e, T229, T234c, T243, T248c, T257, T262c, T271, T276c, T285

THEME BOOKS *See* **The Basics Bookshelf** and **Theme-Related Books**.

THEME-RELATED BOOKS T40k, T56d, T70d, T84d, T98d, T114d, T128d, T142d, T156d, T170d, T184d, T198d, T212d, T228d, T242d, T256d, T270d, T284d

THEMES 10–11

TRANSPARENCIES
  1 Letters and Sounds T15b
  2 Blend Words with Short *a* T17b
  3 Letters and Sounds T19b
  4 Blend Words with Short *i* T21b
  5 Letters and Sounds T23b
  6 Blend Words with Short *o* T25b
  7 Letters and Sounds T27b
  8 Blend Words with Short *e* T29b
  9 Letters and Sounds T33b
  10 Blend Words with Short *u* T35b
  11 Words with Short *a* T50a
  12 Words with Short *o* T50b
  13 Words with Short *a* T50c
  14 Words with Short *o* T50d
  15 Chant: "On the Map" T50
  16 Words with Short *i* T64a
  17 Words with Short *u* T64b
  18 Words with Short *i* and Short *u* T64c
  19 Words with *ch* and *tch* T64d
  20 Chant: "Ice Cream" T64
  21, 22 Words with Short *e* T78a–b
  23 Words that End in *ll, ss, zz, ck* T78c
  24 Words with *sh* T78d
  25 Chant: "Yes, Yes, Yes!" T78
  26, 27, 28 Words with Blends T92a–c
  29 Words with Digraphs T92d
  30 Chant: "Numbers All Around" T92
  31, 32 Words with Short and Long Vowels T108a–b

  33, 34 Multisyllabic Words T108c–d
  35 Chant: "New Friend" T108
  36 Words with Long *a* and Long *o* T122a
  37 Words with Long *i* and Long *u* T122b
  38 Words with Short and Long Vowels T122c
  39 Plurals T122d
  40 Chant: "Family Gifts" T122
  41 Words with Long *a* T136a
  42 Words with Long *e* and Long *o* T136b
  43 Words with Short and Long Vowels T136c
  44 Multisyllabic Words T136d
  45 Chant: "On the Beach" T136
  46, 47, 48, 49 Verbs with *-ed* T150a–d
  50 Chant: "Best Friends" T150
  51, 52 Verbs with *-ing* T164a–b
  53 Chant: "Invitation" T164
  54 Words with Long *i* T178a
  55 Words with Long *u* T178b
  56 Chant: "Night Watch" T178
  57, 58, 59, 60 Words with *R*-Controlled Vowels T192a–d
  61 Chant: "Let Hope Burn Bright" T192
  62, 63 Types of Syllables T206a–b
  64 Chant: "Under the Moon" T206
  65 Words with *y* T222a
  66 Plurals T222b
  67 Chant: "Take a Look at Today" T222
  68 Words with *oi* and *oy* T236a
  69 Words with *ou* and *ow* T236b
  70 Words with *oo* and *ew* T236c
  71 Words with *au, aw, al, all* T236d
  72 Chant: "Tell Me a Tale" T236
  73 Words with Hard and Soft *c* T250a
  74 Words with Hard and Soft *g* T250b
  75 Words with *oo* T250c
  76 Words with Silent Consonants T250d
  77 Chant: "Good Advice" T250
  78, 79, 80, 81 Multisyllabic Words T264a–d
  82 Chant: "Town in the Desert" T264
  83 Suffix *-ly* T278a
  84 Suffix *-y* T278b
  85 Suffixes *-less, -ful* T278c
  86 Prefixes *un-, re-* T278d
  87 Chant: "Young Corn" T278
  88, 89, 90 Types of Syllables T292a–c
  91 Multisyllabic Words T292d
  92 Chant: "Starship Earth" T292

UNIT PLANNERS
  Lakeside School T10a–e
  Unit 1: Glad to Meet You! T40h–k
  Unit 2: Set the Table T56a–d
  Unit 3: On the Job T70a–d
  Unit 4: Numbers Count T84a–d
  Unit 5: City Sights T98a–d
  Unit 6: Welcome Home! T114a–d
  Unit 7: Pack Your Bags! T128a–d
  Unit 8: Friend to Friend T142a–d
  Unit 9: Let's Celebrate! T156a–d
  Unit 10: Here to Help T170a–d
  Unit 11: Make a Difference! T184a–d
  Unit 12: Our Living Planet T198a–d
  Unit 13: Past and Present T212a–d
  Unit 14: Tell Me More T228a–d
  Unit 15: Personal Best T242a–d
  Unit 16: This Land is Our Land T256a–d
  Unit 17: Harvest Time T270a–d
  Unit 18: Superstars T284a–d

WRITING PROJECTS T55, T69, T83, T97, T113, T127, T141, T155, T169, T183, T197, T211, T227, T241, T255, T269, T283, T297

T352 Index

Vocabulary

ABBREVIATIONS T36, T46, T261
ACADEMIC VOCABULARY T54, T68, T82, T96, T112, T126, T131, T140, T154, T160–T161, T168, T182, T188, T190a, T196, T198, T201–T202, T204a, T210, T212, T214–T216, T220a, T226, T228, T230–T232, T240, T242, T244, T248a, T254–T255, T256, T258, T260, T262a, T268, T270, T273, T276a, T282–T283, T284, T288, T290a, T296
ANTONYMS T49, T107, T177, T231
BASIC VOCABULARY
  Actions T20–T21, T32–T33, T38–T39, T61, T72, T76a, T156–T157, T159, T162a, T302
  Animals T198–T199, T201–T203, T204a, T210
  Body parts T28, T242, T244, T248a, T255
  Cardinal numbers *See* **Numbers.**
  Careers T15, T18–T19, T22–T23, T25, T28, T30, T70, T72–T75, T76a, T78, T80, T83, T171, T272, T274, T300
  Classroom activities T20
  Classroom objects and school tools T12, T14–T15, T18–T19, T20–T21, T32–T33
  Clothing T34–T35, T132
  Colors T34–T35, T56, T58–T60, T62a, T67, T301
  Commands T21, T130, T233, T299
  Communication words T41, T47, T48a, T99
  Community workers T170, T176a
  Comparison words T208, T215, T220, T227, T276, T281, T283, T304
  Days of the week T36–T37, T113, T139
  Describing words T58–T60, T131–T132, T160, T201, T203, T275, T301–T302
  Direction words T187, T260
  Family T114, T116–T117, T120a–T120j, T120–T122, T126, T300
  Farming T270, T273, T283
  Feelings T142–T143, T145, T148a, T155, T302
  Food T30–T31, T56, T58, T60–T62, T66–T68, T271–T272, T274–T275, T283
  Greetings and introductions T13, T15
  Habitats T128–T129, T131, T134a, T138–T139, T198, T201–T203, T204a, T208–T210, T300
  Homes and household objects T114, T118–T119, T125, T300
  Landforms T128, T131, T138, T140, T260–T261, T262a, T266–T268, T300
  Library objects T24–T25
  Location words T100–T102, T105, T113, T300
  Money T30–T31, T86, T272, T274
  Months of the year T38–T39, T139
  Negative words T67, T88, T147, T287, T299
  Neighborhood T98, T100–T105, T106a, T300
  Numbers and basic operations T18–T21, T54, T84–T85, T87, T89, T90a, T92–T93, T96–T97, T126, T154, T196, T272, T301–T302
  Opinion words T200, T211, T257, T304
  Opposites T231, T234a
  Order words T49, T52, T89, T302
  Ordinal numbers *See* **Order words.**
  People T48, T116–T117, T120–T122, T160, T172, T178, T180, T182–T183, T215–T216, T226, T240, T258–T259 , T262a *See also* **Careers** and **Family.**
  Personal information T22–T23, T40–T41, T46
  Plants T131, T138, T201–T203, T204a, T278, T280–T283
  Question words T74, T81, T86, T259, T272, T299
  Restaurant words T274
  Rooms *See* **Homes and household objects**
  School locations and objects T12–T13, T14–T15, T16–T17, T18–T19, T20–T21, T22–T23, T24–T25, T26–T27, T28–T29, T30–T31, T32–T33, T34–T35, T36–T37

School subjects T18–T19
Science materials and processes T32, T82
Sensory words T203, T275, T283, T301
Shapes T21, T56, T58–T59, T62a, T67, T301
Sickness and injury T28–T29
Sizes T56, T58–T60, T62a, T67, T301
Social courtesies T13, T42, T246
Sports T26–T27, T242–T243, T246–T247, T252–T255
Story elements T228, T230–T232, T234, T239–T241
Telling time T18–T19, T173, T232
Time order words T304
Tools T14–T15, T18–T19, T22–T23, T24–T25, T26–T27, T28, T32–T33, T70–T71, T75, T80–T81
Transportation T101, T103, T105, T131, T133, T136
Weather T128, T130–T133, T134a, T140, T203, T208, T268, T277, T280
BUILD ORAL VOCABULARY T15b, T17b, T19b, T21b, T23b, T25b, T27b, T29b, T33b, T35b, T50a–d, T64a–d, T78a–d, T92a–d, T108a–d, T122a–d, T136a–d, T150a–d, T164a–b, T178a–b, T192a–d, T206a–b, T222a–b, T236a–d, T250a–d, T264a–d, T278a–d, T292a–d
CLASSIFY WORDS T49, T59–T60, T63, T68, T72, T75, T80, T82, T87, T89, T91, T100–T102, T116, T118–T119, T131–T132, T138, T145, T162, T181, T187, T201–T202, T214, T244, T258, T273, T281, T288, T295
CONTENT-AREA WORDS *See* **Academic vocabulary.**
HIGH FREQUENCY WORDS T13a–b, T15a, T17a, T19a, T21a, T23a, T25a, T27a, T29a, T31a, T33a, T35a, T37a, T39a, T49, T51–T52, T63, T65–T66, T77, T79–T80, T91, T93–T94, T107, T109–T110, T121, T123–T124, T135, T137–T138, T149, T151–T152, T163, T165–T167, T177, T179–T181, T191, T193–T195, T205, T207–T209, T221, T223–T225, T235, T237–T239, T249, T251–T253, T263, T265–T267, T277, T279–T281, T291, T293–T295
MULTIPLE-MEANING WORDS T91, T92c, T121, T192a, T192c, T205, T221, T291
PREFIXES T278–T279, T292–T293
RELATE WORDS T49, T63, T76, T91, T93–T94, T106–T107, T109, T120, T123, T134–T135, T137, T141, T151, T162, T165, T177, T179, T181, T183, T193, T207, T223, T237, T239, T253, T262, T265, T276, T279, T281
SUFFIXES T278–T279, T292–T293
SYNONYMS T100, T107, T135, T177, T200, T215, T239, T253, T276
WORD DIAGRAMS AND WEBS T76, T134, T140–T141, T162, T181, T183, T191, T249

Language Functions

AGREE AND DISAGREE T286
ASK AND ANSWER QUESTIONS T14–T15, T16–T17, T19, T25, T26–T27, T28–T29, T34–T35, T74–T75, T76, T81, T83, T86, T89, T97, T119, T125, T158, T160, T169, T183, T258–T259, T266, T269, T272–T273
ASK AND GIVE PERMISSION T90
ASK FOR AND ACCEPT A FAVOR T231
ASK FOR AND GIVE ADVICE T230

ASK FOR AND GIVE INFORMATION T13, T18–T19, T22–T23, T24–T25, T28, T30–T31, T46, T72, T81, T87, T100–T102, T116, T118, T125, T132, T186, T244, T273, T288
BUY OR SELL AN ITEM T272
DEMONSTRATE NON-VERBAL COMMUNICATION T145
DESCRIBE T38–T39, T58–T61, T62, T67, T69, T82, T131, T133, T141, T144, T146–T147, T155, T159–T161, T166–T167, T169, T174, T180, T201, T203, T208–T209, T232, T238–T239, T241, T267, T275, T283, T289
EXPRESS AND ACKNOWLEDGE GRATITUDE T106
EXPRESS CERTAINTY T176
EXPRESS FEELINGS T28–T29, T145, T155, T188, T197
EXPRESS INTENTIONS T174
EXPRESS LIKES AND DISLIKES T24–T25, T26–T27, T30–T31, T58
EXPRESS NEEDS, WANTS, AND THOUGHTS T22–T23, T32–T33, T89, T188
EXPRESS PROBABILITY T172–T173
EXPRESS REGRETS T162
EXPRESS SOCIAL COURTESIES T12–T13, T14–T15, T16–T17, T36–T37, T42, T47, T55, T246
EXTEND AND ACCEPT AN INVITATION T162
FOLLOW DIRECTIONS T68, T82
GIVE AND CARRY OUT COMMANDS T20–T21, T130, T233
GIVE DIRECTIONS T187, T260
GIVE INFORMATION T13, T18–T19, T28, T31, T43–T46, T54–T55, T62, T72–T73, T75, T82, T87–T88, T95, T97, T103–T105, T111, T113, T116–T118, T120, T126–T127, T131–T133, T134, T139–T141, T154, T162, T186, T189, T190, T194, T196, T197, T204, T216–T219, T220, T245, T247, T248, T252, T254, T255, T261, T262, T269, T273, T276, T287–T289, T294, T297 *See also* **Ask for and give information.**
GIVE OPINIONS T200, T202, T211
GIVE OR ACCEPT COMPLIMENTS T120
GIVE OR EXPRESS PRAISE T120
HAVE A DISCUSSION T214, T224
LISTEN ACTIVELY T13, T14–T15, T17, T19, T21, T23, T25, T26–T27, T29, T30, T33, T35, T37, T39, T42, T46, T50, T58, T60, T62, T64, T72, T75, T78, T86, T89, T92, T100, T102, T108, T116, T118, T122, T128, T130, T132, T136, T144–T145, T150, T158, T160, T164, T172–T173, T178, T186, T188, T192, T200, T202, T206, T214, T215, T222, T230, T231, T236, T244, T246, T250, T256, T258, T260, T264, T272, T274, T278, T286, T292 *See also* **Listening** on page T357.
MAKE A DENIAL T204
MAKE A PROMISE T290
MAKE A SUGGESTION T202, T204
MAKE AND ACCEPT AN APOLOGY T148
MAKE AND SUBSTANTIATE AN EXCUSE T248
MAKE COMPARISONS T208, T215, T220e, T220g, T220, T224, T227, T276c, T276e, T276, T280–T281, T283, T304
ORDER AN ITEM T46, T274
READ A SELECTION T52, T66, T80, T94, T110, T124, T138, T152, T166, T180, T194, T208, T224, T238, T252, T266, T280, T294

Index **T353**

Index, continued

Language Functions, continued

READ ALOUD T42, T49, T50, T54, T58, T63, T64, T72, T77, T78, T86, T91, T92, T100, T104, T106e, T107, T108, T116, T121, T122, T130, T135, T136, T144, T148e, T149, T150, T158, T163, T164, T169, T172, T178, T186, T190e, T192, T200, T205, T206, T214, T220g, T221, T222, T230, T235, T236, T241, T244, T249, T250, T258, T263, T264, T267, T269, T272, T277, T278, T286, T290e, T291, T292

RECITE T42, T50, T58, T64, T72, T78, T86, T92, T100, T108, T116, T122, T130, T136, T144, T150, T158, T164, T172, T178, T186, T192, T200, T206, T214, T222, T230, T236, T244, T250, T258, T264, T272, T278, T286, T292

REPEAT SPOKEN LANGUAGE T13, T14–T15, T17, T19, T21, T23, T25, T26, T29, T30, T33, T35, T37, T39, T42, T50, T58, T62g, T64, T72, T78, T86, T92, T100, T108, T116, T122, T130, T136, T144, T150, T158, T164, T172, T176c, T178, T186, T192, T200, T206, T214, T222, T230, T236, T244, T248e, T250, T258, T264, T272, T276e, T278, T286, T292

RETELL A STORY T48, T62, T76, T90, T106, T148, T176, T234, T290

ROLE-PLAY T102, T148e

STATE A GOAL T190

TELL AN ORIGINAL STORY T232, T241

USE THE TELEPHONE T22–T23, T47, T48

WRITE T42–T45, T53, T55, T58–T61, T67, T69, T72–T75, T81, T83, T86–T89, T95, T97, T100–T105, T106e, T111, T113, T116–T119, T125, T127, T128, T130–T133, T139, T141, T144–T147, T153, T155, T158–T161, T167, T169, T172–T175, T181, T183, T186–T189, T195, T197, T200–T203, T209, T211, T214–T219, T225, T227, T230–T233, T239, T241, T244–T247, T253–T255, T258–T261, T267, T269, T272–T275, T281, T283, T286–T289, T295, T297

Language Patterns and Structures

ABBREVIATIONS T36, T46, T261

ACTION VERBS T61, T72, T161, T174, T302

ADJECTIVES
Demonstrative T34–T35
Descriptive T58–T60, T131–T132, T160, T201, T203, T275, T283, T301–T302
Number words T54, T84, T86–T87, T88–T89, T91, T92–T93, T96–T97, T126, T196, T232, T272, T301–T302
Possessive T175
That appeal to the senses T203, T275, T283, T301

ADVERBS T158–T159, T162a

BASIC SENTENCE PATTERNS
A ___ is in the ___. T24
Can you ___? T26–T27
Carlos ___. (noun + action verb) T38–T39
Do you like ___? T24–T25
Does ___? T24–T25
He/She has ___. T28–T29
Here is/are ___. T14–T15, T18–T19
How do they feel? They feel ___. T28–T29
How do you feel? I feel ___. T28–T29
How does he/she feel? He/she feels ___. T28–T29
I am ___. T12–T13
I can ___. T26–T27
I do not like ___. T30–T31

I have ___. T28–T29
I like ___. T24–T25, T26, T28–T29, T30–T31
I like this/that/these/those ___. T34–T35
I need ___. T32–T33
I need to ___. T22–T23
I think ___. T32–T33
Is this ___? T14–T15
My ___ hurts/hurt. T28–T29
My name is ___. T22–T23
My phone number is ___. T22–T23
Point to ___. T20–T21
See you ___. T36–T37
Show me ___. T20–T21
Some ___ are in the ___. T24
Some ___ are ___./A ___ is ___. T24–T25
They have ___. T28–T29
This/That is ___. T12–T13, T14–T15, T30–T31
What is ___? T23
What is this/that? T30–T31
What time is it? It is ___. It is time for ___. T18–T19
Where is ___? T16–T17, T18–T19, T22–T23
Which ___ do you like? T34–T35
Who is ___? T18–T19
Will you ___? T24–T25
You can ___. T26–T27

CAPITALIZATION
Beginning of sentences T31b, T37b, T39b, T53, T299, T303
Proper adjectives T303
Proper nouns T139, T261, T300, T303

COMMANDS T20–T21, T130, T233, T299

COMMON NOUNS T125, T216, T300

CONTRACTIONS T95, T111, T147, T287, T299, T302, T303

DECLARATIVE SENTENCES See **Statements**.

EXCLAMATORY SENTENCES T39b, T53, T299

IMPERATIVE SENTENCES See **Commands**.

INTERROGATIVE SENTENCES See **Questions**.

IRREGULAR VERBS T146, T186, T189, T217, T303

MODALS
can T26–T27, T74, T133, T303
could, may, might T172, T303
must, should T200

NEGATIVE SENTENCES T30–T31, T67, T88, T95, T147, T299

NOUNS
Capitalization of T139, T261, T303
Common T125, T216, T300
Possessive T153, T300
Plural T125
Proper T139, T261, T300, T303
Singular and plural T24–T25, T125, T300

OBJECT PRONOUNS T218–T219, T247, T301

PHRASES WITH
have to T174
like to T161
need to T22–T23, T174
want to T161

PLURAL NOUNS T24–T25, T125, T300

PLURALS WITH -s T24

PLURAL VERBS T38–T39, T44–T45, T61, T72–T73, T86, T117, T146, T161, T174, T289, T299, T302–T303 See also **Basic sentence patterns**.

POSSESSIVES
Adjectives T175, T301
Nouns T153, T300
Pronouns T175, T301

PREPOSITIONS T100–T102, T105, T113, T187, T232

PROGRESSIVE FORMS OF VERBS T159, T164–T165, T303

PRONOUNS See also **Basic sentence patterns**.
Agreement T42–T43, T74, T218–T219, T300
Demonstrative T12–T13, T14–T15, T30–T31
Object T218–T219, T247, T301
Possessive T175, T301
Singular and plural T42–T43, T74, T175, T218–T219, T300
Subject T42–T43, T247, T301

PROPER ADJECTIVES T303

PROPER NOUNS T139, T261, T300, T303

PUNCTUATION
Apostrophe T95, T111, T147, T153, T287, T299–T300, T302
Exclamation mark T39b, T53, T233, T299
Period T31b, T39b, T53, T233, T299
Question mark T37b, T39b, T74, T299

QUESTIONS See also **Basic sentence patterns**.
with *yes/no* answers T74–T75, T86, T299
with *Who, What, When, Where* T81, T258, T299
with *Do* and *Does* T86, T299
with *How much* or *How many* T272, T299
with *How* T259, T299
with *Why* T259, T299

SENTENCES T53, T105, T130, T233, T299
See also **Basic sentence patterns**, **Questions**, **Commands**, and **Writing**.

SINGULAR VERBS T38–T39, T44–T45, T61, T72–T73, T86, T117, T146, T161, T174, T289, T299, T302–T303 See also **Basic sentence patterns**.

SPELLING T50–T51, T64–T65, T78–T79, T92–T93, T108–T109, T122–T123, T136–T137, T150–T151, T164–T165, T178–T179, T192–T193, T206–T207, T222–T223, T236–T237, T250–T251, T264–T265, T278–T279, T292–T293

STATEMENTS T31b, T53, T299 See also **Basic sentence patterns**.
with infinitives T22–T23, T161, T174
with *There is/are* T105

SUBJECT PRONOUNS T42–T43, T247, T301

SUBJECT-VERB AGREEMENT T38–T39, T44–T45, T61, T72–T73, T86, T117, T146, T161, T174, T289, T299, T302–T303 See also **Basic sentence patterns**.

TENSE, OF VERBS
Present T38–T39, T44–T45, T61, T67, T72–T73, T117, T119, T186, T189, T217, T245, T289, T302–T303 See also **Basic sentence patterns**.
Past T103–T104, T144, T146, T150–T151, T186, T189, T217, T289, T302–T303
Future T287, T289, T303 See also **Basic sentence patterns**.

VERBS
Action T61, T72–T73, T161, T162a, T174, T302
do/does T86
Forms of *be (am, is, are, was, were)* T44–T45, T67, T146, T299, T302
Future tense T287, T289, T303
has, have T117, T119, T303
Irregular T146, T186, T189, T217, T303
Modals T26–T27, T74, T133, T172, T200, T303
Past tense T103–T104, T144, T146, T150–T151, T186, T189, T217, T289, T302–T303
Present tense T38–T39, T44–T45, T61, T67, T72–T73, T117, T119, T186, T189, T217, T245, T289, T302–T303
Progressive forms of T159, T164–T165, T303
Pronoun-verb contractions T111
Singular and plural T38–T39, T44–T45, T61, T72–T73, T86, T117, T146, T161, T174, T289, T299, T302–T303 See also **Basic sentence patterns**.

Learning to Read

ASSOCIATE SOUNDS AND SYMBOLS
Consonants T15b, T19b, T23b, T27b, T33b
Short vowels
/a/ *a* T17b, T21b, T25b, T29b, T35b, T50a, T50–T51
/e/ *e* T29b, T78a, T78–T79
/i/ *i* T21b, T25b, T29b, T64a, T64–T65
/o/ *o* T25b, T29b, T50b, T50–T51
/u/ *u* T35b, T64b, T64–T65
Short vowel phonograms
-at, -an, -ad, -ag, -ap T50c, T50–T51
-et, -en, -ed T78b, T78–T79
-ig, -it, -in T64c, T64–T65
-og, -op, -ot T50d, T50–T51
-un, -ug, -ut T64c, T64–T65
Double consonants and *ck* T78c, T78–T79
Blends T92a–c, T92–T93
Digraphs
/ch/ *ch, tch* T64d, T64–T65, T92d, T92–T93
/ng/ *ng* T92d, T92–T93
/sh/ *sh* T78d, T78–T79, T92d, T92–T93
/th/ *th* T92d, T92–T93
/TH/ *th* T92d, T92–T93
/hw/ *wh* T92d, T92–T93
Long vowels
/ā/ *a_e* T122–T123
ai, ay T136a, T136–T137
/ē/ *ee, ea* T136b, T136–T137
y T222a, T222–T223
/ī/ *i_e* T122–T123
ie, igh T178a, T178–T179
y T222a, T222–T223
/ō/ *o_e* T122–T123
oa, ow T136b, T136–T137
/ū/ *u_e* T122–T123
ui, ue T178b, T178–T179
/yoo͞/ *u_e* T122–T123, T178b, T178
ue T178b, T178–T179
***R*-controlled vowels**
/ä/ *ar* T192a, T192–T193
/ôr/ *or* T192a, T192–T193
/ûr/ *er, ir, ur* T192b, T192–T193
/âr/ *air, ear* T192c, T192–T193
/ir/ *eer, ear* T192d, T192–T193
Variant vowels and diphthongs
/oi/ *oi, oy* T236a, T236–T237
/ou/ *ou, ow* T236b, T236–T237
/ô/ *aw, au* T236d, T236–T237
/ô/ *al, all* T236d, T236–T237
/oo͞/ *oo, ew* T236c, T236–T237
/oo͝/ *oo* T250c, T250–T251
/ə/ *a* T264
Variant consonants
Hard and soft *c* T250–T251
Hard and soft *g* T250–T251
Silent consonants T250d, T250–T251
BOOK CONCEPTS T48a
CONCEPTS OF PRINT
Identify capital letters T76a, T106a
Identify dialogue T148a
Identify end marks T90a, T134c
Identify indentation of paragraphs T234a
Identify quotation marks T234a
Identify types of sentences T31b, T37b, T39b, T90c
Identify title and author T120c
Identify where a story begins and ends T106a
Punctuation T31b, T37b, T39b
Use left-to-right directionality T48c
Use the table of contents and glossary T248a
Use captions T162c

DECODABLE TEXT T51–T52, T65–T66, T79–T80, T93–T94, T109–T110, T123–T124, T137–T138, T151–T152, T165–T167, T179–T181, T193–T195, T207–T209, T223–T225, T237–T239, T251–T253, T265–T267, T279–T281, T293–T295
DECODE WORDS T15b, T17b, T19b, T21b, T23b, T25b, T27b, T29b, T33b, T35b, T50a–d, T50–T52, T64a–T64d, T64–T66, T78a–d, T78–T80, T92a–d, T92–T94, T108a–d, T108–T110, T122a–d, T122–T125, T136a–d, T136–T138, T150a–d, T150–T152, T164a–b, T164–T166, T178a–b, T178–T180, T192a–d, T192–T194, T206a–b, T206–T208, T222a–b, T222–T224, T236a–d, T236–T238, T250a–d, T250–T252, T264a–d, T264–T266, T278a–d, T278–T280, T292a–d, T292–T294
DECODING STRATEGIES
Blending T17b, T21b, T25b, T29b, T35b, T50a–d, T50–T51, T64a–d, T64–T65, T78a–d, T78–T79, T92a–d, T92–T94, T108a, T109, T123, T136a–b, T137, T150a, T151, T165, T178a–b, T178–T179, T192a–d, T192–T193, T207, T222a, T222–T223, T236a–d, T236–T237, T250c–d, T251, T265, T279, T293
Divide words into syllables T108c–d, T108–T109, T136d, T136–T137, T165, T207, T264a–d, T264–T265, T292c, T293
Identify root words and affixes T279, T293
Identify root words and endings T122d, T122, T150b–d, T150–T152, T164a–b, T164–T166, T222b, T293
Identify syllable types T206a–b, T206–T208, T292a–c, T292–T293
Sound out words T51, T65, T79, T93, T109, T123, T137, T151, T165, T179, T193, T207, T223, T237, T251, T265, T279, T293
Use letter patterns T93, T137, T193, T223, T237, T250a–b, T250–T251
Use word patterns T108a–b, T108–T110, T122a–c, T122–T124, T136c, T136–T137
DIVIDE WORDS INTO SYLLABLES *See* **Multisyllabic words.**
HIGH FREQUENCY WORDS T13a–b, T15a, T17a, T19a, T21a, T23a, T25a, T27a, T29a, T31a, T33a, T35a, T37a, T39a, T48c, T49, T52, T63, T66, T77, T80, T91, T94, T106e, T107, T110, T120i, T121, T124, T135, T138, T149, T152, T162g, T163, T166, T177, T180, T191, T194, T204g, T205, T208, T221, T224, T234e, T235, T238, T249, T252, T262e, T263, T266, T277, T280, T290e, T291, T294
INFLECTIONAL ENDINGS
-ed T103–T104, T144, T150a, T150–T151, T217, T289, T293
-ing T159, T164–T165
plurals T122d, T122, T125, T223
MULTISYLLABIC WORDS T292d, T292, T294 *See also* Syllable types.
Compound words T136d, T137–T138
With inflectional endings T103–T104, T125, T144, T150–T151, T159, T164–T165, T217, T223, T289, T293
With one consonant between two vowels T264a, T264c, T264–T266, T292–T293
With two consonants between two vowels T108c, T110, T264a–b, T264–T266, T292–T293
With three consonants between two vowels T108d, T110, T264a–b, T265–T266, T292–T293
With *r*-controlled syllables T206a–b, T206–T208
With roots and affixes T278–T279, T292–T293
With /ə/ *a* in first syllable T264d, T264–T266

PARTNER READING T62g, T106e, T120i, T162g, T190e, T204g, T220g, T234e, T248e, T262e, T276e, T290e
PHONEMIC AWARENESS T15b, T17b, T19b, T21b, T23b, T25b, T27b, T29b, T33b, T35b, T50a–T50, T64a–T64, T78a–T78, T92a–T92, T108a–T108, T122a–T122, T136a–T136, T150a–T150, T164a–T164, T178a–T178, T192a–T192, T206a–T206, T222a–T222, T236a–T236, T250a–T250, T264a–T264, T278a–T278, T292a–T292
PHONICS *See* **Associate sounds and symbols** and **Decoding strategies.**
PLURALS *See* **Inflectional endings.**
PREDICT WORDS T76c, T120i, T220g, T248e, T276e
PREFIXES T278–T279, T292–T293
READING AND SPELLING T50–T51, T64–T65, T78–T79, T92–T93, T108–T109, T122–T123, T136–T137, T150–T151, T164–T165, T178–T179, T192–T193, T206–T207, T222–T223, T236–T237, T250–T251, T264–T265, T278–T279, T292–T293
READING FLUENCY
Automaticity with high-frequency words T13a, T15a, T17a, T21a, T23a, T25a, T29a, T31a, T33a, T35a, T39a, T49, T63, T77, T91, T107, T121, T135, T149, T163, T177, T191, T205, T221, T235, T249, T263, T277, T291
Intonation/expression T52, T80, T110
Phrasing T66, T94, T124, T138, T152
Interactive readings T48c, T62g, T76c, T90c, T106e, T120i, T134c, T148e, T162g, T176c, T190e, T204g, T220g, T234e, T248e, T262e, T276e, T290e
Readers theater T51, T65, T79, T93, T109, T123, T137, T151, T165, T179, T193, T207, T223, T237, T251, T265, T279, T293
Timed fluency passages 18–19, T167, T181, T195, T209, T225, T239, T253, T267, T281, T295
ROOT WORDS T150–T151, T164–T165, T278–T279, T292–T293
SOUNDS FOR *-ed* T150a, T150–T151
SUFFIXES T278–T279, T292–T293
SYLLABLE TYPES *See* **Multisyllabic words.**
Open T108–T109, T264–T265
Closed T108–T109, T264–T265
Consonant + *le* T292a, T292–T293
***r*-controlled** T206a–b, T206–T207
Vowel-silent *e* T292c, T292–T293
Vowel team T136–T137, T292b, T292–T293
TRACK PRINT T48c, T62g, T76a, T76c, T90c, T162a, T162g, T190e, T220g, T262e
WORD ANALYSIS *See* **Associate sounds and symbols, Multisyllabic words,** and **Decoding strategies.**
WORD BUILDING T51, T65, T79
WORD FAMILIES T50c–T50d, T64c, T78b, T92a, T108a, T122a, T136a, T178a, T192a, T192c, T236a, T236c, T250a, T250c, *See also* **Decoding strategies, Use letter and word patterns.**
WORD RECOGNITION T48c, T106e, T120i, T162g, T204g, T234e, T262e, T290e *See also* **High frequency words.**
WORD SORTS T49, T63, T91, T93, T107, T123, T135, T137, T151, T165, T177, T179, T193, T207, T223, T237, T251, T265
WORD WORK T49, T51, T63, T65, T77, T79, T91, T93, T107, T109, T121, T123, T135, T137, T149, T151, T163, T165, T177, T179, T191, T193, T205, T207, T221, T223, T235, T237, T249, T251, T263, T265, T277, T279, T291, T293

Index **T355**

Index, continued

Reading and Learning Strategies, Critical Thinking, and Comprehension

ACTIVATE PRIOR KNOWLEDGE T10, T40–T41, T48a, T56–T57, T62a, T70–T71, T76a, T84–T85, T90a, T98–T99, T106a, T110, T114–T115, T120c, T128–T129, T134a, T142–T143, T148a, T156–T157, T162a, T166, T170–T171, T176a, T180, T184–T185, T190a, T194, T198–T199, T204a, T208, T212–T213, T220a, T224, T228–T229, T234a, T242–T243, T248a, T252, T256–T257, T262a, T270–T271, T276a, T280, T282, T284–T285, T290a, T294

ADJUST READING RATE T266

ANALYZE INFORMATION T38, T68, T82, T84, T154, T182, T196, T242–T243

ANALYZE STORY ELEMENTS T176a, T230–T232, T234, T238–T241

ASK QUESTIONS T14–T15, T16–T17, T26–T27, T28–T29, T34–T35, T74–T75, T81, T86, T119, T125, T158, T180, T258–T259, T272–T273

BUILD BACKGROUND T10, T40–T41, T56–T57, T70–T71, T84–T85, T98–T99, T110, T112, T114–T115, T128–T129, T140, T142–T143, T156–T157, T170–T171, T182, T184–T185, T196, T198–T199, T210, T212–T213, T220a, T226, T228–T229, T240, T242–T243, T256–T257, T270–T271, T282, T284–T285, T296

CAUSE AND EFFECT T96, T112, T140, T148c, T148e, T148, T152, T176c, T176, T180–T181, T208–T210

CHARACTER T230–T231, T234, T238–T241

CLARIFY T180

CLASSIFY T68, T82, T84, T128, T134c, T134, T138, T162e, T162g, T162, T194–T195, T198, T262c, T262e, T262, T266–T267

COMPARE TEXTS T280

COMPARISONS T82, T96, T154, T196, T198–T199, T220e, T220g, T220, T224–T225, T227, T276c, T276e, T276, T280–T281, T283, T297

DETAILS T76c, T76, T80, T94, T106c, T106, T110, T112, T120, T124, T127, T155, T166–T168, T182, T196, T208–T209, T226, T240, T248c, T248e, T248, T252–T255, T268–T269, T296

DRAW CONCLUSIONS T68, T82, T98–T99, T128, T154, T196

FACT AND OPINION T69, T188, T200, T211, T257, T286

FANTASY AND REALITY T240

FOLLOW INSTRUCTIONS T82, T154

FORM OPINIONS T220e

FORMULATE QUESTIONS T83, T97, T169, T183, T269

GENERATE IDEAS T38, T40–T41, T55, T56–T57, T69, T70–T71, T83, T84–T85, T97, T98–T99, T113, T114–T115, T127, T128–T129, T140–T141, T142–T143, T155, T156–T157, T170–T171, T183, T184–T185, T197, T198–T199, T211, T212–T213, T227, T228–T229, T241, T242–T243, T255, T256–T257, T269, T270–T271, T283, T284–T285, T297

GOAL AND OUTCOME T290c, T290e, T290, T294–T295

GRAPHIC ORGANIZERS

  Bar graphs T154

  Category charts T96, T113, T127, T155, T195, T198, T262, T276

  Cause-and-effect charts and maps T148, T152, T176

  Character charts or maps T234

  Charts T197 *See also* **Category charts, Comparison charts,** and **Data charts.**

  Circle graphs T196

  Clusters T76, T94, T134, T162, T181, T183, T267, T281

  Comparison charts T82, T220, T227, T276

  Concept maps and charts T209, T225–T226 *See also* **Clusters.**

  Concept webs *See* **Clusters.**

  Data charts T96, T204

  Detail charts T106, T113

  Diagrams T120, T124, T140, T248

  Goal-and-outcome charts and maps T290, T295

  Graphs *See* **Bar graphs, Circle graphs,** and **Line graphs.**

  Line graphs T210

  Lists T60, T68, T97, T175, T239, T253, T255

  Main idea diagrams T120, T124, T248, T254–T255

  Maps T96, T112, T168, T182, T194, T240, T260, T268

  Mind maps T41, T57, T71, T85, T99, T115, T129, T143, T157, T171, T185, T199, T213, T229, T243, T257, T271, T285

  Observation logs T82

  Pie graphs *See* **Circle graphs.**

  Problem-and-solution charts and maps T90

  Semantic maps/charts *See* **Clusters.**

  Sequence chains, charts, and diagrams T48, T52, T62, T66, T106, T113, T140

  Storyboards T241

  Story maps T239–T241

  Tables T196 *See also* **Category charts** and **Data charts.**

  Time lines T190, T204

  Venn diagrams T283

  Word maps T191, T225, T249

  Word webs *See* **Clusters.**

IDENTIFY CAUSE AND EFFECT *See* **Cause and effect.**

IDENTIFY CHARACTER TRAITS/MOTIVES T234c, T234e, T234

IDENTIFY DETAILS *See* **Details.**

IDENTIFY DETAILS THAT SUPPORT A MAIN IDEA *See* **Main idea and details.**

IDENTIFY PROBLEM AND SOLUTION *See* **Problem and solution.**

IDENTIFY SEQUENCE *See* **Sequence.**

IDENTIFY STEPS IN A PROCESS T62e, T62g, T62, T66, T140, T282

INFERENCES T114–T115, T142–T143, T212, T228–T229

JUDGMENTS T56–T57, T69, T196

MAIN IDEA AND DETAILS T120g, T120i, T120, T124, T248c, T248, T252–T255, T269

MAKE COMPARISONS *See* **Comparisons.**

MAKE OBSERVATIONS T70–T71, T82, T84–T85

MAKE, CONFIRM, AND REVISE PREDICTIONS *See* **Predictions.**

OPINIONS *See* **Fact and opinion.**

ORGANIZE IDEAS T55, T69, T83, T97, T113, T127, T141, T155, T169, T183, T197, T211, T227, T241, T255, T269, T283, T297

PARAPHRASE T224

PARTNER READINGS T62g, T106e, T120i, T162g, T190e, T204g, T220g, T234e, T248e, T262e, T276e, T290e

PLAN T55, T69, T83, T97, T98–T99, T113, T127, T141, T155, T169, T183, T185, T197, T211, T227, T241, T255, T269, T283, T297

PREDICTIONS T52, T80, T94, T124, T152, T238

PREVIEW T40, T48a, T56, T62a, T70, T76a, T84, T90a, T98, T106a, T114, T120c, T124, T128, T134a, T142, T148a, T152, T156, T162a, T170, T176a, T184, T190a, T198, T204a, T212, T220a, T228, T234a, T242, T248a, T256, T262a, T268, T270, T276a, T284, T290a

PROBLEM AND SOLUTION T90c, T90

RELATE EVENTS IN A SEQUENCE T113, T156, T212

RELATE TO PERSONAL EXPERIENCE T10, T40–T41, T44, T56–T58, T61, T68, T100, T113, T114–T115, T117, T155, T158, T188–T189, T212–T213, T227, T245, T247, T252, T255, T268, T275

RETELL T52, T66, T80, T94, T110, T124, T138, T152

SELF-ASSESS T55, T69, T83, T97, T113, T127, T141, T155, T169, T183, T197, T211, T227, T241, T255, T269, T283, T297

SEQUENCE T48c, T48, T52, T61, T66, T113, T157, T190c, T190e, T190, T204e, T204, T213, T240–T241, T271

SET A PURPOSE FOR READING T52, T66, T80, T94, T138, T166, T182, T194, T208, T224, T238, T252, T266, T280, T294

SET GOALS T184

SIGNAL WORDS T52, T215, T276, T281

SOLVE PROBLEMS T54, T126

STEPS IN A PROCESS T62, T69, T140, T282, T184–T185, T270–T271

STORY ELEMENTS T238–T241

STRATEGIES FOR LEARNING LANGUAGE T299

SUMMARIZE T140, T268, T282

TEXT FEATURES T82, T96, T112–T113, T120, T124, T127, T134a, T140, T148, T152, T154–T155, T168, T176, T182, T190a, T190, T194–T196, T204g, T204, T210, T220, T227, T234, T240, T248, T260, T262, T268, T276

TEXT STRUCTURES T140, T154, T168, T190a, T196, T262a, T268, T276a, T290a *See also* **Text Structures and Literary Concepts** on page T357.

USE VISUALS T194, T212

VISUALIZE T60, T69, T72, T119, T155, T166, T175, T197, T203, T208, T232, T294

T356 Index

Text Structures and Literary Concepts

ADVERTISEMENT T183
ARTICLE T96, T112, T138, T166, T168, T196, T268
BIOGRAPHY T190, T194, T204, T269
CAPTIONS T190a
CAREER SKETCH T62
CARTOON T88, T94–T95, T152
CHARACTER T230–T231, T239–T240
DESCRIPTION T69, T131, T155, T169, T211, T275
DIARY T215
ESSAY T96, T112, T134, T138, T166, T168, T248, T268
EXHIBIT CARD T69
EXPOSITORY TEXT *See* **Nonfiction.**
FABLE T234
FACT SHEET T97
FAMILY ALBUM PAGE T127
FANTASY T76, T290
FICTION T48, T52, T66, T76, T124, T232, T234, T238, T240, T290, T294
FOLK TALE *See* **Legend.**
FREE VERSE T192, T206, T264, T278
GOAL AND OUTCOME T290, T295
HISTORICAL ACCOUNT T220
HISTORICAL FICTION T90
HOW-TO ARTICLE T62, T69
IDIOMS T286
INFORMATIONAL TEXT T276, T280
INTERVIEW T83, T154, T160, T169, T172
JOURNAL T113, T148
LEGEND T294
LETTER OR NOTE T219, T231
MANDALA T197
MENU T274
MYTH T240
NARRATIVE POETRY T108, T136, T150, T186, T272
NEWS ARTICLE T110, T180, T252, T265, T279, T293
NONFICTION T62, T69, T83, T96–T97, T110, T112, T120, T134, T138, T140–T141, T154, T160, T162, T166, T168–T169, T172, T180, T190, T194, T196, T204, T208, T210, T220, T248, T252, T265–T266, T268–T269, T276, T279–T280, T282–T283, T293, T296
ORDER FORM T46
PARAGRAPH
  Main idea T254–T255, T269, T320
  Opinion T321
PERSONAL NARRATIVE T124, T155

PHOTO ESSAY T120, T162
PLOT T230, T238–T241
POEM T297
POETRY T42, T58, T78, T86, T108, T122, T130, T150, T158, T172, T192, T206, T222, T230, T244, T258, T278, T286, 297
POSTCARD T55, T131, T267
POSTER T169, T211, T227
PROBLEM AND SOLUTION T90
RAP T78, T222
REALISTIC FICTION T48, T52, T66, T124
REPETITION T50, T58, T64, T78, T92, T108, T158, T164, T178, T192, T206, T236, T272, T278
REPORT T83, T283
RESPOND TO LITERATURE T48, T52, T62, T66, T76, T80, T90, T94, T106, T110, T120, T124, T134, T138, T148, T152, T162, T167, T176, T181, T190, T195, T204, T209, T220, T225, T234, T239, T248, T253, T262, T267, T276, T281, T290, T295
RHYME T42, T50, T64, T72, T78, T86, T92, T100, T108, T116, T122, T130, T136, T144, T150, T158, T172, T178, T186, T200, T214, T222, T230, T236, T244, T250, T258, T272, T286, T292
RHYTHM T42, T50, T58, T64, T72, T78, T86, T92, T100, T108, T116, T122, T130, T136, T144, T150, T158, T164, T172, T178, T186, T192, T200, T206, T214, T222, T230, T236, T244, T250, T258, T264, T272, T278, T286, T292
SCIENCE ARTICLE T140, T210, T280, T282, T296
SENSORY IMAGES T203, T275, T283, T301
SETTING T230, T232, T240
SONG T50, T64, T72, T92, T100, T116, T136, T144, T157, T178, T186, T200, T214, T236, T250, T262, T264, T272, T292
TALL TALE T232
TRAVEL GUIDE T141, T266
WEB SITE T224, T226
WORD CHOICE T69, T113, T155, T183, T211, T239, T253, T275, T283

Listening, Speaking, Viewing, Representing

LISTENING T40–T42, T46, T48a, T49, T50, T52–T53, T56–T58, T60, T62a, T63, T64, T66, T70–T72, T75, T76a, T77, T78, T80, T83, T84–T86, T89, T90a, T91, T92, T94, T96, T98–T99, T100, T102, T106a, T107, T108, T110, T112, T114–T116, T118, T120c, T121, T122, T124, T128–T130, T132, T134a, T135, T136, T138, T140, T142–T145, T148a, T149, T150, T152, T156–T158, T160, T162a, T163, T164, T168–T169, T170–T173, T176a, T177, T178, T182, T184–T186, T188, T190a, T191, T192, T196, T198–T200, T202, T204a, T205, T206, T210, T212–T215, T220e, T221, T222, T228–T231, T234a, T235, T236, T240, T242–T244, T246, T248a, T249, T250, T256–T258, T260, T262a, T263, T264, T268, T270–T272, T274, T276a, T277, T278, T282, T284–T286, T290a, T291, T292, T296
NON-VERBAL COMMUNICATION T42, T47, T73, T75, T102, T118, T145, T158, T174, T202, T231, T246, T272, T274
REPRESENTING T12, T16, T38, T42, T47, T48, T55, T56–T57, T60, T62, T68–T69, T70–T73, T75, T76, T80, T82–T83, T84, T90, T97, T98–T99, T102, T106, T113, T114–T115, T118–T119, T120, T124, T127, T134, T138, T140–T141, T142–T143, T145, T148, T152, T154–T155, T158, T162, T168–T169, T170–T171, T174–T175, T176, T181, T183, T184–T185, T188, T190e, T190, T195, T197, T202–T203, T204, T209, T211, T212–T213, T220, T225, T227, T228–T232, T234, T239, T241, T242, T246, T248–T249, T254–T255, T260, T262, T267, T269, T272, T274–T275, T276, T281–T283, T284–T285, T290, T295, T297
SPEAKING T13, T29, T31, T40–T50, T52, T54, T56–T64, T66, T69, T70–T78, T83, T84–T92, T98–T108, T114–T122, T128–T136, T141, T142–T150, T154, T156–T164, T169, T170–T178, T184–T192, T198–T206, T211, T212–T222, T227, T228–T236, T241, T242–T250, T256–T264, T269, T270–T278, T283, T284–T292
VIEWING T10, T12, T14, T16, T18, T20, T22, T24, T26, T28, T30, T32, T34, T36, T40–T41, T56–T57, T69, T70–T71, T75, T84–T85, T89, T98–T99, T105, T114–T115, T128–T129, T142–T143, T153, T156–T157, T170–T171, T184–T185, T187, T198–T199, T201, T211, T212–T213, T228–T229, T242–T243, T256–T257, T270–T271, T284–T285

Index, continued

Writing

ADVERTISEMENT T183
AUDIENCE T55, T69, T83, T97, T113, T127, T141, T155, T169, T183, T197, T211, T227, T241, T255, T269, T283, T297
BIOGRAPHY T195, T269
CAPTIONS T156, T175, T211, T284
CELEBRATION POSTER T169
CHART T188
CLASS BOOK T162g
CLASS SONG T262e
CLASS THANK-YOU NOTE T148e
CLASS TRAVEL BOOK T141
CLUES T180
COLLECT IDEAS T55, T69, T83, T97, T113, T127, T141, T155, T169, T183, T197, T211, T227, T241, T255, T269, T283, T297
COMMANDS T130, T233
COMPARISON POSTER T227
COMPARISONS T215, T224, T227, T280–T281, T297, T304
DESCRIPTION T59, T69, T131, T141, T158–T160, T166–T167, T169, T201, T203, T208–T209, T232, T238–T239, T275, T288–T289
DETAILS T113, T254–T255, T269
DIRECTIONS T187, T260
DRAFT T55, T69, T83, T97, T113, T127, T141, T155, T169, T183, T197, T211, T227, T241, T255, T269, T283, T297
EDIT AND PROOFREAD T55, T69, T83, T97, T113, T127, T141, T155, T169, T183, T197, T211, T227, T241, T255, T269, T283, T297
EFFECTIVE PARAGRAPHS T254–T255, T269, T304
EFFECTIVE SENTENCES T31b, T39b, T37b, T53, T74, T233, T299, T303
EVALUATE YOUR WRITING T55, T69, T83, T97, T113, T127, T141, T155, T169, T183, T197, T211, T227, T241, T255, T269, T283, T297
EXHIBIT CARD T69
EXPOSITORY WRITING T58, T60, T68–T69, T72, T83, T97, T116, T141, T169, T175, T187, T211, T215–T216, T218, T227, T239, T253–T255, T260, T269, T281, T283, T297, T304
EXPRESSIVE WRITING T55, T113, T131, T219, T231, T267, T297
FACT AND OPINION POSTER T204g, T211
FACT SHEET T97, T211, T244
FAMILY ALBUM T127
FAMILY STORIES T120i
FRIENDLY LETTERS T290e *See also* **Letters and notes.**
FRIENDSHIP BOOK T155
HANDWRITING *See* **Penmanship.**
HEALTHY HABITS POSTER T248e
INFORMATION ABOUT PEOPLE T194
INTERVIEW T83, T154, T160, T169, T172, T227
JOB AD T183
JOB HANDBOOK T83
JOURNAL ENTRY T106e, T113
LABELS T58, T72, T116, T260
LETTERS AND NOTES T219, T231
LIST T60, T68, T97, T175, T239, T253, T255
MAIN IDEA PARAGRAPH T254–T255, T269
MANDALA T197
MORAL T234e
NARRATIVE WRITING T55, T113, T131, T141, T155, T197, T219, T231, T241, T267

NOTE *See* **Letters and notes.**
OPINION POSTER T204g
OPINIONS T200, T211, T286, T304
ORDER FORM T46
ORGANIZATION
  In logical order T83, T97, T127, T141, T169, T183, T211, T255, T269
  In sequential order T61, T69, T113, T155, T304
  To make comparisons T227, T281, T283, T297
  To show goals and outcomes T195
  To show problems and solutions T195, T197
PARAGRAPHS T216, T218, T254–T255, T269, T304
PENMANSHIP T15b, T17b, T19b, T21b, T23b, T25b, T27b, T29b, T33b, T35b, T37b
PERSUASIVE WRITING T183
PLAN T184
POEM T297
POSTCARD T55, T131, T266–T267
POSTER T169, T204g, T211, T227, T248e, T276e
PREWRITE T55, T69, T83, T97, T113, T127, T141, T155, T169, T183, T197, T211, T227, T241, T255, T269, T283, T297
PROOFREAD *See* **Edit and Proofread.**
PUBLISH T55, T69, T83, T97, T113, T127, T141, T155, T169, T183, T197, T211, T227, T241, T255, T269, T283, T297
PURPOSE
  To describe T59, T69, T131, T141, T158–T160, T167, T169, T201, T203, T209, T211, T232, T239, T275, T288–T289, T297
  To entertain T141, T241, T297
  To express your thoughts and feelings T55, T155, T211
  To inform or explain T55, T83, T97, T113, T127, T141, T197, T211, T227, T253, T255, T269, T283, T297
  To learn T42–T46, T53, T55, T58–T61, T67, T69, T72–T75, T81, T83, T86–T89, T95, T97, T100–T105, T111, T113, T116–T119, T125, T127, T130–T133, T139, T141, T144–T147, T153, T155, T158–T161, T167, T169, T172–T175, T181, T183, T186–T189, T195, T197, T200–T203, T209, T211, T214–T219, T225, T227, T230–T233, T239, T241, T244–T247, T253–T255, T258–T261, T267, T269, T272–T275, T281, T283, T286–T289, T295, T297
  To persuade T183, T211
QUESTIONS AND ANSWERS T74–T75, T81, T83, T86, T97, T101, T102, T125, T158, T169, T258, T259, T269, T272–T273
REPORT T83, T283
RESTAURANT ORDER T274
REVISE T55, T69, T83, T97, T113, T127, T141, T155, T169, T183, T197, T211, T227, T241, T255, T269, T283, T297
SENTENCES T42–T45, T53, T59, T61, T67, T73, T87–T89, T95, T100, T103–T105, T111, T117–T119, T127, T132–T133, T139, T144–T147, T153, T155, T159, T161, T167, T169, T172–T174, T181, T186, T189, T197, T198, T209, T211, T214, T217, T230, T239, T241, T245, T247, T259, T261, T287–T288, T295
SPEECH T246
STORY ENDINGS AND SEQUELS T141, T241
SUGGESTIONS T202
SUMMARY SENTENCE T220g

TIME LINE T212
TOPIC
  Choose a T83, T97, T169, T183, T197, T211, T241, T255, T269, T283, T297
  Sentence T254, T269, T304
TRAVEL GUIDE T141
WORD CHOICE T60, T69, T113, T131, T155, T183, T201, T211, T275, T283
WRITE A QUESTION T37b
WRITE A STATEMENT T31b
WRITE AN EXCLAMATION T39b
WRITING CHECKLISTS T55, T69, T83, T97, T113, T127, T141, T155, T169, T183, T197, T211, T227, T241, T255, T269, T283, T297
WRITING PORTFOLIOS T97, T183, T241, T269
WRITING PROJECTS T55, T69, T83, T97, T113, T127, T141, T155, T169, T183, T197, T211, T227, T241, T255, T269, T283, T297
WRITING WITH COMPUTERS T255, T269

Research Skills

BOOKS T255, T269, T283, T297
CHARTS T68, T96, T196, T226, T240
CONDUCT A SURVEY T154
CONDUCT AN INTERVIEW T83, T169
CONDUCT RESEARCH T82, T154, T242–T243
CONTENT AREA CONNECTIONS
  Language Arts and Literature T48, T76, T106, T148, T176, T234, T240, T254, T290
  Mathematics T54, T82, T126, T154, T196, T210
  Science T68, T82, T140, T201, T204, T208, T210, T244, T248, T273, T276, T280–T283, T288–T289, T296
  Social Studies T62, T90, T96, T112, T120, T134, T160, T162, T168, T182, T188, T190, T215, T220, T226, T258–T260, T262, T268, T273, T276
DIAGRAMS T68, T140
FORMULATE QUESTIONS T97
GATHER INFORMATION T68, T82, T97, T169, T212, T269, T283, T297
GRAPHS T154, T196, T210
LOCATE INFORMATION T168
LOCATE RESOURCES T169, T269, T283 *See also* **Gather Information.**
MAPS T96, T112, T168, T182, T240, T268
PHOTOGRAPHS T68, T82, T96, T112, T126, T140, T182, T210, T226, T254, T268, T282, T296
TABLES T196
TAKE NOTES T55, T97, T141, T155, T169, T269, T283, T296
TIME LINES T190, T204
USE THE RESEARCH PROCESS T97, T283, T297

T358 Index

Acknowledgments

TEACHER'S EDITION

Photographs

T114b: by **Carmen Lomas Garza**, courtesy of **Children's Book Press;** T212b: courtesy of National Archives; **AGStockUSA:** T270b ©Timothy Hearsum/AGStockUSA, ©Larry Fleming/ AGStockUSA, ©Ed Young/AGStockUSA; **Allsport:** T242b ©Agence Vandystadt/Syllvain Cazenave/Nikon Janvier 2001; **Artville:** T270b; **Chris Birck:** T184b; **Bridgeman Art Library:** T284b ©Lauros-Giraudon/Bridgeman Art Library Musee d'Orsay, Paris, France; **Bruce Coleman:** T198b ©Frank Krahmer, ©Tom Brakefield, ©Rod Williams, ©John Giustina, ©Joe McDonald, ©Bradley Simmons; **Corbis:** T228b ©Dean Conger/Corbis; T256b ©Kevin Morris, ©Danny Lehman, Annie Griffiths Belt, ©AFP/CORBIS; T284b ©Ralph A. Clevenger/CORBIS, ©Bettmann/CORBIS, ©G rard Degeorge/CORBIS, ©Roman Soumar/CORBIS; **Corbis Stock Market:** T70b ©Mug Shots/The Stock Market, © Bob Rowan; Progressive Image/CORBIS; **Digital Stock:** T198b, T284b; **Robert Hynes:** T128b; **FPG International:** T70b ©Michael Krasowitz, ©Dick Luria; T284b ©Ken Chernis; **Gettyone/Stone:** T2556b ©Zigy Kaluzny; **Image Bank:** T70b ©Stephen Derr; **New Century Graphics:** T114b; **Pacific Stock:** T256b ©William Waterfall; **PhotoDisc:** T56b ©G.K. & Vikki Hart; T70b ©Jack Star/PhotoLink, ©Angela Maynar/Life File, ©Joshua Ets-Hokin, ©Russell Illiq, ©C. Borland/PhotoLink, © C Squared Studios, ©David Hiller; T98b ©John Wang; T284b ©Jules Frazier; **Photo Edit:** T70b ©David Young-Wolff; **PictureQuest:** T84b ©Nick Koudis/PictureQuest, ©S. Meltzer/PhotoLink/PhotoDisc/PictureQuest, ©Corbis Images/PictureQuest, ©Kent Knudson/PhotoLink/PhotoDisc/Picture Quest, T184b ©Mark Richards/PhotoEdit/Picture Quest; T256b©DigitalVision/Picture Quest; **Stockbyte:** T70b; **Stone:** T70b ©Robert E. Daemmrich, ©Hugh Sitton; T198b ©Tom Walker; Digital Stock: T70b; **Liz Garza-Williams:** T40i, T98b, T142b, T170b; T212b, T270b.

PUPIL EDITION

Photographs

83: courtesy of **Brenda Ambrize**; 101, 280, 306: courtesy of **Brown Publishing Network**; 114: by **Carmen Lomas Garza**, courtesy of **Children's Book Press**; 124: courtesy of **Ramiro Ferrey**; 194: courtesy of **Jeffrey Magdar, Free the Children**; 214, 219: courtesy of **National Archives**; 215: written by **Ken Mochizuki**, illustrated by **Dom Lee**, published by **Lee and Low Books**; 216: courtesy of **Moorland Spingarn Research Library**; 220: from the archives of **Yad Vashem, The Holocaust Martyrs' and Heroes' Remembrance Authority, Jerusalem, Israel**; **AGStock USA:** 99; 270 ©Timothy Hearsum/AGStock USA, ©Larry Fleming/AGStock USA, ©Ed Young/AGStock USA; 282 ©B.W. Hoffman/AGStock USA, ©Larry Fleming/AG Stock USA, ©Tom Myers/AGStock USA, ©Jim Jernigan/AG Stock USA; **Allsport:** 242–243 ©Agence Vandystadt/Sylvain Cazenave/Nikon Janvier 2001, 246 ©Ezra Shaw, 249 ©Sylvie Chappaz, 254 ©Shaun Botterill/Allsport; **Animals Animals/ Earth Scenes:** 203 ©Zig Leszczynski; 208 ©Joe McDonald, ©Gary Griffen, ©E.R. Degginger; **AP/Wide World:** 205 ©Obed Zilwa Stringer; **Archive Photos:** 215 ©Anne Frank Fonds-Basel/Anne Frank House-Amsterdam/ Archive Photos, 217 ©Anthony Potter Collection/Archive Photos, 227 ©Anthony Potter Collection/Archive Photos; **Artville:** 14, 30, 31, 54, 57, 59, 67, 206, 236, 244, 250, 270–272, 274–275, 310–311; **Bridgeman Art Library:** 284 by Vincent Van Gogh, Musee d'Orsay, Paris, France ©Lauros-Giraudon/Bridgeman Art Library; **Bruce Coleman, Inc.:** 138 ©S. Nielsen, ©Norman Owen Tomalin, ©John Shaw, ©Rolf Kopfle/KOPFL; 140 ©Roy Morsch; 198 ©Frank Krahmer, ©Tom Brakefield, ©Rod Williams, ©John Giustina, ©Joe McDonald, ©Bradley Simmons; 203 ©John Shaw ©Tom Brakefield, ©Jeff Foott, ©Rodger Wilmshurst; 210 ©Bob & Clara Calhoun; **Bud Endress:** 68–69, 122, 180, 272, 274–275, 286–287, 296, 307, 311; **Cartesia:** 40; **Chris Birck:** 101, 184, 256; **Corbis:** 214, 224, 260; 70 ©Bob Rowan/Progressive Image; 73 ©Reuters NewMedia Inc.; 74 ©Steve Chenn; 77 ©Ales Fevzer; 96 ©Fotografia, Inc., ©Jeremy Horner; 101 ©Kevin Fleming; 105 ©Joseph Sohm/Visions of America; 111 ©Colin Garratt; 116 ©Dave G. Houser, ©Pallava Bagla; 129 ©Michael & Patricia Fogden; 132 ©Sandy Felsentha; 134 ©Eye Ubiquitous; 136 ©Kelly/Mooney Photography, ©Jerry Tobias, ©Forest Johnson, 138 ©Cindy Kassab; 139 ©Kevin Schafer, ©Tom Bean; 140 ©Richard Cummins; 141 ©George W. Wright, ©Catherine Karnow; 160–161 ©Earl & Nazima Kowall; 161 ©Wolfgang Kaehler, ©Stephanie Maze; 163 ©Kelly-Mooney Photography; 166 ©Phil Schermeister; 169 ©Danny Lehman; 175 ©Paul A. Souders; 188 ©Wally McNamee; 189 ©Bettmann, ©Flip Schulke; 190, 214, 216, 217, 221, 258, 261, 269, 284 ©Bettmann ; 191 ©Owen Franken; 214 ©Jeri Cooke; 216 by Joe Rosenthal ©CORBIS; 222 ©M. Dillon; 224 ©Bob Rowan/ Progressive Image, ©Dave Bartruff, 226 ©Hulton-Deutsch Collection; 228 ©Dean Conger, 256 ©Kevin R. Morris, ©Danny Lehman, ©Annie Griffiths Belt, ©AFP; 259 ©Buddy Mays, ©W. Wayne Lockwood, M.D.; 284 ©Ralph A. Clevenger, ©G Rard Degeorge, ©Roman Soumar; 288 ©Premium Stock; 289 ©Dennis di Cicco; 316 ©AFP; **Corbis Stock Market:** 70, 200 ©Mug Shotz/The Stock Market; 72 ©Ed Bock; 73 ©LWA/JDC; 74 ©Ed Wheeler; 78 ©Phillip Wallick/The Stock Market; 132 ©Ariel Skelly, ©Ronnie Kaufman; 136 ©Ariel Skelley; 222 ©corbisstockmarket.com, ©Don Mason/ The Stock Market, ©George B. Diebold/The Stock Market, ©Anthony Redpath/The Stock Market, ©Paul Barton/The Stock Market; **Corel:** 203, 304, 314; **Digital Stock:** 11, 70, 78, 99, 108, 117, 182, 198–199, 200, 284, 288–289, 292, 296, 306, 321; **Digital Studios:** 31, 43, 52; **Doug DeMark:** 194; **EyeWire, Inc.:** 73, 92, 192, 236; **FoodPix:** 68 ©David Bishop, ©Joe Pellegrini, ©Dennis Gottlieb; 206 ©Brian Hagiwara; 275; 310; **FPG International:** 48 ©Michael Simpson; 50 ©Ancil Nance; 70 ©Michael Krasowitz; ©Dick Luria; 73 ©Ancil Nance; 78 ©Kevin Laubacher; 96 ©Harvey Lloyd; 104 ©Rob Gage; 117 ©Peter Gridley; 121 ©John Lawlor; 133 ©John Terence Turner; 136 ©Laurance B. Aiuppy; 158, 164 ©Anthony Nagelmann, ©David Sacks, ©Gary Buss; 159 ©Stephen Simpson, ©Morgan Scott, ©Dennis Galante; 188 ©Sandro Miller; 192 ©Larry West; 259 ©FPG International 1999; **George Ancona:** 162; **Getty Images:** 166 ©David Ball/Stone, 182 ©John A. Rizzo/PhotoDisc, 206 ©PhotoDisc/1999-2000 Getty Images, Inc., ©ImageBank /1999-2000 Getty Images, Inc., ©Stone/1999-2000 Getty Images, Inc., 214 ©Hulton Getty Archive/Liaison Agency, 217-218 ©Hulton Getty Archive/Liaison Agency, 222 ©David Paul Productions/1999-2001 Getty Images, Inc., 236 ©Paul & Lindamarie Ambrose/FPG International, 256 ©Stone/Zigy Kaluzny/1999-2000 Getty Images, Inc., 259 ©J. Chiasson, 261 ©John Freeman/Online USA Inc., 284 ©Ken Chernus/FPG Int'l, 286 ©Ken Chernus/FPG Int'l; **The Granger Collection:** 259 by William Henry Jackson, 262 by N.C. Wyeth; **Grant Heilman Photography:** 273 ©Larry Lefever, ©Alan Pitcairn, ©Grant Heilman; 278 ©Arthur C. Smith III; 280 ©Grant Heilman, ©Barry Runk; 282 ©Grant Heilman, ©Barry Runk, ©Christi Carter, ©Grant Heilman; **Image Bank:** 38 ©Karina Wang, 70 ©Stephen Derr, 72 ©Andrea Pistolesi, 88 ©Dag Sundberg, 116 ©Wendy Chan, 133 ©Mike Brinson, 161, 236 ©Rita Maas; **Index Stock:** 303; **International Stock:** 73 ©Charlie Westerman, 120 ©Frank Priegne; **J. Kevin Wolffe:** 194; **Liaison Agency Int.:** 261 ©Eric Bouvet/Gamma; **Liz Garza Williams:** 11–40, 42–45, 48–50, 52–53, 61, 66, 74, 82–83, 86, 99, 103, 108, 110, 116–119, 124–126, 136, 142, 144–150, 153, 157, 169–170, 172, 182, 186–187, 192, 202–203, 212, 227, 231, 244–248, 250, 255, 264, 270–271, 273, 292, 306, 307, 309, 311–313, 315, 318; **Magnum Photos:** 204 ©Magnum Photos; **NASA:** 288; **New Century Graphics:** 31, 35, 39, 43, 46, 50, 59, 64, 82, 114, 274, 310; **The New York Times:** 215; **Off The Wall:** 284; **Pacific Stock:** 256 ©William Waterfall; **Patrick Tregenza:** 62; **Photonica:** 50 ©Ellen Denuto; **Photo Disc:** 52, 192 ©Siede Preis; 56 ©G.K. & Vikki Hart; 64, 66, 67 ©C Squared Studios; 68, 70 ©Jack Star/Photo Link, ©Angela Maynard/Life File, ©Joshua Ets-Hokin, ©Russell Illiq, ©C. Borland/PhotoLink, ©C Squared Studios, ©David Hiller; 73 ©David Toase; 78, 92 ©Siede Pries; ©Jules Frazier, ©Ryan McVay, ©Donovan Reese, ©C Squared Studios, ©CMCD; 99 ©John Wang; 107 ©John A. Rizzo; 108, 120, 122, 126 ©CMCD; ©C Squared Studios; 127 ©C Squared Studios; 128, 131 ©Karl Weatherly; 136, 166 ©Buccina Studios; 169 ©Siede Preis; 172 ©PhotoLink; 192 ©Ryan McVay, ©Jess Alford, ©Jules Frazier; 200, 203, 206 ©Barbara Penovar, ©Ryan McVay; 222, 236 ©Barbara Penovar, ©C Squared Studios; 236, 242 ©Karl Weatherly; 250, 267 ©Ken Samuelsen; 268 ©Donovan Reese; 271 ©C Squared Studios; 274–275, 277 ©Doug Menuez; 284 ©Jules Frazier; 296, 305 ©Jack Hollingsworth, ©Skip Nall; 310; **Photo Edit:** 38 ©Brian Haimer; 39, 78, 174, 188, 245, 292, 320 ©Tony Freeman; 43, 70, 93, 104, 117, 174, 182, 236, 306, 315 ©David Young Wolff; 55, 74, 105, 117, 174, 182, 305 ©Michael Newman; 72 ©Paul Conklin, ©Jeff Greenberg; 73 ©M. Bridwell; 74 ©Jonathan Nourok, ©Bonnie Kamin, ©Dana White; 80–81 ©Rudi Von Briel; 101 ©Susan Van Etten Lawson; 105 ©Phil McCarten; 133 ©Mark Richards; 174 ©Robert Brenner, ©M. Vincent, ©A. Ramey; 182 ©Susan Van Etten Lawson, ©Spencer Grant; 235 ©Jose Galvez; 245 ©Mark Richards, ©Myrleen Cate, ©Robert W. Ginn; 252 ©Richard Hutchings; 305 ©Rudy Von Briel, ©Jonathan Nourok; 306 ©Phil McCarten, ©Deborah Davis; 311 ©Spencer Grant; 320 ©Deborah Davis; **Photonica:** 50 ©Ellen Denuto; **PictureQuest:** 32 ©DigitalVision/Picture Quest, ©Don Farrall/Photo Disc/PictureQuest, ©Steve Mason/ PhotoDisc/PictureQuest, ©Corbis Images/PictureQuest; 84 ©Nick Koudis/Picture Quest, ©S. Meltzer/PhotoLink/Photo Disc/Picture Quest, ©Corbis Images/PictureQuest, ©PhotoLink/ PhotoDisc/PictureQuest, ©Image Ideas, Inc./PictureQuest, ©Kent Knudson/PhotoLink /PhotoDisc/PictureQuest; 86 ©Ryan McVay/PhotoDisc/Picture Quest; 87 ©Alan Pappe/Rubberball Productions/Picture Quest, ©Corbis Images/PictureQuest; 92 ©Scott Bell/Stock Connection/PictureQuest, ©Corbis Images/ PictureQuest, ©PhotoLink/PhotoDisc/PictureQuest; 111 ©Bonnie Kamin/PhotoEdit/PictureQuest; 117 ©Bob Daemmrich/Stock, Boston Inc./PictureQuest, ©Pictor International/Pictor International, Ltd./PictureQuest; 127 ©Yoav Levy/Phototake/PictureQuest; 131 ©James A. Sugar/Black Star Publishing/PictureQuest; 132 ©Jim Corwin/Stock Connection/PictureQuest; 159 ©Mickey Pfleger/Photo 20–20/ PictureQuest; 180 ©George Hall/Check Six/Picture Quest; 184 ©Mark Richards/PhotoEdit/PictureQuest; 192 ©Fransisco Erize/ Bruce Coleman, Inc./PictureQuest; 214 ©Key Color/Index Stock Imagery/PictureQuest; 226 ©Dennis Brack/Black Star Publishing/PictureQuest; 256 ©Digital Vision/Picture Quest; 264 ©Howard Folsom/Photo Network/PictureQuest, ©PhotoSphere Images/PictureQuest, ©Digital Vision/Picture Quest, ©Jack Deutsch/Stock South/Picture Quest, ©Rick Yamada-Lapides/ Stock Connection/Picture Quest, ©William Schemmel/Stock South/PictureQuest; 291 ©Bob Daemmrich/ Stock Boston, Inc./PictureQuest; **Stockbyte:** 31, 59, 67, 70, 78, 122, 236, 272; **Stone:** 39 ©2000 Stone/Randy Wells; 63 ©Ian O'Leary; 68 ©John Kelly; 70 ©Robert E. Daemmrich, ©Hugh Sitton; 72, 97, 101, 113 ©David Young Wolff, ©Ken Fisher; 87 ©Mike McQueen; 92 ©Jake Rais; 116 ©Seth Kushner, ©Jon Riley, 131 ©Schafer & Hill, ©Glen Allison, ©David Muench; 133 ©Jess Stock, ©Brian Bailey; 135 ©Lori Adamski Peek; 136 ©Kevin Miller; 159 ©Bob Thomas, ©Keren Su, ©Brad Hitz; 160–61 ©Andrea Wells, ©Richard Passmore; 161 ©Rex A. Butcher; 175 ©Chris Cheadle; 192 ©Paul Dance/2000 Stone; 198 Tom Walker; 203 ©Art Wolfe; 263 ©Ken Graham; 266 ©Donovan Reese; 267 ©Hugh Sitton; 268 ©Tom Sheppard; 286 ©Herman Agopian; 298 ©Michel Setboun; 306 ©Schafer & Hill; **Super Stock:** 310; **Supreme Court Historical Society:** 226 ©Richard Strauss, Smithsonian Institution; **U.S. Senate Photo Studio:** 226; **Woodfin Camp & Assoc.:** 177 ©Eastcott/Momatiuk

Illustrations

Andy Adams: 62; **Rick Allen:** 130, 238, 294; **Fian Arroyo:** 232, **Norm Bendell:** 67, 88–89, 94–95, 102; **Michael Bergen:** 192; **Tom Casmer:** 60; **Cathy Diefendorf:** 178; **Rudy Gutierrez:** 175; **Amanda Hayley:** 144, 152; **Marilee Heyer:** 90, 100, 173, 187, 206, 233, 236; **Rober Hynes:** 75, 128, 201; **Barbara Kelley:** 51, 65, 79; **Kathleen Kinkopf:** 122; **Katie Lee:** 276; **Lori Loestoeter:** 58, 64; **Joel Nakamura:** 290; **Tom Newsom:** 106; **Paul Mirocha:** 96, 138, 140; **Michael Slack:** 76; **Kat Thacker:** 234, 240; **Terry Tidwell:** 230; **Lane Yerkes:** 231

TRANSPARENCIES

Photographs

Archive Photos: Tr.65; **Artville:** Tr.2, Tr.3, Tr.5, Tr.7, Tr.11, Tr.18, Tr.19, Tr.26, Tr.29, Tr.33, Tr.34; **Barbara Penovar:** Tr.68; **Bruce Coleman, Inc.:** Tr.44 ©John Shaw; **Corbis:** Tr.1; Tr.5; Tr.31 ©Jack Fields; Tr.6; Tr.12 ©Laura Dewight; Tr.7; Tr.24 ©Sallaz Williams; Tr.9, Tr.12 ©Elaine Soares, ©R. Kessmeyer; Tr.11 ©James Marshall; Tr.12; Tr.14; Tr.46 ©M. Yamashita; Tr.26 ©James L Amos, ©Leonard de Selva; Tr.27, Tr.28, Tr.36 ©Craig Lowell; Tr.37 ©Michael Dunne; Tr.39 ©Kim Bell Art Museum, ©Christine Osborne; Tr.42 ©Forest Johnson, ©Jerry Toblas; Tr.42, Tr.44 ©Ariel Skelley, ©Eric Crichton, ©Tiziana/Gianni Baldizzone; Tr.60, Tr.65 ©Bettmann, ©Bettmann/Corbis; Tr.66 ©Cydney Conger; Tr.68 ©Purcell Team; Tr.70, Tr. 84 ©David Muench, ©David Bartruff; Tr.80 ©Bettmann Archive, ©Nancy Hanks; Tr.90 ©Layne Kennedy; **Corbis Stock Market:** Tr.12 ©Thom Lang, Tr.21, Tr.22 ©Phillip Wallick, Tr.23 ©David D. Keaton, Tr.24, Tr.28 ©Lewis Philppa, Tr.34 ©Alan Schein, Tr.46 ©Cynthia Pringle, Tr.63 ©John Paul Endress, Tr.73 ©Globus Holway Lobel; **Culver Pictures:** Tr.65; **Digital Stock:** Tr.1, Tr.27, Tr.34; **Digital Studio:** Tr.31; **Durmo/Corbis:** Tr.58; **Eye Wire:** Tr.1, Tr.4 ©Ryan McVay, Tr.23, Tr.24 Tr.29, Tr.33; **FPG International:** Tr.36 ©Stephen Simpson, Tr.42 ©Laurence B. Aiuppi, Tr.69 ©Paul and Linda Marie Ambrose; **Freeman Patterson:** Tr.63; **Getty One/Image Bank:** Tr.51 ©Alvis UP I Tis, Tr.65 ©David Paul Prod., Tr.71 ©Rita Maas; **Grant Heilman Photography:** Tr.42 ©Arthur C. Smith III; **Index Stock Imagery:** Tr.49 ©Phil Cantor; **John Paul Endress:** Tr.17, Tr.18, Tr.19, Tr.23, Tr.26, Tr.3, Tr.34, Tr.37, Tr.44, Tr.46, Tr.54, Tr.55, Tr.57, Tr.59, Tr.60, Tr.63, Tr.65, Tr.68, Tr.70, Tr.73, Tr.74; **Liz Garza Williams:** Tr.1, Tr.2, Tr.3, Tr.5, Tr.10, Tr.11, Tr.13, Tr.17, Tr.19, Tr.21, Tr.27, Tr.31, Tr.41, Tr.46, Tr.47, Tr.48, Tr.54, Tr.58, Tr.59, Tr.66, Tr.74; **New Century Graphics:** Tr.33; **Object Gear:** Tr.1, Tr.3, Tr.7, Tr.8, Tr.9, Tr.21, Tr.22; **Peter Arnold, Inc.:** Tr.42 ©Elaine Soares; **Photo Disc:** Tr.1 ©Paul Bread, ©Steve Cole; Tr.1; Tr.6; Tr.36; Tr.59; Tr.73 ©Ryan McVay; Tr.2; Tr.69; Tr.71 ©C. Square Studio; Tr.3 ©Janis Christie; Tr.4; Tr.5; Tr.7; Tr.9; Tr.10; Tr.11; Tr.12; Tr.13; Tr.14; Tr.17; Tr.18; Tr.19; Tr.24 ©Steve Mason; Tr.26 ©Paul Bread; Tr.27; Tr.28 ©Siede Preis, ©Donovan Reese; Tr.29 ©Jules Frazier; Tr.33 ©G.K. Vikki Hakt, ©Russell Illia, ©Siede Preis; Tr.36 ©Nancy R. Cohen; Tr.44 ©Robert Brennel; Tr.57; Tr.63; Tr.66; Tr.68; Tr.70 ©Stockbyte; Tr.74 ©Lawrence Lawry; **Photo Edit:** Tr.5 ©Felisha Martinez, Tr.7, Tr.8, Tr.46, Tr.71 ©David Young Wolff, Tr.23 ©Robert Brennel, Tr.34, Tr.42 ©Felishi Martinez, Tr.51 ©Tony Freeman, Tr.55 ©Jonathan Novrok, Tr.63 ©Eric Fowke, Tr.65 ©Mark Richards, Tr.69, Tr.74 ©Peter Byron; **Photo Research, Inc.:** Tr.39 ©Sylvain Grandadam; Tr.42 ©H. Reinhard/Okapla, ©Joe Munroe; Tr.54; Tr.70 ©John Foster; **Pictor:** Tr.19, Tr.44 ©Randy Napier; **Picture Quest:** Tr.52 ©International Stock Photography, Tr.54 ©IFA/Stock Photography; **Ryan McVay:** Tr.26; **Sports chrome:** Tr.58; **Stock Byte:** Tr.28; **Stock Boston:** Tr.44 ©David J. Sam, Tr.47 ©John Coletti, Tr.57 ©Vincent Van Gogh, Tr.59 ©Mark C. Burnett, Tr.73 ©Lawrence Migdale; **Stock Food:** Tr.23; **StockHouse:** Tr.60 ©Leonard Lee; **Superstock:** Tr.3, Tr.37, Tr.41, Tr.42 ©Elaine Soares, Tr.47 ©John Coletti/Stock Boston, Tr.57, Tr.58; **Image Bank:** Tr.1 ©Harald Sund, Tr.31 ©D. Van Kirk; **Tony Stone:** Tr.21 ©David Hanover, ©Covis Grandadam, ©Myrleen Cate; Tr.23 ©Peter Cortez; Tr.24 ©Joe Cornish; Tr.34 ©Camille Tokerud; Tr.39 ©Hawkins; Tr.41 ©Marce Muench, ©Kevin Miller, ©Bruce Hens; Tr.44 ©W. Bolster, ©Glen Allison; Tr.52 ©Todd Powell; Tr.60 ©Paul Dance/2000 Stone; **Zoran Milich:** Tr.73

Illustrations

Ann Barrow: Tr.36; **Chi Chung:** Tr.31, Tr.57 , Tr.59, Tr.71, Tr.75; **Christina Wald:** Tr.76; **Den Schofield:** Tr.65; **Janice Skivington:** Tr.68; **Joy Allen:** Tr.29, Tr.37, Tr.59, Tr.60; **Judith Love:** Tr.13, Tr.14, Tr.18, Tr.22, Tr.23; **K. Pritchett:** Tr.17, Tr.27; **Liisa Chauncey Guida:** Tr.11, Tr.17, Tr.19, Tr.21, Tr.24, Tr.26, Tr.27, Tr.28, Tr.29, Tr.54, Tr.57, Tr.58, Tr.69, Tr.70, Tr.78, Tr.81; **Misty Maxwell:** Tr.37; **Norman Bendel:** Tr.46, Tr.55, Tr.76; **Robert Hynes:** Tr.31 Tr.41, Tr.42, Tr.46, Tr.62; **S. Schaedler:** Tr.12; **Vivian Rhyan:** Tr.69; **Z. Saunders:** Tr.69, Tr.71

THE BASICS BOOKSHELF BOOKS

A Year Without Rain

Illustrations Marilee Heyer

All Across America

Photographs AP/Wide World: 16 ©Kamenko Pajic Stringer; **Archive Photos:** 1; 20 ©Hulton Getty/John Kobal Foundation; **Art Resource:** 19 ©National Museum of American Art, Washington DC/Art Resource, NY; **CORBIS:** 1, 3, 10–12, 17, 20, 22; cover ©Kevin R. Morris; 22 ©Bettmann/CORBIS; 22 ©Leif Skoogfors, ©Ted Streshinsky; 17 ©Reuters NewMedia Inc./ CORBIS; 17 ©Roger Ressmeyer; 18 ©S.A. Taylor; **Denver Public Library Western History Department:** cover, 8; 16: Courtesy of **DuPont**; 23:

Courtesy of **Estefan Enterprises**; **FPG International LLC:** 2, 11, 17; **George Contorakes:** 24; **The Granger Collection, NY:** 2, 9, 10, 13, 14, 16; 6 by John Trumbull; 7 by N.C. Wyeth; 8 by William Henry Jackson; 15 ©Arnold Genthe; **Liaison Agency, Inc.:** 3 ©John Chiasson/ Gamma Liaiso; 20 ©Kabokov/Liaison, ©Eric Bouvet, ©Tobias Everke; 21 ©Jon Freeman/Online USA Inc; **Liz Garza Williams:** 24; 3: Courtesy of **Lulu Delacre/Photo Assist**; **Michigan Tech University:** 23; **Nebraska State Historical Society:** 2; **NAAS:** 1; **NFL Photos:** 20 James D. Smith/NFL Photos; **PhotoDisc:** cover/back cover,1, 4, 5, 10, 11, 16,17, 22, 23, 24; **PhotoEdit:** 4 ©Michael Newman, ©David Young Wolff; 5 ©Jeff Greenberg; **The Stock Market:** 4 ©90 Clark Mishler/ ALASKA, ©LWA-Dann Tardi; 5 ©Peter Beck, ©Tony Freeman; 1, 20: Courtesy of **Susan Bergholz Literary Services**; 15: Courtesy of **University of Texas Austin Robert Runyon Photograph Collection**
Illustrations **Paul Bachem:** 7

Body Works
Photographs **Corbis Images:** front cover, 12; 23 ©Caroline Penn/Corbis Images; **Eyewire:** 6; **Imagebank:** 16 ©Marc Romanelli/Imagebank, 18 ©Alan Becker/Imagebank; **Kingfisher:** 7, 9; **PhotoDisc:** 2; front cover ©Karl Weatherly/PhotoDisc; **PhotoEdit:** 9; **The Stock Market:** 8 ©Larry Williams & Assoc., 19 ©Ed Bock; **Stone:** 5; 14 ©Ulli Seer/Stone; 21 ©John Kelly/Stone; **Weststock:** covers; **Liz Garza Williams:** 9, 10, 11
Illustrations **Art and Science:** 3; **Bridgeman Art Library:** front/back cover; **Image Bank:** 3 ©Mayo Fundation; **Nucleus Communications, Inc.:** 17; **Photo Researchers:** 15 ©John Bazosil/Photo Researchers

Crops
Photographs **AGStockUSA:** 17 ©Bill Barksdale/AGStockUSA; 20 ©Ed Young/AGStockUSA, ©Jim Jernigan/AGStockUSA; **Animals Animals/Earth Scenes:** 3, 4, 12,14, 24, back cover ©Richard Shiell; 4 ©George Cassidy; 5 ©John Pontier; 5, 22 ©Dani/Jeske; 7 ©E.R. Degginger; 14 ©Richard Kola; 16 ©David Boyle; 18 ©Margot Conte; 21 ©E.R. Degginger; **Artville:** 2, 3, 5, 24, back cover; **DoubleClick Studios:** 7, 11, 15, 18, 21, 23; **Grant Heilman Photography, Inc.:** 9, 17; **Liz Garza Williams:** 24; **PhotoDisc:** covers, 2–5, 7, 10–13, 24; **PhotoEdit:** 6 ©Frank Sitema; 15 ©Jeff Greenberg, ©David Young Wolf; 23 ©Cindy Charle; **Stockbyte:** 2

Explore
Photographs **CORBIS:** 2, back cover; 6 ©Peter Smithers/CORBIS; back cover, 2, 6 ©Michael & Patricia Fogden/CORBIS; 4 ©Gary W. Carter; 6–7 ©Michael T. Sedam; 6 ©Joel W. Rogers/CORBIS; 8–9 ©Eye Ubiquitous/CORBIS; 11 ©Darrell Gulin/CORBIS; **Digital Stock:** 6, 16; **PhotoDisc:** cover, 1, 4, 5, 7, 10, 12, 13, 15 ©Hisham F. Ibrahim, 4–5, 7, 9 ©Adalberto Rios Szalav/Sexto Sol; **Stone:** cover, ©Siegfried Eigstler; cover, 13, 16 ©A. Witte/C. Mahaney; 3, 14, 15, 16 ©D.J. Ball; cover, 3, 10, 11, 16 ©Hugh Sitton; 6 ©David Olsen; 9 ©Wolfgang Kaehler; 10 ©Don and Pat Valenti; 12, 13 ©Mike Severns; 15 ©Robert Van Der Hilst, ©D.C. Lowe; **The Image Bank:** 2, 4; 9 ©Sharon Guynup; 12 ©Cousteau Society; **The Stock Market:** back cover, 4–5 ©Bob Woodward; 4, 16 ©Tim Davis; **Studio photography by Liz Garza Williams.**

Families
Photographs **Artville:** 11; **Ann Morris:** 20, 31; **CORBIS:** 2, 5; 10 ©George H. H. Huey/CORBIS; **Liz Garza Williams:** 2, 27; **Off the Wall:** 1, 4, 8, 17–18; **PhotoEdit:** 18, 30 ©R. Hutchings; **PhotoDisc:** 7, 12, 16, 19, 27, 28; **Viesti Associates, Inc.:** cover ©Martha Cooper; **Woodfin Camp & Associates:** 5, 30 ©Momatuik/Eastcott

Friends Are Like That
Illustrations Amanda Haley
Photographs Liz Garza Williams

Good News
Photographs **Digital Stock:** 2; **FPG International LLC:** 1, 5, 7 ©VCG; 9 ©Harry Bartlet; 11 ©VCG/Imakawa; 13 ©Michael Simpson, 14–15 ©Ken Reid; **PhotoDisc:** 3 ©C Squared Studios, ©Ryan McVay, ©Siede Preis; 16 ©Duncan Smith

I Make Pictures Move!
Photographs **Artville:** 2, 3; **PhotoDisc:** 2; **Stockfood:** 2

Let's Dance!
Let's Dance by George Ancona. Copyright ©1998 by George Ancona. Reprinted by permission of HarperCollins Children's Books

Who Was Martin Luther King, J.R.?
Photographs **Archive Photos:** 6; 4 ©Popperfoto/Archive Photos; 5 ©Archive Photos/Amer. Stock; **Black Star:** 18 ©Charles Moore, 1963; **Bob Fitch:** 17; **CORBIS:** front/back cover, 1, 2, 3, 8–11, 17–18, 20, 24 ©Flip Schulke/CORBIS; 2 ©Underwood& Underwood/CORBIS; 4 ©Bob Krist/CORBIS, 12–16, 19, 21, 22 ©Bettmann/CORBIS; 21 ©Philip James Corwin/CORBIS; 23 ©James L. Amos/CORBIS; back cover ©Reinhard Eisele/ CORBIS; **FPG International LLC:** 6; 3 ©Black Heritage Pitts, 1950; 7 ©F.S. Lincoln; **TimePix:** 23 ©Joseph Louw

More Than A Meal
Illustrated Tom Newsom

Power Out!
Illustrations Rudy Gutierrez

Rachel Carson: A Woman Who Loved Nature
Photographs **Artville:** 16; **Corbis Images:** 16, 21; **Double Click Studios:** interior and exterior book photographs; **Magnum Photos:** front cover, 6, 17, 18; **PhotoDisc:** 12, 15; **Pictor:** 23; **Rachel Carson History Project:** 1, 7, 8, 11, 12, 16; **Stone:** 21

Sunny and Moonshine
Photographs **Center for Information and Research Services:** 24; **PhotoDisc:** 2; **Stockbyte:** 2
Technical Illustrations **Center for Information and Research Services:** 24; **Photri-Microstock:** 2–3 by NASA

The Children We Remember
Photographs **Hulton Getty:** 2; **Painet Inc.:** 2
The Eagle and the Moon Gold Adapted by Yeemay Chan
Illustrations Kat Thacker

What Is It?
Photographs **CORBIS:** 2, 3; **PhotoEdit:** 2 ©Richard Hutchings, ©David Young Wolff, ©Tony Freeman, ©Mary Kate Denny, ©Robert Brenn; 3 ©Michael Newman, ©David Young-Wolff, ©Elena Rooraid, ©Tony Freeman, ©Kate Denny

LANGUAGE PRACTICE BOOK
Photographs
63: Courtesy of **Brown Publishing Network**; 87: Courtesy of **Lawrence Migdale Photography**; **Book Divider Tabs:** 1–2, Liz Garza Williams; **Animals Animals/Earth Scenes:** 65 ©C.C. Lockwood; **Archive Photos:** ©Anne Frank Fonds/ Basel/Anne Frank House; **Art Explosion:** 91; **Artville:** 1, 5, 6, 12, 14, 15, 18, 20, 28, 29, 30, 116, 131; **Cartesia:** 88; **Corbis:** 99, 107, 123; 65 ©James Marshall, ©Richard T. Nowitz; 88 ©Craig Lovell, ©AFP; 89 ©Dean Conger, ©Charles & Josette Lenars, ©Earl & Nazima Kowall; 99, 107, 121, 122, 124 ©Bettmann Archive; 133 ©Premium Stock, ©Dennis di Cicco; **Corbis Stock Market:** 64 ©Ronnie Kaufman, 92 ©Ed Wheeler, 93 ©Ed Bock, 101 ©Mug Shotz; **Digital Stock:** 3, 4, 17, 18, 20, 77, 101, 103, 133; **Digital Studios:** 28, 29, 30 129; **EyeWire:** 117, 131; **FoodPix:**129; 108 ©Burke/Triolo Productions; **FPG International:** 70 ©John Lawlor, 89 ©V.C.L., 93 ©Gary Buss, 108 ©Bob Grant, 117 ©John Giustina, 132 ©E. Dygas; **Getty Images:** 131 ©Karen Moskowitz; **Grant Heilman Photgraphy:** 127 ©Alan Pitcairn, ©Grant Heilman; **Image Bank:** 51 ©AndreaPistolesi, 132 ©Steve Satushek; **John Paul Endress:** 91, 128, 131, 132; **Liz Garza Williams:** 1–14, 16, 18–21, 23–36, 43, 57, 64, 66, 71, 72, 81, 82, 129; **NASA:** 133; **New Century Graphics:** 12, 29, 30; **The New York Times:** 106; **Photo Disc:** 101, 103, 108, 117, 129, 132, 134, 135; 2, 5, 12 ©CMCD; 15, 16, 18; 20 ©Donovan Reese; 46, 67, 76, 77, 78 ©Steve Mason; 94 ©David Buffington; **PhotoEdit:** 4 ©Tony Freeman; 46 ©Felicia Martinez; 51 ©Paul Conklin, ©Jeff Greenberg; 64, 66 ©Susan Van Etten Lawson; 67 ©Jeff Greenberg; 70, 92, 93 ©David Young Wolff, ©Michael Newman, ©Tony Freeman, ©Michael Newman; 77©Richard Hutchings; 78 ©Dana White; 87 ©Deborah Davis, ©Tony Freeman; 91 ©Robert Brenner; 92 ©Robert Brenner; 94 ©Billy E. Barnes; 117 ©Tony Freeman; **Picture Quest:** 12 ©Scott Bell/Stock Connection, ©Corbis Images, ©PhotoLink/ PhotoDisc; 92 ©Bonnie Kamin/PhotoEdit/ Picture Quest; **Stockbyte:** 18, 20, 30; **Stock Food:** 46 **Stone:** 18 ©Donovan Reese, ©Michel Setboun; 51 ©Ken Fisher, ©Walter Hodges; 51, 63, 92 ©David Young Wolff; 77 ©Brian Bailey; 91 ©Sean Murphy; 92 ©Sean Murphy; 127 ©Patrick Bennett
Illustrations
Norm Bendell: 49; **Judith DuFour Love:** 40–42, 44, 47, 48, 52, 53, 54, 62, 69, 72, 74, 75, 76, 84, 86, 97, 98, 109, 111, 113, 114, 118, 119, 122; **Maurie Manning:** 56, 58, 59, 60, 83, 96, 127; **Deborah Miller:** 46; **Karen Morgan:** 102, 104; **Lane Yerkes:** 112

READING PRACTICE BOOK
Photographs
39, 40: Courtesy of **Elaine Soares**; 3: **Zoran Milich**; **Book Divider Tabs:** 1–3, Liz Garza Williams; **Artville:** 2, 4, 6–13, 15, 16, 18, 19, 21, 22, 24–26, 29, 33, 39, 40, 44, 48, 51, 52, 56, 59, 63, 75, 78, 79, 94, 106, 140; **Bruce Coleman Inc.:** 66; **Corbis:** 3, 102; 16, 19, 22, 24, 25 ©Laura Dewight; 19 ©Elaine Soares, 20, 22, 25, 40 ©William Sallaz; 25, 32, 33 ©Elaine Soares; 30, 32, 33 ©Rojer Kessmeyer; 36 ©Dennis di Cicco; 40 ©Michael Yamashita; 47 ©Anthony Nex; 51, 56 ©Leonard de Selva/Corbis, ©Lewis Philppa; 60 ©Michael Dunn; 63 ©Forest Johnson, ©Bruce Hands, ©Ariel Skelley; 65 ©Pat O'Hara/ Corbis; 78 ©Lee Snider; 85 ©M.Dillon/Corbis; 96 ©David Muench/Corbis; 98 ©Bettmann/Corbis; 107 ©Layne Kennedy; 140 ©The Purcell Team; **Corbis Stock Market:** 18 ©Thom Lang; 47 ©Phillip Walker; 47 ©Phillip Warlick; 48 ©David Keaton; 72 ©Ariel Skelley; 82 ©John P. Endress, ©David Sailors; 102 ©Lester Lefkowitz; 103 ©David Pollack; 107 ©Corbis; 63 Corel; **Digital Stock:** 51, 140; **Digital Studios:** 4, 21, 22, 26; **EyeWire:** 48, 55, 85; 3, 4, 7 ©1998–2001 EyeWire, Inc.; 10, 13, 15 ,19 ©Ryan McVay; **Food Pix:** 82 ©Brian Hagiwara; **FPG International:** 64, 65; 59 ©Estephan Simpson; 63 ©Laurence B. Aluppi; 78 ©Larry West; 85 ©Peter Gridley; 97 ©Paul & Lindamarie Ambruse; 101 ©Ken Ross, ©Barbara Peacock; **Getty Images:** 82; 85 ©David Paul Productions; 140 ©Paul & Lindamarie Ambrose; 141 ©Tony Anderson, ©Mike McQueen, ©Photo Disc; **Grant Heilman Photography:** 101; 63 ©Arthur C. Smith III; **Image Bank:** 3 ©Harald Sund, 44 ©Alfred Gescheidt, 48 ©Bob Elsdale, 97, 141 ©Rita Maas; **Image Club:** 47, 93; **John Paul Endress:** 9–13, 15, 16, 18, 19, 22, 25, 28, 30–34, 36, 43, 44, 47, 48, 56, 59, 60, 65, 75, 78, 82, 85, 93, 97, 101, 103, 106, 107, 140, 141; **Liz Garza Williams:** 1, 3, 5–10, 12, 13, 15, 16, 17, 18, 19, 21–25, 28, 30–34, 36, 40, 41, 43–45, 47, 55, 57, 60, 61, 63, 93, 97, 103, 140; **New Century Graphics:** 30, 33, 43, 44; **Object Gear:** 3, 4, 9, 24, 25, 30, 32, 33, 47, 60, 103; **PhotoDisc:** 3 ©Ryan McVay, ©Steve Cole, ©Paul Bread; 4 ©Steve Cole, ©Paul Bread; 6, 7, 8, 9, ©Janis Christie; 10, 12, 13 ©Paul Bread; 15 ©Spike; 16, 18 ©Janis Christie; 19 ©C Squared Studios; 24 ©C Squared Studios, ©Ryan McVay; 25 ©C Squared Studios; 29, 30, 32 ©Ryan McVay; 33 ©C Squared Studios, ©Paul Bread; 39, 40, 43, 44 ©Javier Pierini; 48, 51, 52 ©Steve Mason; 55, 56, 59, 60, 63, 64 ©Nancy R. Cohen; 65, 72, 78 ©Jess Alford; 79 ©Ryan McVay, ©Jules Frazier; 82 ©Ryan McVay; 93 ©Lawrence Lawry; 94, 97, 98, 101, 102, 103, 106, 107, 140 ©Barbara Penovar, ©C Squared Studios; 141 ©C Squared Studios, ©Ryan McVay; **PhotoEdit:** 97; 15 ©Felicia Martinez, ©Michael Newman; 24, 25, 47, 64, 107, 141 ©David Young Wolff; 47, 102, 107 ©Myrleen Ferguson Cate/PhotoEdit, ©Billy E. Barnes; 48 ©Robert Bremnel; 49 ©Rudi Von Briel; 47, 56 ©Michael Newman; 63 ©Felicia Martinez; 102 ©Bonnie Kamin; 107 ©Bill Bachmann; 140 ©Peter Byron, ©Tony Freeman; **Photo Researchers Inc.:** 75; 63 ©Joe Monroe, ©Peter Arnold; 64 ©Okapia Frankfurt; 65 ©Peter Arnold; 98 ©David Ducros; 141 ©John Foster; **PictureQuest:** 79 ©Fransisco Erize/Bruce Coleman, Inc., 94 ©Carol Christenson, 97 ©PhotoSphere Images, 98 ©Digital Vision; **Sports Chrome:** 93; **Stockbyte:** 9, 10, 12, 13, 15, 16, 18, 19, 33, 141; **Stock Food:** 48 ©Eising Food Photography; **Stone:** 22, 25 ©Charles Krebs, 40 ©Stone/Michael Lang, 47 ©Louis Grandadam, 48 ©Peter Cortez, 42, 52 ©Stone/James Balog, 65 ©Waren Bolster, 79 ©Paul Dance, 93 ©Robert Daly, 97 ©Camille Tokerud, 98 ©Robert Daly, 106 ©Stone, 141 ©Mike McQueen; **Super Stock:** 9 59, 60, 63, 64, 140; **Woodfin Camp & Associates:** 15, 30, 32 ©Ken Heyman
Illustrations
Marcia J. Bateman Walker: 151–154;, **Norm Bendell:** 53, 70; **Alex von Dallwitz:** 63, **Liisa Chauncey Guida:** 6–7; **Judith DuFour Love:** 30, 74, 86; **Maurie Manning:** 68–69; **Den Schofield:** 143–146, 179–182; **Michael Slack:** 2, 5, 7, 11, 21; **Dick Smolinski:** 111–114, 115–118, 119–122, 123–126, 127–130, 131–133, 139–142; **Frank Sofo:** 147–150, 167–170; **Ken Stetz:** 159–162; **Stephen Wells:** 171–174; **Lee Woolry:** 135–140, 155–158, 163–166, 175–178

THE HIGH POINT DEVELOPMENT TEAM
Hampton-Brown extends special thanks to the following individuals and companies who contributed so much to the creation of this book.

Design and Production
Jana Abell, Lisa Baehr, Darius Detwiler, Jeri Gibson, Raymond Hoffmeyer, Colette Nichol, Stephanie Rice, Debbie Saxton, Curtis Spitler, Alicia Sternberg, Debbie Wright Swisher, Andrea Erin Thompson, Erika Vinup, Chaos Factory & Associates, Ray Godfrey, Roy Neuhaus, Marcia Bateman Walker, Matthew K. Brown, Aaron D. Busch, Alex von Dallwitz, Terry Harmon, Davis I. Hernandez, Connie McPhedran, Deborah Miller, Russell Nemec, Roger Rybkowski, Margaret E. Tisdale, Donna L. Turner, JR Walker.

Editorial
Alexandra Behr, Susan Blackaby, Janine Boylan, Lisa Cittadino, Shirleyann Costigan, Ramiro Ferrey, Tiina Kurvi, Barbara Linde, Dawn Liseth, Daphne Liu, Sheron Long, Guadalupe López, Jacalyn Mahler, Juan Quintana, Beth Sengel, Virginia Yeater, Lynn Yokoe, Kellie Crain, Phyllis Edwards, Suzanne Gardener, Fredrick Ignacio, Michele McFadden, Debbi Neel, Elizabeth Sengel, Sharon Ursino.